AN INDEX

TO

GENERAL LITERATURE

The "A. L. A." Index

AN INDEX

TO

GENERAL LITERATURE

BIOGRAPHICAL, HISTORICAL, AND LITERARY ESSAYS AND
SKETCHES, REPORTS AND PUBLICATIONS OF BOARDS
AND SOCIETIES DEALING WITH EDUCATION,
HEALTH, LABOR, CHARITIES AND
CORRECTIONS, ETC., ETC.

BY

WILLIAM ISAAC FLETCHER

With the Coöperation of many Librarians

SECOND EDITION

GREATLY ENLARGED AND BROUGHT DOWN TO JANUARY 1, 1900

ISSUED BY THE PUBLISHING BOARD OF THE
AMERICAN LIBRARY ASSOCIATION

Originally published by
HOUGHTON, MIFFLIN AND COMPANY
Boston and New York

BOOKS FOR LIBRARIES PRESS
FREEPORT, NEW YORK

First Published 1901
Reprinted 1971

Reprinted from a copy
in the collections of
The Brooklyn Public Library

INTERNATIONAL STANDARD BOOK NUMBER:
0-8369-2382-0

LIBRARY OF CONGRESS CATALOG CARD NUMBER:
72-165612

PRINTED IN THE UNITED STATES OF AMERICA

PREFACE.

THE character and intent of this work may be best set forth by the following citation from the Preface of the first edition, published in 1893 : —

Dr. William F. Poole, in the preface to his *Index to Periodical Literature*, edition of 1882, repeated the suggestion already made by him at the meeting of the American Library Association in the same year, that a "General Index to books other than periodicals was much needed by students and literary men."

Such a need was generally recognized, and it was hoped that Dr. Poole himself would undertake the task. But when several years had passed, and he, burdened with the care of important library interests in Chicago, persistently declined the undertaking, the "Publishing Section" of the American Library Association was formed to carry out this and other similar work by collaboration ; and the present writer, having had large experience as associate editor on Poole's Index, was summoned to the direction of the work.

The scope of the proposed index was not at first clearly defined, and it was a matter of some difficulty to determine just what books should be included. The general purpose was to index as far as possible all books common in our libraries which treat several subjects under one title, and to the contents of which the ordinary catalogue furnishes no guide, although they are generally treated analytically in the more elaborate library catalogues. To save libraries in the future from the necessity of repeating, each for itself, this analytical work, as well as to place its results within reach of all libraries and of individual literary workers, is the aim of the A. L. A. Index.

A more definite idea of the field covered by this index may be derived from the following statement of the classes of books included : —

1. Essays, so called, and similar collections of critical, biographical, and other monographs.

2. Books in travel, general history, and other subjects, whose chapters or parts are worthy of separate reference, as treating, with some fullness, of individual persons, places, events, or topics.

3. The reports and publications of boards and associations dealing with sociological matters : education, health, labor, statistics, etc. ; also publications of historical and literary societies.

4. A large number of miscellaneous books which for one reason or another seem to deserve such indexing, including some volumes of the U. S. Public Documents, etc.

It will be seen that there is almost no limit to the number of books which might be included under these heads. For the purposes of the present publication it was necessary to establish certain rather stringent limitations, for example the following :

1. Only books in the English language are included — the same rule that has been applied to Poole's Index and supplements.

2. The intention has been to index only such books as are to be found in most of our libraries, the exceptions being generally in favor of books of exceptional value, which may be found in the larger libraries, although they are absent from the smaller ones.

3. Books in history and travel have been sparingly included, as, once entered upon, this field alone would be well-nigh boundless. But under the name of almost any important place will be found references to a few of the best books of travel which give special treatment to that place.

4. The indexing of the sociological reports (education, health, labor, etc.), and of the society publications, is quite general, references being made only to papers of some importance as furnishing monographic treatment of special subjects. The United States public documents have been hardly touched upon, only the Consular Reports and a few other recent series being indexed.

With reference to this new edition it seems necessary to state that the additional matter, which doubles the work in size, is derived from two sources : 1st, the references printed annually from 1893 to 1899 in the Annual Literary Index in the portion called " Index to General Literature," and, 2d, a large number of additional books of the same general character as those covered by the first edition. In this additional indexing the following libraries have collaborated : Amherst College; Auburn, Maine, Public; Boston Athenæum ; Bowdoin College ; Bridgeport, Conn., Public ; Brockton, Mass., Public ; Brooklyn, N. Y., Y. M. C. A. ; Chicago, Ill., Scoville Institute ; Denver, Col., Public ; Detroit, Mich., Public ; Dover, N. H., Public ; Hartford, Conn., Public ; Harvard College ; Jersey City, N. J., Public ; Lowell, Mass., Public ; Madison, Wis., Public ; Medford, Mass., Public ; Newark, N. J., Public ; New Britain, Conn., Institute ; New Haven, Conn., Public ; New Orleans, La., Howard Memorial ; New York, Y. M. C. A. ; Newton, Mass., Public ; Northampton, Mass., Public ; Peoria, Ill., Public ; Philadelphia, Mercantile ; Plainfield, N. J., Public ; St. Paul, Minn., Public ; Salem, Mass., Public ; Saugus, Mass., Public ; Sioux City, Iowa, Public ; Springfield, Mass., City ; University of California ; University of Kansas ; University of Minnesota ; University of Wisconsin ; Wesleyan University ; Wisconsin State Historical Society.

In most respects the character and scope of the new edition correspond with those of the first, the work being brought down to date, and greatly enriched without materially changing the field covered by it. An effort has been made to refer under as many subjects as possible to bibliographies and reading lists, making this work an index to such bibliographies.

The " List of Books Indexed " printed at the end of the volume will serve as a key to the abbreviated forms used in the Index, those forms being merely contractions of the full titles as given in the List ; many references, however, are made to books not in the List because not regularly indexed, and such references are made in a form intended to be self-explanatory. It is believed that all contractions and abbreviations employed will be found intelligible, avoiding the necessity of referring to a list or code.

While much remains to be done in later editions to make this work a complete collection of desirable references on subjects in general literature, and while its shortcomings and defects cannot be more obvious to any one than to its compiler, it is offered in the present form with the confident hope that it will be among the most useful aids in this new era of library development and progress.

W. I. FLETCHER.

AMHERST COLLEGE LIBRARY,
July 1, 1901.

ERRATUM

The following should be added to the list of collaborating libraries: —

Elgin, Ill., Gail Borden; Madison, Wis., State Historical Society; Sacramento, Cal., Public; Scranton, Pa., Public; Springfield, Ill., State.

An imperfect list was accidentally substituted for the correct one.

W. I. F.

A. L. A. INDEX.

dents, 185. — With portrait. Amer. nat. portr. gall. v. 4. — With portrait. Duyckinck. Nat. portr. gall. 2 : 5. — Benton, T. H. 30 years. — Everett. Orat. v. 2. — Curtis, G. T. Life of Buchanan. — Frost. Presidents, 139. — Gallatin, A. Writings. — Griswold. Prose writ. 100. — Lincoln. Lives of pres. 237. — Loring, J. S. 100 Bost. ora. 233. — (C. F. Adams) Mass. Hist. Proc. 2 : 395. — Maury, S. M. Statesm. of Am. 125. — Seward. Works, 3 : 75. — (C. F. Adams) N. E. Hist. Gen. Soc. Biog. 1 : 102. — Brooks, E. S. Hist. Amer. 202. — Griswold, R. W. Sac. poets. — With portrait. Hubbard, E. Lit. jour. 4 : 187. — With portrait. Warner Lib. 1 : 134. — (J. Fiske) Wilson, J. G. Presidents, 120. — Thompson, R. W. Pers. Recoll. 107. — Johnston, A. Amer. ora. 2 : 115. — Lossing. Em. Amer. 309. — Mansfield, E. D. Pers. mem. 204. — Moore, F. Am. eloq. 2 : 247. — Nichol. Amer. lit. 106. — Putnam, A. P. Singers liberal, 9. — Richardson, Amer. lit. 1 : 207. — Upton, Mrs. H. T. Our early pres. 92. — Van Santvoord, C. Disc. 7. — Whittier. Prose, v. 3. — Wise, D. Men of renown, 41.

Adams, John Quincy, and the right of petition. Lodge & Roosevelt. Hero tales, 149.
— Bibliog. of admin. of. Foster, W. E. Ref. lists, 3 : 39.
— Death of. Winthrop. Addresses, 1 : 614.
— Discourse in commem. of. 1826. Webster, D. Works, 1 : 109.
— Home of. (D. L. Child) Homes Am. Statesm. 301.
— Social life during administra. of. Ellet, E. F. Court circles, 123.
— Tribute to. Seward. Works, 3 : 75.
— Unpub. letters of. Mass. Hist. Soc. Proc. 2d ser. 10 : 374.

Adams, Mrs. Louisa Catherine Johnson (wife of J. Q.), with portrait. Holloway, L. C. Ladies, 238. — Amer. nat. portr. gall. v. 4. — Gordon, L. L. Lady Wash'n, 117. — Hanaford. Wom. of cent. 78.

Adams, Josiah. (J. H. Temple) N. E. Hist. Gen. Soc. Biog. 2 : 156.

Adams, Martha. Brockett. Woman's work, 789.

Adams, Phineas, with portrait. Sketches N. H. men, 166.

Adams, Richard. Ivimey. Eng. Bapt. 2 : 331.

Adams, Robert. (E. S. Moseley) N. E. Hist. Gen. Soc. Biog. 2 : 398.

Adams, Samuel, with portrait. Amer. nat. portr. gall. v. 4. — Duyckinck. Nat. portr. gall. 1 : 39. — Lossing. Signers, 33. — Lincoln, R. W. Signers, 1. — Magoon. Orators of rev. 95. — Manning, J. M. Sermons, 483. — Parton. Peop. bk. biog. 553. — Sanderson. Signers, 9. — Brooks, E. S. Hist. Amer. 60. — With portrait. Hubbard, E. Lit. jour. 4 : 117. — Dwight, N. Signers of decl. 44. — Johnston, A. Amer. ora. 1 : 24. — Lossing. Em. Amer. 76. — Moore, F. Am. eloq. 1 : 319. — Richardson. Amer. lit. 1 : 178.
— Charges against, as tax-collector. (A. C. Goodell, jr.) Mass. Hist. Proc. 20 : 213.

Adams, Mrs. Sarah Fuller (Flower). Hatfield, E. F. Poets church, v. 1. — Warner Lib. 1 : 145. — (R. Garnett) Miles, A. H. Poets of cent. 7 : 141. 10 : 215. — Miller, Jos. Singers church, 2d ed. 483.

Adams, Thomas, the merchant. Japp. Noble workers, 391.

Adams, Rev. William. (F. M. Caulkins) Mass. Hist. Coll. 4th ser. 1 : 5.

Adams, William. Bourne, H. R. F. Eng. seamen, 1 : 290.

Adams family in U. S. history. Muzzey. Remin. 48.

Adamson, St. Conyngham, D. P. Irish saints, 431.

Addington, Henry. Earle, J. C. Eng. prem. 2 : 55. — Manning, J. A. Speakers, 465.
— Administration of. Lewis, G. C. Ess. on admin.

Addiscott, Henry. Miller, Jos. Singers church, 2d ed. 485.

Addison, Joseph, with portrait. (H. W. Mabie) Warner Lib. 1 : 148. — (S. Johnson) Chalmers. Eng. poets, 9 : 485. — Collier, W. F. Hist. Eng. lit. 260. — Howitt. Homes Brit. poets, 1 : 39. — Sanborn, K. Eng. poets, 104. — Taine. Eng. lit. 2 : 89. — Thackeray. Humorists. — Tuckerman. Ess. 394. — Wotton. Word portraits, 1. — Hazlitt, W. Eng. com. writ. — Macaulay. Ess. — Anton. Engl. essayists. — Caulfield. Kit-cat, 182. — Crawford, O. Eng. com. dram. 161. — With portrait. Gostwick, J. Eng. poets, 75. — Hatfield, E. F. Poets church, v. 4. — Holland, J. Psalmists, 2 : 157. — (W. Spalding) Macaulay. New biog. 1. — Macdonald, G. England's antiphon, 277. — Miller, Jos. Singers church, 2d ed. 121. — With portrait. Oliphant. Hist. char. Q. Anne, 167. — Russell, W. C. Book of au. 153. — Wrangham. Brit. Plutarch, v. 5.
— Aiken's Life of. Peabody, W. B. O. Lit. rem. 295.
— and Steele. Jones, W. A. Lit. stud. 1 : 1. — Thomson, Mrs. Cel. friend. 1 : 227.
— as an essayist. Drake, N. Ess. Tatler, 2 : 92.
— Biog. sketch of. Drake, N. Ess. Tatler, 1 : 292.
— Cato. Molloy. Famous plays, 39.
— Life and writings of. Macaulay. Ess. 5 : 321.
— Prose style of. Hunt, T. W. Rep. Eng. prose, 288.
— Rosamond, Opera of. Hogarth. Mem. opera, 1 : 194.
— Spectator, Criticisms of operas in. Hogarth. Mem. opera, 1 : 208.
— Works. Perry, T. S. Eng. lit. 18th cent. 130.

Addison, Thomas. Bettany. Em. doctors, 2 : 1.
— Lonsdale. Worthies Cumb. v. 4.

Adela, daughter of William the Conqueror. Green, M. A. E. Princesses, 1 : 34.

Adelaide of Saxe Meiningen. Howitt, M. Queens, 506. — Lancelott. Queens, v. 2.

Adelbert College, Cleveland, O. U. S. Bur. Ed. Circ. '91, no. 5 : 116.

Adeler, Max, *pseud.* *See* Clark, C. H.

Adelicia of Louvaine, queen of Henry I., 1121-1135. Strickland. Queens Eng 1. — Howitt, M. Queens, 24. — Lancelott. Queens, v. 1. — Lawrence, H. Queens, v. 1.

"Adeline," schooner, and the British gunboats. Dawson. Batt. of U. S. 2 : 212.

Adeliza, daughter of William the Conqueror. Green, M. A. E. Princesses, 1 : 14.

Adelphi Theatre. Lennox, W. P. Plays, 1 : 140.

Adelsberg, Cave of. Guild. Over the ocean, 482. — Cobbe, F. P. Hours of work, 131. — Adams, W. H. D. Fam. caverns, 55.

Adie, Louis B. Walker, C. D. Biog. Va. Mil. Inst. 17.

Adirondack region, Destruction of forests in. Chittenden, L. E. Pers. reminis. 159.

Adirondacks, Philosophers' camp in. Stillman, W. J. Old Rome. — Prime, S. I. Under trees, 92.

Adler, Felix. Alviella. Contemp. evol. 191.

Admillan, J. Crauford, Lord. Smith, J. Campbell. Writings, 457.

Administration, Defects of. Helps. Soc. pressure, 247

— in N. Y. State, Centralization of. (J. A. Fairlie) Colum. Univ. Stud. Hist. **9** : no. 8.

— Public, in Massachusetts. (R. H. Whitten) Colum. Univ. Stud. Hist. **8** : no. 4.

— Specialized. Spencer, H. Rec. dis. (N. Y.) 235.

Administrative capacity. Anderson, M. B. Papers, **1** : 152.

Admirals, English. Stevenson, R. L. Virg. puerisque, 179.

Admiralty administration. Brassey, T. Papers, polit. 170.

Admiralty Islands. Chall. voy. narr. 1, pt. 2.

Admiration, Sham, in literature. Payn. Private views, 37.

Adolescence, Initiations into. (G. S. Hall) Am. Antiq. Soc. Proc. n. s. **12** : 367.

— Psychology of. (C. A. Scott) Nat. Ed. Ass. '97 : 843.

Adolph of Nassau, History of. Peake, Eliz. Germ. emperors, 136.

Adolphus Frederick, Prince, Duke of Cambridge. Fitzgerald, P. Royal dukes, **2** : 327.

Adolphus, John. Grant, Jas. Port. pub. char. 1 : 217.

Adoni-Bezek. Hastings, F. Obscure char. 25.

Adopted citizen, The. Pierce, E. L. Addresses, 321.

Adornment of sacred buildings. Parry, T. G. Min. of fine art, 263.

Adrian IV., Eng. pope. Williams, R. F. Eng. card. 1 : 108–475.

Adrian VI., pope. Ranke. Popes, 1 : 91. — Symonds. Age of despots, 440. — Montor. Rom. pont. 1 : 698.

Adulteration of beer. (H. B. Cornwall) Am. Pub. Health, **10** : 106.

— of foods. (A. R. Leeds) Am. Pub. Health, **9** : 166. — (E. Brooks) Am. Pub. Health, **10** : 222. — (A. J. Wolff) Conn. Health, **1886** : 315. — (R. J. Farquharson) Iowa health, **1881** : 265 — (A. Hill) Trans. Soc. Sci. Lond. **1866** : 450. — Wynter. Curios. of toil, **2** : 155. — With bibliography. (S. B. Sharples) Mass. Health, **1882** : 3. — (A. L. Winton, jr.) Conn. Health, **1890** : 289. — Iowa Health, **1893** : 116. — (E. R. Angell) N. H. Health, **1892** : 187. — (D. H. Beckwith) Ohio Health, **1886** : 71, 186. **1887** : 301. — (R. D. Kahle) Ohio Health, **1896** : 15.

— Bibliography of. Battershall. Adultera. 258. — U. S. Comm. Int. Rev. Rept. **1888**.

— Canadian act on. (F. X. Valade) Am. Pub. Health, **24** : 199.

— Continental legislation upon. (E. Richards) Am. Pub. Health, **15** : 114.

— Legislation against. (P. Bevan) Trans. Soc. Sci. Lond. **1870** : 390.

— of coffee, tea, and cocoa. (E. J. Wheeler) N. Y. Health, **1893** : 401.

— of food and drugs. (B. F. Davenport) Am. Pub. Health, **10** : 230. — Mass. Health, **1883** : 91. **1884** : 97. **1885** : 65. **1886** : 73. **1887** : 113. **1888** : 47. — (J. Postgate) Trans. Soc. Sci. Lond. **1857** : 483.

— of groceries. (E. H. Richards) Mass. Health, **1879** (1st) : 57.

— — and drugs. Mass. Health, **1890** : 375. **1891** : 661.

— Our peck of dirt. Wynter, A. Our soc. bees, 1 : 76.

Adventurer, Sketches of occasional contributors to the. Drake, E. Ess. Rambler, **2** : 100.

Adventures of Ernest Alembert : a fairy-tale. (C. Brontë) Nicoll, W. R. Lit. anec. **2** : 49.

Adversity. Bacon. Ess.

— Uses of. Ballantyne. Ess. 127. — Reynolds, G. Papers, 454.

Advertising. Wynter, A. Subtle brains, 44.

— Art of. Wynter, A. Peeps, **2** : 31.

— on natural objects. Appleton, T. G. Sheaf of pap. 119.

Advice. Helps. Essays, 45.

— gratis. Friswell. Better self, 81.

Æd, St. Conyngham, D. P. Irish saints, 336.

Ædan, St. Conyngham, D. P. Irish saints, 316.

Ægean Islands. Warner, C. D. Levant, 249.

Ægina, Marbles of. Pater. Greek stud. 263.

Ælfric. Bibliography. White, C. L. Ælfric.

— Warner Lib. 1 : 172.

Ælinaus, Claudius. Mills. Poets of Greece, 485.

Ængus, St. Conyngham, D. P. Irish saints, 452.

Aerated bread. Wynter, A. Our soc. bees, 1 : 159.

Aerolites. Holland, H. Ess. 265.

— and religion. (A. Harvey) Roy. Soc. Can. 2d ser. 2, § 2 : 69.

Aeronautics ; Bibliography. Aeronautical annual, '95. — Mansfield, C. B. Aerial naviga. 493. — Salem (Mass.) Pub. Lib. Bull. May, '97.

Aeronauts, Heroic. Hodder. Heroes, 1 : 243.

— Real and fabulous. Hunt. Day by fire, 260. — Timbs, J. Inventors, 95. — Verey, J. Open air, 218.

Æschines, with portrait. Warner Lib. 1 : 178. — Mills. Poets of Greece, 454.

Æschylus, with portrait. (J. W. White) Warner Lib. 1 : 183. — (E. Meyers) Abbott, E. Hellenica, 1. — Donaldson. Theatre of Greeks, 62. — (A. W. Schlegel) Donaldson. Theatre of Greeks, 344. — Mills. Poets of Greece, 251. — Symonds. Greek poets, 1 : 372. — Lloyd, W. W. Age of Pericles. — Hundred greatest men, 10.

— Agamemnon, and Sophocles's Trachiniæ. Jenkin, H. C. F. Papers, 1 : 3.

— as poet and teacher. Buchanan, R. Look round, 20.

— Fragments and lost plays of. Symonds. Greek poets, **2** : 76.

— on some modern social problems. Shackford. Soc. & lit. pap. 9.

— Plays. Alford. Poets of Greece, 90.

— Prometheus bound. Buchanan, R. Look round, 1. — Coleridge. Lit. rem. **2** : 323. — Gilfillan, 3d gall. 422. — O'Conor. Ess. 57. — Owen, J. Five skep. dramas, 3. — Blackie, J. S. Horæ Hellen. 60.

— Relig. sent. in. Bunsen. God in hist. **2** : 176.

Æsculapius. Pettigrew. Med. portr. gall. v. 1.

Æsop, with portrait. (H. T. Peck) Warner Lib. 1 : 200. — Newbigging. Fables, 33. — Mills. Poets of Greece, 89. — Bruce, J. Classic port. 9.

Æsthetes. Harrison, F. Choice of bks. 291.

Æsthetical fragments. Jones, W. A. Ess. on authors, 174.

Æsthetics. Bain, A. Emotions, 225. — Chadbourne, P. A. Lec. nat. hist. 52. — Cyples, W. Inquiry hum. exper. 705. — Hall, G. S. Aspects Ger. cult. 101. — McCosh, J. Emotions, 148. — Whittaker, T. Ess. & not. 199.

— Bibliography of. Notes & Q. 6th ser. **8** : 183.

— Grammar and. Gildersleeve. Ess. 127.

— Is it a science ? Hall, G. S. Asp. Ger. 101.

— Notes on. Hamerton. Portfo. pap. 163, 233.

See also Taste.

Agriculture in Massachusetts. Emerson. Nat. hist. intel. 219.
— in New England, 1846. Bushnell. Work, 227.
— in New Jersey, Development of. N. J. Labor. '78:61. '79:3. '81:174. '82:xviii, 399.
— in the period of the Commonwealth and Restoration. Mitchell. Wet days, 169.
— in Scotland, Hindrances to. (G. Hope) Grant, A. Recess, 375.
— in Spain. Prime, S. I. Alhambra, 69.
— in the time of James I. Mitchell. Wet days, 160.
— International trade and. Kempner, W. Common-sense soc. 228.
— Methods of instruction in. U. S. Bur. Ed. Rept. '97–8, 2 : 1575.
— New England. Gray, J. C. Essays, 1.
— Professional teaching of. (E. M. Pendleton) Nat. Educa. Assoc. '76 : 266.
— Progress in. Mitchell. Wet days, 284. — (C. L. Flint) 100 years prog. of U. S. 19. — Everett. Orat. v. 3.
Agrigentum, Siege of. Robson, W. Sieges, 157.
Agrippa von Nettesheim, Heinrich Cornelius. Baldwin, G. C. Rep. men, 265. — Bax. Ethics of socialism, 169.
Agrippina, the mother of Nero. Farrar. Seekers, 111. — Bruce, J. Classic portr. 132.
Agrippina. [A cat.] Repplier. Ess. in idle. 1.
Aguesseau, Henri François d', 1668–1751. Legaré. Writ. 2 : 559. — Vinet. Fr. lit. 18th cent. 45.
Aguilar, Grace. Hall, S. C. Book of mem. 124.
— With portrait. Warner Lib. 1 : 224.
— Grave of. Hall, Mrs. S. C. Pilgr. Eng. shr. 2 : 154.
Aguirre, Lopez d'. Brightwell. Byepaths of biog. 152.
Ahab. Geikie, C. Old Test. char. 305.
Ahithophel. Geikie, C. Old Test. char. 252.
Ahlbeck, Germany. Hall, G. S. Asp. Ger. 80.
Ahlden, castle of, Queen Sophia's imprisonment at. Doran. Queens Hanov. 1.
Ahmed, Syed, khan. Escott, T. H. S. Pillars emp. 165.
Ahriman and Ormuzd. Matheson. Distinc. mess. 171.
Ai, Siege of. Robson, W. Sieges, v. 5.
Aidan, St. Kingsley. Hermits, 289. — Conyngham, D. P. Irish saints, 353.
Aids to Faith. Hunt, J. Rel. thought 19th cent. 212.
Aigues-Mortes. Baring-Gould. Troub.-land, 219. — Larned, W. C. Churches & C. 75. — James, H. Little tour, 173. — Warner, C. D. Roundabout, 46.
Aiken, Lizzie. Moore, F. Women of the war, 478.
Ailbe, St. Conyngham, D. P. Irish saints, 136.
Ailred, abbot of Rievaux. Neale. Mediæv. preachers.
Aim, Ultimate. Mabie. Ess. on work, 127.
Ainos of Japan, with bibliography. (R. Hitchcock) U. S. Nat. Mus. Rept. '90 : 429. — Todd, M. L. Corona, 202.
Ainslie, Hew. Wilson, J. G. Poets of Scot. 2 : 125.
Ainsworth, Henry. Holland, J. Psalmists, 1 : 243.
Ainsworth, William Francis. Smith, C. R. Retrospec. 2 : 83.
Ainsworth, W. Harrison. Friswell. Mod. Men of let. 257. — Wotton. Word portraits, 4. — With photo. Cooper, T. Men of mark, 5 : 8. — Horne, R. H. New spirit, 313. — Warner Lib. 1 : 235.

Ainsworth, W. Harrison, at Little Rockley. Yates, E. H. Celeb. 3 : 297.
— Rookwood. Maginn. Fras. papers, 219.
Ainsworth, William P. Bartlett, J. R. R. I. officers, 446.
Air and life. (H. de Varigny) Smithson. Rept. '93 : 521. '95 : 135.
— and water, Relations to life to. (G. G. Hubbard) Smithson. Rept. '93 : 265.
— expired. Composition of, and its effects upon life. (J. S. Billings and others) Smithson. Rept. '95 : 389.
— free, Exploration of. (A. L. Rotch) Smithson. Rept. '97 : 317.
— in our schoolrooms. (S. Lockwood) N. J. Health, '91 : 85.
— liquid, Researches on. (Prof. Dewar) Smithson. Rept. '96 : 135.
— of towns. (J. B. Cohen) Smithson. Rept. '95 : 349.
— Rebreathed. Nichols, J. R. Fireside sci. 30.
Air moisteners. (E. Atkinson) Am. Pub. Health, 23 : 179.
Aird, Marion. Paul. Wilson, J. G. Poets of Scot. 2 : 389.
Aird, Thomas. Gilfillan. 1st gall. 271. — Wilson, J. G. Poets of Scot. 2 : 243.
Airey, Richard, Lord. With photo. Cooper, T. Men of mark, 3 : 7.
Airy, Sir Geo. B. With photo. Cooper, T. Men of mark, 2 : 15. — Em. persons, 5 : 178. — Ball, R. Great astron. 289.
— at Greenwich. Yates, E. H. Celeb. 3 : 15.
Aitareya-Brahmana, The. Müller, Chips, 1.
αἰτέω and ἐρωτάω, Distinction between. Abbot, E. Auth. 4th gosp. & ess. 107.
Aix. Baring-Gould. Troub.-land, 168. — Freeman. Hist. ess. 4 : 53.
Aix-la-chapelle. Bartley, G. C. D. Rhine, 345. — Buckley, T. A. Great cities, 16.
Aix-les-Bains. Child, T. Summ. holidays, 244.
Ajaccio. Symonds. Sk. so. Eu. 1 : 29.
— Sunday at. Sala. Journey south, 121.
Ajunta, Temples of. Adams, W. H. D. Fam. caves, 67.
Akbar the Great. Adams, W. H. D. Warriors of crescent, 182.
— Palace of. Pidgeon. Engineer's holiday, 398.
— Tomb of. Pidgeon. Engineer's holiday, 397.
Akenside, Mark. Bell, R. Lit. & sci. men, 2 : 364. — (S. Johnson) Chalmers. Eng. poets, 14 : 53. — Tuckermann. Charac. 1 : 228. — (E. Dowden) Ward. Eng. poets, 3 : 341. — With portrait. Warner Lib. 1 : 252. — Pettigrew. Med. portr. gall. v. 1.
Akermann, John Yonge. Smith, C. R. Retrospec. 1 : 276.
Akers, B. P. Tuckerman. Artists, 612.
Akibah, Rabbi, letters of. U. S. Bur. Ed. Rept. '95–96, 1 : 701.
Akoni. Brightwell. Byepaths of biog. 240.
Alabama. Bibliography. (T. M. Owen) Am. Hist. Assoc. Rept. '97, 1 : 777.
Alabama claims. Hobart, V. H. H. Ess. & mis. 2 : 222.
Alabama Polytechnic Institute, Auburn, Ala. U. S. Bur. Ed. Circ. '89, no. 3 : 139.
Alabaster, William. Poems. Drake, N. Noontide, 1 : 242.
Alamanni, Luigi. Symonds. Renais. Ital. lit. 2 : 237. — Stebbing. Ital. poets, v. 2.
Alamo, Battle of the. Lodge & Roosevelt. Herotales, 171.
Alarcon, Pedro Antonio de. Warner Lib. 1 : 262.

Alard, Delphin J., with portrait. Ehrlich, A. Cel. violin. **15**.

Alaric, king of the Visigoths. Utterton, F. A. Biog. sk. 18.

Alaska. Pierrepont. 5th Ave. 141. — Sumner. Works, **11** : 181. — Brockett, L. P. Our west. emp. 1266. — Hartwig, G. Polar world, 277. — (W. W. Kirby) Smithson. Rept. **1864**. — (B. B. Ross) Smithson. Rept. **1866**.

— and Canadian northwest. Bibliography. Providence Pub. Lib. Bull. Sept. '97.

— and its islands. Rutgers, L. On saddle, 20.

— and the Klondike Bibliography, Fitchburg (Mass.) Pub. Lib. Bull. Sept. '97. — Literary news, Sept. '97 : 274.

— as a possible penal colony. (C. Nordhoff) Nat. Pris. Assoc. **1887** : 270.

— Bibliography. Bancroft, H. H. Hist. Alaska. — Scidmore, E. R. Appleton's guide, Alaska.

— Education in. U. S. Bur. Ed. Rept. '97–8, **2** : 1753.

— — Neglect of. (Sheldon Jackson) Nat. Educa. Assoc. **1882** : App. 61.

— Education and gold in. (J. Eaton) Nat. Educa. Assoc. **1898** : 214.

— Ethnography of. Latham. Opuscula, 266.

— Gold fields of. (S. C. Dunham) U. S. Lab. Bull. **3** : 297, 789.

— — Bibliography. Bost. (Mass.) Pub. Lib. Bull. Sept. '97. — Salem (Mass.) Pub. Lib. Bull. Oct. '97.

— Hand Book of. Bur. Am. Rep. Handbook no. 84.

— Introduction of domestic reindeer into. U. S. Bur. Ed. Rept. '97–98, **2** : 1773.

— Southeastern, geographical features of. (W. Libbey, jr.) Am. Geog. Soc. **18** : 279.

— A trip to, 1888. Bates, E. K. Kaleidoscope, 222.

— Yukon river region. (C. W. Raymond) Am. Geog. Soc. **3** : 158. *See also* Yukon river.

Alatri. Freeman. Studies Italy, 206.

Alban, St., Legend of. Charles. Martyrs, 112.

Alban, Mount. Freeman. Studies Italy, 108.

Albani, Mrs. Emma Gye, *called* Madame. Edwards, H. S. Prima don. **2** : 162. — With portrait. Buffen. Mus. celeb. **2** : 1. — Engel. Handel to Hallé, 113.

Albania. Disraeli, B. Home letters, 75. — Curzon. Monast. of the East, 204. — Lear, E. Jour. of lands. painter.

Albany, Louisa, countess of, Alfieri and. Hayward, A. Ess. 2d ser. **2** : 189. — Jesse, J. H. Memoirs of the pretenders. — Wraxall, C. F. L. Historic bye-ways, **1** : 366.

Albany, Alex. Stewart, duke of. Bernard, F. Escapes, 19.

Albany, N. Y. (W. W. Battershall) Powell, L. P. Hist. towns Mid. States, 1.

— Municipal condition of. (J. B. Thacher) Nat. Conf. City Govt. **1896** : 137.

Albany & Susq. R. R., Erie raid upon, 1869. Adams, C. F. Erie, 135.

Albany, House of. Burke, B. Viciss. of fam. **1** : 86.

Albemarle, Anne Clarges, Duchess of. Costello. Englishwomen, **3** : 299.

Albemarle, Geo. Monk, Duke of. James, G. P. R. Commanders, **1** : 193. — Lodge. Portraits (Bohn), **5**. — With portrait. Jesse. Court of Eng. Stuarts, **3** : 41. — Wrangham. Brit. Plutarch, v. **3**.

Albemarle Academy and Central College, Charlottesville, Va. U. S. Bur. Ed. Circ. '88, no. **1** : 55.

Albeniz, Isaac, with portrait. Buffen. Mus. celeb. **2** : 101.

Alberoni, Julius. Crowe & James. For. statesmen, v. **4**. — Maccall. For. biog. **2** : 187. — Smith, G. B. Ambass. 263. — Wraxall, L. Adventurers, v. **1**. — Moore, Geo. Lives. — Maccall, W. For. biog. **2** : 187.

Albert I., of Hapsburg, History of. Peake, Eliz. Germ. emperors, 139.

Albert II., of Austria, History of. Peake, Eliz. Germ. emperors, 199.

Albert, King of Saxony, with portrait. Crowned heads, 11. — Strauss, G. L. M. Men. of Ger. **2** : 106.

Albert, Prince Consort. Dawson, G. Biog. ess. 547. — Duyckinck. Portr. gall. **2** : 93. — Grant, Jas. Port. pub. char. **1** : 1. — Japp, A. H. Leaders of men, 2.

— Death of. Gladstone. Glean. **1** : 1.

— Life of, Martin's. Gladstone. Glean. **1** : 23, 63, 97. — Gladstone. Bulga. 159.

— Memorial to, London. Guild. Abroad again, 111.

— and English monumental sculpture. Palgrave. Ess. on art, 280.

— University days of. Wolff. Odd bits, 219.

Albert Edward, prince of Wales. Field, M. B. Memories, 238. — McCarthy, J. Mod. lead. 35. — Reid, T. W. Politicians, **1** : 21. — With portraits. Lynch, A. Hum. doc's, **1**. — Stead. Char. sk. **5**.

— at home. (A. Forbes) Parton. Princes, 100.

— at Sandringham. Yates, E. H. Celeb. **1** : 3.

— Daughters of. (N. Robinson) Parton. Princes, 107.

— Visit to Washington. Ellet, E. F. Court circles, 502.

Albert N'Yanza River. Barker, Lady. Travel. about, 280.

— Discovery of. Adams, W. H. D. In perils, 248.

Alberti, Henry. Miller, Jos. Singers church, 2d ed. 66.

Alberti, Leon Battista. Milizia. Lives arch. **1** : 192. — Symonds. Renais. It. lit. **1** : 183. — Symonds. Renais. Fine arts, 74. — Symonds. Reviv. of learn. 341. — Vasari. Lives of painters, v. **2**. — Perkins, C. C. Tusc. sculp. **1** : 169.

Albertus *magnus*. Neale. Mediæv. preachers. — Townsend, W. J. Schoolmen, 165.

Albery, James. Archer. Eng. dram. 51.

Albigenses, The. James, G. P. R. Dark scenes. — Shoberl, F. Persecutions, **1** : 44. — Stephen, J. Lec. hist. Fr. 157. — Pennington. Epochs papacy, 102, 156.

— Crusade against. Busk, Mrs. Mediæv. popes, **3** : 123.

— Waldenses and. Maitland, S. R. Eight. ess. 154.

Albin, St. Conyngham, D. P. Irish saints, 449.

Albinus, Matthias. Wallace, R. Anti-Trin. biog. **2** : 238.

Albion College, Albion, Mich., History of. (L. R. Fiske) U. S. Bur. Ed. Circ. '91, no. **4** : 145.

Alboni, Marietta, Comtesse de Pepoli, Italian vocalist. Clayton, E. C. Queens, 439. — Ferris, G. T. Great singers, **2** : 159. — Needham. Queens of song.

Albret, Jeanne d', with portrait. Imbert de St. A. Wom. Valois Ct. 248. — Adams, W. H. D. Noble women, 178. — Owen, Mrs. O. F. Heroines domestic life.

Albuera, Battle of. Adams, W. H. D. Engl. at war, **1** : 308.

— Fusileers at. Fitchett. Deeds, 114.

Albuminoid substances, decomposition of, Sanitary problems of. (P. H. Bryce) Am. Pub. Health, **12** : 133.

Albuquerque, Alfonse d'. Parton. Peop. bk. biog. 311. — Vogel. Cent. of discov. 116.

Alcæus. Arnold, E. Poets of Greece, 102. — Mills. Poets of Greece, 86. — Symonds. Greek poets, 1 : 311. — With portrait. Warner Lib. 1 : 268.

Alcalá de Henares, Spain. Stoughton. Span. ref. 18.

Alcázar, Baltázar de. Warner Lib. 1 : 272.

Alchemists. Heckethorn. Sec. soc. 1 : 215. — Wraxall. Remark. adv. 1 : 168.

Alchemy. Disraeli, I. Curios. (N. Y. 4 v.) 1 : 374. — Mackay, C. Pop. delu. 93. — Davenport, R. A. Delusions, 314.
— and the alchemists. Brown, S. Atom. 1. — Chambers's Papers, no. 66.
— and the dawn of chemistry. Muir, M. M. P. Chemists, 5.
— Bibliography. Waite, A. E. Lives of alch. philos.
— in early New England. Lowell. Writ. 2 : 46.
— Revival of. (H. C. Bolton) Smithson. Rept. **1897** : 207.

Alciate, John Paul. Wallace, R. Anti-Trin. biog. 2 : 112.

Alciatus, Andreas. Emblematum Libellus. Adams, W. D. Famous books, 173.

Alcibiades. Malkin. Class. disq. 84. — Bruce, J. Classic portr. 43. — Plutarch. Lives. — Mombert. Great lives, 41.

Alciphron. (H. T. Peck) Warner Lib. 1 : 275.

Alcman. Arnold, E. Poets of Greece, 142. — Mills. Poets of Greece, 84. — Warner Lib. 1 : 281.

Alcock, John. Campbell. Ld. Chan. 1 : 353.

Alcock, Sir R. With photo. Cooper, T. Men of mark, 2 : 25.

Alcohol. Johnston, J. F. Chem. com. life, 1 : 239. — Calif. Bd. Health, **1884–86** : 137.
— Action of, on human body. (D. Fall) Mich. Health, **1891** : 106. — (E. Smith) Trans. Soc. Sci. Lond. **1860** : 546. — (A. C. Boyden) Nat. Educa. Assoc. **1886** : 108.
— — on vital functions. (A. F. Kinne) Mich. Health, **1881** : 126.
— Bibliography. U. S. Surg.-Gen. Lib. Catalogue.
— Entailments of. (H. O. Hitchcock) Mich. Health, **1874** : 1.
— impure, Consumption of, as a beverage. (J. D. Morales) Am. Pub. Health, **21** : 96.
— Its influence on the human family. (J. G. Jewell) Calif. Health, '84 : 137.
— Moral status of. Scoffern. Stray leaves, 367.

Alcoholic drinks, Abuse of, by the healthy. (S. E. Chaillé) Am. Pub. Health, **12** : 51.
— Abuse of. (S. E. Chaillé) Am. Pub. Health, **12** : 51. — Am. Pub. Health, **21** : 86. — (S. Garciadiego) Am. Pub. Health, **21** : 174.
— — Correcting. (S. Garciadiego) Am. Pub. Health, **21** : 174.
— Effects of. (S. W. Battle) N. C. Health, '95–96 : 198.
— from a sanitary standpoint. Am. Pub. Health, **21** : 86.
— Nature and effects of. Greeley. Hints ref. 257.
— Relations of excessive or habitual use of, to pub. health. (H. O. Hitchcock) Am. Pub. Health, **2** : 257.

Alcoholic medicines. (J. L. Kaine) Wisc. Health, '88 : 163.

Alcoholism. (A. C. Rembaugh) Phila. Soc. Sci. Ass'n, '85.

Alcorn Agricultural and Mechanical College. U. S. Bur. Ed. Circ. '99–00, **2** : 270.

Alcott, A. Bronson. Higginson, T. W. Con-

temp. 23. — With portrait. Mitchell, D. G. Am. lands, **2** : 184. — Frothingham, O. B. Transcend. 249. — Alviella. Contemp. evol. 180. — Nichol. Amer. lit. 257. — Richardson. Amer. lit. 1 : 425.

Alcott, Louisa May. Griswold, H. T. Personal sk. 229. — With portrait. Warner Lib. 1 : 282. — Hamilton, C. J. Wom. writers, **2** : 268. — Brockett. Woman's work, 793. — With portr. (L. C. Moulton) Our fam. wom. 29. — Bolton, S. K. Girls who bec. famous, 104. — Parton, J. Noted wom. 78. — Stearns, F. P. Sk. Concord, 69.

Alcott, W. A. Barnard, H. Educa. biog. 249.

Alcuin. Collier, W. F. Hist. Eng. lit. 24. — Morley. Eng. writ. v. **2**. — Lingard. Anglo-Sax. ch. **2** : 203. — (W. H. Carpenter) Warner Lib. 1 : 295.

Aldegrever, Heinrich. Scott. Little masters, 88. — (A. Rosenberg) Dohme, R. Early mast. 180.

Aldehyde, A formic — its practical use. (F. C. Robinson) Am. Pub. Health, **21** : 356.
— Uses, and experiments with. (F. C. Robinson) Maine Health, '94–95 : 158.

Alden, James. Rogers, A. C. Repres. men, 77.

Alden, Mrs. G. R., with portrait. Bolton, S. K. Succ. women, 72.

Alden, Capt. H. H. Shea, J. G. Fallen brave.

Alden, Henry M. Warner Lib. 1 : 303.

Alden, Leonard Case. (J. E. Wright) Harvard mem. biog. **2** : 207.

Alderley. Croston. Hist. sites Lanc. 50.

Alderney, Isle of. Timbs. Abbeys, 1 : 539.

Alderson, Baron. Grant, J. Bench and bar, 1 : 249.

Aldhelm, St., an Anglo-Saxon saint. Furst, C. Group old auth. 131.

Aldrich, Peleg Emory. Am. Antiq. Soc. Proc. n. s. **9** : 470. **10** : 22. — Am. Bar Assoc. **18** : 508.

Aldrich, Thomas Bailey, with portrait. Warner Lib. 1 : 312. — Bolton, S. K. Amer. au. 286. Derby, J. C. Fifty years, 227. — Nichol. Amer. lit. 388. — Richardson. Amer. lit. **2** : 265. — Rideing, W. H. Boyhood of liv. au. 16. — Stewart, Geo. jr. Evenings in lib. 224. — Stoddard, R. H. Poets' homes, 266. — Vedder, H. C. Amer. writers, 104.
— at home. (W. H. Bishop) Gilder. Authors, 1.
— Flower and thorn. Taylor, B. Crit. ess. 302.
— Sonnets of. Deshler. Afternoons, 303.

Aldringer, John. Cust. Warr. 30 years, **2** : 550.

Aldrovandi, Ulysses. Jardine, W. Nat. library, **17** : 17. — Macgillivray, W. Em. zoöl.

Aldus Manutius. See Manuzio.

Aleander, Jerome. Symonds. Reviv. of learn. 423.

Aleardi, A. Howells. Mod. It. poets, 333.

Alembert, Jean le Rond d'. Brougham. Wks. 1 : 383. — Edgar. Boyhood, 205. — With portraits. Warner Lib. 1 : 354. — Haussonville. Salon of Necker, 1 : 163.

Aleppo. Taylor, B. Lands of Sar. 196.

"Alert," ship, Capture of. Dawson. Batt. of U. S. **2** : 102.

Alesso, Galeazzo. Milizia. Lives arch. 1 : 1.

Aleutian Islands, Explorations in. (W. H. Dall) Am. Geog. Soc. **5** : 243.

Aleutians. Reclus. Prim. folk, 48.

Alexander VI. [Roderigo Borgia], pope. Symonds. Age of despots, 407. — Coffin, C. C. Story of liberty, 159. — Pastor, L. Hist. popes, **5** : 373. **6** : 1.

Alexander VII., Pope. Ranke. Popes, **3** : 51.

Alexander the Great. Freeman. Hist. ess. **2** :

161. — Herbert, H. W. Capt. old world. — Lord, J. Anc. states, 373. — Sterling, J. Ess. 1 : 3. — Bruce, J. Classic portr. 56. — Farmer, L. H. Boys bk. fam. rul. 71. — Ranke. Univ. hist. 1 : 393. — Schlegel. Lec. mod. hist. 311. — Yonge. Bk. worthies. 154. — Huxley. Ess. contro. 155. — Johnson, S. Ori. relig. Persia, 357. — (George Grote) Ferris, G. T. Great leaders, 14. — Gurney, J. H. Hist. sketches, 3 : 6. — Hundred greatest men, 379. — Mahaffy, J. P. Greek life, ch. 2. — Mombert. Great lives, 51. — Yonge, C. M. Book of worthies, 154.

Alexander the Great as a general. Dodge, T. A. Great capt. 1.

— March of, through Gedrosia. Davenport. Narr. peril, 2 : 325.

Alexander I. of Russia. Maccall. For. biog. 2 : 126. — Holland, H. R. For. reminis. 113. — Metternich. Mem.

Alexander II. of Russia, with portr. Crowned heads, 23. — Proctor, E. D. Russ. jour. 313. — Towle, G. M. Certain men, 213. — Em. persons, 2 : 267. — Curtis, W. E. Land of nihilist, 74. — Duyckinck. Portr. gall. 2 : 466.

Alexander III. of Russia. Em. persons, 6 : 144. — With portr. Ann. cyclop. 1880.

— Family life of. Curtis, W. E. Land of nihilist, 204.

Alexander III. of Scotland. Tytler. Scott. worth. v. 1.

Alexander, Prince, of Bulgaria. Em. persons, 6 : 68.

Alexander the Eagle. Brooks, E. S. Gr. men's sons, 17.

Alexander Lycurgus, Greek archbishop. Wordsworth, C. Misc. 1 : 284.

Alexander, martyr of Lyons. Yonge, C. M. Pupils of John, 227.

Alexander of Abonotichus, Cagliostro of 2d cent. Froude. Short stud. 4 : 282.

Alexander of Hales. Townsend, W. J. Schoolmen, 177.

Alexander of Jerusalem. Evans, R. W. Biog. early ch. 1 : 368.

Alexander, Families of. Rogers, C. Mem. Stirling, 1 : 2.

Alexander, Alexander, earl of Stirling, trial for forgery. Townsend, W. C. Mod. state trials, 412.

Alexander, Archibald. Waterbury. Eloq. preach. 14.

Alexander, Cecil Frances (Humphreys). Miles, A. H. Poets of cent. 10 : 433. — Miller, Jos. Singers church, 2d ed. 562. — Hatfield, E. F. Poets of church, 9.

Alexander, James Waddel. Hatfield, E. F. Poets of church, 10.

Alexander, Sir William. (T. H. Ward) Ward. Eng. poets, 2 : 37.

— and the Scottish attempt to colonize Acadia. (G. Patterson) Roy. Soc. Can. 10 : sec. ii.

Alexander, William, Lord. Rogers, C. Mem. Stirling, 1 : 205. — Lossing. Em. Amer. 106.

Alexander, William, of Phila. Miles, A. H. Poets of cent. 10 : 455.

Alexander, William Lindsay. Hatfield, E. F. Poets of church, 13. — Miller, Jos. Singers church, 2d ed. 495.

Alexandria. Moore, Jos. Outl. Eur. 39. — Poole, R. S. Cities of Egypt, 178. — Wright, W. B. Anc. cit. 75. — Stanley. Jewish ch. v. 3. — Buckley, J. M. Trav. 3 cont. 207. — Caldwell, S. L. Cities of faith, 51. — Mahaffy, J. P. Greek life, ch. 9, 10.

Alexandria and Chalcedon. Bright, W. Roman see, 254.

— Bombardment of, 1882. Richards, W. Heroes, 27. — Valentine, L. J. Sea-fights, 283.

— Library of. Delepierre. Hist. diff. 31. — Edwards, E. Mem. of libr.

— Schools of. Moxom. Jerus. to Nicæa, 333. — Kingsley, C. Hist. lec. 3; or Raleigh, 317. — Lewes. Biog. phil. — Martineau, J. Ess. 2 : 293. — Alviella. Contemp. evol. 321.

— Sieges of. Robson, W. Sieges, 262.

Alexis. Mills. Poets of Greece, 394.

Alexis, Grand Duke of Russia, in New York. Ames, M. C. Outlines, 56.

Alexis, Guillaume. Besant. Fr. poetry, 157.

Alfieri, Vittorio. Howells. Mod. Ital. poets, 51. — Montgomery. Men of Italy, 2 : 247. — Tuckerman, Poets, 111. — Ossoli, M. F. Life without, 93. — Longfellow. Poets Eur. — Sismondi. Lit. So. Eur. — With portrait. (L. O. Kuhns) Warner Lib. 1 : 371. — Shelley, Mrs. Lit. men Italy, v. 2. — Stebbing. Ital. poets, v. 3. — Trollope. Ital. poets, 2 : 199. — Vincent, G. E. Ital. authors, 92.

— and the Countess of Albany. Hayward, A. Ess. 2d ser. 2 : 189. See Albany.

— Lester's Autobiography of. Headley, J. T. Miscel. 81.

— Memoirs. Jeffrey, T. Contrib. Ed. Rev. — Symonds. Sk. So. Eur. 2 : 174.

— Tragic poet. Elliot, F. Rom. gossip, 242.

Alfleda, Queen of Peada. Hall. Queens bef. Conq. 261.

Alfonso II. of Ferrara. Ranke. Popes, 2 : 265.

Alfonso I. of Naples, Sicily, and Aragon, the magnanimous. Symonds. Reviv. of learn. 252.

Alfonso I. of Portugal. Parton. Peop. bk. biog. 277.

Alfonso VI. of Portugal. Doran. Monarchs, 1 : 354.

Alfonso X. of Spain, 1252-84, Works of. Montgomery. Men of Ita. 3 : 11. — Ticknor. Span. Lit. 1 : 35. — Warner Lib. 1 : 383.

Alfonso XI. of Spain, 1312-50, Works of. Ticknor. Span. lit. 1 : 76.

Alfonso XII. of Spain, with portrait. Crowned heads, 43.

Alfonsus, Petrus. Disciplina clericalis. Powell, G. H. Excurs. in Libr. 100.

Alford, Henry, with portrait. Hare, A. J. C. Biog. sk. 95. — Japp. Noble workers, 237. — Comegys. Tour, 53. — Miles, A. H. Poets of cent. 10 : 237. — Miller, Jos. Singers church, 2d ed. 508.

— Sonnets of. Deshler. Afternoons, 305.

Alford, Lady Marian Margaret (Compton). Clayton, E. C. Eng. fem. art. 2 : 343.

Alfred the Great. Adams, W. H. D. Worthies, 1. — Collier, W. F. Hist. Eng. lit. 21. — Craik. Pursuit knowl. 2 : 11. — Dunham. Lit. & sci. men, 1 : 60. — Lord, J. Beacon, 2 : 95. — Smith, Gold. Lec. & ess. 267. — Brooks, E. S. Chivalric days, 98. — Farmer, L. H. Boys' bk. fam. rul. 169. — Gilliat, E. Champions, 18. — Tweedie, W. K. Lives earn. men, 225. — Dunham, S. A. Em. liter. men, 1 : 60. — Grube, A. W. Heroes, 162. — (David Hume) Ferris, G. T. Gr. leaders, 107. — Hunt, T. W. Rep. Eng. prose, 16. — Mombert. Great lives, 147. — Hundred greatest men, 398. — Warner Lib. 1 : 389.

— Asser's Life of. Wright, T. Ess. archæol. 1 : 172.

Amazon River, Report of hydrographic commission on. Geog. Soc. **7** : 357.
— Upper. (C. DeKalb) Am. Geog. Soc. **22** : 471. **23** : 1.
Amazon valley, Physical history of. Agassiz. Geol. sk. **2** : 152.
— Resources and trade opportunities of, 1899. U. S. Cons. Rept. **61** : 29.
"**Amazon**," Burning of. Senior, W. Shipwrecks, 126.
Amazons, Eighteenth century. Ashton. 18th cent. waifs, 177.
Amber. Hartwig, G. Subter. 449. — Simmonds, P. L. Comm. prod. 463. — Curtis, W. E. Land of nihilist, 11.
Ambidextry. See Right hand.
Ambition. Bacon. Ess. — Friswell. Gentle life, **1** : 261. — Stevenson, R. L. Virgin. 172.
Amboise, Georges d', Cardinal. Crowe, E. E. For. statesmen, **1** : 1.
Amboise, Chateau of. Larned, W. C. Churches & C. 181.
— Conspiracy of. Cook, T. D. Old Touraine, **2** : 65.
— Early history of. Cook, T. D. Old Touraine, **2** : 36.
Amboyna, Massacre of. Ewald. Stories fr. st. pap. **2** : 73.
Ambrose, St., bishop of Milan. Brigham, C. H. Mem. 59. — Charles. Martyrs, 236. — Farrar. Lives of Fathers, **2** : 84. — Lord, J. Beacon, **1** : 315. — Merivale, C. Four lec. **1**. — (A. Barry) Lefroy, W. Lec. eccl. hist. 375. — With portrait. Blakey, R. Prim. fathers 204. — Broadus. Lec. hist. preach. 79. — Caldwell, S. L. Cities of faith, 129. — Cave. Lives of fathers, **3** : 118. — Hatfield, E. F. Poets of ch. 19. — Ker, J. Lec. hist. preach. 101. — Merivale, C. Four lec. — Miller, Jos. Singers church, 2d ed. 3. — Wilson, Wm. Pop. preach. anc. ch. 51.
— and the empire. Bright, W. Roman see, 214.
— and the music of the early church. Butterworth. Great compos. 27.
— View of Christianity. Newman, J. H. Hist. sk. **1** : 339.
Ambrose, Eleanor, "the dangerous papist." Gerard. Irish beauties, 14.
Ambrosian Church music. Winkworth. Chr. singers Germ. 7.
Ambrosian library (Milan). Child, T. Summ. holidays, 145.
Ambrosian liturgy. Neale. Ess. liturgy.
Ambrosius, Johanna. Warner Lib. **1** : 446.
Ambulance organization in war and peace. Internat. Health Exhib. Sanita.
— of metropolis in epidemic. Internat. Health Exhib. Sanita.
Ambulance system of N. Y. city. Cong. Char. Chic. '93, **5** : 689.
Amelia, Princess, daughter of George II. Doran. Queens Hanov. 2.
Amelia, Princess, daughter of George III. Fitzgerald, P. Royal dukes, **1** : 219.
Amelia Sophia Eleanora of Hanover. Hall, Mrs. M. Princesses, 80.
America, Aboriginal religions of. Bettany. World's relig. 61.
— Advent of man in. (A. de Quatrefages) Smithson. Rept. **1892** : 513.
— Ancient cities of. (F. A. Ober) Am. Geog. Soc. **20** : 39.
— Ancient, Religions of. (J. M. Robertson) Relig. systems, 354.
— Ancient literature of. (J. Campbell) Roy. Soc. Can. 2d ser. **22** : 41.

America and England as subjects of caricature. Everitt, G. Eng. carica. 42.
— Books relating to, in Register of London Company. Am. Hist. Assoc. Rept. **1896** : 1.
— Civilized, Grattan's. Bristed. Pieces, **4** : 88.
— Destiny of. Seward. Works (1884), **4** : 121.
— Discoveries before 1620. Belknap. Amer. biog. **1** : 59.
— Discovery of. Everett. Orat. v. 3.
— — by the Northmen. See Northmen.
— — First. Kingsley, C. Lec. Amer. 65.
— — Pre - Columbian. Chambers's Papers, no. 42.
— — Spanish. (C. F. Adams) Mass. Hist. Soc. Proc. 2d ser. **8** : 24.
— English language in. (C. A. Bristed) Camb. ess. **1855** : 57.
— English writers on. Irving. Sk. book, 41.
— Farewell thoughts on. Farrar. Sermons in Am. 328.
— First Legislative Assembly in. (W. W. Henry) Am. Hist. Assoc. Rept. **1893** : 299.
— for Americans. Godwin, P. Pol. ess. 175.
— Future of. Appleton, T. G. Sheaf of pap. 261.
— History : Four American centuries. Wendell, B. Stelligeri, 21.
— in European literature. Boyesen. Lit. silhouettes, 117.
— Information for settlers in, 1782. Franklin. Works ('87), **8** : 172.
— Internal state of, 1784. Franklin. Works ('87), **9** : 34.
— Is it the best of all possible worlds ? George, H. Soc. prob. 86.
— Languages of northern, western, and central. Latham. Opuscula, 326.
— Mission of. Brownson. Works, **11** : 551.
— Name, Origin of. (T. H. Lambert) Am. Geog. Soc. **15** : 45. — (G. H. Hurlbut) Am. Geog. Soc. **18** : 301. **20** : 183.
— Northwest. (I. Stevens) Am. Geog. Soc. **1** : 3.
— of an American, The. Tartt. Ess. 306.
— the old world. Agassiz. Geol. sk. **1** : 1.
— Prophetic voices concerning. Sumner. Works, **12** : 1.
— Relation of Christianity to. (T. O'Gorman) Barrows, J. H. Parl. relig. **2** : 1152.
— Sketches of travel in. Forbes, E. Lit. papers, 198.
— Thoughts on the progress of. Parker, T. Add. speeches, **2** : 1.
— Travels in. Carlisle, Earl. Lec. 32.
— True glory of. (J. L. Petigru) Charleston book, 89.
— What Christianity has wrought for. (D. J. Burrell) Barrows, J. H. Parl. relig. **2** : 1157.
— What she owes to the Old World. (A. E. Palmer) Factors Amer. civiliz. 55.
American, Evolution of an. Higginson. New world, 221.
— The young. Emerson. Nature, 341.
American agriculture. Winthrop. Addresses, **2** : 54.
American anthropology, Present position of. (J. Campbell) Roy. Soc. Can. 2d ser. **1**, § **2** : 67.
American apples for Belgium. (H. C. Morris) U. S. Cons. Rept. **56** : 431.
American Assoc. of Public Health, Importance of. (M. de Anaya) Am. Pub. Health, **18** : 193.
American authorship. Jones, W. A. Ess. on authors, 22.
— in 1853. Godwin, P. Out of past, 176.
American bar, The, an element of conservatism. Choate. Addr. 153.
American belles. Badeau. Vagabond, 247.

American-Brazilian trade, 1891. (O. H. Dockery) U. S. Cons. Rept. **36** : 600.

American character, Peculiar traits of. Woodbury, L. Writ. **3** : 191.

American characteristics. Temple, R. Cosmop. ess. 439.

— Misrepresentation of. Hatton, J. To-day in Amer. **1** : 24.

American civilization, 1862. Emerson, R. W. Miscell. (1883) : 277.

— contrasted with European. Lowell. Writ. **2** : 274.

— Epochs of. Gammel. Writ. 243.

— Foreign estimates of. Lowell. Writ. **3** : 220.

— Natural factors in. (J. C. Kimball) Factors Amer. civiliz. 23.

American colonial charters. Lucas. Secularia, 250.

American colonies, Comm. policy of Eng. toward. (G. L. Beer) Colum. Univ. Stud. Hist. **3** : no. 2.

— Constitut. relation of, to Eng. gov't. (M. Chamberlain) Am. Hist. Assoc. **3** : 52.

— Foundation of. Smith, Gold. Lec. mod. hist.

— Hist. of elections in. (C. F. Bishop) Colum. Univ. Stud. Hist. **3** : no. 1.

— Naturalization in. (C. Start) Am. Hist. Assoc. Rept. '93 : 317.

— Population in, Estimates of. (F. B. Dexter) Am. Antiq. Soc. Proc. n. s. **5** : 22.

American competition in Europe. (F. H. Mason) 1897. U. S. Cons. Rept. **56** : 164.

American dialect, English sources of. (T. W. Higginson) Am. Antiq. Soc. Proc. n. s. **4** : 159.

American English. Burton, R. Liter. likings, 341.

American ethnography, Contributions to. Latham. Opuscula, 275.

American girl, The. Wallace, S. E. Storied sea, 158.

— in England. Smalley. Lond. lett. **2** : 101.

American history. Reed, W. B. Among books, 238.

— The course of. Wilson, Woodrow. Mere lit. 213.

— education in, Demand for. (J. Jay) Am. Hist. Assoc. **5** : 19.

— English methods of teaching. U. S. Bur. Ed. Rept. '94–95, **2** : 1757.

— Manuscript sources of. (J. Winsor) Am. Hist. Assoc. **3** : 9.

— on the stage. Scudder, H. E. Men & let. **115**.

American humor, Perils of. Higginson. New world, 128.

American imprints, Early. (S. A. Green) Mass. Hist. Soc. Proc. 2d ser. **12** : 273, 380. — (N. Paine) Am. Antiq. Soc. Proc. n. s. **10** : 281.

American independence, True basis of. Seward. Works (1884), **4** : 144.

American institutions, origin of, Written ballot and. (D. Campbell) Am. Hist. Assoc. **5** : 165.

— Vindication of. Everett. Orat. v. **4**.

American Journal of Education, of Dr. Barnard. Nat. Educa. Assoc. **1893** : 822.

American judiciary. (S. F. Miller) Baines, W. H. Sup. court, 3.

American lady, Ideal. Matthews, A. Rumina.

American life and manners. Holland, J. G. Every-day, **1** : 337.

— Dangerous tendencies in. Harrison, J. Dang. tend. 1.

— Pleasantness of. Bryce. Soc. institu. 222.

— Uniformity of. Bryce. Soc. institu. 232.

American literature. Ames, F. Works, 458. — Brownson. Works, **19** : 1, 203. — Griswold. Prose writ. 13. — Lowell, Writ. **6** : 222. — Döl-

linger, Addr. 269. — (C. D. Warner) Shaler. The U. S. **2** : 395. — Matthews, B. Aspects fic. 3. — (B. Matthews) Nat. Educa. Assoc. **1896** : 95. — Wendell, B. Stelligeri, 91.

American literature. Bibliography. Pancoast, H. S. Introd. Amer. lit.

— Conditions of. Lowell. Writ. **2** : 148.

— Development of. Gilman, S. Contrib. 120.

— early, Notes on. (J. F. Hunnewell) Am. Antiq. Soc. Proc. n. s. **11** : 71.

— Founders of. Parton. Triumphs, 279.

— Ideals in. Burton, R. Liter. likings, 131.

— in 1845. Collins, Stephen. Miscel.

— in England. Coan. Stud. lit. 1.

— in England. Warner, C. D. Rela. of lit. 243.

— New fields for. Garland. Crumbling idols. 21.

— The new world and the new book. Higginson. New world, 1.

— Position and prospects of. Ossoli. Art, 298.

— Progress of. Everett. Orat. v. 1.

— Social ideals in, 1840–80. Scudder, V. D. Soc. ideals, 198.

American man, The. Warner, C. D. As we go, 36.

American mind. Whipple. Charac.

American mines and Salt Lake City, 1887. Bates. Year in Gt. Rep. **2** : 196.

American ministers abroad. Ess. from Nation, 69.

American mode of life, Common. Eliot, C. W Five Am. contrib. 103.

American nationality. Choate. Addr. 480.

American orators and statesmen. Hayward, A. Ess. **2** : 34.

American party. Brownson. Works, **10** : 17. *See also* Know-Nothings.

American people, Development of. Seward. Works ('84), **4** : 160. — (W. B. Weeden) Am. Antiq. Soc. Proc. n. s. **13** : 19.

— Physical state of. (D. A. Sargent) Shaler. The U. S. **2** : 452.

American-Peruvian trade. (A. J. Daugherty) 1892. U. S. Cons. Rept. **41** : 109.

American playwrights. Badeau. Vagabond, 128.

American poetry. Has America produced a poet? Gosse, E. Questions, 69.

American political philosophy. Dunning, W. A. Ess. on civ. war, 353.

American politics. Nichol. Amer. lit. 97.

American principles. Whipple. Outlooks, 127.

American products in Italy, 1891. (A. O. Bourn) U. S. Cons. Rept. **36** : 129.

American progress. McMasters. With fathers, 313.

American prose writers, Griswold's. Headley, J. T. Miscel. 284.

American Public Health Association and the science of hygiene. (M. de Anaya) Am. Pub. Health, **18** : 193.

— History of. (S. Smith) Am. Pub. Health, **5** : vii.

American republics and colonies, Foreign commerce of, 1891. Bur. Am. Repub. no. 6.

American reputations in England. Ess. from Nation, 127.

American Revolution. Cairnes. Pol. ess. 59. — Clinton, H. R. Crécy to Assye, 570. — Daly, J. B. Radicals, 154.

— and American progress. Everett. Orat. v. **2**.

— and Quebec Act. (V. Coffin) Am. Hist. Assoc. Rept. '94 : 273.

— and the seven years' war. Everett. Orat. v. 1.

— Augmentation of wages in Europe by. Franklin. Works ('87), **10** : 46.

— British cruelties during. Franklin. Works ('87), **10** : 73.

American Revolution, British parliament and. Burke. Works (Bohn), **5** : 454.
— Carolina loyalist in. Chesney. Ess. mil. biog. 323.
— Causes of. Burke. Works (Bohn), **1** : 306, 450, **2** : 1.
— First battles of. Everett. Orat. v. 1.
— Historical journal of the American war. Mass. Hist. Coll. 1st ser. **2** : 41.
— Influence of, on Eng.'s government of her colonies. (G. B. Alden) Am. Hist. Assoc. Rept. '96, **1** : 373.
— Journal of Ebenezer Wild. Mass. Hist. Proc. 2d ser. **6** : 78.
— Naval history of. (E. E. Hale) Am. Antiq. Soc. Proc. n. s. **5** : 379.
— New England in. Adams, C. F. Three episodes, **2** : 838.
— Negotiations for reconciliation, 1775. Franklin. Works ('87), **5** : 440.
— Northern campaigns of. Reynolds, G. Papers, 54.
— Peace negotiations, 1782. Franklin. Works ('87), **8** : 1. — (J. Jay) Am. Hist. Assoc. **3** : 79.
— Privateering during. (A. B. Ellis) Mass. Hist. Proc. 2d ser. **1** : 15.
— Rise, progress, and consequence of. Webster, N. Ess. 154.
American scholar, The. Emerson. Nature, 81.
— Duty of, to politics and the times. Curtis, G. W. Orations, **1** : 1.
American sculpture. Badeau. Vagabond, 221.
American ship-building and foreign commerce. Greeley. Ess. pol. econ. 214.
American shipping, History of. (J. R. Soley) Shaler. The U. S. **1** · 518.
American society. Forbes, A. Souvenirs, 225.
— as a field for fiction. Bryant. Prose, **2** : 351.
— The individual in. (L. Abbott) Shaler. The U. S. **2** : 579.
American statesmen, Works of. Godwin, P. Out of past, 221.
American temperament, An. Higginson. New world, 19.
American Tract Society and slavery. Lowell. Pol. ess. 1 ; *or* Lowell. Writ. **5** : 1.
American trade negotiations before 1789. (W. C. Fisher) Am. Hist. Assoc. **3** : 467.
American traits. Hatton, J. To-day in Amer. **1** : 39.
American women. Wilde, Lady. Soc. stud. 123.
Americana, Illustrated. (J. F. Hunnewell) Am. Antiq. Soc. Proc. n. s. **6** : 283. **7** : 371.
Americans and Americans. Pidgeon. Old World Ques. 1.
— at home. Wraxall. Scraps, **2** : 34.
-- at home and abroad. Rousiers. Amer. life, 289.
— English press on. Bristed. Pieces, **3** : 37.
— Great, A calendar of. Wilson, Woodrow. Mere lit. 187.
— in England. Phillips, S. Ess. from Times, **2** : 149.
— living abroad, causes of. Bristed. Pieces, **4** : 72.
Americanism in fiction. Hawthorne, J. Confess. 71.
— in literature. Higginson. Atlan. Ess. 49.
— True. Roosevelt, T. Amer. ideals, 15. — Schurz, C. Speeches, 51.
Americanisms. (C. A. Bristed) Camb. ess. **1855** : 57. — Burton, R. Lit. likings, 341.
— and Briticisms. Birrell. Men, women & books, 200.
— Legitimate and illegitimate. Mathews. Lit. style, 320.
— Shakespeare's. Lodge, H. C. Cert. heroes, 95. *See also* Eng. lang. in America.

Amerriques, Amerigho Vespucci, and America. (Jules Marcou) Smithson. Rept. **1888** : 647.
Ames, Ellis. Am. Antiq. Soc. Proc. n. s. **3** : 482.
Ames, Fisher. Griswold. Prose writ. 96. — Harsha. Orators, 338. — Loring, J. S. 100 Bost. ora. 291. — Magoon. Orators of rev. 311. — With portrait, Am. Nat. portr. gall. v. **3**. — With portrait, Duyckinck, Nat. portr. gall. **1** : 204. — Johnston, A. Amer. ora. **1** : 112. — Lossing, Em. Amer. 71. — Moore, F. Am. eloq. **1** : 91.
— Home of. (J. B. Thayer) Homes Am. Statesm. 277.
— Works of. Brownson. Wks. **16** : 379. — Lunt. Three eras, 215.
Ames, Fred. Lothrop, with portrait. (L. Saltonstall) Col. Soc. Mass. Trans. **1** : 258.
Ames, Mary Clemmer, with portrait. (L. Whiting) Our fam. wom. 250.
Ames, William, with portrait. Bartlett, J. R. R. I. officers, 241.
Amherst College. (T. P. Field) U. S. Bur. Ed. Circ. '91, no. **6** : 250.
Amiableness superior to intellect. Hunt, L. Seer, **2** : 134.
Amicis, Edmondo de. Warner Lib. **1** : 453.
Amicus redivivus. Lamb. Elia.
Amiel, Henri Frédéric. (R. Burton) Warner Lib. **1** : 479. — Arnold, M. Ess. **2** : 300.
— and Clough. Hutton, R. H. Criticisms, **2** : 204.
Amiens, Cathedral of. Larned, W. C. Churches & C. 5. — Pater. Miscel. stud. 91.
— Peace of. Coleridge. Friend, 238.
Amish meeting, An. Gibbons, P. E. Penn. Dutch.
Ammanati, Bartolommeo. Symonds. Renais. Fine arts, 173. — Perkins, C. C. Tusc. sculp. **2** : 156.
Ammon, Abbot of Nitria. Hahn-Hahn. Fathers, 165.
Ammon, Moab and, Cities of. Gillett, E. H. Anc. cities, 166.
Ammon Rabbath, Ruins of. Tweedie. Ruined cities, 92.
Ammonia, Carbonate and sulphate of, Decomposition of. Davy. Wks. **2** : 123.
Among the high Alps. Skelton, J. Ess. in romance, 325.
Amory, John, "John Buncle." Hazlitt. Round table, v. 2.
Amory, Thos. Bailey, J. B. Methuselahs, 176.
— Life of John Buncle. Gosse, E. Gossip, 213.
Amory, Thomas C. (A. T. Perkins) Mass. Hist. Proc. 2d ser. **5** : 341. — Am. Antiq. Soc. Proc. n. s. **6** : 104.
Amory, William. (O. W. Holmes) Mass. Hist. Proc. 2d ser. **4** : 414. — With portrait. Sketches N. H. men, 151.
Amoy. Cumming, C. F. G. Wand. in China, **1** : 116.
— Trade of, with the U. S., 1893. U. S. Cons. Rept. no. 154.
Ampère, André Marie. James, H. French poets, 321. — Munro, J. Pioneers elec. 161.
Ampère, Jean Jacques. Hamerton. Mod. French, 234. — James H. French poets, 321.
Ampersand. Van Dyke, H. Little rivers, 59.
Amphilochus, Bishop of Iconium. Blakey, R. Prim. fathers, 245. — Cave. Lives of fathers, **3** : 423.
Amphlett, Sir Richard. Gener. of judges, 128.
Ampoule, Sainte, Knights of the. Doran. Knights, 194.
Amsterdam. Bellows. Old world, **1** : 66. — Guild. Abroad again, 444. — Warner, C. D.

Saunterings, 30. — Amicis. Holland, 244. — Brooks, E. S. Gt. cities, 89.

Amsterdam, Trade and industries of. (T. M. Schleier) 1892. U. S. Cons. Rept. **40**: 314.

Amulets. Jones, W. Credulities, 152.

Amusement as educational means. Clarke, J. F. Self-culture, 381.

Amusements. Dodge, M. A. Stumbl. 260. — Hamerton. Humorist, 383. — Holland, J. G. Every-day, **1** : 241. — Munger. On threshold, 183. — Beecher, H. W. Lec. y. men, 215. — Bushnell, H. Sermons on liv. subj. 374. — Gladden, W. Appl. Christianity, 248. — Jevons, W. S. Meth. of soc. ref. 1.

— and accomplishments, 18th cent. Earle. Colon. dames, 206.

— Christian theory of. Phelps, A. Portfolio, 74.

— Christianity and. Gladden. Appl. Christ'y, 248.

— good, Goodness of. Henry, C. S. Satan, 160.

— How shall we be amused? Stowe, H. B. Chimney, 187.

— Morality of. Woolson. Browsing, 54.

— of my youth. Yates, E. Recollec. **1** : 127.

— of the people. Jevons. Meth. soc. ref.

— Popular. Donne, W. B. Ess. on drama, 207.

— Puritan theory of. Phelps, A. Portfolio, 66.

Anabaptist preachers. Broadus. Lec. hist. preach. 129.

Anabaptists, Early. Wallace, R. Anti-Trin. biog. **3** : 542.

Anacharsis, the Scythian. Fénélon. Philosophers, 107.

Anachronism, Artistic: Apollo, the fiddler. Paget, V. Juvenilia, **1** : 165.

Anacreon. Arnold, E. Poets of Greece, 119. — Hunt, L. Seer, **1** : 108. — Mills. Poets of Greece, 115. — Symonds. Greek poets, **1** : 317. — With portrait. Warner Lib. **1** : 492.

Anæsthesia, Partial. (W. Ramsay) Soc. Psych. Res. **9** : 236.

Anæsthetics, Sir J. Simpson and. Bettany. Em. doctors, **2** : 83.

Anagni. Doellinger, Addr. 181.

Anagrams. Jones, W. Credulities, 251.

— and echo verses. Disraeli, I. Curios. (N. Y. 4 v.) **2** : 415.

Anaheim, California. Nordhoff. Commun. 361.

Analogies, Physical and moral. Blackie. Ess. 60.

Anandibai, Joshee. Chapman, E. F. Sk. Ind. Wom. 48.

Ananias. Baldwin, G. C. Rep. men, 189.

Ananias, Greek poet. Arnold, E. Poets of Greece, 97.

Anarchism. (E. de Laveleye) Coan, T. M. Soc. prob. 198.

Anatolia, Byzantine. Palgrave. Ulysses, 1.

Anatolius. Miller, Jos. Singers church, 2d ed. 9.

Anatomy. Talk concerning the human body. Holmes, O. W. Pages from old vol. 186.

Anatomy bill, 1832. Macaulay. Misc. & spee. 528.

Anaxagoras, the Ionian. Diog. Laertius. Lives, 59. — Fénélon. Philosophers, 130. — Mills. Poets of Greece, 419. — Fairbanks, A. Philos. of Greece, 253.

Anaxandrides. Mills. Poets of Greece, 382.

Anaximander of Miletus. Lewes. Biog. phil. — Osborn. From Greeks, 33. — Mills. Poets of Greece, 416.

Anaximandros. Fairbanks, A. Philos. of Greece, 10.

Anaximenes. Fairbanks, A. Philos. of Greece, 20. — Lewes. Biog. phil. — Mills. Poets of Greece, 417.

Ancæus. Thirlwall, C. Remains, **3** : 106.

Ancestor worship. Maine. Early law, 52.

Ancestors, A man introduced to his. Hunt, L. Men, wom. & books, 54.

— who come after us. Higginson. Conc. all, 15.

Anchieta, Joseph de. Carne, J. Em. mission. **3** : 401.

Anchor stones. (B. F. Snyder) Smithson. Rept. 1887 : 683.

Anchorites, The. Cutts, E. L. Scenes mid. ages, 132. — Hahn-Hahn. Fathers, 52. — Kingsley. Hermits, 329.

Ancient civilization. *See* Civilization.

Ancona, Eligio. Am. Antiq. Soc. Proc. n. s. **9** : 31.

Ancona. Hare. Cities of No. Italy, **2** : 391.

Ancre, Maréchal d'. Wright, T. Nar. Sorcery, **2** : 43.

And, Greek and Latin words for, all of one origin. Key, T. H. Philol. ess. 149.

Andarro. Taylor, B. Byways, 261.

Andersen, H. C. Boyesen. Scand. lit. 155. — With portrait. Brandes. Em. auth. 61. — Seymour, C. C. B. Self-made, 84. — Taylor, B. At home, **2** : 426. — Gosse, E. Stud. lit. No. Eur. 173. — Whittier, J. G. Child-life prose, 253. — With portrait. (B. W. Wells) Warner Lib. **1** : 500.

Anderson, Alexander. Wilson, J. G. Poets of Scot. **2** : 501.

Anderson, Florence. Raymond, I. Southland wr. **1** : 168.

Anderson, G. D. Miller, S. F. Bench of Ga. v. 1.

Anderson, Sir H. Laurier, W. F. B. Dist. Anglo-Ind. **1** : 183.

Anderson, James. Francis, S. W. N. Y. phys. 89.

Anderson, Joseph Gowdy. Am. Bar Assoc. **12** : 351.

Anderson, Martin Brewer. Am. Antiq. Soc. Proc. n. s. **7** : 7.

Anderson, Mary. (J. D. Barry) McKay, F. E. Fam. actors, 51. — Matthews, B. Actors, **5** : 1. — Winter. Shadows, **1** : 90.

— as Juliet. Winter. Shadows, **3** : 252.

— as Rosalind. Winter. Shadows, **3** : 289.

Anderson, Mrs. Ellet. Pioneer wom. 373.

Anderson, Richard Clough. Lossing. Em. Amer. 299.

Anderson, Gen. Robert. Keyes, E. D. Fifty years, 367.

Anderson, Mrs. Sophie. Clayton, E. C. Eng. fem. art. **2** : 7.

Anderson, William, 1805-66. Gilfillan. Mod. lit. 292. — Wilson, J. G. Poets of Scot. **2** : 269. — Taylor, W. M. Scott. pulpit, 248.

Andersonville prison. Abbott, A. O. Prison-life, 192. — Andrews, S. South since war, 301.

Anderton, William. Macaulay. Biog. sk. 304.

Andocides. Mills. Poets of Greece, 442. — Chambers's Repos. no. 15.

Andover House in Boston. (W. J. Tucker) Woods, R. A. Poor, 177.

Andover Theological Seminary, Andover, Mass. (C. F. P. Bancroft) U. S. Bur. Ed. Circ. '91, no. 6 : 236.

Andover Theology. Richardson. Amer. lit. **1** : 305.

Andrássy, Count Julius. Wyatt, W. J. Hunga. celeb. 144.

André, Bernard. Morley, H. Eng. writ. **7** : 58.

André, John, Case of. Stanhope, Earl. Miscel. **2** : 11. — Chandler, P. W. Am. crim. trials, **2** : 155. — Grant, Jas. Constable of Fr. 69.

André, John. Bibliography. Abbott, W. Crisis. of Revol.

Andrea da Barberino. Symonds. Renais. Ital. lit. 1 : 246.

Andrea, Johann Valentin. Winkworth. Chr. singers Germ. 234.

Andrée balloon expedition : Letters from the party. Smithson. Rept. 1897 : 401.

Andreini, Isabella. Trollope, T. A. Dec. Ital. wom. 2 : 205.

Andrew of Crete. Miller, Jos. Singers church, 2d ed. 13.

Andrew, Benjamin. Jones, C. C. jr. Deleg. fr. Georgia, 1.

Andrew, James O. Davidson, J. W. Writ. of South, 22.

Andrew, John A. Long, J. D. After-dinner, 190. — (P. W. Chandler) Mass. Hist. Proc. 18 : 41. — Stowe. Men of time, 325. — Whipple. Success, 306. — Clarke, J. F. Memo. sketches, 1.

Andrew, Sir William. Laurie, W. F. B. Dist. Anglo-Ind. 1 : 260.

Andrewes, Lancelot. (R. W. Church) Barry, A. Masters theol. 61. — McClure. Translators, 78. — Teale. Eng. div. 1. — Morley, H. Eng. writ. 11 : 144.

Andrews, Ebenezer T. (F. W. Andrews) N. E. Hist. Gen. Soc. Biog. 1 : 337.

Andrews, Fanny. Raymond, I. Southland wr. 1 : 512.

Andrews, Israel Ward. (John Eaton) Nat. Educa. Assoc. 1888 : 266.

Andrews, John. Redding. Misers, 2 : 134.

Andrews, Margaret. Burder. Pious wom. 116.

Andrews, Roger. McClure. Translators, 117.

Andrews, Wm. Whiting. Am. Bar Assoc. 21 : 692.

Andromeda [constellation], New star in, 1886. Proctor, R. A. Other suns, 1.

Andronicus, Livius. Dunlop, J. Rom. liter. 1 : 62.

Andros, Sir Edmund. Ferguson, H. Ess. Am. hist. 111. — Gilman. Pathfinders, 145. — Moore, J. B. Am. gov. 403.
— Administration of. Washburn. Jud. hist. Mass. 94.
— Records of. (R. N. Toppan) Am. Antiq. Soc. Proc. n. s. 13 : 237.

Anecdotes of English courts and lawyers. Jeaffreson. Lawyers, 1.

Aneurin. Parry. Camb. Plutarch, 21. — Warner Lib. 1 : 539.

"Angamos," Capture of the "Huascar" by. Rawson, E. K. 20 Nav. Batt. 2 : 569.

Angel, Wm. G. Proctor. Lawy. of N. Y. 728.

Angelico, Fra. Stearns, F. P. Midsum. Ital. art, 27. — Oliphant. Makers of F. 183. — Symonds. Renais. fine arts, 239.
— Coronation of the Virgin. (T. Gautier) Singleton, E. Great pic. 77.

Angell, George T. Bolton, S. K. Givers, 347.

Angell, Mrs. Helen Cordelia (Coleman). Clayton, E. C. Eng. fem. art. 2 : 261.

Angelo, Dominico, Reminis. of. Dobson, A. Miscell. 33.

Angels, Clothing of. Hazard, T. R. Miscel. 363.
— fallen, Existence of. Maitland, S. R. Eruvin, 124.

Angelus, Silesius. Miller, Jos. Singers church, 2d ed. 93.

Anger. Bacon. Ess.
— Laws of. Dodge. Sermons to clergy, 331.

Angers. Dempster. Ess. 39.
— Castle of. Champney, E. W. Feudal chateaux, 74.

Angers; Home of our Angevin kings. Green, J. R. Stray studies, 359.
— in 1866. Musgrave, G. Nooks of Fr. 2 : 1.

Angevin administrative system. (C. W. C. Oman) Wakeman & Hassall. Ess. introd. Eng. Const. 113.

Angkor-Vaht, Temple of, Cambodia. Vincent, F. In and out Cent. Amer.

Anglade, M. d', Trial of. Phillips, S. M. Famous cases, 57.

Anglesea ejectment case. Burke, P. Cel. trials.

Anglesey, Henry William Paget, Marquis of. Martineau, H. Biog. sk. 295. — Cole, J. W. Brit. generals, v. 1.

Anglesey, Earldom of. Burke, B. Viciss. of fam. 3 : 70.

Anglicanism, Romanism, Protestantism. Hutton. Ess. theol. 1 : 375.

Angling, Morality of. Prime, W. C. I go a-fishing, 264.
— Pleasures of. Mathews, Lit. style, 182.

Anglo-American. See English-speaking.

Anglo-Indian words and phrases. Macmillan, M. Globe-trotter, India, 77.

Anglomania and Anglophobia. Higginson. Book & heart, 116.

Anglo-Norman administrative system. (C. W. C. Oman) Wakeman & Hassall. Ess. introd. Eng. Const. 113.

Anglo-Norman Church. Williams, F. Eng. card. 1 : 58.

Anglo-Norman literature. Washburn, E. W. Stud. Eng. lit. 21.

Anglo-Saxon antiquities, Faussett collection. Wright, T. Ess. archæol. 1 : 107.

Anglo-Saxon Church. Williams, F. Eng. card. 1 : 22.

Anglo-Saxon element in English. Rogers, H. Ess. 1 : 368.

Anglo-Saxon language and poetry. Longfellow. Poets Eur. 1.
— Study of. (J. M. Garnett) Nat. Educa. Assoc. 1876 : 141.

Anglo-Saxon literature. Brooks, S. W. Eng. poets, 32. — Longfellow. Prose, 1 : 384. — Washburn, E. W. Stud. Eng. lit. 1. — (Robert Sharp) Warner Lib. 1 : 543.
— Bibliography. Brooke, S. A. Eng. lit. to Norman conq.

Anglo-Saxon race, Contribution of, to modern life. Strong, J. New era, 54.

Anglo-Saxons. Disraeli, I. Amen. (N. Y. 2 v.) 1 : 39. — Milman, H. H. Lat. Christ'y, 2 : 175.
— Americans not. Mathews. Men & bks. 298.
— Ranks and classes among. Allen, W. F. Essays, 293.

Angni. Freeman. Studies Italy, 165.

Angola, Geographic names of. (H. Chatelain) Am. Geog. Soc. 25 : 304.
— The province of. (H. Chatelaine) 1892. U. S. Cons. Rept. 40 : 566.

Angoulême, C. de V., duc de. Taylor, W. C. Rom. biog. v. 2.

Angoulême, Marie Thérèse Charlotte, duchesse d', and Duchesse de Berri. Challice. Illus. wom. 119.

Anguisciola, Sofonisba. Ellet. Women artists, 49.

Anhalt-Dessauk, House of. Baring-Gould. Germany, 12 : 461.

Anicchiarico, Ciro, the priest brigand. Macfarlane, C. Banditti, 64.

Aniline colors in Germany. (F. H. Mason) 1897. U. S. Cons. Rept. 56 : 564.

Arbitration; Treaty of 1897, U. S. and Gr. Brit. Fiske, J. Cent. of science, 166.
Arblay, Frances Burney, Madame d'. Adams, W. H. D. Wom. of fash. 2 : 1. — (M. E. Christie) Coan, J. M. Stud. biog. 89. — Cone & Gilder, Pen-portr. 1 : 45. — Crosland. Mem. women, 53. — Elwood. Lit. ladies, 2 : 33. — Forsyth. Novels, 315.—Jeaffreson. Novelists, 1 : 312. — Kavanagh. Eng. women, 1 : 79. — Macaulay. Ess. 5 : 248. — Darton. Fam. girls, 29. — Duyckinck. Portr. gall. 1 : 139. — Fifty famous women, 134. — Hamilton, C. J. Women writers, 1. Mitchell, D. G. Eng. lands, 3 : 164. — Saintsbury, G. Ess. Eng. lit. 2 : 203. Walford, L. B. Twelve Eng. auth. 21.
— at court. Knight, C. Once on a time, 2 : 97.
— Own story. (M. E. Christie) Coan. Stud. biog. 89.
Arbor day. Ohio Forestry, '87. — U. S. Bur. Educa. Circ. '85.
Arbués, San Pedro, Martyrdom of. (H. C. Lea) Am. Hist. Assoc. 3 : 435.
Arbuthnot, Alexander. Irving, D. Scot. poets, 2 : 169. — Wodrow. Selec. fr. biog. coll.
Arbuthnot, John. Jeaffreson. Doctors, 117. — With portrait. Warner Lib. 2 : 722.
Arc, Joan of. *See* Joan of Arc.
Arcadian Academy, Crescimbeni's. Howells. Mod. It. poets, 11. — Paget, V. Stud. of 18th cent. 7.
Arcesilaus. Diog. Laertius. Lives, 163. — Lewes. Biog. phil. — Mills. Poets of Greece, 430.
Arch, Joseph. Davidson, J. M. Eng. lib. 192. — Hinton. Eng. radicals, 275. — Davidson, J. M. Em. Eng. lib.
Arch of St. Dominic at Bologna. Perkins, C. C. Tusc. sculp. 1 : 18.
Arch of Titus. Spooner, E. Hist. scenes, 29.
Archæology, Bibliography of. Keary, C. F. Dawn of History, 217. — Nottingham (Eng.) Pub. Ref. Lib. Class-List, no. 19, Feb. '94.
— Classic, Study of. Cross lights, 1.
— Field work in Arizona. (J. W. Fewkes) Smithson. Rept. 1897 : 601.
— Fine art in. Parry, T. G. Min. of fine art, 51.
— Mexican: records of Mayas. Brinton. Ess. Amer. 255.
— Phonetic writing. Brinton. Ess. Amer. 213.
— Prehistoric. *See* Prehistoric Archæology.
— research in, Methods of. (Henry Howorth) Smithson. Rept. 1894 : 589.
— Ruins of old world. Dutt. Hist. stud. 2 : 409.
— Scandinavian. (Ingwald Unset) Smithson. Rept. 1889 : 571.
— Stone of the giants. Brinton. Ess. Amer. 274.
— Study of. Newton, C. T. Essays, 1.
— Writing of Mayas and Mexicans. Brinton. Ess. Amer. 195, 230.
Archbishops, English, Lambeth and. Green, J. R. Stray studies, 107.
Archelaus. Mills. Poets of Greece, 421.
Archer, W., as critic. Buchanan, R. Coming terr. 145.
Archery. Depping, G. Strength and skill, 281. — Strutt, J. Sports, 48. — Thompson, M. Boys bk. sports, 174.
— Bibliography. Longman, C. J., and Walrond, H. Archery.
Arches. Baker. Masonry construction. — Berg. Safe building.
— Ribbed. Woodward. St. Louis bridge.
Archias. Mills. Poets of Greece, 230.
Archibald, Sir Thomas D. Gener. of judges, 30.

Archilochus. Arnold, E. Poets of Greece, 83. — Mills. Poets of Greece, 79. — Symonds. Greek poets, 1 : 274.
Archimedes. Hale, E. Stor. inven. 20. — Timbs. Inventors, 15. — Hundred greatest men, 323. — Towle, G. M. Heroes of inven. 7.
Archipelago, Greek. Kinglake. Eothen, 47.
Architectural antiquities, Illustrations of some questions relating to. Wright, T. Ess. archæol. 2 : 129.
Architectural forms, Naturalistic. Kingsley, C. Lit. lec. 260.
Architectural styles. Patmore. Princ. in art, 160.
Architecture. (S. Ferguson) Afternoon lec. 2 : 27. — (M. Schuyler) Butterfield. Lec. Un. Coll. 1 : 171. — Day, H. N. Sci. æsthet. — Samson. Elem. art. crit. — Véron. Æsthetics.
— and restoration. Ruskin. Arrows, v. 1.
— Anglo-Saxon, illus. from illum. MSS. Wright, T. Ess. archæol. 1 : 186.
— Bibliography. Bost. Pub. Lib. Subj. cat. no. 10. — Hamlin, A. D. F. Textbk. hist. architec. — Longfellow, W. P. P. Cyclop. archit. in Italy, &c. — Lowell City Lib. Bull. May, '97. — Mathews, C. T. Story of architec.
— British school of. Alison. Ess. 3.
— Church. Froude, R. H. Remains, 2 : 335.
— Curiosities of. Chambers's Miscel. no. 108.
— Diocletian's place in the history of. Freeman. Hist. ess. 3 : 61.
— French, Early. Pattison. Renais. of art in France, 1.
— Gothic. Lord, J. Beacon, 2 : 402.
— — Development of. Wallace, H. B. Art, 39.
— — in Italy. Symonds. Renais. Fine arts, 50.
— — Principles of. Schlegel. Æsthet. (Bohn) 149.
— — Revival of. Oxenham. Stud. in eccl. hist. 239.
— Grecian. Foster, J. Crit. ess. (Bohn) 2 : 41.
— Health principles of. (C. Pfeiffer) Am. Pub. Health, 1 : 147.
— Ideal and material greatness in. Patmore. Princ. in art, 146.
— in 13th century. (G. E. Street) Afternoon lec. 4 : 1.
— in the U. S. (H. Van Brunt) Shaler. The U. S. 2 : 425.
— "Old English," ancient and modern. Patmore. Princ. in art, 154.
— Origin of "grots and groves." Kingsley. Health, 294.
— Relations of painting and sculpture to. (H. H. Statham *et al.*) Trans. Soc. Sci. Lond. 1881 : 789.
— Renaissance, in Italy. Symonds. Renais. Fine arts, 40.
— Ruskin's views of. Patterson, R. H. Ess. hist. 331.
— Saracenic of Spain. Disraeli, B. Home letters, 50.
— Street, Improvement of. (H. H. Statham) Trans. Soc. Sci. Lond. 1878 : 644.
Archives, Histor., of State Department. (A. H. Allen) Am. Hist. Assoc. Rept. 1894 : 281.
— Value of national. (E. H. Walworth) Am. Hist. Assoc. Rept. 1893 : 25.
Arcisseverius, Tobias. Wallace, R. Anti-Trin. biog. 3 : 314.
Arcissevius, Christopher. Wallace, R. Anti-Trin. biog. 3 : 107.
Arcissevius, Elias. Wallace, R. Anti-Trin. biog. 2 : 425. 3 : 106.
Arcissevius, John. Wallace, R. Anti-Trin. biog. 3 : 284.

Arcissevius, Samuel. Wallace, R. Anti-Trin. biog. 3 : 358.

"**Arctic**," Loss of the. Van Santvoord, C. Disc. 418.

Arctic and Antarctic regions. Bibliography. Bost. Pub. Lib. Bull. Apr. '94.

Arctic Circle, In the. Abercromby. Seas and skies, 175.

Arctic discoveries. (J. E. Davis) Manch. Sci. lec. 7 : 5.

Arctic expeditions, Nordenskiöld's. Frost, T. Mod. expl. 80.

Arctic exploration. (I. I. Hayes) Am. Geog. Soc. 2, pt. 2 : 1. — (B. F. DeCosta) Am. Geog. Soc. 12 : 159. — Chambers's Papers, no. 17.

— Bibliography. Bost. Pub. Lib. Hist. 15. — Foster. Prov. ref. lists, 4 : 5.

— Frost, T. Mod. explorers, 80. — Verne, J. Explor. 3. — Whymper, F. The sea, 3.

— Heroes of. Hodder. Heroes, 1 : 191.

Arctic explorations. (J. Rae) Am. Geog. Soc. 23 : 194. — (A. H. Markham) Smithson. Rept. 1896 : 273.

— Bibliography. Greely, A. W. Hdbk. Arc. disc. — Salem (Mass.) Pub. Lib. Bull. Jul. '95.

Arctic meeting, 1874, Am. Geog. Soc. of N. Y. Am. Geog. Soc. 6 : 93.

— 1878. Am. Geog. Soc. 10 : 276.

— for reception of Lieut. Schwatka, 1880. Am. Geog. Soc. 12 : 237.

— 1884. Am. Geog. Soc. 16 : 311.

Arctic ocean, is it open? Proctor. Light sci. 1.97.

Arctic regions, Explorations, 1700–1880. Winsor. Hist. Amer. 8.

— Geographical discoveries in. (C. F. Hall) Am. Geog. Soc. 3 : 216.

— Landscape of. Reclus. Prim. folk, 3.

— Life and scenery in the far north. (W. Bradford) Am. Geog. Soc. 17 : 79.

— Peary's expedition, 1891. (R. E. Peary) Am. Geog. Soc. 24 : 536.

See also Polar Exploration.

Arctic sea, American expedition to. Everett. Orat. v. 4.

Arctic travelling, Practical hints for. (J. Rae) Am. Geog. Soc. 9 : 149.

Arcy, Grottoes of. Adams, W. H. D. Fam. caverns, 90.

Arden, Alice. (A. H. Coppinger) Vincent, A. Twelve bad women, 33.

Arden, Rambles in. Winter. Gray days, 173.

Ardres, Lords of. Freeman. Hist. ess. 4 : 159. — Round, J. H. Feudal Eng. 462.

Arendrup, Mrs. Edith (Courtauld). Clayton, E. C. Eng. fem. art. 2 : 10.

Arequipa, Peru, Meteor'l station at. (A. L. Rotch) Smithson. Rept. 1893 : 253.

Aretino, Carlo. Symonds. Reviv. of learn. 186.

Aretino, Pietro. Symonds. Renais. It. lit. 2 : 172, 383. — Stebbing. Ital. poets, v. 2.

Aretino, Spinello. Stillman, W. J. Old Ital. mas. 70. — Symonds. Renais. Fine arts, 219.

Aretinus. Arnold, E. Poets of Greece, 74.

Arezzo. Freeman. Studies Italy, 1. — Hare. Cities of No. Italy, 3 : 323.

Argal, Sir Samuel. Belknap. Amer. biog. 2 : 148.

Argaum, Battle of. Adams, W. H. D. Engl. at war, 1 : 246.

Argentine Republic. Clemens, E. J. M. La Plata, 95.

— Col. King on. Senior. Biog. sk. 463.

— Commerce, etc., of, in 1895. (E. L. Baker) U. S. Cons. Rept. 50 : 456.

— Commerce and industries, 1890. U. S. Cons. Rept. 32 : 574.

Argentine Republic, Commercial directory of, 1891. Bur. Am. Rep. no. 26.

— Handbook of. Bur. Am. Rep. Bull. no. 67.

— in 1891. (E. L. Baker) U. S. Cons. Rept. 35 : 37.

— in 1892. (E. L. Baker) U. S. Cons. Rept. 41 : 481.

— Politics and administration of. Child, T. Span. Amer. repub. 326.

— Revolution, 1890. U. S. Cons. Rept. no. 124.

— Trade and finances of, '91. (E. L. Baker) U. S. Cons. Rept. 38 : 385.

— — 1892–93. (E. L. Baker) U. S. Cons. Rept. 44 : 655.

— U. S. trade in 1897. (W. I. Buchanan) U. S. Cons. Rept. 53 : 559.

Argonautic legend. Warner Lib. 2 : 731.

Argos. Mahaffy. Rambles Greece, 263.

— Siege of. Robson, W. Sieges, 188.

"**Argus**," brig, Loss of. Dawson. Batt. of U. S. 2 : 266.

Argyll, Archibald Campbell, 8th earl, 1st marquis. Bayne. Pur. revol. 209. — Lodge. Portraits (Bohn), 5. — Macaulay. Biog. sk. 141.

Argyll, Archibald Campbell, 9th earl of. Lodge. Portraits (Bohn), 6.

Argyll, Archibald Campbell, 1st duke of. Lodge. Portraits (Bohn), 6.

Argyll, George Douglas Campbell, 8th duke of. Higginson, T. W. Engl. statesm. 175. — Hill, F. H. Polit. portr. 270. — Kent, C. Gladst. govt. 255. — Reid, T. W. Cab. portr. 169.

Argyll, John Campbell, 2d duke of. Lodge. Portraits (Bohn), 7. — Georgian era, 2 : 40. — Johns. Nav. & mil. heroes.

Argyll, Margaret Douglas, marchioness of. Chapman, W. Wom. of cov. 39.

Arianism, Dawn of. Farrar. Lives of fathers, 1 : 339.

— Whitaker's Origin of. Coleridge. Lit. rem. 4 : 296.

Arias. Arnold, E. Poets of Greece, 75.

Arion. Arnold, E. Poets of Greece, 39.

Ariosti, Attilio, musician. Hogarth. Mem. opera, 1 : 361.

Ariosto, Lodovico. Longfellow. Poets. Eur. 547. — Montgomery. Men of Italy, 1 : 196. — Shelley, Mrs. Lit. men Italy, v. 1. — Stebbing. Ital. poets, v. 2. — Swanwick, A. Poets, 160. — Trollope. Ital. poets, 1 : 157. — With portrait. (L. O. Kuhns) Warner Lib. 2 : 741.

— Alessandra Strozzi and. Jameson. Loves of poets.

— Ginevra and. Jameson. Loves of poets.

— Giovanni, Stories from. Hunt, L. Stories from Ital. poets, 2 : 109.

— Life and minor writings of. Symonds. Renais. It. lit. 1 : 493.

— Orlando Furioso. Symonds. Renais. It. lit. 2 : 1.

— — epitomized. Dobson, W. T. Class. poets, 186.

— Plays. Symonds. Renais. It. lit. 2 : 148.

Ariphron. Mills. Poets of Greece, 148.

Aristides. Cox. Greek statesmen, 1. — (George Grote) Ferris, G. T. Gr. Lead. 1. — Yonge, C. M. Book of worthies, 70.

— Apology of. (J. A. Robinson) Lefroy, W. Lec. eccl. hist. 25.

Aristippus of Cyrene. Diog. Laertius. Lives, 81. — Fénélon. Philosophers, 185. — Lewes. Biog. phil. — Mills. Poets of Greece, 427.

Aristocracy. Bluntschli. Theory of the state, 412. — Brougham. Polit. phil. 2. — Carlyle. Past & pres. — Emerson. Lec. — Godwin. Polit. justice, 2 : 93. — Woolsey. Polit. sci. v. 2.

Heroes of ind. 9. — Cochrane, R. Gr. thinkers, 36.

"**Armstrong**, General," privateer, Loss of. Dawson. Batt. of U. S. **2** : 209, 396.

Army. *See* Names of Countries.

Army of the Potomac. Everett. Orat. v. 4.

Army supplies, Contracts for European, 1893. U. S. Cons. Rept. **45** : 345.

Armyne, Lady Mary. Burder. Pious wom. 80.

Arnason, Jón. Warner Lib. **2** : 802.

Arnaud, Angélique, abbess of Port Royal. Mackaye. Abbess Pt. Royal, 1.

Arnaud, H., and the Waldenses. Chambers's Repos. no. 28.

Arnaud, Marie J. Yonge. Good wom. **2** : 105.

Arnauld, Antoine. Tollemache. French Jansen. 101.

Arnauld, Isaac. Bernard, F. Escapes, 63.

Arnauld, Jacqueline-M.-A. [Mère Angélique]. Tollemache. French Jansen. 50.

Arndt, Ernst Moritz, with portrait. Warner Lib. **2** : 813. — Baur. Relig. life Germ. **1** : 233.

Arne, Thomas Augustine. Creasy. Etonians, 329. — Keddie. Mus. comp. 292. — Jesse, J. H. Cel. Eton. v. **1**. — Sharp, R. F. Makers of music.
— Inventor of musical form. (Hall) Manchester Lit. Philos. Soc. Mem. 4th ser. **13** : 191.
— Operas of. Hogarth. Mem. opera, **2** : 25, 40.

Arnheim, John George. Cust. Warriors 30 years, **2** : 539.

Arnim, Bettina Von. Grimm, H. Liter. 235.

Arnim, Harry Karl Kurt Eduard, Count von. Tuttle, H. Ger. pol. lead. 73.

Arnim, L. Achim von, 1781–1832. Heine. The romantic school.

Arnobius. Blakey, R. Prim. fathers, 227. — Pressensé. Martyrs, 605. — Cave. Lives of fathers, **3** : 369.

Arnold of Brescia. Brown, J. N. Bapt. martyrs, 40. — Hodgson, Wm. Reformers, 38. — Pennington. Epochs papacy, 85. — Williams, F. Eng. card. **1** : 112.

Arnold, Benedict, with portr. Headley, J. T. Washington, **1** : 46. — Parton. Peop. bk. biog. 521. — Sabine. Loyalists, 130. — Lossing. Em. Amer. 135. — Wise, D. Vanq. victors, 80.
— and André. Chambers's Repos. no. 15.
— Expedition to Quebec, Diary of. (E. Wild) Mass. Hist. Proc. 2d ser. **2** : 265.

Arnold, Edwin. Warner Lib. **2** : 819. — Hatton. Jour. Lond. 111.
— Light of Asia. Hazeltine. Chats, 300.

Arnold, Gottfried. Winkworth. Chr. singers Germ. 291.

Arnold, Isaac N. (E. B. Washburne) Chicago Hist. Soc. Coll. **4** : 27.
— Am. Bar Assoc. **7** : 303.

Arnold, Margaret. Ellet. Women of Revol. **2** : 212.

Arnold, Matthew. Armstrong, R. A. Faith and doubt, 91. — Griswold, H. T. Personal sk. 78. — Stephen, L. Stud. biog. **2** : 76. — Traill. New fiction, 76. — With portrait. (G. E. Woodberry) Warner Lib. **2** : 844. — Austin, A. Poetry, 118. — Cook, Jos. Monday lec. Conscience, 87. — Dawson, W. J. Mod. Engl. 328. — Forman. Liv. poets, 311. — Galton, A. Urbana, 77. — Hutton. Mod. guides, 103. — Nadal, E. S. Ess. 122. — Sharp, A. Vic. poets, 121. — Stedman. Vic. poets, 90. — Swinburne. Ess. 123. — Thorne, W. H. Mod. idols, 1. — Whipple. Recol. 280. — Birrell, A. Res judicatæ, 181. — Cheney, J. V. Golden guess, 75 — Henley. Views, 83. — Robertson, J. M.

Mod. humanists, 137. — Swanwick, A. Poets, 375. — Deshler. Afternoons, 302. — Em. persons, **4** : 87. — Innes, A. D. Seers & s. — Farrar. Men, 73. — Gates, L. E. Three studies, 124. — (G. E. Woodberry) Warner classics, **4** : 97. — Hudson, W. H. Stud. interp. 151. — Jacobs, Jos. Ess. & rev. 77. — Nadal, E. S. Ess. at home. — Roscoe, W. C. Poems & ess. v. **2**. — Payn. Lit. recol. 131. — Saintsbury. Correc. imp. 138. — Walker, H. Gr. Vic. poets, 122. — Smalley. Lond. lett. **1** : 289.

Arnold, Matthew, and the nonconformists. Dale, R. W. Ess. and addr. 236.
— as a critic. Hutton, R. H. Criticisms, **2** : 221.
— Bibliography. Bost. Pub. Lib. Bull. **6** : 84. — Hodgkins. 19th cent. authors.
— Criticism by. Burroughs, J. Indoor, 79.
— His conception of culture. Harrison, F. Choice of bks. 97.
— Ideals of. Scudder, V. D. Soc. ideals, 233.
— Last essays of. Tovey. Rev. & ess. 71.
— Lecture by. Stearns, F. P. Sk. Concord, 117.
— New poems. Swinburne. Essays.
— on the Bible. Hutton, R. H. Criticisms, **2** : 214.
— Poems of. Clough. Prose rem. 362. — Roscoe, W. C. Ess.
— poet of doubt. Scudder, V. D. Life of spirit, 247.
— Poetry. (W. Alexander) Afternoon lec. **4** : 199.

Arnold, Richard, with portrait. Bartlett, J. R. R. I. officers, 363.

Arnold, Smith. Wakeley. Heroes Meth. 309.

Arnold, Thomas, of Rugby. Adams, W. H. D. Good Samar. 66. — Bayne, P. Chr. life, 367. — Edgar. Boyhood, 329. — Mozley. Essays, **2** : 1. — Mozley. Reminis. **2** : 50. — Remark. men. 148. — Benson & Tatham. Men of might, 213. — Bolton, S. K. Fam. leaders, 149. — With portrait. Cochrane, R. Benef. lives, 207. — With portrait. Ewart, H. C. Leaders, 177. — Pierce, B. K. Em. dead, 441. — Smiles. Brief biog. 71. — Smith, G. B. Chr. workers, 201.
— and education. Bibliography. Findlay, J. A. Arnold of Rugby & educ.
— Stanley's Life of. Greg. Ess. pol. **1** : 47. — Martineau, J. Misc. 56. — Martineau, J. Ess. ('91) **1** : 43. — Morley. Ess. **2** : 1.

Arnold, William. Ivimey. Eng. Bapt. **3** : 420.

Arnold, William A. Bartlett, J. R. R. I. officers, 391.

Arnoldi, Alberto. Perkins, C. C. Tusc. sculp. **1** : 70.

Arnolds, The, in the Lake region. Rawnsley. Lit. Assoc. Eng. lakes, v. **1**, **2**.

Arnolfo del Gambio, cathedral builder. Oliphant. Makers of F. 92. — Symonds. Renais. Fine arts, 62. — Perkins, C. C. Tusc. sculp. **1** : 51.

Arnould, Sophie. Clayton, E. C. Queens, 80. — Edwards, H. S. Prima don. **1** : 66. — Ferris, G. T. Great singers, 1. — Houssaye. Men of 18th cent. **1** : 420. — Needham. Queens of Song. — Men & wom. of France, 144.

Arnulph, History of. Peake, Eliz. Germ. emperors, 32.

Arp, Bill, *pseud*. *See* Smith, C. H.

Arpad, 1st Duke of Hungary. Wyatt, W. J. Hunga. celeb. 29.

Arran, James Hamilton, Earl of. Lodge. Portraits (Bohn), v. **2**.

Arras, Siege of. Robson, W. Sieges, 511.

Arria. Owen, Mrs. O. F. Heroines hist. 105.

Arrian. Miills. Poets of Greece, 484.

Arriaza. Kennedy. Poets of Spain, 113.

Arrom, Cecilia B. de F. Zimmern. For. novelists, 183.
Arrow-heads, Flint. Prime, S. I. Under trees, 53.
Arrowpoints, spearheads, and knives of prehistoric times. (T. Wilson) U. S. Nat. Mus. Rept. 1897 : 811.
Arsenic as coloring matter, Effects of. (G. Derby) Mass. Health, 1872 : 17.
— as a domestic poison. (E. S. Wood) Mass. Health, 1883 : 213.
— in paper and fabrics. (F. C. Robinson) Am. Pub. Health, 17 : 219. — Mass. Health, 1891 ; 701.
— Uses of, in industry. Japp. Days w. indus. 128.
Arsenius. Kingsley. Hermits, 149. — Hahn-Hahn. Fathers, 216.
Art. Bartol. Principles, 134. — Calvert, G. H. Brief ess. 55. — Cheney, E. D. Gleanings, 9. — Coleridge. Lit. rem. 1 : 216. — Cozzens-Bushwhacker, 55. — Frieze, H. S. Giov. Dupré, 168. — Hinton. Thinking, 274. — Holland, J. G. Every-day, 2 : 63. — Emerson. Society, 39. — Emerson. Ess. 1 : 325. — Farrar. Soc. & p. day quest. 161.
— Æsthetic school in. Proctor, R. A. Leis. read. 265.
— American. Badeau. Vagabond, 120.
— Among the people. Osgood, S. Amer. leaves, 227.
— Ancient. Fuseli. Life & writ. 2 : 17.
— — in the renaissance. Paget, V. Euphorion, 1 : 169.
— and artists. Tuckerman. Optimist, 88.
— — in England. Ellesmere. Ess. 101.
— and labor. (E. G. Starr) Hull-House maps, 165.
— and language, Difference between. Eastlake. Contrib. 2 : 301.
— and life. Holland, J. G. Plain talks, 271.
— and literature in public schools. (W. T. Harris) Nat. Educa. Assoc. '97 : 261.
— and religion. Hoppin. Early renaiss. 179.
— as developed by culture. (H. Taine) Hundred greatest men, 57.
— Beginning of. (Stanley Lane-Poole) Coan. Art and lit. 56.
— Beginnings of. Crofts, E. Chap. Eng. lit. 56.
— Byzantine. Bury. Later Rom. emp. 2 : 40. — Cheney, E. D. Gleanings, 72.
— Can science help ? Hamerton. Portfo. pap. 285.
— Characteristics of. Cotterill. Introd. study of poetry.
— Christian. Ozanam. Civiliz. v. 2. — Ruskin. Mornings in Flor.
— — and pagan. Oxenham. Stud. in eccl. hist. 9. — Symonds. Renaiss. Fine arts, 6.
— — Early. Cheney, E. D. Gleanings, 61.
— — in England, Plea for school of. Wiseman, N. Ess. 3 : 353.
— — in the middle ages. Trench. Lec. mediæval, 395.
— Contemporaneous. Cheney, E. D. Gleanings, 335.
— Conversations on. Hazlitt. Round table.
— criticism of, Qualifica. for. Jenkin, Fl. Papers, 1 : 93.
— Decay of. Stillman, W. J. Old Rome.
— Decline of. Trail, F. Studies, 294.
— Decorative. See Decorative art.
— Democratic, Walt Whitman and. Symonds. Ess. 2 : 30.
— Dutch. Van Dyke, J. C. Dutch mast. 1.
— Effect of guild system upon. Conway, W. M. Early Flem. artists, 56.

Art, Elementary principles of. Seeley, J. R. Lec. & ess. 155; or Seeley, J. R. Rom. imp. 166.
— an emanation of religious affection. Wallace, H. B. Art, 1.
— Emotional. Patmore. Religio poetæ, 85.
— Encouragement of. Smith, Gold. Lec. & ess. 76.
— Ethics of. Dallas. Gay science, 2 : 143.
— Flemish. Van Dyke, J. C. Dutch mast. 153.
— for the eye. (R. Turner) Nat. Educa. Assoc. '96 : 670.
— French. Cheney, E. D. Gleanings, 168.
— — in 17th cent. Cousin, V. True, beautiful & good. — Dilke. Art in mod. state.
— in education. (E. E. Brown) Nat. Educa. Assoc. '99 : 112.
— in 1883. Quilter. Preferences, 281.
— Landscape. Mollett, J. W. Paint. of Barbizon, 2 : 77.
— Function of : Cherubino at the Scala theatre. Symonds. Ital. byways.
— German, Old. Cheney, E. D. Gleanings, 244.
— Gothic. Thornbury. Brit. art, 2 : 296.
— Government patronage of. (E. M. Gallaudet) Vienna Ex. U. S. Repts. v. 2.
— Greek. Cheney, E. D. Gleanings, 33. — Hegel. Philos. hist. 250. — Mahaffy. Soc. life Gr. ch. 14. — Symonds. Greek poets, 2 : 363. — Thornbury. Brit. art, 2 : 233.
— — and Roman. Bibliography. Newark (N. J.) Pub. Lib. Spec. Read. List, no. 3.
— Hierarchy of. Cobbe, F. P. Studies, 289.
— history and, Varieties of. Hayward, A. Ess. 2d ser. 2 : 1.
— in America. Cheney, E. D. Gleanings, 269.
— in ancient Rome. Jervis, Lady. Painting, 1 : 32.
— in education. Hoppin. Early renaiss. 143.
— in the education of the Amer. citizen. (W. O. Partridge) Nat. Educa. Assoc. '98 : 819.
— in England. Cheney, E. D. Gleanings, 309. — Ward, T. H. Reign of Victoria, 2 : 514. — Zangwill. Without prej. 31.
— — and in Spain, National. Wiseman, N. Ess. 3 : 393.
— — Past and future of. Harris. Theory of the arts, v. 2.
— in Europe. Peabody, A. P. Rem. Eur. 76.
— in industry. (C. D. Wright) Mass. Labor, '86 : 331.
— in magazines. (J. C. Dana) Nat. Educa. Assoc. '95 : 314.
— in public schools. (C. G. Leland) Phila. Soc. Sci. Assoc. '80.
— in Rome. Howe, J. W. Oak to olive, 60.
— in the schoolroom. (L. S. Thompson) Nat. Educa. Assoc. '96 : 678.
— — through decoration and works of art. (Stella Skinner) Nat. Educa. Assoc. '96 : 685.
— in small towns and villages. (T. C. Horsfall et al.) Trans. Soc. Sci. Lond. '78 : 677.
— in the United States (1840). Bethune. Orations, 159.
— in Washington. Sumner. Works, 10 : 540.
— Influence of, on population of large towns. (T. C. Horsfall et al.) Trans. Soc. Sci. Lond. '82 : 577.
— — on social life. Poynter. Ten lec. 252.
— Italian, History of. Fuseli. Life & writ. 3 : 153.
— — Restoration of. Cheney, E. D. Gleanings, 82.
— Japanese. Palgrave. Ess. on art, 185.
— Masterpieces of. Appleton, T. G. Sheaf of pap. 196.
— Means and ends in. Hazlitt. Sket.
— Mediæval. Paget. Euphorion, 167.

Art, Modern. Fuseli. Life & writ. **2** . 73.
— — not imaginative. Lamb. Elia.
— — Patronage of. Hazlitt. Round table.
— — Tendencies of. Hoppin. Early renaiss. 73.
— Moorish. Thornbury. Brit. art, **2** : 275.
— Nature and. Friswell. Gentle life, **2** : 58.
— Nature and aims of. Godwin, P. Out of past, 302.
— Nature of. Day, L. F. Every-day art, 39.
— Observation of works of. Eastlake. Contrib. **2** : 199.
— of savages. Lang. Custom, 276.
—old and new. Poynter. Ten lec. 62.
— Philosophy of. (R. P. Ker) Seth & Haldane. Ess. 159.
— — Taine on. Fiske, J. Unseen world, 280.
— Poetry and prose in. Palgrave. Ess. on art, 203.
— Popularization of. Samuelson, Jas. Civiliz'n, 320.
— Principle in. Patmore. Princ. in art, 1.
— Principles of. Hoppin. Early renaiss. 56.
— — Elementary. Seeley, J. R. Ess.
— — in works of imagination. Bulwer, E. Caxtoniana, 305.
— Progress of. Hazlitt. Round table, 12.
— Realism in. Bunce, O. B. Bach. Bluff, 84.
— Relation of, to education. (Grace Bibb) Nat. Educa. Assoc. **'75** : 32.
— Relation of, to science and morality. Symonds. Ess. **1** : 148.
— Religion and. Robinson, F. S. Connois. 271
— Spalding, J. L. Ess. & rev. 306.
— Religious. Renan. Studies (N. Y.), **2** : 367.
— Religious faith and worship in. Wordsworth, C. Misc. **2** : 384.
— Revival of. Stillman, W. J. Old Rome.
— Sacred and legendary, Jameson's. Kingsley. Raleigh, 196.
— — Poetry of. Kingsley, C. Lit. lec. 187.
— Sanity and. Mabie. My study fire, **2** : 113.
— School of, Foreign competition and. (R. W. Edis *et al.*) Trans. Soc. Sci. Lond. **1883** : 630.
— Science applied to. Sinclair, J. Lec. 26.
— Scriptural and legendary subjects of. Eastlake. Contrib. **1** : 14.
— Sensational. Palgrave. Ess. on art, 193.
— Spanish. Cheney, E. D. Gleanings, 135. — Stoddard, C. A. Span. cit. 67.
— Specific style in. Eastlake. Contrib. **1** : 8.
— Struggle in. Mabie. My study fire, **2** : 143.
— Study of, in academies and colleges. (C. W. Bennett) N. Y. Regents, **79** : app. 146.
— success in, Secret of. Henry, C. S. About men, 222.
— The supernatural in. Paget, V. Belcaro, 70.
— symbolical, not imitative. Wallace, H. B. Art, 21.
— Thoughts on. Bunce, O. B. Bach. Bluff, 185.
— Usefulness of. Calvert. Ess. æsth. 254.
— War and. Robinson, F. S. Connois. 255.
— Work and. Mabie. My study fire, **2** : 46.
Art-chat. Appleton, T. G. Sheaf of pap. 215.
Art collectors. Clayton, E. C. Eng. fem. art. **1** : 78.
Art Congress, An ideal. Patterson, R. H. Ess. hist. 319.
Art criticism, American. Hapgood, N. Lit. statesm. 133.
— and art education. Ruskin. Arrows, v. **1**.
Art criticisms. Miller, H. Hist. ess. 327.
Art department, educa. exhibit, N. E. A. meeting, Chicago, 1887. (Josephine C. Locke) Nat. Educa. Assoc. **'87** : 699.
Art education. Ruskin. Arrows, v. **1**. — (Otto

Fuchs) Nat. Educa. Assoc. **'85** : 275. — (I. E. Clarke) Butler, N. M. Educa. in U. S. 705.
Art education and manual training. (J. L. Tadd) Nat. Educa. Assoc. **'94** : 900.
— Extension of. (C. M. Carter) Nat. Educa. Assoc. **'95** : 810.
— for the cultivation of artistic taste. (J. M. Hoppin) Nat. Educa. Assoc. **'93** : 476.
— High aim in. (A. H. Munsell) Nat. Educa. Assoc. **'88** : 614.
— in America. Wallace, H. B. Art, 295.
— in European and American schools. (W. S. Perry) Nat. Educa. Assoc. **'91** : 765.
— in high and normal schools. (J. A. Greene) Nat. Educa. Assoc. **'99** : 953.
— in Moscow. Atkinson, J. B. Art tour northern, 390.
— in the public schools. (James McAlister ; J. H. Hoose) Nat. Educa. Assoc. **'91** : 456. — (J. McAlister) U. S. Bur. Educa. Rept.' 94, **1** : 793.
— in relation to public education. (W. S. Perry) Nat. Educa. Assoc. **'96** : 694.
— in schools, Results of. (C. G. Leland) Phila. Soc. Sci. Assoc. **'82**.
— Influence of. (Christine Sullivan) Nat. Educa. Assoc. **'94** : 894.
— The library in. Nat. Educa. Assoc. **'98** : 812.
— mechanical, Russian system of. (J. D. Runkle) Nat. Educa. Assoc. **'77** : 231.
— Moral value of. (Ada M. Laughlin) Nat. Educa. Assoc. **'90** : 141.
— Place of, in general education. (J. S. Clark) Nat. Educa. Assoc. **'95** : 830.
— Systems of. Poynter. Ten lec. **'94**.
— true industrial education. (W. T. Harris) Nat. Educa. Assoc. **'89** : 647.
Art exhibitions, annual, Influence of. (Sir T. A. Jones *et al.*) Trans. Soc. Sci. Lond. **'81** : 765.
Art galleries of Paris. Haven, G. Pilgrim. 324.
— Private : lost treasures. Palgrave. Ess. on art, 211.
Art gallery of Madrid. Prime, S. I. Alhambra, 39.
Art instinct, Development of. (J. W. Stimson) Cong. Educa. Chic. ('93) 466.
Art instruction ; æsthetic aim, Importance of. (L. W. Miller) Cong. Educa. Chic. ('93) 462.
— Aim of. (Christine Sullivan) Nat. Educa. Assoc. **'92** : 499.
— Drawing from the flat. (H. T. Bailey) Cong. Educa. Chic. ('93) 458.
— great masters, Study and analysis of. (A. Emerson) Cong. Educa. Chic. ('93) 473.
— in the high school. (Christine Sullivan) Nat. Educa. Assoc. **'90** : 640.
— in normal schools. (Elizabeth H. Perry) Nat. Educa. Assoc. **'92** : 482.
Art-revival in England. Cooke, G. W. Poets, 173.
Art-schools, Early, in England. Cook, D. Art in Eng. 1.
Art-students, Training of. Poynter. Ten lec. 135.
Art study and the public schools. (M. D. Hicks) Cong. Educa. Chic. ('93) 487.
— Methods of, for cultivation of taste. (J. M. Hoppin) Cong. Educa. Chic. ('93) 476.
— treasures of Seville. Prime, S. I. Alhambra, 107.
Art teaching in schools. (W. H. Maxwell) Nat. Educa. Assoc. **'97** : 268.
Art training in American colleges. Anderson, M. B. Papers, **1** : 87.
Art union of London. (G. Godwin) Trans. Soc. Sci. Lond. **'76** : 845.

Asclepiades. Mills. Poets of Greece, 182.
Ascough, William. Fuller. Worthies, **2** : 274.
Ash, John. Ivimey. Eng. Bapt. **4** : 561.
Ashango-land, Du Chaillu's journey to. Forsyth, W. Essays, 247.
Ashantee. Stanley, H. M. Coomassie, v. **1**.
Ashantee war. Congreve, R. Ess. 231. — Adams, W. H. D. Engl. at war, **2** : 223. — Latimer. Eur. in Afr. in 19th cent. 321.
Ashburton, B. Baring, Lord, and Lady. Espinasse. Lit. recoll. 89.
Ashburton, Harriet, Lady. Houghton, Ld. Monog. 217.
Ashburton, J. Dunning, Lord. Brougham : Works, **4** : 325. — Roscoe, H. Em. lawyers, **2** : 85. — Grant, J. Recoll. Lords, 187. — Welsby. Eng. judges.
Ashby, James L. Walker, C. D. Biog. Va. Mil. Inst. 33.
Ashby, John W. Walker, C. D. Biog. Va. Mil. Inst. 46.
Ashby, Richard. Walker, C. D. Biog. Va. Mil. Inst. 36.
Ashby, Turner. Pollard. Life of Lee, 573.
Ashby-de-la-Zouch, Eng. Rimmer, A. Country towns, 32.
Ashdod, Ruins of. Tweedie. Ruined cities, 46.
Ashe, John. Lossing. Em. Amer. 99. — (H. Ellis) Miles, A. H. Poets of cent. **6** : 219.
Ashford, Mary, Murder of, 1817. Thornbury. Old stor. 284.
Ashley, Lord. Horne, R. H. New spirit, 60.
— and the act of 1833. Gibbins. Eng. soc. ref. 129.
— and London thieves. Whittier. Lit. recre. 136.
Ashman, William. Jackson, T. Early Meth. **3** : 221.
Ashmun, Jehudi. Howe, H. Adven. of Amer. 557. — Lossing. Em. Amer. 325.
— Eulogy on. Story, J. Miscell. 599.
Ashton, T. Jesse, J. H. Cel. Eton. v. **1**.
Ashworth, John. Hoare. Nota. workers, 97.
Asia. Barker, Lady. Travel. about, 295. — Frost, T. Mod. expl. — Peebles, J. M. Around the world, 121. — Pumpelly, R. Across Amer. & Asia, 79.
— Ancient home of man in. (O. Street) Am. Geog. Soc. **12** : 193.
— Batuta's travels in, 1320–50. St. John. Cel. travelers, **1** : 64.
— Bell's travels in, 1710–70. St. John. Cel. travelers, **2** : 125.
— Bernier's travels in, 1640–80. St. John. Cel. travelers, **1** : 205.
— Bibliography. Murray. Discov. Asia, v. **3** : app.
— Central. Pumpelly. Amer. & As. 365. — Rawlinson, H. Eng. & Russ. 205.
— — Darwergne's expedition to. Am. Geog. Soc. **24** : 430.
— — Later phases of the C. A. question. Rawlinson, H. Eng. Russ. 293.
— — Notes upon, 1866–68. Strangford. Selec. writ. **2** : 204.
— — Russians in. Rawlinson, H. Eng. & Russ. 136.
— — Vámbéry's travels in. Frost, T. Mod. expl. 9.
— — — and other travels in. Strangford. Selec. writ. **2** : 110.
— Chardin's travels in, 1660–1700. St. John. Cel. travelers, **1** : 233.
— Della Valle's travels in, 1610–50. St. John. Cel. travelers, **1** : 149.
— Forster's travels in, 1770–90. St. John. Cel. travelers, **2** : 198.
— Geography in. Temple, R. Orient. exper. **1**.

Asia, Hanway's travels in, 1735–70. St. John. Cel. travelers, **2** : 301.
— Hasselquist's travels in, 1740. St. John. Cel. travelers, **2** : 52.
— Kaempfer's travels in, 1675–90. St. John. Cel. travelers, **1** : 271.
— Ledyard's travels in. St. John. Cel. travelers, **2** : 163.
— Local transportation in, 1891. U. S. Cons. Rept. **38** : 715.
— Memories of the East. Reed, W. B. Among books, 66.
— Past in the present in. (J. Bellows) Am. Antiq. Soc. Proc. n. s. **9** : 204.
— Pococke's travels in, 1730–50. St. John. Cel. travelers, **2** : 101.
— Tavernier's travels in, 1630–80. St. John. Cel. travelers, **1** : 180.
— Tournefort's travels in, 1675–1700. St. John. Cel. travelers, **2** : 7.
— tribes of, Characteristics of. Brinton. Races & peo. 198.
— Volney's travels in, 1770–1810. St. John. Cel. travelers, **3** : 219.
— Western, Ancient commerce of. Barnes, A. Miscel. **2** : 5.
— World's religious debt to. (P. C. Mozoomdar) Barrows, J. H. Parl. relig. **2** : 1083.
Asia Minor. DeHass, F. S. Buried cities, 457. — Lee, J. S. Sacred cities. — MacGavock. Tennesseean abroad, 282. — Maximilian. On the wing, 198. — Menzies, S. Turkey. — Taylor, B. Land of Saracens.
— and Phœnicia. Lord, J. Anc. states, 100.
Asiatic empires, Ancient. Newman, F. W. Essays, 200.
Asiatic forces in European wars. Greg. W. R. Miscel. **2** : 268.
Asicus, St. Conyngham, D. P. Irish saints, 115.
Aske, Robert. Baring-Gould. Yorks. odd. **2** : 196.
Askelon, Ruins of. Tweedie. Ruined cities, 41.
Askew, Anne. Adams, W. H. D. Heroes, 323. — Hack. Self-sar. 5. — Hodgson, W. Reformers, 406. — Williams, Jane. Lit. wom. 42. — Tayler, C. B. Eng. martyrs, 21. — Adams, W. D. Famous books, 49. — Adams, W. H. D. Noble women, 11. — Brown, J. N. Bapt. martyrs, 270. — Fifty famous women, 93. — Owen, Mrs O. F. Heroines domes. 89.
Asklepios. Bibliography. Walton, A. Cult Asklepios.
Asmus, *pseud. See* Claudius Matthias.
"**Asp**," ship, Defense of. Dawson. Batt. of U. S. **2** : 248.
Aspasia. With portrait. Clarke, M. C. Noted wom. 41. — Owen, Mrs. O. F. Heroines hist. 54.
— Venus appearing to. Doran. New pic. 119.
Asphalt of Trinidad. (W. P. Pierce) U. S. Cons. Rept. **40** : 169.
Aspinwall, Thomas, with portrait. (C. C. Smith) Mass. Hist. Proc. 2d ser. **7** : 32.
Aspinwall, Wm. Am. Bar Assoc. **16** : 428.
Aspirations, Life and its. Rice, H. Nature & cul. 167.
— Vagueness and endlessness of : a sermon. Boyd. Graver tho'ts, 221.
Ass, The. Story, A. T. Vagrom, 79.
Assam. Cooper, T. T. Travels of a pioneer. — Woodthorpe, R. G. Lushai exped.
Assassins. Keightley. Sec. soc. mid. ages.
Assaye. Malleson, G. B. Battles of India, 259.
— Battle of. Adams, W. H. D. Eng. at war, **1** : 242.

Assemanni, Joseph. Carne, J. Em. mission. 3: 176.

Asser Menevensis. Parry. Cam. Plutarch, 86. — True character of. Wright, T. Ess. archæol. 1: 172.

Assessments, Special. (V. Rosewater) Col. Univ. Stud. Hist. 2: 350. — Col. Univ. Stud. Hist. 2: no. 3.

Assheton, John. Wallace, R. Anti-Trin. biog. 2: 122.

Assisi. Hare. Cities of No. Italy, 3: 371. — Taine. Italy, 2: 16.

Association. Brownson. Works, 10.

Associations. Hall, R. Miscel. 178.
— Public, Influence of. Channing. Works, 1: 281.

Assory, Emilia, Countess of, with portrait. Jameson. Beauties, 119.

Assurance. See Insurance.

Assye, Battle of. Clinton, H. R. Crécy to Assye, 647.

Assynt. Watkins, M. G. In country, 140.

Assyria. Sayce, A. H. Fresh light.
— and Greece, connection between. Thirlwall, C. Remains, 3: 154.
— Chaldea and. Lord, J. Anc. states, 80.
— Religion of. Rawlinson. Religions, 48. — (G. Rawlinson) Relig. systems, 26.

Asteroids, Discovery of. Lodge, O. J. Pioneers, 295.

Astley's Amphitheatre. Lennox, W. P. Plays, 1: 143.

Aston family, of Tixhall. Drake, N. Evenings, 1: 139.

Aston, Walter, 1st Lord. Lodge. Portraits (Bohn), v. 4.

Astor family, Story of. Chambers, W. Rem. pers. 105.

Astor, John Jacob. With portrait. Duyckinck. Nat. portr. gall. 2: 30. — Bancroft, H. H. Hist. of N. W. 1: 499. — Gray. Hist. Oregon. — Houghton. Kings, 43. — (D. R. Jaques) Hunt, F. Am. merch. 2: 387. — McCabe, J. D. Great fortunes, 59. — Parton. Fam. Amer. 427. — Lossing. Em. Amer. 379. — With portrait. Stoddard, W. O. Men of bus. 9.
— and S. Girard, Comparison of. Bristed. Pieces, 4: 4.

Astor, William B., house-owner. Parton. Capt. indus. 307.

Astoria. Bancroft, H. H. Hist. of N. W. v. 2.
— Irving's. Poe. Works, 4: 530.

Astrogony, Ancient Babylonian. Proctor. Pleas. ways, 388.

Astrological almanacs. Knight. Once on time, 1: 275.

Astrology. Ashton. Soc. life Q. Anne. — Davenport, R. A. Delusions, 331. — Miller, R. K. Romance of Astronomy. — Proctor. Myths, 1. — Proctor. Pyramid, 312.

Astronomers, Famous. Chambers's Miscel. no. 169.
— Royal, English. Proctor, R. A. Fam. sci. 374.

Astronomy, American, Aspects of. (S. Newcomb) Smithson. Rept. '97: 85.
— American, Beginnings of. (E. S. Holden) Smithson. Rept. '97: 101.
— Ancient. Morton, E. J. C. Heroes astron. 1.
— and the Christian revelation. Foster, J. Crit. Ess. (Bohn) 2: 353.
— and the Jewish festivals. Proctor, R. A. Pyramid, 272.
— Bibliography. Salem (Mass.) Pub. Lib. Bull. Jan. '94. — Berry, A. Short hist. of astron. — Providence Pub. Lib. Bull. Aug. '96. — Todd, D. P. Stars & telescopes.

Astronomy, Copernican system of. Morton, E. J. C. Heroes astron. 32.
— Hindu. Colebrooke. Misc. essays, 2: 374.
— History of. Smith, Adam. Ess. phil. 1.
— Modern. Morton, E. J. C. Heroes astron.
— Myths in. Proctor. Myths, 298.
— of the Brahmins. Playfair, J. Works, v. 3.
— Paradoxes in. Proctor. Myths, 267.
— Problems of. (Simon Newcomb) Smithson. Rept. '96: 83.
— Progress in. 1846-96. (E. S. Holden) Goode. Smithson. Inst. 571.
— Progress of, for 1889-90. (W. C. Winlock) Smithson. Rept. '90: 121.
— Recent discoveries in [1856]. Chambers's Papers, no. 21.
— — Science of. Holland, H. Frag. papers, 113.
— Teaching of. (E. S. Holden) U. S. Bur. Ed. Rept. '97-98, 1: 869.
— Uses of. Everett. Orat. v. 3.
— Wonder of. Chambers's Miscel. no. 175.

Astrophysical observatory, Washington. (S. P. Langley) Goode. Smithson. Inst. 419.

Asuncion, capital of Paraguay. Curtis, W. E. Capitals, 623.

Asylum and extradition among nations. Gammel. Writ. 290.

Athaliah. Geikie, C. Old Test. char. 295. — Maurice, F. D. Theol. ess. 479. — Mozley, J. B. Lec. 183.

Athanasian creed. (C. Gore) Oxf. Ho. papers, 3: 1. — Thirlwall, C. Remains, 2: 247, 317.

Athanasius, St. Blakey, R. Prim. fathers, 150. Broadus. Lec. hist. preach. 63. — Cave. Lives of fathers, 2: 145. — Farrar. Lives of fathers, 1: 331. — Gibbon. Rom. empire, ch. 21. — (W. Ince) Lefroy, W. Lec. eccl. hist. 343. — Milman. Hist. Christianity, 2: 379. — Stanley. Eastern church, 322.

Atharva-Veda. Hopkins. Relig. of India, 151.

Atheism. Farrar. Soc. & p. day quest. 131. — Lilly, W. S. Gr. enig. 35. — Bacon. Ess.
— Causes of. Newman, F. W. Miscel. 2: 180.
— dogmatic, Approach of. Hutton, R. H. Criticisms, 2: 246.
— Moral significance of. Hutton. Ess. theol. 1: 3.
— Necessity of. Shelley. Prose works, 1: 30.
— The newest. Porter, N. Sci. & sent. 331.
— of yesterday. Peabody, E. P. Last evening, 227.
— Perils of, to the nation. Beecher, L. Works, 1: 91.
— Popular view of. Oxenham. Short stud. 349.
— Recent phases of scientific. Thornton, W. T. Old-fash. 199.
— Refutation of. Brownson. Works, 2: 1. — Cudworth. Intel. system.
— Tide of, in the U. S. Grady, H. W. Writings & speech. 230.
— Unreasonableness of. Fisher, G. P. Discus. 468.

Athelney, Isle of, and King Alfred's monastery. Timbs. Abbeys, 1: 540.

Athenæum, London, Mr. Dilke and the. Dilke. Papers, 1: 24.

Athenæus. Warner Lib. 2: 923.

Athenian orators, The. Macaulay: Ess. 1: 139.

Athenian revels: a drama. Macaulay. Ess. 1: 30.

Athenian schools. Newman, J. H. Hist. sk. 3: 77.

Athenians, Literature, arts, and manners of. Shelley. Ess. 1: 63.

Athens. Arnold, R. A. Levant, 1: 44, 147. —

Atonement, The. (R. F. Horton) Faith & crit.: essays. — (Arthur Lyttleton) Gore, C. Lux mundi, 275. — Maurice, F. D. Theol. ess. 127. — Thompson, H. M. Copy, 78. — Pfleiderer. Philos. relig. 4 : 94. — Shedd. Theol. 265.
— Bushnell on. Brownson. Works, 7 : 75.
— Campbell on nature of. Martineau, J. Studies, 147.
— Christian doctrine of. Farrar. Sermons in Am. 259.
— Death of Jesus as an. Godwin, W. Ess. 97.
— Doctrine of. (B. Jowett) Noyes, G. R. Theol. ess. 221. — (J. Stoughton) Liv. papers, v. 8.
— — Levitical illustration of. Newton, W. W. Ess. 149.
— Substitutional. Whedon. Ess. 1 : 197.
— True and false conceptions of. Gladstone. Later gl. 312.
— Vicarious, Inconsistency of. Martineau, J. Studies, 83.
Attalus I. of Pergamum. Mahaffy, J. P. Greek life, ch. 14.
Attalus, the martyr. Bernard, F. Escapes, 10. — Yonge, C. M. Pupils of John, 220.
Attention. Ess. from Sat. R. 236. — Patmore. Religio poetæ, 31.
— concentrated, Difficulty of. Helps. Brevia.
Atterbom, Per Daniel Amadeus. Warner Lib. 2 : 933.
Atterbury, Francis, Bishop. Lodge. Portraits (Bohn), v. 7. — Macaulay. Ess. 6 : 112. — Macaulay. New biographies (Bost. 1857), 19. — Wrangham. Brit. Plutarch, v. 5.
Attila. Curteis. Rom. empire, 136. — Gibbon. Rom. empire, ch. 34, 35. [Same in Ferris, G. T. Gr. leaders, 83.] — Hodgkin. Italy and her Invaders, 2 : 39. — Mombert. Great lives, 106. — Utterton, F. A. Biog. sk. 25.
Attiret, Frère. Brightwell. Byepaths of biog. 246.
Atton II., Bp. of Vercelli. Neale. Mediæv. preachers.
Attucks, Crispus. Phillips, W. Speeches, 2 : 69.
Atuatanas, natives of Copper River, Alaska. (H. T. Allen) Smithson. Rept. '86 : 258.
Atwell, S. F. Walker, C. D. Biog. Va. Mil. Inst. 41.
Aubanel, Theo. Preston, H. W. Troubadours.
Auber, Daniel François. Ferris, G. T. Gr. compos. — Keddie. Mus. comp. 380. — Engel, L Mozart, 1 : 3. — Hogarth. Mem. Opera, 2 : 263.
Auber, Harriet. Miles, A. H. Poets of cent. 10 : 666. — Miller, Jos. Singers church, 2d ed. 353. — Hatfield, E. F. Poets of church, 23.
Aubigné, Agrippa d'. Macdowell, H. C. Henry of Guise, 175.
— Imitation of, by Sterne. Ferrier. Ill. of Sterne, 1 : 53.
Aubrey, John, and his eminent men. Knight. Once on time, 1 : 296.
Aubusson, Peter d'. Maccall. For. biog. 2 : 164.
Aucassin and Nicolette. Lang, A. Let. liter. — Pater. Stud. renais. 1. — (F. M. Warren) Warner Lib. 2 : 943.
— Bibliography. Bost. Pub. Lib. Bull. 4 : 184. — Bourdillon, F. W. Aucassin & Nicolette.
Auckland, England, Chapel of St. Peter and Manor-House of. Lightfoot. Hist. ess. 182.
Auckland castle. Gibson, W. S. Miscel. 1. — Venables, E. Episc. palaces, 73.
Auctioneering, Book. Curwen. Booksellers, 379.

Audiences, Musical. Kingston, W. B. Music & manners, 1 : 324.
Audiffret-Pasquier, C. L. G., Marquis d'. Men of 3d repub. 135.
Audiffret-Pasquier, Edme Armand Gaston, Duc d'. King, E. French pol. lead. 195.
Audley, Thomas, Lord Chancellor. Burke, S. H. Men of reforma. 2 : 3. — Burke, S. H. Hist. portr. Tudor, 2 : 185. — Campbell, Ld. Chan. 2 : 78. — Foss. Judges, 5 : 126.
Audley End. Edwardes, C. Hist. houses. — Jewitt, L. Stately homes, 2 : 112.
Audubon, John Jas. Bolton, S. K. Fam. men of science, 167. — With portrait. Duyckinck. Nat. portr. gall. 2 : 47. — Edgar. Boyhood, 381. — Godwin, P. Out of past, 89. — With portrait. Griswold. Prose writ. 187. — (P. Godwin) Hubbard, E. Little jour. 2 : 237. [Same in Homes Am. authors.] — Lossing. Em. Amer. 272. — Mitchell, D. G. Amer. lands, 1 : 204. — Nichol. Amer. lit. 185. — Smiles. Brief biog. 173. — Parton. Peop. bk. biog. 163. — Saunders, F. Famous books, 141. — Spooner. Biog. fine arts, 1 : 53. — Tuckerman. Ess. 304. — Godwin, P. Comm. addr. 149. — With portrait. Warner Lib. 2 : 956. — Wright, H. C. Child. sto. in Am. lit. 4. — Youmans. Pioneers sci. 152.
Auer, Leopold, with portrait. Ehrlich, A. Cel. violin. 6.
Auerbach, Berthold, with portrait. Warner Lib. 2 : 961. — Zimmern. For. novelists, 1 : 59.
Auerstadt, Battle of. King, C. Battles, 482.
Augereau, Pierre François Charles. Headley. Napoleon, 1 : 86.
Augier, Emile. Pellissier. Lit. move. Fr. 464. — With portrait. Warner Lib. 2 : 998. — Matthews. J. B. Fr. dram. 105. — Mauris, M. Fr. men of lett. 89.
Augment in Sanscrit and Greek. Garnet. Philol. ess. 205.
Augsburg. Hoppin. Notes theol. stud. 53.
Auguries. Jones, W. Credulities, 35.
August. Whiting, C. G. Saunterer, 125.
— Customs and superstitions of. Soane. New curios. 2 : 119.
Augusta, Empress of Germany. With portrait. Crowned heads, 7.
Augusta, Princess, daughter of Prince Frederick, Birth of. Doran. Queens Hanov. 1.
Augusta of Saxe-Gotha. Finch. Princesses of Wales, 2 : 279. 3 : 1.
Augusta Sophia, daughter of George III. Fitzgerald, P. Royal dukes, 1 : 302.
Augusta, Georgia. Sala. Amer. revis. 1 : 266.
Augustan ages. Freeman. Hist. ess. 4 : 258.
Augustine, St. Charles. Martyrs, 260. — Farrar. Lives of fathers, 2 : 298. — Allen, J. H. Chr. hist. 1st per. 122. — Hedge. Atheism, 145. — Shedd, W. G. T. Litt. ess. — Merivale, C. Four lec. 53. — Lord, J. Beacon, 1 : 349. — Osborn. From Greeks, 71. — (H. C. G. Moule) Lefroy, W. Lec. eccl. hist. 479. — (S. Hart) Warner Lib. 2 : 1014. — Blakey, R. Prim. fathers, 260. — Broadus. Lec. hist. preach. 81. — Dale, T. P. Life's motto. — Hundred greatest men, 159. — Ker. J. Lec. hist. preach. 103. — Merivale, C. Four lec. — Wilson, Wm. Pop. preach. anc. ch. 79.
— and Chrysostom. Williams, W. R. Eras, 69.
— and his influence. Brigham, C. H. Mem. 79.
— and his mother. Swing, D. Club ess. 11.
— and his times. Clarke, J. F. Events, 123.
— and the Vandals. Newman, J. H. Hist. sk. 2 : 127.

Automobiles in Europe, 1895. (T. E. Moore) U. S. Cons. Rept. 51 : 552.
— International exposition of, at Berlin, '99. (F. H. Mason) U. S. Cons. Rept. 61 : 517.
Autumn. Guthrie, T. Out of harness, 273. — Ellwanger. Sto. of house, 74. — Holmes, O. W. Old vol. 161. — Mitchell, D. G. Bound toge. 115. — Whiting, C. G. Saunterer, 192.
Autumn days. Curtis. From easy chair, 3 : 37.
Autumn voices. Dodge, M. A. 12 miles, 229.
Autumnal scenery, Influence of. Drake, N. Evenings, 1 : 1.
Autumnal tints. Thoreau. Excursions, 215.
Autun. Freeman. Hist. ess. 4 : 94.
Auvergne, France. Leslie, T. E. C. Ess. pol. econ. 412.
— Geological notes on. (A. Geikie) Vaca. tourists, 2 : 211.
— Tour in. Chambers's Repos. no. 68.
Avalanches in Switzerland, etc. Davenport. Narr. peril. 418.
Avarice. Cowley. Ess. 88.
Aventin, J., and his times. Döllinger. Stud. hist. 139.
Averroës. Warner Lib. 2 : 1079.
Averroism. Lea. Hist. inquis. 3 : 558.
Avery, Captain, pirate. Pyle, H. Buccaneers, 385. — Whitehead, C. Highwaymen, 2 : 19.
Avery, Charles. Parton. Peop. bk. biog. 122.
Avery, David. Headley, J. T. Chaplains Revol. 287.
Avesta, The. Clarke, J. F. Ten great relig. 1 : 171. — Johnson, S. Orient. relig. Pers. — Whitney, W. D. Orient. 1 : 149. — Müller, M. Chips, v. 1. — Johnson, S. Ori. relig. Persia, 53. — (A. V. W. Jackson) Warner Lib. 2 : 1084.
— and Parsi religion. (J. M. Mitchell) Leiv. papers, v. 5.
Avicebron. Warner Lib. 2 : 1099.
Avignon. Baring-Gould. Troub.-land, 261. — James, H. Little tour, 211. — Warner, C. D. Roundabout, 5.
— Papacy at. Leake, F. Hist. bub. 45.
Avirett, James B. Davidson, J. W. Writ. of South, 23.
Avon river, Up and down the. Winter. Gray days, 165.
Ayacucho, Battle of. Knox, T. W. Battles, 1.
Ayer, Richard Hazen. Livingston, J. Hist. Amer. 49.
Aylmer, John, Bishop of London. Hopkins, S. Puritans, 2 : 232.
Aymon, Jean. Baring-Gould. Oddities, 2 : 129.
Aynsley, William. Field, R. S. Prov. courts N. J. 151.
Ayr, Auld. Allingham. Varieties, 2 : 134.
Ayres, Philip. Gosse, E. From Shakesp. 179.
Ayrton, Acton Smee. Hill, F. H. Polit. portr. 301. — Ritchie. Brit. sena. 157.
Aytoun, Sir Robert, 1570-1638. Roy. Hist. Soc. 1 : 105. — Warner Lib. 2 : 1106.
Aytoun, W. Edmondstoune. (M. Bell) Miles, A. H. Poets of cent. 4 : 395. — Lorimer, Jas. Studies, nat'l & internat. — Skelton. Ess. 322. — Warner Lib. 2 : 1109.
Azamgarh, Surprise and ambush of, 1857. Malleson. Ambushes, 394.
Azara, Félice d'. Jardine. Nat. Lib. 19.
Azay-le-Rideau, Château of. Cook, T. D. Old Touraine, 2 : 205. — Larned, W. C. Churches & C. 131.
Azeglio, Massimo d'. Tuckerman. Ess. 342. — Warner Lib. 2 : 1129.
Azores, The. Benjamin, S. G. W. Atlan. isl.

336. — Benjamin, S. G. W. World's paradises, 128.
Azote, Chloride of, a new detonating compound. Davy. Works, 5 : 391.
Aztecs. Bancroft, H. H. Native races. — Foster, J. W. Prehist. Amer. — Prescott, W. H. Conq. Mex. — Short. No. Amer. of antiq.
— Hero-gods of. Brinton. Amer. hero-myths, 63.
— Social organization of. (A. F. Bandelier) Peabody Mus. Repts. 2 : 557.

Baader, Franz B. von. Erdman. Hist. of Phil. 2 : 651.
Ba'albek. (H. H. Jessup) Wilson, C. W. Pictur. Palest. 2 : 215. — Cobbe, F. P. Cities of past, 1. — (DeForest) Jour. Am. Or. Soc. 3 : 349. — Lamartine. Pilg. Holy Land, 2 : 82. — Prime, W. C. Tent life, 456.
— Ruins of. Tweedie. Ruined cities, 105.
Babbage, Charles. Lewis, T. C. Mechanicians, 302. — Timbs. Great inventors, 276.
— Calculating machine. Smiles. Indus. biog.
— Obituary of. Em. persons, 1 : 57.
Babbitt, Jacob, with portrait. Bartlett, J. R. R. I. officers, 265.
Babcock, Daniel Clark, with portrait. Bungay. Pen-portr. 237.
Babcock, Geo. R. Putnam, J. O. Addresses, 310.
Baber, emperor. Adams, W. H. D. Warriors of crescent, 139. — Jeffrey, F. Ess. — (E. S. Holden) Warner Lib. 2 : 1141.
Babington, Anthony, Conspiracy of. Hopkins, S. Puritans, 3 : 72.
Babism. (E. G. Browne) Relig. systems, 333.
Babrius. Arnold, E. Poets of Greece, 200. — Newbigging. Fables, 65. — Warner Lib. 2 : 1148.
— Fables of. Conington. Miscel. 412.
Babson, John J. (C. C. Smith) Mass. Hist. Proc. 2d ser. 3 : 138.
Babthorpes of Babthorpe. Morris, J. Troub. of Cath. v. 1.
Babylas, St., bishop of Antioch. Blakey, R. Prim. fathers, 117. — Cave. Lives of fathers, 1 : 362. — Yonge, C. M. Pupils of John, 250.
Babylon. Duncker. Hist. antiq. v. 1. — Gillett, E. H. Anc. cities, 82. — Patterson, R. H. Ess. hist. 369. — Great rivers of the world, 9.
— Johnson, S. Ori. relig. Persia, 281. — Great sieges, 116. — Keary, A. Nations around. — Myers, P. V. N. Remains of lost emp. 200. — Sayce. Fresh light. — Seven wonders of world, 63. — Wright, W. B. Anc. cities.
— Religion of. Rawlinson. Religions, 48.
— Ruins of. Tweedie. Ruined cities, 141.
— Sieges of. Robson, W. Sieges, 116.
Babylonia, Religion of. (W. St.C. Boscawen) Relig. systems, 15.
Babylonian chronology; meaning of the term "sarus." Latham. Opuscula, 81.
Babylonish captivity, The. Trench. Lec. mediæval, 277.
Babynge, John. Burke, O. J. Cath. Archb. 51.
Babyology. Hazlitt, W. C. Offspring, 273.
Babyshow, Barnum's. Buckland, F. T. Curios. nat. hist. 4 : 87.
Baccarat, Game of, in Paris. Delille, E. Some French wr. 156.
Bacchylides. Arnold, E. Poets of Greece, 128. — Mills. Poets of Greece, 143.
Baccio. See Porta.
Bach, Johann Sebastian. Apthorp. Musicians, 57. — Barnard, C. Tonemasters, 3 : 5. — Bourne, C. E. Gr. compos. 33. — Crowest.

Tone-poets, 1. — Ferris. Germ. composers, 7. — Hale, E. E. Lights 2 cent. 281. — Lillie, L. C. Music, 53. — Parry, C. H. H. Gr. compos. 60. — With portrait. Bie, O. Hist. of piano, 91. — Dole, N. H. Score, 49. — Hundred greatest men, 99. — Ossoli. Art. 250. — With portrait. Rowbotham. Priv. life compos. 78, — Sharp, R. F. Makers of music. — With portrait. Elson, L. Gr. composers, 46. — Statham. Music, 154.

Bach, Johann Sebastian, and family. Keddie. Mus. comp. 14.

— and Handel, scores of, Additions to Apthorp, Musicians, 99.

— Matthew passion and the John. Runciman, J. F. Old scores, 51.

Bach, Leonard E., with portrait. Buffen, F. F. Mus. celeb. 31. — Parry, C. H. H. Gr. comp.

Bach, Philip E., with portrait. Bie, O. Hist. of piano, 138.

Bache, Alex. D. (J. Henry) Smithson. Rept. 1870. — Youmans. Pioneers sci. 436.

Bache, Franklin. Wood, G. B. Hist. mem. 329. — (G. B. Wood) Am. Philos. Soc. Proc. 10: 121.

Bache, Sarah. Ellet. Women of revol. 1: 332.

Bachelors, Poetical old. Jameson. Loves of poets.

Bachman, John. Davidson, J. W. Writ. of South, 23.

Bacilli, the typhoid and colon, Certain agents in destroying. (J. S. Billings and Adelaide W. Peckham) Smithson. Rept. '94: 451.

Bacillus tuberculosis, New stain for. (M. Dorset) Am. Pub. Health, 24: 157.

Background, Need of a. Higginson. New world, 113.

Backhouse, Mrs. Margaret (Holden). Clayton, E. C. Eng. fem. art. 2: 21.

Backhurst, Thomas Sackville, Lord. Collier, W. F. Hist. Eng. lit. 132.

Backus, Elijah. Woollen. Biog. sk. Indians, 373.

Backworth Classical Novel-reading Union. (J. U. Barrow) Moulton, R. G. Four years novel, 17.

Bacon, Ann. Burder. Pious wom. 553. — Williams, Jane. Lit. wom. 60.

Bacon, David William. Clarke, R. H. Cath. bishops, 3: 141.

Bacon, Delia. Hawthorne. Old home, 122.

Bacon, Francis, Lord. Adams, W. H. D. Learned in law, 16. — Adams, W. H. D. Records, 53. — Campbell. Ld. Chan. 3: 1. — Collier, W. F. Hist. Eng. lit. 135. — Disraeli, I. Amen. (N. Y. 2 v.) 2: 322. — Fuller. Worthies, 2: 422. — Ingleby. Ess. 145. — Lewes. Biog. phil. — Lodge. Portraits (Bohn), v. 3. — Lord, J. Beacon, 3: 417. — Maurice, F. D. Mor. & meta. philos. v. 2. — Morris, G. S. Brit. tho't, 114. — Anton. Engl. essayists. — Collins, Stephen. Miscel. — Holland, J. Psalmists, 1: 267. — Hundred greatest men, 222. — Jesse. Court of Eng. Stuarts, 1: 286. — (Wm. Spalding) Macaulay. New biog. 37. — Macdonald, G. England's antiphon, 93. — Mitford, M. R. Recoll. 547. — Morley, H. Eng. writ. 9: 260. 11: 1. — Nasmith. Mak. mod. thought, 1: 139. — Osborn. From Greeks, 90. — Senior. Biog. sk. 384. — Stoughton, J. Worthies of sci. 45. — Taine. Eng. lit. 1: 215. — Washburn, E. W. Stud. Eng. lit. 188. — Weiss, J. Wit, 245. — Whipple. Lit. Eliz. 278. — Whipple. Outlooks, 300. — Wotton. Word portraits, 10. — Russell, W. C. Book of auth. 32. — Senior.

Biog. sk. 384. — With portrait. (C. T. Lewis) Warner Lib. 2: 1155. Same art. Warner classics, 1: 35. — Wrangham. Brit. Plutarch, v. 2.

Bacon, Francis, Lord, and Locke, J., Philosophical genius of. Mackintosh, J. Miscel. 17.

— as a gardener. Hazlitt, W. C. Gleanings, 90.

— as Lord Chancellor. Foss. Judges, 6: 56.

— at home. Disraeli, I. Curios. (N. Y. 4 v.) 4: 224.

— Defense of, by Hepworth Dixon. Lucas. Mornings, 1: 179. — Trotter. Stud. biog. 170.

— A gammon of Bacon. Hutton, L. Other times, 95.

— Life and works of. Barnes, A. Miscel. 1: 123.

— Montagu's life and works of. Macaulay. Ess. 3: 336.

— on inductive reasoning. Webb, T. E. Veil of Isis, 353.

— Philosophy of, in Germany. Müller. Chips, 3: 27.

— Prose style of. Hunt, T. W. Rep. Eng. prose, 210.

— Spedding's Life of. Lucas. Mornings, 1: 203.

— Whately on. Boyd. Crit. ess. 1.

Bacon, Leonard. Burton, N. J. Yale lec. 441. — Hatfield, E. F. Poets of church, 28.

Bacon, Nathaniel. Lossing. Em. Amer. 42.

Bacon, Sir Nicholas. Burke, S. H. Hist. portr. Tudor, 3: 198.

Bacon, Peter Child. Am. Antiq. Soc. Proc. n. s. 4: 75.

Bacon, Roger. Courtney. Studies, 51. — Ewart, H. C. Heroes of sci. 67. — Neil, S. Epoch men, 93. — Johnston, R. M. Stud. 2: 69. — Walters, J. C. Bygone Som. 149.

— the first English freethinker. Maxwell, H. Postmer. 202.

Bacteria. Gall & Robertson, Pop. read. sci. 427.

— and disease. Wisc. Health, 1891–92: 88.

— and temperature. (G. M. Sternberg) Am. Pub. Health, 20: 411.

— colors of, Nomenclature of. (E. B. Shuttleworth) Am. Pub. Health, 20: 403.

— cultivation of, Reaction of media for. (G. W. Fuller) Am. Pub. Health, 20: 381.

— flagella, Nature and value of. (V. A. Moore) Am. Pub. Health, 20: 432.

— found in Connecticut water, Description of. (C. J. Foote) Conn. Health, 1891: 407.

— Genus Cladothrix, Method of branching in. (H. L. Russell) Am. Pub. Health, 20: 408.

— in sewage and water. (G. W. Fuller & W. R. Copeland) Mass. Health, '95: 585.

— Morphological characteristics of. (T. M. Cheesman) Am. Pub. Health, 20: 400.

— Our hidden foes. Iowa Health, '93: 93.

— pathogenic, Origin and sources of. (T. Smith) Am. Pub. Health, 14: 171.

— — Removal of, from drinking water. (G. W. Fuller) Am. Pub. Health, 19: 152.

— Separation of. (J. J. Mackenzie) Am. Pub. Health, 20: 419.

— Variability in. (J. G. Adams) Am. Pub. Health, 20: 415.

— water, Development of. (W. T. Sedgwick) Am. Pub. Health, 20: 450.

— — Grouping of. (W. Johnston) Am. Pub. Health, 20: 445.

Bacteriological diagnosis, Difficulties in. (J. G. Adams) Am. Pub. Health, 20: 324.

Bacteriology. (G. W. Fuller and others) Am. Pub. Health, 20: 58, 381.

— Bibliography. Moore, V. A. Laboratory directions.

Bactra, Siege of. Robson, W. Sieges, 4.

Badajos, Night attack on. Fitchett. Deeds, 39.
— Sieges of. Robson, W. Sieges, 569.
Badby, J. Tayler. Engl. martyrs.
Baden-Baden. Bartley, G. C. T. Rhine, 100.
— and Allerheiligen. (T. A. Trollope) Murphy, Lady B. On Rhine, 75.
Badger, Luther. Livingston, J. Dist. Amer. 117.
Bagdad. Buckley, T. A. Great cities, 421.
— Siege of. Robson, W. Sieges, 422.
Bagehot, W. Hutton, R. H. Criticisms, 1 : 96.
— Leslie, T. E. C. Ess. pol. econ. 251. — With portrait. (F. Morgan) Warner Lib. 2 : 1203.
— Journalism and. Nadal, E. S. Ess. 246.
— a literary politician. Wilson, Woodrow. Mere lit. 69.
Baggallay, Sir R. (Photo.) Cooper, T. Men of mark, 1 : 3.
Baggesen, Jens, with portrait. Warner Lib. 3 : 1235.
Bagot, Elizabeth, with portrait. Jameson. Beauties, 212.
Bahama sponge-fishers. Deming. Byways, 143.
Bahamas, The. Benjamin, S. G. W. Atlantic isl. 13. — Brassey, Lady. In the trades, 285. — Mackie, J. M. Cape Cod, 318. — Benjamin, S. G. W. World's paradises, 157.
— Trade and industries of. (T. J. McLain) 1892. U. S. Cons. Rept. 39 : 370.
Bahia Blanca. Child, T. Span.-Amer. repub. 305.
— in 1890. U. S. Cons. Rept. no. 121.
Bahnmaier, Jonathan F. Miller, Jos. Singers church, 2d ed. 354.
Baif, Jan Antoine de. Cary, H. F. Early Fr. poets, 78.
Bailees, Involuntary. Lang. Leaders, 143.
Bailey, Anna W. Clement, J. Noble deeds, 73.
— Ellet. Pioneer wom. 245. — Ellet. Women of revol. 2 : 251.
Bailey, Jas. M. Clemens. Funny fellows, 100.
Bailey, Philip James, with portrait. Warner Lib. 3 : 1243. — (J. H. Brown) Miles, A. H. Poets of cent. 4 : 467. — Horne, R. H. New spirit, 355. — Gilfillan. Mod. lit. 340. — Whipple. Essays & rev. 1 : 363.
— and the spasmodic school. Nicoll, W. R. Lit. anec. 2 : 411.
— Festus. Ossoli. Life without, 153.
— — comp. with Marlowe's Faustus and Goethe's Faust. Dawson, G. Shakesp. 342.
Bailey, Theodorus, with portrait. Headley, J. T. Farragut, 224.
Baillie, Lady Grisell, 1665-1746. Keddie. Songstresses, 1 : 1. — Robertson. Eng. poetesses, 142. — (C. M. Yonge) Yonge. Good wom. 1 : 128. — Chapman, W. Wom. of cov. 233.
Baillie, Joanna, with portrait. Warner Lib. 3 : 1253. — Cone & Gilder. Pen.-portr. 1 : 223. — Howitt. Homes Br. poets, 2 : 285. — Keddie. Songstresses, 2 : 180. — Oliphant, M. Lit. hist. 2 : 323. — Robertson. Eng. poetesses, 167. — Wilson, J. G. Poets of Scot. 1 : 386. — Wotton. Word portraits, 12. — Bethune, G. W. Brit. fem. poets, 159. — Hamilton, C. J. Women writers, 110. — (W. Whyte) Miles, A. H. Poets of cent. 7 : 1. — Mitford, M. R. Recollec. 152.
Baillie, Matthew. Bettany. Em. doctors, 2 : 51.
— Georgian era, 2 : 442. — Pettigrew. Med portr. gall. v. 2.
Baillie, Robert. Carlyle. Essays. — Irving, D. Scot. writ. 2 : 55. — Miller, H. Lead. articles, 249.
Baillie, Capt. Thomas, Trial of, for libel. Erskine, T. Speeches, 1.

Baillot de Sales, Pierre M. F., with portrait. Ehrlich, A. Cel. violin. 56.
Bailly, Jean Sylvain. Adolphus. Biog. Fr. rev. 1 : 161. — Arago. Sci. Men, 1 : 91. — Jeffrey, F. Contrib. Ed. Rev.
Baily, Francis, Memoir of. Herschel, J. F. W. Essays, 552. — Walker, W., jr. Men. of sci. 2.
Baily, William. Ivimey. Eng. Bapt. 2 : 149, 598.
Bain, Alexander, with portraits. Lynch, A. Hum. doc's, 285. — Munro, J. Heroes of teleg. 277.
Bain, George W., with portrait. Bungay. Pen-portr. 262.
Bainbridge, Christopher, cardinal legate. Williams, R. F. Eng. card. 2 : 195, 536.
Bainbridge, William. Cooper, J. F. Am. nav. off. 1 : 9. — With portrait. Amer. nat. portr. gall. 3. — With portrait. Duyckinck. Nat. portr. gall. 1 : 393. — Lossing. Em. Amer. 340.
Baines, Edward. Ritchie. Brit. sena. 102. — Tartt. Ess. 1 : 25.
Bainville, Theodore de. Henley. Views, 118.
Baird, Sir D. Cole, J. W. Brit. generals, v. 1.
Baird, Henry Carey. Derby, J. C. Fifty years, 558.
Baird, Henry Martyn, with portrait. Warner Lib. 3 : 1272.
Baird, M. Parton, J. Sk. of men of progr.
Baird, Spencer F., with portrait. Goode. Smithson. Inst. 157. — Am. Antiq. Soc. Proc. n. s. 5 : 19. — (Robert Ridgway ; Garrick Mallery ; W. B. Taylor ; W. H. Dall ; J. W. Powell) Smithson. Rept. '88 : 703.
Baird family. Burke, B. Viciss. of fam. 1 : 40.
Baireuth, Wagner festival at. Hueffer. Mus. stud. 188.
Bajazets, The two, of Turkey. Doran. Monarchs, 2 : 373.
Baker, Delphine P. Brockett. Woman's work, 755.
Baker, Edward D., senator and general. Forney. Anec. 42. — Glazier, W. Heroes, 407. — Victor, O. J. Inc. of war, 216. — Sumner, C. Works, 6 : 130. — Johnston, A. Amer. ora. 4 : 51. — (G. Wilkes) Shea, J. G. Fallen brave.
Baker, George E. Derby, J. C. Fifty years, 477.
Baker, Sir G. Jesse, J. H. Cel. Eton. v. 2.
Baker, Sir Henry Williams. Hatfield, E. F. Poets of church, 31. — Miles, A. H. Poets of cent. 10 : 729. — Miller, Jos. Singers church, 2d ed. 558.
Baker, Sir Samuel White, with portrait. Warner Lib. 3 : 1277. — Em. persons, 6 : 86. — (Photo.) Cooper, T. Men of mark, 4 : 8. — Adams, W. H. D. In perils, 248. — Cochrane, R. Fam. travel. 81.
— Exploration of equatorial Africa. Frost, T. Mod. expl. 32.
— Travels of. Adams, W. H. D. Heroes of trav. 365.
Bakewell, John. Hatfield, E. F. Poets of church, 34. — Miller, Jos. Singers church, 2d ed. 229.
Baksar. Malleson, G. B. Battles of India, 164.
Balaam. Maurice, F. D. Patriarchs, 221. — Geikie, C. Old Test. char. 111.
Balaclava, Battle of. Adams, W. H. D. Engl. at war, 2 : 139. — King, C. Battles, 529.
— A version of. Forbes, A. Camps, 67.
Balance of power. Hume. Philos. works, 3 : 364.
Balance of trade. Hume. Philos. works, 3 : 339.
Balboa, Vasco Nuñez de. Maccall. For. biog. 2 : 107. — Coffin, C. C. Story of liberty, 129. — Helps. Span. conq. 1 : 321. — Irving, W. Columbus, 3 : 138. — Vogel. Cent. of discov.

234. — Maccall, W. For. biog. 2: 107. — Murray, J. O'K. Cath. heroes, 209.

Balcarres, Anne Dalrymple, Countess of. (C. M. Yonge) Yonge. Good wom. 1 : 146. — Chapman, W. Wom. of cov. 63.
— House of. Lindsay. Lives, 1 : 326. 2 : 1.

Balceroncius, John. Wallace, R. Anti-Trin. biog 2 : 380.

Balch, Charles E., with portrait. Sketches N. H. men, 113.

Balde, Johann Jacob. Winkworth. Chr. singers Germ. 240.

Baldei, Death of. Matheson. Distinc. mess. 257.

Balduccio, Giovanni, da Fisa. Perkins, C. C. Tusc. sculp. 1 : 73.

Baldung, Hanes (surnamed Grien, Grün). (A. Woltmann) Dohme, R. Early mast. 192.

Baldwin, Archbishop, 1185–90. Hook. Abps. Cant. 2 : 539.

Baldwin, Abraham. With portrait. Amer. Nat. portr. gall. v. 4. — Jones, C. C. jr. Deleg. fr. Georgia, 5. — Lossing. Em. Amer. 256. — Sparks, W. H. Memories, 38.

Baldwin, Charles Candee. Am. Bar Assoc. 18 : 531.

Baldwin, Henry, 1777–1814. Brown, D. P. Forum, 2 : 76.

Baldwin, Henry, Jr. Am. Bar Assoc. 8 : 464.

Baldwin, J. Denison. Worc. Soc. Antiq. Coll. v. 6.

Baldwin, John. Proctor. Lawy. of N. Y. 354.

Baldwin, Joseph G. Shuck. Bench & bar in Calif.

Baldwin, Samuel D. Davidson, J. W. Writ. of South, 30.

Baldwin, Thomas. Edwards, B. B. Self-taught, 121. — Lossing. Em. Amer. 204. — Miller, Jos. Singers church, 2d ed. 315.

Baldwins, The. Doran. Monarchs, 2 : 96.

Bale, John. Dunham. Lit. & sci. men, 1 : 287. — Morley, H. Eng. writ. 8 : 82–112. — Choate, I. B. Wells of Eng. 37. — Minto, W. Eng. poets, 130.

Balearic islands. Taylor, B. Bye-ways, 173. — Vuillier. Forgot. isles, 3.

Balfe, Michael William. Keddie. Mus. comp. 313. — Upton, G. P. Stand. operas, 25. — Spark, W. Mus. mem. 156.
— Violin days of. Phipson. Violinists, 64.

Balfour, Alexander. Wilson, J. G. Poets of Scot. 1 : 434.

Balfour, Arthur James. Warner Lib. 3 : 1287. — Hapgood, N. Lit. statesm. 43. — With portraits. Lynch, A. Hum. doc's, 79. — Smalley. Stud. 17. — Smalley. Lond. lett. 1 : 178. — Stead. Char. sk. 57.
— and his critics. Seth, A. Man's place, 226.
— Criticism of. Pearson, K. Chances, 1 : 173.

Balfour, James. McCosh. Scot. phil. 190.

Balfour, Robert. Irving, D. Scot. writ. 1 : 234.
— Case of. Burke, P. Cel. trials.

Bali, island of. Helms. Pioneering, 1 : 190.

Baliniski, Charles. Soboleski. Poets of Poland, 420.

Balius, Stephen. Wallace, R. Anti-Trin. biog. 2 : 390.

Ball, Sir Alexander. Coleridge. Friend, 479.

Ball, Mrs. Caroline A. Davidson, J. W. Writ. of South, 31. — Raymond, I. Southland writ. 2 : 871.

Ball, John. Gibbins. Eng. soc. ref. 1. — Maurice, C. E. Eng. pop. leaders, v. 2. — Sergeant, L. Wiclif, 259, 290. — Smith, C. R. Retrospec. 3 : 62.

Ballad, The. (F. B. Gummere) Warner Lib. 3 : 1305.
— and song literature. Saunders. Stray leaves, 33.
— the English, The Gregorian chant and. Ritter. Music in Eng. 3.

Ballad-land, Into. Watkins, M. G. In country, 85.

Ballad poetry, Early. Washington, E. W. Stud. Eng. lit. 39.
— Revival of, in 18th cent. Hales. Folia litt. 258.

Ballad singers. Story, A. T. Vagrom, 65.
— Irish and street ballads. Allingham. Varieties, 3 : 137.

Ballads. (A. Lang) Ward. Eng. poets, 1 : 203.
— Ancient Portuguese. Williams, A. M. Stud. folk. 242.
— and lyrics. Rearden. Petrarch, 165.
— Broadside. Baring-Gould, S. Survivals, 179.
— English & Scotch. Bibliography. Child, F. J. Eng. & Scot. ballads.
— Old English. Elson. Realm of music, 95.
— popular, English and Scottish. Williams, A. M. Stud. folk, 71.
— Scottish popular. Walker, H. Three cent. Scot. lit. 1 : 162.

Ballantine, James. Wilson, J. G. Poets of Scot. 2 : 298.

Ballantine, W., with photo. Cooper, T. Men of mark, 6 : 32.

Ballantyne, John. McCosh. Scot. phil. 388.

Ballard, C. R. Hemenway. Poets of Vt. 326.

Ballet, The. Badeau. Vagabond, 143.
— The corps de. Cook, D. On stage, 2 : 1.

Ballets and ballet-dancers. Cook, D. Bk. of play, 2 : 236.

Ballinger, William Pitt. Am. Bar Assoc. 11 : 350.

Balloons. See Aeronautics.

Ballot, The. Foster, R. Comment. on Const. 1 : 344.
— Early history of, in Connecticut. (S. E. Baldwin) Am. Hist. Assoc. 4 : 407.
— Reform essential to free elections. (C. C. Binney) Phila. Soc. Sci. Assoc. '89.
— Speech on the, 1872. (Earl J. Russell) Wagner, L. Mod. pol. ora. 158.
— Written, History of, and origin of Am. inst. (D. Campbell) Am. Hist. Assoc. 5 : 165.
See Suffrage.

Ballou, Hosea. Lossing. Em. Amer. 318.

Ballou, Major Sullivan. Shea, J. G. Fallen brave.
— Bartlett, J. R. R. I. officers, 249.

Balmerino, Arthur Elphinstone, Lord. Jesse. Pretenders, 385.

Balmes, J. Fundamental philosophy. Brownson, Works, 2 : 462.

Balsamo, Joseph. See Cagliostro, Count de.

Baltes, Peter Joseph. Clarke, R. H. Cath. bishops, 3 : 189.

Baltic, Battle of the. Fitchett. Deeds, 211.

Baltic towns. Mahaffy. Holl. & Germ. 179.

Baltimore, C. Calvert, Lord. Belknap. Amer. biog. 3 : 211.

Baltimore, G. Calvert, Lord. Belknap. Amer. biog. 3 : 206.
— Character of. Kennedy, J. P. Occas. addr. 125.

Baltimore, Md. Sala. Amer. revis. 1 : 117. — Brooks, E. S. Gt. cities, 68.
— Bibliography. Peabody. Inst. Lib. Cat. 1 : 227.
— City College. (P. H. Friese) U. S. Bur. Ed. Circ. '94, no. 2 : 207.
— Expedition against. Dawson. Batt. of U. S. 2 : 390.
— Growth of. Kennedy, J. P. Occas. addr. 242.

Baltimore, Md., Medical College. (T. A. Ashby) U. S. Bur. Ed. Circ. '94, no. **2** : 297.
— Recent revolt in city govt. (C. M. Howard) Nat. Conf. City Govt. '96 : 75.
Balzac, Honoré de. Henley. Views, 139. — Peck, H. T. Good English, 147. — Pellissier. Lit. move. Fr. 311. — Wells, B. W. Cent. Fr. fic. 88-165. — With portrait. (W. P. Trent) Warner Lib. **3** : 1348. Same art. Warner classics, **2** : 33. — Challice. French authors, **1** : 1. — Curwen. Sorrow, **2** : 3. — (T. Gautier) Gautier. Fam. Fr. au. 174. — James, H. French poets, 84. — Stephen, L. Hours in lib. **1** : 238. — Zimmern. For. novelists, **2** : 201. — Zola. Exper. novel, 330. — Challice. Fr. authors, **1** : 3. — Collins, W. W. Miscel. 153. — Ste. Beuve. Port. of men, 58.
— Influence of, on literature and morals. Lily. Chapters, **2** : 248.
Bamburgh, Eng., and Dunstanburgh. Freeman. Eng. towns, 324.
Bamford, Samuel. Smiles. Brief biog. 413. — Espinasse. Lanc. worth. v. **2**.
Bampfield, Edward. Ivimey. Eng. Bapt. **1** : 405.
Bampfield, Francis. Ivimey. Eng. Bapt. **2** : 476.
Banana cultivation in Nicaragua. (T. O'Hara) U. S. Cons. Rept. **54** : 556.
Bancroft, Aaron. (A. Hill) Ware, W. Amer. Unita. **1** : 171.
Bancroft, Mrs. Charitie Lees (Smith). Hatfield, E. F. Poets of church, 35.
Bancroft, George. (S. S. Green and others) Am. Antiq. Soc. Proc., n. s. **7** : 138, 237. — Badeau. Vagabond, 301. — Duyckinck. Nat. portr. gall. **2** : 396. — Griswold. Prose writ. 404. — Derby, J. C. Fifty years, 321. — Em. persons, **5** : 8. — Frothingham. Transcend. 117. — (G. W. Greene) Hubbard, E. Little jour. **2** : 361. Same art. Homes Am. authors. — With portrait. Mitchell, D. G. Am. lands, **2** : 33. — Nichol. Amer. lit. 145. — Richardson. Amer. lit. **1** : 459. — With portrait. (A. Scott) Warner Lib. **3** : 1432. — Tuckerman, C. K. Recollec. **1** : 152. — Wright, H. C. Chil. sto. in Am. lit. 123.
— as a historian. Wallis, S. T. Works, **2** : 33.
— at home. (B. G. Lovejoy) Gilder. Authors, 17.
— History of the U. S. Brownson. Works, **19** : 382.
Bancroft, Hubert Howe. With portrait. Publ. Weekly, **38** : 206. — Richardson. Amer. lit. **1** : 481.
Bancroft, Mrs. Marie E. Wilton. Matthews, B. Actors, **5** : 21.
Bancroft, Richard, 1604-10. Hook. Abps. Cant. **10** : 190. — McClure. Translators, 216.
Bancroft, S. B., with portrait. Goddard, A. Players, **1** : 297.
— and Mrs. M. E. Sala, Mrs. Fam. peop. 218.
Bandello, Matteo. Symonds. Renais. Ital. lit. **2** : 63.
Bandiera, Attilio and Emilio. Mazzini. Life & writ. **3** : 263. **5** : 156.
Bandinelli, B. Ottley. Ital. school. — Perkins, C. C. Tusc. sculp. **2** : 144. — Robinson, F. S. Connois. 135. — Symonds. Renais. Fine arts, 173.
Bandits. Appleton, T. G. Sheaf of pap. 183.
Bangkok and its people. Norman, H. Far East, 407.
Bangor, Bishop of, and others, Trial of. Erskine, T. Speeches, 508.
Bangorian controversy, B. Hoadly and. Stephen, L. Eng. thought, **2** : 152.

Bangs, Edward, with portrait. (John Lowell) Mass. Hist. Soc. Proc. 2d ser. **10** : 311.
Banim, John. Hall, S. C. Book of mem. 227. — Mitford, M. R. Recollec. 21. — Murray, J. O'K. Prose & poet. Irel. 412. — Williams, A. M. Poets of Irel.
— and the Irish novelists. Horne, R. H. New spirit, 271.
— and Michael, with portraits. Warner Lib. **3** : 1458.
Bank, The. Dodge, M. A. Country, 21.
Bank of England, Charter of. Peel, R. Speeches, **2** : 724. **4** : 349, 374.
— — History of, 1797-1821. (H. Adams) Adams, C. F. Erie, 225.
— — Restrictive policy of, 1797-1821. — Adams, H. Hist. ess. 178.
— of United States. Benton. 30 years. — Holland. Life of Van Buren, ch. 19. — Madison, J. Letters, **4** : 183, 427. — Paine, R. J. Pol. works, **1** : 365. — Rantoul. Life of Madison, ch. 7. — Williams. Statesman's manual.
— — Charter renewal. Roosevelt. Life of Benton, 114.
— — The currency and. Tilden, S. J. Writ. **1** : 101.
— — On the public deposits. Corwin, T. Life & Speeches, 149.
— — Origin of first. Webster, N. Papers, 163.
— — Removal of the deposits. Schurz. Life of Clay, v. **2**.
— Speeches on, 1815, 1832. Webster, D. Works, **3** : 35, 391.
Bank act of 1844. Hobart, V. H. H. Polit. ess. 110. — Lubbock. Addresses, 25.
Bank-notes, State limitation of issue of. Tilden, S. J. Writ. **1** : 221.
— Government issue. Garfield. Works, **2** : 175, 246.
— Proposed national. Hamilton. Ed. by Lodge, **3** : 61.
— What is a ? (E. Atkinson) Econ. tracts, no. **1**.
Bankes, Henry. Hazlitt. Parl. portr. 49.
Bankes, Sir John. Rawnsley. Lit. Assoc. Eng. lakes, **1** : 118.
Banking. Greene, W. B. Soc. frag. 35. — Atkinson, E. Distrib. of prod. 193. — Gallatin, A. Writings, **3** : 231. — Spencer, H. Ess. 319. — Genin, T. H. Selec. writ.
— and currency. (H. W. Cannon) Butterfield Lec. Un. Coll. **1** : 351.
— Bibliography. Conant, C. A. Hist. modern banks of issue. — Handy, W. M. Banking systems of world. — Providence Pub. Lib. Bull. Oct. '96.
— Good and evil of. Bolles. Chap. pol. econ. 117.
— Scotch. (S. Mason) Trans. Soc. Sci. Lond. 1877 : 686.
Bankrupt law, national, Advantages of a. (S. Wagner) Am. Bar Assoc. **4** : 223.
Bankrupt laws. (R. Wilson ; W. Hawes) Trans. Soc. Sci. Lond. 1866 : 160. — Haven, N. A. Remains, 176. — Filangieri. Sci. of legisla. **2** : 148.
— International aspects of. (J. Westlake) Trans. Soc. Sci. Lond. 1862 : 777.
— of England and Scotland. (H. G. Bell) Trans. Soc. Sci. Lond. 1860 : 183.
— Uniform. Holland. Life of Van Buren, ch. 14.
Bankruptcy. Calhoun. Works, **3** : 506. — (S. W. Dunscomb, jr.) Col. Univ. Stud. hist. **2** : 183.
— Bibliography. 54 Cong. 1st sess. Sen. doc. no. 237.

Bankruptcy, Speeches on, 1840. Webster, D. Works, 5 : 3.
— A study in comparative legislation. (S. W. Dunscomb) Colum. Univ. Stud. Hist. 2 : no. 2.
Banks, John. Dunham. Lit. & sci. men, 3 : 195.
Banks, Sir Joseph. Brougham. Works, 1 : 334.
— Creasy. Etonians, 395. — Jardine. Nat. libr. 38. — Lodge. Portraits (Bohn), v. 8. — Edgar. Boyhood, 375. — Edwards, E. Founders Brit. Mus. 2 : 487. — Walker, W., jr. Men of sci. 4.
Banks, Nath'l P. Bartlett. Pres. candidates, 198. Duyckinck Nat. portr. gall. 2 : 459. — Savage. Liv. rep. men, 17.
Banks, Thos., Eng. sculptor. Spooner. Biog. fine arts, 1 : 67.
Banks, National. See National Banks.
— People's. Lusk, H. H. Foes at home, 26.
— Relations of, to speculators. Bolles. Chap. pol. econ. 149.
Bannantyne, Bp. Adam. Wodrow. Selec. fr. biog. coll.
Bannister, John. Doran. Annals stage, 2 : 342.
— Hunt. Crit. ess. on performers, 60.
Bannister, John, leader of the royal violins. Phipson. Violinists, 32.
Bannockburn, Battle of. Adams, W. H. D. Battle sto. 310. — George, H. B. Battles, 40.
Banquets, English civic. Hawthorne. Old home, 358.
Bantingism, Our once fat friend. Wynter, A. Our soc. bees, 2 : 107.
Bantu notes and vocabularies. (H. Chatelain) Am. Geog. Soc. 26 : 51, 208.
Banville, Théodore de. Lang. Ess. in lit. 51. — Symons, A. Stud. two lit. 264. — With portrait. Warner Lib. 3 : 1474.
Baptism. (W. Clark) Church's ministry. — Stanley. Chr. instit. v. 1.
— Bibliography. Stone, D. Holy baptism.
— Double. Whedon. Ess. 1 : 216.
— English controversy on. Hunt, J. Rel. thought 19th cent. 176.
— Jewish and Christian. (Greene) Roy. Hist. Soc. 10 : 248.
Baptismal regeneration, Gorham controversy on. Stanley. Essays, 1.
Baptist, Father. Ailey Moore. Brownson. Wks. 20 : 73.
Baptist church. (J. Clifford) Relig. systems, 559. — (R. S. McArthur) Why I am, 5.
— Laity of. Anderson, M. B. Papers, 1 : 237.
Baptist churches. Bibliography. Newman, A. H. Hist. Bapt. ch. in U. S.
Baptistry at Florence, Gates of, plate. Perkins, C. C. Tusc. sculp. 1 : 64.
Baptists, Antiquity of the. Brown, J. N. Bapt. martyrs, 17.
— English. Alviella. Contemp. evol. 75.
— 7th day. (A. H. Lewis) Why I am, 141.
Bar, American, Best training for. (J. R. Tucker) Am. Bar Assoc. 19 : 595.
— The Church and the. Lorimer, Jas. Studies, nat'l & internat.
— English, Chances of. Hayward, A. Ess. 1 : 382.
— in the U. S. Bryce. Soc. institu. v. 1.
See also Law.
Barabbas. Hastings, F. Obscure charac. 254.
Baraga, Frederic. Clark, R. H. Cath. bishops, 2 : 468.
Barbadoes. Hill, R. T. Cuba, 373. — Sewell, W. G. Ordeal of free labor, 18. — Trollope, A. West Indies, 199. — Churchill's voyages, 6.
— Commerce and industries of. (E. A. Dimmick) U. S. Cons. Rept. 38 : 6.

Barbarian invaders and the early church. Bright, W. Roman see, 310.
Barbarism and civilization. Higginson. Outdoor, 105.
Barbarossa, Auruck. Utterton, F. A. Biog. sk. 193.
Barbaroux, Charles. Smythe, G. S. Hist. fancies, 260.
Barbary states, Cecil, E. Impress. of life, 79. — Latimer. Eur. in Afr. in 19th cent. 266. — Half-hours in many lands, 251. — Schuyler, E. Amer. diplomacy, 193.
Barbauld, Mrs. Anna Letitia. Elwood. Lit. ladies, 1. 224. Fawcett, M. G. Em. wom. 198. — Oliphant, M. Lit. hist. 2 : 334. — Robertson. Eng. poetesses, 74. — Balfour, C. L. Working women, 87. — Hale, S. J. Less. fr. women, 85. — Williams, Jane. Lit. wom. 281. — With portrait. Warner Lib. 3 : 1481. — Griswold, R. W. Sac. poets. — Hale, S. J. Less. wom. lives, 85. — Hamilton, C. J. Wom. writers, 66. — Hatfield, E. F. Poets of church, 36. — Miles, A. H. Poets of cent. 10 : 659. — Miller, Jos. Singers church, 2d ed. 286.
Barber, Catharine Webb. Davidson, J. W. Writ. of South, 33.
Barber, Edward. Ivimey. Eng. Bapt. 2 : 390.
Barber, Francis. With portrait. Amer. nat. portr. gall. 2.
Barber, John. Wesley & successors, 73, 89.
Barber, Julia A. Hemenway. Poets of Vt. 297.
Barber-shop as a menace to public health. (A. W. Suiter) Am. Pub. Health, 23 : 443.
Barber surgeons. Timbs. Doctors, 165.
Barbers' shops, Hygiene of. (A. Contreras) Am. Pub. Health, 19 : 81.
Barbieri, Giovanni Francesco, called Il Guercino. Symonds. Renais. Cath. reac. 2 : 365.
Barbour, John. Brink. Eng. lit. 2, pt. 2 : 52.
— Legends of the saints. Scott, Mrs. M. M. Abbotsf. 23. — Choate, I. B. Wells of Eng. 21. — Collins, Stephen. Miscel. — Irving, D. Scot. poets, 1 : 253. — Wilson, J. G. Poets of Scot. 1 : 4. — Morley, H. Eng. writ. v. 6. — Minto, W. Eng. poets, 65. — Tytler. Scot. worthies, v. 2.
— The Bruce. Lanier. Music, 212.
Barbour, P. P., Character of. Story, J. Miscel. 825.
Barcelona. Stoddard, C. A. Span. cit. 12.
— in 1892. U. S. Cons. Rept. no. 151.
— Siege of. Robson, W. Sieges, 534.
Barcevicz, Stanislaus, with portrait. Ehrlich, A. Cel. violin. 59.
Barclay, Alex. Brink. Eng. lit. 2, pt. 2 : 98. — Warner Lib. 3 : 1496. — Wilson, J. G. Poets of Scot. 1 : 31.
— The ship of fools. Disraeli, I. Amen. (N. Y. 2 v.) 1 : 326. — Morley, H. Eng. writ. 7 : 90.
Barclay, John. Holland, J. Psalmists, 2 : 243. — Jardine, W. Nat. lib. v. 24. — Irving, D. Scot. writ. 1 : 371.
Barclay, Margaret. Wright, T. Nar. sorcery, 2 : 209.
Barclay, Richard. Rhodes, B. Three apos. Quak.
Barclay, William. Irving, D. Scot. writ. 1 : 210.
Bard, Samuel (1742–1821). (James P. White) Gross. Lives Physicians, 166. — Lossing. Em. Amer. 118.
Bardaxi, Brianda de. Lea. Relig. hist. Spain, 469.
Barebones, Praise-God. Ivimey. Eng. Bapt. 1 : 157.
Barentz, William, in search of Northeast passage. Frost, T. Explorers, 209.

Barère, Bertrand, Memoirs of. Macaulay. Ess. 5 : 423.
— Speeches of. Stephens, H. M. Ora. Fr. Rev. 2 : 1.
Bareze, Cyprian. Carne, J. Em. mission. 3 : 137.
Bargagli, Scipione. Symonds. Renais. It. lit. 2 : 98.
Bargheer, Karl L., with portrait. Ehrlich, A. Cel. violin. 61.
Bargiel, Woldemar. Maitland, J. A. F. Masters Ger. music, 210.
Barham, Nicholas. Woolrych. Serjeants, 1 : 170.
Barham, Richard Harris, with portrait. Warner Lib. 3 : 1503. — Horne, R. H. New spirit, 81. — Jerdan. Men, 11. — (W. Whyte) Miles, A. H. Poets of cent. 9 : 197, 365. — Saintsbury, G. Ess. Eng. lit. 2 : 270. — Smith, C. R. Retrospec. 1 : 13.
Barhebræus, Bishop of Aleppo. Nöldeke, T. Sk. fr. east. hist. 236.
Bari. Freeman. Studies Italy, 295.
Baring, Charles Thomas, bp. of Durham. Arnold, F. Our bishops, 1 : 372.
Baring, Francis T. Grant, J. Recoll. Lords & Comm. 2 : 310.
Baring, Thomas G. See Northbrook, 1st earl of.
Baring-Gould, Sabine. Miles, A. H. Poets of cent. 10 : 755. — Miller, Jos. Singers church, 2d ed. 576. — Warner Lib. 3 : 1529.
Baring Brothers, bankers. Guild. Over the ocean, 165.
Baring family of London. Bourne, H. R. F. Eng. merch. 2 : 234. — Sanford & Townsend. Gov. fam. 2.
Barker, Andrew. Bourne, H. R. F. Eng. seam. 2 : 73.
Barker, Augustus. (A. Lincoln) Harvard mem. biog. 2 : 357.
Barker, Fordyce. Francis, S. W. N. Y. phys. 61.
Barker, George P. Proctor. Lawy. of N. Y. 27.
Barker, Peter. Baring-Gould. Yorks. odd. 1 : 177.
Barker, Mrs. Stephen. Brockett. Woman's work, 200. — Moore, F. Women of the war, 245.
Barking, Eng. Barrett, C. R. B. Essex, 43.
— Abbey. Timbs. Abbeys, 1 : 232.
Barley, John. Burke, O. J. Cath. Abp. 53.
Barlow, Mrs. Arabella G. Brockett. Woman's work, 225.
Barlow, Hannah Bolton. Clayton, E. C. Eng. fem. art. 2 : 303.
Barlow, Jane, with portrait. Warner Lib. 3 : 1543.
Barlow, Joel. With portrait. Amer. nat. portr. gall. 1. — With portrait. Duyckinck. Nat. portr. gall. 1 : 378. — Everest. Poets of Conn. 73. — Greene. Am. revol. 393. — Griswold. Poets Am. 52. — Hatfield, E. F. Poets of church, 41. — Headley, J. T. Chaplains Revol. 207. — Lossing. Em. Amer. 117. — With portrait. Mitchell, D. G. Am. lands, 168. — With portrait. Warner Lib. 3 : 1557.
— Literary shrines of. Tyler, M. C. Three men, 131.
Barlow, Rebecca. Ellet. Women of revol. 2 : 256.
Barlow, William. McClure. Translators, 172.
Barmesyde, Hugh G. The old corner. Fairbanks, O. B. Aguecheek, 212.
Barnabas, St., the apostle. Blakey, R. Prim. fathers, 38. — Cave. Lives of fathers, 1 : 90. — Hastings, F. Obscure charac. 264. — Moxom. Jerus. to Nicæa, 121.

Barnard, Daniel D. Everett. Orat. v. 4 ; also in Mass. Hist. Proc. 5 : 213.
Barnard, David, with portrait. Sketches N. H. men, 304.
Barnard, Edward William. Mitford, M. R. Recollec. 509.
Barnard, Fred'k A. P. Barnard, H. Educa. biog. 407. — N. Y. Regents' rept. 103 : 238.
Barnard, Henry. (A. D. Mayo) U. S. Bur. Ed. Rept. '96–97, 1 : 769.
— Bibliography. (W. S. Monroe) Jour. Educ. N. E. & Nat. Feb. 16, '97.
Barnard, John, of London, 1685–1764. Bourne, H. R. F. Eng. merch. 1 : 404.
Barnard, John, Autobiog. of. Mass. Hist. Coll. 3d ser. 5 : 177.
Barnard, Lady Anne (1750–1825). Keddie. Songstresses, 2 : 1. — Lindsay. Lives, 2 : 382. — Robertson. Eng. poetesses, 155. — Williams, Jane. Lit. wom. 301. — Wilson, J. G. Poets of Scot. 1 : 334. — Bethune, G. W. Brit. fem. poets, 74. — Hamilton. C. J. Women writers, 96. — Mayer, G. T. Wom. of let. 1 : 263.
Barnard, Wm., Mysterious case of. Burke, P. Cel. trials.
Barnardiston, Thomas. Woolrych. Serjeants, 2 : 537.
Barnave, Antoine P. J. M. Smythe, G. S. Hist. fancies, 189.
Barn-burners, New York. Chittenden, L. E. Pers. reminis. 11.
Barnby, Joseph. Engel. Handel to Hallé, 105.
Barnes, Albert. Fish, H. C. Pulp. eloq. 253. — Griswold. Prose writ. 601. — Derby, J. C. Fifty years, 577. — Parton, J. Sk. of men of prog.
— Preaching of. Phelps, A. Portfolio, 205.
Barnes, Barnabe. Bell, R. Lit. & sci. men, 2 : 150. — Griswold, R. W. Sac. poets.
Barnes, D. Parton, J. Sk. of men of prog.
Barnes, W. Dorsetshire poems. Doyle. Lec. on poetry, 53. — (C. Sayle) Miles, A. H. Poets of cent. 3 : 397.
— a modern classic. Patmore. Religio poetæ, 137. — Warner Lib. 3 : 1563.
Barnet, Battlefield of. Winter, W. Shakesp. Eng.
Barnett, John. Keddie. Mus. comp. 318.
Barneveld, Jan van Olden-. Crowe, E. E. For. statesmen, 1 : 153.
— Motley's. Heywood, J.C. How they strike, 236.
Barney, Joshua. With portrait. Amer. nat. portr. gall. 4. — With portrait. Duyckinck. Nat. portr. gall. 1 : 212.
Barney, Timothy (d. 1789). Redding. Misers, 2 : 73.
Barnfield, Richard. (T. H. Ward) Ward. Eng. poets, 1 : 474.
Barnstable, Mass., Settlement of. Everett. Orat. v. 2.
Barnum, Dr. J. P. Brockett. Woman's work, 551.
Barnum, P. T. Bungay. Off-hand, 199. — Wallis, S. T. Works, 2 : 69. — Lossing. Em. Amer. 120.
Barnwell, Annie M. Raymond, I. Southland wr. 2 : 912.
Barolo, Julietta, Marchioness of. Gearey. Dau. of Italy, 169.
Barometer, The. Lardner, D. Mus. of sci. 4 : 177. — Pepper, J. H. Pneumatics, 18. — Timbs. Invent. & discov. 50.
Barometric pressure in the Antarctic zone. Proctor. Light sci. 2 : 277.

Baron, J. Pettigrew. Med. portr. gall. v. 2.

Barres, Maurice. Delille, E. Some French wr. 191.

Barrett, Elizabeth. *See* Browning, Elizabeth B.

Barrett, George. Hutton, L. Plays, 113.

Barrett, Lawrence. (W. M. Laffan) Matthews, B. Actors, 5 : 37. — (B. F. Woolf) McKay, F, E. Fam. actors, 62.

— Acting of. Winter, W. Shadows, 2 : 195.

— as Gringoire. Winter. Shadows, 5 : 47.

— as Lanciotto. . Winter. Shadows, 3 : 186.

— Death of. Winter. Shadows, 1 : 215.

Barrett, Wilson, with portrait. Goddard, A. Players, 1 : 117. — Wilman, G. Sk. liv. celeb. 38.

— as Claudian. Winter. Shadows, 3 : 270.

— as Hamlet. Winter, W. Shadows, 2 : 339.

Barrick, James Russell. Davidson, J. W. Writ. of South, 35.

Barrie, James. Matthew. Griswold, H. T. Personal sk. 336. — With portrait. Warner Lib. 3 : 1571. — Wilson, S. L. Theol. mod. liter.

Barringer, Daniel Moreau. Livingston, J. Em. Am. lawy. 605.

Barrington, Geo. Ashton. 18th cent. waifs, 31.

Barrington, R., with portraits. Goddard, A. Players, 2 : 299.

Barrington, S., bishop of Durham. Jesse, J. H. Cel. Eton. v. 2.

Barritt, Frances Fuller. Coggeshall. Poets of west, 510.

Barron, Edward. Clarke, R. H. Cath. bishops, 2 : 595.

Barron,——. Grant, J. Recoll. Lords & Comm. 2 : 277.

Barrot, Odillon. Loménie. Liv. characters, 249. — Walsh, R. M. Liv. char. France.

Barrow, Elizabeth. Holloway, L. C. Mothers of gr. men, 129.

Barrow, Henry, Independent. Hopkins, S. Puritans, 3 : 445.

Barrow, Isaac. Stoughton, J. Worthies of sci. 111. — Broadus. Lec. hist. preach. 212.

— Prose of. Jones, W. A. Lit. stud. 2 : 1.

Barrow, Sir J. Espinasse. Lanc. worth. v. 2.

Barrowe, Henry. Stoughton, J. Spir. heroes, 42.

Barrows, in East Yorkshire. Wright, T. Ess. archæol. 1 : 22.

— Ogbury. Allen, G. Falling in l. 287.

Barrozzi, Giacomo. Milizia. Lives arch. 2 : 16.

Barry, Anne. Doran. Annals stage, 2 : 103. — Doran. Their maj. serv. 2 : 129.

Barry, Elizabeth. Austin & Ralph. Laureates, 236. — Doran. Annals stage, 1 : 104. — Galt. Players, 1 : 85. — Doran. Their maj. serv. 1 : 138.

Barry, James, Irish hist. painter. Carr, J. C. Papers, 79. — Craik. Pursuit knowl. 2 : 157. — Cunningham, A. Brit. sculp. 2 : 54. — Curran. Irish bar, 2 : 169. — Thornbury. Brit. art, 1 : 156.

— Dwelling of. Hall, Mrs. S. C. Pilgr. Eng. shr. 1 : 209.

Barry, John, Bishop. Clarke, R. H. Cath. bishops, 2 : 551. — Murray, J. O'K. Cath. pioneers, 326. — Murray, J. O'K. Cath. heroes, 615.

Barry, John, Comm. (M. I. T. Griffin) Am. Hist. Assoc. Rept. '95 : 339. — With portrait. Am. nat. portr. gall. v. 2. — Duyckinck. Nat. portr. gall. 1 : 293. — Lossing. Em. Amer. 121.

Barry, John S. (C. C. Smith) Mass. Hist. Proc. 13 : 136.

Barry, Marie J. G. de V., Comtesse du. Imbert de St. A. Wom. last yrs. Louis xv, 91.

Barry, Marie J. G. de V., Comtesse du, Execution of. Imbert de St. A. Wom. last yrs. Louis xv, 199.

Barry, Spranger. Doran. Annals stage, 1 : 357. 2 : 96. — Matthews, B. Actors, 1 : 123. — Doran. Their maj. serv. 1 : 477. 2 : 87, 129.

Barry, William. Am. Antiq. Soc. Proc. n. s. 3 : 487.

Barstow, Nathaniel Saltonstall. (J L. Stackpole) Harvard mem. biog. 2 : 105.

Bart, Jean. Bernard, F. Escapes, 96. — Laughton. Stud. nav. hist. 252. — With portrait. Norman, C. B. Corsairs, 27. — Richards, L. E. Glimpses, 165.

Bartendale, John. Baring-Gould. Yorks. odd. 1 : 117.

Barth, Christian Gottlob. Stevenson. Lives & deeds, 88.

Barth, H., African explorations of. Adams, W. H. D. Heroes of trav. 90.

Bartholdus, Wallace R. Anti-Trin. biog. 3 : 100.

Bartholomew, Erasmus Sherman, with portrait. Bartlett, J. R. R. I. officers, 344. — Tuckerman. Artists, 609.

Bartholomew, William. Miller, Jos. Singers church, 2d ed. 434.

Bartlett, Charles H., with portrait. Sketches N. H. men, 33.

Bartlett, Daniel W. Derby, J. C. Fifty years, 636.

Bartlett, Elisha, 1804-55. (S. H. Dickson) Gross. Lives physicians, 732.

Bartlett, John. (C. T. Thayer) Ware, W. Am. Unita. 2 : 411.

Bartlett, John Russell. Am. Antiq. Soc. Proc. n. s. 4 : 178.

Bartlett, Joseph. Loring, J. S. 100 Bost. ora. 405.

Bartlett, Josiah, 1729-95. Dwight, N. Signers of decl. 1. — Lossing. Em. Amer. 294. — Lincoln, R. W. Signers, 3. — Lossing. Signers, 13. — (R. Frothingham) Mass. Hist. Proc. 1 : 323. — Sanderson. Signers, 3.

Bartlett, Mary E. Brockett. Woman's work, 794.

Bartlett, Shubael. (D. E. Bartlett) N. E. Hist. Gen. Soc. Biog. 2 : 186.

Bartlett, Sydney. Am. Bar Assoc. 12 : 357.

Bartlett, Wm. F., Gen. Brockett. Woman's work, 352.

Bartlett, William H. (I. W. Smith) Memo. of judges fr. Dartm. 41.

Bartlett, Wm. H. C. Am. Acad. A. & S. Proc. 30 : 570.

Bartlett, William S. (E. F. Slafter) Mass. Hist. Proc. 2d ser. 2 : 430.

Bartlett family. Titcomb, S. E. N. Eng. peo. 185.

Bartley, James Avis. Davidson, J. W. Writ. of South, 41.

Bartol, Cyrus Augustus. Frothingham. Transcend. 341. — Putnam, A. P. Singers liberal, 347.

Bartolo, Taddeo di. Symonds. Renais. Fine arts, 218.

Bartolommeo, Fra. (Hermann Lucke) Dohme, R. Early mast. 402.—Oliphant. Makers of Fr. 337. — Stillman, W. J. Old Ital. mas. 183. — Symonds. Renais. fine arts, 304.

Bartolommeo, *di San Marco*. Ottley. Ital. school.

Barton, Andrew. Bourne, H. R. F. Eng. seam. 1 : 50.

Barton, A. S. Hemenway. Poets of Vt. 225.

Baths, Public, needed in London. Meath. Soc. arrows, 347.
— — *versus* disease. (C. H. Shepard) Penn. Health, '92 : 507.
Bathurst, Benjamin. Hazlitt. Parl. portr. 99.
— Disappearance of, 1809. Baring-Gould. Oddities, 1 : 1.
Bathurst, Henry, 2d earl. Campbell. Ld. Chan. 7 : 118. — Foss. Judges, v. 8. — Welsby. Eng. judges.
Bathurst, H., 3d earl. Thornton. For. sec. v. 1.
Bathurst, William Hiley Bragge. Hatfield, E. F. Poets of ch. 48. — Miller, Jos. Singers church, 2d ed. 444.
Batoum, Trade of, 1891. U. S. Cons. Rept. 39 : 16.
— 1893. (J. C. Chambers) U. S. Cons. Rept. 45 : 167.
Batson, James. Whitehead, C. Highwaymen, 1 : 47.
Battell, Andrew. Wanderings in Western Africa. Frost, T. Explorers, 181.
Battell, Philip. Hemenway. Poets of Vt. 205.
Batterley, John. Burke, O. J. Cath. archb. 53.
Battersea. (P. M. Thornton) Clinch, G. Bygone Surrey, 170.
Battie, W. Jesse, J. H. Cel. Eton. v. 1.
Battle, William Horn. Livingston, J. Em. Am. lawy. 144.
Battle Abbey. (Duchess of Cleveland) Malan, A. H. Famous homes, 197. — Timbs. Abbeys, 1 : 360.
Batty, Christopher. Miller, Jos. Singers church, 2d ed. 212.
Batuta, Ibn. St. John. Cel. travelers, 1 : 69.
Baude, Henri. Besant. Fr. poetry, 154.
Baudelaire, Charles. Gautier. Fam. Fr. au. 168.
— Harrison, J. A. Group of poets, 302. — James, H. French poets, 72. — Allingham. Varieties, 3 : 333. — Delille, E. Some French writ. 42. — Pellissier. Lit. move. Fr. 349. — Saintsbury. Misc. ess. 216. — With portrait. (G. King) Warner Lib. 3 : 1617.
Baudin, Pierre Charles Louis, Speech of. Stephens, H. M. Ora. Fr. Rev. 2 : 540.
Baudouin, Pierre Antoine. Dilke. Fr. painters 18th cent. 129.
Baudry, Paul. (K. Cox) Van Dyke, J. C. Mod. Fr. mast. 61.
Baum, Martin. Mansfield, E. D. Pers. mem. 147.
Baur, Ferd. Chr. Gostwick, J. German culture, 446.
— and his theory of Christianity. (A. B. Bruce) Liv. papers, v. 7.
Baux, Les. Baring-Gould. Troub.-land, 114.
Bavaria. Felton, C. C. Europe, 103. — Warner, C. D. Saunterings, 83.
— Beggars in. Rumford. Ess. 1 : 14.
— Public institutions in. Rumford. Ess. 1 : 391.
Baxter, Andrew. McCosh. Scot. phil. 42.
Baxter, Mrs. Margaret (Charlton). Anderson, Jas. Mem. Wom. Pur. 2 : 145. — Kavanagh. Women of Christianity, 236.
Baxter, Richard. Collier, W. F. Hist. Eng. lit. 232. — Dawson, G. Biog. lec. 98. — Grosart. Nonconf. 107. — Neal, D. Hist. Purit. — Stephen. Ess. eccl. biog. 337. — Tulloch, J. Eng. Purit. 281. — Whittier. Old portr. 165. — Broadus. Lec. hist. preach. 204. — Edwards, B. B. Self-taught, 225. — Griswold, R. W. Sac. poets. — Hatfield, E. F. Poets of ch. 50. — Holland, J. Psalmists, 2 : 95. — Macdonald, G. England's antiphon, 232. — Miller, Jos. Singers church, 2d ed. 80. — Pierce, B. K.

Em. dead, 96. — Stoughton, J. Spir. heroes, 292. — Waterbury. Eloq. preach. 173. — Wordsworth, C. Eccles. biog. v. 4.
Baxter, Richard, Autobiography of. Coleridge. Lit. rem. 4 : 70.
— Life and times. Stephen, J. Ess.
Baxwell, James, Trial of. Phillips, S. M. Famous cases, 117.
Bay Psalm Book Nichol. Amer. lit. 56. — Richardson. Amer. lit. 2 : 3.
Bayard, Chevalier. Budd, H. St. Mary's Hall lec. 42. — Hewlett. Heroes, 237. — Hale, E. E. Boys' heroes, 95. — Wilson, J. G. Illus. sol. 29. — Reynolds, G. Papers, 282. — Smith, H. G. Romance of hist. 137.
Bayard, James Asheton. With portrait. Amer. nat. portr. gall. v. 2. — Lossing. Em. Amer. 267. — Moore, F. Am. eloq. 2 : 52.
Bayard, Nicholas, 1702. Chandler, P. W. Am. crim. trials, 1 : 267.
Bayard, Pierre. Utterton, F. A. Biog. sk. 149.
Bayard, Samuel. Carson, H. L. Sup. Ct. of U.S. 572.
Bayard, Thomas Francis. Am. Bar Assoc. 21 : 648. — With portrait. Butterfield Lec. Un. Coll. 1 : 145.
Bayeux and St. Lô, A day at. Dodd, A. B. Three Norm. inns, 266.
Bayfield, R. Tayler. Eng. martyrs.
Bayle, Henri. Hapgood, N. Lit. statesm. 69.
Bayle, P., Characteristics of. Disraeli, I. Curios. (N. Y. 4 v.) 3 : 136.
— Critical dictionary. Disraeli, I. (Curios. N. Y. 4 v.) 3 : 129.
— Skepticism of. Stephen, J. F. Horæ Sabb. 2 : 174.
Bayley, James Roosevelt. Clarke, R. H. Cath. bishops, 3 : 43.
Bayly, Ada E., with portrait. Black, H. C. Wom. authors, 133.
Bayly, Thomas H. Lang. Ess. in lit. 36. — Miles, A. H. Poets of cent. 9 : 241.
Baynard, Mrs. Ann. Burder. Pious wom. 130.
Baynard's Castle, Romance of. Timbs. Abbeys, 1 : 52.
Bayne, Thos. L. Am. Bar Assoc. 15 : 439.
Baynes, Thomas Spencer. Skelton, J. Tabletalk, 38.
Bayreuth in 1897. Runciman J. F. Old scores, 223. — Ehlert. Tone-world, 181. — Hueffer. Mus. stud. 188.
Bazaine, Marshall F. A. Em. persons, 4 : 124.
Bazalgette, Sir J., with photo. Cooper, T. Men of mark, 2 : 19.
Bazan, Emilia Pardo. Warner Lib. 19 : 11038.
Bazin, John S. Clarke, R. H. Cath. bishops, 2 : 370.
Bazzi, Giovanni Antario de', called " Il Soddoma." (R. Vischer) Dohme, R. Early mast. 466.
Bazzini, Antonio. Streatfeild. Masters Ital. mus. 257. — With portrait. Ehrlich, A. Cel. violin. 1.
Beach, Sir Michael Hicks-. Escott, T. H. S. Pillars emp. 122.
Beach, S. Ferguson. Am. Bar Assoc. 16 : 450.
Beach, William A., with portrait. Scott, H. W. Dist. Am. lawy. 33.
Beacons and buoys, Illumination of. Estes. Half-hour, v. 2.
Beaconsfield, Benjamin Disraeli, Lord. Farrar. Men, 237. — Friswell. Mod. Men of l. 195. — Gilfillan. 3d gall. 352. — Hill, F. H. Polit. portr. 22. — Reid, T. W. Politicians, 1 : 37. — Higginson, T. W. Eng. statesm. 35. — Jeaf-

freson. Novelists, **2** : 221. — (F. W. Farrar)
Parton. Princes, 93. — Reid, T. W. Cab. portr.
1. — Skelton. Ess. 240. — Towle. Cert. men,
95. — Walsh, W. S. Pen-pic. Vic. au. 87. — Wotton. Word portraits, 15. — With portrait. (I.
C. Cabell) Warner Lib. **3** : 1633. — Duyckinck.
Portr. gall. **2** : 508. — Bolton, S. K. Fam. Eng.
statesm. — Henley. Views, 20. — Em. persons,
2 : 292. — Collins, M. Pen sketches, **2** : 1. —
Johnston, R. M. Stud. **2** : 24. — Kent, W. C.
M. Derby min. 33. — Skelton, J. Ess. in hist.
240.

Beaconsfield, Benjamin Disraeli, Lord, Administration of. Thornton. For. sec. v. **3**. —
Tyler, M. C. Glimpses Eng. 122.
— and his minor biographers. Espinasse. Lit.
recoll. 407.
— and Louis Napoleon compared. Greg, W. R.
Miscel. **1** : 149.
— at a Guildhall banquet, 1879. Smalley. Lond.
lett. **1** : 52.
— Bibliography. Notes & Quer. 8th ser. **3** : 321.
— Endymion. Scherer. Ess. Eng. lit. 236.
— Foreign policy of. Duff, M. E. G. Miscel. 288.
— Lothair. Harrison, F. Choice of bks. 147.

Beadle, Elias R. (D. H. Agnew) Am. Philos.
Soc. Proc. **22** : 227.

Beal, James. Davidson, J. M. Eng. lib. 231.

Beale, Helen G. Raymond, I. Southland wr. **2** :
809.

Beale, Mrs. Mary (Craddock). Clayton, E. C.
Eng. fem. art. **1** : 40. — Costello. Englishwomen, **3** : 293. — Holland, J. Psalmists, **2** : 75.

Beales, John Charles. Francis, S. W. N. Y.
phys. 195.

Beall, R. A. Miller, S. F. Bench of Ga. v. **1**.

Beamish, Rev. H. H. Grant, Jas. Metropol. pul.
191.

Beane, Sawney. Whitehead, C. Highwaymen,
1 : 30.

Beard, James H. Sheldon, G. W. Amer. painters, 113.

Beard, John, English actor. Hogarth. Mem.
opera, **2** : 26.

Beard, William Holbrook, with portrait. Benjamin, S. G. W. Am. art. v. **1**. — Sheldon.
Amer. painters, 56. — Tuckerman. Artists,
498.

Beards, Concerning. Boyd. Less. of mid. age,
131.
— and their bearers. Doran. Habits, 154.

Beardsley, Samuel. Proctor. Lawy. of N. Y.
365.

Béarn, Churches of. Larned, W. C. Churches
& C. 102.

Bears. Morgan, C. L. Animal sk. 23.

Beasley, Frederick. Wood, G. B. Hist. mem.
403.

Beasley, Peter R. Walker, C. D. Biog. Va. Mil.
Inst. 46.

Beasten, Chas., jr. Am. Bar Assoc. **112** : 355.

Beasts. Bartol. Principles, 228.

Beaton. Boyd. Aut. holid. 275.

Beatoun, Cardinal. Lodge. Portraits (Bohn),
v. **1**.

Beatrice, daughter of Henry III. Green, M. A.
E. Princesses, **2** : 225.

Beatrice, Shakespeare's. Martin. Shaks. female, 289.

Beatrice Portinari and Dante. Goodrich, F. B.
Women, 73. — Jameson. Loves of poets.

Beatson, Wm. F. Laurie, W. F. B. Dist. Anglo-
Ind. **1** : 93.

Beattie, George. Wilson, J. G. Poets of Scot.
2 : 87.

Beattie, James. Chalmers. Eng. poets, **18** : 515.
— McCosh. Scot. phil. 230. — Wilson, J. G.
Poets of Scot. **1** : 254. — Griswold, R. W. Sac.
poets.
— Forbes's Life. Foster, J. Crit. Ess. (Bohn) **1** :
17. — Jeffrey, F. Contrib. Ed. Rev.

Beattie, William. Wilson, J. G. Poets of Scot.
2 : 133.

Beauchamp, Richard, Earl of Warwick. Fuller. Worthies, **3** : 367.

Beauclerk, Topham. Guiney, L. I. Little Eng.
gall, 171.

Beaufort, Duc de. Bernard, F. Escapes, 65.

Beaufort, Sir Francis. Martineau, H. Biog. sk.
207.

Beaufort, Gabrielle d'Estrees, Duchess of. Adams, W. H. D. Fam. beauties, **1** : 255.

Beaufort, H. C. F. Somerset, duke of, at Badminton. Yates, E. H. Celeb. **1** : 105.

Beaufort, Henry. Campbell. Ld. Chan. **1** : 269.
— Williams, R. F. Eng. card. **2** : 70.

Beaufort, Battle of. Dawson. Batt. of U. S. **1** :
480.

Beaujonc mine, Inundation of. Davenport.
Narr. peril. **2** : 360.

Beaulieu Abbey. Timbs. Abbeys, **1** : 399.

Beaumarchais, P. A. C. de. Besant. Fr. humor.
391. — Forster. Fr. & Span. genius, 111. —
Mackaye. Abbess Pt. Royal, 65. — With portrait. (B. Matthews) Warner Lib. **3** : 1657.
— and the French stage. Hawkins. Fr. stage 18th
cent. v. **2**.

Beaumont, Agnes, friend of John Bunyan. Anderson, Jas. Mem. wom. Pur. **2** : 210.

Beaumont, Francis. Chalmers. Eng. poets, **6** :
175. — Hazlitt. Dram. Eliz. — (A. C. Bradley) Ward. Eng. poets, **2** : 43. — Mitford, M.
R. Recollec. 89. — With portrait. Warner
Lib. **3** : 1674.
— and J. Fletcher. Coleridge. Lec. on Shaks. —
Crofts, E. Chap. Eng. lit. 258. — Donne, W.
B. Ess. on drama, 34. — Dunham. Lit. & sci.
men, **2** : 205. — Ward, A. W. Eng. dram. **2** :
155. — Whipple. Lit. Eliz. 157. — Donne. Ess.
on drama. — Crawford, O. Eng. com. dram.
57. — Dunham, S. A. Em. liter. men, **2** : 203.
— Gosse, E. Jacobean poets, 68. — Lowell.
Old Eng. dram. 100. — Morley, H. Eng. writ.
11 : 243. — Swinburne. Stud. prose & p. 53.
— — Bibliography. Harv. Bull. v. **6**. — Harvard
Bibliog. contrib. no. 39.
— — Plots analyzed. Rymer. Tragedies of last
age.
— Notes on. Coleridge. Lit. rem. **2** : 289.

Beaumont, Sir George. Coleridge and Wordsworth. Woodberry. Stud. in lett. 188.

Beaumont, Sir John. Bell, R. Lit. & sci. men,
2 : 162. — Chalmers. Eng. poets, **6** : 3. — Gosse,
E. Jacobean poets, 107. — Griswold, R. W.
Sac. poets. — Macdonald, G. England's antiphon, 142. — Miller, Jos. Singers church, 2d
ed. 506.

Beaumont, Joseph. Poems. Drake, N. Noontide, **1** : 259. **2** : 249.

Beaumont, Thos. Wentworth. Grant, J. Recoll. Lords & Comm. **2** : 66.

Beauregard, Gen. P. G. T. Cooke, J. E. Wearing gray, 83. — Pollard. Life of Lee, 231. —
Snow. So. generals, 199. — (J. C. Ropes)
Dwight, T. F. Fed. & confed. comm. v. **1**.

Beauties and poets. Jameson. Loves of poets.

Beautiful, The. Calvert. Ess. æsth. 7. — Whittier. Lit. recre. 395. — Winchell. Sparks geol.
ham. 100.
— and its rela. to culture. Shedd. Lit. ess. **1**.

Beautiful, the, Educational value of. (N. C. Schaeffer) Nat. Educa. Assoc. '88 : 332.
— Limits of. Schlegel. Æsthet. (Bohn) 413.
— Philosophy of. (J. S. Blackie) Coan. Art & lit. I.
— use of, Christian liberty in. Beecher. Star papers, 293.
Beauty. Bacon. Ess. — Emerson, R. W. Conduct, 265. — Friswell. About, 267. — Hazlitt. Round table, 6. — Holland, E. G. Reviews, 208.
— and religion. King, T. S. Patriotism, 79.
— Artificial. Cobbe, F. P. Re-echoes, 279.
Before Burroughs, Birds and poets, 173.
— composition, expression, characterization in art. Symonds. Ess. 1 : 212.
— female, Criticism on. Hunt, L. Men, wom. & books, 136.
— Metaphysical writers on. Blakey, R. Works, 3 : 419.
— Moral. Peabody. Christian morals.
— Personal. Spencer, H. Ess. (N. Y.) 149.
— Principle of, in works of art. Wallace, H. B. Art. 57.
— Real and ideal. Patterson, R. H. Ess. hist. 44.
— Steps of. Hedge, F. H. Martin Luther, 206.
Beauvais, Cathedral of. Larned, W. C. Churches & C. 18.
— Siege of. Robson, W. Sieges, 447.
Beaux, Chapters on. Doran. Habits, 325.
Beaver, The. Hubbard, B. Memorials, 361.
Beaver-Dams, Battle of. Dawson. Batt. of U. S. 2 : 253.
Beccadelli, Antonio. Il Panormita. Symonds. Reviv. of learn. 254.
Becher, Gen. J. R. Laurie, W. F. B. Dist. Anglo-Ind. 2 : 24.
Beck, Mrs. Brockett. Woman's work, 663.
Beck, John B., 1794-1851. (C. R. Gilman) Gross. Lives physicians, 605.
Beck, Lewis C., 1798-1853. (Alden March) Gross. Lives physicians, 679.
Beck, Theodoric Romeyn. With portrait. Amer. nat. portr. gall. 1. — (Frank H. Hamilton) Gross. Lives physicians, 776.
Becker, Jean, with portrait. Ehrlich, A. Cel. violin. 75.
Becket, Thomas à. See Thomas à Becket.
Beckford, William. Bourne. Lond. merchants, 189. — Griffin, G. W. Stud. liter. 97. — Jeaffreson. Novelists, 1 : 389. — Tuckerman. Charac. 179. — Mitchell, D. G. Eng. lands, 3 : 285. — Robinson, F. S. Connois. 123. — With portrait. Warner Lib. 3 : 1699.
— and Fonthill. Timbs, J. Eng. eccen. 1. — Walters, J. C. Bygone Som. 136.
— Vathek. Griffin, G. W. Stud. in lit. — Saunders, F. Famous books, 124.
Beckner, Volney. Chambers's Miscel. no. 12.
Beckwith, N. W. Parton, J. Sk. of men of progr.
Becuis, John. Wallace, R. Anti-Trin. biog. 3 : 293.
Bed, Advantages of an occasional day in. Arnold, F. 3-cor. ess. 85.
Beddoes, T. Georgian era, 2 : 437.
Beddoes, Thomas Lovell. (E. Gosse) Ward. Eng. poets, 4 : 552. — Gosse, E. Crit. kit-kats. — (R. Garnett) Miles, A. H. Poets of cent. 3 : 521. — Procter, B. W. Autob. 182. — Stoddard, R. H. Under eve. lamp, 200.
Beddome, Benjamin. Hatfield, E. F. Poets of church, 53. — Ivimey. Eng. Bapt. 4 : 461. — Miller, Jos. Singers church, 2d ed. 222.
Bede, The Venerable. Ker, J. Lec. hist. preach. 113. — Charles. Martyrs, 420. — Collier, W.

F. Hist. Eng. lit. 23. — Lloyd, Mrs. W. R. Watchers for dawn, 9. — Montalembert. Monks, 5 : 57. — Milman. Lat. Christianity. — Bayly, J. A. S. New stud. 34. — Morley, H. Eng. writ. v. 2. — Sparvel-Bayly. New stud. 34. — Hunt, T. W. Rep. Eng. prose, 15. — Miller, Jos. Singers church, 2d ed. 14. — Neale. Mediæv. preachers.
Bedell, William, Burnet's life of. Coleridge. Lit. rem. 4 : 71.
Bedford, Anne Carre, countess of. Lodge. Portraits (Bohn), v. 6.
Bedford, Francis Russell, 4th earl of. Lodge. Portraits (Bohn), v. 4.
Bedford, Francis Russell, 5th duke of. Lodge. Portraits (Bohn), v. 8.
Bedford, John, 4th duke of. Brougham. Works, 3 : 384. — Lodge. Portraits (Bohn), v. 7.
Bedford, John Plantagenet, duke of. James, G. P. R. Commanders, 1 : 36. — Edgar. Seakings, 88.
Bedford, John. Wesley & successors, 207.
Bedford, John Russell, 1st earl of. Lodge. Portraits (Bohn), v. 1.
Bedford, Lucy Harrington, countess of. With portrait. Costello. Englishwomen, 2 : 172. — Lodge. Portraits (Bohn), v. 3.
Bedford, William Russell, duke of. Lodge. Portraits (Bohn), v. 6.
Bedford, England, suffering of Baptists at. Ivimey. Eng. Bapt. 1 : 364.
Bedford Park, Eng. Conway, M. D. Trav. So. Kens. 217.
Bedfordshire, Baptists of. Ivimey. Eng. Bapt. 2 : 13.
Bedini, Cagetan. Clarke, R. H. Cath. bishops, 2 : 605.
Bedle, Joseph D. Am. Bar Assoc. 17 : 512.
Beds. Baring-Gould, S. Survivals, 84.
— and bedrooms. Hunt, L. Men, wom. & books, 67.
Bedwell, William. McClure. Translators, 100.
Bee, Bumble-. Whiting, C. G. Saunterer, 176.
— Honey. Morgan, C. L. Animal sk. 251.
Beecham, John. Wesley & successors, 173.
Beecher, Catherine E. Derby, J. C. 50 years.
— Hart, J. S. Fem. prose, 275. — (H. B. Stowe) Our fam. wom. 75. — Hanaford. Wom. of cent. 504.
Beecher, Edward. Bungay. Off-hand, 341.
Beecher, Henry Ward. With portrait. Ann. cyclop. '87. — Bartlett, D. W. Mod. agitators, 203. — Badeau. Vagabond, 279. — Cook, Jos. Curr. relig. perils. — Griswold. Prose writ. 639. — Bungay. Off-hand, 104. — Stowe. Men of our time, 505. — With portrait. Brockett. Men of our day, 590. — Bolton, S. K. Fam. leaders, 217. — Bungay. Repr. men, 44. — Curtis, G. W. Other ess. 110. — Derby, J. C. Fifty years, 461. — Duyckinck. Portrait gall. 2 : 601. — Great mod. preachers. — Johnston, A. Amer. ora. 4 : 93. — McCulloch, H. Men & meas. 140. — Richardson. Amer. lit. 1 : 303. — (Lyman Abbott) Warner Lib. 3 : 1713.
— and his church. Parton. Fam. Amer. 347.
— in his pulpit after the death of Lincoln. Curtis. From easy chair, 3 : 20.
— Influence on relig. thought in England. (C. A. Berry) Abbott, L. New purit. 107.
— Norwood. Brownson. Works, 19 : 533.
— Personality and political influence of. (J. R. Howard) Beecher, H. W. Patriotic addr. 11.
— Speeches of, in England. (O. W. Holmes) Beecher, H. W. Patriotic addr. 422.
— Tilton case. Godkin. Reflections, 192.

dow. Stud. mod. mus. v. 1. — Henley. Views, 124. — Lennox, W. P. Plays, 2 : 232. — Sharp, R. F. Makers of music. — With portrait. Warner Lib. 3 : 1809. — Zola. Exper. novel. 322.

Bermingham, William de. Burke, O. J. Cath. archb. 30.

Bermondsey Abbey and its memories. Timbs. Abbeys, 1 : 41.

Bermudas, The. Benjamin. Atlan. Isl. 161. — Benjamin, S. G. W. World's paradises, 181. — Brassey, Lady. In the trades, 359. — Irving, W. Wolfert's roost, 109. — Mackie. Cape Cod, 385. — Trollope, A. West Indies. — Thomson, W. Voy. of Chall. 1. — Scollard. Und. sum. skies, 239.

Bernadotte, Jean Baptiste Jules. Headley. Napoleon, 2 : 200.

Bernal. Grant, J. Recoll. Lords & Comm. 2 : 124.

Bernard, St., of Clairvaux. Adams, W. H. D. Heroes X'y, 51. — Clarke, J. F. Events, 157. Hewlett. Heroes, 71. — Lloyd, Mrs. W. R. Flower of Chr. chiv. 25. — Lord, J. Beacon, 2 : 175. — Parker, T. Crit. & miscel. — Benson & Tatham. Men of might, 35. — Broadus. Lec. hist. preach. 97. — Brown, J. B. Stoics, 139. — Dale, T. P. Life's motto. — Gurney, J. H. Four eccl. biog. — Hatfield, E. F. Poets of church, 63. — Hundred greatest men, 163. — Hutton, B. Heroes crusades, 225. — Miller, Jos. Singers church, 2d ed. 27. — Pennington. Epochs papacy, 79. — With portrait. Warner Lib. 3 : 1819.

— a type of the 12th century. Harrison, F. Choice of bks. 311.

— as a hymnist, with translations. Schaff. Lit. & poetry, 232.

Bernard of Cluny. Miller, Jos. Singers church, 2d ed. 29. — (W. C. Prime) Warner Lib. 3 : 1828.

Bernard of Morlaix. Hatfield, E. F. Poets of church, 64.

Bernard, Andrew. Austin & Ralph. Laureates, 17.

Bernard, Chas. [Bernard Sugrail de la Villette]. James, H. French poets, 237.

Bernard, P. J. [called Gentil-Bernard]. Houssaye. Men of 18th cent. 1 : 137. — Men & wom. of France, 1 : 140.

Bernardin de St. Pierre, author of "Paul and Virginia." Fields. Underbrush, 251. — With portrait. Warner Lib. 22 : 12695.

— Life and works of. Everett, A. H. Crit. ess. 1 : 67.

Bernardine of Siena, St. Allies, M. H. Three cath. ref. 75.

Bernaud, Nicholas. Wallace, R. Anti-Trin. biog. 2 : 381.

Berne. Bellows. Old World, 1 : 204. — Everett, E. Mt. Vernon, 416. — Prime, S. I. Alhambra, 165.

Berners, John B., Lord. Brink. Eng. lit. 2, pt. 2 : 187. — Morley, H. Eng. writ. 7 : 280.

Berners, or Barnes, Juliana. Bethune, G. W. Brit. fem. poets, 13. — With portrait. Warner Lib. 3 : 1834.

Bernhardt, Sara. Ann. cyclop. '80. — Henry, S. Hours w. Parisians, 159. — With portrait. Lynch, A. Hum. doc's, 232. — Walkley, A. B. Playhouse, 239.

— Acting of. Winter, W. Shadows, 2 : 304.

— in the Avenue de Villiers. Yates, E. H. Celeb. 3 : 159.

— in Phèdre. Stuart, H. Paris days, 224.

Berni, Francesco. Montgomery. Men of Ita. 1 : 188. — Symonds. Renais. Ital. lit. 2 : 356. — Shelley, Mrs. Lit. men Italy, v. 1. — Stebbing. Ital. poets, v. 2. — Trollope. Ital. poets, 2 : 1.

Bernia, F. St. John. Cel. travelers, 1 : 205.

Bernini, Giovanni Lorenzo. Milizia. Lives arch. 2 : 203. — Spooner. Biog. fine arts, 1 : 96.

Bernis, François Joachim de, Cardinal. Houssaye. Men of 18th cent. 2 : 120. — Men & wom. of France, 2 : 305.

Bernward, St., bp. of Hildesheim. (A. Schultz) Dohme, R. Early mast. 34.

Beroalde, Imitation of, by Sterne. Ferrier. Ill. of Sterne, 1 : 49.

Berrettini, Pietro. Milizia. Lives arch. 2 : 173.

Berri, Caroline Ferdinande Louise, duchesse de, and duchesse d'Angoulême. Challice. Illus. wom. 110. — Miller. In ladies' comp. 45.

— Campaign of. Davenport. Narr. peril. 1 : 1.

Berridge, John. Hatfield, E. F. Poets of ch. 66. — Miller, Jos. Singers church, 2d ed. 214. — Ryle, J. C. Chr. leaders, 216.

Berrien, J. M. Miller, S. F. Bench of Ga. v. 1.

Berry, Mrs. Eliza. Burder. Pious wom. 685.

Berry, Mary. Martineau, H. Biog. sk. 259. — Tartt. Ess. 216.

— and Agnes. Adams, W. H. D. Wom. of fash. 1 : 333. — Houghton. Monog. 147. — Mayer, G. T. Wom. of let. 1 : 305.

Berry Pomeroy, Castle of. Timbs. Abbeys, 1 : 473.

Berryer, Antoine Pierre. Cormenin. Orators, 229. — Loménie. Liv. characters, 145. — Parton. Triumphs, 585. — Senior. Biog. sk. 1. — Walsh, R. M. Liv. char. France.

Bersot, Ernest. Fisher, M. Group of Fr. crit. 114.

Bert, Paul. (H. Depasse) Clarétie, J. Fr. celeb. v. 2.

Bertaut, Jean. Cary. French poets, 147.

Bertha, queen of Ethelbert. Hall. Queens bef. conq. 219.

Bertha, queen of France. Bush, A. F. Queens of Fr. 1 : 102.

Bertha, queen of Rudolph II. Bayly, J. A. S. New stud. 24.

Berthier, Louis Alexander. Headley. Napoleon, 1 : 67.

Berthollet, Claude L. Brightwell. Heroes of lab. 9.

Bertillon system of suppressing habitual crime. U. S. Bur Ed. Rept. '96–97, 2 : 1299.

Bertrade de Montford, queen of France. Bush, A. F. Queens of Fr. 1 : 115.

Berwick, James Fitz-James, duke of. Jesse. Court of Eng. Stuarts, 3 : 498. — Leake, F. Hist. bub. 7.

Berwinski, Richard Vincent. Soboleski. Poets of Poland, 358.

Berzelius, J. J., and Davy. Muir, M. M. P. Chemists, 157.

Besant, Annie. Stead. Char. sk. 147.

Besant, Walter, with portrait. Cochrane, R. Benef. lives, 118. — Sala, Mrs. Fam. peop. 136. — With portrait. Warner Lib. 4 : 1837.

Besekirskij, Wasil W., with portrait. Ehrlich, A. Cel. violin. 30.

Besnault, Abbe. Miller, Jos. Singers church, 2d ed. 143.

— Distances of the stars, and discov. of stellar planets. Lodge, O. J. Pioneers, 305.

Bessarion, Joannes, cardinal. Symonds. Reviv. of learn. 246.

Bessel, Friedrich William, Astronomical services of. Herschel, J. F. W. Essays, 507, 532.

Bessemer, Sir Henry. Cochrane, R. Gt. thinkers, 172. — Bolton, S. K. Poor boys famous, 112. — Fortunes made in bus. 1 : 185. — With photo. Cooper, T. Men of mark, 5 : 29. — Hale, E. E. Sto. of inven. 259. — Jeans. Creators, 9. — Parton. Capt. indus. 206.

Bessières, Jean Baptiste. Headley. Napoleon, 2 : 169.

Best, Paul. Wallace, R. Antl-Trin. biog. 2 : 161.

Bestiaries and lapidaries. (L. O. Kuhns) Warner Lib. 4 : 1852.

Betham, Matilda, littérateur and artist. Edwards, M. B. Six women, 229.

Bethany. Little, W. J. K. Sketches, 314.

Bethel, Community of. Hinds. Amer. commun. — Nordhoff. Commun. 324.

Bethel College, Russellville, Kentucky. U. S. Bur. Ed. Circ., '99, 3 : 173.

Bethel, Sir Richard. *See* Westbury.

Bethlehem. Bellows. Old world, 2 : 294. — Lee, J. S. Sac. cities, 29. — Warner, C. D. Levant, 117. — Hoppin. Notes theol. stud. 197. — Kean, J. Among holy places, 92. — Little, W. J. K. Sketches. — Buckley, J. M. Trav. 3 cont. 395. — Wilson, C. W. Pictur. Palest. 1 : 121.

Bethlehem, New Hampshire, Autumn in, 1870. Jackson, H. H. Bits trav. home, 191.

Bethlehem, Pa. Gibbons, P. E. Penn. Dutch.

Bethlen, Francis. Wallace, R. Anti-Trin. biog. 2 : 221.

Bethnal Green, Beggar's daughter of. Timbs. Abbeys, 1 : 56.

Bethune, Geo. W. Bungay. Off-hand, 147. — Fish, H. C. Pulp. eloq. 308. — Griswold. Poets Am. 249. — Griswold, R. W. Sac. poets. — Hatfield, E. F. Poets of ch. 70. — Lanman, C. Haphazard, 250.

Bethune, John. Wilson, J. G. Poets of Scot. 2 : 330.

Betterton, Thomas. Austin & Ralph. Laureates, 231. — Doran. Annals stage, 1 : 79. — Fitzgerald. New hist. Eng. stage, 1 : 284. — Galt. Players, 1 : 8. — Russell, W. Rep. actors, 13. — Brereton, A. Hamlets, 7. — Doran. Their maj. serv. 1 : 101. — Irving, H. Drama, 97. — Irving, H. Eng. actors, 15.

— and his associates. Baker, H. B. Eng. actors, 1 : 50.

Betti, Francis. Wallace, R. Anti-Trin. biog. 2 : 135.

Betting. Collins, M. Pen sketches, 66.

— and mathematics. Proctor, R. A. Leis. read. 271.

— Chances in. Proctor. Light sci. 1 : 274.

— on races. Proctor. Fam. sci. 234.

Betty, Wm. Henry West. Baker, H. B. Eng. actors, 2 : 185. — Doran. Annals stage, 2 : 296. Fitzgerald, P. Rom. of stage, 423. — Hollingshead. Footlights, 139. — Matthews, B. Actors, 2 : 297. — Doran. Their maj. serv. 2 : 411.

Beust, F. F., Count von. Em. persons, 3 : 308.

Beverston Castle. Hodges, Eliz. Anc. Eng. homes, 46.

Beverly, Mass., Settlement of. (A. C. Goodell, jr.) Col. Soc. Mass. Trans. 1 : 77.

Bevis of Hamtoun. Cox & Jones. Romances, 268.

Bewick, Thomas. Fairholt. Eng. artists, 145. — Craik. Pursuit knowl. 2 : 191. — Ewart, H. C. Toilers in art, 323. — Groser, W. H. Men worth imita.

Beyle, Henri (M. de Stendhal, *pseud.*). Hayward, A. Ess. 1 : 327. — Pellissier. Lit. move. Fr. 306. — With portrait. (F. T. Cooper) Warner Lib. 4 : 1861.

— Novels of. Wells, B. W. Cent. Fr. fic. 30.

Beyrout. Bellows. Old world, 2 : 218. — Warner, C. D. Levant, 214.

Beziers. Baring-Gould. Troub.-land, 237.

Bhagavad Gita. Johnson, S. Ori. relig. : India, 409.

— and the New Testament. Ellinwood. Orient. relig. & Chr. 111.

Bharatpúr. Malleson, G. B. Battles of India, 295.

Bhils. Macfarlane, C. Banditti, 203.

Bhotan, India, War in, 1864. Richards, W. Heroes, 65.

Dianoo da Siena. Miller, Jos. Singers church, 2d ed. 37.

Bianconi, Charles. Cochrane, R. Earnest, 221.

Biarritz and Arcachon. Bennett, J. H. Winter on Medit. 425.

Bias of Priene. Fénélon. Philosophers, 77.

Bibb, George M. Livingston, J. Em. Am. lawy. 717.

Bibboni, Cecco. Symonds. Renais.: Cath. reac. 1 : 388.

Bible, The. Everett. Orat. v. 2.

— adapted to the minds of children. Hopkins, M. Miscel. ess. 170.

— and the Bible alone. Thompson, H. M. Copy, 43.

— and its interpretation. Aids to faith, 425.

— and its translators. Friswell. Essays, 168.

— and skepticism. Trail, F. Studies, 253.

— as literature and as revelation. (W. W. Fenn) In spirit & truth.

— as poetry. Whitman. Compl. poetry and prose, 3 : 143.

— as a school book. Rush, B. Ess. 93.

— Authenticity, Evidence on. Taylor. Transm. anc. books.

— Authority and inspiration of. Whedon. Ess. 2 : 192.

— "Authorized" version. Collier, W. F. Hist. Eng. lit. 135. — Mitchell, D. G. English lands, 2 : 44. — Morley, H. Eng. writ. 11 : 85.

— Bibliography. Ayres, S. G. Hist. Eng. Bible. Lib. meth. — Lovett, R. Printed English Bible, 1525-1885. — Prov. Pub. Lib. Bull. Nov. '95. — Sunderland, J. T. Bible, origin, growth. — Wright, Rev. J. Early Bibles America.

— Church, and Antislavery. Phillips, W. Speeches, 2 : 244.

— Columnar truths in. (J. Cook) Barrows, J. H. Parl. relig. 2 : 1072.

— Dictionary of, Brown's. Coleridge, H. Ess. 2 : 269.

— Difficulties of. Ware, H., jr. Works, 3 : 350.

— English, before the Reformation. Gasquet, F. A. Old Eng. Bible, 102.

— — First authorized versions of. Morley, H. Eng. writ. 7 : 306.

— friendly to reason. Thomson, E. Essays, 9.

— Gospel a gift to the imagination. Bushnell. Building eras, 249.

— Hebrew, Text and translations of. Renan. Studies (N. Y.), 2 : 168.

— Holy Scripture. (R. Williams) Noyes, G. R. Theol. ess. 113.

— Homeric poems and. Gladstone. Stud. Homer, 2 : 521.

— How to read. Friswell. Silent hour, 19.

— Impediments to right understanding of. Maitland, S. R. Eruvin, 20.

— in public schools. Brooks, P. Ess. & addr. 519.

— — and state universities. U. S. Bur. Ed. Rept. '97-98, 2 : 1539.

— in Tennyson. Van Dyke, H. Poetry of Tennyson.

Hatfield, E. F. Poets of ch. 78. — Miller, Jos. Singers church, 2d ed. 228.

Blackmar, Miss M. A. Brockett. Woman's work, 429.

Blackmore, Sir Richard. Bell, R. Lit. & sci. men, 2 : 216. — Jeaffreson. Doctors, 122. — (S. Johnson) Chalmers. Eng. poets, 10 : 313. — Griswold, R. W. Sac. poets. — Holland, J. Psalmists, 2 : 165.

Blackmore, Richard Doddridge, with portrait. Warner Lib. 4 : 2011.

Blackmore, Eng., Vale of. Allingham. Varieties, 1 : 149.

Blackshear, Gen. D. Miller, S. F. Bench of Ga. v. 1.

Blackstock's Plantation, S. C., Affair at. Dawson. Batt. of U. S. 1 : 635.

Blackstone, Sir William. Foss. Judges, 8 : 243.

— Commentaries. Reed, W. B. Among books, 119. — Roscoe, H. Em. lawyers, 2 : 28. — Welsby. Eng. judges.

Blackstone, William, hermit of Shawmut. Gilman. Pathfinders, 112.

Blackwater river, Eng., A day on. Barrett, C. R. B. Essex, 25.

Blackwell, Antoinette Brown. Hanaford. Wom. of cent. 422. — (E. C. Stanton) Parton. Em. wom. 389.

Blackwell, Mrs. Elizabeth. Clayton, E. C. Eng. fem. art. 1 : 91. — (H. B. Elliot) Parton. Em. wom. 522.

— and Emily. (L. G. Runkle) Our fam. wom. 134.

Blackwell's Island hospitals. (L. Darche) Conf. char. & correc. '95 : 267.

Blackwood, Adam. Irving, D. Scot. writ. 1 : 161.

Blackwood, Christopher. Ivimey. Eng. Bapt. 2 : 230.

Blackwood, Frederick T. H. *See* Dufferin, Earl of.

Blackwood, William. Curwen. Booksellers, 199.

Bladon, Hyde Wyndham. Miller, Jos. Singers church, 2d ed. 514.

Blaen's Atlas. Maxwell, Sir H. Rainy days, 121.

Blagrove, Henry G., with portrait. Ehrlich, A. Cel. violin. 71.

Blaine, J. G. Em. persons, 6 : 1. — Brooks, N. Statesmen, 281. — Johnston, A. Amer. ora. 4 : 312. — Parton, J. Sk. of men of prog.

Blair, F. P., with portrait. Rogers, A. C. Repres. men, 45.

Blair, Henry W., with portrait. Bungay. Pen-portr. 240. — With portrait. Sketches N. H. men, 285.

Blair, Hugh. Blaikie, W. G. Preachers Scot. 23. — Cross lights, 91. — Taylor, W. M. Scot. pulpit, 154.

— Life and writings of. Foster, J. Crit. Ess. (Bohn) 1 : 81.

Blair, James. Richardson. Amer. lit. 1 : 138.

Blair, Montgomery. Rogers, A. C. Repres. men, 63.

Blair, Robert. Blaikie, W. G. Preachers Scot. 108. — Chalmers. Eng. poets, 15 : 61. — Wilson, J. G. Poets of Scot. 1 : 141. — Griswold, R. W. Sac. poets. — Miller, Jos. Singers church, 2d ed. 159.

Blaise, St., of Armenia, patron of wool-combers. Charles. Martyrs, 128.

Blaise, Jean Louvois Marie. Russell, W. Eccen. 370.

Blake, George. Loring, J. S. 100 Bost. ora. 253.

Blake, Homer Crane. Headley, J. T. Farragut, 271.

Blake, John Lauris. (J. L. Blake) N. E. Hist. Gen. Soc. Biog. 3 : 182.

Blake, John W. Am. Bar Assoc. 18 : 556.

Blake, Joseph. Whitehead, C. Highwaymen, 2 : 145.

Blake, Joseph, jr. Loring, J. S. 100 Bost. ora. 231.

Blake, Pynson. (F. E. Blake) N. E. Hist. Gen. Soc. Biog. 4 : 409.

Blake, Robert, Admiral. Adams, W. H. D. Records, 107. — Dawson, G. Biog. lec. 44. — Edgar. Sea-kings, 200. — Johns. Nav. & mil. heroes. — With portrait. Laughton, J. K. 12 sailors, 81. — Valentine, L. J. Sea fights, 36. — Wrangham. Brit. Plutarch, v. 3. — Yonge, C. D. Our nav. comm.

Blake, William. Benson, A. C. Ess. 147. — Cheney, J. V. That dome, 169. — Collins, M. Pen sketches, 179. — Cunningham, A. Gt. Eng. painters, 275. — Patmore. Princ. in art, 97. — Stoddard, R. H. Under eve. lamp, 164. — Dodge, M. A. Skirmish. 358. — (E. C. Stedman) Ess. from Critic, 21. — Fairholt. Eng. artists, 94. — Oliphant, M. Lit. hist. 2 : 285. — Patmore. Principles in art. — Rossetti, D. G. Works, 1 : 443. — Skelton. Ess. 260. — Tartt. Ess. 192. — Thornbury. Brit. art. 2 : 26. — (J. C. Carr) Ward. Eng. poets, 3 : 596. — Macdonald, G. England's antiphon, 301. — Miles, A. H. Poets of cent. 1 : 85. — Nichol. Amer. lit. 213. — Smetham. Lit. works, 98. — Van Rensselaer, M. G. Six portraits. — With portrait. Warner Lib. 4 : 2041.

— Bibliography. Bost. Lib. Bull. 4 : 335.

— Painter and poet. Timbs, J. Eng. eccen. 339.

— Poems of. Thompson, James (B. V.) Biog. ess. 240.

— Trial of, for sedition. Nicoll, W. R. Lit. anec. 1 : 3.

Blake, William Rufus. Hutton, L. Plays, 118.

Blakesmoor in H—shire. Lamb. Elia.

Blamire, J. C. Lonsdale. Worthies Cumb. v. 4.

Blamire, Susanna. Bethune, G. W. Brit. fem. poets, 81. — Keddie. Songstresses, 1 : 224. — Williams, Jane. Lit. wom. 202. — Wilson, J. G. Poets of Scot. 1 : 318. — Milford, M. R. Recollec. 215. — Lonsdale. Worthies Cumb. v. 4.

Blamire, W. Lonsdale. Worthies Cumb. v. 1.

Blanc, Anthony. Clarke, R. H. Cath. bishops, 2 : 58.

Blanc, Charles. Warner Lib. 4 : 2051.

Blanc, Louis. Challice. French authors, 2 : 202. — Men of 3d repub. 320. — Smalley. Lond. let. 1 : 43.

Blanc, Madame Thérèse. Blanc, T. Wom. U. S. 7. — Simpson, J. P. Pic. revol. Paris, 1 : 17.

Blanc, Samuel. Peters. Am. Bar Assoc. 11 : 333.

Blanc, Mont. Clark, D. W. Fireside read. 71. — Field, H. M. Killarney, 96. — Half-hours in many lands, 215. — Bartol. Pic. of Europe, 373. — Winchell. Sparks geol. ham. 13.

— and its glaciers. Chambers's Repos. no. 81.

— Observations at summit of. (M. J. Janssen) Smithson. Rept. '94 : 237.

— Observatory on. Smithson. Rept. 1893 : 259.

Blanchard, E. L. Wilman, G. Sk. liv. celeb. 96.

Blanchard, Samuel Laman. Hall, S. C. Book of mem. 282. — (A. H. Japp) Miles, A. H. Poets of cent. 3 : 547.

— Recollections of. Patmore. My friends, 3 : 191.

Blanchard, Thos. Howe, H. Em. Mech. 107.

Blanche, Princess, daughter of Edward III. Green, M. A. E. Princesses, 3 : 261.

— Shelley, Mrs. Lit. men Italy, v. **1.** — Stebbing. Ital. poets, v. **2.**

Boiardo, Matteo Maria, School of. Paget, V. Euphorion, **2** : 47.

— Stories from. Hunt, L. Stories from Ital. poets, **2** : 1.

Boieldieu, François Adrien. Ferris, G. T. Ital. & Fr. compos. 195.

Boileau-Despréaux, Nicolas. Besant. Fr. humor. 285. — Hannay. Satire, 94. — Shelley, M. W. Lit. men Fr. 1. — Warner Lib. **4** : 2141.

— Tragedies of. Astié. Louis XIV, 235.

Bois, John McClure, Translators, 199.

Bois Monzil mine, Inundation of. Davenport. Narr. peril. **2** : 369.

Boisrobert, François le Metel de. Besant. Fr. humor. 220.

Boisserée, Sulpiz. Baur. Relig. life Germ. **2** : 260.

Boissier, Gaston, with portrait. Warner Lib. **4** : 2152.

Boito, Arrigo. Streatfeild. Masters Ital. mus. 137.

Boker, Charles S. Winslow, S. N. Biog. Phila. merch. 195.

Boker, George Henry. Griswold. Poets Am. 503. — (G. P. Lathrop) Gilder. Authors, 29. — Parton, J. Sk. of men of prog. — Richardson. Amer. lit. **2** : 249. — With portrait. Warner Lib. **4** : 2163.

Bokhara. Lansdell, H. Russ. Centr. Asia, **2** : 66.

Bol, Ferdinand. Gower. Fig. painters Holl. 27. — Van Dyke, J. C. Dutch mast. 45.

Bolaine, Elizabeth. Redding. Misers, **1** : 236.

Boldness. Bacon. Ess.

Boleyn. Anne. *See* Anne Boleyn.

Bolingbroke, Henry St. John, Viscount (1678–1751). Adams, W. H. D. Men at helm, 85. Brougham. Works, **4** : 461. — Creasy. Etonians, 178. — Georgian era, **1** : 281. — Jones, W. A. Ess. on authors, 210. — Lodge. Portraits (Bohn), v. **7.** — Reed, W. B. Among books, 21. — Skelton. Ess. 165. — Skelton. Impeach. of Mary, 65. — Birrell. Men, women & books, 16. — Mathews, W. Oratory, 226. — Smythe, G. S. Hist. fancies, 118. — Wrangham. Brit. Plutarch, v. **6.**

— and the Barrier treaty. Dilke. Papers, **1** : 361.

— and Harley. Windsor. Ethica, 215.

— and Alexander Pope. Thomson, Mrs. Cel. friendships, **2** : 171.

— — Posthumous quarrel of. Disraeli, I. Calam. v. **2.**

— and Walpole. Stephen, L. Eng. thought, **2** : 167.

— Life of. Goldsmith. Miscel. (N. Y. 4 v.) **3** : 399.

Bolivar of Ponte, Simon. Parton. Peop. bk. biog. 486. — Miller, Gen. J. Memoirs.

Bolivia. Helper, H. R. Oddments of Andean diplomacy, 27. — Matthews, E. D. Up the Amazon.

— Colton claim. Helper, H. R. Andean diplom. 23.

— Commercial directory of, 1891. Bur. Am. Repub. no. 19.

— Constitution, 1821. Miller, Gen. J. Memoirs, **2** : 483.

— Gold mines of, 1891. (T. H. Anderson) U. S. Cons. Rept. **38** : 268.

— Handbook of. Bur. Am. Repub. Bull. no. 55, pt. 6.

— Silver mines of, 1891. (T. H. Anderson) U. S. Cons. Rept. **38** : 519.

Bolland, Baron. Grant, J. Bench & bar, **1** : 241.

Bollandists, The. Neale. Ess. liturg. — (G. T. Stokes) Coan. Stud. lit. 159.

Bolles, Asa Moore. Everest. Poets of Conn. 315.

Bologna, Gain. Perkins, C. C. Tusc. sculp. **2** : 169.

Bologna. Bellows. Old world, **2** : 26. — Hare. Cities of No. Italy, **2** : 246. — Taine. Italy, **2** : 166. — Tuckerman. Ital. sk. 289. — Willis. Pencilings. — Child, T. Summ. holidays, 174. — Sala. Journey south, 185.

— Montilcinus in. Stoughton. Ital. reformers, 171.

— Through the streets of. Scollard, Und. sum. skies, 129.

— University of. Schaff. Lit. & poetry, 262.

Bolswert, Scheltius A., Dutch engraver. Spooner. Biog. fine arts, **1** : 117.

Bolton, Lavinia, duchess of. *See* Fenton, Lavinia.

Bolton, Sarah Tittle. Coggeshall. Poets of west, 367.

Bolton castle. Mackie, C. Castles of Mary.

— Mary, Queen of Scots, at. Strickland. Queens Scot. v. **6.**

Bombay. Brooks, E. S. Gt. cities, 56. — Brooks, J. Seven months, 329. — Burton, Isa. Arabia, 108, 258. — Field, H. M. Egypt to Japan, 115. — Keating. With Grant, 36. — Prime, E. D. G. Around world, 343. — Pidgeon. Engineer's holiday, 422.

— Visit to, 1884. Hübner. Thro' Brit. empire, **2** : 6.

Bommel, Siege of. Robson, W. Sieges, 532.

"Bon Homme Richard" and "Serapis," Battle between. Rawson, E. K. 20 nav. batt. **1** : 221.

Bonaparte, Caroline, queen of Naples, Empress Joséphine, and Queen Hortense. Challice. Illus. wom. 49.

Bonaparte, Joseph, Fête given by, Oct., 1800, in honor of treaty with U. S. Am. Antiq. Soc. Proc. **12** : 240.

Bonaparte, Napoleon Joseph Charles **Paul,** Prince. McCarthy, J. Mod. lead. 77.

Bonaparte, Pauline, Princess Borghese. Elliot, F. Rom. gossip, 210.

Bonaparte, Prince Pierre, Trial of. Morse, J. T., jr. Famous trials.

Bonaparte, Ramoline M. L. Holloway, L. C. Mothers of gt. men, 69.

Bonaparte family, The. Chambers's Papers, no. 1. — Doran. Monarchs, **1** : 248.

Bonapartes, The Roman. Elliot, F. Rom. gossip, 172.

— Vicissitudes of the. Burke, B. Viciss. of fam. **2** : 279.

Bonar, Horatius. Wilson, J. G. Poets of Scot. **2** : 308. — Hatfield, E. F. Poets of church, 82. — (M. Bell) Miles, A. H. Poets of cent. **10** : 247. — Miller, Jos. Singers church, 2d ed. 500.

Bonar, Mrs. Jane Catharine (Lundie). Hatfield, E. F. Poets of church, 85.

Bonaventura. Miller, Jos. Singers church, 2d ed. 32. — Neale. Mediæv. preachers. — Townsend, W. J. Schoolmen, 187.

Bond, Sir Edward A. Garnett, R. Ess. in librarianship, 335.

Bond, George. Woolrych. Serjeants, **2** : 676.

Bond, Henry May. (F. V. Balch) Harvard mem. biog. **2** : 12. — (J. B. Bright) N. E. Hist. Gen. Soc. Biog. **3** : 369.

Bond, Sir Nathaniel. Woolrych. Serjeants, **1** : 413.

Books; Magicians of the shelves. Ellwanger. Sto. of house, 185.
— Making of, in mediæval monasteries. Gasquet, F. A. Old Eng. Bible, 41.
— Notes on. Poe. Works, 5 : 175.
— Obscure. Patmore. Religio poetæ, 111.
— of the people, English. Disraeli, I. Amen. (N. Y. 2 v.) 1 : 294.
— Old. Dawson, G. Shaksp. 176. — Saunders. Stray leaves, 1.
— — and new. Birrell. Men, women & books, 134.
— Origin of celebrated. Saunders. Mosaics, 259.
— Our friends. Repplier. Ess. in min. 11.
— Power and blessedness of. Farrar. Soc. & pres. day quest. 204.
— Preservation of literature. Burton, J. H. Book-hunter, 205.
— published on commission. Spedding, Reviews.
— Rarity of. Powell, G. H. Excurs. in libr. 3.
— Some successful. Shepard, W. Authors, 200.
— Walsh, W. S. Au. & authorship, 200.
— Song of. Lubbock. Pleasures, 53.
— Survival of. Saunders. Stray leaves, 108.
— that have had a great run. Jacox. Aspects, 317.
— that have hindered me. Repplier, A. Points of view.
— Tyranny of. Mabie. My study fire, 2 : 86.
— Unread and unreadable. Jacox. Lit. life, 350.
— War against. Disraeli, I. Amen. (N. Y. 2 v.) 2 : 425.
— World of. Hunt, L. Men, wom. & books, 76. The same in Prose masterpieces, 1 : 25.
Boomerang. U. S. Expl. exped. 2 : 191.
Boon, Ratliff. Woollen. Biog. sk. Indiana, 42.
Boone, Daniel. With portrait. Amer. nat. portr. gall. v. 2. — With portrait. Duyckinck. Nat. portr. gall. 1 : 183. — Everett, E. Mt. Vernon, 471. — Lodge & Roosevelt. Hero-tales, 17. — Lossing. Em. Amer. 192. — Roosevelt. Winning of the west. — With portr. Seymour, C. C. B. Self-made, 191. — Shaler, N. S. Kentucky. — Tuckerman. Ess. 42.
Boone, James Shergold. Mozley. Reminis. 2 : 200.
Boone, Rebecca. Ellet. Pioneer wom. 12.
Boone, Fort, Siege of. Dawson. Batt. of U. S. 1 : 445.
Booth, Abraham. Ivimey. Eng. Bapt. 4 : 365.
Booth, Agnes, with portrait. (L. C. Strang) McKay, F. E. Fam. actors, 231.
Booth, Almeda A., Life and character of. Garfield. Works, 2 : 290.
Booth, Barton. Austin & Ralph. Laureates, 233. — Doran. Annals stage, 1 : 265. — Doran. Their maj. serv. 1 : 367. — Galt. Players, 1 : 163.
Booth, Catherine. Belloc, Mme. Walled garden, 222. — Bolton. Fam. lead. wom. 159.
Booth, Edwin. Badeau. Vagabond, 120, 286. — Houghton. Kings, 599. — Matthews, B. Actors, 5 : 55. — Duyckinck. Portr. gall. 2 : 591. — Godwin, P. Commr. addr. 65. — Hatton, J. To-day in Amer. 2 : 226. — (H. A. Clapp) McKay, F. E. Fam. actors, 26. — Winter. Shadows, 1 : 63.
— and Junius. Badeau. Vagabond, 347.
— and Kean, Edmund. Whyte, F. Actors of cent. 59.
— Character of. Winter. Shadows, 3 : 283.
— in Macbeth. Griffin, G. W. Stud. in lit.
— prince of tragedy in Amer. Bungay. Repr. men, 119.
Booth, Junius Brutus. Brereton, A. Hamlets, 39. — Cook, D. Hours w. players, 2 : 38. —

Matthews, B. Actors, 3 : 91. — Jefferson, Jos. Autobiography. — Murdock. The stage. — Winter, W. Shadows, 2 : 27.
Booth, Junius Brutus; Acting in England and America. Murdock, J. E. Stage, 174.
— as reader. Murdoch, J. E. Stage, 273.
— Love of animals. Clarke, J. F. Memo. sketches, 261.
Booth, Mary Louise, with portrait. Bolton, S. K. Succ. women, 34. — (H. P. Spofford) Our fam. wom. 117.
Booth, Mrs. (in U. S. civil war). Brockett. Woman's work, 769.
Boothby, Louisa Cranstoun (b. Nisbett), Lady. Marston, J. W. Rec. actors, 2 : 151.
Bordigni, Charles de. Besant. Fr. poetry, 191.
Bordoné, Paris. Fisherman presenting ring. (T. Gautier) Singleton, E. Great pic. 1.
Bordoni, Faustina, later Mme. Hasse, Italian vocalist. Clayton, E. C. Queens, 52. — Ferris, G. T. Great singers, 1. — Needham. Queens of song.
Boreel, Adam. Wallace, R. Anti-Trin. biog. 3 : 130.
Bores. Maxwell, H. Post-mer. 115.
— Club. Lang. Leaders, 114.
Borghese, Gwendolin, Princess. Elliot, F. Rom. gossip, 314.
Borghese, Marc Antonio, Prince. Elliot, F. Rom. gossip, 306.
Borghese gallery at Rome. Morelli. Ital. paint. 64.
Borgia, Cesare. (Charles Yriarte) Ferris, G. T. Gt. leaders, 201. — Symonds. Age of despots, 345.
Borgia, Lucretia. Bruce, J. Classic portr. 240. — Symonds. Age of despots, 419. — Tartt. Ess. 289. — Wilson, H. S. Stud. in hist. 1.
Borgne, Lake, Battle of. Roosevelt, T. Naval war 1812, 315.
Bornemisza, Anna. Wyatt, W. J. Hunga. celeb. 176.
Borneo. Abercromby. Seas & skies, 302. — Adams, W. H. D. Eastern archipel. 95. — Hornaday. Two years' jungle, 333. — Wallace, A. R. Malay archipel.
— and Celebes. Ellesmere. Ess. 348.
— Bibliography. Roth, H. L. Natives Sarawak and Brit. N. Borneo.
— Rajah Brooke and. Chambers's Papers, no. 34.
— Travels in. Helms. Pioneering, 123, 204.
Borobridge, Roman race course at. Buckland, F. T. Curios. nat. hist. 3 : 40.
Boroughs, Decayed, in England. Freeman. Hist. ess. 4 : 317.
— English, in the time of Edward IV. Lucas. Secularia, 88.
Borromeo, St. Charles. *See* Charles, St.
Borromini, Francesco. Milizia. Lives arch. 2 : 188.
Borrow, George, with portrait. (J. Hawthorne) Warner Lib. 4 : 2175. — Birrell, A. Res judicatæ, 115. — Henley. Views, 133. — Monkhouse, A. Books, 80. — Smiles. Brief biog. 157. — Saintsbury. Ess. Eng. lit. 403.
Borrowers and lenders. Lamb. Elia.
Borthwick, Jane. Hatfield, E. F. Poets of church, 86. — Miles, A. H. Poets of cent. 10 : 714. — Miller, Jos. Singers church, 2d ed. 574.
Borthwick castle. Mackie, C. Castles of Mary.
— Mary Queen of Scots at. Strickland. Queens Scot. 5.
Boruwlaski, Joseph, Count, the Polish dwarf. Timbs, J. Eng. eccen. 258.

Bosanquet, George William. Memoir of. (C. B. Brackenbury) Bosanquet. Ess. vii.

Bosanquet, Mary. Beiloc. Vignettes, 417. — Wise, D. Heroic Meth. 123. — Withrow. Makers of Meth. 175.

Bosboom-Toussaint, A. L. G. Zimmern. For. novelists, 2 : 311.

Boscan, Juan. Ticknor. Span. lit. 1 : 477. — Warner Lib. 4 : 2203. — Montgomery. Men of Ita. 3 : 21.

Boscawen, Capt. Edw., with portrait. Laughton, J. K. 12 Sailors, 241.

Bosco, General. Malortie. Here, there, 33.

Boscovich, Theory of. (William Thompson) Smithson. Rept. '89 : 435.

Bosio, Angiolina, Italian vocalist. Clayton, E.C. Queens, 451. — Edwards, H. S. Prima don. 2 : 39. — Needham. Queens of song.

Bosnia, English orphanage and training-school in. (A. T. Irby) Nat. Educa. Assoc. 1893 : 900.

— in 1886. Minchin. Balkan peninsula.

— in 1887. Laveleye. Balkan peninsula.

Bosphorus, The. Benjamin, S. G. W. World's paradises, 21.

— Kimmerian, Greek art in. Newton. Essays. 373.

Bossuet, Jacques Bénigne. Flint. Philos. hist. v. 1. — Ste. Beuve. Monday chats, 44. — Lamartine. Cel. char. 2 : 214. — With portrait. (A. Cohn) Warner Lib. 4 : 2209. — Broadus. Lec. hist. preach. 158. — Hundred greatest men, 187.

— and the Protestants. Stephen, J. F. Horæ Sabb. 2 : 88.

— Life and writings of. Butler, Chas. Works, v. 3.

Bostock, J. Pettigrew. Med. portr. gall. v. 3.

Boston, Thomas. Blaikie, W. G. Preach. Scot. 195. — McCosh. Scot. phii. 109. — Taylor, W. M. Scot. pulpit, 160.

Boston, Eng. Hawthorne. Old home, 178. — Rimmer, A. Country towns, 261. — Silloway. Cathedral towns, 270.

Boston, Mass. Arnold, E. Seas & lands, 84. — Badeau. Vagabond, 327. — Faithful, E. Three visits, 102. — Hardy, I. D. Thro' cities, 318. — Blanc, T. Wom. in U. S. 91. — Tuckerman, C. K. Recollec. 1 : 1. — Brooks, E. S. Great cities, 71. — Emerson. Nat. hist. intel. 83. — (T. W. Higginson and E. E. Hale) Powell, L. P. Hist. towns N. E. 167, 187.

— and home again. Dodge, M. A. Country, 246.

— Bibliography. Bost. Pub. Lib. Bull. Feb. '98.

— Charities of. Blanc, T. Wom. in U. S. 132.

— Citizen of; his duties. Pierce, E. L. Addresses, 296.

— Colonial. Bacon, E. M. Hist. pilgrim. 212.

— Continental trenches, 1775. Drake, S. A. Hist. fields Mid. 83.

— Environs of. Winthrop, R. C. Addresses, 3 : 194.

— Epis. Church in, Century of. Brooks, P. Ess. & addr. 119.

— Founding of. Adams, C. F. Three episodes, 1 : 209.

— Life in. Clark, T. M. Reminis. 66.

— — in the early 19th century. Lowell. Writ. 2 : 288.

— Literary. Wolfe. Lit. shr. Am. auth. 83.

— Men of action in. Holyoake. Among Amer. 69.

— Old. Appleton, T. G. Sheaf of pap. 333.

— The old cathedral. Fairbanks, O. B. Aguecheek, 234.

Boston, Mass.; The old corner. Fairbanks, O. B. Aguecheek, 212.

— Old South Meeting-house. Phillips, W. Speeches, 2 : 231.

— past and present. Pidgeon. Old World ques. 296.

— Provincial. Bacon, E. M. Hist. pilgrim. 248.

— Public Library. Winthrop. Addresses, 2 : 213.

— — Dedication of. Everett. Orat. v. 3. — Winthrop. Addresses, 2 : 373.

— Siege of, 1775-76. Dawson. Batt. of U. S. 1 : 74. — Reynolds, G. Papers, 23.

— — Letters illustrating. Mass. Hist. Proc. 14 : 275.

— — Letters of John Andrews. Mass. Hist. Proc. 8 : 316.

— Social and literary (1887). Bates. Year in gt. repub. 1 : 39.

— Streets in, names of. (T. B. Amory) Mass. Hist. Proc. 6 : 23.

— Suburbs of. Howells. Sub. sk. 60, 91.

— Theatre alley. Fairbanks, O. B. Aguecheek, 223.

— Theology in, 1887. Bates. Year in gt. repub. 1 : 129.

— Wayfarers' lodge. (T. F. Ring) Conf. char. & corr. 1885 : 321.

— Women in. Blanc, T. Wom. in U. S. 98.

Boston Bay, Settlement of. Adams, C. F. Three episodes, 1 : 1.

Boston College, Boston, Mass. (A. J. E. Mullan) U. S. Bur. Ed. Circ. '93, no. 6 : 374.

Boston common on a September afternoon. Woolson. Browsing, 80.

Boston culture, The. (J. H. Morse) Ess. from Critic, 133.

Boston fire. Winthrop, R. C. Addr. 3 : 175.

Boston massacre. Chandler, P. W. Am. crim. trials, 1 : 301.

Boston museum, Actors at. Reignolds, Kate. Actors, 122.

Boston road, The old. Nadal, E. S. Ess. 1.

Boston University, Boston, Mass. U. S. Bur. Ed. Circ. '91, no. 6 : 341.

Bostwick, Helen Louisa. Coggeshall. Poets of west, 550.

Bosville, Wm. Sinclair, J. Sketches.

Boswell, Sir Alexander. Burton, J. H. Bookhunter, 292. — Wilson, J. G. Poets of Scot. 1 : 528.

Boswell, James. Henley. Views, 194. — Mitchell, D. G. Eng. lands, 3 : 118. — Russell, W. C. Book of au. 310. — With portrait. (C. F. Johnson) Warner Lib. 4 : 2227. — Wotton. Word portraits, 21.

— Letters. McNicoll. Essays on Eng. lit. 315.

— Predecessors and editors of. Dobson, A. Miscel. 109.

Boswell, Robert. Holland, J. Psalmists, 2 : 242.

Bosworth field. Rimmer, A. Country towns, 96. — Siegvolk. Papers, 209. — Winter. Gray days, 193.

Botanical biology. (W. T. Thiselton-Dyer) Smithson. Rept. '89 : 399.

Botanical garden, A tropical. (M. Treub) Smithson. Rept. '90 : 389.

Botanical science, Educational claims of. (A. Henfrey) Youmans. Culture, 87.

Botany. Goldsmith. Misc. (N. Y. 4 v.) 2 : 549.

— Bibliography. Clark, C. H. Laboratory man. pract. bot. — Cleveland (O.) Pub. Lib. Open Shelf, Mar. '94. — Somerville (Mass.) Pub. Lib. Bull. May, '96. — Waltham (Mass.) Pub. Lib. Bull. June, '95.

Botany, Economic, Some possibilities of. (G. L. Goodale) Smithson. Rept. '91 : 617.
— — Opportunities for study of. (W. Trelease) Smithson. Rept. '97 : 519.
— for children, Bibliography. Salem (Mass.) Pub. Lib. Bull. Apr. '96.
— Progress in, 1846-96. (W. G. Farlow) Goode. Smithson. Inst. 697.
— Study of, Uses of. (M. A. Veeder) N. Y. Regents, '91 : 439.
— Teaching, in secondary schools. (G. F. Atkinson) N. Y. Regents, 206.
— Work of the British Association in. (W. T. Thiselton-Dyer) Smithson. Rept. '95 : 455.
See also Plants.
Bothwell, James Hepburn, Earl of. Burke, S. H. Hist. portr. Tudor, 4 : 485. — (G. G. Smith) Seccombe, T. 12 bad men, 1.
— Queen Mary and. Strickland. Queens Scot. v. 3-7.
Bothy system, The. Miller, H. Hist. ess. 210.
Botta, Anne C. L. Griswold. Fem. poets, 232.
— Hemenway. Poets of Vt. 95.
Bottesini, G. With portrait. Buffen, F. F. Mus. celeb. 37. — (K. Woermann) Dohme, R. Early mast. 341.
Botticelli, Sandro. Rose, G. B. Renais. masters, 150. — Stillman, W. J. Old Ital. mast. 155. — Child, T. Art & criticism, 1. — Oliphant. Makers of Fr. 329. — Pater. Stud. renais. 39. — Symonds. Renais. Fine arts, 240.
— at the Villa Lemmi. Paget, V. Juvenilia, 1 : 77.
— Birth of Venus. (W. Pater) Singleton, E. Great pic. 5.
— Judith. (M. Hewlett) Singleton, E. Great pic. 80.
— Spring. (M. Reymend) Singleton, E. Great pic. 313.
Bottle conspiracy, 1822. Browne, G. L. State trials 19th cent. 2 : 427.
Botts, John Minor. Bartlett. Pres. candidates, 316. — Savage. Liv. repres. men, 57.
Botts, Lawson. Walker, C. D. Biog. Va. Mil. Inst. 53.
Botzen to Landro. Baddeley. Travel-tide, 203.
Boucher, François. Dilke. Fr. painters, 18th cent. 44. — Houssaye. Men of 18th cent. 1 : 292. — Men & wom. of France, 2 : 1.
Boucher, Joan. Brown, J. N. Bapt. martyrs, 281.
Boucher de Crèvecour de Perthes, Jacques. Smith, C. R. Retrospec. 2 : 134.
Bouchet, Jean. Besant. Fr. Poetry, 194.
Boucicault, Dion. Archer. Eng. dram. 38. — Jefferson, Jos. Autobiography. — Matthews, B. Actors, 5 : 77. — (V. Thompson) McKay, F. E. Fam. actors, 81. — Hutton, L. Plays, 208.
Bouck, Wm. C. Jenkins. Gov. of N. Y. 689.
Boudinot, Elias, with portrait. Amer. nat. portr. gall. v. 3. — Lossing. Em. Amer. 133. — Moore, F. Am. eloq. 1 : 262.
Boudon, Henri Marie de. Butler, Chas. Works, v. 3.
Boufflers, Stanislas, Marquis de. Houssaye. Men of 18th cent. 1 : 173. — Men & wom. of France, 1 : 180.
Boughton, G. H. Tuckerman, Artists, 454.
Bougouinc, Simon. Besant. Fr. poetry, 193.
Bouguereau, Adolphe W. Henry, S. Hours w. Parisians, 211. — Hamerton. Contemp. Fr. paint.
Bouilhet, Louis. Du Camp. Recoll. 2 : 323.
Bovillon, H. de la T. d'A. Taylor, W. C. Rom. biog. v. 2.

Boulak Museum. Buckley, J. M. Trav. 3 cont. 319.
Boulanger, Gen. G. E. J. M. Em. persons, 5 : 118.
Boulogne, Our lady of. Doran. New pic. 131.
— Paris to. Fairbanks, O. B. Aguecheek, 163.
Boulton, Matthew, of Birmingham. Bourne, H. R. F. Eng. merch. 2 : 89. — Smiles. Self-help. — Walker, W., jr. Men of sci. 13.
"Bounty," Mutiny of the. Burke, P. Cel. nav. & mil. trials, 200.
Bounty on sugar and fibres, State. N. J. Labor, '81 : 277. '82 : 177, 210. '83 : 319, 327. '84 : 364. 85 : 327.
Bourbon, Charlotte de, princess of Orange. Wittenmeyer. Women Reform. 217.
Bourbon, Constable. Wilson, J. G. Illus. sol. 45.
Bourbon family, The. Chambers's Papers, no. 25.
Bourbons, The, and Charles X. Doran. Monarchs, 1 : 212.
Bourboulon, Catherine de. Adams, W. H. D. Cel. wom. trav. 270.
Bourchier, Thomas. Campbell. Ld. Chan. 1 : 307. — Fuller. Worthies, 1 : 503. — Williams, R. F. Eng. card. 2 : 124. — Hook. Abps. Cant. 5 : 268. — Williams, F. Eng. card. 2 : 124.
Bourdaloue, Louis. Broadus. Lec. hist. preach. 164.
Bourg-en-Bresse. James, H. Little tour. 241.
Bourgeois, Margarite, with portrait. Murray, J. O'K. Cath. heroes, 563.
Bourgeois idols, Some. Bax. Relig. of socialism, 111.
Bourges. James, H. Little tour. 72. — Baring-Gould. Troub. land, 307.
— Cathedral of. Hoppin. Early renais. 199. — Larned, W. C. Churches & C. 201.
Bourget, Paul. Blaze de Bury, Y. French Lit. 107. — With portrait. Warner Lib. 4 : 2252. Delille, E. Some French writ. 1. — Hallard, J. H. Gallica, 110. — Van de Velde. Fr. fic. 1 : 40.
— as critic. Buchanan, R. Coming terr. 145.
— on the U. S. Clemens. How to tell, 181.
Bourignon, Antoinette. Hatfield, E. F. Poets of church, 87. — Miller, Jos. Singers church, 2d ed. 85.
Bourke, Richard S. See Mayo, 6th earl of.
Bourke, Col. Thos. F. Savage, J. Fenian heroes, 121.
Bourne, Hugh. Hatfield, E. F. Poets of church, 90.
Bourne, Vincent. Benson, A. C. Ess. 96.
Boutell, Lewis Henry. Am. Antiq. Soc. Proc. n. s. 13 : 12.
Boutelle family, The. Muzzey, A. B. Prime movers, 300.
Bouts, or Stuerboudt, Dierick. Crowe & Cav. Flem. painters, 321.
Boutwell, George S., with portrait. Brockett. Men of our day, 339.
Bouvé, Thos. Tracy. (W. O. Crosby) Am. Acad. Proc. 32 : 340.
Bouverie, John Augustus Sheil. Burke, B. Viciss. of fam. 3 : 300.
Bovius, John Baptist. Wallace, R. Anti-Trin. biog. 2 : 382.
Bow, Polynesian. (E. Tregear) Smithson. Rept. '92 : 199.
Bowditch, Henry I. (C. F. Folsom) Am. Acad. A. & S. Proc. 28 : 310.
Bowditch, Henry P. Vaille & Clark. Harv. book, v. 1.
Bowditch, Nathaniel. Edwards, B. B. Self-

taught, 325. — Everett. Orat. v. 2. — With portrait. Amer. nat. portr. gall. v. 4. — Hood, E. P. Peerage of poverty, 268. — With portr. Seymour, C. C. B. Self-made, 336. — Lossing. Em. Amer. 246.

Bowditch, Nathaniel I. (S. K. Lothrop) Mass. Hist. Proc. 5 : 500.

Bowdler, John. Miller, Jos. Singers church, 2d ed. 375.

Bowdoin, James. Lossing. Em. Amer. 65.
— Life and services of. Winthrop, R. C. Addresses, 1 : 90.

Bowdoin college. College book, 198.

Bowe, Obadiah A. Hemenway. Poets of Vt. 272.

Bowen, Charles S. C., Lord. Em. persons, 6 : 116. — Smalley. Stud. 238. — Laurence, P. M. Collect. 271.

Bowen, Dennis. Putnam, J. O. Addresses, 314.

Bowen, Francis. Vaille & Clark. Harv. book, v. 1.

Bowen, Sir George. Escott, J. H. S. Pillars emp. 1.

Bowen, Pardon. Goddard, W. G. Pol. & misc. writ. 1 : 296.

Bowen, William. Goddard, W. G. Pol. & misc. writ. 1 : 324.

Bowers, George Hull, Dean of Manchester. Huntington, G. Random recoll. 249.

Bowers, Georgina. Clayton, E. C. Eng. fem. art. 2 : 319.

Bowers, John. Wesley & successors, 189.

Bowlder canyon. Jackson, H. H. Bits trav. home, 300.

Bowles, John. Smith, Syd. Ess. fr. Edin.

Bowles, William Lisle. Hall, S. C. Book of mem. 377. — Jerdan. Men, 23. — Procter, B. W. Autob. 130.
— Sonnets. Deshler. Afternoons, 181.

Bowman, Edward Carson. (E. D. McCarthy) Harvard mem. biog. 2 : 263.

Bowman, James L. Livingston, J. Dist. Amer. 197.

Bowman, Wm. (H. W. Williams) Am. Acad. A. & S. Proc. 28 : 403.

Bowman, Sir William. Bettany. Em. doctors, 2 : 260. — With photo. Cooper, T. Men of mark, 4 : 29.

Bowmen, Mediæval. Cutts, E. L. Scenes mid. ages, 439.

Bowne family of Flushing. Glenn, T. A. Colon. mans. 2 : 91.

Bowring, Sir John. Francis, G. H. Orators, 245. — Hatfield, E. F. Poets of church, 91. — Miles, A. H. Poets of cent. 10 : 147. — Miller, Jos. Singers church, 2d ed. 420. — With portrait. Warner Lib. 4 : 2263.

Bows and arrows in central Brazil. (Hermann Meyer) Smithson. Rept. '96 : 549.
— arrows and quivers, North American. (O. T. Mason) Smithson. Rept. '93 : 631.
— Eskimo, in U. S. Nat. Mus. (John Murdoch) U. S. Nat. Mus. Rept. '84 : 307.

"Boxer," brig, Capture of. Dawson. Batt. of U. S. 2 : 272.

Boxley, Rood of. Bridgett, T. E. Blunders, 159.

Boy and girl out on furlough. (G. Johnston) Conf. Char. & Correc. '98 : 384.

Boy captives of Indian war of 1695. Whittier. Lit. recre. 172.

Boy life in a Mass. town, in 1860. (G. S. Hall) Am. Antiq. Soc. Proc. n. s. 7 : 107.

Boyce, Hector. Irving, D. Scot. writ. 1 : 1.

Boyce, John. Mary Lee. Brownson. Works, 20 : 83.

Boyce, Laura A. Hemenway. Poets of Vt. 125.

Boyce, Sara A. Hemenway. Poets of Vt. 368.

Boycotting. N. Y. Labor, 1885–86.
— in New York, 1885–89. N. Y. Labor, 1889.
— in Wisconsin. Wis. Bur. Lab. '86 : 372.
— Legislation concerning, in U. S. U. S. Labor Rept. v. 3.

Boyd, Alice. Clayton, E. C. Eng. fem. art. 2 : 37.

Boyd, William. See Kilmarnock, W. Boyd, Earl of.

Boyd, Zachary. Holland, J. Psalmists, 2 : 23.

Boyd's Tories, Dispersion of. Dawson. Batt. of U. S. 1 : 485.

Boydell, John (1717–1804), Eng. engraver. Spooner. Biog. fine arts, 1 : 132.

Boyer, Jean Pierre. Maccall. W. For. biog. 2 : 204.

Boyesen, Hjalmar Hjorth, with portrait. Warner Lib. 4 : 2272.

Boyhood. Fields. Underbrush, 277.
— and boys. Fairbanks, O. B. Aguecheek, 258.
— On, and growing up. Friswell. About, 11.

Boyle, Eleanor Vere Gordon. Clayton, E. C. Eng. fem. art. 2 : 346.

Boyle, Richard. See Burlington, Earl of ; also, Stannon, Viscount.

Boyle, Robert. (C. O. Thompson) Am. Antiq. Soc. Proc. n. s. 2 : 54. — Craik. Pursuit knowl. 2 : 73. — Creasy. Etonians, 123. — Garnett. Physicists, 5. — Lodge. Portraits (Bohn), v. 6. — Stoughton, I. Worthies of sci. 130. — Cooper, T. Triumphs of persev. 117. — Crichton, A. Converts, 2 : 7. — Street, G. S. Quales ego, 49. — Thorpe, T. E. Ess. hist. chem. 1. — Wrangham. Brit. Plutarch, v. 4.
— and Bentley. Disraeli, I. Calam. v. 2.
— Character of. Burnet, G. Lives.
— John Evelyn and. Thomson, Mrs. Cel. friend. 1 : 1.

Boylston, Zabdiel. Lossing. Em. Amer. 61.

Boynton, Winthrop Perkins. (H. F. Jenks) Harvard mem. biog. 2 : 363.

Boys, American. Osgood, S. Amer. leaves, 71.
— Bringing up of. Earle, Mrs. C. W. Potpourri, 257.
— Can we save the ? (J. D. Scouller) Conf. char. & corr. 1884 : 102.
— English, in the old times. Wheeler, D. H. Byways, 38.
— What shall we do with ? (J. L. Pickard) Nat. Educa. Assoc. '75 : 172.

Boys' clubs in New York. (E. J. Wendell) Woods, R. A. Poor, 151.

Boyse, S. Chalmers. Eng. poets, 14 : 515.

Bozarth, Experience. Drake, S. G. Trag. of wilderness, 334.

Bozrah, Ruins of. Tweedie. Ruined cities, 95.

Bozzelli [or Bozzolli], Joseph. Redding. Pers. remin. 1 : 299.

Brabacon, Roger le, Chief Justice of England, 1296–1315. Campbell. Ch. just. 1 : 90.

Brabourne, E. H. Knatchbull-Hugessen, Lord. Simson, Jas. Em. men of Kent, 164.

Bracciolini, Poggio. See Poggio Bracciolini.

Bracegirdle, Mrs. Anne. Austin & Ralph. Laureates, 237. — Cook, D. Hours w. players, 1 : 6. — Doran. Annals stage, 1 : 115. — Hogarth. Mem. opera, 1 : 145.

Bracewell, John, with portrait. Sketches N. H. men, 199.

Brackenbury, R. Carr. Miller, Jos. Singers church, 2d ed. 308.

Brackenridge, H. H. Moore, F. Am. eloq. 1 : 356.

Brackley, Thomas Egerton, Viscount. Lodge. Portraits (Bohn), v. 3.

Bracton [or Bretton], Henry de. Foss. Judges, 2 : 249.

Bradberry, David. Miller, Jos. Singers church, 2d ed. 263.

Bradburn, Samuel. Wakeley. Heroes Meth. 269. — Wesley & successors, 51. — Winks. Illus. shoemakers, 47.

Braddon, Mary Elizabeth. Warner Lib. 4 : 2279.

— at home. Hatton, J. Old lamps, 199.

— at Richmond. Yates, E. H. Celeb. 1. 318.

Bradford, Charlotte. Brockett. Woman's work, 731.

Bradford, Gamaliel. (C. Francis) Mass. Hist. Coll. 3d ser. 9 : 75.

Bradford, G. P. Parton, J. Sk. of men of prog.

Bradford, J. Espinasse. Lanc. worth. v. 1. — Tayler. Eng. martyrs.

Bradford, Jonathan, Trial of. Phillips, S. M. Famous cases, 144.

Bradford, Joseph. Wakeley. Heroes Meth. 211. — Wesley & successors, 35, 59.

Bradford, Lewis. (B. Kingman) N. E. Hist. Gen. Soc. Biog. 1 : 282.

Bradford, William. Belknap. Amer. biog. 3 : 7. — Brown, D. P. Forum, 1 : 491. — Moore, J. B. Am. gov. 49. — Richardson, C. F. Amer. lit. 72. — Lossing. Em. Amer. 62. — Richardson. Amer. lit. 1 : 72.

— & Plymouth. Bibliography. Providence Pub. Lib. Bull. May, '97.

— as author, man, and statesman. Blaxland. Mayflower ess. 100.

— Dialogue on church government. (C. Deane) Mass. Hist. Proc. 12 : 306.

— father of Amer. history. Ward, May A. Old col. 9.

— Hist. of Plymouth, Chronological summary of. Blaxland. Mayflower ess. 135.

— — Curious words in. Blaxland. Mayflower ess. 130.

Bradford. Dolman, F. Munic. at work, 85.

Bradford-on-Avon. Freeman. Eng. towns, 134.

Bradlaugh, Charles. Davidson, J. M. Eng. lib. 149. — Hinton. Eng. radicals, 305. — Em. persons, 5 : 14.

— Speech in his defence, 1881. (C. Bradlaugh) Wagner, L. Mod. pol. ora. 242.

Bradley, Amy M. Brockett. Woman's work, 212. — Moore, F. Women of the war, 415.

Bradley, Charles. Davies, G. J. Suc. preach. 138.

Bradley, Charles, Esq. Am. Bar Assoc. 22 : 700.

Bradley, Charles Smith. Am. Bar Assoc. 11 : 346.

Bradley, James. Ball, R. Great astron. 187.

— and the velocity of light. Lodge, O. J. Pioneers, 233.

Bradley, James ; a slave. Child, L. M. Oasis, 106.

Bradley, Joseph P., with portrait. Barnes, W. H. Sup. ct. 107.

Bradley, Randolph. Walker, C. D. Biog. Va. Mil. Inst. 58.

Bradley, William Henry. Everest. Poets of Conn. 307.

Bradley Court. Hodges, Eliz. Anc. Eng. homes, 15.

Bradley family. Titcomb, S. E. N. Eng. peo. 256.

Bradshaw, Henry. Benson, A. C. Ess. 252. — Choate, I. B. Wells of Eng. 44.

Bradshaw, Sir John, chief justice of England,

1649–53. Campbell. Ch. just. 1 : 382. — (T. Cooper) Andrews, W. Bygone Ches. 209.

Bradstreet, Mrs. Anne (Dudley). Anderson, Jas. Mem. wom. Pur. 1 : 156. — Griswold. Fem. poets, 17. — Chapman, W. Wom. of purit. 42. — Richardson. Amer. lit. 2 : 4.

— Poems. Ward, May A. Old col. 249.

Bradstreet, Simon. Moore, J. B. Amer. gov. 377.

Bradwardine, Thomas. Fuller. Worthies, 3 : 246. — Hook. Abps. Cant. 4 : 80. — Sargeant, L. Wiclif, 68, 141.

Brady, James T, Houghton. Kings, 459. — Proctor. Lawy. of N. Y. 238. — With portrait. Scott, H. W. Dist. Am. lawy. 65.

Brady, Mrs. Mary A. Brockett. Woman's work, 647. — Moore, F. Women of the war, 36.

Brady, Nicholas. Hatfield, E. F. Poets of ch. 94. — Holland, J. Psalmists, 2 : 105. — Miller, Jos. Singers church, 2d ed. 113.

Brady, Robert. Lawrence. Brit. historians, 1 : 319.

Bræcan, St. Conyngham, D. P. Irish saints, 328.

Bragadin, Marco, of Cyprus, maker of gold. Brown, H. F. Venet. stud. 259.

Bragadino, Marc Antonio. Rio. Four martyrs.

Bragg, Braxton. Pollard. Life of Lee, 284. — Snow. So. generals, 321.

Braham, John. Jones, W. A. Lit. stud. 1 : 88.

Brahe, Tycho. Ball, R. Great astron. 44. — Craik. Pursuit knowl. 2 : 67. — Morton, E. J. C. Heroes astron. 63. — Nasmith. Mak. mod. thought, 1 : 134.

— and the earliest observatory. Lodge, O. J. Pioneers, 33.

Brahma Dharma and its struggle with Hindu mysticism. Alviella. Contemp. evol. 257.

Brahmanism. Barth, A. Relig. India, 39–100. — Bettany. World's relig. 196. — Hopkins. Relig. of India, 176. — Matheson. Distinc. messages, 124. — (J. Caird) St. Giles lec. 2 : 1. — Clarke, J. F. Ten relig. 77. — Duncker. Hist. antiq. 4. — Hardwick, C. Christ & other mast. 1 : 190. — Parks, L. His star in the east, 57.

— Decline of. Barth, A. Relig. India, 87.

— does not antedate the Mosaic writings. Chatard. Occ. ess. 354.

— Ritual of. Barth, A. Relig. India, 39.

— Vitality of. Müller. Chips, v. 3 ; or Sel. ess. 2 : 87.

Brahmans, Religious ceremonies of the. Colebrooke. Misc. ess. 1 : 123.

Bramante d'Urbino. Milizia. Lives archb. 1 : 203. — Symonds. Renais. fine arts, 81.

Brahmo Somâj. Alviella. Contemp. evol. 234, 241. — (P. C. Mozoomdar) Barrows, J. H. Parl. relig. 1 : 345. — Cobbe, F. P. Hours of work, 59. — Hauser, Mrs. I. L. Orient, 143.

— Spiritual ideas of. (B. B. Nagarkar) Barrows, J. H. Parl. relig. 2 : 1226.

Brahmoism. Alviella. Contemp. evol. 226, 291.

Brahms, Joh. Elson, L. Gt. composers, 252. — Sharp, R. F. Makers of music. — Hadow. Stud. mod. mus. v. 2. — Maitland, J. A. F. Masters Ger. music, 1.

— A note on. Runciman, J. F. Old scores, 241.

Braid, James, work and writings. (J. M. Bramwell) Soc. Psych. Res. 12 : 127.

Brain, The. Calvert, G. H. Brief ess. — Hall, J. A. Glimpses, 149.

— Anthropology of. (D. K. Shute) Smithson. Rept. '92 : 595.

— Building of a. (E. H. Clarke) Nat. Educa. Assoc. '74 : 100.

Brain, Care of the. (A. B. Richardson) Conf. char. & corr. 1888 : 69.
— Functions of the. (D. Ferrier) Manch. Sci. lec. 7 : 105.
— Have we two brains ? Proctor. Sci. byways, 302.
— Physiology of. Carpenter, W. Benj. Nature, 139.
— Unconscious action of the. (W. B. Carpenter) Manch. Sci. lec. 3-4 : 77.
— Weight and size of, relative racial. Wilson, D. Lost Atlantis, 339.
Brain difficulties. Wynter, A. Our soc. bees, 1 : 466.
Brain enigmas. Wynter. Borderl. of insan. 167.
Brain troubles. Proctor, R. A. Nat. stud. 267.
Brain-work, Too much. Ballantyne. Ess. 192.
Brain-workers, Longevity of. (G. M. Beard) Am. Pub. Health, 1 : 54.
Brains and muscles. (W. A. Hammond) Butterfield Lec. Un. Coll. 1 : 265.
Brainard, John Gardner Calkins. Everest. Poets of Conn. 259. — Griswold. Poets Am. 205. — Hood, E. P. Master minds, 13. — Poe. Works, 6 : 28. — Richardson. Amer. lit. 2 : 31.
Brainerd, David. Adams, W. H. D. Good Samar. 202. — Carne, J. Em. mission. 2 : 328. — Collins, Stephen. Miscel. — Graham, W. Ess. 212. — Yonge. Pioneers. — Lossing. Em. Amer. 101. — Pierce, B. K. Em. dead, 195. — Richardson. Amer. lit. 1 : 148. — Thompson, A. Gt. Mission. 31.
Braintree, Mass., Church government in. Adams, C. F. Three episodes, 2 : 581.
Braithwaite, George. Ivimey. Eng. Bapt. 3 : 355.
Braithwaite, Wm. McClure. Translators, 189.
Bramah, Joseph. Seymour, C. C. B. Self-made, 209. — Walker, W., jr. Men of sci. 15.
— Inventions of. Smiles. Indus. biog. 228.
Bramber Castle. Timbs. Abbeys, 1 : 363.
Brampston, Sir John, chief justice of England, 1635-42. Campbell. Ch. just. 1 : 324.
Brampton, Thomas. Holland, J. Psalmists, 1 : 73.
Bramwell, Lord. Em. persons, 5 : 230.
Brand, Henry B. Hazlitt. Parl. portr. 143. — With photo. Cooper, T. Men of mark, 1 : 18. — Ritchie. Brit. sena. 106. — Reid, T. W. Politicians, 2 : 271.
— as Speaker of the Ho. of Commons. Smalley. Lond. let. 2 : 175.
Brand, Sir Mark I. Walker, W., jr. Men of sci. 21.
Brandan, St., Legend of. Am. Geog. Soc. 24 : 321.
Brandebourg, Madame de. Wraxall, C. F. L. Hist. bye-ways, 1 : 120.
Brandes, Georg. Boyesen. Scand. lit. 199. — With portrait. (W. M. Payne) Warner Lib. 4 : 2299.
Brandon, Charles. See Suffolk, Duke of.
Brandon estate, Virginia. Glenn, T. A. Colon. mans. 1 : 401. — Terhune. Colon. homes, 1.
Brandt, Enevold de. Crichton, A. Converts, 1 : 172.
Brandt, Heinrich von. Chesney. Ess. mil. biog. 241.
Brandt, Sebastian. Warner Lib. 4 : 2311.
— Ship of fools. Disraeli, I. Amen. (N. Y. 2 v.) 1 : 326. — Müller. Chips, v. 3.
Brandywine, Battle of. Dawson. Batt. of U. S. 1 : 273.
Brant, Elizabeth. Clement, J. Noble deeds, 459.
Brant, Joseph. Lossing. Em. Amer. 158.

Brantôme, Pierre de, with portrait. Warner Lib. 4 : 2319.
Brasses, Monumental. Sparvel-Bayly. New stud. 165.
Brasseur de Bourbourg, Charles Stephen, Abbé. (H. B. Adams) Am. Antiq. Soc. Proc. n. s. 7 : 274.
Brassey, Anne, Lady. Adams, W. H. D. Cel. wom. trav. 340. — Bolton, S. K. Girls who bec. famous, 300.
Brassey, Thomas. Hinton. Eng. radicals, 161. — Japp, A. H. Golden lives, 136. — Smith, Gold. Lec. & ess. 160. — Smith, G. B. Leaders mod. ind. 301.
Brathwaite, Richard. Alden, R. M. Rise of satire, 216. — Bell, R. Lit. & sci. men, 2 : 168. — Gosse, E. Jacobean poets, 109. — Hales. Folia litt. 192.
Bratiano, Jón. Kingston, W. B. Men, etc. 151.
Bratton, Martha. Clement, J. Noble deeds, 246. — Ellet. Women of revol. 1 : 237.
Braxton, Carter, 1736-97. Dwight, N. Signers of decl. 321. — Lincoln, R. W. Signers, 5. — Lossing. Signers, 197. — Sanderson. Signers, v. 6.
Bray, Charles, Writings of. Stock. Attempts, 213.
Bray, Sir Reginald. Manning, J. A. Speakers, 138.
Bray, William. Bailey, J. B. Methusales, 214.
Braye, Cardinal de, Tomb of, plate. Perkins, C. C. Tusc. sculp. 1 : 52.
Brayton, Charles Ray. Bartlett, J. R. R. I. officers, 331.
Brayton, Mary Clark. Brockett. Woman's work, 545.
Brazil. Bur. Am. Repub. Bull. no. 7.
— and Portugal, Points in history of. Freeman. Hist. ess. 4 : 199.
— Climate and diseases of. (J. Brandao) Am. Pub. Health, 19 : 182.
— Commerce and industries of, 1899. U. S. Cons. Rept. 60 : 1.
— Commercial directory of, 1891. Bur. Am. Repub. Bull. no. 13.
— Condition and prospects of. (G. W. Chamberlain) Am. Geog. Soc. 22 : 537.
— Constitution, 1890. U. S. Cons. Rept. 36 : 1.
— Fiedler claim against. Helper, H. R. Andean diplom. 337.
— Geology of. (C. F. Hartt) Am. Geog. Soc. 2 : pt. 2, 55.
— German colonies in, 1897. (F. D. Hill) U. S. Cons. Rept. 56 : 597.
— Railways of, 1867. (F. D. Hill) U. S. Cons. Rept. 56 : 387.
— Tariff, 1898. U. S. Cons. Rept. 57 : 11.
— Trade with U. S., 1891. (O. H. Dockery) U. S. Cons. Rept. 36 : 600.
Breaca, St. Conyngham, D. P. Irish saints, 130.
Breadstuffs in Latin America. Bur. Am. repub. no. 35.
Breadth of life. Mabie. Books and cul. 154.
Breakfast and how to enjoy it. Hunt, L. Seer, 1 : 73.
Breakspear, Bozon, cardinal. Williams, R. F. Eng. card. 1 : 165, 477.
Breakspear, Nicholas, cardinal-legate. Williams, R. F. Eng. card. 1 : 81.
See also Adrian IV.
Breathing, Healthy. Kingsley. Health, 26.
Brébeuf, John de, with portrait. Murray, J. O'K. Cath. heroes, 405.
Breck, Samuel. Winslow, S. N. Biog. Phila. merch. 61.

Breckenridge, Hugh Henry,1748–1816. Brown, D. P. Forum, 1 : 396.

Breckinridge, James. Walker, C.D. Biog. Va. Mil. Inst. 60.

Breckinridge, John C. Bartlett. Pres. candidates, 336. — Forney. Anec. 41. — Johnston, A. Amer. ora. 4 : 51. — Pollard. Life of Lee, 601 — Savage. Liv. repres. men, 67.

Breckinridge, Margaret E. Brockett. Woman's work, 187. — Moore, F. Women of the war, 75.

Breckinridge, Peachy G. Walker, C. D. Biog. Va. Mil. Inst. 67.

Breckinridge, Robert J. Clarke, J. F. Memo. sketches, 231. — Fish, H. C. Pulpit eloq. 267.

Breckinridge, Samuel Miller. Am. Bar Assoc. 14 : 430.

Bréguet, Abraham L. Brightwell. Heroes of lab. 69.

Bregwin, 759–765. Hook. Abps. Cant. 1 : 234.

Brehan, Madame de. Baker, W. S. Portr. of Wash. 68.

Brehon laws. Maine. Early instit.

Breisgau. Bartley, G. C. T. Rhine, 60.

Brema, Marie, with portrait. Buffen. Mus. celeb. 2 : 109.

Bremen. Fulton, C. C. Europe, 12.

— Free port of. (G. Keenan) 1895. U. S. Cons. Rept. 50 : 195.

Bremer, Frederika. Adams, W. H. D. Cel. wom. trav. 134. — Dix, J. Lions, 237. — Darton. Fam. girls, 189. — Duyckinck. Portr. gall. 2 : 145. — Hall, S. C. Book of mem. 415. — With portrait. Hamilton, C. J. Wom. wr. 2 : 44. — Smith, G. B. Women of renown, 1. — With portrait. Warner Lib. 4 : 2328.

Brendan, St. Kingsley. Hermits, 253.

— Miraculous voyage of. Furst, C. Group of old auth. 95.

Brendley, James. Davenport, R. A. Lives, 310.

Brendon, St., of Birr. Conyngham, D. P. Irish saints, 182.

Brendon, St., of Clonfert. Conyngham, D. P. Irish saints, 232.

Brenius, Daniel. Wallace, R. Anti-Trin. biog. 3 : 77.

Brentano, Clemens. Warner Lib. 4 : 2343.

Brentano, Elizabeth, with portrait. Warner Lib. 4 : 2348.

Brenton, Charles Lancelot Lee. Mozley. Reminis. 2 : 116.

Brenton, Sir Jahleel. Rogers, C. Chr'n heroes, 12.

Brera gallery. Hare. Cities of No. Italy, 1 : 153.

Brereton, Jane. Williams, Jane. Lit. wom. 156.

Brereton, Sir William. Croston. Hist. sites Lanc. 173.

Brereton family. Croston. Hist. sites Lanc. 171.

Brescia. Hare. Cities of No. Italy, 1 : 241.

— Museo patrio at. Stuart, J. M. Reminis. 1.

Brest, sea fight off. Valentine, L. J. Sea fights, 11.

Brethren (and clerks) of the common life (or lot), and the mystics. Ullman. Reformers, 2 : 7.

Breton de los Herreros. Kennedy. Poets of Spain, 249.

Brett, John. Bate, P. H. Eng. Pre-Raph. 87.

Brett, Richard. McClure. Translators, 144. — With photo. Cooper, T. Men of mark, 2 : 31.

Breviary, Roman and Gallican. Neale. Ess. liturg.

Brevity. Coleridge, H. Ess. 1 : 46.

Brevoort, James Carson. Am. Antiq. Soc. Proc. n. s. 5 : 174.

Brewer, David J., with portrait. (W. Watson) Scott, H. W. Dist. Am. lawy. 75.

Brewer, Jehoida. Miller, Jos. Singers church, 2d ed. 308.

Brewer, John S., Memoir of. (H. Wace) Brewer. Eng. stud. vii.

Brewing. Japp & Holmes. Succ. bus. men, 130.

Brewster, Sir David. With portrait. Cochrane, R. Earnest, 175. — Stoughton, J. Worthies of sci. 281.

Brewster, Lot Edw. (D. T. V. Huntoon) N. E. Hist. Gen. Soc. Biog. 1 : 164.

Brewster, William. Belknap. Amer. biog. 3 : 53. — Herrick, S. E. Heretics, 263. — Lossing. Em. Amer. 10.

Briar Creek, Battle of. Dawson. Batt. of U. S. 1 : 489.

Bribery. Hazard, R. G. Econ. & pol. 115.

— Effect on finances in reign of William. Francis, J. Stock exch. 12.

— Law against. Hazard, T. R. Miscel. 234.

Bric-a-brac, Pursuit of. Jarves. Ital. ramb. 285.

Bricher, Alfred T. Sheldon, G. W. Amer. painters, 144.

Bricklayers. (H. R. Taylor) Galton, F. W. Workers, 175.

— and an old book. Hunt, L. Seer, 1 : 145.

Briconnet, Bishop. Wittenmeyer. Women Reform. 88.

Bridge, Horatio. Derby, J. C. Fifty years, 630.

Bridge, Jonathan D. Sherman, D. New Eng. divines, 341.

Bridge, Norman W. Hemenway. Poets of Vt. 148.

Bridge, Britannia, at Montreal. Head, F. B. Descr. ess. 2 : 216.

— Tubular, over the Menai strait. Chambers's Repos. no. 94.

Bridgeman, Sir Orlando. Campbell. Ld. Chan. 4 : 139.

Bridges, Matthew. Hatfield, E. F. Poets of church, 95. — Miles, A. H. Poets of cent. 10 : 684. — Miller, Jos. Singers church, 2d ed. 472.

Bridges, Robert, Poetry of. Dowden. New stud. 61.

Bridges. Story, A. T. Vagrom, 200. — Tuckerman. Collector, 325.

— harbors, and ferries, Early English. Smiles. Engineers, 1 : 237.

— Iron, Fairbairn's. Smiles. Indus. biog.

— Military. Gleig. Ess. 1 : 299.

Bridget, St. Conyngham, D. P. Irish saints, 141.

Bridget, daughter of Edward IV. Green, M. A. E. Princesses, 4 : 44.

Bridgewater, Elizabeth, countess of. Williams, Jane. Lit. wom. 82.

Bridgewater, Francis, duke of (1736–1803). Smiles. Engineers, 1 : 334. — Espinasse. Lanc. worth. v. 1.

Bridgewater, Francis Henry Egerton, 8th earl of. Edwards, E. Founders Brit. Mus. 2 : 446.

Bridgewater castle and the battle of Sedgemoor. Timbs. Abbeys, 1 : 559.

Bridgman, Elijah C. Creegan. Gr. mission. 95. — (P. W. Lyman) Haydn, H. C. Am. miss. heroes, no. 9.

Bridgman, Frederick A. Sheldon, G. W. Amer. painters, 151.

Bridgman, Laura. Chambers's Miscel. no. 52. — Kitto, J. Lost senses, 2 : 41. — Darton. Fam. girls, 55. — Parton. Noted women, 243. Hall, G. S. Asp. Ger. 237.

— Vocal sounds of. Lieber, F. Reminis. 443.

Bridport, Alexander Hood, first viscount. Lodge. Portraits (Bohn), v. 8.

British Museum, Library of, Catalogue of, as basis of a universal catalogue. Garnett, R. Ess. in librarianship, 109.

— — — Past, present, and future of. Garnett, R. Ess. in librarianship, 87.

— — — Printing of. Garnett, R. Ess. in librarianship, 67.

— — Sliding-press at. Garnett, R. Ess. in librarianship, 262.

Britius, St., of Tours. Charles. Martyrs, 362.

Britons, Origin of. Hope. Ess. 93.

Brittany. Church, R. W. Misc. ess. 87.

— Ancient. Field, Mrs. H. M. Sk. France, 57.

— So-called Celtic monuments of. (W. W. Hawkes) Am. Geog. Soc. 10 : 93.

Britton, Alex. Thompson. Am. Bar Assoc. 22 : 669.

Britton, John. Jerdan. Men, 33. — Smith, C. R. Retrospec. 2 : 86.

Broad views. Tuckerman. Optimist, 257.

Broadhead, James O., with portrait. Scott, H. W. Dist. Am. lawy. 89. — Am. Bar Assoc. 21 : 682.

Broadsides, Early Amer. (N. Paine) Am. Antiq. Soc. Proc. n. s. 11 : 455.

Broadstairs and Ramsgate. Zangwill. Without prej. 265.

Brock, Sallie A. Davidson, J. W. Writ. of South, 56. — Raymond, J. Southland writ. 2 : 784.

Brock, Holland. Guild. Abroad again, 457.

— A Dutch paradise. Irving. Crayon pap. 73.

Brockayus, Christopher. Wallace, R. Anti-Trin. biog. 2 : 443.

Broderick, Hon. David C. Forney. Anec. 23.

Brodhead, Jacob. Van Santvoord, C. Disc. 440.

Brodie, Sir Benjamin. Bettany. Em. doctors, 1 : 286. — Pettigrew. Med. portr. gall. v. 2.

Brodsky, Adolph, with portrait. Ehrlich, A. Cel. violin. 17.

Brodzinski, Casimir. Soboleski. Poets of Poland, 228.

Broek. Amicis. Holland, 284.

Broglie, Albert, Duc de. King, E. French pol. lead. 180. — Loménie. Liv. characters, 313. — Men of 3d repub. 96. — Walsh, R. M. Liv. char. France.

Brome, A. Chalmers. Eng. poets, 6 : 637.

Brome, Richard (temp. Charles I). Ward, A. W. Eng. dram. 2 : 337.

Bromfield, John. (J. Quincy) Hunt, F. Am. merch. 2 : 469. — Parton. Capt. indus. 148.

Bromley, Sir Thomas. Campbell. Ld. Chan. 2 : 237.

Bromley, William. Manning, J. A. Speakers, 416.

Bromton Hospital. Disraeli. Sel. Spee. 2 : 633.

Brontë, Anne. Bayne. Ess. v. 2. — Wise, D. Rem. women, 9.

Bronte, Charlotte. Adams, W. H. D. Wom. of fash. 2 : 265. — Badeau. Vagabond, 158. — Balfour, C. L. Work-women, 385. — Bayne, P. Ess. 1 : 393. — Bayne, P. Two great Eng. women. — Cone & Gilder. Pen-portr. 2 : 179. — Goodrich, F. B. Women, 353. — Griswold, H. T. Home-life, 286. — Jeaffreson. Novelists, 2 : 282. — Mason, E. T. Pers. traits, 4 : 233. — Martineau, H. Biog. sk. 44. — Queens of liter. 129. — Roscoe, W. C. Ess. — Stephen, L. Hours in libr. 3 : 325. — Walsh, W. S. Pen. pic. Vict. au. 159. — Wotton. Word portraits, 24. — Adams, W. H. D. Cel. Eng. wom. Vict. 1 : 119. — Adams, W. H. D. Noble women, 249. — Duyckinck. Portr. gall. 2 : 44. — Har-

rison, F. Stud. early Vict. 145. — Saintsbury. Correc. imp. 157. — Skelton, J. Ess. in hist. 296. — Smith, G. B. Poets & nov. — Wise, D. Rem. women, 9. — Fifty famous women, 249. — With portrait. Warner Lib. 4 : 2381. — With portrait. Hamilton, C. J. Wom. writ. 2 : 190. — Walford, L. B. 12 Eng. au. 139. — With portrait. Hubbard, E. Little journeys, 3 : 115.

Brontë, Charlotte, and Emily. Fawcett, M. G. Em. wom. 99.

— in the Lake Country. Rawnsley. Lit. Assoc. Eng. Lakes, 2 : 94, 107.

— Villette, Setting of. Terhune. Where ghosts, 277.

Brontë, Emily. Cone & Gilder. Pen-portr. 2 : 179. — Robertson. Eng. poetesses, 321. — Swinburne. Miscel. 260. — (E. Gosse) Ward. Eng. poets, 4 : 581. — Miles, A. H. Poets of cent. 7 : 283. — Smith, G. B. Poets & nov. — Wise, D. Rem. women, 9.

Brontë, Patrick B., Reminiscences of. Grundy, F. Pictures, 73.

Brontë family. Smith, G. B. Poets & nov. 207.

— Bibliography. (B. Wood) Brontë soc. publica. pt. 1.

Brontë sisters. Kinsley. Views, 303. — Miles, A. H. Poets of cent. 10 : 726. — (M. O. W. Oliphant) Oliphant. Wom. novelists, 1. — Roscoe, W. C. Poems & ess. v. 2. — Smith, G. B. Poets & nov. 207.

Bronze, Age of. Allen, Grant. Science in Arc. 213.

— — in Egypt. (Oscar Montelius) Smithson. Rept. '90 : 499.

— Casting of, in Japan. (W. Gowland) Smithson. Rept. '94 : 609.

Brooches and dress fastenings, Ancient. Fairholt. Rambles, 159.

Brook, A wayside. Abbott, C. C. Outings, 178.

Brook Farm. Cooke, G. W. Life of Emerson, 91. — Frothingham, O. B. Life of Ripley, 108. — Frothingham. Transcend. 159. — Emerson, R. W. Lec. 338. — Curtis. From easy chair, 3 : 1. — Nichol. Amer. lit. 444.

— interp. Christ's idea of society. Peabody, E. P. Last evening, 181.

Brooke, Lady Elizabeth. Burder. Pious wom. 105.

Brooke, Fulke Greville, Lord. Gosse, E. Jacobean poets, 194. — Macdonald, G. England's antiphon, 89. — (M. A. Ward) Ward. Eng. poets, 1 : 365.

Brooke, Gustavus Vaughan. Coleman, G. Players, 2 : 223. — Marston, J. W. Rec. actors, 2 : 171.

Brooke, Henry. Chalmers. Eng. poets, 17 : 329.

— The fool of quality. Kingsley, C. New Misc. 334.

Brooke, Sir James. Adams, W. H. D. In perils, 293.

— and Borneo. Chambers's Papers, no. 34.

Brooke, Robert Greville, 2d Lord. Lodge. Portraits (Bohn), v. 4. — Stoughton, J. Spir. heroes, 98.

Brooke, Stopford A. Great mod. preachers. — Mathews, W. Men, places, and things, 179.

Brooke, William Henry. Smith, C. R. Retrospec. 1 : 281.

Brookfield, W. H. Davies, G. J. Suc. preach. 369.

Brookfield, Mass., in King Philip's war. (G. Reynolds) Am. Antiq. Soc. Proc. n. s. 5 : 77.

Brooklyn, N. Y. Brooks, E. S. Gt. cities, 54.
— (H. Putnam) Powell, L. P. Hist. towns mid.
states, 213.
— Public hospitals of. (L. S. Pilcher) Conf. char.
& corr. 1890 : 177.
— Reservoir of. (A. N. Bell) Am. Pub. Health
Assoc. 41.
— Sanitary work in. Am. Pub. Health, 13 : 56.
Brooks, Charles. (S. Lincoln) Mass. Hist. Proc.
18 : 174.
Brooks, Charles T. Essex Inst. Hist. Coll. v. 21.
— Hatfield, E. F. Poets of ch. 97. — Putnam,
A. P. Singers liberal, 353.
Brooks, Chas. W. Shirley. Miles, A. H. Poets
of cent. 9 : 375.
Brooks, Gorham. (O. B. Frothingham) N. E.
Hist. Gen. Soc. Biog. 2 : 470.
Brooks, James. Lanman, C. Haphazard, 180.
Brooks, James Gordon. Griswold. Poets Am.
240.
Brooks, John. With portrait. Amer. nat. portr.
gall. v. 2. — Loring, J. S. 100 Bost. ora. 184.
— Lossing. Em. Amer. 145.
Brooks, Mrs. Maria Gowen. Griswold. Fem.
poets, 69.
Brooks, Mary E. Griswold. Fem. poets, 139.
Brooks, Peter Chardon. Everett. Orat. v. 3. —
With portrait. (E. Everett) Hunt, F. Am.
merch. 1 : 133.
Brooks, Phillips. Clarke, T. M. Reminis. 206.
Potter, H. C. Scholar & state. 207. — Bolton,
S. K. Fam. leaders, 368. — Mass. Hist. Soc.
Proc. 2d ser. 8 : 80. — (W. R. Huntington)
Am. Acad. A. & S. Proc. 28 : 331. — With
portrait. Warner Lib. 4 : 2417.
— Bibliography. Howe, M. A. D. Phillips
Brooks.
Brooks, Preston S. Johnston, A. Amer. ora. 3 :
121.
Brooks, William G. (C. C. Smith) Mass. Hist.
Proc. 17 : 98.
Brooksbank, Joseph. Morison, J. Fathers of
Lond. Miss. Soc. 2 : 463.
Broome, W. (S. Johnson) Chalmers. Eng. po-
ets, 12 : 3.
Brosamer, Hans. Scott. Little masters, 121.
Broschi, Carlo. Brightwell. Byepaths of biog.
182.
Brotherhood. Hall, John. Papers, 53.
— Doctrine of. Gladden. Ruling ideas, 31.
— Human. (K. Kohler) Barrows, J. H. Parl. re-
lig. 1 : 366.
Brotherhood of the New Life. Hinds. Amer.
commun.
Brotherhood of Purity, The. Poole, S. L. Stud-
ies, 176.
Brotherton, Joseph. Grant, J. Recoll. Lords &
Comm. 2 : 155.
Brough, Lionel, with portrait. Goddard, A.
Players, 2 : 267.
Brougham, H., Lord. Adams, W. H. D. Learned
in law, 339. — Foss. Judges, 9 : 78. — Gilfil-
lan. 1st gall. 171. — Georgian era, 2 : 352. —
Harsha. Orators, 297. — Hazlitt. Spirit. —
Hutton, R. H. Stud. in parl. 116. — McCosh.
Scot. phil. 360. — Martineau, H. Biog. sk.
392. — Miller, H. Lead. articles, 105. — With
portr. Nicoll. Great move. 119. — Sheil, R. L.
Sk. Irish bar, 2 : 349. — Wotton. Word por-
traits, 27. — Browne, I. Gt. Lawyers, 152. —
Duyckinck. Portrait gall. 1 : 444. — Famous
boys, 67. — Goodrich, C. A. Sel. Brit. eloq. —
Grant, Jas. Bench & bar, 1 : 81, 110. — Grant, J.
Recoll. Lords, 314. — Mathews, W. Oratory,
258. — Mitchell, D. G. Eng. lands, 4 : 87. —

Stanton, H. B. Reforms, 85, 116. — Tyler, M.
C. Glimpses Eng. 137.
Brougham, H., Lord, and law reform. Forsyth,
W. Essays, 204.
— Scene between, and Lord Melbourne. Grant, J.
Recoll. Lords & Comm. 1 : 58.
— Speeches of. Forsyth, W. Essays, 1.
— Westmoreland election, 1818. Wordsworth, W.
Prose, 1.
Brougham, John. Hutton. Plays, 49. — Jeffer-
son, Jos. Autob. — Matthews, B. Actors, 3 :
273. — With portrait. Reignolds, Kate. Ac-
tors, 45. — Winter, W. Shadows, 2 : 96.
Brougham Hall. Guild. Over the ocean, 41.
Broughton, Frederick W. Archer. Eng. dram.
87.
Broughton, Rhoda, with portrait. Black, H. C.
Wom. authors, 37. — Heywood, J. C. How
they strike me, 97.
Broughton, Thomas. Jesse, J. H. Cel. Eton.
v. 1. — Tyerman, Oxf. Meth. 334.
Brounker, Henry. Jesse. Court of Eng. Stuarts,
3 : 350.
Broussa. Tuckerman, C. K. Recoll. 2 : 246.
Brouwer, Adriaen. Gower. Fig. painters Holl. 9.
Brown, Aaron V. Livingston, J. Dist. Amer. 62.
Brown, Albert G. Savage. Liv. rep. men, 78.
Brown, Andrew, Dr., and Sydenham. Brown,
J. Locke, etc. 261.
Brown, Charles Brockden. Griswold. Prose
writ. 107. — Prescott. Biog. misc. 1. — Tuck-
erman. Ess. 369. — With portrait. Amer. nat.
portr. gall. 3. — Lossing. Em. Amer. 290. —
With portrait. Mitchell, D. G. Am. lands.
179. — Nichol. Amer. lit. 157. — Ossoli. Art,
322. — Richardson, Amer. lit. 1 : 262. 2 : 286.
— With portrait. Warner Lib. 4 : 2425.
— Novels. Dana. P. & p. writ. 325. — Ossoli.
Life without, 83. — Mitchell, D. G. Amer.
lands, 179.
Brown, Charles Brooks. (W. W. Burrage) Har-
vard mem. biog. 1 : 333.
Brown, David Paul, 1795–1872. Brown, D. P.
Forum, 1 : 27.
Brown, E. Lakin. Hemenway. Poets of Vt.
108.
Brown, Mrs. Eleanor (Fairham). Clayton, E. C.
Eng. fem. art. 2 : 177.
Brown, Ford Madox. Bate, P. H. Eng. Pre-
Raph. 17. — Quilter. Preferences, 8.
— Essay on. (S. Colvin) Atkinson, J. B. Eng.
paint. 31.
— Pictures of. Palgrave. Ess. on art, 168. — Ros-
setti, W. M. Fine art, 178.
Brown, Frances. Bethune, G. W. Brit. fem.
poets, 360. — Smiles. Brief biog. 461.
Brown, Francis. Putnam, A. P. Singers liberal,
153.
Brown, George Loring, with portrait. Benja-
min, S. G. W. Am. art, 1. — Tuckerman.
Artist life, 221. — Tuckerman. Artists, 346.
— Sheldon, G. W. Amer. painters, 111.
Brown, Henry Armitt. Pennypacker. Hist. sk.
293.
Brown, Henry French. (T. W. Higginson) Har-
vard mem. biog. 2 : 372.
Brown, Henry Kirke. Clarke, W. J. Amer.
sculp. 112.
Brown, Henry Stowell. Brown, Hugh S. Lec. 5.
Brown, Mrs. Isabella. Hack. Self-surr. 25. —
Burder. Pious wom. 679.
Brown, Jacob, with portrait. Amer. nat. portr.
gall. v. 2. — With portrait. Duyckinck. Nat.
portr. gall. 1 : 483. — Lossing. Em. Amer. 338.
Brown, James, with portrait. (G. S. Hillard)

Browning, Elizabeth Barrett. Bayne, P. Ess.
1 : 146. — Bayne, P. Two great Eng. women.
— Bolton, S. K. Girls who became famous,
194. — Cone & Gilder. Pen.-portr. 2 : 93. —
Fawcett, M. G. Em. wom. 111. — Gilfillan.
Mod. lit. 2 : 239. — (E. Y. Hincks) Parton.
Em. wom. 221. — Robertson. Eng. poetesses,
255. — Saunders, F. Famous books, 176. —
Sharp, A. Vic. poets, 103. — Smith, G. B.
Poets & nov. 57. — Stedman. Vic. poets, 114.
— Trollope, T. A. What I rem. 2 : 169. —
Tuckerman. Poets, 281. — (W. T. Arnold)
Ward. Eng. poets, 4 : 562. — Walsh, W. S.
Pen pic. 216. — Wotton. Word portraits, 34.
— Benson, A. C. Ess. 205. — Bethune, G. W.
Brit. fem. poets, 452. — Brooks, S. W. Eng.
poets, 426. — Duyckinck. Portr. gall. 2 : 352.
— Griswold, H. T. Personal sk. 114. — With
portrait. Warner Lib. 5 : 2523. — Horne, R. H.
New spirit, 265. — With portrait. Hamilton,
C. J. Wom. writers, 2 : 142. — Innes, A. D.
Seers & s. — Walford, L. B. 12 Eng. auth. 169.
— With portrait. Hubbard, E. Little jour-
neys, 3 : 1. — Macdonald, G. England's anti-
phon, 323. — (J. A. Noble) Miles, A. H. Poets
of cent. 7 : 155. — Mitford, M. R. Recollec.
169. — Ossoli. Art, 198. — Roscoe, W. C.
Poems & ess. v. 2. — Smiles. Brief biog. 449.
— Swanwick, A. Poets, 347.
— and her scarcer books. Nicoll, W. R. Lit. anec.
2 : 81.
— and Robert. Taylor, B. At home, 2 : 410.
— Bibliography. Hodgkins. 19th cent. authors.
— Salem (Mass.) Pub. Lib. Bull. Jan. '97.
— Poems. Poe. Works, 6 : 434.
— Religious opinions of. Nicoll, W. R. Lit. anec.
2 : 123.
— Sonnets from the Portuguese. Gosse, E. Crit.
Kit-kats.
Browning, Orville H. Am. Bar Assoc. 4 :
136.
Browning, Robert. Annual cyclop. '89. — Aus-
tin, A. Poetry, 38. — Cooke, G. W. Poets,
279. — With photo. Cooper, T. Men of mark,
5 : 17. — Dawson, W. J. Mod. Engl. 270. —
Devey, J. Mod. Engl. poets, 376. — Forman.
Liv. poets, 105. — Friswell. Mod. men of let.
119. — Galton, A. Urbana, 59. — Haven, G.
Pilgrim, 209. — Noel. Ess. on poetry. — Os-
soli, M. F. Art, lit., etc. 207. — Sharp, A. Vic.
poets, 40. — Stedman. Vic. poets, 293. —
Taylor, B. At home, 410. — Thorne, W. H.
Mod. idols, 21. — Armstrong, R. A. Faith &
doubt, 114. — Chapman, J. J. Emerson, 185.
— With portrait. (E. L. Burlingame) Warner
Lib. 5 : 2557. — Cheney, J. V. Golden guess,
121. — Swanwick, A. Poets, 387. — Cochrane,
R. Gt. thinkers, 257. — Em. persons, 4 : 196. —
Innes, A. D. Seers & s. — Farrar, Men, 42. —
Forster, J. Four teachers, 103. — Horne, R. H.
New spirit, 278. — Jacobs, Jos. Ess. & rev. 97.
— Mabie. Ess. lit. interp. — (F. J. Furnivall)
Miles, A. H. Poets of cent. 4 : 293. — (J. A.
Noble) Miles, A. H. Poets of cent. 9 : 337. —
Mitford, M. R. Recollec. 180. — Saintsbury.
Correc. imp. 98. — Walker, H. Gt. Vic. poets,
35, 91, 150. — Smalley. Lond. lett. 1 : 309. —
Smiles. Brief biog. 377. — Wilson, S. L.
Theol. mod. lit.
— Alleged obscurity of his poetry. Birrell. Obiter,
1 : 55.
— and Eliz. B. Griswold, H. T. Home-life, 274.
— Walsh, W. S. Pen pic. mod. 216.
— as a humorist. Scudder, V. D. Life of spirit,
201.

Browning, Robert, as a second class poet.
McNicoll, T. Ess. Eng. lit. 298.
— as a thinker. Cooke, G. W. Poets, 345.
— as Wordsworth's successor. Cross lights, 59.
— Bibliography. Hodgkins. 19th cent. authors. —
(T. J. Wise) Athenæum, Sept. 11, 26; Nov.
28 ; Dec. 26, '96. — Nicoll, W. R. Lit. anec. 1 :
361. — Orr, Mrs. S. Hdbk. R. Browning. —
Salem (Mass.) Pub. Lib. Bull. '97.
— Childe Roland. O'Conor. Ess. 1.
— Christmas Eve. MacDonald, G. Orts, 195.
— Death of. Woodberry. Stud. in lett. 276.
— Dramatic poetry of. Cooke, G. W. Poets, 329.
— Ethics of. Boyesen. Lit. silhouettes, 131.
— Genius of. Thomson, Jas. (B. V.) Biog. ess. 437.
— In a balcony. Shackford. Soc. & lit. pap. 116.
— in Florence. Curtis. From easy ch. 197.
— in Westminster abbey. James, H. Ess. in
Lond. 222.
— New Year's eve. Haweis. Poets in pulpit, 117.
— the optimist. Mather, J. M. 19th c. poets, 155.
— Pacchiarotto. Thomson, Jas. (B. V.) Biog. ess.
478.
— Pippa passes. Finlayson, T. C. Ess. 168.
— Plays. Courtney. Stud. 100.
— Poems. Ossoli. Woman, 298.
— Poetry of. M'Cormick, W. S. Three lec. 125.
— — Characteristics of. Cooke, G. W. Poets,
316.
— The poet's poet. Quayle, W. A. Poet, 7.
— Relations of, to his wife. Cooke, G. W. Poets,
289.
— Religion of. Dawson, W. J. Mod. Engl. 288.
— Religious teachings of. Cooke, G. W. Poets,
355.
— Renaissance pictures in poetry of. Burton, R.
Liter. likings, 150.
— Ring and the book. Quayle, W. A. Poet, 292.
— Morley, J. Stud. in lit. 255. — Thomson,
Jas. (B. V.) Biog. ess. 458.
— — Browning's masterpiece. Buchanan. Master
spir. 89.
— — The pope in. Shackford. Soc. & lit. pap.
108.
— Saul, Interpretation of life in. Quayle, W. A.
Poet, 326.
— Sordello. Church, R. W. Dante, 221. — Dow-
den. Transcripts, 474.
— Style and works of. Hutton. Ess. theol. 2 : 190.
— Tennyson and. Dowden. Studies, 191. Same
in Afternoon lec. 5 : 139.
— Theology. Jacobs, J. Jewish ideals, 84.
Browning craze, The. Fawcett, E. Agnost. 100.
Brownlow, William Gannaway, with portrait.
Brockett. Men. of our day, 351.
Brownrigg. Dr. Rawnsley. Lit. Assoc. Eng.
lakes, 1 : 12.
Brownrigg, Elizabeth. (E. Stubbs) Vincent, A.
Twelve bad women, 189. — Wilson, H.
Characters, 340.
Brownrigg, Ralph. Fuller. Worthies, 8 : 171.
Brownrigg, W. Lonsdale. Worthies Cumb. v. 6.
Brown-Sequard, C. E. Am. Acad. A. & S.
Proc. 30 : 589.
— Two-fold brain theory of. Proctor. Sci. byways,
302.
Brownson, Nathan. Jones, C. C. jr. Deleg. fr.
Georgia, 11.
Brownson, Orestes A. Frothingham. Tran-
scend. 128. — Griswold. Prose writ. 422. —
Warner Lib. 5 : 2594.
— His religious autobiography. Brownson. Wks.
5 : 1.
Brownson's Quarterly Review, J. V. H. on.
Brownson. Works, 14 : 317.

Brownswerd, John. Bell, R. Lit. & sci. men, 2 : 96.

Bruce, H. A. *See* Aberdare, Lord.

Bruce, James. Jardine, W. Nat. libr. v. 11. — Kelly, C. Voyages, 586. — St. John. Cel. travelers, 2 : 233.

Bruce, John Collingwood. Smith, C. R. Retrospec. 2 : 164.

Bruce, Michael. Hatfield, E. F. Poets of church, 105. — Miller, Jos. Singers church, 2d ed. 292. — Wilson, J. G. Poets of Scot. 1 : 295.

Bruce, Robert. *See* Robert I., King of Scotland.

Bruce, Robert de, chief justice. *See* Brus, Robert de.

Brucioli, Antonio, in Florence. Stoughton. Ital. reformers, 49.

Bruck, Max. Maitland, J. A. F. Masters Ger. music, 97.

Bruckner, Anton. Maitland, J. A. F. Masters Ger. music, 240.

Bruges. Quilter. Preferences, 165. — Warner, C. D. Saunterings, 24. — Thackeray. Early & late, 167.

— from the belfry-tower. King, R. J. Sk. 427.

Brugsch, Henry. (G. Maspero) Smithson. Rept. '96 : 667.

Bruhmu, Subhâ, Vedantism and. Dutt. Ess. 49.

Brummage, Sergeant. Sinclair, J. Sketches.

Brummel, George, *called* Beau. Dawson, G. Shaksp. 523. — Doran. Habits, 366. — Russell, W. Eccen. 60. — Timbs, J. Eng. eccen. 22. — Winsor, E. Montrose, 39.

Brune, Guillaume Marie Anne. Headley. Napoleon, 2 : 135.

Bruneau, Alfred. Hervey, A. Masters Fr. music, 223.

Brunel, Isambard Kingdom. Arnold, F. Turning points, 183.

— The two Brunels. Tillotson, J. Untit. nobil. 182.

Brunel, Sir Mark Isambard. Jerdan. Men, 47. — Smiles. Indus. biog. — Tartt. Ess. 2 : 118. — Timbs. Inventors, 396.

— a study for engineers. Tillotson, J. Untit. nobil. 163.

Brunelleschi, Filipo, cathedral builder. Milizia. Lives arch. 1 : 179. — Oliphant. Makers of F. 124. — Symonds. Renais. Fine arts, 67, 127.

— Troubles of. Robinson, F. S. Connois. 150.

Brunetière, Ferdinand. Blaze de Bury, Y. French lit. 156. — With portrait. (A. Cohn) Warner Lib. 5 : 2603.

Bruni, Antonio B., with portrait. Ehrlich, A. Cel. violin. 32.

Bruni, Leonardo, of Arezzo. Symonds. Age of despots, 274. — Symonds. Reviv. of learn. 182.

Bruno, Giordano. Erdmann. Hist. philos. 1 : 652. — Lewes. Biog. phil. — Maccall. For. biog. 2 : 88. — Maurice. Mor. & meta. philos. 2 : 163. — Symonds. Renais. Cath. reac. 2 : 126. — Symonds. Renais. It. lit. 2 : 483. — Osborn. From Greeks, 78. — Whittaker, T. Ess. & not. 61 : 249. — Owen, J. Skeptics, Ital. 245. — Warner Lib. 5 : 2613.

— and Galileo. Wilson, J. Stud. mod. mind.

Brunone, St., of Asbi. Neale. Mediæv. preach.

Bruns, John Dickson. Davidson, J. W. Writ. of South, 64.

Brunswick, Augusta, duchess of. Hall, Mrs. M. Princesses, 138.

Brunswick, Charles, Duke of, nephew of Q. Caroline, ward of George IV. Fitzgerald, P. Royal dukes, 1 : 330.

Brunswick, Court of. Baring-Gould. Germany, 467.

Brunswick, Germany. Child, T. Summ. holidays, 199. — Mahaffy. Holl. & Germ. 108.

Brunswick, House of. Doran. Queens Hanov. 1.

Brunswick family. Fitzgerald, P. Royal dukes, 1 : 315.

Brunswick theatre, Destruction of, by fire. Talfourd. Crit. wr.

Brunton, Mrs. Mary, Memoirs of. Elwood. Lit. ladies, 2 : 209.

Brunton, Bishop, Thos., a forgotten 14th cent. preacher. Gasquet, F. A. Old Eng. Bible, 63.

Brus, Robert de, chief justice of England, 1263–1268. Campbell. Ch. just 1 : 80.

Brussels. Brooks, E. S. Gt. cities, 77. — Guild. Over the ocean, 309. — Fairbanks, O. B. Aguecheek, 35.

— Diary at, 1833. Legaré. Writ. 1 : 1.

Brussels international educational congress, Lessons of. (W. T. Harris) Nat. Educa. Assoc. '81 : 165.

Brute, The. Mivart. Less. fr. nature, 192.

Bruté, Simon Gabriel. Clarke, R. H. Cath. bishops, 2 : 7. — Murray, J. O'K. Cath. heroes, 747.

Brute, William. Ivimey. Eng. Bapt. 1 : 74.

Bryan, George. Collier. Actors, 129.

Bryan, Henry H. Am. Bar Assoc. 19 : 652.

Bryan, John. Griswold, R. W. Sac. poets.

Bryan, Mrs. Mary Edwards. Davidson, J. W. Writ. of South, 71. — Freeman, J. D. Wom. of South, 464.

Bryan, Mary E. Raymond, I. Southland wr. 2 : 645.

Bryan, Sallie M. Raymond, I. Southland wr. 1 : 135.

Bryan, Sarah. Ellct. Pioneer wom. 361.

Bryan, William G. Proctor. Lawy. of N. Y. 59.

Bryant, Gridley, with portrait. Stuart, C. B. Am. engineers, 119.

Bryant, Jacob. Creasy. Etonians, 332. — Jesse, J. H. Cel. Eton. v. 1.

Bryant, John Frederick. Southey. Uned. poets, 135.

Bryant, John Howard. Coggeshall. Poets of west, 191. — Griswold. Poets Am. 332.

Bryant, Napoleon B., with portrait. Sk. N. H. men, 187.

Bryant, William Cullen. Annual cyclop. '78. — Bartlett, D. W. Mod. agitators, 183. — Bungay. Off-hand, 309. — Derby, J. C. Fifty years, 150. — Duyckinck. Nat. portr. gall. 2 : 464. — Griswold, H. T. Home life, 122. — Griswold. Prose writ. 324. — Griswold. Poets Am. 157. — Hood, E. P. Master-minds, 203. — Nadal, E. S. Ess. 176. — Poe. Works, 6 : 87. — Powell. Liv. authors (1850), 189. — Stedman. Poets Amer. 62. — Tuckerman. Poets, 303. — Walsh, W. S. Pen pic. mod. 98. — Whipple. Lit. & life. — With portrait. Wilson, J. G. Bryant, 11. — Bungay. Pen-portr. 207. — Cheney, J. V. That dome, 127. — Wright, H. C. Chil. sto. in Am. lit. 69. — Curtis, G. W. Orations, 3 : 323. — Godwin, P. Comm. addr. 195. — Saunders, F. Charac. stud. 133. — Fisher, M. Gen. sur. Am. lit. 85. — Griswold, R. W. Sac. poets. — Hatfield, E. F. Poets of church, 107. — Howe, M. A. D. Am. bookm. 52. — With portrait. (G. P. Lathrop) Warner Lib. 5 : 2623. — (Caroline H. Kirkland) Hubbard, E. Little jour. 2 : 43. The same in Homes Am. authors. — Lanman, C. Haphazard, 109. — Miller, Jos. Singers church, 2d ed. 440. — With portrait. Mitchell, D. G. Am. lands, 366. — Nichol. Amer. lit. 187. — Parton, J. Sk. of men of prog. — Powers, H. N.

Homes of eld. poets, 1. — Putnam, A. P. Singers liberal, 114. — Richardson. Amer. lit. 1 : 288. 2 : 35, 42, 323. — Stewart, Geo., jr. Evenings in lib. 161. — Stoddard, R. H. Poets' homes, 108.
— at Cedarmere. Wolfe, T. F. Lit. haunts, 129.
— Bibliography. Hodgkins. 19th cent. authors.
— County of. Curtis, G. W. Other ess. 23.
— Poems of. Godwin, P. Out of past, 9. — Nichol, J. Amer. lit. 187. — Taylor, B. Crit. ess. 275. — Wilkinson, W. C. Free lance, 184.
— 70th birthday of, 1864. Reply to Hon. G. Bancroft. Bryant. Orations, 303 ; or Prose, 2 : 225.
— Sonnets of. Deshler. Afternoons, 290.
— Translation of the Iliad. Taylor, B. Crit. ess. 258.
Bryant & May. Japp & Holmes. Succ. bus. men, 87.
Bryce, James, with portrait. Warner Lib. 5 : 2643.
Brydson, Thomas. Wilson, J. G. Poets of Scot. 2 : 286.
Brzozovius, Christian. Wallace, R. Anti-Trin. biog. 2 : 146.
Bubastis. See Pi-Beseth.
Bubier, G. B. Miller, Jos. Singers church, 2d ed. 563.
Bucali, Leonardo. Wallace, R. Anti-Trin. biog. 2 : 97.
Buccaneers. Hale, E. E. Stories of the sea, 119. — Hazard, S. San Domingo, 68. — Kelly, C. Voyages, 107. — Whymper, F. The sea, 3. — Macfarlane, C. Banditti, 221.
— Adventures of. Lang. Ess. in lit. 132.
Buccleuch, Charles, duke of. Scott, W. Biog. mem. v. 2.
Bucella, Philip. Wallace, R. Anti-Trin. biog. 2 : 383.
Buchan, David S. Erskine, Lord. Townsend. 12 judges, 2 : 133.
Buchan, John Stuart, earl of. Grant, Jas. Constable of Fr. 1.
Buchanan, Claudius. Carne, J. Em. mission. 2 : 137.
Buchanan, Dugald. Wilson, J. G. Poets of Scot. 1 : 183.
Buchanan, George, 1506-82. Collier, W. F. Hist. Eng. lit. 112. — Drake, S. A. Our great benefactors. — Hannay. Satire, 51. — Irving, D. Scot. writ. 1 : 67. — Kingsley. Health, 326; or Hist. lec. 379. — Nicoll, H. J. Gt. scholars, 1. — Wilson, J. G. Poets of Scot. 1 : 48. — Wrangham. Brit. Plutarch, v. 1. — Morley, H. Eng. writ. 8 : 339. — Walker, H. Three cent. Scot. lit. 1 : 49.
Buchanan, James. Abbott. Lives of Presidents, 352. — Duyckinck. Nat. portr. gall. 2 : 343. — Ellet. Court circles, 62. — Forney. Anec. v. 1. — (H. W. French) Frost. Presidents, 405. — Maury, S. M. Statesm. of Am. 21. — Thompson, R. W. Pers. Recollec. 357. — (G. T. Curtis) Wilson, J. G. Presidents, 277.
— Social life during administration. Ellet, E. F. Court circles, 478.
Buchanan, Robert. (J. A. Noble) Miles, A. H. Poets of cent. 6 : 517. 9 : 547. — Noel. Ess. on poetry. — Smith, G. B. Poets & nov. 307. — Stedman. Vic. poets, 346. — Wilson, J. G. Poets of Scot. 2 : 491. — Walkley, A. B. Playhouse, 157.
— as a poet. Noble, J. A. Sonnet in Eng. 158.
— Poetry of, discussed by himself. Buchanan. David Gray, 289.
— Sonnets of. Deshler. Afternoons, 304.

Buchanan, Sarah. Clement, J. Noble deeds, 346.
Bucharest, Life in. Kingston, W. B. Music & manners, 2 : 182.
Bucheley, Jim. Whitehead, C. Highwaymen, 1 : 169.
Bucher, Lothar. Strauss, G. L. M. Men of Ger. 2 : 307.
Buchtel College, Akron, O. U. S. Bur. Ed. Circ. '91, no. 5 : 165.
Buck, Gordon. Francis. N. Y. surg. 151.
Buckfast, Abbey of. Mivart. Ess. 1 : 250.
Buckingham, Chas. Edward, duke of. Vaille & Clark. Harv. book, v. 1.
Buckingham, Edward Stafford, duke of. Burke, S. H. Hist. portr. Tudor, 1 : 143.
Buckingham, Geo. Villiers, duke of. Disraeli, I. Curios. (N. Y. 4 v.) 3 : 97. — Lodge. Portraits (Bohn), v. 3. — Menzies, S. Roy. fav. 2 : 1. — With portrait. Jesse. Court of Eng. Stuarts, 2 : 61. 3 : 14. — Wrangham. Brit. Plutarch, v. 2. — Grant, J. Recoll. Lords, 97.
— England under. (Sir J. Eliot) Adams, C. K. Rep. Br. orat. 1 : 13.
— The rehearsal. Cook, D. On stage, 2 : 18. — Fitzgerald, P. New hist. Engl. stage, 1 : 129.
Buckingham, George, 2d duke. Street, G. S. Miniatures, 8. — Wrangham. Brit. Plutarch, v. 4.
Buckingham, Joseph S. (S. C. Thacher ; A. Norton) Ware, W. Am. Unita. 2 : 189.
Buckingham, Mary Fairfax, duchess of. Anderson, J. Mem. wom. Pur. 1 : 265.
Buckingham, Mary Villiers, countess of. Jesse. Court of Eng. Stuarts, 1 : 177. 3 : 179.
Buckingham, R. T. N. B. C. Grenville, Duke of. Francis, G. H. Orators, 167.
Buckingham, William Alfred. With portrait. Brockett. Men of our day, 299. — Lanman, C. Haphazard, 288. — Stowe. Men of time, 463.
Buckingham family. Burke, B. Viciss. of fam. 1 : 74.
Buckinghamshire, J. Sheffield, duke of. (S. Johnson) Chalmers. Eng. poets, 10 : 73.
Buckinghamshire, England, Baptists of. Ivimey. Eng. Bapt. 2 : 74.
— Walk through. Collins, M. Pen sketches, 1 : 98.
Buckland, Francis Trevelyan. Bolton, S. K. Fam. men of science, 396. — (W. H. Rideing) Parton. Princess, 25. — Warner Lib. 5 : 2661.
— in Albany street. Yates, E. H. Celeb. 3 : 173.
Buckland, William. Jerdan. Men, 54.
— Museum of. Buckland, F. T. Curios. nat. hist. 2 : 23.
— Verses on. Buckland, F. T. Curios. nat. hist. 2 : 207.
Buckland Abbey. Timbs. Abbeys, 1 : 488.
Buckle, Henry Thomas. Ingleby. Ess. 292. — Warner Lib. 5 : 2673.
— and his theory of averages. Clarke, J. F. 19th cent. ques. 196.
— Biographical sketch of. Buckle. Ess. 7.
— Essay on Spain. Robertson, J. B. Lec. mod. hist. 164.
— History of civilization. Bowen, F. Gleanings, 247.
Buckler, Johann, the Rhine robber. Macfarlane, C. Banditti, 178.
Buckley, William W. Bartlett, J. R. R. I. officers, 405.
Buckman, Rebecca T. Hemenway. Poets of Vt. 137.

Eloq. preach. 173. — Woodberry. Stud. in let. 209.

Bunyan, John, and his prototypes. Hazlitt, W. C. Offspring, 213.

— Birthplace of. Hall, Mrs. S. C. Pilgr. Eng. shr. 1 : 1.

— Life and works Tulloch. Eng. purit. 393.

— Pilgrim's progress. Coleridge. Lit. rem. 3 : 391. — Gilfillan. 3d gall. 289. — Lingsley, C. New misc. 365. — Macaulay. Ess. 2 : 250. — Saunders, F. Famous books, 63.

Bunyiu Nanjió. Müller. Biog. ess 183.

Buonarroti, Michael Angelo. *See* Michael Angelo.

Buonvisi, Lucrezia. Symonds. Renais. Cath. reac. 1 : 330.

Burbadge, Richard. Brereton, A. Hamlets, 1. — Collier, Actors, 1. — Irving, H. Drama, 89. — Irving, H. Eng. actors, 7.

— and his contemporaries. Baker, H. B. Eng. actors, 1 : 3.

Burchard, Rev. S. D. Parton, J. Sk. of men of prog.

Burchillo. Stebbing. Ital. poets, v. 1.

Burckhardt, J. L. Jardine. Nat. library, v. 40. — St. John. Cel. travelers, 3 : 168. — Chambers's Miscel. no. 133.

Burckmair, Hans. (A. Woltmann) Dohme, R. Early mast. 200.

Burde, Samuel Gottlieb. Hiller, Jos. Singers church, 2d ed. 315.

Burden of man, Vision of. Zangwill. Without prej. 1.

Burdens, Bearing of, by human beings. (O. T. Mason) U. S. Nat. Mus. Rept. '87 : 237.

Burder, George. Hatfield, E. F. Poets of ch. 112. — Miller, Jos. Singers church, 2d ed. 309. — Morison, J. Fathers of Lond. Miss. Soc. 2 : 79.

Burdett, Sir F. Georgian era, 1 : 409. — Hazlitt. Spirit. — Hazlitt. Parl. portr. 202. — Grant, J. Recoll. Ho. Comm. 251. — Stanton, H. B. Reforms, 161.

— Motion for parliamentary reform. Southey, R. Ess. 1832, 1 : 1.

Burdett-Coutts, Baroness. Duyckinck. Portr. gall. 2 : 515. — Sala, Mrs. Fam. peop. 11.

Burdette, Robert J. Clemens. Funny fellows, 175.

Burdsall, Richard. Hatfield, E. F. Poets of ch. 115.

Bureau of American Ethnology. (W. J. McGee) Goode. Smithson. Inst. 367.

Burford, Lady. Burder. Pious wom. 572.

Burford, Samuel. Ivimey. Eng. Bapt. 3 : 556.

Bürger, Gottfried August, with portrait. Warner Lib. 5 : 2767.

Burges, Tristam. Moore, F. Am. eloq. 2 : 319.

Burgess, Daniel. Holland, J. Psalmists, 2 : 137.

Burgess, George. Holland, J. Psalmists, 2 : 378. — Miller, Jos. Singers church, 2d ed. 504.

Burgess, Thomas, bishop. Mozley. Reminis. 1 : 419. — Jerdan. Men, 83.

Burgh, Hubert de, chief justice of England, 1215–1239. Campbell. Ch. just. 1 : 66. — Foss. Judges, 2 : 272. — Simson, Jas. Em. men of Kent, 48.

Burghley, William Cecil, Lord. Lodge. Portraits (Bohn), v. 2. — Wrangham. Brit. Plutarch, v. 2.

Burglars. Knox, T. W. Underground, 264.

Burgo, John de, 1441. Burke, O. J. Cath. archb. 54.

Burgo, John de, 1647. Burke, O. J. Cath. archb. 140.

Burgos. Buckley, J. M. Trav. 3 cont. 13. — Lathrop, G. P. Span. vistas, 1. — Prime, S. I. Alhambra, 15.

— Castle of, Siege of. Robson, W. Sieges, 578.

— Cathedral. Thomas, M. Scamper thr. Spain, 13.

Burgoyne, Gen. John. Campaign against, 1777. (J. M. Hughes) Mass. Hist. Proc. 3 : 278. — Creasy. 15 batt. 305.

— in Boston. (G. E. Ellis) Mass. Hist. Proc. 14 : 233.

— Surrender of. Curtis, G. W. Orations, 5 : 133.

Burgoyne, Sir John Fox, Obituary of. Em. persons, 1 : 43.

Burgundy, Marie-Adélaïde, duchess of. Imbert de St. A. Wom. Ct. Louis XIV, 229.

Burgundy, Second house of. Leake, F. Hist. bubb. 75.

Burgwyn, Henry K., jr. Walker, C. D. Biog. Va. Mil. Inst. 73.

Burial. Arnold, M. Last essays. — Bigelow, J. Mod. Inq. 119.

— Curiosities of. Chambers's Repos. no. 79.

— Sanitary entombment. (C. R. Treat) Am. Pub. Health, 15 : 186.

Burial permits and inspection of dead bodies, Necessity of. (C. Horsch) Am. Pub. Health, 13 : 45.

Burial places, Country. Dodge, S. Sk. of N. E. 258.

— Historic, of Boston and vicinity. (J. M. Merriam) Am. Antiq. Soc. Proc. n. s. 7 : 381.

Burial usages. Becker, W. A. Charicles, 383. — Greenwood, J. Savage habits, 337. — Joly, N. Man before metals, 130. — Richardson, B. W. Ministry of health, 230. — Wilkinson, J. G. Anc. Egyptians, 2 : 356.

— Greek. St. John. Anc. Greece, 3 : 414.

Burian, St. Conyngham, D. P. Irish saints, 130.

Burke, Edmund. Adams, C. K. Rep. Br. orat. 1 : 172. — Adams, W. H. D. Eng. party, 1 : 59. — Adams, W. H. D. Learned in law, 216. — Birrell. Obiter, 2 : 149. — Brougham. Works, 3 : 231. — Collier, W. F. Hist. Eng. lit. 375. — Dilke. Papers, 2 : 309. — Edgar. Footpr. 44. — Georgian era, 1 : 318. — Gilfillan. 3d gall. 301. — Gosse, E. 18th cent. liter. ch. 11. — Harsha. Orators, 122. — Lord, J. Beacon, 4 : 287. — Maurice. Friendship, 307. — Mitchell. Wet days, 239. — Rogers, S. Recoll. 105. — Stephen, L. Eng. thought, 2 : 219. — Taylor, W. C. Mod. Brit. Plut. 8. — Tweedie, W. K. Earnest men, 297. — Wotton. Word portraits, 39. — Lossing. Em. Amer. 258. — Hutton, L. Plays, 117. — Burke, B. Viciss. of fam. 1 : 249. — Duyckinck. Portrait gall. 1 : 159. — (W. E. H. Lecky) Ferris, G. T. Gt. leaders, 369. — Goodrich, C. A. Sel. Brit. eloq. — Mathews, W. Oratory, 268. — Murray, J. O'K. Prose & poet. Irel. 294. — Nicoll, H. J. Great orators. — Phillips, C. Irish eloq. — Russell, W. C. Book of au. 284. — Stanton, H. B. Reforms, 57. — With portrait. (E. L. Godkin) Warner Lib. 5 : 2779.

— as agent of N. Y. (C. Stebbins) Am. Antiq. Soc. Proc. n. s. 9 : 89.

— Bibliography. Syle, L. D. P. (ed.) Burke's speech on colonies.

— Character of. Hazlitt. Sketches ; *or* Winterslow.

— Dwelling of. Hall, Mrs. S. C. Pilgr. Eng. shr. 2 : 170.

— interpreter of English liberty. Wilson, Woodrow. Mere lit. 104.

— Pitt, and Fox compared with Calhoun, Clay, and Webster. Burnap. Miscel.

Burke, Edmund, Prose style of. Hunt, T. W. Rep. Eng. prose, 334.
— R. O'Hara, and Wm. J. Wills. Adams, W. H. D. Records, 301.
— the rhetorician. Tuckerman. Charac. 1 : 209.
— Works. Stephen, J. F. Horæ sabb. 93.
Burke, Francis. Burke. O. J. Cath. archb. 187.
Burke, John W. Walker, C. D. Biog. Va. Mil. Inst. 87.
Burke, Rev. Thomas N. Murray, J. O'K. Prose & poet. Irel. 717.
Burlesque. Fitzgerald. Principles of comedy. — Hood. English versification.
Burleigh, Charles C. Bungay. Off-hand, 101.
Burleigh, Francis. McClure. Translators, 98.
Burleigh, George Shepard. Everest. Poets of Conn. 463.
Burleigh, William Cecil, Lord. Burke, S. H. Hist. portr. Tudor, 3 : 186. — Forster. Brit. statesm. 1 : 241. — MacDiarmid. Brit. stat. 1 : 155.
— Nare's Memoirs of. Macaulay. Ess. 3 : 1. — Bungay. Pen-portr. 106.
Burleigh, William Henry. Everest. Poets of Conn. 391. — Griswold. Poets Am. 426. — Miller, Jos. Singers church, 2d ed. 588. — Putnam, A. P. Singers liberal, 315.
Burleigh House. Jewitt, L. Stately homes, 2 : 128.
Burley, William. Manning, J. A. Speakers, 86.
Burlingame, Anson. Bungay. Off-hand, 355.
Burlington, Richard Boyle, 3d earl of, with portrait. Caulfield. Kit-cat, 98. — Lodge. Portraits (Bohn), v. 7.
Burmah. Field, H. M. Egypt to Japan, 292. — Vincent, F., jr. Land of white elephant, 1. — Shoemaker, M. M. Quaint corners, 46.
— British. Keating. With Grant, 104.
— Origin of the war in, 1824. Cobden. Pol. writ. 2 : 23.
— Politics of, 1886. Temple, R. Cosmop. ess. 202.
— Two months in. (F. Vincent, jr.) Am. Geog. Soc. 8 : 162.
Burn, Andrew. Rogers, C. Chr'n heroes, 34.
Burnaby, Capt. F., with photo. Cooper, T. Men of mark, 2 : 33.
— Travels of. Adams, W. H. D. Heroes of trav. 325.
Burnand, Francis Cowley. Archer. Eng. drama. 95. — Sala, Mrs. Fam. peop. 125.
Burnap, George Washington. (N. H. Morison) N. E. Hist.-Gen. Soc. Biog. 3 : 447.
Burne, Sir O. T. Laurie, W. F. B. Dist. Anglo-Ind. 1 : 165.
Burnel, Robert. Campbell. Ld. Chan. 1 : 145.
Burnes, Sir Alexander. Kaye. Indian off. 2 : 1. — Laurie, W. F. B. Dist. Anglo-Ind. 1 : 7.
Burnes, James. Laurie, W. F. B. Dist. Anglo-Ind. 1 : 20.
Burnet, Mrs. Elizabeth. Burder. Pious wom. 184. — Fifty fam. women, 210.
Burnet, Gilbert, bishop. Georgian era, 1 : 196. — Lodge. Portraits (Bohn), v. 7. — Lawrence. Brit. historians, 1 : 232. — Macaulay. Biog. sk. 198. — Wrangham. Brit. Plutarch, v. 5.
— and William and Mary. Macaulay. Biog. sk. 154.
Burnet, Jacob. Livingston, J. Dist. Amer. 1. — Livingston, J. Em. Am. lawy. 684. — Mansfield, E. D. Pers. mem. 155.
Burnet, Rev. John. Grant, Jas. Metropol. pul. 321.
Burnet, Robert. Lossing. Em. Amer. 401.
Burnett, Frances H. (R. H. Stoddard) Ess.

from Critic, 57. — (E. B. Johnston) Our fam. wom. 152. — Vedder, H. C. Amer. writers, 158. — Warner Lib. 5 : 2809.
Burnett, Peter Hardeman, Amer. jurist. Parton. Capt. indus. 126.
— Conversion to Roman Cath. Brownson, O. A. 20 : 93.
Burney, Charles, 1757–1817. Edwards, E. Founders Brit. Mus. 2 : 436.
Burney, Frances. See Arblay, F. d'.
Burnham, Richard. Miller, Jos. Singers church, 2d ed. 300. — Hatfield, E. F. Poets of church, 117.
Burning at the stake, Capital punishment by, in Mass., 1755. (A. C. Goodell, jr.) Mass. Hist. Proc. 20 : 122.
Burning cliff at Holworth, England. Soane. New curios. 1 : 199.
Burns, Agnes B. Holloway, L. C. Mothers of gt. men, 586.
Burns, Anthony, Kidnapping of, in Boston, 1854. Parker, T. Add. speeches, 2 : 71.
— Rendition of. Robinson, W. S. Pen-portr. 206.
Burns, Sir George. Smith, G. B. Leaders mod. indus. 133.
Burns, James Drummond. Hatfield, E. F. Poets of church, 118. — (A. B. Grosart) Miles, A. H. Poets of cent. 10 : 419. — Miller, Jos. Singers church, 2d ed. 561. — Wilson, J. G. Poets of Scot. 2 : 437.
Burns, John, with portrait. Jones, E. R. Heroes of indus. 83. — With portraits. Lynch, A. Hum. doc's, 44.
Burns, Robert. Brooke, S. A. Theol. in Eng. poets, 287. — Carlyle. Essays. — Carlyle. Heroes. — Collier, W. F. Hist. Eng. lit. 369. — Craik. Pursuit knowl. 1 : 388. — Dawson, W. J. Mod. Eng. 17. — Emerson, R. W. Miscel. — Friswell. Essays, 350. — Giles, H. Illus. of gen. 267. — Graham, W. Ess. 227. — Griswold, H. T. Home life, 24. — Hannay. Satire, 172. — Hazlitt. Eng. poets, 171. — Howitt. Homes Br. poets, 1 : 379. — Irving, D. Scot. poets, 2 : 443. — Jameson, A. Loves of poets, ch. 31. — Lang. Let. to dead au. 195. — Miller, H. Tales, 53. — Oliphant, M. Lit. hist. 1 : 98. — Reed, H. Brit. poets, 2 : 9. — Rossetti. Fam. poets. — Russell, A. P. Charac. 132. — Russell, W. Extraor. men, 158. — Sanborn, K. Eng. poets, 267. — Saunders, F. Famous books, 113. — With portr. Seymour, C. C. B. Self-made, 64. — Sterling, J. Ess. 1 : 87. — Taine. Eng. lit. 2 : 228. — Taylor, W. C. Mod. Brit. Plut. 21. — Thorne, W. H. Mod. idols, 62. — Tuckerman. Poets, 193.' — (J. Service) Ward. Eng. poets, 3 : 512. — Wilson, J. G. Poets of Scot. 1 : 349. — Wotton. Word portraits, 42. — Brooks, S. W. Eng. poets, 280. — Deshler. Afternoons, 221. — Dixon, W. M. Eng. poetry, 45. — Curtis, G. W. Orations, 3 : 303. — Duyckinck. Portr. gall. 1 : 204. — With portrait. Gostwick, J. Eng. poets, 123. — Graham, P. A. Nature, 150. — Swanwick, A. Poets, 262. — Holland, J. Psalmists, 2 : 254. — Mitchell, D. G. Eng. lands, 3 : 291. — Quayle, W. A. Poet, 201. — Rosebery. Apprec. 31. — Russell, W. C. Book of au. 351. — Walker, H. Three cent. Scot. lit. 2 : 134. — With portrait. (R. H. Stoddard) Warner Lib. 5 : 2833 ; or Warner Classics, 3 : 157. — Wise, D. Vanq. victors, 106.
— and hero worship. Miller, H. Hist. ess. 144.
— and his school. Kingsley, C. Lit. lec. 127 ; or Raleigh, 119.
— and Hogg. Stuart, J. M. Reminis. 119.

Burns, Robert, and the peasantry of Scotland. Smith, J. Campbell. Writings, 211.
— and Scott. Couch, A. T. Q. Adv. crit. 103.
— Bibliography. Craigie, W. A. Burns primer. — Dow, J. O. (ed.). Selec. R. Burns. — Providence Pub. Lib. Bull. July, '96.
— and Scottish Poetry. Shairp. Aspects.
— as Celt. Japp. Vers de soc. 191.
— as poet and person. Whitman, W. Compl. Works, 3 : 57.
— Biog. and selec. criticism, with portrait. Home Study circle : literature, 3.
— Birthplace of. Terhune. Where ghosts, 17.
— The Bonnie Jean of. Jameson. Loves of poets.
— A Burns pilgrimage. Jackson, H. H. Glimpses of 3 coasts.
— Carnival of. Buchanan, R. Coming terr. 313.
— Chaucer, and Dunbar compared. Drake, N. Mornings, 2 : 1.
— Contemporaries of. Stoddard, R. H. Under eve. lamp, 1.
— festival, 1844. Taylor, B. Views, 55.
— Genius and character of. Wilson, J. Ess. 3 : 1.
— Haunts of. Haven, G. Pilgrim, 55. — Hawthorne. Old home, 225.
— The Highland Mary of. Jameson. Loves of poets.
— Home of, Visit to the. Hawthorne, Mrs. Eng. & It. 119.
— Infirmity of. Madden. Infirm. gen. 133.
— Reliques of. Jeffrey, F. Contrib. Ed. Rev.
— Some aspects of. Stevenson, R. L. Fam. stud. 38 ; or Miscel. 2 : 49.
— Speech at Burns dinner. Dawson, G. Shaksp. 126.
Burns, William. Blaikie, W. G. Leaders, 221.
— With portrait. Japp, A. H. Golden lives, 180.
Burnside, Ambrose Everett, with portrait. Bartlett. J. R. R. I. officers, 9. — Duyckinck. Nat. portr. gall. 2 : 416. — Headley, J. T. Grant & Sherman, 447. — Glazier, W. Heroes, 298. — With portrait. (J. W. de Peyster) Rogers, A. C. Repres. men, 103.
Burntisland castle. Mackie, C. Castles of Mary.
Burr, Aaron. Lossing. Em. Amer. 253. — Parton. Peop. bk. biog. 115. — Hall, J. Romance west. hist. 217. — Victor. Amer. conspiracies, 271. — Wise, D. Vanquished victors, 40. — Sparks, W. H. Memories, 192.
— Bibliography. Merwin, H. C. Aaron Burr.
— Conspiracy of ; Bollman's communication. Madison, J. Letters, 2 : 393.
Burr, Mrs. A. Margaretta (Scobell) Higford. Clayton, E. C. Eng. fem. art. 2 : 408.
Burr, Theodosia. Parton. Fam. Amer. 393.
Burrage, Joseph Perrin. (D. R. Cady) Harvard mem. biog. 2 : 268.
Burrinton, George. Whitehead, C. Highwaymen, 2 : 184.
Burritt, Elihu. Bungay. Off-hand, 301 ; or Repr. men, 126. — Bartlett, D. W. Mod. agitators, 96. — Kirton, J. W. World's Workers, 65. — Parton. Capt. indus. 27. — With portr. Seymour, C. C. B. Self-made, 40. — Famous boys, 201. — Kirton, J. W. Guthrie.
Burroughs, John, with portrait. Warner Lib. 5 : 2867.
— at home. (R. Riordan) Gilder. Authors, 39.
— Ramble with. Ellwanger. Idyllists, 221.
Burroughs, Joseph. Ivimey. Eng. Bapt. 4 : 204.
Burrowes, Peter. Phillips, C. Irish eloq. — Whiteside, J. Early sk. 212.

Burrows, William. Irving. Biog. 60.
Burt, Armistead. Perry, B. F. Biog. sketches, 2 : 5.
Burt, Maria C. Clayton, E. C. Eng. fem. art. 2 : 251.
Burt, Thomas. Reid, T. W. Politicians, 2 : 1. — Davidson, J. M. Eng. lib. 103.
Burton, John. Hatfield, E. F. Poets of church, 122. — Ivimey. Eng. Bapt. 2 : 29. — Miller, Jos. Singers church, 2d ed. 351, 464.
Burton, John H. Masson. Edinb. sk. 372. — Skelton. Ess. 327.
Burton, —— (Justice), 1760–1848 Whiteside, J, Early sk. 238.
Burton, Miss Margaret, of Ceylon. Pitman, Mrs. Heroines mission. 365.
Burton, Mr. and Mrs. Redding. Misers, 2 : 272.
Burton, Capt. Richard (F.), with photo. Cooper, T. Men of mark, 1 : 4. — Cust. Ling. & orient. ess. 4 : 80. — Em. persons, 4 : 288. — With portrait. Warner Lib. 5 : 2883.
Burton, Robert, with portrait. Warner Lib. 5 : 2904.
— Anatomy of melancholy. Jones, W. A. Ess. on authors, 88.
— Imitation of, by Sterne. Ferrier. Ill. of Sterne, 1 : 83.
— Mission to the King of Dahome. Lucas. Mornings, 2 : 53.
— Poetical commonwealth. Knight. Once on time, 1 : 221.
Burton, W. S. Bate, P. H. Eng. Pre-Raph. 79.
Burton, William Evans. Hutton, L. Plays, 236. — Matthews, B. Actors, 3 : 215.
Burton-on-Trent, England. Rimmer, A. Country towns, 221.
Bury, Mrs. Elizabeth. Burder. Pious wom. 189.
Bury, Richard de. Campbell. Ld. Chan. 1 : 191. — Foss. Judges, 3 : 409.
Bury St. Edmunds, Town and abbey of. Green, J. R. Stray studies, 211. — Jessopp, A. Studies, 66.
Busaco, Battle of. Adams, W. H. D. Eng. at war, 1 : 295. — Fitchett. Deeds, 88.
Buscapié, The. Ticknor. Span. lit. 3 : 404.
Buschetto. Milizia. Lives arch. 1 : 125.
Bush, George. Griswold. Prose writ. 354.
Bush, Joshua. Wesley & successors, 253.
Bushe, Sir Charles Kendal. Brougham. Works, 4 : 195. — Phillips, C. Irish eloq. — Sheil, Sk. Irish bar. 1 : 121.
Bush-fruits. Bibliography. Card, F. W. Bushfruits.
Bushnell, David. Howe, H. Em. Mech. 136.
Bushnell, Horace. Bartlett, D. W. Mod. agitators, 266. — Bartol. Principles, 366. — Griswold. Prose writ. 605. — Burton, N. J. Yale lec. 417. — With portrait. Mitchell, D. G. Am. lands, 2 : 75. — Richardson. Amer. lit. 1 : 298.
— God in Christ. Brownson. Works, 7 : 1.
— A vacation with. Phelps, A. Portfolio, 219.
Business. Bartol. Principles, 202. — Ruskin. Crown of wild olive, 47. — Savage, M. J. Mod. sphinx, 36. — Spencer, H. Essays, 107.
— Education for. Helps. Essays, 59.
— Laws and ethics of. (H. M. Rowe) Nat. Educa. Assoc. '97 : 818.
— Morality of. Vaughan, D. J. Questions, 144.
— Nobility in. Potter, H. C. Scholar & state, 197.
— Transaction of. Helps. Essays, 67.
Business colleges, Evolution of. (S. S. Packard) Cong. Educ. Chic. '93 : 788.
— Ideal. (W. J. Amos) Nat. Educa. Assoc. '94 : 971.

Business course of study, disciplinary value of. (A. S. Osborn) Nat. Educa. Assoc. '94 : 989.
Business education. (J. Macalister) Cong. Educ. Chic. '93 : 805. — (D. W. Springer) Nat. Educa. Assoc. '98 : 857.
— and industrial, commercial, and financial interests. (A. D. Wilt) Cong. Educ. Chic. '93 : 793.
— and others. (I. Mayhew) Cong. Educ. Chic. '93 : 803.
— Correlation and coördination of branches. (J. M. Mehan) Nat. Educa. Assoc. '96 : 794.
— Evolution of. (I. O. Crissy) Nat. Ed. Assoc. '99 : 1018.
— Higher aspects of. (R. E. Gallagher) Cong. Educ. Chic. '93 : 796.
— in our public schools. (J. H. Francis) Nat. Ed. Assoc. '99 : 1008.
— Its place in the American curriculum. (S. S. Packard) Nat. Educa. Assoc. '92 : 461.
— Practical advantages of. (G. Soulé) Cong. Educ. Chic. '93 : 791.
— Reasonable expectations concerning. (L. J. Gage) Nat. Educa. Assoc. 98 : 863.
Business Educators' Association, Alliance of, with National Educational Association. (S. A. Spencer) Nat. Educa. Assoc. '95 : 873.
Business high schools, Course of study for. (Allan Davis) Nat. Educa. Assoc. '96 : 804.
Business man, Christian, Duty of. Brooks, P. Addresses, 70.
— of the new school. Whipple. Outlooks, 25.
Business qualities. Smiles. Self-help.
Business training, good and bad. (J. M. Mehan) Nat. Educa. Assoc. '94 : 980.
Business women, World's need of. (S. A. Spencer) Cong. Educ. Chic. '93 : 800.
Buss, Robert William. Everitt, G. Eng. carica. 364.
Bussy, Sir John. Manning, J. A. Speakers, 14.
Busy-body, The. Franklin. Works ('87), 1 : 329.
Busy people. Ess. from Sat. R. 1.
Butcher, Edmund. Miller, Jos. Singers church, 2d ed. 319.
Butcher, The. Hunt, L. Seer, 1 : 180.
Bute, John Stuart, 3d earl of. Earle, J. C. Eng. prem. 1 : 157. — Lodge. Portraits (Bohn), v. 8.
— Jessie, J. H. Cel. Eton. v. 1.
Butler, Alban, Life and writings of. Butler, Chas. Works, v. 3.
Butler, Archer. Davies, G. J. Succ. preach. 69.
Butler, Behethland Foote. Ellet. Women of revol. 2 : 95.
Butler, Benjamin F., of New York. Duyckinck. Nat. portr. gall. 2 : 423. — Proctor. Lawy. of N. Y. 751.
Butler, Benj. F., Gen. Forney, J. W. Anec. 2 : 78. — Am. Bar Assoc. 16 : 429. — Brockett. Men of our day, 448. — With portrait. Scott, H. W. Dist. Am. lawy. 97.
— and Mass. state charities. Mass. Charity, '83 : clxxii.
Butler, Caleb. . (Mrs. F. Brooks) N. E. Hist.-Gen. Soc. Biog. 2 : 266.
Butler, Charles. Am. Bar Assoc. 21 : 687.
Butler, Elizabeth Thompson. Bolton, S. K. Girls famous, 261.
Butler, Mrs. F. A. See Kemble, Mrs. F. A.
Butler, James D. Hemenway. Poets of Vt. 120.
Butler, John Maurice. Am. Bar Assoc. 19 : 645.
Butler, John Maynard. Am. Bar Assoc. 19 : 646.
Butler, Joseph, Bishop. Bagehot. Estimates, 164. — Blunt. Ess. 250. — (Henry Rogers) Macaulay. New biog. 61. — Stephen, J. F. Horæ Sabb. 2 : 280.

Butler, Joseph, Bishop. Analogy of religion. Stephen, L. Eng. thought, 1 : 278.
— Memoirs of. Blunt. Ess. 490.
Butler, Noble. Coggeshall. Poets of west, 225.
Butler, Pierce. Perry, B. F. Biog. sketches, 1 : 459.
Butler, Samuel. Bell, R. Lit. & sci. men, 1 : 264. — (S. Johnson) Chalmers. Eng. poets, 8 : 87. — Collier, W. F. Hist. Eng. lit. 223. — Disraeli, I. Curios. (N. Y. 4 v.) 3 : 255. — Hannay. Satire, 94. — Hazlitt. Comic. — Howitt. Homes Br. poets, 1 : 118. — Saunders, F. Famous books, 146. — (W. E. Henley) Ward. Eng. poets, 2 : 396. — Wotton. Word portraits, 47. — Wrangham. Brit. Plutarch, v. 4. — With portrait. Warner Lib. 5 : 2927.
Butler, Col. Walter. Grant, Jas. Cavaliers, 178.
Butler, Widow. Sinclair, J. Sketches.
Butler, William. Creegan. Gr. mission. 219.
Butler, William Orlando. Coggeshall. Poets of west, 172.
Butler University, Indianapolis, Ind. U. S: Eur. Ed. Circ. '91, no. 1 : 156.
Buttall, Samuel. Ivimey. Eng. Bapt. 2 : 120.
Buttercups. Green, J. R. Stray studies, 198.
— Origin of. (Grant Allen) Proctor, R. A. Nat. stud. 98.
Butterfield, Mrs. Henry J., with portrait. Ellet. Queens Am. soc. 459.
Butterflies, Colors of. Bibliography. (A. G. Meyer) Harv. Mus. Comp. Zoöl. Bull. v. 30 : no. 4.
Butterworth, Joseph Henry. Miller, Jos. Singers church, 2d ed. 511.
Button, Gwinett. Lossing. Signers, 227.
Button industry in Europe, 1898. U. S. Cons. Rept. 58 : 481.
Buxar. See Baksar.
Buxton, G. F., Travels of. Adams, W. H. D. Heroes of trav. 49.
Buxton, Mary Queen of Scots at. Strickland. Queens Scot. 7.
Buxton, Thomas Fowell. Adams, W. H. D. Good Samar. 167. — Edgar. Boyhood, 123. — Smiles. Self-help. — Stanton, H. B. Reforms, 213.
Byblos, Siege of. Robson, W. Sieges, 130.
Byckerdyke, Mrs. Moore, F. Women of the war, 465.
Byers, Albert G. (F. H. Wines and others) Conf. char. & corr. 1891 : 242.
Byles, Sir John B. Gener. of judges, 71.
Byles, Mather. Nichol. Amer. lit. 83. — Sabine. Loyalists, 190.
Byng, George. Grant, Jas. Port. pub. char. 1 : 48.
Byng, John, Admiral. Allen, Jos. Battles Brit. navy, 1 : 172. — Georgian era, 2 : 166.
— Trial of. Burke, P. Cel. nav. & mil. trials, 60.
Bynner, Edwin Lassetter. (B. Wendell) Mass. Hist. Soc. Proc. 2d ser. 9 : 173.
Byrd, William. Lossing. Em. Amer. 31. — With portr. Mitchell, D. G. Am. lands, 75.
Byrds, The, of Westover, Va. Glenn, T. A. Colon. mans. 1 : 17.
Byrhtroth, Death of. Lanier. Music, 136.
Byrne, Andrew. Clarke, R. H. Cath. bishops, 2 : 264.
Byrom, John. Chalmers. Eng. poets, 15 : 177. — (W. E. Henley) Ward. Eng. poets, 3 : 230. — Espinasse. Lanc. worth. v. 1. — Hatfield, E. F. Poets of church, 124. — Macdonald, G. England's antiphon, 287. — Miller, Jos. Singers church, 2d ed. 150. — Stephen, L. Stud. biog, 1 : 74.

Byron, Catharine G. Holloway, L. C. Mothers of gt. men, 194. — Ellis, Mrs. S. S. Mothers.
Byron, G. G. N., Lord. Alger. Solitudes, 289. — Arnold, M. Ess. **2** : 163. — Caine, T. H. Cobwebs, 91. — Castelar. Byron, 9. — Chorley. Authors of Eng. 17. — Collier, W. F. Hist. Eng. lit. 386. — Courthope. Lib. move. in Eng. lit. 111. — Dawson, W. J. Mod. Engl. 26. — Devey, J. Mod. Eng. poets, 184. — Field, M. B. Memories, 209. — Friswell. Essays, 317. — Gilfillan. Mod. lit. 42. — Griswold, H. T. Home life, 94. — Hannay. Satire, 204. — Hayward, A. Em. statesm. **2** : 305. — Hazlitt. Spirit. — Howitt. Homes Br. poets, **1** : 524. — Kingsley, C. New miscel. — Lang. Lett. to dead au. 205. — Mason, E. T. Pers. traits, **3** : 3. — Morley. Crit. miscel. **1** : 203. — Nadal, E. S. Ess. 42. — Oliphant, M. Lit. hist. v. **3**. — Parton. Peop. bk. biog. 288. — Reed, H. Brit. poets, **2** : 163. — Rossetti. Fam. poets. — Russell, W. Extraor. men, 211. — Saunders, F. Famous books, 155. — Scott, W. Biog. mem. v. **2**. — Southey, R. Ess. 1832, **2** : 181. — Swinburne. Ess. 238. — Taine. Eng. lit. **2** : 271. — Taylor, W. C. Mod. Brit. Plut. 28. — Tuckerman. Poets, 165. — Wallace, S. E. Storied sea, 135. — (J. A. Symonds) Ward. Eng. poets, **4** : 244. — Wotton. Word portraits, 47. — Brooks, S. W. Eng. poets, 374. — Deshler. Afternoons, 220. — Dixon, W. M. Eng. poetry, 54. — Duyckinck. Portrait gall. **1** : 507. — Gostwick, J. Eng. poets, 173. — Swanwick, A. Poets, 289. — Holland, J. Psalmists, **2** : 285. — Lennox, W. P. Plays, **2** : 105. — Miles, A. H. Poets of cent. **2** : 363. **9** : 189. — Minto. Georg. era, 253. — Mitchell, D. G. Eng. lands, **4** : 187. — Nadal, E. S. Ess. at home. — Ossoli. Art, 84. — Procter, B. W. Autob. 134. — Russell, W. C. Book of au. 432. — (C. D. Warner) Warner Lib. **5** : 2935 ; *or* Warner classics, **3** : 9.
— and Goethe. Mazzini. Life, etc. **6** : 61.
— and his times. Noel. Essays on poetry.
— and Hucknall-Torkard. Winter. Gray days, 107.
— Are his writings immoral ? Hadley, J. Ess. 346.
— at Newstead Abbey. Gibson, W. S. Miscel. 38.
— Biog. and sel. criticism, with portrait. Home Study circle : literature, **3** : 15.
— Calumniators of. Page, J. Paradoxes, 283.
— Centenary of. Woodberry. Studies in letters.
— Character and writings. Legaré. Writ. **2** : 356.
— Childe Harold's pilgrimage, Canto 3. Jeffrey, F. Contrib. Ed. Rev.
— Disraeli's monument to. Allingham. Varieties, **3** : 279.
— Goethe on. Jameson. Studies.
— Haunts of. Wolfe. Lit. pilg. Brit. au. 62.
— his idea of sin. Mozley, J. B. Lec. 157.
— in Ravenna. Terhune. Where ghosts, 205.
— The infirmity of. Madden. Infirm. gen. 202.
— Italian haunts of. Harrison, J. A. Group of poets, 31.
— Letters and journals of. Legaré. Writ. **2** : 411.
— Manfred, on the stage. Hollingshead. Footlights, 178.
— Moore's Life of. Macaulay. Ess. **2** : 324. — Peabody, W. B. O. Lit. rem. 30.
— Moral philosophy of the life of. Giles, H. Lectures, **1** : 93.
— Moral spirit of the genius of. Giles, H. Lectures, **1** : 136.
— Mother of. *See* Byron, Catharine G.
— Notes for the life of. Moore, T. Prose & verse, 409.

Byron, G. G. N., Lord, the pessimist. Mather, J. M. 19th cent. poets, 75.
— Poetry of. Whipple. Ess. & rev. 1.
— Pope and. Dawson, G. Biog. ess. 225.
— Prisoner of Chillon. Jeffrey, F. Contrib. Ed. Rev.
— Recollections of. Paget, J. Paradoxes, 265. — Winter, W. Shakesp. Eng.
— Revival of interest in. Trent. Authority, 203.
— Thoughts on. Kingsley, C. Lit. lec. 35 ; *or* New miscel. 116.
— Tragedies of. Jeffrey, F. Contrib. Ed. Rev.
— Wordsworth and. Swinburne. Miscel. 63.
Byron, Henry James. Archer. Eng. dram. 119. — Wilman, G. Sk. liv. celeb. 113.
Byron, Lady Noel. Martineau, H. Biog. sk. 282. — Stanton, H. B. Reforms, 352.
Byron, William, 5th baron, duel of, with W. Chaworth, 1765. Thornbury. Old stor. 57.
Byzantine Anatolia. Palgrave. Ulysses, 1.
Byzantine art. Jervis, Lady. Painting, **1** : 47.
Byzantine Cæsars of the iconoclastic period. Doran. Monarchs, **2** : 59.
Byzantine empire. Freeman. Hist. ess. **3** : 231.
— Congreve's "Roman empire of the west." (Goldwin Smith) Oxf. ess. **1856** : 295.
Byzantium. Hahn-Hahn. Fathers, 39. — Mahaffy, J. P. Greek life, ch. 15.
— Battle of. Adams, W. H. D. Battle stories, 13.
— Sieges of. Robson, W. Sieges, 159.

Cabala. *See* Kabbala.
Caballero, Fernan, Spanish novelist. Edwards, M. B. Six women, 1. — Warner Lib. **5** : 3001. — Zimmern. For. novelists, **2** : 67.
Cabannis, Pierre Jean G. Frothingham. Transcend. 63. — Lewes. Biog. phil.
Cabell, William H. Walker, C. D. Biog. Va. Mil. Inst. 92.
Cabinet, Cleveland's. Keim. Society in Washington.
— Responsibility of the. Lowell. Essays on government.
Cable, G. W. Bolton, S. K. Amer. au. 345. — Richardson. Amer. lit. **2** : 429. — Vedder, H.C. Amer. writers, 261. — With portrait. Warner Lib. **5** : 3017.
— at home. (J. K. Wetherill) Gilder. Authors, 49.
Cables. *See* Telegraph Cables.
Cabot, John, and study of sources. (G. P. Winship) Am. Hist. Assoc. Rept. '97 : 35.
— and Sebastian. Coffin, C. C. Sto. of liberty, 123. — Bourne, H. R. F. Eng. seam. **1** : 28. — Murray, J. O'K. Cath. pioneers, 144. — Frost, J. Early explor. 62. — Higginson, J.W. Amer. explorers, 53. — Markham, C. R. Sea fathers, 89. — Parton. Peop. bk. biog. 329.
— — Bibliography. Beazley, C. R. J. & S. Cabot. — (G. P. Winship) Providence Pub. Lib. Bull. June, '97. — Salem Pub. Lib. Bull. May, '97.
— — Controversy about. (J. Winsor) Mass. Hist. Soc. Proc. 2d ser. **11** : 156.
— — Corrections of S. E. Dawson on. (H. Harrisee) Roy. Soc. Can. 2d ser. **4**, § **2** : 103.
— — Discoveries. (J. B. Thacher) Roy. Soc. Can. 2d ser. **3**, § **2** : 279.
— — Home of. Lodge, H. C. Cert. heroes, 189.
— — Voyages of. (S. E. Dawson) Roy. Soc. Can. 2d ser. **3**, § **2** : 139.
— — — in 1497 and 1498. (S. E. Dawson) Roy. Soc. Canada, **12**, § **2** : 51. 2d ser. **2**, § **2** : 3.
Cabot, Sebastian, Re-discovery of America by. Frost, T. Explorers, 62.
Cabot celebration at Halifax, 1897. (E. G. Por-

Calcutta. Brooks, E. S. Gt. cities, 53. — Darmesteter. Eng. stud. 237. — Pidgeon. Engineer's holiday, 359. — Field, H. M. Egypt to Japan, 280. — Keating. With Grant, 94. — Prime, E. D. G. Around world, 203. — Ballou, M. M. Due west, 168. — Barker, Lady. Travel. about, 316. — Brooks, J. Seven months, 292. — Vincent, F. Thro' Tropics, 126.

— Black Hole at, British prisoners in. Davenport. Narr. peril. 1 : 193.

Caldara, P. Ottley. Ital. school.

Calder, Sir Robert, Vice-Admiral. Burke, P. Cel. nav. & mil. trials, 349.

Calderari, Ottone. Milizia. Lives arch. 2 : 371.

Calderon de la Barca, P. Forster. Fr. & Span. genius, 311. — Shelley, Mrs. Lit. men Italy, v. 3. — Swanwick, A. Poets, 207. — Bate, P. H. Eng. Pre-Raph. 87. — With photo. Cooper, T. Men of mark, 6 : 15. — Montgomery. Men of Ita. 3 : 278. — Sismondi. Lit. so. Eur. 4. — Ticknor. Span. lit. 2 : 333. — With portrait. (M. F. Egan) Warner Lib. 6 : 3071.

— El magico prodigioso. Owen, J. Five skep. dramas, 351.

— Essay on. (Tom Taylor) Atkinson, J. B. et al. Eng. paint. 37.

Calderwood, David. Irving, D. Scot. writ. 1 : 306.

Calderwood, Henry. Barrie. Edinburgh eleven, 35.

Caldwell, Lady Barbara. Chapman, W. Wom. of con. 146. — Wittenmeyer. Women Reform. 415.

Caldwell, Elias Boudinot. Carson, H. L. Sup. Ct. of U. S. 573.

Caldwell, Hannah. Ellet. Women of revol. 2 : 106.

Caldwell, Henry C., with portrait. (W. Watson) Scott, H. W. Dist. Am. lawy. 111.

Caldwell, James. Headley, J. T. Chaplain's Revol. 217.

Caldwell, James Fitz-James. Davidson, J. W. Writ. of South, 76.

Caldwell, Merritt. (W. H. Allen) N. E. Hist.-Gen. Soc. Biog. 1 : 136.

Caldwell, Rachel. Clement, J. Noble deeds, 195. — Ellet. Women of revol. 2 : 150.

Caldwell, Samuel Lunt, with portrait. (O. S. Stearns) Caldwell, S. L. Cities of faith, 3.

"Caledonia," brig, Capture of. Dawson. Batt. of U. S. 2 : 139.

Calendar, Mexican. Bancroft, H. H. Native races, 2 : 502.

— Reformation of the, in England, in 1752. Bailey, S. Discourses, 129.

Calendars. Neale. Ess. liturgy.

Calhoun, John C. Baldwin. Party-leaders, 205. — Benton. 30 years. — Brownson. Works, 15 : 451. — Bungay. Off-hand, 82. — Burnap, G. W. Miscel. writ. 93. — With portrait. Duyckinck. Nat. portr. gall. 2 : 162. — Griswold. Prose writ. 172. — Harsha. Orators, 395. — Maury, S. M. Statesm. of Am. 168. — With portrait. Amer. nat. portr. gall. v. 2. — Willis. Hurrygraphs, 179. — Parton. Fam. Amer. 113. — Brooks, E. S. Hist. Amer. 291. — With portrait. Brooks. N. Statesmen, 69. — Duyckinck. Portr. gall. 2 : 203. — Johnston, A. Amer. ora. 1 : 303. 2 : 123. — Lossing. Em. Amer. 326. — Magoon, E. L. Liv. orators, 182. — Mathews, W. Oratory, 312. — Moore, F. Am. eloq. 2 : 471. — Nichol. Am. lit. 108. — Richardson. Amer. lit. 1 : 227. — Trent. South. statesm. 153. — With portrait. (W. P. Trent) Warner Lib. 6 : 3087.

Calhoun, John C., Character of. Dyer, O. Gt. Senators, 147. — Rush, R. Occ. prod. 107.

— Home of. (P. Godwin) Homes Am. statesm. 397.

— Tribute to, 1850. Webster, D. Works, 5 : 368. — Webster, Clay, and. Nichol, J. Amer. lit. 114.

California. Bishop, W. H. Old Mexico, 295. — Bowles, S. Our new west, 317. — Brockett, L. P. Our west. emp. 551. — Chambers's Papers, no. 26. — Dilke. Greater Brit. 156. — Faithful, E. 3 visits, 215. — Gerstaecker, F. Jour. round world, 134. — Howe, J. W. Winter homes, 18. — Jackson, H. H. Bits trav. home. — Jackson, H. H. 3 coasts, 3. — Leighton, C. C. Life at Puget sound, 199. — Leyland, R. W. Round the world, 240. — Miller, Joaq. Memorie, 51. — Simpson, W. Meeting the sun, 347. — Warren, F. R. Dust and foam, 138. — Cumming, C. F. G. Granite crags, 1.

— Admission of. Clay. Life & speeches, 6 : 394, 515. — Hilliard, H. W. Sp. 236.

— and the slavery question. Winthrop, R. C. Addresses, 1 : 654.

— and the gold mania. DeQuincey. Let. to young (Bost.), 199.

— Army life in, 1848–50. Keyes, E. D. 50 years, 223.

— as a home. Taylor, B. At home, 2 : 191.

— Bibliography. (M. T. Pierce) Land sunshine, June, July, '98 : 28. — Providence Pub. Lib. Bull. Jan. '98.

— Christ in. Dodge, M. A. Skirmish, 208.

— Conquest of. Dawson. Batt. of U. S. 2 : 454.

— Early literature of. Bancroft, H. H. Essays, 591.

— Geographical features of. (J. A. Johnson) Am. Geog. Soc. 9 : 84.

— Health resorts. Bibliography. Remondino, P. C. Mediterr. shores of America.

— in 1849–50. Ingram. Hearts of oak, 129.

— in 1850. Helms. Pioneering, 72.

— in 1872. Helms. Pioneering, 302.

— in 1877. Vivian. Tour in Am. 133.

— in 1881. Hardy. Between 2 oceans, 136.

— Kearneyism in. Bryce. American commonwealth, v. 2.

— Languages of. Latham. Opuscula, 300.

— literature, Early. Bancroft, H. H. Works, 38 : 591.

— A night in. Wraxall. Scraps, 1 : 286.

— of the padre. Jordan, D. S. Story, 89.

— Oregon ; Washington. (T. D. Hunt) Am. Geog. Soc. 1 : 137.

— The petrified forest of. Caton. Miscel. 348.

— Schools of, at educa. exhibit, N. E. A. meeting, San Francisco, '88. (J. M. Greenwood) Nat. Educa. Assoc. '88 : 715.

— Southern. Rutgers, L. On saddle, 79.

— University of, in infancy. Gilman, D. C. Univ. prob. 153.

California claims, 1849. Dix. Speeches, 1 : 262.

California, Lower, Explorations in the cape regions of. (G. Eisen) Am. Geog. Soc. 29 : 271.

Californians, Characteristics of. Bancroft, H. H. Essays, 205. — Rae. Westward, 308.

— Social analysis of the. Bancroft, H. H. Essays, 182.

Caligny, A. F. H., Marquis of. (W. Watson) Amer. Acad. A. & S. Proc. 29 : 452.

Caligula, Emperor. Lyman. Rom. emp. v. 1.

Calinorius, James. Wallace, R. Anti-Trin. biog. 2 : 239.

Calixtines, The. Pennington. Epochs papacy, 235.

Calixtus II. Montalembert. Monks, 7 : 513.

Calixtus III. Pastor, L. Hist. Popes, 2 : 344.

Calkins, Norman A. (H. S. Tarbell ; E. C. Hewett) Nat. Educa. Assoc. '96 : 218.

Call, Wathen Mark Wilks. (A. H. Japp) Miles, A. H. Poets of cent. 4 : 523.

Callanan, Jeremiah J. Williams, A. M. Poets of Irel.

Callcott, Sir Augustus Wall. Eng. painters, Georgian, 73. — Redgrave. Century of p. 381.

Callender, John. Loring, J. S. 100 Bost. era. 257.

Callicrates. Milizia. Lives arch. 1 : 45.

Callimachus. Arnold, E. Poets of Greece, 168. — Malkin. Class disq. 118. — Mills. Poets of Greece, 187. — Mahaffy, J. P. Greek life, ch. 11, 12. — Warner Lib. 6 : 3101.

Callinus. Arnold, E. Poets of Greece, 77.

Callis (or Callice), Robert. Woolrych. Serjeants, 1 : 249.

Callissius, Albert. Wallace, R. Anti-Trin. biog. 2 : 422.

Callisthus. Pressensé. Martyrs, 369.

Callistratus. Arnold, E. Poets of Greece, 133. — Mills. Poets of Greece, 150.

Callot, Jacques. Houssaye. Philos. 1 : 192.

Calongue, Adolphe. Davidson, J. W. Writ. of South, 77.

Calotype. Miller, H. Lead. articles, 179.

Caludon Castle. Hodges, Eliz. Anc. Eng. homes, 126.

Calvé, Emma, with portrait. Buffen. Mus. celeb. 2 : 105.

Calverly, Charles Stuart. Payn. Lit. recoll. 137. — Tollemache. Ess. & mock ess. 304. — Warner Lib. 6 : 3107. — (W. Whyte) Miles, A. H. Poets of cent. 9 : 433.

Calvert, Leonard. Belknap. Amer. biog. 3 : 216. — Lossing. Em. Amer. 223.

Calvin, Idelette, wife of John. Chapman, W. Wom. of ref. 199.

Calvin, John. Bancroft, G. Miscel. 405. — Dawson, G. Biog. lec. 461. — Herrick, S. E. Heretics, 207. — Lord, J. Beacon, 3 : 335. — (J. Orr) Reformers. Paisley lec. 241. — Renan. Studies, N. Y. 1 : 285. — Tagart. Sk. reform. 16th cent. 7. — Tulloch. Leaders reform. — Williams, W. R. Eras, 205. — With portrait. (A. C. McGiffert) Warner Lib. 6 : 3117. — Burke, S. H. Hist. portr. Tudor, 3 : 94. — Hundred greatest men, 179. — Pierce, B. K. Em. dead, 26. — Renan. Leaders, 79. — Reynolds, G. Papers, 327. — Russell, J., Earl. Ess. Chr. relig. in W. Eur. 248.

— and Calvinism. Graham, W. Ess. 87.

— and the church of Geneva. Taylor, W. C. Rom. biog. v. 2.

— and Servetus. Wallace R. Anti-Trin. Biog. 1 : 425.

— at Geneva. Pattison. Ess. v. 2.

Calvinism. Froude. Short stud. 2 : 9. — Thompson, H. M. Copy, 263.

— and Puritanism. Tulloch. Eng. purit. 5.

— John W. Fletcher's Conflict with. Larrabee, W. C. Wesley, 2 : 221.

— Fuller's Examination of. Coleridge. Lit. rem. 289.

— Moral argument against. Channing. Works, 1 : 217.

— Scotch, Intolerance of. Oxenham. Stud. in eccl. hist. 248.

Calypso, Opera by J. E. Galliard. Hogarth. Mem. opera, 1 : 345.

Cam, Diogo, and Martin Behaim. Vogel. Cent. of discov. 40.

Camargo, Mademoiselle de. Houssaye. Men of

18th cent. 1 : 372. — Men & Wom. of France, 2 : 90.

Camargue. Baring-Gould. Troub.-land, 177.

Camaroons mountains. Barker, Lady. Travel. about, 214.

Cambodia. (T. G. G. D'Abain) Am. Geog. Soc. 7 : 333. — Vincent, F., jr. Land of white elephant.

— Travels in. Helms. Pioneering, 94.

— Wonderful ruins of. (F. Vincent, jr.) Am. Geog. Soc. 10 : 229.

Cambon, Pierre Joseph, Speech of. Stephens, H. M. Ora. Fr. Rev. 1 : 501.

Cambria Iron Company. Pa. Bur. Indus. Statis. '87.

Cambridge, Ada. Miller, Jos. Singers church, 2d ed. 584.

Cambridge, Adolphus Frederick, Duke of. Grant, Jas. Portr. pub. char. 1 : 16.

Cambridge, George William Frederick, Duke of. McCarthy, J. Mod. lead. 85.

Cambridge, Richard Owen. Chalmers. Eng. poets, 18 : 227. — Dobson, A. 18th cent. vign. 3 : 179. — Jesse, J. H. Cel. Eton. v. 2.

Cambridge, Eng. Haven, G. Pilgrim. 111. — Rimmer, A. Country towns, 232. — Silloway. Cathedral towns, 295.

— Pre-academic. Freeman. Eng. towns, 238.

Cambridge, Mass. Bacon, E. M. Hist. pilgrim. 428. — (S. A. Eliot) Powell, L. P. Hist. towns N. E. 211.

— as village and city. Fiske, J. Cent. of science, 286.

— First church of, and Harvard college. (A. B. Hart) Mass. Hist. Proc. 2d ser. 5 : 396.

— in 1840. Lowell. Writ. 1 : 79.

— in 1852. Clough. Prose rem. 187.

— Old landmarks of. Drake, S. A. Hist. fields Mid. 245.

— 250th anniversary. Long, J. D. After-dinner, 58.

Cambridge Dionysia, a classic dream. Trevelyan, G. O. Ladies in parl. 67.

Cambridge experiment, The. (Francis Cogswell) Nat. Educa. Assoc. '94 : 333.

Cambridge press, The. (A. McF. Davis) Am. Antiq. Soc. Proc. n. s. 5 : 295.

Cambridge University, The building up of. Jessopp, A. Coming of friars, 262.

— Commission of 1850. (W. M. Compton) Camb. ess. 1858 : 165.

— English poets, graduates of. Birrell. Obiter, 275.

— in 1864. Stephen. Life of H. Fawcett.

— Studies of. Mill, J. S. Dissert. (N. Y.) 1 : 121.

Cambridgeshire, England, Baptists of. Ivimey. Eng. Bapt. 2 : 91.

Camden, C. Pratt, 1st earl of. Brougham. Works, 3 : 404. — Campbell. Ld. Chan. 6 : 351. — Creasy. Etonians, 253. — Lodge. Portraits (Bohn), v. 8. — Grant, J. Recoll. Lords & comm. 1 : 82. — Jessie, J. H. Cel. Eton. v. 1. — Welsby. Eng. judges.

Camden, William. Lawrence. Brit. historians, 1 : 164. — Wrangham. Brit. Plutarch, v. 2.

— and Brooke. Disraeli, I. Calam. 2.

Camden, Battle of. Dawson. Batt. of U. S. 1 : 613.

Camelot of history and romance. Walters, J. C. Bygone Som. 90.

Camels. Shaler. Dom. animals, 118.

Camera, Photographic. Buckley, A. B. Thro' magic glass, 47.

Cameron, Emily L., with portrait. Black, H. C. Wom. authors, 96.

Cameron, Sir Ewen Dhu, of Lochiel. Thomson, Mrs. Jacobites, **1** : 313.
Cameron, Col. J. Shea, J. G. Fallen brave.
Cameron, John, of Fassifern. Grant, Jas. Cavaliers, 44. — Irving, D. Scot. writ. **1** : 333.
Cameron, Richard. Blaikie, W. G. Preachers Scott. 171.
Cameron, Simon. Savage. Liv. rep. men, 90. — Character of. Dyer, O. Gt. senators, 132.
Cameron, Verney L., with photo. Cooper, T. Men of mark, **3** : 32. — Am. Geog. Soc. **26** : 121. — Journey across Africa. Frost, T. Mod expl. 152.
Cameron, William. Miller, Jos. Singers church, 2d ed. 301.
Cameroon tribes of West Central Africa. (C. H. Richardson) Cong. Anthrop. Chic. '93 : 199.
"**Camille**," play. Hutton, L. Plays, 157.
Camillus, Marcus Furius. Yonge. Gold. deeds.
Camisards, The. Chambers's Miscel. no. 114.
Camoens, L. de. Shelley, Mrs. Lit. men Italy, v. 3. — Longfellow. Poets Eur. 738. — Montgomery. Men of Ita. **3** : 295. — With portrait. (H. R. Lang) Warner Lib. **6** : 3129.
— Lusiad, epitomized. Dobson, W. T. Class. poets, 239.
— — Spirit of. Chambers's Repos. no. 32.
Campagnés, The, Sketch of. Agnew. Protes. exiles, **2** : 125.
Campaign literature. Bibliography. Literary News, Sept. '96.
Campanella, T. Erdmann. Hist. of philos. **1** : 639. — Heron. Jurisprudence. — Kauffman. Utopias, ch. 2. — Woolsey. Communism. — Ewart, H. C. Heroes of sci. 207.
Campanus, John. Wallace, R. Anti-Trin. biog. **1** : 403.
Campbell, Dr. Alex. Mansfield, E. D. Pers. mem. 272.
Campbell, Archibald. McCosh. Scot. phil. 89.
Campbell, Archibald. See Argyll, 8th earl.
Campbell, Charles. Davidson, J. W. Writ. of South, 77.
Campbell, D. G. Miller, S. F. Bench of Ga. v. 1.
Campbell, Dorothea Primrose. Bethune, G. W. Brit. fem. poets, 325.
Campbell, Edward R. Hemenway. Poets of Vt. 13.
Campbell, Ella G., with portrait. Bolton, S. K. Succ. women, 127.
Campbell, Francis Joseph. Craik, D. D. Plain speaking, 145.
Campbell, George. McCosh. Scot. phil. 239.
Campbell, Sir George. Escott, T. H. S. Pillars emp. 8.
— Administration of, in Bengal. Temple, R. Men in India, 407.
Campbell, Jas. Butler. Am. Bar Assoc. **7** : 319.
Campbell, James C., bishop of Bangor, with photo. Cooper, T. Men of mark, **6** : 9.
Campbell, James Valentine. Am. Antiq. Soc. Proc. n. s. **7** : 9.
Campbell, Jane. Ellet. Women of Revol. **2** : 179.
Campbell, Jane Montgomery. Miles, A. H. Poets of cent. **10** : 725.
Campbell, John, Lord Chancellor, 1859. Foss. Judges, **9** : 155. — With portr. Bennet, W. H. Sel. biog. 153. — Boyd. One life, 227. — Martineau, H. Biog. sk. 241. — Senior. Biog. sk. 162. — Grant, J. Bench & Bar, **2** : 37.
Campbell, John, 1766-1840. Thompson, A. Gt. mission. 135.
Campbell, Mrs. John. Burder. Pious wom. 458.
Campbell, John M. Shairp. Portraits, 169.

Campbell, Miss Letitia A., of Pekin, China. Pitman, Mrs. Heroines mission. 315.
Campbell, Margaret, lady of Towie. Fittis. Heroines of Scot. 167.
Campbell, Margaret Douglas. See Argyll, M. D., Marchioness of.
Campbell, Mungo, Trial of. Burke, P. Cel. trials.
Campbell, Quinton. Winslow, S. N. Biog. Phila. merch. 87.
Campbell, Robert. Hatfield, E. F. Poets of ch. 126. — Miller, Jos. Singers church, 2d ed. 546.
Campbell, Robert Macgregor. See Macgregor, R.
Campbell, Lady Sophia and Lady Henrietta, Wittenmeyer. Women Reform. 429.
Campbell, Thomas. Chambers's Papers, no. 24. — Chorley. Authors of Eng. 81. — Devey. Mod. Eng. Poets, 156. — Gilfillan. 1st gall. 161. — Hazlitt. Spirit. — Howitt. Homes Br. poets, **2** : 231. — Irving. Biog. 115. — Jerdan. Men, 90. — Mason, E. T. Pers. traits, **2** : 101. — (J. T. Fields) Oliphant. Lit. hist. **2** : 152. — Parton. Princes, 157. — Saunders, F. Famous books, 99. — Thompson, K. B. Recoll. 2. — Tuckerman. Ess. 441. — Tuckerman. Poets, 205. — (H. Taylor) Ward. Eng. poets, **4** : 229. — Wilson, J. G. Poets of Scot. **2** : 1. — Wotton. Word portraits, 51. — Brooks, S. W. Eng. poets, 343. — Dixon, W. M. Eng. poetry, 134. — Grant, Jas. Port. pub. char. **2** : 97. — Hall, S. C. Book of mem. 346. — Hatfield, E. F. Poets of ch. 127. — Minto. Georg. era, 217. — Saintsbury, G. Ess. Eng. lit. **2** : 171. — Mitchell, D. G. Eng. lands, **4** : 52. — Miles, A. H. Poets of cent. **2** : 149. — Miller, Jos. Singers church, 2d ed. 358. — Ossoli. Art, 68. — Procter, B. W. Autob. 148. — With portrait. Warner Lib. **6** : 3159.
— and his Scotch contemporaries. Oliphant, M. Lit. hist. **2** : 181.
— Gertrude of Wyoming. Jeffrey, F. Contrib. Ed. Rev.
— Theodoric. Jeffrey, F. Contrib. Ed. Rev.
Campbell, Valeria. Brockett. Woman's work, 594.
Campbell, Wm. H. N. Y. Regents, **105** : 489.
Campbell families. Taylor, J. Fam. of Scot. **1** : 228.
Campden House, Kensington. Timbs. Abbeys, **1** : 178.
Campden Wonder, The. Paget, J. Paradoxes, 337.
Camperdown, A. Duncan, viscount of. Johns. Nav. & mil. heroes.
Camperdown, Battle of. Allen, Jos. Battles Brit. navy, **1** : 458. — Low, C. R. Gt. battles, 229. — Valentine, L. J. Sea fights, 155.
Camphausen, Otto von. Strauss, G. L. M. Men of Ger. **2** : 286. — Tuttle, H. Ger. pol. lead. 49.
Camphuysius, Theodore Raphaelis. Wallace, R. Anti-Trin. biog. **2** : 548.
Campion, E. Taylor, W. C. Rom. biog. v. 2.
Campion, Thos. Gosse, E. Jacobean poets, 89. — (E. Rhys) Warner Lib. **6** : 3184.
Campo Santo at Pisa, with plate. Perkins, C. C. Tusc. sculp. **1** : 39.
Camporese, Violante, later Mme. Giustiniani, Italian vocalist. Clayton, E. C. Queens, 228. — Needham. Queens of song.
Campos Santos. (F. Wurdeman) Charleston book, 328.
Canaan, The blue blood of. Dodge. Sermons to clergy, 63.
Canada. Dilke. Greater Brit. 57. — White, John. Sk. Amer. 3.

Canada, Affairs of. Peel, R. Speeches, 3 : 461.
— and Australia : a study in compar. politics. (J.
G. Bourinot) Roy. Soc. Can. 2d ser. 1, § 2 : 3.
— and the U. S. : an histor. retrospect. (J. G.
Bourinot) Am. Hist. Assoc. 5 : 275.
— Archives of. (D. Drymner) Am. Hist. Assoc.
3 : 395.
— Bibliography. Bourinot. Canada, how gov-
erned. — Providence Pub. Lib. Bull. Oct. '95.
— British policy in. Head, F. B. Descr. ess. 1 :
219.
— Comments on. Warner, C. D. Studies, 407.
— Dairy products of, 1899. (J. L. Bittinger) U. S.
Cons. Rept. 60 : 17.
— Expedition of 1747. (W. P. Upham) Mass.
Hist. Soc. Proc. 2d ser. 12 : 45.
— Expeditions against. Dawson. Batt. of U. S.
1 : 98.
— Folksongs of, Footnotes to. (W. Wood) Roy.
Soc. Can. 2d ser. 2, § 2 : 77.
— Geographical work in, 1894. (G. M. Dawson)
Am. Geog. Soc. 27 : 50.
— — 1896. (G. M. Dawson) Am. Geog. Soc. 29 :
13.
— Government. Bibliography. (J. G. Bourinot)
Am. Hist. Assoc. Rept. '91 : 391.
— in 1863. Ker. Scot. national, 160.
— in 1881. Russell, W. H. Hesper, 1 : 132.
— the land of waterways. (W. Griffin) Am. Geog.
Soc. 22 : 351.
— Local transportation, 1891. U. S. Cons. Rept.
38 : 692.
— Materials for history of. (Sir J. M. LeMoine)
Roy. Soc. Can. 2d ser. 3, § 2 : 309.
— Nationality in. (Robjohns) Roy. Hist. Soc. 7 :
362.
— Nine weeks in. (Capt. R. Collinson) Vaca.
tourists, 2 : 167.
— Northwest. Temple, R. Cosmop. ess. 57.
— Possibilities and future of. Hatton, J. To-day
in Amer. 2 : 69.
— Present and past. Pidgeon. Old World Ques.
351.
— Sault Ste. Marie and the " Soo " canals, 1896.
(C. McCall) U. S. Cons. Rept. 51 : 100.
— Trade with. Dix. Speeches, 1 : 383.
— A Yankee in. Thoreau. Yankee in C. 1.
Canadian French in New England, Condition of.
Mass. Labor, 1882 : 1.
Canal, Middlesex. Lowell Old Res. Assoc. 3 :
273.
Canal excavations, Modern methods of. (I. Ran-
dolph) Deep waterways conven. 1 : 186.
Canal locks, Pneumatic and hydraulic. (C. N.
Dutton) Deep waterways conven. 1 : 222.
Canals, Aqueducts and. Ellesmere. Ess. 201.
— Canadian, 1884. U. S. Cons. Rept. no. 42.
— Early English and continental. Smiles. Engin.
1 : 300.
— New York. Tilden. Writings, 1 : 2.
— in Canada. U. S. Cons. Rept. no. 148.
— — Memoranda of. (G. Johnson) Deep water-
ways conven. 1 : 164.
— Internat. coöperation in construction of. (T. A.
Flower) Deep waterways conven. 1 : 293.
Canaris, Constantine. Em. persons, 2 : 37.
Canary birds, culture of, Curiosities of. Japp.
Days w. indus. 42.
Candahar, Evacuation of. Disraeli. Sel. spee.
2 : 260.
Candle making. Wynter, A. Our soc. bees, 1 :
254.
Candles. Japp & Holmes. Succ. bus. men, 153.
Candlish, Robert S. Blaikie, W. G. Preachers
Scott. 293. — Taylor, W. M. Scott. pulpit, 265.

Candolle, A. P. de. (W. C. Farlow) Am. Acad.
A. & S. Proc. 28 : 406. — Duncan, P. M. Bot-
anists, 98.
Candor, Advent of. Warner, C. D. As we go,
30.
Candy, Manufacture of. Wynter, A. Peeps, 2 :
23.
Canes. Gardner, S. J. Aut. leaves, 87
Canfield, Francesca. Griswold. Fem. poets, 135.
Canfield, Gertrude A. Raymond, I. Southland
wr. 1 : 352.
Canfield, Mrs. S. A. Martha. Brockett. Wo-
man's work, 495.
Canice, St. Conyngham, D. P. Irish saints, 268.
Canisio, Egidio. Symonds. Reviv. of learn. 416.
Canitz, F. R. L. Miller, Jos. Singers church, 2d
ed. 112.
Canna and its people. Buchanan, R. Poet's sk.
book, 267.
Cannæ, Battle of. King, C. Battles, 94.
Canne, John. Ivimey. Eng. Bapt. 2 : 523.
Cannes and St. Honorat. Green, J. R. Stray
studies, 31.
Cannibalism. Simmonds. Animal food, 40.
Canning, C. J., Viscount, Administration of, in
India. Temple, R. Men in India, 164.
Canning, Elizabeth. Paget, J. Paradoxes, 317.
— (W. G. Waters) Vincent, A. Twelve bad
women, 205.
Canning, George. Adams, C. K. Rep. Br. orat.
3 : 1. — Adams, W. H. D. Eng. party, 2 : 97.
— Adams, W. H. D. Men at helm, 227. — Bul-
wer, H. L. Hist. char. 2 : 197. — (R. Therry)
Canning. Speeches, 1 : introd. — Creasy. Eto-
nians, 436. — Earle, J. C. Eng. prem. 2 : 135.
Edgar. Boyhood, 72. — Ewald. Repr. statesm.
2 : 64. — Georgian era, 1 : 401. — Greville me-
moirs (1770–1827). — Harsha. Orators, 281.
— Hazlitt. Spirit. — Jerdan. Men, 101. —
Kebbel. Eng. statesm. 33. — Skelton. Ess.
203. — Taylor, W. C. Mod. Brit. Plut. 41. —
Goodrich, C. A. Sel. Brit. eloq. — Hazlitt.
Parl. portr. 88. — Mathews, W. Oratory, 251.
— (W. Whyte) Miles, A. H. Poets of cent. 9 :
49. — Stanton, H. B. Reforms, 67. — Thorn-
ton. For. sec. v. 1, 2. — With portrait. War-
ner Lib. 6 : 3189.
— Administration of. Lewis, G. C. Ess. on admin.
— as a man of letters. Hayward, A. Ess. 2d ser.
1 : 187.
— as a philosopher and theologian. Fisher, G. P.
Discus. 253.
— Character of. Mackintosh, J. Miscel. 238. —
Rush, R. Occ. prod. 181.
— From Chatham to Canning. Skelton, J. Ess.
in hist. 203.
— Humor of. Timbs, J. Eng. eccen. 451.
Cannon, Henry W., with portrait. Butterfield.
Lec. Un. Coll. 1 : 345.
Cannon, Rifled. Japp & Holmes. Succ. bus.
men, 222.
Cano, Alonzo. Jarvis, Lady. Painting, 2 : 77. —
Washburn, E. Span. mas. 100. — Stirling-
Maxwell. Ann. Art. Spain, 3 : 931.
Cano, Juan Sebastian del, first circumnavigator of
the globe (d. 1526). Markham. Sea-fathers,
46.
Canon law, Feudal law and. Adams, J. Works,
3 : 447.
— in England, History of. Stubbs. Lec. on hist.
292.
— Influence of. (J. G. Phillimore) Oxf. ess. 1858 :
215.
Cañon of the Colorado. Lummis. Strange corners, 1.

Canonbury, and Lady Elizabeth Compton. Timbs. Abbeys, **1 :** 90.

Canonge, Placide. Davidson, J. W. Writ. of South, 79.

Canonicus. Lossing. Em. Amer. 15.

Canonization of saints. Williams, F. Eng. card. 1 : 155.

Canons Park, near Edgware. Timbs. Abbeys, 1 : 194.

Canossa. Hare. Cities of No. Italy, 2 : 225. — Symonds. Sk. So. Eur. 2 : 123.
— Henry IV. at. Archer. Decis. ev. 91.

Canova, Antonia (1757–1822), Ital. sculptor. — Craik. Pursuit knowl. 2 : 186. — Edgar. Boyhood, 304. — Doremus, S. D. Gt. lights, 206. — Hale, E. E. Lights 2 cent. 39. — With portrait. Seymour, C. C. B. Self-made, 323. — Spooner. Biog. fine arts, 1 : 165. — Cooper, T. Triumphs of persev. 51. — Elliot, F. Rom. gossip, 239.
— Birthplace of. Howells. Ital. jour. 280.
— Life and works of. Everett, A. H. Crit. ess. 1 : 234.

Cant, Andrew. Blaikie, W. G. Preachers Scot. 140.

Cant and hypocrisy. Hazlitt. Sk.
— On some forms of modern. Bax. Ethics of socialism, 90.
— Philosophy of. Fairbanks, O. B. Aguecheek, 326.

Cantankerous fool, Advantages of being a. Boyd. Less. of mid. age, 167.

Cantankerousness. Arnold, F. 3-cor. ess. 158.

Cantecroix, Beatrix de Cusance, Princesse de, Portrait of. Wolff. Odd bits, 120.

Canterbury, Eng. Allingham. Varieties, 1 : 192. — Temple, E. L. Old-world, 1 : 231. — Silloway. Cathedral towns, 331.
— Archæological Congress. Smith, C. R. Retrospec. 1 : 8.
— Archbishops of. Gibson, W. S. Miscel. 272.
— — of the Reformation. Wilberforce, S. Ess. Quar. 2 : 185.
— Convocation of. Newman, J. H. Hist. sk. 3 : 341.
— Glimpse of. Winter, W. Shakesp. Eng.
— Pilgrimage to. Stone, J. S. Heart of Eng. 216.
— Shrine of St. Thomas. Bayly, J. A. S. New stud. 65.

Canterbury Castle. Timbs. Abbeys, 1 : 333.

Canterbury Cathedral. (A. P. Stanley) Farrar, F. W. Westm. 89. — Farrar, F. W. Our Eng. minsters, 133. — Stone, J. S. Heart of Eng. 237. — Timbs. Abbeys, 1 : 343. — Van Rensselaer, M. G. Eng. cath. 22.

Canterbury claustral school in 15th century. Gasquet, F. A. Old Eng. Bible, 260.

Canton. Brooks, J. Seven months, 265. — Keating. With Grant, 183. — Prime, E. D. G. Around world, 144. — Cumming, C. F. G. Wand. in China, 1 : 31. — Pidgeon. Engineer's holiday, 325.

Cantor, John A., forger. Clinton, H. L. Extraor. cases, 55.

Cantú, Cesare. Warner Lib. **6 :** 3199.

Canute, King. (J. R. Green) Ferris, G. T. Gt. leaders, 116.
— and the Abbey of St. Bennet. Timbs. Abbeys, 1 : 396.

Canyngs of Bristol, 1360–1475. Bourne, H. R. F. Eng. merch. 1 : 96.

Canyngton Priory and Fair Rosamond. Timbs. Abbeys, 1 : 567.

Cape Breton Island. Benjamin. Atlan. isl. 222.

Cape Cod. *See* Cod, Cape.

Cape Colony. Froude. Oceana, 34. — Gordon, Lady Duff. Last letters, 187. — Trollope, A. So. Africa, 67.
— Commerce and agric. in, 1891. (G. F. Hollis) U. S. Cons. Rept. 37 : 395.
— Commercial conditions in, 1898. (J. G. Stowe) U. S. Cons. Rept. 57 : 351.
— Elementary and secondary education in. (May Bongough) Nat. Educa. Assoc. '93 : 903.
— Life in. Chambers's Miscel. no. 173.
— Rebates on imported goods in, 1898. (J. G. Stowe) U. S. Cons. Rept. 59 : 44.

Cape Fear river, N. C., as a source of watersupply. (T. F. Wood) Am. Pub. Health, 11 : 109.

Cape St. Vincent, Battle of, 1797. Low, C. R. Gt. battles, 210.

Cape Town, Letters from. (Lady Duff-Gordon) Vaca. tourists, 3 : 119.
— Visit to (1883). Hübner. Thro' Brit. empire, 1 : 17.

Capel, Algernon. *See* Essex, Earl of.

Capel, Arthur, 1st lord, with portrait. Lewis, M. T. Clarendon lives, 1 : 247. 2 : 1. — Lodge. Portraits (Bohn), v. 4.

Capel, Thomas J., Monsignor, with photo. Cooper, T. Men of mark, 1 : 32.
— at Kensington. Yates, E. H. Celeb. 3 : 321.

Capell, Catharine (born Stephens), countess of Essex, English vocalist. Clayton, E. C. Queens, 267.

Caper, John, Sr. Wallace, R. Anti-Trin. biog. 2 : 413.

Caper, John, Jr. Wallace, R. Anti-Trin. biog. 3 : 10.

Capernaum. Hoppin. Notes theol. stud. 221.

Capet, The house of, and Louis, the saint. Doran. Monarchs, 1 : 188.

Capgrave, John. Brink. Eng. lit. 2, pt. 2 : 17.

Capillary attraction. Thomson, Sir W. Pop. lec. 1.

Capital. Everett. Orat. 2. — Greeley. Ess. pol. econ. 40. — McClelland, J. Soc. Sci. 79.
— and interest. Bastiat. Ess. on pol. econ. v. 1.
— and its earnings. (J. B. Clark) Am. Econ. Assoc. 3.
— and labor. *See* Labor and Capital.
— Claims of. Kempner, W. Common-sense soc. 148.
— Duties of. Walker, F. A. Discus. in econ. 2 : 341.
— Growth of. Nicol, D. Polit. life, 2 : 71.
— Investment of. Plea for liberty, 227.
— Living, of the United Kingdom. Wagner, L. Mod. pol. ora. 97.
— Progress inherent in. Kempner, W. Common-sense soc. 125.
— Recent accumulations of, in the United Kingdom. Giffen. Ess. finance, 161.
— What is ? Donisthorpe. Individualism.

Capital of the U. S., Absence of a. Bryce. Soc. institu. 203.
— — Locating the. (G. Hunt) Am. Hist. Assoc. Rept. '95 : 289.

Capital punishment. Bentham, J. Works, 1. — Ossoli. Life without, 199. — Shelley. Ess. 1 : 169. — Smith, Alexander. Dreamthorp, 93. — Wordsworth, C. Miscel. 3 : 408. — Phillips, W. Speeches, 2 : 77. — Rush, B. Ess. 164.
— Christianity opposed to. Hazard, T. R. Miscel. 9.
— Crimes by wishers for. Burke, P. Romance of forum.
— for murder. Hobart, V. H. H. Polit. ess. 75.
— Results of abolition of. (W. Tallack) Trans. Soc. Sci. Lond. 1865 : 171.

Capital University, Columbus, Ohio. (G. H. Schodde) U. S. Bur. Ed. Circ. '91, no. **5** : 195.

Capitalist, Career of a. Harrison, J. Dang. tend. 141.

Capitalistic "hearth," The. Bax. Relig. of socialism, 136.

Capito, Wolfgang Fabricius. Wallace, R. Anti-Trin. biog. **1** : 400. **3** : 541.

Capitoline Museum, Rome. Guild. Abroad again, 148.

Cappello, Bianca. *See* Capello.

Capranica, Domenico, cardinal. Pastor, L. Hist. popes, **2** : 483.

Capri, Island of. Craik, M. D. Plain speaking, 191. — Green, J. R. Stray studies, 383. — Hare. Cities of So. Italy, 185. — Howe, J. W. Oak to olive, 110. — Kavanagh, J. Two Sicilies. — Symonds. Sk. So. Eur. **1** : 368. — Taylor, B. Byways, 337.

— and Capriotes. Howells. Ital. jour. 116.

"Captain," Wreck of the. Senior, W. Shipwrecks, 272.

Capture at sea, Court of appeals in cases of. Jameson, J. F. Ess. const. hist. **1**.

— Exemption of private property from. Lawrence. Ess. int. law, 278.

— Law of. Story, J. Miscel. 580.

Car sanitation. (G. P. Conn) N. H. Health, '94-95 : 148.

— Report on. (S. H. Woodbridge; G. P. Conn) Am. Pub. Health, **23** : 242.

Car trust securities. (F. Rawle) Am. Bar Assoc. **8** : 277.

Caracas, capital of Venezuela. Curtis, W. E. Capitals, 257.

Caracci, Agostino. Symonds. Renais. Cath. reac. **2** : 350.

Caracci, Annibale. Ottley. Ital. school. — Symonds. Renais. Cath. reac. **2** : 351.

— Criticisms of his pictures. Guizot. Fine arts, 124.

Caracci, Lodovico. Ottley. Ital. school. — Symonds. Renais. Cath. reac. **2** : 349.

— Criticisms of his pictures. Guizot. Fine arts, 119.

Caracci school, The. Lee, H. F. Old painters, 210.

— History of. Disraeli, I. Curios. (N. Y. 4 v.) **3** : 149.

Caracciolo, Prince, Admiral Nelson and. Paget, J. Paradoxes, 213.

Caravaggio, Michael Angelo. Jervis, Lady. Painting, **1** : 185.

Caravats, The. Browne, G. L. State trials, 19th cent. **1** : 390.

Carberry, John Vaughn, Earl of. Portrait. Caulfield. Kit-cat, 124.

Carbery, Countess of. Burder. Pious wom. 251.

Carbolic acid as a disinfectant. (C. Smart) Am. Pub. Health, **11** : 212.

Carbon Co., Montana, Granites of. (J. P. Kimball) Am. Geog. Soc. **31** : 199.

Carbonari. Fagan. Life of Panizzi. — Heckethorn. Sec. soc. **2** : 91.

Carboniferous period, Fern forests of. Agassiz. Geol. sk. **1** : 66.

Carcano, G. Howells. Mod. It. poets, 360.

Carcassonne. Baring-Gould. Troub.-land, 251. — James, H. Little tour, 141. — Larned, W. C. Churches & C. 61.

Carden, Sir Robert. Ritchie, J. E. City men, 1.

Cardiff castle. Edwardes, C. Hist. houses.

Cardigan, Jas. T., Earl of, Duel of. Burke, P. Cel. trials. — Townsend, W. C. Mod. state trials, **1** : 212.

Cardinal virtues. Bryant, S. Short stud. 3.

Card-playing ; Is it a Christian amusement? Phelps, A. Portfolio, 80.

— and chess : catalogue of games and implements of divination in U. S. Nat. Mus. (Stewart Culin) U. S. Nat. Mus. Rept. **'96** : 665.

Carducci, Giosue. (Frank Sewall) Warner Lib. **6** : 3206.

Carducho, Vicente. Washburn, E. Span. mas. 65.

Cardwell, Edward, Viscount. With photo. Cooper, T. Men of mark, **3** : 10. — Hill, F. H. Polit. portr. 108. — Hutton, R. H. Stud. in parl. 22. — Kent, C. Gladst. govt. 241. — Reid, T. W. Cab. portr. 139. — Ritchie. Brit. sena. 83.

Carefulness. Gray, E. C. Idle musings, 223.

Carême, Marie-Antoine, French cook. Brightwell. Byepaths of biog. 27. — Parton. Capt. indus. 349.

Careri, Gemelli, in India. Macmillan, M. Globe-trotter India, 1.

Carew, Bamfylde Moore, "King of the beggars" (1693–1753). Russell, W. Eccen. 347.

Carew, or Carey, Lady Elizabeth. Bethune, G. W. Brit. fem. poets, 26. — Williams, Jane. Lit. wom. 71.

Carew, John. Ivimey. Eng. Bapt. **2** : 124.

Carew, Sir Nicholas. Lodge. Portraits (Bohn), v. 1.

Carew, Thos. Chalmers. Eng. poets, **5** : 589. — (E. W. Gosse) Ward. Eng. poets, **2** : 111. — Couch, A. T. Q. Adv. crit. 67. — Deshler. Afternoons, 132. — Griswold, R. W. Sac. poets. — Warner Lib. **6** : 3221.

— Loves of. Jameson. Loves of poets.

Carewe, Sir Peter. Knight. Once on time, **1** : 101.

Carey, Henry. Drama, "The dragon of Waultey." Hogarth. Mem. opera, **2** : 32.

Carey, Henry C. (S. D. Gross). Gross, S. D. Autobiog. **2** : 401. — With portr. Griswold. Prose writ. 595.

Carey, Lucius. *See* Falkland, Viscount.

Carey, Mathew. Lossing. Em. Amer. 300. — Murray, J. O'K. Cath. pioneers, 381. — Hunt, F. Am. merch. **1** : 307. — Winslow, S. N. Biog. Phila. merch. 144.

Carey, Philip. Griswold, R. W. Sac. poets. — Ivimey. Eng. Bapt. **2** : 134.

Carey, Rosa N., with portrait. Black, H. C. Wom. authors, 145.

Carey, T., Hermit of Warkworth. Hillhouse. Dramas, **2** : 203.

Carey, Wm. Banks, J. S. Three Ind. heroes. — Brightwell, C. L. Rom. mod. missions, 203. — Creegan. Gt. mission. 45. — Cust. Ling. & orient. ess. 553. — Gurney, J. H. Hist. sk. **3** : 365. — Lives of dist. shoemak. 77. — Thompson, A. Gt. mission. 218. — Tweedie, W. K. Life earn. men, 98. — Winks. Illus. shoemakers, 145. — Yonge. Pioneers.

Cargill, Donald. Blaikie, W. G. Preachers Scott. 169.

Caribbean islands. Churchill. Voyages, v. **5**. — Edwards. West Indies, 1. — Hill, R. T. Cuba, 318.

Cariboo hunting. (Lord Dunraven) Am. Geog. Soc. **11** : 334.

Caricature, English. Everitt, G. Eng. carica. 1.

— the fantastic, the grotesque, in art. Symonds. Ess. **1** : 240.

— Modern English. Lucas. Mornings, **2** : 191.

— Penultimate. Meynell, A. Rhythm, 101.

— Subjects of. Everitt, G. Eng. Carica. 12.

Carlyle, Thomas, Prose style of. Hunt, J. W. Rep. Eng. prose, 479.
— Sartor Resartus, Awakening caused by. Scudder, V. D. Soc. ideals, 143.
— Sunday in Cheyne Row. Burroughs. Fresh fields, 217.
— Works. Thoreau. Yankee in C. 211.
— Writings of. Chambers's Repos. no. 39.
— — Tendency of. Mazzini. Life, etc. **4** : 110.
Carmagnola, F. B. di. Baddeley. Travel-tide, 38. — Oliphant. Makers Venice, 206.—Brown, H. F. Venet. stud. 145.
Carman, Bliss, with portrait. (C. G. D. Roberts) Warner Lib. **6** : 3302.
Carmichael, Gershom. McCosh. Scot. phil. 36.
Carnal, Henri, Trial of, for murder, 1851. Clinton, H. L. Extraor. cases, 97.
Carnan, Thomas, Case of. Erskine, T. Speeches, 17.
Carnarvon, H. H. M. Herbert, 4th earl of. (Photo.) Cooper, T. Men of mark, **4** : 34. — Reid, T. W. Cab. portr. 107. — Em. persons, **4** : 236. — Escott, T. H. S. Pillars emp. 16.— Smalley. Lond. let. **1** : 146.
— at Highclere. Yates, E. H. Celeb. **3** : 251.
Carnarvon, Robert Dormer, 1st earl of. Lodge. Portraits (Bohn), v. 4.
Carn-brea Castle. Timbs. Abbeys, **1** : 505.
Carneades. Lewes. Biog. phil. — Mills. Poets of Greece, 430.
Carnegie, Andrew. With portrait. Cochrane, R. Benef. lives, 95. — With portrait. Butterfield. Lec. Un. Coll. **1** : 315.
— and his libraries. Bolton, S. K. Givers, 58.
Carnessecchi, Pietro, in Florence. Stoughton. Ital. reformers, 49.
Carnival. Dickens. Pic. from Ita. — Yriarte. Venice, ch. 17.
— at Pisa. Crawford. Life in Tuscany, 80.
— in Rome. Moulton, L. C. Rambles, 50.
— on the Cornice. Green, J. R. Stray studies, 44.
Carnochan, John Murray. Francis. N. Y. surg. 75.
Carnot, L. N. M. Arago. Sci. men, **2** : 1. — Brougham. Works, **5** : 172. — Maccall. For. biog. **2** : 255. — Lloyd, E. M. Vauban. — Cranbourne. Hist. sk. **1** : 341.
Carnot, M. F. Sadi-. Smalley. Stud. 258. — Ann. cyclop. '87.
— Mourning for. Stuart, H. Paris days, 113.
Caro, Annibale. Symonds. Renais. It. lit. **2** : 283.
Carolan, The Irish bard. Goldsmith. Miscel. (N. Y. 4 v.) **1** : 208.
Carolina, Queen of Saxony, with portr. Crowned heads, 13.
Caroline of Brandenburg-Anspach, Queen of Eng. Lancelott. Queens, v. **2**. — Finch. Princesses of Wales, **2** : 148.
Caroline Amelia of Brunswick, queen of George IV. Fitzgerald, P. Royal dukes, **1** : 348. — Lancelott. Queens, v. **2**. — Doran. Queens Hanov. **2**. — Finch. Princesses of Wales, **3** : 71. — Georgian era, **1** : 105. — Howitt, M. Queens, 493. — Smith, G. B. Ambass. 299.
— as subject of caricature. Everitt, G. Eng. carica. 62.
— Charges against, Proceedings in parliament. Canning. Speeches, **4** : 228.
— Defense of. Brougham. Works, **9** : 75.
— Example of. Walsh, R. Didactics, **1** : 117.
— Proceedings against. Peel, R. Speeches, **1** : 143.
— Trial of. Browne, G. L. Narr. state tri. **2** : 339.
Caroline Bonaparte, queen of Naples. *See* Bonaparte.

Caroline Elizabeth of Hanover. Hall, Mrs. M. Princesses, 114.
Caroline Matilda, queen of Denmark. Hall, Mrs. M. Princesses, 173. — Smith, G. B. Ambass. 7. — Wilson, H. S. Stud. in hist. 69.
Caroline Wilhelmina, queen of George II. Doran. Queens Hanov. 1. — Georgian era, **1** : 29. — With portrait. Howitt, M. Queens, 484. — Oliphant. Hist. sketches, 1.
Caroline Islands, The, 1898. U. S. Cons. Rept. **58** : 12.
— Bibliography. Salem Pub. Lib. Bull. Sept. '98.
Carp culture. N. J. Labor, **1882** : 135.
Carpaccio, Vittore. Stillman, W. J. Old Ital. mas. 259. — Oliphant. Makers of Venice, 282.
— Dream of St. Ursula. (J. Ruskin) Singleton, E. Great pic. 58.
Carpenter, Frank B. Derby, J. C. Fifty years, 485.
Carpenter, George. Bartlett, J. R. R. I. officers, 178.
Carpenter, George W. Winslow, S. N. Biog. Phila. merch. 124.
Carpenter, Joseph E. Miller, Jos. Singers church, 2d ed. 516.
Carpenter, Josiah, with portrait. Sk. N. H. men, 43.
Carpenter, Mary. Fawcett, M. G. Em. wom. 9. — Japp, A. H. Wise words, 243. — With portrait. Watson, Mrs. R. A. Poet toilers, 57. — Smith, G. B. Women of renown, 271. — Adams, W. H. D. Good Samar. 118. — Adams, W. H. D. Cel. Eng. wom. Vict. **2** : 37.
Carpenter, Matthew H., with portrait. Scott, H. W. Dist. Am. lawy. 125.
Carpenter, Philo, 1805–86. Chicago Hist. Soc. Coll. **4** : 102.
Carpenter, Samuel. Winslow, S. N. Biog. Phila. merch. 34.
Carpenter, William Benjamin. Sketch and portrait, with list of his writings. Carpenter, W. Benj. Nature, **3** : 467.
Carpentry, Wonders and wisdom of. Dodge, M. A. 12 miles, 44.
Carpet-baggers in Louisiana. Dixon, W. H. White conquest, **2** : 101.
Carpets, Manufacture of. U. S. Cons. Repts. Special, '90 : 1.
Carphylides. Mills. Poets of Greece, 240.
Carr, Richard. Doran. Knights, 410.
Carr, Robert. *See* Somerset, Earl of.
Carr, Samuel J. (J. W. Dean) N. E. Hist.-Gen. Soc. Biog. **1** : 63.
Carr, Thomas H. Bartlett, J. R. R. I. officers, 443.
Carracci, Lodovico. Jervis, Lady. Painting, **1** : 288.
Carrara, *or* Carraresi family in Italian history. Brown, H. F. Venet. stud. 90.
Carrel, Armand. Mill, J. S. Dissert. N. Y. **1** : 237.
Carrell, George Aloysius. Clarke, R. H. Cath. bishops, **2** : 505.
Carreno de Miranda, Juan. Stirling-Maxwell. Ann. art. Spain, **3** : 1176.
Carrer, Luigi. Howells. Mod. It. poets, 184.
Carriage and wagon wheels, Manufacture of, in Europe, 1898. U. S. Cons. Rept. **57** : 1.
Carrick-on-Suir. Silloway. Cathedral towns, 59.
Carrier, Indians, Sociology and mythology of. (A. G. Morice) Roy. Soc. Canad. **10** : sec. 2.
Carriera, Rosalba. Ellet. Women artists, 226.
Carriers. Story, A. T. Vagrom, 169.
Carrington, Abram C. Walker, C. D. Biog. Va. Mil. Inst. 98.

Carrion-flower. Abbott, C. C. Outings, 171.

Carrodus, John T., with portrait. Ehrlich, A. Cel. violin. 73.

Carroll, Charles. With portrait. Amer. nat. portr. gall. 1. — Brougham. Works, 5 : 275. — Hilliard, H. W. Sp. 383. — Lossing. Signers, 157. — Lincoln, R. W. Signers, v. 6. — Sanderson. Signers, v. 7. — Boyle, E. Dist. Marylanders. — Dwight, N. Signers, 262. — Lossing. Em. Amer. 146. — With portrait. Murray, J. O'K. Cath. heroes, 729.

Carroll, John, abp. of Baltimore. Boyle, E. Dist. Marylanders. — Clarke, R. H. Cath. bishops, 1 : 32. — With portrait. Murray, J. O'K. Cath. heroes, 635. — Lossing. Em. Amer. 49.

Carroll, Lewis. See Dodgson, C. L.

Carroll, William Thomas. Carson, H. L. Sup. Ct. of U. S. 575.

Carroll family of Maryland. Gleen, T. A. Colon. mans. 1 : 335.

Carroll homestead, Maryland. Terhune, M. V. More colon. homes, 224.

Carswell, Edward, with portrait. Bungay. Pen-portr. 174.

Carswell, Reuben W., with portrait. Rogers, A. C. Repres. men, 121.

Cartandis, queen of Eugenius I. Hall. Queens before Conq. 162.

Carte, Thomas. Lawrence. Brit. historians, 1 : 323.

Carter, Mrs. Elizabeth. Burder. Pious wom. 506. — Edwards, M. B. Six women, 171. — Williams, Jane. Lit. wom. 207. — Bethune, G. W. Brit. fem. poets, 63. — Fifty famous women, 309.
— and Miss Talbot. Thompson, Mrs. Cel. friend. 2 : 145.
— Memoirs of. Elwood. Lit. ladies, 1 : 103.

Carter, Mrs. Major. Ellet. Pioneer wom. 272.

Carter, R. Brudenell. Bettany. Em. doctors, 2 : 267.

Carter, Rev. Mr. Baring-Gould. Yorks. odd. 2 : 14.

Carter, Robert Meek. Hinton. Eng. radicals, 86.

Carter family of Virginia. Glenn, T. A. Colon. mans. 1 : 217.

Carteret, Lord. Earle, C. J. Eng. Prem. 1 : 64.

Cartes-de-Visite and photographic pictures. Wynter. Fruit, 1 : 239.

Cartesian philosophy. See Descartes.

Carthage. Freeman. Hist. ess. 4 : 1.
— and the Carthaginians. Chambers's Papers, no. 20.
— A day in. Wallace, S. E. Storied sea, 56.
— A defense of. Newman, F. W. Essays, 278.
— Punic wars. Dodge. Hannibal.
— Siege of. Robson, W. Sieges, 223.

Carthagena, Siege of. Robson, W. Sieges, 208.

Carthagh, St. Conyngham, D. P. Irish saints, 340.

Carthaginians at Zama, Defeat of the. Archer. Decis. ev. 11.
— Religion of. Rawlinson. Religions, 150.

Carthew, Thomas. Woolrych. Serjeants, 2 : 459.

Carthusian Fathers, The. Burke, S. H. Men of Reforma. 1 : 139. — Burke, S. H. Hist. portr. Tudor, 1 : 282.

Cartier, James. Belknap. Amer. biog. 1 : 230. — Frost. Half-hours with explorers, 95. — Parkman. Pioneers of France, 184. — Parton. Peop. bk. biog. 368.
— Course of. (M. F. Howley) Roy. Soc. Canada, 12, § 2 : 151.

Cartier, James, explorations of, Results of. (J. Winsor) Mass. Hist. Proc. 2d ser. 7 : 298.
— Voyages of. Frost, T. Explorers, 95.
— — Anticipations of. (J. Winsor) Mass. Hist. Soc. Proc. 2d ser. 8 : 67.

Cartismandua, queen of Cymbeline. Hall. Queens bef. Conq. 25.

Cartmel priory. Croston. Hist. sites Lanc. 249.

Cartography, Early history of. (C. P. Daly) Am. Geog. Soc. 11 : 1.
— of America to 1570. (Sophus Ruge) Smithson. Rept. '94 : 281.

Cartouche. Fuller, H. W. Noted trials, 199.

Cartwright, Edmund, 1743–1823. Craik. Pursuit knowl. 2 : 345. — Seymour, C. C. B. Self-made, 234. — Cooper, T. Triumphs of persev. 95. — Towle, G. M. Heroes of inven. 89. — Walker, W., jr. Men of sci. 24. — Woodcroft, B. Biog. invent. 20.

Cartwright, Major John. Coleridge. Friend. 187. — Bourne, H. R. F. Eng. seam. 1 : 300. — Stanton, H. B. Reforms, 147.

Cartwright, Peter. Bungay. Off-hand, 351. — Houghton. Kings, 530. — MacCabe, J. D. Great fortunes, 526.

Cartwright, Thomas. Hopkins, S. Puritans, 3 : 348. — Taylor, W. C. Rom. biog. v. 2.
— and Whitgift. Morley, H. Eng. writ. 8 : 326. — Tulloch. Eng. purit. 19.

Cartwright, Wm. Chalmers. Eng. poets, 6 : 511. — (A. M. Ward) Ward. Eng. poets, 2 : 227. — Choate, J. B. Wells of Eng. 251.

Carver, Capt. Jonathan. Drake, S. G. Trag. of wilderness, 172. — Greely, A. W. Explorers, 71. — Lossing. Em. Amer. 74.

Carver, John. Moore, J. B. Am. gov. 11. — Belknap. Amer. biog. 2 : 205.

Carving. (S. Webb) Morris, W. Arts & crafts, 322.

Carvings; stalls in cathedral and collegiate churches. Wright, T. Ess. archæol. 2 : 111.
— Stone and wood. (S. Clarke) Morris, W. Arts & crafts, 81.

Carvosso, William. Wise, D. Heroic Meth. 230.

Cary, Alice. Derby, J. C. Fifty years, 245. — Hart, J. S. Fem. prose, 489. — Duyckinck. Portr. gall. 2 : 199.
— and Phebe. Coggeshall. Poets of west, 343. — Derby, J. C. Fifty years, 245. — Hatfield, E. F. Poets of ch. 132. — (H. Greeley) Parton. Em. wom. 164.

Cary, Sir Henry. Fuller. Worthies, 2 : 47.

Cary, Henry Francis, Sonnets of. Deshler. Afternoons, 249.

Cary, John W. Am. Bar Assoc. 18 : 501.

Cary, Lott. Edwards, B. B. Self-taught, 179. — Lossing. Em. Amer. 275.

Cary, Thomas Greaves. Loring, J. S. 100 Bost. ora. 653.

Casa, Giovanni della. Galateo. Hunt, L. Men, wom. & books, 232. — Symonds. Renais. It. lit. 2 : 274.

Casanova, Jacques. Smith, H. G. Romance of hist. 288. — Warner Lib. 6 : 3321. — Ellis, H. Affirmations, 86.
— Escape of. Davenport. Narr. peril. 2 : 96.

Casaubon, Isaac, an old-time scholar. Fields. Underbrush, 197.

Case-law, Science of. Pollock. Ess. in juris. 237.

Case, Leonard, and his School of Applied Science. Bolton, S. K. Givers, 297.

Casey, Silas, with portrait. Bartlett, J. R. R. I. officers, 95.

Cashmere, Highlands of. Myers, P. V. N. Rem. lost emp.
See Kashmir.

Casilear, John W. Sheldon, G. W. Amer. painters, 154.

Casimir-Perier, Auguste V. L. King, E. French pol. lead. 308.

Cask-making. (W. Crooks) Galton, F. W. Workers, 115.

Cass, Gen. Geo. W. Parton, J. Sk. of men of prog. — (J. T. King) Rogers, A. C. Repres. men, 117.

Cass, Lewis. With portr. Amer. nat. portr. gall. 1. — Bungay. Off-hand, 92. — Duyckinck. Nat. portr. gall. 2 : 355. — Lanman, C. Haphazard, 184. — Parton. Peop. bk. biog. 545. — Lanman, C. Haphazard, 184. — Magoon, E. L. Amer. orators, 271.

— Influence of, on devel. of Northwest. (A. C. McLaughlin) Am. Hist. Assoc. 3 : 311.

Cassander. Mahaffy, J. P. Greek life, ch. 4.

Cassard, Jacques. Norman, C. B. Corsairs, 105.

Cassel (Germany). Child, T. Summ. holidays, 195.

— Siege of. Robson, W. Sieges, 423.

Cassell, John, publisher. Curwen. Booksellers, 267. — Nicoll. Great move. 204.

Cassiobury. Jewitt, L. Stately homes, 1 : 308.

Cassiodorus. Church, R. W. Miscel. ess. 155.

Cassovia, Siege of. Robson, W. Sieges, 432.

Castagno, Andrea, and Luca Signovelli. Jameson. Ital. painters, 102.

Castaños, Francisco Xavier. Bailey, J. B. Methuselahs, 223.

Caste. Bluntschli. Theory of state, 108. — Bose. Hindoos. — Cust. Pic. Ind. life, 270. — Dilke. Greater Brit. 425. — Müller. Chips, 2.

— Easy lessons in. Higginson. Conc. all, 44.

— Effect of, on the mind. Hamerton. Intellec. 277.

— Effects of. Patterson, R. H. Ess. hist. 444.

— Hindu, Nature and tendency of. Dutt. Ess. 204.

— Question of. Sumner. Works, 13 : 131.

Castel, Jean de. Besant. Fr. poetry, 182.

Castelar, Emilio. Duff, M. E. G. Miscel. 214. — Field, K. Ten days in S. 129. — Towle. Cert. men, 124.

Castellani collection, Bronze head in. Newton. Essays, 400.

Castellejo, Cristóbal. Montgomery. Men of Ita. 3 : 92.

Castelman, M. de. Taylor, W. C. Rom. biog. v. 1.

Castelvetro, Lodovico. Symonds. Renais. It. lit. 2 : 285.

— in Modena. Stoughton. Ital. reformers, 181.

"Casters" and "Chesters." Allen. Gr. Science in Arc. 275.

Castes and clans. Lyall. Asia, 150.

— Indian, Enumeration of. Colebrooke. Miscel. essays, 2 : 177.

Casti, Giambattista. I tre giuli. Hunt, L. Men, wom. & books. 120.

Castiglione, Baldassare. Symonds. Renais. It. lit. 2 : 265. — Symonds. Reviv. of learn. 418. — Jervis, Lady. Painting, 2 : 5. — With portrait. Warner Lib. 6 : 3339.

— as a Latin poet. Symonds. Reviv. of learn. 490.

— Perfect courtier, 1528. Maxwell, Sir H. Rainy days, 11.

Castillejo, C. de. Shelley, Mrs. Lit. men Italy, v. 3.

Castillon, Siege of. Robson, W. Sieges, 444.

Castine, Me. Drake. Nooks of N. E. 58.

Casting, Art of, among Greeks and Romans. Story, W. W. Excursions, 115.

Castle Acre. Jessopp, A. Rand. roam. 46.

Castle Howard. Jewitt, L. Stately homes, 2 : 74.

Castlereagh, Robert Stewart, Lord. Brougham. Works, 4 : 109. — Rush. Residence in Lond. — Capefigue. Diplomats. — Stanton, H. B. Reforms, 65. — Thornton. For. sec. v. 2.

Castles in the air. Jacox. Lit. life, 297.

— in the middle ages. Lucas. Secularia, 78.

-- Norman. Sparvel-Bayly. New stud. 222.

Castleton family. Burke, B. Viciss. of fam. 1 : 197.

Castor bean in India, 1893. (S. Merrill) U. S. Cons. Rept. 42 : 163.

Castorland, Journal de. (J. Appleton) Mass. Hist. Proc. 7 : 326.

Castro, G. de. Ticknor. Span. lit. 2 : 283.

Casuistry. DeQuin. Theo. ess. Bost. 1 : 203. — (B. Jowett) Noyes, G. R. Theol. ess. 299. — Stephen, J. F. Ess. by barr. 1. — Shipley, O. Tracts, 289.

— Common sense. Pollock. Ess. in juris. 261.

— Plea for. Oxenham. Short stud. 89.

— Questions of. Pearson, C. H. Reviews, 78.

Caswall, Edward. Hatfield, E. F. Poets of church, 135. — Miles, A. H. Poets of cent. 10 : 716. — Miller, Jos. Singers church, 2d ed. 519.

Caswell, Richard. Lossing. Em. Amer. 96.

Cat by the fire. Hunt, L. Seer, 2 : 5.

Catacombs. Howe, J. W. Oak to olive, 74. — Knox, T. W. Underground world, 314, 829.

— Church in. (H. Gee) Lefroy, W. Lec. eccl. hist. 415.

— of Rome. Clarke, J. F. Events, 1. — Milman. Savonarola, 468.

— — Paintings in. Woltmann and Woerman. Hist. painting, 1 : 151.

Catalani, Angelica. Clayton, E. C. Queens, 183. — Edwards, H. S. Prima don. 1 : 125. — Ferris, G. T. Great singers, 1. — Hogarth. Mem. opera, 2 : 284. — Needham. Queens of song.

Catalina, Princess. Burke, S. H. Hist. portr. Tudor, 1 : 1.

Catalogues, Educational library. Adams, C. F. New dep. Quincy, 16.

Catalonia in 1886. U. S. Consular Rept. no. 70.

— Journeyings in. Stoddard, C. A. Span. cit. 31.

— Reformers in. Stoughton. Span. ref. 91. — Taylor, B. Byways, 229.

Catania. Warner, C. D. Roundabout, 100.

Catarina in Venice, a romance on the Lagoon. Skelton, J. Ess. in romance, 175.

Catch-pennies. Buckland, F. T. Curios. nat. hist. 4 : 81.

Catechisms, Early N. E. (W. Eames) Am. Antiq. Soc. Proc. n. s. 12 : 76.

Catesby, Wm. Manning, J. A. Speakers, 121.

Catharine. *See* Catherine.

Cathedral, American, Significance of. Potter, H. C. Scholar & state, 321.

Cathedral builders. Oliphant. Makers of F. 92.

Cathedral service, English. Ritter. Music in Eng. 113.

Cathedrals. Boyd. Less. of mid. age, 211, 265.

— Deans and. Arnold, F. Our bishops, 2 : 224.

— English. Van Rensselaer, M. G. Eng. cath. 1.

— French ; Bibliography. Ferree, B. Chronology Cath. churches France.

— German, Builders of. (A. Schultz) Dohme, R. Early mast. 49.

— of Europe. Wallace, H. B. Art, 65.

— Our English. Lucas. Mornings, 2 : 77.

Catherine, St., of Egypt. Charles. Martyrs, 182.

Catherine, St., of Siena. Adams, W. H. D. Heroes Chr. 153.— Hack. Consec. wom. 7.— Kavanagh. Women of Chr. 106. — Trollope, J. A. Dec. Ital. wom. 1 : 1.

— 14th century new woman. Terhune. Where ghosts, 121.

Catherine II., empress of Russia. Bolton. Fam. lead. wom. 55 — Brougham. Works, 5 : 356. — Chambers's Miscel. no. 84.— With portrait. Clarke, M. C. Noted wom. 345.— Fowler, G. Sov. of Russ. 2 : 63, 121. — Jameson. Fem. sov. 2. — Jenkins, J. S. Heroines, 393.— Merivale. Hist. stud. 49. — Parton. Peop. bk. biog. 402. — Russell. Extr. women, 244.

— and Frederick the Great. Wraxall, C. F. L. Hist. bye-ways, 2 : 1.

— Memoirs. Cranbourne. Hist. sk. 1 : 143.

— Twelve favorites of. Menzies, S. Roy. fav. 2 : 434.

Catherine of Braganza, wife of Charles II. With portrait. Jameson. Beauties, 53. — Lodge. Portraits (Bohn), v. 6. — Strickland. Queens Eng. v. 8.— With portrait. Jesse. Court of Eng. Stuarts, 3 : 1.

Catherine de Medicis, queen and regent. Bush, A. F. Queens of F. 1 : 296.— Menzies, S. Roy. fav. 1 : 220. — Cook, T. D. Old Touraine, 2 : 27.— With portrait. Imbert de St. A. Wom. Valois Ct. 123-329. — Owen, Mrs. O. F. Heroines hist. 270.

Catherine of Navarre. Macdowell, H. C. Henry of Guise, 287.

Catherine Parr. Bethune, G. W. Brit. fem. poets, 17.

Catherine, daughter of Edward IV. Green, M. A. E. Princesses, 4 : 15.

Catherine, daughter of Charles I. Green, M. A. E. Princesses, 6 : 396.

Cathode rays. (J. J. Thomson) Smithson. Rept. '97 : 157.

Catholicism, Old. (R. S. Oldham) Relig. systems, 498.

Catholicity, Ancient and modern. Wiseman, N. Ess. 1 : 537.

Catholics. See Roman Catholics.

Catlin, George. Youmans. Pioneers sci. 336.

— Indian gallery, U. S. Nat. Mus. (Thomas Donaldson) U. S. Nat. Mus. Rept. '85 : supp.

Catlyne, Sir Robert, chief justice of England, 1559-74. Campbell. Ch. just. 1 : 175.

Cato, the censor. Warner Lib. 6 : 3347. — Dunlop, J. Rom. liter. 2 : 13. — Vincent, G. E. Ital. authors, 17.

— De re rustica. Mitchell. Wet days, 26.

Cato, the philosopher. Parton. Peop. bk. biog. 424.

Cato street conspiracy, 1820. Browne, G. L. Narr. state tri. 2 : 309. — Thornbury. Old stor. 301.

Cats, Jacob. Warner Lib. 6 : 3353.

Cats. Gosse, E. Gossip, 171. — Sanborn, Kate. Lit. zoo. 75. — Woolson. Browsing, 15.

— Anecdotes of. Chambers's Miscel. no. 55.

— Bibliography. Huidekoper, R. S. The Cat.

— Eccentric. Wynter. Fruit, 2 : 108.

Catskill falls. Curtis, G. W. Lotus, 43.

Catskill mountains. Curtis, G. W. Lotus, 28. — Irving. Biog. 480. — Taylor, B. At home, 2 : 319.

— Heart of the southern. Burroughs, J. Riverby, 33.

Cattell, Alexander G., with portrait. Winslow, S. N. Biog. Phila. merch. 98.

Cattle. Shaler. Dom. animals, 103.

— "Swell-head" in. Am. Pub. Health, 9 : 111.

Cattle, Texas, Characteristics of. (J. R. Smith) Am. Pub. Health, 8 : 125. 9 : 99.

— — Disease among. (J. R. Smith) Am. Pub. Health, 6 : 239. 7 : 114.

— — Fever of : Is it a chimera ? (D. E. Salmon) Am. Pub. Health, 9 : 84.

— transportation of, Sanitary care in. (W. B. Conesy) Am. Pub. Health, 10 : 282.

Cattle and meat inspection, Municipal. (P. II. Bryce) Am. Pub. Health, 22 : 197.
   See also Live-stock.

Cattle diseases in Massachusetts, Testimony on. Bigelow, J. Mod. inq. 295.

Cattle raising in the U. S. Rousiers. Amer. life, 39.

Catullus, Caius Valerius. Collins, M. Pen sketches, 1 : 207. — Dunlop, J. Rom. liter. 1 : 412. — Nettleship. Lec. & essays. — Sellar. Rom. poets repub. 399. — With portrait. (J. W. Mackail) Warner Lib. 6 : 3359.

— and Lucretius, style of. Conington. Miscel. 256.

Catz, Charles. Wallace, R. Anti-Trin. biog. 2 : 169.

Caucasus, Affinities of the languages of the. Latham. Opuscula, 156.

— Eastern, Mountains and mountaineers of. (G. Kennan) Am. Geog. Soc. 5 : 169.

— Languages of the. Cust. Ling. & orient. ess. 3.

— Russia in. Cust. Linguist. essays, 2 : 211.

— Struggle in. Chambers's Repos. no. 9.

Caucus, The, in the U. S. Curtis. From easy ch. 74.

Caucus system, The. (F. Whitridge) Econ. tracts, no. 8.

Caucuses. Haven, N. A. Remains, 236.

Cauls, Superstitions connected with. Jones, W. Credulities, 111.

Caumonts, Refugee, Sketch of the. Agnew. Protes. exiles, 2 : 201.

Caung-Shung. Brightwell. Byepaths of biog. 260.

Caus, Solomon de. Brightwell. Heroes of lab. 174.

Causality, Problem of. Brownson. Works, 1 : 381. — Whittaker, T. Ess. & not. 320.

Causation, Mill on. Ward, W. G. Ess. theism, 1 : 303.

— Principle of. Mozley. Ess. 2 : 414.

Cause and effect, A fragment on. Wright, C. Philos. dis. 408.

— — Law of, as taught by Buddha. (S. Soyen) Barrows, J. H. Parl. relig. 2 : 829.

— — Relation of. Gilman, S. Contrib. 143.

— A chapter in the history of the word. Courtney. Stud. philos. 75.

— First, Argument for. Mill, J. S. Three ess. 143, 176.

— The idea of. Bowen, F. Gleanings, 164.

Causes. Mivart. Less. fr. nature, 356.

— Complexity of. (E. T. Tappan) Nat. Educa. Assoc. '80 : 163.

— final, Chemical. (G. Wilson) Edin. ess. 1856 : 301.

— — Failure of Paley, and fallacy of. Thompson, J. P. Amer. com. 300.

Caution. Gray, E. C. Idle musings, 164.

Cavalcanti, Guido. Symonds. Renais. Ital. lit. 1 : 64.

Cavalier, John, Sketch of. Agnew. Protes. exiles, 2 : 54.

Cavalier and Puritan England, transplanted. Stebbing. Verdicts, 349.

Cavaliers and roundheads. Rands, W. B. Holbeach, 1 : 113.

Cavallero, Lucas. Carne, J. Em. mission. 3 : 214.

Cave, Edward. Knight, C. Old booksel. 171.

Cave, Stephen, with photo. Cooper, T. Men of mark, 3 : 6.

Cave-dwellers of the Sierra Madre. (C. Lumholtz) Cong. Anthrop. Chic. '93 : 100. Same in Am. Geog. Soc. 26 : 299.

Cave dwellings. *See* Pueblos.

Cave-houses. Lummis. Strange corners, 113.

Cave men of Devonshire, The age of. (W. Pengelly) Manch. Sci. lec. 5–6 : 123. 7 : 141.

Cavendish, Henry. Brougham. Works, 1 : 91. — Craik. Pursuit knowl. 2 : 92. — Edgar. Boyhood, 210. — Garnett. Physicists, 125. — Thorpe, T. E. Ess. hist. chem. 70. — Walker, W., jr. Men of sci. 27.

— and his discoveries. (T. E. Thorpe) Manch. Sci. lec. 7 : 84.

Cavendish, John de. Foss. Judges, 4 : 42.

Cavendish, Margaret, duchess of Newcastle. Jeaffreson. Novelists, 1 : 28. — Bethune, G. W. Brit. fem. poets, 35.

Cavendish, Thomas. Bourne, H. R. F. Eng. seam. 2 : 120. — Fuller. Worthies, 3 : 179. — Barrow, J. Nav. worthies, 162. — Southey & Bell. Brit. admirals, v. 3.

Cavendish, William. *See* Devonshire, Duke of.

Cavendish family. Sanford & Townsend. Gov. fam. 1.

— Genealogical sketch of. Jewitt, L. Stately homes, 1 : 119.

Caverns caused by agency of water. Adams, W. H. D. Fam. caverns, 33.

— of volcanic origin. Adams, W. H. D. Fam. caverns, 9.

— Stalactite. Adams, W. H. D. Fam. caverns, 78.

Caves, Bone. Adams, W. H. D. Fam. caverns, 154.

— — in Belgium. Adams, W. H. D. Fam. caverns, 177.

— — of England. Adams, W. H. D. Fam. caverns, 157.

— — of France. Adams, W. H. D. Fam. caverns, 170.

— — of Germany. Adams, W. H. D. Fam. caverns, 178.

— burial, Ancient, in Alabama. (Frank Burns) U. S. Nat. Mus. Rept. '92 : 451.

— Ice, of Washington. Raymond, R. W. Camp. 208.

— of Somersetshire. (E. H. Rann) Walters, J. C. Bygone Som. 28.

Cavour, Count. Hayward, A. Em. statesm. 1 : 133. — Nolan. Liber. of Ita. 406. — Duyckinck. Portrait gall. 2 : 64. — Hitchcock, T. Unhap. loves, 161. — Marriott, J. A. R. Makers mod. It.

Cawdor Castle. (Visct. Emlyn) Malan, A. H. Famous homes, 167. — Edwardes, C. Hist. houses.

Cawnpore. Field, H. M. Egypt to Japan, 210. — Pidgeon. Engineer's holiday, 389.

— of to-day. Forbes, A. Camps, 179.

— Story of. (M. Thompson) Bartlett, D. W. Heroes Ind. rebel. 186.

Cawood, John. Hatfield, E. F. Poets of ch. 138. — Miller, Jos. Singers church, 2d ed. 355.

Caxton, William. Brightwell. Heroes of lab. 26. — Brink. Eng. lit. 2, pt. 2 : 33. — Burke, S. H. Hist. portr. Tudor, 3 : 158. — Collier, W. F. Hist. Eng. lit. 71. — Disraeli, I. Amen. (N. Y. 2 v.) 1 : 247. — Edwards, B. B. Selftaught, 216. — Groser, W. H. Men worth im. — Simson, Jas. Em. men of Kent, 86.

Caxton, William, Printing-office of. Hall, Mrs. S. C. Pilgr. Eng. shr. 1 : 182.

Cayley, E. S. Grant, J. Recoll. Lords & Comm. 2 : 181.

Caylus, M. de M.–V., Marquis de. Imbert de St. A. Wom. Ct. Louis XIV, 143.

— Souvenirs of. Cranbourne. Hist. sk. 1 : 323.

Cayvan, Georgia, with portrait. (R. Edmunds) McKay, F. E. Fam. actors, 274.

Cazanovius, John. Wallace, R. Anti-Trin. biog. 2 : 213.

Cazin, Jean C. Child, T. Art & criticism, 43.

Cazotte, Jacques. Wraxall. Remark. adv. 1 : 321.

Ceba, Ansaldo. Rio. Four martyrs.

Cecil, Arthur, with portrait. Goddard, A. Players, 2 : 151.

Cecil, Lady Mildred. Williams, Jane. Lit. wom. 60.

Cecil, Richard. Seeley, M. Later evang. 118. — Crichton, A. Converts, 1 : 294.

Cecil, Robert A. T. Gascoyne-. *See* Salisbury, Marquis of.

Cecil family. Sanford & Townsend. Gov. fam. v. 2.

— Genealogical sketch of. Jewitt, L. Stately homes, 1 : 297.

Cecilia, Saint, with portrait. Clarke, M. C. Noted wom. 87. — Charles. Martyrs, 154.

Cecilia, daughter of William the Conqueror. Green, M. A. E. Princesses, 1 : 1.

Cecilia, daughter of Edward IV. Green, M. A. E. Princesses, 3 : 404.

Cedar Grove, Estate of. Glen, T. A. Colon. mans. 1 : 97.

Cedar Run, Battle of. Allan, W. Army of N. Va. 165.

Cedar Vale commune. Nordhoff. Commun. 353.

Celebes, Borneo and. Ellesmere. Ess. 348.

Celibacy, Clerical, enforced. Wordsworth, C. Misc. 3 : 257.

— Single blessedness. Saunders. Mosaics, 192.

Cellarius, Martin. Wallace, R. Anti-Trin. biog. 1 : 395.

Cellini, Benvenuto. Dawson, G. Shakesp. 281. — Ossoli. Life without, 93. — Symonds. Renais. Fine arts, 437. — With portrait. Warner Lib. 6 : 3371. — Bernard, F. Escapes, 26. — Brightwell. Heroes of lab. 35. — Harrison, J. A. Group of poets, 148. — Perkins, C. C. Tusc. sculp. 2 : 113.

— Memoirs. Birrell. Obiter, 1 : 154.

— Madrigal by ; trans. by W. W. Story. Perkins, C. C. Tusc. sculp. 2 : 225.

Cellino di Nese. Perkins, C. C. Tusc. sculp. 1 : 101.

Celsus. Froude. Short stud. 4 : 237. — Pressensé. Martyrs, 476. — Wallace, R. Anti-Trin. biog. 3 : 552.

Celtic church, Early. Blaikie, W. G. Preachers Scot. 12.

Celtic churches in the British isles. Bright, W. Roman see, 357.

Celtic heresy, overcome by St. Wilfrid. Montalembert. Monks, 4 : 129.

Celtic languages. Garnett. Philol. ess. 78.

Celtic literature. (W. Sharp and E. Rhys) Warner Lib. 6 : 3403.

Celtic monks, The, and the Anglo-Saxons. Montalembert. Monks, 4 : 1.

Celtic poetry, Sir Samuel Ferguson and. Williams, A. M. Stud. folk. 131.

Celtic studies, Arbois de Joubainville's. Darmesteter. Eng. stud. 181.

Cemeteries of Caliptus and Domatilla. Adams, W. H. D. Fam. caves, 115.
— On graveyards. Guiney. Goose-quill, 130.
— Origin of. Perkins, C. C. Tusc. sculp. 1 : 39.
Cenci family. Symonds. Renais. Cath. reac. 1 : 345.
Cenis, Mont, Tunnel of. Forsyth, W. Essays, 293. — Proctor. Light sci. 1 : 148.
Cennick, John. Hatfield, E. F. Poets of ch. 139.
— Miller, Jos. Singers church, 2d ed. 216.
Censorship. *See* Press.
— of bookstalls. Couch, A. T. Q. Adv. crit. 267.
Census, The, and civilization. Eagles. Ess. 304.
— U. S. (L. Blodget) Phila. Soc. Sci. Assoc. '72.
— Foster, R. Comment. on Const. 410.
— — of 1870. Walker, F. A. Discus. in econ. 2 : 49, 61.
— — of 1890. Walker, F. A. Discus. in econ. 2 : 69–111.
Centenarianism. Bailey, J. B. Methuselahs, 403, 431. — Lankester. Advan. sci. 223.
Centenarians, Unquestionable. Bailey, J. B. Methuselahs, 412.
Centenary College, Jackson, La. U. S. Bur. Ed. Circ. '99, no. 2 : 106.
Centennial of 1876. Oration at Boston, Mass., July 4, 1876. Winthrop, R. C. Addresses, 3 : 373.
Centlivre, Susannah. Costello. Englishwomen, 3 : 380. — Doran. Annals stage, 1 : 167. — Dunham. Lit. & sci. men, 3 : 308. — Galt. Players, 1 : 121. — Williams, Jane. Lit. wom. 151.
Central America, Aborigines of. McLennan. Stud. anc. 2 : 378.
— ancient, Religions of. (J. M. Lang) St. Giles lec. 2 : 289.
— Ancient civilization. (C. H. Berendt) Am. Geog. Soc. 8 : 132.
— Buried cities in. Chambers's papers, no. 13.
— Commercial directory of, 1891. Bur. Am. repub. no. 28.
— explorations in, Anthropological. (J. F. Bransford) Smithson. Rept. '82 : 803.
— Indian settlements in. (C. Sapper) Smithson. Rept. '95 : 537.
— Literature of. Bancroft, H. H. Essays, 455.
— On certain additions to the ethnographical philology of. Latham. Opuscula, 317.
Central College, Fayette, Mo. (T. B. Smith) U. S. Bur. Ed. Circ. '98, no. 2 : 49.
Central park, N. Y., Statues in, 1889. Curtis, G. W. Other ess. 186.
Central Tennessee College, Nashville, Tenn. U. S. Bur. Ed. Circ. '93, no. 5 : 269.
Central University, Richmond, Kentucky. U. S. Bur. Ed. Circ. '99, no. 3 : 193.
Centralization, Against. Grady, H. W. Writings, 142.
— and decentralization. Lorimer, Jas. Studies, nat'l and internat.
Centre College, Danville, Kentucky. U. S. Bur. Ed. Circ. '99, no. 3 : 110.
Century Co. Derby, J. C. Fifty years, 704.
Ceolnoth, 833–870. Hook. Abps. Cant. 1 : 283.
Cephalonia ; Mountain monastery. Barrows, S. J. Isles of Greece, 45.
Ceracchi, Giuseppe. Baker, W. S. Portr. of Wash. 100.
Ceramic ware. Scoffern. Stray leaves, 218.
— Bibliography. Downman, E. A. Eng. pottery. — Ries, H. Clay-working indus. U. S.
Cercopo. Arnold, E. Poets of Greece, 160.
Cerebral development, Bearings of, on child study. (R. P. Halleck) Nat. Educa. Assoc. '97 : 833.

Cerebral development, Laws of. (R. P. Halleck) Nat. Educa. Assoc. '97 : 833.
Cerebration, Unconscious. Cobbe, F. P. Darwinism, 305. — Ireland, W. W. Blot, 215.
Cerebro-spinal meningitis. (H. B. Baker) Mich. Health, '74 : 115.
— Epidemic of, in Massachusetts, 1873. (J. B. Upham) Mass. Health, '74 : 263.
Ceremonials, Costly. Gilbart. Lec. 192.
Ceremonies and respects. Bacon. Ess.
Ceremony and myth, Connection of. (W. Mathews) Cong. Anthrop. Chic. '93 : 246.
Coridwen Williams, Jane. Lit. wom. 23.
Cerne, Abbey of. Timbs. Abbeys, 1 : 440.
Certainty in religion. Taylor, I. Logic in theol. 262.
Certitude. Mr. Mill's reply. Ward, W. G. Ess. theism, 1 : 120.
— in religious assent. Ward, W. G. Ess. theism, 2 : 244.
— Rule and motive. Ward, W. G. Ess. theism, 1 : 7.
Cervantes. Coleridge. Lit. rem. 1 : 113.—Giles, H. Illus. of gen. 7. — Langford. Prison books, 58. — Longfellow. Poets Eur. 688. — Montgomery. Men of Ita. 3 : 120. — Prescott. Biog. Miscel. 123. — Ticknor. Span. lit. 2 : 52. — With portrait. (G. Santayana) Warner Lib. 6 : 3451. — Howells. My lit. passions, 20. — Hundred greatest men, 38. — Matthews, B. Books & play-books. — Shelley, Mrs. Lit. men Italy. v. 3.
— Bibliography. Kelly, J. F. Life Cervantes.
— Cradle and grave of. Hay, J. Castil. days, 282.
— Don Quixote. Dawson, G. Shakesp. 128. — Lowell. Democ. 157 ; *or* Writ. 6 : 115.
— — Translations and imitations of. Ticknor. Span. lit. 3 : 416.
— Zola, Kipling & Co. Matthews, B. Aspects fic. 162.
Cesarotti, Malchior. Stebbing. Ital. poets, v. 3.
Cespedes, Pablo de. Washburn, E. Span. mas. 78.
Cetti. Warner, C. D. Roundabout, 39.
Cettis, John Baptist. Wallace, R. Anti-Trin. biog. 2 : 494.
Ceylon. Abercromby. Seas & skies, 241. — De Quin. Let. to young (Bost.), 245. — Pidgeon. Engineer's Holiday, 340.
— Percival's. Smith, Syd. Ess. fr. Ed.
— Visit to, 1884. Hubner. Thro' Brit. empire, 1 : 389.
Chabrât, Guy Ignatius. Clarke, R. H. Cath. Bishops, 3 : 282.
Chad, St., of Litchfield. Charles. Martyrs, 407.
Chaderton, Lawrence. McClure. Translators, 107.
Chadwick, Sir Edwin. Em. persons, 4 : 244. — Smiles. Brief biog. 386.
Chadwick, John White. Putnam, A. P. Singers liberal, 517.
Chæronea, Greece. Mahaffy. Rambles Greece, 201.
Chaffers, William. Smith, C. R. Retrospec. 2 : 103.
Chagrin. Helps. Brevia.
Chalcedon and Alexandria. Bright, W. Roman see, 254.
Chaldean and Assyrian monarchies. Lord, J. Anc. states, 80.
Chalibbee, Battle at. Dawson. Batt. of U. S. 2 : 323.
Chalk, On a piece of. Huxley. Lay sermons.
Challenger expedition. Carpenter, W. Benj.

Nature, 316. — (J. Murray) Manch. Sci. lec. 9 : 105.

Chalons, Battle of. Creasy. 15 battles, 137. — King, C. Battles, 172.

Chalmers, Mrs. Jane, of Raratonga and New Guinea. Pitman, Mrs. Heroines mission. 186.

Chalmers, Thomas. Bayne, P. Chr. life, 403. — Blaikie, W. G. Leaders, 85. — Davies, G. J. Suc. preach. 454. — Edgar. Boyhood, 347. — Gilfillan. 1st gall. 72. — Gilfillan. 3d gall. 85. — Gleig. Ess. 1 : 1. — McCosh. Scot. phil. 393. — Mason, E. T. Pers. traits, 2 : 127. — Miller, H. Hist. ess. 110. — (D. McLeod) St. Giles lec. 3 : 273. — Stevenson. Lives & deeds, 247. — Blaikie, W. G. Preachers Scot. 276. — Broadus. Lec. hist. preach. 227. — Duyckinck. Portr. gall. 2 : 337. — Mathews, W. Oratory, 400. — Sinclair, J. Sketches. — Stanton, H. B. Reforms, 261. — Taylor, Wm. Scott. pulpit, 194. — Thayer, W. M. Turn. points, 225. — Thomas, R. Lead. of thought, 69. — Van Santvoord, C. Disc. 83. — Waterbury. Eloq. preach. 101.

— and the Cowgate. Guthrie, T. Out of harness, 124.

Chamberlain, Joseph. With photo. Cooper, T. Men of mark, 5 : 28. — Davidson, J. M. — Eng. lib. 89. — Hinton. Eng. radicals, 347. — Reid, T. W. Politicians, 2 : 63. — With portraits. Lynch, A. Hum. doc's, 108. — Smalley. Lond. lett. 1 : 183.

— Liberalism of. Rosebery. Speeches, 209.

Chamberlain, Sir Neville. Escott, T. H. S. Pillars emp. 24.

Chamberlain, Gen. William, Autobiographical letter from. Mass. Hist. Soc. Proc. 2d ser. 10 : 491.

Chamberlaine, James. Holland, J. Psalmists, 2 : 80.

Chamberlayne, William. Choate, I. B. Wells of Eng. 281. — Gosse, E. From Shakesp. 168.

Chambers, Arthur. Whitehead, C. Highwaymen, 1 : 174.

Chambers, John David. Hatfield, E. F. Poets of church, 143. — Miller, Jos. Singers church, 2d ed. 478.

Chambers, Robert. Curwen. Booksellers, 234. — Japp. Noble workers, 96. — Payn. Lit. recoll. 109. — Wilson, J. G. Poets of Scot. 2 : 238. — Smith, S. F. Noble workers, 131.

Chambers, Sir William. Milizia. Lives arch. 2 : 389.

— and Robert, and their publications. Nicoll. Great move. 175.

Chambers, Wm. F. Bettany. Em. doctors, 2 : 59.

Chambers, The. Stanton, H. B. Reforms, 373.

Chambord, Henri C. D., Comte de. Em. persons, 3 : 119. — Field, Mrs. H. M. Sk. France, 188. — James, H. Little tour, 33. — King, E. French pol. lead. 239.

Chambord, Château of. Larned, W. C. Churches & C. 185. — Cook, T. D. Old Touraine, 2 : 183.

Chameleons. Morgan, C. L. Animal sk. 202.

Chamfort, Sébastien R. N. Houssaye. Philos. 2 : 5. — Mathews. Men & bks. 287.

— and Rivarol. Saintsbury. Miscel. ess. 42.

Chamisso, Ludwig, C. A., *called* Adalbert von. Gostwick. Ger. poets, 205. — Hedge. Prose Ger. 544. — Warner Lib. 6 : 3503.

Chamouni. Bellows. Old world, 1 : 230. — Peabody, A. P. Rem. Eur. 124. — Stowe. Sunny mem. 2 : 202 — Thompson. Beaten paths, 206.

— Excursion to. Shelley. Ess. 2 : 60.

Champagne ; was it known to the ancients ? Cozzens. Bushwhacker, 146.

Champfleury, Jules. Henley. Views, 148.

Champion, Anthony. Jesse, J. H. Cel. Eton. v. 2.

Champion, Judah. Headley, J. T. Chaplains Revol. 318.

Champlain, Samuel de. Parton. Peop. bk. biog. 374. — Murray, J. O'K. Cath. heroes, 331.

-- Explorations of. Gilman. Pathfinders, 93.

Champlain, Lake. Pidgeon. Old world ques. 332.

— Battles on. Dawson. Batt. of U. S. 1 : 167. — Allen, Jos. Battles Brit. navy, 2 : 470. — Roosevelt, T. Naval war 1812, 375.

Champlain Valley, Archæolog. researches in. (G. H. Perkins) Cong. Anthrop. Chic. '93 : 84.

Champney, James Wells ; with portrait. Benjamin, S. G. W. Am. art. 2 : 32.

Chance, Laws of. Proctor, R. A. Univ. of suns, 368.

Chancellors, English Lord. Jeaffreson. Lawyers, 1.

— Functions and jurisdiction of. Campbell. Ld. Chan. 1 : 1.

Chancellorsville, Battle of. (H. W. Jackson) Mil. ess. M. O. L. L. U. S. Ills. 49. — Stine, J. H. Army Poto. 309. — Maps. Hotchkiss. Batt.-fields Va. 5.

Chancelor, Richard. Bourne, H. R. F. Eng. seam. 1 : 92.

— Discovery of White Sea by. Frost, T. Explorers, 129.

Chancery, Court of, and the law's delay. Williams, Syd. Forensic, 142.

— — Reforms in. Trans. Soc. Sci. Lond. 1859 : 169.

Chanche, John Mary Joseph. Clarke, R. H. Cath. bishops, 2 : 166.

Chandler, Augustus B. Davidson, J. W. Writ. of South, 85.

Chandler, Elizabeth M. Griswold. Fem. poets, 149.

Chandler, Ellen Louise. Hart, J. S. Fem. prose, 532.

Chandler, George. Am. Antiq. Soc. Proc., n. s. 9 : 25.

Chandler, George Byron, with portrait. Sketches N. H. men, 185.

Chandler, John. Hatfield, E. F. Poets of church, 145. — Miller, Jos. Singers church, 2d ed. 476.

Chandler, John F. Miles, A. H. Poets of cent. 10 : 701.

Chandler, Peleg Whitman. Am. Antiq. Soc. Proc., n. s. 6 : 101. — Loring, J. S. 100 Bost. ora. 613.

Chandler, Thos. Henderson. Vaille & Clark. Harv. book, v. 1.

Chandler, William E., with portrait. Sketches N. H. men, 255.

Chandler, Z., Eulogy of. Blaine. Polit. discus. 272.

Chandos, Marquis of. Grant, J. Recoll. Ho. Comm. 148.

Change, Subjective nature of. Gray, E. C. Idle musings, 234.

Channel islands, The. Benjamin, S. G. W. Atlan. isl. 57. — Benjamin. World's paradises, 138.

Channing, Edward Tyrrel. Loring, J. S. 100 Bost. ora. 384. — Peabody. Harv. rem. 84.

Channing, Francis Dana. Loring, J. S. 100 Bost. ora. 322.

Channing, Walter, and some of his contemporaries. Clarke, J. F. Memo. sketches, 167.

Channing, William Ellery. Alger. Solitudes, 311. — Bancroft, G. Miscel. 436. — Bartol. Principles, 342. — Griswold. Prose writ. 158. — Muzzey. Remin. 169. — Poe. Works, **6**: 163. — Russell, W. Extraor. men, 279. — (W. H. Furness) Ware, W. Am. Unita. **2**: 139. — Alviella. Contemp. evol. 162. — Clarke, J. F. Memo. sketches, 155. — Fisher, M. Gen. sur. Am. lit. 33. — Frothingham. Transcend. 111. — Hedge, F. H. Martin Luther, 164. — Holland, E. G. Reviews, 42. — Lossing. Em. Amer. 373. — Muzzey, A. B. Prime movers, 169. — Nichol. Amer. lit. 132, 184. Ronan, E. Leaders, 1. — Richardson. Amer. lit. **1**: 288. — Thomas, R. Lead. of thought, 25. — With portrait. Warner Lib. **6**: 3513. — Whittier. Prose works, v. **2**. — Woodberry. Stud. in lett. 227.

— and the Unitarian movement. Renan. Studies. N. Y. **1**: 298.

— Death of. Burnap. Miscel.

— Memoir and papers. Martineau, J. Ess. '91, **1**: 81.

— the moralist. Tuckerman. Charac. **1**: 56.

— Philosophical character of. Hazard. Ess. on lang. 158.

— Tribute to. Sumner. Works, **1**: 284.

Channing, William Henry. Frothingham. Transcend. 334.

Chanson, the, Historical sketch of. Besant. Fr. humor. 9.

Chantal, Madame J. F. de. Kavanagh. Women of Christianity, 139.

Chantilly, Château and collections of. Child, T. Art & criticism, 269.

Chantilly, Va., Battle of. Allan, W. Army of N. Va. 311.

Chantrey, Sir Francis. Jerdan. Men, 110. — Edgar. Footpr. 272. — Phillips, S. Ess. from Times, **2**: 166. — Smiles. Self-help. — Thomson, K. B. Recoll. 2. — Cooper, T. Triumphs of persev. 57.

Chanzy, General. Coan. Hist. stud. 179.

Chapin, Edward. (P. B. Olney) Harvard mem. biog. **2**: 425.

Chapin, Edwin H. Badeau. Vagabond, 48. — Bungay. Off-hand, 28. — Bartlett, D. W. Mod. agit. 230. — Parton, J. Sk. of men of prog.

Chapin, Lucy. Ellet. Pioneer wom. 370.

Chapin, Sylva. Ellet. Pioneer wom. 367.

Chaplin, Henry. Reid, T. W. Politicians, **2**: 217.

Chapman, George. Hazlitt. Dram. Eliz. — (A. Lang) Ward. Eng. poets, **1**: 510. — Ward, A. W. Eng. dram. **2**: 1. — Choate, I. B. Wells of Eng. 125. — Lowell. Old Eng. dram. 78. — Gosse, E. Jacobean poets, 39. — Minto, W. Eng. poets, 325. — Morley, H. Eng. writ. **10**: 464. **11**: 298. — With portrait. Warner Lib. **6**: 3523.

— Plays and poems. Lowell. Conv. on old poets, 145.

— Sonnets of. Deshler. Afternoons, 91.

Chapman, John, archdeacon of Sudbury. Jesse, J. H. Cel. Eton. v. **1**.

Chapman, John, D. D. Bungay. Repres. men, 262.

Chapman, John Gadsby. Tuckerman. Artist-life, 146. — Tuckerman. Artists, 216.

Chapman, Jonathan. Loring, J. S. 100 Bost. ora. 571.

Chapman, Nathaniel. (J. B. Biddle) Gross. Lives physicians, 663.

Chapman, William. Walker, W., jr. Men of sci. 30.

Chapone, Mrs. Hester, Memoirs of. Elwood. Lit. ladies, **1**: 181.

Chappelsmith, Margaret Reynolds. Underwood, S. A. Heroines, 243.

Character. Bartol. Rad. prob. 300. — Emerson. Ess. **2**: 87. — Emerson. Lec. & biog. sk. 91. — Lubbock. Use of life, 264. — Mabie. Ess. on work, 208. — Rands, W. B. Holbeach, **2**: 250.

— Christian. Gore, C. Lux mundi, 497.

— — Christian doctrine the mold of. (H. D. Kitchel) Bost. lectures, '72 : 49.

— Corporeal organism and. Dana, A. H. Eth. inq. 176.

— Defects in. Reynolds, G. Papers, 445.

— Effeminacy of. Hazlitt. Table-talk.

— Evidence about. Godkin. Reflections, 249.

— The female. Jameson. Studies.

— Formation of. Greeley. Hints ref. 85.

— in fiction. (M. G. Tuttiet) Art of writ. fict. 60.

— in its bearing on social causation. (B. Bosanquet) Bosanquet. Asp. soc. **9** : 103.

— Inclinations and. Martin, E. S. Windfalls, 239.

— Individual. Bailey, S. Essays, 168.

— Knowledge of. Hazlitt, W. Table-talk, 428.

— Management of. Lecky. Map of life, 235.

— moral, Development of. (G. W. A. Luckey) Nat. Educa. Assoc. '99 : 127.

— Native, of man. Beecher, L. Works, **3** : 53.

— Origin of. Hinsdale, B. A. Schools & stud. v. **1**.

— Religious element in the formation of. (G. Montgomery) Nat. Educa. Assoc. '99 : 121.

— Shreds of. Matthews, A. Rumina.

— Sketches of. Collins, W. W. Miscel. 9.

— Strength of. Hall, John. Papers, 45. — Whipple. Success, 57.

— Study of. Ess. from Sat. R. 151.

— Symmetrical development of. (Ellen Hyde) Nat. Educa. Assoc. '80 : 213.

— Testing, by religious inquiry. Hovey, A. Stud. in ethics, 497.

— Tests of. Anderson, M. B. Papers, **1** : 159. — Helps. Brevia.

— Unseen force in making. (G. H. Martin) Nat. Educa. Assoc. '99 : 276.

— Weakness in. Craik, D. M. Plain speaking, 73.

— Wealth and. Warner, C. D. As we go, 62.

Characteristics. Carlyle. Essays. — Hazlitt. Round table, 445.

Charbon. *See* Anthrax.

Charcot, Jean Martin. Blaze de Bury, Y. French lit. 86.

Chard, Major J. R. M., with photo. Cooper, T. Men of mark, **5** : 3. — Richards, W. Heroes, 72.

Chardin, Sir J. St. John. Cel. travelers, **1** : 233.

Chardin, J. B. S. Dilke. Fr. painters 18th cent. 112. — Wedmore. Masters of genre, 196.

Chardon St. Convention. Emerson. Lec. & biog. sk. 349.

Charing Cross, Changes at. Dobson, A. Miscel. 220.

Charitable agencies and poor laws. (T. Mackay) Cong. char. Chic. '93, **2** : 290.

— Finances of. (F. Tucker) Conf. char. & correc. '99 : 312.

— public and private, Coöperation of. (Alexander Johnson) Cong. char. Chic. '93, **2** : 114.

Charitable and penal institutions, Politics in. Conf. char. & correc. '98 : 237.

Charitable corporation fraud of 1719. Francis, J. Stock exch. 19.

Charitable effort. (Mrs. S. A. Barnett) Barnett, S. A. Prac. socialism, 157.

Charitable institutions and charity. Everett. Orat. v. **3**.

Charles V., of France, the wise. Gurney, J. H. Hist. sketches, **2** : 144.

Charles VI., of France. Gurney, J. H. Hist. sketches, **2** : 147. — Peake, Eliz. Germ. emperors, 403.

Charles VII., of France. Gurney, J. H. Hist. sketches, **2** : 225.

— and Agnes Sorel. Menzies, S. Roy. fav. **1** : 167.

Charles VIII., of France. Gurney, J. H. Hist. sketches, **2** : 242. — Pastor, L. Hist. popes, **5** : 420.

— and Langeais. Cook, T. D. Old Touraine, **1** : 160.

— in Italy. Symonds. Age of despots, 537. — Villari. Life of Savonarola, **1** : 193.

Charles IX., and Elizabeth of Austria. Imbert de St. A. Wom. Valois ct. 281.

Charles the Fat, deposed emperor of Germany. Doran. Monarchs, **1** : 295. — Peake, Eliz. Germ. Emperors, 31.

Charles IV., of Hapsburg, History of. Peake, Eliz. Germ. emperors, 156.

Charles V., emperor. Senior. Biog. sk. 348. — (J. L. Motley) Ferris, G. T. Gt. leaders, 240. — Hundred greatest men, 407. — Peake, Eliz. Germ. emperors, 239.

— abdicating German and Spanish thrones. Doran. Monarchs, **1** : 309.

— after his abdication. Delepiérre. Hist. diff. 128.

— in Italy. Symonds. Renais. Cath. reac. **1** : 18.

Charles VII. (1742–45), History of. Peake, Eliz. Germ. emperors, 405.

Charles II., of Spain, the bewitched, Exorcism of. Hume, M. A. S. Year after Armada, 289.

Charles III., of Spain. Robertson, J. B. Lec. mod. hist. 52.

Charles IV., of Spain. Doran. Monarchs, **2** : 334. — Robertson, J. B. Lec. mod. hist. 68.

Charles X., of Sweden. Cust. Warriors 30 years, **2** : 552.

Charles XII., of Sweden. Brooks, E. S. Hist. Boys, 218. — Parton. Peop. bk. biog. 433. — Schuyler. Peter the Great, **1** : 461. — Wilson, J. G. Illus. sci. 227. — Gurney, J. H. Hist. sketches, **3** : 39.

Charles I., of Roumania, Reminiscences of. Kingston, W. B. Monarchs, **1** : 234.

Charles I., of Württemberg, with portrait. Crowned heads, 15.

Charles the Bold. Freeman. Hist. ess. **1** : 314.

Charles Edward, the Pretender. Adams, W. H. D. Anec. mem. **2** : 235. — Bernard, F. Escapes, 111. — Greene, G. W. Hist. stud. 353. — Jesse. Pretenders, 101. — Oliphant. Hist. sketches, 207.

— Wanderings of. Davenport. Narr. peril. **2** : 1.

Charles of Dunfermline, prince of Wales. Doran. Princes of Wales, 387.

Charles Felix, duke of Savoy. Belloc, Mme. Walled garden, 112.

Charles of Orleans. Stevenson, R. L. Fam. stud. 236. — Cary, H. L. Early Fr. poets, 218. — Stevenson, R. L. Famil. stud. 229.

Charles of St. James, prince of Wales. Doran. Princes of Wales, 410.

Charles, Elizabeth (Rundle). Field, Mrs. H. M. Sk. France, 219.— Miles, A. H. Poets of cent. **10** : 739. — Miller, Jos. Singers church, 2d ed. 536.

Charles, Thos. Lives made sublime, 210. — Smith, C. R. Retrospec. **1** : 141.

Charles City Court-house, Surprise at. Dawson. Batt. of U. S. **1** : 645.

Charleston, S. C. Lanier, S. Florida, 218.

— in 1881. Hardy. Between 2 oceans, 281.

Charleston. S. C., Municipal condition of. (J. F. Ficken) Nat. Conf. City Govt. '97 : 188.

— Tidal drain system of. (L. J. Barbot) Am. Pub. Health, **16** : 236.

Charlestown, Mass. Drake, S. A. Hist. fields Mid. 1.

— Navy yard at. Drake, S. A. Hist. fields Mid. 26.

— Siege of. Dawson. Batt. of U. S. **1** : 570.

— Ursuline convent, Burning of. Winthrop, R.C. Speeches, 174.

Charlotte of Mecklenburg. Howitt, M. Queens, 490. — Lancelott. Queens, v. **2**.

Charlotte of Savoy, Queen. Bush, A. F. Queens of F. **1** : 239.

Charlotte, Princess, dau. of George IV. Fitzgerald, P. Royal dukes, **1** : 367. **2** : 1. — Hall, Mrs. M. Princesses, 366.— Parton. Fam. girls, 171. — Lodge. Portraits (Bohn), v. **8**.

— Funeral of, Free thoughts on. MacCrie, T. Miscel. writ.

— Sermon on death of. Hall, R. Miscel. 291.

Charlotte Augusta, Princess of Saxe-Coburg, with portrait. Ollier, E. Brit. portr. paint. 66.

Charlotte Augusta, queen of Württemberg, dau. of George III. Fitzgerald, P. Royal dukes, **1** : 241. — Hall, Mrs. M. Princesses, 216.

Charlotte Matilda, queen of Denmark. Fitzgerald, P. Royal dukes, **1** : 159.

Charlotte Sophia, queen of George III. Doran. Queens Hanov. v. **2**. — Greville. Journal. — Fitzgerald, P. Royal dukes, **1** : 53.

Charlotte, N. C., Affair at. Dawson. Batt. of U. S. **1** : 626.

Charlton, Jay, *pseud.* See Goldsmith, J. C.

Charm stones or "plummets" from California. (L. G. Yates) Smithson. Rept. '86 : 296.

Charms. Blunt. Anc. customs in mod. Italy, 162. — Grimm. Teutonic mythology, v. **3–4.**

— and fairy faith. Whittier. Lit. recre. 257.

Charolais, C. de Bourbon, Count de. Wraxall, F. C. L. Remark. adv. **2** : 337.

Charon. Mills. Poets of Greece, 465.

Charretie, Mrs. Anna Maria (Kenwell). Clayton, E. C. Eng. fem. art. **1** : 415.

Charrière, Madame de. Kavanagh. Fr. women, 227.

Charron. Owen, J. Skeptics, French, 559.

Charter-house school, London. Staunton, H. Schools, 257.

Charteris, Col. Francis. (A. Vincent) Seccombe, T. 12 bad men, 200.

— Character of. Burnet, G. Lives.

Chartier, Alain. Besant. Fr. poetry, 44.— Cary. Fr. poets, 207.

Chartism. Stanton, H. B. Reforms, 302.

Chartist agitation. Gibbins. Eng. soc. ref. 162, 193.

Chartley castle. Thomson, K. B. Recoll. 2.

— Mary Queen of Scots at. Strickland. Queens Scot. 7.

Chartres. James, H. Portraits, 120.

— Cathedral of. Larned, W. C. Churches & C. 22.

Chartreuse, Grande. Child, T. Summ. holidays, 255. — Taylor, B. Byways, 295.

Chase, Mrs. Elizabeth. Burder. Pious wom. 600.

Chase, Frederick. Am. Bar Assoc. **13** : 356, 183.

Chase, Marion. Clayton, E. C. Eng. fem. art. **2** : 183.

Chase, Nelly M. Moore, F. Women of the war, 536.

Chase, Pliny Earle. (S. S. Green) Am. Antiq. Soc. Proc. n. s. **4** : 316.

Chase, Salmon P., with portrait. Am. Ann.

Chaumont and Louis XII. Cook, T. D. Old Touraine, 1 : 187.

Chauncey, Sir Henry. Woolrych. Serjeants, 1 : 469.

Chauncey, Isaac. Lossing. Em. Amer. 342.

Chauncy, Charles. Peabody. Harv. grad. 239.

Chautauqua. Blanc, T. Wom. in U. S. 220. — Pidgeon. Engineer's holiday, 55. — (J. G. Fitch) Cochrane, R. Benef. lives, 154.
— and the Chautauqua movement. (H. B. Adams) U. S. Bur. Ed. Rept. '94–95, 1 : 977.

Chavannes, Pierre P. du. *See* Puvis de Chavannes.

Chaworth, William, Duel of, with Lord W. Byron. Thornbury. Old stor. 57.

Chawthorne, J. Chalmers. Eng. poets, 14 : 229.

Cheapside, Orchards in. Wynter, A. Our soc. bees, 1 : 143.

Cheare, Abraham. Ivimey. Eng. Bapt. 2 : 103.

Cheatham, Benjamin F. Pollard. Life of Lee, 718.

Cheatham, Mrs. W. A., with portrait. Ellet. Queens Am. soc. 417.

Chedel, Joseph Allen. Bartlett, J. R. R. I. officers, 440.

Cheerfulness. Friswell. Gentle life, 1 : 186.
— The bright side. Saunders. Mosaics, 383.
— in life and art. Patmore. Princ. in art, 31.
— Sources and conditions of. Whipple. Success, 194.
— Three-cornered way of looking at things. Arnold, F. 3-cor. ess. 1.
— Value of. Mathews. Conversers, 186.

Cheesborough, Essie B. Raymond, I. Southland wr. 2 : 877.

Cheese, Poisonous. H. B. Baker. Mich. Health, '84 : 122. — (V. C. Vaughan) Amer. Pub. Health, 10 : 241. — (V. C. Vaughan) Mich. Health, '85 : 221. '86 : 154.

Cheever, David Williams. Vaille & Clark. Harv. book, v. 1.

Cheever, George B. Bungay. Pen-portr. 229. — Griswold. Prose writ. 452.

Chefoo, China, U. S. trade at, 1898. (J. Fowler) U. S. Cons. Rept. 59 : 545.
— — in 1899. (J. Fowler) U. S. Cons. Rept. 61 : 296.

Cheh-Kiang mission, Commencement of. Cumming, C. F. G. Wand. in China, 2 : 50.

Chehocton, N. Y. Willis. Hurry-graphs, 82.

Cheke, Sir J. Wrangham. Brit. Plutarch, v. 1.

Chelas, and lay chelas. 5 years theos. 50.

Chelmius, Martin. Wallace, R. Anti-Trin. biog. 2 : 208.

Chelmius, Remigius. Wallace, R. Anti-Trin. biog. 2 : 207.

Chelmsford, F. Thesiger, Lord, with photo. Cooper, T. Men of mark, 1 : 16.

Chelmsford, Sir F. A. Thesiger, Lord. With photo. Cooper, T. Men of mark, 6 : 7. — Kent, C. M. Derby min. 71.

Chelsea. Wolfe. Lit. pilg. Brit. au. 27.

Chemical energy. (N. Ostwald) Smithson. Rept. '93 : 231.

Chemical final causes. (G. Wilson) Edin. ess. '56 : 301.

Chemical forces. Hunt, R. Poe. of sci. 270.

Chemical phenomena. Hunt, R. Poe. of sci. 295.

Chemical rays and the light of the sky. Tyndall. Frag. sci. 237.

Chemical triad, A : Cavendish, Lavoisier, Dalton. Scoffern. Stray leaves, 20.

Chemist, The American. (G. C. Caldwell) Smithson. Rept. '93 : 239.

Chemist, the American, Life-work of. (H. E. Roscoe) Smithson. Rept. '89 : 491.

Chemistry. Davy. Works, 2 : 307.
— as part of a college course. (Alexander Smith) Nat. Educa. Assoc. '97 : 945.
— Dawn of. Muir, M. M. P. Chemist, 5.
— Elementary; four lect's. (H. E. Roscoe) Manch. Sci. lec. 1 : 1.
— — Teaching of. (P. C. Freer) Nat. Educa. Assoc. '96 : 951.
— Evolution in. Gall & Robertson. Pop. read. sci. 159.
— History of. Brown, S. Atom. 1.
— Industrial. Bibliography. Thorp, F. H. Outlines indust. chemistry.
— Method of teaching, in classes, schools, and colleges. (H. E. Armstrong) Internat. health exh. 14 : 73.
— Modern (1847). Holland, H. Ess. 425. — Muir, M. M. P. Chemists, 294.
— Problems in, of to-day. (Victor Meyer) Smithson. Rept. '90 : 361.
— Progress in, 1846–96. (M. Benjamin) Goode. Smithson. Inst. 611.
— Teaching advanced classes in. (L. C. Cooley) N. Y. Regents, 80 : 603.
— — In the U. S. (F. W. Clarke) U. S. Bur. Ed. Circ. '80, no. 6.

Cheney, Gilman, with portrait. Sketches N. H. men, 215.

Cheney, Person C., with portrait. Sketches N. H. men, 162.

Cheneys and the house of Russell. Froude. Short stud. 4 : 312.

Chénier, André. Curwen. Sorrow, 2 : 169. — Doran. New pic. 73. — Harrison, J. A. Group of poets, 361. — Pellissier. Lit. move. Fr. 44.
— With portrait. (K. Hillard) Warner Lib. 6 : 3601.
— Death of. Houssaye. Philos. 2 : 87.
— Prose writings of. Bristed. Pieces, 1 : 64.

Chenonceaux, Château of. Cook, T. D. Old Touraine, 1 : 240. 2 : 1. — James, H. Little tour, 51. — Larned, W. C. Churches & C. 130.

Chenowith, Joseph H. Walker, C. D. Biog. Va. Mil. Inst. 108.

Chepston Castle ; celebrated prisoners. Hutton, B. Castles, 117.

Chequamegon Bay, Story of. (R. G. Thwaites) Am. Antiq. Soc. Proc. n. s. 10 : 127.

Cherbuliez, Victor. Van de Velde. Fr. fic. 1 : 154. — With portrait. Warner Lib. 6 : 3609.
— Zimmern. For. novelists, 1 : 261. — Saintsbury. Ess. Fr. nov. 419.

Cheri. Dodge, M. A. Gala, 333.

Cherry, Joseph B. Walker, C. D. Biog. Va. Mil. Inst. 114.

Cherry Valley, Massacre of. Dawson. Batt. of U. S. 1 : 464.

Chertsey Abbey. Timbs. Abbeys, 1 : 281.
— and its neighborhood. Hall, Mrs. S. C. Pilgr. Eng. shr. 2 : 231.

Cherubim, Nature of. Parsons, T. Mystery, 307.

Cherubini, M. L. C. Elson, L. Gt. composers, 201. — Keddie. Mus. comp. 254. — Ferris. Great Ital. compos. 120. — Hogarth. Mem. opera, 2 : 258.
— and his predecessors. Ferris, G. T. Ital. & Fr. compos. 120.
— as a violinist. Phipson. Violinists, 38.

Cherubino, the page. Paget, V. Belcaro, 129.

Chersias. Arnold, E. Poets of Greece, 75.

" **Chesapeake** " and " Shannon," Battle of. Allen, Jos. Battles Brit. navy, 2 : 425. — Fitchett

Deeds, 126. — Roosevelt, T. Naval war 1812, 178. — Silliman. Gallop, 64.

"Chesapeake," Loss of. Dawson. Batt. of U. S. 2 : 240.

Chesbro, Frances M. Putnam, A. P. Singers liberal, 484.

Cheshire, Eng. Rimmer, A. Country towns, 1.
— Ancient bridges, fords, and ferries of. (W. Harrison) Andrews, W. Bygone Ches. 181.
— Historic. (T. Frost) Andrews, W. Bygone Ches. 1.
— Plague in. (W. F. A. Axon) Andrews, W. Bygone Ches. 122.
— Proverbial phrases of. (J. P. Briscoe) Andrews, W. Bygone Ches. 189.

Cheshire cat, Origin of the expression. Rimmer, A. Country towns, 49.

Cheshire Cheese Coffee House. Terhune. Where ghosts, 47.

Chess. Jones, W. A. Ess. on authors, 150.
— and playing cards : catalog of games and implements of divination in U. S. Nat. Mus. (S. Culin) U. S. Nat. Mus. Rept. '96 : 665.

Chesshyre, Sir John. Woolrych. Serjeants, 2 : 594.

Chester, Eng. Freeman. Eng. tours, 230. — James. Transatl. — Thompson. Beaten paths, 9. — Silloway. Cathedral towns, 79.
— Festival-time in old. (G. S. Tyack) Andrews, W. Bygone Ches. 60.
— in 1488. Skelton, J. Ess. in hist. 110.
— Old houses. (W. Harrison) Andrews, W. Bygone Ches. 89.
— Origin of the rows. (W. Stevenson) Andrews, W. Bygone Ches. 78.
— Walls of. Smith, C. R. Retrospec. 3 : 158.

Chester Archæological Congress. Smith, C. R. Retrospec. 1 : 64.

Chester castle and walls. (G. C. Yates) Andrews, W. Bygone Ches. 26.

Chester cathedral. (J. A. Clapham) Andrews, W. Bygone Ches. 51. — (J. S. Howson) Farrar, F. W. Westmin. 209.

Chester fair. (Mrs. G. L. Banks) Andrews, W. Bygone Ches. 68.

"Chesters," " Casters " and. Allen, Grant. Science in Arc. 275.

Chesterfield, Elizabeth Butler, countess of. Jesse. Court of Eng. Stuarts, 3 : 275. — With portrait. Jameson. Beauties, 189.

Chesterfield, P. D. Stanhope, 4th earl of. Hayward, A. Ess. 1: 209. — Maceuen. Celeb. 159. — Oliphant. Hist. sketches, 91. — (C. F. Adams) Rice, A. T. Ess. 255. — Ste.-Beuve. Eng. portr. 22. — Tuckerman. Ess. 29. — Wotton. Word portraits, 63. — Wrangham. Brit. Plutarch, v. 6. — With portrait. Warner Lib. 6 : 3625.
— Letters. Adams, W. D. Famous books, 331. — Tovey. Rev. & ess. 51. — Ste.-Beuve. Portr. of men, 36.
— Letters to his son. Ste.-Beuve. Sel. ess. 51.

Cheteagua, Action at. Dawson. Batt. of U. S. 2 : 297.

Chetham, Humphrey, of Manchester, 1580–1653. Bourne, H. R. F. Eng. merch. 1 : 282. — Espinasse. Lanc. worth. v. 1.

Chettle, Henry. Minto, W. Eng. poets, 253.

Chetwynd, Julia B., with portrait. Black, H. C. Wom. authors, 247.

Chevalier, Michel. Em. persons, 2 : 206.

Chevalier, Sulpice Paul. (T. Gautier) Gautier. Fam. Fr. au. 156.

Cheveley. Collins, Stephen. Miscel.

Cheverus, Bishop J. L. de. The old cathedral.

Fairbanks, O. B. Aguecheek, 234. — Clarke, R. H. Cath. bishops, 1 : 164.

Cheviot Hills. Geikie, J. Frag. 62.

Chevreuse, Marie de Rohan, duchesse de. Menzies. Pol. women, 1 : 17. — Menzies. Roy. fav. 2 : 282.

Chevy Chase. Hales. Folia litt. 128.

Chew, Benj., at Cliveden. Terhune. Colon. homes, 104.

Cheyenne Mts., New road over. Jackson, H. H. Bits. trav. home, 331.

Cheyne, J. Pettigrew. Med. portr. gall. v. 3.

Chiabrera, Gabriello Montgomery. Men of Ita. 2 : 163. — Symonds. Renais. Cath. reac. 2 : 286. — Shelley, Mrs. Lit. men Italy, v. 2. — Stebbing. Ital. poets, v. 3.

Chianciano and its mineral springs. Jarves. Ital. ramb. 137.

Chiari, James de. Wallace, R. Anti-Trin. biog. 2 : 120.

Chiaroscuro. Fuseli. Life & writ. 2 : 273.

Chicago. Brooks, E. S. Gt. cities, 44. — Hardy, I. D. Thro' cities, 75. — Marshall, W. G. Thro' Amer. 86. — Rae. Westward, 34. — Sala. Amer. revis. 2 : 114, 318. — Warner, C. D. Studies, 176. — Pidgeon. Engineer's holiday, 85.
— Ancient. Barrows, W. U. S. of yester. 53.
— Bohemians in. (J. H. Zeman) Hull-House maps, 115.
— Charities of. (E. B. McCagg) Conf. char. & corr. '79 : 145.
— Civic Federation of. (A. W. Small) Nat. Conf. City Govt. 2–3 : 474.
— Drainage and sewerage of. (E. S. Chesbrough) Am. Pub. Health, 4 : 18.
— Foreign population of. Blanc, T. Wom. in U. S. 62.
— Growth, destruction, and reconstruction of. Parton. Triumphs, 35.
— in 1877. Vivian. Tour in Am. 86.
— Italian colony in. (A. Mastro-Valerio) Hull-House maps, 131.
— Jewish quarter in. (C. Zeublin) Hull-House maps, 91.
— Massacre at. Dawson. Batt. of U. S. 2 : 103.
— Municipal civil service reform in. (M. Starr) Nat. Conf. City Govt. '96 : 162.
— Municipal history. Bibliography. (S. E. Sparling) Univ. Wis. Bull. '98, no. 23.
— Old. Caton. Miscel. 77.
— Poor of. (J. Kirkland) Woods, R. A. Poor, 195.
— Sanitary problems of, 1877. (J. H. Ranch) Am. Pub. Health, 4 : 3.
— University of. Bolton, S. K. Givers, 357.
— Water supply of. (A. Hazen) Am. Pub. Health, 19 : 146.
— Women in. Blanc, T. Wom. in U. S. 19.
— World's Congresses, '93. (C. C. Bonney) Nat. Educa. Assoc. '92 : 166.
— World's Columbian Exposition, 1893. Zangwill. Without prej. 287.
— — Educational Congress at. (W. T. Harris) Nat. Educa. Assoc. '92 : 591.
— — Educational exhibit at. (John Eaton) Nat. Educa. Assoc. '94 : 515. — (S. H. Peabody) Nat. Educa. Assoc. '92 : 583. '94 : 60.
— — — American views of. (John Eaton and others) U. S. Bur. Ed. Rept. '92–93 : 445.
— — — French views of. (Jules Steeg and others) U. S. Bur. Ed. Rept. '92–93 : 585.
— — — German Criticism of. (Emil Hausknecht and others) U. S. Bur Ed. Rept. '92–93 : 521.
— — — Notes on. (John Eaton) U. S. Bur. Ed. Rept. '92–93 : 1015.

Chicago, World's Columbian Exposition, 1893, educational exhibit at, System of classification for. U. S. Nat. Mus. Rept. '91 : 649.
— — Educational systems represented at. (A. G. Lane) Nat. Educa. Assoc. '92 : 161.
Chicheley, Henry, 1414–43. Fowler, M. Some abps. Cant. 62. — Hook. Abps. Cant. 5 : 1. — Sergeant, L. Wiclif, 354.
Chichester, Eng. Freeman. Eng. towns, 374.
— Cathedral. Timbs. Abbeys, 1 : 380.
Chickering, Jonas. Houghton. Kings, 124. — With portrait. (J. L. Blake) Hunt, F. Am. merch. 1 : 493.
Chief Justices of England, Campbell's. Senior. Biog. sk. 162.
Chiffinch, William. Jesse. Court of Eng. Stuarts, 3 : 345.
Chihuahua, Expedition against. Dawson. Batt. of U. S. 2 : 478.
Child, Calvin Goddard. Am. Bar Assoc. 4 : 124.
Child, David Lee. Loring, J. S. 100 Bost. ora. 420.
Child, Francis J. (C. E. Norton) Am. Acad. Proc. 32 : 333. — Vaille & Clark. Harv. book, v. 1.
Child, Josiah, of London, 1630–99. Bourne, H. R. F. Eng. merch. 1 : 314.
Child, Lydia Maria. Darton. Fam. girls, 266. — Griswold. Fem. poets, 110. — Griswold. Prose writ. 426. — Hart, J. S. Fem. prose, 127. — (S. Coolidge) Our fam. wom. 230. — (T. W. Higginson) Parton. Em. wom. 38. — Higginson, T. W. Contemp. 108. — Whittier. Prose works, v. 2.
Child, The. (F. W. Parker) Nat. Educa. Assoc. '89 : 479.
— and the family. (H. Folks) Conf. char. & corr. '92 : 419.
— and the state, in Michigan. (C. D. Randall) Conf. char. & corr. '88 : 262.
— Autobiography of a. Escott. Politics, 173.
— education of, Problem of. (J. Carhart) Conf. char. & corr. '92 : 183.
— Environment of. (Clara Conway) Nat. Educa. Assoc. '85 : 109.
— First two years of (Milicent W. Shinn) Nat. Educa. Assoc. '93 : 773.
— in the house. Pater. Miscel. stud. 147.
— in Jewish literature. Schechter, S. Stud. Jud. 343.
— Mental and moral development of. (C. C. Van Liew) Nat. Educa. Assoc. '99 : 551.
— modern, Nerves of the. Bridge, N. Penalties of taste, 87.
— problem of, Economic aspect of. (H. H. Hart) Conf. char. & corr. '92 : 191.
Child development, Study of. (Annie H. Barus) Nat. Educa. Assoc. '94 : 996.
Child labor. Conn. Bur. Lab. '94 : 265. — Minn. Labor, 2 : 154. — N. J. Labor, '78 : 10. '79 : 94. '81 : 97. '85 : 264, 353. — Colorado. Labor, '91–92 : 139.
— Bibliography. (M. M. Milner) Am. J. Sociol. '97 : 139.
— in Germany. U. S. Cons. Rept. no. 153.
— in Maryland. Maryland. Labor, '93 : 179.
Child power. Dodge, M. A. Skirmish, 3.
Child-saving. (A. S. White) Conf. char. & corr. '88 : 258.
— Jewish, in U. S. (M. Heymann) Conf. char. & correc. '97 : 108.
Child-saving work. Conf. char. & correc. '94 : 119. — (C. D. Randall) Conf. char. & correc. '93 : 131.
— in England. (T. B. L. Baker) Conf. char. & corr. '84 : 200.

Child-saving in Michigan, Ten years of. (J. N. Foster) Conf. char. & corr. '84 : 132.
— work of the humane societies. (J. G. Shortall) Conf. char. & correc. '97 : 110.
See Children.
Child stealing, Curious cases of. Burke, P. Romance of forum.
Child study. (G. S. Hall) Nat. Educa. Assoc. '94 : 173. — U. S. Bur. Ed. Rept. '92–93 : 357.
— and the science of education. (J. P. Gordy ; R. P. Halleck) Nat. Educa. Assoc. 98 : 348, 354.
— and the teacher. (G. T. W. Patrick) Nat. Educa. Assoc. '95 : 906.
— and training of teachers. (M. K. Smith) Nat. Educa. Assoc. '93 : 447.
— Application of, in the school. (F. W. Parker) Nat. Educa. Assoc. '95 : 418.
— Artistic simplicity of. (Amalie Hofer) Nat. Educa. Assoc. '92 : 279.
— basis of pedagogy. (W. H. Burnham) Cong. Educa. Chic. '93 : 718.
— basis for psychology. (G. S. Hall) Cong. Educa. Chic. '93 : 717.
— Bibliography. Chamberlain, A. F. Child in folk-thought. — (A. Stowell) Journ. Educa. Feb. 25, Mar. 18, '97. — MacDonald, A. Exper. study of child. — Rowe, S. H. Phys. nature of child. — Sully, J. Studies childhood. — Taylor, A. R. Stud. child psychol. — U. S. Bur. Ed. Rept. '92–93 : 385.
— Cautions to be observed in. (O. H. Lang) Nat. Educa. Assoc. '98 : 898.
— A curriculum of applied. (F. Burk) Nat. Educa. Assoc. '99 : 1051.
— Experimental. (A. MacDonald) U. S. Bur. Ed. Rept. 1897–98, 1 : 989.
— for fathers and mothers. (M. V. O'Shea) Nat. Educa. Assoc. '96 : 480.
— for teachers. (M. V. O'Shea) Nat. Educa. Assoc. '95 : 924.
— Froebel's use of. (C. G. O'Grady) Nat. Educa. Assoc. '97 : 593.
— Has it help for the Kindergarten ? (Bertha Payne) Nat. Educa. Assoc. '97 : 586.
— in country schools. (Anna K. Eggleston) Nat. Educa. Assoc. '96 : 887.
— in normal and training schools. (G. Edmund) Nat. Educa. Assoc. '99 : 1032.
— in the U. S. U. S. Bur. Ed. Rept. 1897–98, 2 : 1281.
— Methods of, in the kindergarten. (Jenny B. Merrill) Nat. Educa. Assoc. '97 : 598.
— part of the teacher's art. (C. C. Van Liew) Nat. Educa. Assoc. '96 : 864.
— Practical, for the average teacher. (G. W. A. Luckey) Nat. Educa. Assoc. '97 : 826.
— Practical results. (A. S. Whitney) Nat. Educa. Assoc. '96 : 372.
— Scientific and non-scientific methods. (W. L. Bryan) Nat. Educa. Assoc. '96 : 856.
— special, Plea for. (W. L. Bryan) Cong. Educa. Chic. '93 : 777.
— Systematic and unsystematic. (W. L. Bryan) Nat. Educa. Assoc. '95 : 412.
— Training of teachers for. (M. K. Smith) Cong. Educa. Chic. '93 : 447.
— up to date. (Sarah E. Wiltse) Nat. Educa. Assoc. '96 : 837.
— Work in, at Clark university. (G. S. Hall) Nat. Educa. Assoc. '96 : 860.
Childe, Hattie H. Hemenway. Poets of Vt. 301.
Childe, John, with portrait. Stuart, C. B. Am. engineers, 177.
Childers, Hugh C. E. Escott, T. H. S. Pillars emp. 31. — Kent, C. Gladst. govt. 267. —

With photo. Cooper, T. Men of mark, 3 : 28.
— Higginson, T. W. Eng. statesm. 353.
Childhood. Dodge, M. A. Gala, 411. — Jacox, F. Cues, 1. — Waterston. Culture, 23.
— and nature. Mabie. My study fire, 8.
— Bibliography. Tracy, F. Psychology childhood.
— imitative functions in, Psychology of. (W. T. Harris) Nat. Educa. Assoc. '94 : 637
— Mystery in. Whiting, C. G. Saunterer, 208.
— Religion of. Cobbe, F. P. Darwinism, 65.
— Sorrows of. Boyd. Leis. hours, Bost. 244.
Children. Friswell. Wick. world, 160.
— Acquisition and memory in. (G. P. Brown) Nat. Educa. Assoc. '82 : 183.
— and poetry. Tollemache. Ess. & mock-ess. 140.
— and the state. Field, D. D. Speeches, 3 : 343.
— at the seashore. Green, J. R. Stray studies, 167.
— below school age, Education of. (F. A. Fitzpatrick ; Elizabeth Harrison) Nat. Educa. Assoc. '92 : 626.
— Books for. Jones, W. A. Ess. on authors, 230. — Ossoli. Woman, 310. — Thompson, H. M. Copy, 268. — Burton, R. Liter. likings, 363. — Hawthorne, J. Confess. 100.
— Catholic agencies in U. S. for helping. (T. F. Ring) Conf. char. & correc. '96 : 326.
— Classification and training of. (W. P. Letchworth) Conf. char. & corr. '83 : 344.
— Condition in our civilization. Samuelson, Jas. Civiliz'n, 196.
— crippled and deformed, Care of. (N. M. Shaffer) Conf. char. & correc. '98 : 393.
— defective, Child study as applied to. (W. O. Krohn) Conf. char. & correc. '97 : 308.
— delinquent, Care of. (H. Folks) Conf. char. & correc. '91 : 136.
— Dependent. (C. H. Reeve) Nat. Pris. Assoc. '88 : 101.
— — and delinquent. (E. C. Putnam) Conf. char. & correc. '90 : 190.
— — — Visitation of. (E. C. Putnam) Conf. char. & corr. '81 : 286.
— — — Supplem. work in care of. (Mrs. A. B. Richardson) Conf. char. & correc. '86 : 131.
— — — State and. (Mrs. V. T. Smith) Conf. char. & correc. '87 : 238.
— — and family homes. (W. P. Letchworth) Conf. char. & correc. '97 : 94.
— — Boarding-out of, in Mass. (Mrs. A. A. Calkins) Conf. char. & correc. '86 : 157.
— — Care of. (M. McG. Dana ; Mrs. L. V. Gorgas) Conf. char. & correc. '88 : 237.
— — Country homes for. (E. H. Bailey) Conf. char. & correc. '90 : 202.
— — — in Ohio. (S. J. Hathaway) Conf. char. & correc. '90 : 208.
— — Duty of the state to. (B. C. Mathews) Conf. char. & correc. '98 : 367.
— Desertion of, by parents. (C. Arenal) Conf. char. & correc. '84 : 165. — (E. P. Savage) Conf. char. & correc. '95 : 213. '97 : 317.
— Destitute. (John Hitz) Nat. Educa. Assoc. '79 : 217.
— — and neglected. (E. A. Hall) Conf. char. & correc. '99 : 177.
— — Care of. (J. M. Mulry) Conf. char. & correc. '99 : 166.
— Duties of. Channing. Works, 3 : 287.
— Employment of, in factories. Gibbins. Eng. soc. ref. 112.
  See Child labor.
— Essential studies for. (J. L. Pickard and others) Cong. Educa. Chic. '93 : 251.
— feeble-minded, Care and training of. (F. M. Powell) Conf. char. & correc. '87 : 250.

Children, " Food, fun, and fresh air for." (M. L. Molesworth) Burdett - Coutts. Wom. miss. 13.
— Growth of. (H. P. Bowditch) Mass. Health, '77 : 275. '79 (10th) : 35.
— — studied by Galton's method. Mass. Health, '90 : 479.
— Heights and weights of. (J. M. Greenwood) Am. Pub. Health, 17 : 199.
— Imagination of. Jacox, F. Cues, 310.
— in cities, Problem of. (J. H. Finley) Conf. char. & correc. '91 : 124.
— in factories. (H. K. Oliver) Mass. Labor, '71 : 487.
— — American and European laws on. Mass. Labor, '74 : 1.
— — Education of. (C. D. Wright) Mass. Labor, '75 : 1.
— — — Half-time system. (D. F. Lincoln) Mass. Labor, '78 : 11.
  See Child labor.
— in fiction. Repplier. Ess. in min. 144.
— in London schools, physical and mental condition of. (Francis Warner) U. S. Bur. Ed. Rept. '90-91 : 1081.
— Influence of, in homes, after institutional life. (F. H. Nibecker) Conf. char. & correc. '95 : 216.
— Institution *versus* home. (T. M. Mulry) Conf. char. & correc. '98 : 362.
— Institutions for. (L. P. Alden) Conf. char. & correc. '96 : 318.
— — Problems of. (W. A. Wheeler) Conf. char. & correc. '95 : 204.
— Interference of a municipality in behalf of its wards. (E. B. Bicknell) Conf. char. & correc. '98 : 375.
— Labor of. *See* Child labor.
— Language of. (F. Tracy) Cong. Educa. Chic. '93 : 737.
— Legal rights of. U. S. Bur. Ed. Circ. '80, no. 3. — (W. Addis) U. S. Bur. Ed. Rept. '96-97, 1 : 615.
— Life of, as portrayed by Goethe. Sanborn. Life of Goethe.
— Literature for. *See* Children, Books for.
— Little. Osgood, S. Amer. leaves, 11.
— Mental abnormalities in, occas. by erroneous school methods. Nat. Educa. Assoc. '98 : 162.
— Mental status as indicated by movements in. (F. Warner) Cong. Educa. Chic. '93 : 750.
— Ministering Children's League. Meath. Soc. arrows, 115.
— Mortality of. (S. Garuadiego) Am. Pub. Health, 22 : 309.
— Motor ability of. (J. A. Hancock) Nat. Educa. Assoc. '94 : 1003.
— Naughty. (E. E. Brown) Nat. Educa. Assoc. '99 : 564.
— Neglected. (J. Bone *et al.*) Trans. Soc. Sci. Lond. '80 : 378.
— — and delinquent, school for, Problems of. (W. A. Wheeler) Conf. char. & correc. '95 : 204.
— — Education of. (Mary Carpenter) Trans. Soc. Sci. Lond. '66 : 348. — (M. Carpenter *et al.*) Trans. Soc. Sci. Lond. '69 : 299. — (B. Lambert and A. W. Worthington) Trans. Soc. Sci. Lond. '71 : 342.
— — Reformation of. Boutwell. Educa. topics, 75.
— — Whose is the child ? Brownson. Works, 13 : 400.
— of our cities. (Mary E. McDowell) Nat. Educa. Assoc. '96 : 491.

Children of the state. (W. P. Letchworth) Conf. char. & correc. '86 : 138.
— Outcast. Montgomery, J. Prose, 1 : 87.
— Parents and. Bacon. Ess.
— Past and present. Repplier. Books, 1.
— pauper, Education of. (E. C. Tutnell and M. Carpenter) Trans. Soc. Sci. Lond. '63 : 278.
— — and dependent, Family homes for. (Mrs. C. T. Leonard) Conf. char. & correc. '79 : 170.
— Placing out. (F. M. Gregg) Conf. char. & correc. '92 : 415. — (L. P. Alden) Conf. char. & correc. '85 : 201.
— — Dangers of careless methods. (R. W. Hebberd) Conf. char. & correc. '99 : 171.
— — in the west. (H. H. Hart) Conf. char. & correc. '84 : 143.
— Play of. Stevenson, R. L. Virgin. 222.
— Poets for. Repplier. Ess. in idle. 33.
— Protection of. (M. M'Callum) Bosanquet. Asp. soc. 9 : 46.
— — in Europe. (H. C. Morris) U. S. Cons. Rept. 45 : 609.
— — in Michigan. (C. D. Randall) Conf. char. & correc. '89 : 5.
— Reading of. (R. W. Bullock) Nat. Educa. Assoc. '97 : 1015.
— Rearing of. Holland, J. G. Titcomb's let. 198.
— Religious education of. Laurie, S. S. Educa. addr. 106. — (D. F. Mullany) Barrows, J. H. Parl. relig. 1 : 759.
— Remedial work in behalf of. (M. McG. Dana) Conf. char. & correc. '95 : 230.
— Rescue and relief of. Conf. char. & correc. '96 : 314.
— Rights of. Siegvolk. Papers, 136.
— rights and duties of parents and, Legal. (F. J. Stimson) U. S. Lab. Bull. 2 : 569.
— Saving agencies for, State supervision of. (H. Folks) Conf. char. & correc. '95 : 209.
— — Problems of, in New York City. (C. L. Brace) Conf. char. & correc. '95 : 212.
— School, Anthropometry of Amer. (G. M. West) Cong. Anthrop. Chic. '93 : 50.
— School hours of. Higginson. Out-door, 77.
— State supervision of institutions for care of. (H. Folks) Conf. char. & correc. '95 : 209.
— Temporary homes for, in Conn. (Mrs. V. T. Smith) Conf. char. & correc. '85 : 210.
— Theological life of, in California. (E. Barnes) Cong. Educa. Chic. '93 : 765.
— Training of. (C. H. Dall) Brackett, A. C. Educa. of girls, 149. — Taylor. Notes from life, 90. — Hinsdale, B. A. Schools & stud. 33.
— under five years, Disabilities and mortality of. (C. N. Hewitt) Am. Pub. Health, 23 : 479.
— Very young. Friswell. Better self, 12.
— Wage-earning. (F. Kelley and A. P. Stevens) Hull-House maps, 49.
— What they know. (J. M. Greenwood) Nat. Educa. Assoc. '84 : 195.
— What they read. Repplier. Books, 64.
— Women's work for. (H. Smith) Burdett-Coutts. Wom. miss. 4.
— Working. Bosanquet, Mrs. Standard, 174. — (F. Kelley) Conf. char. & correc. '96 : 161.
— "Writing down to." Hill, G. B. Writers & readers, 186.
— young, Nourishment of. (A. Simard and others) Am. Pub. Health Assoc. 20 : 367.
Children's age, The. Repplier, A. In dozy hours, 190.
Children's interests. (M. V. O'Shea) Nat. Educa. Assoc. '96 : 873.
Children's love of nature. (W. A. Hoyt) Nat. Educa. Assoc. '94 : 1010.

Children's picture-books, New. Peck, H. T. Pers. equa. 193.
Children's Sundays. Butler, E. For furth. consid. 171.
Children's voices. (Linn Marie Hawn) Nat. Educa. Assoc. '95 : 790.
Childs, George W. Am. Antiq. Soc. Proc. n. s. 9 : 125. — Bolton, S. K. Poor boys, 313. — Derby, J. C. Fifty years, 333. — Parton, J. Sk. of men of prog. — Thayer, W. M. Turning points, 36.
Chile. Winsor. Hist. Amer. v. 2.
— Agricultural. Child, T. Span.-Amer. repub. 62.
— Baltimore affair ; Study in American diplomacy. Hart. Am. govt. 98.
— Coal-mining in. Child, T. Span.-Amer. repub. 139.
— Commercial directory of, 1891. Bur. Am. repub. no. 17.
— Financial conditions in, 1898. U. S. Cons. Rept. 58 : 321.
— Growing power of. (A. G. Browne, Jr.) Am. Geog. Soc. 16 : 1.
— History ; Bibliography. Hancock, A. U. Hist. Chile.
— in 1642. Burney. Voyages, v. 3. — Churchill. Voy. v. 1.
— its geography, people, and institutions. (J. Douglas) Am. Geog. Soc. 13 : 59.
— Urban and commercial. Child, T. Span.-Amer. repub. 101.
— War with Peru, 1879–81. Knox, T. W. Decisive battles. — U. S. For. rela. 1880–82.
Chillianwallah, Battle of. Adams, W. H. D. Engl. at war, 2 : 114. — Malleson, G. B. Battles of India, 379.
Chillingham castle. Edwardes, C. Hist. houses.
Chillingworth, William. (E. H. Plumptre) Barry, A. Masters theol. 113. — Stephen, J. F. Horæ Sabb. 1 : 187. — Tulloch. Rational theology.
Chilo, of Lacedæmon. Fénélon. Philosophers, 91.
Chilpancingo, Drinking waters of. (L. Viramontes) Am. Pub. Health, 18 : 118.
Chilton, Robert S. Derby, J. C. Fifty years, 640.
Chimay, Térézia, née Cabarrus. Challice. Illus. wom. 1.
Chimneys, Construction of. Internat. Health Ex. Sanita.
— Smoky, Cause and cure of. Franklin. Works (1887), 9 : 205.
Chimney-sweepers, The praise of. Lamb. Elia. — Smith, Syd. Ess. fr. Ed.
Chimpanzees. Morgan, C. L. Animal sk. 53 : 68.
China. (S. W. Williams) Am. Geog. Soc. 8 : 269. — Brooks, J. Seven months, 129. — Carnegie. Round the world, 75. — Coffin, C. C. New way round, 247. — Curtis, B. R. Dottings, 108. — De Quincey. Avenger, 143. — Field, H. M. Egypt to Japan, 365. — Fogg, W. P. Round the world, 88. — Hübner, J. A. Rambles, 445. — Kingsley, C. Round the world ('69), 2 : 21. — Leyland, R. W. Round the world in 124 days, 100. — Meignan, V. Paris to Pekin, 362. — Peebles, J. M. Around the world, 132. — Prime, E. D. G. Around the world, 132. — Pumpelly. Across America, 203. — Seward, W. H. Travels around, 39. — Simpson, W. Meeting the sun, 99. — Bridges, F. D. Lady's trav. 225. — Tuckermann, C. R. Recollec. 1 : 202.
— America's duty to. (W. A. P. Martin) Barrows, J. H. Parl. relig. 2 : 1137.

China among the great powers. Norman, H. Far East, 260.
— and the Chinese. Whitney, W. D. Orient, 2 : 52.
— and Great Britain, Relations of, 1857. De Quincey. Avenger (Bost.), 143.
— and its progress. (J. H. Wilson) Am. Geog. Soc. 20 : 401.
— and Japan, Brief visit to. Helms. Pioneering, 257.
— — Trade of, 1895. (T. R. Jernigan) U. S. Cons. Rept. 48 : 324.
— and the West. Whitney, W. D. Orient, 2 : 91.
— Bibliography. Providence Pub. Lib. Bull. Feb. '98.
— Corea, Japan. Bibliography. Bost. Pub. Lib. Bull. Jan. '95. — Salem (Mass.) Pub. Lib. Bull. Aug. '94. — Wilkesbarre (Pa.) Osterhout Free Lib. Nov. '94.
— Education in. (A. T. Smith) U. S. Bur. Ed. Rept. '97–98, 1 : 169.
— English in. De Quincey. Uncoll. wr. 2 : 7.
— Future of. Norman, H. Far East, 297.
— Geography of. Pumpelly. Amer. & As. 207.
— Government in. Johnson, S. Ori. relig. China, 265.
— Great Wall of. Norman, H. Far East, 211.
— Japanese influence on. Balfour, F. H. Waifs, 70.
— Manners and customs. Prime, E. D. G. Around world, 160.
— Marco Polo's travels in, 1270–1310. St. John. Cel. travelers, 1 : 30.
— Mistaken application of the ancient name Serica to. Latham. Opuscula, 89.
— National life of. Patterson, R. H. Ess. hist. 235.
— Origin of our political culture in the social life of. Nicol, D. Polit. life, 1 : 58.
— Political lessons of Chinese history. Temple, R. Orient. exper. 43.
— Population of. Temple, R. Cosmop. ess. 260.
— Possible increase of trade with, 1893. (J. A. Leonard) U. S. Cons. Rept. 42 : 295.
— Religions of. Bettany. World's relig. 102.— Brinton. Races & peo. 201.— Matheson. Distinc. mess. 61.— Prime, E. D. G. Around world, 173.— (J. Legge) Relig. systems, 61.
— Rival religious missions of. Balfour, F. H. Waifs, 113.
— State and religion in. Lyall. Asia, 122.
— Summer palace of. Cumming, C. F. G. Wand. in China, 2 : 317.
— Trade and industrial conditions in, 1896. (C. Denby) U. S. Cons. Rept. 51 : 317.
— U. S. trade in, 1899. (J. Fowler) U. S. Cons. Rept. 61 : 71.
— War with, 1840. Macaulay. Misc. & sp. 598. — Regnault. Crim. hist. Eng. govt. — Peel, R. Speeches, 3 : 721.
— — 1857–59. Cobden. Speeches, 370.
— Western policy in. Pumpelly. Amer. & As. 339.
China seas, In the. Abercromby. Seas & skies, 368.
Chinatown, San Francisco. Pidgeon. Engineer's holiday, 197.
Chinch-bugs, Propagation of diseases among. (F. H. Snow) Am. Pub. Health, 17 : 85.
Chinese, The. Norman, H. Far East, 276. — Pumpelly. Amer. & As. 247.
— American origin of. (C. W. Brooks) Cal. Acad. Sci. Proc. 6 : 95.
— Characteristics of. Brinton. Races & peo. 198.
— Immigration to U. S. Phillips, W. Speeches,

2 : 145. — Blaine. Polit. discus. 216. — Smith, R. M. Emigration. — Wharton, F. Digest internat. law. — Bancroft, H. H. Essays, 235. — Dixon, W. H. White conquest, 2 : 208.
Chinese in America. Pidgeon. Engineer's holiday, 197.
— in San Francisco. Hatton, J. To-day in Amer. 1 : 220. — Pierrepont. 5th ave. 45 : 99.
— Labor and mode of life of. Califor. Labor, '85–86.
— Life and customs of. Bancroft, H. H. Essays, 309.
— Time-keeping among (D. J. Magowan) Smithson. Rept. '91 : 607.
Chinese education. (S. L. Baldwin) Nat. Educa. Assoc. '86 : 211.
Chinese ethical system in Japan. Griffis. Relig. Japan, 99.
Chinese games with dice and dominoes. (Stewart Culin) U. S. Nat. Mus. Rept. '93 : 489.
Chinese insect white wax. (G. F. Smithers) U. S. Cons. Rept. 54 : 484.
Chinese labor. Iowa. Labor, '92–93 : 13.
— in Colorado. Colorado. Labor, '91–92 : 129.
Chinese language and literature. Johnson, S. Ori. relig. China, 395, 435.
Chinese mandarin at home. Cumming, C. F. G. Wand. in China, 1 : 250.
Chinese manners. Everett, A. H. Crit. ess. 408.
Chinese marriage, A. Lang. Leaders, 31.
Chinese New Year. Cumming, C. F. G. Wand. in China, 1 : 100.
Chinese secret societies. Balfour, F. H. Waifs, 23.
Chinese social life. Balfour, F. H. Waifs, 153.
Chinese theatre. Keating. With Grant, 210.
Chinon, France, Château of. Cook, T. D. Old Touraine, 1 : 29. — Larned, W. C. Churches & C. 146.
Chintreuil, Antoine. Ewart, H. C. Toilers in art, 137. — Hamerton. Portfo. pap. 102.
Chios. Tozer. Isl. Ægean, 139.
Chipmunk, The. Burroughs, J. Riverby, 145.
Chippewa, Battle of. Dawson. Batt. of U. S. 2 : 348.
Chisholm, Caroline. Darton. Fam. girls, 247. — With portrait. Fifty famous women, 152. — Smiles. Brief biog. 511.
Chisholm, Julian J. Davidson, J. W. Writ. of South, 87.
Chisholm, Walter Scott. Am. Bar Assoc. 14 : 414.
Chiswick House. Balch, E. Old Eng. homes, 130.
Chitral. Younghusband. Heart of cont. 352.
Chittenden, Thomas. Lossing. Em. Amer. 125.
Chitwood, M. Louisa. Coggeshall. Poets of west, 628.
Chivalry. Cleveland, R. E. Eliot, 155. — Hallam. Eur. in mid. ages, v. 3. — Heckethorn. Sec. soc. 1 : 155. — Rands. Chaucer's Eng. 1 : 110. — Scott, W. Ess. on chiv. 1. — Sterling, J. Ess. 1 : 111. — Stillé. Stud. med, 332. — Turner, S. Eng. in mid. ages, 1 : 454.
— Days of. Cutts, E. L. Scenes mid. ages, 353.
— Essay on. Morte d'Arthur, Strachey's edition.
— Heroes of. Grube, A. W. Heroes.
— Is it still possible? Buchanan, R. Coming terr. 183.
— of the middle ages. Schlegel. Æsthet. (Bohn) 309.
— of the period. Cobbe, F. P. Re-echoes, 152.
— Romances of. Ticknor. Span. lit. 1 : 218.
See also Knights.
Chloroform. Timbs. Doctors, 259.

Chlorophyll. (G. C. Caldwell) N. Y. Regents, 93 : 585.

Chlorosis, Necessity for establishing sanitariums for treatment of. (J. E. Monjaras) Am. Pub. Health, 21 : 277.

Choate, Rufus. Boutwell. Lawyer, 1. — Bungay. Off-hand, 167. — With portrait. Duyckinck. Nat. portr. gall. 2 : 253. — Everett. Orat. v. 4. — Loring, J. S. 100 Bost. ora. 588. — Maury, S. M. Statesm. of Amer. 98. — Whipple. Ess. & rev. v. 2. — Whipple. Recoll. 1. — Brown, I. Stud. gt. lawyers, 357. — Congdon, C. T. Trib. ess. 102. — Mathews, W. Oratory, 365. — With portrait. (C. H. Hill) Mass. Hist. Soc. Proc. 2d ser. 11 : 124. — (J. B. D. Coggswell) N. E. Hist. Gen. Soc. Biog. 3 : 383. — Perry, B. F. Biog. sketches, 1 : 506. — With portrait. Scott, H. W. Dist. Am. lawy. 143. — Richardson. Amer. lit. 1 : 233. — With portrait. (A. Stickney) Warner Lib. 6 : 3649.

— College life of. (E. P. Whipple) Parton. Princes, 277.

— His lecture on Rogers and his times. Lunt. Three eras, 249.

— Lawyer and orator. Bungay. Repr. men, 212.

Chocolate. Cozzens. Bushwhacker, 20.

Chodowiecki, D. N., the Berlin Hogarth. Dobson, A. 18th cent. vign. 211.

Chœrilus of Iasus, and Chœrilus of Samos. Arnold, E. Poets of Greece, 165.

Choice. Ess. from Sat. R. 318.

Choir, New England village. Gilman, S. Contrib. 3.

Choiseul, Etienne François, Duc de. Crowe, E. E. For. statesmen, 5 : 217.

Choiseul Gouffier, M. G. A. L. St. John. Cel. travelers, 3 : 154.

Choisy, L'Abbé de. Ste.-Beuve. Portr. of men, 172.

Cholderton, Wiltshire, England, Church at. Mozley. Reminis. 2 : 162.

Cholera. (W. R. Cluness) Calif. Health, '82–'83 : 81.

— and quarantine. (J. H. Rauch) Am. Pub. Health, 13 : 242.

— and U. S. Marine hospital service. (W. Wyman) Am. Pub. Health, 18 : 334.

— Asiatic. (S. W. Abbott) Mass. Health, '84 : 317.

— — in Japan. Arnold, E. Seas & l. 474.

— — Origin and spread of. (J. C. Peters) Am. Pub. Health, 1 : 336.

— Aspects of, in Europe and elsewhere. Internat. Health Ex. Sanita.

— Bacillus of. (A. M. Bleile) Ohio Health, '92 : 368.

— Bibliography. Bost. Pub. Lib. Bull. Oct. '92.

— Causes and preventive measures. (E. Harris) Am. Pub. Health, 1 : 343.

— Coast defences against, in U. S. (J. H. Rauch) Am. Pub. Health, 11 : 125. — Ill. Health, '85 : 19.

— Contagiousness of. Bigelow. J. Mod. inq. 287.

— dead by, Disposal of. (W. F. McLean) Ohio Health, '92 : 343.

— Defence of Mexico against. (E. Liceaga) Am. Pub. Health, 18 : 240.

— Epidemic of 1832. Mansfield, E. D. Pers. mem. 254.

— hospital for, Plan of. (W. Marsden) Am. Pub. Health, 1 : 184.

— in Hull, Eng. (J. W. Mason) Am. Pub. Health, 19 : 25.

— in Russia, 1892. (J. M. Crawford) U. S. Cons. Rept. 40 : 412.

Cholera in St. Louis, History of. (R. Moore) Am. Pub. Health, 10 : 337.

— in the U. S., 1873. (C. B. White et al.) Am. Pub. Health, 1 : 188.

— Local measures to be adopted against. (S. Smith) Am. Pub. Health, 1 : 306.

— Nature, causes, and prevention of. (S. P. Wise) Ohio Health, '87 : 276.

— Power of Congress to prevent importation of. Sumner. Works, 10 : 435.

— Practical conclusions on. (S. P. Wise) Ohio Health, '92 : 331.

— Prevention of. Internat. Health Ex. Sanita.

— — and restriction of. N. H. Health, '92 : 17.

— Refuge from pestilence. Van Santvoord, C. Disc. 123.

— Relations of rain-fall and water supply to. (H. B. Baker) Am. Pub. Health, 11 : 154.

— State's duty in preventing. (B. Stanton) Ohio Health, '92 : 349.

— vs. marine hospital service. (W. Wyman) Am. Pub. Health, 18 : 334.

— Water-supplies as carriers of. (E. T. Nelson) Ohio Health, '92 : 356.

— What we can do against. (M. Von Pettenkofer) Am. Pub. Health, 1 : 317.

Cholera infantum ; its treatment. (M. Septien) Am. Pub. Health, 19 : 39.

Chopin, Frederic F. Engel, L. Mozart, 1 : 111. — Bourne, C. E. Gt. compos. 267. — Ehlert. Tone-world, 265. — Ferris. Germ. compos. 157. — Finck. Chopin, 3. — Haweis. Music & mor. 249. — Keddie. Mus. comp. 345. — Hueffer. Mus. stud. 29. — Dole, N. H. Score, 400. — Elson, L. Gt. composers, 154. — Sharp, R. F. Makers of music. — Hadow. Stud. mod. mus. v. 2. — Lenz. Gt. piano virtuosos, 27. — With portrait. Bie, O. Hist. of piano, 255. — Rowbotham, J. F. Great compos. 173. — Statham. Music, 329.

— and piano music. Butterworth. Great compos. 84.

— Bibliography. Paterson (N. J.) Free Lib. Bull. Feb.–Mar. '97.

Chores. Martin, E. S. Cousin Anthony, 41.

Chotusitz, Battle of. Carlyle. Batt. Fred. the Gt. 25.

Christ. See Jesus Christ.

"**Christ** and Satan," Poem of. Brooke, S. A. Hist. early Eng. lit. 325.

Christ Church, Dublin, State vault of. Cobbe, F. P. Hours of work, 173.

Christchurch Priory. Timbs. Abbeys, 1 : 415.

Christ's Hospital, A day at. Mathews. Men & bks, 327.

Christ's Hospital school, London. Staunton, H. Schools, 442.

Christendom, Creed of, Greg's. Martineau, J. Studies, 266.

— Reunion of. (P. Schaff ; W. H. Fremantle) Barrows, J. H. Parl. relig. 2 : 1192.

— versus Christianity. Curtis, G. W. Other Ess. 216.

Christian IX., King of Denmark, with portrait. Crowned heads, 29.

— and family. (C. Steen de Bille) Parton. Princes, 112.

Christian, Bishop of Prussia. Maclear. Apostles, 264.

Christian, Edmund B. B. Miles, A. H. Poets of cent. 9 : 533.

Christian, The, and the state. Potter, H. C. Scholar & state, 251.

— How to become a. Beecher. New star papers, 304.

Christian, The polite. Butler, E. For good, 178.
Christian character, Evangelistic power of. Finlayson, T. C. Ess. 236.
— Formation of. Ware, H., jr. Works, 4 : 283.
— its own vindication. Manning, J. M. Sermons, 225.
Christian Citizenship League, A. (A. G. Lawson) Nat. Conf. City Govt. '96 : 275.
Christian civilization, Characteristics of. Bayne, P. Ess. 2 : 259.
Christian comprehension, Schemes of. (H. B. Wilson) Oxf. ess. '57 : 94.
Christian comprehensiveness. Bushnell. Building eras, 387.
Christian consciousness, Apologetical value of. (W. F. Warren) Bost. lectures, '72 : 67.
Christian doctrine, Development of. Brownson. Works, 14 : 1.
— history of, Hist. method of writing. (C. J. Little) Am. Hist. Assoc. Rept. '93 : 69.
Christian duty, Theory of. Davies, J. L. Theol. & mor. 41.
Christian Endeavor Societies and better citizenship. (J. W. Baer) Nat. Conf. City Govt. 2-3 : 517.
Christian Evidences. Whedon. Ess. 2 : 168.
Christian experience an argument for Christianity. (Dr. Cairns) Living Papers, 11 : no. 11.
Christian faith, Divine supremacy of. Ellinwood. Orient. relig. & chr. 338.
— Five points of. Martineau, J. Studies, 177.
Christian fidelity, God's witness to. Beecher. New star papers, 322.
Christian hymn, The first. Davis, J. S. Stud. mus. 18.
Christian life and work in the middle ages. Trench. Lec. mediæval, 411.
— Higher, Doctrine of. Hovey, A. Stud. in ethics, 344.
— in 2d & 3d centuries. Lightfoot. Hist. ess. 1.
Christian literature. Porter, N. Books, 111.
— Societies for producing and circulating. Cust. Ling. & orient. ess. 4 : 521.
Christian ministering. Macdonald, G. Orts, 298.
Christian ministry. See Ministry.
Christian optimism. Stephen, J. F. Ess. by barr. 114.
Christian peoples and non-Christian, Intercourse of. Thompson, J. P. Amer. com. 104.
Christian perfection. Whedon. Ess. 2 : 330.
Christian practice. Holland, J. G. Every-day, 1 : 152.
Christian progress, Measuring lives of. Newton, W. W. Ess. 164.
Christian religion and the common law. (P. E. Aldrich) Am. Antiq. Soc. Proc. n. s. 6 : 18.
— Greek philosophy and. (E. M. Müller) Barrows, J. H. Parl. relig. 2 : 935.
— History and effects of. Godwin, W. Ess. 175.
Christian scholar, Position of the. Barnes, A. Miscel. 2 : 96.
Christian science and mind cure. Hovey, A. Stud. in ethics, 71.
Christian system, The. Schopenhauer. Relig. 103.
Christian thought and Hindu thought. (R. A. Hume) Barrows, J. H. Parl. relig. 2 : 1269.
Christian truth, Growth in. Gladden. Ruling ideas, 1.
Christian union. Schaff, P. Christ & Christianity, 292. — Stanley. Essays, 5. — Thomson, E. Essays, 58.
— Bibliography. Huntington, W. R. A national church.

Christian union, Döllinger on. Church, R. W. Occ. pap. 1 : 367.
— The true symbol of. Hodgson. Outcast, 183.
Christian unity, Denominational Christianity and. Schaff, P. Christ & Chr'y, 292.
— Grounds of. Farrar. Sermons in Am. 269.
Christian Worship. Hahn - Hahn. Fathers, 13.
Christiana. Atkinson, J. B. Art tour northern, 82.
Christianity. Bettany. World's relig. 687. — Blackie, J. S. Four phases, 190. — Conway, M. D. Idols, 5. — Grant, G. M. Relig. 183, — (E. Renan ; in French) Hundred greatest men, 149. — Laing, S. Problems, 190.
— Amateur. Mallock. Stud. contemp. sup. 94.
— an experimental science. Patmore. Religio poetæ, 39.
— and ancient Paganism. (J. M. Mitchell) Liv. papers, v. 9.
— and art. Oxenham. Stud. in eccl. hist. 1.
— and the body. Caldwell, S. L. Cities of faith, 328.
— and civilization. Dods, M. Erasmus, 266.
— and the common law. Anderson, M. B. Papers, 2 : 171.
— and common sense. Hole, S. R. Addresses, 13.
— and letters. Newman, J. H. Lec. univ. 1.
— and the life that now is. (W. G. Blaikie) Liv. Papers, v. 1.
— and literature. Brooke, S. A. Hist. early Eng. lit. 189.
— and medical science. Newman, J. H. Lec. univ. 366.
— and Mohammedanism. (G. Washburn) Barrows, J. H. Parl. relig. 1 : 565.
— and other Religions. Matheson. Distinc. mess. 327.
— and our country. Anderson, M. B. Papers, 1 : 252.
— and physical science. Newman, J. H. Lec. univ. 221.
— and politics. (W. J. H. Campion) Gore, C. Lux mundi, 437.
— and popular amusements. Gladden. Appl. Chris. 248.
— and popular education. Gladden. Appl. Chris. 284.
— and " progress." Patmore. Religio poetæ, 57.
— and " the religion of the future." Finlayson, T. C. Ess. 36.
— and the Roman emperors. Grube, A. W. Heroes, 15.
— and science. Holland, J. G. Every-day 1 : 131. — Oxenham. Stud. in eccl. hist. 1.
— and scientific investigation. Newman, J. H. Lec. univ. 262.
— and secularism compared. (W. G. Blaikie) Liv. papers, v. 2.
— and social organization. Blackie. Ess. 1.
— and social science. Gladden. Appl. Chris. 210.
— The argument for. (N. Porter) Bost. lectures, '70 : 340.
— as an organ of political movement. De Quincey. Theo. ess. Bost. 1 : 1.
— as historical religion. (G. P. Fisher) Barrows, J. H. Parl. relig. 2 : 832.
— as history, doctrine, and life. (N. Porter) Liv. Papers, v. 4.
— as interpreted by literature. (T. T. Munger) Barrows, J. H. Parl. relig. 1 : 677.
— as seen by a voyage around the world. (F. E. Clark) Barrows, J. H. Parl. relig. 2 : 1237.
— as a social force. (R. T. Ely) Barrows, J. H. Parl. relig. 2 : 1056.

Christmas, A royal, in the 15th century. Gasquet, F. A. Old Eng. Bible, 226.
— Thoughts about, in Rome. Symonds. Sk. So. Eur. 1 : 275.
Christmas carols, On some. Dempster. Ess. 352.
Christmas customs. Cozzens. Bushwhacker, 174.
Christmas dinner, Versailles, 1870. Kingston, W. B. Men, etc. 53.
Christmas eve. Mabie. My study fire, 35.
— Festival of. Oxenham. Stud. in eccl. hist. 191.
Christmas sentiments. Martin, E. S. Windfalls, 263.
Christmas sermon, A. Stevenson, R. L. Across plains, 302.
Christmastide, Odd experiences of. Arnold, F. Arm-chair, 179.
Christmas-time in India. Arnold, E. Wand. words, 161.
Chroniclers, Early American. Bancroft, H. H. Essays, 1.
— English; first sources of modern history. Disraeli, I. Amen. (N. Y. 2 v.) 1 : 269.
Chronicles, Spanish. Ticknor. Span. lit. 1 : 156.
Chronology. Joyce, J. Fam. introd. to arts, 92.
— Ancient. Nott and Gliddon. Types, 653.
— Books on. Harv. Univ. Bull. 2 : 341.
— Egyptian. Lepsius. Let. from Egypt.
— Greek Legendary. Grote. Hist. of Greece, 2 : 34.
— — Newton's. Gibbon. Miscel. works, 3 : 150.
— Gregorian calendar. Bailey, S. Discourses, 129.
— Hebrew, from Moses to Solomon. Hadley, J. Ess. 385.
— of the human period. (J. W. Davis) Smithson. Rept. '88 : 583.
— Theoretical. Huxley. Ess. contro. 53.
Chrysippus. Mills. Poets of Greece, 429.
Chrysoloras, Manuel. Symonds. Reviv. of learn. 108.
Chrysostom, St., bishop of Constantinople. Portrait. Blakey, R. Prim. fathers, 211. — Broadus. Lec. hist. preach. 73. — Cave. Lives of fathers, 3 : 237. — Farrar. Lives of fathers, 2 : 460. — Kingsley. Hermits, 155. — Lord, J. Beacon, 1 : 279. — Ker, J. Lec. hist. preach. 65, 76. — (J. T. Kingsmill) Lefroy, W. Lec. eccl. hist. 141. — (J. Malone) Warner Lib. 6 : 3665. — Wilson, Wm. Pop. preach. anc. ch. 239.
— and Augustine. Williams, W. R. Eras, 69.
— Last years of. Newman, J. H. Hist. sk. 2 : 217.
Chrystal, George. Barrie. Edinburgh eleven, 65.
Chrystler's Farm, Battle at. Dawson. Batt. of U. S. 2 : 305.
Chubb & Son. Japp & Holmes. Succ. bus. men, 193.
Chudleigh, Lady Mary. Williams, Jane. Lit. wom. 143.
Chunder Sen, Keshub, Lectures of. Müller. Chips, 4.
Church, Benjamin. Loring, J. S. 100 Bost. ora. 37. — Lossing. Em. Amer. 12.
Church, Frederick E. Sheldon, G. W. Amer. painters, 10. — Tuckerman. Artists, 370.
Church, George E., with portrait. Bartlett, J. R. R. I. officers, 293.
Church, Leonard. Livingston, J. Hist. Amer. 72.
Church, Pearson. Am. Bar Assoc. 21 : 700.
Church, R.W. With photo. Cooper, T. Men of mark, 6 : 11. — Em. persons, 4 : 311. — Hutton, R. H. Criticisms, 1 : 221. — Stead. Char. sk. 109.
Church, Sir Richard. Church, R. W. Occ. pap. 2 : 327.

Church, Samuel. Livingston, J. Em. Am. Lawy. 55. — (G. H. Hollister) N. E. Hist.-Gen. Soc. Biog. 2 : 240.
Church, The. Arnold, T. Miscel. 9. — (W. Lock) Gore, C. Lux mundi, 365. — Ullman. Reformers, 122.
— against no church. Brownson. Works, 5 : 331.
— American and primitive. Bacon, L. W. Irenics, 225.
— and the age. Greeley. Hints ref. 385.
— and the bar. Lorimer, Jas. Studies, nat'l & internat.
— and Christianity identical. Brownson. Works, 12 : 59.
— and the common people. (F. D. Huntington) Evang. Alliance, '89 : 205.
— and the democratic idea. (C. L. Marson) Reid, A. New party, 73.
— and dissent. Hole, S. R. Addresses, 298.
— and the masses. Strong, J. New era, 203.
— and modern civilization. Brownson. Works, 12 : 117.
— and political reforms. Commons, J. R. Soc. reform, 71.
— and the problem of poverty. Commons, J. R. Soc. reform, 29.
— and the revolutionary idea. Brownson. Works, 11 : 468.
— and science. Sewall, F. New metaphys. 145.
— and socialism. Vaughan, D. J. Questions, 251.
— and society, Relation of. Hudson. Studies Wordsworth, 313.
— and state. Arnold, T. Lec. on hist. 64, 261. — Brownson. Works, 12 : 216. 13 : 263, 303, 430. — Coleridge, H. Ess. 2 : 355. — Froude. Hist. Eng. ch. 4. — Gladstone. Glean. 5 : 173. 7 : 97. — Lea. Stud. ch. hist. 55 : 316. — Martineau, J. Ess. '91, 2 : 1. — Martineau, J. Miscel. 105. — Mill, J. S. Dissert. v. 1. — Vaughan, R. Ess. 2 : 172. — (T. Raleigh) Faith & crit. essays. — Hunt, J. Rel. thought 19th cent. 56. — (M. Creighton) Oxf. Ho. papers, 3 : 31. — Mazzini. Ess. 107.
— — Connection of. Stanley. Essays, 8.
— — Gladstone on. Burnap. Miscel. — Macaulay. Ess. 4 : 116.
— — in America. (D. H. Greer) Evang. Alliance, '89 : 195.
— — in England, History of connection of. Croly. Hist. sk. 310.
— — in France. Brownson. Works, 12 : 439.
— — in Russia. Wallace. Russia.
— — in the U. S. (P. Schaff) Am. Hist. Assoc. 2 : 385.
— — Separation of. Brownson. Works, 12 : 406.
— — Union of. Brownson. Works, 13 : 127.
— Anglo-American. Newman, J. H. Ess. int. 1 : 308.
— as a teacher of morality. Seeley, J. R. Rom. imp. 259 ; or Lec. & ess. 245.
— as it was, is, and ought to be. Brownson. Works, 7 : 179.
— The broad. Stephen, L. Ess. freeth. 1.
— Catholic and primitive. Thompson, H. M. Copy, 201.
— Constitution of. Brownson. Works, 8 : 527.
— Construction of. Ruskin. Miscel. v. 2.
— Early, Organization of. Moxom. Jerus. to Nicæa, 52.
— The enlarged. Swing. Old pic. 1 : 201.
— Episcopal Observer vs. Brownson. Works, 5 : 389.
— Five theories of. Bacon, L. W. Irenics, 239.
— a historical fact. Brownson. Works, 5 : 457.

Church property. Mill. Early ess. 161; same in Mill, J. S. Dissert. (N. Y.) **1** : 28.
— and secularization, 1867. De Vere. Ess. 197.
— Exemption of. Hazard, T. R. Miscel. 136, 242.
— Mass. Tax Comm'rs Rept. 1875.
— Tenure of, in New York. Putnam, J. O. Addresses, 9.
Church rates. Blunt. Ess. 440. — Peel, R. Speeches, **3** : 373, 414. — Thirlwall, C. Remains, **1** : 231, 347.
Church reform, Principles of. Arnold, T. Miscel. 75.
Church sittings. Dodge, M A Stumbl, 82.
Church unity. Maurice, F. D. Theol. ess. 382.
— and social amelioration. Brownson. Works, **4** : 512.
Churches, American, The period of constitution-making in. (W. P. Trent) Jameson, J. F. Ess. const. hist. 186.
— and clergy in the U. S. Bryce. Soc. institu. 92.
— Battle of. Martineau, J. Miscel. 373; or Essays ('90), **2** : 119.
— English parish. (J. H. Micklethwaite) Poole, R. S. Lec. art, 97.
— Mismanaging. Thompson, H. M. Copy, 110.
— Mission of the. (Dean of Winchester) Reid, A. New party, 55.
— New England, Future of. Eliot, C. W. Five Am. contrib. 347.
Churchill, Arabella. Jesse. Court of Eng. Stuarts, **3** : 510.
Churchill, Charles. Chalmers. Eng. poets, **14** : 265. — Forster, J. Hist. ess. **2** : 209. — Hannay. Satire, 130. — Hitchman. 18th cent. 101.
Churchill, John, bookseller. Curwen. Booksellers, 339.
Churchill, John, Duke of Marlborough. *See* Marlborough.
Churchill, Lord Randolph. Smalley. Lond. let. **1** : 161, 362.
Churchyard, Thomas. Bell, R. Lit. & sci. men, **2** : 110. — Holland, J. Psalmists, **1** : 131. — Minto, W. Eng. poets, 159. — Morley, H. Eng. writ. **8** : 242.
Churchyards. Boyd. Retreat, **2** : 96.
Churton, Edward. Mozley. Reminis. **1** : 63. — Miller, Jos. Singers church, 2d ed. 463.
Ciachorius, George. Wallace, R. Anti-Trin. biog. **3** : 247.
Ciachorius, John. Wallace, R. Anti-Trin. biog. **3** : 141.
Cibber, Colley. Austin & Ralph. Laureates, 246. — Doran. Annals stage, **2** : 15. — Dunham. Lit. & sci. men, **3** : 276. — Galt. Players, **1** : 125. — Russell, W. Rep. actors, 43. — Crawford, O. Eng. com. dram. 109. — Hamilton, Wal. Poets laur. — Mitford, M. R. Recollec. 260.
— and his associates. Baker, H. B. Engl. actors, **1** : 74.
— Apology for his own life. Talfourd. Crit. wr.
Cibber, Susanna Maria. Doran. Annals stage, **2** : 66.
Cibber, Theophilus. Goldsmith. Misc. (N. Y. 4 v.) **1** : 369.
Cibdareal, F. G. de. Ticknor. Span. lit. **3** : 397. **1** : 395.
Cicero. Alger. Solitudes, 208. — Brougham. Works, **7** : 145. — De Quincey. Hist. ess. (Bost.) **2** : 1. — Harsha. Orators, 35. — Lamartine. Cel. char. **1** : 335. — Lord, J. Beacon, **1** : 173. — Dunlop, J. Rom. liter. **2** : 218. — Hundred greatest men, 273. — Vincent, G. E. Ital. authors, 25. — With portrait. (W. C. Lawton) Warner Lib. **7** : 3675.

Cicero and his writings. Malkin. Class. disq. 248.
— Forsyth's life of. Lucas. Mornings, **1** : 82.
— on government. Everett, A. H. Crit. ess. 338.
— Personal and literary character of. Newman, J. H. Hist. sk. **1** : 245.
— Philosophical writings of. Hallam. Remains, 227.
— Pro Cluentio. Nettleship. Lec. & ess.
— Republic of. Legaré. Writ. **2** : 216.
Cicovius, Stanislaus. Wallace, R. Anti-Trin. biog. **2** : 212.
Cid, The. Hewlett. Heroes, 41. — Quintana. Lives Span. 3. — Sismondi. Lit. So. Eur. v. 3. — Ticknor. Span. lit. **1** : 12. — (C. S. Smith) Warner Lib. **7** : 3725.
— epitomized. Dobson, W. T. Class. poets, 95.
Cider making in France, 1896. (C. W. Chancellor) U. S. Cons. Rept. **51** : 576.
Cider songs and customs, English. (Mrs. S. Burgess) Walters, J. C. Bygone Som. 122.
Cieco da Ferrara. *See* Bello, Francesco.
Cigarmaking. Tenement-house in N. Y. City. N. Y. Bur. Lab. '95 : 545.
Cimabue, Giov. Lee, H. F. Old painters, 37. — Symonds. Renais. fine arts, 187. — Jameson. Ital. painters, 7. — Ottley. Ital. school. — Stillman, W. J. Old Ital. mas. 8. — Jervis, Lady. Painting, **1** : 63.
Cimarosa, Domenico. Ferris, G. T. Ital. & Fr. compos. 42. — Hogarth. Mem. Opera, **2** : 103.
Cimbri, The, and the Chersonesus Cimbrica. Latham. Opuscula, 93.
— Rome and. Lord, J. Anc. states, 499.
— A visit to. Howells. Ital. jour. 235.
Cinchona. *See* Quinine.
Cincinnati, Ohio. Brooks, E. S. Gt. Cities, 108.
— Warner, C. D. Studies, 263.
— College. Mansfield, E. D. Pers. mem. 287.
— College of teachers. Mansfield, E. D. Pers. mem. 267.
— Early newspapers of. Mansfield, E. D. Pers. mem. 291.
— Municipal condition of. (C. B. Wilby) Nat. conf. city. govt. **2-3** : 313.
— Observatory. Mansfield, E. D. Pers. mem. 307.
— Social life in, 1826. Mansfield, E. D. Pers. mem. 185.
Cincinnati, Society of. Franklin. Works, '87, **8** : 438. — McMaster. Hist. U. S. **1** : 167. — Muzzey, A. B. Prime movers, 186.
— Draft of orig. articles. Col. Soc. Mass. Trans. **1** : 239.
Cinna, Character of. Malkin. Class. disq. 317.
Cino da Pistoja. Symonds. Renais. It. lit. **1** : 65.
Cinque ports, The. Rimmer, A. Country towns, 166.
Cinthio, Giraldi. Symonds. Renais. It. lit. **2** : 103, 131.
Circle, Squaring the. Proctor. Light sci. **1** : 288.
— (Herman Schubert) Smithson. Rept. '90 : 97.
Circles. Emerson. Ess. **1** : 279.
Circourt, Comte Adolphe de, and his friends. Belloc, Mme. Walled garden, 270.
— Historical conclusions. Mass. Hist. Proc. **15** : 16.
Circuit anecdotes of 18th century. Jeaffreson. Lawyers, 104.
Circuit notes in Ireland. Curran. Irish bar, **1** : 264.
Circumnavigation of the globe, First. Frost, T. Explorers, 69.

Civics, What to teach in fundamental. (S. F. Scovel) Nat. Educa. Assoc. '99 : 616.

Civil government as a science and a study. (W. K. Wickes) N. Y. Regents, 97 : app. 48.

— Resistance to. (H. D. Thoreau) Peabody, E. P. Æsthetic pap. 189.

— Teaching of. (F. A. Hill) Nat. Educa. Assoc. '91 : 657.

Civil law under socialism. Bax. Relig. of socialism, 146.

— as translated in Louisiana. (T. J. Semmes) Am. Bar Assoc. 5 : 243.
See Law, Civil.

Civil polity; duty of Christians and ministers. Hall, R. Miscel. 122.

Civil rights bill. Black, J. S. Ess. & sp. 539. — Sumner. Works, 14 : 355.

Civil service, Appointments for women in. (W. C. Taylor) Trans. Soc. Sci. Lond. '79 : 650.

— Appointments in England. (H. Mann) Trans. Soc. Sci. Lond. '60 : 302.

— Bibliography. Bost. Lib. Bull. 5 : 120. — Prov. Ref. lists, 3 : 1. — U. S. Civ. Ser. 15th Rept. 1898.

— Competitive examination for. (A. Bain ; C. S. Parker) Trans. Soc. Sci. Lond. '77 : 334. — (H. Mann) Trans. Soc. Sci. Lond. '58 : 200. '59 : 274. — (Sir S. Northcote) Trans. Soc. Sci. Lond. '59 : 279. — Bain, A. Prac. ess. 71. — (R. R. Bowker) Econ. tracts, no. 22.

— in England. Rosebery. Apprec. 207.

— in France and Prussia, Schools and requirements for. (W. F. and W. W. Willoughby) U. S. Bur. Ed. Rept. '91–92 : 369.

— in the United States ; Uncle Sam's treatment of his servants. Parton. Topics, 1.

— of states and cities, competitive test for. (E. M. Shepard) Econ. tracts, no 14.

— — Reform of. Morton, O. P. So. Empire, 115.

— University education for. (O. Browning) Internat. health exh. 15 : 191.

Civil service reform. Am. citizen's manual, 116.
— Garfield. Works, 1 : 499. — Stickney. True repub. — (Mrs. C. R. Lowell) Conf. char. & correc. '98 : 256.

— and public schools. (H. R. Waite) Nat. Educa. Assoc. '85 : 122.

— Finance and. Johnston, A. Amer. ora. 4 : 273.

— in England [1780]. Burke. Works (Bohn), 2 : 55.

— in the U. S. ; Do the people wish it ? Hart. Am. govt. 81.

— Presidential elections and. Sumner, W. G. Essays, 140.

— Relation of public schools to. (George William Curtis) Nat. Educa. Assoc. '91 : 481.

— Six years of. Roosevelt, T. Amer. ideals, 134.

Civilization. Brinton. Races & peo. 288. — Elder, W. Questions, 26. — Emerson. Society & sol. — Mill, J. S. Dissert. N. Y. 1 : 186. — Bancroft, G. Miscel. — Smith, Syd. Occ. ess. 1 : 107. — Walsh, J. B. Astron. & geol. 119.

— American. Emerson. Miscel.

— Ancient. Kingsley, C. Lec. Amer. 125; *or* Hist. lec. 289.

— — and modern. Perry. Biog. sk. 217.

— and barbarism. Higginson. Out-door papers.

— and culture. Martin, E. S. Cousin Anthony, 119.

— and decay, Adams on. Roosevelt, T. Amer. ideals, 329.

— and material progress. Harrison, F. Choice of books, 420.

— Barbarisms of. Newman, F. W. Miscel. 3 : 449.

Civilization, Characteristics of. (E. H. Dickson) Charleston book, 70.

— A Christian. (L. T. Chamberlain) Evang. Alliance, '89 : 184. — Maurice. Friendship, 125.

— Christianity and. Lange. Materialism, 3 : 269.

— Curse of. Bax. Ethics of socialism, 106.

— First constituents of. Lieber, C. Miscel. 1.

— History of, Buckle's. Fiske, J. Darwin, 130.
— Pattison. Ess. 2 : 396.

— — Semitic contributions to. Renan. Studies (N. Y.), 1 : 149.

— — Studies in. (A. D. White) Am. Hist. Assoc. 1 · 17.

— in ancient Mexico. Bancroft, H. H. Essays, 26.

— Influence of commerce on. Millar. Eng. govt. 4 : 102.

— Influence of science on. Draper. Conflict of religion and science.

— influences of, Uncivilizing. Alexander, J. M. Isl. Pac. 30.

— Jewish contributions to. (D. G. Lyon) Barrows, J. H. Parl. relig. 2 : 817.

— of future, Relations of Bible to. (Austin Phelps) Bost. lectures, '71 : 11.

— Origin of. Brownson. Works, 9 : 418.

— Process of. Dole, C. F. Theol. of civiliz. 231.

— Progress of, in England. (Sir J. K. Shuttleworth) Trans. Soc. Sci. Lond. '59 : 122.

— — westward. Bancroft, H. H. Essays, 39.

— Relation between it and Christianity. Dods, M. Erasmus, 266.

— Roman Cath. church and. Brownson. Works, v. 12. — Draper. Conflict relig. & sci.

— Ultimate. Taylor, I. Ult. civiliz. 1.

— Watchword of. Thomson, H. M. Copy, 352.

Civitali, Matteo di Giovanni. Perkins, C. C. Tusc. sculp. 1 : 214. — Symonds. Renais. fine arts, 156.

Clack, Mrs. Marie Louise. Davidson, J. W. Writ. of South, 88. — Raymond, I. Southland wr. 1 : 378.

Claflin, Horace B., with portrait. Stoddard, W. O. Men of hist. 212.

Claiborne, John F. H. Davidson. J. W. Writ. of South, 90.

Claiborne, William Charles Cole. Lossing. Em. Amer. 358. — With portrait. Nat. portr. gall. 4. — Sparks, W. H. Memories, 424.

Clairon, Hippolyte. Houssaye. Men of 18th cent. 2 : 392. — Men & wom. of France, 3 : 255.

— and the French stage. Hawkins. Fr. stage 18th cent. v. 1.

Clairvoyance. Mason, R. O. Telepathy, 74.

— denied. Bowen, F. Gleanings, 345.

— Evidence for. (Mrs. H. Sidgwick) Soc. Psych. Res. 7 : 30.

— Experiments in. (A. Backman) Soc. Psych. Res. 7 : 199.

— Normal, of the imagination. Bulwer, E. Caxtoniana.

— Observations on. (Drs. Dufay & Azam) Soc. Psych. Res. 6 : 407.

Clan Gregor, Proceedings against the. Burton, J. H. Crim. tri. 1 : 1.

Clancy, William. Clarke, R. H. Cath. bishops, 2 : 44.

Clapham. (P. M. Thornton) Clinch, G. Bygone Surrey, 170.

Clapham sect, The. Oliphant. Lit. hist. 3 : 308. — Stephen. Ess. eccl. biog. 523.

Clapp, Mrs. Alfred. Brockett. Woman's work, 767.

Clapp, Mrs. Anna L. Brockett. Woman's work, 634.

Clapp, Asa, with portrait. Hunt, F. Am. merch. 1 : 539.

Clare, John. Brooks, S. W. Eng. poets, 405. — Hall, S. C. Book of mem. 107. — Heath, R. Eng. peasant, 292. — (R. Noel) Miles, A. H. Poets of cent. 3 : 79. — Mitford, M. R. Recollec. 115. — Smiles. Brief biog. 432. — Stoddard, R. H. Under eve. lamp, 120.

Clare, Sister Mary Francis. Murray, J. O'K. Prose & poet. Irel. 709.

Clare election. Sheil, R. L. Sketches, 2 : 101.

Clarendon, Edw. Hyde, 1st carl of. Adams, W. H. D. Men at helm, 79. — Bayne. Pur. revol. 435. — Campbell. Ld. chan. 4 : 1. — Collier, W. F. Hist. Eng. lit. 190. — Lawrence. Brit. historians, 1 : 190. — Lodge. Portraits (Bohn), v. 5. — Macdiarmid. Brit. stat. 2 : 281. — Reed, W. B. Among books, 27. — Macaulay. Biog. sk. 100. — Wrangham. Brit. Plutarch, v. 3. — With portrait. Warner Lib. 7 : 3737.
— and his friends. Phillips, S. Ess. from Times, 2 : 118.
— and Lord Falkland. Mitford, M. R. Recollec. 488. — Thomson, Mrs. Cel. friend. 2 : 281.
— History of the rebellion. Disraeli, I. Amen. (N. Y. 2 v.) 2 : 409. — Hunt. Wishing-cap, 360. — Stephen, J. F. Horæ Sabb. 1 : 309.
— Inner life of. Arnold, T. Turning-points, 264.
— Life, by himself. Stephen, J. F. Horæ Sabb. 1 : 329.

Clarendon, George W. F. Villiers, 4th earl of. Grant, Jas. Portr. pub. char. 1 : 25. — Thornton. For. sec. v. 3. — Em. persons, 1 : 16. — Kent, C. Gladst. govt. 209. — Reid, T. W. Cab. portr. 288. — Whitty. Polit. portr.

Clarendon gallery of portraits. Lewis, M. T. Clarendon lives, 1 : 15. 3 : 239.

Clarendon House, Remains of. Hall, Mrs. S. C. Pilgr. Eng. shr. 2 : 191.

Clarendon manuscripts, Disposal of. Lewis, M. T. Clarendon lives, 1 : 67. 3 : 239.

Clarétie, Jules. Van de Velde. Fr. fic. 2 : 221.

Clark, Aaron. (J. Palmer) N. E. Hist.-Gen. Soc. Biog. 4 : 293.

Clark, Abraham, 1726–94. Dwight, N. Signers of decl. 143. — Lincoln, R. W. Signers, 14. — Lossing. Signers, 90. — Sanderson. Signers, v. 6.

Clark, Alexander; the two Mr. Clarks. Miller, H. Lead. articles, 337.

Clark, Alvan G. (O. C. Wendell) Am. Acad. Proc. 33 : 520.

Clark, Sir Andrew, M. D. With photo. Cooper, T. Men of mark, 3 : 29. — Em. persons, 6 : 64.

Clark, Billy J. Bungay. Pen-portr. 102.

Clark, Charles H. Clemens. Funny fellows, 34.

Clark, Charlotte A. Ellet. Pioneer wom. 350.

Clark, Gaylord B. Am. Bar Assoc. 17 : 495.

Clark, George Rogers, with portrait. Amer. Nat. portr. gall. 4. — Lodge & Roosevelt. Hero-tales, 29.

Clark, Jonas. Headley, J. T. Chaplains Rev. 74.

Clark, Joseph Bond, with portrait. Sketches N. H. men, 179.

Clark, Latimer. Munro, J. Heroes of Teleg. 284.

Clark, Ransom. Drake, S. G. Trag. of wilderness, 355.

Clark, Samuel Fulton. (G. F. Clark) N. E. Hist.-Gen. Soc. Biog. 4 : 187.

Clark, W. W. Clemens. Funny fellows, 84.

Clark, Lieut. Wm., with portrait. Greely, A. W. Explorers, 105.

Clark, Mrs. Wm. A. Ellet. Pioneer wom. 359.

Clark, William George. Payn. Lit. recol. 40.

Clark, Willis Gaylord. Griswold. Poets Am. 379.

Clark University, Worcester, Mass. U. S. Bur. Ed. Circ. '91, no. 6 : 379.

Clarke, Dr. Adam. Blunt. Ess. 404. — Taylor, W. C. Mod. Brit. Plut. 71. — Edwards, B. B. Self-taught, 305. — Gorrie. Em. Meth. 107. — Groser, W. H. Men worth im. — Hall, S. C. Book of mem. 79. — Wesley & successors, 67, 87, 107. — Wise, D. Heroic Meth. 142.

Clarke, Sir Andrew. Escott, T. H. S. Pillars emp. 37.

Clarke, Sir C. M. Pettigrew. Med. portr. gall. v. 1.

Clarke, Catherine. Burder. Pious wom. 280.

Clarke, Edward Daniel. St. John. Cel. travelers, 3 : 238.

Clarke, George Rogers. Lossing. Em. Amer. 138.

Clarke, H. J. W. French marshal. Grant, Jas. Cavaliers, 192.

Clarke, James Freeman. Frothingham. Transcend. 343. — (A. P. Peabody) Mass. Hist. Proc. 2d ser. 4 : 320. — Miller, Jos. Singers church, 2d ed. 512. — Putnam, A. P. Singers liberal, 283. — Richardson. Amer. lit. 1 : 309.
— on the church. Brownson. Works, 7 : 179.
— Steps of belief. Brownson. Works, 8 : 378.

Clarke, John. Sparks, W. H. Memories, 78.

Clarke, John B., with portrait. Sketches N. H. men, 311.

Clarke, John S. Matthews, B. Actors, 5 : 95.

Clarke, Marcus A. H. Warner Lib. 7 : 3745.

Clarke, Mary Anne. (W. G. Waters) Vincent, A. Twelve bad women, 289.
— Duke of York and. Browne, G. L. Narr. state tri. 1 : 243.

Clarke, Mrs. Mary Bayard. Davidson, J. W. Writ. of South, 93. — Raymond, I. Southland writ. 2 : 827.

Clarke, Richard. McClure. Translators, 97.

Clarke, Robert. Am. Antiq. Soc. Proc. n. s. 13 : 135.

Clarke, Samuel. Wrangham. Brit. Plutarch, v. 5.
— and Wollaston. Stephen, L. Eng. thought, 1 : 119.

Clarke, Thomas William. Am. Bar Assoc. 18 : 511.

Clarke, William B. Livingston, J. Dist. Amer. 376.

Clarke, William C., with portrait. Sketches N. H. men, 261.

Clarke, William Nash. Ivimey. Eng. Bapt. 4 : 393.

Clarkson, Gertrude. Burder. Pious wom. 357.

Clarkson, Henry Mazyck. Davidson, J. W. Writ. of South, 96.

Clarkson, James. Stanton, H. B. Reforms, 76.

Clarkson, Thomas. Smiles. Self-help, 247. — Stowe. Sunny mem. 2 : 63. — Grant, Jas. Portr. pub. char. 2 : 47. — Gurney, J. H. Hist. sketches, 3 : 431. — Rawnsley. Lit. Assoc. Eng. lakes, 2 : 29.

Clarkson, Wm. Grant, Jas. Portr. pub. char. 1 : 232.

Clason, Isaac Starr. Griswold. Poets Am. 203.

Class, in school, Numbers in a. (W. Emery) Internat. health exh. 16 : 286.

Class legislation, Freedom from. Hazard, T. R. Miscel. 367.

Class management, Practical hints on. Laurie, S. S. Educa. add. 190.

Class system, contrasted with elective system. (Noah Porter) Nat. Educa. Assoc. '77 : 95.

Classes and masses. Higginson. Book & heart, 142.

Clayton, John.   Tyerman. Oxf. meth. 24. — Smith, C. R. Retrospec. 3 : 164, 277.
Clayton, Oscar.   Malortie. Here, there, 270.
Clayton-Bulwer treaty, Panama canal and. Lawrence. Ess. int. law, 89.
Clayton compromise bill.   Corwin, T. Life & speeches, 324.
Cleanliness.   Chambers's Miscel. no. 51.
Cleanthes.   Arnold, E. Poets of Greece, 165. — Mills. Poets of Greece, 206. — Warner Lib. 7 : 3784.
— Hymn of.   Mahaffy, J. P. Greek life, chap. 11.
Clearchus.   Mills. Poets of Greece, 388.
Clearing-house.   Jevons. Money.
Cleasby, Sir Anthony.   With photo. Cooper, T. Men of mark, 4 : 31. — Gener. of judges, 54.
Cleaves, Nathan.   Am. Bar Assoc. 15 : 442.   16 : 424.
Cleburne, Patrick R.   Pollard. Life of Lee, 688.
Clemens, Samuel L. [Mark Twain].   Bolton, S. K. Amer. au. 365. — Haweis. Amer. humorists, 143. — Clemens. Funny fellows, 11. — Vedder, H. C. Amer. writers, 124. — With portrait. Warner Lib. 7 : 3787.
— at home.   Yates, E. H. Celeb. 3 : 135. — (C. H. Clark) Gilder. Authors, 61.
— Best story of.   Matthews, B. Books & playbooks.
Clement VII., Pope.   Ranke. Popes, 1 : 98. — Symonds. Age of despots, 443.
Clement VIII., Pope.   Ranke. Popes, 2 : 235.
Clement IX., Pope.   Ranke. Popes, 3 : 59.
Clement XI., Pope.   Ranke. Popes, 3 : 187.
Clement XIII., Pope.   Ranke. Popes, 3 : 207.
— Works.   Nichol, J. Amer. lit. 426.
Clement XIV., Pope.   Ranke. Popes, 3 : 212.
— and the Jesuits.   Milman. Savonarola, 244.
Clement of Alexandria.   Bigg, C. Chr. Platonists. — Farrar. Lives of fathers, 1 : 261. — Pressensé. Martyrs, 272, 540. — Blakey, R. Prim. fathers, 99. — Cave. Lives of Fathers, 1 : 296. — Evans, R. W. Biog. early church, 1 : 285. — Hort, F. J. A. Ante-N. fathers, 76. — (F. H. Chase) Lefroy, W. Lec. eccl. hist. 255. — Miller, Jos. Singers church, 2d ed. 1.
— and his Apologetic.   Dods, M. Erasmus, 119.
Clement of Rome.   Cave. Lives of Fathers, 1 : 147. — Charles. Martyrs, 28. — Pressensé. Martyrs, 218. — Blakey, R. Prim. fathers, 58. — Evans, R. W. Biog. early ch. 1 : 15. — Hort, F. J. A. Ante-N. fathers, 1. — Moxom. Jerus. to Nicæa, 102.
Clement, John M.   See Kleement.
Clement, Joseph.   Lewis, T. C. Mechanicians, 189.
— Inventions of.   Smiles. Indus. biog.
Clement, Mother Margaret, and the Carthusians.   Morris, J. Troub. of Cath. v. 1.
Clementi, Muzio, Italian pianist. — Ferris, G. T. Great violinists, 177. — Keddie. Mus. comp. 300. — With portrait. Bie, O. Hist. of piano, 218.
Clendenin, Archibald.   Ellet. Pioneer wom. 112.
Clendenin, Mrs.   Drake, S. G. Trag. of wilderness, 284.
Clennell, Luke.   Dobson, A. Bewick and his pupils, 186.
Cleobulus of Rhodes.   Fénélon. Philosophers, 96.
Cleomenes III., King of Sparta.   Mahaffy, J. P. Greek life, chap. 16. — Plutarch. Lives. — Yonge, C. M. Bk. of worthies, 260.
Cleon.   Cox, G. W. Greek statesmen, v. 2.
Cleopatra.   With portrait.   Clarke, M. C. Noted wom. 61. — Jameson. Fem. sov. 1. —

Jenkins, J. S. Heroines, 11. — Lord, J. Beacon, 5 : 23. — Owen, Mrs. O. F. Heroines hist. 76.
Cleopatra, Shakespeare's.   Hazlitt. Charac. Shakes.
Cleopatra of Macedonia.   Mahaffy, J. P. Greek life, chap. 4.
Clergy and churches in the U. S.   Bryce. Soc. institu. 92.
— Are they narrow?   Thompson, H. M. Copy, 100.
— Health of.   Higginson. Out-door, 1.
— in the United States.   Bryce. Amer. commonwealth, v. 2.
— Relation of, to people.   Milman. Savonarola, 374.
— Secular, in the middle ages.   Cutts, E. L. Scenes mid. ages, 195.
— Special education of.   Alford, H. Ess. & addr. 3.
— Usurpations of.   Gilbart. Lec. 173.
    See Ministry, Christian.
Clergymen as health officers.   Wisc. Health, 1891, 2 : 113.
— Country.   Boyd. Recreat. 1 : 7.
— Elizabethan.   Washburn, E. W. Stud. Eng. lit. 158.
— English.   Tuckerman, C. K. Recollec. 2 : 34.
— Salaries of.   Curtis. From easy chair, 3 : 221. — Ess. from Nation, 19.
— Untruthfulness in.   Momerie. Fut. of relig. 109.
Clerical costume.   Cutts, E. L. Scenes mid. ages, 232.
Clerical non-residence, Evils of.   Wordsworth, C. Mis. 3 : 191.
Clerk, Sir George.   Grant, J. Recollec. Lords & Comm. 1 : 292.
Clerk, John, of Edinburgh, Naval tactics of.   Playfair, J. Works, v. 3.
Clerk, The good.   Lamb. Elia.
Clerke, Gilbert.   Wallace, R. Anti-Trin. biog. 3 : 362.
Clermont and the Livingstons.   Glenn, T. A. Colon. mans. 1 : 297.
Clevedon : a literary shrine.   Walters, J. C. Bygone Som. 106.
Cleveland, Aaron.   Everest. Poets of Conn. 23.
Cleveland, Barbara Villiers, Duchess of.   Adams, W. H. D. Fam. beauties, 1 : 35. — With portrait. Jameson. Beauties, 78. — Jesse. Court of Eng. Stuarts, 3 : 182. — Street, G. S. Minia-tures, 40. — (A. Kalisch) Vincent, A. Twelve bad women, 99.
Cleveland, Benj.   Perry, B. F. Biog. sketches, 1 : 577.
Cleveland, Grover, with portrait.   Brooks, N. Statesmen, 333. — Fiske, S. Off-hand portr. 39. — (H. W. French) Frost. Presidents, 537. — Poore, B. P. Reminis. 2 : 483. — Peck, H. T. Pers. equa. 233. — With portrait. Scott, H. W. Dist. Am. lawy. 161. — (W. E. Russell) Wilson, J. G. Presidents, 468.
— and Mrs. Cleveland.   Keim. Soc. in Wash.
Cleveland, Mrs. Grover.   Gordon, L. L. Lady Wash'n, 431.
Cleveland, Henry.   Davidson, J. W. Writ. of South, 98.
Cleveland, John.   Bell, R. Lit. & sci. men, 2 : 188. — Gosse, E. From Shakesp. 157.
Cleveland, Ohio.   Brooks, E. S. Gt. cities, 118.
— City government of.   (E. J. Blandlin) Nat. Conf. City Govt. 2-3 : 112.
Clevenger, S. V.   Tuckerman. Artists, 605.
Clews, Henry.   Barton, J. Sk. of men of prog. — With portrait. Rogers, A. C. Repres. men, 135.

Cleyn sisters. Clayton, E. C. Eng. fem. art. 1 : 30.

Cliefden. Jewitt, L. Stately homes, 2 : 263.

Cliff-dwellers. Bibliography. (Hyla Long) Denver Pub. Lib. '95.

Cliff dwellings of the Mesa Verde. (W. R. Birdsall) Am. Geog. Soc. 23 : 584.

— Origin of. (C. Mendeleff) Am. Geog. Soc. 30 : 111.

Cliff-houses. Lummis. Strange corners, 111.

Cliff villages of the Red Rock Country, Arizona. (J. W. Fewkes) Smithson. Rept '05 : 557.

Clifford, Lady Anne. Coleridge. Northern worthies, 2 : 1. — Gibson, W. S. Miscel. 341.

Clifford, Arthur, Review of Tixhall poetry by. Drake, N. Evenings, 1 : 139.

Clifford, George. See Cumberland, 3d earl of.

Clifford, Henry. See Cumberland, 5th earl of.

Clifford, John H. (R. C. Winthrop) Mass. Hist. Proc. 15 : 368. Same in Winthrop. Addresses, 3 : 343.

Clifford, Lady Margaret. Strickland. Tudor prin. 298.

Clifford, Nathan, with portrait. Barnes, W. H. Sup. ct. 73.

Clifford of Chudleigh, Thomas, first lord. Lodge. Portraits (Bohn), 5.

Clifford, William Kingdon. Porter, N. Sci. & sent. 331. — (F. Pollock) Clifford. Lec. & ess. 1. — Em. persons, 2 : 146. — Hutton, R. H. Criticisms, 2 : 258.

— Lectures and essays. Mallock. Atheism, 1.

Clifford family, of Craven, Annals of. Drake, N. Mornings, 1 : 53, 211. 2 : 65, 237.

Clifton, William. Griswold. Poets Am. 63.

Clifton, Eng., and a lad's love. Symonds. Key of blue, 155.

Climate. Laing, S. Problems, 50.

— and happiness. Warner, C. D. As we go, 99.

— and human life. Martin, E. S. Windfalls, 15.

— Evolution of. Geikie, J. Frag. 349.

— Influence of. Buckle. Hist. civiliza. — Draper. Am. civil war, 1 : 80. — Godwin. Polit. justice, 1 : 95. — Taine. Art in Greece, Art in Netherlands.

— of Great Britain. Jackson, R. M. S. The mountain, 429. — Proctor. Light sci. 2 : 253.

Climatological stations, English. Internat. Health Ex. Sanita.

Climatology, Medical. (C. Smart) Am. Pub. Health, 1 : 129.

— sanitary, Non-periodic changes of heat an element in. (L. Blodget) Am. Pub. Health, 1 : 157.

Clinton, De Witt. Jenkins. Gov. of N. Y. 208. — Tuckerman. Ess. 204. — With portrait. Duyckinck. Nat. portr. gall. 2 : 55. — With portrait. Amer. nat. portr. gall. v. 2. — Lossing. Em Amer. 257. — Mansfield, E. D. Pers. mem. 108. — Moore, F. Am. eloq. 1 : 565.

— Biographical sketch of. Seward. Works (1884), 4 : 206.

— Home of. (T. R. Beck) Homes Am. statesm. 415.

Clinton, George. Jenkins. Gov. of N. Y. 25. — With portrait. Duyckinck. Nat. portr. gall. 1 : 171. — Lossing. Em. Amer. 339.

Clinton, Mrs. George. Clement, J. Noble deeds, 408.

Clinton, Henry. See Lincoln, Earl of.

Clinton, Sir Henry, Secret journal of. (T. C. Amory) Mass. Hist. Proc. 2d ser. 1 : 47.

Clinton, James. Headley. J. T. Washington, 2 : 170.

Clinton family. Sanford & Townsend. Gov. fam. 1.

Clinton, Fort, Capture of. Dawson. Batt. of U. S. 1 : 332.

Clitheron, Margaret, Life of. (J. Mush) Morris, J. Troub. of Cath. v. 3.

Clive, Mrs. Archer. (A. Sergeant) Oliphant. Wom. novelists, 163.

Clive, Caroline. (A. B. Grosart) Miles, A. H. Poets of cent. 10 : 201. — Mitford, M. R. Recollec. 274.

Clive, Catherine. Doran. Annals stage, 2 : 108. — Matthews, B. Actors, 1 : 47. — Hogarth. Mem. opera, 2 : 21. — Doran. Their maj. serv. 2 : 146.

— David Garrick and. Thomson, Mrs. Cel. friend. 2 : 217.

Clive, Robert, Lord. Adams, W. H. D. Memo. batt. 2 : 150. — Chambers's Repos. no. 82. — Foster, E. Heroes of Ind. empire, 9. — Georgian era, 2 : 74. — Gleig. Brit. mil. com. 3 : 1. — Great batt. Brit. army, 149. — Lodge. Portraits (Bohn), 7. — Morgan. Mil. comm. 33. — Neil, S. Epoch men, 211. — Taylor, W. C. Mod. Brit. Plut. 76.

— Malcolm's Life of. Macaulay. Ess. 4 : 194.

Cliveden homestead, Phila. Terhune. Colon. homes, 104.

Cloakmakers, Receipts and expenditures of. (I. Eaton) Hull-House maps, 79.

Clockland [Waterbury, Conn.]. Pidgeon. Old World ques. 27.

Clockmaking. Bibliography. Waltham (Mass.) Pub. Lib. Bull. Mar. '95.

Clocks. Lacroix, P. Arts in mid. ages, 169. — Mateaux, C. L. Wonderland of work, 175. — Smiles, S. Men of inven. 72.

Cloots, Jean-Baptiste. Bax, E. B. Outlooks, 1.

Clootz, Anacharsis. Adolphus. Biog. Fr. rev. 1 : 290.

Clopton, Alfred W. Walker, C. D. Biog. Va. Mil. Inst. 116.

Clopton, John B. Livingston, J. Em. Am. Lawyr. 78.

Close, Rev. Francis, dean of Carlisle, and the evangelicals. Oxenham. Stud. in eccl. hist. 394.

Clothes. Maxwell, H. Post-mer. 1.

— Clothes mania. Parton. Topics, 224.

— Men and coats. Thackeray. Early & late, 36.

— What becomes of them. Wynter, A. Peeps, 2 : 277.

Clothing in its relation to hygiene. (J. F. Hibberd) Am. Pub. Health, 15 : 94.

— What to wear. Nichols, J. R. Fireside sci. 150.

Clotilde, Queen. Bush, A. F. Queens of F. 1 : 20.

Cloud. Meynell, A. Color, 15.

Cloud form, Studies of. Ruskin. Miscel. v. 2.

Clouds, Observations of. Bibliography. (F. H. Bigelow) U. S. Weath. Bur. Bull. no. 20 : 97.

Cloudy condensation, Phenom. of. (J. Aitken) Smithson. Rept. '93 : 201.

Clouet, F. Pattison. Ren. of art in Fr. 1 : 307.

Clouet, Jean-François. Brightwell. Bypaths of biog. 119.

Clough, Arthur Hugh. Armstrong, R. A. Faith & doubt, 43. — (C. C. Norton) Warner Lib. 7 : 3821. — Hudson, W. L. Stud. interp. 71. — Macdonald, G. England's antiphon, 327. — Mabie. My study fire, 2 : 101. — (J. A. Noble) Miles, A. H. Poets of cent. 4 : 597. — Miles, A. H. Poets of cent. 9 : 409. — Bagehot. Lit. studies. — Shairp. Portraits, 195. — (T. H. Ward) Ward. Eng. poets, 4 : 589. — Patmore. Princ. in art, 118. — Swanwick, A. Poets, 367.

— as a writer. Hutton. Ess. theol. 2 : 368.

Clough, Arthur Hugh. Bothie of Toper-na-Fuosich. Bristed. Pieces, 1: 215.
— Memoir of. Clough. Prose rem. 1.
— Poet of doubt. Scudder, V. D. Life of spirit, 265.
Clous, John W., Lieut.-Col. U. S. A., with portrait. Butterfield Lec. Un. Coll. 1: 73.
Cloutt, Mrs. E. Burder. Pious wom. 662.
Clovelly, Eng., and Bideford. Allingham. Varieties, 1: 138.
Clover, Four-leafed. Whiting, C. G. Saunterer, 161.
Cloverdale, Cal. Marshall, W. G. Thro' Amer. 310.
Clovis and Clotilda. Utterton, F. A. Biog. sk. 32.
Clowes, William, sr. Grant, Jas. Port. Pub. char. 2: 204.
Club, Players'. Matthews, B. Stud. stage, 77.
Club and Institute Union, Clubs of. (T. S. Peppin) Knapp, J. M. Univ. 197.
Club bores. Lang. Leaders, 114.
Club talk. Couch, A. T. Q. Adv. crit. 222.
Clubs. Emerson. Society, 211.
— and club life. Croly. Pol. life Burke, 2: 26. — Emerson. Soc. & sol.
— Athletic. Whitney, C. W. Sport. pilg. 301.
— for boys and young men. (V. Brooke-Hunt) Burdett-Coutts. Wom. miss. 56.
— for working girls. (Hon. M. Stanley) Burdett-Coutts. Wom. miss. 49.
— for young men and women, needed in London. Meath. Soc. arrows, 357.
— in general. Burton, J. H. Book-hunter, 243.
— Literary. Mathews. Conversers, 44.
— of London. Goldsmith. Miscel. (N. Y. 4 v.) 1: 168. — Thompson, K. & J. C. Wits & beaux, 95.
— On some, and their ends. Doran. Drury Lane, 2: 105.
— Overclubbableness. Higginson. Book & heart, 224.
Clumber House. Jewitt, L. Stately homes, 2: 317.
Clutterbuck, H. Pettigrew. Med. portr. gall. v. 2.
Clyde, Colin Campbell, baron. Bartlett, D. W. Heroes of Ind. rebel. 447. — Foster, E. Heroes of Ind. empire, 242. — Wilson, J. G. Illus. soldiers, 397.
Clyde, Frith of. Boyd. Recreat. 2: 236.
Clydesdale, Upper ward of. Ker. Scot. national. 144.
Clymer, George. Dwight, N. Signers of decl. 190. — Lincoln, R. W. Signers, 15. — Lossing. Signers, 114. — Sanderson. Signers, v. 4. — Neven, D. R. B. Pennsylvanians, 51.
Coa, Battle of the. Adams, W. H. D. Eng. at war, 1: 291.
Coach, Journey by. Hunt, L. Seer, 2: 249.
Coahuila, Commerce and industries of, 1892. (E. O. Fechet) U. S. Cons. Rept. 40: 591.
Coal. Buckley, A. B. Fairyland sci. 171. — Croll, J. Climate & time, 420. — Dunman. Talks sci. 128. — Knox, T. W. Underground, 37. — (W. B. Dawkins) Manch. sci. lec. 2: 55. — Matéaux. Wonderland, 1. — Page, D. Geol. for gen. readers, 143. — Patton, J. D. Nat. resources U. S. 4. — Sinclair, J. Lec. on popular subjects, 1.
— as a reservoir of power. (R. Hunt) Estes. Half-hour, v. 1.
— A few words about. Proctor. Borderland, 291.
— Formation of. Huxley. Critiques. — (A. H. Green) Manch. Sci. lec. 2: 135.

Coal, Hygroscopicity of. (G. C. Hoffman) Roy. Soc. Can. v. 7.
— in the fire. Kingsley, C. Sci. lec.
— its importance. (W. S. Jevons) Manch. Sci. lec. 1: 103.
Coal colors. (H. E. Roscoe) Manch. Sci. lec. 3-4: 21.
Coal gas from heating apparatus. (F. Winsor) Mass. Health, '79 (10th): 75.
Coal miners, Among the. Nichols, J. R. Fireside sci. 203.
— Hygiene of. (H. C. Sheafer) Buck, A. H. (ed.) Hygiene, 2: 227.
Coal mines and miners. Chambers's Repos. no. 12.
— Disasters in, and their heroes. Hodder. Heroes.
Coal-mining in Chile. Child, T. Span.-Amer. Repub. 139.
Coal supply of England. Proctor. Light sci. 1: 72.
Coal trade of New South Wales. U. S. Cons. Rept. no. 159.
Coalbrookdale, Eng., Iron-works at. Smiles. Indus. biog.
Coan, Titus. Creegan. Gr. mission. 19. — (Rev. S. J. Humphrey) Haydn, H. C. Am. miss. heroes, no. 6.
Coast defence, Economy of. (King) Essayons club, no. 19.
Coast lines, Geogr. development of. (J. Geikie) Am. Geog. Soc. 24: 414. Same in Geikie, J. Frag. 393.
Coast survey operations, 1859. (A. D. Bache) Am. Geog. Soc. 2, pt. 1: 13.
Coates, Samuel. Winslow, S. N. Biog. Phila. merch. 192.
Coates family of Cedar Grove. Glenn, T. A. Colon. mans. 1: 97.
Cobalt, Manufacture of, at Rouen, 1891. (C. P. Williams) U. S. Cons. Rept. 37: 28.
Cobb, Howell. Savage. Liv. Rep. men, 114. — Bartlett. Pres. candidates, 333.
Cobb, Samuel. Holland, J. Psalmists, 2: 132.
Cobb, Samuel C., with portrait. (J. M. Bugbee) Mass. Hist. Proc. 2d ser. 7: 318.
Cobb, Thomas W. Sparks, W. H. Memories, 64.
Cobbe, Frances Power. Miles, A. H. Poets of cent. 10: 730. — Underwood, S. A. Heroines, 285.
— Character of. Hazlitt. Table talk.
Cobbett, William. Bulwer, H. L. Hist. char. 2: 81. — Chambers's Repos. no. 66. — Dawson, G. Biog. ess. 516. — Forsyth, W. Essays, 409. — Gilfillan. Mod. lit. 263. — Hazlitt. Spirit. — Lodge, H. C. Studies, 110. — Mitchell. Wet days, 297. — Oliphant, M. Lit. hist. 2: 355. — Reed, W. B. Among books, 105. — Rogers, J. E. T. Gleanings, 1: 139. — With portrait. Seymour, C. C B. Self-made, 538. — Stebbing. Verdicts, 300. — Wotton. Word portraits, 66. — Grant, J. Recol. Ho. Comm. 191. — Heath, R. Eng. peasants, 245. — Saintsbury, G. Ess. Eng. lit. 2: 38. — Stanton, H. B. Reforms, 155.
— The contentious man. Bulwer, H. L. Hist. char. 2: 99.
— Political works. Stephen, J. F. Horæ sabb. 230.
Cobbin, Ingram. Miller, Jos. Singers church, 2d ed. 360.
Cobblers. Saunders. Pastime, 168.
Cobbold, Thomas S. Bettany. Em. doctors, 2: 254.
Cobden, Richard. Adams, C. K. Rep. Br. orat.

— Mitchell, D. G. Eng. lands, 3 : 309. — With portrait. (G. E. Woodberry) Warner Lib. 7 : 3843. — Brooks, S. W. Eng. poets, 318. — Brooke, S. Theol. Eng. poets, 69. — Deshler. Afternoons, 217. — Devey. Mod. Eng. poets, 104. — Dixon, W. M. Eng. poetry, 74. — Frothingham. Transcend. 76. — Griswold, R. W. Sac. poets. — Hall, S. C. Book of mem. 27. — Hazlitt. Lit. rem. 2 : 359. — Macdonald, G. England's antiphon, 307. — (H. G. Groser) Miles, A. H. Poets of cent. 1 : 435. 9 : 89. — Mitford, M. R. Recoll. 394. — (T. O'Hagan) Afternoon lec. 4 : 229. — Ossoli. Art, 97. — Procter, B. W. Autob. 137. — Russell, W. C. Book of au. 391. — Swanwick, A. Poets, 281.

Coleridge, Samuel Taylor. Aids to reflection. Mozley, J. B. Lec. 142.
— and his school. Tulloch. Movements 19th cent.
— and Charles Lamb. Thomson, Mrs. Cel. friend. 2 : 51.
— and modern theology. Martineau, J. Ess. '91, 1 : 219.
— and opium-eating. DeQuincey. Miscel. pap. (Bost.) 2 : 117.
— and Southey. Saintsbury, G. Ess. Eng. lit. 2 : 415.
— and Wordsworth. Oliphant, M. Lit. hist. 1 : 240. — Woodberry. Studies in let.
— as philosopher and theologian. Shedd. Lit. ess. 271.
— as a philosophical critic. Whipple. Ess. & rev. 1.
— as a poet. Dowden. New stud. 313.
— At the grave of. Winter, W. Shakesp. Eng.
— at Greta Hall. Rawnsley. Lit. assoc. Eng. lakes, 1 : 12.
— Sir George Beaumont, and Wordsworth. Woodberry. Stud. in let. 188.
— Bibliography. (R. H. Shepherd) Notes & Quer. May–July, '95.
— Character of. Birrell. Obiter, 1 : 105.
— Christabel. Sterling, J. Ess. 1 : 102.
— Conversation of. Russell, A. P. Charac. 1.
— Conversations with, on the drama. Hazlitt. Crit. & dram. ess.
— Cottle's Recollections. Foster, J. Crit. ess. (Bohn) 2 : 455. — Phillips, S. Ess. from Times, 1 : 237.
— Country of. Collins, M. Pen sketches, 108.
— The Friend. Foster, J. Crit. ess. (Bohn) 2 : 1.
— his influence on our present theology. Martineau, J. Ess. 1 : 329.
— Home and grave of. Tyler, M. C. Glimpses Eng. 216.
— the metaphysician. Mather, G. M. 19th cent. poets, 51.
— Poet and divine. Ingleby. Ess. 190.
— Poetry of. Dawson, G. Biog. lec. 308. — Caine, H. Cobwebs. — Cotterill. Introd. study of poetry.
— Recollections of. Foster, J. Crit. ess. Ecl. v. 2.
— Supernaturalism of. Watson, W. Excur. in crit. 97.
— Travels of. Hazlitt, W. C. Offspring, 1.

Coleridge, Sara. Adams, W. H. D. Cel. Eng. wom. Vict. 2 : 10. — Bethune, G. W. Brit. fem. poets, 430. — (R. Garnett) Miles, A. H. Poets of cent. 7 : 127.

Coles, Mrs. Clara. Raymond, I. Southland wr. 2 : 718.

Coles, Edward, 2d governor of Illinois. Parton. Capt. indus. p. 117.

Colet, Dr. John. Adams, W. H. D. Worthies church Eng. 1. — Adams, W. H. D. Good Samar. 20. — Broadus. Lec. hist. preach. 191.

— Wordsworth, C. Eccles. biog. v. 1. — Wrangham. Brit. Plutarch, v. 1.

Colfax, Schuyler, with portrait. Brockett. Men of our day, 256. — Bungay. Pen-portr. 142. — Stowe. Men of time, 347.
— How he became Vice-President. Swank. Notes, 202.

Colfax house, Pompton, N. J. Terhune. Colon. homes, 161.

Coligny, Gaspard de, Admiral of France. Herrick, S. E. Heretics, 235. — Myers, F. Lec. gt. men, 382. — Pennington. Epochs papacy, 481.

Coligny, Louise de, Princess of Orange. Wittenmeyer. Women Reform. 237.

Coliseum, The. Guild. Abroad again, 228.
— Last fight in the. Yonge. Gold. deeds.

Collecting. Robinson, F. S. Connois. 1.

Collections, Famous. Robinson, F. S. Connois. 80.

Collectivism, A French economist on. Bax Relig. of socialism, 3.

Collects of the church. Neale. Ess. liturg.

Colleen Bawn, True story of the. Burke, P. Romance of forum.

College, Admission to, by certificate. U. S. Bur. Ed. Rept. '94–95, 2 : 1171.
— — Requisites of. N. Y. Regents, 79 : app. 106. See below, College entrance.
— — The American. (A. F. West) Butler, N. M. Educa. in U. S. 209.
— — past, present, and future. (J. Kennedy) N. Y. Regents, 111 : 333.
— — and university. Butler, N. M. Meaning of Educa. 125.
— and university, Relation between. (G. W. Hemming) Internat. health exh. 15 : 322.
— Christian, Relation of, to public education. (J. W. Strong) Nat. Educa. Assoc. '87 : 152.
— Compulsory attendance in. (N. L. Andrews) N. Y. Regents, 99 : app. 197.
— Distinctive function of the. Stryker. Hamilton, 180.
— Extravagance at. Curtis, G. W. Ars. rec. viv. 1.
— Future of. Stryker. Hamilton, 59.
— Higher life of. (J. E. Bradley) Nat. Educa. Assoc. '96 : 428.
— in the American system of education. (O. Root; S. G. Williams) N. Y. Regents, 100 : app. 135.
— In the recitation-room. (H. A. Frink) N. Y. Regents, 95 : 361.
— of Charleston, S. C. U. S. Bur. Ed. Circ. '88, no. 3 : 56.
— of Physicians and Surgeons, Baltimore, Md. (G. F. Bevan) U. S. Bur. Ed. Circ. '94, no. 2 : 292.
— or university, and the high school graduate. (J. H. Baker) Nat. Educa. Assoc. '96 : 364.
— Preparation for. (I. W. Andrews and others) Nat. Educa. Assoc. '84 : app. 36.
— Preparatory studies for. (F. A. P. Barnard) N. Y. Regents, 80 : 579.
— Religious culture of. (J. Easter) N. Y. Regents, 84 : 487.
— studies in sub-graduate course, Relation of. (C. M. Nairne) N. Y. Regents, 78 : 335.
— What is a ? (M. Pattison) Tollemache. Ess. & mock-ess. 126.

College commencements. Woolson. Browning, 122.

College course, Shortening of. (H. L. Stetson) Nat. Educa. Assoc. '90 : 668.
— — Effect of. (J. M. Coulter) Nat. Educa. Assoc. '91 : 696.

College curriculum. (W. A. Mowry) Nat. Educa. Assoc. '86 : 358.

— Evolution of. Jordan, D. S. Sci. sk. 228.

College discipline. (Anthony) N. Y. Regents, 95 : 328.

— Defects in. (R. C. Burleson) Nat. Educa. Assoc. '90 : 678.

College disorders, treatment of. (J. W. Mears) N. Y. Regents, 92 : 524.

College education, Chatard. Occ. ess. 143. — Diman. Orations, 76. — Garfield. Works, 1 : 265.

— and professional life. (J. C. Hutchinson) Nat. Educa. Assoc. '90 : 702.

— Practical value of. (S. N. Fellows) Nat. Educa. Assoc. '85 : 214.

— Utility of. Hinsdale, B. A. Schools & stud. 332.

College entrance and degrees, Requirements for. (H. A. Thompson and others) Nat. Educa. Assoc. '87 : 461.

— Chicago system. (W. R. Harper) Nat. Educa. Assoc. '96 : 631.

College entrance requirements. (Committee on Secondary Education) Nat. Educa. Assoc. '91 : 306.

— Report of committee on. Nat. Educa. Assoc. '99 : 632.

— Report on. (A. F. Nightingale) Nat. Educa. Assoc. '97 : 647.

— Uniform. (H. A. Fischer) Nat. Educa. Assoc. '90 : 705.

— Yale. (T. D. Seymour) Nat. Educa. Assoc. '96 : 635.

College fellowships. Brodrick. Pol. stud. 548.

College government, Coöperative. (M. C. Fernald) Nat. Educa. Assoc. '90 : 685.

College graduates and public life. Roosevelt, T. Amer. ideals, 47.

— Public and social duties of. Pierce, E. L. Addresses, 214.

College journalism. (O. E. Branch) N. Y. Regents, 88 : 679.

College libraries as aids to instruction. (J. Winsor; O. H. Robinson) U. S. Bur. Ed. Circ. '80, no. 1.

College life at Glasgow. Boyd. Leis. hours (Bost.), 172.

College man, The. Martin, E. S. Windfalls, 65.

College men in Amer. life. Potter, H. C. Scholar & state, 47.

College settlements in Boston. Blanc, T. Wom. in U. S. 144.

College training and morality. (M. D. Hornbeck) Nat. Educa. Assoc. '90 : 690.

College work, ancient and modern. Morley, H. Marot, 2 : 175.

Colleges, Aid to. Everett. Orat. v. 2.

— American, before the country. Sumner, W. G. Essays, 160.

— and academies, Mutual relations of. (W. T. Hewitt) N. Y. Regents, 100 : app. 249.

— Evils of residence in. Bethune. Orations, 144.

— Federation of. (B. A. Hinsdale) Nat. Educa. Assoc. '98 : 720.

— Government in, by students. (S. H. Peabody) Nat. Educa. '89 : 539.

— Hygiene in. Bowditch. Pub. hyg. 279.

— north, and colleges south. (Julius D. Dreher) Nat. Educa. Assoc. '86 : 367.

— Provincial, Relations of, to a university. (S. G. Johnson) Internat. health exh. 15 : 334.

— Relation of, to civilization. (J. J. Keane) Nat. Educa. Assoc. '93 : 161.

— Small, Education in. (R. B. Fairbairn) N. Y. Regents, 95 : 333.

Colleges, Small, Future of. (J. F. Crowell) Nat. Educa. Assoc. '94 : 797.

— training, for teachers, Scotch. (T. Morrison) Internat. health exh. 16 : 153.

— Western, Influence of. White, C. Ess. 177.

— What may people ask of. (C. A. Blanchard) Nat. Educa. Assoc. '90 : 662.

— Workingmen's. (D. Chadwick) Trans. Soc. Sci. Lond. '59 : 323.

Collegiants, Origin of the. Wallace, R. Anti-Trin. biog. 3 : 569.

Colleoni, Bergamo and Bartolommeo. Symonds. Sk. So. Eur. 2 : 201. — Oliphant. Makers of Venice.

Collens, S. Wharton. Davidson, J. W. Writ. of South, 100.

Colles, Christopher. Lossing. Em. Amer. 235.

Collet, Anthelme. Fuller, H. W. Noted trials, 69.

Colley, George Pomeroy. Escott, T. H. S. Pillars emp. 44.

Colleyre, Roger de. Besant. Fr. poetry, 144.

Collier, Arthur. Scheme of idealism. Hamilton. Discus.

Collier, Jeremy, on the English stage. Hogarth. Mem. opera, 1 : 153.

Collier, John. Espinasse. Lanc. worth. v. 1.

Collier, Sir Robert P. (Photo.) Cooper, T. Men of mark, 4 : 33.

Collier, Thomas. Ivimey. Eng. Bapt. 2 : 141.

Collieries. , See Coal Mines.

Collingridge, Elizabeth Campbell. Clayton, E. C. Eng. fem. art. 2 : 334.

Collingwood, Cuthbert, Admiral. Edgar. Footprints, 123. — Edgar. Sea-kings, 350. — Georgian era, 2 : 211.

— Correspondence of. Jeffrey, F. Contrib. Ed. Rev.

Collins, Charles Allston. Bate, P. H. Eng. Pre-Raph. 79.

Collins, Henry. Miles, A. H. Poets of cent. 10 : 744. — Miller, Jos. Singers church, 2d ed. 578. — Hatfield, E. F. Poets of church, 147.

Collins, Hercules. Ivimey. Eng. Bapt. 2 : 435. 3 : 301.

Collins, John. Stanton, H. B. Reforms, 314. — Wakeley. Heroes Meth. 383.

Collins, Mortimer, with portrait. Pen sketches, 1 : vii.

Collins, William, artist. Eng. painters. Georgian, 69. — Fairholt. Eng. artists, 80. — Redgrave. Century of p. 381.

Collins, William, poet. Hazlitt. Eng. poets, 38. — (S. Johnson) Chalmers. Eng. poets, 13 : 191. — Swinburne. Misc. 56. — Tuckerman. Poets, 64. — (A. C. Swinburne) Ward. Eng. poets, 3 : 278. — Mitchell, D. G. Eng. lands, 3 : 160. — With portrait. Warner Lib. 7 : 3871.

— Two poems of. Nadal, E. S. Ess. 166.

Collins, William, Rev. Ivimey. Eng. Bapt. 3 : 331, 397.

Collins, Wm. Wilkie. (Photo.) Cooper, T. Men of mark, 5 : 11. — Wotton. Word portraits, 77. — With portrait. Warner Lib. 7 : 3879. — Quilter. Preferences, 247. — Wilman, G. Sk. liv. celeb. 55. — Swinburne. Stud. prose & p. 110.

— in Gloucester place. Yates, E. H. Celeb. 3 : 145.

Collinson, James. Bate, P. H. Eng. Pre-Raph. 53.

Collinson, Sir R. (Photo.) Cooper, T. Men of mark, 2 : 12.

Collisions at sea, during fog. Proctor. Light sci. 3 : 293.

Collisions, Law of. (J. T. Danson) Trans. Soc. Sci. Lond. '59 : 216.
— Prevention of. Proctor, R. A. Univ. of suns, 204.
Collona, Francesco. Symonds. Renais. It. lit. 1 : 219.
Collyer, Rev. Robert. Bungay. Repr. men, 264. — Grant, Jas. Metropol. pul, 299. — Putnam, A. P. Singers liberal, 476. — Rogers, A. C. Repres. men, 155.
Collyer, William Bengo. Hatfield, E. F. Poets of church, 148. — Miller, Jos. Singers church, 2d ed. 372.
Colman, St., of Cloyne. Conyngham, D. P. Irish saints, 278, 401, 464.
Colman, George, the elder. Timbs. Anec. biog. wits, 1.
Colman, George, the younger. Timbs. Anec. biog. wits, 1. — Miles, A. H. Poets of cent. 9 : 9. — With portrait. Warner Lib. 7 : 3901.
Colman, Samuel. With portrait. Benjamin, S. G. W. Am. art. v. 1. — Sheldon, G. W. Amer. painters, 72.
Cologne. Bartley, G. C. D. Rhine, 329. — Buckley, T. A. Great cities, 384. — Felton, C. C. Europe, 143. — Haven, G. Pilgrim. 384. — Stowe. Sunny mem. 2 : 327.
— Cathedral of. Guild. Over the ocean, 327.
— Commercial directory of, 1891. Bur. Am. Repub. no. 15.
— Congress of Old Catholics at, 1872. Wordsworth, C. Miscel. 1 : 349.
— Import duties of, 1891. Bur. Am. Repub. no. 27.
— University of. Ullman. Reformers, 299.
Colombia. Bur. Am. Repub. no. 33. — Bur. Am. Repub. Rept. '91–92, pt. 8.
— Cotton goods in, 1899. (W. I. Shaw) U. S. Cons. Rept. 60 : 553.
— Foreign commerce of, 1891. (J. T. Abbott) U. S. Cons. Rept. 37 : 514.
— Industrial possibilities of, 1891. (J. T. Abbott) U. S. Cons. Rept. 36 : 330.
— Region of the Magdalena, 1896. (J. Bidlake) U. S. Cons. Rept. 51 : 372.
Colonial governments, Classification of. (H. L. Osgood) Am. Hist. Assoc. Rept. '95 : 617.
Colonies and their government. Helps. Soc. pressure, 347.
— Schemes for Epis. control in. (A. L. Cross) Am. Hist. Assoc. Rept. '96, 1 : 231.
Colonization. Donnelly, I. Atlantis, 348. — Galt, J. Lit. life, 2 : 36. — Hare. Guesses, 1 : 117
— African. Dix. Speeches, 2 : 41. — Hazard, T. R. Miscel. 162.
— and colonial government. Cairnes. Pol. ess. 1.
— as a branch of social economy. (Sir J. Stephen) Trans. Soc. Sci. Lond. '59 : 96.
— Bibliography. Ireland, A. Tropical coloniz.
— Effects of religious disunion on. Miller, H. Lead. articles, 223.
— Necessity for state-directed. Meath. Soc. arrows, 134.
— Wakefield theory of. Spedding. Reviews.
Colonization Society, American. Child, L. M. Oasis, 62, 165.
Colonna, Vittoria. Jameson. Loves of poets. — Montgomery. Men of Ita. 2 : 75. — Ritchie, A. C. Ital. life, 53. — Symonds. Renais. It. lit. 2 : 289. — With portr. Trollope, T. A. Dec. Ital. wom. 1 : 271. — (E. J. Millington) Yonge. Good wom. 2 : 1. — Shelley, Mrs. Lit. men Italy, v. 2. — Stebbing. Ital. poets, v. 2. — Trollope. Ital. poets, 1 : 203.

Colonna, The. Pastor, L. Hist. popes, 4 : 372.
Colonsay, D. McNeill, Lord. Smith, J. Campbell. Writings, 420.
Colophons of the early printers. Garnett, R. Ess. in librarianship, 197.
Color. Hunt, L. Seer, 1 : 34. — (M. Morris) Morris, W. Arts & crafts, 376.
— Distinctions of, Use of. Bushnell. Moral uses, 296.
— Form and. Day, L. F. Every-day art, 134.
— in animals, and sexual selection. Wallace, A. R. Trop. nat. 158.
— in composition. (S. Baring-Gould) Art of writ. Fiction, 35.
— in fresco painting. Fuseli. Life & writ. 2 : 329.
— in nature and art. Patterson, R. H. Ess. hist. 1.
— in nature, in relation to color in the schoolroom. (W. A. Sherwood) Nat. Educa. Assoc. '91 : 789.
— in oil painting. Fuseli. Life & writ. 2 : 353.
— in plants. Wallace, A. R. Trop. nat. 221.
— in pub. schools. (Mary D. Hicks) Nat. Educa. Assoc. '94 : 906.
— Ministry of, to sculpture and architecture. Parry, T. G. Min. of fine art, 62.
— Mission of. (Josephine C. Locke) Nat. Educa. Assoc. '90 : 796.
— of organic beings, Causes of. Davy. Works, 2 : 89.
— Perception of. Hall, G. S. Asp. Ger. 277.
— Photography of. (Otto Wiener) Smithson. Rept. '96 : 167.
Color-blindness. (W. T. Bacon) Conn. Health, '80 : 237.
— Dangers from; with bibliography. (B. J. Jeffries) Mass. Health, '78 : 99.
Color studies, Lombard. Paget, V. Juvenilia, 2 : 65.
Color vision and color blindness. (R. B. Carter) Smithson. Rept. '90 : 687.
Colorado. Dilke. Greater Brit. 101. — Faithful, E. 3 visits, 133. — Marshall, W. G. Thro' Amer. 399. — (A. S. Southworth) Am. Geog. Soc. 6 : 260.
— April days in. Hardy. Betw. two oceans, 229.
— Desert of, and its recent flooding. (B. A. C. Stephens) Am. Geog. Soc. 23 : 367.
— Flowers of. Jackson, H. H. Bits trav. home, 363.
— Sunrises in. Jackson, H. H. Bits trav. home, 407.
Colorado river, Expedition to. (J. C. Ives) Am. Geog. Soc. 1 : 41.
— The great walled river. (F. S. Dellenbaugh) Am. Geog. Soc. 19 : 113.
Colorado Springs. Jackson, H. H. Bits trav. home, 224, 316.
Coloration, Protective, Law which underlies. (A. H. Thayer) Smithson. Rept. '97 : 477.
Colored brigade at battle of Nashville. (H. V. Freeman) Mil. ess. M. O. L. L. U. S. Ills. 399.
Colors from coal. (H. E. Roscoe) Manch. Sci. lec. 3–4 : 21.
— Goethe's theory of. Eastlake. Contrib. 1 : 292.
— of animals. (A. Wilson) Proctor, R. A. Nat. stud. 32.
— Protective, in animals. Allen, Grant. Falling in love, 50.
— used by the ancients. Davy. Works, 6 : 131.
Colossal vestiges [of the older nations]. Tartt. Ess. 2 : 135.
Colporteurs in China. Cumming, C. F. G. Wand. in China, 2 : 230.
Colquhoun, Sir John, and Lady Catherine Graham. Burke, B. Viciss. of fam. 3 : 181.

Common-sense school of philosophy. Lewes. Biog. phil.

Commonplace, The. Watson, E. H. L. Uncon. humor, 69.

— The common and. Davis, L. S. Stud. mus. 152.

Commons, Enclosure of. Fawcett. Sp. pol. ques. 224.

— Town, in New England. Adams, C. F. Three episodes, 2 : 646.

Commonwealths, Growth of. Freeman. Hist. ess. 4 : 353.

Commune, Paris. Bibliography. March, T. Paris Commune.

Communes, Florentine, Origin of. Villari. Two 1st cent. Flor. 1 : 80.

— Italian. Villari. Two 1st cent. Flor. 1 : 15.

— — Family and state in. Villari. Two 1st cent. Flor. 2 : 1.

Communion, Holy. Wordsworth, C. Miscel. 2 : 143.

— Service of, Annot. Book of Prayer on. Conington. Miscel. 479.

Communion cups, Individual. (E. A. Wallace) N. H. Health, '94–95 : 192.

Communipaw. Irving. Biog. 453.

Communism, Lecture on. Davies, J. L. Theol. & mor. 278.

— vs. mutualism. Greene, W. B. Soc. frag. 24.

Communists. Heckethorn. Sec. soc. 2 : 218.

Communities, English, in the middle ages. Allen, W. F. Essays, 300.

— House, East European. Maine. Early law, 232.

Comneni, The. Doran. Monarchs, 2 : 88.

Como. Baddeley. Travel-tide, 160. — Hare. Cities of No. Italy, 1 : 183. — Howells. Ital. jour. 285.

— and Il Medeghino. Symonds. Sk. So. Eur. 2 : 219.

Como, Lake. Fulton, C. C. Europe, 248.

Compagni, Dino. Symonds. Age of despots, 263.

Companions, Our. Friswell. Gentle life, 1 : 196.

Company, How shall we entertain? Stowe, H. B. Chimney, 166.

Compartments in ships, First suggestion of. Franklin. Works ('87), 9 : 5.

Compass. See Magnetic needle.

Compensation. Emerson. Ess. 1 : 89. Also in Prose masterpieces, 1 : 195.

— and expenditure. Holland, J. G. Plain talks, 233.

Competition. Helps. Brevia. — Wasson. Ess. 327.

— Collapse of. Gladden. Tools, 146.

— Foreign. Giffen. Ess. finance, 142.

— Industrial, and commercial freedom. Playfair. Sub. soc. 145.

— Morality of. Stephen, L. Soc. rights, 1 : 133.

— Value of, in medicine. Reynolds, J. R. Ess. 245.

Competitions, Art. (J. Forbes-Robertson) Trans. Soc. Sci. Lond. '77 : 726.

Compiègne. Challice. Fr. palaces, 243.

Complaining. Gray, E. C. Idle musings, 136.

Complatius, George. Wallace, R. Anti-Trin. biog. 2 : 117.

Composers. Mathews, W. S. B. 100 yrs. music, 636.

— First American. Ritter. Music in Amer. 56.

— of the Elizabeth epoch. Ritter. Music in Eng. 30.

Composition in painting. Fuseli. Life & writ. 2 : 237.

— Literary. Disraeli, I. Curios. (N. Y. 4 v.) 2 : 251. — Higginson. Atlan. ess. 69. — Newman, J. H. Lec. univ. 139.

Composition, Literary. Bibliography. Brewster, W. T. Stud. in structure.

— — Labor Limæ. Jacox. Lit. life, 275.

— — Philosophy of. Poe. Works, 5 : 157.

Composure. Meynell, A. Rhythm, 54.

Compromise, Moral. Lecky. Map of life, 92.

Compton, Henry. Marston, J. W. Rec. actors, 2 : 85.

Compton, Spencer. See Wilmington, Earl of.

Compton Castle. Timbs. Abbeys, 1 : 475.

Compulsory education. See Education, Compulsory.

Comstock, Mrs. Ellet. Pioneer wom. 401.

Comte, Auguste. Alger. Solitudes, 372. — Denslow. Mod. think. 285. — Lewes. Biog. phil. — Martineau, J. Ess. ('91) 1 : 331. — Morley. Crit. miscel. 3 : 337. — Arthur, W. Religion without God, 1. — Buchanan, J. Mod. atheism, 84. — Cairnes. Ess. pol. econ. 265. — Ward, L. F. Dynamic sociol. 1 : 82.

— and positivism. Tulloch. Mod. theories, 3.

— and the religion of humanity. (J. R. Thomson) Liv. papers, v. 8.

— Aspirations of. Hutton, R. H. Criticisms, 2 : 303.

— Huxley on. Congreve, R. Ess. 262.

— Life and philosophy of. Martineau, J. Ess. ('91) 1 : 1.

— Philosophy of. Godwin, P. Out of past, 251. — Brimley, G. Ess. 309.

— — Reasons for dissenting from. Spencer, H. Rec. dis. (N. Y.) 113.

— System of. Alviella. Contemp. evol. 129.

Conarroo, George M. Am. Bar Assoc. 19 : 675.

Conaway, Asbury B. Am. Bar Assoc. 21 : 715.

Concanen, Luke. Clarke, R. H. Cath. bishops, 1 : 140.

Conceit. Friswell. Gentle life, 1 : 214.

Conceited folk. Henry, C. S. About men, 57.

Concentration. Mabie. Ess. on work, 149.

— and method. Ballantyne. Ess. 80.

— March of. George, H. Soc. prob. 62.

Concepts, Relation of, to precepts. (G. S. Fullerton) Nat. Educa. Assoc. '92 : 548.

Conciliation. Davis, T. Prose, 254.

— Wisdom of. Bulwer, E. Caxtoniana, 187.

Concini, Concino di, and Marie de Medici. Menzies, S. Roy. fav. 1 : 357.

Concord, Mass. Bacon, E. M. Hist. pilgrim. 360. — (F. B. Sanborn) Powell, L. P. Hist. towns N. E. 243. — Drake, S. A. Hist. fields Mid. 371. — (J. McK. Merriam) Am. Antiq. Soc. Proc. n. s. 9 : 253.

— Address at dedica. of Soldiers' Monument, April 19, 1867. Emerson, R. W. Miscel. ('83), 99.

— Battle of. Dawson. Batt. of U. S. 1 : 9. — Everett. Orat. v. 2.

— — Centen'l celebration of. Curtis, G. W. Orations, 3 : 85.

— Historical discourse at, Sept. 12, 1835. Emerson, R. W. Miscel. ('83) 31.

— Local history of. Reynolds, G. Papers, 104.

— Pilgrimage to. Wolfe. Lit. shr. Am. auth. 17.

— thirty years ago. Stearns, F. P. Sk. Concord, 1.

Concord, N. H. Fellows, H. P. Boating, 17.

Concord River. Thoreau. Selec. 1.

— Boating trip on. Fellows, H. P. Boating, 17.

Concordances, Biblical. Bibliography. Walker, J. B. R. Concordance Scriptures.

Condé, Charlotte Marguerite de Montmorency, Princess of. Holt, E. S. Roy. ladies, v. 2.

Condé, Louis II. de Bourbon, Prince, "the great." Cust. Warriors civ. 1 : 129. — Hewlett. Heroes, 361. — James, G. P. R. Commanders, 2 : 35. — (J. B. Bossuet) Turnbull, R. Pulp. orators France, 22. — Wilson, I. G. Illus. sol. 165.

Condell, Henry. Collier. Actors, 132.

Condensation, cloudy, Phenomena connected with. (John Aitken) Smithson. Rept. '93 : 201.

Conder, Joan Elizabeth. Miller, Jos. Singers church, 2d ed. 445.

Conder, Josiah. Hatfield, E. F. Poets of church, 151. — Holland, J. Psalmists, 2 : 364. — (W. G. Horder) Miles, A. H. Poets of cent. 10 : 95. — Miller, Jos. Singers church, 2d ed. 407.

Condillac, Etienne B. Lewes. Biog. phil. — Rosmini. Origin of ideas, 1.

Condon, Capt. P. J. Savage, J. Fenian heroes, 254.

Condorcet, J. A. N. Caritat de. Adolphus. Biog. Fr. rev. 1 : 296. — Morley. Crit. miscel. 2 : 163. — Shelley, M. W. Lit. Men Fr. 2. — Shelley, Mrs. Fr. authors, v. 2.

Conduct. Hazlitt, W. Lit. remains, 2 : 71, 277. — Russell, A. P. Lib. notes, 325.
— and duty. Proctor. Light sci. 3 : 232.
— The church and. Godkin. Reflections, 146.
— Extremes in. Boyd. Recreat. 2 : 63.
— Intellectual and moral. Bulwer, E. Caxtoniana.
— Religion and. (C. H. Toy) Barrows, J. H. Parl. relig. 2 : 1009.

Conduct of life. Arnold, F. Turning-points, 309.

Confectionery, Art of, Gunter's. Hunt. Wishing-cap, 154.
— Sweets for the million. Wynter, A. Our soc. bees, 2 : 195.

Confederacies, Ancient and modern. Madison, J. Letters, 1 : 293.

Confederacy and union. Senior. Hist. ess. 1 : 359.

Confederate congress. Montgomery, Ala. : a specimen day. Congdon, C. T. Trib. ess. 131.

Confederate flag. "A banner with a strange device." Congdon, C. T. Trib. ess. 121.

Confederate States, Constitutional history of. Foster, R. Comment on Const. 1 : 186.
— Gov't of, Materials for hist. of. (J. O. Sumner) Am. Hist. Assoc. 4 : 331.
— Northern estimate. Congdon, C. T. Trib. ess. 151.
— Southern notions of the North. Congdon, C. T. Trib. ess. 144.
  See United States. History.

Conference wrong side out. Dodge, M. A. 12 miles, 185.

Confession, Auricular. Mahan, M. Works, 3 : 572. — Spalding, M. J. Miscel. 2 : 436.
— and absolution, Doctrine of. Wordsworth, C. Miscel. 2 : 189.
— in the Church of England. Cobbe, F. P. Darwinism, 363; *or*, Re-echoes, 185.

Confessions. *See* Creeds.
— Literary. Shepard, W. Authors, 113.

Confidences. Watson, E. H. L. Uncon. humor. 103.

Confirmation. (W. L. Robbins) Church's ministry. — Thirlwall, C. Remains, 1 : 236.

Conformity. Helps. Friends, 1st ser. 1.

Confucianism. (Kung Hsien Ho) Barrows, J. H. Parl. relig. 1 : 596. — (Pung Kwang Yu) Barrows, J. H. Parl. relig. 1 : 374.
— Christianity and. Barrows, J. H. Chr. conq. Asia, 182. — (J. Legge) Liv. papers, v. 3.

Confucianism in Japan in its philosophical form. Griffis. Relig. Japan, 131. — Matheson. Distinc. mess. 67.

Confucius. U. S. Japan exped. 1. — Alger. Solitudes, 202. — Chambers's Papers, no. 77. — Parton. Peop. bk. biog. 408. — Bettany. World's relig. 102. — Dods, M. Erasmus, 239. — Holland, E. G. Reviews, 1. — Hundred greatest men, 130. — With portrait. (R. K. Douglas) Warner Lib. 6 . 3629.
— and his educational ideas. (Hidesaburo Eudo) Cong. Educa. Chic. ('93) 308.
— Doctrine and influence of. Johnson, S. Ori. relig. China, 571.
— Works of. Müller. Chips, 1 : 300. — Clarke, J. F. Ten relig. 32. — Hardwick, C. Christ & other masters, 2 : 17. — Legge. Relig. of China. — (G. Matheson) Faiths of the world, 61. — Johnson, S. Orient. relig. China. — (G. Matheson) St. Giles lec. 2 : 73. — Grant, G. M. Relig. 52.

Confusions, Mental. Hamerton. Hum. int. 280.

Congo, The, Stanley's descent of. Montefiore, A. Leaders, 215.

Congo basin. Temple, R. Cosmop. ess. 390.

Congo Free State. Bibliography. (J. S. Reeves) Johns Hopk. Univ. Stud. '95 : nos. 11, 12.

Congregationalism. (L. Abbott) Why I am, 57. — Dale, R. W. Ess. and addr. 178. — College and the church, 180. — Where is the city? 51.
— Symbols and. Shedd. Theo. ess. 319.

Congregationalists, English. Alviella. Contemp. evol. 76.

Congregations *de auxiliis*, History of the. Renan. Studies, N. Y. 2 : 380.
— modern, Idea of church in relation to. Dale, R. W. Ess. & addr. 89.

Congress, Continental. (H. Friedenwald) Am. Hist. Assoc. Rept. '94 : 227.
— Journal & Papers of. (H. Friedenwald) Am. Hist. Assoc. Rept. '96, 1 : 83.

Congress, U. S., Cabinet officers in. Garfield. Works, 1 : 61.
— A century of. Garfield. Works, 2 : 463.
— Demands by, upon the executive. (E. C. Mason) Am. Hist. Assoc. 5 : 367.
— 40th. Adams, H. Hist. ess. 366.
— How Congress wastes its time. Parton. Topics, 199.
— Leading speakers in, 1871-81. Monroe, Ja. Oberlin lec. 306.
— library of, Building for the. (B. R. Green) Smithson. Rept. '97 : 625.
— Lobbying in. Parton. Topics, 254.
— members of, Apportionment of. Dix. Speeches, 2 : 279.
— — Qualifications for. Foster, R. Comment on. Const. 1 : 355.
— of 1789. Everett, E. Mt. Vernon, 124.
— Origin, composition, and powers of. Foster, R. Comment on Const. 1 : 306.
— Plea for study of votes in. (O. G. Libby) Am. Hist. Assoc. Rept. '96, 1 : 321.
— relief of, from private legislation, Rept. of committee on. Am. Bar Assoc. 10 : 396.
— Rhode Island members of. Hazard, T. R. Miscel. 59.
— War power of. Blaine. Polit. disc. 18.

Congresses, Early, Pub. Documents of. (A. W. Greely) Am. Hist. Assoc. Rept. '96, 1 : 1109.

Congressional committees. Bibliography. McConachie, L. G. Cong. committees.

Congressional government, Defense of. (F. Snow) Am. Hist. Assoc. 4 : 309.

church, 154. — Miller, Jos. Singers church, 2d ed. 524.

Cook, Thomas, & Son.   Japp & Holmes. Succ. bus. men, 46.

Cook county (Ill.) charities.   (J. C. Lathrop) Hull-House maps, 143.

Cooke, Alexander. Collier. Actors, 182.

Cooke, Elisha, 1637–1715.   Knapp, S. L. Em. lawyers, 273.

Cooke, Elisha, 1678–1737.   Knapp, S. L. Em. lawyers, 281.

Cooke, George Fred. Baker, H. B. Eng. actors, 2 : 52. — Doran, Annals stage, 2 : 288. — Fitzgerald, P. Rom. of stage, 331. — Galt. Players, 2 : 492. — Matthews, B. Actors, 2 : 1. — Russell, W. Rep. actors, 234. — Murdoch, J. E. Stage, 79.

Cooke, Henry. Fish, H. C. Pulp. eloq. 739.

Cooke, Jay. Reid, W. Ohio in the war, 1037. — Pettigrew. Med. portr. gall. v. 1. — With portrait. Brockett. Men of our day, 524.

Cooke, John Esten. Davidson, J. W. Writ. of South, 105. — Derby, J. C. Fifty years, 400. — Richardson. Amer. lit. 2 : 401.

Cooke, Josiah Parsons.   Am. Acad. A. & S. Proc. 30 : 513.

Cooke, Josiah Parsons, jr.   Vaille & Clark. Harv. book, v. 1.

Cooke, Philip Pendleton. Griswold. Poets Am. 455.

Cooke, Rose Terry.   With portrait. (H. P. Spofford) Our fam. wom. 174. — Warner Lib. 7 : 3973.

Cooke, Thomas, Islington miser.   Redding. Misers, 1 : 100. — Wilson, H. Characters, 227.

Cooke, William, 1711–97.   Jesse, J. H. Cel. Eton. v. 1.

Cooke, Sir William Fothergill.   Munro, J. Heroes of Teleg. 273.

Cookery, Schools of.   Wynter, A. Our soc. bees, 2 : 187.

—— in England.   Bolton, S. K. Soc. study in Eng. 63.

Cooking, Art of.   (E. Atkinson) Am. Pub. Health, 15 : 151.

— Practical, in elementary schools.   (F. L. Calder) Internat. Health Exh. 14 : 171.

— Sanitary and economic.   (Mrs. M. H. Abel) Maine Health, '90 : 167.

Cooks and cookery. Gardner, S. J. Aut. leaves, 121.

— Ancient. Disraeli, I. Curios. (N. Y. 4 v.) 2 : 433.

Cook's guide and housekeeper's assistant, Francatelli's. Lucas. Mornings, 1 : 224.

Cook's Islands, Aboriginal. McLennan. Stud. anc. 2 : 189.

Cooley, Thomas M., with portrait.   (H. W. Rogers) Scott, H. W. Dist. Am. lawy. 205. — Am. Bar Assoc. 21 : 674.

Cooly, George.   Miller, Jos. Singers church, 2d ed. 369.

Cooper, Anthony Ashley. See Shaftesbury, Earl of.

Cooper, Sir Astley Parton. Bettany. Em. doctors, 1 : 202. — Edgar. Boyhood, 363. — Pettigrew. Med. portr. gall. v. 1.

Cooper, Edward. Davies, G. J. Suc. preach. 265.

Cooper, Mrs. Emma (Wren).   Clayton, E. C. Eng. fem. art. 2 : 264.

Cooper, James Fenimore. Hall, S. C. Book of mem. 182. — Howe, M. A. D. Am. bookm. 29. — With portrait.   (J. Hawthorne) Warner Lib. 7 : 3985; or Warner classics, 2 : 153. — Lossing. Em. Amer. 344. — Mitchell, D. G. Amer. lands, 1 : 225. — Nichol. Amer. lit. 175.

— Powell, T. Liv. auth. Am. — Fisher, M. Gen. sur. Am. lit. 70. — Wright, H. C. Chil. sto. in Am. lit. 51. — With portrait. Amer. Nat. portr. gall. 1. — Bryant, Prose, 1 : 299. — Charles, P. Anglo-Amer. lit. 42. — With portrait. Duyckinck. Nat. portr. gall. 2 : 199. — With portrait. Griswold. Prose writ. 263. — Greene, G. W. Biog. stud. 9. — Harris, A. B. Amer. authors, 29. — Poe, E. A. Works, 2 : 389. — (F. Parkman) Rice, A. T. Ess. 358. — Richardson, C.F. Amer. lit. 2 : 297. — Sumner, C. Works, 3 : 43. — Willis. Hurrygraphs, 210. — Wilson, J. G. Bryant, 230.

Cooper, James Fenimore, and Sir Walter Scott. Maginn. Fras. papers, 291.

— Centenary of.   Matthews, B. Books & playbooks.

— Life, genius, and writings. Bryant. Orations, 43.

— Literary offenses of. Clemens. How to tell, 93.

— Novels. Nichol, J. Amer. lit. 175. — Winter. Old shrines, 281.

— Redskins. Bristed. Pieces, 1 : 1.

— Shrines and scenes of.   Wolfe, T. F. Lit. haunts, 154.

— Ways of the hour. Brownson. Works, 16 : 326.

Cooper, John.   Wallace, R. Anti-Trin. biog. 3 : 360.

Cooper, John Gilbert.   Chalmers. Eng. poets, 15 : 503.

Cooper, Mrs. Mary. Burder. Pious wom. 634.

Cooper, Peter.   Bolton, S. K. How success is won, 7. — With portrait.   Carroll, H. 12 Amer. 77. — Mills, J. D. Art of money making, 326. — Parton. Capt. indus. 312. — Parton. Triumphs, 26. — Cochrane, R. Benef. lives, 283. — With portrait. Rogers, A. C. Repres. men, 159. — With portrait. Stoddard, W. O. Men of hist. 264.

— In memoriam. Am. Geog. Soc. 15 : 349.

Cooper, Samuel, artist.   Fairholt. Eng. artists, 125.

Cooper, Samuel, Gen.   Snow. So. generals, 288.

Cooper, Susan Fenimore.   Hart, J. S. Fem. prose, 413.

Cooper, Thomas, Dr., 1759–1840. Lossing. Em. Amer. 239.

— South Carolina College and.   U. S. Bur. Ed. Circ. '88, no. 3 : 143.

Cooper, Thomas, chartist. Em. persons, 5 : 239. — Hoare. Nota. workers, 122. — Famous boys, 153. — Hood, E. P. Peerage of pov. 230. — Winks. Illus. shoemakers, 191. — Stanton, H. B. Reforms, 317.

— and his Purgatory of suicides.   Langford. Prison books, 334.

Cooper, Thos. Abthorpe. Dunlap. Am. theatre, 1. — Matthews, B. Actors, 2 : 235.

Cooper, Thomas S.   Wilman, G. Sk. liv. celeb. 138.

Cooper Institute and its founder. Parton. Triumphs, 26.

Cooper's Hill college of engineering.   Temple, R. Orient. exper. 304.

Coöperation.   Samuelson, Jas. Civiliz'n, 159. — Vaughan, D. J. Questions, 67. — About, E. Hdbk. of soc. econ. — Brassey. Work & wages, 247. — Brown, T. E. Stud. mod. soc. 264. — Cairnes. Ess. pol. econ. 166. — Cook, Jos. Socialism, 107. — Elder, W. Questions, 281. — Greeley. Ess. pol. econ. 88, 273. — Hearn. Plutology. — Rylance, J. H. Lec. on soc. ques. 70.

— and labor organizations.   N. J. Labor, '87 : 194.

Coöperation and profit-sharing, 1892. (F. B. Loomis) U. S. Cons. Rept. **41** : 21.
— — in France. U. S. Cons. Rept. no. 148.
— and wages. (H. K. Oliver) Mass. Labor, '73 : 440.
— Development of, American and foreign. N. J. Labor, '78 : 143. '79 : 187. '81 : xii. '82 : 92. '85 : 231. '86 : 317. '87 : 315.
— Godkin on. N. J. Labor, '82 : 92. '85 : xxix.
— in England. Bosanquet. Ess. 252.
— in Germany. (M. Kyllmann) Trans. Soc. Lond. '63 : 630.
— in Minneapolis. (A. Shaw) Am. Econ. Assoc. v. 1.
— in New England. (E. W. Bemis) Am. Econ. Assoc. v. 1.
— in religious work. Evang. Alliance, '89 : 11.
— Industrial. Greg, W. R. Pol. prob. 135. — Mass. Labor, '71 : 452. '73 : 323. — (C. D. Wright) Mass. Labor, '75 : 453. — Mo. Labor, '85. — (M. D. Hill) Trans. Soc. Sci. Lond. '60 : 748. — Walker, F. A. Wages, 262.
— — French coöperative associations. (E. Reclus) Trans. Soc. Sci. Lond. '66 : 695.
— — in Massachusetts. (C. D. Wright) Mass. Labor, '77 : 51.
— — in the U. S., in 1880. Holyoake. Among Amer. 133.
— — in the west, Three phases of. (A. G. Warner) Am. Econ. Assoc. v. 2.
— — Legislation on, in U. S. and England. N. J. Labor, '85 : 407. '89 : 393.
— — Whitwood (Eng.) colliery. (A. Briggs) Trans. Soc. Sci. Lond. '66 : 703.
— Internat. comity and, in canals. (O. A. Howland) Deep waterways conven. 1 : 45.
— the logic of Christianity. Gladden. Tools, 174.
— of men and women, Divine basis of. (L. F. Dickinson) Barrows, J. H. Parl. relig. 1 : 502.
Coöperative associations in Germany. (E. King) Mass. Labor, '72 : 548. — Baring-Gould. Germany, 383.
Coöperative communities. Chambers's Papers, no. 18.
Coöperative distribution. (E. W. Bemis) U. S. Lab. Bull. 1 : 610.
— in Europe, Australia, and U. S. Mass. Labor, '86 : 121.
— in Great Britain. Mass. Labor, '86 : 51.
Coöperative housekeeping; conservation of nerve forces. (Mrs. Coleman Stuckert) Am. Pub. Health, 19 : 116.
Coöperative societies. Bolton, S. K. Soc. stud. in Eng. 175.
Coöperative stores. Wynter, A. Peeps, 2 : 75.
— Retail trades and. (J. Head) Trans. Soc. Sci. Lond. '72 : 444.
Coopwood, Thomas. Livingston, J. Dist. Amer. 445.
Copan, Ruined city of. (G. B. Gordon) Am. Geog. Soc. 31 : 39.
Cope, Thomas Pym, with portrait. (J. R. Chandler) Hunt, F. Am. merch. 1 : 103. — Winslow, S. N. Biog. Phila. merch. 181.
Copeland, T. Pettigrew. Med. portr. gall. v. 4.
Copeland, William J. Miller, Jos. Singers church, 2d ed. 487.
Copenhagen, Battle of. Allen, Jos. Battles Brit. navy, 2 : 26. — Low, C. R. Gt. battles, 293. — Valentine, L. J. Sea-fights, 191.
— Free port of, 1895. (R. J. Kirk) U. S. Cons. Rept. 50 : 203.
— Milk supply of, 1891. (H. B. Ryder) U. S. Cons. Rept. 37 : 558.

Copenhagen, A morning in. Buchanan. Master-spir. 211.
— Museum of northern antiquities at. Atkinson, J. B. Art tour northern, 9.
— a Venice of the Vikings. Harrison, J. A. Group of poets, 155.
Copernicus, Nicholas. Ball, R. Great astron. 30. — Hundred greatest men, 331. — Morton, E. J. C. Heroes astron. 32. — Neil, S. E. Epoch men, 187. — Parton. Peop. bk. biog. — Stoughton, J. Worthies of sci. 26. — Nasmith. Mak. mod. thought, 1 : 47. — Wallace, R. Anti-Trin. biog. 3 : 126. — (C. S. Holden) Warner Lib. 7 : 4040.
— and his work. Brigham, C. H. Mem. 231.
— and the motion of the earth. Lodge, O. J. Pioneers, 5.
Copestake, Lindsay, Crampton & Co. Japp & Holmes. Succ. bus. men, 1.
Copland, J. Pettigrew. Med. portr. gall. v. 1.
Copley, John Singleton, artist. Lossing. Em. Amer. 52. — Ollier, E. Brit. port. paint. 58. — (A. T. Perkins) Mass. Hist. Proc. 11 : 319. — Tuckerman. Artist-life, 20. — Tuckerman. Artists, 71.
Copley, John Singleton, Lord Lyndhurst. See Lyndhurst.
Coppée, François. Henry, S. Hours w. Parisians, 79. — Pellissier. Lit. move. Fr. 378. — With portrait. (R. Sanderson) Warner Lib. 7 : 4045.
— L'Exilée. Buchanan, R. Look round, 333.
— Prose tales. Matthews, B. Books & play-books. — Matthews, B. Aspects fic. 182.
Copper. Bloxam. Metals, 103. — Knox, T. W. Underground, 817. — Scoffern. Useful metals, 524.
— Bibliography. Colby, A. L. Copper in steel.
— Lost art of hardening. Schliemann. Ilios, 737.
— Native, of Michigan. (E. B. Hinsdale) Am. Geog. Soc. 23 : 324.
Copper bowlder, Ontonagon, in U. S. Nat. Mus. (Charles Moore) U. S. Nat. Mus. Rept.' 95 : 1021.
Copper colic. (C. C. Hoyt) Conn. Health, '89 : 242.
Copper implements of America. (H. W. Haynes) Am. Antiq. Soc. Proc. n. s. 3 : 335.
— from Mexico. (F. W. Putnam) Am. Antiq. Soc. Proc. n. s. 2 : 235.
Copper-mine, An Arizona. Todd, M. L. Corona, 357.
Copper-mining, Pre-Columbian, in North America. (R. L. Packard) Smithson. Rept. '92 : 175.
Copper sheathing, Prevention of corrosion of. Davy. Works, 6 : 273.
Coppet Castle. Haussonville. Salon of Necker, 2 : 198.
Coptic church. Gibbon. Decline, chap. 47. — Lane. Mod. Egyp. v. 2.
Coptic language, Intensification in. Abel, C. Ling. ess. 203.
Copyright. Arnold, M. Irish ess. 7. — Carlyle. Ess. — Erskine, T. Speeches, 1 : 201. — Greeley. Ess. pol. econ. 49 — Hood, T. Prose works, 3 : 466. — Macaulay. Miscel. & sp. 609. — Scudder, H. E. Life of N. Webster, ch. 3. — Spencer, H. Var. frag. 18.
— Evolution of. Matthews, B. Books & play-books.
— — in the U. S. 1881. Hatton, J. To-day in Amer. 1 : 207.
— in Canada. (Sir D. Wilson) Roy. Soc. Can. 10 : sec. ii.

Copyright, International. Parton. Topics, 95.
— Thompson, J. P. Amer. com. 151.— (A.
Trollope) Trans. Soc. Sci. Lond. '66 : 119. —
Lodge, H. C. Speeches, 49.
— Law of. Talfourd. Crit. wr. — (T. Webster)
Trans. Soc. Sci. Lond. '59 : 237.
— Question of. Allison. Ess. 2.
— Trade marks and. (C. H. E. Carmichael ; R. A.
Macfie) Trans. Soc. Sci. Lond. '80 : 154.
Copyright-laws, Injustice of. Helps. Brevia.
— United States, Origin of. Webster, N. Papers,
172.
Coq, John. Wallace, R. Anti-Trin. biog. 3 . 19.
Coquelin, B. C. Walkley, A. B. Playhouse, 251.
— and Irving. Winter, W. Shadows, 2 : 285.
— as Tartuffe. Winter, W. Shadows, 2 : 324.
Coquelin, Ernest. Henry, S. Hours w. Pari-
sians, 177.
Coquillart, Guillaume. Besant. Fr. poetry, 163.
Coral and coral reefs. (T. Huxley) Manch. Sci.
lec. 2 : 3. Also in Huxley. Critiques.
Coral-fishers, Feast of. Green, J. R. Stray
studies, 414.
Coral reefs. Holland, H. Ess. 353.
— Structure of. Heilprin. Bermudas.
— Volcanoes and. Dunman. Talks sci. 54.
Coram, Thos., and his foundling asylum. Bolton,
S. K. Givers, 234. — Tillotson, J. Untit. no-
bil. 87.
— in Boston and Taunton. (H. A. Hill) Am. An-
tiq. Soc. Proc. n. s. 8 : 133.
Corbaux, Marie Françoise Catherine Doetyer.
Clayton, E. C. Eng. fem. art. 2 : 68.
Corbet, Richard. Bell, R. Lit. & sci. men, 2 :
159. — Chalmers. Eng. poets, 5 : 553.
— Poems of. Jones, W. A. Lit. stud. 2 : 6.
Corbett, Michael, and others, Boston, 1769.
Chandler, P. W. Am. crim. trials, 1 : 295.
Corbett, Miss. Mitford, M. R. Recoll. 367.
Corbin, Margaret. Clement, J. Noble deeds,
432.
Corbly, John. Drake, S. G. Trag. of wilder-
ness, 335.
Corcoran, Peter [pseud.]. The Fancy. Gosse,
E. Gossip, 269.
Corcoran, Wm. W. Bolton, S. K. Givers, 351.
Corday, Charlotte. Dobson, A. Four French-
women. — Duyckinck. Portr. gall. 1 : 218. —
Fifty famous women, 83. — Hale, S. J. Less.
wom. lives, 168. — Hewitt. Illus. women, 317.
— Russell. Extr. wom. 192. — Watson, H. C.
Heroic wom. 359.
Cordelia and Antigone. Swing. Old pic. 1 : 145.
Cordoba, Gonzalves de, the Great Captain.
James, G. P. R. Commanders, 1 : 55.
Cordon, Grand, How to unhook a. Malortie.
Here, there, 261.
Cordova. Buckley, J. M. Trav. 3 cont. 36. —
Finck, H. T. Spain & Morocco. — Thomas,
M. Scamper thro' Spain, 92. — Hale, E. E.
Seven Span. cit. 40. — Lathrop, G. P. Span.
vistas, 70. — Lee, A. E. Europ. days, 338. —
Prime, S. I. Alhambra, 83. — Stoddard. Red
letter, 16.
— Madrid to. Stoddard, C. A. Span. cit. 94.
— Mosque of. Stoddard, C. A. Span. cit. 100.
— to Seville. Stoddard, C. A. Span. cit. 106.
Corduo, Cremutius. Dunlop, J. Rom. liter. 3 :
506.
Corea. Eden, C. H. China, 281. — Lanman, C.
Lead. men Japan, 326. — U. S. For. rela. '85 :
315. See also Korea.
— and the Coreans. (W. E. Griffis) Am. Geog.
Soc. 29 : 1.
— Bibliography of. Griffis. Hermit.

Corea. The hermit nation. (W. E. Griffis) Am.
Geog. Soc. 13 : 125.
— On horseback across. Norman, H. Far East,
323.
— Question of. Norman, H. Far East, 356.
Corelli, Arcanglo, with portrait. Ehrlich, A.
Cel. violin. 87.
Corfe castle. Freeman. Eng. towns, 149. —
Timbs. Abbeys, 1 : 453.
— and the story of its defence by Lady Bankes.
Hutton, B. Castles, 84.
Corfu. Barrows, S. J. Isles of Greece, 24. —
Freeman. Subj Venice, 343.
— Trip to, in 1887. Baddeley. Travel-tide, 124.
Cori. Freeman. Studies Italy, 123.
Corilla, Maria Maddalena Fernandez. Trollope,
T. A. Dec. Ital. wom. 2 : 393.
Corinna. Arnold, E. Poets of Greece, 150.
Corinth. Freeman. Studies Greece, 183. — Lee,
J. S. Sac. cities, 227. — Mahaffy. Rambles
Greece, 235.
— Gulf of. Freeman. Studies Greece, 202.
— Isthmus of. Arnold, R. A. Levant, 1 : 200.
— of to-day. Buckley, J. M. Trav. 3 cont. 524.
— Sieges of. Robson, W. Sieges, 192.
— to Eleusis. Freeman. Studies Greece, 220.
Corinth, Miss., Battle of. (A. L. Chetlain) Mil.
ess. M. O. L. L. U. S. Ills. 373.
Coriolanus, Shakespeare's. Hazlitt. Char.
Shakes.
Corioli, Siege of. Robson, W. Sieges, 123.
Cork, R. Boyle, earl of. Wrangham. Brit. Plu-
tarch, v. 3.
Cork, Ireland. Silloway. Cathedral towns, 11.
Cork industry. U. S. Cons. Rept. no. 120.
Cormac, King of Cashel. Conyngham, D. P.
Irish saints, 454.
Cormenin, Louis de. Du Camp. Recol. 2 : 299.
Corn, Imports of, into Mexico. (W. P. Sutton)
1893. U. S. Cons. Rept. 42 : 199.
Corn flour. Japp & Holmes. Succ. bus. men, 212.
Corn-law rhymes. Carlyle. Essays.
Corn laws, English. Cobden. Speeches, 8, 23,
188. — Disraeli. Sel. spee. 1 : 46, 111. — Peel,
R. Speeches, 1 : 423, 479, 521. 3 : 587, 709,
822. 4 : 114, 249, 406, 528, 582. — (L. Levi)
Rand. Selec. econ. hist. 207. — Stanton, H. B.
Reforms, 271.
— and protection. Martineau, H. Miscel. 1 : 288.
— Defence of. Rogers, J. E. T. Cobden, 36.
— Repeal of. Nicoll. Great move. 247.
— Speech on, 1842. (R. Cobden) Wagner, L.
Mod. pol. ora. 311.
— Speech on, 1843. (W. J. Fox) Wagner, L. Mod.
pol. ora. 35.
Corn-milling, ancient and modern. (W. Sal-
mon) Galton, F. W. Workers, 81.
Corn starch. See Corn flour.
Cornaro, Catarina. Brooks, E. S. Hist. girls,
134. — Brown, H. F. Venet. stud. 291.
Cornaro, Luigi. Bailey, J. B. Methuselahs, 89.
— Rio. Four martyrs.
Cornazzini dal Borzetti, A. Stebbing. Ital.
poets, v. 1.
Cornbury, Henry Hyde, viscount. Field, R. S.
Prov. courts N. J. 40.
Corneille, P. de, with portrait. Hallard, J. H.
Gallica, 18. — Richards, L. E. Glimpses, 9. —
Shelley, Mrs. Fr. authors, v. 1. — With por-
trait. (F. M. Warren) Warner Lib. 7 : 4065.
— Bibliography. Prov. ref. lists, 4 : 44.
— Poems of. Astie. Louis XIV, 83.
Cornelia. Goodrich, F. B. Women, 43. — Hol-
loway, L. C. Mothers of gt. men, 177. — Owen,
Mrs. O. F. Heroines hist. 64.

Cornelius, Elias. Pierce, B. K. Em. dead, 418.
Cornelius of St. Croix: a negro. Child, L. M. Oasis, 209.
Cornell, Alonzo B., with portrait. Butterfield. Lec. Un. Coll. 1 : 283.
Cornell, Ezra. Bolton, S. K. Poor boys, 238. — Brockett. Men of our day, 619.
Cornell, Samuel G., with portrait. (P. C. Gilbert) Rogers, A. C. Repres. men, 165.
Cornell College, Mount Vernon, Ia. U. S. Bur. Ed. Circ. '93, no. 6 : 148.
Cornell University. College book, 392.
Cornet castle, Guernsey. Timbs. Abbeys, 1 : 533.
Corney, Bolton, and Isaac Disraeli. Hitchman. 18th cent. 254.
Cornice, The [Coast of Italy]. Symonds. Sk. So. Eur. 1 : 9.
Corning, Erastus. Parton, J. Sk. of men of prog.
Cornish miners in America. Head, F. B. Descr. ess. 1 : 1.
Cornplanter. Lossing. Em. Amer. 231.
Cornwall, Barry, pseud. See Proctor, Bryan Waller.
Cornwall, Charles W. Manning, J. A. Speakers, 456.
Cornwall and Devon. Allingham. Varieties, 2 : 44.
— Antiquities of. Müller. Chips, 3.
— Are there Jews in ? Müller. Chips, 3.
— Family traditions of. Timbs. Abbeys, 1 : 527.
— Hill castles in. Timbs. Abbeys, 1 : 510.
— Mines and miners of. Chambers's Repos.no.25.
— Rambles in. Noel. Ess. on poetry.
— Scenery and antiquities of. Merivale. Hist. stud. 355.
Cornwallis, Charles, marquis and earl. Creasy. Etonians, 401. — Foster, E. Heroes Ind. emp. 69. — Gleig. Brit. mil. com. 3 : 115. — Kaye. Indian off. 1 : 1. — Lodge. Portraits (Bohn), v. 8. — With portrait. Caulfield. Kit-cat, 123. — Jesse, J. H. Cel. Eton. v. 2. — Johns. Nav. & mil. heroes.
— and the Indian services. Chesney. Ess. mil. biog. 293.
— Character of. Mackintosh, J. Miscel. 235.
— 100th anniversary of the surrender of. Winthrop. Addresses, 4 : 296.
Cornwallis, F., abp. of Canterbury. Jesse, J. H. Cel. Eton. v. 1. — Ivimey. Eng. Bapt. 2 : 225.
Coronado, Francisco Vasquez de, Explorations of. (J. H. Simpson) Am. Geog. Soc. 5 : 194.
— Expedition of. Bibliography. (G. P. Winship) U. S. Bur. Ethn. 14th rept.
— — True route of. (F. S. Dellenbaugh) Am. Geog. Soc. 29 : 399.
— Seven cities of Cibola, Site of. (E. E. Hale) Am. Antiq. Soc. Proc. n. s. 1 : 236. — (H. W. Haynes) Am. Antiq. Soc. Proc. n. s. 1 : 421.
— Why he went to New Mexico. (G. P. Winship) Am. Hist. Assoc. Rept. '94 : 83.
Coronation, Ceremony of, in England. Strickland. Queens Eng. v. 12.
— of George III. Doran. Queens Hanov. 2.
— of George IV., Queen Caroline and. Doran. Queens Hanov. 27.
Coroner's inquests in London. Wynter. Subtle brains, 46.
Coroners, Jurisdiction of. (H. Cartwright; J. J. Pope) Trans. Soc. Sci. Lond. '66 : 228.
Corot, Camille. Mollett, J. W. Paint. of Barbizon, 2 : 1. — (T. Robinson) Van Dyke, J. C. Mod. Fr. mast. 107. — Van Rensselaer, M. G. Six portraits.

Corporal punishment. Corwin, T. Life and speeches, 139.
Corporate bodies. Hazlitt, W. Table-talk, 369.
Corporation law. (H. Hitchcock) Am. Bar Assoc. 10 : 233.
Corporations and the state. Hoffman, F. S. Sphere, 68.
— in Mass. in colonial times. (A. McF. Davis) Col. Soc. Mass. Trans. 1 : 183.
— in the U. S. (C. F. Adams) Shaler. The U. S. 2 : 191.
— Municipal. Peel, R. Speeches, 3 : 137-388.
— Private, in Amer., Rise and probable decline of. (A. Allison) Am. Bar Assoc. 7 : 241.
Correggio, Antonio. Hundred greatest men, 83. — Jervis, Lady. Painting, 1 : 263. — Jervis, Lady. Sto. of boy-genius, 48. — Lee, H. F. Old painters, 146. — Spooner. Biog. fine arts, 1 : 18. — Symonds. Renais. fine arts, 339. — Jameson. Ital. painters, 290.—Urbino. Princes of art, 162.—Ottley. Ital. school.—Rose, G.B. Renais. masters, 131. — Stearns, F. P. Midsum. Ital. art. 273. — Stillman, W. J. Old Ital. mas. 277. — Van Rensselaer, M. G. Six portraits.
— Criticisms of his pictures. Guizot. Fine arts, 86.
— Magdalen in the desert. (A. Giron) Singleton, E. Great pic. 27.
Correlation. Bartol. Rad. prob. 284.
— Some applications of. (F. M. McMurry) Nat. Educa. Assoc. '96 : 529.
Correlatives, Errors of, suppressed. Bain, A. Prac. ess. 43.
Correspondence [in philosophy]. Peabody, E. P. Æsthetic pap. 112.
Correspondence, Special. Hatton. Jour. Lond. 167.
Correspondents, Distant. Northcote. Lec. & ess. 362.
Corrigan, Sir D. J. Bettany. Em. doctors, 2 : 155.
Corsica, King of. Burke, B. Viciss. of fam. 1 : 144.
Corsica. Benjamin. World's paradises, 74. — Cox, S. S. Search for win. sun, 60. — Sleeper, M. G. Mediter. islands. — Bennett, J. H. Winter on Medit. 255. — Vuillier. Forgot. isles, 143.
— and Maddalena. Taylor, B. Byways, 393.
Corson, Juliet, with portrait. Bolton, S. K. Succ. women, 9.
Corstorphine, Tragedy of. Burke, B. Viciss. of fam. 3 : 202.
Cort, Henry; the story of an inventor. Tillotson, J. Untit. nobil. 233. — Smiles. Indus. biog.
Cort, Richard. Walker, W., jr. Men of sci. 152.
Cortés, Donoso, essay on Catholicism. Brownson. Works, 20 : 279.
Cortez, Hernando. (W. H. Prescott) Ferris, G. T. Gt. leaders, 216. — Hale, E. E. Sto. of adven. 101. — Hewlett. Heroes, 267. — Kelly, C. Voyages, 36. — Murray, J. O'K. Cath. pioneers, 95. — Parton. Peop. bk. biog. 317. — Sands, R. C. Writ. 1. — Tillotson, J. Golden Americas, 59. — Vogel. Cent. of discov. 263. — Winsor. Hist. Amer. v. 2. — With portrait. Murray, J. O'K. Cath. heroes, 237. — Utterton, F. A. Biog. sk. 174.
— Expulsion of, from Mexico. Davenport. Narr. peril. 2 : 208.
— Historical notice of. Sands. Writings, 1 : 1.
Cortona, Pietro da. Criticisms of his pictures. Guizot. Fine arts, 167.
— and Luca Signorelli. E. E. Vari. of fortune, 133.

Country and city, Relative influence of. (J. S. Hough) Am. Pub. Health, 1 : 115.
— — Relative morals of. (W. S. Pierce) Phila. Soc. Sci. Assoc. '75.
— First breath in. Beecher. Star papers, 137.
— Love of. Hazlitt. Round table.
— Sunday in. Dodge, N. S. Sk. of N. E. 55.
Country character. Dodge, M. A. 12 miles, 202.
Country gentleman, The, in England. Jessopp, O. Studies, 184.
Country home in America, A. Taylor, B. At home, 2 : 1.
Country-house, Something like a. Jones, H. L. Ess. 57.
Country-houses and grounds, Sanitary condition of. (G. E. Waring, jr.) Am. Pub. Health, 3 : 130.
Country life. Beecher, H. W. Eyes & ears. — Boyd. Recreat. 1 : 133. — Dodge, M. A. 12 miles, 7.
— compared with city. (J. Stockton-Hough) Phila. Soc. Sci. Assoc. '73.
— Problem of. Strong, J. New era, 164.
— Unsanitary conditions of. (C. Gardner) Conn. Health, '83 : 91.
— Why I prefer. Abbott, C. C. Outings, 190.
    See also Rural life.
Country school, Problem of. (Edward Olney ; W. F. Phelps) Nat. Educa. Assoc. '75 : 7. 76 : 30.
Country schools. (J. P. Slade) Nat. Educa. Assoc. '82 : 17.
— Grading in. (Committee on State School Systems) Nat. Educa. Assoc. '92 : 793.
Country town, Retirement of. Knox. Essays, 3 : 243.
Country wayfarers. Knight. Once on time, 1 : 136.
County franchise and Mr. Lowe. Gladstone. Glean. 1 : 131, 247.
Courage. Bax, E. B. Outlooks, 163. — Brooks, P. Ess. & addr. 319. — Emerson. Soc. & sol. — Higginson. Out-door, 31. — Mathews, W. Men, p. & t. 253. — Emerson. Society, 237. — Starling, E. Noble deeds wom. 291.
— Difficulty of justly estimating. Helps. Brevia.
— Education of. Clarke, J. F. Self-culture, 327.
— Moral and physical. Stephen, J. F. Ess. by barr. 175.
— Self-reliance and. Munger. On threshold, 99.
Courbet, Gustave. (S. Isham) Van Dyke, J. C. Mod. Fr. mast. 199.
Courier, Paul Louis. Maccall. For. biog. 1 : 84.
Courten, William. Edwards, E. Founders Brit. Mus. 1 : 247.
Courtenay, William, 1381–96. Hook. Abps. Cant. 4 : 315. — Sergeant, L. Wiclif, 149, 299.
Courtesy, American : Lady Mavourneen on her travels. Curtis, G. W. Other ess. 155.
— Castiglione on, 1528. Maxwell, Sir H. Rainy days, 11.
Courthope, W. J. (W. Whyte) Miles, A. H. Poets of cent. 9 : 559.
Courting, On going. Friswell. Gentle life, 1 : 96.
Courtney, Leonard Henry. Davidson, J. M. Eng. liberals, 128.
Court of Appeals, The old Federal. (J. F. Jameson) Am. Hist. Assoc. 3 : 383.
Court-of-session. Miller, H. Hist. ess. 282.
Court circles. Godkin. Reflections, 267.
Court life in Germany in the 17th century. Doran. Queens Hanov. 1.
Courts of equity. Grant, Jas. Bench & bar, 1 : 29.
Courts of law. Grant, Jas. Bench & bar, 1 : 9.

Courts of law, Administration of, in Chicago. Altgeld. Live ques. 48.
— Anecdotes of. Grant, Jas. Bench & bar, 2 : 169.
— Delay and uncertainty in, Avoidable causes of. (A. Russell) Am. Bar Assoc. 14 : 197.
— English, Division of the. Foss. Judges, 2 : 160.
— in London, Opening of. Harrison, F. Choice of books, 259.
— — Scenes in. Smalley. Lond. lett. 2 : 447.
Courts-martial and trial of civilians. Davis, H. W. Speeches, 538.
Courtship. Martin, E. S. Windfalls, 25.
Courvoisier, François Benjamin, Trial of, for murder of Lord W. Russell. Townsend, W. C. Mod. state trials, 1 : 267.
Cousin, V. Bowen, F. Crit. ess. — Frothingham. Transcend. 66.
Cousin, Victor, with portrait. Warner Lib. 7 : 4079.
— and his philosophy. Brownson. Works, 2 : 307, 533.
— Reports on German schools. Hamilton. Discus.
Coutances, Dinner at. Dodd, A. B. Three Norm. inns, 276.
Couthon, Georges. Smythe, G. S. Hist. fancies, 278.
Coutts, Baroness Burdett. Bolton, S. K. Girls famous, 320.
Coutts family (bankers) of Edinburgh and Lond. Bourne, H. R. F. Eng. merch. 2 : 120.
Couture, Thomas. (G. P. A. Healy) Van Dyke, J. C. Mod. Fr. mast. 3.
Covenanters, Scottish. Bayne. Pur. revol. 209.
— Blackie, J. S. Lay serm. 236.
— Baillie the covenanter. Carlyle. Crit. ess.
— Proceedings against. Burton, J. H. Crim. tri. 2 : 173.
Covent Garden. Lennox, W. P. Plays, 1 : 131.
— in the 18th century. Dobson, A. 18th cent. vign. 3 : 324.
Coventry, Francis. Pompey the little. Gosse, E. Gossip, 201.
Coventry, Maria, Countess of. Gerard. Irish beauties, 30 : 57.
Coventry, Sir Thomas. Campbell. Ld. Chan. 3 : 206. — Foss. Judges, 6 : 277. — Lodge. Portraits (Bohn), v. 4.
Coventry. Hawthorne. Engl. note-bks. 1 : 175.
Coverdale, Myles. Holland, J. Psalmists, 1 : 88.
— Ivimey. Eng. Bapt. 1 : 100.
Covering, Protective. (L. Cheney-Ward) Brooklyn Eth. Assoc. Life, 247.
Covilham, Pedro de, and Bartholomew Diaz. Vogel. Cent. of discov. 49.
Cow, How to keep one. N. J. Labor, '80 : 227.
Cowbirds, The. (Charles Bendire) U. S. Nat. Mus. Rept. '93 : 587.
Cowdray, England. Freeman. Eng. towns, 367.
Cowdray House. Timbs. Abbeys, 1 : 373.
Cowen, Frederic H. With portrait. Buffen, F. F. Mus. celeb. 63. — With portraits. Willeby, C. Mast. Eng. mus. 173.
Cowen, Joseph. With photo. Cooper, T. Men of mark, 5 : 21. — Davidson, J. M. Eng. lib. 51. — With portr. Jones, E. R. Heroes of ind. 271. — Hinton. Eng. radicals, 77. — Reid, T. W. Politicians, 1 : 169. — Ritchie. Brit. sena. 177.
Cowley, Abraham. Bell, R. Lit. & sci. men, 1 : 38. — (S. Johnson) Chalmers. Eng. poets, 7 : 3. — (J. H. Friswell) Cowley. Ess. vii. — Gosse. Shakes. to Pope. — Gosse. 17th cent.

18th cent. **2** : 38. — Men & wom. of France, **2** : 217.

Crebillon, Prosper Jolyot. Houssaye. Men of 18th cent. **2** : 7. — Vinet. Fr. lit. 18th cent. 100. — Men & wom. of France, **2** : 183. — With portrait. (R. Sanderson) Warner Lib. **7** : 4167. — and the French stage. Hawkins. Fr. stage 18th cent. v. **1**.

Crèche, The. Field, Mrs. H. M. Sk. France, 125.

Crécy, Battle of. Adams, W. H. D. Batt. sto. 39. — Adams, W. H. D. Memo. batt. **1** : 129. — Clinton, H. R. Crécy to Assaye, 28. — George, H. B. Battles, 54. — King, C. Battles, 218. — Low, C. R. Gt. battles, 4.

Credi, Lorenzo di. Stillman, W. J. Old Ital. mas. 205.

Credit. Everett, E. Orat. v. **2**. — Kempner, W. Common-sense soc. 159. — Against state interference with. Bastiat. Ess. on pol. econ. 97. — and bills of exchange. Greene, W. B. Soc. frag. 59. — A broader basis of. (W. S. Logan) Am. Bar Assoc. **21** : 412. — Influence of, on prices. Bolles. Chap. pol. econ. 166. — Public. Hume. Philos. works, **3** . 381.

Credit associations, German, 1897. (J. Muth) U. S. Cons. Rept. **54** : 504.

Credit system, The. Conn. Labor, '**86** : xxxi.

Credit systems. U. S. Cons. Rept. no. 43. — Later American. Bureau Am. Repub. Bull. no. 1.

Credulity; On being cheated. Friswell. About, 276. — Resolute. (F. W. H. Myers) Soc. Psych. Res. **11** : 213.

Creeds. Bain, A. Prac. ess. 257. — Channing. Works, **2** : 289. — Manning, J. M. Sermons, 275. — Stanley, A. P. Chr. inst. 296. — Thompson, J. P. Amer. com. 247. — Stryker. Hamilton, 152. — Ancient, Rights of believers in. Phelps, A. Portfolio, 38. — and confessions of faith. Schaff, P. Christ & Chr. 135. — Crumbling. (R. F. Ingersoll) Why I am, 154. — of principal churches. Butler, Charles. Works, v. **4**. — reformed, Consensus of, and theology. Schaff, P. Christ & Chr. 153. — Subscription to. *See* Subscription.

Crellius, Christopher. Wallace, R. Anti-Trin. biog. **3** : 285. — A providence in the life of. Wallace, R. Anti-Trin. biog. **3** : 590.

Crellius, John, jr. Wallace, R. Anti-Trin. biog. **2** : 558. **3** : 306.

Crellius, Samuel. Wallace, R. Anti-Trin. biog. **3** : 468.

Crema. Symonds. Sk. So. Eur. **2** : 188.

Cremation. Internat. Health Ex. Sanita. — Phila. Soc. Sci. Assoc. '74. — Richardson, B. W. Ministry, 232. — Wordsworth, C. Miscel. **2** : 407. — and burial. (J. F. A. Adams) Mass. Health, '75 : 243. — as a safeguard against epidemics. (J. D. Beugless) Am. Pub. Health, **10** : 140. — Bibliography. Bost. Pub. Lib. Bull. no. 30. — in Siam. Leonowens. Eng. governess, 204. — or earth burial, which ? (E. A. Guilbert) Am. Pub. Health, **21** : 201. — Proper disposal of the dead. (J. Morris) Am. Pub. Health, **11** : 73.

Cremation. Sanitation by fire, Ultimate of. (J. M. Keating) Am. Pub. Health, **10** : 116. — Sir H. Thompson and. Bettany. Em. doctors, **2** : 194.

Cremona. Hare. Cities of No. Italy, **1** : 230. — Sieges of. Robson, W. Sieges, 218.

Creole village in Louisiana; sketch from a steamboat. Irving. Crayon pap. 181.

Crequi, Renée Charlotte, Marchioness. Irving. Crayon pap. 100.

Crescenzi, Pietro. Mitchell. Wet days, 77.

Cresswell, Sir Cresswell. Grant, J. Bench & bar, **2** : 87

Creswell, Mrs. Julia Pleasants. Davidson, J. W. Writ. of South. 113. — Raymond, I. Southland wr. **1** : 255.

Crete. Holland, J. E. Europ. concert in East. ques. 70. — Taylor, B. Trav. in Greece, 89. — Tozer. Islands of the Ægean, 25. — and Greece. Bibliography. Providence Pub. Lib. Bull. Mar. '97. — Salem Pub. Lib. Bull. April, '97. — Waltham (Mass.) Pub. Lib. Bull. Apr.-May, '97. — Bibliography. Pickford-Smith, R. A. H. Cretan sketches. — Insurrections in. Arnold, R. H. Levant, **1** : 127. — Occasional notes on, 1866–68. Strangford. Selec. writ. **2** : 1.

Crétin, Guillaume. Besant. Fr. poetry, 184.

Cretin, Joseph. Clarke, R. H. Cath. bishops, **2** : 415.

Crewdson, Mrs. Jane (Fox). Hatfield, E. F. Poets of ch. 173. — Miller, Jos. Singers church, 2d ed. 502.

Crewe, Lady Frances Anne. Willing. Dames, 69.

Crewe, Sir Randolf, chief justice of England, 1625–26. Campbell. Ch. just. **1** : 303.

Crewe, Sir Thomas. Manning, J. A. Speakers, 294. — Woolrych. Serjeants, **1** : 232.

Crichton, Hugh. Graham, W. Ess. 291.

Crichton, James, "the admirable." Irving, D. Scot. writ. **1** : 258. — Masson, M. Celebrated chil. 315. — (D. Irving) Macaulay. New biog. 305.

Crichton family. Taylor, J. Fam. of Scot. **1** : 174.

Cricket in England. Whitney, C. W. Sport. pilgr. 320.

Criddle, Mrs. Mary Ann (Alabaster). Clayton, E. C. Eng. fem. art. **2** : 70.

Crime. Friswell. About, 141. — Godwin, W. Polit. justice, **2** : 321. — Illinois charity, '72 : 193. — Haweis. Curr. coin. — (J. Hawthorne) Conf. char. & correc. '**85** : 413. — and criminals. (F. M. Voigt) Nat. Pris. Assoc. '88 : 246. — and its causes. (R. Vaux) Pa. Labor, 1875. — and its excuses. (W. Thomson) Oxf. ess. '55 : 177. — and its remedy. (O. Brown) Barrows, J. H. Parl. relig. **2** : 1076. — and punishment, Progress as to. Samuelson, Jas. Civiliz'n, 229. — and transportation in Great Britain. Alison. Ess. 1. — Density of population and. (J. C. Symons) Trans. Soc. Sci. Lond. '57 : 265. — Education and. Boutwell. Educa. topics, 49. — — Common schools and crime. (H. Mann *et al.*) Mass. education, **11** : 39. — — in Massachusetts. Mass. educa. **23** : 59. — Epidemics of. Elam. Phys. prob. 137. — Humanitarianism and. (W. Tallack) N. Y. Pris. Assoc. **26**, app. : 204.

Criticism, Domestic; Critic on the hearth. Payn. Private views, 20.
— Dramatic. *See* Dramatic criticism.
— Educational quality of. Mabie. My study fire, 2 : 158.
— English. Stephen, L. Eng. thought, 1 : 34.
— Function of, at the present time. Arnold, M. Ess. in crit. 1.
— German. Curran. Irish bar, 2 : 55.
— How to bear. Helps. Brevia.
— in French literature. Pellissier. Lit. move. Fr. 267, 385.
— Kinds of. Saintsbury. Ess. Eng. lit. ix.
— Literary. Ruskin. Arrows, v. 2.
— — American. Boyesen. Lit. silhouettes, 97.
— — Bibliography. Gayley, C. M., and Scott, F. N. Meth. lit. crit. — Spingarn, J. E. Lit. crit. in renaissance.
— — in France. Dowden. New stud. 388.
— — in Latin antiquity. Nettleship, H. Lec. 2d ser. 44.
— — Newspaper. Nadal, E. S. Ess. 261.
— — Purpose of. Bristed. Pieces, 4 : 34.
— Modern. Knox. Essays, 1 : 155.
— — Significance of. Mabie. Ess. lit. interp.
— On giving and taking. Helps. Friends, 1st ser. 1.
— Poetry and. Brimley, G. Ess. 184.
— Popular, and Gilfillan. McNicoll, T. Ess. Eng. lit. 204.
— Progress of. Hazlitt, W. C. Offspring, 145.
— Right standard of. Winter, W. Shadows, 2 : 13.
— Sensitiveness to, Folly of. Mathews. Lit. style, 100.
— The slyly-denigrating kind of. Helps. Brevia.
— Some principles of. Symonds. Ess. 1 : 84.
— Vulgarity in. Hazlitt. Crit. & dram. ess.
— Weight, etc. of. Purnell. Liter. 14.
— Whole duty of critics. Matthews, B. Books & play-books.
Criticisms of French and Italian pictures. Guizot. Fine arts, 53.
Critics. Dodge, M. A. Skirmish, 399. — Helps. Brevia. — Maurice. Friendship, 362.
— and criticism. Ess. from Nation, 11. — Tuckerman. Charac. 26.
— and their craft. Watson, W. Excur. in crit. 81.
— and people. Zangwill. Without prej. 114.
— art, Qualifications of. Jenkin, Fl. Papers, 1 : 93.
— British. Whipple. Ess. & rev. v. 2.
— Common-place. Hazlitt. Round table.
— English. Oliphant, M. Lit. hist. 2 : 35.
— — Quarrels of. Caine, T. H. Cobwebs, 232.
— English of. Archer, W. Theatre, 203.
— Mistakes of. Walsh, W. S. Paradox, 45.
— Short essay on. Ossoli. Art, 13.
— Should they be gentlemen? Fawcett, E. Agnost. 194.
Crittenden, John Jordan. Johnston, A. Amer. ora. 3 : 275. — With portrait. Duyckinck. Nat. portr. gall. 2 : 277. — Savage. Liv. repr. men. 128.— With portrait. Scott, H. W. Dist. Am. lawy. 235.
Crittenden, Mrs. John Jordan, with portrait. Ellet. Queens Am. soc. 327.
Crittenden, Llewellyn. Walker, C. D. Biog. Va. Mil. Inst. 133.
Crittenden, Thomas T., with portrait. (F. C. Farr) Scott, N. W. Dist. Am. lawy. 241.
Croakers of society and literature. Whipple. Ess. & rev. v. 2.
Croatia, Tour in. Vaca. tourists, 1 : 76.
Crocker, W. Miller, S. F. Bench of Ga. v. 1.
Crockett, Charles G. Walker, C. D. Biog. Va. Mil. Inst. 137.

Crockett, David. Lossing. Em. Amer. 311. — Parton. Triumphs, 369.
Crockett, Samuel Rutherford, with portrait. Warner Lib. 7 : 4181.
Croft, Marian. Clayton, E. C. Eng. fem. art. 2 : 185.
Croft, William. Keddie. Mus. comp. 291.
Crofters, The. Chamberlain, J. Speeches, 206.
Croke, Sir John. Manning, J. A. Speakers, 273.
Croke, Richard. Creasy. Etonians, 36.
Croker, John Wilson. Grant, J. Recoll. Ho. Comm. 97. — Hazlitt. Parl. portr. 124. — Martineau, H. Biog. sk. 69.
Croker, Thos. Crofton. Smith, C. R. Retrospec. 1 : 251.
Croly, Dr. George (1780-1860). Gilfillan. Mod. lit. 133. — Grant, Jas. Metropol. pul. 144. — Hall, S. C. Book of mem. 232. — Griswold, R. W. Sac. poets. — Procter, B. W. Autob. 133. — Warner Lib. 7 : 4197.
— Tales of the Great St. Bernard. Legaré. Writ. 2 : 205.
Crombie, Alexander. McCosh. Scot. phil. 265.
Crombie, John S. (J. E. Bradley; R. G. Huling) Nat. Educa. Assoc. '94 : 241.
Crome, John, "Old Crome." Redgrave. Century of p. 2 : 361. — Wedmore. Studies, 2d ed. 119.
Crommelin, May, with portrait. Black, H. C. Wom. authors, 210.
Crompton, Samuel. Espinasse. Lanc. worth. v. 2. — Howe, H. Em. merch. 249. — Lewis, T. C. Mechanicians, 156. — Famous boys, 189. — Towle, C. M. Heroes of inven. 84. — Walker, W., jr., Men of sci. 35. — Woodcroft, B. Biog. invent. 12.
Cromwell, Bridget, daughter of Oliver. Anderson, J. Mem. wom. Pur. 1 : 346.
Cromwell, Mrs. Elizabeth Stuart, mother of Oliver. Anderson, Jas. Mem. wom. Pur. 1 : 272.
Cromwell, Mrs. Elizabeth Bourchier, wife of Oliver. Anderson, Jas. Mem. wom. Pur. 1 : 282. — Jesse. Court of Eng. Stuarts, 2 : 337.
Cromwell, Elizabeth. *See* Claypole, Elizabeth.
Cromwell, Frances, daughter of Oliver. Anderson, J. Mem. wom. Pur. 2 : 31.
Cromwell, Mrs. Hannah (Hewling), daughter of Oliver. Anderson, Jas. Mem. wom. Pur. 2 : 372.
Cromwell, Henry. Jesse. Court of Eng. Stuarts, 2 : 362.
Cromwell, Mary, daughter of Oliver. Anderson, J. Mem. wom. Pur. 2 : 1.
Cromwell, Oliver. Adams, W. H. D. Memo. batt. 1 : 261. — Bayne. Pur. revol. 387. — Carlyle. Heroes. — Cust. Warriors civ. 2 : 541. — With portrait. Forster. Brit. statesm. 6 : 7. — Forster. Statesm. of Comm. — Gleig. Brit. mil. com. 1 : 199.— James, G. P. R. Commanders, 1 : 149. — Lamartine. Cel. char. 2 : 119.— Lodge. Portraits (Bohn), v. 5. — Lord, J. Beacon, 4 : 91. — Ossoli. Life without, 179. — Russell, W. Extraor. men, 41. — Smith, G. Three statesm. 67. — Vaughan, R. Ess. 2 : 1. — Wilson, J. G. Illus. sol. 131. — (T. B. Macaulay) Ferris, G. T. Gt. leaders, 315. — Gardiner, S. R. Hist. biog. 152. — Hundred greatest men, 419. — Ivimey. Eng. Bapt. 1 : 220. — Jesse. Court of Eng. Stuarts, 2 : 235.— Myers, F. Lec. gt. men, 243. — Quayle, W. A. Poet, 39. — Stanton, H. B. Reforms, 119.— Thayer, W. M. Turn. points, 282. — Wise, D. Men of renown, 183. — Wrangham. Brit. Plutarch, v. 3.

Crystal-gazing. Mason, R. O. Telepathy, 198.
Crystal palace, London, 1855. Eagles. Ess. 265.
— New York, 1851, and its lessons. Greeley. Hints ref. 401.
— — Opening of. Ruskin. Miscel. v. 2.
Crystalline and molecular forces. J. Tyndall. Manch. sci. lec. 5–6 : 141.
Crystallization. Buckley, A. B. Thro' magic glass, 96. — (G. D. Liveing) Smithson. Rept. '92 : 269.
Crystallogenic forces. Hunt, R. Poe. of sci. 50.
Crystals, Rejuvenescence of. (J. W. Judd) Smithson. Rept. '92 : 281.
Crystal-vision, Recent experiments in. (J. H. Hyslop) Soc. Psych. Res. 5 : 486. 12 : 259.
Ctesias. Mills. Poets of Greece, 480.
Ctesiphon. Milizia. Lives arch. 1 : 23.
Cuba and Anglo-Amer. relations. (J. M. Callahan) Am. Hist. Assoc. Rept. '97 : 193.
— and the Cubans. Bryant. Prose, 2 : 120.
— and Porto Rico, 1898. U. S. Cons. Rept. 57 : 321.
— — Education in. (R. L. Packard) U. S. Bur. Educa. Rept. '97–98, 1 : 909.
— Annexation of, Sanitary interest of U. S. in. (B. Lee) Am. Pub. Health, 15 : 47.
— Bibliography. (A. P. C. Griffin) U. S. Lib. Cong. '98.— Norwich (Ct.) Otis Lib. Bull. Mar. '98. — Newark (N. J.) Lib. News, May, '98. — Paterson (N. J.) Pub. Lib. Bull. Apr. '98. — Pepper, C. M. To-morrow in Cuba. — Providence Pub. Lib. Bull. Mar. '96. — Rowan, A. S. & Ramsey, M. M. Cuba. — Salem (Mass.) Pub. Lib. Bull. May, '95, Apr. '98. — Somerville (Mass.) Pub. Lib. Bull. Feb. '97. — Wilkesbarre (Pa.) Osterhout Free Lib. News letter, July, '96.
— Expeditions against. Brownson. Works, 16 : 272.
— Import duties of, 1891. Bur. Am. Repub. no. 10.
— in war-time. Davis, R. H. Year, 99.
— Shadows in. Deming. By-ways, 124.
— Situation in, in 1825. (Jas. Schouler) Mass. Hist. Soc. Proc. 2d ser. 12 : 360.
— Tariff of, '91. (R. O. Williams) U. S. Cons. Rept. 35 : 5.
— — 1897. U. S. Cons. Rept. 55 : 577.
— U. S. diplomacy in regard to. (J. H. Latané) Am. Hist. Assoc. Rept. '97 : 217.
Cubics, New method of solving. (E. W. Evans) N. Y. Regents, 84 : 605.
Cubitt, Thomas. Jerdan. Men, 139.
Cudworth, Ralph. Tulloch. Rational theol. 17th cent. 2 : 193.
— Intellectual system. Disraeli, I. Amen. (N. Y. 2 v.) 2 : 397.
Cuenca, Reformers in. Stoughton. Span. ref. 50.
Cueva, Conspiracy of. James, G. P. R. Dark sce.
Cujum, On the word. Latham. Opuscula, 60.
Culdee bishops. Blaikie, W. G. Preachers Scot. 34.
Cullen, Paul, Cardinal. Em. persons, 2 : 116.
Cullen, W. Pettigrew. Med. portr. gall. v. 4.
— and revolutions in medicine. Hamilton. Discuss.
— Eulogium on. Rush, B. Ess. 316.
Cullis, Dr. Charles, the consumptive's friend. Japp. Noble workers, 180.
Culloden, Field of. Winter. Old shrines, 98.
Cullom, Shelby M., with portrait. (J. Moses) Scott, H. W. Dist. Am. lawy. 249.
Cullum, Gen. Geo. W. Am. Geog. Soc. 24 : 142.

Cullum geographical medal. Am. Geog. Soc. 29 : 246.
Culmbach, Hans von. (A. Rosenberg) Dohme, R. Early mast. 135.
Culture. Emerson. Conduct, 111.— Holland, J. G. Every-day, 1 : 1. — Hudson. Stud. Wordsw. 259.— Mabie. My study fire, 2 : 34.
— Academic. Diman. Orations, 70.
— Æsthetic, in Troy Female Seminary (Mrs. J. H. Willard) N. Y. Regents, 83 : 539.
— and civilization. Martin, E. S. Cousin Anthony, 119.
— and limitation. (J. J. Lewis) N. Y. Regents, 91 : 429.
— Matthew Arnold's conception of. Harrison, F. Choice of books, 97.
— beyond ordinary school period. (J. H. Vincent) Nat. Educa. Assoc. '87 : 179.
— The common right to. Kempner, W. Commonsense soc. 79.
— Cost of. Giles, H. Illus. of gen. 182.
— General, and professional success. Mackenzie, M. Ess. 288.
— — and special, in American schools and colleges. (W. D. Wilson) N. Y. Regents, 92 : 510.
— higher, Health and. (S. Osgood) Am. Pub. Health, 2 : 201.
— imparted in free schools. (Richard Edwards) Nat. Educa. Assoc. '73 : 51.
— in elementary schools. (G. P. Brown) Nat. Educa. Assoc. '79 : 135.
— in Germany. Baring-Gould. Germany, 438.
— Limits of. Gildersleeve. Ess. 3.
— Meaning and uses of. Symonds. Key of blue, 195.
— Mental. Bulwer, E. Caxtoniana. — (J. Ward) Tollemache. Ess. & mock-ess. 72.
— modern, The part of five great Europ. nations in. Hillebrand. Gen. thought, v. 1.
— — necessary for specialists. Bowen, F. Gleanings, 8.
— Plea for. Higginson. Atlan. Ess. 1. — Ess. from Nation, 215.
— Popular. Morley, J. Crit. miscel. 3 : 1. Same in Prose masterpieces, 1 : 281.
— Relations of, to practical life. (I. G. Greenwood) Owens. College essays, '74 : 1.
— The *summum bonum.* Knight, W. Stud. 225.
— Symmetrical. (J. T. Edwards) N. Y. Regents, '85 : 511.
— What is yours to me ? Warner, C. D. Rela. of lit. 99.
Culturkampf, The, in Germany. Pressensé. Contemp. port. 103.
Culver, Reuben. Livingston, J. Dist. Amer. 371.
Culverwel, Nathaniel. Tulloch. Rational Theol. 17th cent. 2 : 410.
Cumæan Sibyl, The. Macmillan, H. Rom. mosaics, 88.
— Cave of the. Adams, W. H. D. Fam. caves, 146.
Cumberland, Anne, duchess of. Gerard. Irish beauties, 210. — Willing. Dames, 57.
Cumberland, Eleanor Brandon, countess of. Strickland. Tudor prin. 295-297.
Cumberland, George Clifford, 3d earl of. Barrow, J. Nav. worthies, 440. — Bourne, H. R. F. Eng. seam. 2 : 248. — Edgar. Sea-kings, 186. —Lodge. Portraits (Bohn), v. 3.— Burke, S. H. Hist. portr. Tudor, 3 : 408. — Southey & Bell. Brit. admirals, v. 3.
Cumberland, Henry Clifford, 5th earl of. Holland, J. Psalmists, 1 : 299.

Pierce, E. L. Addresses, 343. — Richardson. Amer. lit. **1** : 380. — Smalley. Stud. 386. — With portrait. (E. Cary) Warner Lib. **7** : 4221.

Curtis, George William, at home. (G. P. Lathrop) Gilder. Authors, 73.

Curtis, Joseph Bridgham, with portrait. Bartlett, J. R. R. I. officers, 225.

Curtis, Moses. Goddard, W. G. Pol. & mis. writ. **1** : 315.

Curtis, Russell H. Am. Bar Assoc. **21** : 660.

Curtius, Ernst. Am. Antiq. Soc. Proc. n. s. **11** : 177. — With portrait. Warner Lib. **7** : 4241.

Curves, Greek horizontal, discovery of, in Maison Carrée, at Nîmes. (W. H. Goodyear) Smithson. Rept. '94 : 573.

Curwen, John. With portrait. (N. J. Ross) Ewart, H. C. Leaders, 335. — Lonsdale. Worthies Cumb. v. 1.

Curwen, ——, an Anglo-Indian man of letters. Macmillan, M. Globe-trotter India, 51.

Curwood, ——. Grant, J. Bench & bar, **2** : 147.

Curzon, Robert, cardinal legate. Williams, R. F. Eng. card. **1** : 205.

Cusa, Nicholas of, cardinal. Pastor, L. Hist. popes, **2** : 105.

Cushing, Benjamin Tupper. Coggeshall. Poets of west, 489.

Cushing, Caleb. Bungay. Off-hand, 390. — Loring, J. S. 100 Bost. ora. 513. — Savage. Liv. repres. men, 143.

Cushing, Harry C. Bartlett, J. R. R. I. officers, 424.

Cushing, Joseph. Knapp, S. L. Em. lawyers, 339.

Cushing, Theodore. (W. T. Cushing) N. E. Hist.-Gen. Soc. Biog. **1** : 227.

Cushing, William, 1732–1810. Flanders. Ch. just. **2** : 11.

Cushing, William Barker, with portr. Headley, J. T. Farragut, 383.

— and the "Albemarle." Lodge & Roosevelt. Hero-tales, 291.

Cushman, Charlotte. Badeau. Vagabond, 207. — Cook, D. Hours w. players, **2** : 182. — Matthews, B. Actors, **4** : 137. — With portr. (L. Whiting) Our fam. wom. 207. — With portrait. Reignolds, Kate. Actors, 17. — Duyckinck. Portr. gall. **2** : 554. — Hanaford. Wom. of cent. 556. — Hutton, L. Plays, 226. — Marston, J. W. Rec. actors, **2** : 65. — Winter, W. Shadows, **1** : 206. **2** : 119.

— Play-acting of. Murdoch, J. E. Stage, 233.

Cushman, Miss Major Pauline. Moore, F. Women of the war, 170.

Cushman, Robert. Belknap. Amer. biog. **3** : 70.

Cusins, Sir Wm. Geo., with portrait. Buffen. Mus. celeb. **2** : 73.

Cust, Sir John. Manning, J. A. Speakers, 440.

Custer, Geo. A., Gen. Glazier, W. Heroes, 413. — With portrait. (F. Whittaker) Rogers, A. C. Repres. men, 177.

Custom and education. Bacon. Ess.

— and law. Goldsmith. Miscel. (N. Y. 4 v.) **1** : 132.

Custom-house, Comedy of the. Repplier. Ess. in min. 104.

— Tradition and. Hamerton. Intellec. 193.

Customs of the people, the clubs, and the stock exchange. Williams, Syd. Forensic, 91.

Custozza, Battle of, 1866. Adams, C. Gr. camp. 477.

Cuthbert, St. Kingsley. Hermits, 291. — Montalembert. Monks, **4** : 377.

Cuthbert, Archbishop. Hook. Abps. Cant. **1** : 217.

Cuthbert, Tonstal, bishop of Durham. Burke, S. H. Hist. portr. Tudor, **3** : 280. — Conyngham, D. P. Irish saints, 405.

Cuthell, John, Trial of. Erskine, T. Speeches, 526.

Cutler, Ebenezer, D. D. Am. Antiq. Soc. Proc. n. s. **12** : 226.

Cutler, Mrs. Lizzie Petit. Davidson, J. W. Writ. of South, 121. Raymond, I. Southland wr. **2** : 821.

Cutler, Pliny. Livingston, J. Dist. Amer. 179.

Cutpurse, Moll. (C. Andrews) Vincent, A. Twelve bad women, 49. — Whitehead, C. Highwaymen, **1** : 70.

Cutten, John. Wallace, R. Anti-Trin. biog. **2** : 415.

Cutter, George Washington. Coggeshall. Poets of west, 303.

Cutting, Jonas. (J. A. Peters) Memo. of judges fr. Dartm. 112.

Cutting and carving. Boyd. Every-day, 278.

Cutting-out expeditions, Famous. Fitchett. Deeds, 175.

Cuttle-fish, Gigantic. (W. S. Kent) Estes. Half-hour recr. 16.

Cutts, John, Lord, Letters of. (R. C. Winthrop, jr.) Mass. Hist. Proc. 2d ser. **2** : 171.

Cutts, Lady. Burder. Pious wom. 141.

Cutts, Mary. Hemenway. Poets of Vt. 92.

Cuvier, G. L. C. F. D., Baron. Bolton, S. K. Fam. men of science. — Duncan, P. M. Botanists, 178. — Knox, R. Great artists, 1. — Stoughton, J. Worthies of sci. 234. — Hundred greatest men, 364.

Cuyler, Theodore L., with portrait. Bungay. Pen-portr. 21.

Cuyp, Aelbert. Cundall. Landsc. painters Holl. — Van Dyke, J. C. Dutch mast. 145.

— Country of. Fairholt. Homes Rubens, 119.

Cuzzoni, Francesca, vocalist. Clayton, E. C. Queens, 52. — Edwards, H. S. Prima don. **1** : 42. — Hogarth. Mem. opera, **1** : 297. — Needham. Queens of song.

"Cyane," frigate, Capture of. Dawson. Batt. of U. S. **2** : 422.

Cyclades, The. Barrows, S. J. Isles of Greece, 344.

Cycles, Theory of. (H. P. Blavatsky) Five years theos. 485.

Cycling in England. Whitney, C. W. Sport. pilgr. 310. *See* Bicycling.

Cyclone, Western. Rutgers, L. On saddle.

Cygnus expirans. Prime, W. C. I go a-fishing, 105.

Cymbeline, Shakespeare's. Hazlitt. Char. Shakes.

Cynewulf. Brooke, S. A. Hist. early Eng. lit. 371.

Cynic, Character of the. Malkin. Class. disq. 81.

Cynicism. Finlayson, T. C. Ess. 194. — Mathews, W. Men, p. & t. 283. — Ballantyne. Ess. 107.

— in literature. Pearson, C. H. Reviews, 61.

Cynics, The. Lewes. Biog. phil.

Cynoscephalæ, Battle of. King, C. Battles, 125.

Cyprian, St., of Carthage. Blakey, R. Prim. fathers, 120. — Cave. Lives of fathers, **1** : 374. — Charles. Martyrs, 73. — Farrar. Lives of fathers, **1** : 185. — Pressensé. Martyrs, 414. — Evans, R. W. Biog. early church, **2** : 135. — Hort, F. J. A. Ante-N. fathers, 93. — Ker, J. Lec. hist. preach. 98. — (W. M. Sinclair) Lefroy, W. Lec. eccl. hist. 113. — Wilson, Wm. Pop. preach. anc. church, 11.

— Bibliography. Benson, E. W. Cyprian.

Cyprus. Buckley, J. M. Trav. 3 cont. 497. — Kinglake. Eothen, 55. — Warner, C. D. Levant, 229.
— Ancient. Gardner, P. New chap. Gr. hist.
— Antiquities and inscriptions of. (I. H. Hall) N. Y. Regents, **89** : 523. **90** : 589.
— Mediæval kingdom of. Stubbs. Lec. on hist. 156.
— Researches in. Newton. Essays, 303.
— Trip to. Butler, W. F. Far out, 311.
Cyrenaic School, The. Lewes. Biog. phil.
Cyril, St., bishop of Jerusalem. Portrait. Blakey, R. Prim. fathers, 198. — Cave. Lives of fathers, 3 : 91. — Maclear. Apostles, 201.
Cyrus, the Mede. Hastings, F. Obscure charac. 160. — Johnson, S. Ori. relig. Persia, 281.
— March of, and retreat of the 10,000. Lord, J. Anc. states, 294.
— The servant of the Lord. Kingsley, C. Lec. Amer. 98 ; also in Hist. lec. 265.
Czapska, Comtesse. Van de Velde. Fr. fic. **2** : 143.
Czars, The. Doran. Monarchs, **2** : 168.
Czechovicius, Albert. Wallace, R. Anti-Trin. biog. **3** : 84.
Czechovicius, Martin. Wallace, R. Anti-Trin. biog. **2** : 220.
Czenadius, Paul. Wallace, R. Anti-Trin. biog. **3** : 58.
Czerny, Carl, with portrait. Bie, O. Hist. of piano, 216.

Dabney, Basil G. Walker, C. D. Biog. Va. Mil. Inst. 160.
Dabney, Edward M. Walker, C. D. Biog. Va. Mil. Inst. 161.
Dabney, Robert L. Davidson, J. W. Writ. of South, 123.
Dacebalus, Dacian king. Latham. Opuscula, 175.
Dach, Simon. Winkworth. Chr. singers Germ. 184.
Dacre, Lord. Lower. Contrib. 74.
Dada, Hattie A. Brockett. Wom. Work, 431.
Dadd, B., *pseud.* *See* Williams, J. H.
Dædalus. Milizia. Lives arch. **1** : 13.
Daems, Cornelius. Wallace, R. Anti-Trin. biog. **2** : 414.
Daffodil, The first. (Grant Allen) Proctor, R. A. Nat. stud. 84.
Dagg, John L. Davidson, J. W. Writ. of South, 125.
Daggett, Naphtali, D. D. Headley, J. T. Chaplains Revol. 199.
Dagnan-Bouveret, Pascal A. J. Child, T. Art & criticism, 65. — (W. A. Coffin) Van Dyke, J. C. Mod. Fr. mast. 239.
Daguerre, L. J. M. Drake, S. A. Our great benefactors, 489. — Timbs, J. Great inven. 134.
Daguerreotype, invention of the. Parton. Triumphs, 565.
Dahlgren, John Adolph, with portrait. Headley, J. T. Farragut, 456.
Dahlgren, Ulric, Northern raider in the civil war. Chesney. Ess. mil. biog. 185.
Dahn, Felix, with portrait. Warner Lib. **8** : 4267.
Daily News, London. Hatton. Jour. Lond. 49.
Daily Telegraph and Edwin Arnold. Hatton. Jour. Lond. 111.
Dairying, Italian. U. S. Cons. Rept. no. 10.
Daisies, English. (Grant Allen) Proctor, R. A. Nat. stud. 43.
Dakins, William. McClure. Translators, 183.
Dakota. Brockett, L. P. Our west. emp. 721.
Dakotah Indians, Customs of, Notes on. (Paul Beckwith) Smithson. Rept. '86 : 245.

Dalayrac, N., Works of. Hogarth. Mem. Opera, **2** : 249.
Dale, David, of Glasgow. Bourne, H. R. F. Eng. merch. **2** : 174.
Dale, Richard, with portrait. Amer. nat. portr. gall. 3. — Cooper, J. F. Am. nav. off. **2** : 233.
Dale, Robert William. Davidson, J. M. Eng. lib. 179. — Grant, Jas. Metropol. pul. 129. — Miller, Jos. Singers church, 2d ed. 447.
Dale, Thomas. Belknap. Amer. biog. **2** : 115.
Dalgairns, Rev. John Bernard. Oxenham. Stud. in eccl. hist. 309.
Dalgarno, G. Education of the deaf and dumb. Hamilton. Discus.
Dalhousie, J. A. Ramsay, 10th earl of, Administration of, in India. Temple, R. Men in India, 102.
Dalin, Olof von. (W. H. Carpenter) Warner Lib. **8** : 4278.
Dall, Caroline Healey. Putnam, A. P. Singers liberal, 530.
Dall, Charles H. A. Putnam, A. P. Singers liberal, 525.
Dall, William Cranch Healey. Putnam, A. P. Singers liberal, 534.
Dallas, Alexander James, 1759–1817. Brown, D. P. Forum, **1** : 529. — Carson, H. L. Sup. Ct. of U. S. 560.
Dallas, George M. Savage. Liv. rep. men. 156.
Dalling and Bulwer, Baron, Obituary of. Em. persons, **1** : 92.
Dallond, John, Eng. optician. Craik. Pursuit knowl. **2** : 271.
D'Allonne, Abel Tassin. Agnew. Protes. exiles, **2** : 80.
Dalmatia. Freeman, E. A. Neighbor lands Venice.
Dalrymple, James, 1st viscount Stair. Irving, D. Scot. writ. **2** : 152. — Lancaster, H. H. Ess. & rev. 90. — Macaulay. Biog. sk. 205.
Dalton, John. Espinasse. Lanc. worth. v. 2. — Holland, H. Ess. 389. — Muir, M. M. P. Chemists, 107. — Stoughton, J. Worthies of sci. 249. — Lonsdale. Worthies Cumb. v. 5. — Walker, W., jr. Men of sci. 41.
— and his atomic theory. (H. E. Roscoe) Manch. sci. lec. 5–6 : 152.
Dalton, Tristram (1738–1817). (Stone) Essex. Inst. Hist. Coll. v. 25. — Knapp, S. L. Em. lawyers, 315.
Dalton, Mass. Pidgeon. Old world ques. 104.
Daly, Chas. P. Fiske, S. Off-hand, 79.
Dalyell, Thomas, of Binns. Grant, Jas. Cavaliers, 356.
Damagates. Mills. Poets of Greece, 212.
Damages, Punitive, Doctrine of. (G. Koerner) Am. Bar Assoc. **5** : 211.
Damascenus, John. Browning, E. B. Ess. poets, 80.
Damascus. Bellows. Old world, **2** : 366. — Benjamin, S. G. W. World's paradises, 11. — Curtis, G. W. Howadji, 291. — Gillett, E. H. Anc. cities, 237. — Lee, J. S. Sac. cities, 141. — Porter, J. L. Giant cities, 342. — Taylor, B. Lands of Sar. 121. — Warner, C. D. Levant, 178. — Wright, W. B. Anc. cities, 110. — Buckley, J. M. Trav. 3 cont. 480. — Kean, J. Among holy places, 315. — (Schaff and Rogers) Wilson, C. W. Pictur. Palest. **2** : 143.
— in middle ages. Le Strange. Palestine.
— Sieges of. Robson, W. Sieges, 397.
Damasus, bishop of Rome. Blakey, R. Prim. fathers, 243. — Cave. Lives of fathers, 3 : 413.
Damer, Anne Seymour. Cunningham, A. Brit. painters, 3 : 214. — Ellet, E. F. Women artists.

Darwin, Charles. Bibliography. Bettany. Life of Darwin.
— Critics of. Huxley. Critiques.
— Descent of man. Brownson. Works, **9** : 485.
— Eulogium on. Flower, W. H. Ess. on museums, 290.
— in Westminster Abbey. Smalley. Lond. lett. **1** : 69.
— Life of. Woodberry. Stud. in lett. 240.
— Memorial address on. Fiske, J. Excurs. 337.
— Memorial statute of, So. Kensington. Smalley. Lond. lett. **1** : 76.
— Mistake as to transformation of species. Chatard. Occ. ess. 194.
— or Tennyson? Swinburne. Stud. prose & p. 141.
— Origin of species. Jenkin, Fl. Papers, **1** : 215.
— — 21st anniversary of. Huxley. Sci. & cul. 317.
— Philosophy of language. Müller. Chips, v. **4**.
Darwin, Erasmus. Hitchman. 18th cent. 360.
— Lewes. Biog. phil. — Oliphant, M. Lit. hist. **1** : 217. — Osborn. From Greeks, 139.
— and Miss Anna Seward. Dawson, G. Biog. lec. 191.
Darwinian theory. Gall & Robertson. Pop. read. sci. 123.
Darwinism. Bryant. Prose, **2** : 291. — Jenkin, Fl. Papers, **1** : 215. — Conway, M. D. Idols, 79. — Whedon. Ess. **2** : 92. — Collins, M. Pen sketches, 51.
— and divinity. Stephen, L. Ess. freeth. 72.
— controverted. Bowen, F. Gleanings, 199.
— German. Wright, C. Philos. dis. 399.
— in morals. Cobbe, F. P. Darwinism, 1.
— Mivart, Bateman, and Büchner on. Fiske, J. Darwin, 32.
— verified. Fiske, J. Darwin, 1.
Dascomb, Marianne Parker. (E. B. Huntington) Parton. Em. wom. 286.
Daubenton, L. G. M. Jardine. Nat. lib. 10.
Daubigny, Chas. François. Mollett, J. W. Paint. of Barbizon, **2** : 35. — With portrait. (D. W. Tryon) Van Dyke, J. C. Mod. Fr. mast. 155.
Daudet, Alphonse. Boyesen. Lit. silhouettes, 178. — Crawford, V. M. Stud. for. lit. 49. — Burton, R. Liter. likings, 107. — (P. M. Potter) Ess. from Critic, 121. — Hazeltine, M. W. Chats, 151. — James, H. Par. portr. 195. — Mauris, M. French men of l. 219. — Zimmern. For. novelists, **1** : 155. — Henry, S. Hours w. Parisians, 31. — Pellissier. Lit. move. Fr. 439. — Van de Velde. Fr. fic. **1** : 200. **2** : 1. — Walkley, A. P. Playhouse, 92. — Wells, B. W. Cent. Fr. fic. 305. — With portrait. (A. Filon) Warner Lib. **8** : 4435.
Daugherty, Michael Augustus. Am. Bar Assoc. **10** : 424.
Daughters, Revolt of the. Jeune. Lesser ques. 85.
Daughters of Liberty. Earle. Colon. dames, 240.
Daumier, Honoré. James, H. Picture & t. 116.
Dauphiné, Grottoes of. Adams, W. H. D. Fam. caverns, 66.
Dauphins of France, False. Fuller, H. W. Noted trials, 100.
D'Auvergne, Philip, Story of. Burke, B. Viciss. of fam. **3** : 89.
Davenant, John, Bishop. Fuller. Worthies, **2** : 359.
Davenant, Sir William. Austin & Ralph. Laureates, 109. — Chalmers. Eng. poets, **6** : 341. — Disraeli. Quarrels. — Dunham. Lit. & sci. men, **3** : 70. — Gosse, E. Shakespeare to Pope.

— (E. Gosse) Ward. Eng. poets, **2** : 289. — Hamilton, Wal. Poets laur.
Davenant, Sir William, Dramas of. Hogarth. Mem. opera, **1** : 72. — Hutton, L. Plays, 151.
Davenport, Charles N. Am. Bar Assoc. **5** : 163.
Davenport, Edwin L. Matthews, B. Actors, **4** : 119.
Davenport, Fanny. (Jay B. Benton) McKay, F. E. Fam. actors, 108.
Davenport, Jean Margaret. Hutton, L. Plays, 157.
Davenport, Rev. John. Bacon, L. Thirteen disc. 1st ch. New Haven.
David, St., patron of Wales. Charles. Martyrs, 403. — Kingsley. Hermits, 250. — Parry. Cam. Plutarchs, 71.
David, king of Israel. Geikie. Old Test. char. 212. — Giles, H. Christian thought, 218. — Headley, J. T. Sacred heroes, 268. — Weil, G. Bible, Koran, etc., 171. — Wilberforce, S. Heroes Hebrew, 229. — Williams, H. L. Boys of the Bible, 125. — Yonge, C. M. Book of worthies, 19.
— Statue of, by Michelangelo. Perkins, C. C. Tusc. sculp. **2** : 17.
David ap Gwilym. Parry. Cam. Plutarch, 209.
David, Felicien. Keddie. Mus. comp. 405.
David, Ferdinand, with portrait. Ehrlich, A. Cel. violin. 136.
David, John Baptist. Clarke, R. H. Cath. bishops, **1** : 256.
Davidis, Francis. Wallace, R. Anti-Trin. biog. **2** : 245.
Davidson, John. Blaikie, W. G. Preachers Scot. 90.
Davidson, John. Couch, A. T. Q. Adv. crit. 314.
Davidson, Lucretia Maria. Lossing. Em. Amer. 315.
Davidson, Margaret Miller. Irving. Biog. 163.
— and Lucretia M. Griswold. Fem. poets, 152. — Poe. Works, **6** : 150.
Davidson, Thomas. Japp. Labor, 212.
Davidson, Thomas Fleming. Am. Bar Assoc. **15** : 435.
Davidson, Virginia E. Raymond, I. Southland writ. **2** : 782.
Davie, William Richardson. Lossing. Em. Am. 89. — With portrait. Amer. nat. portr. gall. **3**.
Davies, Mrs. Arabella. Burder. Pious wom. 613.
Davies, Mrs. Christian. Dowie, M. M. Wom. adv. 201.
Davies, Sir John. Bell, R. Lit. & sci. men, **2** : 154. — Parry. Cam. Plutarch, 329. — Chalmers. Eng. poets, **5** : 75. — Deshler. Afternoons, 108. — Griswold, R. W. Sac. poets. — Hatfield, E. F. Poets of church, 180. — Miller, Jos. Singers church, 2d ed. 234. — Jesse, J. H. Cel. Eton. v. **2**. — Macdonald, G. England's antiphon, 105. — (M. A. Ward) Ward. Eng. poets, **1** : 548. — Whipple. Lit. Elizabeth, 238. — Wilmott, R. A. Eng. sac. poets, 45.
— Poems. Hales. Folia litt. 162.
Davies, Samuel D. Davidson, J. W. Writ. of South, 133.
Daviess, Mrs. Marie T. Raymond, I. Southland writ. **1** : 197.
Daviess, Mrs. Samuel. Clement, J. Noble deeds, 114.
Davis, Bliss Nelson. Am. Bar Assoc. **9** : 549.
Davis, Charles. Livingston, J. Em. Am. Lawy. 734.
Davis, Charles Henry, Comm'r., with portrait. Headley, J. T. Farragut, 252.
Davis, Clara [later Mrs. Edward Abbott]. Brockett. Woman's work, 400.

Davis, David, with portrait. Barnes, W. H. Sup. court, 89. — Am. Bar Assoc. 9 : 518.

Davis, Edwin Hamilton, Dr. Am. Antiq. Soc. Proc. n. s. 5 : 368.

Davis, Eliel. Hatfield, E. F. Poets of church, 183. — Miller, Jos. Singers church, 2d ed. 588.

Davis, Mrs. G. T. M. Brockett. Woman's work, 352.

Davis, H. Winter. (J. A. J. Cresswell) Davis, H. W. Speeches, 13. — Johnston, A. Amer. ora. 4 : 129. — With portrait. Scott, H. W. Dist. Am. lawy. 283.

Davis, Isaac P. (G. T. Davis) Mass. Hist. Proc. 12 : 94. — (J. W. Dean) N. E. Hist.-Gen. Soc. Biog. 2 : 327. — Winslow, S. N. Biog. Phila. merch. 121.

Davis, Jefferson. Annual cyclopædia, '89. — Bartlett. Pres. candidates, 295. — Greeley, H. Recollec. 410. — McClure, A. K. The South, 231. — Savage. Liv. rep. men, 168. — Congdon, C. T. Trib. ess. 279. — Derby, J. C. Fifty years, 493. — Em. persons, 4 : 181. — Johnston, A. Amer. ora. 3 : 320. 4 : 32. — Trent. South. statesm. 257.

— Character of. Dyer, O. Gt. senators, 110.

— Imprisonment of. Wallis, S. T. Works, 2 : 3.

Davis, Captain. Whitehead, C. Highwaymen, 2 : 73.

Davis, Capt. John. Barrow, J. Nav. worthies, 49. — Bourne, H. R. F. Eng. seam. 1 : 248. 2 : 143. — Markham. Sea-fathers, 126.

— in search of the Northwest passage. Frost, T. Explorers, 173.

Davis, John. Loring, J. S. 100 Bost. ora. 304. — (C. Francis) Mass. Hist. Coll. 3d ser. 10 : 186. — (S. F. Haven) N. E. Hist.-Gen. Soc. Biog. 2 : 172. — Putnam, A. P. Singers liberal, 3.

Davis, John C. Bancroft. Carson, H. L. Sup. Ct. of U. S. 570.

Davis, J. Lucius, jr. Walker, C. D. Biog. Va. Mil. Inst. 163.

Davis, John W. Woollen. Biog. sk. Indiana, 233.

Davis, Mary. Jesse. Court of Eng. Stuarts, 3 : 388.

Davis, Nathaniel M. (C. Deane) N. E. Hist.-Gen. Soc. Biog. 1 : 141.

Davis, Noah, and the Tweed case. Field, D. D. Speeches, 2 : 322.

Davis, Paulina Wright. Hanaford. Wom. of cent. 667.

Davis, Samuel, B. C. S., F. R. S. Laurie. Anglo-Indians, 2 : 1.

Davis, Samuel. Putnam, A. P. Singers liberal, 7.

Davis, Thomas Osborne. McCarthy, J. H. Em. Irishmen, 134. — Mitford, M. R. Recollec. 15. — Murray, J. O'K. Prose & poet. Irel. 441. — Williams, A. M. Poets of Irel.

Davis, William T. Putnam, A. P. Singers liberal, 8.

Davison, Alexander, and Jones, V., Trials of, 1808–09. Browne, G. L. Narr. state trials, 1 : 223.

Davison, Christopher. Holland, J. Psalmists, 1 : 237.

Davison, Francis. Griswold, R. W. Sac. poets. — Holland, J. Psalmists, 1 : 234.

Davison, John. Newman, J. H. Ess. crit. 2 : 375.

Davos. Symonds, J. A. Ital. byways.

Davoust, Louis Nicolas. Headley. Napoleon, 1 : 114.

Davy, Sir Humphry. Bolton, S. K. Fam. men of science, 139. — Brougham. Works, 1 : 107. — Brown, S. Atom, 1.—Craik. Pursuit knowl. 2 : 111. — DeQuincey. Lit. rem. (Bost.) 1 : 39. — Edgar. Boyhood, 216. — Mitchell. Wet

days, 291. — Parton. Peop. bk. biog. 301. — With portr. Seymour, C. C. B. Self-made, 314. — Taylor, W. C. Mod. Brit. Plut. 112. — Brightwell. Heroes of lab. 44. — Cooper, T. Triumphs of persev. 87.—Edwards, B. B. Self-taught, 290. — (J. D. Forbes) Macaulay. New biog. 361. — Munro, J. Pioneers elec. 105. — Towle, G. M. Heroes of inven. 123.—Walker, W., jr. Men of sci. 44.

Davy, Sir Humphry, and Berzelius. Muir, M. P. Chemists, 157.

Davy, William, Rev. Craik. Pursuit knowl. 1 : 274.

Davy, William, lawyer. Woolrych. Serjeants, 2 : 605.

Davys, Sir John. Woolrych. Serjeants, 1 : 186.

Dawes, Rufus. Griswold. Poets Am. 269. — Poe. Works, 6 : 39.

Dawes, Thomas. Loring, J. S. 100 Bost. ora. 141 : 182.

Dawson, George. Gilfillan. Mod. lit. 177. — Hood, E. P. Brit. pulpit, 356.

Dawson, Henry B., with portrait. Pub. Weekly, 37 : 644.

Dawson, James, and the fatal '45. Croston. Hist. sites Lanc. 397.

Dawson, Matthew, at Health house. Yates, E. H. Celeb. 2 : 133.

Dawson, William. Wakeley. Heroes Meth. 355. — Wise, D. Heroic Meth. 288.

Dawson, W. C. Miller, S. F. Bench of Ga. v. 1.

Day, Miss. Mitford, M. R. Recollec. 279.

Day, James G. Am. Bar Assoc. 21 : 661.

Day, John. Gosse, E. Jacobean poets, 173. — Symons, A. Stud. two lit. 119.

Day, Mrs. Juliana. Brockett. Woman's work, 789.

Day, Martha. Everest. Poets of Conn. 411.

Day, Stephen. Lossing. Em. Amer. 11.

Day, Thomas, author of Sanford and Merton. Hitchman. 18th cent. 334.

Day, Thomas, of Hartford, Conn. (T. M. Day) N. E. Hist.-Gen. Soc. Biog. 2 : 335.

Day *vs*. Day, 1797. Craik, G. L. Eng. causes cel. 153.

Day and night. Saunders. Mosaics, 298. — Saunders. Stray leaves, 185.

Day of the dead in Japan. Arnold, E. Seas & l. 430.

Day of the disasters of Carfington Blundell, Esq. Hunt, L. Men, wom. & books, 19.

Day-dreaming; should i: be indulged in ? Hadley, J. Ess. 369.

Day-fatality. Aubrey, J. Miscel.

Day nursery, Scope of. (M. H. Dewey) Conf. char. & correc. '97 : 105.

— work of. (M. H. Burgess) Conf. char. & correc. '92 : 424.

Dayânanda Saravasti. Müller. Biog. ess. 167.

Dayman, E. Arthur. Miles, A. H. Poets of cent. 10 : 706. — Miller, Jos. Singers church, 2d ed. 481.

Days of good and evil omen. Lawrence, R. M. Magic, 239.

— Superstitions concerning. Jones, W. Credulities, 109, 493.

Dayton, W. L. Savage. Liv. rep. men, 181.

De Anna, Heinrich N. H., with portrait. Ehrlich, A. Cel. violin. 13.

Deacon, Samuel. Miller, Jos. Singers church, 2d ed. 295.

Dead, The, and the living. (B. Lee) Am. Pub. Health, 22 : 176.

— Cultus of, in Sparta. Gardner, P. New chap. Gr. hist.

Dead, Disposal of. (W. H. Curtis) Am. Pub. Health, **7** : 309. — Playfair. Subj. soc. 96. — Richardson, B. W. Ministry, 230. — (C. O. Probst) Am. Pub. Health, **21**: 177. — Internat. Health Ex. Sanita.

— — by embalming. (A. W. Suiter) Am. Pub. Health, **21** : 192.

— Offerings of the, in China. Cumming, C. F. G. Wand. in China, **1** : 277.

— Smile on faces of. Jacox, F. Cues, 328.

— Speaking the truth about : *Siste, viator*. Curtis, G. W. Other ess. 208.

— Transportation and disposal of. Am. Pub. Health, **22** : 131. — (C. O. Probst) Am. Pub. Health, **23** : 452. — (J. D. Griffith) Am. Pub. Health, **20** : 123.

— Treatment of. (B. Lee) Am. Pub. Health, **22** : 176.

Dead bodies, inspection of, Necessity of. (C. Horsch) Am. Pub. Health, **13** : 45.

Dead level, Fear of the. Higginson. New world, 70.

Dead man's sermon. Silliman. Gallop, 231.

Dead Sea, The. Buckley, J. M. Trav. 3 cont. 405.

— A day at. Cobbe, F. P. Cities of past, 107.

Deady, Matthew Paul. Am. Bar Assoc. **16** : 439.

Deaf and dumb, Anecdotes of the. Chambers's Miscel. no. 52.

— Physical education of. (A. Gutzman) Cong. Educa. Chic. '93, 674.

Deaf, The, and their possibilities. (E. M. Gallaudet) Nat. Educa. Assoc. '98 : 207.

— Education and care of. (G. O. Fay) Conf. char. & correc. '86 : 215.

— Education of. (A. G. Bell) Nat. Educa. Assoc. '97 : 96.

— — Dalgarno and. Hamilton. Discus.

— Instruction of. (Mrs. C. Kelsey) N. Y. Regents, 88 : 659.

— Physical education of. (Albert Gutzman) Nat. Educa. Assoc. '93 : 674.

— Public schooling for. (C. S. Perry) Nat. Educa. Assoc. '99 : 1157.

Deafness among school children. (S. Sexton) U. S. Bur. Ed. Circ. '81 : no. 5.

Deak, Francis. Wyatt, W. I. Hungarian celeb. 124.

Deal boatmen, The. Treanor, T. S. Heroes Goodw. sands, 38.

Dean, Benj. Am. Bar Assoc. **20** : 536.

Dean, Henry, 1501–03. Hook. Abps. Cant. **5** : 500.

Dean, Julia. Hutton, L. Plays, 141.

Dean, Nicholas. (H. W. Bellows) N. E. Hist.-Gen. Soc. Biog. **2** : 484.

Dean family. Titcomb, S. E. N. Eng. peo. 129.

Dean, Forest of, Gloucestershire. (J. Bellows) Am. Antiq. Soc. Proc. n. s. **13** : 269.

Dean Priory, Eng., and Robert Herrick. Allingham. Varieties, **1** : 123.

Deane, Charles, with portrait. (J. Winsor) Mass. Hist. Proc. 2d ser. **7** : 45. — Am. Antiq. Soc. Proc. n. s. **6** : 213.

Deane, Silas. (C. Isham) Am. Hist. Assoc. **3** : 40. — Lossing. Em. Amer. 79.

Deaneries, English, Appointments to. Freeman. Hist. ess. **4** : 326.

Dear and cheap. Knight. Once on time, **2** : 180.

Dearborn, Cornelius Van Hess, with portrait. Sketches N. H. men, 195.

Dearborn, Henry, Gen. Lossing. Em. Amer. 328. — James. Mil. occur. v. **1**.

Dearborn, Henry A. S. Loring, J. S. 100 Bost. ora. 360. — (C. K. Dillaway) N. E. Hist.-Gen. Soc. Biog. **1** : 277.

Dearborne, Frances L. H. Hemenway. Poets of Vt. 124.

Deare, Joseph. Thornbury. Brit. art. **2** : 85.

Deas, C. Tuckerman. Artists, 424. — Tuckerman. Artist-life, 202.

Death. Bacon. Ess. — Stevenson, R. I. Virginibus, 153. — Friswell. Gentle life, 292. — Lecky. Map of life, 343.

— and burial. Hunt, L. Seer, **2** : 148.

— and the fear of dying. Smith, Alex. Dreamthorp, 52.

— and marriage. Zangwill. Without prej. 187. Angel of. Conway, M. D. Idols, 201.

— Book of. Disraeli, I. Curios. (N. Y. 4 v.) **4** : 87.

— Causes of, Arrangement of. (C. L. Wilbur) Am. Pub. Health, **20** : 536.

— Certainty of. (Dean Sherlock) Friswell. Silent hour, 73.

— Fear of. Boyd. Our life, **1**. — Hazlitt. Table talk.

— in the country. Beecher. Star papers, 106.

— Is death the end ? Gladden. Burn. ques. 129.

— Life and. Matthews, A. Rumina.

— — Nature of. Whittaker, T. Ess. & not. 267.

— of an angel. Richter. Companer.

— Personal identity after. Thompson, H. M. Copy, 355.

— Phenomena of. Timbs. Doctors, 421.

— Prominence of, in biographies. Meynell, A. Color, 8.

— The riddle of. Cobbe, F. P. Peak in Darien, 274.

— Ruling passion in. Bancroft, G. Miscel. 75.

— Skeleton of. Disraeli, I. Curios. (N. Y. 4 v.) **4** : 95.

— Sudden ; an agnostic's vision. Stephen, L. Ess. freeth. 155.

— — The vision of. DeQuincey. Miscel. ess. (Bost.) 167.

— True and false repose in. Wilks. Chr. ess. **1**.

— Verification of. (W. B. Clarke) Indiana Health, '88 : 195.

Death-rate as a sanitary test. (N. A. Humphreys *et al.*) Trans. Soc. Sci. Lond. '84 : 485.

— of each sex in Michigan. (H. B. Baker) Am. Pub. Health, **2** : 125.

Deaths and infectious diseases, reports of, State and municipal authority concerning. (O. W. Wight) Am. Pub. Health, **8** : 17.

— Records of, Methods of tabulating and publishing. (J. S. Billings) Am. Pub. Health, **11** : 49.

— Registration of. (C. F. Folsom) Mass. Health, '77 : 233.

— — in U. S., Plans for. (E. Harris) Am. Pub. Health, **4** : 135.

— Unlamented. Boyd. Towards sunset, 67.

De Bazzi, Giovanni Antonio. (Robert Vischer) Keane, A. H. Early masters, 466.

De Berenger fraud on the London stock exchange. Browne, G. L. Narr. state trials, **2** : 90.

De Boriot, Charles A., with portrait. Ehrlich, A. Cel. violin. 106.

De Botham, Herbert, cardinal. Williams, R. F. Eng. card. **1** : 165.

De Broen, Miss, Mission work of, in Paris. Bolton, S. K. Soc. stud. in Eng. 115.

De Bruys, Peter. Hodgson, Wm. Reformers, 26.

Debt, Imprisonment for. Ashton. 18th cent. waifs, 227. — Walsh, R. Didactics, **1** : 94.

Debtor class. Godkin. Reflections, 227.

Debts, Burden of small. Bosanquet, Mrs. Standard, 67.

— Early, of England. Francis, J. Stock exch. 6.

Debts, Laws for collection of. Hazard, T. R. Miscel. 174.
— National. *See* National debts.
— of honor ; debts not collectible at law in foreign countries. U. S. Cons. Rept. no. 155.
— of various countries, 1893. U. S. Cons. Rept. 42 : 433.
— of the States. Curtis, B. R. Mem. & writ. v. 2.
De Burgh, Hubert. Bourne, H. R. F. Eng. Seam. 1 : 20.
Decadents and æsthetes. Nordau. Degen. 296.
Decalogue, The. Stanley, A. P. Chr. institu. 372.
Decamps, A. G. Hamerton. Contemp. Fr. painters.
Decatur, Stephen, with portrait. Duyckinck. Nat. portr. gall. 1 : 412. — With portrait. Amer. nat. portr. gall. v. 3. — Frost, J. Pict. hist. U.S. navy, 274. — Parton. Peop. bk. biog. 532. — Lossing. Em. Amer. 343.
Decazes, L. C. E. Amanien, duc de, at the Quai d'Orsay. Yates, E. H. Celeb. 1 : 197.
December, Customs and superstitions of. Soane. New curios. 2 : 281.
Decembrio, Piero Candido. Symonds. Reviv. of learn. 266.
Deceptions. Chambers's Papers, no. 63.
Decimal systems of weights and measures. (R. G. Kimball) N. Y. Regents, 79, app. : 119.
— — Méchain and Delambre on. Playfair, J. Works, v. 4.
Decision. Friswell. Gentle life, 1 : 280.
Decisive men, Mental habit of. Helps. Brevia.
Decius, Nicholas. Miller, Jos. Singers church, 2d ed. 38.
Deck, James George. Hatfield, E. F. Poets of church, 186. — Miller, Jos. Singers church, 2d ed. 473.
Decker, Thos. *See* Dekker.
Declan, St. Conyngham, D. P. Irish saints, 176.
Declaration of independence, Authentication of. (M. Chamberlain) Mass. Hist. Proc. 2d ser. 1 : 273.
— historically considered. Lossing. Signers, 244.
Decomposition and nutrition. Hinton. Thinking, 387.
Decoration and ornament. Bride's room. Baxter, L. E. Tusc. stud. 127.
— Architectural, in the Italian renaissance. Symonds. Renais. fine arts, 78.
— Bibliography. Phila. Drexel Inst. Ref. list, no. 3.
— Decorative. Ellwanger. Sto. house, 92.
— Imitation in. Day, L. F. Every-day art, 113.
— of a villa. Eastlake. Contrib. 1 : 329.
Decorations. Marshall, F. Internat. van. 147.
Decorative art. Poynter. Ten lec. 1. — Samson. Elem. art criticism.
— Ancient. (E. J. Poynter) Poole, R. S. Lec. art, 63.
— Bibliography. Balfour, H. Evol. decor. art.
— Household, Influence of, upon society. (C. E. Eastlake *et al.*) Trans. Soc. Sci. Lond. '76 : 830.
— in connection with modern science. (J. H. Pollen) Afternoon lec. 3 : 155.
Decorative artists. Clayton, E. C. Eng. fem. art. 2 : 334.
Decorative painting and design. (W. Crane) Morris, W. Arts & crafts, 39.
— Rambles of an archæologist. Fairholt. Rambles, 1.
— Recent. Chambers's Papers, no. 65.
— Style suited to public buildings. Eastlake. Contrib. 1 : 127.

De Courcy, Richard. Miller, Jos. Singers ch. 2d ed. 284.
Decretals, The false. Lea. Stud. ch. hist. 43.
Dedham, Mass., Settlement of. Everett. Orat. v. 2.
Dedications of books. Disraeli, I. Curios. (N. Y. 4 v.) 1 : 435.
— Poetical. Hutton, L. From books.
Dee, John, Dr. Disraeli, I. Amen. (N. Y. 2 v.) 2 : 285. — Taylor, W. C. Rom. biog. v. 1. — Waite, A. E. Lives of alchem. 153.
— and his followers. Wright, T. Nar. sorcery, 1 : 226.
Dee mills and the "Miller of the Dee." (T. C. Hughes) Andrews, W. Bygone Ches. 99.
Deems, Charles Force, D. D. Bungay. Repres. men, 208. — Davidson, J. W. Writ. of South, 135. — With portrait. (Dr. Moran) Rogers, A. C. Repres. men, 197.
Deer, American. Caton. Miscel. 146.
— Killing. Curtis. From easy chair, 3 : 28.
Deerfield, Mass. Pidgeon. Old world ques. 161. — (George Sheldon) Powell, L. P. Hist. towns N. E. 403.
— Attack on, 1704. Parkman. Half-cent. 1 : 52.
— Parson Williams's house. Terhune. Colon. homes, 375.
Defective classes. Mass. Charity, '71-'72 : xvii.
— (A. O. Wright) Conf. char. & correc. '91 : 222.
— Education of. (E. E. Allen) Butler, N. M. Education in U. S. 769.
— Treatment of. Illinois Charity, '72 : 11.
Defects, hereditary, Influence of, on health. (J. R. Black) Am. Pub. Health, 2 : 217.
Defence, national, Patriotism and. (C. H. Hall) Econ. tracts, no. 18.
Definition. Bartol. Principles, 3.
De Fleury, Maria. Hatfield, E. F. Poets of ch. 187. — Miller, Jos. Singers church, 2d ed. 381.
De Foe, Daniel. Chambers's papers, no. 56. — Dawson, G. Biog. lec. 125. — Dennis, J. Studies, 77. — Forster, J. Hist. ess. 2 : 1. — Jeaffreson. Novelists, 1 : 65. — Mitchell, D. G. Old story-tellers, 198. — Roscoe, W. C. Essays. — Russell, W. Eccen. 174. — Scott, W. Biog. mem. v. 2. — Taine. Eng. lit. 2 : 152. — Tuckerman. Ess. 285. — Wotton. Word portraits, 83. — With portrait. Oliphant. Hist. char. Q. Anne, 129. — Roscoe, W. C. Poems & ess. v. 2. — With portrait. (C. F. Johnson) Warner Lib. 8 : 4479.
— and the rise of pamphleteering. Windsor. Ethica, 178.
— and Swift. Masson. Brit. novel. 87.
— Novels. Stephen, L. Hours in libr. 1 : 1.
— — Secondary. Lamb. Elia.
— Robinson Crusoe. Adams, W. H. D. Famous books, 299. — Saunders, F. Famous books, 70. — Couch, A. T. Q. Adv. crit. 75. — Dennis, J. Stud. Eng. lit. 77.
Deformation of children, Artificial, among savage and civilized people ; with bibliography. (J. H. Porter) U. S. Nat. Mus. Rept. '87 : 213.
Deformity. Bacon. Ess.
— Fashion in. Flower, W. H. Ess. on museums, 315.
Defrees, John D. Woollen. Biog. sk. Indiana, 485.
Degeneration. Elam. Phys. prob. 89. — Lankester. Advan. sci. 1. — Whedon. Ess. 2 : 124.
De Graaf, H. P. Parton, J. Sk. of men of prog.
Degree-conferring institutions, State supervision of. (H. W. Rogers) Nat. Educa. As-

soc. '97 : 701. — U. S. Bur. Ed. Rept. '97–98, 2 : 1461.

Degrees, Baccalaureate. (E. H. Griffin) Johns Hopk. Univ. circ. 9 : 34.

— College. (D. A. Wallace and others) Nat. Educa. Assoc. '72 : 224.

— Professional, for teachers. (J. C. Gilchrist) Nat. Educa. Assoc. '79 : 114.

Dehon, Arthur. (O. W. Holmes, jr.) Harvard mem. biog. 2 : 219.

Deicola, St. Conyngham, D. P. Irish saints, 325.

Deimanovicius, Stanislaiis. Wallace, R. Anti-Trin. biog. 3 : 310.

Deism. Gostwick. German culture. Pfleiderer. Philos. of relig. 1 : 109. — (M. Pattison) Ess. by Eng. churchmen. — Shelley. Prose works, v. 2.

— and its decay. Stephen, L. Eng. thought, 1 : 74–194.

Deists, English. Alviella. Contemp. evol. 24.

Deity. Bartol. Principles, 66.

De Keyser, Polydore. Ritchie, J. E. City men, 174.

Dekker, Edward Douwes. Warner Lib. 8 : 4513.

Dekker, Thomas. Hazlitt. Dram. Eliz. — Jusserand. Eng. novel. 330. — Ward, A. W. Eng. dram. 2 : 37. — (W. Minto) Ward. Eng. poets, 2 : 55. — Whipple. Ess. & rev. 2 : 38. — Whipple. Lit. Eliz. 131. — Minto, W. Eng. poets, 344.—Morley, H. Eng. writ. 10 : 394. 11 : 290. — Warner Lib. 8 : 4521.

De Kontski, Apollinari, with portrait. Ehrlich, B. Cel. violin. 147.

Delacroix, Eugène. Jervis, Lady. Painting, 2 : 296.

Delafield, Edward. Francis, S. W. N. Y. phys. 177.

De Lancey, James, of New York. Sabine. Loyalists, 245.

De Land University, De Land, Fla. U. S. Bur. Ed. Circ. '88, no. 7 : 50.

Delane, John T. Em. persons, 2 : 187. — Smalley. Lond. let. 1. 61.

Delany, Mrs. Mary (Granville). Clayton, E. C. Eng. fem. art. 1 : 96. — Mayer, G. T. Wom. of let. 1 : 163.

— Memoirs of. Elwood. Lit. ladies, 1 : 81. — Belloc. Vignettes, 365.

De la Pole, Richard. Wolff. Odd bits, 58.

De la Poles of Hull, 1311–66. Bourne, H. R. F. Eng. merch. 1 : 50.

Delaroche, P. Hamerton. Contemp. Fr. painters.

De la Rue, Warren. With photo. Cooper, T. Men of mark, 6 : 26.

Delaune, Thomas. Ivimey. Eng. Bapt. 1 : 395.

Delavan, Edward C., with portrait. Bungay. Pen-portr. 87.

Delavigne, Jean F. C., with portrait. (F. Loliée) Warner Lib. 8 : 4528.

Delaware, Thomas, Lord. Belknap. Amer. biog. 2 : 115.

Delaware College, Wilmington, Del. U. S. Bur. Ed. Circ. '93, no. 3 : 86.

Delaware river, Recent archæol. explor. in valley of. (C. C. Abbott) Univ. Pa. Publ. Philol. 2 : no. 1.

— Ship-building on. Pa. Bur. Indus. Statis. '91.

Delaware valley. Willis. Hurry-graphs, 77.

Delays. Bacon. Ess.

Delbrück, Martin Friedrich Rudolf. Strauss, G. L. M. Men. of Ger. 2 : 295. — Tuttle, H. Ger. pol. lead. 39.

Deléry, Charles. Davidson, J. W. Writ. of South, 136.

Delft. Amicis. Holland, 94.

Delhi. Barker, Lady. Travel. about, 330. — Field, · H. M. Egypt to Japan, 162. — Keating. With Grant, 74. — Prime, E. D. G. Around world, 311. — Pidgeon. Engineer's holiday, 408.

— Siege of. Adams, W. H. D. Eng. at war, 2 : 138. — Adams, W. H. D. Memo. batt. 2 : 362. — Bartlett, D. W. Heroes Ind. rebel. 265. — Robson, W. Sieges, 633.

Deliberative bodies, Procedure in. Bain, A. Prac. ess. 291.

Delilah, Samson and. Geikie, C. Old Test. char. 167.

Delitnoh, Franz. Cheyne. Founders O. T. crit. 155.

Delk, S. Miller, S. F. Bench of Ga. v. 1.

Dell, William. Ivimey. Eng. Bapt. 2 : 55. — Hodgson, W. Reformers, 428.

Della Porta, Giacomo. Milizia. Lives arch. 2 : 89.

De Long, G. W., with portrait. Greely, A. W. Explorers, 212.

Delorme, Philibert, architect. Pattison. Renais. art in France, 1 : 98.

Delos. Tozer. Isl. Æg. 1. — Tuckerman, C. K. Recollec. 2 : 181.

— Excavations at, 1873–88. Diehl, C. Excursions, 130.

Delphi, Hoppin. Notes. theol. stud. 115. — Mahaffy. Rambles Greece, 218.

Delsarte and his contrib. to physical education. (Mrs. A. P. Tucker) Nat. Educa. Assoc. '97 : 880.

— Philosophy of expression. (M. T. Brown) Nat. Educa. Assoc. '82 : 55.

— System, Aims of. (Edna S. Poulson) Nat. Educa. Assoc. '88 : 667.

Del Sarto, Andrea. (D. H. Janitschek) Keane, A. H. Early masters, 422. — Ottley. Ital. school.

Delusions, Epidemic. (W. B. Carpenter) Estes. Half-hour, v. 1. Same in Manch. sci. lec. 3–4 : 101.

Demades. Mills. Poets of Greece, 457.

Demagogism. Brownson. Works, 15 : 434.

Demagogy, Sincere. Harrison, J. Dang. tend. 226.

De Maistre, Joseph. Stephen, J. F. Ess. by barr. 267.

— Minor works. Stephen, J. F. Horæ sabb. 270.

— Principe générateur. Stephen, J. F. Horæ sabb. 287.

— Soirées de St. Petersbourg. Stephen, J. F. Horæ sabb. 250.

Demand and supply, Shibboleth of. Lilly, W. S. Shibboleths, 188.

Demerara in 1856. Ingram. Hearts of oak, 153.

Demeter. Dyer, L. Studies of the gods.

— and Persephone. Pater. Greek stud. 79.

— Homeric hymn to. Lawton, W. C. Succ. of Homer, 154.

Demetrias, Sketch of. Newman, J. H. Hist. sk. 2 : 163.

Demetrius Phalereus. Mills. Poets of Greece, 457.

Demetrius Poliorketes. Mahaffy, J. P. Greek life, ch. 4.

Demetrius Soter. Bernard, F. Escapes, 4.

Demianovicius, John. Wallace, R. Anti-Trin. biog. 3 : 250.

De Milly, Augusta. Raymond, I. Southland wr. 2 : 672.

Deming, Philander. Richardson. Amer. lit. 2 : 419.

Democharis. Mills. Poets of Greece, 242.

Democracies, Ancient. Genin, T. H. Selec. writ. 111.
— Former. Godkin. Unforeseen tend. 1.
Democracy. Arnold, M. Mixed ess. — Brownson. Works, 15 : 1. 18 : 223. — Lowell. Democ. 1 ; or Writ. 6 : 1. — Fullerton, W. M. Patriotism, 117. — Thompson, D. G. Politics in dem. 13.
— and education. (N. M. Butler) Nat. Educa. Assoc. '96 : 86.
— and government. Mill. Early ess. 383.
— and liberty. Brownson. Works, 15 : 258.
— and the U. S. constitution. Lowell, A. P. Essays on government.
— Aristocratic opinions of. Godkin. Problems, 1.
— Catholicity necessary to. Brownson. Works, 10 : 1.
— Colonial. Dilke. Prob. of Greater Britain, 2 : 227.
— Coming, in Great Britain : a democrat on. (H. Labouchère) Coan. Soc. prob. 126.
— Historical aspect of. (J. Bryce) Ess. on reform, '67 : 239.
— in England, Tendencies to. Hazlitt, W. C. Offspring, 170.
— — Limited. Sargant. Ess. 1 : 137.
— in Europe, 1847. Mazzini. Life, etc. 6 : 98.
— in the U. S., Character of. Wilson, W. Old master, 39.
— — Influence of, on thought. Bryce. Soc. institu. 162. — Bryce. Amer. commonwealth, v. 2.
— Maine on. Godkin. Problems, 68. — Laurence, P. M. Collect. 147.
— The mistake of honest democrats. Greg. Rocks, 161.
— Nature of. Williams, A. M. Stud. folk, 56.
— of early Germans. Allen, W. F. Essays, 215.
— Real problems of. Godkin. Problems, 275.
— republicanism, and monarchy. Lorimer, Jas. Studies, nat'l & internat.
— Spirit of. Hamerton. Intellec. 290.
— Ultra-, Dangers of. Mackay. Founders Amer. 353.
Democracy ; an American novel. Hutton, R. H. Criticisms, 2 : 69.
Democratic, The, and aristocratic in literature. Burton, R. Liter. likings, 35.
Democratic government. Brownson. Works, 15 : 405.
Democratic party. Thompson, D. G. Politics in dem. 52.
— Anti-slavery wing, 1856. Field, D. D. Speeches, 3 : 32.
— in 1841. Brownson. Works, 15 : 113.
— Position and policy of. Caton. Miscel. 17.
— Prospects of, in 1839. Brownson. Works, 15 : 34.
Democritus. Diogenes Laertius. Lives, 390. — Fénélon. Philosophers, 138. — Lewes. Biog. phil. — Osborn. From Greeks, 41.
Demography and statistics in their sanitary relations. (C. L. Wilbur) Am. Pub. Health, 24 : 168.
— Medical. (W. A. Haskell) Am. Pub. Health, 18 : 330.
De Moivre, Abraham, Sketch of. Agnew. Protes. exiles, 2 : 83.
Demonology. Emerson. Lec. & biog. sk. 7. — Hunt. Wishing-cap, 160.
— Bibliography. Nevius, J. S. Demon possession.
— In Spain. Lea. Chap. relig. hist. Spain.
— Mediæval. Wraxall, C. F. L. Hist. bye-ways, 2 : 111.

De Morgan, Evelyn. Bate, P. H. Eng. Pre-Raph. 111.
De Mornay, Philip. Pierce, B. K. Em. dead, 32.
Demosthenes. Gray, J. C. Essays, 303. — Hundred greatest men, 270. — Swing. Old pic. 1 : 33. — With portrait. (R. Sharp) Warner Lib. 8 : 4535. — Brougham. Works, 7 : 170. — Cox, G. W. Greek statesm. 2 : 180. — Harsha. Orators, 1. — Legaré. Writ. 1 : 443. — Mills. Poets of Greece, 448.
— Kennedy's translation of. Cracroft. Ess. 2 : 102.
Dempster, Thomas. Irving, D. Scot. writ. 1 : 347.
Denbigh, William Fielding, first earl of. Lodge. Portraits (Bohn), v. 4.
Denck, John. Wallace, R. Anti-Trin. biog. 1 : 417.
Dendera, Temple of. Buckley, J. M. Trav. 3 cont. 266.
De Neckere, Leo Raymond. Clarke, R. H. Cath. bishops, 1 : 518.
Dengue fever. (J. G. Thomas; D. C. Holliday) Am. Pub. Health, 6 : 136, 166. — (H. B. Horlbeck) Am. Pub. Health, 22 : 191.
— in Charleston, S. C., in 1880. (H. B. Horlbeck; F. B. Porcher) Am. Pub. Health, 6 : 165, 368.
Denham, Miss Brooke, Lady. Jesse. Court of Eng. Stuarts, 3 : 306.
Denham, Lady Elizabeth, with portrait. Jameson. Beauties, 138.
Denham, Sir J. (S. Johnson) Chalmers. Eng. poets, 7 : 223. — Gosse, E. Shakespeare to Pope, 95. — (E. Gosse) Ward. Eng. poets, 2 : 279. — Holland, J. Psalmists, 2 : 113.
— Essay on translated verse. Gosse, E. Shakespeare to Pope, 233.
Denia, Trade and industries of, 1894. (R. F. McCrillis) U. S. Cons. Rept. 45 : 415.
"Denigration." Helps. Soc. pressure, 154.
Denis, Mrs. Ellet. Pioneer wom. 111.
Denis, St., patron of France. Charles. Martyrs, 117
Denison, Daniel. (D. D. Slade) Col. Soc. Mass. Trans. 1 : 118.
Denison, Edward. Adams, W. H. D. Good Samar. 373. — Adams, W. H. D. Worthies Ch. Eng. 256. — With portrait. Japp, A. H. Golden lives, 51. — Japp. Good men, 105. — With portrait. Watson, Mrs. R. A. Poet-toilers, 153.
— Work among the poor of London. Green, J. R. Stray studies, v. 1.
Denison, George A., archdeacon of Taunton, with photo. Cooper, T. Men of mark, 1 : 30.
— Mozley. Reminis. 2 : 93.
Denison University, Granville, O. (W. H. Johnson) U. S. Bur. Ed. Circ. '91, no. 5 : 157.
Denman, George, with photo. Cooper, T. Men of mark, 6 : 16.
Denman, Thomas, Lord. Foss. Judges, 9 : 189. — Martineau, H. Biog. sk. 232. — Grant, J. Bench & bar, 1 : 114, 159. — Grant, J. Recoll. Lords, 348. — Whiteside, J. Early sk. 21.
Denmark. Jackson, H. H. 3 coasts, 322. — Moore, Jos. Outl. Eur. 410. — Prime, S. I. Alhambra, 462.
— and Jutland. Gibson, W. S. Miscel. 74.
— Catteau's. Smith, Syd. Ess. fr. Edin.
— Literature of, Poetry of, etc. See Danish literature, poetry, etc.
— Local transportation in. U. S. Cons. Rept. 38 : 619.
Denne, Henry. Ivimey. Eng. Bapt. 2 : 92.
Dennis, John, Works of. Talfourd. Crit. writ.

Denny, Sir Anthony.   Lodge. Portr. (Bohn) v. 1.
Denny, Sir Edward.   Hatfield, E. F. Poets of church, 189. — Miller, Jos. Singers church, 2d ed. 443.
Denominational Christianity and Christian unity. Schaff, P. Christ & Chris. 292.
— Church-life or sect-life ? Martineau, J. Ess. ('91) 2 : 381.
Denominational schools.   (Cardinal Gibbons ; J. J. Keane) Nat. Educa. Assoc. '89 : 111.
Denominations, Comity between. (D. L. Whitman) Barrows, J. H. Parl. relig. 2 : 1215.
Denon, D. V., baron.   St. John. Col. travelers, 3 : 345.
Dent, Caroline.   Miller, Jos. Singers church, 2d ed. 576.
Dental education in the U. S.   U. S. Bur. Ed. Rept. '97–98, 1 : 1235.
Dentatus, Marcus Curius. Yonge, C. M. Book of worthies, 230.
Dentistry in foreign countries, 1896.   U. S. Cons. Rept. 52 : 561.
Denver.   Hardy, I. T. Thro' cities, 261. — Pidgeon. Engineer's holiday, 121.
— Municipal condition of. (P. Rogers) Nat. Conf. City Govt. 2–3 : 424.
Denver and Rio Grande R. R.   Jackson, H. H. Bits trav. home, 386.
Denville, Sir Gosselin.   Whitehead, C. Highwaymen, 1 : 26.
Denys L'Auxerrois.   Pater. Imag. poets, 49.
Deodorants and disinfectants.   (E. M. Hunt) N. J. Health, '92 : 85.
Deor, Widsith, and the scôp.   Brooke, S. A. Hist. early Eng. lit. v. 1.
Deotyma (Hedwige Luszczewska). Soboleski. Poets of Poland, 343.
Departmental teaching in grammar grade. (J. M. Fendley) Nat. Educa. Assoc. '95 : 572.
De Pauw University, Greencastle, Ind.   U. S. Bur. Ed. Circ. '91, no. 1 : 140.
Dependencies, Lewis on.   Senior. Hist. ess. 173.
Dependent children, Education of.   (C. D. Randall) Nat. Educa. Assoc. '80, app.: 19.
Dependents, Alien and non-resident, in Minnesota. (W. A. Gates) Conf. char. & correc. '98 : 276.
Depew, Chauncey M.   Fiske. Off-hand, 91. — With portrait. Scott, H. W. Dist. Am. lawy. 291. — With portrait. Stoddard, W. O. Men of bus. 161.
De Peyster, J. W.   Parton, J. Sk. of men of prog. — With portrait. Rogers, A. C. Repres. men, 183.
Deppe, pianist.   Fay, A. Music study in Germany.
Depravity, Total.   Beecher. New star papers, 178.
De Prez, Justus.   Wallace, R. Anti-Trin. biog. 2 : 412.
De Quincey, Thomas.   Giles, H. Illus. of genius, 300. — Gilfillan. 1st gall. 104. — Griswold, H. T. Home-life, 54. — Ingleby. Ess. 270. — Martineau, H. Biog. sk. 93. — Mason, E. T. Pers. traits, 2 : 217. — Masson, D. Ess. on poets. — Mathews. Men & bks. 9. — Payn. Lit. recol. 48. — Saintsbury. Ess. Eng. lit. 304, 440. — Salt. Lit. sk. 208. — Stephen, L. Hours in libr. 1 : 287. — Wotton. Word portraits, 238. — Anton. Eng. essayists. — Budd, H. St. Mary's Hall lec. 196. — Chancellor, E. B. Lit. types, 1. — Espinasse. Lanc. worth. v. 2. — Mitchell, D. G. Eng. lands, 4 : 28. — With portrait. (G. R. Carpenter) Warner Lib. 8 : 4555.

De Quincey, Thomas, and his works. Bayne, P. Ess. 1 : 15.
— and Lamb. Oliphant, M. Lit. hist. 2 : 1.
— as a political economist. Hodgson. Outcast, 69.
— Genius of. Hodgson. Outcast, 3.
— Prose and verse. Masson. Ess. 447 ; or Wordsworth, 258.
— prose, Style of. Hunt, T. W. Rep. Eng. prose, 417.
Derby, Charles A.   Walker, C. D. Biog. Va. Mil. Inst. 169.
Derby, Charlotte de la Fremoüille, countess of. Lodge. Portraits (Bohn), v. 5. — Yonge, C. D. Seven Heroines, 112.
Derby, Edward G. S. Stanley, 14th earl of. Hutton, R. H. Stud. in parl. 48. — Kebbel. Engl. statesmen, 121. — Reid, T. W. Cab. portr. 267. — Smith, G. Barnett. Prime min. 177. — Kent, W. C. M. Derby min. 1.
Derby, Edward Henry Stanley, 15th earl. (Photo.) Cooper, T. Men of mark, 5 : 34. — Higginson, T. W. Engl. statesmen, 216. — Hill, F. H. Political portr. 92. — Hutton, R. H. Stud. in parl. 61. — Reid, T. W. Cab. portr. 29. — Reid, T. W. Politicians, 1 : 211. — Em. persons, 6 : 26. — Kent, W. C. M. Derby min. 207.
— at Knowsley. Yates, E. H. Celeb. 3 : 309.
Derby, Elias Hasket, with portrait.   (E. H. Derby) Hunt, F. Am. merch. 2 : 17.
Derby, Elizabeth Farren, Countess. Doran. Their maj. serv. 2 : 281.
Derby, George.   Vaille & Clark. Harv. book, v. 1.
Derby, George H. Clemens. Funny fellows, 130.
Derby, James Cephas. Derby, J. C. Fifty years, 21.
Derby, James Stanley, 7th earl of.   Espinasse. Lanc. worth. v. 1. — Lodge. Portraits (Bohn), v. 5. — Coleridge. Nor. worthies, 1 : 363.
Derby, Thomas Stanley, 1st earl of. Espinasse. Lanc. worth. v. 1. — Lodge. Portraits (Bohn), v. 1.
Derby, Eng., Prince Charlie at, 1745. Stanhope, Earl. Miscel. 2 : 94.
Derbyshire, A. J. Winslow, S. N. Biog. Phila. merch. 117.
Derbyshire.   Rimmer, A. Old towns, 25.
Dering, Mrs. Robert.   Mitford, M. R. Recollec. 284.
Dermatosis.   (G. Mendizabal) Am. Pub. Health, 24 : 234.
Dermody, Thomas. Giles, H. Lectures, 2 : 305.
Derne, Capture of.   Dawson. Batt. of U. S. 2 : 56.
Déroulède, Paul, with portrait. Warner Lib. 8 : 4580.
Derr, Temple of.   Adams, W. H. D. Fam. caves, 20.
Dervishes.   Scollard. Und. sum. skies, 23.
— of Constantinople. Arnold, R. A. Levant, 2 : 18, 35.
Derwentwater, James Radcliffe, earl of. Thomson, Mrs. Jacobites, 1 : 224. — Chambers's Miscel. no. 35.
Desaguliers, John Theophilus, Sketch of. Agnew. Protes. exiles, 2 : 89.
Désaugiers, Marie-A.-M. Saintsbury. Miscel. ess. 352.
Des Autels, Guillaume. Cary. Fr. poets, 168.
Descartes, Réné.   Caird. Ess. on lit. & p. 2 : 267. — Nasmith. Mak. mod. thought, 2 : 38. — Hundred greatest men, 228. — With portrait. Warner Lib. 8 : 4585. — Case. Physical

realism, 101. — Erdmann. Hist. philos. 2 : 8. —
Lewes. Biog. phil. — Stoughton, J. Worthies
of sci. 67.

Descartes, Réné, and his theory of vortices.
Lodge, O. J. Pioneers, 137.
— and Princess Elizabeth. Courtney. Stud.
172.
— Cartesian doubt. Brownson. Works, 2 : 358.
— Genius and writings of. Rogers, H. Ess. 3 : 1.
— Mask of. Courtney. Studies, 68.
— on use of reason. Huxley. Lay sermons.
— Philosophy of. Stephen, L. Eng. thought, 1 :
19.

Descent, Ethics of. Guiney. Patrins, 29.

Deschamps, Eustache. Besant. Fr. humor, 82.
— Besant. Fr. poetry, 52.

Descriptive literature. Purnell. Liter. 271.

Desdemona, Shakespeare's. Martin. Shakes.
female, 45.

Desert, Egyptian, A day in the. Wraxall.
Scraps, 1 : 191.
— Great American. Barrows, W. U. S. of yester.
93. — Lummis. Strange corners, 28.

Deserts, Characteristics of. Allen, Grant. Falling in love, 341.
— of the East. Hahn-Hahn. Fathers, 68.

Desiderio da Settignano. Perkins, C. C. Tusc.
sculp. 1 : 173.

Design. (J. D. Sedding) Morris, W. Arts &
crafts, 405.
— in nature, Argument from. Carpenter, W. B.
Nature and man. — McCosh, J. Chris. & positivism. — Mill, J. S. 3 ess. 167. — Mozley.
Ess. 2 : 363. — Stirling. Philos. & theol. —
Whedon. Ess. 2 : 31.
— — equal to nothing. Brown, S. Atom. 2.
— in the organic world. Carpenter, W. Benj.
Nature, 409.
— Meaning of the term. Porter, N. Sci. & sent.
260.

Designs and working drawings. (L. F. Day)
Morris, W. Arts & crafts, 249.

Desjardins, Paul. (G. King) Warner Lib. 8 :
4596.

Des Maizeaux, Pierre, and the secret history of
Anthony Collins's manuscripts. Disraeli, I.
Curios. (N. Y. 4 v.) 3 : 333.
— Sketch of. Agnew. Protes. exiles, 2 : 94.

Desmond, Catherine Fitzgerald, countess of.
Costello. Englishwomen, 3 : 24. — Burke, B.
Viciss. of fam. 2 : 402.

Desmonds, Fall of. Burke, B. Viciss. of fam. 1 :
186.

Desmoulins, Camille. Adolphus. Biog. Fr. rev.
1 : 341. — Chambers, W. Rem. pers. 133. —
Ste.-Beuve. Portr. of men, 99.

Despair. Helps. Friends, 1st ser. 1.

Despard, Edward Marcus. Browne, G. L. State
trials 19th cent. 1 : 43. — Burke, P. Cel. nav.
& mil. trials, 307.

Despencer, Hugh le. Foss. Judges, 2 : 308.

Despencers, The, favorites of Edward II. of
England. Menzies, S. Roy. fav. 1 : 42.

Desportes, Philippe. Cary. Fr. poets, 136.

Despotism. Helps. Friends. 2d ser. 2.
— Beneficent. Rands. Henry Holbeach, 2 : 85.

Dessler, W. C. Miller, Jos. Singers church, 2d
ed. 114.

Destouches, Philippe Néricault. Vinet. Fr. lit.
18th cent. 114.
— and the French stage. Hawkins. Fr. stage 18th
cent. v. 1.

Desty, Robert. Am. Bar Assoc. 19 : 664.

Desvignes, Emily. Clayton, E. C. Eng. fem.
art. 2 : 305.

Deswarte, John, and family. Brown, J. N. Bapt.
martyrs, 151.

De Tabley, Lord. Gosse, E. Crit. kit-kats. —
Miles, A. H. Poets of cent. 6 : 183.

Details, Importance of. Reynolds, G. Papers,
463.

Determinism, The dilemma of. James, W.
Will to believe, 145.

Detonating compound, A new [1812]. Davy.
Works, 5 : 391.

Detraction, Habit of. Russell, A. P. Charac.
281.

Detrianus. Milizia. Lives arch. 1 : 98.

Detroit, Mich., Climate of. Hubbard, B. Me-
morials, 419.
— Founding of. Parkman. Half-cent. 1 : 15.
— Municipal condition of. (D. D. MacLaurin)
Nat. Conf. City Govt. 2–3 : 382.
— Munic. employment scheme proposed for. (J.
A. Porit) Conf. char. & correc. '97 : 217.

Detroit College, Detroit, Mich., History of.
(B. J. Otting) U. S. Bur. Ed. Circ. '91, no. 4 :
166.

"Detroit," brig, Capture of. Dawson. Batt. of
U. S. 2 : 189.

Detroit, Surrender of. Dawson. Batt. of U. S.
2 : 110.

Dettingen, Battle of. Adams, W. H. D. Eng.
at war, 1 : 183.

Deusdedit. Hook. Abps. Cant. 1 : 124.

Deutz, Charles Gonzaga. Wraxall. Remark.
adv. 1 : 240.

De Vaux, James. Lester. Artists, 175.

De Veil, Carolus Maria. Ivimey. Eng. Bapt.
2 : 471.

Development, Harmonious. (W. N. Hailman)
Nat. Educa. Assoc. '89 : 404.
— Dr. Newman on. Thirlwall, C. Remains, 1 : 99.
— Personal. Holland, J. G. Every-day, 1 : 96.

Devens, Charles. Devens. Orations, v. 1. —
With portrait. (J. C. Ropes) Mass. Hist. Proc.
2d ser. 7 : 104.

Devens, David. Livingston, J. Dist. Amer. 133.

De Vere, Aubrey. Austin, A. Poetry, 182. —
Burke, B. Viciss. of fam. 2 : 419. — Macdonald, G. England's antiphon, 321. — (M. Bell)
Miles, A. H. Poets of cent. 2 : 507. 4 : 415.
10 : 479. — With portrait. Warner Lib. 8 :
4609. — Williams, A. M. Poets of Irel.
— on poetry. Woodberry. Stud. in let. 66.
— Poems. Taylor, H. Notes, 187.
— Sonnets of. Deshler. Afternoons, 299.

De Vere, Maximilian Schele. Davidson, J. W.
Writ. of South, 138.

Deverell, Walter H. Bate, P. H. Eng. Pre-
Raph. 53.

Devereux, Robert. *See* Essex, 2d earl of.

Devices and mottoes. Stirling-Maxwell. Miscel.
ess. 201.

Devil, The. Cobbe, F. P. Darwinism, 147. —
Fiske, J. Myths, 104. — Haweis. Curr. coin.
— Maurice, F. D. Theol. ess. 33.

Devils, Luther's, Milton's, and Goethe's. Masson. Three Devils, 1 ; *or* Ess. 53.

Devine, M. le Docteur Eugène. Russell, W.
Eccen. 5.

Devizes, Eng. Freeman. Eng. towns, 142.

Devon and Cornwall. Allingham. Varieties, 2 :
44.

Devonshire, Charles Blount, earl of. Lodge.
Portraits (Bohn), v. 3.

Devonshire, Christian, countess of. Costello.
Englishwomen, 2 : 214.

Devonshire, Edward Courtenay, earl of. Lodge.
Portraits (Bohn), v. 1.

Devonshire, Elizabeth Cecil, countess of. Lodge. Portraits (Bohn), v. 6.

Devonshire, Georgiana Spencer, duchess of. Fifty famous women, 294. — With portrait. Ollier, E. Brit. portr. paint. 11.

Devonshire, Mary Butler, duchess of, with portrait. Jameson. Beauties, 304.

Devonshire, William Cavendish, first duke of. Lodge. Portraits (Bohn), v. 7. — With portrait. Caulfield. Kit-kat, 20.

Devonshire, Wm. C., 7th duke of. Em. persons, 5 : 162. — Smalley. Stud. 48.

Devonshire. King, R. J. Sk. 307. — North, J. Transatl. sk.

— Baptists of. Ivimey. Eng. Bapt. 2 : 102.

— Lanes of, Associations of. Watkins, M. G. In country, 1.

— North. James, H. Transatl. 33.

Devrient, Wilhelmina Schröder. Clayton, E. C. Queens, 288. — Ferris, G. T. Great singers, 2 : 51.

Dew. Estes. Half-hour, v. 2. — Tomlinson, C. Exper. ess. 105.

— and frost. Abbott, C. C. Outings, 227.

— Deposition of. Proctor. Pleas. ways, 357.

Dew, Samuel. Ivimey. Eng. Bapt. 3 : 515.

Dewey, Charles. Woollen. Biog. sk. Indiana, 360.

Dewey, Francis Henshaw. Am. Antiq. Soc. Proc. n. s. 5 : 176.

Dewey, Orville. Griswold. Prose writ. 303.

Dewhurst, Thomas. Ivimey. Eng. Bapt. 3 : 350.

De Wint, Peter. Wedmore. Stud. 2d ed. 193.

De Winton, Julia C. [Mrs. Stretton]. (C. M. Yonge) Oliphant. Wom. novelists, 304.

De Witt, John. Crowe, E. E. For. statesm. 3 : 220.

Dewitt, Thomas, with portrait. (A. R. Thompson) Rogers, A. C. Repres. men, 193.

Dexter, D. Gilbert. Hemenway. Poets of Vt. 347.

Dexter, Franklin. Loring, J. S. 100 Bost. ora. 388.

Dexter, George. (C. C. Smith) Mass. Hist. Proc. 2d ser. 1 : 327.

Dexter, Henry. Tuckerman. Artists, 586.

Dexter, Henry Martyn. Am. Antiq. Soc. Proc. n. s. 7 : 163. — With portrait. (J. E. Sanford) Mass. Hist. Proc. 2d ser. 7 : 90.

Dexter, Samuel. Moore, F. Am. eloq. 2 : 237.

— Character of. Story, J. Miscel. 781.

Dexterity before skill. (G. T. Fairchild) Nat. Educa. Assoc. '82 : 166.

Deyerle, M. P. Walker, C. D. Biog. Va. Mil. Inst. 173.

Deza, Maximilian, 1610–87. Baring-Gould. Preachers, 192.

Dhele. See Hales, Thos.

Diablerêts, The. Cobbe, F. P. Hours of work, 159.

Dial, Papers from the. Emerson. Nat. hist. intel. 175.

Dialect, Home-made. Higginson. Conc. all, 103.

Dialects. See English language, Dialects of.

Diamond fields of South Africa. Latimer. Eur. in Afr. in 19th cent. 345. — Laurence, P. M. Collect. 305.—(W. J. Morton) Am. Geog. Soc. 9 : 66. — Trollope, A. So. Afr. 2 : 161.

Diamond mines of Kimberley. Loomis, E. J. Eclipse party, 107.

Diamond show, Antwerp. Kingston, W. B. Men, etc. 226.

Diamonds. Gillmore, P. Great thirst land, 456. — Knox, T. W. Underground, 372. — (W. Crookes) Smithson. Rept. '97 : 219.

Diamonds and diamond cutting. Nichols, J. R. Fireside sci. 193.

— and pearls. Fields. Underbrush, 209.

— Artificial. Japp. Days w. indus. 274.

— Combustion of. Davy. Works, 5 : 478.

— cutting, at Amsterdam. Bouton, J. B. Round about, 406.

— Famous. Japp. Days w. indus. 240.

Diana de Poitiers. Goodrich, F. B. Women, 155.

— Menzies, S. R. Roy. fav. 1 : 220.

— Capefigue's. Cranbourne. Hist. sk. 1 : 357.

Diaries. Mathews, W. Men, p. & t. 231.

— Moral, historical, critical. Disraeli, I. Curios. (N. Y. 4 v.) 2 : 388.

Diarrhœa, Tropical. (Sir J. Fayrer) Am. Pub. Health, 19 : 38.

Diary, Deadly. Warner, C. D. As we go, 154.

— The deathless. Repplier, A. Varia, 30.

Diaz, Bartolomeo. Frost, T. Explorers, 33. — Parton. Peop. bk. biog. 283.

— and Pedro de Covilham. Vogel. Cent. of discov. 49.

Diaz, Bernal, del Castillo. Warner Lib. 8 : 4613.

Diaz, Henrique. (D. L. Child) Child, L. M. Oasis, 41.

Diaz, Narcisse V. Mollett, J. W. Paint. of Barbizon, 1 : 87. — (A. Hoeber) Van Dyke, J. C. Mod. Fr. mast. 131.

"Dibbarra" epic, Babylonian, A fragment of. (M. Jastrow) Univ. Pa. Publ. Philol. 1 : no. 2.

Dibble, Henry C., with portrait. Rogers, A. C. Repres. men, 211.

Dibdin, Charles. Jerdan. Men, 162. — With portrait. Warner Lib. 8 : 4620.

Dibdin, Thomas Frognall. Hitchman. 18th cent. 272. — Jerdan. Men, 169.

Dibdins, The. Doran. Drury Lane, 2 : 190.

Dice and dominoes, Chinese games with. (Stewart Culin) U. S. Nat. Mus. Rept. '93 : 489.

Dick, Jane. Ellet. Pioneer wom. 193.

Dick, Robert, baker and naturalist. Parton. Capt. indus. 232. — Hoare. Nota. workers, 58.

— Japp, A. H. Leaders of men, 94.

Dick, Thomas, the Christian philosopher. Tillotson, J. Untit. nobil. 225.

Dickens, Charles. Collier, W. F. Hist. Eng. lit. 480. — Fields. Yesterdays, 125. — Friswell. Mod. men of let. 1. — Griswold, H. T. Homelife, 333. — Hale, E. E. Lights 2 cent. 269. — Jeaffreson. Novelists, 2 : 303. — Lang. Ess. in lit. 118. — Lang. Let. to dead au. 10. — (A. W. Ward) Manch. sci. lec. 2 : 69. — Mason, E. T. Pers. traits, 4 : 171. — With portrait. Seymour, C. C. B. Self-made, 353. — Taine. Eng. lit. 2 : 338.—Trollope, T. A. What I rem. 2 : 110. — Walsh, W. S. Pen pic. mod. 236. — Whipple. Lit. & life. — Wotton. Word portraits, 86. — (Percy Fitzgerald) Afternoon lec. 2 : 85. — Buchanan, R. Poet's sk. book, 119. — Henley. Views, 1. — Em. persons, 1 : 8. — Chancellor, E. B. Lit. types, 140. — Harrison, F. Stud. early Vict. 128. — Howells. My lit. passions, 88. — Hubbard, E. Lit. jour. : 259. — Lilly. Four humorists, 3. — Saintsbury. Correc. imp. 117.—Thayer, W. M. Turning points, 82. — Cochrane, R. Gt. thinkers, 93. — Duyckinck. Portrait gall. 2 : 383. — Hall, S. C. Book of mem. 454. — Hodder, G. Memories, 140. — Horne, R. H. New spirit, 9. — Russell, W. C. Book of authors, 2 : 492. — With portrait. Warner Lib. 8 : 4625. — Wise, D. Vanq. victors, 272.

— American Notes. Spedding. Reviews.

— and his children. (Mamie Dickens) Parton. Princes, 30.

Dickens, Charles, and his letters. Clarke, C. C. Recoll. of writ. 295.
— and his philosophy. Van Santvoord, C. Disc. 334.
— and Thackeray. Masson. Brit. novel. 239. — Philips, S. Ess. from Times, 2 : 320.
— and Washington Irving. Lanman, C. Haphazard, 282.
— as an actor. Hutton, L. Plays, 40.
— as a citizen. Parton. Triumphs, 679.
— Barnaby Rudge. Poe. Works, 6 : 532.
— Bibliography. Marzials. Life of D. — Hodgkins. 19th cent. au.
— Bleak House. Brimley. Ess. 281.
— Chapter on. Yates, E. Recollec. 2 : 91.
— A day with. Jerrold, W. B. Good comp. 5.
— Eulogy on. Stanley, A. P. Ser. spec. occ. 127.
— A first meeting with. Payn. Lit. recol. 179.
— Genius of. Hutton, R. H. Criticisms, 2 : 87. — Whipple. Success, 250.
— The "good genie" of fiction. Buchanan. Master-spir. 18.
— Home of. Wolfe. Lit. pilg. Brit. au. 49.
— Mystery of Edwin Drood. (T. Foster) Proctor, R. A. Leis. read. 297.
— Nicholas Nickleby, French dramatization of. Thackeray. Early & late, 95.
— novels of, Educational ideas in. (F. L. Soldan) Nat. Educa. Assoc. '90 : 724.
— Prose style of. Hunt, T. W. Rep. Eng. prose, 444.
— Reading by, in 1867. Curtis. From easy ch. 44.
— Recollections of. (J. T. Fields) Parton. Princes, 48.
— Social pictures by. Scudder, V. D. Soc. Ideals, 128.
— Why a more famous novelist than C. Reade? (E. Cumpston) Moulton, R. G. Four years novel, 43.
— Works of. Kirkus. Miscel. 1.
— Writings; In Dickens-land. Whipple. Outlooks, 314.
Dickerson, Mahlon, with portrait. Amer. Nat. portr. gall. v. 3. — (E. D. Halsey) N. E. Hist.-Gen. Soc. Biog. 2 : 95.
Dickinson, Anna Elizabeth. Hanaford. Wom. of cent. 317. — With portrait. (E. C. Stanton) Parton. Em. wom. 479.
Dickinson, Daniel S. Bartlett. Pres. candidates, 127. — Bungay. Off-hand, 316. — Proctor. Lawy. of N. Y. 534. — Savage. Liv. Rep. men, 200.
Dickinson, John. With portrait. Amer. nat. portr. gall. 3. — Lossing. Em. Amer. 209. — Moore, F. Am. eloq. 1 : 273. — Neven, D. R. B. Pennsylvanians, 202.
Dickinson, William. Miller, Jos. Singers church, 2d ed. 533.
Dickson, David. Blaikie, W. G. Preachers Scot. 102. — Hatfield, E. F. Poets of church, 191. — Miller, Jos. Singers church, 2d ed. 85. — Taylor, W. M. Scott. pulpit, 97.
Dickson, Samuel Henry. Davidson, J. W. Writ. of South, 139.
Diction and style. Bulwer, E. Caxtoniana.
Dictionaries, Eng. *See* English language.
— Modern. Tucker, G. M. Our com. speech, 112.
— Old English. Tucker, G. M. Our com. speech, 95.
Dictionary & grammar, Connection between. Abel, C. Ling. ess. 169.
Didache, The. *See* Teaching of the Twelve.
Diderot, Denis. Carlyle. Essays. — (J. Morley) Gautier. Fam. Fr. au. 307. — Houssaye. Men of 18th cent. 1 : 280. — Vinet. Fr. lit. 18th

cent. 341. — Ellis, H. New spirit. — Forster. Fr. and Span. genius, 85. — Haussonville. Salon of Necker, 1 : 148. — Hundred greatest men, 298. — Men & wom. of France, 1 : 298. — Osborn. From Greeks, 115. — Ste.-Beuve. Portr. of men, 125. — With portrait. Warner Lib. 8 : 4689.
Diderot, Denis, and the French stage. Hawkins. Fr. stage 18th cent. v. 2.
Diego, the Admiral. Brooks, E. S. Gt. men's sons, 221.
Diego y Moreno, Francis Garcia. Clarke, R. H. Cath. bishops, 2 : 157.
Dieppe, Paris days at. Stuart, H. Paris days, 93.
Dies Iræ, with chronological list of English versions. Schaff. Lit. & poetry, 134.
Diet. Kinney, A. Tasks, 154.
— Ethical peculiarities of. Dana, A. H. Eth. inq. 219.
— Importance of, for intellectual effort. Hamerton. Intellec. 14.
Dietetics. Timbs. Doctors, 345.
Dietrich legends. Ludlow. Epics, 1 : 184.
Differences, small, On the perception of. (G. S. Fullerton ; J. McK. Cattell) Univ. Pa. Publ. Philos. no. 2.
Differentials and methods of finding them. (W. D. Wilson) N. Y. Regents, 87 : 604.
Digby, Anastasia Venetia Stanley, Lady. Costello. Englishwomen, 3 : 1.
Digby, G., Baron. Goodrich, C. A. Sel. Brit. eloq.
Digby, Sir Kenelm. Jeaffreson. Doctors, 1 : 47. — Lodge. Portraits (Bohn), v. 5. — Tuckerman. Ess. 75. — With portrait. Jesse. Court of Eng. Stuarts, 2 : 190.
— and Sir Anthony Van Dyck. Thomson, Mrs. Cel. friend. 1 : 319.
Digges, Dudley. Foss. Judges, 6 : 301.
Dilettantism, Modern education tending to. Hamerton. Intellec. 99.
Dilke, Sir Charles Wentworth. With photo. Cooper, T. Men of mark, 5 : 22. — Davidson, J. M. Eng. lib. 36. — Hinton. Eng. radicals, 27. — Reid, T. W. Politicians, 1 : 115.
Dillahunty. Edmund. Livingston, J. Em. Am. lawy. 151.
Dillard, A. W. Davidson, J. W. Writ. of South, 142.
Dillingham, Francis. McClure. Translators, 116.
Dillon, Charles. Coleman, G. Players, 2 : 248. — Marston, J. W. Rec. actors, 2 : 180.
Dillon, Edward. Burke, O. J. Cath. archb. 206.
Dillon, John Brown. Coggeshall. Poets of west, 109.
Dillon, John F., with portrait. Scott, H. W. Dist. Am. lawy. 301.
Dillon, Robert C. Grant, Jas. Metropol. pul. 180.
Dillon, Sidney. Parton, J. Sk. of men of prog.
Diman, Jeremiah L., Discourse on. (J. O. Murray) Diman. Orations, v. 1.
Dime novel, Test of the. Higginson. New world, 198.
Dimitry, Charles. Davidson, J. W. Writ. of South, 143.
Dimock, Susan. Clarke, J. F. Memo. sketches, 211.
Dindall, W. (J. Fox) Wordsworth, C. Eccles. biog. v. 2.
Dinderstadt, Christopher. Wallace, R. Anti-Trin. biog. 2 : 440.
Dingelstedt, Franz von, with portrait. Warner Lib. 8 : 4704.

Dining, Art of. Arnold, F. Arm-chair, v. 1. — Hayward, A. Ess. 2 : 325. — Lang. Leaders, 62.
— Blue-violet salad. Ellwanger. Sto. of house, 152.
— Hayward's Art of. Maxwell, Sir H. Rainy days, 53.
Dining-rooms for the working classes. Wynter. Subtle brains, 14.
Dinner, real and reputed. DeQuincey. Miscel. ess. (Bost.) 205.
Dinner party dialogue, A. Wallace, H. B. Lit. crit. 259.
Dinner question, The. Wraxall. Scraps, 2 : 1.
Dinners. Dodge, M. A. 12 miles, 303.
— and diners. Jeune. Lesser ques. 61.
Dinnies, Anna Peyre. Coggeshall. Poets of west, 198. — Davidson, J. W. Writ. of South, 150. — Freeman, J. D. Wom. of South, 476. — Raymond, I. Southland writ. 1 : 241.
Dinsmore, Robert. Whittier. Old portr. 284.
Diocesan synods. Thirlwall, C. Remains, 2 : 123. 3 : 427.
Diocletian. Doran. Monarchs, 2 : 16.
— Place of, in architectural history. Freeman. Hist. ess. 3 : 61.
Diodorus Siculus. Mills. Poets of Greece, 482.
Diogenes. Lewes. Biog. phil. — Diog. Laertius. Lives, 224. — Fénélon. Philosophers, 220.
Diogenes Laertius. Warner Lib. 8 : 4711.
Diogenes of Apollonia. Lewes. Biog. phil.
Dion Cassius. Mills. Poets of Greece, 485.
Dionysius, St., the Areopagite. Blakey, R. Prim. fathers, 54. — Cave. Lives of fathers, 1 : 130.
Dionysius, St., bishop of Alexandria. Blakey, R. Prim. fathers, 138. — Cave. Lives of fathers, 1 : 417. — Evans, R. W. Biog. early church, 2 : 287. — Pressensé. Martyrs, 342.
Dionysius of Corinth. Evans, R. W. Biog. early church, 1 : 184.
Dionysius of Halicarnassus. Mills. Poets of Greece, 483.
Dionysius of Sicily. Lord, J. Anc. states, 333.
Dionysus, A study of. Pater. Greek stud. v. 1.
Dioscorides. Mills. Poets of Greece, 210.
Diotimus. Mills. Poets of Greece, 182.
Diphilus. Mills. Poets of Greece, 410.
Diptera from a hygienic point of view. (R. Ramirez) Am. Pub. Health, 24 : 257.
Diphtheria. (C. N. Hewitt) Am. Pub. Health, 24 : 88. — (C. A. Ruggles) Califor. Health, '90–92 : 160. — (D. Strock) N. J. Health, '94 : 311.
— Antitoxin treatment of. (C. D. Smith) Maine Health, '94–95 : 182.
— Bacteriological diagnosis of. (E. B. Shuttleworth) Am. Pub. Health, 22 : 68. — A. M. Bleile) Ohio Health, '97 : 260.
— Cause and prevention of. (G. C. Ashmun) Am. Pub. Health, 16 : 97. — Am. Pub. Health, 22 : 56.
— Diagnosis of. (F. J. Tower) Wisc. Health, '91–92 : 73.
— — by staining method. (H. C. Crouch) Am. Pub. Health, 21 : 19.
— Difficulties in dealing with. (P. H. Bryce) Am. Pub. Health, 20 : 94.
— Epidemics of. (C. A. Hodgetts and others) Am. Pub. Health Assoc. 20 : 90.
— in Chihuahua. (M. Marquez) Am. Pub. Health, 22 : 71.
— in Massachusetts. Mass. Health, '78 : 463.
— in the Mexican highlands. (J. Chico) Am. Pub. Health, 17 : 205.

Diphtheria. Management of. (C. A. Hodgetts) Am. Pub. Health, 20 : 89.
— Origin and propagation of. (B. B. Loughead) Ohio Health, '87 : 349.
— Present mortality rate in. (I. N. Snively) Am. Pub. Health, 23 : 162.
— Questions concerning. (A. G. Young) Maine Health, '88 ; 222. '89 : 198.
— Schools and. (H. B. Baker) Am. Pub. Health, 6 : 107.
— Sewer-gas as a cause of. (H. R. Noel) Am. Pub. Health, 2 : 362.
— Use of petroleum products for illuminating, a cause of. (G. H. Wilson) Conn. Health, '86 : 309.
Diphtheria hospitals, Admission and discharge of patients. (E. B. Shuttleworth) Am. Pub. Health, 22 : 68.
Diplomacy, American. (F. W. Seward) Butterfield Lec. Un. Coll. 1 : 117.
— Ceremony and forms in. Marshall, F. Internat. van. 1 : 47.
— Expediency in. Newman, F. W. Miscel. 3 : 13.
— in the early history of the United States. Rush, R. Occa. prod. 141, 161.
Diplomatic appointments, Fitness of. Willis. Hurry-graphs, 213.
Diplomatic privileges. Marshall, F. Internat. van. 234.
Diplomatists, Inadequate recognition of, by historians. (J. B. Angell) Am. Hist. Assoc. Rept. '93 : 13.
— Lady. Wraxall, C. F. L. Hist. byways, 1 : 1.
Dipsomania. Wynter, A. Our soc. bees, 2 : 155.
— a proper subject for legal provision. (A. Peddie) Trans. Soc. Sci. Lond. '60 : 538.
Dirks, Lysken, wife of Jeronimus Segerson. Brown, J. N. Bapt. martyrs, 123.
Disagreeable folk. Henry, C. S. About men, 38.
Disagreeable people, Concerning. Boyd. Everyday, 119.
Disagreeable sayings. Ess. from Sat. R. 128.
Disappointments. Friswell. Gentle life, 1 : 124.
Disciples, Church of the. (B. B. Tyler) Why I am, 128.
Discipline and self-government. (A. V. Storm) Nat. Educa. Assoc. '94 : 764.
— Forms of, and discipline of forms. (B. L. Wiggins) Nat. Educa. Assoc. '90 : 96.
— mental, Dogma of formal. (B. A. Hinsdale) Nat. Educa. Assoc. '94 : 625.
Discontent, Popular. Strong, J. New era, 135.
Discord. Gurney. Power of sound, 549.
Discourse. Bacon. Ess.
Disease, Barbaric theory of. Clodd, E. Myths, 174.
— Causes of. (J. S. Billings) Buck, A. H. ed. Hygiene, 1 : 1.
— Communication of, in public places. (W. T. Corlett) Am. Pub. Health, 18 : 90.
— Definition and nomenclature of. Reynolds, J. R. Ess. 102.
— General causes of. (W. Clendenin) Am. Pub. Health, 1 : 46.
— Inside sources of. (J. J. Speed) Am. Pub. Health, 7 : 274.
— not hereditable. Bowen, F. Gleanings, 232.
— Prevention of. (T. Baker) Trans. Soc. Sci. Lond. '72 : 351. — (G. Derby) Mass. Health, '70 : 42.
— Prevention of, and prolongation of life. (C. G. R. Moutoux) Indiana Health, '93 : 221.

Disease, Registration of. Richardson, B. W. Ministry, 278.
— specific, Etiology of. (R. F. Stone) Indiana Health, '91 : 276.
— Treatment of. Bigelow, J. Mod. inq. 172.
Disease germs and germ diseases. (E. A. Birge) Wisc. Health, '87 : 68.
See Germs.
Diseases, Camp. (C. Smart) Buck, A. H., ed. Hygiene, 2 : 142.
— Classification of. (H. B. Baker) Am. Pub. Health, 14 : 30.
— Contagious. (A. M. Hamilton ; B. M. Emmett) Buck, A. H. ed. Hygiene, 2 : 513.
— Geographic distribution of, in Mass. (S. W. Abbott) Mass. Health, '91 : 759.
— Industrial. Internat. Health Ex. Sanita.
— infectious, Causation of. (H. M. Lyman) Am. Pub. Health, 4 : 88.
— — Prophylactic treatment as a preventive of. (E. M. Hunt) Am. Pub. Health, 4 : 299.
— — Soil factor in the development and prevention of. (E. Playter) Am. Pub. Health, 21 : 54.
— microphytic, Prevention of. (E. M. Hunt) Am. Pub. Health, 13 : 28.
— Nomenclature of. Am. Pub. Health, 20 : 517. 22 : 124.
— Occupational. N. J. Labor, '83 : 81. '84 : 204. '85 : 112. '89 : 1.
— Origin of. (E. M. Hunt) Am. Pub. Health, 13 : 50.
— — of some. (E. M. Hunt) Am. Pub. Health, 13 : 50.
— Registration of. (F. W. Draper) Mass. Health, '76 : 477.
— Self-limited. Bigelow, J. Mod. inq. 143.
— transmission of, Illustrative instances of. Conn. Health, '89 : 210.
Disestablishment of the Irish church. Thirlwall, C. Remains, 2 : 203.
— Policy of. Vaughan, D. J. Questions, 211.
See Church of England.
Disguises. Russell, A. P. Lib. notes, 63.
Disinfectants. Am. Pub. Health, 11 : 189. 12 : 198. 13 : 64.
— and disinfection, Notes on. (A. G. Young) Maine Health, '96–97 : 170.
— Bibliography of. (G. H. Rohe) Am. Pub. Health, 13 : 188. — Am. Pub. Health, 13 : 64. — (E. Waller) Buck, A. H., ed. Hygiene, 2 : 545. — (E. L. Griffin) Wisc. Health, '77 : 19.
— in quarantine work. (F. Montizambert) Am. Pub. Health, 24 : 255.
— Reports on. Am. Pub. Health, 12 : 198. — (F. C. Robinson) Am. Pub. Health, 23 : 101.
— Some standard. (F. C. Robinson) Am. Pub. Health, 24 : 237.
Disinfection. Iowa Health, '95 : 200.
— after diseases. (N. E. Wordin) Conn. Health, '92 : 223.
— and disinfectants. (E. Waller) Am. Pub. Health, 1 : 459. — Ill. Health, '85 : 5.
— by steam. (G. Homan) Am. Pub. Health, 18 : 149.
— — in cities. (H. B. Horlbeck) Am. Pub. Health, 21 : 225.
— Chemical. (F. P. Venable) Am. Pub. Health, 16 : 126.
— Experiment in. (J. Cochran) Maine Health, '92–93 : 216.
— experiments in, Test objects for. (H. W. Hill) Am. Pub. Health, 24 : 246.
— Importance of complete. (W. Hardwicke *et al.*) Trans. Soc. Sci. Lond. '78 : 450.

Disinfection in American cities. (C. V. Chapin) Am. Pub. Health, 21 : 217.
— in cities. (A. Gehrmann) Am. Pub. Health, 24 : 252.
— in quarantine system of Louisiana. (J. Holt) Am. Pub. Health, 13 : 161.
— in yellow fever. (C. B. White) Am. Pub. Health, 3 : 154.
— Methods of practical. (G. H. Rohe) Am. Pub. Health, 13 : 154.
— Methods of testing. (W. Johnston) Am. Pub. Health, 24 : 250.
— Municipal steam. (H. B. Horlbeck) Am. Pub. Health, 21 : 225.
— of dwellings by sulphur dioxide. (C. Edson) Am. Pub. Health, 15 : 65.
— of rooms. (F. G. Novy) Mich. Health, '97 : 129.
— of sewers by ozone. (J. D. Plunket) Am. Pub. Health, 4 : 297.
— Science of. (J. Dougall) Trans. Soc. Sci. Lond. '74 : 708.
Dispatch. Bacon. Ess.
Dispensaries. (C. C. Savage) Cong. Char. Chic. '93, 5 : 630.
Dispensary for chronic diseases of children. Internat. Health Ex. Sanita.
Disraeli, Benjamin. Grant, J. Recoll. Lords & Comm. 2 : 332. — Harrison, F. Stud. early Vict. 88. — Mitchell, D. G. Eng. lands, 4 : 178. — Smiles. Brief biog. 222.
See also Beaconsfield.
Disraeli, Isaac. Jerdan. Men, 178. — Wotton. Word portraits, 91. — Skelton, J. Table-talk, 241. — With portrait. Warner Lib. 8 : 4725.
— and Bolton Corney. Hitchman. 18th cent. 254.
— Life and writings of. (B. Disraeli) Disraeli, I. Curios. (N. Y. 4 v.) 1 : 2.
Disraeli, Maria B. Holloway, L. C. Mothers of gt. men, 387.
Dissent, Characteristics of religious. Vaughan, R. Ess. 1 : 190.
Dissenters. Hall, R. Miscel. 205.
Dissimulation, Simulation and. Bacon. Ess.
Distances in U. S. Barrows, W. U. S. of yester. 9 : 18.
Distant objects, Pleasure from. Hazlitt. Tabletalk.
"**Distinction**," Personal. Patmore. Religio poetæ, 117.
Distortions, Voluntary physical. Chambers's Miscel. no. 93.
D'Istria, Dora (*pseud.*). *See* Koltzoff Massalsky.
Distributed, The word, as used in logic. Latham. Opuscula, 39.
Distribution. Atkinson, E. Indus. prog. 137, 291.
— Is one man's gain another man's loss ? Jenkin, Fl. Papers, 2 : 140.
— A plea for better. (C. M. DuPuy) Phila. Soc. Sci. Assoc. '84.
Distribution bill. Brownson. Works, 15 : 202.
District-school libraries. *See* Libraries.
District visitor in England, Work of. Green, J. R. Stray studies, 313.
Disunion. Dodge, M. A. Skirmish. 245.
— Secret of southern favor of. Lyon, N. Last pol. writ. 169.
Ditches, Animal life in. Abbott, C. C. Outings, 117.
Ditmarsch, Germany, and Klaus Groth. Rearden. Petrarch, 105.
Diver, Jennie. (C. Andrews) Vincent, A. Twelve bad women, 137.
Divers, Bridget. Brockett. Woman's work, 771.

Dogs discovering crime. Burke, P. Romance of forum.

— in public. Wynter, A. Fruit betw. leaves, **2** : 145.

— Muzzling of, and hydrophobia. Romanes. Ess. 226.

— of folk-lore, history, and romance. King, R. J. Sketches, 94.

— "Our Dogs." Brown, J. J. Leech, 449.

Dog Days. Dodge, M. A. Country, 311.

Dogget, Thomas. Galt. Players, **1** : 150.

Dogmas. Jouffroy. Philos. miscel. **2** : 121.

Dogmatist, Our village. Fields. Underbrush, 95.

Doherty, John, chief justice. Sheil. Sk. Irish bar, **1** : 311.

Doig, David. Irving, D. Scot. writ. **2** : 313.

Doing good in the world. Stephen, J. F. Ess. by barr. 78.

Dolce, Carlo; Criticisms of his pictures. Guizot. Fine arts, 175.

Dolce, Lodovico. Symonds. Renais. It. lit. **2** : 133.

Dolet, Stephen. Wallace, R. Anti-Trin. biog. **2** : 1.

Dolley, Sarah R. A. Hanaford. Wom. of cent. 547.

Dollond, J. Groser, W. H. Men worth imita.

Dollond, Peter. Walker, W., jr. Men of sci. 49.

Dolls. Baring-Gould, S. Survivals, 139. — Story, A. T. Vagrom, 111.

Dolph, Joseph N., with portrait. Scott, H. W. Dist. Am. lawy. 309.

Dolphin, Spotted, compared with Prodelphinus doris. (F. W. True) U. S. Nat. Mus. Rept. '84 : 317.

Domanovius, Joseph. Wallace, R. Anti-Trin. biog. **2** : 419.

Domenec, Michael. Clarke, R. H. Cath. bishops, **3** : 583.

Domenichino. Spooner. Biog. fine arts, **1** : 265. — Symonds. Renais. Cath. reac. **2** : 359. — Jervis, Lady. Painting, **1** : 302.

— Criticisms of his pictures. Guizot. Fine arts, 132.

Domesday Book. Ewald, A. C. Paper, 1. — Round, J. H. Feudal Eng. 3.

Domestic animals, Diseases of. (M. Stalker) Iowa Health, '81 : 287. '91 : 349.

— — and their relation to health of man. (M. Stalker) Iowa Health, '81 : 285.

Domestic bliss. Bunce, C. B. Bach. bluff. 13.

Domestic economy. Friswell. Better self, 200.

— as a synthetic study. (Mrs. Ellen H. Richards) Nat. Educa. Assoc. '98 : 766.

— Bibliography. Campbell, H. Household economics. — Salem (Mass.) Pub. Lib. Bull. May, '98.

— Growth and development of. (F. L. Calder) Burdett-Coutts. Wom. miss. 317.

— Teaching of, in schools. (V. J. Germain) Internat. Health Exh. **14** : 334.

Domestic life. Dana. P. & p. writ. 425. — Emerson. Society, 99. — Vaughan, D. J. Questions, 55.

Domestic rule. Helps. Essays, 37.

Domestic servants. Jeune. Lesser ques. 262.

— in colonial times. Earle. Colon. dames, 258.

— Morals and manners of. Godkin. Reflections, 56.

Domestic service. Stowe, H. B. Chimney, 123. — Whipple. Outlooks, 99.

— Bibliography. Salmon, L. M. Domestic service.

— in the millennium. Higginson. Conc. all, 81.

Domestic service in the U. S. Walker, F. A. Discus. in econ. **2** : 225.

Domett, Alfred. (W. Gisborne) Miles, A. H. Poets of cent. **4** : 263.

Domicile, Law of. (J. Westlake) Trans. Soc. Sci. Lond. '80 : 141.

Domingo de Guzman, and the Inquisition. Lawrence, E. Hist. stud. 358.

Dominic, St. Lawrence, E. Hist. stud. 358. — Rule. Inquis. **1** : 20. — Jessopp, A. Coming of friars, 23.

— and St. Francis. Brigham, C. H. Mem. 208.

Dominica, Island of. Hill, R. T. Cuba, 337.

"**Dominica**," schooner, Capture of. Dawson. Batt. of U. S. **2** : 264.

Dominican Friars. Sergeant, L. Wiclif, 46. — Pennington. Epochs papacy, 109, 155, 399.

Dominoes, Chinese games with. (Stewart Culin) U. S. Nat. Mus. Rept. '96 : 489.

Domitian, Emperor. Lynam. Rom. emp. v. **2**.

Domneva, queen of Merowald. Hall. Queens bef. Conq. 283.

Don, Sir Wm. Willis. Hurry-graphs, 230.

Donald, Robert. Holland, J. Psalmists, **2** : 276.

Donaldson, Walter. Irving, D. Scot. writ. **1** : 303.

Donatello, or Donato, the cathedral builder. Ottley. Ital. school. — Perkins, C. C. Tusc. sculp. **1** : 137. — Oliphant. Makers of F. 124. — Symonds. Renais. fine arts, 136.

Donati, Alesso. Symonds. Renais. It. lit. **1** : 157.

Donato. *See* Donatello.

Donellan, Capt., Trial of, for murder. Burke, P. Cel. trials.

Donelson, Fort, Battle of. Swinton, 12 battles, 56.

Doni, Anton Francesco. Symonds. Renais. It. lit. **2** : 87.

Donizetti, Gaetano. Ferris. Great Ital. composers, 85. — Keddie. Mus. comp. 284. — Hogarth. Mem. opera, **2** : 118. — Upton. Stand. operas, 75. — Guerber. Stor. of operas, 157. — With portrait. Rowbotham. Priv. life compos. 272.

Donkin, Bryan. Walker, W., jr. Men of sci. 51.

Donne, John. Alden, R. M. Rise of satire, 75. — Chalmers. Eng. poets, **5** : 115. — (J. W. Hales) Ward. Eng. poets, **1** : 558. — Deshler. Afternoons, 123. — Furst, C. Group old auth. 11. — Gosse, E. Jacobean poets, 47. — Griswold, R. W. Sac. poets. — Ivimey. Eng. Bapt. **2** : 47. — McDonald, G. England's antiphon, 113. — Morley, H. Eng. writ. **11** : 150. — Walton, I. Lives. Same in Wordsworth, C. Eccles. biog. v. **3.** — With portrait. Warner Lib. **8** : 4771.

— and his wife, Story of. Jameson. Loves of poets.

— Death's duel. Gosse, E. Gossip, 53.

— Magdalen Herbert and. Thompson, Mrs. Cel. friend. **1** : 295.

— the poet-preacher. Lightfoot. Hist. ess. 221.

— Poetry of. Dowden. New stud. 90.

— Sermons. 1640. Coleridge. Lit. rem. **3** : 92.

Donoso, Juan Ximenez. Stirling-Maxwell. Ann. art. Spain, **3** : 1202.

Doolittle, Henry Jonas. (L. C. Alden) Harvard mem. biog. **2** : 226.

Doolittle, Mark. (G. A. Oviatt) N. E. Hist.-Gen. Soc. Biog. **2** : 473.

Dooly, J. M. Miller, S. F. Bench of Ga. v. **1.** — Sparks, W. H. Memories, 70.

Dora, Sister. *See* Pattison, Dorothy W.

Doran, John. Comments on Tuckerman's essays. Tuckerman. Collector, 1.

Dorat, Claude Joseph. Houssaye. Men of 18th cent. **2** : 160. — Men & wom. of France, **3** : 1. — Saintsbury. Miscel. ess. 344.

Dorbel, Tom. Whitehead, C. Highwaymen, **1** : 205.

Dorchester, Catharine Sedley, countess of. Jesse. Court of Eng. Stuarts. **3** : 504.

Dorchester, Castle and priory of. Timbs. Abbeys, **1** : 440.

Dorchester, Mass., in 1630, 1776, and 1856. Everett. Orat. v. **3.**

— Pierce house. Terhune. Colon. homes, 346.

Dordogne, Apparitions of the Virgin in (T. Marillier) Soc. Psych. Res. **7** : 100.

Doré, Gustave. With photo. Cooper, T. Men of mark, **2** : 36. — With portrait. Sharp, W. Great minds, 27. — With portrait. Hubbard, E. Little jour. **5** : 469. — Smalley. Lond. let. **1** : 338.

— at home. Yates, E. H. Celeb. **1** : 131.

Dore, James. Ivimey. Eng. Bapt. **4** : 329.

Dorfling, George, the martial tailor. Doran. Habits, 264.

Doria-Pamfili gallery at Rome, The. Morelli. Ital. paint. 250.

Dormer, John, with portrait. Caulfield. Kit-cat, 209.

Dormitories, in colleges. (C. K. Adams) Nat. Educa. Assoc. '79 : 101.

Dornford, Mrs. Eleanor. Burder. Pious wom. 432.

Dornford, Joseph. Mozley. Reminis. **2** : 57.

Dorr, Julia Caroline Ripley. Hart, J. S. Fem. prose, 447. — Hemenway. Poets of Vt. 227.

D'Orsay, Comte. See Orsay, A. G. G., comte d'.

Dorset, Anne Clifford, countess of, with portrait. Costello. Englishwomen, **2** : 228.

Dorset, C. Sackville, earl of. (S. Johnson) Chalmers. Eng. poets, **8** : 339. — Caulfield. Kit-cat, 87. — Jesse. Court of Eng. Stuarts, **3** : 244. — Macaulay. Biog. sk. 179.

Dorset, Edward Sackville, 4th earl of. Lodge. Portraits (Bohn), v. **5.**

Dorset, Henry Gray, marquis of. Burke, S. H. Hist. portr. Tudor, **2** : 495.

Dorset, Lionel C. Sackville, duke of, with portrait. Caulfield. Kit-cat, 66.

Dorset, Thomas Sackville, 1st earl of. Bell, R. Lit. & sci. men, **2** : 91. — Hazlitt. Dram. Eliz. — Lodge. Portr. (Bohn) v. **3.** — Ward. Eng. poets, v. **1.** — Jesse. Court of Eng. Stuarts, **1** : 185. — Wrangham. Brit. Plutarch, v. **2.**

Dorsetshire, England, Baptists of. Ivimey. Eng. Bapt. **2** : 149.

Dorsey, John Syng (1783–1818). (S. D. Gross) Gross. Lives physicians, 139.

Dorsey, Mrs. Sarah A. Davidson, J. W. Writ. of South, 154. — Raymond, I. Southland wr. **1** : 205.

Dorsheimer, William. Am. Bar Assoc. **11** : 337.

Dort, or Dordrecht. Mahaffy. Holl. & Germ. 20.

Dorus-Gras, Julie. See Gras, Julie Dorus.

Dosie, Jaques. Brown, J. N. Bapt. martyrs, 97.

Doss, Louise Woodworth. Hanaford. Wom. of cent. 562.

Dostoyevsky, Feodor M. Vogüé. Rus. nov. 141. — With portrait. (I. F. Hapgood) Warner Lib. **8** : 4779. — Wolkonsky. Lowell lec. 256.

Doten, Lizzie. Austin, A. Poetry, 248.

Double consciousness, A case of. (R. Hodgson) Soc. Psych. Res. **7** : 221.

Doubleday, Thomas. Mitford, M. R. Recollec. 362.

Doubt. (Canon Scott Holland) Wace, H. Lond. mission. 140.

— and faith. Walker, H. Gt. Vic. poets, 292.

— Modern. De Vere, A. Essays, literary, 230.

Douce, Francis. Jerdan. Men, 183.

Doudan, Ximénes. Fisher, M. Group of Fr. crit. 195.

Doudney, Sarah. Miles. A. H. Poets of cent. **10** : 769.

Dougherty, Daniel, with portrait. Scott, H. W. Dist. Am. lawy. 321.

Doughoregan Manor, Maryland. Terhune, M. V. More colon. homes, 224.

Doughty, Thomas. Bourne, H. R. F. Eng. scam. **2** : 83, 87.

Douglas, David Bates, with portrait. Stuart, C. B. Am. engineers, 199.

Douglas, Gavin or Gawin. Irving, D. Scot. poets, **2** : 1. — (A. Lang) Ward. Eng. poets, **1** : 159. — Wilson, J. G. Poets of Scot. **1** : 28. — Brink. Eng. lit. 2, pt. **2** : 79. — Minto, W. Eng. poets. 106. — Morley, H. Eng. writ. **7** : 159. — Tytler. Scot. worthies, v. **3.**

Douglas, James, Lord, and Bishop Lamberton. Shairp. Sk. hist. & poetry, 86.

Douglas, Janet. See Glammis, Lady.

Douglas, Margaret. See Lennox, Countess of.

Douglas, Robert. Blaikie, W. G. Preachers Scot. 137.

Douglas, Stephen A. Bartlett. Pres. candidates, 51. — Boutwell, G. S. Speeches, 9. — Bungay. Off-hand, 383. — With portrait. Duyckinck. Nat. portr. gall. **2** : 273. — Forney. Anec. **1** : 18. — Parton. Peop. bk. biog. 196. — Savage. Liv. rep. men, 215. — Johnston, A. Amer. ora. **3** : 50.

— Traitorous attitude on Kansas question. Lyon, N. Last pol. writ. 134.

— True to his mission of slavery. Lyon, N. Last pol. writ. 151.

Douglas families of Scotland. Taylor, J. Fam. of Scot. **1** : 34.

Douglass, Frederick. Bartlett, D. W. Modern agitators, 38. — Bungay. Repr. men, 179. — With portrait. Carroll, H. 12 Amer. 263. — Ossoli. Life without, 121. — Stowe. Men of time, 380.

Douglass, Samuel Townsend. Am. Bar Assoc. **21** : 679.

Douhault, Madame de, the woman without a name. Fuller, H. W. Noted trials, 29.

Dowro, Passage of the. Adams, W. H. D. Eng. at war, **1** : 278.

Douw, Gerard. Gower. Fig. painters Holl. 34.

— Spooner. Biog. fine arts, **1** : 271.

Dove, Leslie C. Walker, C. D. Biog. Va. Mil. Inst. 175.

Dover, Georgiana Dorothy, with portrait. Ollier, E. Brit. portr. paint. 65.

Dover, Henry Jermyn, Lord. Jesse. Court of Eng. Stuarts, **3** : 272.

Dover, Eng. Rimmer, A. Country towns, 185.

— Siege of. Robson, W. Sieges, 421.

Dover Castle. Timbs. Abbeys, **1** : 323.

Dover, Del., Old houses of. Terhune, M. V. More colon. homes, 315.

Dow, Gerhard. Smetham. Lit. works, 230. — Van Dyke, J. C. Dutch mast. 73.

Dow, Jesse Erskine. Everest. Poets of Conn. 375.

Dow, Neal. Bungay. Off-hand, 263. — Bungay. Pen-portr. 15.

Dow family. Titcomb, S. E. N. Eng. peo. 238.

Dowden, Edward. Warner Lib. **8** : 4806.

Downes, Andrew. McClure. Translators, 198.

Dramatization of novels. Matthews, B. Books & play-books.

Dranesville, Battle of. Stine, J. H. Army Poto. 30.

Draper, John W. Francis, S. W. N. Y. phys. 33. — With portrait. Proctor, R. A. Leis. read. 69. — With portrait. Warner Lib. 9 : 4865.

— Works. Brownson. Works, 9 : 292.

Draper, Lyman Copeland. Am. Antiq. Soc. Proc. n. s. 7 : 307.

Draper, Mrs. Clement, J. Noble deeds, 100.

Draper, Samuel. Redding. Misers, 2 : 301.

Draper, Sir W. Georgian era, 2 : 62. — Jesse, J. H. Cel. Eton. v. 2.

Drawing, Æsthetic aim in. (L. W. Miller) Nat. Educa. Assoc. '93 : 462.

— and color, Use of, in other studies. (Mary D. Hicks ; W. S. Perry) Nat. Educa. Assoc. '87 : 597.

— and coloring, Teaching of, as a prep. for designing and decorative work. (J. Sparks et al.) Internat. health exh. 14 : 200.

— Children's expression through. (M. V. O'Shea) Nat. Educa. Assoc. '94 : 1015.

— Elementary instruction in. (J. P. Seddon et al.) Trans. Soc. Sci. Lond. '84 : 669.

— Elements of. Paget, J. Paradoxes, 413.

— Evolution of, in U. S. (L. S. Thompson) Nat. Educa. Assoc. '89 : 641.

— from the flat. (H. T. Bailey) Nat. Educa. Assoc. '93 : 458.

— High school work in. (Rhoda E. Selleck) Nat. Educa. Assoc. '90 : 790.

— Highest office of. (Frank Aborn) Nat. Educa. Assoc. '91 : 470.

— in advanced industrial education. (C. B. Stetson) Nat. Educa. Assoc. '76 : 273.

— in college education. (J. A. Nichols) N. Y. Regents, 78 : 372.

— in the early years. (H. T. Lukens) Nat. Educa. Assoc. '99 : 946.

— in educa. exhibit, N. E. A. meeting, San Francisco, '88. (L. S. Thompson) Nat. Educa. Assoc. '88 : 699.

— — St. Paul, 1890. (A. C. Fruchte) Nat. Educa. Assoc. '90 : 62.

— — Toronto, 1891. Nat. Educa. Assoc. '91 : 262.

— in graded schools. (Walter Smith) Nat. Educa. Assoc. '72 : 85.

— in high schools. (W. S. Perry) Nat. Educa. Assoc. '85 : 288. '87 : 573.

— in normal schools. (Kate E. Shattuck) Nat. Educa. Assoc. '85 : 295. — (M. Louise Field ; Harriet Cecil Magee) Nat. Educa. Assoc. '87 : 578. 97 : 758.

— in primary and grammar schools. (Mrs. E. F. Dimmock) Nat. Educa. Assoc. '85 : 284. '87 : 558.

— in public schools. (L. M. Godden) Nat. Educa. Assoc. '91 : 767.

— — Supervision of. (W. S. Goodnough) Nat. Educa. Assoc. '91 : 776.

— — What the people want in. (L. M. Godden) Nat. Educa. Assoc. '97 : 767.

— in ungraded schools. (W. S. Goodnough) Nat. Educa. Assoc. '87 : 561.

— Industrial, as a branch of education. (S. E. Warren) N. Y. Regents, 90 : 541.

— — Manual training through. (C. M. Carter) Nat. Educa. Assoc. '86 : 443.

— Instrumental, in scientific education. (S. Edward Warren) Nat. Educa. Assoc. '76 : 282.

Drawing. A new method. (Frank Aborn) Nat. Educa. Assoc. '90 : 858.

— Normal school work in. (Hannah J. Carter) Nat. Educa. Assoc. '90 : 802.

— Relation of, to manual training, (J. C. Miller) Nat. Educa. Assoc. '94 : 872.

— — to other studies. (Mary D. Hicks and others) Nat. Educa. Assoc. '86 : 433.

— Self-correcting system of. (A. R. O. Moore) Cong. Educa. Chic. '93 : 500.

— Study of, as common-school work. (Aaron Gove) Nat. Educa. Assoc. '92 : 495.

— Teaching of, in public schools. (I. E. Clarke) U. S. Bur. Educa. Circ. '74, no. 2. — (J. S. Clark) N. Y. Regents, 93 : 618.

— — Principles for. (M. V. O'Shea) Nat. Educa. Assoc. '98 : 802.

— — Reasons for. (L. S. Thompson) Nat. Educa. Assoc. '77 : 40.

— — with what should it begin ? (J. C. Locke ; H. J. Carter) Cong. Educa. Chic. '93 : 491.

Drawing schools, Free industrial evening. (G. H. Bartlett) Nat. Educa. Assoc. '88 : 607.

Drayton, Michael. Bell, R. Lit. & sci. men, 1 : 1. — Chalmers. Eng. poets, 4 : ix. — Disraeli, I. Amen. (N. Y. 2 v.) 2 : 248. — (G. Saintsbury) Ward. Eng. poets, 1 : 526. — Choate, I. B. Wells of Eng. 151. — Deshler. Afternoons, 104. — Gosse, E. From Shakesp. 29. — Gosse, E. Jacobean poets, 93. — Griswold, R. W. Sac. poets. — Minto, W. Eng. poets, 205. — Morley, H. Eng. writ. 10 : 210-314. 11 : 316. — With portrait. Warner Lib. 9 : 4877.

— Bibliography. Elton, O. Introd. to Michael Drayton.

— Loves of. Jameson. Loves of poets.

Drayton, William Henry. Moore, F. Am. eloq. 1 : 48. — Perry, B. F. Biog. sketches, 1 : 441. — Lossing. Em. Amer. 86.

Dream and the truth. Richter. Campaner.

Dream-life, Thoughts touching. Boyd. Aut. holid. 115.

Dream testimony. Burton, J. H. Crim. tri. 2 : 79.

Dream worlds. Mabie. My study fire, 64.

Dreaming. Griffin, G. W. Stud. in lit.

— and poetic invention. (J. Sully) Cong. Educa. Chic. '93 : 730. — Same in Nat. Educa. Assoc. '93 : 730.

Dreams. Coleridge. Lit. rem. 1 : 201. — (E. Clodd) Proctor, R. A. Nat. stud. 14. — Hazlitt. Plain speaker, v. 1. — Howells. Impressions, 95. — Mason, R. O. Telepathy, 129. — Stevenson, R. L. Miscel. 1 : 317. — Timbs. Doctors, 282. — Wynter, A. Fruit betw. leaves, 2 : 153.

— and dreaming. Smith, Alex. Last leaves, 80.

— and growth of beliefs in the supernatural. Clodd, E. Myths, 143.

— and realities. Stephen, L. Agnos. apol. 86.

— and sleep. Holland, H. Frag. papers, 363. — Jacox, F. Cues, 252.

— as illustrations of unconscious cerebration. Cobbe, F. P. Darwinism, 335.

— as omens and media of communication between gods and men. Clodd, E. Myths, 236.

— Barbaric belief in the reality of. Clodd, E. Myths, 168.

— Chapter on. Stevenson, R. L. Across pl. 229.

— Dreamland. Friswell. About, 229.

— Hallucinations and. Wynter. Borderl. of insan. 208.

— Mysteries. Whiting, C. G. Saunterer, 297.

— presentiments, and visions. Henry, C. S. Satan, 22.

— strangely fulfilled. Proctor, R. A. Fam. sci. 322.

Dred Scott *vs.* Sandford. Curtis, B. R. Mem. & writ. v. 2.
Dredge, New Russian, 1899. (G. F. Lincoln) U. S. Cons. Rept. **61** : 543.
Dredging, Deep sea. Proctor. Light sci. **1** : 142.
Drennan, William. Miller, Jos. Singers church, 2d ed. 315.
Dresden. Bellows. Old world, **1** : 386. — Felton, C. C. Europe, 19. — Guild. Abroad again, 374. — Jameson. Visits, **1** : 203.
— Battle of, 1813. Adams, C. Gt. camp. 156.
Dress. Bunce, O. B. Bach. bluff, 237.
— and its critics. Ess. from Nation, 105.
— beauty in, Sources of. Stowe, H. B. Chimney, 235.
— Extravagance in. Jeune. Lesser ques. 124.
— Extremes of. Mathews, W. Men, p. & t. 289.
— Fashions in. Goldsmith. Misc. (N. Y. 4 v.) **1** : 33.
— female, Proprieties and abuses of. Holland, J. G. Titcomb's let. 85.
— Hygienic relation of, to education. (R. Anna Morris) Nat. Educa. Assoc. '**94** : 880.
— modern, Health endangered by. (L. H. Stone) Brockett, A. C. Educa. of girls, 196.
— Outward adornment. Friswell. About, 44.
— Papers on. Doran. Habits, 7.
— Suitability of. Wilde, Lady. Soc. stud. 108.
— Who makes the fashions? Stowe, H. B. Chimney, 205.
— Women's. Curtis, G. W. Ars rec. viv. 47.
Dressmakers and tailoresses. (F. Hicks) Galton, F. W. Workers, 13.
Drew, Daniel. Brockett. Men of our day, 640.
— Parton, J. Sk. of men of prog.
— and Erie railway war in 1868. Adams, C. F. Erie, 1.
Drew, John. (J. S. Metcalfe) McKay, F. E. Fam. actors, 154.
Drew, Mrs. John. (T. Allston Brown) McKay, F. E. Fam. actors, 127.
Drew, Samuel. Famous boys, 127. — Groser, W. H. Men worth imita. — Smiles. Self-help. — Winks. Illus. shoemakers, 117. — Wise, D. Heroic Meth. 250.
Drew Theological Seminary. U. S. Bur. Ed. Circ. '99, no. **1** : 343.
Drexel, Anthony J., and his Institute. Bolton, S. K. Givers, 285.
Dreyfus case. Bibliography. Bost. Pub. Lib. Bull. July, 1899.
Dreyschock, Raimund, with portrait. Ehrlich, A. Cel. violin. 125.
Dreyse, Johann Nikolaus. Strauss, G. L. M. Men of Germ. **2** : 319.
Dried fruit, Sulphuring or bleaching. (J. W. Smith) Am. Pub. Health, **16** : 199.
Drifting. Friswell. Wick. world, 199.
Driftwood, A flame of. Mabie. My study fire, 60.
Driggs, George. Am. Bar Assoc. **15** : 433.
Drilling, Primitive methods of. (J. D. McGuire) U. S. Nat. Mus. Rept. '**94** : 623.
Drink, Problem of. (T. D. Crothers) Factors Amer. civiliz. 279.
— — Sanitary side of. (T. D. Crothers) Penn. Health, '**92** : 513.
Drink evil, The. (H. N. Raymond) Conf. char. & correc. '**97** : 235.
Drinker, Edward, centenarian. Rush, B. Ess. 288.
Drinking customs in England. Disraeli, I. Curios. (N. Y. 4 v.) **3** : 24.
Drinking songs. Repplier, A. Varia, 130.
Drinking system of Scotland, Extent and cost of.

(J. A. Johnston) Trans. Soc. Sci. Lond. '**66** : 615.
Drinks, Intoxicating; beer-shops and prohibitory laws. (P. E. Aldrich) Mass. Health, '**73** : 134.
— — Effects of. (H. I. Bowditch) Mass. Health, '**72** : 72.
— — in Massachusetts. Mass. Health, '**71** : 246.
— — in foreign countries. Mass. Health, '**71** : 256.
See Liquor.
Drinkwater, Bethune J. Espinasse. Lanc. worth. v. 2.
Driver, S. R. Cheyne. Founders O. T. crit. 248.
Drop, A, a splash, and allied phenomena. (A. M. Worthington) Smithson. Rept. '**94** : 197.
Drouais, François-Hubert. Dilke. Fr. painters 18th cent. 155.
Drowned, Resuscitation of the. (R. C. Kedzie) Mich. Health, '**77** : 131.
Drowning, death from, Mode of. Brodie. Works, **1** : 427.
Drowning scene. Howells. Sub. sk. 190.
Droz, Gustave. Van de Velde. Fr. fict. **2** : 31. — With portrait. Warner Lib. **9** : 4885.
Droz, Joseph, Art of being happy. Everett, A. H. Crit. ess. **1** : 201.
Drozovius, Joachim. Wallace, R. Anti-Trin. biog. **3** : 311.
Drudgery, Problem of. Higginson. Book & heart, 135.
Drugs, Adulteration of. Mass. Health, '**83** : 91. '**84** : 97. '**85** : 65. '**86** : 73. '**87** : 113. '**88** : 47.
Druidical institution, The. Disraeli, I. Amen. (N. Y. 2 v.) **1** : 9.
Drummond, David T. K. Hatfield, E. F. Poets of church, 208.
Drummond, Henry. Ritchie. Brit. sena. 388.
Drummond, Prof. Henry, with portrait. Warner Lib. **9** : 4897.
Drummond, James. See Perth, J. Drummond, duke of.
Drummond, William, of Hawthornden. Chalmers. Eng. poets, **5** : 639. — Drake, N. Mornings, **1** : 247. — Irving, D. Scot. writ. **2** : 10. — (T. H. Ward) Ward. Eng. poets, **2** : 24. — Wilson, J. G. Poets of Scot. **1** : 73. — Deshler. Afternoons, 128. — Gosse, E. Jacobean poets, 102. — Griswold, R. W. Sac. poets. — Macdonald, G. England's antiphon, 146. — Miller, Jos. Singers church, 2d ed. 351. — With portrait. Warner Lib. **9** : 4913.
— Loves of. Jameson. Loves of poets.
— Proposed memorial to. Masson. Edinb. sk. 76.
Drummond, Sir Wm. Academical questions. Jeffrey, F. Contrib. Ed. Rev.
Drummond families. Taylor, J. Fam. of Scot. **2** : 86.
Drumont, E. Henry, S. Hours w. Parisians, 119.
Drunkard, Confessions of a. Lamb. Elia.
Drunkards, Families of. (W. F. Slocum, jr.) Conf. char. & correc. '**88** : 131.
Drunkenness. Haweis. Curr. coin.
— among the poor, Methods and obstacles in repression of. (A. MacLeod) Trans. Soc. Sci. Lond. '**60** : 525.
— and drinking. Dodge, M. A. Skirmishes, 191.
— Causes of. Kingsley, C. San. lec. 167.
— Criminality of. (W. Arnot) Trans. Soc. Sci. Lond. '**59** : 456.
— Habitual drunkards act. (N. Kerr; S. Knaggs) Trans. Soc. Sci. Lond. '**83** : 455.
— Punishment of. (J. W. Horsley) Trans. Soc. Sci. Lond. '**82** : 222.
— a vice, and should be so treated. (A. N. Bell) Am. Pub. Health, **22** : 237.
Drury, Dru. Jardine. Nat. lib. v. 15.

Drury College, Springfield, Mo. (F. A. Hall) U. S. Bur. Ed. Circ. '98, no. 2 : 103.

Drury Lane. Lennox, W. P. Plays, 1 : 133. — In and about. Doran. Drury Lane, 1 : 1.

Druzbacka, Elizabeth. Soboleski. Poets of Poland, 79.

Dry-goods merchant's recollections, An old. Parton. Capt. indus. 392.

Dryburgh Abbey. Stowe. Sunny mem. 1 : 138.

Dryden, John. Austin & Ralph. Laureates, 142. — Bell, R. Lit. & sci. men, 2 : 1. — (S. Johnson) Chalmers. Eng. poets, 8 : 423. — Coleridge, H. Ess. 2 : 28. — Collier, W. F. Hist. Eng. lit. 236. — Doran. Annals stage, 1 : 156. — Gosse, E. 18th cent. lit. chap. 12. — Hannay. Satire, 94. — Hazlitt. Eng. poets. — Howitt. Homes Br. poets, 1 : 126. — Lowell. Writ. 3 : 95. — Macaulay. Ess. 1 : 321. — Masson, D. Ess. on poets. — Mitchell, D. G. English lands, 2 : 227. — Reed, H. Brit. poets, 1 : 267. — Sanborn, K. Eng. poets, 85. — Saunders, F. Famous books, 67. — Skelton. Ess. 143. — Skelton. Impeach. of Mary, 1. — Taine. Eng. lit. 2 : 1. — (A. W. Ward) Ward. Eng. poets, 2 : 437. — Ward, A. W. Eng. dram. 2 : 496. — Wotton. Word portraits, 94. — (W. Rushton) Afternoon lec. 1 : 63. — Gosse, E. From Shakesp. 194. — Hamilton, Wal. Poets laur. — Hatfield, E. F. Poets of church, 210. — Miller, Jos. Singers church, 2d ed. 98. — Russell, W. C. Book of au. 95. — Swanwick, A. Poets, 240. — With portrait. (T. R. Lounsbury) Warner Lib. 9 : 4919. — Wrangham. Brit. Plutarch, v. 4.

— and the comedy of "A mistaken husband." Swinburne. Miscel. 361.

— and the Restoration. Masson. Three devils, 153 ; or Essays, 88.

— Dramas. Hogarth. Mem. opera, 1 : 83, 104, 119.

— Hexastich. DeQuin. Note-book (Bost.) 281.

— Influence of, on the English language. Clough. Prose rem. 325.

— Literary morality of an epoch. Windsor. Ethica, 112.

— Poems and plays. Perry, T. S. Eng. lit. 18th cent. 51.

Dualism in men's lives. Mathews. Conversers, 168.

— in national life. Clarke, J. F. 19th cent. ques. 28.

— in nature and morals. Gladden, W. Ruling ideas, 245.

— materialism, or idealism. Bowen, F. Gleanings, 136.

Duane, William. Mansfield, E. D. Pers. mem. 338.

Dubba, Battle of. Adams, W. H. D. Engl. at war, 2 : 94.

Du Bellay, Joachim. Cary. Fr. poets, 50. — Pater. Stud. renais. 123.

Dublin. Silloway. Cathedral towns, 44. — Courts of justice of. Curran. Irish bar, 1 : 97.

— National agricultural exhibition, 1891. (A. J. Reid) U. S. Cons. Rept. 36 : 237.

— Theatre in, 1700–60. Doran. Their maj. serv. 1 : 489. 2 : 52.

— University of, Ancient. Newman, J. H. Hist. sk. 3 : 203.

Dublin institutions. Davis, T. Prose, 166.

Dubois, Cardinal Guillaume. Crowe, E. E. For. statesmen, 4 : 64.

Dubois, John. Clarke, R. H. Cath. bish. 1 : 414.

Du Bosc. Broadus. Lec. hist. preach. 171.

Dubose, Mrs. Kate A. Davidson, J. W. Writ.

of South, 171. — Freeman, J. D. Wom. of South, 407. — Raymond, I. Southland writ. 1 : 411.

Dubourg, William Louis. Clarke, R. H. Cath. bishops, 1 : 205.

Du Camp, Maxime, with portrait. Warner Lib. 9 : 4951.

Duccio, Buoninsegna. Stillman, W. J. Old Ital. mas. 19. — Symonds. Renais. fine arts, 213.

Du Chaillu, P. B., with portrait. Greely, A. W. Explorers, 330.

Du Châtelet, Madame, Voltaire and. Jameson. Loves of poets.

Duché, Jacob, of Philadelphia. Headley, J. T. Chaplains Revol. 83. — Sabine. Loyalists, 263.

Ducis, Jean, and the French stage. Hawkins. Fr. stage 18th cent. v. 2.

Duck, Stephen. Southey. Uned. poets, 88.

Duckett, Isabella (Smith), Lady. Clayton, E. C. Eng. fem. art. 2 : 371.

Ducks, Wild. Buckland, F. T. Curios. nat. hist. 3 : 122, 130.

Duclos, Charles Pineau, 1704–72. Vinet. Fr. lit. 18th cent. 361.

Du Coudray, T. Senior. Biog. sketches, 94.

Duddlestone, John. Burke, B. Viciss. of fam. 2 : 213.

Du Deffand, Madame. Haussonville. Salon of Necker, 1 : 221. — Hayward, A. Em. statesm. 2 : 129. — Mason, A. G. Wom. of Fr. salons, '96. — Warner Lib. 8 : 4471.

— Correspondence. Jeffrey, F. Contrib. Ed. Rev.

Dudevant, A. L. A. [Geo. Sand]. See Sand, Geo.

Dudgeon, David. McCosh. Scot. phil. 111.

Dudithius, Andrew. Wallace, R. Anti-Trin. biog. 2 : 286.

Dudley, Captain, d. 1681. Whitehead, C. Highwaymen, 1 : 96.

Dudley, Daniel B. Hemenway. Poets of Vt. 357.

Dudley, Dudley, iron worker. Smiles. Indus. biog.

Dudley, James M. Am. Bar Assoc. 15 : 451.

Dudley, J. W., 1st earl of. Sinclair, J. Sketches. — Thornton. For. sec. v. 2.

Dudley, Joseph. Moore, J. B. Am. gov. 390. — Washburn. Jud. hist. Mass. 114.

Dudley, Paul, Commission of. (A. C. Goodell, jr.) Mass. Hist. Soc. Proc. 2d ser. 12 : 51.

Dudley, Robert. See Leicester, Earl of.

Dudley, Governor Thomas. Mass. Hist. Proc. 12 : 207. — Moore, J. B. Am. gov. 273.

Dudley, Thomas. Walker, C. D. Biog. Va. Mil. Inst. 179.

Dudley, Thomas. See Northumberland, Duke of.

Duds. Woolson. Browsing, 68.

Duel, Graves-Cilley. (C. F. Adams) Mass. Hist. Soc. Proc. 2d ser. 12 : 286.

Duelling. Curtis, G. W. Ars rec. viv. 85. — Du Chaillu. Viking age, 1 : 563.

— Casuistry of DeQuincey. Lit. rem. (Bost.) 2 : 295 ; or Uncoll. writ. 2 : 65.

— in the times of chivalry. Doran. Knights, 65.

— Remedy for. Beecher, L. Works, 2 : 33.

— 250 years ago. Carlyle. Essays. — Timbs, J. Romance of Lond. 1 : 200.

Duels and ordeals. Mackay. Delusions, 1 : 160.

Duerer, Agnes. Prime, W. C. I go a-fishing, 74.

Duerer, Albrecht. Cheney, E. D. Gleanings, 209. — Eastlake, E. R. Five painters, 2 : 187. — Grimm, H. Liter. 169. — Lloyd, Mrs. W. R. Watchers, 126. — With portrait. Sharp, W. Great minds, 91. — Spooner. Biog. fine arts,

1 : 281. — (W. Schmidt) Dohme, R. Early mast. 89.

Duerer, Albrecht. Adoration of the Magi. (M. Thausing) Singleton, E. Great pic. 215.
— his works, his compatriots, and his times. Fairholt. Rambles, 185.
— Literary remains of. Dempster. Essays, 1.

Duesseldorf Bartley, G. C. D. Rhine, 355.

Dufaure, Jules Armand Stanislas. King, E. French pol. lead. 202. — Men of 3d repub. 108.

Duff, Grant. Escott, T. H. S. Pillars emp. 56.

Duff, Mary A. Winter, W. Shadows, 2 : 19. — Matthews, B. Actors, 3 . 77.

Duff-Gordon, Lady. Ross, Janet. Three generations.

Dufferin, F. T. Blackwood, Earl. With photo. Cooper, T. Men of mark, 1 : 1. — Escott, T. H. S. Pillars emp. 62. —Sala, Mrs. Fam. peop. 39.

Dufferin, Helen Morton, Lady. Robertson. Eng. poetesses, 246.

Duffie, Alfred N. Portrait. Bartlett, J. R. R. I. officers, 209.

Duffield, Mrs. Ann (Rosenberg). Clayton, E. C. Eng. fem. art. 2 : 272.

Duffield, Dr. Samuel W. Bungay. Off-hand, 392.

Duffield, George, 1732–90. Headley, J. T. Chaplains Revol. 350.

Duffield, George, 1816–88. Hatfield, E. F. Poets of church, 213. — Miller, Jos. Singers church, 2d ed. 544.

Dufour, Amanda L. Ruter. Coggeshall. Poets of west, 404.

Dufour, Cyprien. Davidson, J. W. Writ. of South, 172.

Dufour, Marie Armande Jeanne Gaçon (Humière). Redding. Pers. remin. 1 : 249.

Du Fresnoy C. A., Annotations on poems of. Reynolds. Lit. works, 2 : 297.

Dufresny, C. Rivière. Houssaye. Men of 18th cent. 1 : 11. — Men & wom. of France, 1 : 1.

Dugdale, Richard L. (E. M. Shepard) Econ. tracts, no. 12.

Duguay-Trouin, R. Bernard, F. Escapes, 99. — Laughton. Stud. nav. hist. 287. — With portrait. Norman, C. B. Corsairs, 155.

Dugué, Charles Oscar. Davidson, J. W. Writ. of South, 173.

Duigenan, Patrick. Hazlitt. Parl. portr. 165.

Duilius. Mombert. Great lives, 70.

Dujon, Francis, the younger. Morley, H. Marot, 2 : 285.

Duke, Richard. (S. Johnson) Chalmers. Eng. poets, 9 : 211.

Dulany, D. Boyle, E. Dist. Marylanders.

Dullness as a sensation. Ess. from Sat. R. 81.
— Dignity of. Boyd. Recreat. 1 : 380.

Dumas, Alexandre, the elder. Castelar. Byron, 207. — With portrait. (P. Fitzgerald) Gautier. Fam. Fr. au. 264. — Hayward, A. Ess. 2d ser. 1 : 293. — Lang. Ess. in lit. 1. — Lang. Let. to dead au. 119. — Mathews, W. Men, p. & t. 67. — Matthews, J. B. Fr. dram. 46. — Saintsbury. Ess. Fr. nov. 197. — Henley. Views, 33. — Walkley, A. B. Playhouse, 68. — Saintsbury, G. Ess. Eng. lit. 2 : 328. — With portrait. (A. Lang) Warner Lib. 9 : 4957.
— and the Napoleonic generation. Wells, B. W. Cent. Fr. fic. 68.
— Vicomte de Bragelonne. Stevenson, R. L. Men, 228 ; or Miscel. 1 : 235.

Dumas, Alexandre, the younger. Matthews, J. B. Fr. dram. 136. — Mauris, M. French men of l. 151.—Men of 3d repub. 121.—Pellissier. Lit. move. Fr. 451. — Walkley, A. B. Playhouse,

74. — With portrait. (F. Sarcey) Warner Lib. 9 : 5001.

Dumas, Jean Baptiste André. Thorpe, T. E. Ess. hist. chem. 258.
— Liebig and. Muir, M. M. P. Chemists, 256.

Du Maurier, George. Griswold, H. T. Personal sk. 96. — With portrait. Warner Lib. 9 : 5041. — James, H. Par. portr. 327.
— Bibliography. Providence Pub. Lib. Bull. Mar. '95.
— Society pictures by. Noble, J. A. Impressions, 116.
— Trilby. Couch, A. T. Q. Adv. crit. 384.

Dumb. *See* Deaf and Dumb.

Dumb-shows. Cook, D. On stage, 1 : 23.

Dumbarton. Hawthorne, Mrs. Eng. & It. 156.

Dumbarton castle. Mackie, C. Castles of Mary.
— Scaling of. Davenport. Narr. peril, 2 : 317.

Dumesnil, Marie, and the French stage. Hawkins. Fr. stage 18th cent. v. 1, 2.

Dumler, Nicholas. Wallace R. Anti-Trin. biog. 3 : 1.

Dumont, Julia Louisa. Coggeshall. Poets of west, 43.

Dumont de Bostaquet, Isaac. Agnew. Prot. exiles, 2 : 4.

Du Moulin, Jaques, Trial of. Phillips, S. M. Famous cases, 89.

Dumouriez, Charles F. Adolphus. Biog. Fr. rev. 1 : 350. — Smythe, G. S. Hist. fancies, 217.

Dun, the robber, and the town of Dunstable. Burke, T. Romance of forum.

Dunbar, Charles Franklin. Vaille & Clark. Harv. book, v. 1.

Dunbar, Sophia (Orred), Lady. Clayton, E. C. Eng. fem. art. 2 : 373.

Dunbar, Wm. Brink. Eng. lit. 2, pt. 2 : 65. — Choate, I. B. Wells of Eng. 60. — Morley, H. Eng. writ. 7 : 114.—Minto, W. Eng. poets, 98. — Irving, D. Scot. poets, 1 : 391. — Smith, Alex. Dreamthorp, 72. — (J. Nichol) Ward. Eng. poets, 1 : 147. — Wilson, J. G. Poets of Scot. 1 : 24. — Tytler. Scot. worthies, v. 3. — Warner Lib. 9 : 5064.
— Chaucer and Burns compared. Drake, N. Mornings, 2 : 1.

Dunbar, Battle of. Adams, W. H. D. Eng. at war, 1 : 51. — Adams, W. H. D. Memo. batt. 1 : 344.

Dunbar castle. Mackie, C. Castles of Mary.

Duncan, Adam Duncan, first viscount. Lodge. Portr. (Bohn) v. 8. — Edgar. Sea-kings, 329.

Duncan, John, weaver and botanist. Parton. Capt. indus. 240. — With portrait. Watson, Mrs. R. A. Poet-toilers, 107. — Hoare. Nota. workers, 40. — Japp, A. H. Leaders of men, 220.

Duncan, Mark. Irving, D. Scot. writ. 1 : 295.

Duncan, Mary Lundie. Miller, Jos. Singers church, 2d ed. 523.

Duncan, William. McCosh. Scot. phil. 107.

Dunck, Edmund, with portrait. Caulfield. Kit-cat, 210.

Duncombe, Thomas S. Francis, G. H. Orators, 249. — Ritchie. Brit. sena. 382.

Dundas, Henry. *See* Melville, Lord.

Dundee, John Graham, first viscount of. Lodge. Portraits (Bohn), v. 6. — Skelton. Ess. 135.
— Macaulay on. Paget, J. Paradoxes, 101.

Dunder. Stowe. Sunny mem. 1 : 122.

Dundonald, Thomas Cochrane, earl of. Adams, W. H. D. In perils, 68. — Georgian era, 2 : 247. — Redding. Pers. remin. 2 : 230.
— Trial of, for conspiracy. Townsend, W. C.

Mod. state trials, 2 : 1. — Browne, G. L. State trials 19th cent. 2 : 90.

Dundrennan Abbey. Mackie, C. Castles of Mary.

Dunes, Battle of the. Adams, W. H. D. Eng. at war, 1 : 72.

Dungeness, Battle of. Rawson, E. K. 20 Nav. bat. 1 : 159.

Dunglison, R. Lonsdale. Worthies Cumb. v. 6.

Dunham, Cyrus L. Woollen. Biog. sk. Indiana, 321.

Dunham, Darius. Wakeley. Heroes Meth. 295.

Dunham, Mrs. Ellet. Pioneer wom. 75.

Dunhill, Snowden. Baring-Gould. Yorks. odd. 1 : 62.

Dunker love-feast. Gibbons, P. E. Penn. Dutch.

Dunlap, Andrew. Loring, J. S. 100 Bost. ora. 504.

Dunlap, Archibald Harris, with portrait. Sk. N. H. men, 264.

Dunlap, William. Baker, W. S. Portr. of Wash. 44. — Scilhamer. Amer. theatre, 2 : 273. — Lossing. Em. Amer. 337.

— Autobiography. Dunlap. Am. theatre, 2 : 278.

Dunlevy, Mary. Ellet. Pioneer wom. 226.

Dunman, Thomas. (Charles Welsh) Dunman. Talks sci. v.

Dunmow, Priory of, and the flitch of bacon custom. Timbs. Abbeys, 1 : 222.

Dunn, Ballard S. Davidson, J. W. Writ of South, 174.

Dunn, George G. Woollen. Biog. sk. Indiana, 241.

Dunn, Horace Sargent. (J. C. Dunn) Harvard mem. biog. 2 : 382.

Dunn, John, with portrait. Ehrlich, A. Cel. violin. 257.

Dunn, Rev. John. Sterling, J. Ess. 2 : 188.

Dunn, John Gibson. Coggeshall. Poets of west, 537.

Dunn, Robinson Potter. Hatfield, E. F. Poets of church, 215.

Dunn, Williamson. Woollen. Biog. sk. Indiana, 400.

Dunning, John. See Ashburton, Lord.

Dunnottar castle. Mackie, C. Castles of Mary.

Duns Scotus. Erdmann. Hist. philos. 1 : 485. — Townsend, W. J. Schoolmen, 245.

Dunstable, John. Keddie. Mus. comp. 4.

Dunstan, St., archbishop of Canterbury. Adams, W. H. D. Worthies, 75. — Charles. Martyrs, 429. — Collier, W. F. Hist. Eng. lit. 26. — Hook. Abps. Cant. 1 : 382.

Dunstan, Sir Jeffrey, Reminiscence of. Lamb. Elia.

Dunstanburgh. Freeman. Eng. towns, 324.

Dunster, Henry. Peabody. Harv. grad. 229.

Dunster, Castle and priory of. Timbs. Abbeys, 1 : 546.

Dunster family. Titcomb, S. E. N. Eng. peo. 82.

Dunton, John. Knight, C. Old booksel. 24.

Dupanloup, Félix A. P., bishop. Em. persons, 2 : 112. — King, E. French pol. lead. 122. — Men of 3d repub. 171. — Oxenham. Stud. in eccl. hist. 318. — Pressensé. Contem. portr. 139. — Malortie. Here, there, 72.

Dupee, Mary A. Brockett. Woman's work, 462. — Moore, F. Women of the war, 485.

Dupin, André M. J. J. Cormenin. Orators, 216. — Loménie. Liv. characters, 207. — Walsh, R. M. Liv. char. France.

Dupont, Pierre. Hayward, A. Ess. 1 : 372.

Du Pont, Samuel Francis. Duyckinck. Nat. portr. gall. 2 : 432. — With portrait. Headley, J. T. Farragut, 123.

Duport, John. McClure. Translators, 186.

Dupré, Jules. Mollett, J. W. Paint. of Barbizon, 2 : 59.

Dupuy, Eliza Ann. Davidson, J. W. Writ. of South, 174. — Freeman, J. D. Wom. of South, 376. — Raymond, I. Southland writ. 1 : 87.

Du Quesne, A. Laughton. Stud. nav. hist. 59.

Duquesne, Fort, Braddock's defeat at, 1755. Malleson. Ambushes, 246.

Duran, Carolus, with portrait. (J. C. Beckwith) Van Dyke, J. C. Mod. Fr. mast. 73.

Durand, André, a lost poet. Houssaye. Philos. 2 : 247.

Durand, Asher B. Sheldon, G. W. Amer. painters, 128. — Tuckerman. Artist-life, 79. — Tuckerman. Artists, 187.

Durand, David, Sketch of. Agnew. Protes. exiles, 2 : 87.

Durant, T. C. Parton, J. Sk. of men of prog. — With portrait. Rogers, A. C. Repres. men, 215.

Duras, Claire Lechat de Kersaint, duchesse de. Ste.-Beuve. Portr. women, 248.

Durastanti, M., Italian singer. Hogarth. Mem. opera, 1 : 326.

Durbin, Rev. Dr. Bungay. Off-hand, 382.

Durfee, Job. (Thos. Durfee) N. E. Hist.-Gen. Soc. Biog. 1 : 37.

— Character and writings of. Hazard. Ess. on lang. 203.

D'Urfey, Thomas. Dunham. Lit. & sci. men, 3 : 187.

Durfort-Duras, Claire de Kersaint de. Ste.-Beuve. Cel. wom. 248.

Durham, James. Blaikie, W. G. Preachers Scot. 129.

Durham, John Geo., earl of. Grant, J. Recoll. Lords, 281.

Durham, Joseph, with photo. Cooper, T. Men of mark, 3 : 9.

Durham, England. Silloway. Cathedral towns, 244. — Temple, E. L. Old world, 2 : 166.

— Cathedral. (E. S. Talbot) Farrar, F. W. Westmin. 143. — Farrar, F. W. Our Eng. minsters, 163. — Van Rensselaer, M. G. Eng. cath. 77.

Durham House. Timbs. Abbeys, 1 : 173.

Durham Place, a palace in the Strand. Hume, M. A. S. Year after Armada, 261.

Durie, John. Wodrow. Selec. fr. biog. coll.

Durnford, R., bishop of Chichester, with photo. Cooper, T. Men of mark, 2 : 2.

Duroscius, George. Wallace, R. Anti-Trin. biog. 3 : 307.

Duroure, Louis Henry Scipion Grimoard Beauvoir, comte de. Redding. Pers. remin. 3 : 217.

Duruy, Jean Victor, with portrait. Warner Lib. 9 : 5069.

Duse, Eleanora. Meynell, A. Color, 45. — Hansson, L. M. Six mod. wom. 97.

Du Simitiere, Pierre Eugene. Baker, W. S. Portr. of Wash. 39.

Dust and disease. Tyndall. Frag. sci. 277.

— and house refuse. Wynter, A. Peeps, 1 : 211.

— infectious, Removal of, from the air. (D. Prince) Am. Pub. Health, 12 : 164.

— of particulate material. (D. Prince) Am. Pub. Health, 12 : 164.

— we breathe. Proctor. Light sci. 1 : 265.

Dust-heap, Value of. Wynter, A. Peeps, 2 : 172.

Duste, Jeanne, with portrait. Buffen, F. F. Mus. celeb. 23.

Dustin, Hannah. Clement, J. Noble deeds, 108.

Dusty day, A. Hunt, L. Seer, 1 : 138.

Dutch and Flemish masters. Hamerton. Art ess. 1 : 31.

Dying hour, The. Collins, Stephen. Miscel.

Dyke, Daniel. Ivimey. Eng. Bapt. **2** : 328.

Dykes, John Bacchus. Huntington, G. Random recol. 224.

Dympna, St. Conyngham, D. P. Irish saints, 122.

Dynamics, Speculative. Wright, C. Philos. dis. 385.

Dynamite explosion in Houses of Parliament, 1885. Smalley. Lond. let. **2** : 344.

Dynamo, Invention of. Jeans. Electricians, **1** : 204.

Dynasties, Significance of, in history. Döllinger. Stud. hist. **1**.

Dyre, Mary, Quaker martyr. Watson, H. C. Heroic wom. 84.

Dyslogistic words, Use of. Sargant. Ess. **1** : 204.

Dyspeptic, Letter to a. Higginson. Out-door, 53.

Eadburga, Abbess. Williams, Jane. Lit. wom. 17.

Eadburga, queen of Bertric. Hall. Queens bef. Conq. 307.

Eadie, John. Taylor, W. M. Scot. pulpit, 241.

Eads, James B. Bolton, S. K. Poor boys, 26. — Jones, H. B. Heroes indus. 174. — McCabe, J. D. Great fortunes, 209.

Eagle made of copper. Buckland, F. T. Curios. nat. hist. **4** : 159.

Eames, Emma, with portrait. Buffen. Mus. celeb. **2** : 51.

Ear of Dionysius. Adams, W. H. D. Fam. caves, 144.

"Earl of Abergavenny," Wreck of. Senior, W. Shipwrecks, 52.

Earle, John. Microcosmography. Adams, W. D. Famous books, 165.

Earle, William E. Am. Bar Assoc. **17** : 498.

Earles, John. Benson, A. C. Ess. 19.

Earlham College, Richmond, Ind. Historical sketch. (J. J. Mills) U. S. Bur. Ed. Circ. '91, no. **1** : 173.

Early, Jubal A. Pollard. Life of Lee, 463.

Early, Peter. Miller, S. F. Bench of Ga. v. **1**.

Early closing of shops. Robertson, F. W. Lec. 267. — (J. Lilwall) Trans. Soc. Sci. Lond. '57 : 548.

— and holidays. N. Y. Labor, '87.

Early rising. Hunt, L. Seer, **1** : 67. — Mathews. Men and books, 229.

Earraid, Island of. Stevenson, R. L. Mem. 120.

Ears, A chapter on. Lamb. Elia.

Earth, Age of the. (C. King) Smithson. Inst. Rept. '93 : 335.

— as an abode fitted for life. (Lord Kelvin) Smithson. Rept. '97 : 337.

— Chemistry of ; why it is as it is. (J. N. Lockyer) Manch. Sci. lec. **8** : 106.

— Composition of. (H. E. Roscoe) Estes. Half-hour recr. v. **2**.

— Crust of, Movements of. (A. Blytt) Smithson. Rept. '89 : 325.

— — and their causes. (J. LeConte) Smithson. Rept. '96 : 233.

— Density of, mean, determined by pendulum principle. (J. Wilsing) Smithson. Rept. '88 : 635.

— — Weighing the earth in a coal-pit. Estes. Half-hour recr. 102.

— figure of, Theorems relating to. Playfair, J. Works, v. **3**.

— Limits of our knowledge of. (W. B. Dawkins) Owens College ess. '74 : 129.

Earth, Mathematical theories of. (R. S. Woodward) Smithson. Rept. '90 : 183.

— Motion of, Copernican theory of. Lodge, O. J. Pioneers, 5.

— rotation of, Loss in period of. Proctor. Light sci. **1** : 30.

— Stability of. Shaler. Aspects of earth, v. **1**.

— structure of, Physical. (Henry Hennessy) Smithson. Rept. '90 : 201.

— Succession of life on. (W. C. Williamson) Manch. Sci. lec. **8** : 45.

— Weighing and measuring the. Dunman. Talks sci. 167.

— what composed of. (H. E. Roscoe) Manch. Sci. lec. **8** : 1. Same in Estes. Half-hour recr. 347.

Earthquake in Ohio, 1811. Mansfield, E. D. Pers. mem. 45.

— in Peru, 1868. Proctor. Light sci. **1** : 189.

Earthquakes. Kingsley, C. Madam How, 33. — (S. Sias) N. Y. Regents, **91** : 398. — Proctor. Borderland, 242.

— and volcanoes. (T. S. Hunt) Am. Geog. Soc. 2, pt. **2** : 89.— (W. C. Williamson) Manch. Sci. lec. **5–6** : 220. — Herschel. Fam. lec. v. **1**.

— at Caracas, 1812. Cochrane. Travels in Colombia, 1.

— Bibliography. Foster. Mo. Ref. lists, **4** : 26. — Brit. assoc. 1858. — (E. S. Holden) Smithsonian Miscel. Collec. no. 1087.

— Cause and work of. Proctor, R. A. Univ. of suns, 257.

— Causes of. Franklin. Works ('87), **1** : 462. — Proctor, R. A. Other suns, 287.

— Charleston, 1886. U. S. Geolog. survey, 9th rept. — Annual cyclopædia, '86.

— in the British isles. Proctor, R. A. Univ. of suns, 219.

— in California. Calif. Acad. Sci. v. **1–3**.

— in Java. Proctor, R. A. Univ. of suns, 242.

— in Peru, 1746. Kip. Histor. scenes.

— Usefulness of. Proctor. Light sci. **1** : 211.

Earthworks, Ancient, in Ohio. (J. P. MacLean) Smithson. Rept. '85 : 893.

— at Fort Ancient, Ohio. (W. M. Thompson) Smithson. Rept. '86 : 335.

Easedale. Rawnsley. Lit. assoc. Eng. lakes, **2** : 158.

Easley, William N. Walker, C. D. Biog. Va. Mil. Inst. 181.

East, John. Hatfield, E. F. Poets of church, 222.

East, the Far, The future of. Norman, H. Far East, 589.

— Market in, for dairy products and fruits, 1894. U. S. Cons. Rept. **48** : 193.

— Past and present in. (G. G. Zerffi) Evol. Crys. pal. lec. v. **1**.

— The question of. Gladstone. Bulga. 111.

East India company. Francis, J. Stock exch. 31.

— Abuses under. Burke. Works (Bohn), **2** : 173. **3** : 116. **4** : 1.

— — in India. Kaye. Indian off. **1** : 45, 465.

— and Warren Hastings. Macaulay. Ess. **5** : 7.

— Rise of. Adams, W. H. D. Engl. at war, **1** : 200. — Markham. Sea-fathers, 116.

East India House, Lamb's Reminiscences of. Adams, W. D. Famous books, 360.

East Indian voyages. Bibliography. Harrisse, H. Americus Vespucius.

East Indies, Languages of the. Cust. Ling. ess. 144.

— Ledyard's travels in, 1770. St. John. Cel. travelers, **2** : 163.

East River bridge. Marshall, W. G. Thro' Amer. 5.

East wind, The. Hunt, L. Seer, 1 : 163.
Eastburn, James W. Griswold, R. W. Sac. poets. — Hatfield, E. F. Poets of church, 222.
— and Sands, Robert C. Yamoyden. Drake, N. Evenings, 1 : 237.
Eastburn, Manton. Lanman, C. Haphazard, 201.
Eastburn, Robert. Drake, S. G. Trag. of wilderness, 265.
Easter, English. James, H. Portr. of places.
Easter, John. Wakeley. Heroes Meth. 219.
Easter controversy, The, in the British Isles. Montalembert. Monks, 4 : 149.
Easter flowers. Osgood, S. Amer. leaves, 335.
Easter Island, So. Pacific Ocean. (G. H. Cooke) U. S. Nat. Mus. Rept. '97 : 689.
— Ethnology and antiquities of. (W. J. Thompson) U. S. Nat. Mus. Rept. '89 : 447.
Eastern Church, Preaching of. Ker, J. Lec. hist. preach. 57.
— Prospects of. Neale. Ess. liturg.
Eastern question. Boynton, C. B. Four gt. powers, 49. — Froude. Short stud. 2 : 410. — Hinsdale, B. A. Schools, 254. — Lowe. Life of Bismarck. — Brassey, T. Papers, polit. 1. — Hinsdale, B. A. Schools & stud. 254. — Moltke. Ess. 1 : 261.
— and Eastern Christians. Palgrave. Ess. east. 164.
— Bibliography. Bost. Pub. Lib. Bull. May, '97.
— Hellenic factor in. Gladstone. Glean. 4 : 259.
— in 1877. Bright, Jo. Publ. add. 376, 449, 472.
— Origin of. Döllinger. Stud. hist. 188.
Easthope, Sir John. Grant, Jas. Portr. pub. char. 1 : 76.
Eastlake, Sir Charles Lock. Hall, S. C. Book of mem. 465. — Eastlake. Contrib. 2 : 1.
Eastman, Charles G. Hemenway. Poets of Vt. 62.
Eastman, Mary Henderson. Hart, J. S. Fem.
Eating and drinking. Hunt. Wishing-cap, 89.
Eaton, Amos. Youmans. Pioneers sci. 111.
Eaton, Mrs. Nathaniel. Earle. Colon. dames, 123.
Eaton, Samuel. Headley, J. T. Chaplains Revol. 110.
Eaton, Wyatt. Sheldon, G. W. Amer. painters, 169.
Eaves, Nathaniel Ridley. Livingston, J. Dist. Amer. 226.
Ebed-Melech, Kindness of. Butler, E. Gentle ways, 1.
Eber, Paul. Miller, Jos. Singers church, 2d ed. 47. — Winkworth. Chr. singers Germ. 119.
Eberle, John (1788–1838). (Thomas D. Mitchell) Gross. Lives physicians, 460.
Ebers, Georg Moritz, with portrait. Warner Lib. 9 : 5091.
Eccanachaca, Battle at. Dawson. Batt. of U. S. 2 : 317.
Eccentric character. Whipple. Charac.
Eccentric people specially valuable. Helps. Brevia.
Eccentricity. Craik, D. M. Plain speaking, 33.
Eccles, John. Ivimey. Eng. Bapt. 2 : 594.
— Dramas of. Hogarth. Mem. opera, 1 : 151.
Ecclesiastes. See Bible.
Ecclesiastical history, Epochs in. Washburn, E. A. Epochs, 1.
— Study of. Trench. Lec. mediæval, 1.
Ecclesiastical literature. Bocock. Writings, 236.
Ecclesiasticism. Momerie. Fut. of relig. 55.
Eccleston, Samuel. Clarke, R. H. Cath. bishops, 1 : 525.

Ecclestone, William. Collier. Actors, 245.
Echard, Laurence. Lawrence. Brit. hist. 1 : 316.
Echo lake. Prime, W. C. I go a-fishing, 235.
Ecilaw, Ary. See Czapska, Comtesse. Van de Velde. Fr. fic. 2 : 143.
Eckart, Henry. Ullman. Reformers, 24.
Eckermann, J. P., Goethe and. Jameson. Stud.
Eckford, Henry. Howe, H. Em. mechan. 211.
Eckhoff the actor. Baring-Gould. Germany, 278.
Eclecticism. Knight, W. Ess. 173. — Knight, W. Stud. 44. — Lewes. Biog. philos.
— in morals. Jouffroy. Philos. Miscel. 2 : 94.
Eclipses. Bibliography. Providence Pub. Lib. Bull. Aug. '96.
— of the sun, Great. Proctor. Light sci. 3 : 1.
— — in 1870. Essayons club, no. 18.
Economic and political issues, Present. Econ. tracts, no. 3.
Economic basis of history. Bax, E. B. Outlooks, 125.
Economic history, Relation of teaching of, to teaching of polit. econ. (H. B. Gardner and others) Am. Hist. Assoc. Rept. '97 : 91.
— Importance of the study of. (W. B. Hodgson) Youmans. Culture, 253.
— Instruction of the community in. (W. B. Hodgson) Trans. Soc. Sci. Lond. '77 : 468.
  See also Political economy.
Economic laws: What are they? Ritchie, D. G. Darwin.
"Economic man, The." Godkin. Problems, 156.
Economic policy, Science and sentiment in. (A. T. Hadley) Conf. char. & correc. '95 : 117.
Economic "rocks ahead and harbors of refuge." Greg, W. R. Miscel. 1 : 1.
Economic science and method, Recent controversies on. (W. Westgarth) Trans. Soc. Sci. Lond. '80 : 730.
— and statistics. Leslie, T. E. C. Ess. pol. econ. 375.
Economic world, The known and unknown in. Leslie, T. E. C. Ess. pol. & mor. 221.
Economics. See Polit. economy.
Economy, Community of. Hinds. Amer. commun.
Ecstasy. Aubrey, J. Miscel.
Ecuador, Commercial directory of, 1891. Bur. Am. Repub. Bull. no. 19.
— Handbook of. Bur. Am. Rep. Bull. no. 64.
— Import duties of, 1891. Bur. Am. Repub. Bull. no. 25.
— R. R. extension and customs tariff of, 1894. U. S. Cons. Rept. 46 : 508.
— Rubber culture in, 1898. U. S. Cons. Rept. 57 : 71.
Edda legends. Howitt. Litera. of northern Europe. — Ludlow. Epics, 1 : 64. — Schlegel. Æsthetic works, 243. — (W. H. Carpenter) Warner Lib. 9 : 5112.
— Bibliography. (T. Solberg) Bost. Lib. Bull. 6 : 74.
Eddisbury, Ancient. (Mrs. G. L. Banks) Andrews, W. Bygone Ches. 129.
Eddy, Christian. Hack. Consec. wom. 217.
Eddy, Thomas. Hunt, F. Am. merch. 1 : 329.
Eddystone lighthouse. Towle, G. M. Heroes of inven. 62. — Smiles. Engin. 2 : 15.
Eden, Sir Ashley. Escott, T. H. S. Pillars emp. 70. — Laurie, W. F. B. Dist. Anglo-Ind. 2 : 99.
Eden, Charles P. Burgon. 12 men, 2 : 305.
Edersheim, Alfred. Warner Lib. 9 : 5145.
Edes, Robt. Thaxter. Vaille & Clark. Harv. book, v. 1.
Edessa, Sieges of. Robson, W. Sieges, 365.

Education; Higher branches, Teaching of. (G. Robertson *et al.*) Trans. Soc. Sci. Lond. '80: 454.
— Historical method in. (W. C. Morey) N. Y. Regents, **94** : 599.
— Historical view of. Mann, H. Lec. **1** : 241.
— History of, in U. S., Documents illustrative of. (B. A. Hinsdale) U. S. Bur. Ed. Rept. '92–93 : 1225.
— — its culture value. (B. A. Hinsdale) Nat. Educa. Assoc. '89 : 210.
— — its practical value. (W. H. Payne) Nat. Educa. Assoc. '89 : 218.
— — its value to teachers. (S. G. Williams) Nat. Educa. Assoc. '89 : 223.
— Ideal. Edgar, S. Autob. notes, 227.
— Importance of, in a republic. Everett. Orat. v. **2**.
— in Alabama, History of. (W. G. Clark) U. S. Bur. Ed. Circ. '89, no. 3.
— in Alaska. (Sheldon Jackson) U. S. Bur. Ed. Rept. '90–91 : 923.
— — in 1892. U. S. Bur. Ed. Rept. '91–92 : 873.
— in the Argentine Republic, etc. (F. F. Hilder) U. S. Bur. Ed. Rept. '97–98, **1** : 1205.
— in Belgium. U. S. Bur. Ed. Circ. '75, no. 3.
— — System of. (A. T. Smith) U. S. Bur. Ed. Rept. '92–93 : 157.
— in Bolivia. U. S. Bur. Ed. Circ. '73, no. 1.
— in Boston. Winsor. Hist. Boston, **4** : 235.
— in Brazil, Condition of [1884]. (Baron De Penedo) Internat. health exh. **15** : 374.
— in Cape Colony, Africa. (M. Bengough) Cong. Educa. Chic. '93, 903.
— in Central Europe. U. S. Bur. Ed. Rept. '93–94, **1** : 203.
— in China. Johnson, S. Ori. relig. China, 191. — U. S. Bur. Ed. Circ. '77, no. 1.
— in Denmark. U. S. Bur. Ed. Circ. '77, no. 2. — (Frances G. French) U. S. Bur. Ed. Rept. '96–97, **1** : 71.
— in early New England. Adams, C. F. Three episodes, **2** : 764.
— in Egypt. U. S. Bur. Ed. Circ. '75, no. 3.
— in England. Cobden. Speeches, 589.
— — and Scotland. (Anna T. Smith) U. S. Bur. Ed. Rept. '94–95, **1** : 257.
— — — Systems of, and operations in, '90–91. U. S. Bur. Ed. Rept. '90, **1** : 125.
— — Bill of 1896. (Anna T. Smith) U. S. Bur. Ed. Rept. '95–96, **1** : 79.
— — Elementary. Lubbock. Address, 70.
— — National. Mivart. Ess. **1** : 300. — Dawson, G. Shakesp. 500. — (F. Temple) Oxf. ess. '56 : 218.
— — Rural schools. (H. W. Hulbert) U. S. Bur. Ed. Circ. '80, no. 5.
— — School boards ; what they can do, and what they may do. Huxley. Critiques.
— in Finland. U. S. Bur. Ed. Circ. '77, no. 2. — (Frances G. French) U. S. Bur. Ed. Rept. '93–94, **1** : 413.
— in Florida. (G. G. Bush) U. S. Bur. Ed. Circ. '88, no. 6.
— in France. (M. G. Compayré) Cong. Educa. Chic. '93 : 53. — U. S. Bur. Ed. Circ. '81, no. 4. — U. S. Bur. Ed. Rept. '90–91 : 95. — (A. T. Smith) U. S. Bur. Ed. Rept. '91–92 : 73, 219. 93–94, **1** : 187.
— — Present situation of. (G. Compayré) Nat. Educa. Assoc. '93 : 53.
— — Secondary. Hillebrand. France, 44.
— — System of. Hillebrand. France, 40.
— in Georgia. (C. E. Jones) U. S. Bur. Ed. Circ. '88, no. 4.

Education, in Germany. Baring-Gould. Germany, 175. — U. S. Bur. Ed. Rept. '94–95, **1** : 321.
— — Hist. of German school system. (E. Nohle) U. S. Bur. Ed. Rept. '97–98, **1** : 3.
— in Great Britain. U. S. Bur. Ed. Rept. '93–94, **1** : 165.
— — and Ireland. (A. T. Smith) U. S. Bur. Ed. Rept. '97–98, **1** : 133.
— — Elementary, Concordat of 1840. Sinclair, J. Sketches.
— — National. Miller, H. Lead. articles, 1.
— in Greece. (D. Quinn) U. S. Bur. Ed. Rept. '96–97, **1** : 267.
— in Hawaii. (John Eaton) U. S. Bur. Ed. Rept. '90–91 : 365.
— in India. U. S. Bur. Ed. Rept. '92–93 : 261.
— in Italy. (Alexander Oldrini) U. S. Bur. Ed. Rept. '90–91 : 319. — (Egisto Rossi) Nat. Educa. Assoc. '93 : 907. — (B. A. Hinsdale) U. S. Bur. Ed. Rept. '93–94, **1** : 325.
— in Japan, 1875. U. S. Bur. Ed. Circ. '75, no. 2.
— — 1885. U. S. Bur. Ed. Circ. '85, no. 4.
— — System of. (Frances G. French) U. S. Bur. Ed. Rept. '90–91 : 263.
— in Korea. (Pom K. Soh) U. S. Bur. Ed. Rept. '90–91 : 341.
— in Louisiana. (W. P. Johnston) Nat. Educa. Assoc. '86 : 169.
— — Bibliography. (E. W. Fay) U. S. Bur. Educa. Circ. '98, no. 1.
— in Mexico and Central America. (F. F. Hilder) U. S. Bur. Ed. Rept. '95–96, **1** : 641.
— in the Netherlands. U. S. Bur. Ed. Circ. '77, no. 2. — U. S. Bur. Ed. Rept. '94–95, **1** : 475.
— in New Hampshire. Bibliography. (G. G. Bush) U. S. Bur. Ed. Circ. '98, no. 3.
— in New Jersey. N. J. Labor, '79 : 88. '82 : xx. '84 : 267. '85 : 266, 385. '88 : 621.
— in New Zealand. (Mark Cohen) U. S. Bur. Ed. Rept. '92–93 : 258.
— in the 19th century. Bayne, P. Ess. **2** : 304.
— in North Carolina, History of. (C. L. Smith) U. S. Bur. Ed. Circ. '88, no. 2.
— in the Northwest, 1790–1840. (A. D. Mayo) U. S. Bur. Ed. Rept. '94–95, **2** : 1513.
— in Norway. (Frances G. French) U. S. Bur. Ed. Rept. '96–97, **1** : 103.
— in the Old and New World, Historical Sketch of. (W. H. Bartholomew) Nat. Educa. Assoc. '86 : 512.
— in Ontario. U. S. Bur. Ed. Rept. '92–93 : 239.
— in Portugal. U. S. Bur. Ed. Circ. '73, no. 1. '77, no. 2.
— in relation to religion. Foster, J. Crit. ess. (Bohn) **1** : 372.
— in Russia. U. S. Bur. Ed. Circ. '75, no. 3. — (Frances G. French) U. S. Bur. Ed. Rept. '90–91 : 195. '93–94, **1** : 385.
— in Scotland. (A. C. Sellar) Grant, A. Recess, 261.
— in Servia. U. S. Bur. Ed. Circ. '75, no. 3.
— in the South. (A. D. Mayo) Nat. Educa. Assoc. '82 : app. 44. — (W. T. Harris) Nat. Educa. Assoc. '95 : 1021.
— in So. Carolina, History of. (C. Meriwether) U. S. Bur. Ed. Circ. '88, no. 3.
— in southwestern Virginia. (A. D. Mayo) U. S. Bur. Ed. Rept. '90–91 : 881.
— in Spain. U. S. Bur. Ed. Circ. '73, no. 1.
— in Sweden. (Frances G. French) U. S. Bur. Ed. Rept. '91–92 : 423.
— in Turkey. U. S. Bur. Ed. Circ. '75, no. 3.
— in the U. S. Gilman, D. C. Univ. prob. 289. —

Rousiers. Amer. life, 253. — (W. T. Harris) Shaler. The U. S. **2** : 294.

Education in the U. S. Constit. provisions in states. (F. B. Hough) U. S. Bur. Ed. Circ. '75, no. 7.

— — Downward drift in. Peck, H. T. Pers. equa. 327.

— — European comments on. (C. L. Bodio and others) U. S. Bur. Ed. Rept. '92–93 . 615.

— — Higher and secondary. (G. Compayré) U. S. Bur. Ed. Rept. '96–97, **2** : 1153.

— — Present status of. (W. T. Harris) Nat. Educa. Assoc. '91 : 136.

— in Uruguay. U. S. Bur. Ed. Circ. '73, no. 1. — (Frances G. French) U. S. Bur. Ed. Rept. '92–93 : 337.

— in the western states. Everett. Orat. v. 1.

— in Wisconsin, Higher. (W. F. Allen & D. E. Spencer) U. S. Bur. Ed. Circ. '89, no. 1.

— in Württemberg. U. S. Bur. Ed. Circ. '77, no. 2.

— Influence of scientific discovery on. (W. Whewell) Youmans. Culture, 225.

— Influence of. Davis, T. Prose, 212.

— Intermediate and higher, Taxation for. (Canon Daniel) Internat. health exh. **16** : 373.

— — in Ireland. (G. Molloy et al.) Trans. Soc. Sci. Lond. '81 : 368.

— Jacotot's system of, Payne on. Martineau, H. Miscel. **2** : 150.

— Jefferson on. U. S. Bur. Ed. Circ. '88, no. 1 : 86.

— Larger. Mabie. Ess. on work, 70.

— Liberal. Conington. Miscel. 449. — (C. J. Hinkel) N. Y. Regents, 84 : 493. — Lodge, H. C. Cert. heroes, 157.

— — Ends and means of. Anderson, M. B. Papers, **1** : 3.

— — Essential elements of. (J. R. Buchanan) N. Y. Regents, '92 : 570.

— — Evolution of. (A. F. West) Cong. Educa. Chic. '93, 150.

— — for students in law, medicine, and theology. (Woodrow Wilson) Nat. Educa. Assoc. '93 : 112.

— — Necessity of. Brownson. Works, **19** : 88.

— — of the 19th century. (W. P. Atkinson) Nat. Educa. Assoc. '73 : 141.

— — The truly practical. Mathews. Men & bks. 117.

— — What is a? Eliot, C. W. Educa. reform.

— — Where to find it. Huxley. Lay sermons.

— Liberty in. Eliot, C. W. Educa. reform.

— Limits of. Bigelow, J. Mod. inq. 1. — (W. R. Garrett) Nat. Educa. Assoc. '77 : 33.

— Meaning of. Butler, N. M. Meaning of educ. 3.

— method in, Data of. (J. M. Green) Nat. Educa. Assoc. '97 : 67.

— methods and ends, Relation between. (J. J. Keane) Cong. Educa. Chic. '93, 43.

— Modern; its sphere and its aims. Farrar. Sermons in Am. 236.

— modern system of, Influence upon health. (T. C. Allbutt) Trans. Soc. Sci. Lond. '83 : 354.

— The moral and the secular in. (T. Lewis) N. Y. Regents, 86 : 517.

— moral, Incidental method of. (Lucia Stickney) Nat. Educa. Assoc. '96 : 414.

— — in elementary schools. (E. E. White) Nat. Educa. Assoc. '96 : 407.

— National. Lubbock. Use of life, 94. — Thirlwall, C. Remains, **2** : 98.

— — in France, 18th century. Turgot. Life & wr. 265.

— — in Scotland. (F. C. Stevenson) Cong. Educa. Chic. '93, 874.

Education, National, vs. denominational. Brownson. Works, **13** : 284.

— — Aid to. (J. W. Patterson) Nat. Educa. Assoc. '81 : app. 68.

— Nature and art in. (W. H. Payne) Nat. Educa. Assoc. '80 : 42.

— Nature of. (H. Poesche) Cong. Educa. Chic. '93, 369. — Hinsdale, B. A. Schools & stud. 51.

— Necessity of, in a republic. Mann, H. Lec. **1** : 143.

— Neighborhood as a starting-point in. (R. E. Thompson) Nat. Educa. Assoc. '80 : 28.

— New. Bushnell. Building eras, 35.

— — and old. Ladd, G. T. Ess. higher educa. 75.

— — Is there a? Butler, N. M. Meaning of educa. 69.

— the nurture of the mind. Everett. Orat. v. **2**.

— Obligations of. Bethune. Orations, 283.

— of girls in France. Hillebrand, France, 51.

— of mankind. Everett. Orat. v. **1**.

— of the middle classes in England. Arnold, T. Miscel. 372. — Sargant. Ess. **2** : 183. — (E. Davis) Trans. Soc. Sci. Lond. '57 : 137. — (T. D. Acland, jr.) Trans. Soc. Sci. Lond. '59 : 299.

— of pauper children. (E. C. Tufnell and M. Carpenter) Trans. Soc. Sci. Lond. '63 : 278.

— of the people. Brougham. Works, **8** : 417.

— — Congress and. (W. H. Ruffner) Nat. Educa. Assoc. '80 : app. 73.

— of the poor. Everett. Orat. v. **4**.

— of public opinion. (C. R. Skinner) Nat. Educa. Assoc. '95 : 126.

— of women. See Women, Education of.

— of the young. Turgot. Life & wr. 193.

— of youth in America. Webster, N. Ess. **1**.

— Old, and modern. Wheeler, D. H. By-ways, 55.

— Organizers of the nation and. (Austin Scott) Nat. Educa. Assoc. '94 : 66.

— The outlook in. (N. M. Butler) Nat. Educa. Assoc. '99 : 170.

— Philosophy of. Blackie, J. S. Ess. 228. — (F. L. Soldan) Nat. Educa. Assoc. '87 : 74.

— Physical side of. (W. E. Anderson) Wis. Health, '87 : 99.

— Place and development of purpose in. (W. N. Hailmann) Nat. Educa. Assoc. '99 : 583.

— Place of research in. (H. E. Armstrong) Smithson. Rept. '95 : 743.

— Plato on, in his "Republic." Packard, L. R. Stud. Gr. 65.

— Political. Chambers's Papers, no. 4.

— Popular. Phillips, W. Speeches, **2** : 309. — Thirlwall, C. Remains, **2** : 252.

— — Christianity and. Gladden. Appl. Christianity, 284.

— — in Rhode Island. Goddard, W. G. Pol. & mis. wr. **1** : 213.

— — United States and. (A. S. Draper) Nat. Educa. Assoc. '96 : 201.

— — why it has failed. Eliot, C. W. Five Am. cont. 203.

— Practical. Allen, W. F. Essays, 129. — (S. G. Love) N. Y. Regents, '89 : 554.

— Prenatal. (F. C. Clark) R. I. Health, **4** : 233.

— Preparation for earning a living. (R. K. Buehrle) Nat. Educa. Assoc. '88 : 173.

— a preparation for life. Bethune. Orat. 127.

— Primary. (O. W. Morris) N. Y. Regents, 85 : 551. — Playfair. Subj. soc. 277.

— — in N. Y. State, Annals of. (D. J. Pratt) N. Y. Regents, 96 : 437.

— secondary and collegiate, Harmonizing of. (James McCosh) Nat. Educa. Assoc. '80 : 138.

Education, primary, Progress of. (R. Hamilton) Trans. Soc. Sci. Lond. '77 : 446.
— Principles of. (Mary Carpenter) Trans. Soc. Sci. Lond. '60 : 391.
— The problem of to-day. (Richard Edwards) Nat. Educa. Assoc. '87 : 59.
— Professional and technical, in the university. (N. M. Butler) Nat. Educa. Assoc. '94 : 619.
— Professorships and lectureships on. (J. M. D. Meiklejohn; S. S. Laurie) Internat. health exh. 16 : 97.
— Progress in. (E. W. B. M. Hance) Samuelson, James. Civiliz'n, 252.
— Progress in popular. Hoyt, J. G. Miscel. 147.
— Proper, in a republic. Rush, B. Ess. 6.
— Psychological aspects of. (Bro. Azarias) N. Y. Regents, 91 : 447.
— Psychological view of. (J. H. Baker) Nat. Educa. Assoc. '88 : 166.
— Public ; The Dorian measure. Peabody, E. P. Last evening, 73.
— — in Minnesota. (W. W. Folwell) Nat. Educa. Assoc. '75 : 58.
— — Progress in. (F. L. Soldan) Nat. Ed. Assoc. '99 : 176.
— Quo vadimus ? (Mrs. H. L. Grenfell) Nat. Educa. Assoc. '99 : 99.
— rational, Plea for. Duff, M. E. G. Miscel. 164.
— reform in, Unity of. (C. W. Eliot) U. S. Bur. Ed. Rept. '92–93 : 1465.
— Relation of the drama to. Jones, H. A. Renascence, 287.
— Relation of government to. (G. W. Atherton) Nat. Educa. Assoc. '73 : 60.
— Religious difficulty in. (W. J. Kennedy ; J. Oakley) Trans. Soc. Sci. Lond. '66 : 354.
— Religion an essential part of. White, C. Ess. 7.
— research in, Place of. (H. E. Armstrong) Smithson. Rept. '95 : 743.
— Rudimentary, neglected. Helps. Brevia.
— rural, Difficulties in promoting. (J. P. Hastings) Trans. Soc. Sci. Lond. '57 : 176.
— Scholastic and industrial. (M. E. R. Cobb) Conf. char. & correc. '96 : 347.
— School. (C. A. Walworth) N. Y. Regents, 101 : app. 67.
— Scientific and popular. Shedd. Lit. essays, 187.
— Search of, by an African prince. (Momolu Massaquoy) Nat. Educa. Assoc. '91 : 239.
— Secondary. (G. W. Samson) N. Y. Regents, 94 : 533.
— — in the Netherlands. (J. Bosscha) Internat. health exh. 16 : 197.
— — in Scotland. (J. Black et al.) Trans. Soc. Sci. Lond. '77 : 382.
— — Organization of. (E. L. Stanley) Internat. Health exh. 16 : 363.
— — The state and. (A. B. Watkins) N. Y. Regents, 91 : 401.
— Secular or catholic. Brownson. Works, 13 : 400, 445.
— Secularization of. Hinsdale, B. A. Schools & stud. 230. — (W. W. Folwell) Nat. Educa. Assoc. '82 : 42.
— Self. Lubbock. Use of life, 111.
— Self-activity in. (A. Tompkins) Nat. Educa. Assoc. '99 : 320.
— Shibboleth of. Lilly, W. S. Shibboleths, 126.
— skill, and culture. Kempner, W. Commonsense soc. 72.
— Spiritual element in. (E. F. Bartholomew) Nat. Educa. Assoc. '90 : 696.
— State aid to. (N. W. Benedict) N. Y. Regents, 93 : 613.
— The state and. Hoffman, F. S. Sphere, 35. —

(J. H. Canfield) N. Y. Regents, 111 : 264. — (Frank S. Black) N. Y. Regents, 111 : 190.
Education, the state in, Duty of. (E. E. White) Nat. Educa. Assoc. '98 : 204.
— subsidies to, Economic character of. (C. E. Appleton) Ess. end. research, 64.
— Systematic habit in. (E. H. Cook) N. Y. Regents, 100 : app. 218.
— technical, Relation of, to liberal education. (C. M. Woodward) Nat. Educa. Assoc. '94 : 660.
— Technological. (C. H. Keyes) Nat. Educa. Assoc. '96 : 421.
— True. Hole, S. R. Addresses, 51.
— The true and the false. Partridge, W. O. Art for Amer. 7.
— the true leverage of empire. Rosebery. Speeches, v. 1.
— Twenty years' progress in. (W. T. Harris) Nat. Educa. Assoc. '92 : 56.
— Universal. (Ray Palmer) Hamerton. Higher ed. 84. — (J. L. M. Curry) Nat. Educa. Assoc. '82 : app. 55.
— — the problem of the hour. (Alexander Hogg) Nat. Educa. Assoc. '89 : 299.
— University. See University education.
— Value of. Smiles. Self-help.
— — to labor. (E. Jarvis) U. S. Bur. Ed. Circ. '79, no. 3.
— Waste of labor in. (P. A. Chadbourne) U. S. Bur. Ed. Circ. '75, no. 4.
— Woman's work in. (May Wright Sewall ; F. E. Willard) Nat. Educa. Assoc. '84 : 153.
— World's recent progress in. (J. E. Russell) N. Y. Regents' Rept. 107 : 259.
Educational administration, Recent centralizing tendencies. (W. C. Webster) Colum. Univ. Stud. Hist. 8 : no. 2.
Educational bibliographies, List of. U. S. Bur. Ed. Rept. '93–94, 2 : 1701.
Educational economy. (D. Murray) N. Y. Regents, 81 : 621.
Educational exhibit, N. E. A. meeting, Chicago, 1887. (G. P. Brown, ed.) Nat. Educa. Assoc. '87 : 673.
— — 1888. (W. T. Harris, J. O'Connor, and others) Nat. Educa. Assoc. '88 : 685.
— — 1890. (Mary E. Nicholson) Nat. Educa. Assoc. '90 : 52.
— — 1891. (L. E. Fay) Nat. Educa. Assoc. '91 : 255.
— — 1892. (J. Eaton, J. H. Canfield, and others) Nat. Educa. Assoc. '92 : 391.
Educational extremes. (O. J. Corson) Nat. Educa. Assoc. '97 : 147.
Educational forces, Correlation of. (S. T. Dutton) Nat. Educa. Assoc. '97 : 238.
Educational journalism. (O. H. Lang) Nat. Educa. Assoc. '99 : 210. — (J. Macdonald) Nat. Educa. Assoc. '99 : 304.
— in France. (G. Compayré) Cong. Educa. Chic. '93, 845.
— in Illinois. (J. W. Cook) Cong. Educa. Chic. '93, 833.
— in Indiana. (G. F. Bars) Cong. Educa. Chic. '93, 829.
— in Iowa. (H. Sabin) Cong. Educa. Chic. '93, 840.
— in Michigan. (H. A. Ford) Cong. Educa. Chic. '93, 831.
— in Missouri. (H. A. Gass) Cong. Educa. Chic. '93, 842.
— in New England. (W. A. Mowry) Cong. Educa. Chic. '93, 811.
— in N. Y. (C. W. Bardeen) Cong. Educa. Chic. '93, 826.

Egede, Hans. Carne, J. Em. mission. **1** : 185. —
Stevenson. Lives & deeds, 33.
Eger and Grime. Hales. Folia litt. 40.
Egerton, George. Hansson, L. M. Six mod.
wom. 61.
Egerton, Thomas, Lord Chancellor, 1603. Foss.
Judges, **6** : 136.
Egestorff, Georg Heinrich Christoph. Redding.
Pers. remin. **2** : 292.
Egg, Augustus Leopold. Redgrave. Century of
p. **2** : 326.
Egg, Chemistry of an. Nichols, J. R. Fireside
sci. 18.
— hen's, Life history of a. Dunman. Talks sci.
118.
Eggleston, Edward. Bungay. Repr. men, 241.
— Richardson. Amer. lit. **2** : 422. — Vedder,
H. C. Amer. writers, 248. — With portrait.
Warner Lib. **9** : 5215.
— at home. (O. C. Auringer) Gilder. Authors,
83.
Eggs, Superstitions relating to. Jones, W. Cre-
dulities, 445.
Eglantine, P. F. N. F. de. Adolphus. Biog. Fr.
rev. **1** : 424.
Eglington tournament. Willis. Fam. persons,
188.
Ego, Born with an. Warner, C. D. As we go,
67.
Egoism, altruism, and Christian eudaimonism.
(M. Kaufmann) Living Papers, **11** : no. 64.
Ego-mania, Psychology of. Nordau. Degen.
241.
Egotheism. Peabody, E. P. Last evening, 240.
Egotism. Duhring, J. Gentle folks, 168. — Haz-
litt. Lit. remains, **2** : 1. — Hazlitt. Plain
speaker, v. **1**. — Rands, H. Holbeach, **1** : 176.
Egotist, The. Montgomery, J. Prose, **1** : 159.
2 : 12.
Egypt. (G. W. Cullum) Am. Geog. Soc. **13** : 10.
— Bellows. Old world. **2** : 85. — Bridges, F. D.
Lady's trav. 19. — Duff, M. E. G. Miscel. 12.
— Field, H. M. Egypt to Japan, 1. — Lub-
bock. Addresses, 175.
— Aggression on, and freedom in the East. Glad-
stone. Glean. **4** : 341.
— Ancient and modern. Deutsch. Lit. rem. 173.
— (W. B. Carpenter) Manch. Sci. lec. **3–4** :
304.
— — Literature of. (C. W. Goodwin) Camb. ess.
'58 : 232.
— — Religions of. Rawlinson. Religions, 17. —
(J. Dodds) St. Giles lec. **2** : 145.
— and Abyssinia. Bibliography. Salem (Mass.)
Pub. Lib. Bull. May, '96.
— and Great Britain. Bibliography. Providence
Pub. Lib. Bull. Oct. '98.
— and Thebes. Palgrave. Ulysses, 92.
— Annexation of, by Great Britain. Cust. Ling.
studies, **2** : 281.
— as a type of the priestly kingdom. Newman,
F. W. Essays, 166.
— Bibliography. Ball, E. A. R. Cairo of to-day.
— Wilkesbarre (Pa.) Osterhout Lib. News-
letter, Jan. '95.
— British policy in, Principles of. Temple, R.
Orient. exper. 415.
— Clarke's travels in, 1800–20. St. John. Cel.
travelers, **3** : 238.
— Climate and religion of. Abercromby. Seas &
skies, 24.
— crisis in, 1884, Speech on. (R. Churchill)
Wagner, L. Mod. pol. ora. 261.
— Denon's travels in. St. John. Cel. travelers, **3** :
345.

Egypt, deserts of, Life in the. (R. E. Colston)
Am. Geog. Soc. **11** : 301.
— The English in. Davis, R. H. Rulers Medit.
139.
— Hasselquist's travels in, 1740. St. John. Cel.
travelers, **2** : 52.
— History. Gillett, E. H. Anc. cities, 19.
— — Egypt and the Pharaohs. Lord, J. Anc.
states, 34.
— Impressions of. Disraeli, B. Home letters,
131.
— Khedives of, Reminiscences of. Kingston,
W. B. Monarchs, **2** : 219.
— Modern, and its people. (R. E. Colston) Am.
Geog. Soc. **13** : 133.
— — Bibliography. San Francisco Pub. Lib. Bull.
Nov. '98.
— Nile, The. Hahn-Hahn. Fathers, 49.
— Pococke's travels in, 1730–50. St. John. Cel.
travelers, **2** : 101.
— Political geography of. (C. P. Stone) Am.
Geog. Soc. **15** : 361.
— Pyramids of. Pidgeon. Engineer's holiday, 447.
— Recent discoveries in. (A. B. Edwards) Am.
Geog. Soc. **22** : 555.
— Recent explorations in. (F. Brown) Am. Geog.
Soc. **19** : 164.
— Religion of. Bettany. World's relig. 462. —
Clarke, J. F. Ten relig. 209. — Matheson.
Distinc. mess. 275. — (C. P. Tiele) Relig. sys-
tems, 3.
— research in, Recent. (W. M. F. Petrie) Smith-
son. Rept. '97 : 571.
— Trade conditions of, 1898. (T. S. Harrison)
U. S. Cons. Rept. **58** : 161.
— Upper. Moore, Jos. Outl. Eur. 103.
— War in, 1882, return of troops to London.
Smalley. Lond. let. **2** : 221.
Egyptian grammar. Bibliography. Erman, A.
Egypt. grammar.
Egyptian life and climate. Keating. With Grant,
17.
Egyptian literature. (F. L. Griffith & K. B.
Griffith) Warner Lib. **9** : 5225.
Egyptian rite, An ancient. (S. Y. Stevenson)
Cong. Anthrop. Chic. '93, 298.
Egyptian words compared with Semitic, Aryan,
and Turanian. Cook, F. C. Origins, 343.
Egyptology. Cust. Ling. ess. 314.
Eichendorff, Joseph von. Warner Lib. **9** : 5345.
Eichhorn, J. G. Cheyne. Founders O. T. crit.
13.
Eiffel tower, The. (G. Eiffel; W. A. Eddy)
Smithson. Rept. '89 : 729.
1848; the year of revolutions. Alison. Ess. v. **3**.
1876; *Annus mirabilis*. Curtis, G. W. Other ess.
174.
Eighteenth century, The. Harrison, F. Choice
of books, 351. Same in Coan. Hist. stud. 99.
— Conservatism of. Courthope. Lib. move't, 35.
— Historical estimate of. Lilly. Chapters, **2** : 67.
— Stebbing. Verdicts, 3.
— Last decade of. Hales. Folia litt. 286.
— Schlosser's History of. DeQuincey. Note-
book (Bost.), 81.
Eight-hour law. Walker, F. A. Discus. in econ.
2 : 379.
Eight-hour movement. Altgeld. Live ques.
122. — N. Y. Labor, 1890. — Phillips, W.
Speeches, **2** : 139.
— in Chicago, 1886. Illinois Labor, 1886.
Eight-hour system. Kelley, W. D. Speeches,
278. — Wisc. Bur. Lab. '86 : 314.
Einhart, 770–840. (R. Dohme) Dohme, R. Early
mast. 1.

Eishausen, Mystery of. Wraxall, F. C. L. Remark. adv. **2** : 1.

Eisteddfod, 1888, Speech at. Gladstone. Speeches, **10** : 55.

Elberfeld system of poor relief. (T. Münsterberg) Cong. Char. Chic. '93, **2** : 187. — (Dr. Thoma) Cong. Char. Chic. '93, **2** : 200. — (L. F. Seyffardt) Cong. Char. Chic. '93, **2** : 207.

Elbert, Theodore, Fragments from the travels of. Sterling, J. Ess. **2** : 3.

Elder, Mrs. Susan Blanchard. Davidson, J. W. Writ. of South, 177. — Raymond, I. Southland wr. **1** : 334.

Eldon, J. Scott, Lord. With portrait. Bennet, W. H. Sel. biog. 57. — Brougham. Works, **4** : 50. — Browne, I. Gt. lawyers, 105. — Campbell. Ld. Chan. **6** : 109. — Chambers, W. Rem. pers. 192. — Edgar. Boyhood, 99. — Ewald. Repr. statesm. **2** : 1. — Georgian era, **2** : 318. — Grant, Jas. Bench & bar, **1** : 67. — Grant, J. Recoll. Lords, 119. — Hayward, A. Ess. **1** : 382. — Hazlitt. Spirit of age. — Smiles. Self-help. — Jerdan. Men, 192. — Talfourd. Crit. writ. — Taylor, W. C. Mod. Brit. Plut. 118. — Townsend. 12 judges, **2** : 366.

Eleanor of Aquitaine, queen of Henry II. With portrait. Howitt, M. Queens, 43. — Strickland. Queens Eng. v. **1**. — Lancelott. Queens, v. **1**.

Eleanor, empress of Austria. Kavanagh. Women of Christ'y, 200.

Eleanor of Castile, queen of Edward I. With portrait. Howitt, M. Queens, 96. — Strickland. Queens Eng. v. **2**. — Lancelott. Queens, v. **1**.

Eleanor of Provence, queen of Henry III. With portrait. Howitt, M. Queens, 77. — Strickland. Queens Eng. v. **2**. — Campbell. Ld. Chan. **1** : 123. — Lancelott. Queens, v. **1**.

Eleanor of Austria, queen of France. Bush. Queens of France, **1** : 283.

Eleanor of Guyenne, queen of France. Bush. Queens of France, **1** : 122.

Eleanora, princess of Salms. Townsend. Descend. Stuarts, 257.

Eleanora, daughter of Edward I. Green, M. A. E. Princesses, **2** : 275. **3** : 60.

Eleanora, daughter of Edward II. Green, M. A. E. Princesses, **3** : 65.

Eleanora, daughter of Henry II. Green, M. A. E. Princesses, **1** : 263.

Eleanora, daughter of King John. Green, M. A. E. Princesses, **2** : 48.

Eleatics, The. Lewes. Biog. phil.

Election and reprobation. Whedon. Ess. **1** : 139.

Election laws. (J. F. Duncombe) Am. Bar Assoc. **13** : 291.

Election sermons, Massachusetts. (L. Swift; H. H. Edes) Col. Soc. Mass. Trans. **1** : 388.

Election trials in England. (T. C. Anstey) Grant, A. Recess, 333.

Elections, Bribery at. Hobart, V. H. H. Ess. & miscel. **2** : 165.

— English. Lodge, H. C. Cert. heroes, 203.

— Expense of. Fawcett. Speeches pol. ques. 145.

— — Second reading of the Parliamentary election expenses bill, June 18, 1873. Fawcett. Speeches, 145.

— General. Zangwill. Without prej. 65.

— History of, in Amer. colonies. (C. F. Bishop) Colum. Univ. Stud. Hist. **3** : no. 1.

— Theory and practice of. Sumner, W. G. Essays, 98.

Elective studies in general education. (E. E. White) Nat. Educa. Assoc. '97 : 373.

— in schools and colleges. (W. T. Harris) Nat. Educa. Assoc. '80 : 167.

Elective system, The. (W. L. Broun) Nat. Educa. Assoc. '77 : 87.

— in colleges. (A. P. Peabody) Nat. Educa. Assoc. '74 : 152. — (S. H. Peabody and others) Nat. Educa. Assoc. '80 : 268. — (F. A. P. Barnard) N. Y. Regents, 86 : 611. — (J. McCosh) N. Y. Regents, **100,** app. : 240. — (G. M. Forbes) N. Y. Regents, **103,** app. : 199.

— in college admission, Wider range of. Eliot, C. W. Educa. reform.

Electoral vote. *See* President, Election of.

Electric communications. Chambers's Papers, no. 71.

Electric element, The. Holland, H. Frag. papers, 81.

Electric light, how it is produced. Molloy, G. Gleanings, 235.

— in colleges. U. S. Cons. Rept. no. 150.

Electric lighting. Proctor, R. A. Rough ways, 289.

Electric-spark photographs of flying bullets. (C. V. Boys) Smithson. Rept. '93 : 165.

Electrical and chemical changes, Relations of. Davy. Works, **6** : 305.

Electrical apparatus. Franklin. Works ('87), **2** : 121.

Electrical battery. *See* Battery.

Electrical discovery, Historical sketch of. Davy. Works, **8** : 256.

Electrical distribution. (Louis Duncan) Smithson. Rept. '96 : 207.

— The state and. (F. H. B. Gordon) Plea for liberty, 353.

Electrical energy, Storing of. Molloy, G. Gleanings, 141.

Electrical experiments and researches. Franklin. Works ('87), v. **2, 3, 5.**

Electricity. Hunt, R. Poetry of sci. 193.

— Advance of. (E. Thomson) Smithson. Rept. '97 : 125.

— Age of. (M. Mascart) Smithson. Rept. '94 : 153.

— American work in. (A. E. Kennelly) Shaler. The U. S. **2** : 134.

— Atmospheric. (A. Schuster) Smithson. Rept. '95 : 91.

— Bibliography. Bost. Pub. Lib. Bull. Apr. '92. — Burgoyne, F. J. Lib. World, July, '99 : 22. — Lowell. City Lib. Bull. Apr. '97. — Newark (N. J.) Free Pub. Lib. '94. — Salem (Mass.) Pub. Lib. Bull. Oct. '96. — Springfield (Mass.) Pub. Lib. Bull. Jan. '94. — Thompson, S. P. Polyphase elec. currents.

— Chemical agencies of. Davy. Works, **5** : 1, 225.

— Discharge of, without electrodes. (J. J. Thompson) Smithson. Rept. '92 : 229.

— Force electrically exhibited. (J. W. Phelps) Estes. Half-hour recr. 93.

— History of, Bibliography. Benjamin, P. Intellec. rise in electricity.

— in agriculture. U. S. Cons. Rept. 41 : 321.

— Influence of, in animal life. (Ernest Solvay) Smithson. Rept. '94 : 437.

— Is it energy or matter? (A. Man) Butterfield Lec. Un. Coll. **1** : 197.

— The Leyden phial and Volta's experiments. Franklin. Works ('87), **7** : 487.

— Magnetic phenomena produced by. Davy. Works, **6** : 217.

— Place of, in a college course. (Bro. Potomian) N. Y. Regents, **111** : 216.

— What is? Spencer, H. Rec. dis. (N. Y.) 281. *See* Galvanism.

Electro-chemical science.   Davy. Works, **8** : 274.

Electro-physiology.   Bibliography.   Biederman, W. Electro-physiology.

Electrostatics, Fundamental concepts of. Mach. Pop. sci. lec. 107.

Elegiac poems, The.   Brooke, S. A. Hist. early Eng. lit. 352.

Elegies, Greater English.   Quayle, W. A. Poet, 124.

Elegy, The Alexandrian.   Mahaffy, J. P. Greek life, ch. 11.

Elementary education.   (John Eaton; J. L. Pickard) Nat. Educa. Assoc. '93 : 247. — (W. T. Harris) Butler, N. M. Educa. in U. S. 77.

— and industrial needs.   (A. P. Marble) Nat. Educa. Assoc. '93 : 268.

— and secondary schools, Modifications in.   (J. C. Mackenzie) Nat. Educa. Assoc. '94 : 143.

— Economy in.   (Bettie A. Dutton) Nat. Educa. Assoc. '95 : 447.

— Function of nature in.   (M. G. Brumbaugh) Nat. Educa. Assoc. '96 : 141.

— in England.   Green, T. H. Works, **3** : 413. — (H. Roe) Internat. health exh. **13** : 168. — (William Clark) Nat. Educa. Assoc. '91 : 187. — (Rosamond Davenport-Hill) Nat. Educa. Assoc. '95 : 870.

— in Great Britain and Ireland in 1892.   (A. T. Smith) U. S. Bur. Educa. Rept. '91-92 : 97. '92-93 : 203.

— in London.   U. S. Bur. Educa. Circ. '78, no. 2.

— — in public schools.   Boutwell. Educa. topics, 131.

— — in the U. S.   (J. McClelland) Trans. Soc. Sci. Lond. '60 : 327.

— Learning to do by doing in.   (N. C. Schaeffer) Nat. Educa. Assoc. '87 : 374.

— — Organization of.   (T. E. Heller) Internat. health exh. **13** : 154.

— — Report of Committee of Fifteen.   U. S. Bur. Educa. Rept. '93-94, **1** : 469.

— — Studies best fitted for it.   (F. A. P. Barnard) Youmans. Culture, 309.

— Waste in.   (J. W. Stearns and Z. Richards) Nat. Educa. Assoc. '88 : 300.

Elementary instruction, Modern methods of. (W. N. Hailmann; W. T. Harris) Nat. Educa. Assoc. '87 : 80.

Elementary programs, Correlation of subjects in.   (J. W. Stearns) Nat. Educa. Assoc. '90 : 200.

Elementary school and the child.   (Miss N. Cropsey) Nat. Educa. Assoc. '96 : 345.

Elementary schools and colleges, Gap between. (C. W. Eliot; J. W. Johnson) Nat. Educa. Assoc. '90 : 522.

Changes in.   (E. G. Ward) Nat. Educa. Assoc. '94 : 715.

— Discipline in.   (Bettie A. Dutton) Nat. Educa. Assoc. '89 : 487.

— Enriching the course in.   (E. G. Reveley; H. C. Muckley) Nat. Educa. Assoc. '94 : 418.

— Laboratory methods in.   (C. B. Scott) Nat. Educa. Assoc. '94 : 191.

— Literature in.   (Ella F. Young) Nat. Educa. Assoc. '96 : 111.

— Methods and courses in.   (W. N. Hailmann; N. C. Schaeffer) Nat. Educa. Assoc. '97 : 199.

— Mission of.   (M. G. Brumbaugh) Nat. Educa. Assoc. '98 : 343.

— Preparation in, for citizenship.   (W. A. Mowry) Nat. Educa. Assoc. '93 : 273.

— Relation of, to social virtues.   (Catharine H. Spence) Nat. Educa. Assoc. '93 : 278.

Elementary schools, Subjects studied in.   (Mrs. A. C. Martin) Nat. Educa. Assoc. '74 : 274.

— — Successive differentiation of.   (Z. X. Snyder) Nat. Educa. Assoc. '98 : 632.

Elementary studies.   Newman, J. H. Lec. univ. 116.

Elements, new, Discovery of.   (C. Winkler) Smithson. Rept. '97 : 237.

Eleonor, Queen.   *See* Eleanor.

Elephant, The.   Morgan, C. L. Animal sk. 37.

Elephant hunting in Africa.   Barker, Lady. Travel. about, 285.

Elephanta, Temple of.   Adams, W. H. D. Fam. caves, 47.

Elephants.   Shaler. Dom. animals, 127.

— Anecdotes of.   Chambers's Miscel. no. 61.

— White.   Vincent, F. In & out Cent. Amer.

Eleusinian mysteries.   Dyer. Stud. of the Gods.

Eleusis.   Arnold, R. A. Levant, **1** : 164. — Mahaffy. Rambles Greece, 150.

— and the mysteries.   Gardner, P. New chap. Gr. hist.

— Excavations at, 1882-89.   Diehl, C. Excursions, 300.

Elevated railway in New York city.   Marshall, W. G. Thro' Amer. 24.

Elfgifa, queen of Edmund "the pious."   Hall. Queens bef. Conq. 355.

Elfleda, queen of Wimond.   Hall. Queens bef. Conq. 310.

Elfric, 995-1006.   Hook. Abps. Cant. **1** : 439.

Elfrida, queen of Edgar "the peaceable."   Hall. Queens bef. Conq. 374.

Elgin, James Bruce, 8th earl of.   Martineau, H. Biog. sketch. 346.

Elgin, Thomas Bruce, 7th earl of.   Edwards, E. Founders Brit. Mus. **1** : 380.

Elgin marbles.   Hazlitt. Crit. on art. ser. 1.

— Phidias and.   Story, W. W. Excur. 49.

Eli.   Geikie, C. Old Test. char. 185.

Eliezer of Damascus.   Hastings, F. Obscure charac. 167.

Eligius, or Eloy, St.   Maclear. Apostles, 77.

Elijah.   Geikie, C. Old Test. char. 323. — Wilberforce, S. Heroes Hebrew, 318.

Eliot, Chas. Wm., Pres.   Vaille & Clark. Harv. book, v. 1.

Eliot, George.   Adams, W. H. D. Cel. Eng. wom. Vict. **2** : 86. — Bolton, S. K. Girls famous, 213. — Cone & Gilder. Pen-portr. **2** : 245. — Forman. Liv. poets, 469. — Griswold, H. T. Home-life, 351. — Hazeltine. Chats, 1. — Lanier, S. Eng. novel. — Lord, J. Beacon, **5** : 467. Morley, J. Crit. miscel. **3** : 93. — Myers. Ess. mod. 251. — Paul. Biog. sk. 141. — Robertson. Eng. poetesses, 327. — Thorne, W. H. Mod. idols, 136. — Trollope, T. A. What I rem. **2** : 267. — Underwood, S. A. Heroines, 297. — Walsh, W. S. Pen pic. mod. 41. — Wotton. Word portr. 98. — Em. persons, **2** : 232. — With portrait. Hamilton, C. J. Wom. writers, **2** : 216. — Smith, G. B. Women of renown, 83. Walford, L. B. 12 Eng. auth. 187. — Harrison, F. Stud. early Vict. 205. — Hubbard, E. Lit. jour. **1** : 1. — Lilly. Four humorists, 75. — Saintsbury. Correc. imp. 162. — Henley. Views, 130. — Scherer. Ess. Eng. lit. 251. — Jacobs, Jos. Ess. & rev. 3. — (J. A. Noble) Miles, A. H. Poets of cent. **7** : 293. — (E. L. Linton) Oliphant. Wom. novelists, 61. — Smalley. Lond. let. **1** : 241. — With portrait.   (C. Waldstein) Warner Lib. **9** : 5359; *or* Warner classics, **2** : 83. — Wilson, S. L. Theol. mod. liter.

— Adam Bede.   Mozley, A. Ess. fr. Blackw. 304.

Eliot, George, an ingenious moralist. Heywood, J. C. How they strike, 57.
— and G. H. Lewes. Espinasse. Lit. recoll. 273.
— McCarthy, J. Mod. lead. 136.
— and the novel. (E. Eggleston) Ess. from Critic, 49.
— as author. Hutton. Mod. guides, 151.
— as novelist. Quayle, W. A. Poet, 273.
— as a writer. Hutton. Ess. theol. 2 : 294.
— at home. Field, Mrs. H. M. Sk. France, 208.
— Bibliography. Browning, Life of G. E.— Hodgkins. 19th cent. authors. — Mo. ref. lists, 1 : 15.
Croon'o Lifo of. Jamoo, H. Par. portr. 37.— Buchanan, R. Look round, 314.
— Daniel Deronda. Dowden. Studies, 273. — James, H. Par. portr. 65. — Whipple. Recol. 344. — Scherer. Ess. Eng. lit. 51.
— — A protest. Jacobs, J. Jewish ideals, 61.
— Dorothea Casaubon. Belloc, Mme. Walled garden, v. 1.
— Genius of. (Mrs. S. B. Herrick) Eliot, Geo. Ess. v.
— Life and letters of. Darmesteter. Eng. stud. 97, 111. — Hutton. Mod. guides, 269. — Morley. Crit. miscel. 3 : 93.
— Married people of. Johnston, R. M. Studies, 106.
— Meeting with. (Mrs. J. Lillie) Parton. Princes, 62.
— Middlemarch. Dowden. Studies, 273.
— moralist and thinker. Baildon. Round table.
— Novels. Lancaster, H. H. Ess. & rev. 351.
— — Literary and ethical quality of. Wilkinson, W. C. Free lance, v. 1.
— on the human character. Mallock. Atheism, 147.
— Personal characteristics of. Dowden. Studies, 240.
— Poetry of. Cleveland, R. E. Eliot, 7.
— Private life of. Whipple. Recollec. 380.
— Silas Marner. Scherer. Ess. Eng. lit. v. 1.
— Social conscience and. Scudder, V. D. Soc. ideals, 180.
— A talk with. Buchanan, R. Look round, 218.
Eliot, Sir John. Adams, C. K. Rep. Br. orat. 1 : 1. — With portrait. Forster. Brit. statesm. 2 : 1. — Forster. Statesm. of Comm. — Lucas. Mornings, 1 : 5. — Goodrich, C. A. Sel. Brit. eloq.
Eliot, John, Apostle to the Indians. Adams, W. H. D. Good Samar. 191. — Carne, J. Em. mission. 1 : 1. — (W. H. McDougall) Haydn, H. C. Am. miss. heroes, no. 13. — Lossing. Em. Amer. 17. — (A. Gilman) Lowell Old Residents' Assoc. 3 : 90. — Mass. Hist. Coll. 2d ser. 1 : 211. — Parton. Triumphs, 593. — Yonge. Pioneers. — Parker, H. F. Morning stars, 321. — Richardson. Amer. lit. 1 : 123. — Thomson, A. Gt. mission. 21.
— Bible of, and the Ojibway language. Am. Antiq. Soc. Proc. n. s. 9 : 314.
Eliot, Samuel. (B. Wendell) Am. Acad. A. & S. Proc. 34 : 646.
— Tribute to. (E. F. Slafter ; E. E. Hale) Mass. Hist. Soc. Proc. 2d ser. 12 : 312.
Eliot, Samuel A. Peabody. Harv. grad. 149.
Elisha. Geikie, C. Old Test. char. 331. — Wilberforce, S. Heroes Hebrew, 341.
Elizabeth, St., of Hungary. Kavanagh. Women of Christ'y, 78. — Fifty famous women, 291.
Elizabeth, empress of Austria, with portrait. Crowned heads, 21.
— and Charles IX. Imbert de St. A. Wom. Valois ct. 281.

Elizabeth, queen of Bohemia. With portrait. Costello. Englishwomen, 2 : 1. — Lodge. Portraits (Bohn), v. 5. — Strickland. Queens Scot. v. 8. — Wilson, H. S. Stud. in hist. 118. — Jesse. Court of Eng. Stuarts, 1 : 143.
— and the palatinate. Chambers's Repos. no. 31. — Taylor, T. Leicester Sq. 96.
Elizabeth Woodville, queen of Edward IV. With portrait. Howitt, M. Queens, 204. — Strickland. Queens Eng. v. 3. — Lancelott. Queens, v. 1. — Lawrance. Queens, v. 2.
Elizabeth of York, queen of Henry VII. Burke, B. Viciss. of fam. 3 : 315. — With portrait. Howitt, M. Queens, 225 — Lodge. Portraits (Bohn), v. 1. — Strickland. Queens Eng. v. 4.
Elizabeth, Queen. Bethune, G. W. Brit. fem. poets, 22. — Burke, S. H. Hist. portr. Tudor, 2 : 326. — Dawson, G. Biog. lec. v. 1. — Farmer, L. H. Girls' book of queens, 156. — Howitt, M. Queens, 390. — James, G. P. R. Cel. wom. — Jameson. Fam. sov. v. 1. — Jenkins, J. S. Heroines, 269. — Lodge. Portraits (Bohn), v. 3. — Lord, J. Beacon, 5 : 223. — Russell. Extr. women, 82. — Strickland. Queens Eng. 6 : 7. — Williams, Jane. Lit. wom. 65.— (J. R. Green) Ferris, G. T. Gt. leaders, 265. — Fifty famous women, 279. — Fowler, G. Sov. of Russ. 49. — Hale, S. J. Less. wom. lives, 26. — Holland, J. Psalmists, 1 : 145. — Hunt, L. Men, wom. & books, 185. — Lancellot. Queens, v. 2. — Mombert. Great lives, 183.
— and the Church of England. Gladstone. Later gl. 181.
— death of, Secret history of. Disraeli, I. Curios. (N. Y. 4 v.) 4 : 233.
— English poets and. Jameson. Loves of poets.
— Favorites of. Menzies, S. Roy. fav. 1 : 268.
— Military system of. Adams, W. H. D. Engl. at war, 1 : 20.
— Montalembert's History of. Wiseman, N. Ess. 3 : 223.
— Progresses of. Mitchell, D. G. English lands, 1 : 312.
— Rejected suitors of. Ewald. Studies, 114.
— The Seymour scandal. Burke, S. H. Men of reforma. 2 : 217.
— Spencer's. Jameson. Loves of poets.
Elizabeth of Austria, queen of France. Bush, A. F. Queens of Fr. 1 : 340. — Yonge, C. M. Good women, 2 : 326.
Elizabeth Luise, queen dowager of Prussia. Strauss, G. L. M. Men of Ger. 1 : 33.
Elizabeth, queen of Roumania, "Carmen Sylva." Boyesen, H. H. Ess. Ger. liter. 264. — With portrait. Warner Lib. 24 : 14329. — Kingston, W. B. Monarchs, 1 : 253. — Sherwood, Mrs. M. E. W. Royal girls, 88.
Elizabeth of France, wife of Philip II., with portrait. Imbert de St. A. Wom. Valois ct. 222.
Elizabeth, daughter of Edward I., with portrait. Green, M. A. E. Princesses, 3 : 1.
Elizabeth, Princess, of Hatfield, daughter of Henry VIII. Ewald. Stories fr. st. pap. 1 : 191.
Elizabeth, daughter of Charles I. With portrait. Green, M. A. E. Princesses, 6 : 335.— Jesse. Court of Eng. Stuarts, 2 : 47. — Strickland. Last princ. 155.
Elizabeth, daughter of James I., with portrait. Green, M. A. E. Princesses, 5 : 145. 6 : 1.
Elizabeth, Princess Palatine, Descartes and. Courtney. Stud. 172.
Elizabeth, duchess of Brunswick-Calenberg. Wittenmeyer. Women Reform. 372.

Elizabeth, electress of Brandenburg. Chapman, W. Women Reform. 71. — Wittenmeyer. Women Reform. 366.

Elizabeth, landgravine of Hesse Homburg, daughter of George III. Fitzgerald, P. Royal dukes, 1 : 276. — Hall, Mrs. M. Princesses, 333.

Elizabeth, margravine of Anspach. Williams, Jane. Lit. wom. 307.

Elizabeth Caroline, Princess, of England, 1740-59. Hall, Mrs. M. Princesses, 166.

Elizabeth Charlotte, duchess of Orleans. Townsend. Descend. Stuarts, 167.

Elizabeth Christina, 4th queen of Prussia. Atkinson. Qu. of Prus. 211. — Kavanagh. Women of Christ'y, 303.

Elizabeth, Charlotte. *See* Tonna, Mrs. C. E.

Elizabethan age. Brooks, S. W. Eng. poets, 70.
— Poetic and verse criticism of. (F. E. Schelling) Univ. Pa. Publ. Philol. 1 : no. 1.

Elizabethan art. Crofts, E. Chap. Eng. lit. 113.

Elizabethan poetry. Tovey. Rev. & ess. 169.
— Decline of. Crofts, E. Chap. Eng. lit. 354.
— Minor. Brooks, S. W. Eng. poets, 89.

Elizabethan settlement of religion. Gladstone. Later gl. 159.

Elizabethan thought. Crofts, E. Chap. Eng. lit. 312, 327.

Elizabethtown, N. C., Expedition to. Dawson. Batt. of U. S. 2 : 201.

Ellacombe, Henry Thomas. Mozley. Reminis. 1 : 75.

Ellenborough, E. Law, Lord. With portrait. Bennet, W. H. Select biog. 7. — Brougham. Works, 4 : 174. — Townsend. 12 judges, 1 : 299. — Browne, I. Stud. great lawyers, 76. — Grant, Jas. Bench & bar, 1 : 53. — Grant, J. Recollec. Lords, 181.

Elleray, De Quincey at. Rawnsley. Lit. assoc. Eng. lakes, 2 : 82.

Ellerton, John. Miles, A. H. Poets of cent. 10 : 569.

Ellery, William, 1727–1820. Dwight, N. Signers of decl. 71. — Lincoln, R. W. Signers, 17. — Lossing. Signers, 47. — Muzzey. Remin. 157. — Sanderson. Signers, v. 9.
— on horseback. Higginson, T. W. Travelers, 57.

Ellery family, The. Muzzey, A. B. Prime movers, 157.

Ellesmere, Thomas Egerton, Baron. Campbell. Ld. Chan. 2 : 308. — Fuller. Worthies, 1 : 270.

Ellet, Charles, with portrait. Headley, J. T. Farragut, 209.

Ellet, Charles, jr., with portrait. Stuart, C. B. Am. engineers, 257.

Ellet, Elizabeth F. Griswold. Fem. poets, 199. — Hart, J. S. Fem. prose, 177.

Elley, Sir John. Grant, J. Recollec. Lords & Comm. 2 : 3.

Ellicott, And. Stuart, C. B. Am. engineers, 17.

Ellicott, Charles John, bishop of Gloucester and Bristol, with photo. Cooper, T. Men of mark, 1 : 17.

Ellington murder. Timbs. Abbeys, 1 : 335.

Elliot, Jean. Bethune, G. W. Brit. fem. poets, 76. — Keddie. Songstresses, 1 : 196. — Robertson. Eng. poetesses, 152.

Elliot, Richard. Hatfield, E. F. Poets of ch. 227.

Elliott, Anna. Clement, J. Noble deeds, 338.

Elliott, Charles Loring. Tuckerman. Artists, 300.

Elliott, Charlotte. Hatfield, E. F. Poets of ch. 228. — Japp. Wise words, 124. — Miles, A. H. Poets of cent. 10 : 87. — Miller, Jos. Singers church, 2d ed. 461.

Elliott, Ebenezer. Chambers's Papers, no. 8. —

Giles, H. Lectures, 1 : 166. — Gilfillan. 1st gall. 248. — Hood, E. P. Peerage of pov. 108. — Howitt. Homes Br. poets, 2 : 462. — Stirling, J. H. Jerrold, 225. — Dixon, W. M. Engl. poetry, 71. — Hall, S. C. Book of mem. 97. — Miles, A. H. Poets of cent. 2 : 231. — Smiles. Brief biog. 149. — Stoddard, R. H. Under eve. lamp, 135.

Elliott, Mrs. Julia Anne (Marshall). Hatfield, E. F. Poets of church, 230. — Miller, Jos. Singers church, 2d ed. 482.

Elliott, Melcenia. Brockett. Woman's work, 380.

Elliott, Sabina. Ellet. Women of revol. 2 : 84.

Elliott, Susannah. Clement, J. Noble deeds, 336. — Ellet. Women of revol. 2 : 80.

Ellis, Calvin. Vaille & Clark. Harv. book, v. 1.

Ellis, Geo. Edward. Am. Antiq. Soc. Proc. n. s. 9 : 461. — (J. Winsor and others) Mass. Hist. Soc. Proc. 2d ser. 9 : 254. — (O. B. Frothingham) Mass. Hist. Soc. Proc. 2d ser. 10 : 207.

Ellis, Sir Henry. Edwards, E. Founders Brit. Mus. 2 : 526.

Ellis, John T. Walker, C. D. Biog. Va. Mil. Inst. 190.

Ellis, Sir John Whittaker. Ritchie, J. E. City men, 51.

Ellis, Mrs. Mary M., of the South Seas. Pitman, Mrs. Heroines mission. 160.

Ellis, Robert Leslie. Cracroft. Ess. 2 : 233.

Ellis, William. Japp. Labor, 228.

Ellis family. Titcomb, S. E. New Eng. peo. 5.

Ellison, H. (A. B. Grosart) Miles, A. H. Poets of cent. 10 : 261.

Elliston, Robert William. Baker, H. B. Engl. actors, 2 : 194. — Doran. Annals stage, 2 : 347. — Fitzgerald, P. Rom. of stage, 361. — Hazlitt. Crit. & dram. ess. — Hunt. Crit. ess. on performers, 180. — Matthews, B. Actors, 2 : 159.
— To the shade of. Lamb. Elia.

Ellistoniana. Lamb. Elia.

Ellora, Temples of. Adams, W. H. D. Fam. caves, 53.

Ellsworth, Elmer E. Glazier, W. Heroes, 396. — Shea, J. G. Fallen brave.
— Death of. (E. B. Knox) Mil. ess. M. O. L. L. U. S. Ills. 9.

Ellsworth, Oliver. With portrait. (Amer.) Nat. portr. gall. v. 4. — With portrait. Barnes, W. H. Sup. ct. 27. — With portrait. Duyckinck. Nat. portr. gall. 1 : 345. — Flanders. Ch. just. 2 : 55. — Lossing. Em. Amer. 102. — Moore, F. Am. eloq. 1 : 401. — Perry, B. F. Biog. sketches, 1 : 402. — Van Santvoord. Ch. just.

Ellsworth, William Wolcott. Livingston, J. Em. Am. lawy. 61.

Elmira reformatory. (C. D. Warner) Conf. char. & correc. '85 : 275.

Elmore, Alfred, with photo. Cooper, T. Men of mark, 5 : 33.

Elmore, Franklin H., Tribute to, 1850. Webster, D. Works, 5 : 371.

Elmslie, Alexander. Winslow, S. N. Biog. Phila. merch. 57.

Elmslie, William, and Kashmir. Japp, A. H. Master mission. 145.

El Obeid, Annihilation of Hicks Pasha's army at. Knox, T. W. Battles, 450.

Elocution. Butler, E. For furth. consid. 96. — Emerson. Society, 61. — Emerson. Let. & soc. aims, 107.
— as a part of general education. Newman, F. W. Essays, 316.

Emerson, Ralph Waldo, Home of. Wolfe. Lit. shr. Amer. auth. 45.
— in England. Espinasse. Lit. recol. 156.
— lecturing. Curtis. From easy ch. 21.
— man and teacher. (H. B. Baildon) Baildon. Round table.
— Matthew Arnold's view of. Burroughs, J. Indoor, 128.
— Patriotism of. Muzzey. Remin. 337.
— Poems. Brownson. Works, 19 : 189.
— poet and essayist. Bungay. Repr. men, 154.
— Prose works. Brownson. Works, 3 : 424.
— Reminiscences of. (L. M. Alcott) Parton. Princes, 284.
— Self of. Scudder, H. E. Men lit. 147.
Emerson, Stephen Goodhue. (J. E. Wright) Harvard mem. biog. 2 : 229.
Emerson, William. Loring, J. S. 100 Bost. ora. 311.
Emerson, William Dana. Coggeshall. Poets of west, 284.
Emery, John. Galt. Players, 2 : 289.
Emigrant ships, Hygiene of. (T. J. Turner) Am. Pub. Health, 6 : 17.
— Sanitary service on. (S. H. Durgin) Am. Pub. Health, 16 : 43. — Am. Pub. Health, 19 : 143.
Emigrants to the U. S., Education of. Holyoake. Among Amer. 195.
Emigration. (Hon. Mrs. Stuart Wortley) Burdett-Coutts. Wom. miss. 87. — Kempner, W. Common-sense soc. 89. — Southey, R. Ess. (1832) 2 : 207.
— Coöperative. Holyoake. Among Amer. 153.
— English, Reciprocal duties of state and subjects. Froude. Short stud. 2 : 211.
— Results of. (N. Waterhouse) Trans. Soc. Sci. Lond. '58 : 562.
— State aid to. (R. R. Torrens et al.) Trans. Soc. Sci. Lond. '69 : 524.
Eminent domain, Tenure of land and. Chatard. Occ. ess. 232.
Emlyn, Thomas. Wallace, R. Anti-Trin. biog. 3 : 503.
Emma of Normandy, "the Pearl," queen of Ethelred. Hall. Queens bef. Conq. 394.
Emma, queen of the Netherlands. With portrait. Crowned heads, 37.
Emmanuel, Dom, of Portugal. Wraxall, F. C. L. Remark. adv. 2 : 330.
Emmet, Robert. Thornbury. Old stor. 118.
— Rebellion instigated by. Browne, G. L. State trials 19th cent. 1 : 96.
Emmet, Thomas Addis. Magoon. Orators of rev. 395. — Moore, F. Am. eloq. 1 : 525.
Emmons, Ebenezer. Youmans. Pioneers sci.
Emmons, Henry H. Livingston, J. Dist. Amer. 347.
Emmons, Nathaniel. Dodge, M. A. Skirmishes, 84. — Richardson. Amer. lit. 1 : 146. — Sherman, D. N. Eng. divines, 361.
Emory, John. Gorrie. Em. Meth. 339. — (John McClintock) McClintock, J. Em. Meth. 105.
Emory and Henry College, Washington Co., Va. U. S. Bur. Ed. Circ. '88, no. 1 : 253.
Emory College, Oxford, Ga. U. S. Bur. Ed. Circ. '88, no. 4 : 85.
Emotion. Haweis. Cur. coin.
— Cosmic. Clifford. Lec. & ess. 394.
Emotions, Psychology of. Mivart. Ess. 1 : 423.
Empedocles. Arnold, E. Poets of Greece, 161.
— Diog. Laertius. Lives, 359. — Mills. Poets of Greece, 145. — Lewes. Biog. phil. — Symonds. Greek poets, 1 : 207. — Fénélon. Philosophers, 144. — Fairbanks, A. Philos. of

Greece, 174. — (G. H. Palmer) Warner Lib. 10 : 5467. — Osborn. From Greeks, 37.
Empire. Bacon. Ess.
Empiricism in medicine, Repression of. (A. H. Horton) Am. Pub. Health, 17 : 24.
Employees, Condition of, in Massachusetts, 1888. Mass. Labor, '89 : 231.
Employer and employed. Chambers's Miscel. no. 4.
Employers, Liability of. Brassey, T. Papers, polit. 119. — Minn. Labor, '91–92 : 117. — (C. M. Napton) Missouri. Labor, '93 : 426. — Pa. Bur. Indus. Statis. '91, '97. — (G. P. Macdonell) Trans. Soc. Sci. Lond. '83 : 162. — Pollock. Ess. in juris. 114. — Mass. Labor, '83 : 3. — N. J. Labor, '82 : 89. '88 : 75.
— Relief of employees by. Pa. Bur. Indus. Statis. '87.
— Temple amendment in Iowa. Iowa Bur. Lab. '97 : 94.
Employers' welfare institutions. Bibliography. Gilman, N. P. A dividend to labor.
Employment bureau, Free public. (H. F. Barnes) Conf. char. & correc. '85 : 362.
— — Abuses of. Missouri Labor, 1891. — (C. E. Bartram) Conf. char. & correc. '97 : 207.
— — in Ohio. (P. W. Ayres) Cong. Char. Chic. '93, 1 : 124.
Employment scheme, Municipal, proposed for Detroit, Mich. (J. A. Post) Conf. char. & corr. '97 : 217.
Emuckfau, Battles at. Dawson. Batt. U. S. 2 : 319.
Encina, or Enzina, Juan de la. Montgomery. Men. of Ita. 3 : 17. — Ticknor. Span. lit. 1 : 273.
Encke, Johann Franz. Proctor. Light sci. 1 : 46.
Encyclopædia Britannica. Miller, H. Lead. articles, 315.
End, Art of coming to an. Helps. Comp. of solitude, 238.
— cause and effect, Law of. Sewall, F. New metaphys. 3.
Enda, St. Conyngham, D. P. Irish saints, 180.
Endemoniadas. Lea. Rel. hist. Spain, 423.
Endicott, John. With portrait. Moore, J. B. Am. gov. 347. — Whittier. Prose works, v. 2.
Endowed schools. Thirlwall, C. Remains, 1 : 363.
Endowment of research. See Research.
Endowments. Mill, J. S. Dissert. (N. Y.) 5 : 1.
— Turgot. Life & writ. 219.
— Charitable, Adjustment of. (Sir A. Hobhouse) Trans. Soc. Sci. Lond. '79 : 149.
— — Legal limits to. (T. Hare and L. Fry) Trans. Soc. Sci. Lond. '69 : 132.
— National, for scientific and technical schools. (J. K. Patterson) Nat. Educa. Assoc. '74 : 204.
— of colleges and academies, Voluntary. (J. V. L. Pruyn) N. Y. Regents, 81 : 691.
Enemies, Concerning old. Boyd. Aut. holid. 184.
Energy. Gall & Robertson. Pop. read. sci. 225.
— Chemical. (W. Ostwald) Smithson. Rept. '93 : 231.
— Conservation of. Carpenter, W. Benj. Nature, 350. — Mach. Pop. sci. lec. 137.
Enfield, William. Hatfield, E. F. Poets of church, 232. — Miller, Jos. Singers church, 2d ed. 282.
Enfield palace. Timbs. Abbeys, 1 : 166.
Enfleda, queen of Oswy. Hall. Queens before Conq. 239.
Enforcement act of 1870, Constitutionality of. Field, D. D. Speeches, 1 : 180.
Engel, Mor. Erdm. Roscoe. Germ. novel. 4 : 346.

Engineer, Education of an. (G. Lanza) Cong. Educa. Chic. '93, 569.

Engineering. (J. Swift) Galton, F. W. Workers, 95.

— Bibliography. Milwaukee Pub. Lib. Our Books, Apr. '94. — Smith, A. W. Materials engineering.

— Technical, and scientific education. (T. C. Mendenhall) Butler, N. M. Educa. in U. S. 551.

— Training for. (G. Lanza) Nat. Educa. Assoc. '93 : 569.

— Wonders of. Chambers's Miscel. no. 108.

Engineers, The English. Lucas. Mornings, 1 · 129.

— Great. Hodder. Heroes, 2 : 34.

England, Edward. Whitehead, C. Highwaymen, 2 : 57.

England, John. Clarke, R. H. Cath. bish. 1 : 271. — Murray, J. O'K. Cath. heroes, 783.

England, Samuel S. Miller, Jos. Singers church, 2d ed. 510.

England. Felton, C. C. Fam. let. Eur. 10. — Haven, G. Pilgrim, 1. — Jackson, H. H. 3 coasts, 196. — Taylor, B. Views, 65. — Warner, C. D. Rela. of lit. 207.

— Accounts of, by travelers. Southey, R. Ess. 1832, 1 : 249.

— after the Norman conquest. Stillé. Stud. med. 217.

— Alleged invasion of, 1147. Round, J. H. Feudal England, 491.

— American feeling towards. Peck, H. T. Pers. equa. 213.

— and America. Thompson, H. M. Copy, 302.

— — Kin beyond sea. (W. E. Gladstone) Prose masterpieces, 3 : 151.

— and the continent, in 1845-46, Letters from. Willis. Fam. persons, 345.

— and France compared. Hayward, A. Ess. 3d ser. 123.

— and Germany, Intercourse of, in the middle ages. Pattison. Ess. 1 : 30.

— and India. Pidgeon. Engineer's holiday, 427.

— and the other states, in the middle ages. Adams, G. B. Civil. mid. ages, 339.

— and university education. M'Cormick, W. S. Three lec. 9.

— as it is. Greg. Ess. pol. 1 : 297 ; or Miscel. 2 : 136.

— Augustan age of. Goldsmith. Miscel. (N. Y. 4 v.) 1 : 149.

— Beauty of. Winter, W. Shakesp. Eng.

— Budget and the national debt, 1867-68. Hobart, V. H. H. Ess. & Miscel. 2 : 153.

— a century ago. Doran. New pic. 167.

— Civilization in, in the 9th century. Dunham. Lit. & sci. men, 1 : 60.

— Civil wars in. Freeman. Hist. ess. 4 : 266.

— coast of, Heroes of. Hodder. Heroes, 2 : 34.

— Commercial situation in, 1881. Hatton, J. Today in Amer. 2 : 87.

— Constitution, Burke on. Stephen, J. F. Horæ sabb. 113.

— Constitutional laws of, Dicey on. Laurence, P. M. Collect. 182.

— Cottage homes of. Heath, R. Eng. peasant, 57.

— counties of, Recollections of. Burke, B. Viciss. of fam. 1 : 257.

— Crown of, in relation to the crown of Scotland. Freeman. Hist. ess. 1 : 53.

— Dangers to ; Greg's " Rocks ahead." Duff, M. E. G. Miscel. 57.

— Defenses of. Cairnes. Pol. ess. 199.

— during the commonwealth. Dawson, G. Biog. lec. 60.

England, Economic dangers to. Greg, W. R. Miscel. 1 : 1.

— Emerson on. Godwin, P. Out of past, 441.

— Ethnography of. (J. W. Donaldson) Camb. ess. '56 : 30.

— Expansion of. Froude. Oceana.

— Finances of, 1793-1815. (G. R. Porter) Rand. Selec. econ. hist. 126.

— France and, in 1793. (O. Browning) Coan. Hist. stud. 141.

— — Relations of, 1793-1853. Cobden. Polit. writ. 1 : 355.

— — — 1847-61. Cobden. Polit. writ. 2 : 209.

— Future of. Carlyle. Past & present.

— German traveller in, A. D. 1598. Müller. Chips, v. 3.

— Government of, opportunities and shortcomings of. (A. O. Rutson) Ess. on reform (1867), 279.

— Greatness of. Smith, Goldw. Lec. & ess. 21.

— — is it on the decline ? Vaughan, J. D. Questions, 88.

— History, Abridgment of. Burke. Works (Bohn), 6 : 184.

— — Bibliography. Higginson, T. W., and Channing, E. Eng. hist. for Amer. readers. — Joy, J. R. Twen. cent. Eng. hist. — Traill, H. D. (ed.) Social England. — Wilkesbarre (Pa.) Lib. Newsletter. Jan.–Dec. '97.

— — Continuity of. Freeman. Hist. ess. 1 : 40.

— — Dramas illustrating. Symonds. Shakesp. pred. 363.

— — Dutch invasion, 1667 ; a national scare. Ewald. Stories fr. st. pap. 2 : 232.

— — early, Mythical and romantic elements in. Freeman. Hist. ess. 1 : 1.

— — Commonwealth. Green, T. H. Works, 3 : 277.

— — England and Norway in the 11th century. Dasent. Jest & earnest, 1 : 198.

— — Falsification of. DeQuincey. Note-book (Bost.), 217.

— — Froude's. Kingsley. Plays & p. 209; or Raleigh, 426.

— — Green's Short history of the English people. Brewer. Eng. stud. 50.

— — Hallam's Constitutional. Macaulay. Ess. 1 : 433.

— — in 11th to 15th centuries. Plantagenets and Tudors. Forster, J. Hist. ess. 1 : 177.

— — in 17th cent. ; the " Rump." Disraeli, I. Curios. (N. Y. 4 v.) 4 : 412.

— — — Secret history of Charles I. and his first parliaments. Disraeli, I. Curios. (N. Y. 4 v.) 4 : 372.

— — — Great civil war, 1640-46. Macaulay. Ess. 1 : 112. — Lord, J. Beacon, 4 : 91. — Higginson. Atlan. ess. 125.

— — — — Gathering of the storm. Ewald. Stories from st. pap. 2 : 104.

— — — — Grand remonstrance, Debates on, 1641. Forster, J. Hist. ess. 1 : 1.

— — — — Civil wars and Oliver Cromwell. Forster, J. Hist. ess. 1 : 241.

— — — Revolution of 1688 and its historian. Lucas. Secularia, 268. — Macaulay. Ess. 3 : 251.

— — in 19th cent. Ministry, 1839. Brougham. Works, 9 : 401.

— — Legendary period. Reed, H. Lec. Eng. hist. 46.

— — Macaulay's. Whittier. Lit. recre. 47.

— — New sources of. Brewer. Eng. stud. v. 1.

— — Norman conquest. Chambers's Miscel. no. 132. — Kingsley, C. Hist. lec. 245.

— — Omitted chapters of. Lucas. Mornings, 2 : 302.

England, History; Progress of Protestantism shown in. Croly. Hist. sk. v. 1.
— — Rebellion of 1715. Chambers's Miscel. no. 35.
— — Rebellion of 1745–46. Croston. Hist. sites Lanc. 397.
— — Roman and Saxon periods. Reed, H. Lec. Eng. hist. 78.
— — Smollett's. Goldsmith. Miscel. (N. Y. 4 v.) 3 : 449.
— — Storms in ; Henry VIII. DeQuincey. Uncoll. wr. 1 : 275.
— — Study of. Brewer. Eng. stud. 400. — Maurice. Friendship, 187.
— — Teaching. (J. A. Froude) Oxf. ess. '55 : 47.
— — Tudor period. Bibliography. Busch, W. Eng. under Tudors.
— in 13th century. Lightfoot. Hist. ess. 93.
— in the 17th century. Chambers's Papers, no. 12.
— in the first half of the 19th century. Sterling, J. Ess. 1 : 422.
— Industrial and social dangers in. Greg, W. R. Miscel. 1 : 58.
— Inequality in the conditions of life. Arnold, M. Irish ess. 3.
— Journal kept in, 1820–21. Greenwood, F. W. P. Miscel. v. 1.
— Judicial system ; act of 1873. (J. Bryce) Owens college essays, '74 : 423.
— Judiciary of. The law officers of the crown, May, 1872. Fawcett. Speeches, 239.
— Merry. Hazlitt. Sketches.
— Metal founding in, 1893. U. S. Cons. Rept. 42 : 357.
— National character of. Senior. Hist. ess. 1 : 34.
— National prosperity of, and the reformation. Freeman. Hist. ess. 4 : 284.
— Norman conquest of. Taylor, W. C. Revol. 1 : 313.
— — and literature. Brooke, S. A. Hist. early Eng. lit. 101.
— Old. Peabody, A. P. Rem. Eur. v. 1.
— Peasants' revolt. Sergeant, L. Wiclif, 272, 281.
— Political future of. Brownson. Works, 16 : 489.
— Politics of. *See* Great Britain.
— Pottery trade, 1891. (W. Burgess) U. S. Cons. Rept. 38 : 94.
— Prices in, in 1873. Leslie, T. E. C. Ess. pol. econ. 349.
— Progress in. Froude. Short stud. 2 : 245.
— Rambling in. Appleton, T. G. Chequer-work, 181.
— Religion in, during civil wars. Disraeli, I. Curios. (N. Y. 4 v.) 4 : 356.
— Religious and moral condition, 18th century. Ryle, J. C. Chr. leaders, 11.
— Religious institutions of olden. Burke, S. H. Men of Reforma. 1 : 353. 2 : 29.
— Revival of Christianity in, 18th century. Ryle, J. C. Chr. leaders, 21.
— The road to. Higginson, T. W. Contemp. 349.
— Rural life in. Irving. Sk. book, 49.
— Saxon and Danish. Stillé. Stud. med. 188.
— Second visit to. Willis. Fam. persons, 132.
— South-east, Iron works of. Lower. Contri. 85.
— State of parties at the death of Edward VI. Burke, S. H. Men of Reforma. 2 : 294.
— Taine's. Scherer. Ess. Eng. lit. 70.
— to Cape Town. Froude. Oceana, 18.
— Tour through, 1829. Griffin, E. D. Rem. 2 : 177.
— towns in, Origin and growth of. Jessopp, A. Studies, 112.

England, Trade disputes in, 1892. (H. W. Metcalf) U. S. Cons. Rept. 39 : 721.
— Tramways and waterworks in, 1891. (W. R. Smyth) U. S. Cons. Rept. 37 : 453.
— Travels in. Ossoli. At home, 186.
— two hundred years ago. (B. Chaix) Am. Geog. Soc. 22 : 56.
— under the Saxons. Lord, J. Beacon, 2 : 95.
— Working people of, in 1840. Carlyle. Past & present.
— Young. Saintsbury. Misccl. css. 253.
English, J. E. Patten, J. Sk. of men of prog.
English, Wm. H., with portrait. Rogers, A. C. Repres. men, 221.
English, British and American. Tucker, G. M. Our com. speech, 151.
— College-entrance. (R. Jones) Nat. Educa. Assoc. '97 : 684.
— College study of. (W. H. Crawshaw) N. Y. Regents' Rept. 103 : 775.
— Conference on, of Committee of Ten. (A. F. Nightingale) U. S. Bur. Ed. Rept. '92–93 : 1484.
— the core of a secondary course. (J. C. Hanna) Nat. Educa. Assoc. '98 : 665.
— good, What is ? Peck, H. T. Good English, 3.
— How to write. DeQuincey. Uncoll. wr. 2 : 55.
— in American schools. (E. S. Cox) Nat. Educa. Assoc. '85 : 181.
— in business schools. (S. A. Spencer) Nat. Educa. Assoc. '97 : 797.
— in elementary schools. (M. A. Newell) Nat. Educa. Assoc. '72 : 136.
— in schools of technology. Walker, F. A. Discus. in educa. 111.
— in secondary schools. (C. C. Thach) Nat. Educa. Assoc. '98 : 94.
English admirals. Stevenson, R. L. Virgin. 179.
English and Americans. Fullerton, W. M. Patriotism, 59.
English ballads, Early. Morley. Eng. writ. v. 3.
— Hazlitt. Eng. poets.
English, British and American. Tucker, G. M. Our com. speech, 151.
English cant and slang. Lucas. Mornings, 1 : 334.
English Channel, Battle in, June, 1666. Low, C. R. Great battles.
— Cruise in. Smalley. Lond. lett. 2 . 398.
— Tunnel under. Gladstone. Speeches, 10 : 27.
— Smalley. Lond. lett. 2 : 356. — Freeman. Hist. ess. 4 : 219.
English character. Smiles. Self-help.
— incompatible with the Irish. Arnold, M. Irish ess. v. 1.
English characteristics, Misrepresentation of. Hatton, J. To-day in Amer. 1 : 24.
English charity. Head, F. B. Descr. ess. 1 : 46.
English civilization, Requisites for the progress of. Arnold, M. Irish ess. 3.
English composition. Kingsley, C. Lit. lec. 229.
— in elementary schools. (E. R. Shaw) Nat. Educa. Assoc. '98 : 87.
English drama, religious. Bates, K. L. Eng. relig. drama.
English historians. Morley, H. Eng. writ. 7 : 267.
English home life. Guild. Abroad again, 76.
English homes, Old. Mitchell. Wet days, 177.
English instruction for children. (O. T. Bright) Nat. Educa. Assoc. '84 : 217.
English language. Webster. N. Papers, 289.
— British and American English. Proctor, R. A. Leis. read. 169.
— Dialects of. Garnett. Philol. ess. 41, 147.

English language, Dictionaries of. DeQuincey. Note-book (Bost.), 274.
— Dictionary of, Johnson's, Latham's ed. Dasent. Jest & earnest, 2 : 1.
— Evolution of, 449–1879. (J. A. Weisse) N. Y. Regents, 93 : 553.
— Formation, character, and destiny of. Schaff. Lit. & poetry, v. 1.
— grammar of, Proper construction of a. (A. Brown) N. Y. Regents, 85 : 560.
— — Science of. (W. Harkins) N. Y. Regents, 88 : 615.
— — Study of. (C. S. Halsey) N. Y. Regents, 79, app. : 128.
— History of. Rogers, H. Ess. 3 : 227. — Wright, T. Ess. archæol. 2 : 28.
— in America. (C. A. Bristed) Camb. ess. '55 : 57.
— in elementary schools. (Zalmon Richards) Nat. Educa. Assoc. '77 : 175.
— in schools. Seeley, J. R. Lec. & ess. 217; or Rom. imp. 230.
— in Shakespeare's time. Lowell. Writ. 3 : 7.
— its changes since the 16th cent. Bailey, S. Discourses, 51.
— Lexicography of. Garnett. Philol. ess. 1.
— Logical analysis of. (F. S. Jewell) N. Y. Regents, 78 : 382.
— Modes of teaching. Webster, N. Papers, 307.
— Origin of. Dasent. Jest & earnest, 1 : 310.
— — Disraeli, I. Amen. (N. Y. 2 v.) 1 : 132.
— Orthography and orthoepy of. Disraeli, I. Amen. (N. Y. 2 v.) 2 : 21.
— Our spoken English. Wheeler, D. H. By-ways, 211.
— Pronunciation of. Whitney, W. D. Orient, 2 : 202.
— The Queen's. Cozzens. Bushwhacker, 81.
— — Alford's. Whitney, W. D. Orient, 2 : 166.
— Study of. Latham. Opuscula, v. 1. — (E. Bouton) N. Y. Regents, 98, app. : 275.
— Vicissitudes of. Disraeli, I. Amen. (N. Y. 2 v.) 1 : 151. — (R. Thornton) Evol. Crys. pal. lec. 131.
English law, History of, and politics. Pollock. Ess. in juris. 198.
English life in the 14th century. Lord, J. Beacon, 3 : 59.
English literature. Kingsley, C. Lit. lec. 245.
— Ancient and modern, Spirit of. Hazlitt. Dram. Eliz.
— and French literature, Contrasts of. Saintsbury. Miscel. ess. 300.
— Augustan age of. Hunt, T. W. Rep. Eng. prose, 80.
— Bibliography. Newark (N. J.) Free Pub. Lib. '94.
— Brooke's Primer of.ʿ Arnold, M. Mixed ess.
— Chateaubriand on. Prescott. Biog. miscel. 245.
— Classical and romantic schools of. (W. Rushton) Afternoon lec. 1 : 41.
— compared with French. Arnold, M. Ess. in crit. v. 1.
— Criticism of. Porter, N. Books, 285.
— Development of, from Chaucer to Wordsworth. Clough. Prose rem. 333.
— Early. Mitchell, D. G. English lands, 1 : 1.
— Founders' age. Wheeler, D. H. By-ways, 108.
— Goethe's relation to. Sanborn. Life and genius of Goethe.
— Groundwork of. Budd, H. St. Mary's Hall lec. 138.
— in 18th century. Stephen, L. Eng. thought, 2 : 366, 435.
— in French universities. (A. L. Chevrillon) Cong. Educa. Chic. '93, 168.

English literature in secondary schools. (W. P. Trent) Nat. Educa. Assoc. '96 : 104.
— Influence of the Celt in. Morley, H. Marot, 2 : 248.
— — of foreign literature on. (Ja. Byrne) Afternoon lec. 3 : 35.
— — of Italian works of imagination on. Hallam. Remains, 180.
— — of national character on. (Ja. Byrne) Afternoon lec. 1 : 1.
— — of Protestantism on. Hunt, T. W. Rep. Eng. prose, 63.
Methods of instruction in. (J. H. Gilmore) N. Y. Regents, 96 : 350. — (T. J. Backus) N. Y. Regents, 103, app. : 55.
— Place of, in higher education. (A. B. Stark) Nat. Educa. Assoc. '77 : 24.
— — in popular education. (F. H. Underwood) Nat. Educa. Assoc. '72 : 159.
— Renaissance in. Burton, R. Lit. likings, 313.
— Restoration writers. Gosse, E. From Shakesp. 193.
— Saxon and Norman periods. Washburn, E. W. Stud. Eng. lit. 1 : 21.
— Scottish influence in. Masson. Ess. 391; or Wordsworth, 75.
— Study of. (H. W. Mabie) N. Y. Regents' Rept. 107 : 411.
— — in French universities. (A. L. Chevrillon) Nat. Educa. Assoc. '93 : 168.
— — in public schools. (A. P. Marble) Nat. Educa. Assoc. '94 : 279.
— — Influence and method of. Shedd. Lit. ess. 37.
— — Intensive and extensive. (Mrs. B. S. Pool) N. Y. Regents' Rept. 108 : 770.
— — Introduc. to Greek and Latin. (T. R. Price) Nat. Educa. Assoc. '77 : 262.
— — Thought, not grammar. (Eliz. Weingand) N. Y. Regents' Rept. 108 : 766.
— Teaching of. (M. G. Glazebrook) Thirteen ess. educa.
— — Histor. method in. (J. M. Garnett) Nat. Educa. Assoc. '79 : 87.
— — in high schools. (F. A. March) Nat. Educa. Assoc. '72 : 240.
— — in one high school. (R. G. Huling) Nat. Educa. Assoc. '91 : 632.
— — in secondary schools. (J. B. McChesney) Nat. Educa. Assoc. '88 : 405. — (S. Thurber) Nat. Educa. Assoc. '98 : 671.
— — A term's work in. (H. A. Frink) N. Y. Regents, 97, app. : 189.
— Thoughts on modern. Hobart, V. H. H. Ess. & miscel. 1 : 247.
— to the reign of Charles II. Griffin, E. D. Rem. 2 : 375.
— Victorian. Hales. Folia. litt. 317.
— What the colleges want in. (R. Jones) Nat. Educa. Assoc. '97 : 684.
English lyrical poetry. Dennis, J. Stud. Eng. lit. 288.
English melody. Hogarth. Mem. opera, 1 : 135.
English mind. Whipple. Charac.
English novelists. Hazlitt. Comic.
— of the restoration. Masson. Ess. 88.
English officers in America. (E. E. Hale) Am. Antiq. Soc. Proc. n. s. 1 : 442.
English or British ? (T. Foster) Proctor, R. A. Leis. read. 130.
English peculiarity, An. Hamerton. Human interc. 239.
English people, Ancestors of. (Grant Allen) Proctor, R. A. Nat. stud. 212.
— Character of. Hope. Ess. v. 1.

English people, French idea of. Goldsmith. Miscel. (N. Y. 4 v.) 1 : 140.
— "John Bull." Friswell. About, 22.
— Origin of. (A. S. Wilkins) Manch. Sci. lec. 3–4 : 37. — Proctor. Light sci. 3 : 252.
— Race composition of. (J. W. Donaldson) Camb. ess. '56 : 30.
English periodical essayists. Hazlitt. Comic.
English periodicals. Sterling, J. Ess. 2 : 45.
English poetry, Classical school of. Roscoe, W. C. Poems & ess. v. 2.
— Old. Burton, R. Liter. likings, 173. — Lawrance, H. Queens, v. 2.
— Rousseau's influence on. Texte, J. Rousseau, 292.
English political societies. Daly, J. B. Radicals, 199.
English preachers. Broadus. Lec. hist. preach. 186.
English prose. Washburn, E. W. Stud. Eng. lit. 143. — Saintsbury. Miscel. ess. 1, 81.
— Bibliography. Clark, J. S. Stud. Eng. prose writers.
English race, Origin and political life of. Anderson, M. B. Papers, 2 : 3.
English rural classes in the 11th century. Allen, W. F. Essays, 319.
— in the 13th century. Allen, W. F. Essays, 331.
English rural poetry. Dennis, J. Stud. Eng. lit. 356.
English society, Disraeli's "Endymion" and. (J. W. Howe) Ess. from Critic, 153.
English sonnet. Dennis, J. Stud. Eng. lit. 392.
English-speaking brotherhood. Rosebery. Apprec. 261.
English-speaking nations, Religious mission of. (H. H. Jessup) Barrows, J. H. Parl. relig. 2 : 1122.
English-speaking race, The. Curtis, G. W. Orations, 1 : 391.
English traits and character. Goldsmith. Miscel. (N. Y. 4 v.) 2 : 18.
English verbs of command. Abel, C. Ling. ess. 79.
English verse, The principles of. Hodgson. Outcast, 209.
English village life in 1282. Jessopp, A. Coming of friars, 53.
English weather. Mitchell. Wet days, 155.
— Victorian. Dowden. Transcripts, 153.
English woods ; a contrast. Burroughs. Fresh fields, 37.
English words, Roget's Thesaurus of. Whipple. Lit. & life.
English writers, Old. Hazlitt. Plain speaker, v. 2.
English year, An. Montgomery, J. Prose, 1 : 106.
Englishmen, Character of. Hazlitt. Round table.
— Characteristics of. Stephen, J. F. Ess. by barr. 58.
— in Italy, and Italians in England. Hazlitt, W. C. Offspring, 153.
— their language and countries. Wheeler, D. H. By-ways, 168.
Engravers, Painters and, of New England, Early. (W. H. Whitmore) Mass. Hist. Proc. 9 : 197.
Engraving. Guizot. Fine arts, 43. — Hamerton, P. G. Graphic arts, 398, 449. — Lacroix, P. Arts in mid. ages, 315. — Lossing, B. J. Outline hist. fine arts, 263.
— Bibliography. Singer, H. W., and Strang, W. Etching, engraving, etc.
— White-line, for relief-printing, in XV. and XVI.

centuries. (S. R. Koehler) U. S. Nat. Mus. Rept. '90 : 385.
See also Wood-engraving.
Enjoying one's mind. Mabie. My study fire, 2 : 23.
Enjoyment, Training in. Bosanquet, B. Civil. of Christendom, 237.
Enneking, John Joseph, with portrait. Benjamin, S. G. W. Am. art. v. 1.
Ennius, Quintus. Dunlop, J. Rom. liter. 1 : 78.
— Sellar. Rom. poets repub. 62. — (W. C. Lawton) Warner Lib. 10 : 5475.
Ennui. Bancroft, G. Miscel. 44. — Repplier. Ess. in idle. 137.
— Disappearance of. Higginson. Book & heart, 212.
— Miseries of. Goldsmith. Miscel. (N. Y. 4 v.) 1 : 233.
Enoshima, Island of. Pidgeon. Engineer's holiday, 255.
Enotochopco, Battle of. Dawson. Batt. of U. S. 2 : 321.
Ensilage. N. J. Labor, '79 : 179. '80 : 177.
Enteric or typhoid fever. (G. W. Harrison) Wisc. Health, '95–96 : 91.
Enterkin pass, The. Brown, J. J. Leech, 341.
Enthusiasm, Duty of. Stryker. Hamilton, 48.
— for humanity, Need of. (P. Brooks) Evang. Alliance, '89 : 296.
— Limits of. Newton, W. W. Ess. v. 1.
Enthusiast, The. Watson, E. H. L. Uncon. humor. 173.
Entomological science in the U. S. (J. A. Lintner) N. Y. Regents, 100, app. : 122.
Entomology. Bibliography. Packard, A. S. Textbk. entomol.
— Morals of. (J. Bachman) Charleston book, 30.
Entwisle, Joseph. Wesley & successors, 83 : 115.
Enurchus, or Erortius, St., of Orleans. Charles. Martyrs, 364.
Environment, Influence of, upon human industries. (O. T. Mason) Smithson. Rept. '95 : 639.
— Rela. of institutions to. (W. J. McGee) Smithson. Rept. '95 : 701.
— Rela. of primitive peoples to. (J. W. Powell) Smithson. Rept. '95 : 625.
Envy. Bacon. Ess. — Hazlitt. Sketches ; or Plain speaker, v. 2.
Enyedi, George. Wallace, R. Anti-Trin. biog. 2 : 415.
Enzina. See Encina.
Eon de Beaumont, Chevalier. Russell, W. Eccen. 301. — Smith, G. B. Ambass. 159. — Wilson, H. Characters, 398. — Wraxall, F. C. L. Remark. adv. 2 : 246.
Eons, Christopher. Wallace, R. Anti-Trin. biog. 2 : 440.
Eötövs, Josef. Warner Lib. 10 : 5484. — Wyatt, W. J. Hunga. celeb. 187.
Epaminondas. (E. Curtius) Ferris, G. T. Gr. leaders, 10. — Herbert, H. W. Capt. old world. — Yonge, C. M. Worthies, 141.
— Gustavus Adolphus and. Yonge, C. D. Parallel.
Ephesus. Buckley, J. M. Trav. 3 cont. 509. — Warner, C. D. Levant, 259.
— The chancellor of. Hastings, F. Obscure charac. 275.
— Discoveries at. Newton. Essays, 210.
— Ruins of. Tweedie. Ruined cities, 9.
— St. Paul and. Lee, J. S. Sac. cities, 170.
Ephrata, Pa. Gibbons, P. E. Penn. Dutch.
Ephrem, the Syrian, St. Blakey, R. Prim. fa-

Eratosthenes. Mahaffy, J. P. Greek life, ch. 11.

Erbury, William. Wallace, R. Anti-Trin. biog. 2 : 167.

Ercilla y Zúñiga, Alonso de. Shelley, Mrs. Men of Ita. 3 : 103.

Erckmann-Chatrian, with portraits. (F. Loliée) Warner Lib. 10 : 5538. — Men of 3d repub. 246.

Erfurt, University of. Ullman. Reformers, 217.

Eric VI., king of Denmark. Capgrave. Henries, 167.

Eric IX. [of Denmark] to Christian II. Doran. Monarchs, 2 : 218.

Eric XIV., Story of. Doran. Monarchs, 2 : 240.

Eric, bishop of Garda. Clarke, R. H. Cath. bishops, 1 : 13.

Ericson, Leif, and Norse sagas. (H. W. Haynes) Mass. Hist. Soc. Proc. 2d ser. 7 : 349.

Ericsson, John, with portrait. Hubert, P. G., jr. Inventors, 178. — Youmans. Pioneers sci. 374.

Eridge castle. Balch, E. Old Eng. homes, 99.

Erie canal. Buffalo Hist. Soc. papers, v. 2.

— Enlargement of. (T. P. Roberts) Deep waterways conven. 1 : 241.

Erie, Fort, Siege of. Dawson. Batt. of U. S. 2 : 363.

Erie, Lake, Battle of. Allen, Jos. Battles Brit. navy, 2 : 439. — Dawson. Batt. of U. S. 2 : 274. — Roosevelt, T. Naval war, 1812, 254. — Silliman. Gallop, 56, 104, 314.

— Naval operations on, in 1812. Roosevelt, T. Naval war 1812, 155.

Erie railway war in 1868. Adams, C. F. Erie, 1.

— A great lawsuit and a field fight. Black, J. S. Ess. & sp. 109.

Erigena. See Scotus.

Erinna. Arnold, E. Poets of Greece, 137. — Mills. Poets of Greece, 97.

Erle, Sir Wm. Grant, J. Bench & bar, 2 : 70.

Ermenberge, queen of Egfrid. Hall. Queens bef. Conq. 269.

Ermenilda, queen of Wulphere. Hall. Queens bef. Conq. 273.

Erne river. Allingham. Varieties, 3 : 48.

Ernest II., Duke. Taylor, B. At home, 2 : 243.

Ernestus Augustus, king of Hanover and duke of Wellington. Fitzgerald, P. Royal dukes, 2 : 247. — Malortie. Here, there, 1.

Ernst, Heinrich W., with portrait. Ehrlich, A. Cel. violin. 91.

Ero. Hahn-Hahn. Fathers, 246.

Errata. Disraeli, I. Curios. (N. Y. 4 v.) 1 : 135.

Erratic Enrique, pseud. See Lukens, H. C. Clemens. Funny fellows.

Erring and dependent, Duty of the state to the. (W. R. Stewart) Conf. char. & correc. '98 : 1.

Error. Dodge, M. A. Stumbl. 388.

Errorists, Working with. Beecher. New star papers, 187.

Errors of speech, Common. Mathews. Words, 326.

Erskine, Lady Ann Agnes. Burder. Pious wom. 402.

Erskine, Ebenezer. Blaikie, W. G. Preachers Scot. 204. — (J. Mitchell) St. Giles lec. 3 : 149. — Taylor, W. M. Scot. pulpit, 163.

— and Ralph. Ker. Scot. national, 64.

Erskine, Henry. Jeffrey, F. Contrib. Ed. Rev. — Townsend. 12 judges, 2 : 139.

Erskine, John. Blaikie, W. G. Preachers Scot. 261.

Erskine, John. See Mar, J. Erskine, earl of.

Erskine, Ralph. Blaikie, W. G. Preachers Scot. 205. — McCosh. Scot. phil. 86.

Erskine, Thomas, Lord. Adams, C. K. Rep.

Brit. orat. 2 : 262. — Brougham. Works, 3 : 314. 7 : 209. — Campbell. Ld. Chan. 8 : 223. — Edgar. Footpr. 103. — Foss. Judges, 8 : 268. — Georgian era, 2 : 313. — Harsha. Orators, 211. — Rogers, S. Recol. 187. — Roscoe, H. Em. lawyers, 2 : 136. — Shairp. Portraits, 60. — Taylor, W. C. Mod. Brit. Plut. 128. — Townsend. 12 judges, 1 : 398. 2 : 1. — Browne, I. Gr. lawyers, 90. — Grant, Jas. Bench & bar, 1 : 45. — Goodrich, C. A. Sel. Brit. eloq. — Mathews, W. Oratory, 346. — Sinclair, J. Sketches. — Stanton, H. B. Reforms, 37.

Erskine families. Taylor, J. Fam. of Scot. 2 : 105.

Eruptive diseases, infectious, Sanitary precautions against. (W. Squire) Trans. Soc. Sci. Lond. '75 : 554.

Esau. Geikie, C. Old Test. char. 55.

Eschatology. Whedon. Ess. 2 : 351.

Eschenbach, Wolfram, Sir Percival. Winkworth. Church singers Germ. 54.

Escorial Palace, The. Hay, J. Castil. days, 213. — Stirling-Maxwell. Ann. art. Spain, 1 : 206. — Thomas, M. Scamper thr. Spain, 53. — Stoddard, C. A. Span. cit. 88.

Escovedo. Froude, J. A. Span. Armada, 120.

Esdraelon and Nazareth. (H. B. Tristram) Wilson, C. W. Pictur. Palest. 2 : 25.

— Plain of. Stuart-Glennie. Pilgrim. 328.

Eskimo collection in U. S. Nat. Mus. (T. D. Bolles) U. S. Nat. Mus. Rept. '87 : 335.

Eskimos; Eastern Inoits. Reclus. Prim. folk, 1.

— Graphic art of. (W. J. Hoffman) U. S. Nat. Mus. Rept. '95 : 739.

— Lamps of. (Walter Hough) U. S. Nat. Mus. Rept. '96 : 1025.

— Western Inoits. Reclus. Prim. folk, 48.

— A year among. (F. Boas) Am. Geog. Soc. 19 : 383.

Esoteric, Exoteric and. Godwin, W. Ess. 3.

Esoteric economy. Repplier, A. Points of view.

Espartero, Baldomero. Em. persons, 2 : 125.

Espinel, Vincente de. Shelley, Mrs. Men of Ita. 3 : 239.

Espronceda, José de. Kennedy. Poets of Spain, 291. — (M. J. Serrano) Warner Lib. 10 : 5549.

Espy, James Pollard. Youmans. Pioneers sci. 196.

Esquiros, Henri Alphonse. Warner Lib. 10 : 5556.

Essay, The. Watson, E. H. L. Uncon. humor, 1.

— Farewell to. Hazlitt, Winterslow.

— Passing of the. Repplier, A. In dozy hours, 226.

Essay-writing. Bulwer, E. Caxtoniana. — Hazlitt. Sk. — Jones, W. A. Ess. on authors, 13. — Smith, Alex. Dreamthorp, 27.

Essayists, English. Friswell. Essays, 93.

— Old and new. Smith, Alex. Last leaves, 210.

Essays and essayists. Henley. Views, 188.

Essays and reviews. Thirlwall, C. Remains, 2 : 1. — Hunt, J. Rel. thought 16th cent. 200. — Stanley. Essays, 2. — Wilberforce, S. Ess. Quar. 1 : 104.

— Privy Council judgment on. Stanley, Essays, 3.

Essenes. DeQuincey. Hist. ess. (Bost.) 1 : 29. — DeQuincey. Avenger (Bost.). 107. — Stanley, A. P. Jewish church.

Essex, Algernon Capel, earl of, with portrait. Caulfield. Kit-cat, 94.

Essex, Margaret Elizabeth, countess of. Costello. Englishwomen, 2 : 209.

Essex, Robert Devereux, 2d earl of. Barrow, J. Nav. worthies, 333. — Bourne, H. R. F. Eng. seam. 2 : 256. — Fuller. Worthies, 2 : 76. —

Lodge. Portr. (Bohn) v. **2**. — Burke, S. H. Hist. portr. Tudor, **4** : 551. — Cust. Warriors 17th cent. v. **1**. — Southey & Bell. Brit. admirals, v. **4**. — Wrangham. Brit. Plutarch, v. **2**.

Essex, Robert Devereux, 2d earl of, and Queen Elizabeth. Menzies, S. Roy. fav. **1** : 286. — Strickland. Queens Eng. **7** : 125.
— Rebellion of. Ewald. Stories fr. state pap. **1** : 258.

Essex, R. Devereux, 3d earl of. Cust. Warriors civ. **1** : 271. — Creasy. Etonians, 102. — Lodge. Portraits (Bohn), v, **4**.

Essex, Thomas Cromwell, earl of. Burke, I. H. Hist. portr. Tudor, **2** : 129. — Lodge. Portraits (Bohn), v. **1**.

Essex, Walter Devereux, earl of. Lodge. Portraits (Bohn), v. **2**. — Hopkins, S. Puritans, **2** : 114. — Taylor, W. C. Rom. biog. v. **1**.

" **Essex**," Capture of by "Phoebe" and "Cherub." Dawson. Batt. of U. S. **2** : 330. — Roosevelt, T. Naval war 1812, 291.

Essex House, Siege of. Timbs. Abbeys, **1** : 70.

Estaing, Pierre d', and the lord of Mirabeau. Wright, T. Nar. sorcery, **1** : 85.

Estaugh, Elizabeth. Clement, J. Noble deeds, 284.

Estcourt, Richard. Doran. Ann. stage, **1** : 220.

Este, Anna de, Olympia Morata and. Gearey. Dau. of Italy, **1**.

Este, David K. Mansfield, E. D. Pers. mem. 161.

Este, Guarino and Lionello d'. Symonds. Reviv. of learn. 299.

Estes, Bedford Mitchell. Am. Bar Assoc. **21** : 706.

Estes Park, Colorado. Pidgeon. Engineer's holiday, 113.

Esther. Geikie, C. Old. Test. char. 456.

Esthonian literature. Bibliography. Kirby, W. F. Hero of Esthonia, etc.

Estienne, Family of, French printers. Pattison. Ess. **1** : 66.

Eston, Adam. Williams, F. Eng. card. **1** : 422.

Estrees, Gabrielle d'. *See* Beaufort, Duchess of.

Esturmy, Sir William. Manning, J. A. Speakers, 34.

Etching club, Selection of etchings by the. Cracroft. Ess. **2** : 158.

Eternity, Man's conception of. Mansel. Letters, 111.
— On the supposed scriptural expression for. De Quincey. Theo. ess. Bost. **1** : 127.

Ethelbert I. Simson, Jas. Em. men of Kent, 10.

Ethelburga, "the silent," queen of Edwin "the great." Hall. Queens bef. Conq. 232.

Etheldreda, St. (St. Audrey) Charles. Martyrs, 414.

Ethelfleda, Queen. Williams, Jane. Lit. wom. 19. — Hall. Queens bef. Conq. 343.

Ethelgiva, queen of Edwy "the fair." Hall. Queens bef. Conq. 366.

Ethelhard, 793-805. Hook. Abps. Cant. **1** : 254.

Ethelnoth, 1020-35. Hook. Abps. Cant. **1** : 477.

Ethelred, 870-889. Hook. Abps. Cant. **1** : 297.

Ether, The, and its functions. Lodge. Mod. views of elec.
— Luminiferous. (G. G. Stokes) Smithson. Rept. '93 : 113.

Ether, Application of, in surgery. Cochrane, R. Benef. lives, 174.

Etherege, Sir George. Gosse. 17th cent. stud. 231. — Dunham. Lit. & sci. men, **3** : 175. — Jesse. Court of Eng. Stuarts, **3** : 314. — Street, G. S. Miniatures, 34.

Etheridge, Mrs. Annie. Moore, F. Women of the war, 513. — Brockett. Woman's work, 747.

Etherization, Painless surgery by. Parton. Triumphs.
— Psychical effects of. Bowen, F. Gleanings, 242.

Ethical culture in elementary and secondary schools. (Delia L. Williams) Nat. Educa. Assoc. '92 : 101.
— in elementary schools. (C. De Garmo) Nat. Educa. Assoc. '91 : 170.
— in higher education. (J. H. Canfield) Nat. Educa. Assoc. '92 : 108.
— in the kindergarten. (Irwin Shepard) Nat. Educa. Assoc. '92 : 96.
See Moral training.

Ethical forces, Development of. (T. T. Munger) Conf. char. & correc. '95 : 16.

Ethical ideas, Essential oneness of. (I. C. Hultin) Barrows, J. H. Parl. relig. **2** : 1003.

Ethical movement, The. (S. Coit) Relig. systems, 787.

Ethical philosophy and evolution. Knight, W. Ess. 109.
— Mackintosh's. Everett, A. H. Crit. ess. 283.
— Progress of. Mackintosh, J. Miscel. 94.

Ethical societies, Aims of. Stephen, L. Soc. rights, **1** : 1.

Ethical society, Function of an. Bosanquet, B. Civil. of Christendom, 160.

Ethical systems. Hedge, F. H. Martin Luther, 225.

Ethics. Balfour, A. J. Founda. belief, 11. — Schopenhauer. Selec. ess. 195.
— and morals. Pollock. Ess. in juris. 287.
— and religion, Relation of. Martineau, J. Ess. **4** : 293.
— and the struggle for existence. Stephen, L. Soc. rights, **1** : 221.
— Bibliography. Hyslop, J. H. Elements ethics. — Muirhead, J. H. Elements ethics. — Ryland, F. Manual ethics.
— Christian. (R. L. Ottley) Gore, C. Lux mundi, 467.
— — and the ethics of Christ. Cobbe, F. P. Studies, 3.
— Cosmic evolution and. (L. G. Janes) Brooklyn Eth. Assoc. Life, 3.
— in its bearing on theism. Ward, W. G. Ess. theism, **2** : 83.
— Jouffroy's. Brownson. Works, **14** : 266.
— Mr. Mill on the foundation of morality. Ward, W. G. Ess. theism, **1** : 77.
— Nature and grace. Brownson. Works, **14** : 348.
— The new. Bax. Ethics of socialism, **1**. — Courtney. Stud. philos. 115.
— Object and scope of. Wilson, J. Thoughts sci. 101.
— of Christianity. Martineau, J. Studies, 299.
— Primitive. Brinton. Races & peo. 58.
— Rights and duties. Brownson. Works, **14** : 290.
— Sovereignty of. Emerson. Lec. & biog. sk. 175.
— Spencer's data of. Pollock. Ess. in juris. 352.
— The two enthusiasms. Bax. Relig. of socialism, 128.
— Whewell on. Martineau, J. Ess. **3** : 337.

Ethnic religions, Divine providence and. (T. J. Scott) Barrows, J. H. Parl. relig. **2** : 921.

Ethnography ; earliest migration of nations. Schlegel. Æsthet. (Bohn) 500.
— English. (J. W. Donaldson) Camb. ess. '56 : 30.
— Physical elements of. Brinton. Races & peo. 17.

Ethnological groups, Subjectivity of. Latham. Opuscula, 138.

Ethnologist and historian, Mutual obligations of. (O. T. Mason) Am. Hist. Assoc. **4** : 205.

Europe, Politics of, in 1829. Croly. Hist. sk. 75.
— — in 1873. Brownson. Works, 18 : 502.
— Primacy of the great powers. Lawrence. Ess. internat. law, 208.
— Revolutions of 1848. Brownson. Works, 16 : 102.
— Schools of. Mann, H. Lec. 2 : 230.
— Shadow of. Higginson. New world, 27.
— Sheep and wool in, 1892. (A. O. Bourn) U. S. Cons. Rept. 39 : 395.
— Tavernier's travels in, 1630–80. St. John. Cel. travelers, 1 : 180.
— Things and thoughts in. Ossoli. At home, 120.
— Tournefort's travels in, 1675–1700. St. John. Cel. travelers, 2 : 7.
— tribes of, Characteristics of. Brinton. Races & peo. 154, 211.
— Union within. Congreve, R. Ess. 127.
— Wars of, 1851–95. Laing, S. Problems, 340.
Eusden, Laurence. Austin & Ralph. Laureates, 239. — Hamilton, Wal. Poets laur.
Eusebius, bishop of Cæsarea. Broadus. Lec. hist. preach. 63. — With portrait. Blakey, R. Prim. fathers, 143. — Cave. Lives of fathers, 2 : 95. — Lang. Lett. to dead au. 162. — (H. M. Gwatkin) Lefroy, W. Lec. eccl. hist. 325.
— Silence of. Lightfoot. Ess. Super. relig. 32.
Eusebius, bishop of Emisa. Blakey, R. Prim. fathers, 239. — Cave. Lives of fathers, 3 : 400.
Eustis, Henry L. Vaille & Clark. Harv. book, v. I.
Eutaw Springs, S. C., Battle of. Dawson. Batt. of U. S. 1 : 711.
Euthanasia. Scoffern. Stray leaves, 460.
Evangelical Alliance. Brownson. Works, 8 : 461.
— Aim of. (W. E. Dodge) Evang. Alliance, '89: 1.
— Methods of. (F. Russell; J. L. Phillips) Evang. Alliance, '89 : 101.
Evangelical movement, History of. Gladstone. Glean. 7 : 201.
Evangelical revival. Brooke, S. Theol. Eng. poets, 11.
"Evangelical" succession, The. Stephen. Ess. eccl. biog. 379.
Evangelical teaching. Eliot, G. Ess. 118.
Evangelicalism, Spirit of. Kirkus. Miscel. 387.
Evangelicals, Characteristics of the. Taylor, W. M. Scott. pulpit, 176.
Evangelism, Christian, in American Christianity. (J. Brand) Barrows, J. H. Parl. relig. 2 : 984.
Evans, Augusta J. Raymond, I. Southland writ. 2 : 566.
Evans, Caleb. Ivimey. Eng. Bapt. 4 : 274.
Evans, Captain. Whitehead, C. Highwaymen, 1 : 201.
Evans, Christmas. Broadus. Lec. hist. preach. 226. — Pierce, B. K. Em. dead, 338.
Evans, Hugh. Ivimey. Eng. Bapt. 4 : 270.
Evans, Israel. Headley, J. T. Chaplains Revol. 300.
Evans, James Harington. Hatfield, E. F. Poets of church, 234. — Miller,·Jos. Singers church, 2d ed. 389.
Evans, John. Smith, C. R. Retrospec. 3 : 126.
Evans, Jonathan. Hatfield, E. F. Poets of church, 236. — Miller, Jos. Singers church, 2d ed. 297.
Evans, Joseph R. Winslow, S. N. Biog. Phila. merch. 107.
Evans, Oliver. Howe, H. Em. mech. 68. — Seymour, C. C. B. Self-made, 440.
Evans, Thomas Edward. Smith, C. R. Retrospec. 3 : 137.

Evarts, Jeremiah. Pierce, B. K. Em. dead, 364.
Evarts, William M. Bungay. Repr. men, 82. — With portrait. Scott, H. W. Dist. Am. lawy. 341.
Eve, Milton's, Character of. Hazlitt. Round table.
Eve, Maria Lou. Raymond, I. Southland writ. 1 : 455.
Evelyn, John. Adams, W. H. D. Worthies Ch. Eng. 168. — Choate, I. B. Wells ot Eng. 294. With portrait. Warner Lib. 10 : 5591.
— and Robert Boyle. Thomson, Mrs. Cel. friend. 1 : 1.
— Diary of. Saunders, F. Famous books, 45.
Evelyn, Mrs. John. Burder. Pious wom. 310. — Costello. Englishwomen, 2 : 305.
Evening schools. (A. P. Marble) Nat. Educa. Assoc. '87 : 186.
Evenus. Mills. Poets of Greece, 147.
Everett, Alexander Hill. Griswold. Prose writ. 284. — Loring, J. S. Hundred Bost. ora. 480.
— Essays of. Jones, W. A. Ess. on authors, 32.
Everett, Charles C. Vaille & Clark. Harv. book, v. I.
Everett, David. Loring, J. S. Hundred Bost. ora. 337.
Everett, Edward, with portrait. Am. nat. portr. gall. v. 4. — Badeau. Vagabond, 213. — Bungay. Off-hand, 59. — Duyckinck. Nat. portr. gall. 2 : 400. — Griswold. Prose writ. 330. — Harsha. Orators, 491. — Loring, J. S. Hundred Bost. ora. 525. — Peabody. Harv. rem. 91. — Savage. Liv. rep. men, 240. — (R. C. Winthrop et al.) Mass. Hist. Proc. 8 : 101. — Tuckerman. Charac. 239. — Whipple. Charac. — Willis. Hurry-graphs, 166. — (G. S. Hillard) Hubbard, E. Little jour. 2 : 335 ; Same in Homes Am. authors. — Johnston, A. Amer. ora. 3 : 32. — Lanman, C. Haphazard, 130. — Magoon, E. L. Amer. orators, 65. — Mathews, W. Oratory, 337. — Nichol. Amer. lit. 129. — Richardson. Amer. lit. 1 : 236. — With portrait. Warner Lib. 10 : 5605. — Whittier. Prose works, v. 2. — (E. E. Hale) Vaille & Clark. Harv. book, v. I.
— in 1862. Curtis. From easy ch. v. I.
— Orations of. Jones, W. A. Ess. on authors, 32.
— Oratory of. Gilman, S. Contrib. 231.
Everett, John. Loring, J. S. Hund. Bost. ora. 407.
Everett, William. Putnam, A. P. Singers liberal, 504.
Evergreen, The. [Periodical.] Zangwill. Without prej. 289.
Everheart, Lawrence. Balch, T. Maryland line, 42.
Eversley, Charles Sharo-Lefevre, Viscount. Em. persons, 4 : 129.
Evertsen, Johan. DeLiefde. Dutch adm. 268.
Evesham, John Somers, Baron of, with portrait. Caulfield. Kit-cat, 125.
Evidence, Circumstantial. Godkin. Reflections, 119. See Circumstantial.
Evidences. Mozley, J. B. Lec. I.
Evil, Agency of. Whittier. Lit. recre. 288.
— and good, in Parsism. Matheson. Distinc. mess. 171.
— and misery, Proposals for the speedy extinction of. Thomson, J. Ess. 51.
— Encouragement of. Comfort to Sodom : a sermon. Boyd. Graver tho'ts, 236.
— Existence of. Holland, H. Frag. papers, 162.
— for good. Thompson, H. M. Copy, 298.
— Good and. Conway, M. D. Idols, 163.
— The great cure for. Thomson, E. Essays, 314.

Evil in matters extraordinary, Nature of. Gurney. Tertium, 1 : 227.
— legal, Nature of. Williams, Syd. Forensic, 234.
— Mystery of. Baring-Gould. Mod. diff. 145.
— of life, The great. Reynolds, G. Papers, 428.
— — The use to be made of the. Reynolds, G. Papers, 437.
— Problem of. Kinsley, W. W. Views, 191.
— Rules of, as applicable to history. Forsyth, W. Essays, 438.
— Theory of. Maine. Vilb. com. 295.
— Utilization of. Blackie, J. S. Lay serm. 138.
Evil doers, Charity for. Mathews. Lit. style, 207.
Evil eye, Charms against the. Jones, W. Credulities, 167.
— Fascination and. Story. St. Angelo, 147.
Evolution. Allen, Grant. Falling in love, 31.
— Huxley. Amer. addr. v. 1. — Wilson, J. M. Ess. 236. — Whedon. Ess. 2 : 92. — Wilson, J. M. Ess. & addr. 236.
— and Christianity. (H. Drummond) Barrows, J. H. Parl. relig. 2 : 1316.
— and ethics. (S. T. Skidmore) Nat. Educa. Assoc. '99 : 136.
— and heredity, Problems in. (H. F. Osborn) Smithson. Rept. '92 : 313.
— and its consequences. Mivart. Ess. 2 : 60.
— and its religious bearings. Anderson, M. B. Papers, 1 : 208.
— and religion. Fiske, J. Excurs. 294.
— and theism. Carpenter, W. Benj. Nature, 384.
— Bibliography. Cope, E. D. Organic evolution.
— King, H. C. Selec. bibliog. of evol. — Osborn. From Greeks, 251. — Salem (Mass.) Pub. Lib. Bull. Mar. '96. — Shute, D. K. 1st book in organ. evol.
— Books relating to. Wright, C. Philos. dis. 394.
— by natural selection. Wright, C. Philos. dis. 168.
— Cosmic, as related to ethics. (L. G. Janes) Brooklyn Eth. Assoc. Life, 3.
— defined and applied to history. Shedd. Theo. ess. 121.
— Derivation of man from the monkey. Whipple. Outlooks, 47.
— Development of theory of. Osborn. From Greeks, 1.
— Divergent, through cumulative segregation. (J. T. Gulick) Smithson. Rept. '91 : 269.
— doctrine of, Rise of. Royce, J. Spir. mod. phil. 265.
— — Scope and purport of. Fiske, J. Cent. of science, 39.
— Effect of the theory of, on education. (J. Le Conte) Nat. Educa. Assoc. '95 : 149.
— Ethical philosophy and. Knight, W. Ess. 109; or Studies.
— Ethics of, examined. (J. Iverach) Liv. papers, v. 8.
— Found links of animal life. (A. Wilson) Proctor, R. A. Nat. stud. 105.
— from the religious side. Edgar, S. Autob. notes, 243.
— Grounds and consequences of. Winchell. Sparks geol. ham. 332.
— Has evolution banished God? Gladden. Burn. ques. 1.
— Huxley and. Winchell. Sparks geol. ham. 319.
— in biology. Huxley. Sci. & cul. 281.
— in the light of recent researches. (C. M. O'Leary) N. Y. Regents, 97, app. : 143.
— A limit to. Mivart. Ess. 2 : 289.
— Man and the ape. Wake. Serpent wor. 278.
— Martineau on. Spencer, H. Rec. dis. (N. Y.) 329.

Evolution, Nature and. Royce, J. Spir. mod. philos. 311.
— of man. Smith, Goldwin. Lec. & ess. 89.
— organic, Factors of. (H. L. Bailey) Smithson. Rept. '97 : 453.
— — Method of. (A. R. Wallace) Smithson. Rept. '94 : 413.
— Palæontological evidences of. (H. S. Williams) N. Y. Regents, 95 : 319.
— Palæontology and. Huxley. Critiques.
— Philosophical basis of. Whittaker, T. Ess. & not. 336.
— Philosophy of. Alviella. Contemp. evol. 35. — Symonds. Ess. 1 : 1.
— Relation to psychology. Sully. Sensa.
— Relation to theism. Carpenter. Nature & man.
— Tait on the formula of. Spencer, H. Var. frag. 75.
— Theory of. Alviella. Contemp. evol. 217. — Rice, W. N. 25 years sci. prog. 59.
— — Moral and religious bearings of. (Miss Bevington) Relig. systems, 768.
Evolutionary ethics. Spencer, H. Var. frag. 111.
Evolutionary principles, Application of, to art and literature. Symonds. Ess. 1 : 42.
Evolutionists, Objections of, against sanitary reform. (S. E. Chaillé) Am. Pub. Health, 6 : 279.
— of 18th century. Osborn. From Greeks, 106.
Ewald, Heinrich. Cheyne. Founders, O. T. crit. 66.
Ewald, Johannes, with portrait. (W. M. Payne) Warner Lib. 10 : 5614.
Ewell, Benjamin S., Col. Pollard. Life of Lee, 457.
Ewell, Richard Stoddart, Gen. Snow. So. generals, 343.
Ewer, Charles. (S. H. Riddel) N. E. Hist.-Gen. Soc. Biog. 2 : 113.
Ewer, Peter Folger. (F. C. Ewer) N. E. Hist.-Gen. Soc. Biog. 2 : 319.
Ewer, Samuel. Ivimey. Eng. Bapt. 2 : 178.
Ewing, Alexander, bishop. (J. C. Lees) St. Giles lec. 3 : 353.
Ewing, Charles, with portrait. [Amer.] Nat. portrait gall. v. 2.
Ewing, John, of Glasgow. Bourne, H. R. F. Eng. merch. 2 : 321.
Ewing, Julia Horatia. (Emily Marshall) Oliphant. Wom. novelists, 298.
Ewins, Thomas. Ivimey. Eng. Bapt. 2 : 530.
Exaggeration. Friswell. Gentle life, 1 : 224. — Gardner, S. J. Aut. leaves, 83.
Examination halls, China. Cumming, C. F. G. Wand. in China, 2 : 206.
Examinations. Laurie, S. S. Educa. add. 144.
— and education. Pollock, F. Oxf. lec. 216.
— as tests for promotions. (H. S. Tarbell) Nat. Educa. Assoc. '87 : 107. — (W. H. Maxwell; G. S. Albee) Nat. Educa. Assoc. '90 : 127.
— Competitive. Todhunter, I. Conflict stud.
— — Chinese. (E. Wentworth) N. Y. Regents, 97, app. : 115.
— — Civil service. Bain, A. Prac. ess. 71. — (H. Mann) Trans. Soc. Sci. Lond. '58 : 200. '59 : 274. — (Sir S. Northcote) Trans. Soc. Sci. Lond. '59 : 279.
— — in general knowledge. (J. Heywood) Trans. Soc. Sci. Lond. '60 : 311.
— — Preparatory training for, in Scotland. (W. G. Blackie) Trans. Soc. Sci. Lond. '60 : 318.
— Higher. (E. O. Haven) N. Y. Regents, 91 : 407.
— school, Arrangement of course of study for. (R. B. Poole) Internat. health exh. 16 : 203.

Eyesight in schools, Hygiene of. (T. D. Reed)
Am. Pub. Health, **20** : 257. — (E. Jackson)
Am. Pub. Health, **21** : 141.
— Industries and. (B. J. Jeffries) Mass. Health,
'82 : 89.
Eyes. Meynell, A. Color, 96.
— Care of the. (C. F. Clark) Ohio Health, '89 :
261.
— Student life and. (A. W. Calhoun) U. S. Bur.
Ed. Circ. '81 : no. 6.
— Why has man two? Mach. Pop. sci. lec. 66.
Eyre, John, with portrait. Morison, J. Fathers
of Lond. Miss. Soc. **1** : 241.
Eyre, Manuel. Winslow, S. N. Biog. Phila.
merch. 227.
Ezekiel. Geikie, C. Old Test. char. 437.

Faber, Frederick William. Hatfield, E. F. Poets
of church, 238. — Macdonald, G. England's
antiphon, 317. — Miles, A. H. Poets of cent.
10 : 299. — Miller, Jos. Singers church, 2d ed.
518.
Faber, Geo. Stanley. Hunt, J. Rel. thought 19th
cent. 40.
Faber, Matthias, 1586–1653. Baring-Gould.
Preachers, 100.
Faber, Peter. Rose. Loyola.
Fabian, St., bishop and martyr, of Rome.
Charles. Martyrs, 70.
Fabiola. Hahn-Hahn. Fathers, 428.
Fable, Definition of. Newbigging. Fables, 1.
Fables, Characteristics of. Newbigging. Fa-
bles, 7.
— Migration of. Müller. Chips, 4; or Sel. ess. **1** :
500.
— Moral and application of. Newbigging. Fables,
13.
— Origin and use of. O'Conor. Ess. 169.
Fabre d'Eglantine, P. F. N., Amours de voyage
of. Dowden. New stud. 121.
Fabriano, Gentile da. Stillman, W. J. Old Ital.
mas. 76. — Symonds. Renais. fine arts, 238.
— Adoration of the Magi. (F. A. Gruyer) Single-
ton, E. Great pic. 98.
Fabulists as censors. Newbigging. Fables, 19.
Faces. Mathews. Conversers, 85.
Facey, William. Ivimey. Eng. Bapt. **2** : 68.
Faction. Bacon. Ess.
Factories, Employment of girls in. (R. S.
Baker) Trans. Soc. Sci. Lond. '68 : 537.
— Inspection of, in the U. S. U. S. Lab. Bull. **2** :
549.
— Mothers in, and infant mortality. (W. C. Tay-
lor *et al.*) Trans. Soc. Sci. Lond. '74 : 569. —
(T. M. Dolan *et al.*) Trans. Soc. Sci. Lond.
'82 : 357.
— Sanitary requirements in. (L. F. C. Garvin)
Am. Pub. Health, **3** : 69.
Factory, A German. Whitman, S. Teuton stud.
131.
Factory education. (E. Akroyd) Trans. Soc. Sci.
Lond. '57 : 151.
Factory girls. (Frances Hicks) Reid, A. New
party, 315.
Factory labor in New England, Early. Mass.
Labor, '83 : 379.
Factory legislation, English, History of. (C. D.
Wright) Mass. Labor, '75 : 115.
Factory operatives in Massachusetts, Intelligence
of. Mass. Educa. **23** : 39.
Factory reformers. Gibbins. Eng. soc. ref. 111.
Factory system, English and American. (H. K.
Oliver) Mass. Labor, '70 : 106.
— in New England. Pidgeon. Old world ques.
253.

Factory town in New England, Study of a. Har-
rison, J. Dang. tend. 156.
Facts and inferences. Bailey, S. Essays, 131.
Fadette. Raymond, I. Southland wr. **2** : 905.
Faed, Thomas, with photo. Cooper, T. Men of
mark, **4** : 30. — Ewart, H. C. Toilers in art,
245.
Faidherbe, L. L. C. Men of 3d repub. 160.
Failings. Friswell. Wick. world, 187.
Failure. Force of adverse circumstances. Ar-
nold, F. Turning-points, 300.
Failures, and what they prove. Thompson,
H. M. Copy, 330.
Fair Oaks, Battle of. Keyes, E. D. 50 years, 450.
Fair trade in England, Depression of agriculture
and. Playfair. Subj. soc. 107.
Fairbairn, Sir Wm. Smith, G. B. Leaders mod.
ind. 335. — Em. persons, **1** : 244. — Chambers,
W. Rem. pers. 146.
— Inventions of. Smiles. Indus. biog.
Fairbairns, The, of Manchester and Leeds. For-
tunes made in bus. **2** : 231.
Fairbanks, Gerry. Loring, J. S. Hundred Bost.
ora. 398.
Fairfax, Lady Anne (Vere). Anderson, J. Mem.
wom. Pur. **1** : 242. — Chapman, W. Women of
purit. 123.
Fairfax, Thos., Lord. Cust. Warriors 17th cent.
v. **2**. — Coleridge. Nor. worthies, **1** : 279. —
Cust. Warriors civ. **2** : 391. — Sabine. Loyal-
ists, 277.
Fairfield, Sumner Lincoln. Griswold. Poets
Am. 265.
Fairholt, Frederick William. Smith, C. R. Re-
trospec. **1** : 218.
Fairies. Jones, W. Credulities, 30.
— and Genii of the East. Hunt. Day by fire, 124.
Fairs, statute, Abolition of. (N. Stephenson)
Trans. Soc. Sci. Lond. '60 : 797.
Fairy tale, Faith, fact, and. Conway, M. D.
Idols, 49.
Fairy tales, Barbaric philosophy in. Clodd, E.
Myths, 188.
— Bibliography. (F. J. Olcott) N. Y. State Lib.
Bull. no. **13** : '98. — Salem (Mass.) Pub. Lib.
Bull. Mar. '96. — Roscoe, W. C. Poems & ess.
v. **2**.
Faith, St. (Fides Foi) of Aquitaine. Charles.
Martyrs, 175.
Faith. Bartol. Rad. prob. 210. — Blackie, J. S.
Lay serm. 113. — Dawson, G. Shakesp. 393.
— Munger. On Threshold, 209. — (H. S. Holland) Gore, C. Lux mundi, 3. — Lubbock. Use
of life, 228. — Wace, H. Lond. mission. 1.
— Aids to. Wilberforce, S. Ess. Quar. **1** : 205.
— and doubt. Walker, H. Gt. Vic. poets, 292.
— and reason, Harmony of. Brownson. Works,
3 : 257.
— — their claims and conflicts. Rogers, H. Reason, 339 ; *or* Ess. **2** : 250. — Rands. Henry Holbeach, **2** : 108.
— and science. (F. Guizot) Noyes, G. R. Theol.
ess. 1.
— and the sciences. Brownson. Works, **9** : 268.
— and sight, Antithesis of. Picton. Mystery, 131.
— and theology. Brownson. Works, **8** : 1.
— and works. Godwin, W. Ess. 137.
— Collapse of. Porter, N. Sci. and sent. 452.
— Essay on. Coleridge. Lit. rem. 425.
— Full assurance of. Wilks. Chr. ess. 56.
— Human certitude and divine faith. Chatard.
Occ. ess. 309.
— impossible without the church. Brownson.
Works, **5** : 417.
— Mysteries of. Brownson. Works, **8** : 28.

Faith needed in political reform. Mazzini. Ess. 25.
— New defense of. Kirkus. Miscel. 213.
— On the life of. Butler, E. For furth. consid. 131.
— Phases of, Newman's. Martineau, J. Miscel.216.
— Protestant rule of. Brownson. Works, 8 : 418.
— rule of, Philosophy of. De Vere. Ess. 253.
— Weak : " Not quite sure." Boyd. Towards sunset, v. 3.
Faith cure. Jeaffreson. Doctors, 162.
Falaiseau, Peter, Sketch of. Agnew. Protes. exiles, 2 : 77.
Falckenstein, Ernst Friedrich Edward Vogel von. Strauss, G. L. M. Men of Ger. 2 : 181.
Falcon, Marie Cornelie, French vocalist. Clayton, E. C. Queens, 323. — Needham. Queens of song.
Falconberg, Mary Cromwell, countess of. Jesse. Court of Eng. Stuarts, 2 : 379.
Falconer, W. Chalmers. Eng. poets, 14 : 381. — Seymour, C. C. B. Self-made, 310. — Wilson, J. G. Poets of Scot. 1 : 235. — Edwards, B. B. Self-taught, 406.
Falconet, Étienne. Brightwell. Byepaths of biog. 38.
Falconius, John. Wallace, R. Anti-Trin. biog. 2 : 230.
Falconius, Thomas. Wallace, R. Anti-Trin. biog. 2 : 230.
Falerii, Siege of. Robson, W. Sieges, 126.
Fales, Mrs. Almira. Brockett. Woman's work, 279.
Fales, Stephen. (A. H. Hoyt) N. E. Hist. Gen.-Soc. Biog. 2 : 234.
Faliero, Marino. Smith, H. G. Romance of hist. 118.
Falk, J. Cobb, J. F. Heroes of charity.
Falk, Paul L. A. Tuttle, H. Ger. pol. lead. 25.
Falkirk. George, H. B. Battles, 40.
Falkland, Lettice, Countess. Burder. Pious wom. 258.
Falkland, Lucius Cary, Viscount. Arnold, M. Mixed ess. 6. — With portrait. Lewis, M. T. Clarendon lives, 1 : 1. — Lodge. Portraits (Bohn), v. 4. — Smith, Gold. Lec. & ess. 219. — Thomson, Mrs. Cel. friend. 2 : 281. — Jesse. Court of Eng. Stuarts, 2 : 172. — Teale, W. H. Laymen, 1. — Tulloch. Rational theol. 17th cent. 1 : 76. — Wallace, R. Anti-Trin. biog. 2 : 148.
— Pym *versus*. Bulwer. Ess. 317.
Falkland islands. (G. C. Hurlbut) Am. Geog. Soc. 19 : 254.
Falkland palace. Mackie, C. Castles of Mary.
Fall of man. Dodge. Sermons to clergy, 33.
— and its consequences. Maitland, S. R. Eruvin, 79 : 113.
— Arminian view of. Whedon. Ess. 1 : 78.
Fall River, Mass., labor troubles at, Causes of. (C. D. Wright) Mass. Labor, '82 : 195.
Fallacies. Bailey, S. Essays. 131. — Proctor, R. A. Leis. read. 278.
— Bentham on. Smith, Syd. Ess. from. Ed. R.
— Popular. Hoyt, J. G. Miscel. 59. — Lamb. Elia. — Mathews. Conversers, 72.
Fallacy, A popular. Lamb. Elia.
Fallen women, Helping. Jeune, Lady. Lesser ques. 156.
Falling out. Friswell. Better self, 255.
Falloux, Comte de. Mémoires. Mivart. Ess. 1 : 95.
Fallows, Rev. F. Lonsdale. Worthies Cumb. v. 6.
Falmouth, Edward Boscawen, 1st earl. Grant, J. Recoll. Lords & Comm. 1 : 104.

Falmouth and Dorset, Elizabeth Bagot, countess of. Jesse. Courts of Eng. Stuarts, 2 : 281.
False pretences. Friswell. Better self, 279.
Falsehood and deceit. Goldsmith. Miscel. (N. Y. 4 v.) 1 : 143.
— An unrecognized form of. Hamerton. Hum. int. 233.
Falstaff, Sir John. Birrell. Obiter, 1 : 200. — Doran. Knights, 276. — Giles, H. Lectures, 1 : 1.
— Merry wives of Windsor and. Winter. Shadows, 243.
— Shakespeare's, Historical element in. (J. Gairdner) Gairdner & Spedding. Stud. 55.
Fame. Goldsmith. Miscel. (N. Y. 4 v.) 1 : 94. — Saunders. Mosaics, 321. — Schopenhauer. Wisdom, 116.
— Different sorts of. Hazlitt. Round table. — Hazlitt, W. C. Offspring, 87.
— Equation of. Higginson. New world, 88.
— Parini on. Leopardi. Ess. 80.
— Penalties of. Zangwill. Without prej. 236.
— Posthumous. Hazlitt. Round table.
— true, Traces and tokens of. Jacox. Lit. life, 390.
— Value of. Mathews, W. Men, p. & t. 355.
Familiar, Charm of the. Repplier. Ess. in min. 171.
Familiar spirit, Michael Scott's. Boyd. Aut. holid. 206.
Familiarity. Hazlitt. Table talk.
Families, great, Rise of. Wynter, A. Fruit betw. leaves, 1 : 139.
— illustrious, Extinction of. Burke, B. Rise of gt. fam. 289.
— past and present. (Lewis Felméri) Nat. Educa. Assoc. '75 : 16.
— Vicissitudes of. Hayward, A. Ess. 3d ser. 258.
Familistère, Society of, Guise, France. N. J. Labor, '82 : 92.
Familists. Bibliography. (A. C. Thomas) Haverford Coll. Stud. May, '93.
Family, The. Maurice, F. D. Soc. morality, 227. — (Canon Furse) Wace, H. Lond. mission. 125.
— and the state. Hoffman, F. S. Sphere, 207.
— Christian and pagan. Brownson. Works, 13 : 526.
— Development of. Wake. Serpent wor. 192.
— Early history of. Lang. Custom, 245.
— Idea of, in modern society. Lorimer, Jas. Studies, nat'l & internat.
Family life, On some historical aspects of. (C. H. Pearson) Butler. Woman's work, 152.
— Right of the state in regard to. Green, T. H. Works, 2 : 536.
— Roman. Duruy. Hist. Rome, 5 : 233.
— Scriptural ideal of. (W. G. Blaikie) Liv. papers, v. 10.
Family religion. Hall, John. Papers, 118.
Family reunions. Cobbe, F. P. Re-echoes, 323.
Family stocks in a democracy. Eliot, C. W. Five Am. cont. 135.
Family ties, Looseness of, in England. Hamerton. Hum. int. 63.
Family worship. Maurice, F. D. Soc. morality, 83.
Famine in Bengal in 1770. Fiske, J. Unseen world, 190.
Fanaticism. Stephen, J. F. Ess. by barr. 123.
— Whittier. Lit. recre. 107.
Fanch, James. Miller, Jos. Singers church, 2d ed. 202.
Fane family. Sanford & Townsend. Gov. fam. 1.

Fate. Emerson. Conduct, 1. — Friswell. Wick. world, 226.

Fatherhood, Doctrine of. Gladden. Ruling ideas, 17.

Fathers and sons. Hamerton. Hum. int. 78.

Fathers, The. Boyd's translations from. Moore, T. Prose & v. 55.

— Opinions and. Thompson, H. M. Copy, 57

Fathers of the U. S., Political depravity of. McMaster. With fathers, 71.

Fatigue in the school-room: how to reduce it. (H. E. Kratz) Nat. Educa. Assoc. '99 : 1090.

— in study. (E. R. Shaw) Nat. Educa. Assoc. '98 : 550.

Faubin-Janson, Charles A. M. J. de. Clarke, R. H. Cath. bishops, 2 : 601.

Faucit, Helena. *See* Martin, Helena F.

Fauconberg, Mary (Cromwell) Belasyse, Lady. Anderson, Jas. Mem. wom. Pur. 2 : 1.

Faugères, Mrs. Margaretta V. Bleecker. Griswold. Fem. poets, 35.

Fauntleroy, H., forger, Trial and execution of, 1824. Thornbury. Old stor. 359.

Faust, Dr. Johann. Dawson, G. Shakesp. 342.

— Hain, J. Varia, 79.

— and his contemporaries. Bax. Ethics of socialism, 147.

— Facts and fancies about. Wilson, H. S. Stud. in hist. 206.

— Legend of. Symonds. Reviv. of learn. 53. — Wright, T. Nar. sorcery. 1 : 133.

Faust, Play of, by W. G. Wills. Winter. Shad. stage, 3 : 162.

Faustina, Bordone. Edwards, H. S. Prima don. 1 : 42.

Fauveau, Felicie de. Ellet. Women artists, 247.

Favart, C. S., ballad opera writer. Hogarth. Mem. opera, 2 : 219.

Faversham Abbey. Timbs. Abbeys, 1 : 321.

Favre, Jules. Em. persons, 2 : 212. — King, E. French pol. lead. 224.

Fawcett, E. Stoddard, R. H. Poets' homes, 75.

Fawcett, Henry. Bolton, S. K. Fam. Eng. statesm. — With photo. Cooper, T. Men of mark, 1 : 15. — Davidson, J. M. Eng. lib. 75. — Hinton. Eng. radicals, 11. — Reid, T. W. Politicians, 2 : 103. — Davidson, J. Mor. Em. Eng. lib. — Em. persons, 3 : 160. — Pembroke, Earl. Polit. lett. 440. — Smalley. Lond. lett. 1 : 81.

Fawcett, John, D. D. Foster, J. Crit. ess. (Bohn) 2 : 430. — Hatfield, E. F. Poets of ch. 243. — Ivimey. Eng. Bapt. 4 : 568. — Miller, Jos. Singers church, 2d ed. 271.

Fawkes, Francis. Chalmers. Eng. poets, 16 : 233.

Fawkes, Guy. Doran. Knights, 410. — Lamb. Elia.

— the 5th of November. Hutton, L. Other times, 148.

— — Decline of celebration of. Cobbe, F. P. Reechoes, 287.

Fay, Elizabeth G. Yonge. Good wom. 1 : 389.

Fay, Richard Sullivan. Loring, J. S. Hundred Bost. ora. 524.

Fay, Theodore Sedgwick. Griswold. Prose writ. 447.

Fayal and the Portuguese. Higginson. Atlan. ess. 225.

Fayrer, Sir Joseph. Laurie, W. F. B. Dist. Anglo-Ind. 2 : 81.

Fayûm, The. (L. Dickerman) Am. Geog. Soc. 24 : 173.

Fear, Nervous. Boyd. Recreat. 1 : 204.

Feasts and fasts. Hahn-Hahn. Fathers, 28.

Featly, Isaac. Ivimey. Eng. Bapt. 1 : 163.

February, Customs and superstitions of. Soane. New curios. 1 : 49.

Fécamp, Fort, Surprisal of. Davenport. Narr. peril, 2 : 321.

Fechin, St. Conyngham, D. P. Irish saints, 386.

Fechter, Charles. Brereton, A. Hamlets, 44. — Coleman, G. Players, 2 : 295. — Cook, D. Hours with players, 2 : 256. — Matthews, B. Actors, 4 : 207.

— in Hamlet and Othello. Lewes. Actors, 130. — Marston, J. W. Rec. actors, 2 : 193.

Feckenham, John Baptist, Burke, S. H. Hist. portr. Tudor, 3 : 163.

Federal convention, A new. (J. Schouler) Am. Hist. Assoc. Rept. '97 : 19.

Federal judicial system, The. (W. B. Hill) Am. Bar Assoc. 12 : 289.

Federalism of Carl Marlo. Rae, J. Contem. soc. 172.

Federalist, The. Richardson. Amer. lit. 1 : 197. — Stephen, J. F. Horæ sabb. 172.

— Authorship of. (H. C. Lodge) Am. Antiq. Soc. Proc. n. s. 3 : 409.

Federations. Kempner, W. Common-sense soc. 87.

Fee, John G., and the freedmen of America. Japp, A. H. Master mission. 363.

Feeble-minded, The. (G. H. Knight) Conf. char. & correc. '95 : 150.

— and epileptics, Progress in care of. (M. J. Dunlap) Conf. char. & correc. '99 : 255.

— Care of. (F. M. Powell) Conf. char. & correc. '97 : 289.

— — Hist. of. (W. E. Fernald) Conf. char. & correc. '93 : 203.

— Colony plan for. (G. H. Knight; W. B. Fish) Conf. char. & correc. '92 : 155.

— Education of. (J. B. Richards) Conf. char. & correc. '85 : 174.

— Growth and arrested development. (F. M. Fowell) Conf. char. & correc. '99 : 259.

— Institutions for, in the U. S. (C. T. Wilbur) Conf. char. & correc. '88 : 106.

— Manual training for. (I. C. Barrows) Conf. char. & correc. '94 : 179.

— Permanent care of. (A. Johnson) Conf. char. & correc. '96 : 207.

— school for, Functions of. (A. C. Rogers) Conf. char. & correc. '88 : 101.

— Training of. (M. W. Barr) Nat. Educa. Assoc. '98 : 1045.

— Training of an idiotic hand. (S. J. Fort) Conf. char. & correc. '95 : 155.

Feeble-minded women, Protection and training of. (C. W. Winspear) Conf. char. & corr. '95 : 160.

Feeble-mindedness as an inheritance. (E. Bicknell) Conf. char. & correc. '96 : 219.

— Prevention of, from a moral and legal standpoint. (J. C. Carson) Conf. char. & correc. '98 : 294, 304.

Feeling for others. Friswell. Better self, 58.

Feelings and the intellect. Mivart. Ess. 1 : 423.

— Delicate. Friswell. Better self, 146.

— Influence of reason on. Bailey, S. Essays, 140.

— Mutability of. Bailey, S. Essays, 210.

— Right and wrong in. Bosanquet, B. Civil. of Christendom, 208.

Fehrenbatch, John. Ohio Labor, '88.

Felbinger, Jeremiah. Wallace, R. Anti-Trin. biog. 3 : 273.

Felinski, Aloizy. Soboleski. Poets of Poland, 188.

Felix, Rachel. *See* Rachel.

Fellenberg, P. E. von. (W. de Fellenberg)
Trans. Soc. Sci. Lond. '53 : 323.
Felling colliery, Explosions at. Davenport. Narr.
peril, **2** : 348.
Fellow-crafts. Heckethorn. Sec. soc. **2** : 61.
Fellows, Sir Charles. Edwards, E. Founders
Brit. Mus. **2** : 643.
Fellows, John. Hatfield, E. F. Poets of church,
246. — Miller, Jos. Singers church, 2d ed. 299.
Fellowship. Mabie. Ess. on work, 79.
Fellowships in English universities, Intentions
of founders of. (J. S. Cotton) Ess. end. re-
search, 26.
— Post-graduate. Hovey, A. Stud. in ethics, 513.
— university, Functions of. (D. K. Dodge) N. Y.
Regents, **102** : app. 135.
Felt, Joseph B. (H. M. Dexter) Mass. Hist. Proc.
14 : 113.
Feltham, Owen. Resolves. Saunders, F. Fa-
mous books, 48.
Felton, Cornelius C. Everett. Orat. v. **4**. — Pea-
body. Harv. rem. 168. — (G. S. Hillard) Mass.
Hist. Proc. **10** : 352. — (A. P. Peabody) N. E.
Hist.-Gen. Soc. Biog. **4** : 444. — (W. W. Good-
win) Vaille & Clark. Harv. book, v. **1**.
Felton, John, political assassin. Disraeli, I. Cu-
rios. (N. Y. 4 v.) **3** : 115.
Feltre, Vittorino de' Rambaldoni, calling himself.
Symonds. Reviv. of learn. 289.
Female education. *See* Women, Education of.
Female novelists. Jones, W. A. Lit. stud. **2** : 71.
Female sovereigns. Walsh, R. Didactics, **2** : 136.
Feminine, The eternal. Repplier, A. Varia, 1.
Feminine conquerors. Higginson. Conc. all,
60.
Feminine reserve, New. Warner, C. D. As we
go, 109.
Fencing. Bibliography. Castle, E. Schools &
masters fence.
Fendall, Reginald. Am. Bar Assoc. **22** : 671.
Feneberg, Michael. Stevenson. Lives & deeds,
154.
Fénelon. Astié. Louis XIV, 151. — Chambers's
Papers, no. 28. — Channing. Works, **1** : 167.
— Fénelon. Philosophers, 9. — Lamartine.
Cel. char. **2** : 303. — Ste.-Beuve. Monday
chats, 22. — Shelley, M. W. Lit. men Fr. **1**. —
Thomson, Mrs. Cel. friend. **2** : 99. — Benson
& Tatham. Men of might, 111. — Broadus.
Lec. hist. preach. 170. — Taylor, W. C. Rom.
biog. v. **1**. — With portrait. (T. J. Shahan)
Warner Lib. **10** : 5641.
— at the court of Queen Elizabeth. Strickland.
Queens Eng. v. **6**.
— Bibliography. Ramsay, A. M. Life of Fénelon.
— Letters of Mary Queen of Scots to. Strick-
land. Queens Scot. v. **7**.
— Life of. Butler, Chas. Works, v. **3**.
— Mysticism of. Church, R. W. Occ. pap. **1** : 286.
Fenian idea, The. Cobbe, F. P. Hours of work,
117.
Fenians. Heckethorn. Sec. soc. **2** : 200.
— of Ballybogmucky. Cobbe, F. P. Hours of
work, 253.
Fenn, Augustus H. Am. Bar Assoc. **21** : 646.
Fenn, Mrs. Curtis T. Brockett. Woman's work,
666.
Fenn, George M. Wilman, G. Sk. liv. celeb. 81.
Fenne, Samuel. Ivimey. Eng. Bapt. **2** : 31.
Fenner, Capt. Thomas. Barrow, J. Nav. wor-
thies, 316.
Fenning, Eliza. Paget, J. Paradoxes, 373.
— Questionable conviction of. Burke, P. Ro-
mance of forum.
— Trial of. Phillips, S. M. Famous cases, 73.

Fens, The, and fen-men. Heath, R. Eng. peasant,
109.
— Reclamation of. Smiles. Engin. **1** : 17.
Fenton, Capt. Edward. Barrows, J. Nav. wor-
thies, 152. — Bourne, H. R. F. Eng. seam. **2** :
117.
Fenton, Elijah. Jones, W. A. Lit. stud. **1** : 111.
— (S. Johnson) Chalmers. Eng. poets, **10** : 385.
Fenton, John Lyman. (G. W. Crocker) Har-
vard mem. biog. **2** : 234.
Fenton, Lavinia. Needham. Queens of song.
— Clayton, E. C. Queens, 35. — Edwards, H.
S. Prima donnas, **1** : 13.
Fenton, Reuben E., with portrait. Brockett.
Men of our day, 306.
Fenton, Roger. McClure. Translators, 180.
Fenwick, Bishop B. J. Brownson. Works, **14** :
470. — Clarke, R. H. Cath. bishops, **1** : 374.
Fenwick, Edward D. Clarke, R. H. Cath. bish-
ops, **1** : 328.
Ferabosco, Alfonse, as a musician. Hogarth.
Mem. opera, **1** : 52.
Ferberinus. Wallace, R. Anti-Trin. biog. **3** :
136.
Ferdinand I., deposed monarch of Austria.
Doran. Monarchs, **1** : 341. — Peake, Eliz.
Germ. emperors, 293.
Ferdinand II., of Austria. Abbott. Kings &
queens, 113. — Peake, Eliz. Germ. emperors,
341.
Ferdinand III., king of Hungary. Cust. War-
riors 30 years, **2** : 558. — Peake, Eliz. Germ.
emperors, 363.
Ferdinand V. and Isabella. Burke, S. H. Hist.
portr. Tudor, **1** : 30.
Ferdinand VI., of Spain. Robertson, J. B. Lec.
mod. hist. 42.
Ferdinand VII., of Spain. Robertson, J. B.
Lec. mod. hist. 87.
Ferentino. Freeman. Studies Italy, 185.
Ferguson, Adam. Lawrence. Brit. hist. **2** : 242.
— McCosh. Scot. philos. 255.
Ferguson, Catherine. Lossing. Em. Amer. 404.
Ferguson, Elizabeth. Ellet. Women of revol.
1 : 189. — Griswold. Fem. poets, 24.
Ferguson, James, Scotch astronomer. Craik.
Pursuit knowl. **1** : 196. — Edgar. Boyhood,
157. — Howe, H. Em. mech. 237. — Edwards,
B. B. Self-taught, 436.
Ferguson, Sir Samuel. Miles, A. H. Poets of
cent. **4** : 229. — Williams, A. M. Poets of
Irel.
— and Celtic poetry. Williams, A. M. Stud. folk,
131.
— Poems. De Vere. Ess. 98.
Fergusson, David. Blaikie, W. G. Preachers
Scot. 88.
Fergusson, Robert. Miller, H. Tales, **1**. — Wil-
son, J. G. Poets of Scot. **1** : 327. — Irving, D.
Scot. poets, **2** : 413.
Fergusson, Sir William. Bettany. Em. doctors,
2 : 71. — With photo. Cooper, T. Men of
mark, **2** : 11. — Em. persons, **2** : 19.
Ferme, Charles. Wodrow. Selec. fr. biog. coll.
Fern, Fanny. *See* Parton, Mrs. S. P.
Fern forests of the carboniferous period. Agassiz.
Geol. sk. **1** : 66.
Ferns. Bibliography. Atkinson, G. F. Biol. ferns.
Ferozeshuhur, Battle of. Adams, W. H. D.
Eng. at war, **2** : 102.
Ferrar, Nicholas. (P. Peckard) Wordsworth, C.
Eccles. biog. v. **4**.
Ferrar, Robert, Bishop. Tayler. Eng. martyrs.
Ferrara, Renée of France, duchess of. Stough-
ton. Ital. reformers, 193.

fiction. — (F. J. Teggart) San Fran. Pub. Lib. Bull. Sept.–Oct. '97.

Fiction, fair and foul. Ruskin. Miscel. v. 2.
— for children. (Mrs. Molesworth) Art of writ. fict. 84.
— Greek & Roman. Bibliography. Peck, H. T. Trimalchio's dinner.
— Hero in. Boyesen. Lit. Silhouettes, 79.
— Historical. Alison. Ess. 3. — Allen, W. F. Essays, 112.
— — American. Bibliography. Norwich (Ct.) Otis Lib. Bull. Nov. '95. — Waltham (Mass.) Pub. Lib. Bull. May, '95. — Bost. Pub. Lib. Bull. Jan., Apr., July, Oct. '92.
— — Eastern Empire. Bibliography. Bost. Pub. Lib. Bull. July–Oct. '95.
— — Germany. Bibliography. Bost. Pub. Lib. Bull. July, Oct. '94.
— — New England. Bibliography. Springfield (Mass.) Lib. Bull. July, '94.
— — Poland. Bibliography. Bost. Pub. Lib. Bull. June–Oct. '95.
— — Russia. Bibliography. Bost. Pub. Lib. Bull. July–Oct. '95.
— — Scandinavia, etc. Bibliography. Bost. Pub. Lib. Bull. Apr. '95.
— — Servia. Bibliography. Bost. Pub. Lib. Bull. July–Oct. '95.
— — Spain and Portugal. Bibliography. Bost. Pub. Lib. Bull. Jan. '96.
— — Switzerland and Netherlands. Bibliography. Bost. Pub. Lib. Bull.
— A humble remonstrance. Stevenson, R. L. Miscel. 1 : 267.
— in public libraries. Adams, C. F. New dep. Quincy, 16.
— Italian. Symonds. Renais. It. lit. 2 : 51.
— Lamps of. Smith, Gold. Lec. & ess. 69.
— Local. Higginson. Book & heart, 60.
— Modern. Bunce, O. B. Bach. bluff, 139. — Walsh, W. S. Paradox, 105. — Warner, C. D. Rela. of lit. 133.
— — English. Bayne, P. Ess. 1 : 363.
— — Permanent types in. Burton, R. Liter. likings, 91.
— Moral aim in. Hawthorne, J. Confess. 128.
— Morality of works of. Foster, J. Crit. ess. (Bohn) 1 : 417.
— Penny. Payn. Private views, 90.
— Personality in. Jacox. Lit. life, 428.
— A prophecy. Mill, J. S. Dissert. (N. Y.) 1 : 309.
— prose, Goldsmith and the history of, in England. Windsor. Ethica, 285.
— — railway, English. Repplier, A. Points of view.
— Reading of. Porter, N. Books, 72, 210.
— Realism in. (Legendre) Roy. Soc. Can. v. 8.
— — Limits of. Gosse, E. Questions, 135.
— Romantic, Spanish. Ticknor. Span. lit. 1 : 218.
— Royal road of. Repplier, A. Varia, 185.
— Study of. (R. G. Moulton) Moulton, R. G. Four years novel, 1.
— Value and influence of. Green, T. H. Works, 3 : 20.
— Writing. Rands. Henry Holbeach, 1 : 251.
— — from editor's standpoint. (L. T. Meade) Art of writ. fict. 124.

Fiction market, The glut in the. Ess. from Nation, 1.

Fiddlers. Cook, D. On stage, 2 : 87.
Fidenæ. Freeman. Studies Italy, 77.
Field, Mrs. Benj. H., with portrait. Ellet. Queens Am. soc. 175.
Field, Cyrus West. Houghton. Kings, 223. — With portrait. Stoddard, W. O. Men. of bus. 131. — Thayer, W. M. Turn. points, 74.

Field, Cyrus West, Master of the ocean cable. Bungay. Repr. men, 89.
Field, David Dudley. Am. Bar Assoc. 17 : 517. — Parton, J. Sk. of men of prog. — Scott, H. W. Dist. Am. lawy. 359.
Field, Eugene. Clemens. Funny fellows, 193. — With portrait. Warner Lib. 10 : 5687.
— Bibliography. (W. O. Comstock) Below, I. C. E. Field in his home.
Field, George Wilde. Bartlett, J. R. R. I. officers, 261.
Field, Henry Martyn. Derby, J. C. Fifty years, 610.
Field, Mrs. H. M. Field, Mrs. H. M. Sk. France, 9, 20.
Field, James G. Pollard. Life of Lee, 520.
Field, John. Keddie. Mus. comp. 309.
Field, Kate, Death of, with portrait. Todd, M. L. Corona, 97.
Field, Marshall. With portrait. Stoddard, W. O. Men of bus. 281. — Houghton. Kings, 185.
Field, Nathan. Collier. Actors, 206.
Field, Nathaniel. Gosse, E. Jacobean poets, 87.
Field, Stephen J. With portrait. Barnes, W. H. Sup. ct. 95. — With portrait. Scott, H. W. Dist. Am. lawy. 373.
Field of the cloth of gold. Ewald. Studies, 54.
Field of forty footsteps. Timbs. Abbeys, 1 : 106.
Field sports, British. Hayward, A. Ess. 2 : 230.
Field studies and scientific excursions. (D. R. Ford) N. Y. Regents, 89 : 623.
Fieldens, The, of Todmorden. Fortunes made in bus. 1 : 411.
Fielding, Bean, Trial of, for bigamy. Burke, P. Cel. trials.
Fielding, Copley, and George Robson. Ruskin. Art of Eng. 137.
Fielding, Henry. Collier, W. F. Hist. Eng. lit. 311.—Creasy. Etonians, 281.—Forsyth. Novels, 255. — Jeaffreson. Novelists, 1 : 91. — Lang. Let. on lit. 29. — Lowell. Democ. 65; or Writ. 6 : 51. — Scott, W. Biog. mem. v. 1. — Taine. Eng. lit. 2 : 170. — Thackeray. Humorists. — Whipple. Ess. & rev. 2. — Wotton. Word portraits, 102. — Henley. Views, 229. — Jesse, J. H. Cel. Eton. v. 1. — Mitchell, D. G. Eng. lands, 3 : 67. — Russell, W. C. Book of au. 215. — Smith, G. B. Poets & nov. 251. — With portrait. (L. Stephen) Warner Lib. 10 : 5693.
— and Smollett. Masson. Brit. novel. 133.
— Library of. Dobson, A. 18th cent. vign. 3 : 164.
— Novels. Stephen, L. Hours in libr. 3 : 50.
— Tom Jones. Rees, J. R. With friend, 46.
Fielding, Joseph, the champion. Jones, W. A. Ess. on authors, 19.
Fielding, Robert, Beau. Doran. Habits, 335.
Fielding, Sarah. David Simples. Kavanagh. Eng. women, 1 : 49.
Fields, James Thomas. Derby, J. C. Fifty years, 619. — Griswold. Poets Am. 474. — Willis. Hurry-graphs, 204. — Putnam, A. P. Singers liberal, 437.
Fields, Mrs. J. T. Blanc, T. Wom. in U. S. 122.
Fieri, Ludovico. Wallace, R. Anti-Trin. biog. 2 : 169.
Fieschi and his infernal machine. Thornbury. Old. stor. 453.
Fiesole. Howells. Tuscan cities, 247.
— and Florence. Zangwill. Without prej. 294.
— A walk to. Scollard. Und. sum. skies, 139.
Fife, Lord. Grant, J. Recoll. Lords, 301.
Fife, Coast of. Stevenson, R. L. Miscel. 1 : 289.
Fifteen puzzle, The. Proctor, R. A. Fam. sci. 273.

Fire-making, Methods of. (Walter Hough) U. S. Nat. Mus. Rept. '90 : 395.

Firenzuola, Agnolo. Symonds. Renais. It. lit. 2 : 82. — Warner Lib. 10 : 5755.

Fire-places, Chimney. Rumford. Ess. 1 : 305. 3 : 387, 457.

— Franklin's. Franklin. Works ('87), 1 : 490.

Fire-worship. Müller, M. Phys. relig. 115.

Fires and fireside. Mitchell, D. G. Bound together, 207.

Fires and fire-engines in London. Wynter, A. Peeps, 2 : 200.

— in public buildings, How to prevent. Miller, H. Hist. ess. 89.

— Inquests into. (P. M'Lagan) Trans. Soc. Sci. Lond. '74 : 240.

Fireside industries in colonial times. Earle. Colon. dames, 276.

Firmilian. Maxwell, Sir H. Rainy days, 33.

Firmin, Thomas. Wallace, R. Anti-Trin. biog. 3 : 372.

First aid to injured. (J. B. Pine) Conf. char. & correc.

— Papers on. Cong. char. Chic. '93, 5 : 651–693.

First cause. See Cause, First.

First Maryland University, The, Chestertown and Annapolis. U. S. Bur. Ed. Circ. '94, no. 2 : 69.

First step into the world. Knight. Once on time, 2 : 280.

Firúzshahar. Malleson, G. B. Battles of India, 337.

Fischer, Heinrich. Am. Antiq. Soc. Proc. n. s. 4 : 74.

Fischer, Kuno, with portrait. (R. Jones) Warner Lib. 10 : 5766.

Fischers, Giambernardo. Milizia. Lives arch. 2 : 299.

Fish, Hamilton. Jenkins. Gov. of N. Y. 816.

— Tribute to. (J. G. Wilson) Am. Hist. Assoc. Rept. '94 : 55.

Fish. Goldsmith. Miscel. (N. Y. 4 v.) 2 : 529.

— and fishing. Buckland, F. T. Curios. nat. hist. 1 : 227.

— Bibliography. N. Y. Pub. Lib. Bull. July–Aug. '99. — (Louise R. Albee) Harv. Coll. Lib. Bibliog. Contrib. no. 51.

— Curious. Allen, Grant. Falling in love, 302.

— Geographical distribution of. (R. R. Roosevelt) Am. Geog. Soc. 7 : 93.

— Parental habits of. Allen, Grant. Science in Arc. 154.

Fish culture in France. (J. G. Bertram) Vaca. tourists, 3 : 49.

Fish Dam Ford, S. C., Affair at. Dawson. Batt. of U. S. 1 : 633.

Fish farming. Wynter. Curios. of toil, 2 : 100.

Fish hatching. Wood, J. G. Out of doors, 260.

Fish legends. Jones, W. Credulities, 48.

Fish supply of Gt. Britain. (W. M. Adams) Trans. Soc. Sci. Lond. '83 : 562.

Fishcraft, oddities of. Deming. Byways, 227.

Fisher, Charles, with portrait. (L. Hutton) McKay, F. E. Fam. actors, 204.— Winter. Shadows, 1 : 367.

Fisher, Clara. Matthews, B. Actors, 3 : 259.

Fisher, James L. Wood, G. B. Hist. mem. 409.

Fisher, John, bishop of Rochester. Burke, S. H. Men of Reforma. 1 : 154.— Burke, S. H. Hist. portr. Tudor, 1 : 301. — Coleridge. Nor. worthies, 2 : 161. — Wrangham. Brit. Plutarch, v. 1.

Fisher, Joshua. Peabody. Harv. Grad. 1.

Fisher, Payne. Bell, R. Lit. & sci. men, 2 : 208.

Fisher, Samuel. Ivimey. Eng. Bapt. 2 : 245, 599.

Fisheries, American. Seward. Works, 1 : 254.

— in Connecticut. Conn. Labor, '89 : 154.

— Newfoundland, Treaty of 1818 in relation to the. Rush, R. Occ. prod. 269.

— North American. (A. Gesner) Am. Geog. Soc. 1 : 288.

— Norwegian, 1892. (F. G. Gade) U. S. Cons. Rept. 39 : 244.

Fisheries exhibition, 1883, Scientific results of. Lankester. Advan. sci. 193.

Fishes. Bibliography. Dean, B. Living & foss. fish.

— Food, Artificial propagation of. (M. Harvey) Roy. Soc. Can. 10 : sec. iv.

— fresh water, Dispersion of. Jordan, D. S. Sci. sk. 83.

— in the U. S., Geographical distribution of. (R. R. Roosevelt) Am. Geog. Soc. 7 : 93.

Fishing. Fly-fisher and his library. (H. R. Francis) Camb. ess. '56 : 233.

— in Wessex co., England. Kingsley, C. New miscel. 24.

— Jack. Buckland, F. T. Curios. nat. hist. 3 : 143.

— Morals of. Beecher. Star papers, 231.

Fishing Creek, S. C., Surprise of Gen. Sumter at. Dawson. Batt. of U. S. 1 : 622.

Fishing match, Yorkshire. Buckland, F. T. Curios. nat. hist. 3 : 49.

Fisk, James, jr., Erie raid of 1869. Adams, C. F. Erie, 135.

— Gold conspiracy of 1869. (H. Adams) Adams, C. F. Erie, 100.

Fisk, Wilbur. Gorrie. Em. Meth. 360. — (O. H. Tiffany) McClintock, J. Em. Meth. 241. — Pierce, B. K. Em. dead, 452. — Sherman, D. N. Eng. divines, 238.

Fisk University, Nashville, Tenn. U. S. Bur. Ed. Circ. '93, no. 5 : 261.

Fiske, Fidelia. Hack. Consec. wom. 239. — Pitman, Mrs. Heroines mission. 140.

Fiske, John. Richardson. Amer. lit. 1 : 325. — With portrait. Warner Lib. 10 : 5777.

Fiske, Rev. John, Note-book. (S. A. Green) Mass. Hist. Soc. Proc. 2d ser. 12 : 317.

Fiske, Theophilus. Loring, J. S. Hundred Bost. ora. 555.

Fisons and Forsters, The, of Burley in Wharfedale. Fortunes made in bus. 1 : 381.

Fitch, Edward Hubbard. Am. Bar Assoc. 21 : 693.

Fitch, Eleazer Thompson. Hatfield, E. F. Poets of church, 247.

Fitch, John. Drake, S. G. Trag. of wilderness, 139. — Howe, H. Em. mech. 13. — Parton. Peop. bk. biog. 146. — Seymour, C. C. B. Selfmade, 394. — Lossing. Em. Amer. 93.

Fitch, William Stevenson. Smith, C. R. Retrospec. 1 : 245.

Fitting school, Place of, in American education. Ladd, G. T. Ess. higher educa. 53.

Fitton, Mary, Was she Shakespeare's "dark lady"? (W. E. A. Axon) Andrews, W. Bygone Ches. 144.

Fitts, Henry C. Bartlett, J. R. R. I. officers, 425.

Fitz, Reginald Heber. Vaille & Clark. Harv. book, v. 1.

Fitzgeffrey, Henry. Alden, R. M. Rise of satire, 207.

Fitz Gerald, Edward. Gosse, E. Crit. kit-kats. — Stoddard, R. H. Under eve. lamp, 245. — With portrait. (N. H. Dole) Warner Lib. 10 : 5797.

— Old commonplace book of. Nicoll, W. R. Lit. anec. 2 : 385.

Fitzgerald, George R. Ashton. 18th cent. waifs,

135. — (G. L. G. Norgate) Seccombe, T. 12 bad men, 265.

Fitzgerald, Horatio A. Winslow, S. N. Biog. Phila. merch. 221.

Fitzgerald, James. Hazlitt. Parl. portr. 34.

Fitzherbert, Sir Anthony. Burke, S. H. Hist. portr. Tudor, 2 : 216. — Mitchell. Wet days, 154.

Fitzherbert, Mrs. Maria Anne. Willing. Dames, 113.

Fitzhugh, Anne. Clement, J. Noble deeds, 258.

Fitzhugh, George. Davidson, J. W. Writ. of South, 186.

Fitzhugh, Samuel H. Proctor. Lawyers of N. Y. 508.

Fitz-James, Anna Maria. Clayton, E. C. Eng. fem. art. 2 : 274.

Fitzjames, Sir John, chief justice. Burke, S. H. Hist. portr. Tudor, 2 : 218. — Campbell. Ch. just. 1 : 150. — Foss. Judges, 5 : 170.

Fitzpatrick, John Bernard. Clarke, R. H. Cath. bishops, 2 : 310.

Fitzroy, Charles. See Grafton, Duke of.

Fitzroy, Henry. Burke, S. H. Hist. portr. Tudor, 2 : 213.

Fitzroy family. Sanford & Townsend. Gov. fam. 1.

FitzWarine, Fulk. Ewald, A. C. Paper, 42.

Fitzwilliam, Charles William Wentworth, earl. Grant, J. Recoll. Lords, 306. — Hazlitt. Parl. portr. 128.

Fitzwilliam, Sir William. Bourne, H. R. F. Eng. seam. 1 : 75.

Fitzwilliam family. Sanford & Townsend. Gov. fam. 1 : 1.

Five coördinate groups of studies in the schools, Necessity for. (W. T. Harris) Nat. Educa. Assoc. '96 : 287.

Five days' peregrination of Hogarth and others. Dobson, A. 18th cent. vign. 3 : 134.

Five Forks, Battle of. King, C. Battles, 646. — Knox, T. W. Battles, 289. — Stine, J. H. Army Poto. 699. — Swinton. 12 battles, 478.

Flade, Dietrich, Fate of. (G. L. Burr) Am. Hist. Assoc. 5 : 189.

Flag, U. S., Lessons of. Osgood, S. Amer. leaves, 139.

Flag-bearer, The. Lodge & Roosevelt. Hero-tales, 197.

Flag episode, A. (T. C. Mendenhall) Am. Antiq. Soc. Proc. n. s. 12 : 425.

Flagellants, The. Winkworth. Chr. singers Germ. 71.

Flaget, Benedict Joseph. Clarke, R. H. Cath. bishops, 1 : 144.

Flagg, Edmund. Coggeshall. Poets of west, 201.

Flagg, Geo. W. Tuckerman. Artists, 404. — Tuckerman. Artist-life, 215.

Flambard, Ranulph, bishop of Durham. Foss. Judges, 1 : 61.

Flame. (T. H. Core) Manch. Sci. lec. 3–4 : 215. — (T. E. Thorpe) Manch. Sci. lec. 9 : 40. — Poetry of. Mabie. My study fire, 2 : 12.

Flamel, Nicholas. Waite, A. E. Lives of alchem. 95.

Flamininus, Titus Quintius. Herbert, H. W. Capt. Rom.

Flaminio, Marcantonio. Symonds. Reviv. of learning, 498.

Flamsteed, John. Ball, R. Great astron. 147. — Wrangham. Brit. Plutarch, v. 5.

Flanders, Commerce and industries of, 1894. (H. C. Morris) U. S. Cons. Rept. 46 : 224.

Flandrin, Hippolyte. Palgrave. Ess. on art, 144.

Flannan, St. Conyngham, D. P. Irish saints, 368.

Flannel under-clothing, Importance of. (F. W. Hatch) Calif. Health, '77–79 : 104.

Flash, Henry Lyndon. Davidson, J. W. Writ. of South, 184.

Flatman, Thomas. Bell, R. Lit. & sci. men, 2 : 214. — Griswold, R. W. Sac. poets.

Flaubert, Gustave. With portrait. Brandes. Em. auth. 259. — James, H. French poets, 6 : 237. — Saintsbury. French novelists, 334. — Du Camp. Recol. 1 : 154. — James, H. Ess. in Lond. 121. — Pellissier. Lit. move. Fr. 411. — Wells, D. W. Cent. Fr. fic. 242. — With portrait. (P. Bourget) Warner Lib. 10 : 5815.

Flavel, John. Broadus. Lec. hist. preach. 207.

Flavoring substances, Character of. (H. K. Oliver) Mass. Health, '73 : 146.

Flax, Cultivation of. (J. D. Reid) U. S. Cons. Rept. 42 : 265. — U. S. Cons. Rept. special, 1891.

— — in Russia, 1891. (T. E. Henan) U. S. Cons. Rept. 35 : 361.

Flaxman, Ann Denman, wife of John (d. 1820). Child. Good wives, 113.

Flaxman, John. Ewart, H. C. Toilers in art, 355. — Fairholt. Eng. artists, 101. — Hall, S. C. Book of memo. 466. — Smiles. Self-help. — Wedmore. Studies, 2d ed. 97.

— Lectures on sculpture. Hazlitt. Crit. on art, ser. 1.

— Monument of. Hall, Mrs. S. C. Pilgr. Eng. shr. 2 : 198.

Fleas, Performing. Buckland, F. T. Curios. nat. hist. 4 : 115.

Fleet marriages. Ewald, A. C. Paper, 227.

Fleet St. as journalistic headquarters. Hatton. Jour. Lond. 1.

Fleetwood, Mrs. Bridget (Cromwell), daughter of Oliver Cromwell. Anderson, James. Mem. wom. Pur. 1 : 346.

Fleetwood, William. Woolrych. Serjeants, 1 : 132.

Fleischer, Heinrich Leberecht, Memoir of. (A. Müller) Smithson. Rept. '89 : 507.

Fleming, Marjorie. Brown, J. J. Leech, 199 ; or Spare hours, 2 : 47.

Fleming, Paul, with portrait. Warner Lib. 10 : 5844.

Fleming, Sir Thomas, chief justice of England, 1607–13. Campbell. Ch. just. 1 : 202.

Flemish art in 15th century. Conway, W. M. Early Flem. artists, 89.

— Influence of. Conway, W. M. Early Flem. artists, 196.

Flemish school of music. Elson, L. Gr. composers, 11.

Flemming, James. Am. Bar Assoc. 18 : 522.

Flemming, Paul. Winkworth. Chr. singers Germ. 174.

Flesh-worm disease. Wynter, A. Our soc. bees, 2 : 444.

Fletcher, Abraham. Lonsdale. Worthies Cumb. v. 6.

Fletcher, Rev. Alexander. Grant, Jas. Metropol. pul. 272.

Fletcher, Calvin. Woollen. Biog. sk. Indiana, 464.

Fletcher, Giles. Deshler. Afternoons, 137. — Fuller. Worthies, 2 : 146. — Chalmers. Eng. poets, 6 : 51. — (J. W. Hales) Ward. Eng. poets, 2 : 104. — Gosse, E. Jacobean poets, 137. — Griswold, R. W. Sac. poets. — Macdonald, G. England's antiphon, 150. — Morley, H. Eng. writ. 11 : 311.

Florida Blanca, José Moñino, count of. Crowe, E. E. For. statesm. 5 : 157.

Florida war. Dawson. Batt. of U. S. 2 : 439.

Flotner, Peter. (A. Rosenberg) Dohme, R. Early mast. 176.

Flotow, Fred. von. Keddie. Mus. comp. 397.
— Martha. Guerber. Stor. of operas, 121.

Flour, American extension of markets for (Canada), 1893, 1894. U. S. Cons. Rept. 44 : 399.
— — — in various countries, '94. U. S. Cons. Rept. 44 : 713, 491. 45 : 83, 257.
— — in foreign markets, 1894. U. S. Cons. Rept. 46 : 20.
— — in China and Japan, 1897. U. S. Cons. Rept. 55 : 519.
See Corn flour.

Flour-making machinery, History of. Minn. Labor, '91–92 : 156.

Flower, George, pioneer. Parton. Capt. indus. 104.

Flower, Thomas. Ivimey. Eng. Bapt. 3 : 426.

Flower farms of Europe. Wynter, A. Peeps, 2 : 94.

Flowers. Beecher. Star papers, 93. — Tuckerman. Optimist, 238.
— and insects, Relations of. Lubbock. Sci. lec. 1.
— for pleasure in cities. Meath. Soc. arrows, 49.
— How fertilized. (A. W. Bennett) Manch. Sci. lec. 5–6 : 22.
— Names of. Hunt, L. Seer, 1 : 59.
— Old-fashioned. Woolson. Browsing, 109.
— The procession of the. Higginson. Out-door, 317.
— Sacred. King, R. J. Sketches, 34.

Flowers, Symbolism of. Saunders. Stray leaves, 147.
— Wild, British. Burroughs. Fresh fields, 173.

Flower bed, My. Dodge, M. A. Country, 351.

Flower culture. Chambers's Miscell. no. 37.

Flowerdew, Mrs. Alice. Hatfield, E. F. Poets of church, 249. — Miller, Jos. Singers church, 2d ed. 327.

Floyd, Chas., sergeant under Captains Lewis and Clark, Journal of. (J. D. Butler) Am. Antiq. Soc. Proc. n. s. 9 : 225.

Floyd, John B. Black, J. S. Essays, 470. — Pollard. Life of Lee, 783.

Floyd, Robert. See Fludd, R.

Floyd, William. Dwight, N. Signers of decl. 97.
— Lincoln, R. W. Signers, 18. — Lossing. Signers, 63. — Sanderson. Signers, 4.

Fluorine. (H. Moissan) Smithson. Rept. '97 : 259.

Fly, Autobiography of a. Wilson, A. Nat. notebook, 194.

Fly-fisher, The, and his book of flies. (H. R. Francis) Camb. ess. '56 : 233.

Flygare-Carlen, E. Zimmern. For. novelists, 1 : 243.

Flying. (F. H. Wenham) Smithson. Rept. '89 : 303.
— of birds. (L. P. Mouillard) Smithson. Rept. '92 : 397.
— Problem of. (O. Lilienthal) Smithson. Rept. '93 : 189.

Flying-machines. Proctor, R. A. Borderland, 328. — Proctor, R. A. Univ. of suns, 198.
See also Aeronautics.

Focqué, Louis. Dilke. Fr. painters 18th cent. 152.

Fodor, Josephine, vocalist. Clayton, E. C. Queens, 213.

Foecler, Isaac. Wallace, R. Anti-Trin. biog. 3 : 100.

Fog. Whiting, C. G. Saunterer, 70.
— in New York harbor. Beecher. Star papers, 226.

Fogazzaro, Antonio. Crawford, V. M. Stud. for. lit. 219.

Fogg, Francis Brinley. Livingston, J. Em. Am. lawy. 538.

Fogg, Mrs. Isabella. Brockett. Woman's work, 505. — Moore, F. Women of the war, 113.

Foggy morning. Abbott, C. C. Outings, 89.

Foix, Gaston Phœbus, Comte de. Powell, G. H. Excurs. in Libr. 49.

Folengo, Girolamo. Symonds. Renais. It. lit. 2 : 312.

Foley, Paul Manning, J. A. Speakers, 395.

Foley, Richard. Smiles. Self-help.

Foley, Thomas. Clarke, R. H. Cath. bishops, 3 : 171.

Folger, Charles J. Bungay. Repr. men, 173.

Folgore de San Gemignano. Symonds, J. A. Ital. byways. — Symonds. Renais. It. lit. 1 : 54.

Folk-lore. Davis, L. S. Stud. mus. 131. — Keary, C. F. Dawn of history, 254. — Müller. Chips, 2.
— African. Bibliography. Chatelain, H. (ed.). Folk-tales Angola.
— and language of Delaware Indians. Brinton. Ess. Amer. 181.
— Bibliography. (I. C. Chamberlain) Jour. Am. Folk-lore, Ja.–Mar. '99. — Cox, M. R. Introd. folk-lore.
— Method of. Lang. Custom, 10.
— of Yucatan Indians. Brinton. Ess. Amer. 163.
— Origin of. Fiske. Myths, v. 1.

Folk-song. (F. B. Gummere) Warner Lib. 10 : 5853.

Folk-songs, Hungarian. Williams, A. M. Stud. folk, 282.
— of the civil war. Williams, A. M. Stud. folk, 36.
— of lower Brittany. Williams, A. M. Stud. folk, 189.
— of Poitou. Williams, A. M. Stud. folk, 220.
— of Roumania. Williams, A. M. Stud. folk, 309.

Folk-tales, Jewish diffusion of. Jacobs, J. Jewish ideals, 135.

Folkes, William C. Am. Bar Assoc. 14 : 453.

Folkestone, Eng. Rimmer, A. Country towns, 183.
— Castle and nunnery. Timbs. Abbeys, 1 : 327.

Follen, Carl, and the German liberal movement. (K. Francke) Am. Hist. Assoc. 5 : 65.

Follen, Charles. Peabody. Harv. rem. 116.
— Death of. Channing. Works, 5 : 231.

Follen, Eliza Lee. Griswold. Fem. poets, 121. — Putnam, A. P. Singers liberal, 55.

Follett, Sir William Webb. Brougham. Works, 4 : 296. — Grant, Jas. Bench & bar, 2 : 49, 62.
— Grant, J. Recoll. Ho. Comm. 371.

Followers and friends. Bacon. Ess.

Folly. Ess. from Sat. R. 270. — Gray, E. C. Idle musings, 203.
— human, Wonders of. Chambers's Papers, no. 63.
— of mankind a constant quantity. Helps. Soc. pressure, 121.
— Problem of. Dixon, T. Liv. prob. 144.

Folsom, Charles. (T. Parsons) Mass. Hist. Proc. 13 : 26. — Peabody. Harv. rem. 100.

Fonblanque, Albany. Horne, R. H. New spirit, 166.

Fontaine, James. Agnew. Protes. exiles, 2 : 16.

Fontaine, John. Agnew. Protes. exiles, 2 : 26.

Fontaine, Lamar. Davidson, J. W. Writ. of South, 194.
See La Fontaine.

Fontainebleau. Challice. Fr. palaces, 313. — Mollett, J. W. Paint. of Barbizon, 1 : xi. — Stevenson, R. L. Across pl. 108.

Fontana, Carlo. Milizia. Lives arch. 2 : 64.

Fontana, Domenico. Milizia. Lives arch. 2 : 72.

Fonte, Gaja. Perkins, C. C. Tusc. sculp. 1 : 105.

Fontenelle, Bernard le Bovier de. Men & wom. of France, 1 : 40. — Ste.-Beuve. Port. of men, 200. — Bailey, J. B. Methuselahs, 164. — Houssaye. Men of 18th cent. 1 : 46. — Vinet. Fr. lit. 18th cent. 131.

Fontenoy, Battle of. Adams, W. H. D. Engl. at war, 1 : 176. — Clinton, H. R. Crécy to Assye, 514.

Fontevrault, Abbey of. Cook, T. D. Old Touraine, 1 : 70.
— in 1866. Musgrave, G. Nooks of Fr. 2 : 172.

Fonthill Abbey. Hazlitt. Crit. on art, ser. 1.
— and W. Beckford. Walters, J. C. Bygone Som. 136.

Foo-Chow city. Cumming, C. F. G. Wand. in China, 1 : 179.

Food. Laing, S. Problems, 389. — (H. E. Armstrong) Manch. Sci. lec. 7 : 125.
— Adulteration of. (E. Richards) Am. Pub. Health, 15 : 114. — (S. P. Sharples) Buck, A. H. (ed.). Hygiene, 2 : 349.
— Adulterations and impurities of. (H. B. Hill) Mass. Health, '72 : 132. '73 : 390.
See also Adulterations.
— and the distribution of wealth. (A. Blue) Am. Pub. Health, 12 : 145.
— and drink. (J. Tyson) Buck, A. H. (ed.). Hygiene, 1 : 143.
— — Cost and consumption of. N. J. Labor, '78 : 119. '80 : 319. '86 : 1. 87 : 76.
— — Preservatives of. (H. B. Cornwall) N. J. Health, '93 : 327.
— and feeding. Allen, Grant. Falling in love, 193.
— and health. (W. O. Atwater) Am. Pub. Health, 15 : 208.
— and physical culture. Holland, J. G. Titcomb's let. 54.
— as related to life and survival. (W. O. Atwater) Brooklyn Eth. Assoc. Life, 115.
— Bibliography. U. S. Dept. Agric. Exper. Stat. Office, Circ. 43.
— chemistry and economy of. N. J. Labor, '80 : 319. '85 : 184.
— Falsification of. Wynter, A. Fruit betw. leaves, 2 : 1.
— Food-materials, Quantities, costs, and nutrients of. (C. D. Wright) Mass. Labor, '86 : 239.
— for the million. Wynter, A. Peeps, 2 : 139.
— Fossil. Allen, Grant. Falling in love, 271.
— in its relation to wealth. (A. Blue) Am. Pub. Health, 12 : 145.
— Influence of, on civilization. Proctor, R. A. Univ. of suns, 268.
— of the people. (R. Bannister) Samuelson, Jas. Civiliz'n, 26.
— of the people of Massachusetts. (G. Derby) Mass. Health, '73 : 237.
— Prophylactic and therapeutic value of. (E. H. Richards) Am. Pub. Health, 19 : 161.
— Relation of, to health. Am. Pub. Health, 3 : 1.
— Use and abuse of. Proctor. Pleas. ways, 330. Also in Estes. Half-hour recr. 249.

Food-animals, Inspection of. (C. H. Horsch) Am. Pub. Health, 13 : 34.

Food supply, Sanitary control of. (W. K. Newton) Am. Pub. Health, 9 : 149.
— Tuberculosis and. (D. E. Salmon) N. H. Health, '93 : 238.

Foods. Bibliography. Blyth, A. W. Foods, compos. and anal.
— Chemistry and economy of. (W. O. Atwater) Conv. Labor Bur. '85 : 85.

Foolish things. Ess. from Sat. R. 35.

Fools. Mathews. Lit. style, 173.
— Court. Jesse. Court of Eng. Stuarts, 1 : 311.
— Philosophers and. Walsh, W. S. Paradox, 12.

Foot-ball. Hutton, L. Other times, 1.
— Club, in England. Whitney, C. W. Sport. pilgr. 203.
— University, in England. Whitney, C. W. Sport. pilgr. 179.

Foote, Albertus B. Hemenway. Poets of Vt. 219.

Foote, Andrew Hull. Duyckinck. Nat. portr. gall. 2 : 340. — With portrait. Headley, J. T. Farragut, 151.

Foote, Henry W. Am. Antiq. Soc. Proc. n. s. 6 : 103.

Foote, Samuel. Baker, H. B. Engl. actors, 1 : 234. — Doran. Annals stage, 2 : 119. — Forster, J. Hist. ess. 2 : 293. — Galt. Players, 1 : 290. — Matthews, B. Actors, 1 : 139. — Russell, W. Rep. actors, 134. — Timbs. Anec. biog. wits, v. 1. — Warner Lib. 10 : 5878.
— Audacity of. Russell, A. P. Charac. 234.

Foote, Wm. Henry. Davidson, J. W. Writ. of South, 202.

Foot-lights. Cook, D. Bk. of play, 1 : 158.

Footmen. Hazlitt. Sk.

Footprints. Conway, M. D. Idols, 105.

Forbes, Alexander. Forbes, A. Souvenirs, 290.

Forbes, Archibald, at Maida Vale. Yates, E. H. Celeb. 3 : 39.

Forbes, Sir Charles. Grant, Jas. Port. pub. char. 2 : 66.

Forbes, Edward. Jerdan. Men, 198. — Brown, J. Locke, etc. 285.

Forbes, Eli, Brookfield, Mass., Diary, 1762. Mass. Hist. Proc. 2d ser. 7 : 384.

Forbes, James David. Chambers, W. Rem. pers. 248. — Japp. Noble workers, 358.

Forbes, John. Irving, D. Scot. writ. 2 : 43.

Forbes, Bp. Patrick. Wodrow. Selec. fr. biog. coll.

Forbes, Robert B., with portrait. (L. Saltonstall) Mass. Hist. Proc. 2d ser. 6 : 197.

Forbes, William. Irving, D. Scot. writ. 2 : 1.

Forbes, William A. Walker, C. D. Biog. Va. Mil. Inst. 194.

Force, Peter. Lanman, C. Haphazard, 160. — Parton. Capt. indus. 140.

Force. Hall, J. A. Glimpses, 9.
— and matter. Holland, H. Frag. papers, 32.
— Conservation of. Faraday, M. Researches in chem. 443. — Helmholtz. Pop. lec. 1 : 317.
— distinct from matter. Carpenter, W. Benj. Nature, 173.
— electrically exhibited. (J. W. Phelps) Estes. Half-hour, v. 2.
— energy and will. Mivart. Ess. 2 : 226.
— law, and design. Porter, N. Sci. & sent. 260.
— Mind and. Carpenter. Nature and man, 173.
— Origin of. Herschel. Famil. lec. 460.

Forces, doctrine of, Natural theology of. (B. N. Martin) N. Y. Regents, 85 : 701.
— Modern theory of. (R. B. Welch) N. Y. Regents, 88 : 569.
— natural, Interaction of. Helmholtz. Pop. lec. 1 : 153.
— physical, Theories of. Clifford. Lec. & ess. 74.

Ford, Charles E. Walker, C. D. Biog. Va. Mil. Inst. 203.

Ford, David Everard. Hatfield, E. F. Poets of church, 250.

Ford, John. Dunham. Lit. & sci. men, **2** : 299. — Hazlitt. Dram. Eliz. — Swinburne. Ess. 276. — (W. Minto) Ward. Eng. poets, **2** : 60. — Ward, A. W. Eng. dram. **2** : 295. — Whipple. Lit. Eliz. 185. — Minto, W. Eng. poets, 360. — Warner Lib. **10** : 5889.

— Dramatic works. Jeffrey, F. Contrib. Ed. Rev.

— Massinger and. Lowell. Old Eng. dram. 113.

— Plays. Lowell. Conv. on old poets, 236.

Ford, Richard, with portrait. Stirling-Maxwell. Mis, ess. 101.

Ford, Sally Rochester. Raymond, I. Southland wr. **1** : 182. — Davidson, J. W. Writ. of South, 203. — Freeman, J. D. Wom. of South, 291.

Ford, Simon. Holland, J. Psalmists, **2** : 90.

Ford, Wm. Hemenway. Poets of Vt. 177.

Fordun, J. de. Tytler. Scot. worthies, v. **2**.

Fordyce, David. McCosh. Scot. phil. 106.

Fordyce, Col. John. Rogers, C. Chr'n heroes, 90.

Foreclosure executions, Mortgages and. N. J. Labor, '89 : 307.

Forefather's Day. Lodge, H. C. Speeches, 41. — Long, J. D. After-dinner, **17** : 124.

Foreign-born children in primary grades. (Jane Addams) Nat. Educa. Assoc. '97 : 104.

Foreign-born population of Massachusetts, 1885, Statistics of. Mass. Labor, '88 : 119.

Foreign languages, Changes in methods of teaching. (J. Krug) Nat. Educa. Assoc. '96 : 575.

Foreign policy, Doctrines of. Brougham. Works, **8** : 51.

Foreign relations, Liberalism in. Ess. in liberalism, 131.

Foreigners, Assimilation of, in the U. S. Eliot, C. W. Five Am. cont. 30.

— On a certain condescension in. Lowell. Writ. **3** : 220. Also in Prose masterpieces, **2** : 115.

Foreknowledge. Whedon. Ess. **1** : 118.

Forest, John. Stone, J. M. Faithful, 46.

Forest, William S. Davidson, J. W. Writ. of South, 204.

Forest corporations. N. J. Labor, '78 : 275.

Forest phenomena. Thoreau. Selec. 118.

Forest trees. Gray, J. C. Essays, 75. — American. Peabody, W. B. O. Lit. rem. 62.

Forest trees, Succession of. Thoreau. Excursions, 135.

Forestry. Bibliography. Fernow, B. E. U. S. 55th C. 3d S. H. D. 181. — Newark (N. J.) Pub. Lib. News, Apr. '95. — U. S. Dept. Agric. Lib. Bull. Oct. '98. — Bost. Pub. Lib. Bull. Oct. '98.

— Education in. (C. W. Parks) U. S. Bur. Ed. Rept. '93–94, **1** : 809.

— for the British dominions. Temple, R. Cosmop. ess. 92.

— Instruction in. (Sir R. Temple) Trans. Soc. Sci. Lond. '83 : 343.

— Japanese. Rein. Indus. of Japan.

— Rural and village adornment. N. J. Labor, '78 : 123.

— Question of. Econ. tracts, no. 30.

— Schools of. (F. B. Hough) Nat. Educa. Assoc. '81, app. : 40.

Forests. Shaler. Aspects of the earth.

— and trees as sanitary factors. (J. S. Caulkins) Mich. Health, '81 : 61. — (G. L. Andrew) Am. Pub. Health, **4** : 31.

— German. Whitman, S. Teuton. stud. 60.

— Hygienic influence. (S. Garciadiego) Am. Pub. Health, **23** : 473.

— of the U. S. (N. S. Shaler) Shaler. The U. S. **1** : 485.

— of North America. Shaler. Aspects of earth, 257.

Forests of the public domain, Administration of. (H. Gannett) Am. Geog. Soc. **29** : 181.

— preservation of, Health interests in. (F. B. Hough) Am. Pub. Health, **3** : 176.

— Sanitary influence of. (J. M. Anders) Phila. Soc. Sci. Assoc. '85.

Forgeries, Literary. Dawson, G. Shakespeare, 142. — Disraeli, I. Curios. (N. Y. 4 v.) **4** : 205. — Lang. Books & bookm. 69.

Forgetfulness; a neglected gift. Mabie. My study fire, **2** : 29.

Forgiveness. Dodge, M. A. Stumbl. 375.

Forkenbreck, Wildebrand. Wallace, R. Anti-Trin. biog. **2** : 541.

Form and color at educa. exhibit, N. E. A. meeting, St. Paul, 1890. (Hannah J. Carter) Nat. Educa. Assoc. '90 : 58.

— and design. (Fannie S. Comings) Nat. Educa. Assoc. '84 : 207.

— in literature. Mabie. Short stud. lit. 79.

— in subject-matter, mental effects of. (J. M. Hoose) Nat. Educa. Assoc. '90 : 753.

— Instruction in. (Mary D. Hicks) Nat. Educa. Assoc. '91 : 796.

— Poetry of. Hazlitt, W. C. Offspring, 120.

Form-study in the common schools. (J. H. Brown) Nat. Educa. Assoc. '89 : 655.

Formaldehyde. Iowa Health, '97 : 233.

— Fumigation with. (S. Burrage) Am. Pub. Health, **23** : 110.

— The new disinfectant. (A. M. Bleile) Ohio Health, '96 : 20.

— Practical use of. (F. C. Robinson) Am. Pub. Health, **21** : 356.

Formaldehyde gas, Amount of, yielded by lamps and generators. (E. A. De Schweinitz) Am. Pub. Health, **23** : 118.

— Experiments with. (J. F. McShane) Am. Pub. Health, **23** : 114.

— Lamp for generating. (E. A. De Schweinitz) Am. Pub. Health, **21** : 362.

Formalities, needless, Obstructiveness of. Helps. Brevia.

Formes, Carl. Badeau. Vagabond, 256.

Formosa. (J. B. Steere) Am. Geog. Soc. **6** : 302.

— Sugar industry of, 1896. (J. W. Davidson) U. S. Cons. Rept. **51** : 530.

— Trade of, and tea industry in, 1899. (J. W. Davidson) U. S. Cons. Rept. **60** : 301.

Forms, Diplomatic. Marshall, F. Internat. van. 47.

Fornova. Symonds. Sk. So. Eur. **2** : 154.

Forrer, Samuel. Stuart, C. B. Am. engin. 286.

Forrest, Edwin. Badeau. Vagabond, 71. — Matthews, B. Actors, **4** : 33. — With portrait. Reignolds, Kate. Actors, 29. — Jefferson, Jos. Autob. — Murdoch. The stage, 252. — Hutton, L. Plays, 127. — Winter, W. Shadows, **2** : 47.

— and his social relations. Murdoch, J. E. Stage, 294.

— as an amateur actor. Murdoch, J. E. Stage, 317.

— as reader. Murdoch, J. E. Stage, 281.

— divorce case. Clinton, H. L. Extraor. cases, 71.

— Greeley and. Ames, M. C. Outlines, 116.

Forrest, Nathan B. Pollard. Life of Lee, 748.

Forrest, William. Holland, J. Psalmists, **1** : 163.

Forrester, Alfred Henry. Everitt, G. Eng. carica. 368, 410.

Forrester, C. Robert. Miles, A. H. Poets of cent. **9** : 293.

Forster, Anthony. (M. L. Hurlbut) Ware, W. Am. Unita. **2** : 379.

Forster, George. Eliot, Geo. Ess. 94. — St. John. Cel. travelers, 2 : 198.

Forster, John. Espinasse. Lit. recol. 113.

Forster, J. P., Trial of. Feuerbach. Crim. trials.

Forster, Nathaniel, 1718–57. Jesse, J. H. Cel. Eton. v. 2.

Forster, Wm. Edw. Bolton, S. K. Fam. Eng. statesm. — With photo. Cooper, T. Men of mark, 3 : 8. — Higginson, T. W. Engl. statesm. 292. — Hill, F. H. Polit. portr. 197. — Hutton, R. H. Stud. in parl. 150. — Reid, T. W. Cab. portr. 230. — Reid, T. W. Politicians, 2 : 197. — Em. persons, 3 : 286. — Smalley. Lond. let. 1 : 94.

Forsyth, J. Miller, S. F. Bench of Ga. v. 2.

Forsyth, William. Miller, H. Tales, 295.

Fort Fisher expedition. (E. J. Harkness) Mill. ess. M. O. L. L. U. S. Ills. 145.

Fort Hamilton, Ride to. Beecher. Star papers, 201.

Fort Wayne College, Fort Wayne, Ind. U. S. Bur. Ed. Circ. '91, no. 1 : 186.

Fortebraccio, Captain, Perugia and. E. E. Vari. of fortune, 33.

Fortescue, Chichester S. Kent, C. Gladstone govt. 309.

Fortescue, Sir John. Brink. Eng. lit. 2, pt. 2 : 21. — Campbell. Lord chan. 1 : 317. — Foss. Judges, 4 : 308. — Morley. Eng. writ. 6 : 196.

Fortescue, Lucy, Lord Lyttleton and. Jameson. Loves of poets.

" Forth," wreck of the. Senior, W. Shipwrecks, 109.

Forth bridge, Builders of. Cochrane, R. Gt. thinkers, 243.

Fortification, Origin of the modern art of. Ferrier. Ill. of Sterne, 2 : 131.

Fortifications. Bibliography. Mahan, D. H. Permanent fortifica.

Fortiguerra, N. Stebbing. Ital. poets, v. 3.

Fortitude. Starling, E. Noble deeds wom. 268.

Fortress Monroe in 1861. Winthrop, T. Open air, 293.

Fortunate Islands. Baring-Gould. Curious myths.

Fortunatus, V. H. C. Miller, Jos. Singers ch. 2d ed. 11.

Fortune. Bacon. Ess. — Osgood, S. Amer. leaves, 117.

— and luck. Lawrence, R. M. Magic, 140.

— Wheel of. Friswell. Wick. world, 40.

Fortune-tellers. Mackay. Delusions, 2 : 288.

Fortuny, Mariano, with portrait. Hubbard, E. Little Jour. 5 : 285.

Forty, Henry. Ivimey. Eng. Bapt. 2 : 66.

Forza Maggiore. Howells. Ital. jour. 178.

Foscari, Doge of Venice. Utterton, F. A. Biog. sk. 139.

Foscolo, Ugo. Howells. Mod. Ital. poets, 116. — Montgomery. Men of Ita. 2 : 354. — Redding. Pers. remin. 1 : 117. — Hall, S. C. Book of mem. 450. — Stebbing. Ital. poets, v. 3.

Fosdick, William Whiteman. Coggeshall. Poets of west, 471.

Foskett, Bernard. Ivimey. Eng. Bapt. 4 : 266.

Fossils, Oldest, and discovery of the bottom of the ocean. (W. K. Brooks) Smithson. Rept. '94 : 359.

Fossil man in the Delaware valley. Abbott, C. C. Outings, 260.

Foster, Birket, with photo. Cooper, T. Men of mark, 4 : 27.

Foster, Dwight. Am. Antiq. Soc. Proc. n. s. 3 : 108. — Am. Bar Assoc. 7 : 314.

Foster, Mrs. Eliza Ann, of Jamaica. Pitman, Mrs. Heroines mission. 350.

Foster, James. Ivimey. Eng. Bapt. 3 : 399.

Foster, John. Bayne, P. Chr. life, 303. — De Quincey. Ess. poets (Bost.), 217. — Jesse, J. H. Cel. Eton. v. 2. — Gilfillan. 1st gall. 110. — Gilfillan. Mod. lit. 78. — Vaughan, R. Ess. 1 : 217.

— Life and writings. (E. Whately) Afternoon lec. 1 : 181.

Foster, John Leslie. Sheil. Sk. Irish bar, 2 : 235.

Foster, Judith Ellen. Hanaford. Wom. of cent. 654.

Foster, Lafayette Sabine. Am. Bar Assoc. 4 : 128. — Lanman, C. Haphazard, 277. — Livingston, J. Dist. Amer. 203.

Foster, Leslie. Sheil, R. L. Sketches, 1 : 167.

Foster, Sir Robert, chief justice of England, 1660–1662. Campbell. Ch. just. 1 : 392.

Foster, Stephen Collins. Richardson. Amer. lit. 2 : 225.

Foster, Thos. F. Miller, S. F. Bench of Ga. v. 2.

Fosters, The, of Queensbury. Fortunes made in bus. 2 : 1.

Fothergill, Jessie, with portrait. Black, H. C. Wom. authors, 184.

Fothergill, John. Coleridge. Nor. worthies, 3 : 341. — Georgian era, 2 : 385.

Fotheringhay castle. Sparvel-Bayly. New stud. 86.

— Last days of Mary Queen of Scots, at. Strickland. Queens Scot. 7. — Mackie, C. Castles of Mary.

Fouché, Joseph, duke of Otranto. Brougham. Works, 5 : 103.

" Foudroyant " and " Guillaume Tell," Battle between. Rawson, E. K. 20 nav. batt. 1 : 287.

Foulques family. Burke, B. Viciss. of fam. 3 : 373.

Foundations of buildings, Superstitious. Baring-Gould, S. Survivals, 1.

Foundling hospital. Wynter, A. Peeps, 1 : 200. — Wynter, A. Our soc. bees, 2 : 296.

Foundlings and deserted children. (Mrs. S. I. Lesley) Conf. char. & correc. '81 : 282.

— Care of. Mass. Charity ('69), 5 : 48.

— Laws of Belgium relative to. (J. B. Curgenven) Trans. Soc. Sci. Lond. '67 : 531.

Fountain, John. Miller, Jos. Singers church, 2d ed. 231.

Fouqué. See La Motte Fouqué.

Fouquet, J. Pattison. Renais. Fr. 1 : 254.

Fourier, Charles. Denslow. Mod. think. 169. — Greeley. Hints reform. 272.

Fourier, Joseph. Arago. Sci. men, 1 : 374.

Fourierism. Brownson. Works, 10 : 38. — Peabody, E. P. Last evening, 202.

Fourteenth-century parson. Jessopp, A. Rand. roam. 122.

Fourth of July. Everett. Orat. v. 3. — Walsh, R. Didactics, 2 : 108. — Long, J. D. After-dinner, 196.

— orations on, Hints for. Ess. from Nation, 119.

Fowle, Mrs. Elida Rumsey. Moore, F. Women of the war, 91.

Fowler, John, with photo. Cooper, T. Men of mark, 6 : 5.

Fowler, Mary. Drake, S. A. Trag. of wilderness, 140.

Fowler, Sir Robert Nicholas. Ritchie, J. E. City men, 271.

Fowlkes, Eusebius. Walker, C. A. Biog. Va. Mil. Inst. 222.

Fownes, George. Ivimey. Eng. Bapt. 2 : 536.

Francis Joseph, Emperor of Austria. With portrait. Crowned heads, 19. — Wyatt, W. J. Hunga. celeb. 154.
— Coronation of. Kingston, W. B. Men, etc. 38.
— Reminiscences of. Kingston, W. B. Monarchs, 1 : 79.
Francis, Benjamin. Hatfield, E. F. Poets of church, 252. — Ivimey. Eng. Bapt. 4 : 475. — Miller, Jos. Singers church, 2d ed. 260.
Francis, Charles S. Derby, J. C. Fifty years, 580.
Francis, Convers. (W. Newell) Mass. Hist. Proc. 8 : 203.
Francis, James B. (W. E. Worthen) Am. Acad. A. & S. Proc. 28 : 333.
Francis, John W. With portrait. (Amer.) Nat. portr. gall. 4. — Bungay. Off-hand, 364. — (H. R. Storer) N. E. Hist.-Gen. Soc. Biog. 4 : 181.
Francis, John Wakefield, jr. Lossing. Em. Amer. 406.
Francis, Sir Philip. Murray, J. O'K. Prose & poet. Irel. 274. — Brougham. Works, 4 : 80. — Georgian era, 1 : 336.
— and the Junius letters. Dilke. Papers, 2 : 1. — Macaulay. Ess. 5 : 36.
Franciscan friars. Sergeant, L. Wiclif, 52. — Lea. Inquis. 3 : 1. — Westcott. Soc. aspects, 101.
— Dante and. Liddon. Ess. and add. 178.
Franck, Adam. Wallace, R. Anti-Trin. biog. 3 : 102.
Franck, John. Wallace, R. Anti-Trin. biog. 2 : 541.
Francke, August Hermann. Cobb, J. F. Heroes of charity. — Ker, J. Lec. hist. preach. 201, 219. — Winkworth. Chr. singers Germ. 264.
Francken, Christian. Wallace, R. Anti-Trin. biog. 2 : 370.
Franco-German war. Lorimer, Jas. Studies, nat'l and internat.
— Adventures of a war correspondent. Oliphant, L. Traits, 298.
— A chapter of. Belloc, Mme. Walled garden, 179.
— Cost of. Giffen. Ess. finance, 1.
Franconia mountains, Among the. Prime, W. C. I go a-fishing, 178.
Franconius, Daniel. Wallace, R. Anti-Trin. biog. 2 : 498.
Frank, Johann. Miller, Jos. Singers church, 2d ed. 87. — Winkworth. Chr. singers Germ. 226.
Frank, Solomon. Miller, Jos. Singers church, 2d ed. 113.
Frankfort-on-the-Main. Bartley, G. C. D. Rhine, 167. — Child, T. Summ. holidays, 186. — Lee, A. E. Europ. days, 13. — Fulton, C. C. Europe, 136. — Prime, S. I. Alhambra, 264. — Stowe. Sunny mem. 2 : 318. — Taylor, B. Views, 125.
— Electro-technical exhibition at, 1891. (F. H. Mason) U. S. Cons. Rept. 36 : 442.
Franking privilege, Abolition of. Sumner. Works, 13 : 387.
Frankish conquests and Charlemagne. Stillé. Stud. med. 70.
Frankland, E., with photo. Cooper, T. Men of mark, 4 : 12.
Franks, Rebecca. Ellet. Women of revol. 1 : 178.
Franks, The. Grube, A. W. Heroes, 125.
— and Charlemagne. Adams, G. B. Civil. mid. ages, 137.
— and the Gauls. Freeman. Hist. ess. 1 : 161.

Franklin, Benjamin. With portrait. (Amer.) Nat. portr. gall. 2. — Brougham. Works, 5 : 291. — Craik. Pursuit. knowl. 1 : 217. — Duyckinck. Nat. portr. gall. 1 : 9. — Edgar. Boyhood, 186. — Foster, J. Crit. ess. (Bohn) 2 : 411. — Garnett. Physicists, 38. — With portrait. Griswold. Prose writ. 57. — Howe, H. Em. mech. 37. — Lincoln, R. W. Signers, 18. — Lossing. Signers, 104. — Mackay. Founders Amer. 293. — Nichol, J. Amer. lit. 61. — Parker, T. Hist. Amer. 13. — Parton. Peop. bk. biog. 128. — Russell, W. Extraor. men, 89. — Ste.-Beuve. Eng. portr. 47. — Sanderson. Signers, 2. — With portrait. Seymour, C. C. B. Self-made, 428. — Stebbing. Verdicts, 255. — Taylor, W. C. Mod. Brit. Plut. 152. — Tuckerman. Ess. 456. — Brooks, E. S. Hist. Amer. 18. — Dwight, N. Signers of decl. 171. — With portrait. Hubbard, E. Lit. jour. 4 : 41. — With portrait. (J. Bigelow) Warner Lib. 10 : 5925. — With portrait. Hubert, P. G., jr. Inventors, 9. — Hundred greatest men, 469. — Lossing. Em. Amer. 39. — With portrait. Mitchell, D. G. Am. lands, 98. — Mombert. Great lives, 240. — Munro, J. Pioneers elec. 45. — Neven, D. R. B. Pennsylvanians, 26. — Richardson. Amer. lit. 1 : 154. — Thayer, W. M. Turn. points, 258. — Wynne. Lit. men of Amer. — Youmans. Pioneers sci. 1.
— and Archimedes. Winthrop, R. C. Addresses, 2 : 102.
— and Joseph De Maistre. Merivale. Hist. stud. 204.
— and Slidell at Paris. Sumner. Works, 8 : 1.
— Anecdotes of. Jefferson. Works, 8 : 497.
— as a poet. Bryant. Prose, 2 : 329.
— Autobiography. Franklin. Works ('87), 1 : 3. — Saunders, F. Famous books, 149.
— Bibliography. (W. A. Wetzel) Johns Hopk. Univ. Stud. 13 : no. 9.
— the Boston boy. Everett. Orat. v. 4.
— Extract from private journal of. Franklin. Works ('87), 8 : 509.
— Fragment of diary by, 1789. Franklin. Works ('87), 7 : 172.
— Home of. (C. F. Briggs) Homes Am. statesm. 65.
— House of, Boston. Everett, E. Mt. Vernon, 21.
— in France. McMasters. With Fathers, 253.
— Inauguration of statue of, at Boston, Mass. Winthrop, R. C. Addresses, 2 : 258.
— Works of. Jeffrey, F. Contrib. Ed. Rev.
— Youth of. Everett. Orat. v. 2.
Franklin, Sir John. With portrait. Bolton, S. K. Fam. voyag. 235. — (Sir J. Richardson) Macaulay. New biog. 166. — Jerdan. Men, 220. — Parton. Peop. bk. biog. 390. — Thayer, W. M. Turn. points, 139.
— Markham's. (J. Rae) Am. Geog. Soc. 23 : 339.
— Search for. Am. Geog. Soc. 1 : 247. — Chambers's Repos. no. 45.
Franklin, Thomas Emlen. Am. Bar Assoc. 9 : 539.
Franklin, William. Lossing. Em. Amer. 129. — Sabine. Loyalists, 294.
Franklin College, Franklin, Ind.; Historical sketch. (John W. Moncrief) U. S. Bur. Ed. Circ. '91, no. 1 : 163.
Franklin College, New Athens, O. (W. A. Williams) U. S. Bur. Ed. Circ. '91, no. 5 : 203.
Franklin Fund. (S. F. McCleary) Mass. Hist. Soc. Proc. 2d ser. 12 : 17.
Franz, Robert. Ferris. Germ. composers, 153. — Hueffer, F. Wagner, 240.
— and Drexel, Otto. Apthorp. Musicians, 203.

Fraser, Mrs. Alexander, with portrait. Black, H. C. Wom. authors, 234.

Fraser, Campbell. Barrie. Edinburgh eleven, 57.

Fraser, James, 2d bishop of Manchester. Huntington, G. Random recol. 37. — Arnold, F. Our bishops, 2 : 119. — Church, R. W. Occ. pap. 2 : 373. — Photo. Cooper, T. Men of mark, 3 : 16. — (W. Harrison) Ewart, H. C. Leaders, 157. — Yates, E. H. Celeb. 2 : 323.

Fraser, Simon. *See* Lovat, S. Fraser, Lord.

Fraser families. Taylor, J. Fam. of Scot. 2 : 269.

Fraser's Magazine, Election of editor of. Maginn. Fras. papers, 1.

Fraternities, college, Influence of. (J. T. M'Farland) Nat. Educa. Assoc. '90 : 707.

Fraunce, Abraham. Holland, J. Psalmists, 1 : 224.

Frazer, Philip F. Walker, C. D. Biog. Va. Mil. Inst. 208.

Frazier's Farm, Battle of. Allan, W. Army of N. Va. 106.

Frechette, Louis Honoré. (M. F. Egan) Warner Lib. 10 : 5964.

Fredegonde, queen and regent. Bush, A. F. Queens of Fr. 1 : 46.

Frederic, Harold, with portrait. Warner Lib. 10 : 5971.

Frederica, Louisa, 5th queen of Prussia. Atkinson. Queens of Prussia, 299.

Frederica, Sophia Wilhelmina. Memoirs. Jeffrey, F. Contrib. Ed. Rev.

Frederick I., Barbarossa. Duffy, B. Tuscan repub. 41, 57.—Hewlett. Heroes, 82. — Winkworth. Chr. singers Germ. 31.

— as king of Italy. Freeman. Hist. ess. 1 : 252.

— History of. Peake, Eliz. Germ. emperors, 95.

— Reign of. Busk, Mrs. Mediæv. popes, 2 : 1.

Frederick II., Emperor. (T. Carlyle) Ferris, G. T. Gt. leaders, 357.

— Literature at the court of. Symonds. Renais. It. lit. 1 : 21.

— Reign of. Busk, Mrs. Mediæv. popes, 3 : 217.

Frederick III., emperor of Germany. Kingston, W. B. Men, etc. 133. — Pastor, L. Hist. popes, 2 : 138.

Frederick, deposed king of Bohemia. Doran. Monarchs, 1 : 348.

Frederick II., Suabian emperor, History of. Peake, Eliz. Germ. emperors, 109.

Frederick III. (the Handsome), Archduke of Austria. Peake, Eliz. Germ. emperors, 152.

Frederick III. (of Austria), History of. Peake, Eliz. Germ. emperors, 200.

Frederick II., of Prussia, the Great. Adams, W. H. D. Gt. names, 269. — Brougham. Works, 5 : 309. — Craik. Pursuit knowl. 1 : 114. — Hewlett. Heroes, 105. — Lord, J. Beacon, 4 : 249. — Ste.-Beuve. Monday chats, 248. — Trotter. Stud. biog. 89. — Wilson, J. G. Illus. sol. 267. — Dover, G. J. W. A. Em. sov. — Duyckinck. Portr. gall. 1 : 60. — (T. Carlyle) Ferris, G. T. Gt. leaders, 357. — Gurney, J. H. Hist. sketches, 3 : 59. — Hundred greatest men, 430. — Lancaster, H. H. Ess. & rev. 229. — Mombert. Great lives, 204. — Morris, W. O. Commanders, 68.

— and Catherine II. Wraxall, C. F. L. Hist. byeways, 2 : 1.

— and his times. Macaulay. Hist. 5 : 148.

— and Macaulay. Grimm, H. Liter. 131.

— and Philip of Macedon. Yonge, C. D. Parallel.

— and Voltaire. Grimm, H. Liter. 93. — Wraxall, C. F. L. Hist. bye-ways, 2 : 25.

— as a general. Dodge, T. A. Great capt. 140.

— Bibliography. Lavisse, E. Youth Fred. Great.

Frederick II., Carlyle on. Lancaster, H. H. Ess. 229.

— Domestic life of. Wraxall, C. F. L. Hist. byeways, 2 : 53.

— Last years of. Stanhope, P. H. Hist. essays.

Frederick III., king of Prussia and emperor of Germany. Strauss, G. L. M. Men of Ger. 2 : 33. — Em. persons, 4 : 97.

Frederick of Hohenstaufen, with portrait. Utterton, F. A. Biog. sk. 79.

Frederick, Prince, duke of York, son of George III. Fitzgerald, P. Royal dukes, 2 : 99.

Frederick Augustus, duke of York, and Mary Ann Clarke. Browne, G. L. State trials 19th cent. 1 : 243.

Frederick Charles, prince of Prussia, and White Horse of Hanover. Malortie. Here, there, 170. — Strauss, G. L. M. Men of Ger. 2 : 82.

Frederick Louis of Hanover, prince of Wales. Adams, W. H. D. Anec. mem. 2 : 303. — Doran. Princes of Wales, 476. — Georgian era, 1 : 47.

— Marriage of. Doran. Queens Hanov. 1.

Frederick William I., Carlyle's last pet. Wraxall, C. F. L. Hist. bye-ways, 1 : 46.

— Anecdote of. Wraxall, C. F. L. Hist. bye-ways, 2 : 247.

Frederick William IV., of Prussia. Baur. Relig. life Germ. 1 : 80. — Lucas. Secularia, 295. — Martineau, H. Biog. sk. 434. — Sybel. Found. of Ger. emp. 1 : 108.

Frederick, Empress. *See* Victoria Louisa.

Frederick College, Fredericktown, Md. U. S. Bur. Ed. Circ. '94, no. 2 : 175.

Fredericksburg, Battle of. Cooke, J. E. Life of R. E. Lee, 172. — Allan, W. Army of N. Va. 459. — Stine, J. H. Army Poto. 244.

Frederikshall, Siege of. Robson, W. Sieges, 521.

"Fredrik Carl," Wreck of the. Treanor, T. S. Heroes Goodw. sands, 101.

Free and equal, Are men born ? Buchanan, R. Coming terr. 41.

Free agency, Dependence and. Beecher, L. Works, 3 : 13.

Free Church of Scotland. Stanton, H. B. Reforms, 259.

Free for the day. Abbott, C. C. Outings, 66.

Free government, Tyrannies of. (R. W. Parker) Am. Bar Assoc. 18 : 295.

Free judges. Heckethorn. Sec. soc. 1 : 199.

Free-religion. Clarke, J. F. 19th cent. ques. 90.

— Criticism of. Brownson. Works, 3 : 407.

Free Religious Association. Alviella. Contemp. evol. 183. — Emerson, R. W. Miscel. '83 : 379-385.

Free schooling. Laurie, S. S. Educa. add. 19.

Free schools and free governments. Winthrop. Addresses, 1 : 137.

See Public schools.

Free soil organization, First. Chittenden, L. E. Pers. reminis. 1.

Free-soil party, 1848–52. Robinson, W. S. Penportr. 183, 400. — Pierce, E. L. Addresses, 311. — Tilden. Writ. 1 : 232. 2 : 535.

Free speech. Davis, H. W. Speeches, 397. — Schurz, C. Speeches, 222.

— Limitations of. (T. Erskine) Adams, C. K. Rep. Brit. orat. 2 : 273.

Free thinking, History and tendencies of. Mansel. Letters, 293.

Free trade. Appleton, T. G. Chequer-work, 281. — Bright, Jo. Publ. add. 367. — Bryant. Orations, 313. — Cobden. Speeches, 1. — Disraeli. Sel. spee. 1 : 182. — Kempner, W. Common-sense soc. 97.

Free trade and protection. Alison. Ess. 1 : 3. — Chamberlain, J. Speeches, 141. — Elder, W. Questions, 190. — Johnston, A. Amer. ora. 4 : 191.

— British policy of. Swank. Notes, 48.

— Defense of. Kingsley, C. New miscel. 149.

— Exposition of. Kennedy, J. P. Occas. addr. 65.

— General principles of. Woodbury, L. Writ. 1 : 510.

in England, Effects of, 1881. Hatton, J. To-day in Amer. 0 : 131

— in Great Britain. Alison. Ess. 1.

— Story of. Dasent. Jest & earnest, 2 : 121.

— what it is doing. Greeley. Hints ref. 348.
   See Fair trade.

Free will. Thornton, W. T. Old-fash. 84. — Whedon. Ess. 1 : 111. — Whittaker, T. Ess. & not. 274. *See* Will.

Freed, David. Winslow, S. N. Biog. Phila. merch. 149.

Freedman; "Contrabands" at Fortress Monroe, 1861. Pierce, E. L. Addresses, 19.

— at Port Royal, S. C., 1862. Pierce, E. L. Addresses, 54.

— Enfranchisement and protection of. Sumner. Works, 10 : 55.

— John G. Fee and. Japp, A. H. Master mission. 363.

Freedom. Müller. Chips, 5.

— and authority : how far consistent, in church and state. Oxenham. Stud. in eccl. hist. 49.

— and equality in the United States in 1830. Whittier. Lit. recre. 69.

— Civil and religious. Brownson. Works, 20 : 308.

— Human. Holland, E. G. Reviews, 350.

— Literature of. Stanton, H. B. Reforms, 359.

— of the press, Rom. Cath. church and. Brownson. Works, 6 : 520.
   See also Press.

— of the will and Parsism. Matheson. Distinct. mess. 186.

— Sense of, in morality. Green, T. H. Works, 2 : 309.

— Spiritual. Channing. Works, 4 : 67.

Freeke, William. Wallace, R. Anti-Trin. biog. 3 : 389.

Freeling, Sir Sanford. Escott, T. H. S. Pillars emp. 76.

Freeman, Alice E., with portrait. Bolton, S. K. Succ. women, 223.

Freeman, Edward Augustus. Davidson, J. M. Eng. lib. 288. — Em. persons, 5 : 221. — Fiske, J. Cent. of science, 265. — With portrait. (J. B. McMaster) Warner Lib. 10 : 5977.

— Reminiscences of. Tollemache. Ess. & mock ess. 264.

Freeman, James. Clarke, J. F. Memo. sketches, 67. — (F. W. P. Greenwood) Mass. hist. Coll. 3d ser. 5 : 255; also in Ware, W. Am. Unita. 1 : 139. — Putnam, A. P. Singers liberal, 1.

Freeman, James Edward. Tuckerman. Artist-life, 163.

Freeman, Richard. Ivimey. Eng. Bapt. 2 : 100.

Freemasonry in Indiana. Woollen. Biog. sk. Indiana, 489.

— Origin and tendency of. Robertson, J. B. Lec. mod. hist. 405.

— Rosicrucianism and. Soane. New curios. 2 : 35.

Freemasons. Heckethorn. Sec. soc. 1 : 239.

Freerks, Sicke Snyder or. Brown, J. N. Bapt. martyrs, 65.

Freiligrath, Ferdinand, with portrait. Warner Lib. 10 : 6002.

Fréjus. Baring-Gould. Troub.-land, 31.

Frémont, Jessie Benton, with portrait. Ellet. Queens Am. soc. 428.

Frémont, John C. Bartlett. Pres. candidates, 346. — Bungay. Off-hand, 37. — Glazier, W. Heroes, 352. — Savage. Liv. rep. men, 273. — Duyckinck. Nat. portr. gall. 2 : 329. — Annual cyclop. 1890. — With portrait. Greely, A. W. Explorers, 212.

French, Alice (*pseud.* Octave Thanet). Warner Lib. 25 : 14733.

French, Benjamin Vinton. (M. P. Wilder) N. E. Hist.-Gen. Soc. Biog. 4 : 49.

French, Ebenezer. Loring, J. S. Hundred Bost. ora. 322.

French, John C., with portrait. Sketches N. H. men, 157.

French, Jonathan. (Joseph Dow) N. E. Hist.-Gen. Soc. Biog. 3 : 140.

French, Mrs. L. Virginia. Davidson, J. W. Writ. of South, 205. — Freeman, J. D. Wom. of South, 439. — Raymond, I. Southland writ. 2 : 687.

French, Thomas V., bishop of Lahore. Escott, T. H. S. Pillars emp. 84.

French, A day with the. Appleton, T. G. Sheaf of pap. 92.

French Academy, The. Hunt, T. W. Rep. Eng. prose, 94.
   See also Académie française.

French and Indian border war of 1708. Whittier. Lit. recre. 113.

French anti-clerical novels. Dempster. Ess. 75.

French Canadians in Holyoke, Mass. Pidgeon. Old world ques. 172.

— in New England. (E. C. Smyth) Am. Antiq. Soc. Proc. n. s. 7 : 316.

— in United States. (C. E. Amaron) Evang. Alliance, '89 : 239.
   See also Canadian French.

French colonial administration. Norman, H. Far East, 103.

French drama. Hillebrand. France, 126.

French fiction. Hillebrand. France, 111.

— Historical. Bibliography. Bost. Pub. Lib. Bull. Jan., Apr. '94.

— Lowest depth of. Greg. Lit. & soc. judg. 146.

— under Napoleon I. Wells, B. W. Cent. Fr. fic. 1.

French language and German, Should they be required for admission to colleges? (H. C. G. Brandt) N. Y. Regents, 102, app. 51.

— — in colleges and schools. (H. S. White) N. Y. Regents, 96 : 394.

— and poetry. Longfellow. Poets Eur. 403.

— Composition of. (H. C. G. Brandt) N. Y. Regents, 90 : 575.

— in American life. Swing, D. Club. ess. 86.

— Some reasons for learning. Hallard, J. H. Gallica, 3.

— Spoken by those who do not speak French. Matthews, B. Pen & ink, 168.

French literature. (S. Gilman) Charleston book, 61.

— and English literature, Contrasts of. Saintsbury. Miscel. ess. 300.

— Bibliography. Brunetière, F. Hist. French lit. — Dowden, E. Hist. French lit. — Lemcke, E. Catal. world literat. — Pelissier, G. Liter. move. France 19th cent. — Salem (Mass.) Pub. Lib. Bull. Apr. '95.

— Decadence in. Crawford, V. M. Stud. for. lit. 1.

French literature, Glimpses into. Trail, F. Studies, 38.
— Modern. Brownson. Works, 19 : 48.
French memoirs. Dawson, G. Shakesp. 248.
French models. Morley, J. Stud. in lit. 156.
French noblesse. Field, Mrs. H. M. Sk. France, 199.
French novel, the, Present state of, 1890. Saintsbury. Ess. Fr. nov. 1.
See French fiction.
French official life. Moore, T. Prose & v. 92.
French oratory. Stephens, H. M. Ora. Fr. Rev. 1 : 1.
French people, Characteristics of. Hillebrand. France, 1.
— Traits of. Mathews. Conversers, 121.
French poetry, History of, to 1628. Cary, H. F. Early Fr. poets, ix.
French poets, Chronological table of, to 1628. Cary, H. F. Early Fr. poets, v.
— Some recent. Dowden. Stud. 392.
French political life. Hillebrand. France, 135.
French preachers. Broadus. Lec. hist. preach. 135.
French provincial society. Hillebrand. France, 77.
French Revolution. *See* France, History.
French ruralisms. Mitchell. Wet days, 115.
French settlers in America. Hubbard, B. Memorials, 109.
French singers, Early. Clayton, E.C. Queens, 43.
French spoliations. Dix. Speeches, 1 : 60.
— Indemnities for. Seward. Works, 1 : 131.
French women before the revolution. Mackaye. Abbess Pt. Royal, 93.
Frenchtown, Battle at. Dawson. Batt. of U. S. 2 : 191.
Frendraught, Burning of. Burton, J. H. Crim. tri. 1 : 202.
Freneau, Philip. Griswold. Poets Am. 31. — Mansfield, E. D. Pers. mem. 337. — With portrait. Mitchell, D. G. Am. lands, 215. — Nichol. Amer. lit. 93. — Richardson. Amer. lit. 2 : 13.
Frere, Sir Bartle. With photo. Cooper, T. Men of mark, 1 : 23. — Temple, R. Cosmop. ess. 171.
— and western India. Temple, R. Men in India, 254. — Em. persons, 3 : 149. — Escott, T. H. S. Pillars emp. 92. — Laurie, W. F. B. Dist. Anglo-Ind. 1 : 180.
Frère, E. Hamerton. Contemp. Fr. painters.
Frere, John Hookham. (W. Whyte) Miles, A. H. Poets of cent. 9 : 23. — Mitford, M. R. Recollec. 474.
Fresco painting, Color in. Fuseli. Life & writ. 2 : 329.
— Origin of the modern German school of. Eastlake. Contrib. 1 : 21.
— Spirit. Parry, T. G. Min. of fine art, 363.
Frescoes, Recovered. Baxter, L. E. Tusc. stud. 140.
Fresh air charities. Bibliography. Ufford, W. S. Fresh air charity in U. S.
Fresh-air fund. (W. Parsons) Woods, R. A. Poor, 131.
Fresnel, Augustine John. Arago. Sci. men, 2 : 171.
Freyburg, A day at the barricades in. Wraxall. Scraps, 1 : 118.
Freylinghausen, J. Anastasius. Miller, Jos. Singers church, 2d ed. 120. — Winkworth. Chr. singers Germ. 267.
Freytag, Gustav Zimmern. For. novelists, 2 : 37.
— With portrait. Warner Lib. 10 : 6011.

Frezzi, Federigo, bishop of Foligno. Symonds. Renais. It. lit. 1 : 168.
Friars, Order of. Cutts, E. L. Scenes mid. ages, 36.
— Preaching. Ker, J. Lec. hist. preach. 139.
Frick, Chas. (F. Donaldson) Gross. Lives physicians, 815.
Frick, Otto. De Garmo. Herbart, 187.
Friday ; days of omen. Lawrence, R. M. Magic, 239.
Fridolin, St. Conyngham, D. P. Irish saints, 437.
Fridolinus, St. Conyngham, D. P. Irish saints, 121.
"Friedenheim," London. (Mrs. E. Charles) Burdett-Coutts. Wom. miss. 178.
Friedland, Albrecht von Wallenstein, duke of. Cust. Warriors 30 years, 1 : 239.
Friedland, Battle of, 1809. Adams, C. Gt. camp. 139.
Friedrich. *See* Frederick.
Friendly Islands, Aboriginal. McLennan. Stud. anc. 2 : 241.
Friendly societies. Hole, S. R. Addresses, 156.
— Pembroke, Earl. Polit. let. 161.
— Government control of. (J. Y. Stratton *et al.*) Trans. Soc. Sci. Lond. '73 : 566.
— in England. Mass. Labor, '71 : 639.
Friendly visiting. Cong. Char. Chic. '93, 2 : 15.
— (Mrs. Roger Wolcott) Cong. Char. Chic. '93, 2 : 108. — (F. C. Prideaux) Cong. Char. Chic. '93, 2 : 369. — (M. E. M'Dowell) Conf. char. & correc. '96 : 253.
— as a social force. (C. F. Weller) Conf. char. & correc. '97 : 199.
Friendly visitor, The. (Mrs. L. P. Rowland) Conf. char. & correc. '96 : 256.
Friends and companions. Munger. On threshold, 31.
— and no friends. Friswell. Better self, 69.
— Blessing of. Lubbock. Pleasures, 94.
— A complaint of. Dodge, M. A. Country, 285.
— The death of. Procter, B. W. Ess. 1 : 62.
— Followers and. Bacon. Ess.
Friendship. Bacon. Ess. — Ballantyne. Ess. 174. — Goldsmith. Miscel. (N. Y. 4 v.) 1 : 389. — Walsh, R. Didactics, 1 : 46. — Bryant, S. Short stud. 46. — Emerson. Ess. 1 : 181. — Friswell. Gentle life, 1 : 205. — Thoreau. Selec. 29.
— between men and women. Matthews, A. Ruminations.
— Conduct of. Maxwell, H. Post-mer. 146.
— death of, Causes of the. Hamerton. Hum. int. 110.
— Intellectual. Hamerton. Intellec. 301.
Friendships, Celebrated and common. Johnston, R. M. Stud. 2 : 222.
Friesland. Amicis. Holland, 355.
Frietchie, Barbara. Brockett. Woman's work, 761.
Frisbee, *pseud.* *See* Clark, W. W.
Frisbie, Levi. Griswold. Poets Am. 83. — (A. Norton) Ware, W. Am. Unita. 2 : 231.
Frisch, C., Trial of. Feuerbach. Crim. trials.
Frith, W. P., with photo. Cooper, T. Men of mark, 4 : 21. — Rossetti, W. M. Fine art, 262.
— Wilman, G. Sk. liv. celeb. 129.
Frobisher, Sir Martin. Barrow, J. Nav. worthies, 17. — Bourne, H. R. F. Eng. seam. 1 : 120. — Parton. Peop. bk. biog. 306. — Southey & Bell. Brit. adm. v. 5.
— in search of Northwest passage. Frost, T. Explorers, 151.
Frobisher Bay revisited. (R. W. Porter) Am. Geog. Soc. 30 : 97.

Frodsham, Bridge. Coleman, G. Players, **2**: 202.

Frodsham, William J. Walker, W., jr. Men of sci. 53.

Froebel, Friedrich W. A. Quick. Educ. ref. 384. — With portrait. (N. A. Smith) Warner Lib. **10**: 6022.

— and Herbart: Educational theories compared. (J. L. Hughes) Nat. Educa. Assoc. '95: 538.

— Bibliography. Bowen, H. C. Froebel & educa. by self-activity.

— Educational principles of, in England. (E. A. E. Shirrell) Cong. Char. Chic. '93, 360.

— Message of, to parents. (Alice H. Putnam) Nat. Educa. Assoc. '89 : 473.

— Method of. (Mrs. John Kraus-Boelte) Nat. Educa. Assoc. '76 : 211.

— Principles of, applied to primary schools. (W. N. Hailmann) Nat. Educa. Assoc. '86 : 504. — (Kate L. Brown) Nat. Educa. Assoc. '87 : 339.

— System of. (J. W. Dickinson ; Mrs. Kraus-Boelte) Nat. Educa. Assoc. '73 : 230.

— — adapted to American institutions. (W. N. Hailmann) Nat. Educa. Assoc. '72 : 141.

— What he did for young children. (Miss Manning) Internat. health exh. **13** : 78.

Frog, The common. Dunman. Talks sci. 222.

Frogs. Buckland, F. T. Curios. nat. hist. **1** : 1. — Morgan, C. L. Animal sk. 213.

Frohn, Joseph. Wraxall, F. C. L. Remark. adv. **2**: 283.

Froissart, Jean, with portrait. (G. M. Harper) Warner Lib. **10**: 6035.

— Chronicles. Repplier, A. Varia, 155. — Stephen, J. F. Horæ Sabb. **1** : 22.

— Poetry of. Besant. Fr. poetry, 42.

"**Frolic**," brig, Capture of. Dawson. Batt. of U. S. **2** : 168.

Fronde, Wars of the. Higginson. Atlan. ess. 157.

Frost, John, Trial of, for sedition. Erskine, T. Speeches, 289. — Townsend, W. C. Mod. State trials, **1** : 1.

Frost, John, U. S. historian. (J. Palmer) N. E. Hist.-Gen. Soc. Biog. **3** : 478.

Frothingham, Nathaniel L. (F. H. Hedge) Mass. Hist. Proc. **12**: 371. — Putnam, A. P. Singers liberal, 87.

Frothingham, Octavius Brooks. Allen, J. H. Sequel, 146. — Buchanan, R. Look round, 140. — (E. J. Young) Mass. Hist. Proc. 2d ser. **10** : 363. — With portrait. (J. P. Quincy) Mass. Hist. Proc. 2d ser. **10**: 507. — Putnam, A. P. Singers liberal, 454.

Frothingham, Richard. (C. Deane) Mass. Hist. Proc. 2d ser. **1** : 381.

Froude, Jas. Anthony, with photo. Cooper, T. Men of mark, **1** : 14. — McCarthy, J. Mod. lead. 222. — Mozley. Reminis. **1** : 225. **2** : 30. — Smalley. Stud. 287. — Skelton, J. Table-talk, **119**: 167. — With portrait. (C. F. Johnson) Warner Lib. **11**: 6059.

— as a lecturer. Godkin. Reflections, 40.

— on progress. Warner, C. D. Rela. of lit. 169.

Froude, Richard Hurrell, Life of. Stephen, J. Ess. — Church. Oxf. move.

— Remains of. Wiseman, N. Ess. **2** : 73.

Froude, William. Mozley. Reminis. **2** : 15.

Frozen-meat trade in Australasia and the Argentine, 1898. U. S. Cons. Rept. **57** : 161.

Frugality and luxury, True effects of. Bastiat. Ess. on pol. econ. 107.

— in God's service. Thompson, H. M. Copy, 155.

Frugoni, C. I. Stebbing. Ital. poets, v. 3.

Fruit, Birds as preservers of, in Malta. U. S. Cons. Rept. no. 149.

— dried, Sulphuring, a mistake. (J. W. Smith) Am. Pub. Health, **16** : 199.

— vegetables and, Packing, sale, and inspection of. (S. C. Bussey) Am. Pub. Health, **2** : 60.

Fruits and flowers of the U. S. Bryant. Prose, **2** : 194.

— native, Improvement of. Bryant. Ora. 267.

Fry, Sir E., with photo. Cooper, T. Men of mark, **5** : 26.

Fry, Elizabeth. Blaikie, W. G. Leaders, 61. — Fawcett, M. G. Em. wom. **1**. — Kavanagh. Women of Chr. 330. — Russell. Extr. wom. 15. — Walford, L. B. Four biog. 73. — Adams, W. H. D. Good Samar. 317. — Bolton, S. K. Girls famous, 240. — Duyckinck. Portr. gall. **1** : 529. — Fifty famous women, 275. — Hall, S. C. Book of mem. 171. — Hubbard, E. Little jour. **3** : 251. — Owen, Mrs. O. F. Heroines domes. 319. — Stanton, H. B. Reforms, 348. — Starling, E. Noble deeds wom. 253. — Thayer, W. M. Turn. points, 161.

Fry, John. Wallace, R. Anti-Trin. biog. **2** : 206.

Frye, William P., with portrait. Scott, H. W. Dist. Am. lawy. 379.

Fuca, Juan de. Belknap. Amer. biog. **2** : 7.

Fuel, Conglomerate, Manufacture of, in France, 1891. (C. P. Williams) U. S. Cons. Rept. **36** : 449.

Fuels. Bibliography. Poole, H. Calorific power fuels.

Fuentes d'Onor, Battle of. Adams, W. H. D. Engl. at war, **1** : 304.

Fuga, Ferdinando. Milizia. Lives arch. **2** : 361.

Fugitive slave law, The. Emerson, R. W. Miscel. '83 : 205. — Robinson, W. S. Pen-portr. 189.

— in Boston. Parker, T. Add. sp. **1** : 17. **2** : 71.

— Remarks on, 1850. Webster, D. Works, **5** : 373.

— Slavery in Massachusetts. Thoreau. Yankee in C. 97.

Fugitive slaves, Extradition of alleged kidnappers of. Seward. Works, **2** : 449.

— Law of 1793. Seward. Works, **1** : 476.

Fuji-San, Ascent of. Arnold, E. Seas and l. 448.

Fulbert of Chartres. Hatfield, E. F. Poets of ch. 253. — Miller, Jos. Singers church, 2d ed. 22.

Fulburn, Stephen de. Burke, O. J. Cath. archb. 28.

Fulgoso, A. Stebbing. Ital. poets, v. 1.

Fulham Palace. Arnold, F. Our bishops, **1** : 340. — (W. S. Simpson) Venables, E. Epis. palaces, 49.

Fulkerson, Samuel V. Walker, C. D. Biog. Va. Mil. Inst. 210.

Fuller, Andrew. Ivimey. Eng. Bapt. **4** : 527.

— Ryland's Memoirs of. Foster, J. Crit. ess. (Bohn) **2** : 396.

Fuller, Arthur Buckminster. (T. W. Higginson) Harvard mem. biog. **1** : 72.

Fuller, Elisha. (N. Paine) N. E. Hist.-Gen. Soc. Biog. **2** : 353.

Fuller, George. Sheldon, G. W. Amer. painters, 186. — Van Rensselaer, M. G. Six portraits.

Fuller, Henry B. Warner Lib. **11** : 6101.

— By-way in fiction. Repplier. Ess. in min. 87.

Fuller, Henry Holton. Livingston, J. Dist. Amer. 121. — (H. H. Fuller) N. E. Hist.-Gen. Soc. Biog. **1** : 410.

Fuller, Margaret. *See* Ossoli, M. F.

Fuller, Melville W., with portrait. Scott, H. W. Dist. Am. lawy. 387.

Fuller, Richard. Davidson, J. W. Writ. of South, 212.

Fuller, Thomas. Choate, I. B. Wells of Eng. 244. — Collier, W. F. Hist. Eng. lit. 181. — Lawrence. Brit. historians, 1 : 312. — With portrait. Warner Lib. 11 : 6129.

— Life and writings of. Rogers, H. Ess. 1 : 1; or Reason, 1.

— Sermons. Tovey. Rev. & ess. 39.

— Works. Butler, E. Gentle ways, '87.

Fuller, Timo. Loring, J. S. Hundred Bost. ora. 494.

Fuller, William. Macaulay. Biog. sk. 259. — Redding. Misers, 1 : 229.

Fuller family. Titcomb, S. E. N. Eng. peo. 274.

Fullerton, Lady Georgiana. Belloc, Mme. Walled garden, 100. — (C. M. Yonge) Oliphant. Wom. novelists, 193. — Grantley manor. Brownson. Works, 19 : 244.

— Mrs. Gerald's niece. Brownson. Works, 19 : 544.

Fullerton, Joseph Scott. Am. Bar Assoc. 21 : 655.

Fullerton, William, with portrait. Scott, H. W. Dist. Am. lawy. 393.

Fulton, Robert, with portrait. Amer. nat. portr. gall. v. 3. — With portrait. Duyckinck. Nat. portr. gall. 1 : 439. Houghton. Kings, 275. — Howe, H. Em. mech. 156. — Nicoll. Great move. 435. — Parton. Peop. bk. biog. 153. — With portrait. Seymour, C. C. B. Self-made, 460. — Tuckerman. Ess. 121. — With portrait. Hubert, P. G., jr. Inventors, 45. — Lossing. Em. Amer. 155. — Neven, D. R. B. Pennsylvanians, 223. — Smith, S. F. Noble workers, 342. — Towle, G. M. Heroes of inven. 160. — Wynne. Lit. men Amer.

Fulwell, Ulpian. Bell, R. Lit. & sci. men, 2 : 102.

Fundy, Giant tides of. Deming. Byways, 61.

Funerals, Classic. Wallace, S. E. Storied sea, 145.

— Dangers to health arising from. Califor. Health, '90–92 : 152.

— in the Apennines. Baxter, L. E. Tusc. stud. 245.

Fungi. Buckley, A. B. Through magic glass, 55.

— Bibliography. Underwood, L. M. Moulds, mildews, mushrooms.

Fur trade in Canada. Chambers's Repos. no. 65.

Furman, Richard. Davidson, J. W. Writ. of South, 212.

Furnaces, air, Experiments with. Nichols, J. R. Fireside sci. 228.

Furness, William Henry. Putnam, A. P. Singers liberal, 159.

Furnishing. Earle, Mrs. C. W. Pot-pourri, 276.

Furniture. (S. Webb) Morris, W. Arts & crafts, 89.

— and the room. (E. S. Prior) Morris, W. Arts & crafts, 261. — Wynter, A. Our soc. bees, 2 : 93.

— Bibliography. Providence Pub. Lib. Bull. May, '95.

— Carpenters'. (W. R. Lethaby) Morris, W. Arts & crafts, 302.

— Decorated. (J. H. Pollen) Morris, W. Arts & crafts, 310.

— English tradition in. (R. Blomfield) Morris, W. Arts & crafts, 289.

— Manufacture of, in Michigan. Mich. Labor, 1890.

Fursey, St. Conyngham, D. P. Irish saints, 361.

Furz, John. Jackson, T. Early Meth. 2 : 325.

Fuseli, Henry. Spooner. Biog. fine arts, 1 : 332. — Timbs. Anec. lives painters, 179. — Thornbury. Brit. art. 1 : 137.

Fusinato, A. Howells. Mod. It. poets, 362.

Fussy people. Gray, E. C. Idle musings, 171.

Future, Past and. Hazlitt, W. Table-talk, 25.

Future life, The. Calvert. Br. ess. 96. — Channing. Works, 4 : 217. — Greg. Enig. 261.

— A crumb for the "modern symposium." Fiske, J. Darwin, 55.

— Frederic Harrison on. Greg, W. R. Miscel. 1 : 248.

— Physical theory of. Stephen, J. Ess.

— Preparation for a. Hall, John. Papers, 349.

— Primitive ideas of. Clodd. Story prim. man, 103. — Keary, C. F. Dawn of history, 236.

— Science and. Myers. Sci. and fut. life, 1.

— Spirits of just men made perfect. Boyd. Towards sunset, 109.

— Vedic doctrine of. Whitney, W. D. Orient, 1 : 46.

Future punishment. Brownson. Works, 20 : 187.

— History of the doctrine of. Fisher, G. P. Discus. 410.

Future state. Hume. Philos. works, 4 : 151. — Shelley. Ess. 1 : 182.

— Egyptian doctrine of a. Mozley, J. B. Lec. 301.

— Figuier on. Fiske, J. Unseen world, 59.

— Jewish and heathen ideas of a. Mozley, J. B. Lec. 26.

— Physical speculations on. Clifford. Lec. & ess. 161.

— True conception of another world. Bosanquet. Ess. 92.

Future years. Boyd. Recreat. 2 : 386.

Fye, Eelken and. Brown, J. N. Bapt. martyrs, 69.

Fytche, Albert. Laurie, W. F. B. Dist. Anglo-Ind. 1 : 118.

Gá, The, and the shire. Freeman. Eng. towns, 103.

Gabb, James. Miller, Jos. Singers church, 2d ed. 579.

Gables of houses. Baring-Gould, S. Survivals, 36.

Gaboriau, Emile. Warner Lib. 11 : 6137. — Zimmern. For. novelists, 2 : 255.

Gabrias. See Babrius.

Gabrielle d'Estrees and Henry of Navarre. Menzies, S. Roy. fav. 1 : 328.

Gabrielli, Caterina, Italian vocalist. Clayton, E. C. Queens, 71. — Edwards, H. S. Prima don. 1 : 53. — Ferris, G. T. Great singers, 1. — Hogarth. Mem. opera, 1 : 332. — Needham. Queens of song.

Gabriel's defeat [Virginia negro insurrection]. Higginson, T. W. Travellers, 185.

Gaddi, Gaddo. Stillman, W. J. Old Ital. mas. 47.

Gaddi, Taddeo. Stillman, W. J. Old Ital. mas. 51.

Gadsden, Christopher. Lossing. Em. Amer. 109. — Perry, B. F. Biog. sketches, 1 : 264.

Gaelic poetry. Shairp. Aspects.

Gage, F. B. Hemenway. Poets of Vt. 315.

Gage, Mrs. Frances Dana. Brockett. Woman's work, 683. — Coggeshall. Poets of west, 393. — (E. C. Stanton) Parton. Em. wom. 382.

Gagging in plays. Cook, D. Bk. of play, 2 : 214.

Gailingen, Eppelein von. Wilson, H. S. Stud. in hist. 174.

Gaillard, Château, Siege of. Champney, E. W. Feudal châteaux, 285.

Gaines, Edmund Pendleton, with portrait. Amer. nat. portr. gall. 4.

Gaines, Myra Clark. Ellet, E. F. Court circles, 572.
Gaines's Mill, Battle of. *See* Cold Harbor.
Gainesville, Va., Battle of. Allan, W. Army of N. Va. 230.
Gainsborough, Thomas. Cunningham, A. Gt. Eng. painters, 253. — Buxton, H. J., *et al.* Eng. paint. 55. — Carr, J. C. Papers, 159 — Fairholt. Eng. artists, 46. — Redgrave. Century of p. 1 : 154. — Eng. painters Georgian, 9. — Thornbury. Brit. art. 1 : 1. — Timbs. Anec. lives painters, 156. — Wedmore. Studies, 2d ed. 1. — Hall, Mrs. S. C. Pllgr. Eng. shr. 1. 255.
— The market-cart. (R. & S. Redgrave) Singleton, E. Great pic. 268.
Galapagos Islands, The. (G. Baur) Am. Antiq. Soc. Proc. n. s. 7 : 418.
Galba, Emperor. Lynam. Rom. emp. v. 2.
Galberry, Thomas. Clarke, R. H. Cath. bishops, 3 : 128.
Galdós, Bénito Perez. (W. H. Bishop) Warner Lib. 11 : 6153.
Gale, John. Ivimey. Eng. Bapt. 4 : 212.
Gale, William. Loring, J. S. Hundred Bost. ora. 381.
Gale, A winter. Guthrie, T. Out of harness, 36.
Galen, C. Hundred greatest men, 327. — Pettigrew. Med. portr. gall. v. 4.
Gales, Joseph. Lanman, C. Haphazard, 41.
Galiani, Ferdinand. Haussonville. Salon of Necker, 1 : 169. — Ste.-Beuve. Monday chats, 227.
Galicia, Gold mines of. (J. Harmony) U. S. Cons. Rept. 53 : 310.
Galilee. (S. Merrill) Wilson, C. W. Pictur. Palest. 2 : 49.
— and the sea-coast. Porter, J. L. Giant cities, 227.
— Sea of. Buckley, J. M. Trav. 3 cont. 467.
Galileo. Ball, R. Great astron. 67. — Bolton, S. K. Fam. men of science, 1. — Craik. Pursuit knowl. 1 : 8. — Delepierre. Hist. diff. 148. — Edgar. Boyhood, 133. — Lord, J. Beacon, 8 : 461. — Montgomery. Men of Ita. 2 : 1. — Morton, E. J. C. Heroes astron. 115. — Parton. Peop. bk. biog. 261. — Brewster. Martyrs sci. — Ewart, H. C. Heroes of sci. 89. — Gurney, J. H. Hist. sketches, 1 : 291. — Hundred greatest men, 339. — Hutton, L. Landm. Florence, 31. — Nasmith. Mak. mod. thought, 1 : 220.
— and the inquisition. Lodge, O. J. Pioneers, 108.
— and the invention of the telescope. Lodge, O. J. Pioneers, 84.
— and Milton, Interview of. Drake, N. Mornings, 2 : 313.
— Trial of. Renan. Leaders, 72. — Renan. Studies (N. Y.), 2 : 407.
Gall, Richard. Wilson, J. G. Poets of Scot. 1 : 551.
Gall, St. Conygham, D. P. Irish saints, 347. — Montalembert. Monks, 2 : 456.
Gallagher, William Davis. Coggeshall. Poets of west, 132. — Griswold. Poets Am. 355.
Gallantry, Modern. Lamb. Elia.
Gallas, Matthias von. Cust. Warriors 30 years, 2 : 375.
Gallatin, Albert. Duyckinck. Nat. portr. gall. 1 : 405. — Lodge, H. C. Studies, 263. — Maury, S. M. Statesm. of Am. 136. — Johnston, A. Amer. ora. 1 : 84. — Lossing. Em. Amer. 321. — Moore, F. Am. eloq. 2 : 130. — (H. Adams) N. E. Hist.-Gen. Soc. Biog. 1 : 203.
Gallaudet, Thomas Hopkins. Lossing. Em. Amer. 381. — With portrait. Rogers, A. C. Repres. men, 235.

Gallican Church. Wilberforce, S. Ess. Quar. 2 : 42.
— Present state of, 1867. Neale. Ess. liturgy.
Gallicanism, True origin of. Châtard. Occ. ess. 9.
Gallison, John. Channing. Works, 5 : 343.
Gallitzin, Demetrius Augustine. Murray, J. O'K. Cath. heroes, 765.
Galloway, Joseph. Lossing. Em. Amer. 72. — Sabine. Loyalists, 308.
Gallows, The. Baring-Gould, S. Survivals, 238.
Gallus, Caius Cornelius. Dunlop, J. Rom. liter. 3 : 409.
Galt, John. Douglas, G. Blackwoods, 47. — Hall, S. C. Book of mem. 396. — Jerdan. Men, 229. — Thomson, K. B. Recoll. v. 2.
— Novels. Jeffrey, F. Contrib. Ed. Rev.
Galt, William. Walker, C. D. Biog. Va. Mil. Inst. 223.
Galton, Francis. Warner Lib. 11 : 6174.
Galuppi, B., musician. Hogarth. Mem. opera, 1 : 292.
— Immortality of. Paget, V. Juvenilia, 2 : 1.
Galvanic apparatus, Volta's. Davy. Works, 2 : 139.
Galvanic electricity, Experiments on. Davy. Works, 2 : 211.
Galvanism, Outlines of a view of. Davy. Works, 2 : 188.
— Progress of. Davy. Works, 2 : 221.
Galvanized iron, Drinking-water in. (W. E. Boardman) Mass. Health, '74 : 489.
Galway, Henri de Ruvigne, earl of, Life of. Agnew. Protes. exiles, 1 : 144.
Gama, Vasco da. Parton. Peop. bk. biog. 266. — Vogel. Cent. of discov. 57.
— Voyage to India. Frost, T. Explorers, 52.
Gamache, Louis Oliver, of Anticosti. Lanman, C. Recoll. 22.
Gamain, F., locksmith, Attempted poisoning of, by Louis XVI. Baring-Gould. Oddities, 1 : 83.
Gambara, Veronica. Jameson. Loves of poets. — Symonds. Renais. Ital. lit. 2 : 288.
Gambetta, Leon. Bolton, S. K. Poor boys famous, 204. — (F. Harrison) Coan. Stud. biog. 1. — With photo. Cooper, T. Men of mark, 6 : 31. — King, E. French pop. lead. 75. — Men of 3d repub. 33. — Reid, T. W. Politicians, 1 : 55. — Towle. Cert. men, 66. — Washburne. Recoll. of min. 1 : 174. — Yates, E. H. Celeb. 2 : 195. — Smalley. Lond. lett. 1 : 34. — Em. persons, 3 : 80.
Gambling. Gladden. Appl. Christ'y, 180. — Walsh, R. Didactics, 2 : 190.
— and betting. Hole, S. R. Addresses, 273.
— at Baden-Baden. Wraxall. Scraps, 1 : 150.
— In defense of. Zangwill. Without prej. 86.
— Melodramas against. Talfourd. Crit. ess.
Gambling games of Chinese in America. (S. Culin) Univ. Pa. Publ. Philol. 1 : no. 4.
Gambling-houses of Paris. Willis. Pencillings.
Gambling superstitions. Proctor, R. A. Fam. sci. 254. — Proctor. Borderland, 349.
Gambold, John. Tyerman. Oxf. meth. 155.
Game; Is it property? Miller, H. Hist. ess. 262.
Game laws, English, 1819, 1823. Smith, Syd. Ess. fr. Ed.
Game Park, Corbin. (J. R. Spears) Smithson. Rept. '91 : 417.
Game preservation in Germany, 1891. (F. H. Mason) U. S. Cons. Rept. 35 : 261.
Gamekeeper, Museum of. Buckland, F. T. Curios. nat. hist. 2 : 109.
Games. Maxwell, H. Post-mer. 27.

Gamin, London. Wynter. Curios. of toil, 1 : 82.

Gammer Gurton's needle. Dunham. Lit. & sci. men, 2 : 5. — Hogarth. Mem. opera, 1 : 38. — Lennox, W. P. Plays, 1 : 11.

Gamond, Blanche. Bernard, F. Escapes, 90.

Gananoqui, Canada, Expedition to. Dawson. Batt. of U. S. 2 : 135.

Gandy, Samuel Whitlock. Miller, Jos. Singers church, 2d ed. 368.

Ganges, Wreck of the. Treanor, T. S. Heroes Goodw. sands, 79.

Gannett, Deborah Samson. Clement, J. Noble deeds, 450. — Ellet. Women of revol. 2 : 122.

Gannett, Ezra S. Clarke, J. F. Memo. sketches, 187.

Gannett, William Channing. Putnam, A. P. Singers liberal, 510.

— His views of science and religion. Alviella. Contemp. evol. 219.

Gannon, Mary. Hutton, L. Plays, 254.

Gano, John. Headley, J. T. Chaplains Revol. 250.

Gano Sanese, Maestro. Perkins, C. C. Tusc. sculp. 1 : 99.

Garaschianin, Gospodin. Kingston, W. B. Men, etc. 168.

Garbage, Collection and disposal of, in large cities. (W. F. Morse) Am. Pub. Health, 20 : 187.

— Collection and transportation of. (E. Clark ; W. F. Morse) Am. Pub. Health, 17 : 104.

— Destruction of. (L. Laberge) Am. Pub. Health, 13 : 233.

— — by fire. (G. Baird) Am. Pub. Health, 12 : 119.

— Disposal of. Am. Pub. Health, 17 : 90. — (T. H. McKenzie) Am. Pub. Health, 20 : 184, 196. — (R. Hering) Am. Pub. Health, 22 : 105.

— — at World's Columbian Exposition. (W. F. Morse) Am. Pub. Health, 19 : 53.

— — Domestic. N. H. Health, '94-95 : 127. — (N. E. Wordin) Am. Pub. Health, 20 : 278. 22 : 79. — (W. F. Morse) Am. Pub. Health, 22 : 109.

— — Plea for. (N. E Wordin) Am. Pub. Health, 22 : 78.

— — Health officers' reports on. Am. Pub. Health, 17 : 120.

— — in Boston. (E. C. Clarke) Am. Pub. Health, 5 : 24.

— — in Europe. (R. Hering) Am. Pub. Health, 17 : 140.

— — in Milwaukee. (R. Martin) Am. Pub. Health, 15 : 63. — (U. O. B. Wingate) Am. Pub. Health, 19 : 49.

— — in New Orleans. (H. M. Thompson) Am. Pub. Health, 5 : 32.

— — in Providence, R. I. (C. V. Chapin) Am. Pub. Health, 18 : 259.

— — in St. Paul, Minn. (H. F. Hoyt) Am. Pub. Health, 18 : 115.

— — Merz or Vienna system of. (E. Clark) Am. Pub. Health, 17 : 127.

— — Reports on. Am. Pub. Health, 17 : 90. 23 : 206.

— Refuse of cities, Sanitary care and utilization of. (C. A. Leas) Am. Pub. Health, 1 : 454.

— Sanitary treatment of, by the Simonin process. (I. M. Simonin) Am. Pub. Health, 18 : 405.

Garbage cremator, The Engle. (W. F. Morse) Am. Pub. Health, 17 : 136.

Garbage furnace, The Rider. (C. Gray) Am. Pub. Health, 17 : 130.

Garbage furnaces. (S. S. Kilvington) Am. Pub. Health, 14 : 156.

Garbage reduction by steam. (M. A. Veeder) Am. Pub. Health, 24 : 296.

Garber, Michael C. Woollen. Biog. sk. Indiana, 480.

Garborg, Arne. Warner Lib. 11 : 6185.

Garcia, Michello Ferdinande Pauline. See Viardot, M. F. P.

Garczynski, Stephen. Soboleski. Poets of Poland, 290.

Garden, My indoor. Ellwanger. Sto. of house, 127.

Garden beds of moundbuilders. Hubbard, B. Memorials, 243.

Garden party, Queen's, 1889. Smalley. Lond. lett. 2 : 262.

Garden philosophy. Osgood, S. Amer. leaves, 307.

Gardener, An old Scotch. Stevenson, R. L. Mem. 77.

Gardeners, English, Early. Mitchell. Wet days, 189.

Gardeners' schools in Russia, 1898. U. S. Cons. Rept. 57 : 511.

Gardening. (C. Fraser) Charleston book, 165.

— Bibliography. Van Rensselaer, Mrs. Schuyler. Art gardening.

Gardens. Maxwell, H. Post-mer. 270. — Bacon. Ess. — Cowley. Ess. — Dodge, M. H. Country, 38. — Story, A. T. Vagrom, 11.

— Art in embellishing. Drake, N. Noontide, 1 : 101. 2 : 112.

— Market, near London. Early. Hazlitt, W. C. Gleanings, 169.

— Public. Hill, O. Our comm. land, 105.

Gardiner, Allen, the sailor martyr. Rogers, C. Chr'n heroes, 140. — Yonge. Pioneers, 255.

Gardiner, Sir Christopher. (C. F. Adams, jr.) Mass. Hist. Proc. 20 : 60.

Gardiner, Col. James. Rogers, C. Chr'n heroes, 79.

Gardiner, John. Loring, J. S. Hundred Bost. ora. 168.

Gardiner, Stephen, bishop of Winchester. Burke, S. H. Hist. portr. Tudor, 1 : 521.—Campbell. Ld. chan. 2 : 171. — Burke, S. H. Men of Reforma. 1 : 317. — Foss. Judges, 5 : 362. — Fuller. Worthies, 8 : 168.— Oxenham. Stud. in eccl. hist. 151. — Wrangham. Brit. Plutarch, v. 1.

Gardner, Augustus K. Francis, S. W. N. Y. phys. 119.

Garfield, Mrs. Eliza Ballou. With portrait. Holloway, L. C. Ladies, 688. — Holloway, L. C. Mothers of gt. men, 398.

Garfield, James A. Burton, N. J. Yale lec. 430. — Farrar. Soc. & p. day quest. 254. — With portrait. Brooks, N. Statesm. 313. — Em. persons, 2 : 337. — (H. W. French) Frost. Presidents, 505.— Lowell. Democ. 43; or Writ. 6 : 38.— Pennypacker. Hist. sk. 285. — Blaine. Polit. discuss. 503. — Long, J. D. After-dinner, 152. — Thayer, W. M. Turn. points, 126. — (W. W. Phelps) Wilson, J. G. Presidents, 426.

— Death of. Whittier. Prose Works, v. 2.

— — English sympathy for. Smalley. Lond. lett. 2 : 289.

— New England ancestry of. (G. F. Hoar) Am. Antiq. Soc. Proc. n. s. 1 : 386.

Garfield, Mrs. Lucretia Rudolph. Gordon, L. L. Lady Wash'n, 408. — Hanaford. Wom. of cent. 105. — With portrait. Holloway, S. C. Ladies, 665.

Gargrave family. Burke, B. Viciss. of fam. 1 : 142.

Garibaldi, G. Bolton, S. K. Poor boys famous, 172. — Duyckinck. Portrait gall. 2 : 624. — Elliot, F. Rom. gossip, 141. — Em. persons, 3 : 12. — Farrar. Soc. & p. day quest. 324. — Marriott, J. A. R. Makers mod. It. — Nolan. Liber. of Ita. 19. — Parton. Peop. bk. biog. 492.

Garin the Lorrainer. Ludlow. Epics, 2 : 12.

Garland, Augustus Hill. Am. Bar Assoc. 22 : 672. — With portrait. Scott, H. W. Dist. Am. lawy. 401.

Garland, Hamlin, with portrait. Warner Lib. 11 . 6195.

Garland, Hugh A. Livingston, J Dist. Amer. 286.

Garland, Samuel, jr. Walker, C. D. Biog. Va. Mil. Inst. 227.

Garnets, Bohemian. U. S. Cons. Rept. no. 153.

Garnett, Henry Wise. Am. Bar Assoc. 20 : 533.

Garnett, Richard. Garnett. Philol. ess. v. 2. — (C. Monkhouse) Miles, A. H. Poets of cent. 6 : 165.

Garnett, Thomas S., M. D. Walker, C. D. Biog. Va. Mil. Inst. 238.

Garnier, Francis. Exploration in Indo-China. Frost, T. Mod. expl. 101.

Garnier, Robert. Cary. Fr. poets, 176.

Garnier-Pages, Etienne Joseph Louis. Cormenin. Orators, 151.

Garret, The, Genius and poverty. Guiney. Goose-quill, 172.

Garretson, Catharine. Stevens, A. Women of Meth. 256.

Garrett, Charles. Wesley & successors, 241.

Garrett, Mary Elizabeth. Bolton, S. K. Givers, 326.

Garrettson, Freeborn. McClintock, J. Em. Meth. 223. — With portrait. Withrow. Makers of Meth. 284.

Garrick, David. Baker, H. B. Eng. actors, 1 : 133. — Brereton, A. Hamlets, 12. — Duyckinck. Portrait gall. 1 : 106. — Doran. Annals stage, 1 : 333. 2 : 75. — Fitzgerald. New hist. Eng. stage, 2 : 122. — Galt. Players, 1 : 247. — Hitchman. 18th cent. 136. — Irving, H. Drama, 106. — Irving, H. Eng. actors, 24. — Matthews, B. Actors, 1 : 59. — Murdoch. The stage, 62, 462. — Russell, W. Rep. actors, 107. — Russell, W. C. Book of au. 240.

— and Mrs. Clive. Thomson, Mrs. Cel. friend. 2 : 217.

— and his wife, with portrait. Ollier, E. Brit. portr. paint. 25.

— as an actor. Murdoch, J. E. Stage, 59.

— "Exit Roscius." Dobson, A. 18th cent. vign. 3 : 1.

— Strictures upon his acting. Murdoch, J. E. Stage, 490.

Garrick, Eva Maria. Bailey, J. B. Methuselahs, 227.

Garrick Club. Yates, E. Recollec. 2 : 1.

Garrison, Cornelius K. Parton, J. Sk. of men of prog.

Garrison, Helen Eliza. Phillips, W. Speeches, 2 : 454.

Garrison, Wm. Lloyd. Bacon, L. W. Irenics, 145. — Bartlett, D. W. Mod. agit. 111. — Bartol. Principles, 413. — Bolton, S. K. Poor boys famous. 156. — Loring, J. S. Hundred Bost. ora. 577. — Stowe. Men of time, 154. — With portrait. Brockett. Men of our day, 568. — Higginson, T. W. Contemp. 244. — Nichol. Amer. lit. 139. — Phillips, W. Speeches, 2 : 459. — Richardson. Amer. lit. 1 : 248. — Whittier. Prose, v. 3.

Garrow, Sir William. Hazlitt. Parl. portr. 75.

Garter, Order of the. Doran. Knights, 148.

— — Foreign knights of. Doran. Knights, 170.

— — Ladies of. Burke, B. Rise of gt. fam. 182.

Garth, Sir Samuel. Portrait. Caulfield. Kit-cat, 152. — (S. Johnson) Chalmers. Eng. poets, 9 : 419. — Jeaffreson. Doctors, 44. — Hunt, L. Men, wom. & books, 215.

Gartland, Francis Xavier. Clarke, R. H. Cath. bishops, 2 : 408.

Garway, Sir Henry. Bourne. Lond. merchants, 132.

Gas, coal and water, Relative poisonous effects of. (W. T. Sedgwick ; W. R. Nichols) Mass. Health, '84 : 275.

— — and public health. (S. W. Abbott) Mass. Health, '84 : 249.

— illuminating, Danger to health from. (S. H. Durgin) Am. Pub. Health, 24 : 196.

— — Introduction of, into England. Nicoll. Great move. 366.

— — Question of, in Phila. (E. J. James) Phila. Soc. Sci. Assoc. '86.

— — Relations of, to health. (E. S. Wood) Am. Pub. Health, 3 : 62.

— Liquefaction of. Faraday. Researches in chem. 96.

— Natural, at Finlay, Ohio. Warner, C. D. Studies, 256.

— rock-pressure of, Origin of. (Edward Orton) Smithson. Rept. '91 : 155.

— An undiscovered. (W. Ramsay) Smithson. Rept. '97 : 247.

Gases. Bibliography. Barus, C. Laws of gases.

— from decay, Effects of, in dwellings. (W. H. Brewer) Am. Pub. Health, 3 : 199.

Gas lamps, Plea for. Stevenson, R. L. Virgin. 271.

Gas-supply, The modern municipality and. (E. J. James) Am. Econ. Assoc. 1.

Gascoigne, Geo. Alden, R. M. Rise of satire, 67. — Chalmers. Eng. poets, 2 : 447. — Dunham. Lit. & sci. men, 2 : 15. — (J. W. Hales) Ward. Eng. poets, 1 : 263. — Criswold, R. W. Sac. poets. — Holland, J. Psalmists, 1 : 182. — Macdonald, G. England's antiphon, 57. — Miller, Jos. Singers church, 2d ed. 48. — Minto, W. Eng. poets, 153. — Morley, H. Eng. writ. 8 : 261.

— Life and writings of. (F. E. Schelling) Univ. Pa Pub. Philol. 2 : no. 3.

Gascoigne, Sir William, chief justice. Campbell. Ch. jus. 1 : 122. — Foss. Judges, 4 : 163.

Gascoigne-Cecil. See Cecil.

Gasendi, Pierre. Edgar. Boyhood, 181. — New biographies (Bost. 1857), 289.

Gaskell, Mrs. E. C. With portrait. Hamilton, C. J. Wom. writers, 2 : 166. — Walford, L. B. 12 Eng. auth. 755. — (A. E. Bayly) Oliphant. Wom. novelists, 117. — With portrait. Warner Lib. 11 : 6205.

— Molly Gibson. (C. Coleridge) Townsend, M. E. Gt. char. fic. 199.

Gast, Pierre du (sieur De Monte), Biography of. Belknap. Amer. biog. 2 : 15.

Gaston, Esther. Clement, J. Noble deeds, 261.

Gaston, James McFadden. Davidson, J. W. Writ. of South, 215.

Gaston, Margaret. Ellet. Women of revol. 2 : 136.

Gaston, William. Am. Bar Assoc. 17 : 507. — With portrait. [Amer.] Nat. portr. gall. v. 2. — Lossing. Em. Amer. 350. — Moore, F. Am. eloq. 2 : 533.

Gastronomy. Bristed. Pieces, 1 : 126.

Genevan church, The, and Christianity. (H. B. Wilson) Ess. & rev.

Genga, Fabius. Wallace, R. Anti-Trin. biog. 2: 380.

Genghis (or Zingis) Khan. (E. Gibbon) Ferris, G. T. Gt. leaders, 142. — Utterton, F. A. Biog. sk. 101.

Geniality. Stephen, J. F. Ess. by bari. 89.

Genitive case, Origin and import of. Garnett. Philos. ess. 214.

Genius. Bethune. Orations, 3. — Calvert. Biog. essays. — Ferrier. Illus. of Sterne, 2 : 163. — Hedge. Atheism, 354. — Hinton. Thinking, 225. — Holland, E. G. Reviews, 169. — (Sampson Reed) Peabody, E. P. Æsthetic pap. 58. — Veron. Æsthetics. — Whipple. Lit. & life.

— and common sense. Hazlitt. Table talk.

— and expression. Rees, J. R. With friend, 57.

— and liberty. Patterson, R. H. Ess. hist. 351.

— and marriage. Wilde, Lady. Soc. stud. 28.

— and misery, Connection of. (A. Wilson) Edin. ess. '56 : 132.

— and morality. Trail, F. Studies, 152.

— and religion. Trail, F. Studies, 109.

— and talent. Siegvolk. Papers, 108.

— Before. Burroughs. Birds & poets, 161.

— Causes of. Fiske, J. Excurs. 175.

— conscious of its powers. Mathews. Lit. style, 85.

— Early difficulties of. Arnold, F. Turning-points, 162.

— Early maturity of. Jones, W. A. Lit. stud. 2 : 23.

— Failings of. Mabie. My study fire, 29.

— Fortunes of. Hunt, L. Seer, 2 : 232.

— Influence of civilization on. Green, T. H. Works, 3 : 11.

— Last moments of men of. Madden. Infirm. gen. 70.

— Limitations of. Patmore. Princ. in art, 67.

— Method of. Mabie. My study fire, 140.

— Punishment of. Watson, W. Excur. in crit. 23.

— Recipe for. Allen, Grant. Falling in love, 328.

— Solitude of. Alger. Solitudes, 65.

— Specific. Mivart. Ess. 2 : 103.

— true, Sanity of. Lamb. Elia.

— Two kinds of. Salt. Lit. sk. 1.

— Unconsciousness of. Hare. Guesses, 2 : 151.

Genlis, Madame de. Dobson, A. Four French-women. — Kavanagh. Fr. women, 190. — Russell, W. Eccen. 390. — Russell. Extr. women, 232.

Genoa. Buckley, J. M. Trav. 3 cont. 143. — Buckley, T. A. Great cities, 187. — Duffy, B. Tuscan repub. 11 : 28, 106. — Sala. Journey south, 172. — Fairbanks, O. B. Aguecheek, 45. — Fulton, C. C. Europe, 188. — Hare. Cities of No. Italy, 1 : 29. — Howells. Ital. jour. 52. — Tuckerman. Ital. sk. 270. — Pfirshing. Mem. Ital. 33.

— and Paris. Moulton, L. C. Rambles, 23.

— from 1288 to 1410. Duffy, B. Tuscan repub. 223.

— in the time of Barbarossa. Duffy, B. Tuscan repub. 57.

— Italian-American exposition in, 1891. (J. Fletcher) U. S. Cons. Rept. 36 : 625.

— Suburbs of, and country about London. Hunt. Wishing-cap, 213.

— to Naples by sea. Howells. Ital. jour. 65.

Genotin, Mrs. Mary. Burder. Pious wom. 622.

Gensonné, Armand, Speeches of. Stephens, H. M. Ora. Fr. Rev. 1 : 385.

Gent, Thomas, printer. Dobson, A. 18th cent. vign. 3 : 104. — Knight, C. Old booksel. 76.

Genth, Fred. A. (W. Gibbs) Am. Acad. A. & S. Proc. 28 : 393.

Gentiles, Fullness of the. Maitland, S. R. Eight ess. 135.

Gentileschi, Artemisia. Clayton, E. C. Eng. fem. art. 1 : 21.

Gentilis, John Valentine. Wallace, R. Anti-Trin. biog. 2 : 103

Gentility. Friswell. Gentle life, 1 : 1.

— Decayed. Curtis, G. W. Other ess. 142.

Gentils, Philippe de. Wraxall, F. C. L. Remark. adv. 2 : 292.

Gentleman, Character of the. Lieber, F. Rom inis. 225.

— He is a. Siegvolk. Papers, 7.

— The look of a. Hazlitt. Plain speaker, v. 2.

— Qualities of. Gray, E. C. Idle musings, 102. — Mathews. Lit. style, 287.

— Soul of the. Curtis, G. W. Ars rec. viv. 30.

— Who is ? Hole, S. R. Addresses, 255.

Gentlemanliness. Ballantyne. Ess. 59.

Gentlemen, English and American. Higginson. Book & heart, 123.

Gentz, F. von. Hayward, A. Ess. 2d ser. 1 : 71.

Geodetic operations in Russia, History of. (B. Witskowski and J. H. Gore) Smithson. Rept. '90 : 305.

Geoffrey of Monmouth. Collier, W. F. Hist. Eng. lit. 31.

— Literary history of his history. Wright, T. Ess. archæol. 1 : 202.

Geoffrin, Madame Marie Thérèse Rodet. Haussonville. Salon of Necker, .1 : 197. — Ste.-Beuve. Monday chats, 162.

— and the philosophers. Mason, A. C. Wom. of Fr. salons, 168.

Geoffroy St. Hilaire, Etienne. Knox, R. Great artists, 51.

Geographic environment, Influence of. (C. Mindeleff) Am. Geog. Soc. 29 : 1.

Geographical names, Definition of. (K. Ganzenmüller) Am. Geog. Soc. 19 : 355. 21 : 516. 22 : 211, 566.

Geographical work of the U. S. during 1871. (D. C. Gilman) Am. Geog. Soc. 4 : 119.

— — in 1872. (C. P. Daly) Am. Geog. Soc. 4 : 63.

— — in 1873. (C. P. Daly) Am. Geog. Soc. 5 : 49.

— — in 1874. (C. P. Daly) Am. Geog. Soc. 6 : 53.

— — in 1875. (C. P. Daly) Am. Geog. Soc 7 : 31.

— — in 1876. (C. P. Daly) Am. Geog. Soc. 8 : 45.

— — in 1877. (C. P. Daly) Am. Geog. Soc. 10 : 21.

— — in 1878-79. (C. P. Daly) Am. Geog. Soc. 12 : 1.

— — Recent. (C. P. Daly) Am. Geog. Soc. 20 : 1.

Geography from nature. (R. E. Dodge) Am. Geog. Soc. 28 : 146.

— Function and field of. (J. S. Keltie) Smithson. Rept. '97 : 381.

— in the middle ages; Ancient map of the world preserved in Hereford cathedral. Wright, T. Ess. archæol. 2 : 1.

— in the school, Method applied to the teaching of. Laurie, S. S. Educa. addr. 83.

— Marine, Progress of, 1860. Am. Geog. Soc. 2, pt. 1 : 1.

— Modern. (F. Galton) Camb. ess. '55 : 79.

— of the Greeks and Romans. Cust. Ling. studies, 2 : 483.

— Present standpoint of. (C. R. Markham) Smithson. Rept. '93 : 395.

— Present trend of. (W. M. Davis) N. Y. Regents, 111 : 192.

— Progress in, 1846-96. (G. G. Hubbard) Goode. Smithson. Inst. 773.

Geography, Relation of, to history. (Edward Channing) Nat. Educa. Assoc. '95 : 192.
— Reports of a Conference on. (I. C. Russell) Am. Geog. Soc. 27 : 30.
— scientific study of, Plea for. (W. A. Hales) Evol. Crys. pal. lec. 47.
— Teaching of. (V. L. Cameron) Internat. health exh. 13 : 481.
— — How to enliven. (K. Ganzenmüller) Am. Geog. Soc. 19 : 355.
— — in Central Europe. U. S. Bur. Educa. Rept. '92–93 : 279.
— — New departure in. (L. R. Klemm) Nat. Educa. Assoc. '85 : 330.
— — Scientific methods in. (C. F. Palmer) Nat. Educa. Assoc. '88 : 382.
— Value of. (J. P. Thompson) Am. Geog. Soc. 1 : 98.
Geok Tepe, Capture of. Knox, T. W. Battles, 413.
Geologic spaces and periods. Miller, H. Hist. ess. 386.
Geologic time as indicated by sedimentary rocks of No. America. (C. D. Walcott) Smithson. Rept. '93 : 301.
Geological contemporaneity. Huxley. Lay sermons.
Geological history of America. Agassiz. Geol. sk. 1 : 1.
Geological middle age, The. Agassiz. Geol. sk. 1 : 148.
Geological phenomena. Hunt, R. Poe. of sci. 332.
Geological reform. Huxley. Lay sermons.
Geological seasons. Winchell. Sparks geol. ham. 175.
Geological surveys, govt., Utility of. (J. P. Lesley) Phila. Soc. Sci. Assoc. '74.
Geologies, Two. (W. S. Lewis) Living Papers, 11 : no. 63.
Geology. (W. Hopkins) Camb. ess. '57 : 172. — Davy. Works, 8 : 180.
— and Christianity, Defence of Miller's Testimony of the rocks. Bayne, P. Ess. 2 : 356.
— and culture. (A. Winchell) N. Y. Regents, 102 : app. 69.
— and religion. Forbes, E. Lit. papers, v. 1.
— Application of physics and mathematics to. (C. Chree) Smithson. Rept. '91 : 127.
— Bibliography. (J. M. Clarke) Albany State Mus. Rept. no. 47. — Salem (Mass.) Pub. Lib. Bull. Apr. '94.
— Change and time in. (Archibald Geikie) Smithson. Rept. '92 : 111.
— Continental problems of. (G. K. Gilbert) Smithson. Rept. '92 : 163.
— department of, in U. S. Nat. Mus., Handbook of. (G. P. Merrill) U. S. Nat. Mus. Rept. '90 : 503.
— Glacial. (James Geikie) Smithson. Rept. '90 : 221.
— Heroes of. Duncan, P. M. Botanists, 209.
— in early education. (Alexander Winchell) Nat. Educa. Assoc. '90 : 587.
— North American. Bibliography. (N. H. Darton) U. S. Geol. Surv. Bull. no. 127. — (F. B Weeks) U. S. Geol. Surv. Bull. nos. 149. 156.
— of Oxford and its neighborhood. (J. Phillips) Oxf. ess. '55 : 196.
— Progress in, 1846–96. (W. N. Rice) Goode. Smithson. Inst. 631.
— Relation of, to water-supplies of the U. S. (E. Orton) Am. Pub. Health, 2 : 292.
— Romance of. Chambers's Miscel. no. 18.
— Teaching of, in colleges and univ. of U. S. (J.

C. Hopkins) U. S. Bur. Ed. Rept. '93–94, 1 : 819.
Geology, Town. Kingsley, C. Sci. lec.
— vs. astronomy. Miller, H. Hist. ess. 370.
Geometrical axioms, Origin and significance of. Helmholtz. Pop. lec. 2 : 27.
Geometry and algebra. (C. T. R. Smith) N. Y. Regents, 100 : app. 227.
— in our schools. (Matilda T. Karnes) Nat. Educa. Assoc. '91 : 651.
— Postulates of. Clifford. Lec. & ess. 210.
"Geoponica Geoponicorum;" collection of agricultural opinions. Mitchell. Wet days, 71.
Georg, Jean Michel. Brightwell. Byepaths of biog. 168.
George, St., of England. Baring-Gould. Myths, 266. — Charles. Martyrs, 132. — Doran. Knights, 113.
— calumniated by Gibbon. Helps. Brevia.
George Pisida, St. Browning, E. B. Ess. poets, 76.
George I., of England. Georgian era, 1 : 17.
— Character of. Doran. Queens Hanov. 1.
George II., of England. Georgian era, 1 : 29.
George III., of England. Brougham. Works, 3 : 9. — Georgian era, 1 : 63. — Scott, W. Biog. mem. v. 2. — Edwards, E. Founders Brit. Mus. 2 : 464. — Fitzgerald, P. Royal dukes, 1 : 1. — Mitchell, D. G. Eng. lands, 3 : 181.
— Coronation of. Doran. Queens Hanov. v. 2. — Goldsmith. Miscel. (N. Y. 4 v.) 1 : 248.
— Daughters of. Hall, Mrs. M. Princesses, 305.
— Death of. Doran. Queens Hanov. v. 2.
— Insanity of, proceedings in parliament. Canning. Speeches, 3 : 50.
— Letters to Lord North. Brougham. Works, 3 : 67.
George IV., of England. Brougham. Works, 4 : 5. — Georgian era, 1 : 105.
— and his Queen. Browne, G. L. State trials 19th cent. 2 : 339.
— as prince of Wales. Doran. Queens Hanov. v. 2.
— as prince regent. Mitchell, D. G. Eng. lands, 4 : 118, 165.
— Coronation of Queen Caroline and. Doran. Queens Hanov. v. 2.
George I., king of Greece, with portr. Crowned heads, 57.
George Augustus of Hanover, prince of Wales. Doran. Princes of Wales, 445.
George Augustus Frederick of St. James, prince of Wales. Doran. Princes of Wales, 513.
George William Frederick of Norfolk House, prince of Wales. Doran. Princes of Wales, 496.
George, David. Wallace, R. Anti-Trin. biog. 3 : 544.
George, Mrs. E. E. Brockett. Woman's work, 511. — Moore, F. Women of the war, 333.
George, Enoch. Gorrie. Em. Meth. 244. — Wakeley. Heroes Meth. 137.
George, Henry, Progress and poverty. Rae, J. Contem. ess. 380.
— Schemes of. Kempner, W. Common-sense soc. 113.
George, John Hatch, with portrait. Sketches N. H. men, 98.
George, Leopold. Erdmann. Hist. philos. 3 : 219.
George, Fort, Capture of. Dawson. Batt. of U. S. 2 : 231.
George, Lake. Badeau. Vagabond, 194. — Benjamin, S. G. W. World's paradises, 170. — Curtis, G. W. Lotus, 127. — Pidgeon. Old world ques. 332.

Germany. Evolution of the German state. Lee, A. E. Europ. days, 32.

— Exports to the U. S., 1892. (F. H. Mason) U S. Cons. Rept. **39** : 647.

— Federal constitution of. (E. J. James) Univ. Pa. Pub. Pol. Econ. **1** : no. 7.

— Federal system in. Bibliography. Hart, A. B. Stud. of. Fed. gov.

— Feudal and imperial. Stillé. Stud. med. 158.

— Foreign commerce and industrial progress of. (F. H. Mason) U. S. Const. Rept. **59** : 119.

— France, and England, 1870. Gladstone. Gleam. **4** : 197.

— Grain question in, 1891. (J. H. Smith) U. S. Cons. Rept. **36** : 635.

— How the Germans educate. Lee, A. E. Europ. days, 88.

— in 1887. Dilke. Eur. politics.

— Intoxicating liquors in, 1892. (W. H. Edwards) U. S. Const. Rept. **39** : 755.

— Iron and coal trade of, 1891. (W. H. Edwards) U. S. Cons. Rept. **37** : 215.

— Life in. Bellows. Old world, **1** : 91.

— Local transportation in, 1891. U. S. Cons. Rept. **38** : 633.

— Making of. Lilly, W. S. Ess. 143.

— Manufacture of wood pulp in, 1893. (F. H. Mason) U. S. Cons. Rept. **42** : 123.

— Metal founding in, 1893. U. S. Cons. Rept. **42** : 373.

— Modern, Starting-point and first stages of. Hillebrand. Ger. thought, 37.

— The new. (A. D. White) Am. Geog. Soc. **14** : 205.

— of the past and of to-day. Whitman, S. Teuton. stud. 1.

— Old towns of. Mahaffy. Holl. & Germ. 106.

— Parliamentary experiment in. (K. Francke) Am. Hist. Assoc. **3** : 133.

— Prices in, in 1872. Leslie, T. E. C. Ess. pol. econ. 326.

— Reformation in. Wittenmeyer. Women Reform. 361.

— Religion in. Bellows. Old world, **1** : 100.

— Religious opinion in. Hall, G. S. Asp. Ger. 7.

— Religious state of, in 1893. (Count A. Bernstorff) Barrows, J. H. Parl. relig. **2** : 986.

— Revolutions in history of. Butler, Chas. Works, v. **2**.

— Rome and, in middle ages. Döllinger. Stud. hist. 58.

— society in, Aspects of. Taylor, B. At home, **1** : 458.

-- Underground conduits in, 1891. U. S. Cons. Rept. **38** : 764.

— Western boundary of. Moltke. Ess. **1** : 165.

Germs, Disease. (G. M. Sternberg) Am. Pub. Health, **10** : 69. — Nichols, J. R. Fireside sci. 255. — (A. Wilson) Proctor, R. A. Nat. stud. 250. — Proctor, R. A. Other suns, 313.

— in dust. Tyndall. Frag. sci. 277.

— Micro-organisms in air of a hospital. (G. R. Tucker) Mass. Health, '88 : 161.

See also Bacteria.

Gérôme, Jean L. Hamerton. Contem. Fr. painters. — (W. H. Low) Van Dyke, J. C. Mod. Fr. mast. 31.

Gerona and its cathedral. Stoddard C. A. Span. cit. 6.

Geronimo, St. Little, W. J. K. Sketches, 1.

Gerry, Elbridge, 1744–1814. Dwight, N. Signers of decl. 58. — Lincoln, R. W. Signers, 22. — Lossing. Signers, 40. — Sanderson. Signers, 8.

Gerson, Jean Charlier. Townsend, W. J. Schoolmen, 291.

Gervinus, G. G., and instrumental music. Ehlert. Tone world, 57.

Gesenius, Justus. Miller, Jos. Singers church, 2d ed. 66.

Gesenius, Wilhelm. Cheyne. Founders O. T. crit. 54.

Gesner, Conrad. Duncan, P. M. Botanists, 125. — Jardine, W. Nat. lib. v. **20**. — Morley, H. Marot, **2** : 97. — Macgillivray, W. Em. zoöl.

Gesner, Solomon, Swiss poet. Craik. Pursuit knowl. **1** : 153. — Winkworth. Chr. singers Germ. 239.

Gesta Romanorum. Warner Lib. **11** : 6261.

Geste, Guillaume de. Miller, Jos. Singers church, 2d ed. 143.

Gesticulation. Cook, D. On stage, **1** : 48.

— Italian. Wiseman, N. Ess. **3** : 531.

Gesture, descriptive, Psychology of. (S. H. Clark) Nat. Educa. Assoc. '96 : 497.

— A method of teaching. (H. B. Sprague) N. Y. Regents, **89** : 597.

Gethin, Lady Grace. Williams, Jane. Lit. wom. 129.

Gethsemane, Garden of. Hoppin. Notes theol. stud. 231.

Getting on. Boyd. Every-day, 183.

Gettings, William. Whitehead, C. Highwaymen, **2** : 100.

Getty, Archibald. Winslow, S. N. Biog. Phila. merch. 175.

Gettysburg, Battle of. (H. P. Goodnow) Am. Hist. Assoc. Rept. '95 : 413. — Cooke, J. E. Life of Lee, 281. — King, C. Battles, 587. — Knox, T. W. Battles, 230. — Swinton. 12 battles, 311. — Pennypacker. Hist. sk. 305. — Stine, J. H. Army Poto. 447.

— The charge at. Lodge & Roosevelt. Herotales, 225.

— First gun at. (J. L. Beveridge) Mill. ess. M. O. L. L. U. S. Ills. 79.

Geysers, The. Jackson, H. H. Bits trav. home, 41. — (W. H. Weed) Smithson. Rept. '91 : 163.

— of California. Marshall, W. G. Thro' Amer. 307. — Taylor, B. At home, **2** : 65.

— Soaping. (Arnold Hague) Smithson. Rept. '92 : 153.

Ghent. Thackeray. Early and late, 167.

— Amer. products in, 1893. (J. B. Osborne) U. S. Cons. Rept. **43** : 165.

— Horticulture at. (H. C. Morris) U. S. Cons. Rept. **50** : 51.

— Industries and working people of, 1896. (H. C. Morris) U. S. Cons. Rept. **52** : 303.

— Trade and industries of, 1892. (J. B. Osborne) U. S. Cons. Rept. **40** : 1.

Ghetto, Story of the. Wraxall, C. F. L. Hist. bye-ways, **2** : 88.

Ghibeline, Origin of the name. Pennington. Epochs papacy, 91.

Ghiberti, Lorenzo. Brightwell. Heroes of lab. 74. — Jameson. Ital. painters, 64. — Oliphant. Makers of Fr. 124. — Symonds. Renais. fine arts, 127. — Perkins, C. C. Tusc. sculp. **1** : 124. — Gates of. Jarves. Ital. ramb. 263.

Ghirlandajo, Domenico. (K. Woermann) Dohme, R. Early mast. 356. — Jameson. Ital. painters, 106. — Symonds. Renais. fine arts, 258. — Stillman, W. J. Old Ital. mas. 194.

Gholson, William Yates. (W. P. Garrison) Harvard mem. biog. **2** : 237.

Ghost-seeing. Hedge, F. H. Martin Luther, 250.

Ghost stories. Jameson. Studies. — Zangwill. Without prej. 145.

Ghost-world, The primeval. Fiske. Myths, 269.

Ghosts and ghost-seers. Brown, S. Atom, 2.
— and goblins. Proctor. Borderland, 406.
— The argument in favor of. Arnold, F. Armchair, 236.
— of old and new school. Roscoe, W. C. Poems & ess. v. 2.
— Primeval. Fiske. Myths, 209.
— Stage. Cook, D. Book of play, 1 : 293.

Giant rabbit, Myth of. Brinton. Amer. hero-myths, 37.

Giant's causeway. Taylor, B. Views, 33.

Giants. Buckland, F. T. Curios. nat. hist. 4 : 1–19. — Wilson, A. Nat. note-book, 215.
— Ogres, and cyclops. Hunt. Day by fire, 231.

Gibbes, Sarah R. Ellet. Women of revol. 1 : 208.

Gibbon, Edward. Anton. Masters in hist.
— Bagehot. Estimates, 104. — Brougham. Works, 2 : 378. — Collier, W. F. Hist. Eng. lit. 363. — Cooper, T. Triumphs of persev. 42.
— Duyckinck. Portrait gall. 1 : 75. — Edgar. Boyhood, 35. — Lawrence. Brit. historians, 2 : 244. — Ste.-Beuve. Eng. portraits, 116. — Wotton. Word portraits, 107. — Birrell, A. Res judicatæ, 39. — Stephen, J. F. Horæ Sabb. 2 : 386, 402. — Hundred greatest men, 308. — (Henry Rogers) Macaulay. New biog. 242. — Mitchell, D. G. Eng. lands, 3 : 122. — Ste.-Beuve. Sel. ess. 139. — Russell, W. C. Book of au. 303. — With portrait. (W. E. H. Lecky) Warner Lib. 11 : 6271. Same in Warner classics, 4 : 9.
— and Madame Necker. Haussonville. Salon of Necker, 1 : 32. — Hitchcock, T. Unhap. loves, 1.
— Autobiography. Stephen, L. Stud. biog. 1 : 147.
— Bibliography. Roy. Hist. Soc. Proc. Gibbon commemor. '95.
— Works. Stephen, L. Eng. thought, 1 : 446.

Gibbons, Abby Hopper. (L. G. Runkle) Brockett. Woman's work, 467. — Our fam. wom. 316.

Gibbons, Orlando. Keddie. Mus. comp. 8.

Gibbons, Sarah H. (afterwards Mrs. Emerson). Brockett. Woman's work, 467.

Gibbons, Simeon B. Walker, C. D. Biog. Va. Mil. Inst. 266.

Gibbons, Thomas. Hatfield, E. F. Poets of ch. 258. — Miller, Jos. Singers church, 2d ed. 225.

Gibbons, William. Jones, C. C., jr. Deleg. fr. Georgia, 40.

Gibbs, James E. A., with portrait. Rogers, A. C. Repres. men, 255.

Gibbs, John. Ivimey. Eng. Bapt. 2 : 79.

Gibbs, Philip. Ivimey. Eng. Bapt. 4 : 298.

Gibbs, Sir Vicary. Brougham. Works, 3 : 215.
— Creasy. Etonians, 463. — Foss. Judges, 8 : 287. — Townsend. Twelve judges, 1 : 239.

Gibbs, Wolcott. Vaille & Clark. Harv. book, v. 1.

Giberne, Maria. Mozley. Reminis. 2 : 44.

Gibraltar. Buckley, J. M. Trav. 3 cont. 103. — Congreve, R. Ess. 1. — Davis, R. H. Rulers Medit. 1. — Moore, Jos. Outl. Eur. 280. — Smith, Goldw. The empire, 204. — Stoddard. Red letter, 56. — Utterton, F. A. Biog. sk. 239. — Warner, C. D. Roundabout, 144. — Pfirshing. Mem. Ital. 23. — Stoddard, C. A. Span. cit. 186. — Thomas, M. Scamper through Spain, 203.
— Impressions of. Disraeli, B. Home letters, 6.
— Siege of. Robson, W. Sieges, 235.

Gibson, Gen. George. Neven, D. R. B. Pennsylvanians, 153.

Gibson, George Stacey, with portrait. Smith, C. R. Retrospec. 3 : 111.

Gibson, John. Smiles. Self-help.

Gibson, John, of Indiana. Woollen. Biog. sk. Indiana, 11.

Gibson, Gen. John. Neven, D. R. B. Pennsylvanians, 153.

Gibson, John Bannister, 1780–1853. Brown, D. P. Forum, 1 : 418.

Gibson, Susanna. Hack. Self-surr. 303.

Gibson, Thos. Milner. Francis, G H Orators, 224. — With portrait. Nicoll. Great move. 291. — Ritchie. Brit. sena. 239.

Giddings, Joshua R. Bartlett, D. W. Mod. agit. 170.
— Tribute to. Garfield. Works, 1 : 593.

Gideon. Geikie, C. Old Test. char. 150.

Giffard, William, bishop of Winchester. Foss. Judges, 1 : 118.

Gifford, Andrew. Ivimey. Eng. Bapt. 1 : 412. 2 : 541. 3 : 574, 592.

Gifford, Emanuel. Ivimey. Eng. Bapt. 2 : 552.

Gifford, John. Ivimey. Eng. Bapt. 2 : 18.

Gifford, Robert Swain. With portrait. Benjamin, S. G. W. Am. art. 1. — Sheldon, G. W. Amer. painters, 93.

Gifford, Sanford Robinson. With portrait. Benjamin, S. G. W. Am. art. 1. — Sheldon, G. W. Amer. painters, 14. — Tuckerman. Artists, 524.

Gifford, William. Austin & Ralph. Laureates, 49. — Cooper, T. Triumphs of persev. 35. — Craik. Pursuit knowl. 1 : 398. — Davenport, R. A. Lives, 1. — Devey. Mod. Eng. poets, 136. — Edwards, B. B. Self-taught, 110. — Hazlitt. Spirit. — Jerdan. Men, 237. — Lives of dist. shoemak. 166. — Seymour, C. C. B. Self-made, 374. — Winks. Illus. shoemakers, 77.
— and the Quarterly. Mitchell, D. G. Eng. lands, 4 : 113.
— Early years of. Stoddard, R. H. Under eve. lamp, 91.
— Letter to. Hazlitt. Spirit.

Gifts. Emerson. Ess. 2 : 151. — Repplier, A. In dozy hours, 85.
— Limitation of the right to receive. Kempner, W. Common-sense soc. 279.
— Selection of. Woolson. Browsing, 91.

Gignoux, F. R. Tuckerman. Artists, 507.

Gigs, Margaret. Williams, Jane. Lit wom. 42.

Gilbert, Adrian. Bourne, H. R. F. Eng. seam. 1 : 248.

Gilbert, Ann. Miller, Jos. Singers church, 2d ed. 374.

Gilbert, Bartholomew. Belknap. Amer. biog. 2 : 237.

Gilbert, Dr. Daniel. (D. D. Gilbert) N. E. Hist.-Gen. Soc. Biog. 1 : 199.

Gilbert, Davies G. Walker, W., jr. Men of sci. 53.

Gilbert, Mrs. G. H. Winter. Shadows, 374.

Gilbert, Sir Humphrey. Barrow, J. Nav. worthies, 61. — Belknap. Amer. biog. 1 : 272. — Bourne, H. R. F. Eng. seam. 1 : 109, 178. — Creasy. Etonians, 55 — Gilman. Pathfinders, 51. — Higginson, T. W. Amer. explorers, 167. — Payne, E. J. Voyages of Eliz. seamen, 171.
— Death of. (D. Brymner) Roy. Soc. Can. 2d ser. 2, sec. 2 : 33.
— Expedition of, Termination of. (G. Patterson) Roy. Soc. Can. 2d ser. 3, sec. 2 : 113.

Gilbert, Sir J., with photo. Cooper, T. Men of mark, 2 : 28.

Gilbert, John, with portrait. Carroll, H. Twelve
Amer. 169. — (S. Fiske) McKay, F. E. Fam.
actors, 170. — Winter, W. Shadows, 2 : 81.
Gilbert, William. Munro, J. Pioneers elec. 33.
Gilbert, William Schwenck. Archer. Eng. dram.
148. — Miles, A. H. Poets of cent. 9 : 501. —
— With portrait. Warner Lib. 11 : 6333. —
Wilman, G. Sk. liv. celeb. 91.
Gilburne, Samuel. Collier. Actors, 189.
Gilchrist, Anne. Scudder, H. E. Men & let.
195.
Gilchrist, J. C. (H. Sabin) Nat. Educa. Assoc.
'98 : 291.
Gilder, R. W. Bolton, S. K. Amer. au. 309. —
Richardson. Amer. lit. 2 : 243. — With por-
trait. Warner Lib. 11 : 6347.
— The new day. Taylor, B. Crit. ess. 308.
Gildersleeve, Basil L. Davidson, J. W. Writ.
of South, 223.
Gildon, Charles. Crichton, A. Converts, 1 : 281.
Gilds. Brentano. Rela. of labor to law. —
Gomme. Literature of local instit. 146. —
Howell. Capital and labor. — Weeden. Social
law of labor.
Giles, St., patron of lepers. Charles. Martyrs,
376.
— Bibliography. Rembry. St. Giles, 1 : xxiii.
Giles, Charles. Hatfield, E. F. Poets of church,
261.
Giles, Joel. Loring, J. S. Hundred Bost. ora.
656.
Giles, John Eustace. Miller, Jos. Singers church,
2d ed. 482.
Giles, William B. Moore, F. Am. eloq. 2 : 189.
Gilfillan, Robert. Wilson, J. G. Poets of sci. 2 :
177.
Gilhooley, pseud. See Clark, W. W.
Gill, John. Ivimey. Eng. Bapt. 3 : 272. 3 : 430.
Gill, Thomas Hornblower. Hatfield, E. F. Poets
of church, 263. — (W. G. Horder) Miles, A. H.
Poets of cent. 10 : 361.
Gill, William. Wakeley. Heroes Meth. 199.
Gillespie, George. Blaikie, W. G. Preachers
Scot. 137.
Gillies, Margaret. Clayton, E. C. Eng. fem. art.
2 : 87.
Gillon, ——. Grant, J. Recoll. Lords & Comm.
2 : 256.
Gilman, Mrs. Caroline Howard. Davidson, J.
W. Writ. of South, 224. — Freeman, J. D.
Wom. of South. — Griswold. Fem. poets, 52.
— Hart, J. S. Fem. prose, 49. — Putnam, A.
P. Singers liberal, 76.
Gilman, Samuel. Putnam, A. P. Singers liberal,
721.
Gilman, Virgil C., with portrait. Sketches N. H.
men, 148.
Gilmer, John A. Livingston, J. Em. Am. lawy.
591.
Gilmore, Thomas. Am. Bar Assoc. 14 : 419.
Gilmore's Peace Jubilee, 1869. Howells. Sub.
sk. 195.
Gilpin, Bernard. Adams, W. H. D. Worthies
Ch. Eng. 79. — Gilpin. Reformers, v. 2. —
Pierce, B. K. Em. dead, 66. — (G. Carleton)
Wordsworth, C. Eccles. biog. v. 3.
Gilpin, Charles. Ritchie. Brit. sena.
Gilpin, H. D. Everett. Orat. v. 4.
Gilray, James, and his caricatures. Timbs, J.
Eng. eccen. 330. — Wright, J. Hist. carica.
464.
Gilson, Helen Louise. Brockett. Woman's
work, 133.
Ginevra, Ariosto and. Jameson. Loves of poets.
— Tale of. Terhune. Where ghosts, 147.

Ginseng, American, in China, 1898. (R. Wildman) U. S. Cons. Rept. 56 : 514.
— in Korea, 1898. (H. N. Allen) U. S. Cons. Rept.
56 : 517.
Gioberti, Vicenzo. Brownson. Works, 2 : 101.
— Political influence of. Wrightson. Mod. Italy,
159.
Giocondo, Fra. Milizia. Lives arch. 1 : 237.
Giordano, Luca. Jervis, Lady. Painting, 2 :
29. — Stirling-Maxwell. Ann. art. Spain, 3 :
1147.
Giorgione, G. Barbarelli, called. Jervis, Lady.
Painting, 1 : 209. Ottley. Ital. school. — Still-
man, W. J. Old Ital. mas. 246. — Jameson.
Ital. painters, 310. — Keddie, H. Old masters,
181. — Lee, H. F. Old painters, 177. — Oli-
phant. Makers of Venice, 294. — Symonds.
Renais. fine arts, 366.
Giotto. Jameson. Ital. painters, 25. — Jarves.
Art stud. 122. — Jervis, Lady. Painting, 1 : 67.
— Lee, H. F. Old painters, 37. — Oliphant.
Makers of Fr. 101. — Ottley. Ital. school. —
Ruskin. Miscellanea, 1. — Symonds. Renais.
fine arts, 189. — Stillman, W. J. Old Ital. mas.
28.
— and his works in Padua. Ruskin. Miscel. v. 1.
— St. Francis before the Soldan. (J. Ruskin)
Singleton, E. Great pic. 202.
Giovanbatista of Toledo. Milizia. Lives arch.
1 : 330.
Gipsies, The. Chambers's Miscel. no. 139.
See Gypsies.
Giraffe, The. Morgan, C. L. Animal sk. 37.
Giraldus Cambrensis. Morley. Eng. writers, 3 :
64. — Parry. Cam. Plutarch, 146. — Purnell.
Liter. 96.
Girard, Regnault, Journey to Scotland in 1435.
Jusserand. Eng. Ess. 24.
Girard, Stephen. With portrait. Duyckinck.
Nat. portr. gall. 1 : 467. — Houghton. Kings,
15. — Hunt, F. Am. merch. 1 : 227. — Los-
sing. Em. Amer. 271. — McCabe, J. D. Great
fortunes, 33. — With portrait. Seymour, C.
C. B. Self-made, 165. — Wise, D. Vanq. vic-
tors, 133.
— and Girard College. Bolton, S. K. Givers, 29.
— Parton. Fam. Amer. 221.
— and J. J. Astor, Comparison of. Bristed.
Pieces, 4 : 4.
Girard College. Comegys. Tour, 179.
— Contributions to history of. Wood, G. B. Hist.
mem. 485.
— Course of study. Webster, N. Papers, 291.
— Speech on, 1844. Webster, D. Works, 6 : 133.
Girardin, Delphine de. Challice. French au-
thors, 1 : 105. — (Imbert de Saint-Amand) Gau-
tier. Fam. Fr. au. 56.
— and Geo. Sand. Challice. Fr. authors, 2 :
53.
Girardin, Emile de. Castelar. Byron, 237. —
Men of 3d repub. 221.
— in the Rue de La Pérouse. Yates, E. H. Celeb.
3 : 123.
Girardin, Saint-Marc. See Saint-Marc Girardin.
Girgenti. Hare. Cities of So. Italy, 462. — Symonds. Sk. So. Eur. 2 : 36. — Warner, C. D.
Roundabout, 93.
Girl, The American. Curtis, G. W. Other ess.
166.
Girlhood and girls. Fairbanks, O. B. Aguecheek, 270.
— to womanhood, Transition from. Holland, J.
G. Titcomb's let. 94.
Girls, American. Osgood, S. Amer. leaves, 93.
— at home. Friswell. Better self, 23.

—Giles, H. Lectures, 1 : 218. — Howitt. Homes Br. poets, 1 : 322. — Jeaffreson. Novelists, 1 : 223. — Lawrence. Brit. historians, 2 : 318. — Macaulay. Ess. 6 : 151. — Mitchell. Wet days, 242. — Sanborn, K. Eng. poets, 218. — Scott, W. Biog. mem. v. 1. — Taylor, W. C. Mod. Brit. Plut. 163. — Timbs. Anec. biog. wits, v. 1. — Thackeray. Humorists. — Tuckerman. Poets, 30. — (E. Dowden) Ward. Eng. poets, 3 : 368. — Wotton. Word portraits, 112. — Gostwick, J. Eng. poets, 107. — Macaulay, Biog. Encyc. Brit.; or Biog. sk. 37; or New biog. 224. — Murray, J. O'K. Prose & poet. Irel. 192. — Russell, W. C. Book of au. 278. — With portrait. (C. M. Gayley) Warner Lib. 11 : 6501. — Wise, D. Vanq. victors, 224. — Wrangham. Brit. Plutarch, v. 6.

Goldsmith, Oliver, and the history of prose fiction in England. Windsor. Ethica, 285.
— Bibliography. (J. P. Anderson) Dobson. Life of G.
— Deserted village. Quayle, W. A. Poet, 265.
— his friends and his critics. Whiteside, J. Ess.
— Poems and plays of. Dobson, A. Miscel. 7.
— She stoops to conquer. Molloy. Famous plays, 127.
— Vicar of Wakefield. Saunders, F. Famous books, 102.
— — and its illustrators. Dobson, A. Miscel. 165.

Goldsmith and silversmith, Art of the. Robinson, F. S. Connois. 238.
Goldsmiths, French. Perkins, C. C. Tusc. sculp. 2 : 124.
Goldthwaite, Alfred. Am. Bar Assoc. 15 : 441.
Golf. Hutton, L. Other times, 32. — Lang. Leaders, 53. — Whitney, C. W. Sport. pilgr. 331, 363.
Goliath. Geikie, C. Old Test. char. 221.
Golightly, Charles Portalis. Mozley. Reminis. 2 : 110.
Gomanton. Abercromby. Seas & skies, 337.
Gomersall, Robert. Bell, R. Lit. & sci. men, 2 : 180.
Gomez, Miss Louisa, of Calcutta. Pitman, Mrs. Heroines mission. 356.
Goncharof, Ivan Alexandrovitch, with portrait. (N. H. Dole) Warner Lib. 11 : 6533.
Goncourt, Edmond de. Blaze de Bury, Mme. French lit. 53. — Van de Velde. Fr. fic. 2 : 138. — With portrait. Warner Lib. 11 : 6549.
— and Jules de. Journal. James, H. Ess. in Lond. 186. — Pellissier. Lit. move. Fr. 422.
Goncourt, Jules de. Warner Lib. 11 : 6549.
Gondokoro. Barker, Lady. Travel. about, 269.
Gondolier's wedding, The. Symonds, J. A. Ital. byways.
Gondomar, Diego Sarmiento de Acuña. Smith, G. B. Ambass. 123.
"Gone." Boyd. Leis. hours, Bost. 93.
Gonesius, Peter. Wallace, R. Anti-Trin. biog. 2 : 171.
Gongora y Argote, Luis de. Montgomery. Men of Ita. 3 : 243. — Ticknor. Span. lit. 2 : 521. — Shelley, Mrs. Lit. men Italy, v. 2.
Gonorrhœa, Protection of the innocent from. (F. C. Valentine) Am. Pub. Health, 22 : 234.
Gonzalo Fernandez de Córdova. Quintana. Lives Span. 224. — Utterton, F. A. Biog. sk. 129. — Wilson, J. G. Illus. sol. 11.
Good, John Mason, Biographical notice of. Drake, N. Mornings, 1 : 322. — Georgian era, 2 : 448.
Good and evil. Jouffroy. Philos. miscel. 2 : 102.

Good and evil, Knowledge of. Martin, E. S. Cousin Anthony, 103.
— On doing good. Friswell. Gentle life, 2 : 120.
Good Hope, Cape of, Census, 1891. U. S. Cons. Rept. 38 : 504.
Good Friday. Hutton, L. Other times, 128.
Good Government Clubs and Municipal Leagues. (H. Welso) Nat. Conf. City Govt. 2-3 : 146.
Good-humor and ill. Thompson, H. M. Copy, 285.
Good-nature. Hazlitt. Round-table.
Good-natured and ill-natured people. Helps. Brevia.
Good old times. Ess. from Nation, 41.
Goodall, F., with photo. Cooper, T. Men of mark, 3 : 13.
Goode, Edmond. Walker, C. D. Biog. Va. Mil. Inst. 248.
Goode, George Brown. (D. S. Jordan) Goode. Smithson. Inst. 501.
Goode, William. Hatfield, E. F. Poets of church, 266. — Miller, Jos. Singers church, 2d ed. 331.
Goodell, Constans L. Hemenway. Poets of Vt. 132.
Goodell, David H., with portrait. Sketches N. H. men, 233.
Goodell, Rev. William. Creegan. Gt. mission. 31. — With portrait. (Rev. S. C. Bartlett) Haydn, H. C. Am. miss. heroes, no. 5.
Goodenough, John G. Japp, A. H. Leaders of men, 140.
Goodenow, Daniel. Livingston, J. Em. Am. lawy. 615.
Goodere, Capt., Trial of, for murder. Burke, P. Cel. trials.
Goodford, Charles O., with photo. Cooper, T. Men of mark, 3 : 27.
Goodhart, Morris. Am. Bar Assoc. 20 : 548.
Goodhue, Jonathan. Hunt, F. Am. merch. 1 : 345.
Goodman, Cardell. Doran. Annals of stage, 1 : 73.
Goodness of nature. Bacon. Ess.
— Negative. Oxenham. Short stud. 28.
Goodrich, Frank Boot. Derby, J. C. Fifty years, 123.
Goodrich, John Franklin. (T. W. Higginson) Harv. mem. biog. 1 : 126.
Goodrich, Mrs. Ellet. Pioneer wom. 400.
Goodrich, Samuel Griswold. Derby, J. C. Fifty years, 110. — Everest. Poets of Conn. 213. — Griswold. Prose writ. 593. — Griswold. Poets Am. 200. — With portrait. Mitchell, D. G. Am. lands, 1 : 330.
Goodrich, Thomas. Campbell. Ld. chan. 2 : 160.
Goodrich Court and Castle. Smith, C. R. Retrospec. 1 : 41.
Goodridge, Richard. Holland, J. Psalmists, 2 : 53.
Goodsir, Sir J. Arnold, F. Turning-points, 175.
Goodwin, Harvey, bishop of Carlisle. Arnold, F. Our bishops, 2 : 57.
Goodwin, Ichabod, with portrait. Sketches N. H. men, 133.
Goodwin, John Noble, with portrait. Rogers, A. C. Repres. men, 267.
Goodwin, Mehetable. Drake, S. G. Trag. of wilderness, 111.
Goodwin, Nathaniel. (H. Barnard) N. E. Hist.-Gen. Soc. Biog. 2 : 358.
Goodwin, Nat. C., with portrait. (F. E. Chase) McKay, F. E. Fam. actors, 377.
Goodwin, Richard Chapman. (L. N. Goodwin). Harvard mem. biog. 1 : 273.

Goodwin, Wm. Watson. Vaille & Clarke. Harv. book, v. 1.

Goodwin Sands, The. Treanor, T. S. Heroes Goodwin Sands, 13.

Goodwyn, Robert H. Livingston, J. Dist. Amer. 81.

Goodyear, Charles. Houghton. Kings, 302. — Parton. Fam. Amer. 307. — Parton. Peop. bk. biog. 215. —, With portrait. Hubert, P. G., jr. Inventors, 155. — Towle, G. M. Heroes of inven. 170.

Googe, Barnaby. Morley, H. Eng. writ. 9: 21.

Goold, Thomas, Sergeant. Curran. Irish bar, 1: 183. — Sheil. Sk. Irish bar, 1: 232.

Goose, Mother. Bibliography. Whitmore, W. H., ed. Orig. Moth. Goose melody.

Gorboduc, Tragedy of. Lennox, W. P. Plays, 1: 11.

Gordon, C. P. Miller, S. F. Bench of Ga. v. 2.

Gordon, Chas. G., Gen. Adams, W. H. D. In perils oft, 472. — Charles, E. Three martyrs. — Benson & Tatham. Men of might, 257. — Em. persons, 3: 191. — Malortie. Here, there, 180.

— and the Mahdi. Latimer. Eur. in Afr. in 19th cent. 66.

— and Taiping rebellion. Chesney. Ess. mil. biog. 350.

— Death of. Pembroke, Earl. Polit. let. 428.

— in the Soudan. Cust. Ling. ess. 3: 580.

— War in Soudan for rescue of. (R. E. Colston) Am. Geog. Soc. 17: 125.

Gordon, Lady Duff. Mayer, G. T. Wom. of let. 2: 261.

Gordon, George, Lord, Trial of, for high-treason. Erskine, T. Speeches, 51.

Gordon, George H. Livingston, J. Dist. Amer. 499. — Livingston, J. Em. Am. lawy. 673.

Gordon, Jane, Duchess of. Willing. Dames, 87.

Gordon, Jane Campbell. See Kenmure, J. C., viscountess of.

Gordon, John B. Pollard. Life of Lee, 535.

"Gordon, Lord," adventurer and swindler. Chambers, W. Rem. pers. 71.

Gordon, Lucie Austin Duff. Japp. Wise words, 31.

Gordon, General P. Diary. Ellesmere. Ess. 433.

Gordon, Thomas. Field, R. S. Prov. courts, N. J. 86.

Gordon, William. Lossing. Em. Amer. 166.

Gordon, Sir William, of Gordon's battery. Chesney. Ess. mil. biog. 341.

Gordon, William. See Kenmure, W. Gordon, earl of.

Gordon families. Taylor, J. Fam. of Scot. 2: 292.

Gore, Catherine Grace. Horne, R. H. New spirit, 137.

— Quid pro quo. Cook, D. On stage, 2: 273.

Gore, Christopher. Mass. Hist. Coll. 3d ser. 3: 191.

Gorecki, Anton. Soboleski. Poets of Poland, 413.

Gorges, Ferdinando. Belknap. Amer. biog. 2: 47.

— and the Council for N. England. Adams, C. F. Three episodes, 1: 105, 294.

Gorham, Geo. C., Controversy in case of. Stanley. Essays, 1.

— vs. the Bishop of Exeter. Thirlwall, C. Remains, 1: 151.

Goring, George, Lord. Lodge. Portraits (Bohn), v. 4.

Gormandizing. Thackeray. Early & late, 1.

Gortchakoff, Prince Alexander. Em. persons, 3: 98. — Reid, T. W. Politicians, 2: 159.

Goschen, Geo. J. With photo. Cooper, T. Men of mark, 2: 35. — Higginson, T. W. Eng. statesm. 347. — Hutton, R. H. Stud. in parl. 139. — Kent, C. Gladst. govt. 319. — Reid, T. W. Politicians, 2: 235. — Ritchie. Brit. sena. 87.

Goshen. Poole, R. S. Cities of Egypt, 89.

— Land of. (Lane-Poole) Wilson, C. W. Pictur. Palest. 4: 121.

Goslavius, Adam. Wallace, R. Anti-Trin. biog. 2: 501.

Goslawski, Maurice. Soboleski. Poets of Poland, 408.

Gosnold, Bartholomew. Belknap. Amer. biog. 2: 206.

Gosnold, John. Ivimey. Eng. Bapt. 2: 440.

Gospel, Liberalizing influence of. Hopkins, M. Miscel. ess. 147.

— visible, The. Thompson, H. M. Copy, 340.

— What is the? Hall, John. Papers, 248.

Gospels; are they fairy tales? Gladden. Burn. ques. 195.

— Criticism confirmatory of. (J. H. Thayer) Bost. lectures, '71: 324.

— Historical element in. Laing, S. Problems, 232.

— Proof of the genuineness of. Griffin, E. D. Rem. 2: 425.

— Prophetic element in. Greg, W. R. Miscel. 1: 221.

See also Bible: New Test. Gospels.

Goss, John. Spark, W. Mus. mem. 137.

Gosse, Edmund. Warner Lib. 11: 6565.

— Poetry of. Benson, A. C. Ess. 292.

Gosse, François Joseph. Bailey, J. B. Methuselahs, 208.

Gosse, Mrs. Nellie (Epps). Clayton, E. C. Eng. fem. art. 2: 87.

Gossip. Boyd. Aut. holid. 280.

— and scandal. Friswell. Gentle life, 2: 100.

Gossner, John E. Stevenson. Praying & w. 251.

Gosson, Stephen. Morley, H. Eng. writ. 8: 389.

Goszczynski, Severin. Soboleski. Poets of Poland, 371.

Gothic and Getæ, The terms. Latham. Opuscula, 129.

Gothic churches, About. Thompson, H. M. Copy, 122.

Gothic mind, literature, and art. Coleridge. Lit. rem. 1: 67.

Gothic romances. Disraeli, I. Amen. (N. Y. 2 v.) 1: 98.

Goths at Ravenna. Freeman. Hist. ess. 3: 121.

Gott, Benj., of Leeds. Bourne, H. R. F. Eng. merch. 2: 211.

Göttingen University, Amer. Colony at, 1815–1898. (Prof. Goodwin) Mass. Hist. Proc. 2d ser. 12: 366.

Gottschalk, Louis Moreau, pianist. Ferris, G. T. Great violinists, 249.

— and Thalberg. Badeau. Vagabond, 15.

Gottschall, Rudolf von. Warner Lib. 11: 6571.

Gottsched, Johann Christopher. Bancroft, J. Miscel. 129.

Gough, Benjamin. Hatfield, E. F. Poets of church, 268. — Miller, Jos. Singers church, 2d ed. 408.

Gough, John B. Bartlett, D. W. Mod. agitators, 128. — Bolton, S. K. How success is won, 22. — Cook, Jos. Current relig. perils, 423. — Dix, J. Lions, 65. — With portrait. Bungay. Penportr. 24. — Parton, J. Sk. of men of prog.

Gough, Prudence. Stevens, A. Women of Meth. 235.

Goughe, Robert. Collier. Actors, 265.

Goujon, Jean Pattison. Renaissance of art, 1 : 170.

Goulburn, Edward M., with photo. Cooper, T. Men of mark, 4 : 36.

Gould, Albert P. Am. Bar Assoc. 12 : 353.

Gould, Benjamin Apthorp. (S. C. Chandler) Am. Acad. Proc. 32 : 355. — Am. Antiq. Soc. Proc. n. s. 11 : 268.

Gould, Hannah F. Griswold. Fem. poets, 45.

Gould, Jacob. Livingston, J. Dist. Amer. 46.

Gould, Jay. Houghton, Kings, 261. — Parton, J. Sk. of men of prog.

— Gold conspiracy of 1869. (H. Adams) Adams, C. F. Erie, 100.

Gould, Mary. Clement, J. Noble deeds, 143.

Gould, Samuel Shelton. (E. P. Gould) Harvard mem. biog. 2 : 385.

Gould, Thomas R. Clarke, W. J. Amer. sculp. 124.

Goulding, F. R. Davidson, J. W. Writ. of South, 227.

Gounod, Charles F. With portrait. Buffen, F. F. Mus. celeb. 53. — Engel, L. Mozart, 1 : 146. — Ferris, G. T. Ital. & Fr. compos. 228. — Hervey, A. Masters Fr. music, 37. — Keddie. Mus. comp. 395. — Em. persons, 6 : 58. — Elson, L. Gt. composers, 207. — Sharp, R. F. Makers of music.

— Faust. Guerber. Stor. of operas, 1.

— Polyeucte. Hueffer. Mus. stud. 213.

Goupil, Ernest. Redding. Misers, 2 : 229.

Gournay, Marie le Jars de. Kavanagh. Fr. women, 7.

Gournay, Vincent de. Turgot. Life & writ. 229.

Gout. Jacox, F. Cues, 273. — Timbs. Doctors, 320.

— Dialogue between Franklin and. Franklin. Works ('87), 7 : 140.

Gove, Lorenzo D. Bartlett, J. R. R. I. officers, 441.

Governesses, mothers and, Relative social position of. Jameson. Mem. & ess. 155.

Government. Helps. Friends, 1st ser. 2, 2d ser. 2. — Maurice, F. D. Soc. morality, 153. — Webster, N. Ess. 49.

— Anarchy or regimentation. Huxley. Method, 383.

— and commerce, principles of. Webster, N. Ess. 38.

— and Protestantism. Brownson. Works, 10 : 411.

— bad, Use of. Bushnell. Moral uses, 52.

— Cicero on. Everett, A. H. Crit. ess. 338.

— Dialogue on, Franklin and Montesquieu. Everett, A. H. Crit. ess. 382.

— Function of. George, H. Soc. prob. 234.

— — Extension of. Rogers, J. E. T. Econ. interp. 501.

— Ground and forms of. Beecher, H. W. Patriotic add. 382.

— Hobbes on. Stephen, J. F. Horæ Sabb. 2 : 1.

— Idea of a perfect form of. Hume. Philos. works, 3 : 546.

— in Canada and U. S. compared. (G. F. Hoar) Am. Antiq. Soc. Proc. n. s. 7 : 178.

— Local. See Local government.

— Locke on. Stephen, J. F. Horæ Sabb. 2 : 140.

— Methods of. Linton, W. J. Eng. repub. 104.

— Mill's essay on. Macaulay. Ess. 2 : 5.

— Origin of. Hume. Philos. works, 2 : 306.

— — and first principles of. Hume. Philos. works, 3 : 28.

— — and ground of. Brownson. Works, 15 : 296.

— — Three theories. Coleridge. Friend. 153.

Government. Original contract. Hume. Philos. works, 3 : 495.

— Popular, by divine right. Bushnell. Building eras, 286.

— — Maine on. Morley, J. Stud. in literature.

— Present scope of. (E. Wambaugh) Am. Bar Assoc. 20 : 307.

— Province of. Amos. Science of politics, 371.

— Representative, Popular discontent with. (G. F. Hoar) Am. Hist. Assoc. Rept. '95 : 21.

— Republican and monarchical. Brougham. Works, 5 : 375.

— Science of. Story, J. Miscel. 614.

— True function of. Bastiat. Ess. on pol. econ. 119, 173.

— Utilitarian theory of. Macaulay. Ess. 2 : 92.

Governmental powers, Separation of. (W. Bondy) Colum. Univ. Stud. Hist. 5 : no. 2.

Governor of a State of the U. S., Office of. (A. H. Rice) Butterfield Lec. Un. Coll. 1 : 45.

Gow, Captain. Whitehead, C. Highwaymen, 2 : 129.

Gow, Mary L. Clayton, E. C. Eng. fem. art. 2 : 189.

Gowdie, Isabel, Confessions of. Wright, T. Nar. sorcery, 2 : 224.

Gower, G. G. L. See Granville, Earl.

Gower, John. Chalmers. Eng. poets, 2 : iii. — Collier, W. F. Hist. Eng. lit. 61. — Disraeli, I. Amen. (N. Y. 2 v.) 1 : 206. — Minto, W. Eng. poets, 54. — Morley, H. English writers, v. 4. — (T. Arnold) Ward. Eng. poets, 1 : 102. — With portrait. Warner Lib. 11 : 6579.

— Confessio amantis. Hales. Folia litt. 114.

— — Rhymes of. (M. W. Easton) Univ. Pa. Publ. Philol. 4 : no. 1.

Gowrie conspiracy under James I. Bisset, A. Ess. on hist. 109.

Goya, Francis Joseph. Hamerton. Portfo. pap. 119. — Stirling-Maxwell. Ann. art. Spain, 4 : 1471.

Gozzi, C., and Venetian fairy comedy. Paget, V. Stud. of 18th cent. 275.

Gozzoli, Benozzo. Jameson. Ital. painters, 95. — Symonds. Renais. fine arts, 241. — Stillman, W. J. Old Ital. mas. 109.

— Rape of Helen. (C. Monkhouse) Singleton, E. Great pic. 138.

Gracchi, The. Dunlop, J. Rom. liter. 2 : 184. — (Plutarch) Ferris, G. T. Gt. leaders, 23. — Ihne. Hist. of Rome, v. 4.

— Daughters of the. Hahn-Hahn. Fathers, 418.

Grace, Wm. G., at Down End. Yates, E. H. Celeb. 1 : 119.

Grace, William P. Livingston, J. Dist. Amer. 295.

Grace, Nature and. Brownson. Works, 3 : 350.

Grâce-Dieu, Ice cave of. ✓ Adams, W. H. D. Fam. caverns, 138.

Gracian, Balthazar, "Oraculo manual" of. Duff, M. E. G. Miscel. 144.

Grade meeting, Use of. (E. C. Delano) Nat. Educa. Assoc. '96 : 251.

Graded schools, management of, Problems in. (E. E. White) Nat. Educa. Assoc. '74 : 254.

Grading and classification. (Ella F. Young) Nat. Educa. Assoc. '93 : 83.

— and promotion in schools. (E. R. Shaw, J. T. Prince, and others) Nat. Educa. Assoc. '98 : 422.

Graduating system for country schools. (A. L. Wade) Nat. Educa. Assoc. '79 : 164.

Grady, Henry W. (H. Watterson ; J. C. Harris ; M. Verdery) Grady, H. W. Writings and speech. 5.

Graefenberg, Life at. Chambers's Papers, no. 59.

Graeme Park, Phila. Glenn, T. A. Colon. mans. 1 : 367.

Grafton, Charles Fitzroy, duke of, with portrait. Caulfield. Kit-cat, 18.

Grafton, James Ingersoll. (T. W. Higginson) Harvard mem. biog. 2 : 270.

Grafton, Richard. Morley, H. Eng. writ. 8 : 357.

Graham, Lady Catherine, and Sir John Colquhoun. Burke, B. Viciss. of fam. 3 : 181.

Graham, Miss Clementina Stirling. Brown, J. J. Leech, 117, 169. — Chambers, W. Rem. pers. 289.

Graham, George, dramatist. Jesse, J. H. Cel. Eton. v. 2.

Graham, George, clockmaker. Brightwell. Heroes of lab. 63. — Parton. Capt. indus. 51. — Lonsdale. Worthies Cumb. v. 6.

Graham, Hector, of Lea Castle. Burke, B. Viciss. of fam. 3 : 129.

Graham, Isabella. Clement, J. Noble deeds, 213. — Hack. Consec. wom. 315. — Lossing. Em. Amer. 332.

Graham, James. See Montrose, 5th earl and 1st marquis of.

Graham, Sir James R. G. Francis, G. H. Orators, 142. — Grant, J. Recoll. Ho. Comm. 163. — Lonsdale. Worthies Cumb. v. 2. — Ritchie. Brit. sena. 351.

Graham, John, of Claverhouse. Street, G. S. Miniatures, 15.

Graham, Mary J. Hack. Self-surr. 175.

Graham, Mrs. Pierce, B. K. Em. dead, 239.

Graham, Robert (1786–1845). Chambers, W. Rem. pers. 116.

Graham, Sir Robert. Grant, J. Bench & bar, 1 : 75.

Graham, Thomas. Cooke, J. P., jr. Sci. cul. 127. — Muir, M. M. P. Chemists, 234. — Thorpe, T. E. Ess. hist. chem. 160.

Graham, Wm., D. D. Morison, J. Fathers of Lond. Miss. Soc. 2 : 495.

— Reminiscences of. (W. M. Taylor) Graham, W. Ess. 1.

Graham, William Grenville. Redding. Pers. remin. 2 : 102.

Graham families. Taylor, J. Fam. of Scot. 2 : 141.

Grahame, James, poet. Griswold, R. W. Sac. poets. — Wilson, J. G. Poets of Scot. 1 : 402.

Grahame, James, historian. (J. Quincy) Mass. Hist. Coll. 3d ser. 9 : 1.

Grahame, Kenneth. The golden age. Street, G. S. Quales ego, 77.

Grain crops of the world, 1891. (J. Goldschmidt) U. S. Cons. Rept. 37 : 161.

Grain trade and waterways. (L. R. Hurd) Deep waterways conven. 1 : 155.

Grainger, J. Chalmers. Eng. poets, 14 : 469.

Grammar. Newman, J. H. Lec. univ. 120.

— and æsthetics. Gildersleeve. Ess. 127.

— as a natural science. (C. T. R. Smith) N. Y. Regents, 87 : 647.

Grammar school, An average Massachusetts. Eliot, C. W. Educa. reform.

— of the future. Eliot, C. W. Educa. reform.

Grammar school course, Shortening and enriching of. (C. W. Eliot) Nat. Educa. Assoc. '92 : 617.

Grammar school curriculum, Reconstruction of. (C. B. Gilbert) Nat. Educa. Assoc. '94 : 323.

Grammatical revolution. Wheeler, D. H. Byways, 188.

Grammont, Chevalier. Street, G. S. Miniatures, 3.

Grammont, Elizabeth Hamilton, countess de. Adams, W. H. D. Fam. beauties, 1 : 67. — With portrait. Jameson. Beauties, 102. — Jesse. Court of Eng. Stuarts, 3 : 284.

Gran Chaco, Paraguay, Bewohner des. (E. Hassler) Cong. Anthrop. Chic. '93, 349.

Granada, Spain. Buckley, J. M. Trav. 3 cont. 58. — Buckley, T. A. Great cities, 369. — Finck, H. T. Spain and Morocco. — Hale, E. E. Seven Spanish cit. 93. — Stoddard, C. A. Span. cit. 171. — Thomas, M. Scamper thr. Spain, 164. — Prime, S. T. Alhambra, 1 : 129.

— Cadiz to. Stoddard, C. A. Span. cit. 140.

— Conquest of. Irving. Biog. 378.

— — Irving's. Prescott. Biog. miscel. 88.

— Impressions of. Irving. Biog. 471.

— Letter from. Irving. Crayon pap. 148.

— Religious persecutions in. Stoughton. Span. ref. 114.

— Siege of. Robson, W. Sieges, 449.

— to Malaga. Stoddard, C. A. Span. cit. 177.

Granby, John Manners, marquis of. Cooper, T. Men of mark, 3 : 4. — Hill, F. H. Polit. portr. 212. — James, G. P. R. Commanders, 2 : 195. — Jesse, J. H. Cel. Eton. v. 2. — Johns. Nav. & mil. heroes. — Lodge. Portraits (Bohn), v. 7. — Reid, T. W. Cab. portr. 126. — Kent, W. C. M. Derby min. 247. — Sheil. Sk. Irish bar, 2 : 172.

Grand Remonstrance, Debates on. Foster, J. Hist. ess. 1 : 1.

Grand River, Labrador. (A. Carey) Am. Geog. Soc. 24 : 1.

Grand River of Canada. (B. Sulte) Roy. Soc. Can. 2d ser. 4 : § 2, 107.

Grand style, The. Pearson, C. H. Reviews, 89.

Grand tour, The. Curtis, G. W. Other ess. 193.

Grande Mademoiselle. See Montpensier, Duchess de.

Grandeur, worldly, Instability of. Goldsmith. Miscel. (N. Y. 4 v.)1 : 117.

Grandfathers, and grandchildren. Eagles. Ess. 84.

Grandison, William Villiers, viscount. Lodge. Portraits (Bohn), v. 4.

Grandval, his plot against William III. Macaulay. Biog. sk. 278.

Grange, Origin and progress of the. N. J. Labor, '86 : 333.

Granger, Gordon. Shanks. Rec. of generals, 268.

Granger cases and the police power. (J. K. Edsall) Am. Bar Assoc. 10 : 288.

Grangerism and Grangerites. Hutton, L. From books.

Granite industry in Maine. Maine Labor, 1889.

Grant, Mrs. Anne, of Laggan. Bethune, G. W. Brit. fem. poets, 156. — DeQuincey. Lit rem. (Bost.) 1 : 55.—Williams, Jane. Lit. wom. 519. — Wilson, J. G. Poets of Scot. 1 : 338. — Yonge. Good wom. 1 : 207.

— Memoirs of. Elwood. Lit. ladies, 2 : 66.

Grant, Asahel. (T. Laurie) Haydn, H. C. Am. miss. heroes, no. 4. — Thompson, A. Gt. mission. 171.

Grant, James. Miller, Jos. Singers church, 2d ed. 200.

Grant, Moses. Bungay. Off-hand, 245. — Bungay. Pen-portr. 170.

Grant, Richard, 1229–34. Hook. Abps. Cant. 3 : 105.

Grant, Sir Robert. Griswold, R. W. Sac. poets.

Gray, Edward. Loring, J. S. Hundred Bost. ora. 229.

Gray, Elisha. Munro, J. Heroes of teleg. 288.

Gray, Eliz. C. Clement, J. Noble deeds, 381.

Gray, Francis C. Loring, J. S. Hundred Bost. ora. 385.

Gray, Frederick Turell. (L. C. Pray) N. E. Hist.- Gen. Soc. Biog. 2 : 340.

Gray, Henry. *See* Dorset, Marquis of.

Gray, Henry Peter. Tuckerman. Artists, 442.

Gray, Mrs. Jane L. Griswold. Fem. poets, 104. — Hatfield, E. F. Poets of church, 272.

Gray, John Chipman. Loring, J. S. Hundred Bost. ora. 398. — (J. C. Ropes) Mass. Hist. Proc. 2d ser. 4 : 22.

Gray, Mary, Bessie Bell and. Fittis. Heroines of Scot. 247.

Gray, Miss (of Teases, North Britain). Burder. Pious wom. 539.

Gray, Capt. Robert. Greely, A. W. Explorers, 88.

Gray, Thomas. Arnold, M. Ess. 2 : 69. — (S. Johnson) Chalmers. Eng. poets, 14 : 137. — Collier, W. F. Hist. Eng. lit. 321. — Creasy. Etonians, 299. — Howitt. Homes Br. poets, 1 : 308. — Sanborn, K. Eng. poets, 178. — Tuckerman. Poets, 51. — (M. Arnold) Ward. Eng. poets, 3 : 302. — Wotton. Word portraits, 116. — Bell, C. D. Some Eng. poets, v. 1. — Benson, A. C. Ess. 119. — Mitchell, D.G. Eng. lands, 3 : 79. — Brooke, S. Theol. Eng. poets, 38. — Brooks, S. W. Eng. poets, 251. — Jesse, J. H. Cel. Eton. v. 1. — Lowell. Latest ess. v. 1. — Roscoe, W. C. Poems & ess. v. 2. — Wrangham. Brit. Plutarch, v. 6. — With portrait. (G. P. Lathrop) Warner Lib. 11 : 6623.

— and Cowper. Jones, W. A. Lit. stud. 2 : 58.

— and music. Krehbiel. Music & man, 3.

— and Stoke-Pogis. Winter, W. Shakesp. Eng.

— at Keswick. Rawnsley. Lit. assoc. Eng. lakes, 1 : 113.

— Bibliography. Phelps, W. L. (ed.). Selec. T. Gray.

— Elegy. Saunders, F. Famous books, 95.

— — Evolution of. Clarke, J. F. 19th cent. ques. 60.

— Sonnets of. Deshler. Afternoons, 172.

— Tomb of. Hall, Mrs. S. C. Pilgr. Eng. shr. 1 : 88.

— Works. Bulwer. Ess. 135.

Gray, Thomas, jr. Putnam, A. P. Singers liberal, 171.

Gray, William. Lossing. Em. Amer. 214.

Gray's Inn. Foss. Judges, 4 : 272. 5 : 119.

Gray's Peak, Ascent of. Raymond, R. W. Camp, 225.

Grayling, Catching the. Deming. Byways, 258.

Grayson, William. Balch, T. Maryland line, 99.

Grazzini, Anton Francesco, *called* Il Lasca. Symonds. Renais. It. lit. 2 : 79.

Great and little things. Hazlitt. Table talk.

Great Britain, Administration of, 1827. Macaulay. Ess. 6 : 405.

— and France, 1853. Disraeli. Sel. spee. 2 : 3.

— and Germany, New commercial treaty between. (J. Faucher) Cobden Club Ess. 2 : 261.

— and the United States. Winthrop. Addresses, 1 : 464.

— — Treaty of amity, commerce, and navigation. Webster, N. Papers, 179.

— — Walsh's appeal from judgments of Gt. Brit. Jeffrey, F. Contrib. Ed. Rev.

— army of, Examinations of candidates for officers in. Bosanquet. Ess. 135.

— — Irish regiments of the new era. Carlyle. Resc. ess. 89.

Great Britain, Army of. Peace enlistments and war salaries. Scoffern. Stray leaves, 162.

— — Promotions in. Bosanquet. Ess. 180.

— — Purchase system in. Hayward, A. Ess. 3d ser. 396.

— — Reform of. Rogers, J. E. T. Cobden, 146.

— — Sanitary reform in, due to Dr. H. Marshall. Brown, J. Locke, etc. 165.

— Christian origins in. Montalembert. Monks, 3 : 3.

— Colliery strike in, 1893. (C. Meeker) U. S. Cons. Rept. 43 : 368.

— Colonial question, 1871. (J. E. T. Rogers) Cobden Club ess. 2 : 399.

— Colonies of. Froude. Short stud. 2 : 149, 280, 382.

— — Bibliography. Egerton, H. E. Hist. Brit. col. policy.

— — Colonial government and the W. India question. Alison. Ess. 1.

— — Colonial policy, 1880. (Sir D. Wedderburn) Howard, Jas. Prac. pol. 239.

— — Colonial question, The. (E. Jenkins) Trans. Soc. Sci. Lond. '72 : 142.

— — England and the. (J. E. Gorst *et al.*) Trans. Soc. Sci. Lond. '69 : 97.

— — Independence of. Rogers, J. E. T. Cobden, 222.

— — inferior races in, Treatment of. (C. S. Roundell) Trans. Soc. Sci. Lond. '66 : 126.

— — Shall we retain them? Gregg. Ess. pol. 2 : 219.

— Constitution of. Brougham. Works, v. 11.

— Constitutional history. (H. Henson) Wakeman & Hassall. Ess. introd. Eng. const. 1.

— Defensive armament of. Gleig. Ess. 1 : 126.

— Empire of. Smith, G. Ess. on ques. of day, 127.

— — in 1884. Temple, R. Cosmop. ess. 1.

— — Imperial federation. Smalley. Lond. let. 2 : 361, 367. — Temple, R. Cosmop. ess. 36.

— Exports to U. S., 1892. (J. C. New) U. S. Cons. Rept. 39 : 404.

— Farm holdings in, 1891. (W. Bruce) U. S. Cons. Rept. 35 : 139.

— Finances. Cobden. Speeches, 233. — Hobart, V. H. H. Ess. & mis. 2 : 140. — Hobart, V. H. H. Polit. ess. 141.

— — in 1816. (H. Adams) Adams, C. F. Erie, 269.

— — Reform of. Rogers, J. E. T. Cobden, 183.

— Fishing industry of, 1892. (B. G. Daniels) U. S. Cons. Rept. 38 : 457.

— Foreign affairs, 1853–81. Disraeli. Sel. spee. 2 : 1.

— Foreign policy of. (J. Bright) Adams, C. K. Rep. Br. orat. 3 : 159. — Cobden. Speeches, 389. — Congreve, R. Ess. 1. — Peel, R. Speeches, 2 : 516.

— — 1880. (Joseph Cowen) Wagner, L. Mod. pol. ora. 190. — (M. E. Grant Duff) Howard, Jas. Prac. pol. 59.

— — Imperial or economic? Greg, W. R. Miscel. 1 : 29.

— Foreign relations of. Brougham. Works, 8 : 103.

— — Liberalism in. Ess. in liberalism, 131.

— Future of. Smith, J. Campbell. Writings, 65.

— Future political position. Greg, W. R. Pol. prob. 27.

— Government, Law officers of the crown. Fawcett. Sp. pol. ques. 239.

— — Lecky on. Jeffrey, F. Contrib. Ed. Rev.

— History during the 18th century. Alison. Ess. 3.

Religions, 199. — (W. Milligan) St. Giles lec. 2 : 181.

Greece, Ancient, Rural life in. Chambers's Repos. no. 34.

— and Assyria, Connection between. Thirlwall, C. Remains, 3 : 154.

— and England; the quarrel of, 1850. Dasent. Jest & earnest, 2 : 110.

— and the Greeks, Occasional notes on, 1866-68. Strangford. Selec. writ. 1 : 275.

— and Turkey in 1869. (C. E. Trevelyan) Grant, A. Recess, 55.

— Archæology; recent discoveries at Athens & Olympia. (T. Davidson) Am. Geog. Soc. 2 : 217.

— as it is. (J. M. Francis) Am. Geog. Soc. 6 : 138.

— Bibliography. Botsford, G. W. Hist. of Greece.

— City life of the 3d cent. B. C., and its effect upon the civilization of the age. Mahaffy, J. P. Greek life, ch. 13.

— Constitution. Bibliography. Greenidge, A. H. J. Greek const. hist.

— Constitutional history of. Legaré. Writ. 1 : 367.

— Golden age of. Mahaffy, J. P. Greek life, ch. 8.

— historians of, Earlier. Mahaffy. Prob. Gr. hist. 1.

— History. Bibliography. Myers, P. V. N. Hist. Greece for coll.

— — Curtius's. Freeman. Hist. ess. 2 : 148.

— — Grote's. Phillips, S. Ess. from Times, 1 : 270.

— — Macedonian supremacy. Freeman. Hist. ess. 2 : 207.

— — Post-Alexandrian. Huxley. Ess. contro. 168.

— — Revolution of 1821-28. Phillips, S. Ess. from Times, 2 : 287.

— in 1885. Temple, R. Cosmop. ess. 316.

— Influence of, in the development of humanity. Jouffroy. Philos. miscel. 2 : 186.

— Mediæval and modern. Freeman. Hist. ess. 3 : 303.

— Mining and metallurgy, 1891. (I. J. Manatt) U. S. Cons. Rept. 35 : 20.

— Mitford's history of. Macaulay. Ess. 1 : 172.

— Modern. Bellows. Old world, 2 : 435. — De Quincey. Theo. ess. (Bost.) 2 : 157. — Field, H. M. Killarney, 291.

— — Bibliography. Samuelson, J. Greece; pres. condit. & prog.

— — Popular poetry of. Blackie, J. S. Horæ Hellen. 297.

— Notes in, 1833. Wordsworth, C. Miscel. 1 : 34.

— People and government. Arnold, R. A. Levant, 1 : 111.

— poets of, Lost. Alford. Poets of Greece, 70.

— — Pastoral. Alford. Poets of Greece, 205.

— Religion of. Bettany. World's relig. 371. — Matheson. Distinc. messages, 193.

— revisited. Howe, J. W. Is polite soc. pol. ? 77.

— revolution in, Speech on, 1824. Webster, D. Works, 3 : 60.

— Revolution of, 1821-28. DeQuincey. Memo. (Bost.) 1 : 287.

— Romans in. Huxley. Ess. contro. 187.

— Speech on difficulty with, 1850. (Alex. Cockburn) Wagner, L. Mod. pol. ora. 60.

— Trade and products of. U. S. Cons. Rept. 39 : 345.

— under the Romans. DeQuincey. Theo. ess. (Bost.) 1 : 273.

— War of 1897. With the Greek soldiers. Davis, R. H. Year, 193.

— What we owe to. Butcher, S. H. Greek genius, 1.

Greek anthology. Alford. Poets of Greece, 223. — Cracroft. Ess. 2 : 79. — Symonds. Greek poets, 2 : 281. — (T. Williams) Warner Lib. 11 : 6637.

Greek art. Lord, J. Beacon, 1 : 99.

Greek character. Hare. Guesses, 1 : 91.

— Development of, illustrated by use of the word *Entrapetos.* Arnold, M. Irish ess. 5.

Greek church. (D. Latas) Barrows, J. H. Parl. relig. 1 : 352. — Lawrence, E. Hist. stud. 455.

— (N. Orloff) Relig. systems, 405.

— in Greece. Arnold, R. A. Levant, 1 : 133.

— Latin church and. French. Lec. mediæval, 366.

— Mysticism in. Vaughan, R. A. Mystics, 1 : 109.

Greek comedy, Age of. (R. Bentley) Donaldson. Theatre of Greeks, 197.

— Athenian. Donne, W. B. Ess. on dram v. 1.

Greek composition. (W. E. Waters) Nat. Educa. Assoc. '97 : 664.

Greek culture, Influence of, on western world, in middle ages. Döllinger. Stud. hist. 164.

Greek dialects. Bibliography. Smyth, H. W. Sounds and inflec. Greek dialec.

Greek drama, choral element, History of. Donaldson. Theatre of Greeks, 5.

Greek dress, Antique, for women. Jenkin, H. C. F. Papers, 1 : 35.

Greek fire. Proctor, R. A. Univ. of suns, 192.

Greek goddesses. Higginson. Atlan. ess. 269.

Greek ideal, The. Hoppin. Notes theol. stud. 139.

Greek language, Accent of. Hadley, J. Ess. 110.

— ancient, Pronunciation of. (N. W. Benedict) N. Y. Regents, 85 : 485. — (J. A. Spencer) N. Y. Regents, 85 : 563.

— and Latin, Importance of better preparation in, for college. (B. Stanton) N. Y. Regents, 79, app. : 49.

— and methods of teaching the classics. (M. Anagostopoulos) Nat. Educa. Assoc. '70, app. : 13.

— Byzantine, Pronunciation in 10th century. Hadley, J. Ess. 128.

— Genitive as an ablative case in. Hadley, J. Ess. 44.

— modern, Philological character of. Blackie, J. S. Horæ Hellen. 111.

— Requirement of, for degree of A. B. (W. G. Hale) Cong. Educa. Chic. '93, 118.

— — Should older colleges require ? N. Y. Regents, 99, app. : 105.

— Rhythm and metre of. Hadley, J. Ess 81.

— Study of, Homer and. Lang. Ess. in lit. 77.

— — In behalf of. (T. Field) Thirteen ess. educa.

— — in preparatory schools. (M. E. Gates) N. Y. Regents, 87 : 669.

— Teaching of. (M. J. Rendall) Thirteen ess. educa.

Greek legends. Müller. Chips, 2 ; *or* Sel. ess. 1 : 465.

Greek literature. Swing. Old pic. 1 : 105.

— and art, Relation to social life. Mahaffy, J. P. Greek life, ch. 6.

— Brief appraisal of. DeQuincey. Uncoll. wr. 1 : 23.

— Five periods of. Symonds. Greek poets, 1 : 15.

— Influence of, on western world, in middle ages. Döllinger. Stud. hist. 164.

— of Alexandria. Mahaffy, J. P. Greek life, ch. 11, 12.

Greek philosophy. Lord, J. Beacon, 1 : 65.

— and modern education. (Leroy D. Brown) Nat. Educa. Assoc. '88 : 365.

— and religion. Mahaffy, J. P. Greek life, ch. 7.

Greek play at Harvard. *See* Sophocles. Œdipus Tyrannus.

Greek plays, Representation of. Donaldson. Theatre of Greeks, 131.

Greek poetry. Bibliography. Appleton, W. H. (ed.). Greek poets in Eng. verse.

Greek privative, so-called. Key, T. H. Philol. ess. 127.

Greek religions and Latin religions. (Sir G. W. Cox) Relig. systems, 216.

Greek scholars in Italy. Morley, H. Eng. writ. 7 : 1.

Greek social life. Mahaffy, J. P. Greek life, ch. 1.

Greek statuary, Polychromy in. (M. Collignon) Smithson. Rept. '95 : 601.

Greek Testament, Story of the. Hall, John. Papers, 102.

Greek tragedy, Age of. (R. Bentley) Donaldson. Theatre of Greeks, 214.

— Nemesis in. Shackford. Soc. & lit. pap. 89.

— Theory of. DeQuincey. Lett. to young (Bost.), 101.

Greek tragic poets, lost, Fragments of. Symonds. Greek poets, 2 : 113.

Greek type, Permanence of the. (E. A. Grosvenor) Am. Antiq. Soc. Proc. n. s. 11 : 338.

Greek verse, Value of accent in. (I. Flagg) N. Y. Regents, 92 : 549.

Greeks, ancient, Every-day life of. Chambers's Papers, no. 29.

— — Social development. (J. P. Mahaffy) Afternoon lect. 5 : 1.

— and Romans, Plutarch's lives of. Stephen, J. F. Ess. by barr. 280.

— — relationship between, Ross on. Hadley, J. Ess. 141.

— Melancholy of the. Butcher, S. H. Greek genius, 130.

— Taste for the picturesque among. (E. M. Cope) Camb. ess. '56 : 115.

Greeley, Horace. Bartlett, D. W. Mod. agita. 315. — Bolton, S. K. Poor boys famous, 138. — With portrait. Brockett. Men of our day, 546. — With portrait. Bungay. Pen-portr. 91. — Bungay. Off-hand, 237. — Chambers, W. Rem. pers. 203. — Derby, J. C. Fifty years, 127. — Famous boys, 1. — Field, M. B. Memories, 116. — Griswold. Prose writ. 626. — Stowe. Men of time, 293. — Parton. Capt. indus. 254. — Godkin. Reflections, 48. — Lanman, C. Haphazard, 155. — With portrait. Mitchell, D. G. Am. lands, 2 : 359. — With portrait. (C. C. Buel) Warner Lib. 12 : 6653.

— and E. Forrest. Ames, M. C. Outlines, 116.

— Talmadge vs. Clinton, H. L. Extraor. cases, 190.

Greely, A. W. Bolton, S. K. Fam. voyag. 455.

Green, Edwin P. Am. Bar Assoc. 18 : 533.

Green, Mrs. Frances H. Whipple. Griswold. Fem. poets, 123.

Green, Horace. Francis, S. W. N. Y. phys. 217.

Green, John Richard, with portrait. Warner Lib. 12 : 6663.

Green, Joseph. Knapp, S. L. Em. lawyers, 129. — Lossing. Em. Amer 130.

Green, Matthew. Chalmers. Eng. poets, 15 : 157. — (A. Dobson) Ward. Eng. poets, 3 : 194.

Green, Nathan. Livingston, J. Em. Am. lawy. 88.

Green, Thomas. Diary of a lover of literature. Gosse, E. Gossip, 239.

Green, Capt. Thomas, Trial of. Burton, J. H. Crim. tri. 1 : 101.

Green, Prof. Thos. Hill. Lilly, W. S. Ess. 29. — Warner Lib. 12 : 6683.

— Memoir. Green, T. H. Works, 3 : pref.

Green, Prof. Thos. Hill, Political philos. of. Ritchie. State interference.

Green, William J. Walker, C. D. Biog. Va. Mil. Inst. 251.

Green Springs, S. C., Affair at. Dawson. Batt. of U. S. 1 : 606.

Greene, Albert G. Griswold. Poets Am. 246.

Greene, Catharine. Ellet. Wom. of revol. 1 : 62.

Greene, Charles Gordon. Loring, J. S. Hundred Boston ora. 477.

Greene, Francis V., with portrait. Butterfield. Lec. Un. Coll. 1 : 371.

Greene, George Sears, with portrait. Bartlett, J. R. R. I. officers, 139.

Greene, Howard. Bartlett, J. R. R. I. officers, 370.

Greene, Nathanael. With portrait. [Amer.] Nat. portr. gall. 1. — With portrait. Duyckinck. Nat. portr. gall. 1 : 196. — Glazier, W. Heroes, 54. — With portrait. Headley, J.T. Washington, 2 : 7. — Loring, J. S. Hundred Bost. ora. 449. — Hamilton. Ed. by Lodge, 7 : 23. — Lossing. Em. Amer. 59.

Greene, Robert. Choate, I. B. Wells of Eng, 132. — Collier. Eng. dram. poetry, 2 : 322. — Dunham. Lit. & sci. men, 2 : 22. — Jeaffreson. Novelists, 1 : 7. — Jusserand. Eng. novel. 150. — Minto, W. Eng. poets, 240. — Symonds. Shakes. pred. 534. — Ulrici. Shakespeare's dram. art, 1 : 139. — Ward, A. W. Eng. dram. 1 : 214. — (E. Gosse) Ward. Eng. poets, 1 : 402. — Morley, H. Eng. writ. 10 : 90. — Warner Lib. 12 : 6691.

— Novels. Morley, H. Eng. writ. 9 : 215, 268.

Greene, Ruhama. Ellet. Pioneer wom. 196.

Greene, Thomas. Miller, Jos. Singers church, 2d ed. 314.

Greenaway, Kate, and Mrs. Allingham. Ruskin. Art of Engl. 81.

Greenland, Nansen's first crossing of. Montefiore, A. Leaders, 271.

— North, Proposed explorations of. (R. E. Peary) Am. Geog. Soc. 23 : 157, 256.

— — Work in, 1894-95. (R. E. Peary) Am. Geog. Soc. 28 : 21.

— Peary's Expedition to, 1891-92. (R. E. Peary) Am. Geog. Soc. 24 : 536.

Greenland inland ice, Reconnaissance of. (R. E. Peary) Am. Geog. Soc. 19 : 261.

Greenland scientific expedition. Am. Geog. Soc. 27 : 126, 221.

Greenleaf, Daniel. (R. C. Greenleaf) N. E. Hist.-Gen. Soc. Biog. 2 : 34.

Greenleaf, Simon. (G. Dexter) Mass. Hist. Proc. 2 : 563. — (S. G. Croswell) N. E. Hist.-Gen. Soc. Biog. 2 : 106.

Greenock, Mortality in. (J. Wallace) Trans. Soc. Sci. Lond. '60 : 607.

Greenough, Horatio. Clarke, W. J. Amer. sculp. 45. — Lossing. Em. Amer. 393. — Tuckerman. Artists, 247.

Greenough, William Whitwell. Loring, J. S. Hundred Bost. ora. 658.

Greenville, Sir R. Southey & Bell. Brit. adm. v. 3.

Greenwell, Dora. (A. H. Japp) Miles, A. H. Poets of cent. 7 : 341. — Whittier. Prose, v. 3.

Greenwich, England. Hawthorne. Old home, 260.

— Ancient palace of. Thomson, K. B. Recoll. 1.

Greenwich Castle and Queen Elizabeth. Timbs. Abbeys, 1 : 120.

Greenwood, Grace, pseud. See Lippincott, Sarah J. C.

Grey, Henry G., 3d earl. Earle, J. C. Eng. prem. 2 : 231. — Hutton, R. H. Stud. in parl. 94. — Kent, C. Gladst. govt. 152.—Miller, H. Hist. ess. 70.

Grey, Lady Jane. Adams, W. H. D. Noble women, 124. — Burder. Pious wom. 1. — Burke, S. H. Men of reforma. 2 : 373. — Burke, S. II. Hist. portr. Tudor, 2 : 471. — With portrait. Clarke, M. C. Noted wom. 263.—Hale, S. J. Less. wom. lives, 190. — With portrait. Howitt, M. Queens, 334. — James, G. P. R. Cel. wom.—Lodge. Portraits (Bohn), v. 1. — Russell. Extr. women, 122. — Williams, Jane. Lit. wom. 49. — With portrait. Fifty famous women, 66.—Owen, Mrs. O. F. Heroines hist. 301. — Wittenmeyer. Women Reform. 300.

— and her sisters (Lady Katharine and Lady Mary). Strickland. Tudor prin. 94–292.

— and Northumberland's treason. Burke, S. H. Men of reforma. 2 : 301.

— Execution of. Starling, E. Noble deeds wom. 279.

Grey, Lady Mary, Prison of. Hall, Mrs. S. C. Pilgr. Eng. shr. 1 : 243.

Grey, Samuel. Japp, A. H. Leaders of men, 264.

Grey family, of Howick. Sanford & Townsend. Gov fam. 1.

Greyfriars, Order of. Mivart. Ess. 1 : 288.

Gribaldus, Matthew. Wallace, R. Anti-Trin. biog. 2 : 98.

Gridley, Albert Gallatin. Livingston, J. Dist. Amer. 483.

Gridley, Jeremiah. Knapp, S. L. Em. lawyers, 199.

Gridley, Richard. Lossing. Em. Amer. 122.

Grief in print. Jacox. Lit. life, 244.

Griefs, Great, as a medicine to less. Jacox, F. Cues, 195.

Grieg, Edvard. Sharp, R. F. Makers of music.

— Bibliography. Paterson (N. J.) Pub. Lib. Bull. Feb.–Mar. '97.

Grien, Hans Baldung. (Alfred Woltman) Keane, A. H. Early masters, 192.

Grier, Mrs. Maria C. Brockett. Woman's work, 597.

Grier, Robert Cooper, 1794–1846. Brown, D. P. Forum, 2 : 91 — Livingston, J. Em. Amer. lawy. 41.

Grievances. Friswell. Better self, 136. — Gray, E. C. Idle musings, 136.

Griffin, Ebenezer. Proctor. Lawy. of N. Y. 602.

Griffin, Edward Dorr. (J. McVickar) Griffin, E. D. Rem. 1 : 11. — Griswold. Poets Amer. 273. — Waterbury Eloq. preach. 82.

— Sermon on death of, 1837. Hopkins, M. Miscel. ess. 288.

Griffin, Gerald. Forgotten English poet. — Fitzgerald, P. Rom. of stage, 401. — Hall, S. C. Book of mem. 229. — Lanier. Music, 115.— M'Carthy, J. H. Hours w. em. Irish. 39. — Mitford, M. R. Recollec. 457. — Murray, J. O'K. Prose and poet. Irel. 383. — Oliphant, M. Lit. hist. 3 : 225. — Warner Lib. 12 : 6699. — Williams, A. M. Poets of Irel..

Griffin, Mrs. Josephine R. Brockett. Woman's work, 707.

Griffin, Simon G., with portrait. Sketches N. H. men, 58.

Griffith, John. Creegan. Gt. mission. 75.

Griffith, Walter. Wesley & successors, 85.

Griffith, William. Carson, H. L. Sup. Ct. of U. S. 574.

Griffiths, John. Ivimey. Eng. Bapt. 1 : 408.

Griffiths, Ralph. Knight, C. Old booksel. 182.

Grigg, John. Miller, Jos. Singers church, 2d ed. 197. — Winslow, S. N. Biog. Phila. merch. 17.

Grigg, Joseph. Hatfield, E. F. Poets of church, 276.

Grigg, Wesley P. Walker, C. D. Biog. Va. Mil. Inst. 254.

Grimald, Nicholas. Morley, H. Eng. writ. 8 : 214.

Grimaldi, Joseph, the clown. Timbs, J. Eng, eccen. 382.

Grimbald, St., and St. Robert. Doran. New pic. 143.

Grimké, Angelina. Wise, D. Rem. women, 191.

Grimké, Sarah. Wise, D. Rem. women, 191.

— and Angelina. (E. C. Stanton) Parton. Em. wom. 363.

Grimké, Thomas Smith. Mansfield, E. D. Pers. mem. 273.

Grimm, Frédéric Melchior, Baron. Haussonville. Salon of Necker, 1 : 133.

— and P. H. T. d'Holbach. Vinet. Fr. lit. 18th cent. 352.

— Correspondence of. Jeffrey, F. Contrib. Ed. Rev.

Grimm, Hermann. Stearns, F. P. Real & ideal, 109. — With portrait. Warner Lib. 12 : 6723.

Grimm, Jacob Ludwig Carl, with portrait. (B. W. Wells) Warner Lib. 12 : 6733.

Grimm, Wilhelm C., with portrait. (B. W. Wells) Warner Lib. 12 : 6733.

— and Jacob. Grimm, H. Liter. 213.

Grimm's law. Skeat. English etymol. 1 : 104.

Grimshaw, Rev. William. Adams, W. H. D. Worthies Church Eng. 201. — Pierce, B. K. Em. dead, 186. — Ryle, J. C. Chr. leaders, 106.

Grimston, Sir Harbottle. Manning, J. A. Speakers, 346.

Grindal, Edmund, 1575–83. Hook. Abps. Cant. 10 : 1.

Grindrod, Edmund. Wesley and successors, 141.

Gringore, Pierre. Cary. Fr. poets, 268.

Grip. See Influenza.

Griscom, John H. Francis, S. W. N. Y. phys. 43.

Griselda, The tale of. Furst, C. Group old auth. 61.

Grisi, Giulia, vocalist. Edwards, H. S. Prima don. 1 : 267. — Clayton, E. C. Queens, 363. — Ferris, G. T. Great singers, 2 : 67. — Q. You have heard of them, 46. — Needham. Queens of song.

— and Mario. Spark, W. Mus. mem. 235.

Grisons. Guild. Abroad again, 346.

Griswold, A. M. Clemens. Funny fellows, 113.

Griswold, Hiram. Livingston, J. Em. Amer. lawy. 677.

Griswold, Mary Caroline. Davidson, J. W. Writ of South. 230. — Raymond, I. Southland writ. 2 : 918.

Griswold, John A. Parton, J. Sk. of men of prog.—With portrait. Rogers, A. C. Repres. men, 273.

Griswold, Rufus W. Hemenway. Poets of Vt. 39. — Wallace, H. B. Lit. crit. 227.

— and the poets. Poe. Works, 6 : 243.

Grit. Whipple. Success, 57.

Grobianus. Herford. Lit. rela. of Eng. and Ger. 379.

Grocyn, W., and Linacre, at Oxford. Morley, H. Eng. writ. 7 : 20.

Groningen. Amicis. Holland, 382.

Groot, Gerhard. Hodgson, Wm. Reformers, 170. — Ullmann. Reformers, 59.

Grosart, Alexander Balloch. Miles, A. H. Poets of cent. 10 : 611.

Groser, William. Miller, Jos. Singers church, 2d ed. 585.

Gross, Joseph P. Am. Bar Assoc. 9 : 543.

Gross, Samuel D. (A. Flint) Gross, S. D. Autobiog. 1 : xiii.

Grossi, T. Howells. Mod. It. poets, 178.

Grossmith, George, with portrait. Goddard, A. Players, 2 : 229.

Grosvenor family. Sanford & Townsend. Gov. fam. 1.

Grote, George. Anton. Masters in hist. — Friswell. Mod. men of l. 183.

— Eulogy on. Stanley, A. P. Ser. spec. occ. 158.

— History of Greece. Ste.-Beuve. Sel. ess. 183.

— Obituary of. Em. persons, 1 : 37.

Grotesque design, as exhibited in ornamental and industrial art. Fairholt. Rambles, 45.

Groth, Klaus. Rearden. Petrarch, 105.

Grotius, Hugo. Bernard, F. Escapes, 60. — Craik. Pursuit knowl. 1 : 119. — Oxenham. Stud. in eccl. hist. 281. — Nasmith. Mak. mod. thought, 1 : 247. — Wallace, R. Anti-Trin. biog. 3 : 574.

— as a reformer of international law. Lawrence. Ess. int. law, 163.

Grotkovius, John. Wallace, R. Anti-Trin. biog. 2 : 543.

Groton, Conn., Massacre, 1781. Winthrop, R. C. Addresses, 2 : 84.

Grotta del cane. Adams, W. H. D. Fam. caverns, 18.

Grottaferrata, abbey of, St. Nilus and. E., E. Vari. of fortune, 9.

Grotto des demoiselles. Adams, W. H. D. Fam. caverns, 84.

Grotto of Bonifacio. Adams, W. H. D. Fam. caverns, 39.

Grottoes, Famous. Adams, W. H. D. Fam. caverns.

Grouchy, Emmanuel. Headley. Napoleon, 2 : 257.

Ground, The, as affecting health. (R. C. Kedzie) Am. Pub. Health, 18 : 27.

Grout, Lieut. J. W. (E. Cotter) Shea, J. G. Fallen brave.

Grove, Sir W. R., with photo. Cooper, T. Men of mark, 2 : 20.

Groveton, Va., Battle of. Allan, W. Army of N. Va. 244.

Grow, Galusha A. Brockett. Men of our day, 363. — Parton, J. Sk. of men of prog.

Growth and inheritance, Eimer on. Mivart. Ess. 2 : 417.

— Lines of, in maturing. (R. G. Boone) Nat. Educa. Assoc. '97 : 173.

Grub Street, Revolution in. Traill. New fiction, 226.

Gruber, Jacob. Wakeley. Heroes Meth. 407.

Grumbling and discontent. Friswell. Better self, 114.

Grundtvig, N. F. S. Gosse. Nor. studies, 199.

Grundy, Felix. With portrait. [Amer.] Nat. portr. gall. 3. — Lossing. Em. Amer. 366. — Perry, B. F. Biog. sketches, 1 : 546.

Grundy, Mrs., Memorials of. Fairbanks, O. B. Aguecheek, 295.

Grundy, Sidney. Archer. Eng. dram. 182.

Grünewald, Matthias. (A. Woltmann) Dohme, R. Early mast. 186.

Grunzig, Otto, Trial of, for murder, 1851. Clinton, H. L. Extraor. cases, 137.

Grymeston, Elizabeth. Williams, Jane. Lit. wom. 70.

Gryphius, Andreas. Winkworth. Chr. singers Germ. 176.

Guadalajara, Mex., Phthisis in. (J. M. Benitez) Am. Pub. Health, 18 : 210.

Guadalupe, Legend of Our Lady of. Doran. New pic. 154.

Guadeloupe island. Norman. Colon. France, 162. — Hill, R. T. Cuba, 337.

Guadet, Marguerite Elie, Speeches of. Stephens, H. M. Ora. Fr. Rev. 1 : 415.

Gualterus, P. Alexandreis. A curiosity of literature. Sumner. Works, 9 : 503.

Gualther, Mark. Wallace, R. Anti-Trin. biog. 3 : 73.

Guanches, The : ancient inhabitants of Canary. (J. W. Gambier) Smithson. Rept. '94 : 541.

Guano. Andersson, C. J. Okawango river, 388. — Dickens, C. (ed.). Sunshine, 168. — Knox, T. W. Underground, 561. — Peck, G. W. Melbourne, 138.

— Statistics of. Am. Geog. Soc. 1 : 181.

Guaranteeing teaching positions. (J. W. Warr) Nat. Educa. Assoc. '95 : 879.

Guarantyism. Elder, W. Questions, 247.

Guardato, Masuccio. Symonds. Renais. It. lit. 1 : 178.

Guardian, Sketches of occasional contributors to the. Drake, N. Ess. Tatler, 3 : 1.

Guardian societies. (J. Morel) Conf. char. & correc. '99 : 204.

Guarini, Giambattista. Montgomery. Men of Ita. 2 : 82. — Stebbing. Ital. poets, v. 2. — Symonds. Renais. Cath. reac. 2 : 243. — Trollope. Ital. poets, 2 : 47.

Guarneri, Two Josephs, of Cremona. Phipson. Violinists, 97.

Guatemala. Bur. Am. Rep. Rept. '91–92, pt. 7.

— and the U. S., Trade between, 1893. U. S. Cons. Rept. no. 152.

— British loan of 1825. Francis, J. Stock exch. 103.

— Trade and commerce, 1891. (S. Kimberley) U. S. Cons. Rept. 36 : 353.

Guatemala City, capital of Guatemala. Curtis, W. E. Capitals, 60.

Guatuso Indians of Costa Rica. (Leon Fernandez and J. F. Bransford) Smithson. Rept. '82 : 675.

Guaymas, Commerce and industries, 1891. (A. Willard) U. S. Cons. Rept. 35 : 151.

Gubbio. Hare. Cities of No. Italy, 2 : 432. — Symonds, J. A. Ital. byways.

Gudrun. Ludlow. Epics, 1 : 193.

— Analysis and history of the poem. Dippold. Epics, 159.

Guebriant, Jean Baptiste Budes, Count de. Cust. Warriors 30 years, 2 : 563.

Guelphs and Ghibellines. Villari. Two 1st cent. Flor. 1 : 173.

— Early ancestors of our Queen. Wolff. Odd bits, 91.

— Page from history of. Malorite. Here, there, 11.

Guenever I., II., and III., queens of Arthur. Hall. Queens bef. Conq. 189.

Guercino. Criticisms of his pictures. Guizot. Fine arts, 163.

Guerilla warfare. Mazzini. Life & writ. 1 : 369.

Guérin, Mrs. Anna Maria (Edmonds). Clayton, E. C. Eng. fem. art. 2 : 277.

Guérin, Eugénie de. Alger. Solitudes, 365. — Arnold, M. Ess. in crit. v. 1. — Forsyth, W. Essays, 273. — Yonge. Good wom. 2 : 557.

— and Maurice. Warner Lib. 12 : 6761.

Guerin, Maurice de. (M. Arnold) Gautier. Fam.

Fr. au. 272. — Alger. Solitudes, 338. — Arnold, M. Ess. in crit. v. 1.

Guernsey. Bibliography. Lewis, E. S. Guernsey peop. & dialect.

Guerre, Martin, the false. Fuller, H. W. Noted trials, 5.

Guerric, abbot of Igny. Neale. Mediæv. preachers.

"Guerrière," frigate, Capture of. Dawson. Batt. of U. S. **2** : 119.

Guest, Benjamin. Miller, Jos. Singers church, 2d ed, 531.

Guests. Repplier, A. In cozy hours, 158.

Guevara, A. de. Ticknor. Span. lit. **1** : 540.

Guevara, L. V. de. Ticknor. Span. lit. **2** : 293.

Guiana and Venezuela. Cartography. (P. L. Phillips) Am. Hist. Assoc. Rept. '97 : 681.

— Bibliography. Salem (Mass.) Pub. Lib. Bull. Jan. '96.

— French. Norman. Colon. France, 191.

— in 1596. (L. Keymis) Hakluyt. Voyages, v. **3.**

— Three colored republics of. (D. L. Child) Child. L. M. Oasis, 113.

Guicciardini, Francesco. Church, R. W. Occ. pap. **1** : 167. — Montgomery. Men of Ita. **2** : 63. — Owen, J. Skeptics Ital. 179. — Robertson, W. Charles V. — Symonds. Age of despots, 295. — Symonds. Renais. It. lit. **2** : 447. — Yriarte. Florence, 168.

— and his golden maxims. Wilson, J. Stud. mod. mind.

Guides : a protest. Repplier, A. Varia, 63.

Guidi, Carlo Alessandro. Stebbing. Ital. poets, v. **3.**

Guido Reni. Jervis, Lady. Painting, **1** : 323.

— Aurora. (C. A. Eaton) Singleton, E. Great pic. 114.

— Beatrice Cenci. (P. B. Shelley) Singleton, E. Great pic. 239.

— the Caracci school. Lee, H. F. Old painters, 234.

— Criticisms of his pictures. Guizot. Fine arts, 151.

Guiet, Charles. Miller, Jos. Singers church, 2d ed. 143.

Guignet, Adrien. Hamerton. Portfo. pap. 110.

Guilbert, Yvette. Henry-S. Hours w. Parisians, 199.

Guild, Reuben Aldridge. Am. Antiq. Soc. Proc. n. s. **13** : 126.

Guild of St. George. Gibbins. Eng. soc. ref. 220.

Guild system and its effect upon art. Conway, W. M. Early Flem. artists, 56.

Guilds. Baring-Gould. Germany, 34, 386, 409. — Heckethorn. Secret soc. **1** : 330. — Brentano. Rela. of labor to law. — Gomme. Literature of local instit. 146. — Howell. Capital and labor. — Weeden. Social law of labor.

— and trades-unions. Mass. Labor, '71 : 12.

— Bibliography. Ashley, W. J. Introd. Eng. econ. hist. 67.

— Florentine. Villari. Two 1st cent. Flor. **1** : 232.

— Mediæval, of England. (E. R. A. Seligman) Am. Econ. Assoc. v. **2.**

— of minstrels. Cutts, E. L. Scenes mid. ages, 298.

— Religious. Bayly, J. A. S. New stud. 193.

— Working, and work societies. (Mrs. G. A. Sala) Burdett-Coutts. Wom. miss. 72.

Guilford, Francis North, Baron. Campbell. Ld. chan. **4** : 280. — Georgian era, **1** : 315. — Jesse, J. H. Cel. Eton. v. **2.** — Lodge. Portraits (Bohn), v. **6.** — Roscoe, H. Em. lawyers, **1** : 106.

Guilford, Francis North, Baron, North's Life of. Talfourd. Crit. writ.

Guilford, Frederick North, 2d earl of. Lodge. Portraits (Bohn), v. **8.**

Guilford, Eng. (F. Lasham) Clinch, G. Bygone Surrey, 204.

Guilford Castle. Timbs. Abbeys, **1** : 266.

Guilford, N. C., Battle at. Dawson. Batt. of U. S. **1** : 663.

Guilpin, Edward. Alden, R. M. Rise of satire, 148.

Guimard, Marie Madeleine. Houssaye. Men of 18th cent. **1** : 396. — Men & wom. of France, **2** : 117.

Guinea, Aborigines of. McLennan. Stud. anc. **2** : 405.

Guinicelli, Guido. Symonds. Renais. It. lit. **1** : 46.

Guinness, Sir Edward. Cochrane, R. Benef. lives, 69.

Guion, Madame. *See* Guyon.

Guiscard, Robert. (E. Gibbon) Ferris, G. T. Gt. leaders, 126.

Guise, Charles de, 1591. Bernard, F. Escapes, 54.

Guise, Family of. Doran. Knights, 228.

Guiteau, C. J., Trial of. Ann. Cyclop. '81 : 381.

Guittone of Arezzo. Symonds. Renais. It. lit. **1** : 45.

Guizot, Mme. E. C. P., a French journalist. Ames, M. C. Outlines, 95. — Ste.-Beuve. Cel. wom. 344.

Guizot, F. P. G. Adams, C. K. Democ. & mon. in France. — Alison. Ess. **3.** — Ann. Cyclop. '74 : 390. — Cormenin. Orators, 263, 373. — Flint. Philos. of hist. **1** : 219. — Loménie. Liv. characters, 87. — Q. You have heard of them. — Ste.-Beuve. Monday chats, 295. — Duyckinck. Portr. gall. **2** : 346. — Walsh, R. M. Liv. char. France. — With portrait. (C. Gross) Warner Lib. **12** : 6771.

— as a historian. Pellissier. Lit. move. Fr. 250.

— Dismissal of. Simpson, J. P. Pic. revol. Paris, **1** : 28.

— Memoirs of. Cranborne. Hist. sk. **1** : 3. — Wilson, J. Stud. mod. mind.

— Obituary of. Em. persons, **1** : 247.

Gujerat, Battle of. Adams, W. H. D. Eng. at war, **2** : 118. — Knox, T. W. Battles, 117. — Malleson, G. B. Battles of India, 379.

Gulager, Christian. Baker, W. S. Portr. of Wash. 71.

Gulf States, Public instruction in. (Joseph Hodgson) Nat. Educa. Assoc. '72 : 274.

Gulf-stream, The. (Alexander Agassiz) Smithson. Rept. '91 : 189. — Agassiz. Cruises of the Blake. — Proctor. Light sci. **2** : 188.

— Chart of. Franklin. Works ('87), **9** : 6.

— a myth? Proctor. Light sci. **1** : 114.

— Pillsbury on. Am. Geog. Soc. **24** : 300.

— Recent investigations of. (J. R. Bartlett) Am. Geog. Soc. **13** : 29. **14** : 69.

Gull, Sir William. Bettany. Em. doctors, **2** : 159. — With photo. Cooper, T. Men of mark, **3** : 35. — Em. persons, **4** : 233.

Gun-cotton. (F. A. Abel) Manch. sci. lec. **5–6** : 57.

Gundred, supposed daughter of William the Conqueror. Green, M. A. E. Princesses, **1** : 72.

Gunn, H. Mayo. Miller, Jos. Singers church, 2d ed. 535.

Gunn, James. Jones, C. C., jr. Deleg. fr. Georgia, 44.

Halévi, Jehuda, poet and pilgrim. Jacobs, J. Jewish ideals, 103. — (R. Gottheil) Warner Lib. **12** : 6869.

Halévy, Jacques François Fromental. Ferris, G. T. Ital. & Fr. compos. 186. — Hogarth. Mem. opera, **2** : 270. — Keddie. Mus. comp. 383. — Upton, G. P. Stand. operas, 127.

Halévy, Ludovic. Van de Velde. Fr. fic. **2** : 217. — With portrait. Warner Lib. **12** : 6831.
— Meilhac and. Matthews, J. B. Fr. dram. 243.
— Short stories of. Matthews, B. Aspects fic. 196 ; *or* Books & play-books.

Halford, Sir Henry. Bettany. Em. doctors, **2** : 55. — Pettigrew. Med. portr. gall. v. **1**.

Half-time system in schools. (W. N. Molesworth) Trans. Soc. Sci. Lond. '66 : 371.
— Factory, and the educational test. (G. Anderson) Trans. Soc. Sci. Lond. '60 : 379.

Haliburton, Thomas Chandler [Sam Slick]. Grant, Jas. Port. pub. char. **1** : 291. — With portrait. Warner Lib. **12** : 6848.

Halifax, Charles Montague, earl of, with portrait. Caulfield. Kit-cat, 107. — (S. Johnson) Chalmers. Eng. poets, **9** : 331. — Ewald. Rep. statesm. — Rogers, J. E. T. Gleanings, **1** : 1.

Halifax, C. Wood, Viscount. Hill, F. H. Polit. portr. 254.

Halifax, G. Montagu, earl of. Jessie, J. H. Cel. Eton. v. **1**.

Halifax, George Savile, marquis of. Ewald. Rep. statesmen, **1** : 60. — Wrangham. Brit. Plutarch, v. **4**. — Macaulay. Biog. sk. 111 ; Same in Ferris, G. T. Gt. leaders, 322.

Halir, Karl, with portrait. Ehrlich, A. Cel. violin. 47.

Halket, Lady Anne. Williams, Jane. Lit. wom. 130.

Hall, B., Travels in North America. Legaré. Writ. **2** : 254.

Hall, Catherine. Whitehead, C. Highwaymen, **2** : 167.

Hall, Sir Charles, with photo. Cooper, T. Men of mark, **1** : 24. — Gener. of judges, 128.

Hall, Capt. Charles F. With portrait. Bolton, S. K. Fam. voyag. 319. — With portrait. Greely, A. W. Explorers, 293.
— Reception to, 1871. Am. Geog. Soc. **3** : 401.

Hall, Daniel, with portrait. Sketches N. H. men, 229.

Hall, Edward. Creasy. Etonians, 41.

Hall, Henry Ware. (N. Hall) Harvard mem. biog. **2** : 124.

Hall, James. Coggeshall. Poets of west, 71. — Griswold. Prose writ. 289. — Headley, J. T. Chaplains Revol. 245.

Hall, Sir James. Thomson, K. B. Recoll. 2.

Hall, John, D. D., preacher, lecturer, and writer. Bungay. Repr. men, 53.

Hall, John, M. D. Holland, J. Psalmists, **1** : 178.

Hall, John J. Am. Bar Assoc. **21** : 695.

Hall, Joseph, Bp. Alden, R. M. Rise of satire, 97. — Chalmers. Eng. poets, **5** : 221. — Fuller. Worthies, **2** : 230. — (J. G. Collins) Ward. Eng. poets, **1** : 537. — Macdonald, G. England's antiphon, 125. — Holland, J. Psalmists, **2** : 27. — Wordsworth, C. Eccles. biog. v. **4**.
— Imitation of, by Sterne. Ferrier. Ill of Sterne. **1** : 123.

Hall, Joseph. Loring, J. S. Hundred Bost. ora. 307.

Hall, Mrs. Louisa Jane Park. Griswold. Fem. poets, 111. — Putnam, A. P. Singers liberal, 155.

Hall, Lyman. Dwight, N. Signers of decl. 362. — Lincoln, R. W. Signers, 26. — Lossing. Sign-

ers, 229. — Sanderson. Signers, 3. — Jones, C. C., jr. Deleg. fr. Georgia, 88.

Hall, Maria M. C. Brockett. Woman's work, 449. — Moore, F. Women of the wär, 397.

Hall, Marshall. Bettany. Em. doct. **1** : 264. — Smiles. Self-help. — Pettigrew. Med. portr. gall. v. **4**. — Tillotson, J. Untit. nobil. 203.

Hall, Martha J. Hemenway. Poets of Vt. 299.

Hall, Nathan K. Putnam, J. O. Addresses, 264.

Hall, Newman. With photo. Cooper, T. Men of mark, **2** : 5. — Hatfield, E. F. Poets of ch. 286. — Miller, Jos. Singers church, 2d ed. 532.

Hall, Robert. Blunt. Ess. 361. — Georgian era, **1** : 463. — Gilfillan. 1st gall. 39. — Gilfillan. 3d gall. 76. — Mathews, W. Oratory. — Vaughan, R. Ess. **1** : 217. — Broadus. Lec. hist. preach. 224. — Hall, S. C. Book of mem. 77. — Ivimey. Eng. Bapt. **4** : 280, 603. — (Henry Rogers) Macaulay. New biog. 144. — Mathews, W. Oratory, 391. — Pierce, B. K. Em. dead, 267. — Stanton, H. B. Reforms, 114. — Van Santvoord, C. Disc.83. — Waterbury. Eloq. preach. 90.
— as a preacher. (J. Foster) Hall, R. Miscel. 65.
— Memoir of. (O. Gregory) Hall, R. Miscel. 1.

Hall, Robert Pleasants. Miller, S. F. Bench of Ga. v. **2**.

Hall, Samuel. Livingston, J. Dist. Amer. 494.

Hall, Samuel Romilly. Wesley & successors, 209.

Hall, Sarah. Hart, J. S. Fem. prose, 58.

Hall, Sarah E. Hemenway. Poets of Vt. 275.

Hall, Susan E. Brockett. Woman's work, 431.

Hall, Westley. Tyerman. Oxf. Meth. 386.

Hall, William Ware. Bartlett, J. R. R. I. officers, 207.

Hallam, A. H. Brown. Spare hours, **1** : 241. — Hallam. Remains, 9. — Tennyson. In memoriam. — (A. H. Japp) Miles, A. H. Poets of cent. **4** : 103.
— and the Tennysons. Nicoll, W. R. Lit. anec. 21.
— as advocate of Alfred and Charles Tennyson. Nicoll, W. R. Lit. anec. **1** : 21.

Hallam, Henry. Everett, E. Mt. Vernon, 276. — Everett. Orat. v. **4**. — Gilfillan. 3d gall. 182. — Oliphant, M. Lit. hist. **3** : 240. — Jerdan. Men, 243. — Martineau, H. Biog. sk. 77. — Stephen, J. F. Ess. by barr. 16. — Wotton. Word portraits, 118. — Warner Lib. **12** : 6853.
— Literature of Europe. Jones, W. A. Lit. stud. **1** : 17.

Hallam, Henry Fitzmaurice. Hallam. Remains, 53.

Hallam, Lewis, "the second." Dunlap. Am. theatre, v. **1**. — Matthews, B. Actors, **1** : 243.

Hallam, Robert, cardinal priest. Williams, R. F. Eng. card. **2** : 59.

Hallberg-Broich, Theodore M. H. von, Sketch of. Wraxall, C. F. L. Hist. bye-ways, **2** : 202.

Halle, Sir Charles. Engel. Handel to Hallé, 227. — With portrait. Buffen, F. F. Mus. celeb. 107.

Halleck, Fitz-Greene. Bryant. Prose, **1** : 369. — Everest. Poets of Conn. 221. — Griswold. Poets Am. 193. — Poe. Works, **5** : 483. — Powell. Liv. authors, 1850, 222. — Whipple. Essays. — With portr. Wilson, J. G. Bryant, 245. — Mitchell, D. G. Amer. lands, **1** : 280. — Mitford, M. R. Recollec. 340. — Powell, T. Liv. auth. Am. — Richardson. Amer. lit. **2** : 26. — Howe, M. A. D. Amer. bookm. 99. — With portrait. Warner Lib. **12** : 6861.
— Dedication of monument to. Taylor, B. Crit. ess. 233.
— Life and writings. Bryant. Orations, 155.

Halleck, Fitz-Greene. Statue in Central Park, N. Y. Taylor, B. Crit. ess. 245.

Halleck, Henry Wager. Duyckinck. Nat. portr. gall. 2 : 412.

Haller, Albert von. Crichton, A. Converts, 2 : 218. — Jardine, W. Nat. lib. v. 13. — Bancroft, G. Miscel. 132. — Pettigrew. Med. portr. gall. v. 1.

Halley, Edmund. Ball, R. S. Great astron. 162.

Halliwell-Phillips, J. O. Jeaffreson, J. C. Book of recoll. 2 : 167. — Smith, C. R. Retrospec. 3 : 75.

Hallowell, Mrs. M. M. Brockett. Woman's work, 710.

Hallucinations. Ireland, W. W. Blot, 1. — (E. Gurney) Soc. Psych. Res. 3 : 151. — (H. Sidgwick and others) Soc. Psych. Res. 10 : 25.

— and dreams. Wynter. Borderl. of insan. 208; or Fruit betw. leaves, 2 : 153.

— Illusions and. Elam. Phys. prob. 256.

Halpine, George Graham. Derby, J. C. Fifty years, 426.

Hals, Franz. Van Dyke, J. C. Dutch mast. 17.

"Halsewell," Wreck of. Senior, W. Shipwrecks, 43.

Halsey, Jeremiah. Am. Bar Assoc. 19 : 625.

Halsted, Oliver Spencer. Livingston, J. Em. Am. lawy. 112.

Halyburton, Thomas. Blaikie, W. G. Preachers Scot. 246. — Pierce, B. K. Em. dead, 126.

Ham House. Thomson, K. B. Recoll. 1. — Timbs. Abbeys, 1 : 159.

Hamann, Johann Georg. Hedge. Prose Ger. 119. — Pfleiderer, O. Philos. of religion, 1 : 196.

Hamath and the northern border of Israel. Porter, J. L. Giant cities, 307.

Hamblen, David. (W. B. Trask) N. E. Hist.-Gen. Soc. Biog. 2 : 480.

Hambrick, Joseph A. Walker, C. D. Biog. Va. Mil. Inst. 261.

Hamburg. Bellows. Old world, 1 : 322. — Howard, B. W. One year, 1 : 239. — Brooks, E. S. Gt. cities, 112. — Buckley, T. A. Great cities, 399. — Mahaffy. Holl. & Germ. 225. — Wikoff, H. Reminis. 199.

— and its sanitary reforms. Shaw, A. Munic. govt. Eur. 378.

— Foreign commerce of, for 1894–96. (W. H. Robertson) U. S. Cons. Rept. 55 : 254.

— Free port of, 1895. (W. H. Robertson) U. S. Cons. Rept. 50 : 137.

— Industries in the free port of, 1897. (W. H. Robertson) U. S. Cons. Rept. 54 : 533.

— Seamen's bureau of, 1897. (W. H. Robertson) U. S. Cons. Rept. 54 : 511.

Hamerton, Philip Gilbert, with portrait. Warner Lib. 12 : 6875.

Hamilcar. Dodge. Hannibal, 122.

Hamilton, Alexander. Am. Antiq. Soc. Proc. n. s. 3 : 41. — With portrait. [Amer.] Nat. portr. gall. 2. — Baldwin. Party leaders. — Duyckinck. Nat. portr. gall. 1 : 147. — Griswold. Prose writ. 89. — Lodge, H. C. Studies, 132. — Lord, J. Beacon, 4 : 367. — Magoon. Orators of rev. 283. — Parton. Peop. bk. biog. 463. — Perry, B. F. Biog. sketches, 289. — Brooks, E. S. Hist. Amer. 115. — Bullock, A. H. Addresses, 287. — Hubbard, E. Lit. jour. 4 : 71. — With portrait. (D. C. Gilman) Warner Lib. 12 : 6891. — Johnston, A. Amer. ora. 1 : 39. — Lossing. Em. Amer. 213. — Moore, F. Am. Eloq. 1 : 183. — Nichol. Amer. lit. 73. — Richardson. Amer. lit. 1 : 201.

Hamilton, Alexander, and John Adams, Controversy between. Hamilton, ed. by Lodge, 6 : 391.

— and Jefferson, Controversy between. Hamilton, ed. by Lodge, 6 : 314.

— and William Patterson. (C. Parker) Am. Bar Assoc. 3 : 149.

— Defence of, as secretary of the treasury. Hamilton, ed. by Lodge, 6 : 449.

— Home of. (J. C. Carter) Homes Am. statesm. 235.

— in favor of protection. Swank. Notes, 107. Philosophy Prov. Ref. lists, 1 ; 11.

— Sketch of the character of. Ames, F. Works, 282.

Hamilton, Allen. Livingston, J. Dist. Amer. 485.

Hamilton, Anne, Duchess. Chapman, W. Wom. of cov. 167.

Hamilton, Anthony, Count. Saintsbury. Ess. Fr. nov. 31. — With portrait. Warner Lib. 12 : 6913.

Hamilton, Elizabeth, duchess of. Gerard. Irish beauties, 30, 80.

See Grammont, Countess de.

Hamilton, Elizabeth, Memoirs of. Elwood. Lit. ladies, 2 : 98. — Keddie. Songstresses, 1 : 290.

Hamilton, Frank H. Francis. N. Y. surg. 59.

Hamilton, George, Lord. With photo. Cooper, T. Men of mark, 1 : 21. — Escott, T. H. S. Pillars emp. 98.

Hamilton, James. See Abercorn, Duke of.

Hamilton, James, 1st duke of. Lodge. Portraits (Bohn), v. 4.

Hamilton, James, 2d marquis of. Lodge. Portraits (Bohn), v. 3.

Hamilton, Janet. Cochrane, R. Earnest, 155.

Hamilton, John, 1st marquis of. Lodge. Portraits (Bohn), v. 3.

Hamilton, James. Blaikie, W. G. Preachers Scot. 294. — Tuckerman. Artists, 565.

Hamilton, La Belle, with portrait. Ollier, E. Brit. portr. paint. 18.

Hamilton, Lady Emma. Paget, J. Paradoxes, 229. — With portrait. Ollier, E. Brit. portr. paint. 46.

— Nelson and. Doran. Drury Lane, 2 : 222. — Phillips, S. Ess. from Times, 1 : 1.

Hamilton, Patrick. Blaikie, W. G. Preachers Scot. 49. — MacCrie, T. Miscel. writ.

— and George Wishart. (J. Kidd) Reformers. Paisley lec. 344.

Hamilton, R. Winter. Miller, Jos. Singers church, 2d ed. 437.

Hamilton, Samuel. Wakeley. Heroes Meth. 337.

Hamilton, Thos. Douglas, G. Blackwoods, 151.

Hamilton, Walter Kerr. Bp. of Salisbury. Arnold, F. Our bishops, 1 : 213.

Hamilton, William, 2d duke of. Lodge. Portraits (Bohn), v. 5.

Hamilton, William, 1665–1751. Wilson, J. G. Poets of Scot. 1 : 92.

Hamilton, William, 1704–54. Chalmers. Eng. poets, 15 : 595. — Holland, J. Psalmists, 2 : 184. — Wilson, J. G. Poets of Scot. 1 : 169.

Hamilton, Sir Wm. DeQuincey. Phil. writ. (Bost.) 1 : 1 or Works (Masson), v. 5. — (T. S. Baynes) Edin. ess. '56 : 241. — Edwards, E. Founders Brit. Mus. 1 : 346. — McCosh. Scot. phil. 415. — Masson. Rec. Brit. philos. — Morris, G. S. Brit. tho't, 265. — Sinclair, J. Sketches. — Smith, H. B. Faith & philos. 297. — Smith, J. Campbell. Writings, 231. —

Spencer, H. Essays, 383. — Webb, T. E. Veil of Isis, 235. — Whipple. Ess. & rev. 2 : 117.

Hamilton, Sir Wm. Bibliography. Monck. Sir W. Hamilton, 165.

— Edinburgh and. Innes, A. T. Studies, 161.

— Lectures. Anderson, M. B. Papers, 2 : 74.

— Mill's examination of. Bowen, F. Gleanings, 288.

— Philosophy of. Martineau, J. Ess. 2 : 227. 3 : 439.

Hamilton, Wm. Rowan. Ball, R. S. Great astron. 303.

Hamilton families. Taylor, J. Fam. of Scot. 1 : 208.

Hamilton-King, Harriet Eleanor. (E. H. Hickey) Miles, A. H. Poets of cent. 7 : 475.

Hamilton College. College book, 238.

Hamlet among the graves. Whittier. Prose, v. 3.

— Character of. Maudsley. Body & mind, 145.

— Madness of. Radford, G. H. Shylock, 77.

— Shakespeare's. Hazlitt. Char. Shakes. — O'Conor. Ess. 108.

— Sources of. Radford, G. H. Shylock, 57.
See also Shakespeare.

Hamlin, Hannibal, with portrait. Brockett. Men of our day, 223. — With portrait. Carroll, H. Twelve Amer. 117.

Hammersmith ghosts. Burke, P. Romance of forum.

Hammett, Charles D. Bartlett, J. R. R. I. officers, 184.

Hammon, George. Ivimey. Eng. Bapt. 2 : 220.

Hammond, Abram A., with portrait. Woollen. Biog. sk. Indiana, 113.

Hammond, Charles. Coggeshall. Poets of west, 68. — Mansfield, E. D. Pers. mem. 174.

Hammond, George N. Walker, C. D. Biog. Va. Mil. Inst. 263.

Hammond, Henry. Creasy. Etonians, 145. — Teale. Eng. divines, 99. — (J. Fell) Wordsworth, C. Eccles. biog. v. 4.

Hammond, James H. Bartlett. Pres. candidates, 322. — Perry, B. F. Reminis. 104. — Savage. Liv. rep. men, 304.

Hammond, Lawrence, Charlestown, Mass., Diary, 1677–94. (S. A. Green) Mass. Hist. Soc. Proc. 2d ser. 7 : 144.

Hammond, Capt. Maximilian M. Rogers, C. Chr'n heroes, 168.

Hammond, Nathaniel J. Am. Bar Assoc. 22 : 674.

Hammond, Thomas. Knapp, S. L. Em. lawyers, 343.

Hammond, William. Hatfield, E. F. Poets of church, 289.

Hammond, William A., with portrait. Butterfield. Lec. Un. Coll. 1 : 263. — Derby, J. C. Fifty years, 697. — Miller, Jos. Singers church, 2d ed. 200. — Francis, S. W. N. Y. phys. 209.

Hammond, William Gardner. Am. Bar Assoc. 17 : 511.

Hamon, Jean Louis. Hamerton. Contemp. Fr. painters.

Hamont, Matthew. Wallace, R. Anti-Trin. biog. 2 : 364.

Hampden, Henry B. W. B., Viscount. Em. persons, 5 : 216.

Hampden, John (1594–1643). Adams, W. H. D. Men at helm, 34. — Forster. Statesm. of Comm. — With portrait. Forster. Brit. statesm. 3 : 306. — Tweedie, W. K. Earnest men, 251.

— Burial-place of. Hall, Mrs. S. C. Pilgr. Eng. shr. 1 : 25.

Hampden, John, Controversy about. Wiseman, N. Ess. 2 : 1.

— Nugent's memorials of. Macaulay. Ess. 2 : 427.

Hampden, Renn Dickson, bishop of Hereford. Hunt, J. Rel. thought 19th cent. 98.

— Bampton lectures. Mozley. Reminis. 1 : 351.

Hampden-Sidney College, Prince Edward Co., Va. (C. R. McIlwaine) U. S. Bur. Ed. Circ. '88, no. 1 : 227.

Hampshire, England, Baptists of. Ivimey. Eng. Bapt. 2 : 210.

— Walk through. Collins, M. Pen sketches, 1 : 120.

Hampstead. Wolfe. Lit. pilg. Brit. au. 13.

Hampton, Wade. Perry, B. F. Biog. sketches, 1 : 564. 2 : 108. — Pollard. Life of Lee, 738. — Snow. So. generals, 466.

Hampton court and palace. Thomson, K. B. Recoll. 1. — Eagles. Ess. 66. — Guild. Over the ocean, 223. — Stone, J. S. Heart of Eng. 382. — Timbs. Abbeys, 1 : 139.

Hampton Roads, Battle at. Lodge & Roosevelt. Hero-tales, 183.

Hampton, Va., Descent on. Dawson. Batt. of U. S. 2 : 255.

Hamstead, Hadrian Cornelius. Wallace, R. Anti-Trin. biog. 2 : 137.

Hanaford, Phebe A. Hanaford. Wom. of cent. 427.

Hanby, Thomas. Jackson, T. Early Meth. 1 : 275. — Wesley & successors, 33.

Hancock, Cornelia. Brockett. Woman's work, 284.

Hancock, Dorothy. Ellet. Women of revol. 1 : 143.

Hancock, John. With portrait. [Amer.] Nat. portr. gall. 2. — With portrait. Duyckinck. Nat. portr. gall. 1 : 92. — (G. Mountfort) Hunt, F. Am. merch. 2 : 583. — Lincoln, R. W. Signers, 27. — Loring, J. S. Hundred Bost. ora. 72. — Lossing. Signers, 22. — Magoon. Orators of rev. 139. — Sanderson. Signers, 1. — Dwight, N. Signers, 18. — Lossing. Em. Amer. 159. — Moore, F. Am. eloq. 1 : 224. — (S. H. Peabody) Nat. Educa. Assoc. '91 : 287. — (W. E. Sheldon) Nat. Educa. Assoc. '92 : 602.

— Home of. (R. Hildreth) Homes Am. statesm. 97; Same in Hubbard, E. Lit. journeys, 4 : 145.

Hancock, Mrs. John, with portrait. Ellet. Queens Am. soc. 114.

Hancock, Mrs. Susan J. Raymond, I. Southland wr. 2 : 855.

Hancock, Gen. Winfield S. (F. A. Walker) Dwight, T. F. Fed. & confed. comm. 47. — Glazier, W. Heroes, 347. — McCulloch, H. Men & meas. 293.

Hancock's Bridge, Skirmish at. Dawson. Batt. of U. S. 1 : 383.

Hand, Daniel. Bolton, S. K. Givers, 336.

Handel, Georg Friedrich. Balfour, A. J. Ess. 111. — With portrait. Rowbotham. Priv. life compos. 98. — Barnard, C. Tonemasters, 2 : 5. — Bourne, C. E. Gt. compos. 11. — Crowest. Tone-poets, 32. — Cooper, T. Triumphs of persev. 77. — Dole, N. H. Score, 81. — Dawson, G. Shakesp. 444. — Edgar. Boyhood, 259. — Engel. Handel to Hallé, 1. — Ferris. Germ. composers, 15. — Haweis. Music & mor. 125. — Hogarth. Mem. opera, 1 : 207. — Hundred greatest men, 103. — Keddie. Mus. comp. 25. — Lillie, C. C. Story of music, 79. — Parry. Stud. Gt. compos. 22. — With portrait. Elson, L. Gt. composers, 57. — Sharp, R. F. Makers

Harris, John. Miller, Jos. Singers church, 2d ed. 466.

Harris, Mrs. John. Brockett. Wom. work, 149. — Moore, F. Wom. of the war, 176.

Harris, Miriam Coles. Derby, J. C. Fifty years, 568.

Harris, Thaddeus Mason. (N. L. Frothingham) Mass. Hist. Coll. 4th ser. 2 : 130. — (N. Hall) Ware, W. Am. Unita. 1 : 259.

Harris, Thaddeus William. Higginson, T. W. Contemp. 192.

Harris, Thomas Lake. Austin, A. Poetry, 227.

Harris, Miss W. F. Brockett. Woman's work, 742.

Harris, Wiley P., with portrait. Scott, H. W. Dist. Am. lawy. 421.

Harris, William Thaddeus. (E. D. Harris) N. E. Hist.-Gen. Soc. Biog. 2 : 294.

Harrison, Mrs. Anna Symmes. Hanaford. Wom. of cent. 82. — Holloway, L. C. Ladies, 346.

Harrison, Benjamin, 1740–91. Dwight, N. Signers of decl. 297. — Lincoln, R. W. Signers, 29. — Lossing. Signers, 184. — Sanderson. Signers, v. 8. — Lossing. Em. Amer. 103.

Harrison, Benjamin, Pres., with portrait. Scott, H. W. Dist. Am. lawy. 435. — (W. P. Fishback) Wilson, J. G. Presidents, 492.

Harrison, Mrs. Benj. Gordon, L. L. Lady Wash'n, 185.

Harrison, Carter H., 1831–61. Walker, C. D. Biog. Va. Mil. Inst. 271.

Harrison, Christopher. Woollen. Biog. sk. Indiana, 160.

Harrison, Mrs. Constance Cary. Raymond, I. Southland writ. 2 : 775.

Harrison, Frederic. Alviella. Contemp. evol. 136. — Warner Lib. 12 : 6975.

Harrison, James A., at home. (W. M. Baskerville) Gilder. Authors, 125.

Harrison, John, exquisite watchmaker. Brightwell. Heroes of lab. 207. — Parton. Capt. indus. 58.

Harrison, Maria. Clayton, E. C. Eng. fem. art. 2 : 280.

Harrison, Mary. Clayton, E. C. Eng. fem. art. 1 : 411.

Harrison, Major-General, of England. Ivimey. Eng. Bapt. 1 : 282.

Harrison, Thomas. Ivimey. Eng. Bapt. 2 : 407. 3 : 568. — McClure. Translators, 118.

Harrison, Thomas, Major-Gen. U. S. A. (C. H. Firth) Am. Antiq. Soc. Proc. n. s. 8 : 390. — James. Mil. occur. v. 1.

Harrison, William Henry. Abbott. Lives of presidents, 253. — Amer. nat. portr. gall. v. 3. — Benton. Thirty years. — Bethune. Orations. — With portrait. Duyckinck. Nat. portr. gall. 2 : 211. — Frost. Presidents, 271. — Goddard, W. G. Pol. & miscel. wr. 1 : 49. — Hilliard, H. W. Speeches, 39. — Julian. Polit. recollec. — Lincoln. Lives of pres. 357. — Lossing. Em. Amer. 240. — (A. E. Bostwick) Wilson, J. G. Presidents, 185. — Thompson, R. W. Pers. Recollec. 189. — Woollen. Biog. sk. Indiana, 1.

— Death of. (W. Adams) Amer. nat. preacher, v. 15. — Burnap. Miscel.

— Election to presidency. Mansfield, E. D. Pers. mem. 317.

— Social life during administration of. Ellet, E. F. Court circles, 282.

Harrison family of Brandon, Va. Glenn, T. A. Colon. mans. 1 : 401.

Harrison, Fort, Siege of. Dawson. Batt. of U. S. 2 : 127.

Harrow school. Staunton, H. Schools, 302.

Harrowby, D. Ryder, 2d baron. Thornton. For. sec. v. 3.

Harsdorffer. Winkworth. Chr. singers Germ. 237.

Hart, Abraham. Derby, J. C. Fifty years, 551.

Hart, Charles. Galt. Players, 1 : 5.

Hart, James McDougal. Sheldon, G. W. Amer. painters, 46. — Tuckerman. Artists, 547.

Hart, John. Dwight, N. Signers, 138. — Lincoln, R. W. Signers, 30. — Lossing. Signers, 87. — Sanderson. Signers, v. 9.

Hart, Joseph. Hatfield, E. F. Poets of church, 294. — Miller, Jos. Singers church, 2d ed. 204.

Hart, Nancy. Ellet. Women of revol. 2 : 226.

Hart, Sir Robert, and his work. Norman, H. Far East, 231.

Hart, William. Sheldon, G. W. Amer. painters, 84.

Harte, Bret. Haweis. Amer. humorists, 197. — — Hazeltine. Chats, 287. — Nichol, J. Amer. lit. 434. — Heywood, J. C. How they strike, 197. — Richardson. Amer. lit. 2 : 423. — Vedder, H. C. Amer. writers, 212. — With portrait. (W. H. Hudson) Warner Lib. 12 : 6985.

Harte, Walter. Chalmers. Eng. poets, 16 : 311. — Holland, J. Psalmists, 2 : 219.

Hartford, Conn. Pidgeon. Old world ques. 197. — (M. K. Talcott) Powell, L. P. Hist. towns N. E. 507.

— Author's homes at. Wolfe, T. F. Lit. haunts, 193.

Hartford convention. Adams, H. Hist. of U. S. 8 : 287.

— Origin of. Webster, N. Papers, 311.

Hartford Theological Seminary, Hartford, Conn. U. S. Bur. Ed. Circ. '93, no. 2 : 284.

Hartigveld, John. Wallace, R. Anti-Trin. biog. 3 : 280.

Hartington, S. C. Cavendish, Lord. Smalley. Lond. lett. 1 : 152. — Higginson, T. W. Engl. statesm. 279. — Kent, C. Gladst. govt. 329. — Reid, T. W. Cab. portr. 92. — Reid, T. W. Politicians, 2 : 23.

— at Hardwick Hall. Yates, E. H. Celeb. 3 : 3.

Hartley, David. Lewes. Biog. philos. — Ribot. Eng. psychology.

— Adam Smith and. Stephen, L. Eng. thought, 2 : 63.

Hartley, Jona. Swift. Benjamin, S. G. W. Am. artists, 2 : 41.

Hartlib, Samuel. Mitchell. Wet days, 165.

Hartmann, Jakob. Strauss, G. L. M. Men of Ger. 2 : 266.

Hartmann, K. R. E. von. Erdmann. Hist. philos. 3 : 237.

— Pessimistic ethics of. Hall, G. S. Asp. Ger. 175.

— Pessimistic philosophy of. Hedge. Atheism, 123.

Hartop, Job. Bourne, H. R. F. Eng. seam. 2 : 60.

Hartshorne, Joseph. (E. Hartshorne) Gross. Lives physicians, 563.

Hartung, Philip von, 1629–82. Baring-Gould. Preachers, 116.

Hartz mountains. Hoppin. Notes theol. stud. 81. — Taylor, B. Views, 180.

Harvard, John. Everett. Orat. v. 1.

Harvard College and University. U. S. Bur. Ed. Circ. '91, no. 6 : 21. — Arnold, E. Seas & l. 97. — College book, 1. — Dilke. Greater Brit.

Hawthorne, Julian. Novels. Nichol, J. Amer. lit. 379.

Hawthorne, Nathaniel. Alcott, A. Concord days, 193. — Bungay. Off-hand, 210. — Cheney, J. V. Golden guess, 255. — Courtney. Studies, 77. — Curtis, G. W. Lit. & soc. ess. 31. — Fields. Yesterdays, 39. — Fischer, M. Gen. sur. Am. lit. 176. — Griswold, H. T. Home-life, 207. — Griswold. Prose writ. 470. — Hall, S. C. Book of mem. 184. — Heywood, J. C. How they strike me, 161. — Higginson. Sh. studies, 3. — Hood, E. P. Master minds. — Houghton. Kings, 587. — Howe, M. A. D. Am. bookm. 200. — (G. W. Curtis) Hubbard, E. Little jour. 2 : 197; Same in Homes Am. authors. — Hutton. Ess. theol. 2 : 392. — Johnson, C. F. Three Amer. 132. — Lawton, W. C. N. E. Poets, 48. — MacCabe, J. D. Great fortunes, 578. — With portrait. Mitchell, D. G. Am. lands, 2 : 202. — Mitford, M. R. Recollec. 515. — Nichol. Amer. lit. 322. — Poe. Works, 6 : 103. — (G. W. Curtis) Rice, A. D. Ess. 334. — Richardson. Amer. lit. 1 : 390. 2 : 230. — Saunders, F. Famous books, 186. — Smiles. Brief biog. 256. — Smith, G. B. Poets & nov. — Stearns, F. P. Sk. Concord, 29. — Stephen, L. Hours in libr. 1 : 204. — Walsh, W. S. Pen-pic. mod. 150. — With portr. (H. James, jr.) Warner Lib. 12 : 7053; Same in Warner classics, 2 : 9. — Whipple. Charac. — Wise, D. Men of renown, 94. — Wright, H. C. Chil. sto. in Am. lit. 108.

— and Berkshire. Wolfe. Lit. shr. Am. auth. 155.

— and Brook Farm. Curtis. From easy chair, 3 : 1.

— and family. Bolton, S. K. Amer. au. 104.

— at college. (G. P. Lathrop) Parton. Princes, 312.

— Bibliography. Conway. Life of H. — Hodgkins. 19th cent. au.

— Connection with Brook Farm. Frothingham. Transcend. 171.

— Home of. Wolfe. Lit. shr. Am. auth. 58.

— in the shadow of S. Johnson. Nicoll, W. R. Lit. anec. 1 : 281.

— James's Life of. Cheney. Golden guess, 255. — Hazeltine. Chats, 260.

— Marble Faun. Peabody, E. P. Last evening, 293.

— — Theology of. Phelps, A. Portfolio, 130.

— Mosses from an old manse. Ossoli. Art, 319.

— Paradox of. Noble, J. A. Impressions, 65.

— the philosopher of crime. Heywood, J. C. How they strike, 161.

— Psychology of. Quayle, W. A. Poet, 217.

— Romances. Salt. Lit. sk. 189.

— Scarlet letter. Giles, H. Illus. of gen. 66. — Griffin, G. W. Stud. in lit.

— Twice-told tales. Gilman, S. Contrib. 476. — Longfellow. Prose, 1 : 372.

— Works of. Curtis, G. W. Lit. & soc. ess. 61.

Hawthorne, Mrs. Sophia P., an evening with. Higginson, T. W. Contemp. 102.

Hay, Sir Andrew Leith. Grant, J. Recoll. Ho. Comm. 236.

Hay, John, with portrait. Warner Lib. 12 : 7097.

— at home. (B. G. Lovejoy) Gilder. Authors, 135.

Hay, Mrs. M. B. Raymond, I. Southland writ. 1 : 346.

Hay, Malcolm. Am. Bar Assoc. 8 : 467.

Hay families. Taylor, J. Fam. of Scot. 2 : 370.

Hay-fever. Bibliography. Hollopeter, W. C. Hay-fever & treat.

Hayden, Ferdinand Vandeveer, Prof. Am. Antiq. Soc. Proc. n. s. 5 : 180.

Haydn, Franz Joseph. Barnard, C. Tone-masters, 2 : 144. — Bourne, C. E. Great compos. 77. — Butterworth. Great compos. 50. — Crowest. Tone-poets, 104. — Dole, N. H. Score, 146. — Elson, L. Great compos. 66. — Ferris. Germ. composers, 74. — Fuller, S. M. Liter. & art, 2 : 45. — Haweis. Music & mor. 209. — Keddie. Mus. compos. 57. — Ossoli. Art, 226. — Parry. Gt. compos. 91. — Sharp, R. F. Makers of music. — With portrait. Rowbotham. Priv. life compos. 56.

— Creation. Runciman, J. F. Old scores, 85.

— in London. Krehbiel. Music & man, 57.

Haydon, Benjamin R. Buxton, H. J., et al. Eng. paint. 150. — Hall, S. C. Book of mem. 468. — Procter, B. W. Autob. 184. — Redgrave. Century of p. 2 : 164. — Wise, D. Vanq. victors, 197.

Hayes, Albert H., with portrait. Sketches N. H. men, 202.

Hayes, Catherine, later Mrs. Bushnell, Irish vocalist. Clayton, E. C. Queens, 423. — Needham. Queens of song.

Hayes, Isaac I., with portrait. Greely, A. W. Explorers, 272.

— Biographical sketch of. (G. W. Cullum) Am. Geog. Soc. 13 : 110.

Hayes, Lucy Webb. Hanaford. Wom. of cent. 102. — With portrait. Holloway, L. C. Ladies, 628.

Hayes, Rutherford B., with portrait. Bungay. Pen.-portr. 66. — (H. W. French) Frost. Presidents, 497. — Poore, B. P. Reminis. v. 2 : 336. — Gordon, L. L. Lady Wash'n, 391. — (C. Schurz) Wilson, J. G. Presidents, 397.

Hayes-Tilden electoral commission. Monroe, Ja. Oberlin lec. 254.

Haymarket Theatre. Lennox, W. P. Plays, 1 : 138.

Haymond Creed. Shuck. Bench and bar in California, 324.

Hayn, H. Louisa von. Miller, Jos. Singers church, 2d ed. 234.

Hayne, Paul H. Bungay. Repr. men, 280. — Davidson, J. W. Writ. of South, 242. — Richardson. Amer. lit. 2 : 229. — Stoddard, R. H. Poets' homes, 172. — With portrait. Warner Lib. 12 : 7110.

— Review of poetry of Lanier. Music, 197.

Hayne, Robert Young, with portrait. Amer. nat. portr. gall. 2. — Moore, F. Am. eloq. v. 2 : 555. — Perry, B. F. Reminis. 68. — Johnston, A. Amer. ora. 1 : 233. — Lossing. Em. Amer. 280.

Haynes, Ann. Ellet. Pioneer wom. 145.

Haynes, John. Moore, J. B. Am. gov. 297.

Haynes, Joseph. Galt. Players, 1 : 30.

Haynes, Lemuel. Sherman, D. N. Eng. divines, 267.

Hayti, Republic of. Chambers's Miscel. no. 57.

— Hill, R. T. Cuba, 263.

— and Liberia, Independence of. Sumner. Works, 6 : 445.

— Commercial directory of, 1891. Bur. Am. re-pub. no. 29.

— Faithful slaves of, 1790. Yonge. Gold. deeds.

— or, the Black Republic. Pearson, C. H. Reviews, 305.

— Recognition of. Legaré. Writ. 1 : 322.

Hayward, Abraham. Escott. Politics, 189. — Smalley. Lond. lett. 1 : 270.

Haywood, Elizabeth. Forsyth. Novels, 203.

— Novels of. Gosse, E. Gossip, 159.

Haywood, William H. Maury, S. M. Statesm. of Am. 46.

Hazard, A. G. Parton, J. Sk. of men of prog.
Hazard, Jeffrey. Bartlett, J. R. R. I. officers, 418.
Hazard, John G., with portrait. Bartlett, J. R. R. I. officers, 383.
Haziness in speech. Watson, E. H. L. Uncon. humor, 141.
Hazing, College. Curtis, G. W. Ars rec. viv. 20.
Hazledine, William C. Am. Bar Assoc. 15 : 449.
Hazlitt, William. Birrell, A. Res judicatæ, 224. — Rees, J. R. With friend, 38. — DeQuincey. Ess. on poets, Bost. 225; or Works (Masson), 11 : 34. — Gilfillan. 1st gall. 25. — Gilfillan 3d gall. 175. — Mason, E. T. Pers. traits, 1 : 175. — Patmore. My friends, 2 : 249. 3 : 1. — Saintsbury. Ess. Eng. lit. 135. — Stephen, L. Hours in libr. 2 : 290. — Wotton. Word portraits, 120. — Guiney, L. I. Little Eng. gall. 229. — Hall, S. C. Book of mem. 65. — Procter, B. W. Autob. 167. — With portrait. Warner Lib. 12 : 7115.
— and Charles Lamb. Birrell. Obiter, 2 : 224.
— and Sarah Walker. O'Connor, T. P. Love-stories.
— the critic. Tuckerman. Charac. 216.
— Intellectual character of. Talfourd. Crit. writ.
— Lectures on the English poets. Dana. P. & p. writ. 156.
Hazlitt, Wm. Carew, as an editor. Lowell. Writ. 314.
Heacock, Grosvenor W. Putnam, J. O. Addresses, 307.
Head, Natt., with portrait. Sketches N. H. men, 223.
Head, The, and the hand. (Oscar Clute) Nat. Educa. Assoc. '97 : 737.
— heart, and hand. Saunders. Stray leaves, 159.
Headley, Joel Tyler. Griswold. Prose, 540.
— Sacred mountains. Poe. Works, 6 : 193.
Heads in groups, Comparison of. Taylor, I. Ult. civiliz. 289.
Heald, Rebecca. Ellet. Pioneer wom. 281.
Healing by royal touch. Baring-Gould. Oddities, 1 : 164. — Scoffern. Stray leaves, 411. — Strickland. Queens Eng. v. 12.
Health. Brown, J. Spare hours, 2 : 141. — Dana, A. H. Eth. inq. 69. — Munger. On threshold, 123. — Earle, Mrs. C. W. Pot-pourri, 296. — Lubbock. Use of life, 78.
— and disease, Progress as to. (J. Pinkerton) Samuelson, Jas. Civiliz'n, 202.
— and education. Richardson, B. W. Ministry, 110.
— and the higher culture. (S. Osgood) Am. Pub. Health, 2 : 201.
— and happiness. McSherry. Ess. 113.
— and physique of city populations. Meath. Soc. arrows, 1.
— and religion. (S. Means) Conn. Health, '84 : 237.
— boards of, modern, Functions of. (W. H. Brewer) Conn. Health, '72 : 21.
— — Relations of, to prosperity of community. (W. H. Brewer) Conn. Health, '80 : 23.
— — Usefulness of. (J. E. Reeves) Am. Pub. Health, 9 : 171.
— Bodily. (A. Van Harlingen) Buck, A. H. (ed.). Hygiene, 1 : 367. — Clarke, J. F. Self-culture, 53.
— Conditions of, and management of the body. Holmes, O. W. Old vol. 208.
— English and American. Higginson. Conc. all, 117.
— Germs of. (E. T. Nelson) Ohio Health, '95 : 332.

Health, Good ; bodily religion, a sermon on. Stowe, H. B. Chimney, 142.
— Influence of altitude upon. (S. E. Solly) Am. Pub. Health, 21 : 129.
— — of occupation upon. (R. S. Tracy) Buck, A. H. (ed.). Hygiene, 2 : 1. — Ohio Health, '87 : 311. — Conn. Labor, '85 : 85. — (C. H. Brigham) Mich. Health, '75 : 41. — N. J. Labor, '83 : 81. '84 . 204. '85 : 112. '89 : 1
— Maritime health ordinances. (E. Licéaga) Am. Pub. Health, 19 : 137.
— Mexican Board of. (D. Orvananos) Am. Pub. Health, 17 : 38.
— National Board of, Operations of. (J. L. Cabell) Am. Pub. Health, 8 : 71.
— of American cities. (E. Harris) Trans. Soc. Sci. Lond. '74 : 628.
— of coal-miners. (H. C. Sheafer) Buck, A. H. (ed.). Hygiene, 2 : 227.
— of metal miners. (R. W. Raymond) Buck, A. H. (ed.). Hygiene, 2 : 251.
— of schools and school-children. (D. F. Lincoln) Buck, A. H. (ed.). Hygiene, 2 : 595.
— of towns, Manners, and habits affecting. Vaughan, D. J. Questions, 22.
— of villages. (R. S. Tracy) Buck, A. H. (ed.). Hygiene, 2 : 571.
— of women. (C. H. Dall) Brackett, A. C. Educa. of girls, 151.
— — benefited by housework. Brackett, A. C. Educa. of girls, 320.
— — improved by mental development. (L. H. Stone) Brackett, A. C. Educa. of girls, 179, 194, 201, 228, 375.
— Plain words on, addressed to working people. Brown, J. Locke, etc.
— Political economy of. (E. Jarvis) Mass. Health, '74 : 335.
— Public. (J. S. Billings) Buck, A. H. (ed.). Hygiene, 1 : 34. — Playfair. Subj. soc. 3.
— — Advancement of. (H. A. Johnston) Am. Pub. Health, 15 : 1.
— — and legislation. (W. C. Cook) Am. Pub. Health, 10 : 269.
— — Effect of poverty on. (W. P. Alison) Trans. Soc. Sci. Lond. '58 : 434.
— — Essentials in promotion of. (C. N. Hewitt) Am. Pub. Health, 14 : 1.
— — Fundamental conditions of. (G. Homas) Am. Pub. Health, 18 : 143.
— — Necessity for analytical study of. (E. H. Greenhow) Trans. Soc. Sci. Lond. '57 : 365.
— — of Gt. Britain. (H. W. Acland) Trans. Soc. Sci. Lond. '72 : 64.
— — Public health questions in the U. S., Leading. (J. M. Toner) Am. Pub. Health, 2 : 1.
— — Public health service, American, Municipal organization of. (E. Foster) Am. Pub. Health, 7 : 96.
— — — in principal cities of U. S. (E. Harris) Am. Pub. Health, 2 : 151.
— — — Relation of highest medical education to. (S. Smith) Am. Pub. Health, 2 : 187.
— — Public health studies, Topographical surveys and maps and. (J. T. Gardner) Am. Pub. Health, 3 : 100.
— The state and. (E. Brooks) Am. Pub. Health, 6 : 299.
— — State preventive medicine. (J. S. Butler) Conn. Health, '78 : 29.
— — Syphilis and. (F. R. Sturgis) Am. Pub. Health, 2 : 439.
— — What the people owe to the state. (E. Brooks) Am. Pub. Health, 7 : 331.
— Regimen of. Bacon. Ess.

Health, Science of. Kingsley. Health, 1; *or* San. lec. 21.
— the true nobility. (A. L. Gihon) Am. Pub. Health, 7 : 342.
— Value of, to the state. (W. E. Boardman) Mass. Health, '75 : 57.
Health associations and the practice of medicine. (J. J. Speed) Am. Pub. Health, 8 : 39.
Health laws and sanitary organizations. (E. Harris) Am. Pub. Health, 1 : 472.
— Uniform and coöperative. (S. P. Heilman) Am. Pub. Health, 23 : 379.
Health offices, Proposed system for administration of. Richardson, B. W. Ministry, 1.
Health resorts. Benjamin, S. G. W. Atlan. islands. — Benjamin. World's paradises. — Denison, C. Rocky Mt. health res. — Howe, J. W. Winter homes. — Mackenzie, M. Ess. 49. — Merryless, J. Carlsbad. — Ulyat, W. C. Life at the seashore.
Health-work in Indiana, History of. (T. M. Stevens) Am. Pub. Health, 8 : 63.
Heard, Elizabeth. Clement, J. Noble deeds, 76.
— Drake, S. G. Trag. of wilderness, 71.
Hearing. Allen. Physiolog. æsthetics.
— and eyesight, How to obtain and preserve the best. Mich. Health, '82 : 176.
— Defective, of pupils. (Ephraim Cutter) Nat. Educa. Assoc. '94 : 947.
Hearn, Lafcadio, with portrait. Warner Lib. 12 : 7131.
Hearn, Wm. E., on the Aryan household. Leslie, T. E. C. Ess. pol. econ. 469.
Heartlessness, Disadvantage of. Henry, C. S. About men, 13.
Heat. Cracroft. Ess. 2 : 174.
— and light. Davy. Works, 2 : 3.
— as a cause of chemical change. Meyer. Modern theories of chemistry.
— Conversion into mechanical effect. Siemens. Works, v. 1.
— excited by friction. Rumford. Ess. 2 : 469.
— from chemical action. Andrews, T. Scientific papers, 70, 190.
— Latent, of liquids. Molloy, G. Gleanings, 1.
— — of vapors. Andrews, T. Sci. papers, 163. — Molloy, G. Gleanings, 28.
— Progress of, in spherical bodies. Playfair, J. Works, v. 3.
— Propagation of, in fluids. Rumford. Ess. 2 : 200.
— — in various substances. Rumford. Ess. 2 : 391.
— Radiant. Tyndall. Frag. sci. 213.
— Solar and terrestrial. Hunt, R. Poe. of sci. 62.
— Utilization of. Siemens. Sci. works, 3 : 182.
Heath, George, the moorland poet. Buchanan. Master-spir. 303.
Heath, Henry. Stone, J. M. Faithful, 154.
Heath, Job. Ivimey. Eng. Bapt. 3 : 485.
Heath, Nicholas. Burke, S. H. Hist. portr. Tudor, 3 : 288. — Campbell. Ld. chan. 2 : 200.
Heath, Sir Robert, chief justice of England, 1642–1644. Campbell. Ch. just. 1 : 332.
Heathen systems, Indirect tributes of, to doctrines of Bible. Ellinwood. Orient. relig. and Chr. 266.
Heathenism, Heavenly. Dodge. Sermons to clergy, 207.
— Methods of early church with. Ellinwood. Orient. relig. and chr. 39.
Heather, Amongst the. Watkins, M. G. In country, 33.
Heathfield, G. A. Elliott, 1st Lord. Georgian era, 2 : 58. — Lodge. Portraits (Bohn), v. 8.

Heating and ventilation. (T. C. Miller) Ohio Health, '86 : 105.
— — of school buildings. (J. S. Billings ; Charles Smart) Nat. Educa. Assoc. '82, app. : 11.
Heaton colliery, Inundation of. Davenport. Narr. peril. 2 : 364.
Heaven, Ideas of. Whittier. Lit. recre. 161.
— Where is ? Stock. Attempts, 238.
Heavenly life, What do we know of ? Phelps, A. Portfolio, 271.
Heavens, Mechanism of the. Herschel, J. F. W. Essays, 21.
  See Astronomy.
Heavysege, Charles. Lanman, C. Haphazard, 259. — Taylor, B. Crit. ess. 112.
Hebbe, G. C. Bungay. Off-hand, 162.
Hebel, Johann Peter. Taylor, B. Crit. ess. 55.
Heber, R., Bishop. (J. T. Page) Andrews, W. Bygone Ches. 231. — Caldwell, H. Art of doing best, 221. — Griswold, R. W. Sac. poets. — Hatfield, E. F. Poets of church, 308. — Miles, A. H. Poets of cent. 10 : 49. — Miller, Jos. Singers church, 2d ed. 378. — St. John. Cel. travellers, 3 : 356. — Taylor, W. C. Mod. Brit. Plut. 205. — Yonge. Pioneers, 171. — With portrait. Warner Lib. 12 : 7153.
Heberden, Wm. Pettigrew. Med. portr. gall. v. 3.
Hébert, Jacques Réné. Smythe, G. S. Hist. fancies, 249.
Hebich, Samuel, and the Hindus. Japp, A. H. Master mission. 113.
Hebrew books in the British Museum. Schlechter, S. Stud. Jud. 306.
Hebrew lady, Toilette of. DeQuincey. Theo. ess. (Bost.) 2 : 59.
Hebrew religion, Origin of. (E. P. Conder) Liv. papers, v. 5.
Hebrew theocracy, The. (L. Bacon) Bost. lectures, '71 : 171.
Hebrew thought, Influence of physical geography of Palestine on. (F. Adler) Am. Geog. Soc. 7 : 149.
Hebrews, Myth among the. Clodd, E. Myths, 131.
Hebrides, Birds of the. Buchanan. Master-spir. 187.
— Long Island, or Outer. Geikie, J. Frag. 125.
Hebron. Kean, J. Among holy places, 65.
— Cave of Machpelah and. Lee, J. S. Sac. cities, 45.
— Trip to. Wallace, S. E. Bosphorus, 79.
Hecatæus. Mills. Poets of Greece, 464.
Heck, Barbara. Stevens, A. Women of Meth. 175.
Heckendorf. Redding. Misers, 2 : 190.
Hecker, I. T. Aspirations of nature. Brownson. Works, 14 : 548.
— Questions of the soul. Brownson. Works, 14 : 538.
Heckewelder, Mary. Ellet. Pioneer wom. 193.
Heckmann, Georg J. R., with portrait. Ehrlich, A. Cel. violin. 142.
Hector. Gladstone. Studies on Homer, 3 : 555.
— Yonge, C. M. Book of worthies, 53.
Hector, Annie (French) [Mrs. Alexander], with portrait. Black, H. C. Wom. authors, 58.
Hedderwick, James. Wilson, J. G. Poets of Scot. 2 : 378.
Hedding, Elijah. Lossing. Em. Amer. 382. — (M. L. Scudder) McClintock, J. Em. Meth. 159. — Sherman, D. N. Eng. divines, 183.
Hedge, Frederic Henry. Allen, J. H. Sequel, 63. — Vaille & Clark. Harv. book, v. 1. — Putnam, A. P. Singers of the lib. faith, 205.

Hedge, Levi. Peabody. Harv. rem. 37.
Hedges, James Neville. (A. G. Sedgwick) Harvard mem. biog. **2** : 438.
Hedingham Castle, Eng. Barrett, C. R. B. Essex, 56. — Timbs. Abbeys, **1** : 229.
Hedonism. Peabody. Chr. morals.
— Ancient. Courtney. Stud. philos. 23.
"Hedvig Sophia," Wreck of the. Treanor, T. S. Heroes Goodw. sands, 196.
Heemskerk, Jacob van. De Liefde. Dutch adm. v. **1**.
Heermann, Hugo, with portrait. Ehrlich, A. Cel. violin. 134.
Heermann, Johann. Winkworth. Chr. singers Germ. 194.
Hegel, G. W. F. Alger. Solitudes, 350. — Erdmann. Hist. philos. v. **2**, **3**. — Frothingham. Transcend. 43. — Hedge. Prose Ger. 446. — Lewes. Biog. phil. — Royce, J. Spir. mod. philos. 190. — With portrait. (W. T. Harris) Warner Lib. **12** : 7161. — Webb, T. E. Veil of Isis, 275.
— and Darwin. Ritchie, D. G. Darwin.
— as an educator. (F. L. Luqueer) Colum. Univ. Contrib. Philos. **2**: no. **1**.
— Doctrine of the will. (J. A. MacVannel) Colum. Univ. Contrib. Philos. **2**: no. **2**.
— his followers and critics. Hall, G. S. Asp. Ger. 153.
— Philosophy of right. (T. C. Sandars) Oxf. ess. '85 : 213.
Hegelianism. Ker, J. Lec. hist. preach. 371.
Hegelians, New, on Christianity. Renan. Studies (N. Y), **1** : 331.
Hegelisms, On some. James, W. Will to believe, 263.
Hegesias. Mahaffy, J. P. Greek life, ch. 14.
Hegesippus. Evans, R. W. Biog. early church, **1** : 199.
Hegesistratus. Bernard, F. Escapes, 2.
Hegg, Mrs. Teresa (de Lauderset). Clayton, E. C. Eng. fem. art. **2** : 281.
Heginbothom, Ottiwell. Hatfield, E. F. Poets of church, 313. — Miller, Jos. Singers church, 2d ed. 287.
Hegner, Otto. Engel. Handel to Hallé, 242.
Heidelberg. Bartley, G. C. T. Rhine, 115. — Bellows. Old world, **1** : 308. — Fulton, C. C. Europe, 126. — Howard, B. W. One year, 12. — Temple, E. L. Old-world, **1** : 53.
— Princess Elizabeth at. Strickland. Queens Scot. v. **8**.
— to Nuremberg on foot. Taylor, B. At home, **1** : 66.
— University of. Ullman. Reformers, 328.
Heidelberg College, Tiffin, O. U. S. Bur. Ed. Circ. '91, no. **5** : 190.
Heigham, Sir Clement. Manning, J. A. Speakers, 208.
Heilly, Mlle. Anne de, and Francis I. Menzies, S. Roy. fav. **1** : 216.
Heilmann, Joshua. Wooncroft, B. Biog. invent. 41.
Hein, Piet. De Liefde. Dutch adm. 30.
Heine, Heinrich. Arnold, M. Ess. in crit. v. **1**. — Eliot, G. Ess. & leaves, 65 ; or Ess. 69. — Ellis, H. New spirit. — Gostwick. Ger. poets, 243. — Hedge. Prose Ger. 568. — Hosmer, J. K. Ger. literature, 505. — Magnus. Jew. poet, 45. — Henley. Views, 79. — Howells. My lit. passions, 165. — Wells, B. W. Mod. Ger. lit. 324. — Selss. Lit. Germ. 185. — With portrait. (R. Burton) Warner Lib. **12** : 7185.
— and de Musset. Buchanan, R. Poet's sketchbook, 152.

Heine, Heinrich, and Judaism. Karpeles. Jew. lit. 340.
— Bibliography. Sharp. Life of Heine.
— Last days of. Houghton, Ld. Monog. 283.
— Poems of, Martin's translation. Buchanan, R. Look round, 210.
— Sorrows of. Harrison, J. A. Group of poets, **1**.
— Tennyson, De Musset and. Buchanan. Masterspir. 54.
Heintzelman, S. P. Parton, J. Sk. of men of prog.
Heister, Joseph, with portrait. Armor. Gov. of Pa. 333.
Heldenbuoh, Tho. Longfellow. Poets Eur. 203.
Helder. Amicis. Holland, 326.
Hele, Sir John. Woolrych. Serjeants, **1** : 172.
Helen in Homer's poems. Gladstone. Studies on Homer, **3** : 571. — Symonds. Greek poets, **1** : 124.
Helen, Fair, of Ardoch. Fittis. Heroines of Scot. 195.
Helen, Fair, of Kirkconnel. Fittis. Heroines of Scot. 148.
Helena, Empress. Brockett. Woman's work, 67.
Helena, St., queen of Constantius Chlorus. Hall. Queens bef. Conq. 163.
Helena ap Eudda, empress of Maximus. Hall. Queens bef. Conq. 195.
Helfta, convent of, History of. Robinson, A. M. F. End of mid. age, 45.
Heliand. Taylor, B. Stud. Ger. 15.
Heligoland. Wraxall. Scraps, **2** : 130.
Heliodorus. Arnold, E. Poets of Greece, 204. — Warner Lib. **12** : 7221.
— Adventures of Theogenes and Chariclea. Hunt, L. Men, wom. & books, 240.
Heliopolis, Present condition of. Buckley, J. M. Trav. **3** cont. 219.
See On.
Hell, Madame Hommarie de. Adams, W. H. D. Cel. wom. trav. 66.
Hell, The question of. Dixon, T. Liv. prob. 71.
Hellanicus. Mills. Poets of Greece, 466.
Hellas. Hoppin. Early renais. 275.
Hellenes. Gladstone. Stud. Homer, v. **1**.
Hellenism and its revival. Oxenham. Stud. in eccl. hist. 35.
— Christianity in conflict with. Hedge, F. H. Martin Luther, 64.
— Decaying, in Egypt. Mahaffy, J. P. Greek life, ch. 21.
— — in Syria. Mahaffy, J. P. Greek life, ch. 20.
— Gradual subjection of, to Rome. Mahaffy, J. P. Greek life, ch. 19.
— Importation of, to Rome. Mahaffy, J. P. Greek life, ch. 23.
— in Rome. Duruy. Hist. of Rome, **2** : 202. — Mahaffy. Greek world under Roman sway.
— in South Kensington. (H. D. Traill) Coan. Art. & lit. 40.
— Jewish. Mahaffy, J. P. Greek life, ch. 20.
Hellmesberger, Josef, with portrait. Ehrlich, A. Cel. violin. 3.
Helm, Mrs. L. J. Ellet. Pioneer wom. 302.
Helmboldt, Louis. Winkworth. Chr. singers Germ. 153.
Helmbrecht, Meier, German farmer of 13th cent. McLaughlin, E. T. Stud. mediæv. 100.
Helmholtz, Hermann Ludwig Ferdinand von. Am. Acad. A. & S. Proc. **30** : 592. — (A. W. Rucker) Smithson. Rept. '94 : 709. — (T. C. Mendenhall) Smithson. Rept. '95 : 787.
— Investigations of, on principles of mathematics

and mechanics. (Leo Koenigsberger) Smithson. Rept. '96 : 93.
Helmstedt, Germany. Mahaffy. Holl. & Germ. 131.
Heloïse. Clarke, M. C. Noted wom. 113. — Lamartine. Cel. char. 1 : 103. — Lord, J. Beacon, 5 : 101. — McLaughlin, E. T. Stud. mediæv. 152.
Helper, Hinton Rowan. Davidson, J. W. Writ. of South, 251.
Helps, Arthur. Friends in council. Boyd. Crit. ess. 167; *or* Recreat. 2 : 326.
— Obituary of. Em. persons, 1 : 289.
— Oulita, the serf. Boyd. Crit. ess. 282; *or* Leis. hours (Bost.), 371.
Helsingfors. Atkinson, J. B. Art tour northern, 143.
Helst, Bartholomeus van der. Gower. Fig. painters Holl. 31. — Van Dyke, J. C. Dutch mast. 67.
Helvetius, Claude Adrien, 1715–71. Vinet. Fr. lit. 18th cent. 349.
Helvetius, John Frederick. Waite, A. E. Lives of alchem. 201.
Hemans, Mrs. Felicia Dorothea. Bethune, G. W. Brit. fem. poets, 188.
Hemans, Felicia. Brooks. English, 413. — Chorley. Authors of Eng. 1. — Darton. Fam. girls, 72. — Elwood. Lit. ladies, 2 : 225. — Gilfillan. Mod. lit. 229. — With portrait. Hamilton, C. J. Wom. writers, 2 : 1. — Howitt. Homes Brit. poets, 2 : 122. — Queens of literature, 261. — Robertson. Eng. poetesses, 182. — Tuckerman. Poets, 262. — Walford, L. B. Twelve Eng. auth. 85. — With portrait. Warner Lib. 12 : 7229. — Williams, Jane. Lit. wom. 389. — Wotton. Word portraits, 125. — Duyckinck. Portrait gall. 1 : 566. — Espinasse. Lanc. worth. v. 2. — Griswold, R. W. Sac. poets. — Hall, S. C. Book of mem. 363. — (Browne) Hatfield, E. F. Poets of church, 315. — (M. Bell) Miles, A. H. Poets of cent. 7 : 53. — Miller, Jos. Singers church, 2d ed. 435. — Wise, D. Rem. women, 164.
— Poetry of. Jeffrey, F. Contrib. Ed. Rev.
— Sonnets of. Deshler. Afternoons, 255.
Hemenway, Mrs. A. D. Hemenway. Poets of Vt. 393.
Heminge, John. Collier. Actors, 57.
Hemi-Speos of Nubia. Adams, W. H. D. Fam. caves, 23.
Hemlock and pine trees. Dodge, M. A. Twelve miles, 23.
Hemp culture. N. J. Labor, '78 : 246. '79 : 157. '82 : 177.
Hempstead, Stephen, 1812–83. Iowa Hist. Record, 1 : 3.
Henault, Charles Jean François, 1685–1770. Vinet. Fr. lit. 18th cent. 171.
Hendee, Mrs. Clement, J. Noble deeds, 95.
Henderson, E. Y. W., Colonel, at Scotland Yard. Yates, E. H. Celeb. 3 : 79.
Henderson, John. Doran. Annals stage, 2 : 235. — Galt. Players, 2 : 21. — Matthews, B. Actors, 1 : 253.
Henderson, Richard. Lossing. Em. Amer. 180. — MacCrie, T. Miscel. writ. — Taylor, W. M. Scot. pulpit, 79.
Hendricken, Thomas Francis. Clarke, R. H. Cath. bishops, 3 : 153.
Hendricks, Abram W. Am. Bar Assoc. 11 : 327.
Hendricks, Thomas A. Am. Bar Assoc. 9 : 524.
Hendricks, William. Woollen. Biog. sk. Indiana, 51.

Hengham, Ralph de, chief justice of England, 1278–89. Campbell. Ch. just. 1 : 85.
Henley, David, Colonel, 1778. Chandler, P. W. Am. crim. trials, 2 : 59.
Henley, Joseph W. Hill, F. H. Polit. portr. 240. — Kent, W. C. M. Derby min. 239. — Reid, T. W. Cab. portr. 162.
Henley, Samuel. (M. Chamberlain) Mass. Hist. Proc. 15 : 230.
Henley, William Ernest, with portrait. Warner Lib. 12 : 7236.
Henner, Jean J. Henry, S. Hours w. Parisians, 217.
Hennessy, Sir John Pope. Escott, T. H. S. Pillars emp. 106.
Henotheism. Renouf. Religion of Egypt.
Henri, John Martin. Clarke, R. H. Cath. bishops, 3 : 324.
Henrietta Anne, daughter of Charles I. Green, M. A. E. Princesses, 6 : 399. — Strickland. Last princ. 209.
Henrietta Maria, queen of Charles I. Bayne. Pur. revol. 101. — With portrait. Howitt, M. Queens, 433. — Lodge. Portraits (Bohn), v. 5. — Strickland. Queens Eng. 8. — Jesse. Court of Eng. Stuarts, 2 : 1. — Lancelott. Queens, v. 2.
Henry I., emperor of Germany. Capgrave. Henries, 7. — Peake, Eliz. Germ. emperors, 39.
Henry II., emperor of Germany. Capgrave. Henries, 14. — Peake, Eliz. Germ. emperors, 51.
Henry III., emperor of Germany. Capgrave. Henries, 19. — Peake, Eliz. Germ. emperors, 61.
Henry IV., emperor of Germany. Capgrave. Henries, 27. — Doran. Monarchs, 1 : 299. — Peake, Eliz. Germ. emperors, 63.
Henry V., emperor of Germany. Capgrave. Henries, 35. — Peake, Eliz. Germ. emperors, 68.
Henry VI., emperor of Germany. Capgrave. Henries, 43. — Peake, Eliz. Germ. emperors, 103.
Henry VII., of Hapsburg, History of. Peake, Eliz. Germ. emperors, 149.
Henry I., *Beauclerc.* Brooks, E. S. Gt. men's sons, 160. — Capgrave. Henries, 53.
— Charter of. Round, J. H. Feudal Eng. 482.
Henry II., of England. Capgrave. Henries, 69. (D. Hume) Ferris, G. T. Gt. leaders, 138.
— Learning and literature under. Stubbs. Lecture on history, 132.
Henry III., of England. Capgrave. Henries, 88.
— Ellis, W. Royal jubilees, 42.
Henry IV., of England. Capgrave. Henries, 102.
— Reign of. Reed, H. Lec. Eng. hist. 181. — Warner, B. E. Eng. hist. 93.
Henry V., of England. Adams, W. H. D. Memo. batt. 195. — Capgrave. Henries, 125. — James, G. P. R. Commanders, 1 : 13. — Warner, B. E. Eng. hist. 134.
— Cradle of. (W. W. Old) Roy. Hist. Soc. 4 : 231.
— Imprisonment by Gascoign. (Solly-Ford) Roy. Hist. Soc. 11. 3 : 47.
— Reign of. Reed, H. Lec. Eng. hist. 213.
— Youth of. Ewald. Stories fr. st. pap. 1 : 18.
— War in Wales, 1402–05. — (Solly-Ford) Roy. Hist. Soc. 11. 4 : 125. — Busk, Mrs. Mediæv. popes, 2 : 316.
Henry VI., of England. Capgrave. Henries, 144. — Creasy. Etonians, 1. — Warner, B. E. Eng. hist. 169.

Henry VI., of England, Reign of. Reed, H. Lect. Eng. hist. 245.

Henry VII., of England. Redding. Misers, 1: 32.

— Matrimonial negotiations of. Ewald. Studies, 39.

— Mother of, Ellis, Mrs. S. S. Mothers.

— Reign of. Stubbs. Lec. hist. 382.

Henry VIII., of England. Burke, S. H. Hist. portr. Tudor, 1 : 66. — Coffin, C. C. Story of liberty, 140. — Johnston, R. M. Stud. 2 : 205. — Lodge. Portraits (Bohn), v. 1, — Lee, F. G. Hist. sk. reforma. 51 — Stubbs, W. Seventeen lect. 241. — Warner, B. E. Eng. hist. 244.

— Anne Boleyn and the reformation. Burke, S. H. Men of reforma. 1 : 7.

— Church under. Gladstone. Later gl. 219.

— Death of. Burke, S. H. Men of reforma. 2 : 172.

— Defender of the faith. (Brown) Roy. Hist. Soc. 8 : 242.

— Divorce of. Pennington. Epochs papacy, 309.

— His literary character. Disraeli, I. Amen. (N. Y. 2 v.) 1 : 287.

— Manuscript sonnets of. Deshler. Afternoons, 46.

— Military system of. Adams, W. H. D. Eng. at war, 1 : 1.

— Political character of the reformation of. Alviella. Contemp. evol. 16.

— Reign of. DeQuincey. Uncoll. 1 : 275. — Stubbs. Lec. hist. 277. — Reed, H. Dec. Eng. hist. 327.

— Valor ecclesiasticus. Ewald, A. C. Paper, 71.

Henry I., of France. Capgrave. Henries, 171.

Henry II., of France, Reign of. Cook, T. D. Old Touraine, 1 : 240. 2 : 1. — Gurney, J. H. Hist. sketches, 2 : 275.

Henry III., of France, and Louise de Vaudemont. Imbert de St. A. Wom. Valois ct. 293.

— and the minions. Menzies, S. Roy. fav. 1 : 241.

Henry IV., of France. Chambers's Miscel. no. 78. — Hewlett. Heroes, 318. — (J. L. Motley) Ferris, G. T. Gt. leaders, 284. — Gurney, J. H. Hist. sketches, 2 : 287. — Lord, J. Beacon, 8 : 383.

— and the fair Gabrielle. Menzies, S. Roy. fav. 1 : 328.

— and Marguerite de Valois. Imbert de St. A. Wom. Valois ct. 304.

— Mother of. Ellis, Mrs. S. S. Mothers.

Henry, prince of Wales. Lodge. Portraits (Bohn), v. 3. — Edwards, E. Founders Brit. Mus. 1 : 153. — Jesse. Court of Eng. Stuarts. — With portrait. Court of Eng. Stuarts, 1 : 118.

— Anecdotes of, when a child. Disraeli, I. Curios. (N. Y. 4 v.) 2 : 364.

— Death of. Bisset, A. Ess. on hist. 357.

Henry of Monmouth, prince of Wales. Doran. Princes of Wales, 201.

Henry of Greenwich, prince of Wales. Doran. Princes of Wales, 332.

Henry of Stirling, prince of Wales. Doran, Princes of Wales, 350.

Henry, prince of Portugal, the navigator. Markham. Sea fathers, 1. — Vogel, T. Cent. of discov. 6.

Henry, Prince of Spain, Death of, in duel. Hay, J. Castil. days, 371.

Henry Plantagenet, duke of Lancaster. Capgrave. Henries, 186.

Henry, archdeacon of Huntingdon. Capgrave. Henries, 205.

Henry, archdeacon of Ghent. Capgrave. Henries, 209.

Henry, archbishop of Sens. Capgrave. Henries, 184.

Henry, count of Champagne, king of Jerusalem. Capgrave. Henries, 180.

Henry de Beaumont. Capgrave. Henries, 194.

Honry de Bohun, earl of Hereford. Capgrave. Henries, 192.

Henry de Urimaria. Capgrave. Henries, 212.

Henry le Despenser, bishop of Norwich. Capgrave. Henries, 198.

Henry the minstrel. Irving. Scot poets, 1 ; 339.

Henry of Almayne. Capgrave. Henries, 175.

Henry of Lausanne. Hodgson, Wm. Reformers, 30.

Henry of Lonfenburg. Winkworth. Chr. singers Germ. 91.

Henry of Stirling. Adams, W. H. D. Anec. mem. 1 : 319.

Henry Frederick, duke of Cumberland, son of George II., 1745–90. Fitzgerald, P. Royal dukes, 1 : 182.

Henry, Alexander. Drake, S. G. Trag. of wilderness, 286. — (S. A. Allibone) Hunt, F. Am. merch. 1 : 473. — Winslow, S. N. Biog. Phila. merch. 132.

Henry, I. M. Porter. Raymond, I. Southland writ. 2 : 584.

Henry, John. Dunlap. Am. theatre, 1.

Henry, Joseph. Bolton, S. K. Fam. men of science, 275. — Garfield. Works, 2 : 627. — With portrait. Goode. Smithson. Inst. 1117. — Lanman, C. Haphazard, 7. — Youmans. Pioneer sci. 354.

Henry, Mrs. Katharine (Matthews). Anderson, J. Mem. Wom. Pur. 2 : 236.

Henry, Matthew. Grosart. Nonconf. 263.

Henry, Matthew Schropp. N. E. Hist.-Gen. Soc. Biog. 4 : 439.

Henry, Patrick, with portrait. [Amer.] Nat. portr. gall. v. 2. — Baldwin. Party leaders, 162. — Brooks, E. S. Hist. Amer. 73. — Duyckinck. Nat. portr. gall. 1 : 27. — Edwards, B. B. Selftaught, 614. — Harsha. Orators, 308. — Johnston, A. Amer. ora. 1 : 18. — Lossing. Em. Amer. 126. — Magoon. Orators of rev. 234. — Mathews, W. Oratory, 301. — Moore, F. Am. eloq 1 : 8. — Perry, B. F. Biog. sketches, 1 : 279. — Richardson. Amer. lit. 1 : 188. — With portrait. Seymour, C. C. B. Self-made, 401. — Smith, S. F. Noble workers, 280. — With portrait. Warner Lib. 12 : 7241.

— and relig. liberty in Virginia. (C. J. Stillé) Am. Hist. Assoc. 3 : 205.

— Home of. (E. W. Johnston) Homes Amer. statesm, 153.

Henry, Philip. Walker, W., jr. Men of sci. 58.

Henry, Wm. Pierce, B. K. Em. dead, 106.

Henrys, The, of Manchester and Bradford. Fortunes made in bus. 3 : 199.

Henry, Fort, Siege of. Dawson. Batt. of U. S. 1 : 267.

Henry, The, of electrical measure. (T. C. Mendenhall) Smithson. Rept. '94 : 141.

Henryson, Robert. Choate, I. B. Wells of Eng. 67. — Irving, D. Scot. poets, 1 : 375. — Minto, W. Eng. poets, 97. — Tytler. Scot. worth. v. 3. — (W. E. Henley) Ward. Eng. poets, 1 : 137. — Wilson, J. G. Poets of Scot. 1 : 18.

Henschel, George, with portrait. Buffen, F. F. Mus. celeb. 99.

Hensel, Louise. Baring-Gould. Germany, 162. Hatfield, E. E. Poets of church, 321.

Henselt, Adolph. Lenz. Gt. piano virtuosos, 119.

Henshaw, David. Loring, J. S. Hundred Bost. ora. 564. — (A. H. Ward) N. E. Hist.-Gen. Soc. Biog. 1 : 483.

Henshaw, Joshua Sidney. (Mrs. J. Henshaw) N. E. Hist.-Gen. Soc. Biog. 3 : 364.

Henshaw, Colonel William. (E. Washburn) Mass. Hist. Proc. 15 : 65.

Henslow, J. Stevens. Arnold, F. Turning-points, 179.

Hensol, C. Talbot, 1st baron. Welsby. Eng. judges.

Hentz, Mrs. Caroline Lee. Freeman, J. D. Wom. South, 265. — Griswold. Prose writ. 613. — Hart, J. S. Fem. prose, 162. — Mansfield, E. D. Pers. mem. 266.

Hepburn, James. *See* Bothwell, Earl of.

Hepburn family. Taylor, J. Fam. of Scot. 2 : 247.

Hepworth, Geo. H. Parton, J. Sk. of men of prog.

Heraclas. Pressensé. Martyrs, 341.

Heraclitus of Ephesus. Diog. Laertius. Lives, 376. — Fénélon. Philosophers, 125. — Hall, G. S. Aspects, 194. — Lewes. Biog. phil. — Mills. Poets of Greece, 418. — Fairbanks, A. Philos. of Greece, 28. — With portrait. Warner Lib. 13 : 7247.

Heraclius, Roman emperor. Bury. Later Roman empire, 2 : 207.

Heraldry. Burke, B. Viciss. of fam. 1 : 340.
— Bibliography. Salem (Mass.) Pub. Lib. Bull. July, '95.

Herat, Defence of. Hodder. Heroes, 1 : 117.

Herbart, Joh. F. Erdmann. Hist. philos. 2 : 607.
— Bibliography. Dodd, C. I. Introd. Herbartian prin. teach. — Garmo, C. de. Herbart & Herbartians.
— Pedagogy of, for normal schools. (Frank McMurray) Nat. Educa. Assoc. '92 : 421.

Herbeck, Johann von. Kingston, W. B. Music & mann. 1 : 13.

Herbert, Auberon. Davidson, J. M. Eng. lib. 275.

Herbert, Daniel. Miller, Jos. Singers church, 2d ed. 301.

Herbert, Sir Edward. Campbell. Ld. chan. 3 : 397. — Campbell. Ch. just. 2 : 72.

Herbert, Edward, of Cherbury, 1st Lord Herbert. Jesse. Court of Eng. Stuarts, 1 : 299. — Lodge. Portraits (Bohn), v. 4. — Ossoli. Art, 25. — (J. C. Collins) Ward. Eng. poets, 2 : 188.

Herbert, George. Adams, W. H. D. Gt. churchm. 265. — Brown, S. Atom, 2. — Haweis. Poets in the pulpit, 195. — (G. A. Simcox) Ward. Eng. poets, 2 : 192. — Deshler. Afternoons, 142. — Griswold, R. W. Sac. poets. — Holland, J. Psalmists, 1 : 279. — Macdonald, G. England's antiphon, 174. — Miller, Jos. Singers church, 2d ed. 61. — Ossoli. Art, 25. — Pierce, B. K. Em. dead, 87. — Walton, I. Lives. — With portrait. Warner Lib. 13 : 7253. — (I. Walton) Wordsworth, C. Eccles. Biog. v. 4.
— and his poetry. Haweis. Poets in pulpit, 195.
— his love of nature. Japp. Vers de soc. 225.
— Mother of. Guiney, L. I. Little Eng. gall. 1.

Herbert, Henry Howard Molyneux. *See* Carnarvon, Earl of.

Herbert, John Rogers, "Delivery of the law." Palgrave. Ess. on art, 151.

Herbert, Lady Magdalen. Costello. English-women, 1 : 380.

Herbert, Lady Magdalen, and Dr. Donne. Thomson, Mrs. Cel. friend. 1 : 295.

Herbert, Robert G. W. Escott, T. H. S. Pillars emp. 115.

Herbert, Sidney, Baron Herbert of Lea. Martineau, H. Biog. sk. 316. — Ritchie. Brit. sena. 417.

Herbert, Wm. Griswold, R. W. Sac. poets.

Herbert family. Sanford & Townsend. Gov. fam. v. 2.

Herbeson, Massy. Drake, S. G. Trag. of wilderness, 349.

Herbs of the field. Abbott, C. C. Outings, 215.

Herculaneum and Pompeii. Arnold, H. P. Eur. mosaic, 291.
— A half-hour at. Howells. Ital. jour. 106.
— Visit to. Chambers's Miscel. no. 28.

Hercules. Mombert. Great lives, 1.

Herdegen, Adolf. Am. Bar Assoc. 11 : 355.

Herder, Johann Gottfried von. Bancroft, G. Miscel. 167. — DeQuincey. Phil. wr. (Bost.) 1 : 159; *or* Writings (Masson), 4 : 380. — Gostwick. Ger. poets, 111. — With portrait. Hedge. Prose Ger. 231. — Hillebrand. Ger. thought, 117. — Hurst. Hist. rationalism, 171. — Pfleiderer, O. Philos. relig. 204. — Taylor. Stud. Ger. 256. — Baring-Gould. Germany, 150. — Edwards, B. B. Self-taught, 206. — Japp. German life, 211. — With portrait. (K. Francke) Warner Lib. 13 : 7259. — Wells, B. W. Mod. Ger. lit. 38.
— and Goethe. Scherer. Germ. lit. 2 : 82.

Heredia, José-Maria de. Gosse, E. Crit. kitcats. — Kennedy. Poets of Spain, 265. — Pellissier. Lit. move. Fr. 362. — With portrait. (M. F. Egan) Warner Lib. 13 : 7277.

Hereditary defects, Influence of, on health. (J. R. Black) Am. Pub. Health, 2 : 217.

Hereditary disease. (W. W. Godding) Nat. Educa. Assoc. '82 : app. 75.

Hereditary entailments. (J. Law) Am. Pub. Health, 2 : 239.

Hereditary genius. Brownson. Works, 9 : 401.

Hereditary legislators. Rosebery. Speeches, 58.

Hereditary piety. Cobbe, F. P. Darwinism, 35.

Hereditary tendencies as exhibited in history. (H. E. Malden) Evol. Crys. pal. lec. 74.

Hereditary traits. Proctor, R. A. Rough ways, 205.

Heredity. Elam. Phys. prob. 1. — Morgan. Animal life, 123. — Wallace. Darwinism, ch. 14. — (A. E. Tyng) R. I. Health, 3 : 247. — (C. W. Chancellor) Penn. Health, '86 : 234. — (William Turner) Smithson. Rept. '89 : 541. — Stephen, L. Soc. rights, 2 : 1.
— and environment : a study of adolescence. (E. J. Swift) Nat. Educa. Assoc. '98 : 910.
— and hybridity. Wilson, D. Lost Atlantis, 307.
— as a factor in knowledge. Ritchie, D. G. Darwin.
— Degenerative. (C. Denison) Am. Pub. Health, 21 : 245.
— Lessons of. Bridge, N. Penalties of taste, 119.
— A theory of. Lankester. Advan. sci. 271.
— — controverted. Bowen, F. Gleanings, 232.
— — Weismann's. (G. J. Romanes) Smithson. Rept. '90 : 433.

Hereford, Nicholas. Sergeant, L. Wiclif, 308.

Hereford, Eng. Silloway. Cathedral towns, 92.

Hereford map, The, and St. Brandan. Am. Geog. Soc. 24 : 321.

Herefordshire, England, Baptists of. Ivimey. Eng. Bapt. 2 : 202.

Heresbach, Conrad. Mitchell. Wet days, 101.

Heresies. Moxom. Jerus. to Nicæa, 276.

Higginson, T. W., at home. (G. W. Cooke) Gilder. Authors, 147.

High church bishops. Arnold, F. Our bishops, 2 : 64.

High life. Friswell. Gentle life, 1 : 243.

— and low life. Holland, J. G. Plain talks, 156.

High school, The. (A. F. Nightingale) Nat. Educa. Assoc. '89 : 501.

— and the citizen. (H. C. Missimer ; Laura Donnan) Nat. Educa. Assoc. '89 : 507.

— and the elementary school graduate. (F. L. Soldan) Nat. Educa. Assoc. '96 : 354.

— and university, Severance of. (J. W. Johnson) Nat. Educa. Assoc. '90 : 629.

— as a finishing school. (J. H. Baker) Nat. Educa. Assoc. '90 : 633.

— as a fitting-school. (A. F. Bechdolt) Nat. Educa. Assoc. '90 : 617.

— college-preparatory, Influence of, on lower grades. (C. W. Bardeen) Nat. Educa. Assoc. '90 : 624.

— Course in, as business preparation. (C. H. Thurber) Nat. Educa. Assoc. '97 : 808.

— Discipline in. (R. E. Denfeld) Nat. Educa. Assoc. '92 : 341.

— a factor in mass education. (E. A. Steere) Nat. Educa. Assoc. '90 : 645.

— for girls in England. (Mary Gurney and Rose Kingsley) Nat. Educa. Assoc. '93 : 225.

— Future of. (J. R. Bishop) Nat. Educa. Assoc. '94 : 788.

— of the future. (F. E. Plummer) Nat. Educa. Assoc. '91 : 620.

— Pupils in, Study of first-year. (F. W. Atkinson) Nat. Educa. Assoc. '98 : 903.

— Question of. (J. W. Dickinson) Nat. Educa. Assoc. '79 : 18.

— Relation of, to training-school. (Olive A. Evers) Nat. Educa. Assoc. '88 : 427.

— Studies in, Order and relation of. (Samuel Thurber) Nat. Educa. Assoc. '87 : 428.

— teachers for, Training of. (Eoline Clark) Nat. Educa. Assoc. '94 : 781.

— Township. (C. J. Baxter) Nat. Educa. Assoc. '98 : 308.

— western, Province of. (L. H. Austin) Nat. Educa. Assoc. '91 : 677.

High school system, The. Boutwell. Educa. topics, 164.

High-school work, Electives in. (W. L. Steele) Nat. Educa. Assoc. '99 : 331.

High schools and colleges, Conference between. (R. B. Fulton) Nat. Educa. Assoc. '99 : 147.

— and the state. (J. E. Seaman) Nat. Educa. Assoc. '85 : 173.

— Curriculum in, and college entrance requirements. (J. G. Schurman) N. Y. Regents, 111 : 64.

— Electives in, by courses or subjects ? (O. D. Robinson) Nat. Educa. Assoc. '95 : 586.

— For what do they prepare ? (G. B. Morrison) Nat. Educa. Assoc. '99 : 603.

— Public. Conn. Educa. '80 : 93.

— — and endowed academies. Boutwell. Educa. topics, 152.

— — Relations of, to colleges. (S. Thurber) N. Y. Regents, 89 : 603. — (E. W. Coy and others) Nat. Educa. Assoc. '87 : 282.

— teachers in, Equipment of. (A. Leonard and others) N. Y. Regents, 111 : 26.

— — Training of. (M. V. O'Shea) Nat. Educa. Assoc. '98 : 709.

— Uniform course of study for. (E. W. Coy) Nat. Educa. Assoc. '89 : 524.

High schools, What studies to review in. (J. W. Crabtree) Nat. Educa. Assoc. '99 : 611.

High station in life. Bacon. Ess.

High treason. *See* Treason.

High-water marks. Higginson. New world, 97.

Highclere Castle. Balch, E. Old Eng. homes, 196.

Higher Institutions, Necessity of. (A. L. Chapin) Nat. Educa. Assoc. '86 : 285.

Higher mathematics, Modern theories in. (William Thornton) Nat. Educa. Assoc. '76 : 129.

Highgate. Wolfe. Lit. pilg. Brit. au. 21.

Highlands of Scotland. Paget, J. Paradoxes, 77. — Chambers's Miscel. no. 141.

— West, Tales of. Müller. Chips, 2.

Highland clearing, A. Miller, H. Lead. articles, 136.

Highland Mary, Burns's. Jameson. Loves of poets.

Hight, B. W. Hemenway. Poets of Vt. 185.

Highwayman, The — real and ideal. Hain, J. Varia. 309.

Highways and parks. Mitchell, D. G. Bound together, 228.

— British, 1896. (T. F. Bayard) U. S. Cons. Rept. 52 : 157.

— in early New England. Adams, C. F. Three episodes, 2 : 666.

Hilarion. Hahn Hahn. Fathers, 139. — Kingsley. Hermits, 104.

Hilary, St., bishop of Poictiers. With portrait. Blakey, R. Prim. fathers, 161. — Cave. Lives of fathers, 2 : 365. — Charles. Martyrs, 346. — Farrar. Lives of fathers, 1 : 426.

Hilda, Abbess. Williams, Jane. Lit. wom. 16.

Hildebert, archbishop of Tours. Miller, Jos. Singers church, 2d ed. 25. — Neale. Mediæv. preachers.

Hildebrand. *See* Gregory VII., Pope.

Hildebrand, Lay of. Ludlow. Epics, 1 : 98. — Taylor, B. Stud. Ger. 10.

Hildegarde, Saint. Miller, Jos. Singers church, 2d ed. 30.

Hilderferth, St. Sparvel-Bayly. New stud. 42.

Hildesheim, Germany. Mahaffy. Holl. & Germ. 130.

Hildreth, Richard. Griswold. Prose writ. 615.

— Richardson. Amer. lit. 1 : 471. — With portrait. Warner Lib. 13 : 7371.

Hildrop, John. Baring-Gould. Yorks. odd. 2 : 1.

Hilf, Arno, with portrait. Ehrlich, A. Cel. violin. 140.

Hill, Ambrose Powell. Pollard. Life of Lee, 440.

— Snow. So. generals, 375.

Hill, Clement H., Tribute to. (T. K. Lothrop ; G. B. Chase) Mass. Hist. Proc. 2d ser. 12 : 373.

Hill, Daniel H. Davidson, J. W. Writ. of South, 257. — Pollard. Life of Lee, 448.

Hill, Ellen G. Clayton, E. C. Eng. fem. art. 2 : 257.

Hill, George. Woolrych. Serjeants, 2 : 634.

Hill, George, b. 1796. Everest. Poets of Conn. 277. — Griswold. Poets Am. 237.

Hill, Hamilton Andrews. Am. Antiq. Soc. Proc. n. s. 10 : 205. — Mass. Hist. Proc. 2d ser. 10 : 139. — With portrait. (S. E. Herrick) Mass. Hist. Proc. 2d ser. 11 : 188.

Hill, Harry R. W. With portrait. (W. K. King) Hunt, F. Am. merch. 2 : 501.

Hill, James, the dockyard incendiary. Burke, P. Cel. nav. & mil. trials, 118.

Hill, John, and the Royal Society. Disraeli, I. Calam. v. 2.

Hill, Matthew. Grant, Jas. Bench & bar, 2 : 93.

Hill, Nicholas. Proctor. Lawy. of N. Y. 618.
Hill, Sir Richard. Larrabee, W. C. Wesley, 2 : 243.
Hill, Robert. Craik. Pursuit knowl. 1 : 347.
Hill, Rowland, 1st viscount. Johns. Nav. & mil. heroes. — Cole, J. W. Brit. generals, v. 2.
Hill, Sir Rowland, with portrait. Nicoll. Great move. 209. — Parton. Capt. indus. 342. — Stanton, H. B. Reforms, 246. — Timbs, J. Great inventors, 267. — Em. persons, 2 : 168. — at Hampstead. Yates, E. H. Celeb. 1 : 209.
Hill, Rev. Rowland. Grant, Jas. Metropol. pul. 72. — Hatfield, E. F. Poets of church, 326. — Miller, Jos. Singers church, 2d ed. 289. — With portrait. Morison, J. Fathers of Lond. Miss. Soc. 2 : 118. — Sprague, W. B. Europ. celebrities, 20. — Waterbury. Eloq. preach. 119.
Hill, Sylvester G. Bartlett, J. R. R. I. officers, 447.
Hill, Theophilus H. Davidson, J. W. Writ. of South, 258.
Hill, Thomas, with portrait. Benjamin, S. G. W. Am. art. 2 : 22.
Hill, Thos., Pres. Harv. Coll. Allen, J. H. Sequel, 120. — Putnam, A. P. Singers liberal, 410. — Vaille & Clark. Harv. book, v. 1.
Hill, Sir Wm. Laurie, W. F. B. Dist. Anglo-Ind. 1 : 253.
Hill-digging and magic. Jessopp, A. Rand. roam. 84.
Hillard, George Stillman. Loring, J. S. Hundred Bost. ora. 546. — (F. W. Palfrey) Mass. Hist. Proc. 19 : 339. — Pierce, E. L. Addresses, 185.
Hiller, Philip Frederick. Winkworth. Chr. singers Germ. 279.
Hillhouse, Augustus Lucas. Hatfield, E. F. Poets of church, 331.
Hillhouse, James Abraham. Everest. Poets of Conn. 169. — Griswold. Poets Am. 114. — Griswold. Sac. poets. — Moore, F. Am. eloq. 2 : 144.
— The judgment, Critical remarks on. Drake, N. Evenings, 2 : 100.
Hilliard, Henry W. Davidson, J. W. Writ. of South, 267.
Hillibee towns, Massacre at. Dawson. Batt. of U. S. 2 : 309.
Hillis, David. Woollen. Biog. sk. Indiana, 173.
Hillsdale College, Hillsdale, Mich. (S. W. Norton) U. S. Bur. Ed. Circ. '91, no. 4 : 124.
Hillyer, Wm. S., with portrait. (W. L. Stone) Rogers, A. C. Repres. men, 289.
Hilo, Island of Hawaii, Surf bathing at. Caton. Miscel. 242.
Hilton, Martha. (L. I. Guiney) Spofford, H. P. Three heroines, 109.
Hilton, William. Redgrave. Century of p. 2 : 164.
Himalayan brothers; Do they exist? (R. K. Brahmachari) Five years theos. 459.
Himalayas, The. Abercromby. Seas and skies, 265. — Field, H. M. Egypt to Japan, 182. — Prime, E. D. G. Around world, 320. — Younghusband. Heart of cont. 170.
— In the. Pidgeon. Engineer's holiday, 364.
— Journeys in. Forbes, E. Lit. papers, 238.
— Visit to. Chambers's Repos. no. 85.
Hinchingbrooke. Balch, E. Old Eng. homes, 64.
Hinckley, George. Richards, W. Heroes, 17.
Hinckley, Thomas. Moore, J. B. Am. gov. 201.
Hind, James. Whitehead, C. Highwaymen, 1 : 59.

Hinderer, Mrs. Anna, of Ibadan, West Africa. Pitman, Mrs. Heroines mission. 198.
Hindersin, Gustav Edward. Strauss, G. L. M. Men of Ger. 2 : 271.
Hindley, Charles. Grant, J. Recoll. Lords & Comm. 2 : 197.
Hinds, Samuel. Miller, Jos. Singers church, 2d ed. 429.
Hindu idolatry and Christianity. Foster, J. Crit. ess. (Bohn) 1 : 110.
Hindu religion. (J. M. Mitchell) Liv. papers, v. 6.
Hindu sects. Barth, A. Relig. India, 159.
Hindu thought and Christian thought. (R. A. Hume) Barrows, J. H. Parl. relig. 2 : 1269.
Hindu widow, Duties of a faithful. Colebrooke, H. T. Miscel. ess. v. 1.
Hindu women, Education of. (Pundita Ramabai) Nat. Educa. Assoc. '88 : 665.
Hindu worship. Barth, A. Relig. India, 252.
Hinduism. (M. D'Vivedi) Barrows, J. H. Parl. relig. 1 : 316. — (Swami Vivekananda) Barrows, J. H. Parl. relig. 2 : 968. — Barth, A. Religions of India, 153. — Draper. Intel. devel. 1 : 56. — Foster, J. Crit. ess. 1 : 110. — Hardwick, C. Christ & other mas. 1 : 165. — Parks, L. His star in the east, 178. — Grant, G. M. Relig. 93. — Hopkins. Relig. of India, 348. — (Sir A. Lyall) Relig. systems, 112.
— Concession to native ideas. (T. E. Slater) Barrows, J. H. Parl. relig. 1 : 456.
— Modern. Bettany. World's relig. 213.
— Philosophic. Barrows, J. H. Chr. conq. Asia, 92.
— Popular. Barrows, J. H. Chr. conq. Asia, 60.
— Successive developments of. Ellinwood. Orient. relig. and Chr. 73.
Hindus, Philosophy of the. Colebrooke. Miscel. essays, 1 : 227.
— Religious ceremonies of. Colebrooke. Miscel. essays, 1 : 123.
— Sacred laws of. Maine. Early law, 1.
— Sacred writings of. Colebrooke. Miscel. essays, 1 : 9.
— Truthful character of. Müller, M. India, 52.
Hinkley, Edward Otis. Am. Bar Assoc. 19 : 653.
Hinsdale, Mrs. Grace Webster (Haddock). Hatfield, E. F. Poets of church, 334.
Hinton, J. Howard. Miller, Jos. Singers church, 2d ed. 417.
Hinton, James. Bettany. Em. doctors, 2 : 277.
Hippocrates. Hundred greatest men, 319. — Pettigrew. Med. portr. gall. v. 3.
Hippolytus, St. Hort, F. J. A. Ante-N. fathers, 76. — Pressensé. Martyrs, 360.
— and his age, Bunsen's. Martineau, J. Studies, 201.
— Homily against Noetus. Dods, M. Erasmus, 94.
Hippolytus veiled. Pater. Greek stud. 156.
Hipponax of Ephesus. Arnold, E. Poets of Greece, 97. — Symonds, Greek poets, 1 : 283.
Hippopotamus, The. Morgan, C. L. Animal sk. 37.
— Our last. Wood, J. G. Out-of-doors, 331.
— Petherick's. Buckland, F. T. Curios. nat. hist. 3 : 108.
Hiram College, Hiram, O. U. S. Bur. Ed. Circ. '91, no. 5 : 185.
Hirsch, Maurice de. Bolton, S. K. Givers, 312.
Hirschvogel, Augustine. (A. Rosenberg) Dohme, R. Early mast. 174.
Hirst, Henry Beck. Griswold. Poets Am. 439.
Hirst, Jemmy. Baring-Gould. Yorks. odd. 1 : 191.

Hissing in theatres. Cook, D. Bk. of play, **2** : 295. — Lamb. Elia.

Histology, Physiological : Processes of life revealed by the microscope. (S. H. Gage) Smithson. Rept. '**96** : 381.

Historian and ethnologist, Mutual obligations of, (O. T. Mason) Am. Hist. Assoc. **4** : 205.

Historians, American. Richardson. Amer. lit. **1** : 446.

— English. Ferrier. Ill. of Sterne, **2** : 101.

— Greek, The great. Huxley. Ess. contro. 91.

Historic truth, perversion of, Pernicious influence of. Henry, C. S. Satan, 172.

Historical cycles. Freeman. Hist. ess. **4** : 249.

Historical difficulties. Fiske, J. Unseen world, 169.

Historical evidence. Forsyth, W. Essays, 438.

— Mode of handling. McLennan. Stud. anc. **2** : 27.

Historical grouping. Schouler, Jas. Hist. briefs, 16. Same in Am. Hist. Assoc. **3** : 48.

Historical industries. Schouler, Jas. Hist. briefs, 34.

Historical inquiries, The most important. Woodbury, L. Writ. **3** : 131.

Historical material, Organization of. (W. H. Mace) Am. Hist. Assoc. **5** : 143.

Historical monographs. Schouler, Jas. Hist. briefs, 48.

Historical portraits by romantic painters. Doran. New pic. 198.

Historical progress, Supposed consequences of doctrine of. Smith, Gold. Lec. mod. hist.

Historical research, Spirit of. (J. Schouler) Am. Hist. Assoc. **4** : 297.

Historical sciences, Needs of. (A. H. Sayce) Ess. end. research, 197.

Historical societies, Bibliography of. (A. P. C. Griffin) Am. Hist. Assoc. Rept. '**95** : 675.

— Functions of. (J. F. Jameson) Am. Hist. Assoc. Rept. '**97** : 51.

— State-supported, Functions of. (R. G. Thwaites) Am. Hist. Assoc. Rept. '**97** : 61.

Historical studies in Canada. (G. Stewart) Am. Hist. Assoc. **4** : 433. **5** : 257.

— in the South, Outlook for. (W. P. Trent) Am. Hist. Assoc. **4** : 383.

Historical style, Varieties of. Stirling-Maxwell. Miscel. ess. 277.

Historical testimony. Schouler, Jas. Hist. briefs, 60.

Historical work, Aspects of. Scudder, H. E. Men & let. 171.

— Recent, in colleges and universities of Europe and America. (C. K. Adams) Am. Hist. Assoc. **4** : 39.

History. Carlyle. Essays ; also in Prose masterpieces, **2** : 161. — Cleveland, R. E. Eliot, 63. — Helps. Friends, 1st ser. 1. — Holland, H. Frag. papers, 229. — Emerson. Ess. **1** : 7. — Farrar. Soc. & p. day quest. 148. — Macaulay. Ess. **1** : 376 ; also in Prose masterpieces, **2** : 185. — (D. W. Thompson) Afternoon lec. **3** : 1.

— Ancient. Dutt. Hist. stud. **1** : 1. — Maurice. Friendship, 159.

— and historical reading. Porter, N. Books, 125.

— and its philosophy. Henry, C. S. Satan, 62.

— and literature, coördination in. (C. A. McMurry) Nat. Educa. Assoc. '**95** : 104.

— — in grammar grades. (J. H. Phillips) Nat. Educa. Assoc. '**92** : 606.

— and political science necessary studies in free countries. Lieber, F. Reminis. 179, 329.

— and politics, Essays upon. Lucas. Mornings, **2** : 327.

History as an aid to moral culture. (C. M. Andrews) Nat. Educa. Assoc. '**94** : 397.

— as development. Shackford. Soc. & lit. pap. 283.

— Connection of. Harrison, F. Mean. of hist. 24.

— Definition of. (W. P. Johnston) Am. Hist. Assoc. Rept. '**93** : 43.

— early, Method of inquiry in. McLennan. Stud. anc. **2** : 6.

— Economic interpretation of. (E. A. Bryan) Nat. Educa. Assoc. '**99** : 186.

— English, Need of its cultivation. Jessopp, A. Studies, 278.

— Fallacies of. (A. P. Peabody) Am. Antiq. Soc. Proc. n. s. **4** : 12.

— for children. Bibliography. Rice, E. J. Courses stud. hist. & lit.

— for secondary schools. (E. V. Robinson) Nat. Educa. Assoc. '**97** : 679.

— General. Bibliography. Barnes, M. D. Stud. Gen. hist. — Larned, J. N. Hist. ready ref.

— — Methods of teaching. Mary S. Barnes) Nat. Educa. Assoc. '**91** : 673.

— — Studies in. (A. D. White) Am. Hist. Assoc. **1** : 47.

— Guizot's Essays and lectures on. Mill, J. S. Dissert. (N. Y.) **2** : 297.

— How to study. Hart, A. B. Stud. Am. educa. 75.

— Illusions of. Mathews. Men & bks. 171.

— in elementary education. (M. A. Newell) Nat. Educa. Assoc. '**92** : 310.

— in elementary education, Ethical value of. (J. F. Millspaugh) Nat. Educa. Assoc. '**96** : 410.

— in the German Gymnasia. (L. M. Salmon) Am. Hist. Assoc. Rept. '**97** : 73.

— in the high school. (W. M. West) Nat. Educa. Assoc. '**90** : 648.

— in literature. Trail, F. Studies, 219.

— in the secondary schools. (H. M. Stephens) Nat. Educa. Assoc. '**96** : 623.

— — How to teach. Hart, A. B. Stud. Am. educa. 91.

— Is it a science ? (R. H. Dabney) Am. Hist. Assoc. **5** : 263.

— Literature and. Masson. Three devils, 301.

— Mediæval and modern, differences between. Stubbs. Lec. on hist. 208.

— Method of. Birrel, A. Obiter, 2.

— Modern. Dutt. Hist. stud. **1** : 195.

— — Arnold's lectures on. Gregg. Ess. pol. **1** : 1.

— Museums of. (G. B. Goode) Am. Hist. Assoc. **3** : 497.

— Nature and influence of the historic spirit. Shedd. Theo. ess. 53.

— New spirit in. Lilly, W. S. Ess. 193.

— of the earth in libraries and museums. (G. E. Ellis) Am. Antiq. Soc. Proc. n. s. **8** : 24.

— Patriotic force in the schools. (H. B. Carrington) Nat. Educa. Assoc. '**89** : 333.

— Pearls and mock pearls of. Hayward, A. Ess. 2d ser. **1** : 1.

— Philosophic aspects of. (W. T. Harris) Am. Hist. Assoc. **5** : 247.

— Philosophy of. Brownson. Works, **4** : 361. — Gilbart. Lec. 347. — Jouffroy. Philos. miscel. **2** : 161. — (E. P. Powell) Factors Amer. civiliz. 363. — Whittaker, T. Ess. & not. 1.

— Plea for study of, in No. Europe. (A. C. Coolidge) Am. Hist. Assoc. Rept. '**95** : 445.

— Rationality of. (D. G. Ritchie) Seth & Haldane. Ess. 126.

— Reconstruction of. Am. Hist. Assoc. **2** : 79.

— Relation of, to politics. (J. Macy) Am. Hist. Assoc. Rept. '**93** : 179.

History, Relations of, to practical life. (S. Howell) N. Y. Regents, **90** : 557.
— Romance of. Macaulay. Ess. **1** : 376.
— Science of. Froude. Short. stud. **1** : 7 ; also in Prose masterpieces, **3** : 3.
— Scientific method applied to. Froude. Short stud. **2** : 445.
— Scientific pretensions of. Thornton, W. T. Old-fash. 84.
— Some great books of. Harrison, F. Mean. of hist. 77.
— Source study method of teaching, in high schools. (H. W. Caldwell) Nat. Educa. Assoc. '97 : 670.
— — To what extent may undergraduate students be trained in the use of sources ? (J. A. Woodburn) Am. Hist. Assoc. Rept. '97 : 43.
— Study of. Brewer. Eng. stud. 379. — Friswell. Essays, v. **12**. — Reed, H. Lec. Eng. hist. 13. — Royal Hist. Soc. **1** : 9. **8** : 1. — Stubbs. Lec. on hist. — Smith, Gold. Lec. mod. hist.
— — at Oxford. Stubbs. Lec. on hist. 26.
— — Chief aim in. (W. A. Edwards) Nat. Educa. Assoc. '92 : 348.
— — in Amer. colleges. (H. B. Adams) U. S. Bur. Ed. Circ. '87, no. 2.
— — in public schools. (N. C. Dougherty) Nat. Educa. Assoc. '97 : 58.
— — in secondary schools. (H. P. Judson) N. Y. Regents, **99**, app. : 81.
— — Methods of. Stubbs. Lec. on hist. 93.
— — Purposes of. Stubbs. Lec. on hist. 71.
— Style in writing. Schouler, Jas. Hist. briefs, 71.
— universal, Notes on. Turgot. Life & writ. 174.
— Teaching of. (H. B. Adams) Am. Hist. Assoc. Rept. '96, **1** : 243. — (J. R. Seeley) Internat. health exh. **15** : 33.
— — Bibliography. Am. Hist. Assoc., Comm. of Seven Report.
— — in schools. (B. A. Hinsdale) Nat. Educa. Assoc. '95 : 360.
— — in state schools. Pearson, C. H. Reviews, 202.
— — to children. (M. H. Peabody) Cong. Educa. Chic. '93, 284.
— Teaching of European, in college. (T. H. Robinson) Am. Hist. Assoc. Rept. '96, **1** : 265.
— Tendency of. (H. Adams) Am. Hist. Assoc. Rept. '95 : 17.
— True and the false in. Smith, J. Campbell. Writings, 115.
— True function of. Birrell. Obiter, **2** : 196.
— True sources of. Disraeli, I. Curios. (N. Y. 4 v.) **4** : 293.
— Truth of. Hare. Guesses, **1** : 368.
— Truth in. Wilson, Woodrow. Mere lit. 161.
— Uncertainty of. Woodbury, L. Writ. **3** : 169.
— U. S., in elementary schools. (W. F. Gordy) Nat. Educa. Assoc. '98 : 70.
— — in secondary schools. (H. H. Seerley) Nat. Educa. Assoc. '98 : 77.
— Universal, from a socialist standpoint. Bax. Relig. of socialism, **1**, 164.
— — Scientific treatment of. (G. G. Zerffi) Roy. Hist. Soc. **3** : 380.
— Use of. Harrison, F. Mean. of hist. **1**.
— — made by framers of Constitution. (E. G. Bourne) Am. Hist. Assoc. Rept. '96, **1** : 221.
— Veracity of. (A. P. Stanley) Hundred greatest men, 259.
— Voltaire's ideas on. (G. G. Zerffi) Roy. Hist. Soc. **10** : 344.
— What can it teach us ? Lilly. Chapters, **1** : 1.
— Writing of. Bancroft, H. H. Works, **38** : 75.

39 : 592. — (J. P. Baxter) Am. Antiq. Soc. Proc. n. s. **13** : 138. — Bancroft, H. H. Essays, 75.
History doctorate in America, Requirements for the. (E. Emerton) Am. Hist. Assoc. Rept. '93 : 77.
Hitcham, Sir Robert. Woolrych. Serjeants, **1** : 220.
Hitchcock, Edward, Pres. Amherst College. Griswold. Prose writ. 591. — Youmans. Pioneers sci. 290.
— on the union of religion and science. Phelps, A. L. Rev. & ess. 270.
Hitchcock, Lucy A. Hemenway. Poets of Vt. 118.
Hitchcock, Peter. Livingston, J. Em. Am. lawy. 630.
Hitopadesa, The. Colebrooke, H. T. Miscel. ess. v. **2**.
Hittites. (L. Dickerman) Am. Geog. Soc. **21** : 325. — Perrot and Chipiez. History of art in Sardinia, v. **2**.
— Bibliography. Conder, C. R. Hittites & their lang.
— Historical connections. (Conder) Roy. Hist. Soc. **11**, **4** : 41.
— Religion of. (T. Tyler) Relig. systems, 10.
Hitz, Mrs. Ann. Moore, F. Women of the war, 472.
Hitzig, Ferdinand. Cheyne. Founders O. T. crit. 119.
Hoadley, D. Parton, J. Sk. of men of prog.
Hoadly, Benj., Bishop. Wrangham. Brit. Plutarch, v. **6**.
— and the Bangorian controversy. Stephen, L. Eng. thought, **2** : 152.
Hoar, Ebenezer R. (J. Winsor and others) Mass. Hist. Proc. 2d ser. **9** : 301.
— Tribute to. Pierce, E. L. Addresses, 373.
Hoar, Samuel. Emerson. Lec. & biog. sk. 405. — (W. Minot) Mass. Hist. Proc. **5** : 367. (G. F. Hoar) N. E. Hist. Gen. Soc. Biog. **3** : 105.
Hobab. Hasting, F. Obscure charac. 189.
Hobart, Augustus C. [Hobart Pasha], with photo. Cooper, T. Men of mark, **6** : 35.
Hobart, Lady Frances. Burder. Pious wom. 134.
Hobart, J. H., Bishop. Wilson. Centennial history Protestant Episcopal Church in New York.
Hobart, Vere Henry Hobart, baron ; biographical sketch. Hobart, V. H. H. Ess. & Miscel. **1** : 1.
Hobbema, Myndert. Cundall. Landsc. painters Holl. — Van Dyke, J. C. Dutch mast. 131.
— Avenue of Middelharnais. (P. Lafond) Singleton, E. Great pic. 88.
Hobbes, Thomas. Bisset, A. Ess. on hist. 53. — Courtney. Stud. **1**. — Disraeli. Quarrels. — Evelyn. Diary, **2** : 118. — Lewes. Biog. phil. — Lange. Materialism, **1** : 270. — Maurice, F. D. Mor. & meta. philos. **2** : 235. — Morris, G. S. Brit. tho't, 141. — Green, T. H. Works, **2** : 366. — Nasmith. Mak. mod. thought, **2** : 1. With portrait. Warner Lib. **13** : 7381.
— and his quarrels. Disraeli, I. Calam. **2**.
— Ethics, Bibliography of. Sneath, E. H. Ethics Hobbes in selec. from Works.
— Leviathan. Saunders, F. Famous books, 59. — Stephen, J. F. Horæ Sabb. **2** : 19.
— Minor works. Stephen, J. F. Horæ Sabb. **2** : 36.
— on general reasoning. Webb, T. E. Veil of Isis, 344.
— political system of. Coleridge. Friend, 154.
— Writings of. Hazlitt. Lit. remains, **1** : 113.

Homicide, Justifiable. Grahame, K. Pagan papers, 147.
Homœopathy. Brodie. Works, **1** : 645. — Brown, S. Atom, 2. — Bunce, O. B. Bach. bluff, 178.
— and its kindred delusions. Holmes, O. W. Currents, 51 ; *or* Med. ess. 1.
— criticised. (W. T. Gairdner) Edin. ess. '56 : 95.
— Epistle on. McSherry. Ess. 78.
— Report on, to Mass. Medical Society. Bigelow, J. Mod. inq. 326.
Honduras. (E. W. Perry) Am. Geog. Soc. **25** : 224.
— Handbook of. Bur. Am. Rep., Bulletin no. 57.
— Import duties of, 1891. Bur. Am. Repub. Bulletin, no. 24.
Hone, William. Hall, S. C. Book of mem. 62. — Routledge, J. Pop. prog. in Eng. 267, 364.
Honesty. (J. W. Horsley) Wace, H. Lond. mission. 60.
— as a marketable commodity. Whipple. Success, 156.
Honeywood, St. John. Griswold. Poets Am. 60.
Honfleur, New and old. Dodd, A. B. Three Norm. inns, 127.
Hong Kong. Brooks, J. Seven months, 255. — Keating. With Grant, 165. — Palgrave. Ulysses, 200. — Cumming, C. F. G. Wand. in China, **1** : 5, 109. — Pidgeon. Engineer's holiday, 323.
— and Shanghai. Norman, H. Far East, 3.
— Increase of U. S. trade with, 1898. (R. Wildman) U. S. Cons. Rept. **59** : 279.
— Statistics of, 1892. (O. H. Simons) U. S. Cons. Rept. **40** : 366.
Honolulu, Life in. Todd, M. L. Corona, 42.
Honor. Schopenhauer. Wisdom, 73.
— and reputation. Bacon. Ess.
— due to all men. Channing. Works, **3** : 299.
— Law of. Oxenham. Short stud. 230. — Ware, H., jr. Works, **3** : 141.
— Marks of. Friswell. Gentle life, **2** : 91.
Honorary degrees as conferred in American colleges. (C. F. Smith) Nat. Educa. Assoc. '89 : 291.
Honorius. Hook. Abps. Cant. **1** : 110.
Honthorst, Gerard van. Gower. Fig. painters Holl. 5.
Hooch, Pieter de. Gower. Fig. painters Holl. 69. — Wedmore. Masters of genre, 50. — Van Dyke, J. C. Dutch mast. 109.
Hood, John B., Gen. Pollard. Life of Lee, 663. — Snow. So. generals, 384.
Hood, Robin. *See* Robin Hood.
Hood, Samuel, first viscount. Lodge. Portraits (Bohn), v. **8**. — Johns. Nav. & mil. heroes. — Laughton, J. K. Twelve sailors, 359.
— Sea fight of. Valentine, L. J. Sea fights, 101.
Hood, Thos. Brooks, S. W. Eng. poets, 472. — Dawson, G. Biog. lec. 451. — Gilfillan. Mod. lit. 96. — Hall, S. C. Book of mem. 135. — Henley. Views, 165. — Mather, J. M. 19th cent. poets, 99. — Horne. New spirit, **2** : 51. — Mason, E. T. Pers. traits, **4** : 1. — (R. Garnett) Miles, A. H. Poets of cent. **3** : 215. **9** : 249. — Ossoli. Life without, 61. — (J. T. Fields) Parton. Princes, 151. — Parton. Triumphs, 255. — Rossetti. Famous poets. — Saintsbury, G. Ess. Eng. lit. **2** : 109. — Saunders, F. Famous books, 173. — Stedman. Vic. poets, 72. — (A. Dobson) Ward. Eng. poets, **4** : 531. — With portrait. (L. G. Runkle) Warner Lib. **13** : 7589. — Whipple. Ess. & rev. v. **2**. — Wotton. Word portraits, 130.

Hood, Thos., Sonnets of. Deshler. Afternoons, 295.
Hooft, Pieter Corneliszoon, with portrait. Warner Lib. **13** : 7610.
Hook, James C., with photo. Cooper, T. Men of mark, **4** : 32.
Hook, Theodore E. Jeaffreson. Novelists, **2** : 108. — Smiles. Brief biog. 165. — Thompson. Wits & beaux, 405. — Timbs. Anec. biog. wits, v. **2**. — Wotton. Word portraits, 134. — Hall, S. C. Book of mem. 147, 163. — Horne, R. H. New spirit, 223. — Miles, A. H. Poets of cent. **9** : 375. — Saintsbury, G. Ess. Eng. lit. **2** : 270. — Warner Lib. **13** : 7613.
Hook, Walter Farquhar. Davies, G. J. Suc. preach. 164. — Huntington, G. Random. recol. 151.
Hooke, John. Woolrych. Serjeants, **2** : 466.
Hooke, Nathaniel. Lawrence. Brit. historians, **2** : 239.
Hooker, David G. Am. Bar Assoc. **11** : 357.
Hooker, Herman. Griswold. Prose writ. 417.
Hooker, Sir J. D., with photo. Cooper, T. Men of mark, **5** : 15.
Hooker, Joseph, Gen. Duyckinck. Nat. portr. gall. **2** : 419. — Glazier, W. Heroes, 314. — Headley. Grant and Sherman, 360. — Shanks. Rec. of generals, 165. — Parton, J. Sk. of men of prog. — With portrait. (J. W. De Peyster) Rogers, A. C. Repres. men. 295.
Hooker, Richard. Barry, A. Masters theol. 1. — Coleridge. Lit. rem. **3** : 18. — Collier, W. F. Hist. Eng. lit. 129. — Disraeli, I. Amen. (N. Y. 2 v.) **2** : 86. — Fuller. Worthies, **1** : 423. — Hopkins, S. Puritans, **3** : 39. — Tulloch. Eng. purit. 24. — Washburn, E. A. Epochs, 199. — Whipple. Lit. Eliz. 340. — Morley, H. Eng. writ. **9** : 415. — (I. Walton) Walton, I. Lives ; Same in Wordsworth, C. Eccles. biog. v. **3**.
— Ecclesiastical polity. Stephen, J. F. Horæ Sabb. **1** : 145.
— Prose style of. Hunt, T. W. Rep. Eng. prose, 231.
Hooker, Thomas. Lossing. Em. Amer. 26. — Richardson. Amer. lit. **1** : 118.
Hooper, John, bishop, 1495–1555. Hopkins, S. Puritans, **1** : 1. — Pierce, B. K. Em. dead, 54. — Tayler, C. B. Eng. martyrs. — Tulloch. Eng. purit. 8. — Wordsworth, C. Eccles. biog. v. **2**. — Burke, S. H. Hist. portr. Tudor, **3** : 46.
Hooper, John, d. 1789. Redding. Misers, **2** : 66.
Hooper, Lucy. Griswold. Fem. poets, 288.
Hooper, Robert L. Field, R. S. Prov. courts N. J., 126.
Hooper, Sue C. Raymond, I. Southland wr. **2** : 792.
Hooper, William. Dwight, N. Signers of decl. 325. — Lincoln, R. W. Signers, 34. — Lossing. Signers, 201. — Sanderson. Signers, v. **7**.
Hooper, William Sturgis. (S. L. Thorndike) Harvard mem. biog. **1** : 189.
Hoopskirts. Jeune, Lady. Lesser ques. 143.
Hope, George, Scotch farmer. Parton. Capt. indus. 288.
Hope, Henry Joy McCracken. Hatfield, E. F. Poets of church, 338.
Hope, James. Hemenway. Poets of Vt. 277.
Hope, James Barron. Davidson, J. W. Writ. of South, 279.
Hope, John, Lord justice-clerk. Smith, J. Campbell. Writings, 319.
Hope, Lady Henrietta. Burder. Pious wom. 532.
Hope, Mrs. Mary, of Kunnunkulum, India. Pitman, Mrs. Heroines mission. 267.
Hope family. Titcomb, S. E. N. Eng. peo. 102.

House of Commons, Indirect representation in. (B. Cracroft) Ess. on reform, '67 : 155.
— Judges in. Macaulay. Miscel. & sp. 763.
— Redistribution of seats in. (J. B. Kinnear) Ess. on reform, '67 : 127.
— Speaker of, Change of, 1884. Smalley. Lond. let. 2 : 175.
House of Lords. (R. Peel) Stanhope, Earl. Miscel. 1 : 60. — Fawcett. Ess. & lec. 292. — Freeman. Hist. ess. 4 : 425. — Pembroke, Earl. Polit let, 363.
— Appellate jurisdiction of, from courts of Scotland. (J. Anderson) Trans. Soc. Sci. Lond. '60 : 239.
— Functions of. Newman, F. W. Miscellanies, 3 : 198.
— Reform of. Buxton. Political questions. — Geffcken. British empire, 293. — Rosebery. Speeches, 267.
House of Representatives, U. S. Foster, R. Comment. on Const. 1 : 316, 355, 369, 447, 451.
— in 1826. Quincy, J. Figures, 280.
— Speaker of. Foster, R. Comment. on Const. 1 : 451.
House of superstition; a poem. (Thomas Denton) Gilpin, W. Lives, 5.
House-breakers, Familiar letter to. Fields. Underbrush, 83.
House decoration as work for women. Bolton, S. K. Soc. stud. in Eng. 74.
House decorations, Poisonous. (W. B. Clarke) Indiana Health, '90 : 191.
House-hunting in London and suburbs. Wynter. Curios. of toil, 2 : 209.
House interiors. Mitchell, D. G. Bound toge. 252.
House warming. Thoreau. Selec. 80.
Housekeeping. Ames, M. C. Outlines, 188.
Houses, construction of, Necessity of filing plans for, in a public office. (E. G. Janeway) Am. Pub. Health, 5 : 44.
— for the poor. (Raffalovich) Mackay. Plea for liberty.
— for working men. (C. H. Hartshorne) Trans. Soc. Sci. Lond. '57 : 437. — Pa. Labor, 1886.
— Sanita. arrangements of, in London. Internat. Health Ex. Sanita.
— Sanitary condition of. (A. Hill et al.) Trans. Soc. Sci. Lond. '78 : 471.
Housework beneficial to health. Brackett, A. C. Educa. of girls, 320.
Housing the poor. Gibbins. Eng. soc. ref. 174, 217.
    See Dwellings.
Houseman, Mrs. Burder. Pious wom. 366.
Housman, H. Pierce, B. K. Em. dead, 203.
Houssaye, Arsène. (E. C. J. B. Jacquot) Gautier. Fam. Fr. au. 70. — Van de Velde. Fr. fic. 2 : 195.
Houston, Lock E. Am. Bar Assoc. 20 : 547.
Houston, Samuel. Bungay. Off-hand, 219. — Glazier, W. Heroes, 212. — Savage. Liv. rep. men, 318.
— Bibliography. Williams, A. M. S. Houston & independence Tex.
— Character of. Dyer, O. Gt. senators, 110.
Houstoun, John. Jones, C. C., jr. Deleg. fr. Georgia, 106. — Miller, S. F. Bench of Ga. v. 2.
Houstoun, Mrs. M. C., with portrait. Black, H. C. Wom. authors, 223.
Houstoun, William. Jones, C. C., jr. Deleg. fr. Georgia, 118.
Hovenden, Thomas. Sheldon, G. W. Amer. painters, 189.

Hovey, Joseph. Knapp, S. L. Em. lawyers, 233.
How, Henry Jackson. (J. Schouler) Harvard mem. biog. 2 : 30.
How, Nehemiah. Drake, S. G. Trag. of wilderness, 127.
How, William Walsham. Hatfield, E. F. Poets of church, 341. — Miles, A. H. Poets of cent. 10 : 445. — Miller, Jos. Singers church, 2d ed. 563.
Howard, Benjamin Chew. Carson, H. L. Sup. Ct. of U. S. 566.
Howard, Bronson. Archer. Eng. dram. 209.
Howard, Catherine. Burke, S. H. Men of reforma. 2 : 88.
Howard, Charles. See Carlisle, Earl of.
Howard, Charles. See Nottingham, Charles, 1st earl of.
Howard, Edward C. Walker, W., jr. Men of sci. 63.
Howard, Sir Edw. With portrait. Laughton, J. K. Twelve sailors, 315. — Bourne, H. R. F. Eng. seam. 1 : 49.
Howard, Henrietta, wife of John (d. 1765). Child. Good wives, 154.
Howard, Henry. See Surrey, Earl of.
Howard, Henry. Redgrave. Century of p. 2 : 164.
Howard, Jacob M. Bungay. Repr. men, 255.
Howard, John, the philanthropist. Adams, W. H. D. Good Samar. 273. — Bayne, P. Chr. life, 96. — Blaikie, W. G. Leaders, 19. — Chambers's Miscel. no. 112. — Cobb, J. F. Heroes of charity. — Cooper, T. Triumphs of persev. 134. — Gurney, J. H. Hist. sketches, 3 : 408. — Hodder. Heroes, 1 : 163. — Hundred greatest men, 477. — (H. Dixon) Macaulay. New biog. 85. — With portrait. Nicoll. Great move. 11. — Parton. Peop. bk. biog. 30. — Phillips, S. Ess. from Times, 1 : 127. — Rio. Four martyrs. — Taylor, W. C. Mod. Brit. Plut. 211.
Howard, John, Capt. Bourne, H. R. F. Eng. seam. 1 : 48.
Howard, John Eager. With portrait. [Amer.] Nat. portr. gall. 2. — Lossing. Em. Amer. 141.
Howard, Gen. Oliver Otis. With portrait. Brockett. Men of our day, 168. — Bungay. Pen-portr. 166. — Glazier, W. Heroes, 357. — Stowe. Men of time, 447.
— as a general. Shanks. Rec. of generals, 299.
Howard, Philip. See Arundel, Earl of.
Howard, Philip John. Grant, J. Recoll. Lords & Comm. 2 : 140.
Howard, Sir R. Indian Queen; a drama. Hogarth. Mem. opera, 1 : 116.
Howard, Thomas. Bourne, H. R. F. Eng. seam. 1 : 48.
Howard, Thomas. See Norfolk, 4th duke of.
Howard, Thomas. See Suffolk, Earl of.
Howard, Tilghman A. Woollen. Biog. sk. Indiana, 262.
Howard family. Lonsdale. Worthies Cumb. v. 3. — Sanford & Townsend. Gov. fam. 2.
— Genealogical sketch of. Jewitt, L. Stately homes, 1 : 158.
Howard Castle. Edwardes, C. Hist. houses.
Howard College, Birmingham, Ala. U. S. Bur. Ed. Circ. '89, no. 3 : 172.
Howe, Abbie J. Brockett. Woman's work, 465.
Howe, Elias, jr. Bolton, S. K. Success, 132. — Houghton. Kings, 343. — Parton. Triumphs, 411. — With portrait. Hubert, P. G., jr. Inventors, 99. — Rogers, A. C. Repres. men, 301. — Towle, G. M. Heroes of inven. 180.
Howe, Jemima. Drake, S. G. Trag. of wilderness, 156.

Hugh Lupus, 1st earl of Chester. (J. L. Thornely) Andrews, W. Bygone Ches. 105.
Hughes, Arthur. (W. M. Rossetti) Atkinson, J. B., *et al.* Eng. paint. 44. — Bate, P. H. Eng. Pre-Raph. 71.
Hughes, David Darwin. Am. Bar Assoc. 6 : 338.
Hughes, David Edwin. Munro, J. Heroes of Teleg. 251.
Hughes, George. Adams, W. H. D. Worthies Church Eng. 271
Hughes, Hughes. Grant, J. Recoll. Lords & Comm. 1 : 294.
Hughes, John. (S. Johnson) Chalmers. Eng. poets, 10 : 3.
Hughes, John. Mitford, M. R. Recollec. 499.
Hughes, John, archbishop. Brownson. Works, 14 : 485. — Clarke, R. H. Cath. bishops, 2 : 73. — Maury, S. M. Statesm. of Amer. 228. — With portrait. Murray, J. O'K. Cath. heroes, 807.
Hughes, Margaret. Doran. Annals stage, 1 : 58.
Hughes, Thomas, with photo. Cooper, T. Men of mark, 4 : 35. — Hinton. Eng. radicals, 99. — Ritchie. Brit. sena. 151. — With portrait. Warner Lib. 13 : 7695.
— and the Arnolds. Tollemache. Ess. & mock-ess. 254.
Hugo of Avalon, St., bishop in 12th century. Froude. Short stud. 2 : 54.
Hugo of St. Victor. Townsend, W. J. Schoolmen, 126.
Hugo, Victor Marie. Amicis. Stud. Paris, 108. — Archer, W. About theatre, 287. — Castelar. Byron, 185. — Challice. French authors, 2 : 73. — With photo. Cooper, T. Men of mark, 2 : 7. — Friswell. Mod. men of let. 61. — (E. C. J. B. Jacquot) Gautier. Fam. Fr. au. 119. — Griswold, H. T. Home-life, 150. — Hale, E. E. Lights 2 cent. 473. — Hazletine, M. W. Chats, 14. — King, E. French pol. lead. 9. — Loménie. Liv. characters, 185. — Mauris, M. French men of letters, 5. — Men of 3d repub. 343. — Myers. Ess. mod. 105. — (J. Parton) Parton. Princes, 204. — Taylor, B. Crit. ess. 37. — Towle. Cert. men, 154. — Buchanan, R. Poet's sk. book, 157. — Henley. Views, 63. — Swanwick, A. Poets, 356. — Em. persons, 3 : 207. — Forster. Fr. & Span. genius, 211. — Griffin, G. W. Stud. in lit. — Hatton, J. Old lamps, 30. — Hubbard, E. Lit. jour. 167. — Pellissier. Lit. move. Fr. 173, 233, 295, 339. — Walsh, R. M. Liv. char. France. — With portrait. (A. Cohn) Warner Lib. 13 : 7709.
— and Wagner. Archer, W. Theatre, 321.
— L'année terrible. Swinburne. Ess. 17.
— as a dramatist. Matthews, J. B. Fr. dram. 15.
— as a novelist. Buchanan, R. Look round, 32.
— at home. (R. Lesclide) Parton. Princes, 188.
— Bibliography. Marzials. Life of H.
— Character of his verse. Arnold, M. Irish ess.
— L'homme qui rit. Swinburne. Ess. 1.
— Household gods of. Stuart, H. Paris days, 3.
— in 1872. Buchanan. Master-spir. 143.
— in the Rue de Clichy. Yates, E. H. Celeb. 2 : 53.
— La légende des siècles. (W. Alexander) Afternoon lec. 2 : 197.
— Ninety-three. Morley. Stud. in lit. 229.
— Le Pape, A study from. Wilde, Lady. Soc stud. 249.
— Plays. Archer, W. Theatre, 287.
— Poems. Mazzini. Life, etc. 2 : 257. — Dowden. Studies, 428.
— Posthumous works of. Swinburne. Stud. prose & p. 161.

Hugo, Victor Marie. Romances. Stevenson, R. L. Fam. stud. 1 ; *or* Miscel. 2 : 17.
— Toilers of the sea. Buchanan. Look round, 10.
— Works of : A malformed giant. Burroughs, J. Indoor, 177.
— Writings of. Hazeltine. Chats, 14.
Huguenots, The. Clarke, J. F. Events, 326. — Lawrence, E. Hist. stud. 247. — Lord, J. Beacon, 8 : 383. — Parkman, F. Pioneers of France, 1. — Merson. Heroic days, 129. — Pennington. Epochs papacy, 370. — Punshon, W. M. Lectures, 235.
— and the edict of Nantes. Gammel. Writ. 221 ; also in R. I. Hist. Soc. Proc. 1885–90.
— Historical sketch of. Agnew. Protes. exiles, 1 : 1.
— in Rhode Island. (E. B. Carpenter) R. I. Hist. Soc. Proc. 1885–86.
Huie, Richard. Miller, Jos. Singers church, 2d ed. 443.
Huillard-Bécholles, J. L. A. Oliphant, T. L. K. Duke, 61.
Hulburd, Calvin T., with portrait. Parton, J. Sk. of men of prog. — Rogers, A. C. Repres. men, 315.
Hulburd, H. R. Parton, J. Sk. of men of prog.
Hull, Amelia Matilda. Miller, Jos. Singers church, 2d ed. 582.
Hull, E. L. Great mod. preachers.
Hull, William. Clarke, J. F. Memo. sketches, 403. — Loring, J. S. Hundred Bost. ora. 218. — Lossing. Em. Amer. 219.
Hull House. Blanc, T. Wom. in U. S. 67. — Hull-House maps, 207.
— a factor in labor movement. (J. Addams) Hull-House maps, 183.
Hulton, Mrs. Ann. Burder. Pious wom. 327.
Human beings, Concerning the estimate of. Boyd. Aut. holid. 80.
Human body, Chemistry of. Nichols, J. R. Fireside sci. 215.
— Perfection of structure in, a leading element of hygiene. (N. Allen) Am. Pub. Health, 1 : 36.
— a subject of study for teachers. (J. L. Pickard) Nat. Educa. Assoc. '70 : 41.
Human development, Direction of. Greg. Enig. 155.
Human faculty, Origin of. Romanes. Ess. 86.
Human form, The. Parsons, T. Ess. 1 : 86.
Human nature. Thompson, H. M. Copy, 357.
— Dignity or meanness of. Hume. Philos. works, 3 : 86.
— Scientific study of. Youmans. Culture, 371.
— Two fundamental laws of. Strong, J. New era, 114.
Human race, Told off from. Higginson. Conc. all, 183.
Human sacrifices, Did the Romans use ? Stanhope, Earl. Miscel.
Human wishes, Vanity of. Stephen, J. F. Ess. by barr. 183.
Humanism. Sinclair, T. Humanities, 112.
— in Italy. Symonds. Reviv. of learn. 510.
Humanists in Florence. Duffy, B. Tuscan repub. 334.
Humanitarians. Alviella. Contemp. evol. 114.
Humanity. Greeley. Hints ref. 396. — Starling, E. Noble deeds wom. 174.
— Faith in. Farrar. Soc. & p. day quest. 69. — Holland, J. G. Lessons, 236.
— Modern conception of. Maurice, F. D. Soc. morality, 350.
— Present state of. Jouffroy. Philos. miscel. 2 : 195.

Humanity, Religion of. Brownson. Works, **4** : 100. — Congreve, R. Ess. 278, 391.
— Spirit of. (J. H. Barrows) Conf. char. & correc. '99 : 16.
— to man and beast. Swing. Old pic. **2** : 119.
Humayun. Adams, W. H. D. Warriors of crescent, 168.
Humbert, King of Italy, with portrait. Crowned heads, 51.
— Reminiscences of. Kingston, W. B. Monarchs, **2** : 150.
Humboldt, Alexander von. Alison. Ess. 3. — Bolton, S. K. Fam. men of science, 107. — Jardine, W. Nat. lib. v. **37.** — Everett, E. Mt. Vernon, 284. — Houghton, Lord. Monog. 19. — Ingersoll, R. G. Gods, 93. — Martineau, H. Biog. sk. 146. — Tuckerman. Charac. 56. — Anderson, M. B. Papers, **2** : 203. — Duyckinck. Portr. gall. **1** : 466. — (J. P. Thompson and others) Graham & Collar. Pulpit and rost. v. **1.** — Lieber, F. Reminis. 389. — With portrait. Warner Lib. **13** : 7768.
— at the court of Berlin. Houghton, Lord. Monog. 19.
— Commemorative oration on, 1859. Am. Geog. Soc. **1** : 225.
— Cosmos. Herschel, J. F. W. Essays, 257.
— Eulogy on. (E. Everett) Mass. Hist. Proc. **4** : 314 ; also in Everett. Orat. v. **4.**
— Visit to. Taylor, B. At home, **1** : 351.
Humboldt, Marie E. Holloway, L. C. Mothers of gt. men, 411.
Humboldt, Neb. Marshall, W. G. Thro' Amer. 247.
Hume, Sir Abraham, with portrait. Ollier, E. Brit. port. paint. 78.
Hume, Alexander. Wilson, J. G. Poets of Scot. **1** : 59. **2** : 313.
Hume, David. Brougham. Works, **2** : 168. — Case. Phys. realism. — Collier, W. F. Hist. Eng. lit. 325. — Edgar. Footpr. 180. — Lawrence. Brit. historians, **2** : 9. — Lewes. Biog. phil. — McCosh. Scot. phil. 113. — Morris, G. S. Brit. tho't, 234. — Oliphant. Hist. sketches, 416. — Pünjer. Chr. philos. relig. 359. — Wotton. Word portraits, 136. — Foster, J. Crit. ess. Ecl. v. **1.** — Grant, J. Recoll. Ho. Comm. 275. — Hundred greatest men, 250. — (H. Rogers) Macaulay. New biog. 379. — Mitchell, D. G. Eng. lands, **3** : 145. — Russell, W. C. Book of au. 224. — Sinclair, J. Sketches. — With portrait. (M. A. Mikkelsen) Warner Lib. **13** : 7777. — Webb, F. E. Veil of Isis, 67, 360.
— as a historian. Bisset, A. Ess. on hist. 136.
— as a metaphysician. Thornton, W. T. Old fash. 113.
— Essays. Stephen, J. F. Horæ Sabb. **2** : 367.
— Philosophy of, expounded by Huxley. Porter, N. Sci. & sent. 293.
— Treatise of human nature, Introductions to. Green, T. H. Works, **1** : 1.
— Works. Stephen, L. Eng. thought, **1** : 309.
Hume, Joseph. Martineau, H. Biog. sk. 302. — Smiles. Self-help. — Stanton, H. B. Reforms, 298.
Hume, Lady Grisell. Wittenmeyer. Women Reform. 443.
Hume family. Taylor, J. Fam. of Scot. **1** : 391.
Humidity, atmospheric, Drainage and. (S. B. Hunt) Am. Pub. Health, **2** : 357.
Humility. Friswell. Silent hour, 188.
— Independence and. Taylor. Notes from life, 29.
Hummel, Johann Nepomuk, with portrait. Bie,

O. Hist. of piano, 211. — Keddie. Mus. comp. 329.
Humming-birds. (Robert Ridgway) U. S. Nat. Mus. Rept. '90 : 253.
— of the tropics. Wallace, A. R. Trop. nat. 124.
Humor. Bailey, S. Discourses, 241. — Tuckerman. Optimist, 175.
— American. Lang. Leaders, 70, 181. — Nichol, J. Amer. lit. 402.
— — Perils of. Higginson. New world, 128.
— and realism. Stearns, F. P. Real & ideal, 40.
— Charity and. Thackeray. Humorists.
— English and American. Repplier, A. In dozy hours, 94.
— English, Future of. Hutton, R. H. Criticisms, **2** : 103.
— Future of. Traill. New fiction, 283.
— in the schoolroom. (H. C. Kirk) N. Y. Regents, **93** : 577.
— of various nations. Cobbe, F. P. Hours of work, 233.
— Penalty of. Matthews, B. Aspects fic. 43.
— Plea for. Repplier, A. Points of view.
— realism and romance. Stearns, F. P. Real, 40.
— A word about. Mabie. Ess. lit. interp.
Humorist, The. Walsh, W. S. Paradox, 81.
Humorists, American, with portraits. Howe, M. A. D. Am. bookm. 153.
Humorous, The, in literature. (J. H. Shorthouse) Coan. Stud. lit. 120.
Humorous literature, Worth of. Mathews. Conversers, 159.
Humphreys, A. A., Gen. (J. H. Wilson) Dwight, T. F. Fed. & confed. comm. 69. — (J. W. de Peyster) Rogers, A. C. Repres. men, 321.
Humphreys, David. With portrait. [Amer.] Nat. portr. gall. v. **2.** — Everest. Poets of Conn. 59. — Griswold. Poets Am. 50. — Lossing. Em. Amer. 215. — With portrait. Mitchell, D. G. Am. lands, 163.
Humphreys, John C. Livingston, J. Em. Am. lawy. 115.
Humphreys, Joseph. Hatfield, E. F. Poets of church, 343. — Miller, Jos. Singers church, 2d ed. 227.
Hundred years ago, A. Doran. Drury Lane, **1** : 285.
Hungarian types and Austrian pictures. (C. E. King) Murphy, Lady B. On Rhine, 276.
Hungary. Zangwill. Without prej. 271.
— and Austria. Brownson. Works, **16** : 209.
— Revolution in. Brownson. Works, **16** : 178.
— under Matthias Corvinus. (G. G. Zerffi) Roy. Hist. Soc. II., **1** : 260.
Hungerford, James. Davidson, J. W. Writ. of South, 288.
Hungerford, Margaret (H.), with portrait. Black, H. C. Wom. authors, 107.
Hungerford family. Burke, B. Viciss. of fam. **1** : 194.
Hunila, empress of Bonosus. Hall. Queens bef. Conq. 101.
Hunnis, William. Holland, J. Psalmists, **1** : 152.
Huns. Bury. Later Roman empire, **1** : 161. — Hodgkin. Dynasty of Theodosius. — Wyatt, W. J. Hunga. celeb. 11.
See also Attila.
Hunt, Benjamin Faneuil. Livingston, J. Dist. Amer. 144.
Hunt, Cornelius E. Davidson, J. W. Writ. of South, 288.
Hunt, Freeman. Bungay. Off-hand, 368. — N. E. Hist.-Gen. Soc. Biog. **3** : 200.

Hunt, Harriot Kesia. Belloc. Vignettes, 389. — (H. B. Elliot) Parton. Em. wom. 528.

Hunt, Henry. Grant, J. Recoll. H. Comm. 173.

Hunt, Holman. Bate, P. H. Eng. Pre-Raph. 25. — Quilter. Preferences, 23, 95. — Rossetti, W. M. Fine art, 233.

— and D. G. Rossetti. Ruskin. Art of Engl. 3.

— Recent pictures by, 1864. Palgrave. Ess. on art, 160.

— "The light of the world," and "The shadow of death." Dawson, G. Shakesp. 450.

Hunt, Leigh. Brooks, S. W. Eng. poets, 440. — Caine, T. H. Cobwebs, 123. — Gilfillan. Mod. lit. 303. — Hall, S. C. Book of mem. 243. — Hawthorne. Old home. — Hazlitt. Spirit. — Hodder, G. Memories, 160. — Horne. New spirit, 1 : 305. — Howitt. Homes Brit. poets, 2 : 396. — Langford. Prison books, 316. — Mason, E. T. Pers. traits, 1 : 215. — Miles, A. H. Poets of cent. 2 : 301. 9 : 157. — Mitchell, D. G. Eng. lands, 4 : 142. — Mitford, M. R. Recollec. 308. — Noble, J. A. Sonnet in Eng. 93. — Redding. Pers. remin. 2 : 184. — Saintsbury. Ess. Eng. lit. 201. — Smiles. Brief biog. 300. — Taylor, B. At home, 2 : 421. — Thayer, W. M. Turn.-points, 205. — Tuckerman. Poets, 154. — (E. Dowden) Ward. Eng. poets, 4 : 340. — With portrait. (E. Rhys) Warner Lib. 13 : 7791. — Wotton. Word portraits, 139.

— and Keats. Procter, B. W. Autob. 195.

— and his letters. Clarke, C. C. Recoll. of writ. 190.

— and his second journal. Espinasse. Lit. recol. 338.

— Letters to. Moore, T. Prose & v. 391.

— Poems. Whipple. Ess. & rev. 2.

— Recollections of. (J. T. Fields) Parton. Princes, 138.

— Reminiscences of. Grundy, F. Pictures, 162.

— Sonnets of. Deshler. Afternoons, 270.

— Ultra-crepidarius. Gosse, E. Gossip, 283.

Hunt, Peter, with portrait. Bartlett, J. R. R. I. officers, 171.

Hunt, Mrs. Sallie Ward, with portrait. Ellet. Queens Am. soc. 228.

Hunt, Thomas P., with portrait. Bungay. Penportr. 139.

Hunt, Ward. With portrait. Barnes, W. H. Sup. ct. 113. — Hill, F. H. Polit. portr. 226.

Hunt, Wm. Ruskin. Miscel. v. 1.

— and William Dyer. Palgrave. Ess. on art, 135.

— and Prout. Wedmore, F. Studies, 2 : 153.

Hunt, William Henry. Quilter. Preferences, 177.

Hunt, Wm. Holman. See Hunt, Holman.

Hunt, William M. Bartol. Principles, 435. — Bolton, S. K. How success is won, 114. — Sheldon, G. W. Amer. painters, 88.

Hunter, Mrs. Anne. Bethune, G. W. Brit. fem. poets, 78. — Williams, Jane. Lit. wom. 265. — Wilson, J. G. Poets of Scot. 1 : 282.

Hunter, Henry. Morison, J. Fathers of Lond. Miss. Soc. 2 : 435.

Hunter, Henry W. Walker, C. D. Biog. Va. Mil. Inst. 282.

Hunter, John. Bettany. Em. doctors, 1 : 133. — Craik. Pursuit knowl. 1 : 45. — Edgar. Boyhood, 358. — Edwards, B. B. Self-taught, 415. — Georgian era, 2 : 395. — Jardine, W. Nat. lib. v. 22. — Pettigrew. Med. portr. gall. v. 2. — Smiles. Self-help. — Taylor, T. Leicester Sq. 381.

— Discovery of remains of. Buckland, F. T. Curios. nat. hist. 4 : 215.

Hunter, John Dunn. Redding. Pers. remin. 3 : 42.

Hunter, Joseph. (H. M. Dexter) N. E. Hist.-Gen. Soc. Biog. 4 : 280. — (C. Deane) Mass. Hist. Proc. 17 : 300.

Hunter, R. M. T. Bartlett. Pres. candidates, 244. — Savage. Liv. rep. men, 329.

Hunter, Thomas, Trial of, for conspiracy and murder. Townsend, W. C. Mod. state trials, 2 : 162.

Hunter, Wm. Jackson, T. Early Meth. 1 : 305. — Tayler. Eng. martyrs.

Hunter, William, M. D. Bettany. Em. doctors, 1 : 119. — Edgar. Footpr. 305. — Pettigrew. Med. portr. gall. v. 2.

Hunter, William, Amer. statesman. Moore, F. Am. eloq. 2 : 335.

Hunterian Museum at the College of Surgeons. Wynter, A. Our soc. bees, 1 : 106.

Hunting in France ; a day with the French emperor's hounds, 1864. Higgins, M. J. Ess. 194.

— in North America. Barker, Lady. Travel. about, 131.

— in Wyoming. Pierrepont. Fifth ave. 265.

Huntingdon, Selina Hastings, countess of. Burder. Pious wom. 396. — Newman, J. H. Ess. crit. 1 : 386. — Miller, Jos. Singers church, 2d ed. 180. — Stevens, A. Women of Meth. 145. — Wise, D. Heroic Meth. 84. — Withrow. Makers of Meth. 150.

Huntingdon, Theophilus Hastings, Earl of, with portrait. Caulfield. Kit-cat, 84.

Huntington, Daniel, b. 1788. Everest. Poets of Conn. 163. — Sheldon, G. W. Amer. painters, 106.

Huntington, Daniel, d. 1816. With portrait. Benjamin, S. G. W. Am. art. 2 : 17. — Tuckerman. Artist-life, 185.

Huntington, Samuel, 1731–96. Dwight, N. Signers of decl. 85. — Edwards, B. B. Self-taught, 146. — Lincoln, R. W. Signers, 37. — Lossing. Signers, 53. — Sanderson. Signers, v. 4.

Huntington, William, preacher, 1745–1813. Georgian era, 1 : 455. — Heath, R. Eng. peasant, 320. — Timbs, J. Engl. eccen. 219.

Huntley, Stanley. Clemens. Funny fellows, 200.

Huntly, George Gordon, second marquis of. Lodge. Portraits (Bohn), v. 4.

Hunton, Logan. Livingston, J. Em. Am. lawy 126.

Huntoon, Mary A. Hemenway. Poets of Vt. 341.

Huntsman, Benj., inventor of cast steel. Smiles. Indus. biog.

Hunyadi, Demetrius. Wallace, R. Anti-Trin. biog. 2 : 367.

Hunyady, John. Wyatt, W. J. Hunga. celeb. 67.

Hunza. Younghusband. Heart of cont. 341.

Hupa reservation, Ray collection from. (O. T. Mason) Smithson. Rept. '86 : 205.

Hupfeld, Hermann. Cheyne. Founders O. T. crit. 149.

Hupton, Job. Hatfield, E. F. Poets of church, 345. — Miller, Jos. Singers church, 2d ed. 332.

Hurd, Frank Hunt. Am. Bar Assoc. 20 : 550. — Johnston, A. Amer. ora. 4 : 238.

Hurd, Mrs. Phineas B. Moore, F. Women of the war, 65.

Hurley Hall. Hodges, Eliz. Anc. Eng. homes, 157.

Hurn, William. Hatfield, E. F. Poets of church, 346. — Miller, Jos. Singers church, 2d ed. 316.

Huron-Iroquois, a typical race. Wilson D. Lost Atlantis, 246.

Hurry and leisure. Boyd. Recreat. **1** : 267.
Hurst coal-pit, Fall in. Davenport. Narr. peril,
2 : 359.
Hurstmonceux Castle. Timbs. Abbeys, **1** :
370.
Hurtado de Mendoza, Diego. Montgomery.
Men. of Ita. **3** : 58.
Husband, Mrs. Mary Morris. Brockett. Wo-
man's work, 287. — Moore, F. Women of the
war, 313.
Husbands. Friswell. Gentle life, **1** : 114.
Hushai the Archite. Hastings, F. Obscure
charac. 61.
Huskisson, William. Hazlitt. Parl. portr. 210.
— Jerdan. Men, 268.
Huss, John. Gilpin, W. Lives, 129. — Herrick,
S. E. Heretics, 45. — (D. McLean) Reform-
ers. — Paisley lec. 49. — Stevenson. Lives &
deeds, 181.— Hodgson, Wm. Reformers, 123.
— Mears, J. W. Heroes Bohem.—Miller, Jos.
Singers church, 2d ed. 38. — Williams, F.
Eng. card. **2** : 35. — Wittenmeyer. Women
Reform. 60.
— and the reformation in Bohemia. Merson.
Heroic days, 84. — Trench. Lec. mediæval,
321.
— Story of. Rogers, H. Ess. fr. G. W. 90.
— Wycliffe and Savonarola. Williams, W. R.
Eras, 110.
Hussey, Mrs. Henrietta (Grove). Clayton, E. C.
Eng. fem. art. **2** : 411.
Hussey, Sir John, chief justice of England, 1482–
1492. Campbell. Ch. just. **1** : 147.
Hussites. Pennington. Epochs Papacy, 234. —
Ullman. Reformers, 334.
Hutchens, Jesse T. Am. Bar Assoc. **13** : 349.
Hutcheson, Francis. McCosh. Scot. phil. 49.
— Martineau, J. Types, **2** : 474.
Hutchins, Harvey. Whitehead, C. Highway-
men, **1** : 184.
Hutchins, Waldo. Am. Bar Assoc. **14** : 438.
Hutchinson, Anne. Adams, C. F. Three epi-
sodes, **1** : 380. **2** : 533. — (Marbury) Ander-
son, Jas. Mem. wom. pur. **1** : 185.—Chandler,
P. W. Am. crim. trials, **1** : 1. — Chapman, W.
Wom. of purit. 57. — Earle. Colon. dames,
111.—Stedman. Lib. Amer. literature, **1** : 233.
— Trial of. (E. Stiles) Mass. Hist. Proc. 2d ser.
4 : 159.
Hutchinson, Col. J., Memoirs. Jeffrey, F.
Contrib. Ed. Rev. — Wrangham. Brit. Plu-
tarch, v. 3.
Hutchinson, John A. Am. Bar Assoc. **19** : 680.
Hutchinson, Mrs. Lucy (Apsley). Anderson, J.
Mem. wom. Pur. **2** : 54. — Burder. Pious wom.
292.— Child. Good wives, 25.— Cochrane, R.
Earnest, 9.— Costello. Englishwomen, **3** : 57.
— Crosland. Mem. women, 244. — Knight.
Once on time, **1** : 266. — Russell. Extr. women,
74.— Williams, Jane. Lit. wom. 87. — Yonge.
Good wom. **1** : 38. — Ewald, A. C. Paper, 140.
— With portrait. Johnstone, G. Lead. women,
129. — Fifty famous women, 118.— Hale, S. J.
Less. wom. lives, 46.— Owen, Mrs. O. F. He-
roines domes. 151.
Hutchinson, Ralph. McClure. Translators, 183.
Hutchinson, Sylvester. Wakeley. Heroes
Meth. 287.
Hutchinson, Thomas. Lossing. Em. Amer. 58.
— Richardson. Amer. lit. **1** : 447. — Sabine.
Loyalists, 376.
— Franklin and. Franklin. Works ('87), **5** : 292,
378.
— Historical publications of. (C. Deane) Mass.
Hist. Proc. **3** : 134.

Hutchinson, Thomas. Pamphlet on Bills of
Credit, 1736. (A. M. Davis) Mass. Hist. Proc.
2d ser. **12** : 429.
Hutten, Leonard. McClure. Translators, 210.
Hutten, Ulrich von. Doran. Knights, 420. —
Maccall. For. biog. **1** : 176. — Jordan, D. S.
Story, 205.
Hutton, Henry. Alden, R. M. Rise of satire,
213.
Hutton, James. Duncan, P. M. Botanists, 221.
— McCosh. Scot. phil. 261. — Miller, Jos.
Singers church, 2d. ed. 211.
— Biog. account of. Playfair, J. Works, v. 4.
Hutton, Richard Holt. Watson, W. Excur. in
crit. 115.
Hutton, William. Chambers's Miscel. no. 69. —
Craik. Pursuit knowl. **1** : 172. — Davenport,
R. A. Lives, 56. — Knight, C. Old booksel.
154. — Seymour, C. C. B. Self-made, 289.
Huxham, J. Pettigrew. Med. portr. gall. v. **2**.
Huxley, T. H. With portrait. Clodd. Pioneers
evol. 201. — With photo. Cooper, T. Men of
mark, **4** : 25. — Engel. Handel to Hallé, 121.
— Flower, W. H. Ess. on museums, 381. —
Griswold, H. T. Personal sk. 152.— With portrait. (E. R. Lancaster) Warner Lib. **13** : 7805.
— and evolution. Winchell. Sparks geol. ham.
319.
— and his work. (T. Gill) Smithson. Rept. '95 :
759.
— and Salvation Army. Buchanan, R. Coming
terr. 336.
— Bibliography. Providence Pub. Lib. Bull. Aug.
'95.
— Lectures. Godkin. Reflections, 104.
— Protoplasm. Whedon. Ess. **2** : 139.
Huxleyism. Thornton, W. T. Old fash. 158.
Huysmans, Joris Karl. Crawford, V. M. Stud.
for. lit. 78. — Ellis, H. Affirmations, 158. —
Henry, S. Hours w. Parisians, 113.
— as a mystic. Symons, A. Stud. two lit. 299.
— En route. Peck, H. T. Pers. equa. 135.
Hyacinth bulbs. (G. Allen) Proctor, R. A. Nat.
stud. 69.
Hybrias. Arnold, E. Poets of Greece, 134. —
Mills. Poets of Greece, 155.
Hybridity and heredity. Wilson, D. Lost At-
lantis, 307.
Hyde, Mrs. Abigail. (Bradley) Hatfield, E. F.
Poets of church, 349.
Hyde, Andrew J. Hemenway. Poets of Vt. 339.
Hyde, Ann Beadley. Miller, Jos. Singers church,
2d ed. 463.
Hyde, Anne. See York, Duchess of.
Hyde, Edward. See Clarendon, Earl of.
Hyde, Sir Nicholas, chief justice of Eng., 1626–
1631. Campbell. Ch. just. **1** : 312.
Hyde, Sir Robert, chief justice of England, 1663.
Campbell. Ch. just. **1** : 398.
Hyde Park. Wynter, A. Our soc. bees, **1** : 43.
Hyderabad in the Deccan. Burton, Isa. Ara-
bia, 155.
Hydrophobia. Scoffern. Stray leaves, 392. —
(S. Marks) Wisc. Health, '77 : 31.
— and muzzling of dogs. Romanes. Ess. 226.
— in Mexico, Prophylaxis of. (A. Reyes) Am.
Pub. Health, **18** : 138.
— Pasteur's treatment of. Lankester. Advan. sci.
119.
— Protection against. (J. M. Partridge) Am. Pub.
Health, **10** : 293.
Hygeiolatry. Cobbe, F. P. Peak in Darien,
79.
Hygiene, Ancient and modern, contrasted. (C.
T. Lewis) Am. Pub. Health, **3** : 165.

Hygiene and higher education. (J. M. Gregory) Am. Pub. Health, **4** : 57.
— and sanitary science, Teaching of, in secondary schools. (D. Fall) Mich. Health, **'97** : 114.
— and sanitation, Municipal. (E. S. Kelly) Am. Pub. Health, **19** : 169.
— as a branch of military education. (Sir J. Richardson) Trans. Soc. Sci. Lond. **'57** : 449.
— at Amherst College. (E. Hitchcock) Am. Pub. Health, **4** : 46.
— Bibliography. Galbraith, A. M. Hygiene & phys. cult. for women.
— Camp. (C. Smart) Buck, A. H. (ed.). Hygiene, **2** : 79.
— Civil public, Importance of. (C. A. Cameron) Am. Pub. Health, **19** : 186.
— in Italy. (G. H. F. Nuttall) Am. Pub. Health, **20** : 26.
— in medical education. (J. I. Desroches) Am. Pub. Health, **20** : 298.
— in the public schools. (H. P. Yeomans) Am. Pub. Health, **12** : 99.
— in schools and family education. (C. N. Hewitt) Am. Pub. Health, **4** : 81.
— Instruction in, in schools and colleges. (C. O. Probst) Am. Pub. Health, **20** : 251.
— International, Rise and progress of. (J. L. Cabell) Am. Pub. Health, **7** : 16.
— Irregularities of habits, Rational, not harmful. Am. Pub. Health, **16** : 183.
— Lecture on. McSherry. Ess. 95.
— Means of spreading knowledge of, among the people. U. S. Bur. Ed. Rept. '97-98, **1** : 257.
— Naval. (T. J. Turner) Buck, A. H. (ed.). Hygiene, **2** : 175.
— of the household. (J. W. Hervey) Indiana Health, **'80** : 15.
— personal and public. Bibliography. Bost. Pub. Lib. Bull. July, '94.
— Public, Importance to the state. (Sir C. A. Cameron) Am. Pub. Health, **19** : 186.
— — in the U. S. (S. W. Abbott) Shaler. The U. S. **2** : 556.
— Questions of. (A. G. Young) Maine Health, **'91** : 142.
— Railroad, Contribution to the discussion of. (T. Noriega) Am. Pub. Health, **21** : 80.
— School. (F. Formento) Am. Pub. Health, **10** : 38. — (H. I. Jones) Am. Pub. Health, **7** : 241. — (C. J. Lundy) Am. Pub. Health, **9** : 137. — (J. C. Cameron) Am. Pub. Health, **20** : 268. — (M. T. Brennan) Am. Pub. Health, **20** : 278.
— — Principles of. (Aaron Gove) Nat. Educa. Assoc. **'97** : 891.
— Study of. (A. de Garay) Am. Pub. Health, **21** : 263.
— Teaching of, in elementary schools. (S. Gauthier) Am. Pub. Health, **20** : 259.
— — in public schools. (H. P. Yeomans) Am. Pub. Health, **12** : 99. — (C. O. Probst and others) Am. Pub. Health Assoc. **20** : 251.
— — to the young. (G. G. Groff) Am. Pub. Health, **20** : 263.
Hygienic institutes. (G. A. Smyth) Conn. Health, **'83** : 63.
Hygrometer, A slowly sensible. Franklin. Works ('87), **7** : 151.
Hymnology. Bibliography ; Paine hymnol. collec. Hartford Sem. Rec. Feb. '92.
— Latin. Oxenham. Stud. in eccl. hist. 74.
— — Bibliography. Providence Pub. Lib. Bull. Aug. '98.
Hymn-writers. Butterworth. Great compos. 114, 124.
— Biography of. Stevenson. Lives & deeds, 267.

Hymns and hymn-writers. (C. B. Pearson) Oxf. ess. **'58** : 124.
— Ancient. Posnett. Compar. literature, 99.
— First Christian hymn. Davis, L. S. Stud. mus. 18.
— German. Taylor, B. Crit. ess. 333.
— of the populace. Mozley, A. Ess. 27.
— St. Bernard's translations of. Schaff. Lit. & poetry, 233.
— Tinkering. Ess. from Nation, 55.
Hypatia. Vaughan, R. A. Ess. & rev. v. **2.**
— History of. Goldsmith. Miscel. (N. Y. 4 v.) **1** · 57
Hyperæsthesia, Cases of hypnotic. Soc. Psych. Res. **4** : 532
Hyperbole, Social. Mozley, A. Ess. fr. Blackw. v. **1.**
— Use of. Goldsmith. Miscel. (N. Y. 4 v.) **1** : 320.
Hyperides. Mills. Poets of Greece, 456.
Hypnotic phenomena, Personally observed. (J. M. Bramwell) Soc. Psych. Res. **12** : 176.
Hypnotism. Hall, G. S. Asp. Ger. 134. — (W. B. Clarke) Indiana Health, **'90** : 144. — Mason, R. O. Telepathy, 28. — Romanes. Ess. 213.
— and spiritualism, Connection of. Soc. Psych. Res. **5** : 279.
— and telepathy. (E. Gurney) Soc. Psych. Res. **5** : 216.
— Certain post-hypnotic states. (E. Gurney) Soc. Psych. Res. **4** : 268.
— Recent experiments in. (E. Gurney) Soc. Psych. Res. **5** : 3.
— Stages of. (E. Gurney) Soc. Psych. Res. **2** : 61, 265.
— Telepathic. (F. W. H. Myers) Soc. Psych. Res. **4** : 127.
— What is ? (J. M. Bramwell) Soc. Psych. Res. **12** : 204.
Hypochondriacs. Lang. Leaders, 158.
Hypocrisy. Hazlitt. Sketches.
— Religious. Hazlitt. Round table.
Hypocrite of fiction. Noble, J. A. Impressions, 105.
Hyslop, James. Wilson, J. G. Poets of Scot. **2** : 181.
Hythe, Eng. Rimmer, A. Country towns, 170.

Ibar, St. Conyngham, D. P. Irish saints, 128.
Ibn Gînî. (T. Davidson) Warner Lib. **14** : 7835.
Ibrahim, the baby. Brooks, E. S. Gt. men's sons, 98.
Ibsen, Hendrik. With portrait. Brandes. Em. auth. 405. — Gosse. Stud. lit. No. Eur. 35. — Ellis, H. New spirit. — James, H. Ess. in Lond. 230. — Walkley, A. B. Playhouse, 47. — With portrait. (W. H. Carpenter) Warner Lib. **14** : 7839.
— Influence of. Garland. Crumbling idols, 99.
— Peer Gynt. Couch, A. T. Q. Adv. crit. 283.
— Prose dramas. Watson, W. Excur. in crit. 127.
— Social dramas. Courtney. Studies, 25.
— Social plays of. Monkhouse, A. Books, 155.
Ibsen drama. Winter. Shad. stage, **3** : 330.
Ibsenism. Nordau. Degen. 338.
Ibuin, Temples of. Adams, W. H. D. Fam. caves, 20.
Ibycus. Arnold, E. Poets of Greece, 147. — Mills. Poets of Greece, 100. — Symonds. Greek poets, **1** : 326.
Icaria, Community of. Hinds. Amer. commun. — Nordhoff. Commun. 333.
Icarians. Nordhoff. Commun. soc. 333.
Ice and glaciers. Helmholtz. Pop. lec. **1** : 107.

Ignorance. Ess. from Sat. R. 24.
— Genteel. Hamerton. Hum. int. 253.
— of the learned. Hazlitt. Table-talk.
— Patriotic. Hamerton. Hum. int. 264.
— Political, as safeguard of absolute govt. Curtis, B. R. Mem. & wr. v. 2.
Ilaria del Caretto. Perkins, C. C. Tusc. sculp. 1 : 107.
Ilgen, Karl D. Cheyne. Founders O. T. crit. 26.
Illegitimate children, Laws of Belgium relative to. (J. B. Curgenven) Trans. Soc. Sci. Lond. '67 . 531.
Illinois ; an Amer. state and its architecture. Caton. Miscel. 53.
— Early lead mining in. (R. G. Thwaites) Am. Hist. Assoc. Rept. '93 : 189.
— in 1832. Bryant. Prose, 2 : 3.
— Industrial training school. (O. L. Dudley) Conf. char. & correc. '91 : 145.
Illiteracy in America. Dixon, W. H. White conquest, 2 : 340.
— in the U. S. in 1870 and 1880. (C. Warren) U. S. Bur. Ed. Circ. '84, no. 3.
Ill-nature and sneers. Friswell. Better self, 101.
Illness as a mental stimulant. Proctor, R. A. Rough ways, 236.
Ill-tempered folk. Henry, C. S. About men, 48.
Illuminati, The. Heckethorn. Sec. soc. 2 : 31.
— Lillie, A. Mod. mystics, 45.
— Account of. Robertson, J. B. Lec. mod. hist. 465.
— in Spain. Lea. Chap. relig. hist. Spain, 251.
Illumination, Mental, vs. acquisition. Maurice. Friendship, 342.
Illuminism, Preaching of. Ker, J. Lec. hist. preach. 241, 286.
Illusions. Emerson. Conduct, 271. — Friswell. Gentle life, 1 : 272. — Marion, F. Wonders of optics, 160. — (T. Foster) Proctor, R. A. Leis. read. 78. — Rands, W. B. Holbeach, 1 : 153.
— Hallucinations and. Elam. Phys. prob. 256.
— Spectral. Chambers's Miscel. no. 70.
Illustrated London News. Hatton. Jour. Lond. 221.
Illustration, Literary. Mozley, A. Ess. fr. Blackw. 69.
— of books. Hamerton. Portfo. pap. 293.
— Philosophy of, in elementary teaching. (J. J. Burns) Nat. Educa. Assoc. '81 : 218.
Illustrators, English. Buxton, H. J., et al. Eng. paint. 85.
— of Harper's Magazine, with portraits. James, H. Picture & t. 1.
Illyria and its emperors. Freeman. Hist. ess. 3 : 22.
Iltut, St. Kingsley. Hermits, 249.
Image, Selwyn. Miles, A. H. Poets of cent. 10 : 653.
Image worship. Thompson, H. M. Copy, 205.
Imagery, Mental. (W. Lay) Colum. Univ. Contrib. Philos. 4 : no. 2.
Imagination. Clarke, J. F. Self-culture, 175. — Dallas. The gay science, 1 : 179. — Everett. Poetry, comedy, and duty. — Mabie. Books and cul. 143. — Patmore. Princ. in art, 43.
— Culture of. Jones, W. A. Ess. on authors, 129. — Waterston. Culture, 219.
— Force of. Walsh, R. Didactics, 2 : 78.
— Functions and culture of. Macdonald, G. Orts, 1.
— The gospel a gift to. Bushnell. Building eras, 249.
— in art. Harris. Theory of the arts, 2 : 122. — Patmore. Principle in art, etc.

Imagination in religion. Morison, J. H. Great poets, 15.
— Normal clairvoyance of the. Bulwer, E. Caxtoniana.
— Play of. Mabie. Ess. on work, 219.
— the power which liberates. Mabie. My study fire, 2 : 128.
— Practical uses of. Finlayson, T. C. Ess. 128.
— — in the ministry. Finlayson, T. C. Ess. 154.
— Scientific use of. Tyndall. Frag. sci. 127.
— Tricks of. Whipple. Success, 185.
Imbecile, The moral. (I. N. Kerlin) Conf. char. & correc. '90 : 244.
Imbecile children, Training of. Wynter, A. Peeps, 1 : 251.
Imbeciles, Education and custody of. (A. J. Mott) Conf. char. & correc. '94 : 168.
— Educability of. (B. Brodie) Trans. Soc. Sci. Lond. '60 : 409.
— Training of. Wynter. Borderl. of insan. 148.
Imitation. Hazlitt. Round table.
— as psychological tendency. (Anna T. Smith) U. S. Bur. Ed. Rept. '96–97, 1 : 671.
— and similarities, Poetical. Disraeli, I. Curios. (N. Y. 4 v.) 2 : 260.
— Laws of. Whittaker, T. Ess. & not. 309.
Imitations, by Frederick Yates. Lennox, W. P. Plays, 2 : 61.
Imitative arts. Allen, C. G. B. Physiolog. æsthetics.
Immaculate Conception. Thirlwall, C. Remains, 1 : 251. — Williams, F. Eng. card. 1 : 145.
Immanence, Divine. Bibliography. Wood, C. J. Survivals in Christianity.
Immaturity. Boyd. Leis. hours (Bost.), 16.
Immermann, Karl Lebrecht, with portrait. Warner Lib. 14 : 7896.
Immigrant inspection and the public health. (H. R. Mills) Am. Pub. Health, 8 : 102.
Immigrants and tramps, Law affecting. (H. A. Millis) Conf. char. & correc. '97 : 355.
— Our debt and duty to. (E. J. Wolf) Evang. Alliance, '89 : 217.
Immigration. Altgeld. Live ques. 104. — (C. S. Hoyt) Conf. char. & correc. '95 : 245. — (A. White) Cong. Char. Chic. '93, 1 : 191. — Greeley. Ess. pol. econ. 306. — U. S. Consular reports, special, v. 2.
— Alien paupers, insane, and crim. in N.Y. (C. S. Hoyt) Conf. char. & correc. '87 : 197.
— and crime. (H. H. Hart) Conf. char. & correc. '96 : 307.
— and interstate migration. (R. Guenther) Conf. char. & correc. '98 : 262.
— and the labor problem. N. J. Labor, '84 : 282.
— and migration. (F. B. Sanborn) Conf. char. & correc. '86 : 253.
— and sale of public lands, Laws of Amer. Republics relating to. Bur. Am. Rep. Bulletin, no. 53, pt. 4.
— British. Bibliography. Board Trade Rept. Alien immigration.
— Dumping garbage. George, H. Soc. prob. 147.
— Educational test for. Higginson. Book & heart, 160.
— Effect of. Everett. Orat. v. 8.
— — in New England. Adams, C. F. Three episodes, 2 : 944.
— — on American national character. Tiffany, O. H. Pulpit & p.
— — on the community. (S. C. Wrightington) Conf. char. & correc. '90 : 281.
— Evils of. Keyes, E. D. Fifty years, 92.

Immigration, History of. (C. S. Hoyt) Conf. char. & correc.' **93** : 106.
— in the U. S. (P. C. Garrett) Conf. char. & correc. '**88** : 185.
— — Defects in system of. (P. C. Garrett) Conf. char. & correc. '**87** : 206.
— — Regulation of. (F. B. Sanborn) Conf. char. & correc. '**87** : 212.
— Increase of social pressure. George, H. Soc. prob. 36.
— Its objects and objections. (P. C. Garrett) Conf. char. & correc. '**99** : 158.
— of contract laborers. U. S. Ho. Miscel. Doc. '87–88, v. **15.**
— Progress, extent, and effect of. N. Y. Bur. Lab. '**98** : 954.
— Restriction of. (C. Biddle) Conf. char. & correc. '**91** : 197. — Swank. Notes, 177. — Walker, F. A. Discus. in econ. **2** : 417.
— to U. S. Everett. Orat. v. **3.**
— U. S. legislation respecting. (R. Guenther) Conf. char. & correc. '**96** : 302.
Immigration service of U. S., Defects in. (J. M. Woodworth) Am. Pub. Health, **1** : 441.
Immortality. Bax. Ethics of socialism, 180. — Buchanan, R. Look round, 148. — Channing. Works, **4** : 169. — Greg. Enig. 231. — Hazard, T. R. Miscel. 329. — Hume. Philos. works, **4** : 547. — Knight, W. Ess. 283. — Emerson. Let. & soc. aims, 305. — Schopenhauer. Stud. pres. 53.
— Argument for. (P. S. Moxom) Barrows, J. H. Parl. relig. **1** : 476.
— Can it be shown from the light of nature ? Hadley, J. Ess. 373.
— Egyptian belief in. Buckley, J. M. Trav. 3 cont. 231.
— Egyptian tombs and. Poole, R. S. Lec. art.
— Evidences of. Mill, J. S. Three ess. 196.
— Feeling of, in youth. Hazlitt. Sketches ; or Winterslow.
— Fragment on. Green, T. H. Works, **3** : 159.
— from the point of view of natural science. Shaler. Interp. of nat. 278.
— Is death the end ? Gladden. Burn. ques. 129.
— Is there another life ? Smith, Goldw. Guesses, 97.
— Natural science and. Shaler. Interpre. 287.
— Our knowledge of. Whedon. Ess. **2** : 382.
— Plato's Arguments in " Phædo." Packard, L. R. Stud. Gr. 41.
— Plato's views of. King, T. S. Patriotism, 113.
— Struggle for. Phelps, E. S. Struggles, 119.
— Thoughts and things. King, T. S. Patriotism, 164.
Imogen, Shakespeare's. Martin. Shakesp. female, 157.
Impeachment. Tilden, S. J. Writings, **1** : 472.
— of U. S. officials. Foster, R. Comment. on Const. **1** : 566, 606.
Impeachment trials in States. Foster, R. Comment. on Const. **1** : 633.
Impeachments before U. S. Senate. Foster, R. Comment. on Const. **1** : 508, 529.
— Origin of. Foster, R. Comment. on Const. **1** : 506.
Imperial Federalism, Rise of. (G. B. Adams) Am. Hist. Assoc. Rept. '**95** : 25.
Imperialism. Lord, J. Beacon, **1** : 133.
— Bibliography. Boston Pub. Lib. Spec. Bibliog.
— Roman. Seeley, J. R. Rom. imp. 5 ; or Lec. & ess. 1.
— vs. socialism. Bax. Relig. of socialism, 123.
Impermeable construction with ref. to ventila. and warming. Internat. Health Ex. Sanita.

Implements of war. Sparvel-Bayly. New Stud. 1.
Importance of a man to himself. Smith, Alex. Dreamthorp, 171.
Imports, Excess of. Giffen. Ess. finance, 151.
Impostors, Literary. Davenport, R. A. Delusions, 163.
— Religious. Chambers's Miscel. no. 14.
— Royal. Davenport, R. A. Delusions, 83.
Impostures. Davenport, R. A. Delusions, 140.
— Literary. Dawson, G. Shakesp. 142. — Disraeli, I. Curios. (N. Y. 4 v.) **1** : 198.
Impressionism. Garland. Crumbling idols, 121.
— The point of honor. Meynell, A. Rhythm, 49.
Impressionists, The. (F. Wedmore) Coan. Art and lit. 134.
Impressions, Justification of. Noble, J. A. Impressions, 1.
Impressments of American sailors by British men of war, Negotiations with Mr. Rose. Madison, J. Letters, **2** : 410.
Imprisonment, Cellular system of. (W. Tallack & J. Field) Trans. Soc. Sci. Lond. '**71** : 264.
— false, Indemnification for. (M. A. Corne) N. Y. Pris. Assoc. **26,** app. 244.
— Unnecessary. (J. P. Altgeld) Nat. Pris. Assoc. '**85** : 408.
    See Cumulative sentences ; Sentences, Indeterminate, etc.
Improvement, Permanent, of neighborhoods. (C. DeGraffenried) Conf. char. & correc. '**95** : 101.
Improvements, Modern. Talfourd. Crit. writ.
Improvidence of authors. Madden. Infirm. gen. 79.
Impudence and modesty. Hume. Philos. works, **4** : 497.
Impulse. Galt, J. Lit. life, **2** : 196.
Impulses, Natural. Mill, J. S. Three ess. 56.
Imputation of Adam's sin. (B. Jowett) Noyes, G. R. Theol. ess. 265.
In, preposition, and related words. Key, J. H. Philol. ess. 57.
Incarnation, The. Brownson. Works, **14** : 141.
— Green, T. H. Works, **3** : 207. — Johnson, S. Ori. relig. India, 481. — Maurice, F. D. Theol. ess. 98.
— as the basis of dogma. (R. C. Moberley) Gore, C. Lux mundi, 217.
— as the great moral force. (T. M. Post) Bost. lectures, '**72** : 122.
— Bushnell on. Brownson. Works, **7** : 49.
— Heresy and. Brownson. Works, **8** : 186.
— Idea of, in history and in Christ. (J. J. Keane) Barrows, J. H. Parl. relig. **2** : 882.
— in the Ramayana. Williams, M. Indian wisdom, 321.
— in relation to development. (J. R. Illingworth) Gore, C. Lux mundi, 181.
Incas of Peru. (C. R. Markham) Winsor's America, v. **1.** — Réville. Religions of Mexico and Peru, 127.
Inchbald, Mrs. Elizabeth. Adams, W. H. D. Noble women, 90. — Adams, W. H. D. Wom. of fash. **2** : 123. — Elwood. Lit. ladies, **1** : 310. — Hamilton, C. J. Women writers, 24. — Jeaffreson. Novelists, **1** : 340. — Kavanagh. Eng. women, **2** : 1. — Mayer, G. T. Wom. of let. **2** : 1. — Wotton. Word portraits, 143.
Inchmahome. Mackie, C. Castles of Mary.
Incognito, Delights of an. Guiney. Patrins, 63.
Income, Definition of, for purposes of taxation. (Dr. Chadwick) Trans. Soc. Sci. Lond. '**80** : 716.

strong) Nat. Educa. Assoc. '84 : 177. — (T. J. Morgan) Nat. Educa. Assoc. '90 : 491. — (Dr. Oronhyatekha) Nat. Educa. Assoc. '91 : 234.

Indians, Education of, in the Indian Territory. (R. L. Owen) Nat. Educa. Assoc. '86: 192.

— — Next step in. (W. N. Hailman) Nat. Educa. Assoc. '95 : 80.

— Employment of, in War of 1812. (E. Cruikshank) Am. Hist. Assoc. Rept. '95 : 321.

— Folk-lore of Delaware tribe. Brinton. Ess. Amer. 181.

— Food of certain. (L. Carr) Am. Antiq. Soc. Proc. n. s. 10 : 155.

— George Catlin Indian gallery in U. S. Nat. Mus. (Thomas Donaldson) U. S. Nat. Mus. Rept. '85 : supp.

— Government policy toward. Hubbard, B. Memorials, 187.

— in Central America, Settlements of. (C. Sapper) Smithson. Rept. '95 : 537.

— in Michigan. Hubbard, B. Memorials, 179.

— in the United States, Architecture of. (C. Mindeleff) Am. Geog. Soc. 30 : 414.

— in the west. Ossoli. At home, 87.

— Indian's view of difficulties besetting him. (J. M. Stuart) Conf. char. & correc. '92 : 66.

— Languages of, on N. W. coast, Classification of. (F. Boas) Cong. Anthrop. Chic. '93 : 339.

— Legal status of. (W. B. Hornblower) Am. Bar Assoc. 14 : 261.

— Legislation on, Rept. of committee on. Am. Bar Assoc. 16 : 351.

— Massachusetts, Condition of. (F. B. Sanborn) Mass. Charity, '68 : 20.

— Massacre of, in Lancaster county, Pa., 1764. Franklin. Works ('87), 3 : 260.

— Mechanics among. (O. T. Mason) Cong. Anthrop. Chic. '93 : 69.

— Methods of burying dead among. Webster, N. Ess. 205.

— Mingling with whites, Advantages of. (R. H. Pratt) Conf. char. & correc. '92 : 45.

— Myths of. Brinton. Amer. hero-myths, 37.

— not Mongolian. Brinton. Ess. Amer. 56.

— of British Columbia. (F. Boas) Am. Geog. Soc. 28 : 229.

— of New England, 1630–1700. (J. Winsor) Mass. Hist. Proc. 2d ser. 10 : 327.

— of the Quinaielt Agency, Washington Terr. (C. Willoughby) Smithson. Rept. '86 : 267.

— Our dealings with. (J. E. Greene) Am. Antiq. Soc. Proc., n. s. 11 : 23.

— Philosophy of. (J. W. Powell) Am. Geog. Soc. 8 : 231.

— Pipes and smoking customs of. (J. D. McGuire) U. S. Nat. Mus. Rept. '97 : 351.

— Policy of U. S. toward. (P. C. Garrett) Conf. char. & correc. '92 : 23.

— Religion of. (A. C. Fletcher) Barrows, J. H. Parl. relig. 2 : 1078.

— Sacred symbols and numbers of. (F. Parry) Am. Geog. Soc. 26 : 163.

— Supposed Asian relations. (D. G. Brinton) Cong. Anthrop. Chic. '93 : 145.

— Treatment of. Reynolds, G. Papers, 394.

— — in U. S. Bancroft, H. H. Essays, 65.

— Tribes of. Brinton. Races & peo. 248.

— Twana, Chemakum, and Klallam, of Washington. Terr. (Myron Eells) Smithson. Rept. '87 : 605.

— What shall we do with ? (F. H. Head; D. M. Riordan) Sunset Club Echoes, 222.

— Wrongs of. Marshall, W. G. Thro' Amer. 242.

Indifference. Friswell. Wick. world, 213.

— Religious, in Germany. Baring-Gould. Germany, 338.

Individual, The, and a crowd. Hunt, L. Seer, 1 : 326. — Leslie, T. E. C. Ess. pol. econ. 16.

— and society. Gladden. Ruling ideas, 63.

— in American society. (L. Abbott) Shaler. The U. S. 2 : 579.

Individual development, Sketch of. Macdonald, G. Orts, 43.

Individualism. Bartol. Rad. prob. 28. — Donisthorpe. Individualism. — Erdmann, History of philosophy, 2 : 93. — Morell, J. D. Philos. tend. — Thomson, H. M. Copy, 72.

— and state-action. Whittaker, T. Ess. & not. 111.

— Force of, in religious movements. Oxenham. Stud. in eccl. hist. 259.

— in art. Van Dyke. Principles of art, 278.

— in mass education. (P. W. Search) Nat. Educa. Assoc. '95 : 398.

— of Herbert Spencer. Ritchie, D. G. State interf. 3.

— sustained. Bastiat. Ess. on pol. econ. 74, 102, 173.

— *vs.* socialism. Bosanquet, B. Civil. of Christendom, 304.

Individuality. Ingersoll, R. G. Gods, 169.

— Necessity and means of developing. (S. B. Todd) Nat. Educa. Assoc. '91 : 665.

— of character. Helps. Brevia.

Individuals, Importance of. James, W. Will to bel. 255.

Indo-China, French. Norman, H. Far East, 71.

— Garnier's Explorations in. Frost, T. Mod. expl. 101.

Indo-European languages, Aspirate mutes in. Hadley, J. Ess. 168.

— Philological classification of. Latham. Opuscula, 143.

— Study of. (T. Raftery) N. Y. Regents, 94 : 580.

Indo-European philology and ethnology. Whitney, W. D. Orient. 1 : 198.

Indo-Germanic languages, chronology of, Curtius on. Müller, M. Sci. ess. 1 : 79; *or* Chips, v. 1.

Indolence. Friswell. Gentle life, 1 : 252.

— a moral essay. Thompson, J. Ess. 142.

Inductive philosophy. Lord, J. Beacon, 8 : 417.

Indulgences, John of Wesel and. Ullman. Reformers, 243.

Industrial action, The state and. (H. C. Adams) Am. Econ. Assoc. v. 1.

Industrial and manual training in grammar schools. (T. O. Crawford) Nat. Educa. Assoc. '88 : 570.

— — in school course. (W. B. Powell) Nat. Educa. Assoc. '93 : 606.

Industrial and social revolution. Smith, G. Ess. on ques. of day, v. 1.

Industrial and technical schools at educ. exhibit, N. E. A. meeting, San Francisco, '88. (J. M. Ordway) Nat. Educa. Assoc. '88 : 704.

Industrial and technical training, National need of. Meath. Soc. arrows, 383.

Industrial art ; Art and industry. Gladstone. Speeches, 10 : 301.

— in public schools. (C. G. Leland) Phila. Soc. Sci. Assoc. '80 ; also in U. S. Bur. Ed. Circ. '82 : no. 4.

Industrial art education in U. S. (E. S. Drone) Hamerton. Higher ed. 106.

Industrial college, National. (E. E. White) Nat. Educa. Assoc. '82 : 131.

Industrial communities. (W. F. Willoughby) U. S. Lab. Bull. 1 : 223–609.

Industrial conflict, Lines of. Bosanquet, Mrs. Standard, 162.

Infants, Management of.   Chambers's Miscel. no. 6.
— Nourishment of.   (A. Simard) Am. Pub. Health, **20** : 367.
— Sanitary care of.   Kingsley, C. San. lec. 257.
Infectious and contagious diseases, Management of, in Milwaukee.   (O. W. Wight) Am. Pub. Health, **6** ; 86.
Infectious disease and its prevention.   Internat. Health Ex. Sanita.
Infectious diseases, Cause and prevention of. (P. H. Bryce) Am. Pub. Health, **24** : 73.
— Compulsory notification of.   (W. H. Michael et al.) Trans. Soc. Sci. Lond. '**81** : 532.   '**82** : 448. — Internat. Health Ex. Sanita.
— eruptive, Precautions against.   (W. Squire) Trans. Soc. Sci. Lond. '**70** : 554.
— The government and.   (W. Budd and W. Hardwicke) Trans. Soc. Sci. Lond. '**69** : 386.
— How spread.   Internat. Health Ex. Sanita.
— Isolation hospitals for.   (S. W. Abbott) Mass. Health, '**93** : 691.
— Notification of.   Internat. Health Ex. Sanita.
— of Saltillo, Mex.   (D. G. Fuertes) Am. Pub. Health, **18** : 389.
— Periods of incubation, etc.   N. H. Health, '**93** : 263.
— Removal from air of dust supposed to produce. (D. Prince) Am. Pub. Health, **12** : 164.
— Sanitary management of.   (G. C. Ashmun) Ohio Health, '**87** : 357.
— Transportation of persons ill with.   (G. P. Conn) N. H. Health, '**93** : 204.
Infectious fevers, Legislation relative to.   (F. T. Bond) Trans. Soc. Sci. Lond. '**76** : 478.
Inferences and facts.   Bailey, S. Essays, 131.
Inferior races, Treatment of.   (C. S. Roundell) Trans. Soc. Sci. Lond. '**66** : 126.
Infernal machine of Fieschi.   Thornbury. Old stor. 453.
Infidelity.   Hall, R. Miscel. 247.
— European democracy and.   Thomson, H. M. Copy, 21.
— A form of, at the present day.   Newman, J. H. Lec. univ. 296.
— Unreasonable.   (Isaac Barrow) Friswell. Silent hour, 29.
Infidels, Testimony of, in courts of law.   Winthrop, R. C. Addresses, **1** : 187.
Infinite, the, Personality and.   Knight, W. Ess. 211.
Infinites, Our knowledge of.   Hovey, A. Stud. in ethics, 1.
Infinity.   Holland, H. Frag. papers, 190. — McCosh. First truths.
— Notes on.   Proctor, R. A. Fam. sci. 1.
Infirmaries, County, Buildings for.   (R. Brinkerhoff) Conf. char. & correc. '**79** : 104.
Infirmities, Our often.   Craik, D. M. Serm. 41.
Inflection, Evolution of.   Latham. Opusc. 57.
Influences, Indirect.   King, T. S. Patriotism, 194.
Influenza.   Mackenzie, M. Ess. 245. — (A. G. Young) Maine Health, '**89** : 230.
— Causes and prevention of.   (H. B. Baker) Mich. Health, '**94** : 160.
— Epidemic, in Connecticut, 1889–90.   (C. P. Lindsley) Conn. Health, '**90** : 269.
Informers and spies in England in 1817.   Routledge, J. Pop. prog. in Eng. 315.
Ingalls, John J., with portrait.   (H. Inman) Scott, H. W. Dist. Am. lawy. 457.
Ingalls, Wm.   (W. Ingalls) N. E. Hist.-Gen. Soc. Biog. **1** : 328.

Ingborge of Denmark and Agnes de Maranie, queens.   Bush, A. F. Queens of F. **1** : 144.
Ingelow, Jean, with portrait.   Black, H. C. Wom. authors, 299.—Bolton, S. K. Girls, 331. — Forman. Liv. poets, 89.— Robertson. Eng. poetesses, 359. — (M. Bell) With portrait. Warner Lib. **14** : 7968. — Miles, A. H. Poets of cent. **7** : 385.
Ingemann, Bernhardt Severin.   Miller, Jos. Singers church, 2d ed. 577. — With portrait. Warner Lib. **14** : 7982.
Ingersoll, Charles Jared.   Maury, S. M. Statesm. of Am. 155.
Ingersoll, Jared, 1750–1822.   Brown, D. P. Forum, **1** : 470.
Ingersoll, Col. Robert G.   Alviella. Contemp. evol. 204. — Buchanan, R. Look round, 135. — Peck, H. T. Good English, 227. — With portrait. Scott, H. W. Dist. Am. lawy. 473.
— Answer to.   Black, J. S. Ess. & sp. 76.
— "The apostle of unbelief."   Hatton, J. To-day in Amer. **1** : 122, 155.
— Reply to.   Gladstone. Later gl. 118.
Ingham, Benjamin.   Tyerman. Oxf. meth. 57.
Inglis, Sir Robert.   Grant, J. Recoll. Ho. Comm. 131.
Inglis, Samuel D.   (E. C. Hewett) Nat. Educa. Assoc. '**98** : 288.
Ingoldsby, Thomas.   Horne. New spirit of the age, **1** : 127.
Ingomar.   Hutton, L. Plays, 137.
Ingratestone Hall, hiding place of priests. Timbs. Abbeys, **1** : 235.
Ingrès, J. A. D.   Hamerton. Contemp. Fr. painters.
Inheritance, Ancestor-worship and.   Maine. Early law, 78.
— Limitation of the rights of.   Kempner, W. Common-sense soc. 762.
Inheritance tax.   (M. West) Colum. Univ. Stud. Hist. **4** : no. 2.
Inhibition.   (B. B. Breese) Colum. Univ. Contrib. Philos. **5** : no. 3.
Injunction and organized labor.   (C. C. Allen) Am. Bar Assoc. **17** : 299.
Injuries, Factors of disease and death after. (S. D. Gross) Am. Pub. Health, **2** : 400.
Inkerman, Battle of.   Adams, W. H. D. Eng. at war, **2** : 151. — Adams, W. H. D. Memo. batt. **2** : 343. — Malleson. Ambushes, 333.
Inman, Henry.   Lester. Artists, 35. — Tuckerman. Artists, 233. — Tuckerman. Artist-life, 105. — Lossing. Em. Amer. 386.
Inner life, Rediscovery of.   Royce, J. Spir. mod. philos. 68.
Inner light, The.   Lilly, W. S. Gt. enig. 254.
"Inner Mission," German.   (C. R. Henderson) Conf. char. & correc. '**95** : 72.
Inness, George.   With portrait.   Benjamin, S. G. W. Am. art. **2** : 36.—Tuckerman. Artists, 527. — Sheldon, G. W. Amer. painters, 29.
Inness, George, jr.   Sheldon, G. W. Amer. painters, 203.
Innis, Anna.   Ellet. Pioneer wom. 61.
Innocent III., Pope.   Gurney, J. H. Four eccl. biog. — Milman. Latin Christianity. — Oliphant. Frederick II. **1** : 70. — Oliphant. Makers Mod. Rome, 307.
Innocent VIII. [Giambattista Cibo], Pope.   Pastor, L. Hist. popes, **5** : 227. — Symonds. Age of despots, 403.
Innocent IX., Pope.   Ranke. Popes, **2** : 233.
Innocent X., Pope.   Ranke. Popes, **3** : 41.
Innocent XI., Pope.   Ranke. Popes, **3** : 173.
Innocent XII., Pope.   Ranke. Popes, **3** : 183.

Intellectual pursuits, Healthfulness of. (J. E. Bradley) N. Y. Regents, 88 : 723.
— Variety of. Bailey, S. Essays, 186.
Intellectual superiority. Hazlitt. Table-talk.
Intelligence. Bowen, F. Gleanings, 328.
— Taine on. Mill, J. S. Dissert. (N. Y.) 5 : 122.
Intemperance. Gladden. Appl. Chr. 180. — Hazard. Ess. on lang. 323. — Kingsley. Health, 52. — Wynter, A. Our soc. bees, 2 : 155.
— and immorality in early New England. Adams, C. F. Three episodes, 2 : 783.
— and war. Van Santvoord, C. Disc. 144.
— Efforts to suppress. Samuelson, Jas. Civiliz'n, 222.
— Evils of. Beecher, L. Works, 1 : 379.
— Nature and occasions of. Beecher, L. Works, 1 : 347.
— Remedy of. Beecher, L. Works, 1 : 401.
— Signs of. Beecher, L. Works, 1 : 362.
Interest. Ashley. Introd. to Engl. econ. history. — Greeley. Ess. pol. econ. 79.
— and profit, History and future of. Leslie, T. E. C. Ess. pol. & mor. 243.
— Capital and. Bastiat. Ess. on pol. econ. 1.
— Cause of low rate. Hume. Philos. works, 3 : 324.
— Immorality of. Carpenter, E. Eng. ideal, 20.
— Rate of. Haven, N. A. Remains, 163.
— Theory of, Böhm-Bawerk's. Walker, F. A. Discus. in econ. 1 : 439.
Interludes. Hogarth. Mem. opera, 1 : 8. — Lennox, W. P. Plays, 1 : 11.
Intermediate or upper schools. (G. P. Hays and others) Nat. Educa. Assoc. '74 : 10.
Intermediate state maintained by the fathers. Evans, R. W. Biog. early ch. 1 : 322, 365.
Internal improvements. Seward. Works, 3 : 128.
Internal Revenue. Bibliography. Howe, F. C. Taxation.
International association of working people. Greene, W. B. Soc. frag. 237.
International comity and coöperation. (O. A. Howland) Deep waterways conven. 1 : 45.
International copyright. *See* Copyright.
International equity. Nicol, D. Polit. life, 2 : 375.
International exhibitions. Zangwill. Without prej. 257.
International Geographical Congress, 7th. Am. Geog. Soc. 31 : 151, 282, 490.
International law. Cairnes. Pol. ess. 109. — Coleridge. Friend, 252. — Senior. Hist. ess. 1 : 138. — (W. V. Harcourt) Trans. Soc. Sci. Lond. '68 : 137.
— Bibliography. Walker, T. A. Sci. internat. law.
— Case of A. McLeod. Seward. Works, 2 : 547.
— Code of. Field, D. D. Speeches, 1 : 384. — International American Conference, 1890. Reports.
— Develop. of, as to newly organized territory. (W. B. Scaife) Am. Hist. Assoc. 4 : 269.
— Institute of, at Ghent. Lorimer, Jas. Studies, nat'l & internat.
— Is there a true ? Lawrence. Ess. int. law, 1.
— Nations and. Leslie, T. E. C. Ess. pol. econ. 111.
— Reports of committee on. Am. Bar Assoc. 15 : 395. 16 : 323. 19 : 385. 20 : 393. 21 : 425. 22 : 418.
International questions, disputed, Settlement of. (Sir S. Baker *et al.*) Trans. Soc. Sci. Lond. '81 : 169.
Internationalism. Kempner, W. Common-sense soc. 84.

Interoceanic canal, Commercial geography of. (C. H. Stockton) Am. Geog. Soc. 20 : 75.
— Congress on, Paris, 1879. Am. Geog. Soc. 11 : 113, 153.
— Surveys, 1870–75. (D. Ammen) Am. Geog. Soc. 8 : 188.
Interoceanic communication, Problem of. (A. de Gogorza) Am. Geog. Soc. 20 : 502. 21 : 526.
Interstate commerce. Garfield. Works, 1 : 42.
— Congressional power over. (J. R. Tucker) Am. Bar Assoc. 11 : 247.
Intervention, American. Seward. Works, 1 : 196
Intervention, material and moral. Hobart, V. H. H. Ess. & Miscel. 2 : 36.
— Perils of. Harcourt, W. V. Letters fr. Times.
Interviews. Helps. Essays, 83.
"**Interviewing,**" Propagandist uses of. Holyoake. Among Amer. 55.
Intolerance, Religious, in Germany. Baring-Gould. Germany, 335.
Intoxication. Timbs. Doctors, 320.
— Ether-drinking and extra-alcoholic. Richardson, B. W. Ministry, 306.
Intrusiveness. Helps. Soc. pressure, 83.
Intuition. Clarke, J. F. Self-culture, 155. — McCosh. First truths.
— Review of McCosh on. Wright, C. Philos. dis. 329.
Invalid. Payn. Private views, 198.
Invalids, Migration of. (S. A. Eliot) Conf. char. & correc. '92 : 90.
Invective, Economy of. Whipple. Success, 114.
Invention. Greeley. Ess. pol. econ. 4.
— Birth of. (O. T. Mason) Smithson. Rept. '92 : 603.
— Early history of, in England. Francis, J. Stock exch. 89.
— in painting. Fuseli. Life & writ. 2 : 131.
Inventions, American. Dodge, M. A. Twelve miles, 94.
— as agents in history. Hare. Guesses, 1 : 85.
— Great. (S. Walpole) Rand. Selec. econ. hist. 31.
— Influence of, upon civilization. (C. Smith) Conv. Lab. Bur. '85 : 12.
— Mechanical, and inventors. Smiles. Indus. biog.
Inventors, Great. Hodder. Heroes, 2 : 143.
— Lay. Taylor, I. Ult. civiliz. 191.
Inverness, "Character" fair at. Forbes, A. Camps, 217.
Invertebrates. Bibliography. (S. Weller) U. S. geol. surv. bull. no. 153.
Investigation, General principles of physical. Bailey, S. Discourses, 153.
— Social value and dangers of. (E. T. Devine) Conf. char. & correc. '97 : 193.
Investment. (T. Mackay) Plea for liberty, 227.
— Bibliography. Aubrey, W. H. S. Stock exchange invest.
Iodine and oxygen, A solid compound of. Davy. Works, 5 : 492.
— Experiments and observations on. Davy. Works, 5 : 457.
Iona, Storm-bound in. Winter. Old shrines, 107.
— A visit to, in 1862. Montalembert. Monks, 3 : 461.
Ionian islands. Smith, Goldwin. The empire, 232.
— in the year 1863. Lucas. Mornings, 1 : 281.
Ionians, Migration of the. Hadley, J. Ess. 1.
Ios. Tozer. Isl. Ægean, 78.

Ireland, Scenery in. Davis, T. Prose, 184.
— Schools for the middle classes. Arnold, M. Irish ess. 2.
— societies in, Unlawful. Peel, R. Speeches, 1 : 322.
— Society in. Foster, J. Crit. ess. (Bohn) 2 : 139.
— State of. Peel, R. Speeches, 1 : 56. 4 : 268, 316.
— Taxation and representation of. Giffen. Ess. finance, 280.
— union with, Repeal of, 1833. Macaulay. Miscel. & sp. 535.
— University education in. Fawcett. Sp. pol. ques. 182, 196, 217. — (C. Dawson) Trans. Soc. Sci. Lond. '81 : 433.
— university question in, Present position of, 1873. Cairnes. Pol. ess. 323.
— Wrongs of. Black, J. S. Essays, 158.
Irenæus, St., bishop of Lyons. Blakey, R. Prim. fathers, 88. — Cave. Lives of Fathers, 1 : 258. — Evans, R. W. Biog. early church, 1 : 212. — Hort, F. J. A. Ante-N. fathers, 49. — (S. Leathes) Lefroy, W. Lec. eccl. hist. 81.
Ireton, Bridget Cromwell. Jesse. Court of Eng. Stuarts, 2 : 371.
Iriarte. See Yriarte.
Irish in America, The. White, John. Sk. Amer. 351.
— in Spain. Grant, Jas. Cavaliers, 233.
Irish ballad history. Davis, T. Prose, 201.
Irish ballad poetry. Davis, T. Prose, 192.
Irish bar. Sheil, R. L. Sketches, 1 : 197.
Irish brigade. Davis, T. Prose, 104.
Irish character, The. Ossoli. Woman, 320.
Irish cottier, The. Cairnes. Pol. ess. 151.
Irish elections. Sheil, R. L. Sketches, 2 : 329.
Irish exchequer in 1829. Whiteside, J. Early sk. 268.
Irish genius. Maginn. Fras. papers, 197.
Irish historical paintings, Hints for. Davis, T. Prose, 155.
Irish language, National. Davis, T. Prose, 158.
Irish literature. Oliphant, M. Lit. hist. 3 : 209.
Irish lyric poetry. Johnston, R. M. Stud. 2 : 138.
Irish music and poetry. Davis, T. Prose, 188.
Irish political ballads. Darmesteter. Eng. stud. 217.
Irish portraits. Curran. Irish bar, 2 : 273.
Irish question in America, 1881. Hatton, J. To-day in Amer. 1 : 60.
Irish race, Thébaud on the. Brownson. Works, 13 : 547.
Irish societies. Heckethorn. Sec. soc. 181.
Irishman, The. Guiney. Patrins, 153.
Iron and civilization. Smiles. Indus. biog.
— and tools, American, in England, 1898. U. S. Cons. Rept. 59 : 242.
— Cast. (W. R. Lethaby) Morris, W. Arts & crafts, 184.
— Manufacture of, in Germany, Economy in. U. S. Cons. Rept. no. 155.
— — in Gt. Britain, Beginning of. Smiles. Indus. biog.
— in Scotland. Smiles. Indus. biog.
Iron and steel industries, Devel. of, since 1860. Swank. Notes, 145.
Iron industry in the American colonies. Swank. Notes, 137.
— in Ohio. Ohio Labor, 1878-80.
Iron making and waterways. (A. J. Moxham) Deep waterways conven. 1 : 77.
Iron mask, Man with the. Chambers's Miscel. no. 131. — Davenport, R. A. Delusions, 254. — Wraxall. Remark. adv. 1 : 106.
Iron-smelting by pit-coal. Smiles. Indus. biog.

Iron workers, Our great. Wynter, A. Our soc. bees, 2 : 161.
Irons, Joseph. Miller, Jos. Singers church, 2d ed. 390, 515.
Irons, W. Josiah. Miles, A. H. Poets of cent. 10 : 465.
Irony. Hedge. Atheism, 306.
Iroquois condoling council, An. (H. Hale) Roy. Soc. Can. 2d ser. § 2 : 45.
Iroquois confederacy, Consolidation of the. (J. Douglas) Am. Geog. Soc. 29 : 41.
Irrawaddy river. Shoemaker, M. M. Quaint corners, 60.
Irreligion, Apparent causes of. Hamerton. Hum. int. 205.
Irrigation. N. J. Labor, '80 : 197.
— Bibliography. (J. W. Powell) U. S. Geolog. Surv. Rept. '89-90, pt. 2.
— in Spain. U. S. Cons. Rept. no. 148.
— Its influence on health, etc. (H. S. Orme) Calif. Health, '82-83 : 51.
— Relations of, to geography. (H. M. Wilson) Am. Geog. Soc. 30 : 1.
Irvine, William. Neven, D. R. B. Pennsylvanians, 117.
Irving, Edward. Carlyle. Reminis. 55. — De Quin. Lit. rem. Bost. 2 : 236. — Gilfillan. 1st gall. 130. — Gilfillan. 3d gall. 52. — Hazlitt. Spirit. — Newton, W. W. Ess. 80. — Paul. Biog. sk. 1. — (R. H. Story) St. Giles lec. 3 ; 225. — Dale, T. P. Life's motto. — (N. J. Ross) With portrait. Ewart, H. C. Leaders, 193. — Grant, Jas. Metropol. pul. 101. — Hall, S. C. Book of mem. 48. — Procter, B. W. Autob. 158. — Saunders, F. Charac. studies, 1.
— and Mrs. Carlyle. Hitchcock, T. Unhap. loves, 183.
— Death of. Carlyle. Essays.
Irving, Henry. Matthews, B. Actors, 5 : 131. — Hatton, J. Old lamps, 1. — Walkley, A. B. Playhouse, 256. — With portr. Goddard, A. Players, 1 : 13. — Wilman, G. Sk. liv. celeb. 1.
— and Coquelin. Winter, W. Shadows, 2 : 285.
— and Ellen Terry. Winter, W. Shadows, 3 : 148.
— — in Macbeth. Winter, W. Shadows, 2 : 277.
— — in " Merchant of Venice." Winter. Shadows, 1 : 178.
— — in " Olivia." Winter. Shadows, 1 : 119.
— — in " Ravenswood." Winter. Shadows, 1 : 226.
— as Eugene Aram. Winter. Shadows, 1 : 348.
— as Hamlet. Winter. Shadows, 3 : 101.
— as Mathias. Winter. Shadows, 3 : 55.
— as Othello. Morris. Essays in theatrical criticism.
— as Shylock. Winter. Shadows, 3 : 242.
— as Wolsey. Winter. Shadows, 3 : 199.
— Era of. Whyte, F. Actors of cent. 163.
— in Bond street. Yates, E. H. Celeb. 1 : 59.
— in Faust. Winter. Shadows, 1 : 30.
Irving, Washington. With portrait. [Amer.] Nat. portr. gall. v. 1. — Bolton, S. K. Amer. au. 58. — Bryant. Prose, 1 : 332. — Bungay. Off-hand, 141. — Curran. Irish bar, 2 : 213. — With portrait. Duyckinck. Nat. portr. gall. 2 : 99. — Everett. Orat. v. 4. — Greene, G. W. Biog. stud. 155. — Griswold, H. T. Home-life, 112. — With portrait. Griswold. Prose writ. 201. — Haweis. Amer. humorists, 1. — Hazlitt. Spirit. — Mitchell, D. G. Bound toge. 3. — With portraits. Mitchell, D. G. Am. lands, 300. — Saunders, F. Famous books, 179. — Tartt. Ess. 2 : 1. — Walsh, W. S. Pen pic. Vic. au. 208. — Wilson, J. G. Bryant, 157. — Curtis, G. W. Lit. & soc. ess. 237. — Saunders, F.

Charac. studies, 65. — Howe, M. A. D. Am. bookm. 1. — With portrait. (E. W. Morse) Warner Lib. 14 : 7991 ; *or* Warner Classics, 4 : 143. — Howells. My lit. passions, 28. — Wright, H. C. Chil. sto. in Am. lit. 28. — Brooks, E. S. Hist. Amer. 263. — Fisher, M. Gen. sur. Am. lit. 52. — Duyckinck. Portr. gall. 2 : 150. — (H. T. Tuckerman) Hubbard, E. Little jour. 2 : 265. Same art. Homes Am. authors. — Lanman, C. Haphazard, 75. — (C. D. Warner) N. E. Hist.-Gen. Soc. Biog. 3 : 461. — Nichol. Amor. lit. 170. — (E. Everett and J. A. Todd) Graham & Collar. Pulpit and rost. v. 1. — Richardson. Amer. lit. 1 : 258. 2 : 289.

Irving, Washington, at Sunnyside. Tartt. Ess. 2 : 60.

— — and Sleepy Hollow. Wolfe, T. F. Lit. haunts, 174.

— Bibliography. Hodgkins. 19th cent. authors.

— Bracebridge Hall. Jeffrey, F. Contrib. Ed. Rev.

— Eulogies on. (H. W. Longfellow, E. Everett *et al.*) Mass. Hist. Proc. 4 : 393.

— Life, character, and genius. Bryant. Orations, 93.

— Rip Van Winkle, Moral of. Curtis. From easy ch. 106.

— Services to Amer. history. Burton, R. Liter. likings, 247.

— Sketch book. Dana. P. & p. writ. 268.

— Works, genius, and character. Wallace, H. B. Lit. crit. 67.

Irvingism. (E. Miller) Relig. systems, 594.

Irwin, Anne, viscountess. Williams, Jane. Lit. wom. 194.

Irwin, Thomas. Williams, A. M. Poets of Irel.

Isaac. Geikie, C. Old Test. char. 23.

Isaacson, Stephen. Smith, C. R. Retrospec. 1 : 20.

Isaaks, Jorge. Warner Lib. 14 : 8046.

Isabella of Angoulême, with portrait. Howitt, M. Queens, 71. — Strickland. Queens Eng. v. 2. — Lancelott. Queens, v. 1. — Lawrance. Queens, v. 1.

Isabella of France, queen of Edward II. With portr. Howitt, M. Queens, 112. — Strickland. Queens Eng. v. 2. — Lancelott. Queens, v. 1. — Lawrance. Queens, v. 2.

— Favorites of. Menzies, S. Roy. fav. 1 : 53.

Isabella of Valois, queen of Richard II. With portr. Howitt, M. Queens, 147. — Strickland. Queens Eng. v. 3. — Lancelott. Queens, v. 1.

Isabella of Bavaria, queen and regent. Bush, A. F. Queens of F. 1 : 207.

Isabella I., queen of Castile. Owen, Mrs. O. F. Heroines hist. 237. — Fifty famous women, 236.

Isabella II., of Spain. Abbott. Kings & queens, 239. — With portrait. Clarke, M. C. Noted wom. 237. — Goodrich, F. B. Wom. 129. — Jameson. Fem. sov 1. — Russell. Extr. women, 104. — Yonge, C. D. Seven heroines, 82.

Isabella, daughter of King John, with portrait. Greene, M. A. E. Princesses, 2 : 1.

Isabella, daughter of Edward III. Greene, M. A. E. Princesses, 3 : 163.

Isæus. Mills. Poets of Greece, 446.

Isaiah, the prophet. (J. Lord) Bost. lectures, '71 : 196. — (M. Arnold) Coan. Stud. lit. 182. — Geikie, C. Old Test. char. 376.

Ischia. Pfirshing. Mem. Ital. 105. — Taylor, B. By-ways, 367.

Iseran, Mount. (J. J. Cowell) Vaca. tourists, 1 : 239.

Ishmael. Geikie, C. Old Test. char. 32.

Ishmaelites. Heckethorn. Sec. soc. 1 : 161.

Iskander Effendi. Prime, W. C. I go a-fishing, 37.

Islam. Carlyle. Heroes. — Trench. Lec. mediæval, 46. — Deutsch, E. Lit. rem. 59. — Nöldeke, T. Sk. fr. east. hist. 60.

— Ethics of. (G. E. Post) Barrows, J. H. Parl. relig. 2 : 1096.

— Influence of, on social conditions. (A. R M. Webb) Barrows, J. H. Parl. relig. 2 : 1046.

— Religion of. Hoppin. Notes theol. stud. 165.

— Rise and decline of. (W. Muir) Liv. papers, v. 3.

— Spirit of. (A. R. M. Webb) Barrows, J. H. Parl. relig. 2 : 989.

Island sanctuaries in Somersetshire. Walters, J. C. Bygone Som. 169.

Islands and the geographical distribution of animals. (A. R. Wallace) Manch. Sci. lec. 11 : 1.

— Fortunate. Baring-Gould. Myths, 524.

— Natural history of. Allen, Grant. Science in Arc. 1.

— Oceanic. (A. R. Wallace) Am. Geog. Soc. 19 : 1.

Isle of Wight, The. Benjamin. Atlan. isl. 234.

Isles of Shoals. Benjamin. Atlan. isl. 205. — Drake. Nooks of N. E. 153.

Islington congregation. Stoughton, J. Spir. heroes, 11.

Islip, Simon, 1349–66. Hook. Abps. Cant. 4 : 111. — Sergeant, L. Wiclif, 142.

Ismail, Siege of. Robson, W. Sieges, 525.

Isobel, countess of Buchan. Fittis. Heroines of Scot. 6.

Isocrates. Mills. Poets of Greece, 444.

Isocratio party, The. (Grant Allen) Reid, A. New party, 1.

Israel, Hannah E. Clement, J. Noble deeds, 164. — Ellet. Women of revol. 1 : 155.

Israel, Heroic age of. (W. S. Tyler) Bost. lectures, '71 : 132.

— Preparation for Christ in. Gore, C. Lux mundi, 150.

Israels, Josef. Ewart, H. C. Toilers in art, 261.

Issus battle, B. C. 333. Dodge. Alexander, 295.

Ita, St. *See* Ida, St.

Italian academies, Ridiculous titles assumed by. Disraeli, I. Curios. (N. Y. 4 v.) 3 : 242.

Italian book trade, Early. Garnett, R. Ess. in librarianship, 141.

Italian domestics. Jarves. Ital. ramb. 381.

Italian gesticulation. Wiseman, N. Ess. 3 : 531.

Italian historians. Disraeli, I. Curios. (N. Y. 4 v.) 4 : 61.

Italian journeyings. Tuckerman. Ital. sk. 172.

Italian lakes, The. Bennett, J. H. Winter on Medit. 399. — (R. A. McLeod) Murphy, Lady B. On Rhine, 133.

Italian language and poetry. Longfellow. Poets Eur. 501.

— Formation of. Symonds. Renais. It. lit. 1 : 28.

Italian literature. Griffin, E. D. Rem. 2 : 321.

— Bibliography. Garnett, R. Hist. Ital. lit.

— Debt of English literature to. Symonds. Sk. So. Eur. 1 : 101.

— Earliest. Nettleship. Lec. & ess.

— in first half of 19th century. Greene, G. W. Hist. stud. 120.

— in 1837. Mazzini. Life, etc. 2 : 159.

— Influence on English literature. Hallam. Remains, 180.

— Influence upon Spain. Ticknor. Span. lit. 1 : 346.

— Popular, in the 15th century. Symonds. Renais. It. lit. 1 : 234.

Italian literature, Renaissance. Woodberry. Studies in letters, 112.
Italian nationality. Everett, E. Mt. Vernon, 293.
Italian poetry, ancient, Indigenous. Sellar. Rom. poets repub. 28.
— narrative, Da Ponte on. Prescott. Biog. miscel. 596.
— Pastoral and didactic. Symonds. Renais. It. lit. **2** : 194.
— Popular, of the Renaissance. Symonds. Sk. So. Eur. **1** : 118.
— Satirical and burlesque. Symonds. Renais. It. lit. **2** : 309.
Italian poets, Recent. Hueffer. Ital. stud. v. **1**.
Italian rural life. Mitchell. Wet days, 91.
Italian training. Jarves. Ital. ramb. 392.
Italian women, A decade of. Tartt. Ess. **1** : 114.
Italians, The. Taine. Italy, **2** : 28.
— Character of, during the Renaissance. Symonds. Reviv. of learn. **1**.
— in England and Englishmen in Italy. Hazlitt, W. C. Offspring, 153.
Italy. Addison. Works (Bohn), **1** : 356. — Felton, C. C. Fam. lett. Eur. 130. — Fulton, C. C. Europe, 188. — Howe, J. W. Oak to olive, 45. — James. Transatl. 75. — Moulton, L. C. Rambles, 33. — Wikoff, H. Reminis. 152.
— American researches in. Irving. Crayon pap. 96.
— Ancient, as seen in Pompeiian paintings. Merivale. Hist. stud. 416.
— and France in 1787. Jefferson. Works, **9** : 313.
— and her church. Gladstone. Bulga. 209; *or* Gleanings, **6** : 193.
— and Palermo, Trade of, 1892. (H. C. Pugh) U. S. Cons. Rept. **39** : 464.
— and the Pope. Brownson. Works, **18** : 445.
— — Growth of anti-papal spirit. Hallam. Remains, 319.
— and the western powers. Congreve, R. Ess. 111.
— by diligence. Willis. Pencillings.
— central, Dwindling cities of. Jarves. Ital. ramb. 145.
— Cities of. James. Transatl. 212.
— Civilization in, Early. Nettleship. Lec. & ess.
— The Cornice. Symonds. Sk. So. Eur. **1** : 9.
— From Como to Milan during war of 1848. Curtis. From easy chair, **3** : 43.
— Germany and, after 1848. Greg. Ess. pol. **2** : 113.
— Guide-books to. Wiseman, N. Ess. **3** : 461.
— Historical romance of. Greene, G. W. Hist. stud. 253.
— History of, 476–1500. Symonds. Age of despots, 32.
— History. Bibliography. King, B. Hist. of Ital. unity.
— — Dante on recent. Grimm, H. Liter. 253.
— — Invasion by the barbarians. Stillé. Stud. med. 41.
— — — by Charles VIII., of France. Symonds. Age of despots, 537.
— — Republics of middle ages in. Symonds. Age of despots, 193.
— — in 16th century (1515–59). Symonds. Renais. Cath. reac. **1** : 1.
— — Revolution of 1848. Ossoli. At home, 301.
— — 1859–60. Forsyth, W. Essays, 61.
— Holidays in, 1856. Taylor, B. At home, **1** : 304.
— Hopes of, 1848. Greene, G. W. Hist. stud. 208, 436.
— in the 15th century. Taine. Italy, **2** : 108.
— in the 17th century. Taine. Italy, **1** : 204.
— in 19th century. Bibliography. Salem (Mass.) Pub. Lib. Bull. Mar. '96.

Italy in 1861. Brownson. Works, **18** : 431.
— in 1862. Wordsworth, C. Miscel. **1** : 140.
— in 1877. James. Portraits of places.
— in 1887. Dilke. European politics.
— in 1889. U. S. Consular report, no. 120.
— Leaves from my journal in. Lowell. Writ. **1** : 120.
— Letters from. Shelley. Ess. **2** : 79.
— Mediæval. Stearns, F. P. Midsum. Ital. art, **1**.
— — and ancient Greece. (E. A. Freeman) Oxf. ess. '57 : 129; also in Freeman. Hist. ess. **2** : 1.
— Modern. Tuckerman. Ital. sk. 405.
— Moral and religious condition during the Renaissance. Pastor, L. Hist. popes, **5** : 1.
— nationality of, Struggle for. Stillé. Stud. med. 305.
— north, Art notes in. Pater. Miscel. stud. 74.
— of the Elizabethan dramatists. Paget, V. Euphorion, **1** : 57.
— Palaces of. Taine. Italy, **1** : 218.
— Politics of, 1846. Ossoli. At home, 242.
— Program for republican unity of. Mazzini. Ess. 139.
— Reformation in. Blunt. Ess. 89.
— Religion of. Taine. Italy, **1** : 316. — Wiseman, N. Ess. **3** : 507.
— Revisited. Gammel. Writ. 315.
— Social and domestic morals of, in 16th century. Symonds. Renais. Cath. reac. **1** : 301.
— Society in, in the last days of the Roman republic. Froude. Short stud. **3** : 185.
— Statistics of, 1891. (A. O. Bourn) U. S. Cons. Rept. **39** : 45.
— Technical education in, 1893. U. S. Cons. Rept. **43** : 244.
— Tour through, 1829. Griffin, E. D. Rem. **1** : 135. **2** : 9.
— Two Rivieras. Bennett, J. H. Winter on Medit. 228.
— Union of. Bibliography. Stillman, W. J. Union Italy, 1815–95.
— Unity of. Bryant. Orations, 351. — Whittier. Prose, v. **3**.
— University system in. (A. De Gubernatis) Hamerton. Higher ed. 71.
Ithaca, Greece. Barrows, S. J. Isles of Greece, 56.
Itzamna, God of the Mayas. Brinton. Amer. hero-myths, 146.
Ivan the great. Fowler, G. Sov. of Russ. **1** : 74.
Ivan IV., the Terrible, czar of Russia. Fowler, G. Sov. of Russ. **1** : 92. — Ireland, W. W. Blot, 129.
Ivan VI., deposed czar. Doran. Monarchs, **2** : 175.
Ivara, Filippo. Milizia. Lives arch. **2** : 307.
Iverson, Alfred. Johnston, A. Amer. ora. **3** : 325.
Ives, St., Bp. of Chartres. Neale. Mediæv. preachers.
Ives, Jeremiah. Ivimey. Eng. Bapt. **2** : 603.
Ives, Robert H. Bartlett, J. R. R. I. officers, 350.
Ives, Thomas Poynton. Bartlett, J. R. R. I. officers, 273. — Goddard, W. G. Pol. & miscel. wr. **1** : 288.
Ivison, Henry. Derby, J. C. Fifty years, 49.
Ivory, James. Walker, W., jr. Men of sci. 155.
Ivory carving, 14th century. Wright, T. Ess. archæol. **2** : 88.
Ivy, Richard. Wakeley. Heroes Meth. 206.
Izard, Ralph. Lossing. Em. Amer. 282.

Jabez : his life and his prayer; a sermon. Boyd. Graver tho'ts, 77.
Jaca. Hale, E. E. Seven Spanish cit. 279.

Jachowicz, Stanislaus.   Soboleski. Poets of Poland, 303.

Jack, Gilbert.   Irving, D.   Scot. writ. 1 : 323.

Jack Abbott's breakfast.   Hunt, L.   Men, wom. & books, 84.

Jackson, Alfred E.   Walker, C. D.   Biog. Va. Mil. Inst. 283.

Jackson, Andrew.   Abbott.   Lives of presidents, 207. — With portrait. [Am.] Nat. portr. gall. v. 1. — Baldwin.   Party leaders, 277. — Bethune.   Orations, 321. — With portrait.   Duyckinck.   Nat. portr. gall. 2 : 116. — Frost. Presidents, 187. — Keyes, E. D.   Fifty years. — Lincoln.   Lives of pres. 273. — Parton.   Peop. bk. biog. 469. — Poore.   Reminis. 1 : 88. — With portr.   Seymour, C. C. B.   Self-made, 9. — Brooks, E. S.   Hist. Amer. 231. — Duyckinck.   Portr. gall. 1 : 615. — James.   Mil. occur. v. 2. — Lossing.   Em. Amer. 244. — Muzzey, A. B.   Prime movers, 285. — Nichol.   Amer. lit. 108. — Sparks, W. H.   Memories, 151. — Thompson, R. W.   Pers. recoll. 141. — (J. Fiske) Wilson, J. G.   Presidents, 137.—Upton, Mrs. H. T.   Our early pres. 337.

— Appointment as brigadier in the army.   Madison, J.   Letters, 3 : 373.

— Canvass of.   Mansfield, E. D.   Pers. mem. 228.

— Eulogy on.   Black, J. S.   Ess. & sp. 189.

— Home of.   (P. Godwin) Homes Am. statesm. 341.

— in Massachusetts.   Quincy, J.   Figures, 352.

— Life and character of.   Woodbury, L.   Writ. 3 : 362.

— Oration on the death of.   Bancroft, G.   Miscel. 444.

— Social life during administration of.   Ellet, E. F.   Court circles, 143.

Jackson, Mrs. Andrew.   Gordon, L. L.   Lady Wash'n, 134.

Jackson, Charles, Eulogy on.   Lunt.   Three eras, 233.

Jackson, Clement.   Ivimey.   Eng. Bapt. 2 : 146.

Jackson, Francis.   Phillips, W.   Speeches, 2 : 440.

Jackson, Helen Hunt.   Bolton, S. K.   Girls famous, 18. — Higginson, T. W.   Contemp. 142. — Higginson.   Sh. stud. 40. — Richardson.   Amer. lit. 2 : 248. — Thayer, W. M.   Turn. points, 61. — With portrait.   Warner Lib. 14 : 8057.

Jackson, Henry.   Am. Bar Assoc. 19 : 634.

Jackson, Henry R.   Davidson, J. W.   Writ. of South, 289.

Jackson, James.   Am. Antiq. Soc. Proc. n. s. 10 : 210. — With portrait. [Am.] Nat. portr. gall. 3. — Lossing.   Em. Amer. 131.

Jackson, John, bp. of London.   Arnold, F.   Our bishops, 1 : 340. — With photo.   Cooper, T.   Men of mark, 1 : 11.

Jackson, John B. S.   Vaille & Clark.   Harv. book, v. 1.

Jackson, Julia N.   Holloway, L. C.   Mothers of gt. men, 241.

Jackson, Patrick Tracy, with portrait.   (J. A. Lovell) Hunt, F.   Am. merch. 1 : 555.

Jackson, Mrs. Rachel Donelson.   Hanaford.   Wom. of cent. 80. — With portrait.   Holloway, L. C.   Ladies, 272. — Parton.   Peop. bk. biog. 593.

Jackson, Samuel.   Wesley & successors, 167.

Jackson, Serjeant.   Grant, J.   Recoll. Lords & Comm. 2 : 230.

Jackson, Thomas.   Wesley & successors, 143, 171. — Wise, D.   Heroic Meth. 268.

Jackson, Thomas J., "Stonewall."   Duyckinck.   Portr. gall. 2 : 487. — (H. McGuire) With portrait.   Hotchkiss.   Battfields Va. 118. — Pollard.   Life of Lee, 177. — Snow.   So. generals, 156. — Rogers, C.   Chr'n heroes, 51. — (F. H. Smith) Walker, C. D.   Biog. Va. Mil. Inst. 543.

— Death of.   Lodge & Roosevelt.   Hero-tales, 211.

Jackson, William, composer.   Smiles.   Self-help.

Jaco, Peter.   Jackson, T.   Early Meth. 1 : 137.

Jacob, Geikie, C.   Old Test. char. 40. — Wilberforce, S.   Heroes Hebrew, 30.

Jacob of Jüterbock.   Ullman.   Reformers, 209.

Jacob, Henry.   Stoughton, J.   Spir. heroes, 88.

Jacobi, Friedrich Heinrich.   (N. Wilde) Colum. Univ. Contrib. Philos. 1 : no. 1. — Frothingham.   Transcend. 23. — Hodge.   Prose Ger. 206. — Pünjer.   Christian philos. religion, 621.

Jacobinism.   Mivart.   Ess. 1 : 1.

Jacobins, Account of.   Robertson, J. B.   Lec. mod. hist. 476.

— Club of.   Farmer, J. E.   Ess. Fr. hist. 57.

Jacobite family, A.   Brown, J. J.   Leech, 83.

Jacobite insurrection, Chiefs of.   Bernard, F.   Escapes, 108.

Jacobson, William.   Burgon.   Twelve men, 2 : 238.

Jacobus de Benedictis.   Miller, Jos.   Singers church, 2d ed. 36.

Jacobus, Mrs. Rebecca.   Raymond, I.   Southland writ. 1 : 504.

Jacoby, Johann.   Tuttle, H.   Ger. pol. lead. 160.

Jacopone da Todi.   Symonds.   Renais. It. lit. 1 : 283.

Jacotot.   Quick.   Educa. ref. 414.

Jacquard, Jos. M.   Bolton, S. K.   Poor boys famous, 130. — Brightwell.   Heroes of lab. 80. — Chambers's Miscel. no. 158. — Lamartine.   Cel. char. 2 : 17. — Woodcroft, B.   Biog. invent. 27.

Jacque, Charles Emile.   Hamerton.   Contem. Fr. painters.

Jacquemart, Jules.   Wedmore.   Four masters, 12.

Jacquemont, Victor.   Hamerton.   Mod. Fr. 1.

Jacques Cartier, Salmon-fishing on the river.   Lanman.   Recol. 147.

Jael.   Geikie, C.   Old Test. char. 134. — Hastings, F.   Obscure charac. 128. — Owen, Mrs. O. F.   Heroines hist. 11.

Jaenbert, 766–790.   Hook.   Abps. Cant. 1 : 242.

Jaffa.   *See* Joppa.

Jago, Richard.   Chalmers.   Eng. poets, 17 : 281.

Jahanger.   Adams, W. H. D.   Warriors of crescent, 221.

Jahel.   *See* Jael.

Jail construction, Simplicity in.   (E. Bicknell) Conf. char. & correc. '97 : 58.

Jails and poorhouses, Administration of.   (A. G. Byers) Conf. char. & correc. '86 : 31.

— Construction and management of.   (A. O. Wright) Conf. char. & correc. '85 : 304.

— County.   (E. Smith) Nat. Pris. Assoc. '85 : 240. — (R. Brinkerhoff) Nat. Pris. Assoc. '85 : 89.

— — and city.   (E. A. Meredith) Nat. Pris. Assoc. '87 : 242.

— — prisoners in, Treatment of.   (J. T. Hibbert) Trans. Soc. Sci. Lond. '75 : 333.

— — System of.   Illinois Charity, '72 : 207.   '76 : 175.

— Notes on the construction of.   Illinois Charity, '70 : 212.

Jainism.   Barth, A.   Relig. India, 140. — Hopkins.   Relig. of India, 280.

Jains, Sect of. Colebrooke. Miscel. essays, **2** : 191.

— in 1890. U. S. Consular Report, no. 113.

— Philosophy and ethics of. (V. A. Ghandi) Barrows, J. H. Parl. relig. **2** : 1222.

Jakubowski, A. A. Soboleski. Poets of Poland, 458.

Jamaica. Hill, R. T. Cuba, 185.

— Foreign trade of, 1891. (W. R. Estes) U. S. Cons. Rept. **37** : 321.

— Fruits of, 1891. (W. R. Estes) U. S. Cons. Rept. **36** : 321.

— Maroons of. Higginson, T. W. Travellers, 116.

— Mobs in. Child, L. M. Oasis, 262.

— Pirates' paradise. Powell, G. H. Excurs. in Libr. 123.

— Tariff of, effect upon trade, 1899. (L. A. Dent) U. S. Cons. Rept. **91** : 1.

Jamaica government bill, 1839. Peel, R. Spee. **3** : 623.

James, St., the greater. Kingsley. Hermits, 156.

James I., of Scotland. Collier, W. F. Hist. Eng. lit. 64. — Craik. Pursuit knowl. **2** : 15. — Irving, D. Scot. poets, **1** : 287. — Oliphant. Royal Edinburgh, 38. — Veitch. Feeling for nature in Scottish poetry, **1** : 186. — (T. H. Ward) Eng. poets, 129. — Wilson, J. G. Poets of Scot. **1** : 12. — Minto, W. Eng. poets, 94. — Tyler. Scot. worth. v. **2, 3.**

— and the king's quail. Shairp. Sk. hist. & poetry, 240.

— A royal poet. Irving. Sk. book, 65.

James V., of Scotland. Bernard, F. Escapes, 22. — Wilson, J. G. Poets of Scot. **1** : 51.

James I., of England (VI. of Scotland). Bayne. Pur. recol. 25. — Disraeli, I. Curios. (N. Y. 4 v.) **2** : 143. — Irving, D. Scot. poets, **2** : 209. — Wilson, J. G. Poets of Scot. **1** : 63. — Holland, J. Psalmists, **1** : 250. — Macaulay. Biog. sk. 89.

— and the duke of Buckingham. Menzies, S. Roy. fav. **2** : 10.

— and Sir T. Overbury. (J. Spedding) Gairdner & Spedding. Stud. 175.

— and witchcraft. Wright, T. Nar. sorcery, **1** : 180.

— as a father and a husband. Disraeli, I. Curios. (N. Y. 4 v.) **4** : 239.

— Era of. Deshler. Afternoons, 115.

— Farewell of, to Holyrood. Masson. Edinb. sk. 61.

— Favorites of. Menzies, S. Roy. fav. **1** : 391.

— Military system of. Adams, W. H. D. Eng. at war, **1** : 35.

James II., of England. Jesse. Court of Eng. Stuarts, **3** : 407. — Smythe, G. S. Hist. fancies, 93.

— and Magdalen College, Oxford. Pattison. Ess. **1** : 320.

— and St. Germain's. Doran. Monarchs, **1** : 101.

— Fox's Reign of. Jeffrey, F. Contrib. Ed. Rev.

— Military system of. Adams, W. H. D. Eng. at war, **1** : 95.

James III., of England. Townsend. Descend. Stuarts, 126.

James, duke of Monmouth. Adams, W. H. D. Anec. mem. **2** : 26.

James, duke of York. Adams, W. H. D. Anec. mem. **2** : 103.

James Francis Edward, the first Pretender. Adams, W. H. D. Anec. mem. **2** : 189. — Jesse. Pretenders, 1.

— at Bar-le-Duc. Wolff. Odd bits, 1.

James, George Payne Rainsford. Field, M. B. Memories, 186. — Hall, S. C. Book of mem.

263. — Horne, R. H. New spirit, 127. — Mitchell, D. G. Eng. lands, **4** : 283.

James, George Payne Rainsford. Novels. Whipple. Ess. & rev. 1.

James, Henry. Burton, R. Liter. likings, 107. — Hapgood, N. Lit. statesm. 193. — Hazeltine. Chats, 347. — Higginson. Short stud. 51. — Heywood, J. C. How they strike, 183. — Vedder, H. C. Amer. writers, 69. — With portrait. Warner Lib. **14** : 8071.

— " The American." Hazeltine. Chats, 72.

— as critic. Buchanan, R. Coming terr. 145.

— Novels. Nichol, J. Amer. lit. 389.

James, John. Ivimey. Eng. Bapt. **1** : 320.

James, John Angell. Stanton, H. B. Reforms, 224.

James, John H. Wesley & successors, 213.

James, John Warren. Loring, J. S. Hundred Bost. ora. 460.

James, Maria. Griswold. Fem. poets, 66.

James, Ralph. Ivimey. Eng. Bapt. **2** : 283.

James, Thomas C. (1766-1835). (Casper Morris) Gross. Lives physicians, 338.

James, Thomas L., with portrait. Butterfield. Lec. Un. Coll. **1** : 401.

James, Sir William M. Davenport, R. A. Lives, 308. — With photo. Cooper, T. Men of mark, **4** : 15. — Gener. of judges, 95. — Grant, J. Recoll. Lords & Comm. **2** : 221.

Jameson, Mrs. Anna. Belloc. Vignettes, 439. — Martineau, H. Biog. sk. 113. — Duyckinck. Portrait gall. **2** : 12. — Hall, S. C. Book of mem. 374. — With portrait. Hamilton, C. J. Wom. writers, **2** : 24. — Horne, R. H. New spirit, 233. — Saunders. Charac. studies, 31.

Jameson, Mrs., In Rome with. Belloc, Mme. Walled garden, 64.

— Memoirs and essays. Ossoli. Woman, 288.

Jamestown Ford, Va., Action at. Dawson. Batt. of U. S. **1** : 701.

Jamestown, Va. Terhune. Colon. homes, 471.

Jāmī. (A. V. W. Jackson) Warner Lib. **14** : 8110.

Jamieson, George W. Winter, W. Shadows, **2** : 113.

Jamieson, John. Blaikie, W. G. Preachers Scot. 214.

Jamieson, Robert. Wilson, J. G. Poets of Scot. **2** : 37.

Jamison, David. Field, R. S. Prov. courts N. J. 91.

Jamrach, Animal-dealer. Buckland, F. T. Curios. nat. hist. **4** : 111.

Jamyn, Amadis. Cary. Fr. poets, 264.

Janauschek, Madame. Griffin, G. W. Stud. in lit. — (P. Hale) McKay, F. E. Fam. actors, 18.

Jane Beaufort, queen of Scotland. Holt, E. S. Roy. ladies, v. **1.**

Jane Seymour, Queen. With portrait. Howitt, M. Queens, 300. — Lodge. Portraits (Bohn), v. **1.** — Strickland. Queens Eng. v. **4.** — Lancelot. Queens, v. **1.**

Jane of Navarre, Queen. Bush, A. F. Queens of F. **1** : 282.

Jane of France, Queen. Bush, A. F. Queens of F. **1** : 259.

Janes, Edm. S., bishop. Bungay. Off-hand, 377.

Janes, Heman, with portrait. Rogers, A. C. Repres. men, 331.

Janeway, John. Pierce, B. K. Em. dead, 112.

Janin, Jules, and Balzac. Zola. Exper. novel. 342.

Janissaries, The. Utterton, F. A. Biog. sk. 214.

Jansen, Cornelius. Tollemache. French Jansen, 1.

Jansen, Ellert. Brown, J. N. Bapt. martyrs, 67.

Johnston, Peyton, jr. Walker, C. D. Biog. Va. Mil. Inst. 294.

Johnston, Richard M. Davidson, J. W. Writ. of South, 298. — With portrait. Warner Lib. 14 : 8317.

— Bibliography. (S. B. Weeks) South. Hist. Assoc. Pub. Oct. '98 : 318.

Johnston, Chancellor Samuel. Livingston, J. Em. Am. lawy. 72.

Johnston, Mrs. Sarah R. Brockett. Woman's work, 269.

Johnston, William Freame, with portrait. Armor. Gov. of Pa. 403.

Johnstone, Chevalier de, Adventures of. Davenport. Narr. peril, 2 : 47.

Johnstone, Charles. Scott, W. Biog. mem. v. 1.

Johnstone, Robert. Irving, D. Scot. writ. 1 : 291.

Johnstone family. Taylor, J. Fam. of Scot. 2 : 54.

Johnstoun, John. Wodrow. Selec. fr. biog. coll.

Johnstown flood, 1889. Godbey. Great disasters, 324.

— A lesson in value of organized charity. (L. S. Emery) Conf. char. & correc. 90 : 43.

Johonnot, Andrew. (J. W. Dean) N. E. Hist.-Gen. Soc. Biog. 4 : 118.

Joint-stock companies of 1807–8. Francis, J. Stock exch. 72.

Joint-stock company (limited), Autobiography of. Oliphant, L. Traits, 106.

Joint-stock undertakings, Protection of shareholders in. (J. O. Chadwick) Trans. Soc. Sci. Lond. 79 : 567.

Joinville, Jean de, and St. Louis. Stephen, J. F. Horæ Sabb. 1 : 1.

Jókai, Maurus. With portrait. (E. Reich) Warner Lib. 14 : 8331. — Zimmern. For. novelists, 1 : 329.

Jokers, A chapter on. Hazlitt, W. C. Offspring, 240.

— Royal and imperial. Doran. Drury Lane, 2 : 327.

Joliet, Louis. Greely, A. W. Explorers, 9.

Jomelli, Nicolo, Italian musician. Hogarth. Mem. opera, 2 : 72.

Jonah. Geikie, C. Old Test. char. 360.

Jones, Agnes Eliz. Hack. Self-surr. 321. — Blaikie, W. G. Leaders, 301. — Fawcett, M. G. Em. wom. 91. — Japp, A. H. Golden lives, 314.

Jones, Chas. A. Coggeshall. Poets of west, 203.

Jones, Charles Colcock. Am. Antiq. Soc. Proc. n. s. 9 : 27. — Am. Bar Assoc. 16 : 417.

Jones, David. Lossing. Em. Amer. 140.

Jones, Mrs. Dorothy, of the West Indies. Pitman, Mrs. Heroines mission. 175.

Jones, Capt. E. W. (A. J. Bates) Shea, J. G. Fallen braves.

Jones, Edmund. Hatfield, E. F. Poets of ch. 353. — Miller, Jos. Singers church, 2d ed. 333.

Jones, Sir Edward Burne-. Monkhouse, C. Brit. contemp. artists, 119. — Bate, P. H. Eng. Pre-Raph. 103. — Smalley. Stud. 180. — Wedmore, F. Studies, 2 : 203.

— and G. F. Watts. Ruskin. Art of Eng. 29.

— Essay on. (S. Colvin) Atkinson, J. B., et al. Eng. paint. 7.

Jones, Ernest C. Miles, A. H. Poets of cent. 4 : 547.

Jones, Francis B. Walker, C. D. Biog. Va. Mil. Inst. 299.

Jones, George. Derby, J. C. Fifty years, 363.

Jones, H. Bolton. Sheldon, G. W. Amer. painters, 180.

Jones, Henry, bp. of Meath, 1660. Morgan, J. Four biog. sk.

Jones, Henry A. Archer. Eng. drama. 220. — Walkley, A. B. Playhouse, 111.

Jones, Henry J. Walker, C. D. Biog. Va. Mil. Inst. 310.

Jones, Hetty H. Brockett. Woman's work, 783.

Jones, Inigo. Milizia. Lives arch. 2 : 158. — Wrangham. Brit. Plutarch, v. 1.

Jones, Isaac D. Am. Bar Assoc. 16 : 426.

Jones, James Athearn. (R. L. Pease) N. E. Hist.-Gen. Soc. Biog. 2 : 204.

Jones, John, Attempts in verse ; with an account of his life, by himself. Southey. Uned. poets, 169.

Jones, John Paul. With portrait. [Amer.] Nat. portr. gall. v. 3. — Cooper, J. F. Am. nav. off. 2 : 5. — With portrait. Duyckinck. Nat. portr. gall. 1 : 157. — Glazier, W. Heroes, 118. — With portrait. Headley, J. T. Washington, 2 : 326. — Laughton. Stud. nav. hist. 363. — Parton. Peop. bk. biog. 334. — With portrait. Seymour, C. C. B. Self-made, 303. — Johnston, A. Amer. ora. 4 : 347. — Lossing. Em. Amer. 95. — Wise, D. Vanq. victors, 13.

Jones, J. Rice, 1759–1824. Chicago Hist. Soc. Coll. 4 : 230. — Woollen. Biog. sk. Indiana, 373.

Jones, John Winter. Garnett, R. Ess. in librarianship, 304.

Jones, Joseph. Am. Antiq. Soc. Proc. n. s. 11 : 17.

Jones, Major Joseph, of Pineville, pseud. See Thompson, W. T.

Jones, Justus. Winkworth. Chr. singers Germ. 115.

Jones, Lieut. L. L. Shea, J. G. Fallen brave.

Jones, Rev. M. Redding. Misers, 1 : 107.

Jones, Nathaniel. Field, R. S. Prov. courts N. J. 151.

Jones, Noble W. Jones, C. C., jr. Deleg. fr. Georgia, 124.

Jones, Samuel. Pollard. Life of Lee, 530.

Jones, Thomas. Great mod. preachers.

Jones, Tom. Whitehead, C. Highwaymen, 1 : 172.

Jones, Walter Restored. (W. A. Jones) Hunt, F. Am. merch. 1 : 415.

Jones, Sir William. Adams, W. H. D. Learned in law, 291. — Chambers's Miscel. no. 152. — Chalmers. Eng. poets, 18 : 427. — Craik. Pursuit of knowl. 1 : 107. — Edgar. Boyhood, 323. — Lodge. Portraits (Bohn), v. 8. — Nicoll, H. J. Gr. scholars, 199. — Roscoe, H. Em. lawyers, 2 : 109. — With portrait. Seymour, C. C. B. Self-made, 469. — Taylor, W. C. Mod. Brit. Plut. 222. — Cooper, T. Triumphs of Persev. 4. — Edwards, B. B. Self-taught, 594. — Wrangham. Brit. Plutarch, v. 6.

Jones, William, curate of Nayland. Teale. Eng. div. 343.

Jonkovsky. Wolknosky. Lowell lec. 181.

Jonson, Ben. Alden, R. M. Rise of satire, 192. — Austin and Ralph. Poets laureate, 49. — Collier, W. F. Hist. Eng. lit. 162. — Chalmers. Eng. poets, 5 : 443. — Crofts, E. Chap. Eng. lit. 232. — Dunham. Lit. & sci. men, 2 : 31. — Fuller. Worthies, 2 : 424. — Hazlitt. Comic. — Hazlitt. Dram. Eliz. — Taine. Eng. lit. 1 : 267. — (A W. Ward) Ward. Eng. poets, 2 : 1. — Ward, A. W. Eng. dram. 1 : 514. — Whipple. Lit. Eliz. 85. — Wotton. Word portraits, 152. — Crawford, O. Eng. com. dram. 11. —

Gosse, E. Jacobean poets, 213. — Hamilton, Wal. Poets laureate. — Griswold, R. W. Sac. poets. — Hunt, L. Men, wom. & books, 196. — Macdonald, G. England's antiphon, 131. — Minto, W. Eng. poets, 337. — Mitford, M. R. Recollec. 240. — Morley, H. Eng. writ. 10 : 387. 11 : 218. — Russell, W. C. Book of au. 44. — Thomson, Jas. (B. V.) Biog. ess. 80. — With portrait. (B. Wendell) Warner Lib. 14 : 8341. — Wrangham. Brit. Plutarch, v. 2.

Jonson, Ben, and Decker. Disraeli, I. Calam. 2.
— and his school. Ulrici. Shakespeare's dramatic art, 1 : 280.
— his mother. Knight. Once on time, 1 : 194.
— Humors of. Disraeli, I. Amen. (N. Y. 2 v.) 2 : 241.
— Masques of. Hogarth. Mem. opera, 1 : 49.
— Notes on. Coleridge. Lit. rem. 2 : 268.
— Skull of. Buckland, F. T. Curios. nat. hist. 4 : 238.
— Sonnets of. Deshler. Afternoons, 84.

Joppa. Warner, C. D. Levant, 1.

Jordan, Mrs. Cornelia J. M. Davidson, J. W. Writ. of South, 299. — Raymond, I. Southland wr. 2 : 811.

Jordan, Mrs. Dorothy Bland. Baker, H. B. Engl. actors, 2 : 98. — Doran. Annals stage, 2 : 344. — Galt. Players, 2 : 234. — Hunt. Crit. ess. on performers, 161. — Matthews, B. Actors, 2 : 133. — Doran. Their maj. serv. 2 : 478. — Lennox, W. P. Plays, 1 : 45.

Jordan, John. Winslow, S. N. Biog. Phila. merch. 24.

Jordan, Thomas. Davidson, J. W. Writ. of South, 304.

Jordan, The river. Bellows. Old world, 2 : 305.
— Lee, J. S. Sac. cities, 112.
— and the Dead Sea. Porter, J. L. Giant cities, 99.
— Valley of the. Kean, J. Among holy places, 145.

Jörgensen, Jörgen. Wraxall, F. C. L. Remark. adv. 2 : 184.

Jortin, John. Wrangham. Brit. Plutarch, v. 6.
— Works. Knox. Essays, 2 : 282.

Joseph, Patriarch. Geikie, C. Old Test. char. 68. — Wilberforce, S. Heroes Hebrew, 57.
— as a statesman. Monroe, Ja. Oberlin lec. 348.
— Story of : sacred idyl. Henry, C. S. Satan, 12.

Joseph I., emperor of Germany. Peake, Eliz. Germ. emperors, 387.

Joseph II., emperor of Germany. Brougham. Works, 5 : 344.
— History of. Peake, Eliz. Germ. emperors, 446.

Joseph II., of Austria. Merivale. Hist. stud. 1.

Joseph of Arimathea. Hastings, F. Obscure charac. 248.
— Garden of. Hoppin. Notes theol. stud. 231.

Joseph of the studium. Miller, Jos. Singers church, 2d ed. 19.

Josephine, Empress. Bush, A. F. Queens of F. 2 : 289. — Imbert de Saint-Amand. Famous women of the French court. — Russell. Extr. wom. 26. — With portrait. Fifty famous women, 22. — Gearey, C. Three empresses. — With portrait. Hubbard, E. Little journeys, 3 : 355.
— and Maria Louisa. Abbott. Kings & queens, 13.
— Queen Hortense and Caroline Bonaparte. Challice. Illus. wom. 49.

Josephus. (E. K. Mitchell) Warner Lib. 14 : 8361.
— Historical writings of. Malkin. Class. disq. 187.

Joshua. Geikie, C. Old Test. char. 126. — Wil-

berforce, S. Heroes Hebrew, 131. — Yonge, C. M. Book of worthies, 1.

Joshua (Book of) and Judges. (W. S. Tyler) Bost. lectures, '71 : 132.

Josiah. Geikie, C. Old Test. char. 387.

Josselyn, Robert. Hemenway. Poets of Vt. 86.

Joubert, Joseph. Arnold, M. Ess. in crit. v. 1.
— Ste.-Beuve. Monday chats, 185. — (T. W. Higginson) Warner Lib. 14 : 8385.

Jourdan, Jean B. Headley. Napoleon, 2 : 188.

Journal des savants and Journal des Trévoux. Müller. Chips, v. 3.

Journalism. Chaney, G. L. Every-day, 161. — Godwin, P. Out of past, 75. — Nordau. Conventional lies of civilization, 328.
— Catholic. Brownson. Works, 19 : 269.
— German. Spalding, J. L. Ess. & rev. 278.
— in France. Hayward, A. Ess. 2 : 99.
— Literary. Espinasse. Lit. recollec. 366.
— Protestant. Brownson. Works, 13 : 567.
— Truth in. Higginson. Book & heart, 87.

Journalist, young, Letter to. Lang. Ess. in lit. 191.

Journalistic life in London, Personal retrospect of. Escott. Politics, v. 1.

Journalists ; born or made. (E. M. Camp) Phila. Soc. Sci. Assoc. '88.

Journals, Class and trade. Hatton. Jour. Lond. 203.

Journey around the world. (B. R. Curtis) Am. Geog. Soc. 12 : 131.

Journeyings. Hazlitt. Table-talk.

Jovellanos. Kennedy. Poets of Spain, 3.

Jovius, Paulus, *or* Giovio. Symonds. Reviv. of learn. 417.

Jowett, Benjamin. Smalley. Lond. lett. 1 : 320.
— (W. W. Goodwin) Am. Acad. A. & S. Proc. 29 : 460. — Em. persons, 6 : 36. — Smalley. Stud. 151.
— and his personal influence. Tollemache. Ess. and mock-ess. 243.
— at Balliol College. Yates, E. H. Celeb. 3 : 95.
— Recollections of. Swinburne. Stud. prose & p. 26

Jowett, Mrs. Martha, of Malta. Pitman, Mrs. Heroines mission. 322.

Jowett, William. Miller, Jos. Singers church, 2d ed. 391.

Joy, Henry, Chief-baron. Sheil. Sk. Irish bar, 1 : 170.

Joy, Jansen. Redding. Misers, 2 : 86.

Joy, Emotion of. (G. V. N. Dearborn) Colum. Univ. Contrib. Philos. 4 : no. 4.
— of the moment. Mabie. My study fire, 2 : 74.

Joyce, James. Miller, Jos. Singers church, 2d ed. 449.

Joyce, Matthias. Jackson, T. Early Meth. 2 : 275.

Joyce, Thomas, Cardinal legate. Williams, R. F. Eng. card. 1 : 368.

Joyce, William. Burke, O. J. Cath. archb. 59.

Juana de Navarre, queen of Spain. Holt, E. S. Roy. ladies, v. 1.

Juarez, Benito. Duyckinck. Portr. gall. 2 : 124.

Juba, Col. Chaillé-Long on the. Am. Geog. Soc. 19 : 194.

Jubilee of 1450. Pastor, L. Hist. popes, 2 : 74.

Jubilee singers. Chambers, W. Rem. pers. 261.

Jucundus, Brother. Baring-Gould. Yorks. odd. 2 : 220.

Judæo-Arabic metaphysics. Deutsch. Lit. rem. 191.

Judah. Geikie, C. Old Test. char. 61.
— and Ephraim. (C. R. Conder) Wilson, C. W. Pictur. Palest. 1 : 193.

Junius, Woodfall's. Foster, J. Crit. ess. (Bohn) 2 : 72.

Junks and sampans. Cumming, C. F. G. Wand. in China, 1 : 369.

"**Junon**," frigate, Attack on. Dawson. Batt. of U. S. 2 : 250.

Jupiter, Planet, with bibliography. Todd, D. P. Stars and tel. 150.

— Cloud masses of. Proctor, R. A. Fam. sci. 60.

— the giant of the solar system. Proctor. Borderland, 86.

— Red spot on. Proctor, R. A. Other suns, 196.

— Satellites of. Proctor, R. A. Mysteries, 259.

— Temperature of. Proctor. Light sci. 3 : 177.

Juries ; Are they judges of the law ? Curtis, B. R. Mem. & writ. v. 2.

— deciding by majority. Genin, T. H. Selec. writ.

Jurisprudence. Pollock. Oxford lectures, 1 : 37.

— American. Baldwin. Mod. polit. inst. 239.

— and law reform, Report of committee on. Am. Bar Assoc. 2 : 193.

— Austin on. Mill, J. S. Dissert. (N. Y.) 4 : 210.

— British. (Sir R. J. Phillimore) Trans. Soc. Sci. Lond. '65 : 17. — (Sir J. D. Coleridge) Trans. Soc. Sci. Lond. '72 : 28.

— comparative, Study of. (W. W. Howe) Am. Bar Assoc. 22 : 567.

— considered as a branch of social science. (J. M. Woolworth) Am. Bar Assoc. 11 : 279.

— English opportunities in historical and comparative. Pollock, F. Oxf. lec. 37.

— Evolution of. (W. W. McFarland) Am. Bar Assoc. 16 : 271.

— in U. S., Opportunity for development of. (J. T. Platt) Am. Bar Assoc. 9 : 215.

— medical, Importance of, in law schools. (N. S. Davis) Am. Bar Assoc. 18 : 469.

— Methods of. Pollock, F. Oxf. lec. 1.

— Nature of. Pollock. Ess. in juris. 1.

— Reasons for study of. Lorimer, Jas. Studies, nat'l & internat.

— study of, The East and. Maine. Vill.-com. 1.

Jurkievicius. Wallace, R. Anti-Trin. biog. 3 : 127.

Jury, Trial by. (J. H. Choate) Am. Bar Assoc. 21 : 285. — Bancroft, H. H. Essays, 280. — Budd, H. St. Mary's Hall lec. 94. — (J. Brown et al.) Trans. Soc. Sci. Lond. '82 : 147. — Bancroft, H. H. Works, 38 : 280.

— — in England, 1784. Hopkinson, F. Miscel. 2 : 194.

— — Right of. Black, J. S. Ess. & sp. 510.

— — Should verdicts be unanimous ? (W. Forsyth et al.) Trans. Soc. Sci. Lond. '74 : 164.

Jury laws, British. (J. Brown ; J. G. S. MacNeil) Trans. Soc. Sci. Lond. '81 : 139.

Jury system, European modifications of. (W. B. Scaife) Am. Hist. Assoc. Rept. '94 : 125.

— of U. S., How can it be improved ? (S. Zeisler ; I. N. Stiles) Sunset Club Echoes, 210.

Justice. Bryant, S. Short stud. 17. — Goldsmith. Miscel. (N. Y. 4 v.) 1 : 61. — Hume. Philos. works, 2 : 240. 4 : 244. — Holland, E. G. Reviews, 375. — Bax. Ethics of socialism, 75.

— Natural. Bunce, O. B. Bach. bluff, 269.

— Theory of. Whittaker, T. Ess. & not. 186.

Justification, Doctrine of. (B. Jowett) Noyes, G. R. Theol. ess. 239. — Green, T. H. Works, 3 : 190. — Maurice, F. D. Theol. ess. 189. — Whedon. Ess. 1 : 131.

Justin the martyr, St. With portrait. Blakey, R. Prim. fathers, 79. — Cave. Lives of fathers, 1 : 228. — Evans, R. W. Biog. early

church, 1 : 122. — Farrar. Lives of fathers, 1 : 93. — Pressensé. Martyrs, 243, 531. — Bury. Later Roman empire, 1 : 333. — Hort, F. J. A. Ante-N. fathers, 49. — (Canon Meyrick) Lefroy, W. Lec. eccl. hist. 53.

Justinian. Mombert. Great lives, 115.

Justus, 624–627. Hook. Abps. Cant. 1 : 99.

Jute culture. N. J. Labor, '78 : 90. '79 : 157. '82 : 177. '83 : 319.

Jutland. Gibson, W. S. Miscel. 74.

Juvenal. Hannay. Satire, 7. — Vincent, G. E. Ital. authors, 54. — (T. B. Lindsay) Warner Lib. 14 : 8411.

— Bibliography. West. Reserve Univ. Bull. Oct. '95.

— Life and poems of. Nettleship. Lec. & ess. 117.

Juvenile crime, Police and. (F. L. Jenkins) Conf. char. & correc. '84 : 285.

Juvenile criminals, Reform of. Whittier. Lit. recre. 29.

Juvenile delinquency. (C. Scott et al.) Trans. Soc. Sci. Lond. '80 : 357. — (G. W. Goler) Conf. char. & correc. '96 : 352.

Juvenile delinquents, Christian duty of caring for. (F. Merrick) N. Y. Pris. Assoc. 26, app. : 429.

— Duty of the State to. (P. Caldwell) Conf. char. & correc. '98 : 494.

— Education, training, etc. of. (J. Allison) Conf. char. & correc. '98 : 411.

— Family visitation of, in Mass. (G. Tufts) N. Y. Pris. Assoc. 26, app. : 359.

— Obligation of State to. (W. G. Fairbanks) Conf. char. & correc. '95 : 238.

— Physical training of. (H. D. Wey) Nat. Pris. Assoc. '88 : 181.

— Schools of discipline for. (A. Hill et al.) Trans. Soc. Sci. Lond. '84 : 246.

— Treatment of. Mass. Charity, 1869, 6 : 9. — (A. G. Madison) Conf. char. & correc. '84 : 195.

— — in courts. (T. C. S. Kynnersley) Trans. Soc. Sci. Lond. '60 : 465.

Juvenile reformatory, Seven years in a. (F. H. Briggs) Conf. char. & correc. '97 : 121.

Juventus mundi. Fiske. Myths, 174. — Warner, C. D. As we go, 73.

Juxon, William, Bishop, 1660–63. Fuller. Worthies, 3 : 250. — Hook. Abps. Cant. 11 : 394.

Kabbala, The. Heckethorn. Sec. soc. 1 : 119. (S. A. Binion) Warner Lib. 15 : 8425.

Kabir-Pauthis. Barth, A. Relig. India, 239.

Kaempfer, E. St. John. Cel. travellers, 1 : 271.

Kaercher, George R. Am. Bar Assoc. 14 : 447.

Kaffraria, Visit to, 1883. Hübner. Thro. Brit. empire, 1 : 70.

— War in. Chambers's Repos. no. 33.

Kaibar, Siege of. Robson, W. Sieges, 371.

Kailasa, Temple of. Adams, W. H. D. Fam. caves, 54.

Kaiserswerth, Fleidner's institutions at. Stevenson. Praying & w. 107.

Kalamazoo College, Mich. (S. Haskell) U. S. Bur. Ed. Circ. '91, no. 4 : 133.

Kalb, Johann de. Headley, J. T. Washington, 2 : 318. — Lossing. Em. Amer. 291. — Wraxall. Remark. adv. 1 : 191.

Kalevala ; Finnish national epic. Lang. Custom, 156. — (W. Sharp) Warner Lib. 15 : 8443.

Kālidāsa. (A. V. W. Jackson) Warner Lib. 15 : 8455.

Kalisch, M. M. Cheyne. Founders, O. T. crit. 204.

Kamakura, Japan. Pidgeon. Engineer's holiday, 263.

Kames, Henry Home, Lord. McCosh. Scot. phil. 173. — Mitchell. Wet days, 221. — Foster, J. Crit. ess. (Bohn) 1 : 63.

Kamtschatka, Dog-sledge journey in. (G. Kennan) Am. Geog. Soc. 8 : 96.

Kane, Elisha Kent. With portrait. Bolton, S. K. Fam. voyag. 290. — With portrait. Greely, A. W. Explorers, 240. — Bungay. Off-hand, 205. — Duyckinck. Nat. portr. gall. 2 : 284. — Lanman, C. Haphazard, 243. — Thayer, W. M. Turn.-points, 93.

— The rescue party. Yonge. Gold. deeds.

Kangaroos. Wilson, A. Nat. note-book, 203.

Kankakee river, Sanitary problem of. (J. L. Campbell) Am. Pub Health, 7 : 279.

Kansas. Whittier. Prose, v. 3.

— Admission of. Seward. Works (1884), 4 : 479. — Kansas. Hist. Soc. Collec. *passim.*

— — Against the. Davis, H. W. Speeches, 83.

— The crime against. Sumner. Works, 4: 125.

— Immigration into, 1855. (Goodnow) Kansas Hist. Soc. Coll. 4 : 244.

— must be free, 1856. Godwin, P. Pol. ess. 307.

— the saviour of freedom. Seward. Works ('84), 4 : 385.

— Speech on affairs in, 1856. Emerson, R. W. Miscel. ('83) 241.

Kansas City. Warner, C. D. Studies, 348.

— Municipal condition of. (H. Hopkins) Nat. Conf. City. Govt. '97 : 233.

— Sewer system of. (E. Butts) Am. Pub. Health, 17 : 44.

Kant, Immanuel. Frothingham. Transcend. 5 : 14. — Hedge. Atheism, 271. — Hedge. Prose Ger. 57. — Lewes. Biog. phil. — Seymour, C. C. B. Self-made, 101. — Hundred greatest men, 255. — Osborn. From Greeks, 98. — Royce, J. Spir. mod. philos. 101. — With portrait. (J. Royce) Warner Lib. 15 : 8477. — Webb, T. E Veil of Isis, 165.

— and his English critics, J. Watson on. Green, T. H. Works, 3 : 147.

— and his essays. DeQuincey. Phil. writ. (Bost.) 1 : 101 ; *or* Works (Masson), 2 : 81.

— and the Kantian revival. Tulloch. Mod. theories, 377.

— as a logician and moralist. Courtney. Stud. philos. 164.

— "Back to." Courtney. Stud. philos. 135.

— Bibliography [German works]. Philos. Rev. '93–94.

— Centen'l of, 1881. Porter, N. Sci. & sent. 412.

— Critic of pure reason. Brownson. Works, 1 : 130.

— DeQuincey and Coleridge on. Stirling, J. H. Jerrold, 172.

— Ethics of. (W. M. Washington) Colum. Univ. Contrib. Philos. 3 : no. 1.

— German language and philosophy of. De Quincey. Uncoll. writ. 1 : 91.

— Goethe, and Schiller, Triumvirate of. Hillebrand. Ger. thought, 173.

— Habits of. Hamerton. Intellec. 10.

— Inaugural dissertation, 1770. (W. J. Eckoff) Colum. Univ. Contrib. Philos. 1 : no. 2.

— Last days of. DeQuincey. Miscel. pap. (Bost.) 2 : 233.

— Lectures on the philosophy of. Green, T. H. Works, 2 : 1.

— Philosophy of. Green, T. H. Works, 3 : 126. Mansel. Letters, 157.

— Spinoza to. Royce, J. Spir. mod. philos. 68.

Karamsin, N. M. Wolkonsky. Lowell lec. 175.

Karcher, Théo. Rienzi. Cracroft. Ess. 2 : 152.

Karlstein, Castle. Schlegel. Æsthet. (Bohn) 400.

Karnak. Bellows. Old world, 2 : 180.

— Temples at. Buckley, J. M. Trav. 3 cont. 280.

Karnievius, Peter. Wallace, R. Anti-Trin. biog. 3 : 141.

Karpinski, Francis. Soboleski. Poets of Poland, 111.

Karr, Alphonse. Van de Velde. Fr. fic. 2 : 225.

Karslake, Sir John. Gener. of judges, 183.

Käsegrotto, Die. Adams, W. H. D. Fam. caverns, 15.

Kashgar. Younghusband. Heart of cont. 306.

Kashmir. Myers, P. V. N. Rem. lost empires, 341.

Katahdin, Mt. Winthrop, T. Open air, 88.

Kater, Capt. Henry. Waiker, W., jr. Men of sci. 75.

Katharine, princess of Schwartzburg. Chapman, W. Wom. of ref. 129.

Katherine of Valois, queen of Henry V. Strickland. Queens Eng. v. 3. — With portrait. Howitt, M. Queens, 169.

Katharine of Arragon. Burke, S. H. Hist. portr. Tudor, 1 : 370. — Finch. Princesses of Wales, 1 : 191. 2 : 1. — With portrait. Howitt, M. Queens, 241. — Strickland. Queens Eng. v. 4. — Lancelott. Queens, v. 1.

— and her divorce. Burke, S. H. Men of reforma. 1 : 23.

— Marriages of. Gairdner & Spedding. Stud. 78 : 142.

Katherine Howard, Queen. Howitt, M. Queens, 313. — Strickland. Queens Eng. v. 4. — Lancelott. Queens, v. 1.

Katherine Parr, Queen. Bethune, G. W. Brit. fem. poets, 17. — Burder. Pious wom. 22. — With portrait. Howitt, M. Queens, 318. — Lodge. Portraits (Bohn), v. 1. — Strickland. Queens Eng. v. 5. — Williams, Jane. Lit. wom. 44. — Burke, S. H. Hist. portr. Tudor, 2 : 183. — Lancelott. Queens, v. 1.

Katherine of Braganza. *See* Catherine.

Katherine of France, queen of England. Lancelott. Queens, v. 1. — Lawrance. Queens, v. 2.

Katherine, daughter of Henry III. Green, M. A. E. Princesses, 2 : 270.

Kavanagh. Julia. (Mrs. K. S. Macquoid) Oliphant. Wom. novelists, 251.

Kávéripak. Malleson, G. B. Battles of India, 18.

Kauffman, Andrew John. Am. Bar Assoc. 22 : 698.

Kauffman, Angelica, Swiss painter. Clayton, E. C. Eng. fem. art. 1 : 233. — Ellet. Women artists, 144. — Spooner. Biog. fine arts, 1 : 434.

— Bibliography. Gerard, F. A. Angel. Kauffmann.

Kauffman, Benj. F. Am. Bar Assoc. 16 : 422.

Kaunitz, Wenceslaus Anthony von. Wraxall. Remark. adv. 1 : 296.

Kay, John. Austin & Ralph. Laureates, 17. — Espinasse. Lanc. worth. v. 1. — Towle, G. M. Heroes of inven. 72. — Woodcroft, B. Biog. invent. v. 1.

Kaye, John. *See* Caius.

Kaye, Sir J. W., with portrait. Laurie, W. F. B. Dist. Anglo-Ind. 1 : 153.

Keach, Benjamin. Ivimey. Eng. Bapt. 1 : 339. 2 : 360. 3 : 409.

Keach, Elias. Ivimey. Eng. Bapt. 2 : 467. 3 : 534.

Kean, Charles John. Cook, D. Hours w. players, 2 : 232. — Lewes. Actors, 12. — Matthews,

Kellogg, Clara Louise. (H. P. Spofford) Our fam. wom. 359. — (W. Winter) Parton. Em. wom. 462.

Kellogg, Prof. Ebenezer, Sermon on death of. Hopkins, M. Miscel. ess. 311.

Kelly, Benjamin Eddy. Bartlett, J. R. R. I. officers, 439.

Kelly, Charles Henry. Wesley & successors, 255.

Kelly, Dennis. Winslow, S. N. Biog. Phila. merch. 158.

Kelly, Edward (1855–80). (J. W. Allen) Seccombe, T. Twelve bad men, 322.

Kelly, Sir Fitzroy. With photo. Cooper, T. Men of mark, 4 : 11. — Gener. of judges, 38.

Kelly, Henry B. Am. Bar Assoc. 17 : 499.

Kelly, Jas. Madison. Miller, S. F. Bench of Ga. v. 2.

Kelly, Oliver. Burke, O. J. Cath. archb. 229.

Kelly, Patrick. Clarke, R. H. Cath. bishops, 1 : 268.

Kelly, Thomas. Curwen. Booksellers, 363. — Famous boys, 269. — Hatfield, E. F. Poets of church, 362. — Miles, A. H. Poets of cent. 10 : 664. — Miller, Jos. Singers church, 2d ed. 337.

Kelly, Thos. J. Savage, J. Fenian heroes, 163.

Kelsey, Ambrose Parsons. (E. North) N. Y. Regents, 105 : 494.

Kelynge, Sir John, chief justice of England, 1663–71. Campbell. Ch. just. 1 : 401. — Woolrych. Serjeants, 1 : 396.

Kemble, Adelaide. Jameson. Studies.

— and the lyrical drama, Aug. 1843. Jameson. Mem. & ess. 43.

Kemble, Charles. Donne, W. B. Ess. on drama, 156. — Doran. Annals stage, 2 : 279. — Hunt. Critical essays on the performers, 223. — Matthews, B. Actors, 2 : 217. — Russell, W. Rep. actors, 309. — Marston, J. W. Rec. actors, 1 : 109.

— and Mrs. Charles, Notes on. Murdoch, J. E. Stage, 198.

Kemble, Frances Anne. Bethune, G. W. Brit. fem. poets, 434. — Duyckinck. Portr. gall. 2 : 633. — James, H. Ess. in Lond. 81. — Matthews, B. Actors, 3 : 239. — (J. Parton) Parton. Em. wom. 102. — (A. H. Japp) Miles, A. H. Poets of cent. 7 : 253.

— First appearance of. Talfourd. Crit. wr.

— Readings. Willis. Hurry-graphs, 182.

Kemble, Mrs. Maria Theresa Decamp. Badeau. Vagabond, 242. — Doran. Annals stage, 2 : 281.

Kemble, John Philip. Brereton, A. Hamlets, 21. — Doran. Annals stage, 2 : 264. — Duyckinck. Portr. gall. 1 : 240. — Galt. Players, 2 : 250. — Hunt. Crit. ess. on performers, 5. — Matthews, B. Actors, 2 : 65. — Russell, W. Rep. actors, 239.

— Retirement of. Hazlitt. Crit. & dram. ess.

— Tieck's remarks on. Murdoch, J. E. Stage, 387.

Kemble family. Baker, H. B. Engl. actors, 2 : 3.

Kembles, Days of the. Whyte, F. Actors of cent. 7, 17, 36.

Kemp, George, architect. Smiles. Self-help.

Kemp, John, cardinal bishop. Campbell. Ld. chan. 1 : 292. — Hook. Abps. Cant. 5 : 188. — Williams, R. F. Eng. card. 2 : 110. — Simson, Jas. Em. men of Kent, 96. — Williams, F. Eng. card. 2 : 110.

Kemp, William. Collier. Actors, 89.

Kempenfelt, Richard, Admiral. Hatfield, E. F. Poets of church, 365. — Rogers, C. Chr'n heroes, 1.

Kempis, Thomas à. Hodgson, Wm. Reformers, 179. — Ullman. Reformers, 114. — (J. Malone) Warner Lib. 15 : 8529.

— Imitation of Christ. Renan. Leaders, 93. — Farrar, F. W. Great books, 291.

— — Spiritual sense of. Mullany. Phases of tho't, 89.

— Life and writings of. Butler, Chas. Works, v. 3.

Kempthorne, John. Hatfield, E. F. Poets of church, 368.

Ken, Thomas, bishop. Adams, W. H. D. Gt. churchm. 418. — Edgar. Boyhood, 337. — Strickland. Bishops, 234. — Hatfield, E. F. Poets of church, 369. — Macdonald, G. England's antiphon, 268. — Miller, Jos. Singers church, 2d ed. 103.

Kendal, Madge Robertson [Mrs. W. H.]. Winter. Shadows, 3 : 264.

Kendal, W. H., with portraits. Goddard, A. Players, 2 : 85.

Kendall, George W. Bungay. Off-hand, 218.

Kendall, May. Miles, A. H. Poets of cent. 9 : 613.

Kenilworth, Eng. Silloway. Cathedral towns, 175. — Stowe. Sunny mem. 1 : 243. — Thomson, K. B. Recollec. 1. — Winter, W. Shakespeare's Eng.

Kenilworth castle. Stone, J. S. Heart of Engl. 386.

Kenjin Kasawara. Müller. Biog. ess. 211.

Kenmure, Jane Campbell, viscountess of. Chapman, W. Wom. of cov. 9.

Kenmure, William Gordon, earl of. Thomson, Mrs. Jacobites, 2 : 71.

Kenna, John E., with portrait. Scott, H. W. Dist. Am. lawy. 495.

Kennard, John E. Am. Bar Assoc. 10 : 410.

Kennard, Mary E., with portrait. Black, H. C. Wom. authors, 172.

Kennedy, Andrew. Woollen. Biog. sk. Indiana, 281.

Kennedy, B. Hall. Miller, Jos. Singers church, 2d ed. 478.

Kennedy, Captain. Whitehead, C. Highwaymen, 2 : 93.

Kennedy, Henry W., the blind officer. Silliman. Gallop, 283.

Kennedy, J. Leland. Davidson, J. W. Writ. of South, 306.

Kennedy, John Pendleton. Davidson, J. W. Writ. of South, 307. — Griswold. Prose writ. 341. — Richardson. Amer. lit. 2 : 397.

Kennedy, William. Wilson, J. G. Poets of Scot. 2 : 213.

Kennet, Basil. Holland, J. Psalmists, 2 : 126.

Kenrick, Francis Patrick. Clarke, R. H. Cath. bishops, 1 : 473.

Kenrick, John. Martineau, J. Ess. '91, 1 : 397.

Kensett, J. F. Tuckerman. Artists, 510.

Kensington Palace. Timbs. Abbeys, 1 : 151.

Kent, Elizabeth, countess of. Williams, Jane. Lit. wom. 82.

Kent, Henry O., with portrait. Sketches N. H. men, 21.

Kent, James. With portrait. [Amer.] Nat. portr. gall. v. 2. — With portrait. Duyckinck. Nat. portr. gall. 2 : 39. — Griswold. Prose writ. 575. — Browne, I. Stud. gt. lawyers. 218. — Lossing. Em. Amer. 335. — (J. Kent) N. E. Hist.-Gen. Soc. Biog. 1 : 67. — With portrait. Scott, H. W. Dist. Am. lawy. 511.

— Commentaries on American law. Legaré. Writ. 2 : 102.

Kent, John. Miller, Jos. Singers church, 2d ed. 333.

Killinghall, John. Miller, Jos. Singers church, 2d ed. 156.

Kilmaine, C. J., French general. Grant, Jas. Cavaliers, 213.

Kilmarnock, William Boyd, earl of. Jesse. Pretenders, 399. — Thomson, Mrs. Jacobites, 3 : 381.

Kilpatrick, Hugh J. Glazier, W. Heroes, 375. — Headley, J. T. Grant & Sherman, 310.

Kilwardby, Robert, 1273–78. Hook. Abps. Cant. 3 : 304. — Williams, R. F. Eng. card. 1 : 345.

Kimball, Alonzo S. (T. C. Mendenhall) Am. Acad. Proc. 33 : 524.

Kimball, Charles P., with portrait. (B. D. Verrill) Rogers, A. C. Repres. men, 351.

Kimball, H. I. Parton, J. Sk. of men of prog.

Kimball, John, with portrait. Sketches N. H. men, 89.

Kimber, Isaac. Ivimey. Eng. Bapt. 4 : 217.

Kimberley, John Wodehouse, earl of. Escott, T. H. S. Pillars emp. 171. — Kent, C. Gladst. govt. 165.

Kimberley, Diamond mines of. Loomis, E. J. Eclipse party, 107.

Kimmont, Alex. Mansfield, E. D. Pers. mem. 270.

Kincheloe, James M. Walker, C. D. Biog. Va. Mil. Inst. 316.

Kinchin, Charles. Tyerman. Oxf. meth. 363.

Kindergarten. Hailman, W. N. Twelve lec. on pedagogy, 114. — Hurst, J. F. Life & lit. in fatherl. 82. — Newton, R. H. Social stud. 215. — Payne, J. Lec. sci. educa. 385. — Royce, S. Deterioration, 133.

— Allies of. (Caroline T. Haven) Nat. Educa. Assoc. '96 : 504.

— and prevention of crime. (R. H. Newton) Conf. char. & correc. '86 : 53.

— and primary school, Organic connection between. (Miss N. Cropsey) Nat. Educa. Assoc. '91 : 538. — (S. B. Cooper) Nat. Educa. Assoc. '93 : 336.

— as a basis for life. (Henrietta Schrader) Nat. Educa. Assoc. '93 : 346.

— as a character builder. (Mrs. S. B. Cooper) Conf. char. & correc. '85 : 222.

— as a child-saving work. Conf. char. & correc. '82 : 130.

— at educa. exhibit, N. E. A. meeting, St. Paul, 1890. (Josephine C. Locke) Nat. Educa. Assoc. '90 : 66.

— Bibliography. (A. Brooks) Cleveland (O.) Pub. Lib. Open Shelf, Nov. '94. — Osterhout (Wilkesbarre) Free Lib. Sept. '94.

— Character study in. (T. P. Bailey) Nat. Educa. Assoc. '99 : 541.

— city, The problem of. (Ellise B. Payne) Nat. Educa. Assoc. '96 : 510.

— Duty of the State in relation to. (A. S. Draper) Nat. Educa. Assoc. '92 : 174.

— Essential principles of. (Angeline Brooks) Nat. Educa. Assoc. '94 : 696.

— Essentials of. (Eudora Hailmann) Nat. Educa. Assoc. '85 : 364.

— Eye and ear cultivated by. (Lucy F. Wheelock) Nat. Educa. Assoc. '90 : 560.

— for blind children. Poulsson. How to learn.

— Games and plays in. (S. A. Stewart) Cong. Educa. Chic. '93, 328.

— in Austria. (O. Bondy) Cong. Educa. Chic. '93, 366.

— in the mother's work. (Elizabeth P. Bond) Nat. Educa. Assoc. '85 : 352.

— in relation to industrial products. (E. Heerwart) Internat. health exh. 13 : 96.

Kindergarten in its relation to motherhood. (Sarah B. Cooper) Nat. Educa. Assoc. '89 : 467.

— in St. Louis, History of. U. S. Bur. Ed. Rept. '96–97.

— Music in. (A. M. Stovall) Nat. Educa. Assoc. '99 : 559.

— Plea for. Peabody, E. P. Last evening, 331.

— Practical psychology in. (Constance Mackenzie) Nat. Educa. Assoc. '92 : 285.

— Practical results of ten years' work. (S. B. Cooper) Conf. char. & correc. '89 : 186.

— Preparation of. (L. P. Hopkins) Cong. Educa. Chic. '94, 344.

— Relation of imitation to originality. (M. F. Ledyard) Nat. Educa. Assoc. '99 : 547.

— Relation of, to history and literature in higher grades. (Sarah E. Wiltse) Nat. Educa. Assoc. '94 : 691.

— — to primary school. (J. W. Dickinson) Nat. Educa. Assoc. '85 : 360.

— — to public schools. (J. L. Hughes) Nat. Educa. Assoc. '94 : 483.

— — to social reform. (K. D. Wiggin) Conf. char. & correc. '88 : 247.

— — to the school. (W. T. Harris ; Lelia E. Patridge) Nat. Educa. Assoc. '79 : 142.

— Schoolishness in. (W. N. Hailmann) Nat. Educa. Assoc. '90 : 565.

— Social settlement and. (Amalie Hofer) Nat. Educa. Assoc. '95 : 514.

— Some criticisms of. (N. M. Butler) Nat. Educa. Assoc. '99 : 536.

— Song in. (C. Mackenzie) Cong. Educa. Chic. '93, 331.

— Story-telling in. (M. T. Hotchkiss) Cong. Educa. Chic. '93, 351.

— symbolism in, Use of. (E. Barnes and E. L. Hailmann) Cong. Educa. Chic. '93, 355, 356.

— teachers for, Training of. (Maria Kraus-Boelte) Nat. Educa. Assoc. '77 : 207.

— Use and abuse of, in America. (John Kraus) Nat. Educa. Assoc. '77 : 186.

Kindergarten child physically. (F. L. Burk) Nat. Educa. Assoc. '99 : 570.

Kindergarten education. (S. E. Blow) Butler, N. M. Educa. in U. S. 33.

Kindergarten exhibit at Cotton Centennial Exposition, New Orleans, '85. (W. N. Hailmann) Nat. Educa. Assoc. '85 : 546.

Kindergarten exhibits. (Mrs. L. T. Newcombe) Nat. Educa. Assoc. '91 : 49.

Kindergarten idea, Morality and intelligence in. (L. T. Newcomb) Nat. Educa. Assoc. '94 : 686.

Kindergarten methods in intellectual training. (Mrs. J. L. Hughes) Nat. Educa. Assoc. '91 : 533.

Kindergarten plays and games, Changes in. (Sarah A. Stewart) Nat. Educa. Assoc. '93 : 328.

Kindergarten spirit, Influence of, on higher education. (J. L. Hughes) Nat. Educa. Assoc. '96 : 378.

Kindergarten training, Influence of, on primary school. (Irwin Shepard) Nat. Educa. Assoc. '90 : 554.

— Value of, in normal schools. (Clara A. Burr) Nat. Educa. Assoc. '87 : 335.

Kindergarten training-school, Ideal. (C. H. M'Grew ; Mrs. Dohrmann ; Kate D. Wiggin) Nat. Educa. Assoc. '88 : 339.

Kindergarten work and principles in schools. (K. Beebe) Nat. Educa. Assoc. '97 : 604.

— at educa. exhibit, N. E. A. meeting, San Francisco, '88. (Nora A. Smith) Nat. Educa. Assoc. '88 : 710.

Kindergarten, Letter killeth in. (Anna E. Bryan) Nat. Educa. Assoc. '90 : 573.

Kindergartens, Free. (C. Mackenzie) Conf. char. & correc. '86 : 48.

— from an outsider's standpoint. (Helen E. Starrett) Nat. Educa. Assoc. '90 : 547.

— public, and écoles gardiennes in Europe, History and status of. (W. N. Hailmann) U. S. Bur. Ed. Rept. '90–91 : 676.

King, Daniel. Ivimey. Eng. Bapt. **2** : 577.

King, Daniel P. (B. C. Perkins) N. E. Hist.-Gen. Soc. Biog. **1** : 255.

King, David. Taylor, W. M. Scott. pulpit, 244.

King, Gen. Edward. Mansfield, E. D. Pers. mem. 263.

King, Miss E. M. Brockett. Woman's work, 789.

King, Geoffrey. McClure. Translators, 99.

King, Grace E., with portrait. Warner Lib. **15** : 8573.

King, Harriet M. Robertson. Eng. poets, 367.

King, Henry, bishop of Chichester. Griswold, R. W. Sac. poets. — Holland, J. Psalmists, **2** : 60.

King, Capt. James. Espinasse. Lanc. worth. v. 2.

King, James Gore, with portrait. (C. King) Hunt, F. Am. merch. **1** : 185.

King, Col. John Anthony. Senior. Biog. sk. 463.

King, Jonas. Edwards, B. B. Self-taught, 273.

King, Katharine. Clayton, E. C. Eng. fem. art. **2** : 307.

King, Peter, Lord. Brougham. Works, **4** : 155. — Campbell. Ld. chan. **6** : 59.— Senior. Biog. sk. 415. — Grant, J. Recoll. Lords, 70. — Welsby. Eng. judges.

King, Robert. Wallace, R. Anti-Trin. biog. **2** : 130.

King, Rufus. Am. Bar Assoc. **14** : 440. — With portrait. Amer. nat. portr. gall. 3. — With portrait. Duyckinck. Nat. portr. gall. **1** : 349. — Lossing. Em. Amer. 150.— Moore, F. Am. eloq. **2** : 33.

— Home of. (C. King) Homes Am. statesm. 355.

King, Mrs. Sue Pettigru. Davidson, J. W. Writ. of South, 313. — Raymond, I. Southland writ. **2** : 861.

King, Thomas. Cook, D. Hours w. players, **1** : 97. — Galt. Players, **2** : 128.

King, Thos. Starr. Allen, J. H. Sequel, 103. — (R. Frothingham) King, T. S. Patriotism, 13. — Loring, J. S. Hundred Bost. ora. 676. — Whipple. Charac.

— Character and genius of. Whipple. Amer. lit. 299.

King, Wm. (S. Johnson) Chalmers. Eng. poets, **9** : 237.

King, Wm. R. Everett. Orat. v. 3.

King, The. Doran. Monarchs, **1** : 1.

— and early civil justice. Maine. Early law, 160.

Kingdom coming. Dodge, M. A. Summer rest, 219.

Kingdom of God on earth, True nature of. Bosanquet. Ess. 108.

— Where is it ? Gladden. Burn. ques. 221.

Kinglake, Alexander W. Couch, A. T. Q. Adv. crit. 141. — Em. persons, **5** : 1. — With portrait. Warner Lib. **15** : 8599.

King's College, London, and Professor Momerie. Momerie. Fut. of relig. 77.

King's evil. *See* Healing by royal touch.

King's Mountain, S. C., Battle of. Dawson. Batt. of U. S. **1** : 628. — Lodge & Roosevelt. Hero-tales, 69.

King's peace. Pollock, F. Oxford lectures, 65.

Kings, British and Saxon, Dethroned. Doran. Monarchs, **1** : 70.

— Canonized. Doran. Monarchs, **1** : 60.

— Divine right of. (J. Gairdner) Gairdner & Spedding. Stud. 245. — Oxenham. Stud. in eccl. hist. 180.

— of England, as knights. Doran. Knights, 329.

— — Deposed. Doran. Monarchs, **1** : 85.

— of Hungary, Four deposed. Doran. Monarchs, **1** : 354.

— of Sardinia, Three crownless. Doran. Monarchs, **2** : 205.

— of Scotland, Deposed. Doran. Monarchs, **1** : 155.

— of Sweden. Doran. Monarchs, **2** : 233.

— Right of. Hume. Philos. works, **3** : 495.

— Scripture, and eastern monarchs. Doran. Monarchs, **1** : 31.

Kingsbury, William. Hatfield, E. F. Poets of church, 379. — Miller, Jos. Singers church, 2d ed. 288. — Morison, J. Fathers of Lond. Miss. Soc. **2** : 518.

Kingsbury Hall. Hodges, Eliz. Anc. Eng. Homes, 157.

Kingship, Constitutional. (A. Hassall) Wakeman & Hassall. Ess. introd. Eng. Const. 224.

Kingsley, Charles. Bayne, P. Ess. **2** : 9. — Davies, G. J. Suc. preach. 309.— Friswell. Mod. men of l. 313. — Griswold, H. T. Home-life, 363. — Japp. Good men, 197. — Lang. Ess. in lit. 153. — McCarthy, J. Mod. lead. 211. — Masson. Brit. novelists. — Müller. Biog. ess. 363. — (E. P. Whipple) Parton. Princes, 230. — Paul. Biog. sk. 115. — Stephen, L. Hours in libr. **3** : 365.— Tulloch. Movements in relig. thought, 286. — (W. E. Henley) Ward. Eng. poets, **4** : 608. — Wotton. Word portraits, 164. — Bolton, S. K. Fam. leaders, 261. — Cochrane, R. Gt. thinkers, 224.—(A. H. Japp) With portrait. Ewart, H. C. Leaders, 17. — Harrison, F. Stud. early Vict. 163.— Putnam, J. O. Addresses, 215.— With portrait. Warner Lib. **15** : 8611.

— Alton Locke. Phillips, S. Ess. from Times, **2** : 200.

— and Carlyle. Greg. Lit. & soc. judg. 115.

— and the Christian Socialists. Gibbins. Eng. soc. ref. 155.

— and F. D. Maurice. Tulloch. Movements 19th cent.

— Eulogy on. Stanley, A. P. Ser. spec. occ. 184.

— Obituary of. Em. persons, **1** : 268.

— Phaethon. Martineau, J. Ess. **2** : 192.

— Westward ho ! Brimley, G. Ess. 294.

Kingsley, Henry. Couch, A. T. Q. Adv. crit. 131.

Kingsley, James L. (W. L. Kingsley) N. E. Hist.-Gen. Soc. Biog. **1** : 396.

Kingsnorth, Richard. Ivimey. Eng. Bapt. **2** : 233.

Kingston, Earl of, Trial for shooting Col. Fitzgerald. Burke, P. Cel. trials.

Kingston, Elizabeth Chudleigh, duchess of. Baring-Gould. Oddities, **1** : 26.

— Trial for bigamy. Burke, P. Cel. trials. — (W. G. Waters) Vincent, A. Twelve bad women, 225.

Kingston, Evelyn Pierpoint, duke of. Portrait. Caulfield. Kit-cat, 51.

Kingston, Mass. Bacon, E. M. Hist. pilgrim. 68.

Kinney, Coates. Coggeshall. Poets of west, 527.

Kinney, Mrs. Elizabeth Clementine (Dodge) Stedman. Derby, J. C. Fifty years, 526. — Hart, J. S. Fem. prose, 237.

Kinnison, David. Lossing. Em. Amer. 403.

Kinsman, Henry Willis. Loring, J. S. Hundred Bost. ora. 564.

Kioto, Japan. Palgrave. Ulysses, 217. — Pidgeon. Engineer's holiday, 306. — Todd, M. L. Corona, 194.

Kipling, Rudyard. Griswold, H. T. Personal sk. 266. — With portrait. Warner Lib. 15 : 8633. — Lynch, A. Hum. doc's, 203.

— at Brattleboro. Wolfe, T. F. Lit. haunts, 206.

— Bibliography. Clemens, W. M. A ken of Kipling. — Knowles, F. L. A Kipling primer. — Biog. and bibliog. notes about Kipling.

— Short stories of. Gosse, E. Questions, 255.

— Stories. Lang. Ess. in lit. 198.

— Suppressed books by. Nicoll, W. R. Lit. anec. 2 : 403.

Kippis, Andrew. Hatfield, E. F. Poets of church, 380. — Miller, Jos. Singers church, 2d ed. 236.

Kirby, Edmund. Walker, C. D. Biog. Va. Mil. Inst. 319.

Kirchner, Theodor Maitland, J. A. F. Masters Ger. music, 199.

Kirchoff, Gustav Robert, Memoir of. (R. von Helmholtz) Smithson. Rept. '89 : 527.

Kirk, Edward N. Lanman, C. Haphazard, 238.

Kirk, John Foster. Nichol. Amer. lit. 155. — Richardson. Amer. lit. 1 : 501.

Kirkham, Robert. Tyerman. Oxf. meth. 1.

Kirkland, Caroline Matilda. Griswold. Prose writ. 463. — Hart, J. S. Fem. prose, 116. — Powell. Liv. authors, 1850, 319. — Powell, T. Liv. auth. Am.

Kirkland, John Thornton. Loring, J. S. Hundred Bost. ora. 287. — Lowell. Writ. 1 : 83. — Peabody. Harv. rem. 9. — Ware, W. Am. Unita. 1 : 273. — (J. Pierce) Mass. Hist. Proc. 2d ser. 9 : 144.

Kirkland, Samuel. Headley, J. T. Chaplains Revol. 239. — Lossing. Em. Amer. 66.

Kirkland family, The. Muzzey, A. B. Prime movers, 143.

— in U. S. history. Muzzey. Remin. 143.

Kirkpatrick of Closeburne. Burke, B. Viciss. of fam. 1 : 46.

Kirkstall, Eng. Freeman. Eng. towns, 294.

Kirschner, Mary Louisa. Clayton, E. C. Eng. fem. art. 2 : 311.

Kissing, Reichenbach's theory of. Scoffern. Stray leaves, 291.

Kissingen. Whitman, S. Teuton stud. 146.

Kistler, Cyril. Maitland, J. A. F. Masters Ger. music, 281.

Kiszka, Lady Barbara. Wallace, R. Anti-Trin. biog. 2 : 236.

Kiszka, John. Wallace, R. Anti-Trin. biog. 2 : 342.

Kitchen, The farmer's. Knight. Once on time, 2 : 111.

Kitchen fireplaces and utensils. Rumford. Ess. 3 : 3.

Kitchens ; make them attractive. Ames, M. C. Outlines, 200.

Kitchener, William. Jerdan. Men, 282. — Hitchman. Eighteenth cent. 233.

Kitsons, The, of Leeds. Fortunes made in bus. 3 : 313.

Kitten, A. Repplier, A. In dozy hours, 16.

Kittery Point, Me. Drake. Nooks of N. E. 141.

Kitto, John. Famous boys, 81. — Miller, H. Hist. ess. 425. — Smiles. Brief biog. 325. — Thayer, W. M. Turn.-points, 48.

Klagenfurt. Jarves. Ital. ramb. 330.

Kleement, John Michael von. Wraxall, F. C. L. Remark. adv. 2 : 70.

Kleinschrot family, The. Feuerbach. Crim. trials.

Kleist, Heinrich von, with portrait. (C. H. Genung) Warner Lib. 15 : 8665.

Klimo, George. Wyatt, W. J. Hunga. celeb. 122.

Klingenstierna, Samuel. Bailey, J. B. Methuselahs, 205.

Klondike. *See* Alaska.

Klonowicz, Fabian Sebastin. Soboleski. Poets of Poland, 54.

Klootz. *See* Cloots.

Klopstock, Friedrich Gottlieb. Bancroft, G. Miscel. 135. — Gostwick. Ger. poets, 63; also Ger. culture, 248. — Hedge. Hours w. Ger. cl. 121. — Jameson. Loves of poets, 369. — MacCallum. Stud. Ger. 291. — Taylor. Stud. Ger. 234. — Miller, Jos. Singers church, 2d ed. 232. — With portrait. (K. Francke) Warner Lib. 15 : 8691. — Wells, B. W. Mod. Ger. lit. 38. — Winkworth. Chr. sing. Germ. 323.

— The Meta of. Jameson. Loves of poets.

Klopstock, Madame. Yonge. Good wom. 2 : 255.

Knapp, Albert. Miller, Jos. Singers church, 2d ed. 453.

Knapp, Frederick N. Allen, J. H. Sequel, 115.

Knapp, Samuel Lorenzo. Loring, J. S. Hundred Bost. ora. 445.

Knaresborough, Dropping-well of. Buckland, F. T. Curios. nat. hist. 3 : 34.

— Local museum and bells of. Buckland, F. T. Curios. nat. hist. 3 : 63.

Kneass, Samuel Honeyman. Stuart, C. B. Am. engineers, 173.

Knebworth, England, Description of. Bulwer. Student, 1 : 35.

Kneller, Sir Godfrey. With portrait. Caulfield. Kit-cat, v. 1. — Spooner. Biog. fine arts, 1 : 441.

Knevet, Sir Edmond, Trial of. Burke, P. Cel. trials.

Kniaznin, Francis Dionysius. Soboleski. Poets of Poland, 99.

Knickerbocker literature. Wilson, J. G. Bryant, 376.

Knife, The man's, among the No. Amer. Indians. (O. T. Mason) U. S. Nat. Mus. Rept. '97 : 725.

Knight, Charles. Cochrane, R. Earnest, 203. — Curwen. Booksellers, 251. — Japp. Noble workers, 66. — Smith, G. B. Leaders mod. ind. 73. — Smith, S. F. Noble workers, 94.

— as a publisher. Nicoll. Great move. 195.

Knight, Edward C. Winslow, S. N. Biog. Phila. merch. 46.

Knight, Ellis Cornelia. Belloc. Vignettes, 279.

— Autobiography of. Lucas. Mornings, 2 : 134.

— Reliques of. Tartt. Ess. 2 : 89.

Knight, Gally. Grant, J. Recollec. Lords & Comm. 2 : 104.

Knight, Henry Edmund. Ritchie, J. E. City men, 185.

Knight, Rev. Jas. Morison, J. Fathers of Lond. Miss. Soc. 2 : 551.

Knight, Joel A., with portrait. Morison, J. Fathers of Lond. Miss. Soc. 2 : 407.

Knight, Jonathan. Stuart, C. B. Am. engineers, 222.

Knight, Richard Payne. Edwards, E. Founders Brit. Mus. 1 : 402.

Knight, Sarah. Earle. Colon. dames, 135.

— Journey to N. Y., 1704. Mitchell, D. G. Am. lands, 82.

Knight, Sophia. Brockett. Woman's work, 794.

Knight service in England. Round, J. H. Feudal Eng. 225.

Knighthood, Orders of. Woodhouse. Mil. rel. orders, 295.
— Recipients of. Doran. Knights, 388.
Knights, Female. Doran. Knights, 104.
— Home life of. Doran. Knights, 36.
— of the middle ages. Cutts, E. L. Scenes mid. ages, 311.
— of the stage. Doran. Knights, 295.
— Poor, of Windsor. Doran. Knights, 184.
— Sham. Doran. Knights, 439.
— Teutonic. Woodhouse. Mil. rel. orders, 263.
Knights Hospitallers. *See* Knights of St. John of Jerusalem.
Knights of Labor. N. J. Labor, '85 : 269. '87 : 3. — McNeill. Labor movement, 397. — Walker, F. A. Discus. in econ. 2 : 321.
— in Pennsylvania, History of. (J. L. Butler) Penna. Labor, 1887.
Knights of St. John of Jerusalem, or Hospitallers. Cutts, E. L. Scenes mid. ages, 29. — Woodhouse. Mil. rel. orders, 11.
— In London. Timbs. Abbeys, 1 : 117.
Knights Templars. Cutts, E. L. Scenes mid. ages, 26. — Heckethorn. Sec. soc. 1 : 181. — Pennington. Epochs papacy, 179. — Woodhouse. Mil. rel. orders, 207.
— in London. Timbs. Abbeys, 1 : 112.
Knipp, or Knep, Mrs. Doran. Ann. stage, 1 : 59.
Kniphausen, Dodon de. Cust. Warriors thirty years, 2 : 568.
Knives and forks, Manufacture of. Japp. Days w. indus. 222.
— Manufacture of, in Europe, Hours of labor and wages in. U. S. Cons. Rept. no. 153.
Knockdowns, mental, Benefits of. Arnold, F. Three-cor. ess. 40.
Knole House. Edwardes, C. Hist. houses. — Jewitt, L. Stately homes, 2 : 56.
Knole Park. Timbs. Abbeys, 1 : 308.
Knollys, Hansard. Ivimey. Eng. Bapt. 2 : 347.
Knorr von Rosenrath, Christian. Miller, Jos. Singers church, 2d ed. 102.
Knowledge, Advantages of, to the lower classes. Hall, R. Miscel. 373.
— and activity. Seth, A. Man's place, 114.
— and feeling. Clifford. Lec. & ess. 200.
— and opinion, Philosophical distinction between. Bosanquet. Ess. 181.
— and probability. Hume. Philos. works, 1 : 95.
— Cheap. Grahame, K. Pagan papers, 55.
— Delights of. (H. L. Pinckney) Charleston book, 320.
— Divisions and mutual relations of. Arnold, T. Miscel. 290.
— Elementary and scientific. (J. W. Dickinson) Nat. Educa. Assoc. '73 : 172.
— elements of, Nature and origin of. (W. D. Wilson) N. Y. Regents, 100, app. : 159.
— human, Progress of. Holland, H. Frag. papers, v. 1.
— Is it worth having? Friswell. Gentle life, 1 : 297.
— Nobility of. Cooke, J. P., jr. Sci. cul. 45.
— of the world. Bulwer. Student, 2 : 133.
— — in authors. Bulwer, E. Caxtoniana, 357.
— On improving. Huxley. Method, 18.
— Praise of. Bacon. Ess.
— Range of. Arnold, E. Seas & lands, 244.
— Secondhand. Stephen, J. F. Ess. by barr. 215.
— Superficial. DeQuincey. Note-book, Bost. 267.
— Theory of. Ladd. Introd. to philosophy. — Stuckenberg. Introd. to philosophy.
— universal, Passion for. Bulwer. Student, 1 : 147.
— What is of most worth? Butler, N. M. Meaning of educa. 37 ; Same in Nat. Educa. Assoc. '95 : 69.
Knowledge, A word about. Abbott, C. C. Outings, 203.
— Worth of a love of. Sterling, J. Ess. 1 : 465.
Knowles, Herbert. Griswold, R. W. Sac. poets. — Miles, A. H. Poets of cent. 10 : 683.
Knowles, James Davis. Goddard, W. G. Pol. & mis. wr. 1 : 303. — Loring, J. S. Hundred Bost. ora. 455.
Knowles, James Sheridan. Collier, W. F. Hist. Eng. lit. 468. — Horne. New spirit of the age, 2 : 83. — Grant, Jas. Port. pub. char. 2 : 251. — Hall, S. C. Book of mem. 236. — Hodder, G. Memories, 170. — Marston, J. W. Rec. actors, 2 : 122. — Miles, A. H. Poets of cent. 2 : 261.
— The Hunchback. Hutton, L. Plays, 141.
— Virginius and the Hunchback. Molloy. Famous plays, 219.
Knowles, John. Wallace, R. Anti-Trin. biog. 2 : 211.
Knowles, John Adams. Livingston, J. Dist. Amer. 492.
Knowles, John K. Bartlett, J. R. R. I. officers, 451.
Know-nothing party. Robinson, W. S. Penportr. 214.
— Riotous career of. McMasters. With Fathers, 87.
See American party.
Knox, Alex., DeQuincey and. Birrell. Men, women, and books, 59.
Knox, Elizabeth, wife of John Welsh. Wittenmeyer. Women Reform. 378.
Knox, Henry. With portrait. [Amer.] Nat. portr. gall. v. 2. — With portrait. Duyckinck. Nat. portr. gall. 1 : 288. — Headley, J. T. Washington, 2 : 99. — Parton. Peop. bk. biog. 457. — Lossing. Em. Amer. 274.
Knox, Isa Craig. Wilson, J. G. Poets of Scot. 2 : 477.
Knox, John. Blaikie, W. G. Preachers Scot. 44, 54. — Broadus. Lec. hist. preach. 194. — Burke, S. H. Hist. portr. Tudor, 4 : 367. — Carlyle. Heroes. — Graham, W. Ess. 111. — Herrick, S. E. Heretics, 181. — Irving, D. Scot. writ. 1 : 35. — Lodge. Portraits (Bohn), v. 2. — Oliphant. Royal Edinburgh, 258. — (J. Brown) Reformers. Paisley lec. 412. — (M. C. Taylor) St. Giles lec. 3 : 1. — Tagart. Sk. ref. 16th cent. 121. — Tulloch. Leaders reform. — Williams, W. R. Eras, 217. — (J. A. Froude) Ferris, G. T. Gt. leaders, 255. — Ker. Scot. nationality, 23. — Morley, H. Eng. writ. 8 : 132, 335. — Pierce, B. K. Em. dead, 45. — Walker, H. Three cent. Scot. lit. 1 : 83. — Wrangham. Brit. Plutarch, v. 1.
— and his relations to women. Stevenson, R. L. Fam. stud. 328 ; *or* Miscel. 2 : 300.
— as a preacher. Taylor, W. M. Scott. pulpit, 44.
— at the court of Mary, queen of Scots. Strickland. Queens Scot. v. 3, 4, 5.
Knox, John C. Brown, D. P. Forum, 2 : 140.
Knox, Lucia. Ellet. Women of revol. 1 : 107.
Knox, Thos. W. Fiske, S. Off-hand portr. 222.
— Rideing. Boyhood.
Knox, Wm. Griswold, R. W. Sac. poets. — Wilson, J. G. Poets of Scot. 2 : 106.
Knox College, Galesburg, Illinois. Blanc, T. Wom. in U. S. 191.
Knoxville College, Knoxville, Tenn. U. S. Bur. Ed. Circ. '93, no. 5 : 274.
Kochanowski, John. Soboleski. Poets of Poland, 41.

Kock, Charles Paul de. Gautier, T. Fam. Fr. au. 139.

Kögel, R. Ker, J. Lec. hist. preach. 379.

Köln. See Cologne.

Kömpel, August, with portrait. Ehrlich, A. Cel. violin. 149.

Königgratz, Battle of, 1866. Adams, G. Gt. camp. 341. — Knox, T. W. Battles, 308.

Koenigsmark, John Christopher, count de. Cust. Warriors thirty years, 2 : 572.— Wraxall, F C. L. Remark. adv. 2 : 148.

— Trial of, for murder, 1682. Craik, G. L. Eng. causes cel. v. 1.

Koenigsmark family, The. Doran. Queens Hanov. 1.

Koerner, Carl Theodor. Gostwick. Ger. poets, 195. — Tuckerman. Ess. 103. — With portrait. Warner Lib. 15 : 8725.

Koerner, Gustave. Am. Bar Assoc. 19 : 637.

Kogalniceanu, Michel. Kingston, W. B. Men, etc. 151.

Koitsch, C. J. Miller, Jos. Singers church, 2d ed. 156.

Kojiki, The, and its teachings. Griffis. Relig. Japan, 59.

Kolariaus of Bengal. Reclus. Prim. folk. 242.

Kolin, Battle of. Carlyle. Batt. Fred. the Gt. 92.

Koltzoff. Wolkonsky. Lowell lec. 212.

Konarscius, Alexander. Wallace, R. Anti-Trin. biog. 3 : 308.

Konarski, Stanislaus Hieronim. Soboleski. Poets of Poland, 88.

Kondratowicz, Louis. Soboleski. Poets of Poland, 387.

Kondur. Malleson, G. B. Battles of India, 72.

Kontz, Balthazar. Wallace, R. Anti-Trin. biog. 2 : 222.

Kootenay and Tshimsian languages. (J. Campbell) Roy. Soc. Can. 2d ser. 4, sec. 2 : 23.

Kootenay Indians, Tales of. (A. F. Chamberlain) Cong. Anthrop. Chic. '93 : 282.

Kopp, Herman. Thorpe, T. E. Ess. hist. chem. 299.

Koran, The. Nöldeke, T. Sk. fr. east. hist. 21. — Poole, S. L. Studies, 115. — (H. P. Smith) Warner Lib. 15 : 8707.

— does it supply ethical base for political structure? Lorimer, Jas. Studies, nat'l & internat.

Korea. Bibliography. Providence Pub. Lib. Bull. Jan. '95.

— Collections from, in U. S. Nat. Mus. (Walter Hough) U. S. Nat. Mus. Rept. '91 : 429.

— Journey through. (W. Grinnell) Am. Geog. Soc. 3 : 283.

— Mortuary pottery of, in U. S. Nat. Mus. (P. L. Jouy) U. S. Nat. Mus. Rept. '88 : 589.

— Opening of ports in, 1897. (H. N. Allen) U. S. Cons. Rept. '56 : 228.

— Trade of, 1898. (H. N. Allen) U. S. Cons. Rept. '60 : 411.

See also Corea.

Korsak, Julian. Soboleski. Poets of Poland, 401.

Korsak, Raymund. Soboleski. Poets of Poland, 411.

Korzeniowski, Joseph. Soboleski. Poets of Poland, 309.

Kosa, John. Wallace, R. Anti-Trin. biog. 2 : 418.

Kosciusko, Thaddeus. Glazier, W. Heroes, 140. — Lossing. Em. Amer. 306.

— Biographical sketch of. Jefferson. Works, 8 : 494.

Kossuth, Louis. Brace, C. L. Hung. in 1851. — Bryant. Prose, 2 : 189. — Stiles, W. H. Aus-

tria in '48. — Em. persons, 6 : 100. — Godwin, P. Comm. addr. 107.

Kossuth, Louis, Address to. Emerson, R. W. Miscel. '83 : 359.

— and intervention. Putnam, J. O. Addresses, 320.

— in New York ; the Kossuth day. Willis. Fam. persons, 433.

— in U. S., and slavery. Phillips, W. Speeches, 2 : 40.

— Press banquet to. Bryant. Orations, 259.

Koster, L., vs. Gutenberg, as inventor of printing. Blades. Books in chains, 171.

Koszta, Martin. Brownson. Works, 16 : 226.

Kovalevsky, Sonya. Hansson, L. M. Six mod. wom. 3.

Krakatoa. (G. C. Hurlbut) Am. Geog. Soc. 19 : 233.

Krapf, Mrs. Rosine D., of Mombas, East Africa. Pitman, Mrs. Heroines mission. 343.

Krasicki, Ignatz. Soboleski. Poets of Poland, 123.

Krasinski, Sigismund. Soboleski. Poets of Poland, 257. — With portrait. Warner Lib. 15 : 8735.

Kraszewski, Joseph Ignatz. Soboleski. Poets of Poland, 437. — Zimmern. For. novelists, 2 : 121.

Kraus, John. (H. S. Tarbell) Nat. Educa. Assoc. '96 : 229.

Krause, C. C. F. Erdmann. Hist. philos. 2 : 669.

Krautbauer, Francis Xavier. Clarke, R. H. Cath. bishops, 3 : 346.

Kremlin of Moscow. Prime, S. I. Alhambra, 332.

Kreutzer, Rudolph, with portrait. Ehrlich, A. Cel. violin. 20.

Krilof, Ivan Andreivitch. Newbigging. Fables, 119.

Krishna. Barth, A. Relig. India, 167.

Kristo Das Pal. Escott, T. H. S. Pillars emp. 51.

Krochmal, N. Guide of the perplexed. Schechter, S. Stud. Jud. 56.

Krokier, Paul. Wallace, R. Anti-Trin. biog. 2 : 526.

Kropiński, Louis. Soboleski. Poets of Poland, 191.

Krotovius, John. Wallace, R. Anti-Trin. biog. 2 : 305.

Kru coast. (W. Durrant) Vaca. tourists, 2 : 293.

Kruedener, Barbara Juliede. Baur. Relig. life Germ. 2 : 81. — Kavanagh. Fr. wom. 241. — Ste.-Beuve. Cel. wom. 309.

Krug, Ludwig. (A. Rosenberg) Dohme, R. Early mast. 157.

Krummacher, Friedrich Wilhelm. Ker, J. Lec. hist. preach. 357, 367.

Krupp, Alfred. Strauss, G. L. M. Men of Ger. 2 : 328.

Kruse, Mrs., of Egypt. Pitman, Mrs. Heroines mission. 328.

Kruythoff, Joanna, a slave. Child, L. M. Oasis, 65.

Kryle, John, Town of. Hall, Mrs. S. C. Eng. shrines, 263.

Krzyskievicius. Wallace, R. Anti-Trin. biog. 3 : 137.

Kublai Khan, In the footprints of. (C. C. Long) Am. Geog. Soc. 22 : 219.

Kuegeigen, Gerhard von, Murder of. Baring-Gould. Oddities, 2 : 39.

Kuenen, Abraham. Cheyne. Founders O. T. crit. 185.

Ku-Klux Klan. Garfield. Works, 1 : 702. — Tourgee. Fool's errand.

Kukulcan, God of the Mayas. Brinton. Amer. hero-myths, 159.

Kulturkampf in Germany. Baring-Gould. Germany, 294. — Lowe. Bismarck, v. 2. — Müller. Polit. hist. recent times.

Kunersdorf, Battle of. Carlyle. Batt. Fred. the Gt. 179.

Kuo Sung-Tao, with photo. Cooper, T. Men of mark, 4 : 18.

Kuroscius, Gratian. Wallace, R. Anti-Trin. biog. 3 : 145.

Kushan monastery. Cumming, C. F. G. Wand. in China, 1 : 257.

Kuyper, Francis. Wallace, R. Anti-Trin. biog. 3 : 312.

Kwakiutl nation. (F. Boas) Am. Geog. Soc. 19 : 225.
— Social organization and secret societies of. (Franz Boas) U. S. Nat. Mus. Rept. '95 : 311.

Kwakiutl-Nootka tribes, Oceanic origin of. (C. Hill-Totu) Roy. Soc. Can. 2d ser. 4, § 2 : 187.

Kyd, Thomas. Dunham. Lit. & sci. men, 2 : 59.
— Minto, W. Eng. poets, 251. — Ward, A. W. Eng. dram. 1 : 169.

Kynane. Mahaffy, J. P. Greek life, ch. 4.

Kynaston, Edward. Doran. Annals stage, 1 : 53. — Galt. Players, 1 : 24.

Kynaston, Herbert. Miller, Jos. Singers church, 2d ed. 505.

Kyrle, John, Town of. Hall, Mrs. S. C. Pilgr. Eng. shr. 1 : 263.

Kyteler, Lady Alice. Wright, T. Nar. sorcery, 1 : 25.

Labadie, Jean de. Ker, J. Lec. hist. preach. 199.

Labadists, Colony of. Bibliography. James, B. B. Labadist col. in Maryland.

Labauve, Zenon. Livingston, J. Dist. Amer. 364.

Laberius, Decimus. Dunlop, J. Rom. liter. 1 : 502.

Labiche, Eugène M. Henley. Views, 143. — Matthews, J. B. Fr. dram. 224.

Labor. Edgar, S. Autob. notes, 259. — Greeley. Ess. pol. econ. 13. — McClelland, J. Soc. sci. 57.
— Accidents to work. people. (F. B. Loomis) U. S. Cons. Rept. 38 : 259.
— and art. (E. G. Starr) Hull-House maps, 165.
— and capital. Aikman, W. Life at home, 198. — Eliot, G. Ess. & leaves, 251. — Giffen, R. Ess. in finance, 365. — Holland, J. G. Everyday, 1 : 333. — Jones, Rich. Lit. remains. — Mill, J. S. Dissert. 2 : 260. 5 : 28. — Rainsford, W. S. Sermons at St. G. 89. — Robertson, F. W. Life, etc. 739. — Stillé, C. J. Stud. med. hist. 385.
— — Conciliation and arbitration. Samuelson, Jas. Civiliz'n, 154.
— — Is it peace or war? Gladden. Appl. Chr. 102.
— — Relative strength of. Wagner, L. Med. pol. ora. 117.
— — Two opposing tendencies. George, H. Soc. prob. 49.
— and intellectual attainments. Carlisle, Earl. Lec. 108.
— and its attendant legislation, History of. (H. K. Oliver) Mass. Labor, '70 : 39.
— and labor insurance in Europe, 1894. U. S. Cons. Rept. 46 : 425.
— as a commodity. Nicol, D. Polit. life, 2 : 209.
— as a factor in evolution. (D. A. Gorton) Brooklyn Eth. Assoc. Life, 219.

Labor as a legislative force. Nicol, D. Polit. life, 2 : 289.
— Bibliography. Providence Pub. Lib. Bull. Aug. '96. — Salem (Mass.) Pub. Lib. Bull. Aug. '94, Aug. '96.
— Cheap. Conn. Labor, '85 : 44.
— Child and woman, in Germany, 1893. (A. H. Washburn) U. S. Cons. Rept. 42 : 172.
— Claims of. Mill, J. S. Dissert. (N. Y.) 2 : 260.
— Combinations of, and competition. Wagner, L. Mod. pol. ora. 22.
— Convict. See Convict labor.
— Dignity of. Blackie, J. S. Lay serm. 221.
— Division of. Hinsdale, B. A. Schools & stud. 68.
— Educated. (L. S. Thompson) Nat. Educa. Assoc. '79 : 203.
— — Steps to secure. (W. C. Russell) Nat. Educa. Assoc. '76 : 257.
— Emancipation of. Greeley. Hints ref. 13.
— Employers and employed, The relation between. Greg. Ess. pol. 2 : 252.
— Ethics of. Chambers's Miscel. no. 170.
— European and American, Comp. of condition of. (T. Tonge) Nat. Conven. Lab. Bur. v. 9.
— Exploitation of. Carpenter, E. Eng. ideal, 1.
— Foreign, in New York. N. Y. Labor, '85.
— Gospel of. Ballantyne. Ess. 187.
— Hist. of labor employment in France, 1893. (F. B. Loomis) U. S. Cons. Rept. 42 : 179.
— Hours of. Gunton. Wealth and prog. — Ills. Labor, '84. — N. Y. Labor, '88. — Hazard, R. G. Econ. & pol. 249.
— — effect on production. Conn. Bur. Lab. '94 : 293.
— — in factories. Peel, R. Speeches, 4 : 341, 366, 717.
— — Long hours of London saleswomen. Meath. Soc. arrows, 284.
— — Lubbock's shop-hours regulation bill. Meath. Soc. arrows, 332.
— — Reduction of. N. Y. Labor, '85.
— — Shop-hours league of London. Meath. Soc. arrows, 271.
— — State regulation of. Fawcett. Ess. & lec. 107.
    See Eight-hour movement.
— in Amoy, 1891. (E. Bedloe) U. S. Cons. Rept. 38 : 137.
— in Australasia, 1891. (G. N. Griffin) U. S. Cons. Rept. 35 : 285.
— in England, Organization of. Espinasse. Lit. recol. 177.
— in France, 1894. (S. H. Angell) U. S. Cons. Rept. 47 : 313.
— in Spain, 1893. U. S. Cons. Rept. no. 150.
— Influence of learning upon. Boutwell. Educa. topics, 9.
— Insufficiency of the reward of. Kempner, W. Common-sense soc. 16.
— Is it a commodity? Gladden. Appl. X'ty, 38.
— Laws of supply and demand appl. to. Jenkin, Fl. Papers, 2 : 76.
— Legislation affecting, in France. Nat. Assoc. Soc. Sci. Rept. on strikes, 1860, 588.
— — in Massachusetts. (H. K. Oliver) Mass. Labor, '73 : 397.
— Liberals and. Ess. in Liberalism, 97.
— Liberty for. (G. Howell) Plea for liberty, 109.
— 100 years ago. (T. Williams) Econ. tracts, no. 24.
— Plea for industrial liberty. Wagner, L. Mod. pol. ora. 137.
— Political economy of. Greeley. Hints ref. 232.

Labrador, Physical geography of. (A. S. Packard) Am. Geog. Soc. **19** : 403.

— A summer's cruise to northern. (A. S. Packard) Am. Geog. Soc. **20** : 337, 445.

Labrunie, G. [Gérard de Nerval]. Lang. Letters on literature, 170.

La Bruyère, Jean de. Jones, W. A. Ess. on authors, 147. — Mozley, A. Ess. 108. — Ste.-Beuve. Portr. of men, 148. — With portrait. Warner Lib. **15** : 8760.

Labyrinth of Crete. Adams, W. H. D. Fam. caves, 73.

La Cava and Pæstum. Scollard. Und. sum. skies, 185.

Lace. Morey, H. Wonder stories, 342. — (A. S. Cole) Morris, W. Arts & crafts, 224.

Lace-making. Bibliography. Brazza, C. S. di. Old & new lace at Chicago, '93.

Lacedæmon, Siege of. Robson, W. Sieges, 187.

Lacedemonian empire. Lord, J. Anc. states, 304.

Lacépède, Comte de. Jardine, W. Nat. lib. v. **26**.

Lacey, John. Ivimey. Eng. Bapt. **4** : 486.

La Chaumière du Prairie, Ky. Terhune, M. V. More colon. homes, 65.

La Chaussée, Pierre Claude Nivelle de, 1692–1754. Vinet. Fr. lit. 18th cent. 168.

Lachovius, Andrew. Wallace, R. Anti-Trin. biog. **3** : 249.

Lackington, James, bookseller. Cooper, T. Triumphs of persev. 126. — Curwen. Booksellers, 70. — Davenport, R. A. Lives, 214. — Knight, C. Old booksel. 282. — Parton. Capt. indus. 247. — Winks. Illus. shoemakers. 15. — Lives of dist. shoemak. 12.

Lackland, Francis. Walker, C. D. Biog. Va. Mil. Inst. 323.

Laclos, Pierre Ambroise François Choderlos de. Houssaye. Men of 18th cent. **1** : 225. — Men & wom. of France, **1** : 237.

La Colle River, Canada, Action at the mill on. Dawson. Batt. of U. S. **2** : 336.

La Condamine, C. M. de. Wraxall, F. C. L. Remark. adv. **2** : 129.

Lacordaire, Jean B. H., abbé. Maceuen. Celeb. 87. — Newton, W. W. Ess. 108 — Skelton. Ess. 268. — Turnbull, R. Pulpit orators, 275.

— and Catholic progress. Brownson. Works, **20** : 249.

Lacquer work. Rein. Industries of Japan, 338.

Lactantius, Blakey, R. Prim. fathers, 230. — Cave. Lives of fathers, **3** : 373.

Lacy, F. A., count de, Spanish general. Grant, Jas. Cavaliers, 164.

Lacy, J. F. M., count, Austrian marshal. Grant, Jas. Cavaliers, 148.

Lacy, John. Doran. Annals stage, **1** : 70.

Lacy, Louis. Grant, Jas. Cavaliers, 169.

Lacy, Peter, Russian marshal. Grant, Jas. Cavaliers, 142.

Ladd, Mrs. Catharine. Raymond, I. Southland writ. **2** : 896.

Ladd, Marie S. Hemenway. Poets of Vt. 352.

Ladd, William Spencer. Am. Bar Assoc. **14** : 432.

Ladenspelder, Hans. Dohme. Early masters, 177.

Ladies in Parliament. Trevelyan, G. O. Ladies in parl. 3.

Ladoga, A cruise on. Taylor, B. Byways, 23.

Ladrone Islands. Bibliography. Salem (Mass.) Pub. Lib. Bull. Sept. '98.

Lætus, Julius Pomponius, his academy at Rome. Symonds. Reviv. of learn. 359.

Lafarge, John, with portrait. Benjamin, S. G. W. Am. art. **2** : 7.

Lafayette, Marquis de. Adolphus. Biog. Fr. rev. **1** : 437. — Brougham. Works, **5** : 195. — Cormenin. Orators, 192. — With portrait. Duyckinck. Nat. portr. gall. **1** : 315. — Everett. Orat. v. **1**. — Glazier, W. Heroes, 61. — With portrait. Headley, J. T. Washington, **2** : 271. — Muzzey. Remin. 308. — Parton. Peop. bk. biog. 475. — Duyckinck. Portrait gall. **1** : 263. — (C. Sumner) Graham & Collar. Pulpit & rost. v. **2**. — Lossing. Em. Amer. 287. — Muzzey, A. B. Prime movers, 308. — Smith, S. F. Noble workers, 307.

— and Washington. Clark, W. G. Lit. rem. 387.

— Life and services of. Hillhouse. Dramas, **2** : 145.

— Tour in, 1824. Schouler, Jas. Hist. briefs, 85.

— Tributes to. Seward. Works, **3** : 25. — Sumner. Works, **5** : 369.

— Visit to Massachusetts. Quincy, J. Figures, 101, 147.

La Fayette, Louise Angelique de, and Louis XIII. Menzies, S. Roy. fav. **1** : 466.

La Fayette, Madame de. Kavanagh. Fr. women, 94. — Ste.-Beuve. Cel. wom. 24. — Mason, A. G. Wom. of Fr. salons, 96. — Ste.-Beuve. Portr. women, 24. — With portrait. Warner Lib. **15** : 8767.

Lafayette College. College book, 282.

La Ferte-Imbault, Marie Thérèse Geoffrin, Marquise de. Haussonville. Salon of Necker, **1** : 235.

Laffan, Bertha, with portrait. Black, H. C. Wom. authors, 286.

Lafitte, Jacques. Lomenie. Liv. characters, 65. — Tuckerman. Ess. 83. — Walsh, R. M. Liv. char. France.

Lafont, Charles P., with portrait. Ehrlich, A. Cel. violin. 120.

La Fontaine, Jean de. Astié. Louis XIV, 189. — Besant. Fr. humor. 262. — Gautier: Fam. Fr. au. 319. — Hogarth. Mem. opera, **1** : 29. — Shelley, M. W. Lit. men Fr. **1**. — Newbigging. Fables, 96. — With portrait. (G. M. Harper) Warner Lib. **15** : 8779.

La Fontaine, Peter de, Adventures of. Burke, P. Romance of forum.

La Force, Caumont de. Bernard, F. Escapes, 45. — Wraxall, F. C. L. Remark. adv. **2** : 311.

La Garaye, Comtesse de. Yonge. Good wom. **2** : 242.

Lagniel, John. Miller, Jos. Singers church, 2d ed. 156.

Lagrange, Joseph L. Morton, E. J. C. Heroes astron. 249.

— and Laplace. Lodge, O. J. Pioneers, 255.

La Grange College, La Grange, Ala. (J. E. Saunders) U. S. Bur. Ed. Circ. '89, no. **3** : 164.

La Granja, Castle of. Hay, J. Castil. days, 158.

Laguerre, Louis, and A. Verrio. Cook, D. Art in Eng. 15.

Laguette, Jacqueline de. Smith, H. G. Romance of hist. 190.

La Harpe, Jean François de. Crichton, A. Converts, **2** : 289.

La Hire, Laurent de. Criticisms of his pictures. Guizot. Fine arts, 205.

La Hogue, Battle of. Rawson, E. K. Twenty nav. batt. **1** : 189. — Valentine, L. J. Sea fights, 76.

Laifield, John. McClure. Translators, 97.

Laighton, Albert. Putnam, A. P. Singers liberal, 489.

Lambert, Francis, of Avignon. MacCrie, T. Miscel. writ.

Lambert, Geo., with portrait. Morison, J. Fathers of Lond. Miss. Soc. 2 : 259.

Lambert, John. Tayler. Eng. martyrs.

Lamberton, W., Bishop, and Edward James Douglas. Shairp. Sk. hist. & poetry, 86.

Lambeth and the archbishops. Green, J. R. Stray studies, 107.

Lambeth Palace. (J. Cave-Browne) Clinch, G. Bygone Surrey, 10. — (J. Cave-Browne) Venables, E. Episc. palaces, v. 1.

— Lollards at. Timbs. Abbeys, 1 : 58.

Lamennais, Félicité de. Challice. French authors, 2 : 141. — Dowden. Studies, 311. — Loménie. Liv. characters, 165. — Mazzini. Life, etc., 6 : 1. — Church, R. W. Occ. pap. 1 : 301. — Walsh, R. M. Liv. char. France. — With portrait. (G. King) Warner Lib. 15 : 8845.

— Fall of. Newman, J. H. Ess. crit. 1 : 102.

Lamia, Ælius. DeQuincey. Avenger (Bost.), 131.

La Mothe-le-Vayer. Owen, J. Skeptics, Fr., 649.

La Motte, Antoine H. de. Houssaye. Men of 18th cent. 2 : 64. — Men & wom. of France, 2 : 245. — Vinet. Fr. lit. 18th cent. 156.

La Motte Fouqué, Friedrich de. Carlyle. Essays. — With portrait. Warner Lib. 10 : 5895.

Lamoureux, Charles, and his orchestra. Runciman, J. F. Old scores, 271.

Lampe, J. F., Musician and writer. Hogarth. Mem. opera, 2 : 39.

Lamprocles, the street boy. Brooks, E. S. Gt. men's sons, v. 1.

Lamson, Alvan. (A. P. Peabody) Mass. Hist. Proc. 12 : 258.

Lamson, Charles Marion, D. D. Am. Antiq. Soc. Proc., n. s. 13 : 132.

Lancashire, England, Baptists of. Ivimey. Eng. Bapt. 2 : 253.

Lancaster, James. Barrow, J. Nav. worthies, 484. — Bourne, H. R. F. Eng. seam. 1 : 281.

Lancaster, Joseph. Leitch, J. Prac. educa.

Lancaster and York, Houses of, Genealogy of. Warner, B. E. Eng. hist. 307.

Lancaster, Mass. Fellows, H. P. Boating, 146.

Lancasterian system of education. Adams, W. H. D. Good Samar. 53.

Lancastrian usurpation. Warner, B. E. Eng. hist. 57, 307.

Lancret, Nicolas. Dilke. Fr. painters 18th cent. 101. — Houssaye. Men of 18th cent. 2 : 221. — Wedmore. Masters of genre, 182. — Men & wom. of France, 3 : 68.

Land, Agricultural tenure of. (W. E. Bear) Samuelson, Jas. Civiliz'n, v. 1.

— and its owners in past times. Jessopp, A. Studies, 143.

— and labor. (M. Reed) Nat. Conven. Lab. Bur. v. 9.

— Bibliography. (T. E. Will) Arena, Aug. '96 : 380.

— Common. Hill, O. Our comm. land, 1.

— Community in, Survival of, in New England. Allen, W. F. Essays, 345.

— Condition of. Kempner, W. Common-sense soc. 104.

— The, for the people. McClelland, J. Soc. sci. 125.

— Free trade in. Arnold, A. Soc. pol. — Rogers, J. E. T. Cobden, 73.

— in England, Land laws and the land question. Williams, Syd. Forensic, 42.

— — Questions connected with. Pembroke, Earl. Polit. let. 255–358.

Land in Great Britain, Freedom of. (G. S. Lefevre) Howard, Jas. Prac. pol. 113.

— in Scotland ; land-rights Registration of. (A. M. Bell ; J. S. More) Trans. Soc. Sci. Lond. '60 : 217.

— in the U. S., Degradation of. Lusk, H. H. Foes at home, 63.

— Leslie on. Mill, J. S. Dissert. (N. Y.) 5 : 95.

— Liberation of, as a public health measure. (G. Homan) Am. Pub. Health, 17 : 80.

— Monopoly of. (W. Jameson) Reid, A. New party, 145.

— — and health. (G. Homan) Am. Pub. Health, 16 : 153. 17 : 80.

— Municipal ownership of. (G. A. Black) Col. Univ. Stud. hist. 1 : 173.

— Nationalization of. Coan. Soc. prob. 229.

— Ownership and occupation of. (F. Hill et al.) Trans. Soc. Sci. Lond. '69 : 152.

— A piece of. (F. A. Shaw) George, H. Soc. prob. 361.

— Property in. Gladden. Tools, 55.

— Question of. Lorimer, Jas. Studies, nat'l & internat. — (H. George) McNeill. Labor.

— — Aspect of, 1871. (W. Fowler) Cobden Club ess. 2 : 117.

— — in England. Chamberlain, J. Speeches, 106, 249.

— Reform in. Lusk, H. H. Foes at home, 87.

— Right of property in. Mill, J. S. Dissert. (N.Y.) 5 : 279.

— Surveying of, in New York state. (A. White) N. Y. Regents, 90 : 617.

— system of, Econ. Hist. of, in the South. (J. C. Ballagh) Am. Hist. Assoc. Rept. '97 : 99.

— in Ireland. (W. O. Morris) Oxf. ess. '55 : 193.

— Taxation of, as proposed by Henry George. (E. O. Brown ; M. L. Scudder) Sunset Club echoes, 63.

— Taxes on. Giffen. Ess. finance, 234.

— Tenure of. Mill, J. S. Dissert. (N. Y.) 5 : 225.

— — and eminent domain. Chatard. Occ. ess. 232.

— — in the middle ages. Allen, W. F. Essays, 312.

— — in village communities. Maine. Vill. com. 65.

— — Reform in. Greeley. Hints ref. 311.

— — The state and the land-owner. (J. T. Danson) Trans. Soc. Sci. Lond. '64 : 129.

— Transfer of. (Sir R. R. Torrens) Trans. Soc. Sci. Lond. '72 : 159. — (E. T. Wakefield ; W. Fawcett) Trans. Soc. Sci. Lond. '57 : 80.

— — in Australia. U.S. Cons. Rept. nos. 154, 155.

— — Reform in. (D. H. Olmstead) Am. Bar Assoc. 13 : 265.

See Torrens system.

— Use of ; Obligations of the soil. Greg, W. R. Miscel. 1 : 98.

Land Bank of 1740, The. (A. McF. Davis) Am. Antiq. Soc. Proc. n. s. 11 : 86. — Greene, W. B. Soc. frag. 70.

— General court and. (A. Mc.F. Davis) Am. Antiq. Soc. Proc. n. s. 11 : 351.

Land credit association, in Saxony, 1896. (T. W. Peters) U. S. Cons. Rept. 52 : 87.

Land grants for education in the N. W. Terr. (G. W. Knight) Am. Hist. Assoc. 1 : 73.

Land laws, British. (F. J. Kingsley) Trans. Soc. Sci. Lond. '79 : 601. — Howard, Jas. Prac. pol. 3.

— of our time. Nicol, D. Polit. life, 2 : 1.

Land titles and town commons in New England. Adams, C. F. Three episodes, 2 : 646.

Land values in Michigan. Mich. Labor, 1892.

Langford, John. Miller, Jos. Singers church, 2d ed. 242.

Langham, Lady Elizabeth. Burder. Pious wom. 83.

Langham, Samuel, cardinal legate. Williams, R. F. Eng. card. 1 : 384.

Langham, Simon, archbishop of Canterbury. Sergeant, L. Wiclif, 147. — Williams, F. Eng. card. 1 : 384. — Foss. Judges, 3 : 453. — Hook. Abps. Cant. 4 : 163.

Langhorne, John. Chalmers. Eng. poets, 16 : 407.

Langhorne, Richard. Pierce, B. K. Em. dead, 501.

Langland, William. Choate, I. B. Wells of Eng. 29. — Swanwick, A. Poets, 147.
— Middle ages and. Scudder, V. D. Soc. ideals, 7.

Langland, Wm. Piers Ploughman. Disraeli, I. Amen. (N. Y. 2 v.) 1 : 213. — Mitchell, D. G. Wet days, 126. — Morley. Eng. writers, 4 : 285. — (W. W. Skeat) Ward. Eng. poets, 1 : 91. — Gibbins. Eng. soc. ref. v. 1. — Minto, W. Eng. poets, 45.

Langles, Louis Mathieu. Redding. Pers. remin. 1 : 283.

Langley, Samuel P., with portrait. Goode, Smithson. Inst. 201.

Langston, Dicey. Clement, J. Noble deeds, 125. — Ellet. Women of revol. 1 : 284.

Langton, Bennet. Guiney, L. I. Little Eng. gall. 171.

Langton, John de. Campbell. Ld. chan. 1 : 155. — Foss. Judges, 3 : 272.

Langton, Stephen, Cardinal. Maurice, C. E. Eng. pop. leaders, v. 1. — Williams, F. Eng. card. 1 : 205, 482. — Simson, Jas. Em. men of Kent, 65. — Adams, W. H. D. Gt. churchm. 163. — Fuller. Worthies, 2 : 182. — Hook. Abps. Cant. 2 : 657. — Williams, R. F. Eng. card. 1 : 205.

Language. Maurice, F. D. Soc. morality, 133. — Mivart. Less. fr. Nature, 82. — Peabody, E. P. Æsthetic pap. 214. — DeQuincey. Lett. to young (Bost.), 161. — Dodge, M. A. Skirmish. 200. — Peabody, E. P. Last evening, 138.
— and art. Eastlake. Contrib. 2 : 301.
— and education. Whitney, W. D. Orient. 1 : 376.
— and race. Freeman. Hist. ess. 3 : 173.
— and style in relation to thought. Shedd. Lit. ess. 149.
— as the art of expression. Hazard. Ess. on lang. 7.
— as an educator. (Z. Richards) Nat. Educa. Assoc. '85 : 322.
— as the expression of national modes of thought. Abel, C. Ling. ess. v. 1.
— as a means of classifying man. Anderson, M. B. Papers, 236.
— barbaric, Limitations of. Clodd, E. Myths, 148.
— Bibliography. Salem (Mass.) Pub. Lib. Bull. Sept. '94.
— Elements of. Garnett. Philol. ess. 78.
— Influence of, on opinions. Webster, N. Ess. 222.
— — on thought. (W. D. Wilson) N. Y. Regents, 93 : 487.
— International communication by. Hamerton. Higher ed. 1.
— Lessons in elementary schools. (Miss H. A. Keeler) Nat. Educa. Assoc. '74 : 264.
— Müller and Whitney controversy. Stearns, F. P. Real & ideal, 187.

Language, Müller's Lectures on. Whitney, W. D. Orient. 1 : 239.
— No common primeval. Fiske, J. Excurs. 147.
— Origin of. Abel, C. Ling. ess. 223. — Whitney, W. D. Orient. 1 : 279.
— — Theories of. Bailey, S. Discourses, 53.
— Periods in the development of. Hare. Guesses, 1 : 306.
— Philosophy of. Mansel. Letters, 3. — Tuckerman. Charac. 107.
— Race and. (E. A. Freeman) Prose masterpieces, 3 : 55.
— Science of. (E. S. Gallup) N. Y. Regents, 79, app. : 15.
— — Historical results. (A. S. Wilkins) Owens college essays, '74 : 291. — Müller. Chips, 4.
— Stratification of. Müller, M. Sel. ess. 1 : 27 ; or Chips, v. 4.
— The study of. Latham. Opuscula, 27.
— — as an intellectual discipline. (W. L'Amoreux) N. Y. Regents, 78 : 366.
— — Importance of, in a liberal education. (John Bascom) Nat. Educa. Assoc. '85 : 273.
— Teaching of, in elementary schools. (H. F. Harrington) Nat. Educa. Assoc. '75 : 153.
— Usage the authority in. (Brainerd Kellogg) Nat. Educa. Assoc. '92 : 357.
— Use of. Goldsmith. Miscel. (N. Y. 4 v.) 1 : 51.

Languages, Acquisition of. Hamerton. Hum. int. 148.
— American. Brinton. Ess. Amer. 390.
— — Characteristics of. Brinton. Ess. Amer. 349.
— — Humboldt's study of. Brinton. Ess. Amer. 328.
— Ancient and modern. Cook, F. C. Origins, 261.
— — Precedence between. (H. F. Burton) N. Y. Regents' Rept. 108.
— foreign, First difficulties with. Taylor, B. At home, 1 : 24.
— Foreign, On the study of. Lieber, F. Reminis. 499.
— Grammatical structure of. Brinton. Races & peo. 62.
— Growth of. Sinclair, T. Humanities, 100.
— Modern. See Modern languages.
— Origin of. Brinton. Races & peo. 61.
— Study of. Hamerton. Intellec. 112.
— teaching, J. Hamilton's method of. Smith, Syd. Ess. fr. Ed. Rev.
— — "Natural method" of. (G. C. Sawyer) N. Y. Regents, 101 : app. 199.

Langworthy, Edward. Jones, C. C., jr. Deleg. fr. Georgia, 137.

Lanier, Clifford Anderson. Davidson, J. W. Writ. of South, 319.

Lanier, Sidney. Davidson, J. W. Writ. of South, 321. — (E. C. Stedman) Ess. from Critic, 141. — Taylor, B. Crit. ess. 312. — Higginson, T. W. Contemp. 85. — Richardson. Amer. lit. 2 : 231. — With portrait. (R. Burton) Warner Lib. 15 : 8891.
— Bibliography. (M. Calloway, jr.) Lanier, S. Poems ; ed. Calloway.
— Centennial Cantata. Lanier. Music, 80.

Laniere, Nicolo, as a musician. Hogarth. Mem. opera, 1 : 53.

Lannes, Jean. Headley. Napoleon, 1 : 177.

Lansdowne, Henry Petty Fitz-Maurice, 3d marquis of. Martineau, H. Biog. sk. 329. — Grant, J. Recoll. Lords, 223. — Edwards, E. Founders Brit. Mus. 2 : 422. — Lodge. Portraits (Bohn), v. 8.

Lantara, Simon Mathurin. Dilke. Fr. painters 18th cent. 183. — Houssaye. Men of 18th cent. 1 : 334. — Men & wom. of France, 2 : 48.

Law schools, Teaching practice in. (B. Lee) Am. Bar Assoc. **19** : 507.

Lawes, Henry, Music of. Hogarth. Mem. opera, **1** : 63.

Lawless, Mather Jones. Bate, P. H. Eng. Pre-Raph. 79.

Lawrence, Abbott. Bungay. Off-hand, 116. — With portrait. Duyckinck. Nat. portr. gall. **2** : 110. — Everett. Orat. 3. — With portrait. (N. Appleton) Hunt, F. Am. merch. **2** : 331. — (N. Appleton) Mass. Hist. Coll. 4th ser. **11** : 495. — (N. Appleton) Mass. Hist. Proc. **3** : 68. — (H. A. Hill) N. E. Hist.-Gen. Soc. Biog. **2** : 401. — Wise, D. Men of renown, 71.

Lawrence, Albert Gallatin. Parton, J. Sk. of men of prog.

Lawrence, Amos. Houghton. Kings, 101. — With portrait. Hunt, F. Am. merch. **2** : 223. — McCabe, J. D. Great fortunes, 115. — With portr. Seymour, C. C. B. Self-made, 76. — (W. M. Cornell) N. E. Hist.-Gen. Soc. Biog. **1** : 500. — Wise, D. Men of renown, 71.

Lawrence, Amos A., Memoir of, with portrait. (W. Lawrence) Mass. Hist. Proc. 2d ser. **12** : 130.

Lawrence, Sir Henry. Banks, J. S. Three Ind. heroes. — Bartlett, D. W. Heroes Ind. rebel. 390. — Holmes, F. M. Four heroes. — Laurie, W. F. B. Dist. Anglo-Ind. **1** : 33. — Smith, S. F. Noble workers, 165. — Kaye. Indian off. **2** : 275. — Japp. Noble workers, 301.

— and John, in India. Temple, R. Men in India, 51, 310.

— Eulogy on. Stanley, A. P. Ser. spec. occ. 241.

Lawrence, James. Lossing. Em. Amer. 352. — With portrait. Duyckinck. Nat. portr. gall. **2** : 74. — Irving. Biog. 37. — Parton. Peop. bk. biog. 526.

Lawrence, Sir James Clarke. Ritchie, J. E. City men, 26.

Lawrence, James Robbins. Livingston, J. Em. Am. lawy. 58.

Lawrence, John (d. 1879). Japp, A. H. Leaders of men, 367.

Lawrence, John L. M., 1st baron. Cust. Pic. Indian life, 244. — Em. persons, **2** : 162.

Lawrence, Jonathan. Griswold. Poets Am. 335.

Lawrence, Sir Thomas. Buxton, H. J., *et al.* Eng. paint. 117. — Craik. Pursuit knowl. **2** : 170. — Edgar. Boyhood, 276. — Eng. painters Georgian, 33. — Jerdan. Men, 287. — Redgrave. Century of p. v. **2**. — With portr. Seymour, C. C. B. Self-made, 368. — Russell, W. Extraor. men, 175. — Thornbury. Brit. art. **1** : 64. — Timbs. Anec. lives painters, 228. — Ollier, E. Writ. port. paint. 37.

— and J. Hoppner. Cook, D. Art in Eng. 260.

Lawrence, Sir William. Bettany. Em. doctors, **1** : 303. — Ritchie, J. E. City men, 37.

Lawrence, William, with portrait. (S. K. Lothrop) Hunt, F. Am. merch. **2** : 365. — Livingston, J. Hist. Amer. 218.

Lawrence, Wm. Beach. Parton, J. Sk. of men of prog.

Lawrence, Mass., Fall River and Lowell, Condition of labor in. (C. D. Wright) Mass. Labor, '82 : 195.

Lawrence University, Appleton, Wis. U. S. Bur. Ed. Circ. '89, no. **1** : 51.

Laws of Lauriston. Burke, B. Viciss. of fam. **2** : 380.

Laws, civil and criminal, New theory of. Hazlitt. Sket.

— Higher. Thoreau. Selec. 64.

Laws, Natural, difference from political. Carpenter, W. Benj. Nature, 365.

— — and laws of man. Pollock. Ess. in juris. 42.

— of succession in Germany. Baring-Gould. Germany, 47.

Lawson, Albert G., with portrait. Bungay. Pen-portr. 232.

Lawson, Edward. Sala, Mrs. Fam. peop. 230.

Lawson, Prof. George, Memoir of. (A. H. Mackay) Roy. Soc. Can. 2d ser. **2** : app. B.

Lawson, James. Blaikie, W. G. Preachers Scot. 71. — Wilson, J. G. Poets of Scot. **2** : 208. — Wodrow. Selec. fr. biog. coll.

Lawson, Mrs., with portrait. Jameson. Beauties, 186.

Lawson, Sir Wilfrid, with portrait. Bungay. Pen-portr. 160. — With photo. Cooper, T. Men of mark, **6** : 13. — Davidson, J. M. Eng. lib. 64. — Hinton. Eng. radicals, 211. — Reid, T. W. Politicians, **2** : 179. — Davidson, J. Mor. Em. Eng. lib.

Lawsuit, A modern, 1786. Hopkinson, F. Miscel. **2** : 247.

Lawton, Alexander Robert. Am. Bar Assoc. **19** : 635.

Lawton, Charles E. Bartlett, J. R. R. I. officers, 452.

Lawyer, Character of. Haven, N. A. Remains, 227.

— Responsibilities of. (J. B. Warner) Am. Bar Assoc. **19** : 319.

Lawyers. Tuckerman. Collector, 176. — Tuckerman. Criterion, 171.

— American, Responsibilities of. Lowell, A. L. Ess. gov't, 118.

— as horsemen. Jeaffreson. Lawyers, 92.

— as lovers. Jeaffreson. Lawyers, 167.

— become authors. Jacox. Aspects, 202.

— Circuit riding in England in 18th century. Jeaffreson. Lawyers, 104.

— Corruption among. Jeaffreson. Lawyers, 240.

— Courts of justice and. Hazard, T. R. Miscel. 177.

— Fees of. Jeaffreson. Lawyers, 215.

— Homes of. Jeaffreson. Lawyers, 125.

— in arms. Jeaffreson. Lawyers, 60.

— Successful. Arnold, F. Turning-points, 191.

— Wigs and gowns of. Jeaffreson. Lawyers, 280.

Lay, Benj., Biographical anecdotes of. Rush, B. Ess. 296.

Lay preaching, Christian. Bibliography. Telford, J. Hist. lay preach.

— in the primitive church. Broadus. Lec. hist. preach. 47.

Lay workers in the churches. (G. Taylor) Evang. Alliance, '89, 264.

Layamon's Brut. Garnett. Philol. ess. 128. — Morley. Eng. writ. ('88) v. **2**.

Layard, Austen Henry, with photo. Cooper, T. Men of mark, **2** : 16. — Ritchie. Brit. sena. 75. — Edwards, E. Founders Brit. Mus. **2** : 626. — Em. persons, **6** : 130.

Layards, refugee, Sketch of the. Agnew. Protes. exiles, **2** : 202.

Laying on of hands, Healing by, in the 19th century. Hazard, T. R. Miscel. 379. *See* Healing by royal touch.

Laynez, Diego. Rose. Loyola.

Laziness, Advantages and disadvantages of. Butler, E. For furth. consid. 65.

Lazzaretti, David, the prophet of Monte Labbro. Elliot, F. Rom. gossip, 339.

Lea, Isaac. Youmans. Pioneers sci. 260.

Lead mines of Sierra Mojada, Mex. U. S. Cons. Rept. no. 148.

Lead mines of the Mendips. (J. T. Page) Walter, J. C. Bygone Som. 39.

Lead-pipe, Poisoning by, with bibliography. (W. R. Nichols) Mass. Health, '71 : 32.

— Poisoning from use of tinned, glazed, and enameled ware. (R. C. Kedzie) Mich. Health, '78 : 25.

Leadbeater, Mary Shackelton. Yonge. Good wom. 2 : 480.

Leadbeater papers, The. Lucas. Mornings, 2 : 212.

Leader, Benj. W. Grant, J. Recoll. Lords & Comm. 2 : 211.

Leadville, Colorado. Pidgeon. Engineer's holiday, 150.

Leah and Rachel. Geikie, C. Old Test. char. 47.

Leamington Spa. Hawthorne. Old home, 49.

Lear, King, Shakespeare's. Hazlitt. Char. Shakes.

Lear, Edward. (W. Whyte) Miles, A. H. Poets of cent. 9 : 343.

Learned, Ignorance of the. Hazlitt, W. Tabletalk, 93.

Learning, Democracy of. (Lyman Abbott) Nat. Educa. Assoc. '97 : 190.

— How to learn. (A. D. Mayo) Nat. Educa. Assoc. '85 : 102.

— Liberty and. Boutwell. Educa. topics, 274.

— Nature and value of, and its influence upon labor. Boutwell. Educa. topics, 9.

— polite, State of, in 1759. Goldsmith. Miscel. (N. Y. 4 v.) 1 : 395.

— Relations of, to labor. Greeley. Hints ref. 112.

— Revival of, in the middle ages. Trench. Lec. mediæval, 382.

— Unity of. Butcher, S. H. Greek genius, 200.

Leaseholds, Enfranchisement of. (J. T. Emmett; J. S. Rubinstein) Trans. Soc. Sci. Lond. '84 : 535.

Leaves, Arrangement of, in plants. Wright, C. Philos. dis. 126.

Leaves from sketch-books of Philip Evergreen, painter. Skelton, J. Ess. in romance, 149.

Leaving off, Art of. Helps. Soc. pressure, 106.

Leavitt, Thomas Joseph. (C. Leavitt) Harvard mem. biog. 2 : 243.

Lebanon, Porter, J. L. Giant cities, 285. — Stuart-Glennie. Pilgrim. 405. — (H. H. Jessup) Wilson, C. W. Pictur. Palest. 3 : 1.

— Heights and hollows of. Little, W. J. K. Sketches, 281.

Le Brun, Charles. Dilke. Art in mod. state. — (C. A. Regnet) Dohme, R. Early mast. 511.

Le Brun, Elizabeth. Darton. Fam. girls, 117. — Ellet, E. F. Women artists, 206.

Le Brun, M., Trial of. Phillips, S. M. Famous cases, 65.

Lebuin, St. Maclear. Apostles, 138.

Lechmere's Point, Cambridge, Mass. Drake, S. A. Hist. fields Middlesex, 179.

Lecky, William E. H., with portrait. (J. W. Chadwick) Warner Lib. 15 : 8929.

— Rationalism in Europe. Eliot, G. Ess. & leaves, 157.

Leclaire, Jean. Bosanquet. Ess. 1. — With portrait. Ehrlich, A. Cel. violin. 67.

Le Clerc, Clara. Raymond, I. Southland writ. 1 : 487.

Le Conte, Joseph. Davidson, J. W. Writ. of South, 324.

Leconte de Lisle. Symons, A. Stud. two lit. — Pellissier. Lit. move. Fr. 353.

Lecouvreur, Adrienne (1690–1730). Maceuen. Celeb. 181.

— and the French stage. Hawkins. Fr. stage 18th cent. v. 1.

Lecture, The. Jones, W. A. Ess. on authors, 62.

— Vicissitudes of a. Hunt, L. Seer, 2 : 224.

Lecture lyceum. Curtis, G. W. Other ess. 39.

Lectures. Repplier, A. In dozy hours, 123.

— Popular. Holland, J. G. Every-day, 1 : 72 ; or Plain talks, 309.

Leczinski, Stanislaus. Bernard, F. Escapes, 118.

"Leda," Wreck of the. Treanor, T. S. Heroes Goodw. sands, 181.

Ledyard, John, American traveler. Craik. Pursuit knowl. 2 : 373. — Seymour, C. C. B. Self-made, 138. — St. John. Cel. travelers, 2 : 163. — Lossing. Em. Amer. 82. — Prime, W. C. I go a-fishing, 343.

Lee, Ann. Lossing. Em. Amer. 68.

Lee, Arthur. Lossing. Em. Amer. 234.

Lee, Gen. Charles. With portrait. Headley, J. T. Washington, 2 : 126. — Lossing. Em. Amer. 307.

— Headquarters at Somerville, Mass. Drake, S. A. Hist. fields Middlesex, 141.

Lee, Mrs. Eleanor Percy. Freeman, J. D. Wom. of South, 150.

Lee, Fitzhugh. Pollard. Life of Lee, 549.

Lee, Francis Lightfoot, 1734–97. Dwight, N. Signers of decl. 318.— Lincoln, R. W. Signers, 38. — Lossing. Signers, 194. — Sanderson. Signers, v. 9.

Lee, Frederick George. Miller, Jos. Singers church, 2d ed. 574.

Lee, Gideon. (C. M. Leupp) Hunt, F. Am. merch. 1 : 401.

Lee, Henry. With portrait. [Amer.] Nat. portr. gall. 3. — With portrait. Duyckinck. Nat. portr. gall. 1 : 235. — Lossing. Em. Amer. 152. — Moore, F. Am. eloq. 1 : 447.

— Tribute to. (C. F. Adams ; C. W. Eliot) Mass. Hist. Soc. Proc. 2d ser. 12 : 342.

Lee, James Prince, 1st bishop of Manchester. Huntington, G. Random recoll. 9.

Lee, Jesse. Gorrie, Em. Meth. 224. — Sherman, D. N. Eng. divines, 115. — Wakeley. Heroes Meth. 229. — Withrow. Makers of Meth. 290.

Lee, Leroy M. Davidson, J. W. Writ. of South, 325.

Lee, Mary Elizabeth. Freeman, J. D. Wom. of South, 485. — Hart, J. S. Fem. prose, 458.

Lee, Mrs. Mary W. Brockett. Woman's work, 480. — Moore, F. Women of the war, 148.

Lee, Nath'l. Dunham. Lit. & sci. men, 3 : 134.

Lee, Richard. Hatfield, E. F. Poets of church, 384.

Lee, Richard Henry. With portrait. Duyckinck. Nat. portr. gall. 1 : 53. — Dwight, N. Signers, 270.—Lincoln, R. W. Signers, 40. — Lossing. Signers, 166. — Magoon. Orators of rev. 266. — Sanderson. Signers, v. 9. — Lossing. Em. Amer. 186. — Moore, F. Am. eloq. 1 : 40. — Perry, B. F. Biog. sketches, 1 : 362.

Lee, Robert, Rev. (J. Cunningham) St. Giles lec. 3 : 390. — Skelton. Impeach. of Mary, 305. — Skelton. Ess. 317. — Duyckinck. Portrait gall. 2 : 449.

Lee, Robert E., Gen. Pollard. Life of Lee, 33. — Snow. South. generals, 9. — Wilson, J. G. Illus. sol. 431. — Wallis, S. T. Works, 1 : 151.

— and Grant. Keyes, E. D. Fifty years, 204.

— Bibliography. Trent, W. P. Robt. E. Lee.

— Cooke's Life of. Chesney. Ess. mil. biog. 81.

Lee, Samuel. Cooper, T. Triumphs of persev. 18. — Cust. Ling. & Orient. ess. 4 : 562. — Edwards, B. B. Self-taught, 1 : 104.

Lee, Samuel Phillips. Headley, J. T. Farragut, 416.

Lee, Sophia and Harriet. Jeaffreson. Novelists, 1 : 262.

Lee, Thomas. Jackson, T. Early Meth. 2 : 191.

Lee, Sir Wm. Campbell. Ch. just. 2 : 168.

Lee, William. Towle, G. M. Heroes of inven. 52.

Lee, William F. Walker, C. D. Biog. Va. Mil. Inst. 338.

Lee, William Raymond. (J. C. Ropes) Am. Acad. A. & S. Proc. 28 : 346.

Lee & Shepard. Derby, J. C. Fifty years, 517.

Leech, John. Brown, J. J. Leech, 3 ; *or* Spare hours, v. 2. — Paget, J. Paradoxes, 465. — Rossetti, W. M. Fine art, 282. — Everitt, G. Eng. carica. 277. — Hodder, G. Memories, 43.

— and John Tenniel. Ruskin. Art of Eng. 111.

— Illustrative work of. Everitt, G. Eng. carica. 407.

— Pictures of life and character. Thackeray. Early & late, 122.

Leechdoms, wort-cunning, and starcraft of early England. Lucas. Mornings, 1 : 165.

Leeds, Edward. Woolrych. Serjeants, 2 : 539.

Leeds, Thomas Osborne, first duke of. Lodge. Portraits (Bohn), v. 7.

Leeds, Eng. Dolman, F. Munic. at work, 105. — Silloway. Cathedral towns, 191.

— American trade, 1891. (F. H. Wigfall) U. S. Cons. Rept. 37 : 545.

— Labor in, 1892. (F. H. Wigfall) U. S. Cons. Rept. 39 : 186.

Leeds Castle. Timbs. Abbeys, 1 : 314.

Leeson, Jane E. Hatfield, E. F. Poets of church, 385. — Miller, Jos. Singers church, 2d ed. 547.

Leeward Islands, The, and the "boiling lake." Palgrave. Ulysses, 112.

Le Fanu, Joseph Sheridan. Miles, A. H. Poets of cent. 9 : 357.

Lefebre, François Joseph. Headley. Napoleon, 2 : 36.

Lefevre, Peter Paul. Clarke, R. H. Cath. bishops, 2 : 191.

Lefevre, Shaw. Grant, J. Recoll. Lords & Comm. 2 : 177.

Lefferts, Marshall. Parton, J. Sk. of men of prog.

Le Franc, Martin. Besant. Fr. poetry, 177.

Lefroy, E. C. Symonds. Key of blue, 87.

Lefroy, Thomas, Chief-justice. Grant, J. Recoll. Lords & Comm. 2 : 237. — Sheil. Sk. Irish bar, 1 : 216.

Left-handedness and right-headedness. Ireland, W. W. Blot, 299.

Leftwich, James C. Walker, C. D. Biog. Va. Mil. Inst. 341.

Legal administration and admission to the bar. Am. Bar Assoc. 19 : 376.

Legal education. (S. Williston) Am. Bar Assoc. 16 : 391. — (H. W. Rogers) Am. Bar. Assoc. 17 : 389. — (J. B. Thayer) Am. Bar Assoc. 18 : 409. — Am. Bar Assoc. 20 : 419.

— and admission to the bar. Am. Bar Assoc. 20 : 349.

— — Rept. of committee on. Am. Bar Assoc. 2 : 209. 4 : 237.

— better, The great need of the profession. (D. J. Brewer) Am. Bar Assoc. 18 : 441.

— Bibliography of. U. S. Bur. Ed. Rept. '90–91 : 565.

— Common-law procedure in. (C. M. Campbell) Am. Bar Assoc. 19 : 493.

— Existing questions of. (A. Abbott) Am. Bar Assoc. 16 : 371.

— in Canada. (N. W. Hoyles) Am. Bar Assoc. 22 : 579.

Legal education in Canada, Australia, etc. U. S. Bur. Ed. Rept. '90–91 : 549.

— in England. (G. H. Emmott) Am. Bar Assoc. 19 : 605.

— In Europe. (L. R. Klemm) U. S. Bur. Ed. Rept. '90–91 : 447.

— in France. Hillebrand. France, 59.

— in United States. (L. Dimscha) Cong. Educa. Chic. '93, 48. — (L. R. Klemm) U. S. Bur. Ed. Rept. '90–91 : 376.

— in a university. (T. E. Holland ; Prof. Lorimer) Internat. health exh. 15 : 102.

— in the West, Standards of. (J. D. Lawson) Am. Bar Assoc. 17 : 423.

— Inductive method in. (W. A. Keener) Am. Bar Assoc. 17 : 473.

— Limitations and requirements of. (E. Wetmore) Am. Bar Assoc. 17 : 461.

— of undergraduates. (W. Wilson) Am. Bar Assoc. 17 : 439.

— orthodox, A principle of. (J. H. Wigmore) Am. Bar Assoc. 17 : 453.

— Report of committee on. Am. Bar Assoc. 13 : 327. 14 : 301. 15 : 317. 17 : 351. 18 : 309. 19 : 433.

— Roman law and. Maine. Vill.-comm. 330 ; also in Camb. ess. '56 : 1.

— "The true professional ideal." (J. F. Dillon) Am. Bar Assoc. 17 : 409.

Legal fictions, Decadence of. Baldwin. Mod. polit. inst. 266.

Legal history, Uses of. (M. Crackanthorpe) Am. Bar Assoc. 19 : 343.

Legal maxims, New use for. Butler, E. For good, 1.

Legal procedure, Reform of. Curtis, B. R. Mem. & writ. v. 2.

Legal profession, The. Johnston, R. M. Studies, 31. — Williams, Syd. Forensic, 257.

Legal rules, Classifications of. Maine. Early law, 362.

Legal science, Magnitude and importance of. Field, D. D. Speeches, 1 : 517.

Legal studies in England, Early history of. (J. Walton) Am. Bar Assoc. 22 : 601.

— Necessity of collegiate education as a preparation for. (E. Evans) N. Y. Regents, 79, app. : 39.

— value and importance of. Story, J. Miscel. 503.

Legal-tender act of 1862. (F. A. Walker and H. Adams) Adams, C. F. Erie, 303. — Adams, H. Hist. ess. 279.

Legal-tender decisions. (E. J. James) Am. Econ. Assoc. v. 3.

Le Gallienne, R., with portrait. Warner Lib. 15 : 8957.

Legaré, Hugh Swinton. Griswold. Prose writ. 390. — Lossing. Em. Amer. 308.

— and James Louis Petigru. (A. R. Lawton) Am. Bar Assoc. 5 : 180.

— Character of. Story, J. Miscel. 820.

— Death of. (R. Yeadon) Charleston book, 142.

— Memoir of. Legaré. Writ. v. 1.

— Mental structure of. (B. S. Carroll) Charleston book, 266.

Legaré, Mary Swinton. Ellet. Women artists, 301.

Legate, Bartholomew. Wallace, R. Anti-Trin. biog. 2 : 530.

Legends. Disraeli, I. Curios. (N. Y. 4 v.) 1 : 148.

Leggett, William. Griswold. Poets Am. 251. — Whittier. Old portr. 211.

— Political writings of. Field, D. D. Speeches, 2 : 209.

Lenox, Charles. *See* Richmond, Duke of.

Lenox, Margaret Douglas, Countess of. Burke, S. Hist. portr. Tudor, **4** : 145. — Strickland. Queens Scot. v. **2**.

Lenox, Mass., Literary associations of. Wolfe. Lit. shr. Am. auth. 176.

Lens, John. Woolrych. Serjeants, **2** : 734.

Lenten dinners and fasts. Cobbe, F. P. Re-echoes, 41.

Lenthall, William. Manning, J. A. Speakers, 312.

Lentils in foreign countries, 1894. U. S. Cons. Rept. 45 : 505.

Leo, St., pope, the Great. Blakey, R. Prim. fathers, 274.

— and the rise of the papacy. Merivale, C. Four lec.

Leo X., Pope. Church, R. W. Ess. & rev. — Crowe & James. Em. for. statesm. **1** : 70. — Duffy, B. Tuscan repub. 395. — Gebhart, E. Rom. cameos, 221. — Lawrence, E. Hist. stud. 56. — Lord, J. Beacon, **1** : 427. — Ranke. Popes, **1** : 80. — Symonds. Age of despots, 435. — Oliphant. Makers Mod. Rome, 592.

— and Luther. Lawrence, E. Hist. stud. 56.

Leo XII., Pope. Gavazzi. Four popes, 79. — Wiseman. Four popes, 131.

Leo XIII., Pope. With portrait. Crowned heads, 55. — Elliot, F. Rom. gossip, 76. — Kingston, W. B. Men, etc. 289.

— Bull on the study of the Bible. Cust. Ling. & Orient. ess. **4** : 530.

— The encyclical "Immortale Dei," 1885. Chatard. Occ. ess. 223.

Leo Africanus. *See* Hasan Ibn Muhammad.

Leo, Leonardo, Italian opera writer. Hogarth. Mem. opera, **1** : 274.

Leon, Elizabeth Jane. Williams, Jane. Lit. wom. 71.

Leon, Luis de. Montgomery. Men of Ita. **3** : 70. — Ticknor. Span. lit. **2** : 40.

Leonard, St. (patron of prisoners), of the Limousin. Charles. Martyrs, 370.

Leonard, Agnes. Raymond, I. Southland writ. **1** : 115.

Leonard, Elkanah. Knapp, S. L. Em. lawyers, 327.

Leonard, George. Knapp, S. L. Em. lawyers, 341.

Leonard, Hubert, with portrait. Ehrlich, A. Cel. violin. 84.

Leonardo da Vinci. *See* Vinci.

Leoncavallo, Ruggiero. Streatfeild. Masters Ital. mus. 215.

Leonidas. Mills. Poets of Greece, 203. — Mombert. Great lives, 27.

Leonine verses. Malkin. Class. disq. 346.

Leonor, St., Legend of. Lanier. Music, 91.

Leonora Baroni, Milton and. Jameson. Loves of poets.

Leonora de Este, Tasso and. Jameson. Loves of poets.

Leopardi, Giacomo. Gebhart, E. Rom. cameos, 297. — Gladstone. Glean. **2** : 65. — Howells. Mod. It. poets, 244. — Tuckerman. Ess. 267. — With portrait. (K. Hillard) Warner Lib. **15** : 8977.

— Birthplace of. Jarves. Ital. ramb. 119.

Leopold I. (1657–1705), History of. Peake, Eliz. Germ. emperors, 381. — Wraxall, C. F. L. Hist. bye-ways, **1** : 68.

Leopold I., of Belgium. Abbott. Kings & queens, 197.

Leopold II., of Belgium, with portrait. Crowned heads, 39.

Leopold, Prince, duke of Albany. Myers. Sci. and fut. life, 211.

Leopold of Dessau. Baring-Gould. Germany, 461.

Leopold William, archduke. Cust. Warriors thirty years, 575.

Lepanto, Battle of. Rawson, E. K. Twenty nav. batt. **1** : 59.

Lepelletier, Michel. Adolphus. Biog. Fr. rev. **2** : 1.

Leper asylums, Ought we to reopen the? (J. Ramirez) Am. Pub. Health, **24** : 180.

Lepers and leprosy in the East. Wallace, S. Bosphorus, 69.

— How shall our, be cared for? (B. Lee) Am. Pub. Health, **19** : 246.

— of Molokai. Todd, M. L. Corona, 111.

"**L'Epervier**," brig, Capture of. Dawson. Batt. of U. S. **2** : 338.

L'Epine, Francesca Margaret de, vocalist. Clayton, E. C. Queens, 15. — Hogarth. Mem. opera, **1** : 183.

Le Poule, Robert, cardinal. Williams, R. F. Eng. card. **1** : 141.

Leprosy. Cust. Linguistic essays, **3** : 571. — Murray, E. C. G. Turkey, 192. — Nordhoff. No. Califor. 192. — (K. Hoegh) Wisc. Health, '88 : 154. '90–91 : 92.

— and its management in Minnesota. (C. N. Hewitt) Am. Pub. Health, **16** : 172.

— as related to public health, with bibliography. Mass. Health, '82 : 121.

— Dreadful revival of. Mackenzie, M. Ess. 109.

— in India, and prevention of its increase. Internat. Health Ex. Sanita.

— in mediæval Britain. Creighton, C. Epidem. 69.

— in Minnesota. (H. M. Bracken) Am. Pub. Health, **24** : 186.

— Maracaibo hospital. U. S. Cons. Rept. no. 119.

Leray, Francis Xavier. Clarke, R. H. Cath. bishops, **3** : 371.

Lerida to Saragossa. Stoddard, C. A. Span. cit. 37.

Lerma, Duke of. Crowe, E. E. For. statesmen, **1** : 262.

Lermolieff, Ivan, *pseud. See* Morelli, Giovanni.

Lermont, Thomas. Irving, D. Scot. poets, **1** : 225.

Lermontov, M. I. Wolkonsky. Lowell lec. 209.

Leroux, Pierre. Simpson, J. P. Pic. revol. Paris, **2** : 85.

Lesage, Alain René. Saintsbury. Ess. Fr. nov. 66. — Scott, W. Biog. mem. v. **1**. — Vinet. Fr. lit. 18th cent. 107. — With portrait. (J. G. Cooke) Warner Lib. **15** : 8984.

— and the French stage. Hawkins. Fr. stage 18th cent. v. **1**.

— Who wrote Gil Blas? Everest, A. H. Crit. ess. **1** : 28.

Les Banx. James, H. Little tour, 201.

Lesbos island. Tozer. Islands of the Ægean.

Lescot, Pierre, architect. Pattison. Renaissance of art in France, **1** : 143.

Lesley, Sir David. Cust. Warriors civ. **2** : 622.

Lesley, John. Irving, D. Scot. writ. **1** : 122.

Leslie, Charles Robert. Buxton, H. J., *et al.* Eng. paint. 170. — Eng. painters Georgian, 81. — Tuckerman. Artists, 171. — Tuckerman. Artist-life, 123. — Redgrave. Century of p. **2** : 213, 326. — Taylor, B. At home, **2** : 407. — Wedmore. Masters of genre, 231.

Leslie, Eliza. Griswold. Prose writ. 385. — Hart, J. S. Fem. prose, 26. — Taylor, B. At home, **2** : 404.

Leslie, George D. (Tom Taylor) Atkinson, J. B.

109. — Lincoln, R. W. Signers, 42. — Lossing. Signers, 71. — Sanderson. Signers, v. 6.

Lewis, Sir Geo. Cornewall. Aspects of statesmanship. Arnold, F. Turning-points, 273. — Ritchie. Brit. sena. 410.

— at Ely place. Yates, E. H. Celeb. 2 : 267.

Lewis, Ida. Hanaford. Wom. of cent. 136.

Lewis, James. Winter. Shadows, 379.

Lewis, John. Wallace, R. Anti-Trin. biog. 2 : 366.

Lewis, John Fred. Bate, P. H. Eng. Pre-Raph. 87.

Lewis, John Travers, 1st bishop of Ontario. Bungay. Repr. men, 271.

Lewis, M. G., "Monk." Jeaffreson. Novelists, 2 : 88. — Oliphant, M. Lit. hist. 3 : 136. — Wotton. Word portraits, 179.

— Castle spectre. Morris. Essays in theat. criticism, 125.

Lewis, Meriwether, with portrait. Greely, A. W. Explorers, 105.

— Biographical sketch of. Jefferson. Works, 8 : 480.

Lewis, Morgan, with portrait. [Amer.] Nat. portr. gall. 3. — Jenkins. Gov. of N. Y. 132.

Lewis, Robert Byrd. Am. Bar Assoc. 21 : 659.

Lewis, Sir W. T., with portrait. Jones, E. R. Heroes of ind. 134.

Lewis, William, 1750–1819. Brown, D. P. Forum, 1 : 444.

Lexden, Eng. Barrett, C. R. B. Essex, 164.

Lexicography and lexicons. Gilman, S. Contrib. 450.

Lexington, Mass. Bacon, E. M. Hist. pilgrim. 332.

— Battle of. Bacon, E. M. Hist. pilgrim. 379. — Drake, S. A. Hist. fields Mid. 354. — Everett. Orat. 1. — Everett. Mt. Vernon, 425. — Dawson. Batt. of U. S. 1 : 9. — Muzzey, A. B. Prime movers, 360.

— — Men engaged in. Muzzey. Remin. 360.

Ley, Sir James, chief justice of England, 1621–1624. Campbell. Ch. jus. 1 : 297.

Leyden. Amicis. Holland, 205. — Mahaffy. Holl. & Germ. 47.

Leyden, John. Brooks, S. W. Eng. poets, 389. — Chambers's Miscel. no. 152. — Hood, E. P. Peerage of poverty, 416. — Scott, W. Biog. mem. v. 2. — Wilson, J. G. Poets of Scot. 1 : 514. — Edwards, B. B. Self-taught, 490.

— Scenes of infancy : a poem. Drake, N. Winter nights, v. 1.

Leyden, Lucas van. (A. Rosenberg) Dohme, R. Early mast. 231. — Spooner. Biog. fine arts, 1 : 472.

Leyden, Holland, Explosion at. Davenport. Narr. peril, 2 : 342.

— Siege of. Davenport. Narr. peril, 444. — Great sieges, 475. — Tillotson. Stories of wars, 9. — Robson, W. Sieges, 475.

Leyson, Thomas. Bell, R. Lit. & sci. men, 2 : 118,

Leyva, Virginia Maria de. Symonds. Renais. Cath. reac. 1 : 317.

Lhermitte, Léon Augustin. Ewart, H. C. Toilers in art, 41.

L'Hôpital, M. de. Foster, J. Crit. ess. (Bohn) 2 : 278.

— Essay on life of. Butler, Chas. Works, v. 2.

Liars, Big. Clark, W. G. Lit. rem. 381.

Libel. Coleridge. Friend. 75.

— and slander. Williams, Syd. Forensic, 69.

— Law of. Seward. Works, 1 : 391.

— — Newspaper press and. Field, D. D. Speeches, 1 : 547.

Libel, Powers of juries in prosecutions for. Burke. Works (Bohn), 6 : 154.

Liberal education, Modern. Ladd, G. T. Ess. higher educ. 111.

— *See* Education, Liberal.

Liberal party in England, and Irish catholicism. Arnold, M. Mixed ess.

— Future of. Arnold, M. Irish ess. v. 4.

— Speech on aims of, 1885. (J. Chamberlain) Wagner, L. Mod. pol. ora. 267.

— Value of. Goddard, W. G. Pol. & miscel. wr. 1 : 1.

Liberal studies. Brownson. Works, 19 : 431.

Liberal thought, Origins of, in America. Fiske, J. Cent. of science, 122.

Liberalism and catholicity. Brownson. Works, 5 : 476.

— and progress. Brownson. Works, 20 : 342.

— *vs.* Socialism. Bax, E. B. Outlooks, 67.

Liberation. Mabie. Ess. on work, 62.

Liberia, Republic of. Hazard, T. R. Miscel. 130. — Howe, H. Adven. & achiev. 357. — Williams, G. W. Hist. negro race, 1 : 95.

— and Hayti, Independence of. Sumner. Works, 6 : 445.

— and Maryland's own colony. Latimer. Eur. in Afr. in 19th cent. 290.

— Büttikofer's. (G. C. Hurlbut) Am. Geo. Soc. 23 : 295.

Liberty. Burgess, J. W. Pol. sci. v. 1. — Cowley. Ess. 1. — Godwin, W. Ess. 217. — Thompson, D. G. Soc. prog.

— American doctrine of. Curtis, G. W. Orations, 1 : 95.

— and the church. Brownson. Works, 10 : 69.

— and equality. Linton, W. J. Eng. repub. 190.

— and genius. Patterson, R. H. Ess. hist. 351.

— and legislation. Bosanquet, B. Civil. of Christendom, 358.

— and necessity. Hazlitt. Lit. rem. 1 : 169. — Hume. Philos. works, 4 : 91.

— Civil, and absolute government. Hume. Philos. works, 3 : 94.

— — and political. Brownson. Works, 18 : 201.

— Constitutional. Gilbart. Lec. 210.

— History of. Everett. Orat. v. 1.

— Limits of. (W. Donisthorpe) Plea for liberty, 63.

— Mill on. Buckle. Ess. 39. — Müller, M. Sel. ess. 2 : 479. — Ritchie. State interference.

— Nature of. Clough. Prose rem. 405.

— of conscience. Brownson. Works, 7 : 479.

— of the press : Policy in war. Congdon, C. T. Trib. ess. 187.

— — in England. Daly, J. B. Radicals, 95. *See also* Press.

— Patriotism and. Beecher. New star papers, 264.

— Progress of. Hazard, T. R. Miscel. 99.

— Religious. Brownson. Works, 13 : 222.

— — in the U. S. Brownson. Works, 12 : 103.

— The renaissance and. Lilly. Chapters, 1 : 254.

— Shibboleth of. Lilly, W. S. Shibboleths, 49.

— State guardianship of. Lusk, H. H. Foes at home, 234.

— State interference and. Ritchie, D. G. State interf. 33.

— True. Brooks, P. Addresses, 96.

— True love of. Coleridge. Friend. 296.

— under laws. Beecher, H. W. Patriotic add. 403.

— Well-being and. Lusk, H. H. Foes at home, 213.

— Worth of. Giles, H. Lectures, 2 : 51.

Librarian's work, A. Fiske, H. Darwin, 237.

Life after death. Hunt, L. Seer, **2** : 140.
— Aims of. Bax. Ethics of socialism, 138. — Greeley. Hints ref. 374.
— and death. Matthews, A. Ruminations. — Platt, J. Excelsior, 171.
— — Nature of. Whittaker, T. Ess. & not. 267.
— and its arts, Mystery of. (John Ruskin) Afternoon lec. **5** : 91.
— and its aspirations. Rice, H. Nature & cul. 167.
— and letters in N. E., Historic notes of. Emerson. Lec. & biog. sk. 305.
— and liberty, Right to. Green, T. H. Works, **2** : 460.
— and organization. Holland, H. Ess. 50.
— and thought. Whittaker, T. Ess. & not. 303.
— Answer of. Mabie. My study fire, 16.
— a better, Glimpses of. Greeley. Hints ref. 367.
— Controversy of. Gurney. Tertium, **1** : 100.
— A conveyancer's meditation on the lease of. Butler, E. For furth. consid. 178.
— Divine human. (G. A. Gates) Conf. char. & correc. '92 : 223.
— Essay on. Shelley. Ess. **1** : 176.
— Eternal, and eternal death. Maurice, F. D. Theol. ess. 442.
— Facts and laws of. Reynolds, J. R. Ess. 36.
— Government of. Mivart. Ess. **1** : 352.
— how to live. Lubbock. Use of life, v. **1**.
— Human ; a lecture. Greeley. Hints ref. 149.
— Humdrum aspect of. Woolson. Browsing, 31.
— The ideal and the actual. Greeley. Hints ref. 51.
— Immortal. Holland, E. G. Reviews, 320.
— Is it worth living ? James, W. Will to bel. 32.
— Joy in. Mabie. My study fire, **2** : 51.
— Laws of. Parsons, T. Ess. **1** : 5.
— Little days of. Saunders. Stray leaves, 121.
— Love of. Hazlitt. Round table.
— Meaning of. Mivart. Ess. **1** : 315.
— Meridian of. Boyesen. Lit. silhouettes, 205.
— modern, Demands of. Anderson, M. B. Papers, **1** : 166.
— more than meat. King, T. S. Patriotism, 207.
— Mysteries of. Martin, E. S. Windfalls, 149.
— Mystery of. Parsons, T. Mystery, 5.
— not so miserable after all. Helps. Friends, 2d ser. 2.
— Object of. Romanes. Ess. 152.
— Philosophy of. Fairbanks, O. B. Aguecheek, 306.
— Practical. Laing. Mod. sci. 298.
— Preservation of, at sea. (T. B. M. Mason) Am. Geog. Soc. **11** : 59.
— Prolongation of, in 18th century. (S. Smith) Trans. Soc. Sci. Lond. '57 : 498.
— Protection to human. Minn. Labor, '91–92 : 42.
— Retributions of. Dana, A. H. Eth. inq. 279.
— Rhythm of. Meynell, A. Rhythm, 1.
— Right conduct of. Anderson, M. B. Papers, **1** : 139.
— Serious time of. Martin, E. S. Windfalls, 183.
— Shortness of. Cowley. Ess. 106.
— Significance of. Greg. Enig. 199.
— — What makes it significant ? James, W. Talks psychol. 265.
— Standard of. Bosanquet, Mrs. Standard, 1.
— Sweetness of. Friswell. Silent hour, 264.
— a true, Ideal of. Greeley. Hints. ref. 392.
— Vicissitudes of. Bailey, S. Essays, 176.
— without principle. Thoreau. Yankee in C. 248; *or* Selec. 301.
— Worries of. Boyd. Recreat. **1** : 309.
Life-boat heroes. Hodder. Heroes, **1** : 99.

Life-boats. Wynter, A. Our soc. bees, **2** : 404.
— and those who man them. Wynter. Fruit, **1** : 195.
Life insurance. *See* Insurance, life.
Life processes. Bibliography. (S. H. Gage) Smithson. Inst. Rept. '96, publica. 1109.
Life sentences, Treatment of prisoners under. (M. D. Hill) Trans. Soc. Sci. Lond. '66 : 213.
Life story in six short chapters. Hall, John. Papers, 62.
Light. Gall & Robertson. Pop. read. sci. 253. — Herschel. Famil. lec. 219. — Hunt, R. Poe. of sci. 118.
— Absorption of, by colored media. Herschel. Famil. lec. 476.
— and electricity, according to Maxwell and Hertz. (H. Poincaré) Smithson. Rept. '94 : 129.
— and its artificial production. (O. Lummer) Smithson. Inst. Rept. '97 : 273.
— Combinations of. Davy. Works, **2** : 3.
— Concealing power of. Finlayson, T. C. Ess. 230.
— Modern theory of. (O. J. Lodge) Smithson. Rept. '89 : 441.
— Physiological. (R. Dubois) Smithson. Inst. Rept. '95 : 413.
— Polarization of. (W. Spottiswoode) Manch. Sci. lec. **5–6** : 9.
— Striking a. Baring-Gould, S. Survivals, 110.
— Velocity of. Mach. Pop. sci. lec. 48.
— Waves of. Tyndall. New frag. 78.
— — and the measurement of motion of bodies. Proctor. Pleas. ways, 77.
Lightfoot, Joseph B., bishop of Durham. With photo. Cooper, T. Men of mark, **4** : 7. — Em. persons, **4** : 203.
Light-houses. Everett, E. Mt. Vernon, 310. — Chambers's Repos. no. 17. — Faraday, M. Various forces, 173. — Sci. lec. So. Kens. **2** : 201. — Sauzay. Wonders of glass, 309. — Whymper. The sea, **2** : 156. — Wonder stories sci. 233.
Lightning and thunder. Molloy, G. Gleanings, 53.
— Danger from. Proctor. Sci. byways, 262.
— Death by. Tyndall. Frag. sci. 397.
— — how produced. Brodie. Works, **1** : 439.
— Effects of, at Cremona. Franklin. Works ('87), **7** : 476.
Lightning conductors. Molloy, G. Gleanings, 93, 339. — Franklin. Works ('87), **4** : 40, 175, 508.
Lights, Shining. Hall, John. Papers, 71.
Ligne, Karl Joseph, Prince de. Doran. Habits, 358.
Ligoniers, refugee, Sketch of the. Agnew. Protes. exiles, **2** : 191.
Ligouri, Alphonse. Miller, Jos. Singers church, 2d ed. 154.
Liguost, Pierre Laclede, pioneer. Parton. Capt. indus. 89.
Li Hung Chang. Norman, H. Far East, 244.
Likel. Redding. Misers, **2** : 149.
Likeness, Law of, and its working. Wilson, A. Leisure, 205.
Likenesses. Mivart. Ess. **2** : 250.
Likes and dislikes. Friswell. Better self, 245.
Lilburne, John, and agreement of the people. Foster, R. Comment. on Const. **1** : 46.
Lille, Abbé de, Observations on a version of his "Les Jardins." Drake, N. Noontide, **1** : 101. **2** : 112.
Lilliard of Ancrum. Fittis. Heroines of Scot. 134.
Lillington, John Alexander. Lossing. Em. Amer. 94.

Lillo, George, dramatist. Craik. Pursuit knowl. **1** : 192.
— George Barnwell. Morris. Essays in theat. criticism, 118.
Lima, capital of Peru. Curtis, W. E. Capitals, 355.
— Description of, 1724. (B. Swartz) Mass. Hist. Proc. **8** : 202.
— in 1820. Miller, Gen. J. Memoirs, **1** : 382.
Lime and slate in Maine. Maine Labor, 1889.
— in the mortar, The. Kingsley, C. Sci. lec.
Limerick. Silloway. Cathedral towns, 40.
Limited liability acts, British. (G. L. Browne) Trans. Soc. Sci. Lond. '**84** : 565.
Limits. Russell, A. P. Lib. notes, 157.
Limoges, France. Child, T. Summ. holidays, 219.
Limoges china, Manufacture of, 1897. (W. T. Griffin) U. S. Cons. Rept. **54** : 426.
Linacre, Thomas. Bettany. Em. doctors, **1** : 1.
— Jeaffreson. Doctors, 10. — Simpson, J. Em. men of Kent, 94.
— and Grocyn at Oxford. Morley, H. Eng. writ. **7** : 20.
Lincoln, Abraham. Abbott. Lives of presidents, 375. — Blaine. Twenty years. — Boutwell. Lawy. 90. — Duyckinck. Nat. portrait gall. **2** : 373. — Everett. Orat. v. **4.** — Field, M. B. Memories, 321. — Forney. Anec. 244. — (H. W. French) Frost. Presidents, 427. — Garfield. Works, **1** : 202. **2** : 533. — Hawthorne. Old home, 167. — Lyon, N. Last pol. writ. 112. — Beecher, H. W. Patriotic add. 701. — Bullock, A. H. Addresses, 76. — With portrait. Scott, H. W. Dist. Am. lawy. 521. — Bolton, S. K. Poor boys famous, 342. — Brooks, E. S. Hist. Amer. 335. — With portrait. Brooks, N. Statesmen, 175. — Brooks, P. Addresses, 149. — Chittenden, L. E. Pers. reminis. 340. — Tiffany, O. H. Pulpit & p. — Lodge & Roosevelt. Hero-tales, 323. — Thayer, W. M. Turn.-points, 148. — Tuckerman, C. K. Recollec. **1** : 101. — With portrait. Hubbard, E. Lit. jour. **4** : 395. — With portrait. (H. W. Mabie) Warner Lib. **16** : 9059. — Emerson, R. W. Miscel. ('83) 307. — Johnston, A. Amer. ora. **3** : 154. **4** : 16, 123. — Mombert. Great lives, 273. — Phillips, W. Speeches, **2** : 446. — Piatt, D. Men who saved Union, 27. — Stryker. Hamilton, 25. — Richardson. Amer. lit. **1** : 238, 254. — (J. Hay) Wilson, J. G. Presidents, 300. — Thompson, R. W. Pers. recoll. 389. — Wise, D. Men of renown, 11.
— and his wife, Love-story of. O'Connor, T. P. Love-stories.
— and emancipation. Garfield. Works, **2** : 533.
— as presidential candidate, 1864. Lowell. Pol. ess. 153; *or* Writ. **5** : 177.
— Bibliography. Salem (Mass.) Pub. Lib. Bull. Feb. '96.
— Character of. Keyes, E. D. Fifty years, 421.
— Death of. Caton. Miscel. 10. — Chittenden, L. E. Pers. reminis. 236.
— Douglas Debate. Johnston, A. Amer. ora. **3** : 184.
— Early years of. Smith, Gold. Lec. & ess. 240.
— Election of. Phillips, W. Sp. 294. — Robinson, W. S. Pen-portr. 241.
— Emancipation proclamation. Brownson. Works, **17** : 510. — Congdon, C. T. Trib. ess. 325, 374.
— Eulogy on. Sumner. Works, **9** : 367.
— Message to Congress, 1862. Brownson. Works, **17** : 386.

Lincoln, Abraham, Recollections of. (B. P. Poore) Parton. Princes, 347.
— Social life during administration of. Ellet, E. F. Court circles, 520.
Lincoln, Benjamin. Lossing. Em. Amer. 298. — With portrait. [Amer.] Nat. portr. gall. v. **2.** — With portrait. Duyckinck. Nat. portr. gall. **1** : 222. — With portrait. Headley, J. T. Washington, **2** : 104. — Mass. Hist. Coll. 2d ser. **3** : 233.
Lincoln, Daniel Waldo. Loring, J. S. Hundred Bost. ora. 351.
Lincoln, Edward Clinton, earl of. Lodge. Portraits (Bohn), v. **2.**
Lincoln, Elizabeth, countess of. Williams, Jane. Lit. wom. 80.
Lincoln, Henry Clinton, earl of. Caulfield. Kitcat, 61.
Lincoln, James (1826–62). Rogers, C. Chr'n heroes, 247.
Lincoln, Levi. Bullock, A. H. Addresses, 176. — (E. Washburn) Mass. Hist. Proc. **12** : 47.
Lincoln, Mary Todd. Gordon, L. L. Lady Wash'n, 314. — Hanaford. Wom. of cent. 91. — With portrait. Holloway, L. C. Ladies, 526.
Lincoln, Nancy H. Holloway, L. C. Mothers of gt. men, 111.
Lincoln, William. (C. A. Chase) Am. Antiq. Soc. Proc. n. s. **7** : 424. — (J. Willard) Mass. Hist. Coll. 3d ser. **10** : 225.
Lincoln family, The. Muzzey, A. B. Prime movers, 101.
— in U. S. history. Muzzey. Remin. 101.
Lincoln, Eng. Rimmer, A. Country towns, 163. — Freeman. Eng. towns, 191. — Silloway. Cathedral towns, 265.
Lincoln cathedral. Farrar, F. W. Our Eng. minsters, 231. — (E. Venables) Farrar, F. W. Westmin. 163. — Freeman. Eng. towns, 222. — Hawthorne, Mrs. Eng. & It. 31. — Van Rensselaer, M. G. Eng. cath. 159.
Lincoln palace. (A. R. Maddison) Venables, E. Episc. palaces, 189.
Lincolnshire, England, Baptists of. Ivimey. Eng. Bapt. **2** : 261.
Lind, Jenny. Clayton, E. C. Queens, 461. — Edwards, H. S. Prima don. **2** : 1. — Field, M. B. Memories, 216. — Hogarth. Mem. opera, **2** : 334. — (J. Parton) Parton. Em. wom. 250. — Tuckerman. Ess. 222. — Willis. Fam. persons, 429. — Ferris, G. T. Great singers, **2** : 181. — Curtis. From easy ch. 145. — Bolton. Famous types, 196. — Duyckinck. Portrait gall. **2** : 472. — Needham. Queens of song. — Smith, G. B. Wom. of renown, 119.
— and Daniel Webster. Willis. Hurry-graphs, 189.
— the Consuelo of George Sand. Ossoli. Woman, 241.
— Kindness of. Parton. Princes, 252.
— Likenesses of. Willis. Hurry-graphs, 257.
Lindsay, Lady Anne. Wittenmyer. Women Reform. 421.
Lindsay, Sir David. Minto, W. Eng. poets, 109. — Morley, H. Eng. writ. **7** : 239. **8** : 131. — Tytler. Scot. worth. v. **3.** — Walker, H. Three cent. Scot. lit. **1** : 1.
Lindsay, Bp. David. Wodrow. Selec. fr. biog. coll.
Lindsay, Sir James, of Crawford. Lindsay. Lives, **1** : 69.
Lindsay, John, Journal of, in prison at Seringapatum, 1780–86. Lindsay. Lives, **3** : 261.
Lindsay, Sophia, Lady. Fittis. Heroines of Scot. 312.

Lindsay, William S. Ritchie. Brit. sena. 280.
Lindsay family and Mary Queen of Scots. Lindsay. Lives, 1 : 263.
— Norman origin of. Lindsay. Lives, 1 : 1.
— of Edzell. Burke, B. Viciss. of fam. 1 : 113.
Lindsey, Montagu Bertie, 2d earl of. Lodge. Portraits (Bohn), v. 5.
Lindsey, Robert Bertie, first earl of. Cust. Warriors civ. 2 : 608. — Lodge. Portraits (Bohn), v. 4.
Lindsey survey (1115-18). Round, J. H. Feudal Eng. 181.
Lingley, James. Miller, Jos. Singers church, 2d ed. 485.
Lingurius, Alfonso. Wallace, R. Anti-Trin. biog. 2 : 168.
Links of animal life, Found. (A. Wilson) Proctor, R. A. Nat. stud. 105.
Linley, George, poet and musician. Spark, W. Mus. mem. 216.
Linley, Rev. Ozias. Sinclair, J. Sketches.
Linley, Thomas, musical composer. Hogarth. Mem. opera, 2 : 344.
Linlithgow palace. Mackie, C. Castles of Mary.
Linnæus, Carl. Bolton, S. K. Fam. men of science, 49. — Duncan, P. M. Botanists, 52. — Jardine, N. Nat. lib. v. 6. — Groser, W. H. Men worth imita. — Hundred greatest men, 352. — Macgillivray, W. Em. zoöl. — With portrait. (J. Muir) Warner Lib. 16 : 9077.
Linseed oil trade in foreign countries, 1896. U. S. Cons. Rept. 51 : 611.
Linsley, Charles. Hemenway. Poets of Vt. 253.
Linthicum, Thales A. Am. Bar Assoc. 4 : 137.
Lintol, Bernard. Curwen. Booksellers, 33.
Linton, E. Lynn, with portrait. Black, H. C. Wom. authors, 1.
Linton, Wm. James. (A. H. Bullen) Miles, A. H. Poets of cent. 4 : 377.
Lion, The. Morgan, C. L. Animal sk. 9.
Lion-hunting in Africa, Gordon Cumming's. Phillips, S. Ess. from Times, 2 : 87.
Lions at the Zoölogical Gardens. Buckland, F. T. Curios. nat. hist. 3 : 192-235.
Lipinski, Carl J., with portrait. Ehrlich, A. Cel. violin. 79.
Lippi, Filippino. (K. Woermann) Dohme, R. Early mast. 330. — Stillman, W. J. Old Ital. mast. 149. — Symonds. Renais. fine arts, 247.
Lippi, Fra Filippo. (H. Woermann) Dohme, R. Early mast. 316. — Ottley. Ital. school. — Stillman, W. J. Old Ital. mast. 101. — Symonds. Renais. fine arts, 245.
— and Fra Angelico. Jameson. Ital. painters, 84.
Lippincott, Joshua Ballinger. Derby, J. C. Fifty years, 382.
Lippincott, Sara J. Griswold. Fem. poets, 390. — Griswold. Prose writ. 676. — Hart, J. S. Fem. prose, 334. — (J. B. Lyman) Parton. Em. wom. 147. — Willis. Hurry-graphs, 207.
Lipscomb, Abner S. Livingston, J. Em. Am. lawy. 622.
Liquids and gases. (William Ramsay) Smithson. Rept. '92 : 303.
— Forms of. Mach. Pop. sci. lec. 1.
— Latent heat of. Molloy, G. Gleanings, 1.
Liquor laws in Amer. commonwealths, Centralized adminis. of. (C. M. L. Sites) Colum. Univ. Stud. Hist. 10 : no. 3.
— English, What reform is desirable ? (J. W. Horsley ; A. J. Mott) Trans. Soc. Sci. Lond. '86 : 6.
Liquor licenses, Conditions of. Trans. Soc. Sci. Lond. '66 : 609.

Liquor licenses in England, 1890. Gladstone. Speeches, 10 : 201.
— Preventive and protective design of. (D. Burns) Trans. Soc. Sci. Lond. '60 : 532.
— revocation of, Compensation for. (E. W. Norfolk et al.) Trans. Soc. Sci. Lond. '86 : 53.
Liquor question. Arnold, A. Soc. pol.
— Bibliography. Koren, J. Econ. aspects of liq. problem.
— Economic aspects of. U. S. Lab. Bull. 3 : 509.
— in politics. (G. Iles) Econ. tracts, no. 26.
Liquor traffic, Legislation and. Jevons. Meth. soc. ref.
— Relation to pauperism, crime, and insanity. Mass. Bur. Lab. '95 : 1.
Lisbon. Crawfurd, O. Trav. in Portugal, 187.
— Recollections of. Talfourd. Crit. writ.
— Siege of. Robson, W. Sieges, 396.
Lisle, Lady Alicia. Adams, W. H. D. Noble women, 59. — Anderson, Jas. Mem. wom. Pur. 2 : 328.
Lisle, Charles M. R. L. de, with portrait. Warner Lib. 15 : 8952.
Lismaninus, Francis. Wallace, R. Anti-Trin. biog. 2 : 147.
Lismore castle. Edwardes, C. Hist. houses.
Lissa, Battle of. Rawson, E. K. Twenty nav. batt. 2 : 533.
Listeners, Good. Jacox, F. Cues, 236.
Listening, Art of. Mathews. Lit. style, 279.
Lister, Sir Joseph. Bettany. Em. doctors, 2 : 135. — Cochrane, R. Benef. lives, 198.
Lister, S. C. Fortunes made in bus. 1 : 45.
Liston, John. Hunt. Crit. ess. on performers, 97. — Matthews, B. Actors, 2 : 253.
— Biographical memoir of. Lamb. Elia.
Liston, Robert. Bettany. Em. doctors, 2 : 24.
Liszt, Franz. Butterworth. Great compos. 94. — Fay. Music study. — Ferris, G. T. Great violinists, 287. — Haweis. My mus. life, 609. — Haweis. My mus. memo. 250. — Hueffer, F. R. Wagner, 267. — Keddie. Mus. comp. 407. — With portrait. Bie, O. Hist. of piano, 271. — Lenz. Gt. piano virtuosos, 1. — Dole, N. H. Score, 489. — Kingston, W. B. Men, etc. 118. — Rowbotham, J. F. Great compos. 211. — Statham. Music, 349.
— Goethe and. Krehbiel. Music & man. 243.
Litchfield, Conn. Mansfield, E. D. Pers. mem. 122.
Literary ambassadors. Jones, W. A. Lit. stud. 1 : 31.
Literary bishops. Arnold, F. Our bishops, 2 : 1.
Literary blunders. Disraeli, I. Curios. (N. Y. 4 v.) 1 : 415.
Literary calling, The, and its future. Payn. Private views, 106.
Literary centre, Do we need a? Higginson. New world, 77.
Literary centres. Garland. Crumbling idols, 145.
Literary character. Hazlitt. Round table.
Literary coincidences. Cozzens. Bushwhacker, 59.
Literary confessions. Walsh, W. S. Au. & authorship, 113.
Literary controversy. Disraeli, I. Curios. (N. Y. 4 v.) 1 : 401.
Literary criticism, Newspaper. Nadal, E. S. Ess. at home.
Literary deans. Arnold, F. Our bishops, 2 : 278.
Literary ethics. Emerson. Nature, 149.
Literary exercises in academies. (S. G. Love) N. Y. Regents, 81 : 647.
Literary follies. Disraeli, I. Curios. (N. Y. 4 v.) 1 : 385.

Literary heroes. Walsh, W. S. Au. & authorship, 180.

Literary hero-worship. Purnell. Liter. 63.

Literary idolatries. Watson, W. Excur. in crit. 1.

Literary journals. Disraeli, I. Curios. (N. Y. 4 v.) 1 : 60.

Literary life, The. Walsh, W. S. Au. & authorship.

Literary matter and manner. Hazlitt. Sket.

Literary men. Purnell. Liter. 1.

— Claims of the country upon. Bethune. Orations, 383.

— English. Tuckerman, C. K. Recollec. 2 : 1.

— in parliament. Purnell. Liter. 47.

Literary morality. Buchanan. David Gray, 239.

Literary novitiate. DeQuincey. Lit. rem. (Bost.) 1 : 11.

Literary pendulum, The. Higginson. New world, 213.

Literary portraits. Jones, W. A. Ess. on authors, 196.

Literary prophecy. Garland. Crumbling idols, 39.

Literary pursuits, Abuses of. Madden. Infirm. gen. 16.

— Advantages of. Madden. Infirm. gen. 11.

— Effects of. Madden. Infirm. gen. 1.

Literary quarrels from personal motives. Disraeli, I. Calam. 2.

Literary shibboleths. Repplier, A. Points of view.

Literary society. Jacox. Aspects, 128. — Shepard, W. Authors, 237. — Walsh, W. S. Au. & authorship, 237.

Literary success, Uncertainty of. Goldsmith. Miscel. (N. Y. 4 v.) 1 : 67.

Literary tendencies of the times [1842]. Story, J. Miscel. 740.

Literary tonics. Higginson. New world, 62.

Literary tradition. Ste.-Beuve. Sel. ess. 21.

Literary work, Personality in. Mabie. Ess. lit. interp.

Literature. Newman, J. H. Lec. univ. 29. — Platt, J. Excelsior, 155.

— Amenities of. Miller, H. Hist. ess. 412.

— and art. (Joseph Napier) Afternoon lec. 2 : 1.

— — in public schools. (W. T. Harris) Nat. Educa. Assoc. '97 : 261.

— and the fine arts. (J. R. Poinsett) Charleston book, 306.

— and history. Masson. Three devils, 301.

— and life. Brooks, P. Ess. & addr. 454.

— and literary men. Holland, J. G. Every-day, 1 : 16. 2 : 81.

— and morals. Trent. Authority, 97.

— and national life. Lilly, W. S. Ess. 183.

— and natural science. Nettleship. Lec. & ess. 235.

— and science. Arnold, M. Disc. Amer. 72.

— — Relations between. Nettleship, H. Lec. 2d ser. 235.

— as an art. Higginson. Atlan. ess. 23.

— as a crutch. Walsh, W. S. Au. & authorship, 93.

— as a staff. Walsh, W. S. Au. & authorship, 81.

— as a trade. Jacox. Lit. life, 160.

— Attitude of public towards. Couch, A. T. Q. Adv. crit. 2.

— Catholic Church and. Brownson. Works, 10 : 357. 19 : 447.

— Censorship of. Lea. Chap. relig. hist. Spain.

— Chances of. Walsh, W. S. Au. & authorship, 18.

Literature, Children's interest in. (I. Lawrence) Nat. Educa. Assoc. '99 : 1044. *See* Children.

— Christianity and. Brooke, S. A. Hist. early Eng. lit. 189. — Newman, J. H. Lec. univ. 1.

— Comparative. (C. C. Shackford) N. Y. Regents, 90 : 754.

— Consolations of. Walsh, W. S. Au. & authorship, 248.

— Conversations on. Hazlitt. Round table.

— Domestic. Sands. Writings, 1 : 101.

— An English academy of. Disraeli, I. Curios. (N. Y. 4 v.) 3 : 157.

— Ethical element in. (J. A. McLellan) Nat. Educa. Assoc. '94 : 71.

— European, 1829. Mazzini. Life, etc. 2 : 4.

— for schools, Duty of normal school toward. (C. C. Van Liew) Nat. Educa. Assoc. '94 : 833.

— for teachers. (H. W. Mabie) Nat. Educa. Assoc. '92 : 157.

— good, Practical value of taste for. (Mary L. Beecher) Nat. Educa. Assoc. '88 : 78.

— History in. Traill, F. Studies, 219.

— Imaginative. Porter, N. Books, 81.

— in account with life. Caldwell, S. L. Cities of faith, 305.

— in the high school. (Minnie C. Clark) Nat. Educa. Assoc. '89 : 265.

— in school work. (R. Jones and others) N. Y. Regents, 111 : 15.

— Influence of democracy on. Gosse, E. Questions, 33.

— Influence of money in. Zola. Exper. novel, 161.

— Influence of the republic in. Zola. Exper. novel, 373.

— Influence of, upon society. Vaughan, R. Ess. 1 : 141.

— Interpretation of. Dowden. Transcripts, 237.

— Its value to men of business. Disraeli. Sel. spee. 2 : 617.

— Lynch's Essays on some of the forms of. Macdonald, G. Orts, 218.

— Making a name in. Gosse, E. Questions, 113.

— Ministration of. (Minnie Caroline Clark) Nat. Educa. Assoc. '87 : 417.

— Modern. Emerson. Nat. hist. intel. 177.

— — Some aspects of. Mabie. Ess. lit. interp.

— Monasticism and. Brooke, S. A. Hist. early Eng. lit. 218.

— Moral influence of. Nettleship, H. Lec. 2d ser. 191.

— Morals in. Bunce, O. B. Bach. bluff, 219. — Cobbe, F. P. Studies, 261.

— Mutability of. Irving. Sk. book, 96; also in Prose masterpieces, 1 : 3.

— Nature of. Trent. Authority, 141.

— not ill-paid. Mathews. Conversers, 224.

— of the people. Miller, H. Hist. ess. 300.

— of Scotland before Burns. Oliphant, M. Lit. hist. 1 : 168.

— Office of. Birrell. Obiter, 2 : 256.

— Organization of. Espinasse. Lit. recol. 28.

— Place of, in college course. (H. B. Sprague) Nat. Educa. Assoc. '87 : 448.

— — in common school education. (H. E. Scudder) Nat. Educa. Assoc. '88 : 57.

— Politics of. Traill. New fiction, 52,

— Pre-Islamic. (J. G. Lansing) N. Y. Regents, 90 : 763.

— Profession of. Tuckerman. Optimist, 195.

— pure and sound, Value of. White, C. Ess. 99.

— Relations of, to a republican government. Hillhouse. Dramas, 2 : 101.

— Rewards of. Walsh, W. S. Au. & authorship, 66.

Literature, Rights of. Wallace, H. B. Art, 363.
— Social aspects of. DeVere. Ess. 1.
— Study of. Hill, G. B. Writers & readers, 143.
— Morley, J. Stud. in lit. 189. — (R. G. Moulton) Nat. Educa. Assoc. '94 : 210.
— Teaching the spirit of. Trent. Authority, 237.
— Use of, in teaching children to read. (Le Roy Halsey) Nat. Educa. Assoc. '88 : 70.
— Uses of, in elementary education. (Committee on elementary education) Nat. Educa. Assoc. '92 : 766.
— Value of, in moral training. (C. De Garmo) Nat. Educa. Assoc. '94 : 388.
— Vanity and glory of. Rogers, H. Ess. 1 : 456; or Reason, 241.
See also Letters.
Lithgow, William. Smith, H. G. Romance of hist. 166.
Lithography. Bibliography. Curtis, Atherton. Some masters lithog. — Grolier Club cat. '96.
Little, Harvey D. Coggeshall. Poets of west, 116.
Little, Mrs. Sophia L. Griswold. Fem. poets, 107.
Little, Brown & Co. Derby, J. C. Fifty years, 670.
"Little Belt," sloop, Action with. Dawson. Batt. of U. S. **2** : 63.
Little iron soldier, The. Whittier. Lit. recre. 308.
Little masters of Germany. (A. Rosenberg) Dohme, R. Early mast. 132.
Little Rock, Ark. Warner, C. D. Studies, 303.
Little Sodbury Manor. Hodges, Eliz. Anc. Eng. homes, 191.
Little things. Hazlitt. Table-talk.
— Helpfulness of. Boyd. Our life, 79.
Little touches, The. Peck, H. T. Good English, 33.
Little Turtle, Indian chief. Mansfield, E. D. Pers. mem. 22.
Littledale, Richard F. Miles, A. H. Poets of cent. **10** : 752. — Miller, Jos. Singers church, 2d ed. 571.
Littleton, Edward, Baron. Campbell. Ld. chan. **3** : 273.
Littleton, Sir Thomas. Fuller. Worthies, **3** : 366. — Manning, J. A. Speakers, 400.
Liturgical growth. Brooks, P. Ess. & addr. 96.
Liturgies, Antiquity of existing. Froude, R. H. Remains, **2** : 383.
Liturgy, Congregational. Beecher. New star p.
— Growth of a. Thompson, H. M. Copy, 288.
— Revision of. Thirlwall, C. Remains, **1** : 283, 374.
— Use of, in worship. (J. Tunis) In spirit & truth.
Liuchiu, Kingdom of. Balfour, F. H. Waifs, 55.
Liuder, St. Maclear. Apostles, 144.
Livadia. Mahaffy. Rambles Greece, 189.
Lively, Edward. McClure. Translators, 103.
Livermore, Abiel Abbot. Putnam, A. P. Singers liberal, 312.
Livermore, Edward St. Loe. Loring, J. S. Hundred Bost. ora. 367.
Livermore, George. (C. Deane) Mass. Hist. Proc. **10** : 415.
Livermore, Mrs. Mary A. Brockett. Woman's work, 577. — With portrait. (E. S. Phelps) Our fam. wom. 386. — Hanaford. Wom. of cent. 305. — Bolton, S. K. Girls famous, 50. — Putnam, A. P. Singers liberal, 61.
Liverpool, Charles, 1st earl of. Brougham. Works, **4** : 118.
Liverpool, Robt. B. Jenkinson, 2d earl of. Earle, J. C. Eng. prem. **2** : 134. — Lodge. Por-

traits (Bohn), v. **8**. — Stanton, H. B. Reforms, 67. — Thornton. For. sec. v. 1.
Liverpool, Robt. B. Jenkinson, 2d earl of, Administration of. Lewis, G. C. Ess. on admin.
Liverpool, Eng. Allingham. Varieties, **1** : 225.
— Brooks, E. S. Gt. cities, 62. — Dolman, F. Munic. at work, 42. — Fulton, C. C. Europe, 299. — Guild. Over the ocean, 28. — Hawthorne. Engl. note-books, **1** : 353. — Howe, J. W. Oak to olive, 9. — Stowe. Sunny mem. **1** : 14. — Silloway. Cathedral towns, 75.
— docks of, Extension of, 1898. (J. Boyle) U. S. Cons. Rept. **56** : 45.
— Pavements, sewers, artisans' dwellings. U. S. Cons. Rept. no. 117.
— Street life in, 340.
— Trade of, with U. S., 1898. (J. Boyle) U. S. Cons. Rept. **59** : 415.
Liverseege, Henry. Espinasse. Lanc. worth. v. 2.
Livesey, James. Kirton, J. W. Guthrie.
Live-stock, Transportation of. (J. C. Hoadley) Mass. Health, '75 : 79.
Livin, St. Conyngham, D. P. Irish saints, 375.
Living, Art of. Helps. Friends, 1st ser. 1. — Russell, A. P. Charac. 309.
— beyond one's means. Greeley. Hints ref. 326.
— Cost of. Ohio Labor, 1878. — U. S. Labor, 1890, 1891.
— — in Massachusetts and Gt. Britain, 1860–83. Mass. Labor, '84 : 435.
— good, Morality of. Matthews. Men & books, 159.
— to one's self. Hazlitt, W. Table-talk, 121.
— together, Art of. Siegvolk. Papers, 33.
— with others, Art of. Helps. Friends, 1st ser. 1; also in Prose masterpieces, **2** : 3.
Livingston, Edward. With portrait. [Amer.] Nat. portr. gall. v. 1. — Lossing. Em. Amer. 174. — Moore, F. Am. eloq. **2** : 218. — Perry, B. F. Biog. sketches, 1 : 555. — Sparks, W. H. Memories, 426.
— and his code of law. Godwin, P. Out of past, 56. — Hayward, A. Ess. 2d ser. **2** : 59.
Livingston, Mrs. Edward. Ellet, E. F. Court circles, 204.
Livingston, John Henry. Lossing. Em. Amer. 200.
Livingston, Philip. Dwight, N. Signers, 104. — Lincoln, R. W. Signers, 43. — Lossing. Signers, 67. — Sanderson. Signers, v. 3.
Livingston, Robert R. With portrait. [Amer.] Nat. portr. gall. v. 4. — With portrait. Duyckinck. Nat. portr. gall. **1** : 372. — Lossing. Signers, 238. — Lossing. Em. Amer. 105. — Moore, F. Am. eloq. **1** : 350.
Livingston, William. Moore, F. Am. eloq. **1** : 82.
Livingston family of Clermont, N. Y. Glenn, T. A. Colon. mans. **1** : 297.
Livingston manor. Terhune. Colon. homes, 201.
Livingstone, David. Benson & Tatham. Men of might, 237. — Em. persons, 1 : 225. — Blaikie, W. G. Leaders, 201. — Charles, E. Three martyrs. — Frost, T. Mod. explorers, 57. — Hodder. Heroes, **2** : 76. — Smiles. Self-help.
— With portrait. Bolton, S. K. Fam. voyag. 336. — Cochrane, R. Famous trav. 5. — Creegan. Great mission. 385. — Thayer, W. M. turn.-points, 106. — Duyckinck. Portrait gall. **2** : 605. — Famous boys, 237.
— and Stanley. Latimer. Eur. in Afr. in 19th cent. 123.
— Eulogy on. Stanley, A. P. Ser. spec. occ. 169.

London, Life in, Shakespeare's time. Hudson, W. H. Idle hours, 1.
— Literary, in 1835. Walsh, W. S. Pen pic. Vic. au. 1.
— Little Britain. Irving. Sk. book, 182.
— Lord Mayor of. Hatton, J. Old lamps, 336.
— Metropolitan improvement. Wynter, A. Fruit betw. leaves, 2 : 129.
— Modern and ancient Rome. Escott. Politics, 109.
— Newspapers of. Hatton. Jour. Lond. 155.
— Noise of. Cobbe, F. P. Re-echoes, 88.
— November day in. Everett, A. H. Ess. 2 : 452.
— Old theatres of. Winter. Shadows, 3 : 116.
— Omnibus system in. Wynter, A. Peeps, 1 : 220.
— out of season. Cobbe, F. P. Re-echoes, 179.
— Parks of. Doran. Drury Lane, 2 : 134.
— Pauperism in. (A. Foster) Reid, A. New party, 271.
— Plague in. See Plague.
— Pleasure grounds of. Cook, D. On stage, 2 : 291.
— Poetry of. Adams, W. D. With poet, 49.
— Post-office. Wynter, A. Our soc. bees, 1 : 1.
— Progressive party platform. Shaw, A. Munic. gov. Gt. Brit. 349.
— — Mechanism of. Head, F. B. Descr. ess. 2 : 286.
— Pulpit of ; Farrar, Liddon, Parker, Brooke. Mathews, W. Men, p. & t. 150.
— Quiet. Guiney. Patrins, 191.
— Red roofs of. Jefferies, R. Open air, 259.
— Riots in. Smalley. Lond. lett. 2 : 315, 332.
— Riverside parish in. (Sir W. Besant) Woods, R. A. Poor, 240.
— Sanitary legislation in. (E. Lankester) Trans. Soc. Sci. Lond. '60 : 666.
— Smoke in. Wynter, A. Our soc. bees, 1 : 24. — Wynter, A. Peeps, 2 : 214.
— Social awakening in. Woods, R. A. Poor, 1.
— Social condition, one hundred years ago. Bosanquet, Mrs. Standard, 191.
— Society in. Jeune. Lesser ques. 38.
— — Invitations sought. Smalley. Lond. lett. 2 : 16.
— — Politics as affecting. Smalley. Lond. lett. 2 : 3.
— Steelyard. Zimmern. Hansa towns, 179.
— Streets of, how lighted formerly. Knight. Once on time, 1 : 109.
— — Scenes in. Sterling, J. Ess. 2 : 15.
— Street traffic in. Wynter. Curios. of toil, 1 : 222.
— Bayard Taylor's first experiences in. Taylor, B. At home, 1 : 35.
— Temple. Bibliography. Baylis, T. H. Temple ch. & chap. St. Anne.
— Thackeray's. Lang. Leaders, 166.
— Theatres in. Kings and Dukes Theatre. Hogarth. Mem. opera, 1 : 76.
— Thieves of, and Lord Ashley. Whittier. Lit. recre. 136.
— Thoroughfares in, Congested condition of. Wynter, A. Fruit betw. leaves, 2 : 206.
— Thoughts on. Sterling, J. Ess. 2 : 3.
— Tower. Harrison. Choice of books, 275. — Wallace, S. E. Bosphorus, 129.
— Transformation of. Harrison, F. Mean. of hist. 412.
— Transit in. Wynter. Fruit, 2 : 206.
— Trees of. Maxwell, H. Post-mer. 254.
— Unification of. Shaw, A. Munic. govt. Gt. Brit. 354.
— Water supply of. Kingsley, C. New miscel. 203. — Wynter, A. Fruit betw. leaves, 1 : 218. 2 : 249. — Wynter, A. Our soc. bees, 2 : 27.

London Zoölogical Gardens. Wynter, A. Our soc. bees, 2 : 338.
"London," Wreck of the. Senior, W. Shipwrecks, 256.
London and Northwestern railway. Head, F. B. Descr. ess. 2 ; 76.
London Bridge, Old, Stories and ballads of. Timbs. Abbeys, 1 : 33.
— to Cabourg. Allingham. Varieties, 2 . 146.
London Cathedral. Van Rensselaer, M. G. Eng. cath. 361.
London Magazine, The. DeQuincey. Lit. rem. (Bost.) 2 : 257.
— and its staff. Procter, B. W. Autob. 204.
London Quarterly Review. Stanton, H. B. Reforms, 369.
London stout. Wynter, A. Our soc. bees, 1 : 208.
London Times. See Times.
London university, The. Macaulay. Ess. 6 : 331.
Londonderry, C. W. V. Stewart, marquis of. Georgian era, 2 : 144. — Martineau, H. Biog. sketch, 182. — Grant, J. Recoll. Lords, 107.
Londonderry, Robert Stewart, marquis of. Adams, W. H. D. Men at helm, 199. — Hazlitt. Parl. portr. 11.
Long, Elizabeth. Hack. Self-surr. 157.
Longborough, A. Wedderburn, Lord. Brougham. Works, 3 : 167.
Long-bow, The. George, H. B. Battles, 51.
Longchamp, William. Campbell. Ld. chan. 1 : 96. — Foss. Judges, 389.
Longevity. Bailey, J. B. Methuselahs, v. 1. — Holland, H. Ess. 102. — Jackson, R. M. S. The mountain, 270. — (G. L. Curtiss) Indiana Health, '80 : 37. — Wynter, A. Our soc. bees, 2 : 282.
— Curiosities of. Ess. from Nation, 223.
— Effect of climate on. Bryant. Prose, 2 : 373.
— The elixir of life. Five years theos. 1.
— Influence of civilization on. (C. T. Lewis) Am. Pub. Health, 3 : 165.
— Length of our days. Friswell. About, 249.
— Limitations and modifying conditions of. (S. Smith) Am. Pub. Health, 1 : 1.
— Marriage as affecting. Proctor, R. A. Univ. of suns, 354.
— of brain-workers. (G. M. Beard) Am. Pub. Health, 1 : 54.
— of men of genius. Madden. Infirm. gen. 47.
— Secret of. Mathews. Lit. style, 214.
— Signs and prerequisites of. (N. Allen) Am. Pub. Health, 1 : 39.
Longfellow, Henry Wadsworth. Badeau. Vagabond, 362. — Bolton, S. K. Amer. au. 28. — Devy. Mod. Eng. poets, 360. — Duyckinck. Nat. portr. gall. 2 : 444. — Friswell. Mod. men of let. 285. — Gilfillan. Mod. lit. 328. — Griswold, H. T. Home life, 220. — Griswold. Poets Am. 315. — With portrait. Griswold. Prose writ. 495. — Haweis. Poets in the pulpit. — Hazeltine. Chats, 169. — Houghton. Kings, 569. — Johnson, C. F. Three Amer. 213. — Lang. Lett. on lit. 43. — (J. T. Trowbridge) Parton. Princes, 289. — Powell. Liv. authors, 1850, 135. — Saunders, F. Famous books, 189. — Stedman. Poets Amer. 180. — Taylor, B. Crit. ess. 296. — Walsh, W. S. Pen pic. mod. 119. — Brooks, E. S. Hist. Amer. 354. — Fisher, M. Gen. sur. Am. lit. 198. — With portrait. Mitchell, D. G. Am. lands. 2 : 282. — Fields, A. Authors, 1. — Cheney, J. V. That dome, 116. — Wright, H. C. Chil. sto. in Am. lit. 156. — (H. E. Scudder) Mass. Hist. Proc. 2d ser. 8 : 152. — Curtis, G. W.

Louisiana, Settlement of. Parkman. Half-cent.
1 : 288.
Louisville, Ky. Warner, C. D. Studies, 279.
— Charity Organization Society. (W. T. Rolph)
Conf. char. & correc. '95 : 93.
— Medical College. U. S. Bur. Ed. Circ. '99, 3 :
288.
— Municipal condition of. (F. N. Hartwell) Nat.
Conf. City Govt. 2-3 : 391.
— Presbyterian Theological Seminary. U. S. Bur.
Ed. Circ. '99, 3 : 306.
— Tornado, March 27, 1890, Relief system after.
(W. T. Rolph) Conf. char. & correc. '90 :
'49.
Loupouloff, Prasca. Owen, Mrs. O. F. Hero-
ines domes. 337.
Lourdes. Buckley, J. M. Trav. three cont. 4.
— Miracles of, mind-cure, faith-cure, and the. (A.
T. and F. W. H. Myers) Soc. Psych. Res. 9 :
160.
— Our lady of. Brownson. Works, 8 : 104.
— Shrines of, and Zaragossa. Cust. Ling. &
orient. ess. 4 : 568.
Loutherbourg, Philip James de, scene-painter.
Cook, D. Art in Eng. 201.
Louvain, Historical sketch of. King, R. J. Sk.
404.
Louvain university, Degree of arts in. Hamil-
ton. Discus.
L'Ouverture, Toussaint. Gurney, J. H. Hist.
sketches, 3 : 194. — Chambers's Miscel. no.
57. — Phillips, W. Sp. 469.
Louvet de Couvray, Jean Baptiste. Smythe,
G. S. Hist. fancies, 267.
— Speeches of. Stephens, H. M. Ora. Fr. Rev.
1 : 454.
Louvois, François Michel Letellier, Marquis de.
Crowe, E. E. For. statesmen, 3 : 282.
Louvre, The. Guild. Over the ocean, 261. —
Stowe. Sunny mem. 2 : 159.
— and the Tuileries. Challice. Fr. palaces, 95.
— Gallery of. Beecher. Star papers, 56, 70.
— in 1802-4. Schlegel. Æsthetic works.
Lovat, Simon, Lord. Jesse. Pretenders, 77. —
Thomson, Mrs. Jacobites, 2 : 208. — Sec-
combe, T. Twelve bad men, 155.
Love, John. Morison, J. Fathers of Lond. Miss.
Soc. 2 : 59.
Love, Mrs. Mary. Anderson, Jas. Mem. wom.
Pur. 1 : 324.
Love. Bacon. Ess. — Bartol. Principles, 157. —
Dixon, T. Liv. prob. 158. — Emerson. Ess.
1 : 159. — Street, G. S. Miniatures, 96. —
Watson, E. H. L. Uncon. humor. 189. —
Simpson, R. Philos. of Shakespeare's son-
nets.
— and hatred. Hume. Philos. works, 2 : 66.
— and poetry. Patmore. Princ. in art, 72.
— Conception of, in some ancient and modern
languages. Abel, C. Ling. ess. 23.
— Courts of. Rutherford. Troubadours. — Pa-
get. Euphorion.
— Dantesque and Platonic ideals of. Symonds,
Key of blue, 55.
— Divine. Maurice, F. D. Theol. ess. 1.
— Essay on. Shelley. Ess. 1 : 136.
— Ethics of. Osgood, S. Amer. leaves, 281.
— Expressions of, in American languages. Brin-
ton. Ess. Amer. 410.
— Falling in. Allen, G. Falling in love, 1. — Gray,
E. C. Idle musings, 33. — Stevenson, R. L.
Virgin. 44.
— the foolish passion. Friswell. Gentle life, 2 :
181.
— History of. Swing, D. Club ess. 127.

Love, Human and divine. Patmore. Religio
poetæ, 213. — Holland, E. G. Reviews, 385.
— in life and literature. Zangwill. Without prej.
179.
— in ye olden time. Stone, J. S. Heart of Eng.
82.
— Infidelity in. Bulwer. Student, 1 : 61.
— Lyrists of. Adams, W. D. With poet, 110.
— Metaphysics of. Schopenhauer. Sel. ess. 55.
— The passion of. Hamerton. Hum. int. 33.
— Primitive. Bibliography. Finck, H. T. Prim.
love.
— Rationale of. Tuckerman. Optimist, 262.
— Religion of. Heckethorn. Sec. soc. 1 : 135.
— Sphere of. Rands, W. B. Holbeach, 2 : 34.
— Supremacy of. Caldwell, S. L. Cities of faith,
336.
— Third-. Matthews, A. Ruminations.
Love-charm. DeQuincey. Uncoll. writ. 2 : 113.
Love-songs, English. Repplier, A. Points of
view.
Lovejoy, Elijah Parish. Coggeshall. Poets of
west, 79.
— Murder of. Phillips, Wend. Sp. 1.
Lovejoy, Mrs. Ellet. Pioneer wom. 368.
Lovejoy, Owen. Dodge, M. A. Skirmish, 53.
Lovelace, Richard. Bell, R. Lit. & sci. men, 2 :
210. — Langford. Prison books, 189. — (E.
W. Gosse) Ward. Eng. poets, 2 : 181. — Wot-
ton. Word portraits, 181. — Choate, I. B.
Wells of Eng. 273. — Mitford, M. R. Recol-
lec. 287.
— Grave of. Hall, Mrs. S. C. Pilgr. Eng. shr. 2 :
143.
— Hazlitt's edition. Lowell. Writ. 1 : 302.
Lovell, James. Loring, J. S. Hundred Bost. ora.
29.
Lovell, John. Lossing. Em. Amer. 97.
Lovell, Mansfield. Pollard. Life of Lee, 621.
Lover, Samuel. (A. J. Symington) Miles, A. H.
Poets of cent. 9 : 229. — Willis. Hurry-graphs,
196. — With portrait. Warner Lib. 16 : 9216.
— as actor. Hutton, L. Plays, 115.
Lovering, Joseph. Vaille & Clarke. Harv.
book, v. 1.
Lovett, William. Stanton, H. B. Reforms, 311.
Lovewell, John, Campaigns of, against the In-
dians. Parkman. Half-cent. 1 : 241.
Lovibond, Edward. Chalmers. Eng. poets, 16 :
283.
Low, Abiel Abbott. Brockett. Men of our day,
520.
Low, Edward. Whitehead, C. Highwaymen, 2 :
132.
Low countries. See Netherlands.
Low Moor Company, The. Fortunes made in
bus. 1 : 87.
Lowe, Helen. Bethune, G. W. Brit. fem. poets,
432.
Lowe, Col. J. W. (J. O. Lowe) Shea, J. G.
Fallen brave.
Lowe, Martha Perry. Putnam, A. P. Singers
liberal, 497.
Lowe, Robert. See Sherbrooke, Viscount.
Lowe, Wilhelm, called Löwe-Kalbe. Tuttle, H.
Ger. pol. lead. 139.
Lowell, Anna. Brockett. Woman's work, 792.
Lowell, Charles. (W. Jenks) Mass. Hist. Proc.
5 : 427. — Peabody. Harv. grad. 98. — (Mrs.
M. L. Putnam) N. E. Hist.-Gen. Soc. Biog.
4 : 134.
Lowell, Charles Russell, Col. (J. M. Peirce)
Harvard mem. biog. 1 : 275. — Lodge & Roose-
velt. Hero-tales, 261.
Lowell, Edward J. (A. L. Lowell) Mass. Hist.

Soc. Proc. 2d ser. **9** : 541. — Am. Acad. A. &
S. Proc. **30** : 562.

Lowell, James Jackson. (F. J. Child) Harvard
mem. biog. **1** : 395.

Lowell, James Russell. (H. E. Scudder) Am.
Acad. A. & S. Proc. **29** : 423. — Curtis, G. W.
Orations, **3** : 365. — Bolton, S. K. Amer. au.
156. — Bungay. Off-hand, 394. — Griswold,
H. T. Home life, 262. — Griswold. Poets
Amer. 485. — Griswold. Prose writ. 660. —
Haweis. Amer. humorists, 73, — Rideing.
Boyhood. — Stedman. Poets Amer. 304. —
Taylor, B. Crit. ess. 298. — Walsh, W. S. Pen
pic. mod. 135. — Cheney, J. V. That dome,
61. — Wright, H. C. Chil. sto. in Amer. lit.
203. — James, H. Ess. in Lond. 44. — Mey-
nell, A. Rhythm, 68. — Bartlett, D. W. Mod.
agit. 307. — Em. persons, **5** : 100. — Fisher,
M. Gen. sur. Am. lit. 310. — (C. F. Briggs)
Hubbard, E. Little jour. **2** : 123. Same art.
Homes Amer. authors. — Nichol. Amer. lit.
220, 413. — (F. B. Sanborn) Powers, H. N.
Homes of eld. poets, 162. — Richardson.
Amer. lit. **1** : 409, 478. **2** : 186. — Stead. Char.
sk. 121. — Stewart, Geo., jr. Evenings in lib.
74. — Stewart, G. Ess. from Rev. — Stoddard,
R. H. Poets' homes, 84. — Vaille & Clark,
Harv. book, v. **1**. — Howe, M. A. D. Amer.
bookm. 242. — With portrait. (H. James)
Warner Lib. **16** : 9229.

— as a critic. Watson, W. Excur. in crit. 89.

— as a prose writer. Whipple. Outlooks, 306.

— as a teacher. Wendell, B. Stelligeri, 203.

— at home. (G. E. Woodberry) Gilder. Authors,
227.

— Bibliography. Hale, E. E., jr. Jas. Russell
Lowell. — Hodgkins. Nineteenth cent. authors.

— in England. Smalley. Lond. let. **1** : 217.

— Last years in Cambridge. Higginson. Book
& heart, 47. — With portrait. (A. L. Lowell)
Mass. Hist. Soc. Proc. 2d ser. **11** : 75.

— Letters. Mabie. My study fire, **2** : 79. — Stillman, W. J. Old Rome.

— Poems. Nichol, J. Amer. lit. 220, 412. — Wilkinson, W. C. Free lance, 50.

— poet and statesman. Bungay. Repr. men, 11.

— Prose works. Wilkinson, W. C. Free lance,
105.

— Sonnets of. Deshler. Afternoons, 300.

— Vision of Sir Launfal. Brownson. Works, **19** :
308.

Lowell, John. Am. Bar Assoc. **20** : 537. —
Loring, J. S. Hundred Bost. ora. 278. — (J.
Lowell) Mass. Hist. Proc. **2** : 160.

Lowell, John, jr., and the Lowell Lectures. Bolton, S. K. Givers, 1. — Everett. Orat. v. **2**.

Lowell, John A., Memoir of, with portrait. (C.
C. Smith) Mass. Hist. Soc. Proc. 2d ser. **12** :
113.

Lowell, Mass., Cemetery of. Whittier. Lit.
recre. 335.

— Condition of labor in. (C. D. Wright) Mass.
Labor, '82 : 195.

— Founders of. Parton. Capt. indus. 170.

— in 1843. Whittier. Lit. recre. 316.

— "Lighting up night" in the mills. Whittier.
Lit. recre. 403.

— past and present. Pidgeon. Old World ques.
234.

— Sunday in. Whittier. Lit. recre. 381.

Lowenberg, Moses, Murder case of. Clinton,
H. L. Extraor. cases, 263.

Lower California, Geology and natural history of.
(G. P. Merrill) U. S. Nat. Mus. Rept. '95 : 969.

Lower grades, Educational burdens upon. (Abbie Low) Nat. Educa. Assoc. '91 : 599.

Lower life, A study of. Wilson, A. Leisure, 45.

Lowin, John. Collier. Actors, 165.

Lowndes, William. Perry, B. F. Biog. sketches,
1 : 371.

Lowry, Mrs. Ellen J. Brockett. Woman's work,
736.

Lowry, Walter Hoge. Brown, D. P. Forum, **2** :
143.

Lowther, Captain. Whitehead, C. Highwaymen, **2** : 119.

Lowther Castle. Jewitt, L. Stately homes, **2** :
291.

Lowther family. Sanford & Townsend. Gov.
fam. 1.

Loyalists, The. Ferguson, H. Ess. Am. hist.
161.

Loyalty. Henry, C. S. Satan, 189. — Starling,
E. Noble deeds wom. 366.

— to country, Doctrine of. Bushnell. Work,
343.

Loyola, Ignatius. Brigham, C. H. Mem. 299. —
Hewlett. Heroes, 302. — Lord, J. Beacon, **3** :
299. — Ranke. Popes, **1** : 181. — Church, R.
W. Occ. pap. **1** : 238. — (Sir J. Stephen) Ferris, G. T. Gt. leaders, 230. — Hundred greatest men, 183. — Nasmith. Mak. mod. thought,
1 : 79.

— and his associates. Stephen, J. Ess.

— and the Jesuits. Lawrence, E. Hist. stud. 99.
— Taylor, W. C. Rom. biog. v. **2**.

Loyola College, Baltimore, Md. U. S. Bur. Ed.
Circ. '94, no. **2** : 175.

Loyson, C. J. M., Père Hyacinthe. With photo.
Cooper, T. Men of mark, **1** : 26.

— at Geneva. Yates, E. H. Celeb. **2** : 17.

— at Nôtre Dame. Field, Mrs. H. M. Sk. France,
87.

Lozier, Clemence Sophia, with portrait. (H. B.
Elliot) Parton. Em. wom. 517.

Lubbock, Sir John. With photo. Cooper, T.
Men of mark, **2** : 22. — Hinton. Eng. radicals.
— Ritchie, J. E. City men, 206. — With por-
trait. Warner Lib. **16** : 9279.

Lubieniecius, Andrew. Wallace, R. Anti-Trin.
biog. **2** : 386.

Lubieniecius, Christopher. Wallace, R. Anti-
Trin. biog. **2** : 389.

Lubieniecius, Christopher, jr. Wallace, R.
Anti-Trin. biog. **3** : 117.

Lubieniecius, Gabriel. Wallace, R. Anti-Trin.
biog. **3** : 143.

Lubieniecius, Stanislaüs. Wallace, R. Anti-
Trin. biog. **2** : 388.

Lubieniecius, Stanislaüs, jr. Wallace, R. Anti-
Trin. biog. **3** : 294.

Luby, Thos. Clarke. Savage, J. Fenian heroes,
317.

Lucas, Daniel Bedinger. Davidson, J. W. Writ.
of South, 343.

Lucca, Pauline. Edwards, H. S. Prima don. **2** :
125.

Lucca. Hare. Cities of No. Italy, **2** : 490. —
Howells. Tuscan cities, 221. — Tuckerman.
Ital. sk. 214. — Duffy, B. Tuscan repub. **22** :
106.

— Vermigli, Pietro Martin, in. Stoughton. Ital.
Reformers, 37.

Luce, Eugénie (Berlan) Allix. Belloc. Vignettes,
181.

Lucerne. Prime, S. I. Alhambra, 186.

Luci, Richard de. Foss. Judges, **1** : 264.

Lucian, St., of Beauvois, priest and martyr.
Charles. Martyrs, 123.

Lucian. Arnold, E. Poets of Greece, 204. — Gildersleeve. Ess. 299. — Froude. Short stud. 3 : 210. — Lang. Let. to dead au. 55. — Pressensé. Martyrs, 450. — Traill. New fiction, 196. — With portrait. (E. J. Smith) Warner Lib. 16 : 9285.

— a satirist of the 2d century. Shackford. Soc. & lit. pap. 31.

— true history, Note on. Besant. Fr. humor. 129.

Lucidity or clairvoyance. (C. Richet) Soc. Psych. Res. 6 : 66.

Luciennes, Pavilion of. Imbert de St. A. Wom. last yrs. L. xv, 177.

Lucilius, Caius. Dunlop, J. Rom. liter. 1 : 359. — Sellar. Rom. poets repub. 217.

Luck. Friswell. Gentle life, 1 : 57. — Gray, E. C. Idle musings, 217. — Lawrence, R. M. Magic, 140.

— Belief in. Jones, W. Credulities, 115.

— Dangers and successes. Arnold, F. Turning-points, 53.

Lucknow. Barker, Lady. Travel. about, 326. — Field, H. M. Egypt to Japan, 222. — Pidgeon. Engineer's holiday, 384.

— and Cawnpore. Knox, T. W. Battles, 154.

— Defense of. Bartlett, D. W. Heroes Ind. rebel. 390.

— Relief of. Bartlett, D. W. Heroes Ind. rebel. 70.

— Siege of. Robson, W. Sieges, 657.

— to-day, 1879. Forbes, A. Camps, 271.

Lucretia, with portrait. Clarke, M. C. Noted wom. 23.

Lucretia Donati, Lorenzo de Medici and. Jameson. Loves of poets.

Lucretius Caius, Titus. Dunlop, J. Rom. liter. 1 : 379. — Hundred greatest men, 25. — Lang. Let. on lit. 102. — Sellar. Rom. poets repub. 274. — Symonds. Sk. So. Eur. 1 : 339. — Osborn. From Greeks, 60. — With portrait. (P. Shorey) Warner Lib. 16 : 9304.

— and the atomic theory. Jenkin, H. C. F. Papers, 1 : 177.

— and Catullus, Style of. Conington. Miscel. 256.

— and the poetic characteristics of his age. (W. Y. Sellar) Oxf. ess. '55 : 1.

— De rerum natura. Buchanan, R. Look round, 96.

— Munro's. Conington. Miscel. 229.

Lucy, St., of Syracuse. Charles. Martyrs, 169.

Lucy, Lady Alice. Burder. Pious wom. 123.

Luddite rioters, 1812. Thornbury. Old stor. 196. — Browne, G. L. State trials 19th cent. 2 : 64.

Ludewig, Hermann Ernst. (H. C. Murphy) N. E. Hist.-Gen. Soc. Biog. 3 : 136.

Ludicrous side of life. Whipple. Lit. & life.

Ludlow, Edmund. Macaulay. Biog. sk. 237.

Ludlow castle. The lord marchers of Wales. Hutton, B. Castles, 263.

Ludlow station, Cincinnati. Mansfield, E. D. Pers. mem. 21.

Ludwig I., deposed king of Bavaria. Doran. Monarchs, 1 : 364.

Ludwig II., of Bavaria. (Mrs. J. Lillie) Parton. Princes, 121.

Ludwig, M'lle, of the Comédie français. Stuart, H. Paris days, 237.

Ludwig, Hubert, and modern physiology. (J. Burdon-Sanderson) Smithson. Rept. '96 : 365.

Luebeck, Germany. Mahaffy. Holl. & Germ. 212.

Lueneburg, Germany. Mahaffy. Holl. & Germ. 221.

Luers, John Henry. Clarke, R. H. Cath. bishops, 2 : 555.

Luetzen, Battle of. King, C. Battles, 265.

— in 1862. Merivale. Hist. stud. 286.

Luini, Bernardino. Stillman, W. J. Old Ital. mast. 255. — Symonds. Renais. fine arts, 484.

Luini, Bernardo. Bibliography. Williamson, G. C. Bernardo Luini.

Luke, St., Writings, their existence and origin. Zeller. Acts, 1 : 93.

Luke, Jemima. Miller, Jos. Singers church, 2d ed. 519.

Lukens, Henry Clay. Clemens. Funny fellows, 150.

Lull, Raymund. Maclear. Apostles, 269.— Waite, A. E. Lives of alchem. 68.

Lullworth Castle. Timbs. Abbeys, 1 : 452.

Lully, Giovanni Battista. Chambers's Miscel. no. 29. — Hogarth. Mem. opera, 1 : 20. — Richards, L. E. Glimpses, 40. — Ferris, G. T. Ital. & Fr. compos. 120.

Lumber industry in the U. S. (N. S. Shaler) Shaler. The U. S. 1 : 485.

Lumber trade, British. Galt, J. Lit. life, 2 : 64.

Lumley, Lady Jane. Williams, Jane. Lit. wom. 57.

Lumpkin, Joseph H. Sparks, W. H. Memories, 174.

Lunacy. See Insanity.

Lundy, Benj. Birney. J. G. Birney, 389.

Lundy's Lane, Battle of. Dawson. Batt. of U. S. 2 : 352. — Silliman. Gallop, 112, 314.

Lungs and air-passages, Diseases of. (H. B. Baker) Mich. Health, '91 : 127.

Lunt, George. Griswold. Poets of Amer. 329.

Lunt, Rev. William P. (N. L. Frothingham) Mass. Hist. Coll. 4th ser. 4 : 508. — Putnam, A. P. Singers liberal, 194.

Luray caverns. Hovey, H. C. Cel. Am. cav. 163.

Lush, Sir Robert. With photo. Cooper, T. Men of mark, 5 : 16. — Gener. of judges, 21.

Lushington, Charles. Grant, J. Recoll. Lords & Comm. 2 : 216.

Lushington, Stephen. Georgian era, 2 : 359.

Lushington, Thomas. Wallace R. Anti-Trin. biog. 2 : 170.

Lusk, Sir Andrew. Ritchie, J. E. City men, 74. — Ritchie. Brit. sena. 182.

Lussan, Zélie de, with portrait. Buffen. Mus. celeb. 2 : 47.

Luther, Madame Martin (Catherine de Bora). Chapman, W. Wom. of ref. 41. — Child. Good wives, 129. — Wittenmeyer. Women Reform. 361.

Luther, Margaret L. Holloway, L. C. Mothers of gt. men, 221.

Luther, Martin. Brigham, C. H. Mem. 244. — Carlyle. Heroes. — Coleridge. Friend, 724. — Dawson, G. Biog. lec. 458. — Graham, W. Ess. 67. — Headley, J. T. Miscel. 251. — With portrait. Hedge. Prose Ger. 9. — Hewlett. Heroes, 254. — Lord, J. Beacon, 8 : 217. — Mozley. Ess. 1 : 320. — Reformers. Paisley lec. 191. — Russell, W. Extraor. men, 18. — Stephen. Ess. eccl. biog. 189. — Tagart. Sk. ref. 16th cent. 3. — Taylor. Stud. Ger. 149. — Tulloch. Leaders reform. — Brooks, P. Ess. & addr. 375.— Cooke, F. E. Guid. lights. — (T. Carlyle) Ferris, G. T. Gt. leaders, 222. — Gurney, J. H. Hist. sketches, 1 : 147. — Hatfield, E. F. Poets of ch. 387. — Hedge, F. H. Martin Luther, 1. — Hundred greatest men, 175. — Miller, Jos. Singers church, 2d ed. 39. —Mombert. Great lives, 175. — Morley, H. Eng. writ. 7 : 215. — Nasmith. Makers mod. thought, 53. — Myers, F. Lec. gt. men, 1. — Pennington. Epochs papacy, 278. — Scherer.

Germ. lit. 1 : 272. — Waterbury. Eloq. preach. 214. — With portrait. (C. D. Hartranft) Warner Lib. 16 : 9319.

Luther, Martin, and Calvin, Contrast between. Broadus. Lec. hist. preach. 118.
— and Erasmus, Times of. Froude. Short stud. 1 : 37.
— and his friends. Winkworth. Chr. singers Germ. 98.
— and his times. Williams, W. R. Eras, 182.
— and his work. (F. H. Hedge) Mass. Hist. Proc. 20 : 364.
— and Leo X. Lawrence, E. Hist. stud. 56.
— and the reformation. Clarke, J. F. Events, 241. — Stephen, J. Ess.
— as a preacher. Ker, J. Lec. hist. preach. 147. — Broadus. Lec. hist. preach. 122.
— Correspondence and character of. Rogers, H. Ess. 1 : 104; or Reason, 90.
— Ein feste Burg. Carlyle. Essays.
— French revolution and its relation to. Farmer, J. E. Ess. Fr. hist. 3.
— Hallucinations of. Ireland, W. W. Blot, 37.
— Hans, son of. Brooks, E. S. Gt. men's sons, 244.
— Memoir of. Croly. Hist. sk. 225.
— Table-talk. Coleridge. Lit. rem. 4 : 1.

Lutheran Church. (G. F. Krotel) Why I am, 106.
— Bibliography. Jacobs, H. E. Hist. Luther. ch. U. S.
— modern, Preaching of. Ker, J. Lec. hist. preach. 376.

Lutomirscius, Stanislaüs. Wallace, R. Anti-Trin. biog. 2 : 177.

Luttrell, Henry, Letters to Julia. Dobson, A. Miscel. 203.

Luttrell, Narcissus, Diary of. Ewald, A. C. Paper, 173.

Luxembourg, Madeleine Angélique de N. V., Maréchale de. Haussonville. Salon of Necker, 1 : 206.

Luxembourg, Grand duchy of. U. S. Cons. Rept. 43 : 352.

Luxembourg gallery. Beecher. Star papers, 64.

Luxuries. Woolson. Browsing, 135.

Luxury. Filangieri. Science of legislation, 2 : 259. — Stephen, L. Soc. rights, 2 : 95.
— and the Fine Arts, in some of their moral and historical relations. Winthrop. Addresses, 2 : 451.
— and refinement. Bosanquet, B. Civil. of Christendom, 268.
— Discomforts of. Repplier, A. In dozy hours, 112.
— frugality and, True effects of. Bastiat. Ess. on pol. econ. 107.
— Our love of. Ess. from Nation, 205.
— What is culpable ? Smith, Gold. Lec. & ess. 147.

Luynes, Charles, Duc de, favorite of Louis XIII. Menzies, S. Roy. fav. 1 : 433.

Luynes, H. T. P. J. D'Albert, Duc de. Oliphant, T. L. K. Duke, v. 1.

Luz, Templar church of St. Jean de. Larned, W. C. Churches & C. 90.

Luzenberg, Charles Aloysius (1805–48). (Thos. M. Logan) Gross. Lives physicians, 545.

Lyall, Alfred C. Escott, T. H. S. Pillars emp. 177.

Lyall, Edna, pseud. See Bayly, Ada E.

Lycanthropy, Were-wolves and. Wynter. Fruit, 1 : 106.

Lyceum, English. Lennox, W. P. Plays, 1 : 139.

Lycia, Travels in. Vaughan, R. Ess. 1 : 284.

Lycophron. Arnold, E. Poets of Greece, 167. — Mills. Poets of Greece, 161. — Mahaffy, J. P. Greek life, ch. 12.

Lycurgus. Mombert. Great lives, 9. — Duruy. Hist. of Greece, 1 : 443.
— Institutions of. Ames, F. Works, 439.

Lycurgus, poet. Mills. Poets of Greece, 447.

Lydda and Ramleh. (Warren) Wilson, C. W. Pictur. Palest. 3 : 145.

Lydford, Castle of. Timbs. Abbeys, 1 : 474.

Lydgate, John. Disraeli, I. Amen. (N. Y. 2 v.) 1 : 226. — Fuller. Worthies, 3 : 183. — Morley. Eng. writ. 6 : 101. — (T. Arnold) Ward. Eng. poets, 1 : 114. — Macdonald, G. England's antiphon, 45. — Minto, W. Eng. poets, 75.

Lydiat, Thomas. Fuller. Worthies, 3 : 21.

Lyell, Sir Charles. Bolton, S. K. Fam. men of science, 246. — Duncan, P. M. Botanists, 307.
— Eulogy on. Stanley, A. P. Ser. spec. occ. 198.

Lying. Friswell. Gentle life, 2 : 157.
— A few remarks on the rare vice called. Hunt, L. Men, wom. & books, 129.

Lykewake, The. Miller, H. Tales, 201.

Lyle, Alexander. Walker, C. D. Biog. Va. Mil. Inst. 346.

Lyly, John. Collier. Eng. dram. lit. 3 : 1. — Dunham. Lit. & sci. men, 2 : 67. — Hazlitt. Dram. Eliz. — Jusserand. Eng. novel. 103. — Symonds. Shakes. pred. 499. — Ulrici. Shakespeare, 1 : 84. — Ward, A. W. Eng. dram. 1 : 151. — (W. Minto) Ward. Eng. poets, 1 : 394. — Minto, W. Eng. poets, 228. — Morley, H. Eng. writ. 8 : 305. 9 : 196. — Vincent, L. H. Bibliotaph, 137.

Lyman, Phineas. Lossing. Em. Amer. 113.

Lyman, Theodore. (H. P. Bowditch) Am. Acad. A. & S. Proc. 34 : 656. — Loring, J. S. Hundred Bost. ora. 391, 704. — (T. Lyman) N. E. Hist.-Gen. Soc. Biog. 1 : 169.

Lyme house, England. (Lady Newton) Malan, A. H. Famous homes, 263.
— and the Leghs. Croston. Hist. sites Lanc. 278.

Lymne, Excavations at. Smith, C. R. Retrospec. 1 : 205.

Lynch, Anne C. See Botta, Anne C. L.

Lynch, James. Burke, O. J. Cath. archb. 171.

Lynch, Patrick Niesen. Clarke, R. H. Cath. bishops, 3 : 68.

Lynch, Thomas, jr. Dwight, N. Signers of decl. 347. — Lincoln, R. W. Signers, 45. — Lossing. Signers, 219. — Sanderson. Signers, v. 5.

Lynch, Thomas Toke. Miller, Jos. Singers church, 2d ed. 560. — (W. G. Horder) Miles, A. H. Poets of cent. 10 : 313.

Lynch law. Barrows, W. U. S. of yester. 221.

Lyndhurst, J. S. Copley, Lord. With portrait. Bennet, W. H. Sel. biog. 177. — Foss. Judges, 9 : 178. — Francis, G. H. Orators, 111. — Lucas. Mornings, 2 : 5. — Martineau, H. Biog. sk. 338. — Laurence, P. M. Collect. 135. — Grant, Jas. Bench & bar, 1 : 101. — Grant, J. Recoll. Lords, 165.
— Scene between him and Lord Melbourne. Grant, J. Recoll. Lords, 1 : 58.

Lyndsay, Sir David. Hannay. Satire, 51. — Irving, D. Scot. poets, 2 : 71. — Lindsay. Lives, 1 : 87. — Veitch. Feeling for nature. — Wilson, J. G. Poets of Scot. 1 : 34. — Ward. Eng. poets, 1 : 192.

Lyndsay, Margaret Keith, Lady. Fittis. Heroines of Scot. 67.

Lyne, Joseph L. [Father Ignatius], at Llanthony. Yates, E. H. Celeb. 2 : 207.

Lynedoch, Lord. Cole, J. W. Brit. generals, v. **2**.

Lynn, Eng. Silloway. Cathedral towns, 279.

Lyon, Hanford, with portrait. Rogers, A. C. Repres. men, 357.

Lyon, Mary. Bolton, S. K. Girls famous, 122. — Hanaford. Wom. of cent. 499.

Lyon, Merrick. (W. A. Mowry) Nat. Educa. Assoc. '89 : 362.

Lyon, Nathaniel, Gen. Duyckinck. Nat. portr. gall. **2** : 351. — Glazier, W. Heroes, 391. — Shea, J. G. Fallen brave.

— Memoir of. Lyon, N. Last pol. writ. 11.

— Reminiscences of. Lyon, N. Last pol. writ. 233.

Lyons, Richard B. Penell, Earl. Em. persons, **4** : 17.

Lyons. Everett, E. Mt. Vernon, 301. — Fairbanks, O. B. Aguecheek, 89.

— Exposition of 1894. (C. W. Parks) U. S. Bur. Ed. Rept. '93–94, **2** : 1729.

— Sieges of. Robson, W. Sieges, 269.

Lyons's Creek, Canada, Action at. Dawson. Batt. of U. S. **2** : 398.

Lyric and dramatic. Clarke, J. F. Nineteenth cent. ques. 3.

Lyric poetry. Tuckerman. Optimist, 103.

— of Alexandria. Mahaffy, J. P. Greek life, ch. 11.

Lyric poets, Greek. Symonds. Greek poets, **1** : 287.

Lyrics, sacred, of the 13th cent. Macdonald, G. England's antiphon, 5.

Lysias. Mills. Poets of Greece, 442.

— Bibliography. Morgan, M. H. (ed.). Lysias eight orat.

Lysimachus. Mahaffy, J. P. Greek life, ch. 3.

Lysons, Sir D., with photo. Cooper, T. Men of mark, **6** : 17.

Lyte, Henry Francis. Hatfield, E. F. Poets of church, 391. — Miles, A. H. Poets of cent. **10** : 157. — Miller, Jos. Singers church, 2d ed. 431. — Wilson, J. G. Poets of Scot. **2** : 137.

Lytle, William Haines. Coggeshall. Poets of west, 565.

Lyttelton, Edward, Lord keeper, 1641. Foss. Judges, **6** : 343.

Lyttelton, George, Lord. (S. Johnson) Chalmers. Eng. poets, **14** : 161. — Creasy. Etonians, 268. — Lawrence. Brit. historians, **1** : 366. — Crichton, A. Converts, **1** : 188. — Jesse, J. H. Cel. Eton. v. **1**.

Lyttelton, Thomas. Foss. Judges, **4** : 436.

Lyttleton, Anne Temple, Lady. Jesse. Court of Eng. Stuarts, **3** : 304.

Lyttleton, C., bp. of Carlisle. Jesse, J. H. Cel. Eton. v. **1**.

— and Lucy Fortesque. Jameson. Loves of poets.

Lytton, Sir Edward Bulwer, Lord. *See* Bulwer-Lytton.

Lytton, Robert, Lord. Em. persons, **5** : 147. — Farrar. Men, 257. — Smalley. Lond. lett. **1** : 326. — With portrait. Warner Lib. **16** : 9348.

Maartens, Maarten, with portrait. (W. Sharp) Warner Lib. **16** : 9357.

Maas, Joseph. Smith, C. R. Retrospec. **3** : 100.

Mabinogion, The. Warner Lib. **16** : 9373.

Macadam, John. Parton. Triumphs, 571.

MacAlexander, Families of. Rogers, C. Mem. Stirling, **1** : 1.

McAll, Robert Stephens. Hatfield, E. F. Poets of church, 395.

MacAll mission. Loomis, S. L. Mod. cities, 163. — Pierson, A. T. Evangelistic work, 277.

McAnally, D. R. Davidson, J. W. Writ. of South, 344.

Macao. Norman, H. Far East, 183.

Macaroneana. Cracroft. Ess. **2** : 166.

Macaroni, Manufacture of. U. S. Cons. Rept. no. 125.

Macaroni industry of Italy, 1891. (A. O. Bourn and others) U. S. Cons. Rept. **35** : 199.

M'Arthur, William. Ritchie. Brit. sena. 233. — Ritchie, J. E. City men, 85.

Macartin, St. Conyngham, D. P. Irish saints, 131.

Macaulay, Catherine. Lawrence. Brit. historians, **2** : 230.

Macaulay, Thos. Babington. Adams, C. K. Rep. Br. orat. **3** : 50. — Alison. Ess. 3. — Bagehot. Estimates, 410. — Bayne, P. Ess. **2** : 52. — Canning. Lit. infl. in Brit. history. — Collier, W. F. Hist. Eng. lit. 461. — Gilfillan. First gall. 262. — Gilfillan. Third gall. 233. — Gilfillan. Mod. lit. 110. — Gladstone. Glean. **2** : 265. — Griswold, H. T. Home life, 177. — Horne. New spirit of the age, **2** : 33. — Maginn. Fras. papers, 112. — Martineau, H. Biog. sk. 102. — Mason, E. T. Pers. traits, **4** : 33. — Morley. Crit. miscel. **1** : 253. — Russell, A. P. Charac. 74. — Skelton. Ess. 279. — Stephen, J. F. Ess. by barr. 97. — Stephen, L. Hours in libr. **3** : 279. — Stirling, J. H. Jerrold, 112. — Taine. Eng. lit. **2** : 402. — Tuckerman. Charac. **1** : 171. — Walsh, W. S. Pen pic. Vic. au. 136. — Whipple. Ess. & rev. 1. — Wotton. Word portraits, 187. — Anton. Masters in hist. — Brooks, S. W. Eng. poets, 497. — Duyckinck. Portr. gall. **2** : 104. — Francis, G. H. Orators, 64. — Harrison, F. Stud. early Vict. 64. — Howells. My lit. passions, 114. — Saintsbury. Correc. imp. 79. — Lancaster, H. H. Ess. & rev. 178. — Miles, A. H. Poets of cent. **3** : 277. — Mitchell, D. G. Eng. lands, **4** : 259. — Punshon. Lec. 39. — With portrait. (J. B. McMaster) Warner Lib. **16** : 9381 ; also in Warner Classics, **4** : 127.

— and the duke of Marlborough. Paget, J. Paradoxes, 3.

— as a translator. Tartt. Ess. **1** : 162.

— at college. (E. P. Whipple) Parton. Princes, 164.

— Biog. sketch of. (E. P. Whipple) Macaulay. Ess. (Bost.) **1** : vii.

— Bibliography of. Hodgkins. Nineteenth cent. authors.

— Connection with Edinburgh. Macaulay. Biog. Encyc. Brit. ix.

— Frederick the Great and. Grimm, H. Liter. 131.

— History of England. Cobb, J. B. Leis. labors, 248.

— Mornings with. Stuart, J. M. Reminis. 15.

— Place in Eng. literature. Lancaster, H. H. Essays, 178.

— Prose style of. Hunt, T. W. Rep. Eng. prose, 387.

— Writings of. Chambers's Repos. no. 20.

Macaulay, Zachary. Blaikie, W. G. Leaders, 107. — Stanton, H. B. Reforms, 217.

M'Auley, Alexander. Wesley & successors, 229.

McAvoy, Margaret, the blind girl. Wilson, H. Characters, 202.

Macbeth, John W. V. Might and mirth of literature. Heywood, J. C. How they strike, 251.

McCabe, James D., jr. Davidson, J. W. Writ. of South, 345.

McCabe, W. Gordon. Davidson, J. W. Writ. of South, 347.

Maccabees; brave brethren of Judah. Yonge. Gold. deeds.

McCafferty, John. Savage, J. Fenian heroes, 177.

McCalla, Daniel. Headley, J. T. Chaplains Revol. 276.

McCalla, Mrs. Thomas. Clement, J. Noble deeds, 146.

McCance, Robert G. Walker, C. D. Biog. Va. Mil. Inst. 373.

McCartee, Mrs. Jessie G. Bethune. Griswold. Fem. poets, 131.

McCarthy, Denis F. Williams, A. M. Poets of Irel.

McCarthy, Justin, with portrait. Warner Lib. 16 : 9440. — Wilman, G. Sk. liv. celeb. 68.

MacCarthy family. Burke, B. Viciss. of fam. 2 : 312.

MacCarthy-More. Burke, B. Viciss. of fam. 1 : 162.

McCarty, Nicholas. Woollen. Biog. sk. Indiana, 457.

McCheyne, Robert Murray. Hatfield, E. F. Poets of church, 297. — Miller, Jos. Singers church, 2d ed. 517.

Macchiavelli, Niccolo. Greene, G. W. Hist. stud. 46. — Hewlett. Heroes, 225. — Montgomery. Men of Ita. 1 : 256. — Symonds. Age of despots, 308. — Symonds. Renais. It. lit. 2 : 157, 431. — Vincent, G. E. Ital. authors, 84. — With portrait. (C. P. Neill) Warner Lib. 16 : 9479. — Nasmith. Mak. mod. thought, 1 : 38. — Owen, J. Skeptics Ital. 160. — Shelley, Mrs. Lit. men Italy, v. 1.

— Works of. Macaulay. Ess. 1 : 267. — Mackintosh, J. Miscel. 245.

Machlipatanam. Malleson, G. B. Battles of India, 72.

McClellan, George, 1796-1847. (J. H. B. McClellan) Gross. Lives physicians, 498.

McClellan, George B., Gen. Duyckinck. Nat. portr. gall. 2 : 408. — Glazier, W. Heroes, 287. — Keyes, E. D. Fifty years observa. 437. — (J. C. Ropes) Dwight, F. F. Fed. & confed. comm. 97. — Lanman, C. Haphazard, 370.

— as presidential candidate, 1864. Lowell. Pol. ess. 153.

— — Nomination of. Winthrop. Addresses, 2 : 590.

— Bibliography. Campaigns in Va. Mass. Milit. Hist. Soc. v. 1.

— Comments on Peninsula Campaign of. (C. A. Whittier) Dwight, T. F. Camp. Va. 277.

— Own story, reviewed. Piatt, D. Men who saved Un. 280.

— Plans for the Peninsula Campaign. (J. C. Ropes) Dwight, T. F. Camp. Va. 59.

— Report on army of the Potomac, July, 1861, to Nov. 1862. Lowell. Pol. ess. (Writ.) 5 : 92.

— Retreat to Harrison's Landing. Allan, W. Army of N. Va. 139.

Macclesfield, Thomas Parker, earl of. Campbell. Ld. chan. 6 : 1. — Welsby. Eng. judges.

McClintock, Andrew Todd. Am. Bar Assoc. 15 : 463.

McClintock, Sir F. L., with photo. Cooper, T. Men of mark, 3 : 19.

McCloskey, John, Cardinal. Clarke, R. H. Cath. bishops, 3 : 412. — With portrait. (J. A. Patten) Rogers, A. C. Repres. men, 365.

MacColl, Evan. Wilson, J. G. Poets of Scot. 2 : 303.

McComb, Henry S., with portrait. Rogers, A. C. Repres. men, 361.

McCook, Capt. C. M. (D. McCook) Shea, J. G. Fallen brave.

McCord, Mrs. Louisa S. Davidson, J. W. Writ.

of South, 351. — Freeman, J. D. Wom. of South, 480. — Hart, J. S. Fem. prose, 198.

McCormick, Cyrus H. Houghton. Kings, 393. With portrait. Hubert, P. G., jr. Inventors, 207. — Patton, J. Sk. of men of prog.

McCosh, James. Richardson. Amer. lit. 1 : 318. — Christianity and positivism. Brownson. Wks. 2 : 428.

McCoy, Isabella. Drake, S. G. Trag. of wilderness, 143.

McCrary, George W. Am. Bar Assoc. 13 : 354.

M'Crea, Jane. Ellet. Wom. of revol. 2 : 221.

M'Crie, Thomas. Blaikie, W. G. Preachers Scot. 269. — Taylor, W. M. Scott. pulpit, 234.

McCrimmon, Mrs. Mary A. Raymond, I. Southland writ. 1 : 508.

M'Cullagh, Thomas. Wesley & successors, 243.

McCulloch, Ben. Pollard. Life of Lee, 637.

McCulloch, Hugh, with portrait. Brockett. Men of our day, 539.

McCulloch, Oscar C. (I. C. Barrows and others) Conf. char. & correc. '92 : 230.

McCullough, John. Matthews, B. Actors, 4 : 265. — Morris. Ess. in theatr. crit. 68. — Winter. Shadows, 185.

MacDiarmid, John. Wilson, J. G. Poets of Scot. 2 : 114.

Macdonald, Alexander. Hinton. Eng. radicals, 142. — Wilson, J. G. Poets of Scot. 1 : 166.

M'Donald, Annie, and the Fifeshire forester. Miller, H. Lead. articles, 123.

McDonald, Craig W. Walker, C. W. Biog. Va. Mil. Inst. 377.

Macdonald, Étienne Jacques Joseph. Headley. Napoleon, 1 : 234.

Macdonald, Flora. Chambers's Miscel. no. 50. — Ellet. Women of revol. 2 : 142. — Jesse. Pretenders, 421. — Thomson, Mrs. Jacobites, 3 : 310. — Yonge, C. D. Seven heroines, 169. — Owen, Mrs. O. F. Heroines domes. 249. — Starling, E. Noble deeds wom. 408. — Wharton, A. H. Colon. days, 226.

MacDonald, George. Miles, A. H. Poets of cent. 10 : 525. — Paladin. Glances, 187. — With portrait. Warner Lib. 16 : 9455. — Wilson, J. G. Poets of Scot. 2 : 449. — Wilson, S. L. Theol. mod. liter.

Macdonald, Hugh, 1817-60. Wilson, J. G. Poets of Scot. 2 : 398.

Macdonald, James, 1807-48. Wilson, J. G. Poets of Scot. 2 : 202.

Macdonald, John. Wilson, J. G. Poets of Scot. 1 : 87.

Macdonald, Sir John A. Bungay. Repr. men, 219. — Em. persons, 5 : 90.

Macdonald, S. J. J., French Marshal. Grant, Jas. Cavaliers, 308.

Macdonell, of Glengarry. Burke, B. Viciss. of fam. 1 : 54.

McDonogh, John. Wallis, S. T. Works, 1 : 195.

Macdonough, Thomas. With portrait. Duyckinck. Nat. portr. gall. 2 : 82. — With portrait. [Amer.] Nat. portr. gall. 1. — Lossing. Em. Amer. 323.

McDowell, Ephraim. (Samuel D. Gross) Gross. Lives physicians, 207.

McDowell, Silas. Davidson, J. W. Writ. of South, 357.

Macduff, John Robert. Miller, Jos. Singers church, 2d ed. 516. — Wilson, J. G. Poets of Scot. 2 : 417.

McDuffee, John, with portrait. Sketches N. H. men, 153.

McDuffie, George. Magoon, E. L. Amer. orators, 244.

Mace, Jean, with portrait. Warner Lib. 16: 9473.

"Macedonian," frigate, Capture of. Dawson. Batt. of U. S. 2 : 175.

Macedonian and Roman schools. Newman, J. H. Hist. sk. 390.

— in 1887. Laveleye. Balkan peninsula.

McElrath, Thomas. Derby, J. C. Fifty years, 141.

McEntee, Jervis. Sheldon, G. W. Amer. painters, 51. — Tuckerman. Artists, 543.

Macerata. Jarves. Ital. ramb. 114.

M'Evilly, John. Burke, O. J. Cath. archb. 375.

McEwen, Mrs. Hetty M. Brockett. Woman's work, 764.

Macfarlan, James. Wilson, J. G. Poets of Scot. 2 : 482.

McFarland, Francis Patrick. Clarke, R. H. Cath. bishops, 3 : 117.

Macfarren, Geo. Alex. With photo. Cooper, T. Men of mark, 5 : 30. — Keddie. Mus. comp. 319.

— and Walter Cecil Macfarren. Spark, W. Mus. mem. 269.

M'Flynn, Florence. Burke, O. J. Cath. archb. 24.

MacGahan, Januarius Aloysius. Forbes, A. Souvenirs, 120.

— Travels of. Adams, W. H. D. Heroes of trav. 260. — Marvin, C. Reconnoitring, 95.

McGarrahan, W., Land claim of. U. S. 50th Cong., 1st Sess. Sen. Repts. v. 6. — Black, J. S. Ess. 565.

McGee, Thomas D'Arcy. Murray, J. O'K. Prose & poet. Irel. 653.

McGill, John. Clarke, R. H. Cath. bishops, 3 : 81. — Davidson, J. W. Writ. of South, 360.

MacGillivray, William. Smiles. Brief biog. 198.

MacGowan, John. Ivimey. Eng. Bapt. 4 : 318.

McGowan's Ford, Action at. Dawson. Batt. of U. S. 1 : 653.

Macgregor, Robert (called Rob Roy). Chambers's Miscel. no. 117. — Thomson, Mrs. Jacobites, 2 : 155.

Macgregors, History of the. Burton, J. H. Crim. tri. 1 : 1.

M'Grigor, Sir J. Pettigrew. Med. portr. gall. v. 4.

McGuffey, Dr. William H. (Daniel Read) Nat. Educa. Assoc. 73 : 15.

McGuire, Francis Howe. Am. Bar Assoc. 18 : 546.

McGuire, Mrs. John P. Davidson, J. W. Writ. of South, 361.

MacHale, John. Burke, O. J. Cath. archb. 240. — Murray, J. O'K. Prose & poet. Irel. 670.

Macham, Robert. Bourne, H. R. F. Eng. seam. 1 : 25.

McHenry, James. Winslow, S. N. Biog. Phila. merch. 72.

Machias, Action off. Dawson. Batt. of U. S. 1 : 44.

Machiavelli. See Macchiavelli.

Machine tool-makers. Wynter. Peeps, 2 : 124.

Machinery, Accidents by. Missouri Labor, 1880.

— Displacement of labor by. Playfair. Subj. soc. 126.

— Early English. Wynter. Curios. of toil, 1 : 240.

— Effects of. George, H. Soc. prob. 192.

— — on labor. Bolles. Chap. pol. econ. 41. — Marx. Capital, 365.

— efficiency of, Graphic methods of determining. Jenkins, H. C. F. Papers, 2 : 271.

Machinery, labor-saving, Moral and economic consequences of using. (A. S. Bolles) Conv. Labor Bur. '88 : 70.

— Objections to, answered. Bastiat. Ess. on pol. econ. 90.

McHugh, Malachy. Burke, O.-J. Cath. archb. 39.

Machutus, St. (St. Malo), of Brittany. Charles. Martyrs, 373.

Machyn, Henry, Diary of. Ewald, A. C. Paper, 87.

Maciliowoscius. Wallace, R. Anti-Trin. biog. 3 : 135.

McIlroy, Archibald. Wakeley. Heroes Meth. 345.

McIlroy, Samuel. Bartlett, J. R. R. I. officers, 223.

McIlvaine, Charles P. Lanman, C. Haphazard, 334.

McIntosh, Lachlan. With portrait. [Amer.] Nat. portr. gall. v. 3. — Jones, C. C., jr. Deleg. fr. Georgia, 139. — Lossing. Em. Amer. 279.

McIntosh, Maria J. Davidson, J. W. Writ. of South, 362. — Freeman, J. D. Wom. of South, 163. — Hart, J. S. Fem. prose, 63.

McIntosh, William. Woollen. Biog. sk. Indiana, 373.

Macintosh, William, of Borlum. Chambers, W. Rem. pers. 303.

Macintyre, Duncan. Wilson, J. G. Poets of Scot. 1 : 227.

McIntyre, Joseph. Bartlett, J. R. R. I. officers, 452.

Mackay, Alex. M. Creegan. Gt. mission. 273.

Mackay, Charles. Lanman, C. Haphazard, 326. — Miles, A. H. Poets of cent. 4 : 455. — Wilson, J. G. Poets of Scot. 2 : 381.

McKay, Mrs. Charlotte E. Brockett. Woman's work, 514. — Moore, F. Women of the war, 278.

Mackay, Margaret. Hatfield, E. F. Poets of church, 400. — Miller, Jos. Singers church, 2d ed. 464.

Mackay, Robert. Wilson, J. G. Poets of Scot. 1 : 180.

McKean, Joseph. Mass. Hist. Coll. 2d ser. 8 : 157.

McKean, Thomas. With portrait. [Amer.] Nat. portr. gall. v. 4. — Brown, D. P. Forum, 1 : 323. — Dwight, N. Signers of decl. 237. — Lincoln, R. W. Signers, 46. — Lossing. Signers, 141. — Sanderson. Signers, v. 6. — With portrait. Armor. Gov. of Pa. 289. — Lossing. Em. Amer. 203. — Neven, D. R. B. Pennsylvanians, 175.

McKendree, William. Gorrie. Em. Meth. 271. — (B. St. J. Fry) McClintock, J. Em. Meth. 69. — Wakeley. Heroes Meth. 93.

M'Kenna, Edward. Richards, W. Heroes, 125.

McKenney, James Hall. Carson, H. L. Sup. Ct. of U. S. 576.

McKenny, Barbara. Clement, J. Noble deeds, 410.

Mackenzie, Alex. C., with portrait. Willeby, C. Mast. Eng. Mus. 103.

Mackenzie, Lady Anne. Wittenmyer. Women Reform. 429.

Mackenzie, Charles Frederick. Dale, T. P. Life's motto. — Yonge. Pioneers, 285.

Mackenzie, Sir George. Innes, A. T. Studies, 63.

Mackenzie, Henry. Jeaffreson. Novelists, 1 : 276. — Scott, W. Biog. mem. v. 2. — Wilson, J. G. Poets of Scot. 1 : 285.

— Novels of. Talfourd. Crit. writ.

Mackenzie, John K. Creegan. Gt. mission. 143.

Mackenzie, Kenneth. A Highland seer and Scotch superstitions. Jeune. Lesser ques. 13.

Mackenzie, Morell. Bettany. Em. doctors, 2; 249.

Mackenzie families. Taylor, J. Fam. of Scot. 1 : 185.

Mackenzie River. (A. J. Russell) Am. Geog. Soc. 8 : 305.

McKernan, J. H., with portrait. (J. A. Patten) Rogers, A. C. Repres. men, 371.

Mackey, Albert Gallatin. Davidson, J. W. Writ. of South, 364.

Mackinaw. Pidgeon. Engineer's holiday, 78.

McKinley, William, Inauguration of. Davis, R. H. Year, 137.

McKinney, Robert M. Walker, C. C. Biog. Va. Mil. Inst. 380.

Mackintosh, Sir James. Adams, C. K. Rep. Brit. orat. 2 : 176. — DeQuincey. Phil. writ. (Bost.) 1 : 63; or Writ. (Masson) 8 : 127. — Edgar. Boyhood, 43. — Georgian era, 2 : 331. — Hazlitt. Spirit. — Jerdan. Men, 298. — Mc-Cosh. Scot. phil. 347. — Oliphant, M. Lit. hist. 3 : 266. — Redding. Pers. remin. 2 : 271. — Taylor, W. C. Mod. Brit. Plut. 229. — Thomson, K. B. Recoll. v. 2. — Mitchell, D. G. Eng. lands, 4 : 103. — Stanton, H. B. Reforms, 107. — Whiteside, J. Early sk. 77.

— and his ethical philosophy. Everett, A. H. Crit. ess. 283.

— Life of. Ossoli. Art, 53.

— the man of promise. Bulwer, H. L. Hist. char. 2 : 3.

— Memoirs. Jeffrey, F. Contrib. Ed. Rev.

Mackintosh, John, of Geddes. Shairp. Portraits, 182.

Macklin, Charles. Baker, H. B. Eng. actors, 1 : 174. — Doran. Annals stage, 2 : 184. — Galt. Players, 2 : 1. — Matthews, B. Actors, 1 : 1.

— Manslaughter by. Burke, P. Romance of forum.

M'Lachlan, Alexander. Wilson, J. G. Poets of Scot. 2 : 403.

Maclachlan, Ewen. Wilson, J. G. Poets of Scot. 1 : 533.

Maclagan, Alexander. Wilson, J. G. Poets of Scot. 2 : 340.

Maclagan, W. D., bishop of Lichfield, with photo. Cooper, T. Men of mark, 5 : 19.

Maclaine, James. (G. T. Drury) Seccombe, T. Twelve bad men, 246.

McLane, Louis, with portrait. [Amer.] Nat. portr. gall. v. 1.

Maclaren, A. Great mod. preachers.

McLaughlin, Edward Augustus. Coggeshall. Poets of west, 247. — Everest. Poets of Conn. 289.

Maclaurin, John. Blaikie, W. G. Preachers Scot. 255. — Taylor, W. M. Scott. pulpit, 167.

McLaws, L. Pollard. Life of Lee, 487.

McLean, John. With portrait. [Amer.] Nat. portr. gall. v. 4. — Bartlett. Pres. candidates, 218. — Livingston, J. Em. Am. lawy. 33. — (M. F. Force) N. E. Hist.-Gen. Soc. Biog. 4 : 270. — Maury, S. M. Statesm. of Am. 89. — Savage. Liv. rep. men, 373.

Maclean, Sir John. Thomson, Mrs. Jacobites, 2 : 124.

MacLean, Lauchlan. Galt, J. Lit. life, 1 : 192.

Maclean, Letitia Elizabeth. See Landon, Letitia Elizabeth.

Maclellan family. Taylor, J. Fam. of Scot. 2 : 409. See McClellan.

McLeod, A. Case of the Caroline. Seward. Works, 2 : 547.

Macleod, Sir Donald, the Christian governor. Japp. Noble workers, 225.

McLeod, Mrs. Georgiana A. Hulse. Davidson, J. W. Writ. of South, 365. — Freeman, J. D. Wom. of South, 490. — Raymond, I. Southland writ. 2 : 943.

Macleod, Norman. Blaikie, W. G. Preachers Scott. 292. — (W. C. Smith) With portrait. Ewart, H. C. Leaders, 221. — With portrait. Japp. Good men, 13. — (R. Flint) St. Giles lec. 3 : 427. — Shairp. Portraits, 149. — Wilson, J. G. Poets of Scot. 2 : 361. — Miles, A. H. Poets of cent. 10 : 712. — Taylor, W. M. Scot. pulpit, 260. — Warner Lib. 16 : 9595.

McLeod, Wm. B. Hemenway. Poets of Vt. 257.

Maclise, Daniel. Rossetti, W. M. Fine art, 145.

Macmahon, Marshal. Em. persons, 6 : 47. — King, E. French pol. lead. 114. — Men of 3d repub. 17.

— at the Elysée. Yates, E. H. Celeb. 1 : 251.

McMahon, Thomas W. Davidson, J. W. Writ. of South, 367.

McMaster, John Bach, with portrait. Warner Lib. 16 : 9503.

McMeens, Mrs. Anna C. Brockett. Woman's work, 491.

Macmillan, Daniel. Watson, Mrs. R. A. Poet-toilers, 23.

McMillan, Mary. Ellet. Pioneer wom. 338.

McMullen, John. Clarke, R. H. Cath. bishops, 3 : 592.

M'Naughton, Daniel, Trial of, for murder of Edward Drummond. Townsend, W. C. Mod. state trials, 1 : 326.

M'Neill, Rev. Hugh. Grant, Jas. Portr. pub. char. 1 : 239.

McNeill, D. See Colonsay, Lord.

Macneill, Hector. Wilson, J. G. Poets of Scot. 1 : 307.

Macneven, Wm. Jas. (J. W. Francis) Gross. Lives physicians, 479.

Macomb, Alexander. With portrait. [Amer.] Nat. portr. gall. v. 1. — Lossing. Em. Amer. 303.

Macon, Nathaniel. Lossing. Em. Amer. 312.

Macovius, Samuel. Wallace, R. Anti-Trin. biog. 3 : 127.

MacPherson, Sir H. Laurie, W. F. B. Dist. Anglo-Ind. 1 : 290.

Macpherson, James. Lawrence. Brit. historians, 2 : 235. — Wilson, J. G. Poets of Scot. 1 : 271. — Mitchell, D. G. Eng. lands, 3 : 221.

— Life and letters of. Tovey. Rev. & ess. 138.

— Ossian's poems. Cross lights, 33. — Montgomery, H. R. Impost. 38.

McPherson, James B. Glazier, W. Heroes, 337.

Macpherson family of Mt. Pleasant. Glenn, T. A. Colon. mans. 2 : 443.

Macready, William C. Whyte, F. Actors of cent. 76. — Baker, H. B. Eng. actors, 2 : 253. — Doran. Drury Lane, 1 : 82. — Horne. New spirit, 2 : 104. — Lewes. Actors, 32. — Matthews, B. Actors, 4 : 1. — Murdoch. The stage, 114. — (J. Parton) Parton. Princes, 247. — Russell, W. Rep. actors, 366. — Coleman, G. Players, 1 : 15. — Grant, Jas. Portr. pub. char. 2 : 215. — Marston, J. W. Rec. actors, 1 : 25.

— Acting of. Hazlitt. Crit. and dram. ess.

— Anecdotes about. Murdoch, J. E. Stage, 93.

— as Hamlet. Murdoch, J. E. Stage, 114.

— Early training of. Murdoch, J. E. Stage, 252.

— Obituary of. Em. persons, 1 : 157.

McRee, William. Stuart, C. B. Am. engineers, 170.

McSherry, Richard. Davidson, J. W. Writ. of South, 367.

McTyeire, H. N. Davidson, J. W. Writ. of South, 368.

M'Vickar, John, the professor. Japp. Noble workers, 155.

MacWhirter, Agnes C. Clayton, E. C. Eng. fem. art. **2** : 283.

McWhorter, Alexander. Headley, J. T. Chaplains Revol. 327.

Macy, William G. Sheldon, G. W. Amer. painters, 204.

Maczynski, Peter. Wallace, R. Anti-Trin. biog. **2** : 353.

Madách, Emerich, with portrait. (G. A. Kohut) Warner Lib. **16** : 9515.

Madagascar. Latimer. Eur. in Afr. in 19th cent. 425. — Norman. Colonial France, 217.

— Gold traffic and gold mining in, 1896. (E. T. Wetter) U. S. Cons. Rept. **53** : 180.

— in 1889. U. S. Ho. Ex. Docs. '88–89, v. **26**.

— King of. Wraxall, F. C. L. Remark. adv. **2** : 292.

Madan, Mrs. Judith (Cowper). Hatfield, E. F. Poets of church, 401.

Madan, Martin. Hatfield, E. F. Poets of church, 402. — Miller, Jos. Singers church, 2d ed. 248.

Maddern-Fiske, Minnie, with portrait. (M. Aldrich) McKay, F. E. Fam. actors, 328.

Madeira Islands. Benjamin. Atlan. isl. 94. — Benjamin, S. G. W. World's paradises, 198. — (J. F. Healy) U. S. Cons. Rept **41** : 604.

— as a health resort. Mackenzie, M. Ess. 49.

— Discovery of. Knight. Once on time, **1** : 54. — Parton. Triumphs, 585.

— Visit to. Chambers's Miscel. no. 64.

Madeira, Rio. (C. Young) Vaca. tourists, **2** : 121.

Madeley, Eng. Rimmer, A. Country towns, 208.

Maderno, Carlo. Milizia. Lives arch. **2** : 137.

Madison, Dorothy Payne. With portrait. [Amer.] Nat. portr. gall. v. **3**. — Ellet. Queens Am. soc. 238. — Parton. Peop. bk biog. 574. — With portrait. Holloway, L. C. Ladies, 171. — Bolton. Fam. lead. wom. 123. — Duyckinck. Portr. gall. **1** : 488.

Madison, Mrs. James. Gordon, L. L. Lady Wash'n, 87. — Hanaford. Wom. of cent. 75. — Upton, Mrs. H. T. Our early pres. 192.

Madison, James. Abbott. Lives of presidents, 148. — With portrait. [Amer.] Nat. portr. gall. v. **3**. — With portrait. Duyckinck. Nat. portr. gall. **1** : 385. — Frost. Presidents, 91. — Griswold. Prose writ. 79. — Mackay. Founders Amer. 323. — Lincoln. Lives of pres. 131. — (J. W. Stevenson) Am. Bar Assoc. **6** : 269. — Brooks, E. S. Hist. Amer. 175. — Johnston, A. Amer. ora. **1** : 53. — Lodge, H. C. Hist. & pol. ess. — Lossing. Em. Amer. 296. — Moore, F. Am. eloq. **1** : 125. — Nichol. Amer. lit. 79. — Richardson. Amer. lit. **1** : 198. — Thompson, R. W. Pers. recoll. 64. — (J. Fiske) Wilson, J. G. Presidents, 88. — Upton, Mrs. H. T. Our early pres. 191. — With portrait. Warner Lib. **16** : 9531.

— Home of. (E. W. Johnston) Homes Amer. statesm. 181.

— Social life during administration of. Ellet, E. F. Court circles, 80.

Madison, James, D. D. Lossing. Em. Amer. 255.

Madison, Indiana, 1844–52. Woollen. Biog. sketch Indiana, 513.

Madison, Fort, Attack on. Dawson. Batt. of U. S. **2** : 133.

Madoc. Belknap. Amer. biog. **1** : 129.

Madras. Pidgeon. Engineer's holiday, 354. — Shoemaker, M. M. Quaint corners, 36.

— Visit to, 1884. Hübner. Through Brit. empire, **1** : 398.

Madrid. Brooks, E. S. Gt. cities, 92. — Finck, H. T. Spain & Morocco. — Stoddard, C. A. Span. cit. 51. — Thomas, M. Scamper through Spain, 25. — Hale, E. E. Seven Spanish cit. 155. — Lathrop, G. P. Span. vistas, 16. — Prime, S. I. Alhambra, 29.

— al fresco. Hay, J. Castil. days, 1.

— and the Escorial. Buckley, J. M. Trav. three cont. 19.

— Museums in. Hale, E. E. Seven Spanish cit. 218.

— Out-door life in. Hale, E. E. Seven Spanish cit. 228.

— Reiigious persecutions in. Stoughton. Span. ref. 226.

— to Cordova. Stoddard, C. A. Span. cit. 94.

Madura. Shoemaker, M. M. Quaint corners, 23.

Madvig, Johan N. Nettleship, H. Lec. 2d ser. v. **1**.

Mæcenas, Caius Cilnius. Dunlop, J. Rom. liter. **3** : 26.

Maedchenstein, The ; a tradition of the Saxon Sweitz. Gleig. Ess. **2** : 326.

Maedler, John H. [German astronomer], Courtship of. Baring-Gould. Oddities, **1** : 234.

Maertz, Louisa. Brockett. Woman's work, 390.

Maes, Nicolaas. Gower. Fig. painters Holl. 61. — Wedmore. Masters of genre, 63. — Van Dyke, J. C. Dutch mast. 59.

Maestricht, Sieges of. Robson, W. Sieges, 482.

Maeterlinck, Maurice. Crawford, V. M. Stud. for. lit. 139. — With portrait. (W. Sharp) Warner Lib. **16** : 9541.

Magalhaes, Fernão de. *See* Magellan.

Magazines, American, in 1847. Bristed. Pieces, **3** : 14.

Magazine literature. Dodge, M. A. Skirmish. 225.

Magdalen College, Oxford, and James II. Pattison. Ess. **1** : 320.

Magdalen islands, The. Benjamin. Atlan. isl. 78.

Magdalena River and valley, The, 1892. (J. Nicheus) U. S. Cons. Rept. **40** : 121.

— Trip up. (J. A. Bennett) Am. Geog. Soc. v. **9**.

Magdalene of France, queen of James V., 1537. Strickland. Queens Scot. **1**.

Magdeburg, Siege of. Robson, W. Sieges, 505.

Magee, Wm. C., archbishop. With photo. Cooper, T. Men of mark, **2** : 34. — Em. persons, **5** : 83. — Hutton, R. H. Criticisms, **1** : 297.

— and Anglican oratory. Arnold, F. Our bishops, **2** : 139.

Magellan, Fernando. With portrait. Bolton, S. K. Fam. voyag. 120. — Parton. Peop. bk. biog. 298. — Vogel. Cent. of discov. 244.

— First voyage round the world. Wraxall, C. F. L. Hist. bye-ways, **1** : 186.

Magellan, Strait of. Child, T. Span.-Amer. repub. 227.

Magenta, Andrea. Symonds. Renais. fine arts, 269.

Magenta, Battle of, 1859. Adams, C. Gt. camp. 271.

— Day at, after the battle. Cranbourne. Hist. sketch, **1** : 221.

Magic and witchcraft, History of. Wright, T. Nar. sorcery, 1 : 1.
— in England at the time of the Reformation. Wright, T. Nar. sorcery, 1 : 198.
— Natural. Chambers's Miscel. no. 82.
— — Bibliography. Hopkins, A. H. (ed.). Magic.
Magic circle. Franklin. Works ('87), 2 : 160.
Magic lanterns in schools. (G. Serrurier) Cong. Educa. Chic. '93, 314.
Magic square. Franklin. Works ('87), 2 : 156.
Magicians and witch folk. Whittier. Lit. recre. 273.
Maginn, William. Hall, S. C. Book of mem. 158. — Saintsbury, G. Ess. Eng. lit. 2 : 270. — Thompson, K. B. Recoll. 1. — Wotton. Word portraits, 190. — With portrait. Warner Lib. 16 : 9564.
— Memoir of. (S. Mackenzie) Maginn. Fras. papers, ix.
Magistracy, The, in France. Hillebrand. France, 74.
Magliabecchi, Antonio, Ital. bibliographer and scholar. Brightwell. Byepaths of biog. 145. — Craik. Pursuit knowl. 1 : 343.
Magna Charta. Stanton, H. B. Reforms, 18. — Signing of. Archer. Decis. ev. 115.
Magnanimity. Cracroft. Ess. 1 : 182.
Magnard, Francis. Smalley. Stud. 355.
Magnesia, Battle of. King, C. Battles, 136.
Magnetic induction, Molecular process in. (J. A. Ewing) Smithson. Rept. '92 : 255.
Magnetic needle, Declination of the. Proctor. Light sci. 1 : 14.
    See also Compass.
Magnetic observations, General bearings of. (E. W. Creak) Smithson. Rept. '95 : 107.
Magnetism. Hunt, R. Poe. of sci. 235.
— Animal. Brown, S. Atom, 2. — Laing, S. Problems, 163. — Timbs. Doctors, 251.
— — Modern magic. Hawthorne, J. Confess. 218.
— Elementary lecture on. Tyndall. Frag. sci. 357.
— Polar. (J. A. Parker) Am. Geog. Soc. 2, pt. 2 : 70.
— Terrestrial. (B. G. Jenkins) Am. Geog. Soc. 10 : 267. — Herschel, J. F. W. Essays, 63. — Proctor, R. A. Mysteries, 272. — (A. W. Rucker) Smithson. Rept. '94 : 173.
Magnetizers, Noted. Mackay. Delusions, 2 : 311.
Magnus, St., of the Orkneys. Scott, Mrs. M. M. Abbotsf. 76.
Magnus the Good. Dasent. Jest & earnest, v. 2.
— and Harold Hardrada. Dasent. Jest & earnest, 2 : 154.
Magnus, H. Gustav. Helmholtz. Pop. lec. 2 : 1.
Magny, Olivier de. Cary. Fr. poets, 46.
"Magpie" Schooner, Loss of. Yonge. Gold. deeds.
Magra, Major. Sinclair, J. Sketches.
Magruder, John B. Pollard. Life of Lee, 840.
Maguaga, Action at. Dawson. Batt. of U. S. 2 : 98.
Maguelonne. Baring-Gould. Troub.-land, 227. — Warner, C. D. Roundabout, 59.
Maguire, Adelaide A. Clayton, E. C. Eng. fem. art. 1 : 420.
Maguires of Tempo. Burke, B. Viciss. of fam. 1 : 171.
Magyars, Origin of. Leger. Austro-Hungary.
Máhábáleshwar, the sanitaria of western India. Burton, Isa. Arabia, 276.
Mahabharata, The. Reed. Hindu literature, 272. — Williams. Indian wisdom, 371.
— Morality of. Macmillan, M. Globe-trotter, India, 193.

Mahaffy, John P. Warner Lib. 16 : 9569.
Mahan, Alfred Thayer, with portrait. Warner Lib. 16 : 9580.
Maharani of Kuch Behar. Chapman, E. F. Sketch Ind. wom. 71.
Mahdi, The, and Gordon. Latimer. Eur. in Afr. in 19th cent. 66.
Mahmud the Sultan. Adams, W. H. D. Warriors of crescent, 3.
Mahomet. See Mohammed.
Mahony, Francis. Hall, S. C. Book of mem. 237. — Williams, A. M. Poets of Irel. — Wotton. Word portraits, 195.
Mahopac, Lake. Willis. Hurry-graphs, 101.
Mahrattas. Temple, R. Orient. exper. 337.
Mai, Angelo, Cardinal. (C. W. Russell) Afternoon lec. 4 : 95.
Maid and the writ, The. Curtis. From easy chair, 3 : 112.
Maidalchini-Pamfili. See Pamfili.
Mail-coach, English. DeQuincey. Miscel. ess. (Bost.) 127.
Maillefer, Nicolas, An unknown sculptor. Houssaye. Philos. 2 : 215.
Maillet, Benôit. Osborn. From Greeks, 109.
Mailly, Louis J. de M.-N., Comtesse de. Imbert de St. A. Wom. Ct. Louis xv, 46, 59.
Maimon, Solomon, Autobiography of. Hallard, J. H. Gallica, 143.
Maimonides, Moses. Karpeles. Jew. lit. 145. — (Rabbi Gottheil) Warner Lib. 16 : 9589.
Main street. (N. Hawthorne) Peabody, E. P. Æsthetic pap. 145.
Maine, Anne-L.-B. de Bourbon, duchesse du. Mason, A. G. Wom. of Fr. salons, 146.
Maine, Sir Henry Sumner. Escott, T. H. S. Pillars emp. 197. — Em. persons, 4 : 24. — With portrait. (D. MacG. Means) Warner Lib. 16 : 9605. — Laurence, P. M. Collect. 203. — and his work. Pollock, F. Oxf. lec. 112.
— Early history of institutions. Leslie, T. E. C. Ess. pol. econ. 448.
Maine de Biran. Frothingham. Transcend. 65.
Maine law, The. Phillips, W. Speeches, 2 : 178.
Maintenon, Frances d'Aubigny, Mme. de. Adams, W. H. D. Fam. beauties, 1 : 151. — Bolton. Fam. lead. wom. 1. — Bush, A. F. Queens of F. 2 : 182. — Döllinger. Stud. hist. 325. — James, G. P. R. Cel. wom. — Lord, J. Beacon, 5 : 267. — With portrait. Fifty famous women, 162. — Imbert de St. A. Wom. Ct. Louis xiv, 117-198. — Owen, Mrs. O. F. Heroines hist. 350.
— and her times. Phelps, A. L. Rev. & ess. 119.
— and Louis XIV. Menzies, S. Roy. fav. 2 : 406.
Mainville, Fodor J. Needham. Queens of song.
Maisters, Joseph. Ivimey. Eng. Bapt. 2 : 183.
Maistre, Joseph de. Maccall. For. biog. 1 : 1. — Morley. Crit. miscel. 2 : 256. — Franklin and. Merivale. Hist. stud. 204.
Maistre, Pierre Pathelin, the earliest French comedy. Besant. Fr. poetry, 200.
Maistre, Xavier de, with portrait. Warner Lib. 17 : 9617.
Maitani, Lorenzo. Symonds. Renais. fine arts, 117.
Maitland family. Taylor, J. Fam. of Scot. 1 : 347.
Maitland, F. L. Georgian era, 2 : 268.
Maitland, John, first lord. Lodge. Portraits (Bohn), v. 2.
Maitland, Sir Richard. Irving, D. Scot. poets, 2 : 147. — Wilson, J. G. Poets of Scot. 1 : 38.

Malthus on population, Principle of. Southey, R. Ess. 1832, 1 : 77.
Malthusianism, Darwinism, and pessimism. Bowen, F. Gleanings, 351.
Malus, Stephen Louis. Arago. Sci. men, 2 : 117.
Malvern Hill, Battle of. Allan, W. Army of N. Va. 122. — (F. W. Palfrey) Dwight, T. F. Camp. Va. 253.
Mammals, Geographical distribution of. (P. L Sclater) Manch. Sci. lec. 5-6 : 202. — (C. H. Merriam) Smithson. Rept. '91 : 365.
Mammon worship. Farrar, Soc. & p. day quest. 108.
Mammoth Cave. Adams, W. H. D. Fam. caverns, 106. — Burroughs, J. Riverby, 242. — Hovey, H. C. Cel. Am. cav. 53. — (H. C. Hovey) Am. Geog. Soc. 23 : 47. — Taylor, B. At home, 1 : 180.
Mammoths and mastodons. Winchell. Sparks geol. ham. 234.
Man, Albon, with portrait. Butterfield Lec. Un. Coll. 1 : 195.
Man. Friswell. Gentle life, 2 : 1. — Mivart. Less. fr. nature, 128.
— Age and origin of, geologically considered. (S. R. Pattison and F. Pfaff) Liv. Papers, v. 3.
— Ancient home of, in Asia. (O. Street) Am. Geog. Soc. 12 : 193.
— and ape, Cranial affinities of. (R. Virchow) Estes. Half-hour, v. 1.
— and brute. Romanes. Ess. 59.
— and his dwelling-place. Boyd. Recreat. 2 : 261.
— and lower animals, Moral distinctions between. Mill, J. S. Three ess. 48.
— and nature. Foster, J. Crit. ess. Ecl. v. 2. — Holland, H. Frag. papers, 251.
— and nature, Huxley on. Seth, A. Man's place, 1.
— Antiquity of. Kinsley, W. W. Views, 151. — (John Evans) Smithson. Rept. '90 : 467. — Laing. Mod. sci. 105.
— — His arrival in Europe. Fiske, J. Excurs. 41.
— — in America. Winsor. Hist. Amer. 1 : 369.
— — in western Europe. (E. Clodd) Proctor, R. A. Leis. read. 34.
— — When did the race begin ? Kinsley. Views, 151.
— as distinguished from animals. Swing. Old pic. 2 : 163.
— Ascent of. Smith, Gold. Lec. & ess. 89. — (Frank Baker) Smithson. Rept. '90 : 447.
— Birthplace of. Brinton. Races & peo. 82.
— Descent of, Darwin on. Mivart. Ess. 2 : 1.
— Destiny of humanity. Wilde, Lady. Soc. stud. 175.
— Duties of. Mazzini. Life, etc. 4 : 209.
— Fallen. Ames, M. C. Outlines, 144.
— from a Catholic point of view. (T. S. Byrne) Barrows, J. H. Parl. relig. 1 : 360.
— genealogy of, Last steps in. (Paul Topinard) Smithson. Rept. '89 : 669.
— Godwin's thoughts on. Martineau, H. Miscel. 2 : 118.
— The healthy. (C. N. Hewitt) Am. Pub. Health, 24 : 270.
— in America, Pre-Aryan. Wilson, D. Lost Atlantis, 130.
— in the light of revelation and science. (Thos. Dwight) Barrows, J. H. Parl. relig. 2 : 950.
— in nature. Wasson. Ess. 127.
— in North America, in paleolithic period of stone age. (Thomas Wilson) U. S. Nat. Mus. Rept. '88 : 677.
— Is man only a machine ? Gladden. Burn. ques. 67.

Man. Is man the machine, or man the inventor: which ? (J. W. Glenn) Nat. Educa. Assoc. '82 : 118.
— — *not* a machine. (Prebendary Row) Liv. papers, v. 5.
— Mystery of. Baring-Gould. Mod. diffi. 56.
— Natural history of. Holland, H. Ess. 465.
a noble animal. Friswell. Gentle life, 2 : 1.
— Origin of. Laing, S. Problems, 131.
— Origin of human faculty. Romanes. Ess. 86.
— physiologically considered. (A. Macalister) Liv. papers, v. 7.
— Place of, in nature. Laing. Mod. sci. 166, — (A. B. Bruce) Barrows, J. H. Parl. relig. 2 : 938.
— Pre-adamite. Scoffern. Stray leaves, 117.
— Prehistoric. Buckley, A. B. Through magic glass, 209. — Dunman. Talks sci. 36. — Keary, C. F. Dawn of hist. 1 : 28, 113.
— — Social life of. Keary, C. F. Dawn of history, 135, 156.
— Primeval. Baring-Gould. Mod. diff. 71. — Peabody, E. P. Last evening, 153.
— — Argyll on. Brownson. Works, 9 : 318.
— — not a savage. Brownson. Works, 9 : 457.
— Primitive. Clodd. Story prim. man, 9.
— — was he a modern savage ? (Talcott Williams) Smithson. Rept. '96 : 541.
— Relation of, to nature. Foster, J. Crit. ess. (Bohn) 2 : 223.
— Savage and civilized. Clodd, E. Myths, 143.
— Service of, J. C. Morison on. Hutton, R. H. Criticisms, 2 : 271.
— — and service of Christ. Courtney. Stud. 225.
— Solitudes of. Alger. Solitudes, 31.
— Unity of the human races. Miller, H. Hist. ess. 394. — (Marquis De Nadaillac) Smithson. Rept. '97 : 549.
Man-haters, Modern. Linton, E. L. Girl of per. 2 : 173.
Man of letters, The. Emerson. Lec. & biog. sk. 229.
Man with the cloaks, The : a Vermont legend. Austin, W. Lit. papers, 77.
Man, Isle of, Monarchs of. Doran. Monarchs, 1 : 176.
Manæn. Hastings, F. Obscure charac. 15.
Managua, capital of Nicaragua. Curtis, W. E. Capitals, 138.
Manassas, Battle of. *See* Bull Run.
— Second battle of. Allan, W. Army of N. Va. 262.
Manasseh ben Israel. Magnus. Jew. portr. 99.
Manatee, The. Morgan, C. L. Animal sk. 98.
Mancala : the national game of Africa. (Stewart Culin) U. S. Nat. Mus. Rept. '94 : 595.
Mance, Jane. Murray, J. O'K. Cath. heroes, 495.
Manchester, Charles Montagu, duke of. With portrait. Caulfield. Kit-cat, 63.
Manchester, Edward Montagu, 2d earl of. Lodge. Portraits (Bohn), v. 5.
Manchester, Eng. Chambers's Repos. no. 1. — Dolman, F. Munic. at work, 23. — Hawthorne. Engl. note-books, 2 : 305.
— Athenæum. Disraeli. Sel. spee. 2 : 617.
— Municipal activities of. Shaw, A. Munic. govt. Gt. Brit. 145.
— Opening of the town hall. Bright, Jo. Publ. add. 398.
— Rioters of, 1810. Browne, G. L. State trials 19th cent. 2 : 264.
Manchester School of politicians. Hobart, V. H. H. Ess. & mis. 2 : 242.

Manchuria. Younghusband. Heart of cont. 1.
— and Korea, Journey through. (W. Grinnell)
Am. Geog. Soc. 3 : 283.
Mancinelli, Luigi. Streatfeild. Masters Ital.
mus. 262.
Mancini, F. Hydaspes, opera. Hogarth. Mem.
opera, 1 : 201.
Mandalay. Shoemaker, M. M. Quaint corners,
60.
"Mandalay," Wreck of the. Treanor, T. S.
Heroes Goodw. sands, 166.
Mandeville, Bernard de. Stephen, J. F. Horæ
Sabb. 2 : 193.
— Earl of Shaftesbury and. Stephen, L. Eng.
thought, 2 : 15.
— Fable of the bees. Robertson. Ess. towards a
crit. method. — Stephen, L. Ess. freeth. 243.
Mandeville or Maundeville, Sir John. Collier,
W. F. Hist. Eng. lit. 44. — Disraeli, I. Amen.
(N. Y. 2 v.) 1 : 176. — Lang. Lett. to dead au.
110. — Morley. Eng. writ. 4 : 276. — Frost, T.
Explorers, 24. — Warner Lib. 17 : 9655.
Mandrake root, Myth of. Lang. Custom, 143.
Manet, Edouard. (J. C. Beckwith) Van Dyke,
J. C. Mod. Fr. mast. 215.
Manetti, Giannozzo. Symonds. Reviv. of learn.
188.
Manfred, Reign of. Busk, Mrs. Mediæv. popes,
274.
Manfred of Sicily. Utterton, F. A. Biog. sk.
118.
Mangan, James Clarence. (J. H. Ingram)
Miles, A. H. Poets of cent. 3 : 453. — Wil-
liams, A. M. Poets of Irel. — Warner Lib. 17 :
9664.
Manganese mining in New Brunswick, 1898.
(G. Beutelspacher) U. S. Cons. Rept. 57 : 84.
Manheim, Frederick. Drake, S. G. Trag. of
wilderness, 333.
Manheim, Louise. Raymond, I. Southland wr.
1 : 496.
Manhood in art. Partridge, W. O. Art for
Amer. 90.
— True. Giles, H. Lectures, 2 : 80.
Maniacs, Among the. Deming. Byways, 237.
Manichæism. Johnson, S. Ori. relig. Persia,
441. — Moxom. Jerus. to Nicæa, 319.
Manifest destiny of the U. S. Fiske. Am. polit.
ideas, 101.
Manin, Daniele. Castelar. Byron, 261.
— and "the theory of the dagger." Mazzini.
Life, etc. 6 : 266.
Manila. Norman, H. Far East, 169. — Shoe-
maker, M. M. Quaint corners, 116.
— Markets of, 1899. (O. S. Williams) U. S. Cons.
Rept. 60 : 295.
Manila Bay, Battle of. Rawson, E. K. Twenty
nav. batt. 2 : 607.
Manipur, War in. Richards, W. Heroes, 201.
Manisty, Sir H., with photo. Cooper, T. Men
of mark, 4 : 26.
Manitoba, School question in. (Anna T. Smith)
U. S. Bur. Ed. Rept. '94–95, 1 : 275.
Manitou, Colorado. Pidgeon. Engineer's holi-
day, 139.
Mankind, Perfectibility of. Hare. Guesses,
2 : 41.
Manley, Mrs. Mary de la Riviere. Forsyth.
Novels, 196. — Jeaffreson. Novelists, 1 : 85.
— Williams, Jane. Lit. wom. 152. — Street,
G. S. Miniatures, 44.
— and Mrs. Behn. Hudson, W. H. Idle hours,
125.
Manley, John. Lossing. Em. Amer. 114.
Manliness. Manning, J. M. Sermons, 308.

Manlius, George. Wallace, R. Anti-Trin. biog.
2 : 522.
Manly, Alice Alfrida. Clayton, E. C. Eng. fem.
art. 2 : 189.
Manly, Basil, jr. Miller, Jos. Singers church,
2d ed. 572.
Mann, Horace. Brooks, E. S. Hist. Amer. 320.
— Bungay. Off-hand, 175. — Griswold. Prose
writ. 597. — Loring, J. S. Hundred Bost. ora.
598. — Bungay. Pen-portr. 72. — (W. T. Harris, N. C. Schaefer, H. Sabin, J. M. Green-
wood, and others) Nat. Educa. Assoc. '96 : 52.
— (W. T. Harris) U. S. Bur. Ed. Rept. '96–97,
1 : 887. — Nichol. Amer. lit. 186.
— and the educational revival, 1830–50. (A. D.
Mayo) U. S. Bur. Ed. Rept. '96–97, 1 : 715.
— at Antioch College. (W. A. Bell) Nat. Educa.
Assoc. '96 : 72.
— Bibliography. (B. P. Mann) U. S. Bur. Ed.
Rept. '95–96, 1 : 897. — Hinsdale, B. A. H.
Mann & common sch. reviv.
— his country school. (Henry Sabin) Nat. Educa.
Assoc. '94 : 204.
Mann, Sir Horace, Walpole's letters to. Ma-
caulay. Ess. 3 : 143.
Mann, Maria R. Brockett. Woman's work,
697.
Mann, Tom, with portrait. Lynch, A. Hum.
doc's, 59.
Manner. Hazlitt. Round table. — Tuckerman.
Optimists, 231.
— and man. Mabie. My study fire, 2 : 119.
— A homily for self and friends. Hall, John.
Papers, 309.
Manners, John. See Granby, Marquis of.
Manners family. Sanford & Townsend. Gov.
fam. 1.
— Genealogical sketch of. Jewitt, L. Stately
homes, 1 : 272.
Manners. Cracroft. Ess. 1 : 275. — Hazlitt.
Sket. — Munger. On threshold, 51. — Walsh,
R. Didactics, 2 : 5. — Willis. Hurry-graphs,
290, 321. — Emerson. Ess. 2 : 115. — Friswell.
Gentle life, 1 : 25.
— and customs. Müller. Chips, 2.
— — Obsolete. Knight. Once on time, 2 : 240.
— and dress of young men. Holland, J. G. Tit-
comb's let. 31.
— and morals. Hazard, T. R. Miscel. 154.
— Anecdotes of European. Disraeli, I. Curios.
(N. Y. 4 v.) 2 : 188.
— Codes of. Hayward, A. Ess. 2 : 269.
— Contagion of. Higginson. Conc. all, 197.
— 18th century. Earle. Colon. dames, 189.
— French and English. DeQuincey. Lett. to
young (Bost.), 187.
— Good. Henry, C. S. Satan, 143.
— — and good breeding. Ballantyne. Ess. 68.
— Greek comedy of. Shackford. Soc. & lit. pap.
126.
— Mind and, Schools of. Mozley, A. Ess. 261.
— New and old world. Jarves. Ital. ramb. 402.
— Novel of. Traill. New fiction, 137.
— Petrie's Rules, 1720. Maxwell, Sir H. Rainy
days, 3.
— Schools of mind and. Mozley, A. Ess. fr.
Blackw. 261.
Manning, Anne. (C. M. Yonge) Oliphant.
Wom. novelists, 211.
Manning, Cardinal H. E. Belloc, Mme. Walled
garden, 209. — Em. persons, 5 : 190. — Stead.
Char. sket. 135. — With photo. Cooper, T.
Men of mark, 1 : 13. — McCarthy, J. Mod.
lead. 175.
— at Westminster. Yates, E. H. Celeb. 2 : 243.

Manual training, Methods of, in Philadelphia schools. (J. L. Tadd) Nat. Educa. Assoc. '94: 886.

— New demands upon schools. (C. M. Woodward) Cong. Educa. Chic. '93, 594.

— Pedagogical value of. (S. H. Peabody and others) Nat. Educa. Assoc. '86: 305.

— Purpose and value of. (J. Barnard) Nat. Educa. Assoc. '98: 989.

— Relations of normal schools to. (W. D. Parker) Nat. Educa. Assoc. '97 : 749.

— Rise and progress of. (G. M. Woodward) U. S. Bur. Ed. Rept. '93–94, 1 : 877.

— Typical institutions offering. U. S. Bur. Ed. Rept. '96–97, 2 : 1001.

— Ways, means, and maxims in. (J. D. Walters) Nat. Educa. Assoc. '89 : 621.

See also Industrial training.

Manual training school, at St. Louis, Results of. (C. M. Woodward) Nat. Educa. Assoc. '89 : 73.

— Function of. (C. M. Woodward) Nat. Educa. Assoc. '82 : 140.

— Work of. (W. F. M. Goss) Nat. Educa. Assoc. '85 : 263.

Manual training schools. Internat. health exh. 14 : 53.

— in Europe, 1893. U. S. Cons. Rept. no. 157.

— Relation to technical schools. (C. M. Woodward) Nat. Educa. Assoc. '88 : 583.

— Teacher in. (W. A. Edwards) Nat. Educa. Assoc. '99 : 905.

Manucy, Dominic. Clarke, R. H. Cath. bishops, 3 : 388.

Manuel Eugène. Pellissier. Lit. move. Fr. 365.

Manuel, Jacques Antoine. Cormenin. Orators, 146.

Manuel, Juan. Ticknor. Span. lit. 1 : 61.

Manuel, Pierre. Adolphus. Biog. Fr. rev. 2 : 12.

Manufacturers, English, Characteristics of. Sargant. Ess. 1 : 1.

— of the eastern U. S. Rousiers. Amer. life, 189.

Manufactures, American. Everett. Orat. v. 2.

— — Early. Hazard, T. R. Miscel. 186.

— Curiosities of. Chambers's Miscel. no. 113.

— English. Bright, Jo. Publ. add. 188.

— Growth of, in Massachusetts. Mass. Labor, '89 : 287.

— in the U. S., Economic condition of. Rousiers. Amer. life, 225.

— Report on, 1791. Hamilton, ed. by Lodge, 3 : 294.

Manufacturing, Government establishments. Bright, Jo. Publ. add. 139.

Manufacturing centres of New Jersey, Five. N. J. Labor, '86 : 401.

Manufacturing establishments in Missouri. Missouri Labor, 1890.

Manufacturing system and the poor. Southey, R. Ess. 1832, 1 : 110.

Manuscript treasures of England, How can they be made available ? (G. Harris) Trans. Soc. Sci. Lond. '57 : 241.

Manuscripts of the classics, Discovery of, in Italy. Symonds. Reviv. of learn. 131.

— Recovery of. Disraeli, I. Curios. (N. Y. 4 v.) 1 : 67.

— Rejected. Shepard, W. Authors, 49.

— Study of. Bibliography. Madan, F. Books in MS., stud. & use.

— Suppressors and dilapidators of. Disraeli, I. Curios. (N. Y. 4 v.) 3 : 200.

Manuzio, Aldo. Craik. Pursuit knowl. 1 : 156.

— Oliphant. Makers of Venice. — Phillimore. Stud. Ital. lit. 95. — Symonds. Reviv. of learn. 373.

Manzoni, Alessandro. Greene, G. W. Hist. stud. 171. — Howells. Mod. It. poets, 126.

— Phillimore. Stud. Ital. lit. 228. — Tuckerman. Charac. 13. — With portrait. (M. F. Egan) Warner Lib. 17 : 9671. — Em. persons, 1 : 160.

Maori manuscript, A remarkable. Winchell. Sparks geol. ham. 282.

Maori wars in New Zealand. Jenks, E. Hist. Aust. col. 271.

Map *or* Mapes, Walter. Foss. Judges, 1 : 275.

— Poems. Bristed. Pieces, 1 : 262. — Morley. Eng. writers ('88), 3 : 120.

Maps, How they are made. (W. B. Blakie) Smithson. Inst. Rept. '93 : 419.

— Value of, in boundary disputes. (P. L. Phillips) Am. Hist. Assoc. Rept. '96, 1 : 455.

See Cartography.

Mar, John Erskine, Earl of. Thomson, Mrs. Jacobites, 1 : 1.

Mar, Ancient earldom of. Taylor, J. Fam. of Scot. 1 : 6.

Mar Saba, Convent of. Buckley, J. M. Trav. 3 cont. 400. — Warner, C. D. Levant, 129.

Mara, Gertrude Eliz., German vocalist. Clayton, E. C. Queens, 97. — Edwards, H. S. Prima don. 1 : 112. — Ferris, G. T. Great singers, 1. — Hogarth. Mem. opera, 2 : 154. — Needham. Queens of song.

— as a child violinist. Phipson. Violinists, 150.

Marana and Cyra. Hahn-Hahn. Fathers, 283.

Marat, Jean P. Adolphus. Biog. Fr. rev. 2 : 24.

— (H. A. Taine) Ferris, G. T. Gt. leaders, 396. — Smythe, G. S. Hist. fancies, 245.

Marathis (Mahrattees), Subjugation of the. Adams, W. H. D. Engl. at war, 1 : 239.

Marathon. Freeman. Studies Greece, 52. — Mahaffy. Rambles Greece, 143.

— and its brigands. Stillman, W. J. Old Rome.

— The battle of. Archer. Decisiv. ev. 1. — Arnold, R. A. Levant, 1 : 173. — Creasy. Fifteen battles, 1. — King, C. Battles, 25.

Marblehead, Mass. Bacon, E. M. Hist. pilgrim, 189. — Drake. Nooks of N. E. 228.

Marburg, Germany. Mahaffy. Holl. & Germ. 153.

Marcel, dancing-master to Louis XIV. Brightwell. Byepaths of biog. 55.

Marcello, B. Satire " Il Teatro alla moda." Hogarth. Mem. opera, 1 : 159.

Marcellus II., Pope. Ranke. Popes, 1 : 284.

Marcellus, Nonius. Nettleship. Lec. & ess.

Marcet, Jane Haldimand. Martineau, H. Biog. sket. 70.

March, Henry. Miller, Jos. Singers church, 2d ed. 414.

March. Whiting, C. G. Saunterer, 5.

— Customs and superstitions of. Soane. New curios. 1 : 109.

March of the ideal ; poem. (C. Scollard) Nat. Educa. Assoc. '97 : 139.

Marchais, Madame Julie de Laborde. Haussonville. Salon of Necker, 1 : 242.

Marchant, Jacques, about 1600. Baring-Gould. Preachers, 155.

Marchbanks, Andrew J. Livingston, J. Dist. Amer. 170.

Marcion. Evans, R. W. Biog. early church, 1 : 93.

Marckant, John. Miller, Jos. Singers church, 2d ed. 46.

Marco Polo. *See* Polo, M.

Marcou, Jules. (A. Hyatt) Am. Acad. A. & S. Proc. 34 : 651.

Marcoy, Paul. Travels in valleys of lower Peru. Frost, T. Mod. expl. 126.

Marie Josèphe of Saxony, dauphiness of France. Imbert de St. A. Wom. ct. Louis xv, 258.

Marie Leckzinsky, Queen. Bush, A. F. Queens of F. **2** : 211. — Kavanagh, J. Women of Christ. 289. — With portrait. Imbert de St. A. Wom. ct. Louis xv, 23–269.

Marie-Louise, Empress. Gearey, C. Three empresses.

Marie C. C. Sobieski, queen of England. Holt, E. S. Roy. ladies, v. **2**.

Marie Thérèse of Savoy. Gearey. Dau. of Italy, 99.

Marienbad. Moulton, L. C. Lazy tours, 279.

Marietta College, Ohio. (I. W. Andrews) U. S. Bur. Ed. Circ. '91, no. **5** : 101.

Marine biological stations. (B. Dean) Smithson. Inst. Rept. '93 : 505.

Marine geography, Progress of, 1860. Am. Geog. Soc. **2** : 1.

Marine hospital service *vs.* cholera. (W. Wyman) Am. Pub. Health, **18** : 334.

— of the U. S. and quarantine. (A. N. Bell) Am. Pub. Health, **18** : 349.

Marine life. Bibliography. Providence Pub. Lib. Bull. Aug. '95.

Marini, Giambattista. Montgomery. Men of Ita. **2** : 174. — Shelley, Mrs. Lit. men Italy, v. **2**. — Stebbing. Ital. poets, v. **3**.

Marino, Giovanni. Symonds. Renais. Cath. reac. **2** : 259.

Mario, Conti di Candida. Engel, L. Mozart, **2** : 332. — Spark, W. Mus. mem. 235.

Marion, Francis. With portrait. [Amer.] Nat. portr. gall. v. **3**. — With portrait. Duyckinck. Nat. portr. gall. **1** : 177. — Glazier, W. Heroes, 106. — With portrait. Headley, J. T. Washington, **2** : 225. — Lossing. Em. Amer. 184.

Marischal, Earls, Fate of. Burke, B. Viciss. of fam. **3** : 239.

Maritime bill of lading, Rept. of committee on. Am. Bar Assoc. **12** : 339.

Maritime capture and blockade. Hobart, V. H. H. Polit. ess. 59.

See Capture.

Maritime contracts, Law affecting. (R. Lowndes *et al.*) Trans. Soc. Sci. Lond. '76 : 264.

Maritime police, International, Principles of. (E. Liceaga) Am. Pub. Health, **19** : 137.

Maritime sanitation at ports of arrival. (H. B. Horlbeck) Am. Pub. Health, **16** : 110.

— Canadian system of. (F. Montizambert) Am. Pub. Health, **14** : 116.

— Value of steam heat in. (H. B. Horlbeck) Am. Pub. Health, **18** : 363.

Marius, Caius. Bernard, F. Escapes, 6. — (J. A. Froude) Ferris, G. T. Gt. leaders, 27. — Herbert, H. W. Capt. Rom.

— Campaign of. Baring-Gould. Troub.-land, 130.

Marivaux, Pierre C. de. Forster. Fr. & Span. genius, 1. — Houssaye. Men of 18th cent. **1** : 76. — Vinet. Fr. lit. 18th cent. 162. — Men & wom. of France, **1** : 75.

— and the French stage. Hawkins. Fr. stage 18th cent. v. **1**.

Marivaux, Mademoiselle de. Houssaye. Philos. **1** : 292.

Marjouram, William. Rogers, C. Chr'n heroes, 236.

Market gardens. *See* Gardens.

Markets, Need of. Wynter, A. Peeps, **1** : 286.

Markham, Rev. George, *vs.* John Fawcett. Erskine, T. Speeches, 605.

Markham, Gervase. Mitchell. Wet days, 146.

Markham, Sir John, chief justice of England, 1461–64. Campbell. Ch. just. **1** : 137.

Marking system, The. (B. Kellogg) N. Y. Regents, **103** : app. 219.

Marks, Cornelius. Wallace, R. Anti-Trin. biog. **3** : 5.

Marks, David L. Pierce, B. K. Em. dead, 473.

Marks, Elias. Davidson, J. W. Writ. of South, 368.

Marks, Henry S. Atkinson, J. B., *et al.* Eng. paint. 50. — Wilman, G. Sk. liv. celeb. 135.

Marlborough, John Churchill, 1st duke of. Adams, W. H. D. Memo. batt. **2** : 31. — Caulfield. Kit-cat, 26. — George, H. B. Battles, 153. — Edgar. Boyhood, 239. — Georgian era, **2** : 9. — Gleig. Brit. mil. com. **1** : 318. **2** : 1. — James, G. P. R. Commanders, **2** : 82. — Lodge. Portraits (Bohn), v. **7**. — With portrait. Mongan. Mil. comm. 11. — Russell, W. Extraor. men, 69. — Wilson, J. G. Illus. sol. 189. — (W. E. H. Lecky) Ferris, G. T. Gt. leaders, 344. — Johns. Nav. & mil. heroes. — Morris, W. O. Commanders, 36. — Wrangham. Brit. Plutarch, v. **5**.

— and Lord Macaulay. Page, D. Paradoxes, 3.

— and Queen Anne. Strickland. Queens Eng. v. **12**.

— Estimate of. (Duke of Wellington) Stanhope, Earl. Miscel. **1** : 81.

Marlborough, J. W. S. Churchill, duke of, with photo. Cooper, T. Men of mark, **5** : 7.

— at Dublin castle. Yates, E. H. Celeb. **3** : 263.

Marlborough, Sarah Jennings, duchess of. Adams, W. H. D. Wom. of fash. **1** : 151. — With portrait. Costello. Englishwomen, **4** : 1. — Lodge. Portraits (Bohn), v. **7**. — Lord, J. Beacon, **5** : 303. — Macaulay. Biog. sk. 173. — Adams, W. H. D. Fam. beauties, **2** : 185. — With portrait. Fifty famous women, 112. — Willing. Dames, 3.

— at court of Queen Anne. Strickland. Queens Eng. v. **12**.

Marlitt, E. *See* John, Eugenia.

Marlo, Karl, Federalism of. Rae, J. Contemp. soc. 172.

Marlowe, Christopher. Collier, W. F. Hist. Eng. lit. 167. — Collier. Eng. dram. poetry, **2** : 486. — Crofts, E. Chap. Eng. lit. 171. — Dowden. Transcripts, 431. — Dunham. Lit. & sci. men, **2** : 49. — Hazlitt. Dram. Eliz. — Ulrici. Shakes. dram. art, **1** : 150. — Symonds. Shakes. pred. 581. — Ward, A. W. Eng. dram. **1** : 173. — (A. C. Bradley) Ward. Eng. poets, **1** : 411. — Whipple. Lit. Eliz. 25. — Choate, I. B. Wells of Eng. 166. — Lowell. Old Eng. dram. 28. — Morley, H. Eng. writ. **9** : 245. **10** : 111. — Minto, W. Eng. poets, 230. — Simson, Jas. Em. men of Kent, 109. — Warner Lib. **17** : 9714.

— Faustus, and Bailey's Festus. Dawson, G. Shakesp. 342.

Marlowe, Julia. (E. Fuller) McKay, F. E. Fam. actors, 159.

Marmont, Auguste Frédéric Louis Viesse. Headley. Napoleon, **2** : 92.

Marmontel, Belisarius. Griffin, G. W. Stud. in lit.

— and the French stage. Hawkins. Fr. stage 18th cent. v. **1, 2**.

Marmontel, Jean François. Haussonville. Salon of Necker, **1** : 118.

Marochetti, sculptor, bust of Thackeray in Westm. Abbey. Palgrave. Ess. on art, 299.

Maroons. Scoffern. Stray leaves, 154.

Maroons of Jamaica and Surinam. Higginson, T. W. Travelers, 116, 150.
— of Jamaica in Nova Scotia. (D. Brymner) Roy. Soc. Can. 2d ser. 1, § 2 : 81.
Maroon war, 1795-96. (Alexander, earl of Balcarres) Lindsay, Lives, 3 : 1.
Marot, Clement. ^ary. Fr. poets, 1. — With portrait. Warner Lib. 17 : 9729.
— and his family. Besant. Fr. poetry, 248.
— Diana of Poictiers and. Jameson. Loves of poets.
Marquesas Islands. Alexander, J. M. Isl. Pac. 215.
Marquette, Jacques. Milburn. Pioneers, 67. — Murray, J. O'K. Cath. pioneers, 251. — Parkman. Discov. gt. west, 49. — Shea. Discov. Miss. valley, 41. — Murray, J. O'K. Cath. heroes, 511.
Marable, Madeline Cockburn. Clayton, E. C. Eng. fem. art. 2 : 192.
Marr, John Q. Walker, C. D. Biog. Va. Mil. Inst. 359.
Marriage. Arnold, F. Turning-points, 128. — De Vere. Ess. 2 : 265. — Ossoli. Women, 72. — Friswell. Gentle life, 1 : 288. — Gray, E. C. Idle musings, 71. — Lecky. Map of life, 300. — Martin, E. S. Cousin Anthony, 53. — Stevenson, R. L. Virgin. 1.
— among primitive peoples. Wake. Serpent wor. 165.
— and divorce. Du Chaillu. Viking age, v. 2. — Martin, E. S. Windfalls, 49.
— — in the U. S. Rousiers. Amer. life, 271.
— and free thought. Mallock. Stud. contemp. sup. 139.
— and single life. Bacon. Ess.
— Bond of, Roman Catholic Church and. (M. J. Wade) Barrows, J. H. Parl. relig. 1 : 743.
— by capture. Wake. Serpent wor. 180.
— Choice in. Taylor. Notes from life, 43.
— Companionship in. Hamerton. Hum. int. 44.
— Consanguineous, Explanation of laws against. Webster, N. Ess. 322.
— History of. Greene, W. B. Soc. frag. 183.
— in Germany. Baring-Gould. Germany, 96.
— Influence of, on death and crime. Proctor. Light sci. 3 : 281.
— — on the death-rate. Proctor. Light sci. 1 : 238.
— Is the marriage contract eternal? Buchanan, R. Coming terr. 259.
— Kindred group. Pearson, K. Chances, 2 : 92.
— Laws and customs of. Kirkus. Miscel. 79. — Newman, F. W. Miscel. 3 : 222.
— Love in. Walsh, R. Didactics, 1 : 32.
— Mésalliances. Linton, E. L. Girl of per. 1 : 147.
— Mutuality as the law of. Greene, W. B. Soc. frag. 5.
— Partners for life. Friswell. Gentle life, 2 : 192.
— Philosophy and poetry of. Collins, M. Pen sketches, 62.
— Primitive, Rejoinder to McLennan on. Spencer, H. Var. frag.'63.
— Remarriage of native converts. Maine, H. Life & sp. 130.
— Socialist view of. Bax, E. B. Outlooks, 151.
— State regulation of. (Mrs. K. G. Wells) Conf. char. & correc. '97 : 302.
— Women and. Hamerton. Intellec. 226.
Marriage customs. Jones, W. Credulities, 481.
Marriage law in England and Scotland. (J. Boyd-Kinnear) Trans. Soc. Sci. Lond. '77: 231.
— of England and Ireland. (M. H. Cookson) Trans. Soc. Sci. Lond. '63 : 164.

Marriage law of Scotland. (G. H. Palmer) Trans. Soc. Sci. Lond. '63 : 176.
— — Instance of. Burke, P. Romance of forum.
Marriage laws, Discrepancies in. (A. Waddilove) Trans. Soc. Sci. Lond. '82 : 206.
Marriage question in Gt. Britain. (W. O'C. Morris) Trans. Soc. Sci. Lond. '62 : 199.
Marriage relation, First essential duties of. Holland, J. G. Titcomb's let. 167.
Marriage-ring, The. (Jeremy Taylor) Friswell. Silent hour, 228.
Marriages, Fleet. Ewald, A. C. Paper, 227.
— International. Higginson. Book & heart, 148.
— Morganatic. Baring-Gould. Germany, 11 : 23.
Married life; Kisses and caresses. Cobbe, F. P. Re-echoes, 61.
— Purity in ; white life for two. (F. E. Willard) Barrows, J. H. Parl. relig. 2 : 1230.
Married people, Behavior of. Lamb. Elia.
Marriott, Charles. Burgon. Twelve men, 1 : 296.
Marriott, George Robert. Mozley. Reminis. 1 : 166.
Marriott, John. Hatfield, E. F. Poets of church, 409. — Miller, Jos. Singers church, 2d ed. 368.
Marryatt, Florence, with portrait. Black, H. C. Wom. authors, 81.
Marryat, Frederick. Horne, R. H. New spirit, 142. — With portrait. Warner Lib. 17 : 9737. — Wotton. Word portraits, 199.
— Bibliography. Hannay. Life of M.
Mars, Mdlle. Stuart, H. Paris days, 211.
Mars, the planet. Proctor, R. A. Univ. of suns, 160.
— Views of Schiaparelli on. (W. H. Pickering) Smithson. Rept. '94 : 113.
— Whewellite essay on. Proctor. Borderland, 130.
— with bibliography. Todd, D. P. Stars & tel. 178.
Marsden, George. Wesley & successors, 105, 129.
Marsden, Joshua. Miller, Jos. Singers church, 2d ed. 412.
Marsden, Samuel. Yonge. Pioneers, 216.
Marseilles. Baring-Gould. Troub.-land, 42. — Fairbanks, O. B. Aguecheek, 89. — Fulton, C. C. Europe, 184. — Howe, J. W. Oak to olive, 42. — Sala. Trip to Barbary, 71.
— Life at. Sala. Journey south, 28.
— Sieges of. Robson, W. Sieges, 259.
Marsh, Catherine. Darton. Fam. girls, 219.
Marsh, Charles, with portrait. Sketches N. H. men, 184.
Marsh, G. Tayler. Eng. martyrs.
Marsh, George Perkins. Am. Antiq. Soc. Proc. n. s. 2 : 108. — Griswold. Prose writ. 414. — Lanman, C. Haphazard, 91. — With portrait. Mitchell, D. G Am. lands, 2 : 59.
Marsh, Herbert, Bishop. Hunt, J. Rel. thought 19th cent. 30.
Marsh, John. Bungay. Pen-portr. 178.
Marsh, Jonathan. (E. W. Marsh) N. E. Hist.-Gen. Soc. Biog. 4 : 375.
Marsh, Mrs. M. M. Brockett. Woman's work, 621.
Marsh, Othniel Charles. Am. Antiq. Soc. Proc. n. s. 13 : 124.
Marsh, William. Newton, W. W. Ess. 139.
Marsh warbler in Oxfordshire and Switzerland. Fowler, W. N. Sum. stud. 69.
Marshall, Alfred, Economics of industry. Leslie, T. E. C. Ess. pol. & mor. 73.
Marshall, Henry, and military hygiene. Brown, J. Locke, etc. 165.
Marshall, James K. Walker, C. D. Biog. Va. Mil. Inst. 369.

recol. 78. — Queens of liter. Vic. era, 33. — Underwood, S. A. Heroines, 153. — Walsh, W. S. Pen-pic. Vic. au. 279. — Wotton. Word portraits, 202. — Bolton. Famous types, 150. — Clarke, J. F. Nineteenth cent. quest. 284. — With portrait. Hubbard, E. Little journeys, 3 : 79. — Duyckinck. Portrait gall, 2 : 370. — Em. persons, 2 : 1. — With portrait. Hamilton, C. J. Wom. writers, 2 : 72. — Walford, L. B. Twelve Eng. auth. 49. — Phillips, W. Speeches, 2 : 473 — Putnam, J. O. Addresses, 221. — Rawnsley. Lit. Assoc. Eng. lakes, 2 : 107. — Smiles. Brief biog. 499. — Stanton, H. B. Reforms, 353.

Martineau, Harriet, and Atkinson, H. G., Correspondence of. Forbes, E. Lit. papers, 119.

Martineau, James. Great mod. preachers. — Hunt, J. Rel. thought 19th cent. 246. — Hutton, R. H. Criticisms, 1 : 1. — Miles, A. H. Poets of cent. 10 : 699. — With portrait. Warner Lib. 17 : 9750.
— Ethical system of. (J. H. Hertz) Colum. Univ. Contrib. Philos. 1 : no. 3.
— Theology of. Courtney. Studies, 203.

Martineau, Robert. Bate, P. H. Eng. Pre-Raph. 79.

Martinez de la Rosa. Kennedy. Poets of Spain, 169.

Martini, Simone. Symonds. Renais. fine arts, 216

Martinique. Hill, R. T. Cuba, 345. — Norman. Colonial France, 133.
— Business depression, resources, etc., 1895. (J. G. Tucker) U. S. Cons. Rept. 49 : 478.

Martino, Anna Blunden. Clayton, E. C. Eng. fem. art. 2 : 196.

Martinus, Severinus. Wallace, R. Anti-Trin. biog. 2 : 522.

Martyn, Henry. Adams, W. H. D. Good Samar. 218. — Adams, W. H. D. Heroes Chr. 415. — Dana. P. & p. writ. 418. — Kaye. Indian off. 1 : 321. — Seeley, M. Later evang. 286. — Taylor, W. C. Mod. Brit. Plut. 237. — Benson & Tatham. Men of might, 188. — Collins, Stephen. Miscel. — Cust. Ling. & Orient. Ess. 4 : 547. — Dale, T. P. Life's motto. — Gurney, J. H. Hist. sketches, 3 : 371. — Thompson, A. Gt. mission. 229. — Tillotson, J. Untit. nobil. 117.

Martyrdom. Brown, J. N. Bapt. martyrs, 3.

Martyrologies. Charles. Martyrs, 7.

Martyrs. Cobbe, F. P. Re-echoes, 34.
— A group of. Hodder. Heroes, 2 : 223.
— of Scotland and Sir W. Scott. Bocock. Writings, 273.
— Virgin, Legends of. Charles. Martyrs, 151.

Marvell, Andrew. Benson, A. C. Ess. 68. — Choate, I. B. Wells of Eng. 287. — Coleridge. Nor. worthies, 1 : 1. — Dawson, G. Biog. lec. 89. — Rogers, H. Ess. 1 : 48. — Rogers, H. Reason. 42. — (G. Smith) Ward. Eng. poets, 2 : 380. — Gosse, E. From Shakes. 181. — Griswold, R. W. Sac. poets. — Macdonald, G. England's antiphon, 247. — Mitford, M. R. Recollec. 532. — Wrangham. Brit. Plut. v. 4. — With portrait. Warner Lib. 17 : 9770.
— House of. Hall, Mrs. S. C. Pilgr. Eng. shr. 1 : 133.

Marvin, Dudley. Proctor. Lawy. of N. Y. 440.

Marwedel, Emily. (Elizabeth Harrison) Nat. Educa. Assoc. '94 : 238.

Mary, Virgin. Coleridge, H. Ess. 2 : 326.
— House of. Jarves. Ital. ramb. 121.
— Superstitions of sailors concerning. Jones, W. Credulities, 34.

Mary, Virgin, Worship of. Brownson. Works, 8 : 59.
— — Moral and social influence of. Brownson. Works, 8 : 86.

Mary, Mother of the Incarnation. (Marie Guyard) With portrait. Murray, J. O'K. Cath. heroes, 473.

Mary I., queen of England. Burke, S. H. Hist. portr. Tudor, 2 : 446. — With portrait. Howitt, M. Queens, 360. — Lodge. Portraits (Bohn), v. 2. — Strickland. Queens Eng. v. 5. — Strickland. Tudor prin. 1 : 93. — Williams, Jane. Lit. wom. 55. Hunt, L. Men, wom. & books, 183. — Lancelott. Queens, v. 1.
— and Elizabeth. Burke, S. H. Men of reforma. 2 : 358.
— Reign of. Burke, S. H. Men of reforma. 2 : 301.

Mary II. Burder. Pious wom. 45. — Howitt, M. Queens, 470. — Strickland. Queens Eng. 10 : 11. — Fifty famous women, 217. — Lancelott. Queens, v. 2. — Burnet, G. Lives.
— Death of. Macaulay. Biog. sk. 322.
— Letters of. Ewald, A. C. Paper, 205.

Mary of Lorraine, queen of James V. of Scotland. Burke, S. H. Hist. portr. Tudor, 390.
— Strickland. Queens Scot. 1 : 2.

Mary Beatrice of Modena, queen of James II. Howitt, M. Queens, 464. — Strickland. Queens Eng. 9 : 10. — Jesse. Court of Eng. Stuarts, 3 : 483.

Mary, Queen of Scots. Bayly, J. A. S. New stud. 74. — Bush, A. F. Queens of F. 1 : 323. — Goodrich, F. B. Women, 187. — Jameson. Fem. sov. 1. — Lodge. Portraits (Bohn), v. 2. — Russell. Extr. women, 131. — Ste.-Beuve. Engl. portr. 1. — Strickland. Queens Scot. v. 3. — Swinburne. Miscel. 323. — Williams, Jane. Lit. wom. 58. — Bernard, F. Escapes, 41. — Bethune, G. W. Brit. fem. poets, 20. — Burke, S. H. Hist. portr. Tudor, 4 : 70. — Cook, T. D. Old Touraine, 2 : 19. — (D. Hume) Ferris, G. T. Gt. leaders, 275. — With portrait. Fifty famous women, 284. — With portrait. Imbert de St. A. Wom. Valois ct. 190. — Owen, Mrs. O. F. Heroines hist. 318. — Scott, Mrs. M. M. Abbotsf. 248. — Stanhope, P. H. Hist. essays.
— and Chastelar. Menzies, S. Roy. fav. 1 : 293.
— Defense of. Skelton. Ess. 1.
— The Edinburgh of. Masson. Edinb. sket. 1.
— Execution of. Starling, E. Noble deeds wom. 281.
— Her last prayer. Smythe, G. S. Hist. fancies, 56.
— Impeachment of. Skelton. Impeach. of Mary, 133.
— in Holyrood Palace. Terhune. Where ghosts, v. 1.
— Last hours of. Ewald. Studies, 154.
— Portraits of. Hutton, L. From books.
— Trial and execution of. Strickland. Queens of Eng. v. 7.

Mary of Anjou, Queen. Bush, A. F. Queens of F. 1 : 222.

Mary of Brabant, Queen. Bush, A. F. Queens of F. 1 : 177.

Mary of England, Queen. Bush, A. F. Queens of F. 1 : 270.

Mary of France. Williams, Jane. Lit. wom. 23.
— Love match of. Ewald. Stories fr. st. pap. 1 : 96.

Mary Tudor, queen of Louis XII. Burke, S. H. Hist. portr. Tudor, 1 : 127.

Massachusetts Bay. Bacon, E. M. Hist. pilgrim. 5. — Richardson. Am. Lit. 1 : 89.

Massachusetts Bay currency, 1690–1750. (A. McF. Davis) Am. Antiq. Soc. Proc. n. s. 12 : 410.

Massachusetts bill of rights. (E. Washburn) Mass. Hist. Proc. 8 : 294.

Massachusetts company, King Charles's charter of. Adams, C. F. Three episodes, 1 : 240.

Massachusetts Institute of Technology, Boston, Mass. (S. W. Holman) U. S. Bur. Ed. Circ. '91, no. 6 : 280.

Massachusetts Militia, 15th regiment. Devens. Orations, 179.

Massacre of St. Bartholomew. See St. Bartholomew.

Massart, Lambert J., with portrait. Ehrlich, A. Cel. violin. 104.

Masséna, André. Headley. Napoleon, 2 : 53.

Massenet, H. Henry, S. Hours w. Parisians, 223.

Massenet, Jules. Hervey, A. Masters Fr. music, 173.
— Le Cid. Guerber. Stor. of operas, 241.
— Roi de Lahore. Hueffer. Mus. stud. 228.

Masses, Reaching the. Hall, John. Papers, 218.

Massey, Charles, jr. Winslow, S. N. Biog. Phila. merch. 227.

Massey, Gerald. Gilfillan. Third gall. 163. — Russell, W. Eccen. 90. — Smiles. Brief biog. 440.

Massie, Richard. Hatfield, E. F. Poets of ch. 415. — Miles, A. H. Poets of cent. 10 : 686.

Massillon, Jean Baptiste. Broadus. Lec. hist. preach. 174. — Ste.-Beuve. Monday chats, 84. — Waterbury. Eloq. preach. 204. — With portrait. (J. F. Bingham) Warner Lib. 17 : 9780.

Massimi family. Symonds. Renais. Cath. reac. 1 : 353.

Massinger, Philip. Choate, I. B. Wells of Eng. 204. — Dunham. Lit. & sci. men, 2 : 252. — Hazlitt. Dram. Eliz. — Stephen, L. Hours in libr. 3 : 1. — Ward, A. W. Eng. dram. 2 : 263. — Whipple. Lit. Eliz. 178. — Gosse, E. Jacobean poets, 202. — Minto, W. Eng. poets, 363. — Symons, A. Stud. two lit. 92. — With portrait. (A. M. Sholl) Warner Lib. 17 : 9797.
— and Ford. Lowell. Old Eng. dram. 113.
— and his plays. Budd, H. St. Mary's Hall lec. 166.

Masson, David. Barrie. Edinburgh eleven, 17.

Master of the ceremonies, Diary of a. Disraeli, I. Curios. (N. Y. 4 v.) 2 : 374.

Masters, Mary. Miller, Jos. Singers church, 2d ed. 175.

Masters in literature. Garland. Crumbling idols, 165.

Masters, The old. Saunders. Pastime, 53.

Master-singers, The. Winkworth. Chr. singers Germ. 76.
See Meistersingers.

Mastodons and mammoths. Winchell. Sparks geol. ham. 234.

Mastricht, Gerhard von. Abbot, E. Auth. 4th gosp. & ess. 184.

Masulipatam. See Macchlípatanam.

Matabeleland, English war with, 1893. Latimer. Eur. in Afr. in 19th cent. 370.
— Invasion of, by the English unjustifiable. Cust. Ling. & orient. ess. 4 : 330.

Matches. Japp & Holmes. Succ. bus. men, 87.
— Manufacture of. Wynter, A. Peeps, 2 : 159.

Match-box, Death in the. Wynter, A. Our soc. bees, 2 : 209.

Materialism. Calvert. Br. ess. 90. — Flint.

Anti-theistic, 39. — Holland, H. Frag. papers, 206. — Haweis. Curr. coin. — Hutton, R. H. Criticisms, 2 : 310. — Romanes. Mind & motion, 55, 119.

Materialism and modern spiritualism. Stock. Attempts, 157.
— and spiritualism. Brownson. Works, 9 : 379.
— Common sense and. Stephen, L. Eng. thought, 1 : 59.
— Dualism, or idealism. Bowen, F. Gleanings, 136.
— Modern. (W. F. Wilkinson) Liv. papers, v. 3.
— — and theology. Martineau, J. Ess. 4 : 165.
— Modern scientific. Tulloch. Mod. theories, 125.
— Scientific. Tyndall. Frag. sci. 109.
— Theism and. Thompson, J. P. Amer. com. 257.
— What is ? Stephen, L. Agnos. apol. 127.

Maternal schools in France. U. S. Bur. Ed. Circ. '82, no. 5.

Mathematics, Antipathy to. Guiney. Goosequill, 113.
— applied, Educational value of. (F. R. Hutton & others) Cong. Educa. Chic. '93, 560.
— Bibliography. Cajori, F. Hist. mathemat.
— Elementary, and education. (L. W. Colwell) Nat. Educa. Assoc. '97 : 637.
— higher, Cultural value of. (W. B. Smith) Nat. Educa. Assoc. '98 : 178.
— Liberal teaching of. Newman, F. W. Essays, 305.
— Methods of teaching and studying. (O. H. Robinson) N. Y. Regents, 82 : 744.
— Nature and method of teaching. (W. D. Wilson) N. Y. Regents, 81 : 659.
— Poetry of. Ware, H., jr. Works, 1 : 107.
— Positive and negative terms in. (W. D. Wilson) N. Y. Regents, 88 : 652.
— Progress in, 1846–96. (R. S. Woodward) Goode. Smithson. Inst. 561.
— Study of. (G. B. Docharty) N. Y. Regents, 81 : 591.
— — as an exercise of mind. Hamilton. Discus.
— — in Oxford Univ., Encouragement of. Froude, R. H. Remains, 2 : 325.
— Teaching, in academies. (T. H. Safford) N. Y. Regents, 95 : 298.
— Teaching and history of, in the U. S. (F. Cajori) U. S. Bur. Ed. Circ. '90, no. 3.

Mathematical instruction, Economy in. (J. L. Patterson) Nat. Educa. Assoc. '96 : 588.

Mathematical tripos. Todhunter, I. Conflict stud.

Mather, Alexander. Jackson, T. Early Meth. 1 : 367. — Wesley & successors, 25.

Mather, Cotton. Holland, J. Psalmists, 2 : 140. — Lossing. Em. Amer. 27. — With portrait. Mitchell, D. G. Am. lands, 51. — Pierce, B. K. Em. dead, 120. — Richardson. Amer. lit. 1 : 130. — Sherman, D. N. Eng. divines, 76.
— and his slaves. (H. W. Haynes) Am. Antiq. Soc. Proc. n. s. 6 : 191.
— Diary of, and the "Magnalia." (C. Deane) Mass. Hist. Proc. 6 : 404.

Mather, Eleazer. Sherman, D. N. Eng. divines, 107.

Mather, Increase. Lossing. Em. Amer. 48. — Richardson. Amer. lit. 1 : 126. — Sherman, D. New Eng. divines, 57.

Mather, Increase. Remarkable providences; Offor's edition. Lowell. Writ. 1 : 256.

Mather, Richard. Sherman, D. N. Eng. divines, 26.

— With portrait. Ewart, H. C. Leaders, 95.
— Gibbins. Eng. soc. ref. 159. — Hutton, R.
H. Criticisms, 1 : 80. — Haweis. Sermons, 325.
— Hutton. Mod. guides, 311. — Mozley, J. B.
Ess. v. 2. — Stanley, A. P. Westm. sermons,
191. — Tulloch. Move. of relig. thought, 263.
— Wotton. Word portraits, 205 — Thomas,
R. Lead. of thought, 166. — With portrait.
Warner Lib. 17 : 9828.

Maurice, Frederic Denison, a modern prophet.
Scudder, H. E. Men & let. 70.
— Obituary notice of. Kingsley, C. Lit. lec. 337.
— Theological essays. Mozley. Ess. 2 : 255.

Mauritius. Abercromby. Seas & skies, 223.

Maury, D. H. Pollard. Life of Lee, 837.

Maury, Matthew Fontaine. Davidson, J. W.
Writ. of South, 379. — With portrait. Sey-
mour, C. C. B. Self-made, 51. — Youmans.
Pioneers sci. 464.

Maury family. Agnew. Protes. exiles, 2 : 30.

Maverick family. Agnew. Protes. exiles, 2 : 30.
— Titcomb, S. E. N. Eng. peo. 244.

Maxen, Surprise of the Prussian army at, 1759.
Malleson. Ambushes, 271.

Maxfield, Rufus A., with portrait. Sketches
N. H. men, 289.

Maximian to Romulus Augustus, From. Doran.
Monarchs, 2 : 30.

Maximilian I., of Austria. Peake. Eliz. Germ.
emperors, 222.

Maximilian I., of Mexico. Bryant. Prose, 2 :
237. — (St. Maurice) Roy. Soc. Canada, v. 7.
— U. S. For. rela. 1867.
— His travels and his tragedy. Gildersleeve.
Ess. 453.
— Reminiscences of. Kingston, W. B. Monarchs,
1 : 278.

Maximilian II., 1564-76. Peake, Eliz. Germ.
emperors, 306.

Maxims, moral and spiritual, A collection of.
Wordsworth, C. Miscel. 3 : 29.
— of Balthazar Gracian. Duff, M. E. G. Miscel.
144.

Maxse, Fred. Augustus. Davidson, J. M. Eng.
liberals, 263.

Maxwell, Lady Darcy. Burder. Pious wom.
534. — Wise, D. Heroic Meth. 162.

Maxwell, James. Holland, J. Psalmists, 2 : 227.
— Chambers's Miscel. no. 12.

Maxwell, James Clerk. Garnett. Physicists,
278. — Watson, Mrs. R. A. Poet toilers, 73. —
Munro, J. Pioneers elec. 223.

Maxwell, Lady Stirling. See Norton, Caroline.

Maxwell, William. See Nithsdale, W. Maxwell, earl of.

Maxwell, William Stirling. Wilson, J. G.
Poets of Scot. 2 : 407.

Maxwell, Winifred, countess of Nithsdale.
Owen, Mrs. O. F. Heroines domes. 219.

Maxwell family. Taylor, J. Fam. of Scot. 2 : 1.

May, Abby W. Brockett. Woman's work, 554.

May, Caroline. Hart, J. S. Fem. prose, 441.

May, Charles. Glazier, W. Heroes, 230.

May, E. H. Tuckerman. Artists, 501.

May, Joseph, with portrait. Hunt, F. Am. merch.
1 : 443.

May, Samuel J. Clarke, J. F. Memo. sketches,
197.

May, Month of. Hunt, L. Men, wom. & books,
113.
— Customs and superstitions of. Soane. New
curios. 1 : 222.
— A little tour in. Boyd. Less. of mid. age, 265.
— The three cold days in. Proctor, R. A. Univ.
of suns, 318.

Maya pottery and implements, Copies of. (E. H.
Thompson) Am. Antiq. Soc. Proc. n. s. 6 :
358.

Mayan hieroglyphics, Primer of. (D. G. Brinton)
Univ. Pa. Publ. Philol. 3 : no. 2.

Mayan inscriptions. (A. Le Plongeon) Am. Antiq. Soc. Proc. n. s. 1 : 246.

Mayas, Hero gods of the. Brinton. Amer. hero-
myths, 143.

Mayday. Hutton, L. Other times, 139.

May-day, Evil. Knight. Once on time, 1 : 126.

May fair. Knight. Once on time, 1 : 283.

May-morning : its poetry and its prose. Knight.
Once on time, 1 : 177.

May-pole of Merry-Mount, 1627. Adams, C. F.
Three episodes, 1 : 174.

Maydole, David, hammer-maker. Parton. Capt.
indus. 9.

Mayence. Bartley, G. C. D. Rhine, 142.

Mayer, Brantz. Davidson, J. W. Writ. of South,
383.

Mayer, Joseph. Smith, C. R. Retrospec. 1 : 67.

Mayfield House. (M. Corbett) Knapp, J. M.
Univ. 107.

"Mayflower," Ship, Note on. Blaxland. Mayflower ess. 42.

Mayhew, Henry. Hodder, G. Memories, 39.

Mayhew, William Edwards. (N. H. Chamberlain) N. E. Hist.-Gen. Soc. Biog. 4 : 40.

Maynard, Sir John. Foss. Judges, 7 : 325. —
Campbell. Ld. chan. 5 : 2. — Woolrych. Serjeants, 1 : 1.

Maynard, Margaret, Lady, with portrait. Johnstone, G. Lead. women, 121.

Mayne, John. Wilson, J. G. Poets of Scot. 1 :
373.

Maynooth College. Peel, R. Speeches, 4 : 479,
516.

Maynooth grant, 1845. Disraeli. Sel. spee. 1 :
82. — Thirlwall, C. Remains, 1 : 69.

Mayo, Charles. (W. B. Trask) N. E. Hist.-Gen.
Soc. Biog. 3 : 272.

Mayo, R. S. Bourke, 6th earl of, Administration
of, in India. Temple, R. Men of India,
365.
— Obituary of. Em. persons, 1 : 76.

Maynwaring, Arthur, with portrait. Caulfield.
Kit-cat, 228.

Mayseder, Joseph, with portrait. Ehrlich, A.
Cel. violin. 69.

Mazarin, Giulio, Cardinal. Crowe, E. E. For.
statesm. 2 : 269. — Maceuen. Celeb. 51-67.

Mazarin, Hortensia Mancini, duchess of. Jesse.
Court of Eng. Stuarts, 3 : 207.

Mazatlan. 1891. (R. Lambert) U. S. Cons.
Rept. 37 : 388.

Mazeppa, Ivan Stepanovitch. Parton. Peop.
bk. biog. 439.

Mazzini, Giuseppe. Bryant, W. C. Prose, 2 :
343. — Myers. Ess. mod. v. 1. — Nolan. Liber.
of Ita. 308. — Schuyler. Peter the Great, 2 :
115. — Marriott, J. A. R. Makers mod. It. —
Pearson, C. H. Reviews, 187. — Thayer, W. R.
Dawn Ital. 1 : 379. — Tyler, M. C. Glimpses
Eng. 24. — With portrait. (F. Sewall) Warner
Lib. 17 : 9843.
— and the Carlyle brotherhood. Espinasse. Lit.
recol. 103.
— as a patriot. Purnell. Liter. 253.
— Letters to the pope. Ossoli. At home, 284.
— Obituary of. Em. persons, 1 : 83.

Mazzola, Francesco, called Parmigiano. Jameson. Ital. painters, 302.

Mazzola-Bedoli, Girolamo. Ricci. Correggio,
369.

Mead, Edward C. Davidson, J. W. Writ. of South, 385.

Mead, Richard. Georgian era, 2 : 372. — Jeaffreson. Doctors, 152. — Pettigrew. Med. portr. gall. v. 1.

— Library of, 18th century. Dobson, A. Eighteenth cent. vign. 3 : 29.

Meade, Gen. George Gordon. With portrait. Brockett. Men of our day, 159. — Devens. Orations, 27. — Glazier, W. Heroes, 326.

Meade, William. (P. Slaughter) N. E. Hist.-Gen. Soc. Biog. 4 : 454.

Meadows, Kenny. Everitt, G. Eng. carica. 355. — Hodder, G. Memories, 98.

Meagher, Thomas Francis. Bungay. Off-hand, 288. — Forney. Anec. 2 : 67. — McCarthy, J. H. Hours w. em. Irishmen, 141.

Mealy-face, John, Old. Baring-Gould. Yorks. odd. 2 : 102.

Meanee, Battle of. Adams, W. H. D. Engl. at war, 2 : 90.

Means, William Gordon, with portrait. Sketches N. H. men, 103.

Means and ends. Hazlitt. Winterslow.

Meany, Stephen Jos. Savage, J. Fenian heroes, 231.

Measles and smallpox, History of. Creighton, C. Epidem. 439.

— and whooping-cough ; should they be quarantined ? (F. T. Miles) Ohio Health, '95 : 372.

— Quarantine of. (H. M. Bracken) Am. Pub. Health, 22 : 297.

Measurement, exact, Educational value of. (A. M. Mayer) Cong. Educa. Chic. '93, 558.

Measures ; fundamental units. (T. C. Mendenhall) Smithson. Inst. Rept. '93 : 135.

— Lineal, of American nations. Brinton. Ess. Amer. 433.

Meat, Diseased. (H. P. Wenzel) Wisc. Health, '80 : 74.

— A few words on our. Wynter, A. Our soc. bees, 2 : 216.

— Food-supply of the nation. (A. Ames) Am. Pub. Health, 13 : 37.

— — inspection of, Necessity of. (C. H. Horsch) Am. Pub. Health, 13 : 34. — (D. E. Salmon) Am. Pub. Health, 15 : 174. 21 : 12.

— — — Bibliography. (A. Hassall) U. S. Bur. Animal Indust. '98 : 145.

— — — Methods of. (L. Pearson) Am. Pub. Health, 23 : 332.

— — of England. Wynter. Cu.ios. of toil, 1 : 206.

— — Our, and public health. (C. F. Folsom) Mass. Health, '75 : 136.

— frozen, Exportation of, from Australasia, 1892. U. S. Cons. Rept. no. 149.

— Preserved. Wynter, A. Our soc. bees, 1 : 191.

Mecca, Burton's Pilgrimage to. Montefiore, A. Leaders, 59.

Mechanic art, Development of. Story, J. Miscel. 475.

Mechanical arts, Relation to preventive medicine. (A. N. Bell) Am. Pub. Health, 16 : 227.

— Progress of Britain in. (J. Sime) Edin. ess. '56 : 169.

Mechanical inventions and inventors. Smiles. Indus. biog.

Mechanics' institutions. Chambers's Papers, no. 23.

— for working women. (F. Hertz) Trans. Soc. Sci. Lond. '59 : 347.

— Utility of. Carlisle, Earl. Lec. '73 : 112.

Mechanics, Curiosities of. Chambers's Miscel. no. 113.

Mechanicsville, Battle of. Allan, W. Army of N. Va. 75.

Mechanism in thought and morals. Holmes, O. W. Old vol. 160.

Mecherino, De Beccafumi, called. Ottley. Ital. school.

Mechi, J. J., at Tiptree hall. Yates, E. H. Celeb. 2 : 255.

Mechlin, Historical sketch of. King, R. J. Sk. 378.

Med, Slave, Case of. Curtis, B. R. Mem. & writ. v. 2.

Medals, American. (J. F. Fisher) Mass. Hist. Coll. 3d ser. 6 : 286.

— Dialogues upon. Addison. Works (Bohn), 1 : 253.

Mede, Joseph. Fuller. Worthies, 1 : 519.

Medes and Persians, Empire of. Lord, J. Anc. states, 88.

Medford, Mass., Plantation at Mystic side. Drake, S. A. Hist. fields Mid. 119.

Mediæval feeling for nature. McLaughlin, E. T. Stud. mediæv. 1.

Mediæval literature, Childhood in. McLaughlin, E. T. Stud. mediæv. 123.

Mediæval society. Grube, A. W. Heroes, 319.

Mediæval towns. Cutts, E. L. Scenes mid. ages, 529.

Medical associations. (W. H. Prescott) Conf. char. & correc. '95 : 285.

Medical attendance and other parochials. Eagles. Ess. 33.

Medical College of Alabama. U. S. Bur. Ed. Circ. '89, no. 3 : 147.

Medical College of Georgia. U. S. Bur. Ed. Circ. '88, no. 4 : 122.

Medical delusions. Davenport, R. A. Delusions, 342.

Medical demography. (W. A. Haskell) Am. Pub. Health, 18 : 330.

Medical education. Everett. Orat. v. 2. — Huxley. Critiques. — (A. E. Miller) U. S. Bur. Ed. Rept. '92–93 : 1617.

— Advantages of apprenticeship. Brown, J. Locke, etc. 95.

— and medical licensure. (W. H. Watson) N. Y. Regents, 99, app. : 229.

— in France. Hillebrand. France, 62.

— in the U. S., French views of. (Marcel Baudouin and M. Bonet-Maury) U. S. Bur. Ed. Rept. '92–93 : 601.

— Objects and requirements of. (F. R. Sturgis) N. Y. Regents. 98 : app. 291.

— of the future. Eliot, C. W. Educa. reform.

— Practical views on. Bigelow, J. Mod. inq. 263.

Medical ethics, Best books on. Brown, J. Locke, etc. 370.

Medical inspection of schools. U. S. Bur. Ed. Rept. '97–98, 2 : 1489.

Medical libraries. Holmes, O. W. Med. ess. 396.

Medical mission work in China. Cummings, C. F. G. Wand. in China, 2 : 288.

Medical practice, Art and science in. Brown, J. Locke, etc. 225.

— Free competition in. Brown, J. Locke, etc. 277.

Medical profession and its relationship to the clerical. Richardson, B. W. Ministry, 78.

Medical reformers. Platt, J. Excelsior, 107.

Medical science, Christianity and. Newman, J. H. Lec. univ. 366.

— Currents and counter-currents in. Holmes, O. W. Med. ess. 173.

— in Massachusetts, Historical sketch of. (J. Bartlett) Mass. Hist. Coll. 2d ser. 1 : 105.

Medical science, Limits of. Holmes, O. W. Med. ess. 209.

— Valedictory address, Harvard medical school, 1858. Holmes, O. W. Currents, 383.

Medical student, Position and prospects of. Holmes, O. W. Currents, 279.

Medical teaching, Scholastic and bedside. Holmes, O. W. Med. ess. 273.

Medical topography. (J. S. Billings) Am. Pub. Health, 2 : 47.

Medici, Cosimo de. Duffy, B. Tuscan republics, 287. — Perkins, C. C. Tusc. sculp. 2 : 109. — Hewlett. Heroes, 172. — Symonds. Reviv. of learn. 168.

— Bibliography. Ewart, K. D. Cosimo de Medici.

Medici, Lorenzo de. Crowe & James. Em. for. statesmen, 1 : 314. — Montgomery. Men of Ita. 1 : 151. — Symonds, J. A. Ital. byways. — Symonds. Renais. It. lit. 1 : 369. — Symonds. Reviv. of learn. 311. — Villari. Savonarola, 1 : 38. — Pastor, L. Hist. popes, 4 : 288. — Perkins, C. C. Tusc. sculp. 2 : 5. — (J. A. Symonds) Ferris, G. T. Gt. leaders, 190. — Stebbing. Ital. poets, v. 1. — Terhune. Where ghosts, 231.

— Cajano farm of. Mitchell. Wet days, 81.

— Lucretia Donati and. Jameson. Loves of poets.

Medici, Piero de, Flight of, 1494. Robinson, A. M. F. End of mid. ages, 314.

Medici family, and Florence. Symonds. Sk. So. Eur. 1 : 46.

— Crimes of. Symonds. Renais. Cath. reac. 1 : 382.

Medicine. Helmholtz. Pop. lec. 2 : 199.

— and surgery, Progress of. Wynter, A. Peeps, 1 : 152.

— the art of healing, rather than the science of diseases. Brown, J. Locke, etc. 61.

— as a science; address, 1840. Hopkins, M. Miscel. ess. 197.

— Biological sciences and. Huxley. Sci. & cul. 333.

— Ethics of. Brown, J. Spare hours, 3 : 261.

— History of, Miller's disquisitions on. Bigelow, J. Mod. inq. 271.

— Inventions and discoveries in, American. (J. S. Billings) Smithson. Rept. '92 : 613.

— Is it a progressive science? Mackenzie, M. Ess. 36.

— Modern progress in. Gilman, D. C. Univ. prob. 213.

— Mysteries of. Saunders. Salad for solitary, 199.

— practice of, Art of rising in. Winslow. F. Physic. 1 : 244.

— Present position of knowledge in. Reynolds, J. R. Ess. 139.

— Preventive. Wynter. Fruit, 2 : 65.

— Progress of. Reynolds, J. R. Ess. 290.

— rational, Brief expositions of. Bigelow, J. Mod. inq. 216.

— Recent advances in science and their bearing on medicine. (Michael Foster) Smithson. Rept. '96 : 339.

— revolutions in, W. Cullen and. Hamilton. Discus.

— Roman, Ancient. Middleton, C. Miscel. works (1752), v. 4.

— Russell's History and heroes of. Macdonald, G. Orts, 236.

— Science and. (A. Gamgee) Owens college essays, '74 : 257.

— Science of. Dana, A. H. Eth. inq. 206.

— Specialists in. Holmes. Over the teacups, 124.

— The study of. Latham. Opuscula, 15.

Medicine, Thought in. Helmholtz. Pop. lec. 2 : 199.

Meditation, Religious. Thomson, E. Essays, 31.

Mediterranean ports and gardens. Lathrop, G. P. Span. vistas, 153.

Mediterranean sea, The. Bennett, J. H. Winter on Medit. 129. — Gibson, W. S. Miscel. 89. — Holland, H. Ess. 228. — Howe, J. W. Winter homes, 164. — Wallace, S. E. Storied sea, 9.

— physical and historical. (R. L. Playfair) Smithson. Rept. '90 : 259.

— Yachting in. Mackenzie, M. Ess. 259.

Medley, Samuel. Hatfield, E. F. Poets of church, 416. — Ivimey. Eng. Bapt. 4 : 590. — Miller, Jos. Singers church, 2d ed. 269.

Medoc, Wines of the, 1891. (H. G. Knowles) U. S. Cons. Rept. 37 : 281.

Medusa, Wreck of the. Davenport. Narr. peril, 444. — Thornbury. Old stor. 263.

Medway floods. Smith, C. R. Retrospec. 3 : 119.

Meffreth, German priest, about 1443. Baring-Gould. Preachers, 81.

"**Megæra**," Wreck of the. Senior, W. Shipwrecks, 292.

Megario school, The. Lewis. Biog. phil.

Meek, George Henry. Davidson, J. W. Writ. of South, 386.

Meeker, Bradley B. Livingston, J. Dist. Amer. 480.

Meeker, Joseph R. Sheldon, G. W. Amer. painters, 135.

Meekness. Finlayson, T. C. Ess. 212.

Meem, J. Lawrence. Walker, C. D. Biog. Va. Mil. Inst. 363.

Meer, Jan Van der, of Delft. Van Dyke, J. C. Dutch mast. 115. — Wedmore. Masters of genre, 56.

Meeting-house, The, in early New England. Adams, C. F. Three episodes, 2 : 732.

Megerlin, Johann Ulrich. *See* Abraham á Sancta Clara.

Mehadia. Arnold, R. A. Levant, 2 : 245.

Mehemet Ali. Latimer. Eur. in Afr. in 19th cent. 9.

— Medal to. Smith, C. R. Retrospec. 1 : 132.

Mehul, Étienne Henri. Ferris, G. T. Ital. & Fr. compos. 175. — Hogarth. Mem. opera, 2 : 255.

Meigs, Return Jonathan. Lossing. Em. Amer. 362.

Meigs, Fort, Siege of. Dawson. Batt. of U. S. 2 : 221.

Meinhard, Bishop of Yxhull. Maclear. Apostles, 251.

Meinhold, John William. Miller, Jos. Singers church, 2d ed. 446.

Meissonier, J. L. E. Bolton, S. K. Poor boys famous, 303. — Hamerton. Contem. Fr. painters. — Van Dyke, J. C. Mod. Fr. mast. 93.

Melancas, The two. Hahn - Hahn. Fathers, 475.

Melancholy. Bunce, O. B. Bach. bluff, 205.

— Exercise a remedy for. Mathews. Lit. style, 72.

— of the Greeks. Butcher, S. H. Greek genius, 130.

Melanchthon, Philip. Herrick, S. E. Heretics, 155. — (S. E. Herrick ; A. V. G. Allen) Mass. Hist. Proc. 2d ser. 11 : 254. — Pierce, B. K. Em. dead, 13.

Melanesia. Alexander, J. M. Isl. Pac. 408.

Melba, Nellie, with portrait. Buffen. Mus. celeb. 2 : 7.

Melbourne, Wm. Lamb, 2d viscount. Earle, J. C. Eng. prem. 2 : 261. — Hayward, A. Em. statesm. 1 : 329. — Hayward, A. Ess. 1 : 254. — Smith, G. Barnett. Prime min. 3. — Grant, J. Recoll. Lords, 204.
— Fall of his ministry. Walpole. Life of Lord J. Russell, 1.
— Scenes between him and Lords Lyndhurst and Brougham. Grant, J. Recoll. Lords & comm. 1 : 58.
Melbourne, Australia. Brooks, E. S. Gt. cities, 82.
— exhibition, 1888. U. S. Sen. Docs. 1889-90, v. 4.
Melbourne, Derbyshire. Rimmer, A. Old towns, 116.
Melbourne Hall. Jewitt, L. Stately homes, 2 : 186.
Melcher, Joseph. Clarke, R. H. Cath. bishops, 3 : 339.
Meleager. Mills. Poets of Greece, 231.
Melendez Valdes. Kennedy. Poets of Spain, 61.
Melissos. Fairbanks, A. Philos. of Greece, 129.
Melito, St., bishop of Sardis. Blakey, R. Prim. fathers, 94. — Cave. Lives of fathers, 1 : 280. — Yonge, C. M. Pupils of John, 205.
Mell, St. Conyngham, D. P. Irish saints, 117.
Mell, P. H. Davidson, J. W. Writ. of South, 387.
Mellen, Grenville. Griswold. Poets Am. 234.
Mellish, Sir George. Gener. of judges, 95.
Mellitus. Hook. Abps. Cant. 1 : 90.
Mellon, Harriet, duchess of St. Albans. Hunt, L. Men, wom. & books, 287.
Mellor, Sir J., with photo. Cooper, T. Men of mark, 4 : 5.
Melly, George. Ritchie. Brit. sena. 145.
Melodrama. Cook, D. On stage, 2 : 190. — Walkley, A. B. Playhouse, 190.
Melrose Abbey. Silloway. Cathedral towns, 238. — Stowe. Sunny mem. 1 : 151.
Melton Mowbray, England. Rimmer, A. Old towns, 121.
Melvill, James. Morley, H. Eng. writ. 8 : 352.
Melvill, Capt. Philip. Rogers, C. Chr'n heroes, 163.
Melville, Andrew. Irving, D. Scot. writ. 1 : 170. — (C. Campbell) St. Giles lec. 3 : 37. — Taylor, W. M. Scot. pulpit, 72.
Melville, H. Dundas, Lord. Brougham. Works, 3 : 306.
— Impeachment of, 1806. Browne, G. L. Narr. state trials, 1 : 170.
Melville, Rev. Henry. Grant, Jas. Metropol. pul. 200. — Waterbury. Eloq. preach. 112.
Melville, Herman. Griswold. Prose writ. 665. — Richardson. Amer. lit. 2 : 403. — With portrait. Warner Lib. 17 : 9867.
Melvin, James. Nicoll, H. J. Gt. scholars, 227.
Memling, Hans. Conway, W. M. Early Flem. artists, 235. — Crowe & Cav. Flem. painters, 251.
Memmi, Simone. See Martini.
Memnon. Thirlwall, C. Remains, 3 : 58. — Colossus of. Buckley, J. M. Trav. three cont. 297. — Stanhope, P. H. French retreat.
Memoirs, contemporary, Difficulties of writers of. Disraeli, I. Amen. (N. Y. 2 v.) 2 : 407.
— A medley of. Powell, G. H. Excurs. in Libr. 151.
— Personal. Pearson, C. H. Reviews, 39.
— — Elements of interest in. Birrell. Obiter, 1 : 154.
— Writing of. Foster, J. Crit. ess. Ecl. v. 1.

Memorial day. Long, J. D. After-dinner, 72.
— Bibliography. Salem (Mass.) Pub. Lib. Bull. May, '95. — Somerville (Mass.) Pub. Lib. Bull. May, '96.
— in New York. Marshall, W. G. Thro' Amer. 48.
Memories, Random. Stevenson, R. L. Across pl. 168.
Memoriter instruction. (T. Lewis) N. Y. Regents, 78 : 404.
Memory. Allen, Grant. Common-sense sci. 19. — Emerson. Nat. hist. intel. 61. — Grahame, K. Pagan papers, 123.
— and its marvels. Mathews. Lit. style, 150.
— Bibliography. (F. Kennedy) Psycholog. Rev. Sept. '98 : 477.
— Cultivation of. Friswell. About, 160.
— Effects of age on. Holland. Mental physiol. 150.
— Fallacies of. Cobbe, F. P. Hours of work, 87.
— hypnotic, Stages of. (E. Gurney) Soc. Psych. Res. 4 : 515.
— Marvels of. Saunders. Pastime, 147.
Memphis, Egypt. (S. Lane-Poole) Wilson, C. W. Pictur. Palest. 4 : 167. — Buckley, J. M. Trav. three cont. 243. — Poole, R. S. Cities of Egypt, 1.
Memphis, Tenn. Warner, C. D. Studies, 292.
— Municipal condition of. (J. H. Malone) Nat. Conf. City Govt. '96 : 110.
— Six years' sanitary work in. (G. B. Thornton) Am. Pub. Health, 12 : 109.
— System of sewerage. (G. E. Waring) Am. Pub. Health, 18 : 153.
Men, and women. Dodge, M. A. Country, 80.
— False estimate of. Gardner, S. J. Aut. leaves, 26.
— Famous. Hazlitt. Sketches.
— Female. Gray, E. C. Idle musings, 15.
— Great. Friswell. Gentle life, 252.
— — Uses of. Emerson. Repr. men, 7.
— Influence of women upon; give the men a chance. Warner, C. D. As we go, 20.
— judged by women. Higginson. Conc. all, 146.
— made, self-made and unmade. (E. G. Robinson) Phillips Ex. lec. '85-86 : 125.
— Nature in. Bacon. Ess.
— Notable. Platt, J. Excelsior, 57.
— of letters. Smith, Alex. Dreamthorp, 141.
— — and unlettered wives. Jacox. Lit. life, 176.
— — and science, Brougham's Lives of. Peabody, W. B. O. Lit. rem. 199.
— — on themselves. Escott. Politics, 64.
— — of one idea. Holland, J. G. Lessons, 208.
— vs. classes. Bax. Ethics of socialism, 99.
Mena, Juan de. Montgomery. Men of Ita. 3 : 14. — Ticknor. Span. lit. 1 : 379.
Menander. Hundred greatest men, 22. — Mills. Poets of Greece, 401.
Mencius. Johnson, S. Ori. relig. China, 637.
Mendeleef, Dmitri Ivanovich. Thorpe, T. E. Ess. hist. chem. 350.
Mendelssohn Bartholdy, Felix. Barnard, C. Tone masters, 1 : 99. — Bourne, C. E. Gt. compos. 243. — Butterworth. Great compos. 76. — Crowest. Tone-poets, 315. — Dawson, G. Shakesp. 439. — Ferris. Germ. compos. 189. — Hale, E. E. Lights two cent. 353. — Haweis. Music & mor. 283. — Keddie. Mus. comp. 206. — Parry, C. H. H. Studies, 255. — With portrait. Bie, O. Hist. of piano, 249. — Dole, N. H. Score, 347. — Rowbotham, J. F. Great compos. 152. — Sharp, R. F. Makers of music. — With portrait. Elson, L. Gt. composers, 172. — With portrait. Warner Lib. 17 : 9886. — Spark, W. Mus. mem. 30.

Mérimée, Prosper, as a critic. Hapgood, N. Lit. statesm. 115.
— Letters of. James, H. French poets, 390.
Merit, Unfortunate. Goldsmith. Miscel. (N. Y. 4 v.) 1 : 103.
Merit system in public institutions. (L. L. Flower) Conf. char. & correc. '96 : 388. — (P. C. Garrett) Conf. char. & correc. '96 : 368. — (C. R. Henderson) Conf. char. & correc. '96 : 382.
Merivale, Charles. (S. M. MacVane) Am. Acad. A. & S. Proc. 29 : 462.
Merivale, Herman C. Archer. Eng. dram. 233. — (J. A. Blaikie) Miles, A. H. Poets of cent. 6 : 371. — Wilman, G. Sk. liv. celeb. 106.
Merlin. Cox & Jones. Romances, 234.
Mermaids. Jones, W. Credulities, 20.
— and Nondescripts. Buckland, F. T. Curios. nat. hist. 4 : 134, 140.
Merovingian race, The, and the lazy kings. Doran. Monarchs, 1 : 178.
Merriam, G. & C., & Co. Derby, J. C. Fifty years, 377.
Merrick, Edwin T. Am. Bar Assoc. 20 : 534.
Merrick, James. Griswold, R. W. Sac. poets. — Hatfield, E. F. Poets of church, 420. — Holland, J. Psalmists, 2 : 209. — Miller, Jos. Singers church, 2d ed. 224.
Merrick, Pliny. Livingston, J. Dist. Amer. 134. — Loring, J. S. Hundred Bost. ora. 635.
Merrick, Richard Thomas. Am. Bar Assoc. 8 : 453.
Merrill, James Cushing. (J. W. Preston) N. E. Hist.-Gen. Soc. Biog. 2 : 88.
Merrill, Mrs. John. Clement, J. Noble deeds, 118.
Merrimac river, Scenery on. Whittier. Lit. recre. 390.
Merriott, Wharton Booth. Adams, W. H. D. Worthies Ch. Eng. 249.
Merritt, Paul. Archer. Eng. dram. 226. — Wilman, G. Sk. Liv. celeb. 116.
Merritt, Timothy. Sherman, D. N. E. divines, 312.
Merry masks and sad faces. Jacox. Lit. life, 235.
Merton, Bygone. (E. A. Kempson) Clinch, G. Bygone Surrey, 239.
Merton Priory. Timbs. Abbeys, 1 : 284. — Freeman. Eng. towns, 181.
Merv, O'Donovan's Ride to. Adams, W. H. D. In perils, 393.
Meryon, Charles. Wedmore, F. Studies, 2 : 169.
Mésalliances. Linton, E. L. Girl of per. 1 : 147.
Mescal; a new artificial paradise. (H. Ellis) Smithson. Rept. '97 : 537.
Meschinet, Jean. Besant. Fr. poetry, 173.
Mesmerism, Experiences in. Trollope, T. A. What I rem. 1 : 362.
— Methodology of. Brown, S. Atom. 2.
— Reports on. Soc. Psych. Res. 1 : 217, 251. 2 : 12.
    See Clairvoyance.
Mesomedes. Arnold, E. Poets of Greece, 130.
Mesopotamia. Cust. Ling. ess. 289.
Messalla Corvinus, Marcus Valerius. Dunlop, J. Rom. liter. 3 : 53.
Messenger, Lilian Rozell. Raymond, I. Southland writ. 2 : 554.
Messiah, Kingdom of the. Maitland, S. R. Eruvin, 198.
Messiahs, False. Davenport, R. A. Delusions, 24.
Messianic ideas, Early history of. Martineau, J. Ess. 3 : 219.

Messina. Hare. Cities of So. Italy, 384.
— Sieges of. Robson, W. Sieges, 189.
Meszlenyi, Susanne Kossuth. Peabody, E. P. Last evening, 253.
Metal founding in Europe, 1893. U. S. Cons. Rept. no. 154.
Metal work. (W. A. S. Benson) Morris, W. Arts & crafts, 68.
Metal-working, Educational value of. (V. S. Paessler) Nat. Educa. Assoc. '99 : 911.
Metallic tractors of Dr. Perkins. Holmes, O.W. Currents, 73.
Metamorphoses of matter. Scoffern. Stray leaves, 102.
Metals. Chambers's Miscel. no. 155.
— The age of. Clodd. Story prim. man, 160.
— Bibliography. (J. L. Howe) Smithson. Miscel. Coll. No. 1084.
— Earliest use. Schrader. Prehist. antiq. of Aryans, 150.
— Origin of deposits of. (T. S. Hunt) Estes. Half-hour, v. 1.
— Rarer, and their alloys. (W. C. Roberts-Austen) Smithson. Rept. '96 : 497.
— Use of. Goldsmith. Miscel. (N. Y. 4 v.) 1 : 301.
Metaphysic. Caird. Ess. on lit. & p. 2 : 384.
Metaphysical systems, Worth of. Thomson, J. Ess. 296.
Metaphysical writers, English. Friswell. Essays, 249.
Metaphysics, Ancient history of. Smith, Adam. Ess. phil. 113.
— and debating societies. Bain, A. Prac. ess. 139.
— Future. Renan. Philos. dialogues, 140.
— Hume as a metaphysician. Thornton, W. T. Old-fash. 113.
— Mansel's. Stephen, J. F. Ess. by barr. 320.
— of the future. McCosh. Scot. phil. 455.
— of science. Winchell. Sparks geol. ham. 358.
— Physiological. Porter, N. Sci. & sent. 222.
— Plea for. Porter, M. Sci. & sent. 38.
— Speculations in. (A. White) N. Y. Regents, 87 : 699. — Shelley. Ess. 1 : 187.
— Swedenborgian. Sewall, F. New metaphys. 3.
Metastasio, Pietro Bonaventura. Montgomery. Men of Ita. 2 : 185. — Stebbing. Ital. poets, v. 3.
— and the opera. Paget, V. Stud. of 18th cent. 141.
— Life and works. Hogarth. Mem. opera, 1 : 225.
Metaurus, Battle of. Creasy. Fifteen battles, 81.
Metcalf, Edwin. Bartlett, J. R. R. I. officers, 252.
Metcalf, Frederick. Bartlett, J. R. R. I. officers, 442.
Metcalf, John, "the blind roadmaker." Smiles. Engin. 1 : 208. — Baring-Gould. Yorks. odd. 1 : 120.
Metcalf, John George. Am. Antiq. Soc. Proc. n. s. 8 : 17.
Metcalfe, Sir Charles. Kaye. Indian off. 1 : 375.
Metempsychosis, Doctrine of. Knight, W. Ess. 316; *or* Stud. 119.
"Meteor," Steamship, case of. Morse, J. T., jr. Famous trials.
Meteoric dust. Proctor, R. A. Fam. sci. 47.
Meteorites. Bibliography. Farrington, O. C. Hdbk. meteorite coll. Field Col. Mus.
Meteorological observations as respects disease prevalence. (W. W. Payne) Am. Pub. Health, 14 : 179.
Meteorological station, The highest in the

Mexico, En route through. Rutgers, L. On saddle, 94.
— Finances and industries of, 1898. U. S. Cons. Rept. **56** : 469.
— Guatemala boundary question. (M. Romero) Am. Geog. Soc. **29** : 123, 281.
— gulf coast of, Survey of. (F. H. Baker) Am. Geog. Soc. **5** : 237.
— Health, Board of. (D. Orvañanos) Am. Pub. Health, **17** : 38.
— Import duties of. Bur. Am. Repub. no. 5.
— — 1891. Bur. Am. Repub. no. 21.
— in 1872. Bryant. Prose, **2** : 148.
— Literature of, in 19th century. Bancroft, H. H. Essays, 537.
— Maximilian. Bryant. Prose, **2** : 237.
— Message of President Diaz, 1895. (E. C. Butler) U. S. Cons. Rept. **48** : 133.
— Myths of. Brinton. Amer. hero-myths, 64.
— National railroad, 1891. (W. P. Sutton) U. S. Cons. Rept. **36** : 217.
— negotiations with, Three million bill for expenses of. Dix. Speeches, **1** : 179.
— Northern, Explorations in. (C. Lumholtz) Am. Geog. Soc. **23** : 386.
— Orange cultivation in, 1896. (W. J. Crittenden) U. S. Cons. Rept. **53** : 209.
— Pacific coast of, Hygienic conditions of. (J. Revueltas) Am. Pub. Health, **18** : 101.
— Physical geography. (A. R. Conkling) Am. Geog. Soc. **15** : 319.
— plateau of, Over the, in a diligence. (A. S. Packard) Am. Geog. Soc. **18** : 215.
— Policy of the United States in regard to, 1860. Davis, H. W. Speeches, 472.
— Production of coffee in, 1896. (T. T. Crittenden) U. S. Cons. Rept. **52** : 103.
— Sanitary legislation in the state of. (M. Alvarez) Am. Pub. Health, **22** : 301.
— Territories acquired from. Dix. Speeches, **1** : 413.
— Topography of. (H. M. Wilson) Am. Geog. Soc. **29** : 249.
— United States and France in. Davis, H. W. Speeches, 456.
— Visit to. Bryant. Prose, **2** : 148.
— Yellow fever on Gulf coast of. (G. Mendizabal) Am. Pub. Health, **17** : 193.
Mexico, City of. (C. Pullen) Am. Geog. Soc. **20** : 153. — Rutgers, L. On saddle, 119. — Curtis, W. E. Capitals, 1.
— after the drainage of the valley. (R. Macouzet) Am. Pub. Health, **23** : 195.
— Climate of. (D. Orvañanos) Am. Pub. Health, **18** : 367.
— Drainage of. (R. Gayol) Am. Pub. Health, **17** : 53.
— Mortality statistics in. (E. Liceaga) Am. Pub. Health, **18** : 378.
— Vaccination and small-pox in, 1872–95. (J. Ramirez) Am. Pub. Health, **22** : 328.
Meyer, Johann F. von. Ker, J. Lec. hist. preach. 366.
Meyer, Konrad Ferdinand, with portrait. Warner Lib. **17** : 9965.
Meyer, Waldemar, with portrait. Ehrlich, A. Cel. violin. 167.
Meyerbeer, Giacomo. Apthorp. Musicians, 139. — Badeau. Vagabond, 35. — Engel, L. Mozart, **1** : 181. — Ferris, G. T. Great comp. 205. — Keddie. Mus. comp. 384. — Hogarth. Mem. opera, **2** : 264. — Dole, N. H. Score, 327. — With portrait. Elson, L. Gt. composers, 204. — With portrait. Rowbotham. Priv. life compos. 294. — Spark, W. Mus. mem. 62.

Meyerbeer, Giacomo. The Huguenots. Guerber. Stor. of operas, 51.
Meynell, Mrs. Alice. Poems. Patmore. Religio poetæ, 199. — Robertson. Eng. poetesses, 356.
Mhar, Temples of. Adams, W. H. D. Fam. caves, 68.
Miall, Edward. Hinton. Eng. radicals, 224. — Ritchie. Brit. sena. 267. — Stanton, H. B. Reforms, 319.
Miami University, Oxford, O. (E. D. Warfield) U. S. Bur. Ed. Circ. '91, no. **5** : 30.
Miamis, Battle on. Dawson. Batt. of U. S. **2** : 19.
Miantonomoh. Lossing. Em. Amer. 20.
Miaskowski, Kaspar. Soboleski. Poets of Poland, 58.
Miazzi, Giovanni. Milizia. Lives arch. **2** : 379.
Micah and the young Levite. Hastings, F. Obscure charac. 68.
Micaiah. Wilberforce, S. Heroes Hebrew, 294.
Michabo, Algonkin myth of. Brinton. Amer. hero-myths, 37.
Michael, Prince, of Servia, Reminiscences of. Kingston, W. B. Monarchs, **2** : 278.
Michael Angelo. Benson & Tatham. Men of might, 76. — Stillman, W. J. Old Ital. mas. 218. — Bolton, S. K. Fam. Europ. art. 7. — Cheney, E. D. Gleanings, 102. — Eastlake, E. R. Five painters, **1** : 101. — Jameson. Ital. painters, 191. — Lee, H. F. Old painters, 76. — Lord, J. Beacon, **8** : 183. — Milizia. Lives arch. **1** : 259. — Story, W. W. Excur. 1. — Spooner. Biog. fine arts, **1** : 148. — Symonds. Renais. fine arts, 342, 384. — Taine. Italy, **1** : 186. — Wallace, H. B. Art, 217. — Cooke, F. E. Guid. lights. — With portrait. Hubbard, E. Little jour. **5** : 1. — Hundred greatest men, 75. — Emerson. Nat. hist. intel. 113. — Jarves. Art stud. 412. — Ottley. Ital. school. — Pastor, L. Hist. popes, **6** : 503. — Ruskin. Miscel. v. 1. — Trollope. Ital. poets, **1** : 255. — Jervis, Lady. Painting, **1** : 105. — Perkins, C. C. Tusc. sculp. **2** : 1. — With portrait. Warner Lib. **17** : 9977. — Rose, G. B. Renais. masters, 42.
— and V. Colonna, Busts of. Jarves. Ital. ramb. 319.
— and his works. Oliphant. Makers of F. 353.
— and the renaissance. Lilly. Chapters, **2** : 1.
— as an architect. Symonds. Renais. fine arts, 86.
— as a sculptor. Symonds. Renais. fine arts, 171.
— Hartford's life of. Tartt. Ess. **1** : 90.
— Homer, Dante and. Allison. Ess. v. **2**.
— The house of, at Florence. Fairholt. Homes Rubens, 229.
— Last Judgment. (A. Dumas) Singleton, E. Great pic. 18.
— Life and works of. Knox, R. Great artists, 171.
— Poems of. Cheney, E. D. Gleanings, 124. — Pater. Stud. renais. 62. — Symonds. Renais. It. lit. **2** : 296.
— Ruskin on. Poynter. Ten lec. 217.
— Sonnets of. Chapman, J. J. Emerson, 153. — Symonds. Renais. fine arts, 512.
— Works of. Stearns, F. P. Midsum. Ital. art, 71.
Michault, Pierre. Besant. Fr. poetry, 182.
Michelet, Jules, with portrait. (G. King) Warner Lib. **17** : 9982.
— as a historian. Pellissier. Lit. move. Fr. 260.
Michelson, Researches of, in light. (Joseph Lovering) Smithson. Rept. '**89** : 449.
Michelozzo. Perkins, C. C. Tusc. sculp. **1** : 163.
— Symonds. Renais. fine arts, 76.
Michie, Peter Smith, with portrait. Butterfield Lec. Un. Coll. **1** : 11.

Michieli family. Oliphant. Makers of Venice.
Michigan, Birds of. Hubbard, B. Memorials, 281.
— Colonists of. Hubbard, B. Memorials, 109.
— Fauna of. Hubbard, B. Memorials, 323.
— Geological expedition in 1837. Hubbard, B. Memorials, 65.
— in 1835–39. Hubbard, B. Memorials, 93.
— lower peninsula of, Climate and topog. of. (H. F. Lyster) Mich. Health, '78 : 167.
— Seasons in. Hubbard, B. Memorials, 485.
— State Agricultural College Lansing, Mich. (O. Clute) U. S. Bur. Ed. Circ. '91, no. 4 : 105.
— University of. Dilke. Greater Brit. 68.
— — Women at. (S. D. Hamlin) Brackett, A. C. Educa. of girls, 307, 314.
Michigan Mining School, Houghton, Mich. (M. E. Wadsworth) U. S. Bur. Ed. Circ. '91, no. 4 : 116.
Michigan wilds, Logging in. Deming. By-ways, 285.
Michilimacinac, Expedition against. Dawson. Batt. of U. S. 2 : 346.
— Surprise of. Dawson. Batt. of U. S. 2 : 88.
Michoacan, Mexico, Archæology of. (Nicolas Leon) Smithson. Rept. '86 : 306.
Mickiewicz, Adam. Soboleski. Poets of Poland, 203. — With portrait. (C. H. Genung) Warner Lib. 17 : 9995.
Mickle, Wm. Julius. Chalmers. Eng. poets.
Microbes, War with. (E. A. de Schweinitz) Smithson. Rept. '96 : 485.
Micronesia. Alexander, J. M. Isl. Pac. 306. — (L. H. Gulick) Am. Geog. Soc. 1 : 129.
Micro-organisms and their relation to disease. (S. P. Wise) Ohio Health, '89 : 245.
— Beneficent and malignant. (R. F. Frankland) Maine Health, '87 : 305.
Microphytic diseases, Prevention of. (E. M. Hunt) Am. Pub. Health, 13 : 28.
Microscope, The. Buckley, A. B. Through magic glass, 37.
— and its marvels. Chambers's Papers, no. 41. — Chambers's Miscel. no. 150.
— in public schools. (W. H. Skinner) Nat. Educa. Assoc. '97 : 935.
Middle-aged, Becoming. Arnold, F. Three-cor. ess. 14.
Middle ages. Bibliography. Emerton, E. Mediæval Europe. — Getchell, M. Stud. mediæv. hist. by lib'y method.
— Church in. Brownson. Works, 10 : 239.
— General characteristics of. Stillé. Stud. med. 13.
— Heroes of. Grube, A. W. Heroes, 265.
— Modern conception of. Dawson, G. Shakesp. 190.
— Society in England in. Lawrance, H. Queens, v. 2.
— The true, and the false. Montalembert. Monks, 1 : 193.
— Turning-point in. Lilly. Chapters, 1 : 98.
Middle classes, Education of. Arnold, T. Miscel. 372.
— Pride and luxury of. Goldsmith. Miscel. (N. Y. 4 v.) 1 : 135.
Middlemass, Jean, with portrait. Black, H. C. Wom. authors, 260.
Middlesex, Lionel Cranfield, first earl of. Lodge. Portraits (Bohn), v. 4.
Middleton, Arthur. Dwight, N. Signers, 353. — Lincoln, R. W. Signers, 47. — Lossing. Signers, 323. — Sanderson. Signers, v. 5. — Perry, B. F. Biog. sketches, 1 : 454.
Middleton, Clara, Meredith's portrayal of char-

acter of. (J. Fairney) Moulton, R. G. Four years' novel. 59.
Middleton, Conyers, Miscel. works of. Stephen, J. F.
Middleton, Daniel Webster. Carson, H. L. Sup. Ct. of U. S. 576.
Middleton, Henry. Davidson, J. W. Writ. of South, 388.
Middleton, Sir Hugh. Lodge. Portraits (Bohn), v. 3.
Middleton, Mrs. Jane, with portrait. Jameson. Beauties, 252.
Middleton, Thomas. Choate, I. B. Wells of Eng. 174. — Gosse, E. Jacob. in poctry 109 — Hazlitt. Dram. Eliz. — Ward, A. W. Eng. dram. 2 : 67. — Yonge. Pioneers. — Minto, W. Eng. poets, 347.
Middleton, T. Fanshaw. Miller, Jos. Singers church, 2d ed. 335.
Midlane, Albert. Hatfield, E. F. Poets of ch. 422. — Miller, Jos. Singers church, 2d ed. 572.
Midsummer outing. Abbott, C. C. Outings, 197.
Midwives, Plea for. Brown, J. Locke, etc. 23.
Miége, John Baptist. Clarke, R. H. Cath. bishops, 3 : 611.
Mieris, Frans van. Gower. Fig.-painters Holl. 73.
Mifflin, Thomas. With portrait. [Amer.] Nat. portr. gall. 4. — With portrait. Armor. Gov. of Pa. 273. — Neven, D. R. B. Pennsylvanians, 110.—Winslow, S. N. Biog. Phila. merch. 199.
Mifflin, Fort, Attack on. Dawson. Batt. of U. S. 1 : 360.
Migdol. Poole, R. S. Cities of Egypt, 112.
Might and right. Rands, W. B. Holbeach, 2 : 85.
Mignard, Pierre. (C. A. Regnet) Dohme, R. Early mast. 527.
Mignet, F. M. A., as a historian. Pellissier. Lit. move. Fr. 253.
Migration and the food quest. (O. T. Mason) Smithson. Rept. '94 : 523.
— Interstate. (H. H. Hart) Conf. char. & correc. '95 : 248.
— — considered historically. (James Bryce) Smithson. Rept. '93 : 567.
— Laws of. Elder, W. Questions, 33.
— of races. Grube, A. W. Heroes, 43.
Migrations in the Pacific Ocean, Compulsory. (O. Sittig) Smithson. Rept. '95 : 519.
Mikó, Count Emerich. Wyatt, W. J. Hunga. celeb. 135.
Milan. Fulton, C. C. Europe, 246. — Guild. Over the ocean, 438. — Hare. Cities of No. Italy, 1 : 121. — Taine. Italy, 2 : 342.
— and the Italian lakes. Arnold, H. P. Eur. mosaic, 61.
— Art notes in. Child, T. Summ. holidays, 138.
— Cathedral of. Symonds. Renais. fine arts, 57.
— Claim of house of Orleans to. Robinson, A. M. F. End of mid. a. 179.
— during the renaissance. Symonds. Reviv. of learn. 265.
— Exposition of 1894. (C. W. Parks) U. S. Bur. Ed. Rept. '93–94, 2 : 1723.
— Ladies of, in 15th century. Robinson, A. M. F. End of mid. a. 300.
— Municipal government in. Shaw, A. Munic. govt. Eur. 258.
— Reformers in. Stoughton. Ital. reform. 259.
— Sieges of. Robson, W. Sieges, 287.
Milanollo, Therese and Marie, with portraits. Ehrlich, A. Cel. violin. 169.

Milbourne, Luke. Holland, J. Psalmists, **2** : 116.

Miles, Elizabeth Appleton. Putnam, A. P. Singers liberal, 232.

Miles, George H. Boyle, E. Dist. Marylanders. — Davidson, J. W. Writ. of South, 391.

Miles, Helen Jane Arundel. Clayton, E. C. Eng. fem. art. **2** : 110.

Miles, John, Trial of. Phillips, S. M. Famous cases, 125.

Miles, Richard Pius. Clarke, R. H. Cath. bishops, **2** : 147.

Miles, Sarah. Miller, Jos. Singers church, 2d ed. 545.

Miles, Sarah S. Hemenway. Poets of Vt. 234.

Milestones, Suburban. Knight. Once on time, **2** : 209.

Milicz, John. Hodgson, Wm. Reformers, 108.

Military and naval expenditure. Rogers, J. E. T. Cobden, 146.

Military art among the Greeks and Romans. Herbert, H. W. Capt. old world. — and science. Morris, W. O. Commanders, 1. — Bibliography. U. S. War dept. Milit. Inform. Div. Oct. '97 ; May, '98. — Wagner, A. L. Organization & tactics.

Military clothing establishment at Pimlico. Wynter, A. Our soc. bees, **1** : 229.

Military commissions, Jurisdiction of. Garfield. Works, **1** : 143.

Military drill in academies. (C. J. Wright) N. Y. Regents, **90** : 623. — in colleges and academies. (E. P. Waterbury) N. Y. Regents, **96** : 385.

Military education. Gleig. Ess. **2** : 390. — in United States. (Allen Allensworth) Nat. Educa. Assoc. '91 : 221.

Military government of states, Constitutionality of. Field, D. D. Speeches, **1** : 118.

Military history : Marmont, Alison, Siborne. Ellesmere. Ess. 273.

Military hygiene, Dr. H. Marshall's contributions to. Brown, J. Locke, etc. 165.

Military law. (J. W. Clous) Butterfield Lec. Un. Coll. **1** : 75. — Bibliography. Davis, G. B. Milit. law of U. S.

Military orders. Cutts, E. L. Scenes mid. ages, 26.

Military science and tactics in universities and colleges. (A. D. Schenck) Nat. Educa. Assoc. '75 : 124.

Military stratagems. Davenport, R. A. Delusions, 122.

Military training in schools. (D. A. Sargent) Nat. Educa. Assoc. '96 : 920. — of boys. (Sir W. Crofton et al.) Trans. Soc. Sci. Lond. '79 : 248.

Military tribunals for civilians, Constitutionality of. Field, D. D. Speeches, **1** : 3.

Militia ; duties of the citizen soldier. Burnap. Miscel. — Enrolling and calling out the. Garfield. Works, **1** : 19. — Importance of. Everett. Orat. v. **2**. — in early New England. Adams, C. F. Three episodes, **2** : 764. — of the United Kingdom, Organization of. (R. A. S. Adair) Camb. ess. '58 : 28. — of U. S., Gen. Knox's plan for arrangement of. (J. Willard) Mass. Hist. Proc. **6** : 364. — — Organization of, Remarks on, 1846. Webster, D. Works, **5** : 151.

Militia system, Report on. Dix. Speeches, **2** : 116.

Milk. Iowa Health, '97 : 71.

Milk, Adulteration of. (A. H. Nichols ; J. F. Babcock) Mass. Health, '73 : 279. — and products. Bibliography. Irving, H. H. Milk and m. products. — as a vehicle of infection. (J. J. Berry) N. H. Health, '93 : 194. — Composition and infectiousness of. (J. F. Kennedy) N. H. Health, '95-96 : 150 ; also in Am. Pub. Health, **21** : 333. — — and properties of. (E. E. Calder) R. I. Health, **5** : 261. — Infectious diseases conveyed by. Internat. Health Ex. Sanita. — Infectiousness of. (J. F. Kennedy) Conn. Health, '96 : 272.

Milk supplies, Infected. (B. Lee) Am. Pub. Health, **24** : 281. — of cities. (J. C. Morris) Phila. Soc. Sci. Assoc. '84. — (J. H. Kellogg) N. H. Health, '94-95 : 164. — of large cities, Adulteration of. (J. C. Morris) Am. Pub. Health, **10** : 246. — Problem of. (P. H. Bryce) Am. Pub. Health, **17** : 144. — Zymotic diseases and. (F. Vacher et al.) Trans. Soc. Sci. Lond. '83 : 395.

Milkin' time, a song. Baring-Gould. Yorks. odd. **2** : 100.

Milky way, Figure of the. Proctor, R. A. Other suns, 80.

Mill, James. Bissett, A. Ess. on hist. 103. — McCosh. Scot. phil. 370. — Oliphant, M. Lit. hist. **3** : 282. — Essay on government, Defense of, by J. Bentham. Macaulay. Ess. **2** : 52.

Mill, John Stuart. With portrait. Brandes. Em. auth. 123. — Hinsdale, B. A. Schools, 103. — Martineau, J. Ess. **1** : 63. — McCarthy, J. Mod. leaders, 106. — Morris, G. S. Brit. tho't, 302. — Rands, W. B. H. Holbeach, **2** : 3. — Ribot, T. Eng. psychol. 78. — Ritchie. Brit. sena. 295. — Taine. Eng. lit. **2** : 477. — Tulloch. Move. relig. thought, 209. — Wright, C. Philos. dis. 414. — Em. persons, **1** : 195. — Robertson, J. M. Mod. humanists, 62. — Scherer. Ess. Eng. lit. 13. — Godkin. Reflections, 67. — Hinsdale, B. A. Schools & Stud. 103. — Hutton, R. H. Criticisms, **2** : 171, 193. — Leslie, T. E. C. Ess. pol. econ. 243. — Smalley. Lond. lett. **1** : 232. — With portrait. (R. T. Ely) Warner Lib. **17** : 10007. — and his school. Tulloch. Movements 19th cent. — as a statesman. Purnell. Liter. 51. — as a stump speaker. Tyler, M. C. Glimpses Eng. 13. — Autobiography. Morley. Crit. miscel. **3** : 53. — Porter, N. Sci. & sent. 96, 127. — Bibliography. Courtney, Life of M. — Death of. Morley. Crit. miscel. **3** : 37. — in the House of Commons. Tyler, M. C. Glimpses Eng. 54. — Inaugural address. Mill, J. S. Dissert. N. Y. **4** : 385. — Individualism of. Ritchie, D. G. State interf. 83. — Influence on modern education. (C. M. O'Leary) N. Y. Regents, **87** : 707. — Logic of. Green, T. H. Works, **2** : 195. — Philosophical position of. Ward, W. G. Ess. theism, **1** : 185. — Philosophy of. Martineau, J. Ess. **3** : 489.

Millais, John Everett. Bate, P. H. Eng. Pre-Raph. 33. — Monkhouse, C. Brit. contemp. artists, 43. — Cochrane, R. Gt. thinkers, 271. — With photo. Cooper, T. Men of mark, **1** :

Milton, John. Comus. Hogarth. Mem. opera, 1 : 62.
— English criticisms of. Arnold, M. Mixed ess. 7.
— Idealism of. Dowden. Transcripts, 454.
— Leonora Baroni and. Jameson. Loves of poets.
— Life and works. Tulloch. Eng. purit. 170.
— the Londoner. Knight. Once on time, 1 : 233.
— Lycidas. Hazlitt. Round table.
— Macbeth of. Hales. Folia litt. 198.
— Notes on. Hales. Folia litt. 231.
— Paradise lost, epitomized. Dobson, W. T. Class. poets, 394.
— — Spirit of. Chambers's Repos. no. 8.
— Paradise regained, epitomized. Dobson, W. T. Class. Poets, 446.
— Pattison's Life of. Smith, Gold. Lec. & ess. 320.
— Poetry. Seeley, J. R. Lec. & ess. 120 ; *or* Rom. imp. 129.
— Political opinions of. Seeley, J. R. Lec. & ess. 89 ; *or* Rom. imp. 96.
— Politics, prose writings, and biographers of. Windsor. Ethica, 51.
— Prose. (Justice Keogh) Afternoon lec. 3 : 129.
— Prose style of. Hunt, T. W. Rep. Eng. prose, 246.
— Prose works of. Greenwood, F. W. P. Miscel. 208. — Ossoli. Art, 45.
— Sacred poetry of. McNicoll, T. Ess. Eng. lit. 65.
— Scherer's criticism of. Arnold, M. Mixed ess. 7.
— Sonnets of. Deshler. Afternoons, 160. — Hazlitt. Table talk.
— The supernatural in. Hodgson. Outcast, 129.
— Versification of. Hazlitt. Round table.
— *versus* Southey and Landor. DeQuincey. Note-book (Bost.), 193.
— Youth of. Masson. Ess. 37 ; *or* Three devils, 125.
Milton, Mary P. Holloway, L. C. Mothers of gt. men, 457.
Milton, Viscount. *See* Fitzwilliam, Earl.
Milton, Mass., Address at dedica. of Town Hall, 1876. Pierce, E. L. Addresses, 195.
Milton College, Milton, Wis. U. S. Bur. Ed. Circ. '89, no. 1 : 62.
Milwaukee, Wisconsin. Brooks, E. S. Great cities, 154.
— City government of. (F. C. Winkler) Nat. Conf. City Govt. 2-3 : 119.
— Disposal of animal and vege. waste in. (U. O. B. Wingate) Am. Pub. Health, 19 : 49.
— Flushing tunnel at. (G. H. Benzenberg) Am. Pub. Health, 14 : 186.
— Police system of. (F. J. Ries) Conf. char. & correc. '87 : 115.
Mimicry. Gall & Robertson. Pop. read. sci. 149.
— and imitation among actors. Murdoch, J. E. Stage, 42.
Mimms, Fort, Massacre at. Dawson. Batt. of U. S. 2 : 269.
Mimnermus. Arnold, E. Poets of Greece, 89. — Mills. Poets of Greece, 99. — Symonds. Greek poets, 1 : 244.
Min River, On the. Cumming, C. F. G. Wand. in China, 1 : 122.
Minas Geraes, Brazil, diamond and gold mining in, 1899. U. S. Cons. Rept. 60 : 535.
Minasowicz, Joseph Dionisius. Soboleski. Poets of Poland, 186.
Minchmoor. Brown, J. J. Leech, 239.
Mind, Godefroi. Brightwell. Byepaths of biog. 9.

Mind. Hall, J. A. Glimpses, 57.
— Abnormal conditions of. Soc. Psych. Res. 1 : 238.
— and body. Clifford. Lec. & ess. 244. — Elam. Phys. prob. 199. — Maudsley. Body & mind, 1. — Proctor, R. A. Rough ways, 376.
— and manners, Schools of. Mozley, A. Ess. 261.
— and matter. Picton. Mystery, 61.
— and motive. Hazlitt. Sket.
— and music. (T. H. Johnston) Nat. Educa. Assoc. '95 : 795.
— Avenues to. (W. M. Giffin) Nat. Educa. Assoc. '85 : 339.
— the basis of the universe. Fiske, J. Excurs. 320.
— Common errors on. Bain, A. Prac. ess. 3.
— Discipline of. Newman, J. H. Lec. univ. 330.
— — in education. Youmans, E. L. Culture, 1.
— Greatness of. Hume. Philos. works, 2 : 374.
— Growth of. Waterston. Culture, 41.
— — and decay of. Proctor. Sci. byways, 272.
— Health of. Friswell. Gentle life, 2 : 69.
— human, Advances of. Turgot. Life & writ. 159.
— The human and the brute. Bowen, F. Gleanings, 328.
— in form. Taylor, I. Ult. civiliz. 134.
— in men and animals. Romanes. Ess. 75.
Mind-cure and Christian science. Hovey, A. Stud. in ethics, 71.
Mind-reading. (P. Frazer) Phila. Soc. Sci. Assoc. 75. *See* Thought-reading.
Mind-stuff, historically treated. Whittaker, T. Ess. & not. 43.
Minds, Vital and mechanical. Whipple. Success, 94.
Minden, Battle of. Adams, W. H. D. Eng. at war, 1 : 191.
Mine labor in the Hocking Valley, Ohio. (E. W. Bemis) Am. Econ. Assoc. 3.
Mine Run, Battle of. Stine, J. H. Army Poto. 581.
Miner, Alonzo A., with portrait. Sketches N. H. men, 16.
Miner, Hiram J. Livingston, J. Dist. Amer. 314.
Mineral resources and waterways. (C. R. Van Hise) Deep waterways conven. 1 : 71.
Mineral springs, medicine and mythology. Gibson, W. S. Miscel. 162.
— of California. (F. W. Hatch) Calif. Health, 79-80 : 27.
Mineral substances. Chambers's Miscel. no. 130.
Minerals. Bibliography. Chester, A. B. Dict. minerals.
Mineralogy, Collections of, in U. S. Nat. Mus. (Wirt Tassin) U. S. Nat. Mus. Rept. '95 : 995.
Mines and mining laws of Latin America. Bur. Am. repub. no. 40.
— Coal, in Illinois. Ills. Labor, '84, '86, '88.
— in Greece. U. S. Cons. Repts. no. 124.
— Swindles in. Murphy. Prac. mining.
Miners, Condition of, in Illinois. Ills. Labor, 1884.
— Superstitions of. Jones, W. Credulities, 120.
Mingotti, Caterina (or Regina). Clayton, E. C. Queens, 63. — Edwards, H. S. Prima don. 1 : 53. — Hogarth. Mem. opera, 1 : 327. — Needham. Queens of song.
Miniatures, English painters of. Buxton, H. J. *et al.* Eng. paint. 92.
Mining and health. (R. W. Raymond) Buck, A. H. (ed.). Hygiene, 2 : 251.
— and minerals in the U. S. (N. S. Shaler) Shaler. The U. S. 1 : 417.
— Cornish, in America. Head, F. B. Descr. ess. 1 : 1.

Miracles, Special providences and. Tyndall. Frag. sci. 45, 418.
— A word about. Fiske, J. Unseen world, 129.
Miraculous, Value of witness to the. Huxley. Ess. contro. 294.
Miraculous element in Christianity. Smith, Goldw. Guesses, 135.
Miraflores, Battle of. Knox, T. W. Battles, 431.
Miramion, Madame M. B. de R. de. Kavanagh. Women of Chr. 168.
Miranda, Saa de. Montgomery. Men of Ita. 3 : 88.
Mirehouse, John. Grant, Jas. Portr. pub. char. 1 : 111. — Rawnsley. Lit. Assoc. Eng. lakes, 1 : 160.
Miremont, Armand de Bourbon, Marquis de, Sketch of. Agnew. Protes. exiles, 2 : 42.
Miriam. Geikie, C. Old Test. char. 119.
Mirror for magistrates. Gosse, E. Gossip, 25.
Mirrors. Repplier, A. In dozy hours, 76.
Mirror-writing. Ireland, W. W. Blot, 309.
Mirthfulness. Hare. Guesses, 1 : 345.
Misanthrope, Character of the. Malkin. Class. disq. 63.
Misanthropy. Bulwer, E. Caxtoniana, 219.
Miscegenation. Brinton. Races & peo. 283.
Misers, Remarkable. Wilson, H. Characters.
Miseries of human life, The. Helps. Friends, 2d ser. 2.
Misfortune. Dawson, G. Shakesp. 289.
— Origin and nature of. Illinois Charity, '72 : 11.
Misplaced men, Thoughts on. Boyd. Aut. holid. 38.
Missing people. Wilson, A. Nat. note-book, 22.
Mission field of the middle ages. Maclear. Apostles, 10.
Mission Indians of California. (Mrs. O. J. Hiles) Conf. char. & correc. '87 : 187.
Missionaries in the Pacific. Hübner. Thro. Brit. empire, 2 : 414.
— Necessity of entire devotion to their work. Cust. Ling. & orient. ess. 4 : 393.
Missionary and non-missionary religions. Lyall. Asia, 99.
Missionary bishops. Arnold, F. Our bishops, 2 : 88.
Missionary enterprise. Thomson, E. Essays, 104.
Missionary literature. Cust. Ling. & orient. ess. 4 : 505.
Missionary work. Brassey, T. Papers polit. 272.
Missions, Christian. (E. Armitage) Faith & crit. essays. — Japp, A. H. Master mission. — Thompson, H. M. Copy, 94.
— American medical, in Japan, 1881. Hatton, J. To-day in Amer. 1 : 237.
— ancient and modern, Comparative progress in. Lightfoot. Hist. ess. 71.
— and the social ideal. Manning, J. M. Sermons, 463.
— as seen by candidates for the ministry. Phelps, A. Portfolio, 172.
— Bibliography. Dennis, J. S. Missions & soc. prog.
— Debate on, in 1796. Taylor, W. M. Scott. pulpit, 175.
— Difficulties of. Cust. Ling. & orient. ess. 4 : 592.
— Failure of modern. Oxenham. Short stud. 423.
— Foreign. Müller, M. Sel. ess. 2 : 46.
— — of the Jesuits. Carne, J. Em. mission. 3 : 9.
— — of the Moravians in Greenland. Carne, J. Em. mission. 1 : 223.

Missions, Foreign, to Japan. Carne, J. Em. mission. 3 : 279.
— — to Labrador. Carne, J. Em. mission. 2 : 252.
— — to Madagascar. Carne, J. Em. mission. 2 : 124.
— — to Tranquebar, Coromandel. Carne, J. Em. mission. 1 : 82.
— — Work of. Anderson, M. B. Papers, 1 : 189.
— Heroes of. Hodder. Heroes, 1 : 53. 2 : 303.
— history of. Bibliography. Bliss, E. M. Hist. missions.
— in Africa and the Anglican Church. Cust. Ling. & orient. ess. 4 : 386.
— in China, Failures and fruits of. Johnson, S. Ori. relig. China, 837. — Younghusband. Heart of cont. 377.
— in India, 1808. Smith, Syd. Ess. fr. Ed.
— in the Pacific, Origin of. Alexander, J. M. Isl. Pac. 55.
— Lecture on. Müller. Chips, 4.
— Limited range of appeal of. Phelps, A. Portfolio, 181.
— Missionary musings. Dodge. Sermons to clergy, 291.
— Religious unity and. (G. T. Candlin) Barrows, J. H. Parl. relig. 2 : 1179.
— Remunerative. Thomson, E. Essays, 117.
— Roman Catholic. Ranke. Popes, 2 : 503.
— Stanley on. Müller. Chips, 4.
— Wm. Wilberforce on. Foster, J. Crit. ess. (Bohn) 2 : 237.
— Women's work in. Pitman, Mrs. Heroines mission. 1.
Mississinneway towns, Expedition against. Dawson. Batt. of U. S. 2 : 180.
Mississippi, State of, A political retrospect. Deming. Byways, 321.
— Spanish policy in, after treaty of San Lorenzo. (F. L. Riley) Am. Hist. Assoc. Rept. '97 : 175.
Mississippi College. U. S. Bur. Ed. Circ. '99, no. 2 : 80.
Mississippi River as a sewer. (J. Hartzell) Am. Pub. Health, 21 : 22.
— The father of waters. Deming. Byways, 303.
— Navigation of. Madison, J. Letters, 4 : 558.
— — Negotiations with Spain for. Jefferson. Works, 7 : 568.
— Physical geography. (E. Fontaine) Am. Geog. Soc. 3 : 343.
Mississippi scheme, Law's. Chambers's Miscel. no. 172. — Irving. Crayon pap. 38. — Mackay. Delusions, 1 : 15.
Mississippi valley. (H. P. Judson) Shaler. The U. S. 1 : 273.
— Flood of 1890 in. Godbey. Gt. disasters, 296.
— History of explorations in. (S. D. Peet) Am. Antiq. Soc. Proc. n. s. 11 : 124.
— Prehistoric inhabitants of. (D. A. Robertson) Am. Geog. Soc. 5 : 256.
Mississippi voyage. Martineau. Retrosp. 2 : 161.
Misson, Maximilian. Agnew. Protes. exiles, 2 : 10.
Missouri and Louisiana territory. Bibliography. St. Louis Mercan. Lib. '98.
Missouri campaign, 1861–62. (J. B. Leake) Mil. ess. M. O. L. L. U. S. Ills. 269.
Missouri compromise. McLaughlin. Lewis Cass, 287. — Schurz. Life of H. Clay, 1 : 172. — Mansfield, E. D. Pers. mem. 84. — Putnam, J. O. Addresses, 337.
— Historical significance of. (J. A. Woodburn) Am. Hist. Assoc. Rept. '93 : 249.
Missouri River, Utmost waters of the. (J. V. Brower) Am. Geog. Soc. 28 : 387.

Missouri State University, Boone Co., Mo. (T. J. Lowry) U. S. Bur. Ed. Circ. '98, no. 2 : 9.

Mistakes. Boyd. Our life, 266.

— in life. Ess. from Sat. R. 92.

Mistassini, Lake. (G. C. Hurlbut) Am. Geog. Soc. **20** : 469.

Misti, Ascent of the. (H. C. Cochrane) Am. Geog. Soc. **6** : 212.

Mistral, Frédéric, with portrait. (H. W. Preston) Warner Lib. **17** : 10097.

— Calendan. Preston, H. W. Troubadours.

Mistress of the Robes, How to become a. Malortie. Here, there, 244.

Mists, Formation of. Davy. Works, **6** : 182.

Mitchel, John. Bungay. Off-hand, 400.

— Pro-slavery sympathies. Congdon, C. T. Trib. ess. 20, 50.

Mitchel, Ormsby McKnight. Duyckinck. Nat. portr. gall. **2** : 362. — Griswold. Prose writ. 623. — Parton. Peop. bk. biog. 79. — Mansfield, E. D. Pers. mem. 277.

Mitchell, Donald Grant. Griswold. Prose writ. 672. — Howells. My lit. passions, 82. — With portrait. Warner Lib. **17** : 10110.

— at home. (H. A. Beers) Gilder. Authors, 237.

Mitchell, Elisha. Youmans. Pioneers sci. 279.

Mitchell, Mrs. Elizabeth (Rolls). Clayton, E. C. Eng. fem. art. **2** : 414.

Mitchell, Ellen E. Brockett. Woman's work, 420.

Mitchell, Maggie, with portrait. (L. L. Holden) McKay, F. E. Fam. actors, 309.

Mitchell, Maria. Bolton, S. K. Girls famous, 89. — Hanaford. Wom. of cent. 252. — With portrait. (J. W. Howe) Our fam. wom. 437.

Mitchell, Nahum. (A. M. Alger) N. E. Hist.- Gen. Soc. Biog. **2** : 69.

Mitchell, S. Weir, with portrait. Warner Lib. **17** : 10123.

Mitchell, T. D. Miller, S. F. Bench of Ga. v. 2.

Mitchell, Thomas. Jackson, T. Early Meth. **1** : 65.

Mitchell, William, actor. Hutton, L. Plays, 23.

Mitchill, Samuel Latham. With portrait. [Amer.] Nat. portr. gall. v. **1**. — (S. D. Gross) Gross, S. D. Autobiog. **2** : 236. — (J. W. Francis) Gross. Lives physicians, 267.

Mitford, Sir John. Manning, J. A. Speakers, 473.

Mitford, J. F. *See* Redesdale, Lord.

Mitford, Mary Russell. Adams, W. H. D. Cel. Eng. wom. Vict. **1** : 189. — Bethune, G. W. Brit. fem. poets, 318. — Chorley. Authors of Eng. 77.— Cone & Gilder. Pen-portr. **1** : 269. — Duyckinck. Portrait gall. **2** : 116. — Fields. Yesterdays, 261. — Jeaffreson. Novelists, **2** : 142. — Martineau, H. Biog. sket. 37. — (J. T. Fields) Parton. Princes, 142. — Payn. Lit. recol. 61. — Robertson. Eng. poetesses, 253. — Wotton. Word portraits, 211. — Hall, S.C. Book of mem. 438.— Hamilton, C. J. Women writers, 243. — Mayer, G. T. Wom. of lett. **2** : 163.— Payn. Lit. recol. 74.— Repplier. Ess. in min. 157. — With portrait. Warner Lib. **17** : 10143.

Mithraism. (J. M. Robertson) Relig. systems, 194.

Mithridates. (T. Mommsen) Ferris, G. T. Gt. leaders, 32.

Mitla, Notes on. (L. H. Aymé) Am. Antiq. Soc. Proc. n. s. **2** : 82.

Mivartism. Whedon. Ess. **2** : 98.

Mnasalcas. Mills. Poets of Greece, 155.

Mnason. Hastings, F. Obscure charac. 35.

Mnemonics, Relation of, to power of thought.

(Committee on Psychological Inquiry) Nat. Educa. Assoc. '92 : 789.

Mnesimachus. Mills. Poets of Greece, 391.

Moab and Ammon, Cities of. Gillett, E. H. Anc. cities, 166.

Moak, Nathaniel Cleveland. Am. Bar Assoc. **15** : 457.

Mob patriotism. Dodge, M. A. Skirmish, 170.

Moborly, G., bishop of Salisbury, with photo. Cooper, T. Men of mark, **2** : 26.

Mobile Bay, Battle of. Rawson, E. K. Twenty nav. batt. **2** : 491.

Mobs and education. Phillips, Wend. Sp. 319.

— The Boston mob, 1835. Phillips Wend. Sp. 213.

Mochelloc, St. Conyngham, D. P. Irish saints, 185.

Mock auctions. Wynter, A. Our soc. bees, **1** : 35.

Model, The, in art. Symonds. Ess. **1** : 199.

Modeling in public school work. (Mrs. E. M. Kent) Nat. Educa. Assoc. '94 : 915.

Modena. Hare. Cities of No. Italy, **2** : 233. — Tuckerman. Ital. sk. 154.

— Castelvetro in. Stoughton. Ital. reformers, 181.

Moderates and Evangelicals. Taylor, W. M. Scott. pulpit, 148, 190.

Moderation : "Easy does it, Guv'ner." Curtis, G. W. Other ess. 203.

Modern government, Centenary of. (S. E. Baldwin) Am. Bar Assoc. **12** : 235.

Modern languages, Place of, in higher education. (E. S. Joynes) Nat. Educa. Assoc. '76 : 111.

— Should they be substituted for ancient, in college courses? (S. G. Ashmore) N. Y. Regents, 102, app. : 63.

— — Study of. Lowell. Latest ess. 131. — Mathews. Men & bks. 263.

— — Committee of Twelve on. U. S. Bur. Ed. Rept. '97–98, **2** : 1391.

— — teaching of, in Germany. Bibliography. Brebner, M. Meth. teach. mod. lang. in Germany.

Modern life. The electric way. Warner, C. D. As we go, 41.

Modjeska, Helena. Matthews, B. Actors, **5** : 193. — Winter, W. Shadows, **2** : 330. — (C. E. L. Wingate) McKay, F. E. Fam. actors, 72.

Modrevius, Andrew Fricues. Wallace, R. Anti-Trin. biog. **2** : 155.

Moeris, Lake. (F. C. Whitehouse) Am. Geog. Soc. **11** : 85.

— The Raiyān. (F. C. Whitehouse) Am. Geog. Soc. **21** : 530.

Moeser, Justus. Hedge. Prose Ger. 51.

Moffat, Mrs. Mary, of the Kuruman, So. Africa. Pitman, Mrs. Heroines mission. 42.

Moffat, Robert. Creegan. Gt. mission. 305. — Cust. Ling. & orient. ess. **4** : 556. — Cochrane, R. Earnest, 108.

— and South Africa. Japp, A. H. Master mission. 226.

Moffatt, Geo. Tufton. Vaille & Clark. Harv. book, v. **1**.

Mogridge, G. Groser, W. H. Men worth im.— Miller, Jos. Singers church, 2d ed. 399.

Moguls, The great. Adams, W. H. D. Warriors of crescent, 139.

Mohammed. Arbuthnot. Arabic authors, 119. — Carlyle, T. Heroes. — Lord, J. Beacon, **2** : 23. — Poole, S. L. Studies, 34. — Renan. Studies (N. Y.), **1** : 226. — Trotter. Stud. biog. v. **1**. — Benson & Tatham. Men of might, 18. — Johnson, S. Ori. relig. Persia, 525. — Carlyle. Heroes. — Bettany. World's relig. 500. — (E. Gibbon) Ferris, G. T. Gt. leaders, 92. — Hundred greatest men, 140. — Mombert. Great lives, 122. — Utterton, F. A. Biog. sk. 39.

Mohammed and his religion. Brigham, C. H. Mem. 144.

— and his system. Stillé. Stud. med. 98.

— Hallucinations of. Ireland, W. W. Blot, 37.

— Ibrahim, son of. Brooks, E. S. Gt. men's sons, 98.

Mohammed II. (E. Gibbon) Ferris, G. T. Gt. leaders, 187.

Mohammed Toghlak, sultan of India. Ireland, W. W. Blot, 110.

Mohammedan revival. Palgrave. Ess. east. 111.

Mohammedan sects. Colebrooke, H. T. Miscel. ess. v. 2,

Mohammedanism. Clarke, J. F. Ten relig. 448. — Clodd. Childh. of relig. 204. — Kuenen. National religions, v. 1. — Kingsley, C. Hist. lec. 103. — St. Giles lec. 2 : 361. — Williams, W. R. Eras, 138. — Grant, G. M. Relig. 13. — (G. W. Leitner) Relig. system, 292. — Matheson. Distinc. mess.152. — Temple, R. Orient. exper. 312.

— Bibliography. Salem (Mass.) Pub. Lib. Bull. Jan. '96.

— Christianity and. (G. Washburn) Barrows, J. H. Parl. relig. 1 : 565.

— Destiny of. Wordsworth, C. Miscel. 3 : 83.

— in India. Lyall. Asia, 228.

— in the Levant. Palgrave. Ess. east. 1 : 110.

— Origins of. Renan. Studies (N. Y.), 1 : 226.

— past and present. Ellinwood. Orient. relig. & chr. 178.

Mohaves, Manners and customs of. (G. A. Allen) Smithson. Rept. '90 : 615.

Mohl, Julius. Müller. Biog. ess. 272.

Mohr, Andrew and Samuel. Wallace, R. Anti-Trin. biog. 3 : 136.

Mohun, Charles, Lord, with portrait. Caulfield. Kit-cat, 120. — Cook, D. Hours w. players, 1 : 12.

— Two trials of. Burke, P. Cel. trials.

Mohun, Michael. Doran. Annals stage, 1 : 72.

Moir, David Macbeth. Douglas, G. Blackwoods, 94. — Miller, Jos. Singers church, 2d ed. 450. — Gilfillan. Third gall. 200. — Wilson, J. G. Poets of Scot. 2 : 166.

— Sonnets of. Deshler. Afternoons, 303.

Molecular forces. Hunt, R. Poe. of sci. 35.

Molecules and molecular force. Gall & Robertson. Pop. read. sci. 415.

— Atoms and. Dunman. Talks sci. 73.

— atoms, and ether waves. Tyndall. New frag. 78.

— habits, etc. Bibliography. (F. W. True) U. S. Nat. Mus. Proc. 19 : 107.

Molesworth, Sir William. Grant, J. Recoll. Lords & Comm. 2 : 202. — Redding. Pers. reminis. 2 : 1.

Molière, Jean B. P. de. Besant. Fr. humor. 310. — (C. K. Watson) Camb. ess. '55 : 1. — Lang. Lett. to dead au. 184. — Northcote. Lec. & ess. 384. — Prescott. Biog. miscel. 361. — Russell, W. Extraor. men, 51. — Scott, Sir W. Essays. — Shelley, W. M. Lit. men Fr. 1. — Hundred greatest men, 47. — With portrait. (B. Matthews) Warner Lib. 17 : 10153.

— Character of his verse. Arnold, M. Irish ess. 6.

— Comedies of. Astié. Louis xiv, 325.

— Influence upon Congreve and Sheridan. Syle. Ess. in dram. 3.

Molière, Jean B. P. de, Life and genius of. (C. K. Watson) Camb. ess. '55 : 1.

— Tartuffe. Hunt. Wishing-cap, 298.

Molina, T. de. Ticknor. Span. lit. 2 : 308.

Molinet, Jean. Besant. Fr. poetry, 173.

Molinists. See Quietists.

Molinos, Michael de. Hodgson, W. Reformers, 321. — E., E. Vari. of fortune, 90.

Molique, Wilhelm B., with portrait. Ehrlich, A. Cel. violin. 10.

Molle, Rebecca. Clement, J. Noble deeds, 129.

Mollwitz, Battle of. Carlyle. Batt. Fred. the Gt. 10.

Molocus, St., of Cong. Conyngham, D. P. Irish saints, 183.

Molokai, Lepers of. Todd, M. L. Corona, 111.

Moltke, Helmuth K. B. von. Duyckinck. Portrait gall. 2 : 360. — Em. persons, 5 : 54. — Morris, W. O. Commanders, 274. — Strauss, G. L. M. Men of Ger. 1 : 54. — Wilson, J. G. Illus. sci. 415. — Whitman, S. Teuton. stud. 159.

— at headquarters in Berlin. Yates, E. H. Celeb. 3 : 69.

Molva, St. Conyngham, D. P. Irish saints, 279.

Molza, Francesco Maria. Symonds. Renais. It. lit. 2 : 224. — Symonds. Reviv. of learn. 488.

Momerie, A. W., Removal of, from King's College. Momerie. Fut. of relig. 77.

Mommsen, Theodor, with portrait. (W. C. Lawton) Warner Lib. 17 : 10206.

Mompesson, Roger. Field, R. S. Prov. courts N. J. 56.

Monachism, Import of. Ullman. Reformers, 106.

Monaco in 1864. Higgins, M. J. Ess. 163.

Monad. Leibnitz. Philos. works (1890), 218.

Monaghan, Robert Emmet. Am. Bar Assoc. 18 : 544.

Monaldeschi, Death of. Wraxall, C. F. L. Historic bye-ways, 323.

Monarchs among the monks. Doran. Monarchs, 2 : 77.

— of the Eastern empire (A. D. 395 to 716). Doran. Monarchs, 2 : 46.

— of Rome, retired, Incidents in lives of. Doran. Monarchs, 2 : 1.

Monarchy. Thompson, D. G. Politics in dem. v. 1.

— republicanism, and democracy. Lorimer, Jas. Studies, nat'l & internat.

— Spirit of. Hazlitt. Lit. rem. 2 : 441.

— Universal. Galt, J. Lit. life, 2 : 106.

Monasteries, Austrian, Visit to. Mivart. Ess. 1 : 262.

— in England, Dissolution of. Froude. Short stud. 1 : 324.

— — Effects of the confiscation of. Burke, S. H. Men of reforma. 2 : 122.

— — in the 16th century. Burke, S. H. Men of reforma. 2 : 29.

— — Spoliation of. Disraeli, I. Amen. (N. Y. 2 v.) 1 : 361.

— of Ireland, List of. Conyngham, D. P. Irish saints, 537.

Monastery, The. Cleveland, R. E. Eliot, 129.

— Buildings of the. Cutts, E. L. Scenes mid. ages, 70.

Monastic inquisitors of Thomas Cromwell, Character of. Burke, S. H. Men of reforma. 1 : 337.

Monastic institutions. Gilbart. Lec. 158. — Lord, J. Beacon, 2 : 175.

— Nature of. Montalembert. Monks, 1 : 9.

Monastic Italy in the 6th century. Montalembert. Monks, 2 : 71.

Monastic life in England in the 13th century. Jessopp, A. Coming of friars, 113.

Monastic orders, Influence of, on feudal society. Montalembert. Monks, 6 : 3.

Monastic precursors in the west. Montalembert. Monks, 1 : 381.

Monastic scriptorium. Gasquet, F. A. Old Eng. Bible, 41.

Monastic spirit, Fundamental tendency of. Montalembert. Monks, 6 : 247.

Monastic vows. Ullman. Reformers, 117.

Monasticism. Clarke, J. F. Events and epochs, 82. — Stillé. Stud. med. 332. — Taylor, I. Nat. hist. of enthusiasm, 208. — Trench. Lec. mediæval, 102. — Williams, W. R. Eras, 45.

— and the life of the church. Brown, J. B. Stoics, 93.

— and literature. Brooke, S. A. Hist. early Eng. lit. 218.

— eastern, Beginning of. Montalembert. Monks, 1 : 287.

— Origin of. Cutts, E. L. Scenes mid. ages, 1.

Monazite in foreign countries, 1895. U. S. Cons. Rept. 48 : 541.

Monboddo, James Burnett, Lord. McCosh. Scot. phil. 245.

Moncacht-Apé, Journey of. (A. McF. Davis) Am. Antiq. Soc. Proc. n. s. 2 : 321.

Moncel, Theodose Achille Louis, comte du. Munro, J. Heroes of Teleg. 285.

Moncey, Bon Adrien Jeannot de. Headley. Napoleon, 1 : 215.

Monck, George. Fuller. Worthies, 1 : 415.

Mondonville, J. J. C., opera Daphius et Alcimadur. Hogarth. Mem. opera, 2 : 215.

Monet, Claude, with portrait. (T. Robinson) Van Dyke, J. C. Mod. Fr. mast. 169.

Money. Greeley. Ess. pol. econ. 54. — Hume. Philos. works, 3 : 308. — Taylor. Notes from life, 1. — Hoffman, F. S. Sphere, 133.

— Abolition of. Zangwill. Without prej. 124.

— and banks, State tamperings with. Spencer, H. Ess. (N. Y.) 319.

— and its functions. (Clinton Furbish; L. J. Gage) Sunset club echoes, 183.

— and its substitutes. (H. White) Econ. tracts, no. 6.

— and its uses. Bolles. Chap. pol. econ. 81.

— as an exchanger of values. Elder, W. Questions, 106.

— as a producer. Elder, W. Questions, 120.

— Bibliography. Delmar, A. Hist. Monet. systs. — Fisher, I. Monetary appreciation. — White, H. Money & banking in Amer. hist. — Cincinnati Pub. Lib. Bull. Apr.–Jun. '96. — New Haven (Ct.) Pub. Lib. Bull. Aug. '96. — Newark (N. J.) Pub. Lib. Rec. Sept. 15, '96. — Salem (Mass.) Pub. Lib. Bull. Sept. '96. — Springfield (Mass.) Pub. Lib. Bull. Sept. '96. — Waltham (Mass.) Pub. Lib. Bull. Sept. '96.

— a commodity. Smart, W. Stud. econ. 141.

— Ethics of. (J. de Soyres) Wace, H. Lond. mission. 22.

— Fluctuations in the value of. Kempner, W. Common-sense soc. 179.

— in relation to character. Lecky. Map of life, 268.

— Influences of. Hamerton. Intellec. 168.

— its use and abuse. Smiles. Self-help.

— Love of. Leslie, T. E. C. Ess. pol. econ. 1.

— Management of. Bulwer, E. Caxtoniana.

— of the future. Bolles. Chap. pol. econ. 113.

— of the U. S. and other countries. U. S. Lab. Bull. 1 : 181.

Money, Quantity-theory of. Walker, F. A. Discus. in econ. 1 : 211.

— True nature and function of. Bastiat. Ess. on pol. econ. 97, 136.

— Unification of. (R. N. Toppan) Am. Antiq. Soc. Proc., n. s. 5 : 283.

— usury, and banking. Greene, W. B. Soc. frag. 35.

— Value of. Walker, F. A. Discus. in econ. 1 : 193.

— Want of. Ess. from Sat. R. 341. — Hazlitt. Lit. rem. 2 : 227.

— weights and measures of Amer. republics. Bur. Am. repub. no. 4.

Money-getting. Greene, W. B. Soc. frag. 111.

Money matters. Lubbock. Use of life, 41.

Money-worship and railway novels. Phillips, S. Ess. from Times, 1 : 34.

Money-worthness. Henry, C. S. About men, 108.

Mongolia and Tibet, Explorations in. (W. W. Rockhill) Smithson. Rept. '92 : 659.

Mongolians. See Yellow races.

Monica, mother of St. Augustine. Holloway, L. C. Mothers of gt. men, 91. — Kavanagh. Women of Chris. 37.

Monism. Gurney. Tertium, 1 : 316. — Romanes. Mind & motion, 79, 129.

"Monitor" and "Merrimac," Battle between. Knox, T. W. Battles, 210. — Swinton. Twelve battles, 226. — Rawson, E. K. Twenty nav. batt. 2 : 421.

Monk, George. See Albemarle, duke of.

Monk, Mary. Williams, Jane. Lit. wom. 143.

Monkey, May a, possess genius. Appleton, T. G. Chequer-work, 113.

Monkeys, Anecdotes of. Senior. Biog. sk. 511.

— My monkey Jacko. Buckland, F. T. Curios. nat. hist. 1 : 291.

Monkhouse, Cosmo. (R. Le Gallienne) Miles, A. H. Poets of cent. 6 : 453.

Monks, Buddhist, of central Asia. Clarke, J. F. Events, 46.

— Celtic, and Anglo-Saxons. Montalembert. Monks, 4 : 1.

— Christian, and monastic life. Clarke, J. F. Events, 82.

— of ancient England. Carlyle. Past & present.

— Social and political influence of, among the Anglo-Saxons. Montalembert. Monks, 5 : 137.

— Their services to society, and to science, etc. Montalembert. Monks, 6 : 109, 130.

— under the first Merovingians. Montalembert. Monks, 2 : 217.

Monkshood. (G. Allen) Proctor, R. A. Nat. stud. 335.

Monmouth, Anne Scott, duchess of, with portrait. Costello. Englishwomen, 3 : 327.

Monmouth, James Scot, 1st duke, with portrait. Jesse. Court of Eng. Stuarts, 3 : 112. — Lodge. Portraits (Bohn), v. 6. — Macaulay. Biog. sk. 118.

Monmouth rebellion. (K. Parkes) Walters, J. C. Bygone Som. 6.

Monmouth, N. J., Battle of. Dawson. Batt. of U. S. 1 : 394.

Monnier, Henri. (E. C. J. B. Jacquot) Gautier. Fam. Fr. au. 259.

Monod, Adolphe. Pressensé. Contem. port. 149.

Monograms used by artists. Spooner. Biog. fine arts, 1 : lxv.

Monologues among the mountains. Wallace, H. B. Lit. crit. 399.

Monte Carlo. Field, H. M. Killarney, 227.
— A day at. Arnold, F. Arm-chair, 143.
Monte-Casino, Abbey of. Baddeley. Travel-tide, 1.
Monte Generoso. Symonds. Sk. So. Eur. **2** : 273.
Monte Oliveto. Hare. Cities of No. Italy, **3** : 299. — Symonds, J. A. Ital. byways.
Montecuculi, Raymond de. Cust. Warriors thirty years, **2** : 523.
Montefiore, Sir Moses. Bailey, J. B. Methuselahs, 327. — Parton. Capt. indus. 379. — Em. persons, **3** : 253. — Simson, Jas. Em. men of Kent, 167.
Monteith, Florence, with portrait. Butten. Mus. celeb. **2** : 37.
Monteiths of Glasgow. Bourne, H. R. F. Eng. merch. **2** : 174.
Montelupo, Raffaello da. Perkins, C. C. Tusc. sculp. **2** : 72.
Monte-mór, or Montemayer, Jorge de. Montgomery. Men of Ita. **3** : 89.
Montenegro. Gladstone. Glean. **4** : 305. — Minchin. Balkan penin. 1886. — Vaca. tourists, **2** : 357.
— and the Montenegrins. Chambers's Repos. no. 47.
— in 1843. Ingram. Hearts of oak, 33.
Montenotte, Battle of, 1796. Adams, C. Gr. camp. 1.
Montepulciano. Symonds, J. A. Ital. byways.
Monterey. Hardy, I. D. Through cities, 221.
— the old Pacific capital. Stevenson, R. L. Across pl. 77.
— Palustric infection in. (R. G. Cantu) Am. Pub. Health, **18** : 198.
— Santa Cruz and San Francisco. Bates. Year in Gt. Rep. **2** : 112.
— Siege of. Dawson. Batt. of U. S. **2** : 463.
Montespan, Madame de, and Louis XIV. Menzies, S. Roy. fav. **2** : 391.
— in 1682, with portrait. Imbert de St. A. Wom. Ct. Louis XIV, 67.
— Old age of. Imbert de St. A. Wom. Ct. Louis XIV, 207.
Montesquieu, Charles de S. de. Alison. Ess. **2**. — Hundred greatest men, 289. — Maceuen. Celeb. 103. — Vinet. Fr. lit. 18th cent. 199. — Carlyle, T. Montaigne, 20. — With portrait. (F. N. Thorpe) Warner Lib. **18** : 10249.
Monteverde, Claudio. Use of instruments. Hogarth. Mem. opera, **1** : 10.
Montevideo, capital of Uruguay. Curtis, W. E. Capitals, 591.
— Defense of, 1846. Ingram. Hearts of oak, 83.
Montez, Lola. Ames, M. C. Outlines, 124.
Montezuma castle. Lummis. Strange corners, 134.
Montezuma's well. Lummis. Strange corners, 122.
Montfaucon, B. Carlyle, T. Montaigne, 34.
Montford, Mrs. Lennox, W. P. Plays, **1** : 32.
Montfort, Jane, countess de. Owen, Mrs. O. F. Heroines hist. 139.
Montfort, Simon de. Adams, W. H. D. Memo. batt. **1** : 95. — (J. R. Green) Ferris, G. T. Gt. leaders, 148. — Gardiner, S. R. Hist. biog. 3.
Montgolfier, Adelaide de. Belloc, Mme. Walled garden, 270.
Montgolfier, Joseph. Hundred greatest men, 473. — Parton. Peop. bk. biog. 134.
Montgolfier, Stephen. Parton. Peop. bk. biog. 134. — Towle, G. M. Heroes of inven. 113.
Montgomery, Alexander. Holland, J. Psalmists, **1** : 241. — Irving, D. Scot. poets, **2** : 183. — Wilson, J. G. Poets of Scot. **1** : 54.

Montgomery, Anne, Barbara, and Elizabeth Gerard. Irish beauties, 162.
Montgomery, James. Baillie, J. Life stud. 178. — Boyd. Crit. ess. 124. — Gilfillan. Mod. lit. 277. — Howitt. Homes Br. poets, **2** : 334. — Langford. Prison books, 287. — Miller, H. Lead. articles, 146. — Wilson, J. G. Poets of Scot. **1** : 485. — Deshler. Afternoons, 223. — Devey. Mod. Eng. poets, 355. — Griswold, R. W. Sac. poets. — Hall, S. C. Book of mem. 81. — Hatfield, E. F. Poets of church, 437. — Holland, J. Psalmists, **2** : 300. — Miles, A. H. Poets of cent. **10** : 1. — Miller, Jos. Singers church, 2d ed. 341.
Montgomery, Martin V. Am. Bar Assoc. **22** : 684.
Montgomery, Richard. With portrait. [Amer.] Nat. portr. gall. v. 4. — With portrait. Duyckinck. Nat. portr. gall. **1** : 135. — With portrait. Headley, J. T. Washington, **1** : 132. — Lossing. Em. Amer. 157.
Montgomery, Sir Robert. Hall, S. C. Book of mem. 89. — Horne, R. H. New spirit, 322. — Laurie, W. F. B. Dist. Anglo-Ind. **1** : 202.
— Poems of. Macaulay. Ess. **2** : 188.
Montgomery castle, The Herbert family at. Hutton, B. Castles, 291.
Montgomery, Fort, Capture of. Dawson. Batt. of U. S. **1** : 332.
Months, The. Lamb. Elia.
— Procession of. Mitchell, D. G. Bound toge. 61.
Monti, G. B., Teresa Richler, wife of. Jameson. Loves of poets.
Monti, Vincenzo. Howells. Mod. Ital. poets, 102. — Montgomery. Men of Ita. **2** : 303. — Stebbing. Ital. poets, v. 3.
Montilcinus in Bologna. Stoughton. Ital. reformers, 171.
Montmirail, Battle of, 1814. Adams, C. Gt. camp. 171.
Montmorency, Maria Felicia, duchess of. Belloc, Mme. Walled garden, 302.
Montorsoli, Fra Giovan Angelo. Perkins, C. C. Tusc. sculp. **2** : 95.
Montpellier. James, H. Little tour, 160. — Warner, C. D. Roundabout, 29.
Montpensier. A. M. L. d'Orleans, M'lle de. Higginson. Atlan. ess. 157. — Menzies. Pol. women, **2** : 69. — Mason, A. G. Wom. of Fr. salons, 49.
Montpensier, Duke de, duel with Prince Henry. Hay, J. Castil. days, 371.
Montreal. Hardy, I. D. Through cities, 27. — Taylor, B. At home, **2** : 366.
— and Toronto. Arnold, E. Seas & l. 28.
— Drainage of. (A. Brittain) Am. Pub. Health Assoc. **20** : 319.
— Incomes, wages, and rents in. (H. B. Ames) U. S. Lab. Bull. **3** : 39.
— Sanitation in. (L. Laberge) Am. Pub. Health, **20** : 301.
Montrose, James Graham, 5th earl and 1st marquis of. Bayne. Pur. revol. 257. — Cust. Warriors civ. **2** : 431. — Lodge. Portraits (Bohn), v. 4. — Mitford, M. R. Recollec. 299. — Skelton. Ess. 123. — Wilson, J. G. Poets of Scot. **1** : 84. — Stanhope, P. H. Hist. essays.
Monts, Sieur de. See Gast, P. du.
Montucla, J. E. Carlyle, T. Montaigne, 293.
Montyon, A. de, baron. Coffy, J. F. Heroes of charity.
Montyon prizes. Kavanagh. Women of Chr. 318. — Yonge. Gold. deeds.
Monumenta ritualia ecclesiæ Anglicanæ, Maskell's. Mivart. Ess. **1** : 242.

Monuments. Ess. from Nation, 193.
— National. Alison. Ess. v. 2.
— — Preservation of English. Lubbock. Addresses, 154.
Monvel, Maurice Boutet de. (W. H. Low) Van Dyke, J. C. Mod. Fr. mast. 251.
Monza. Hare. Cities of No. Italy, 1 : 79.
Mood, Ease of. Mabie. Ess. on work, 180.
Moods and frames of mind. Holland, J. G. Lessons, 9.
Moodus noises. Hovey, H. C. Cel. Am. Cav. 199.
Moody, Fanny, with portrait. Buffen. Mus. celeb. 2 : 65.
Moody, Dwight L. Bolton, S. K. Poor boys famous, 323. — Holland, J. G. Every-day, 1 : 147.
Moon, April. Abbott, C. C. Outings, 105.
— Birth of. Proctor, R. A. Mysteries, 30.
— Crater Tycho. (A. C. Ranyard) Smithson. Inst. Rept. '93 : 89.
— A dead world. Proctor, R. A. Other suns, 214.
— Has it an atmosphere? (A. C. Ranyard) Proctor, R. A. Leis. read. 22.
— History of. Proctor, R. A. Rough ways, 81.
— Man in. Baring-Gould. Myths, 190.
— New crater in. Proctor, R. A. Rough ways, 98.
— News from. Proctor. Borderland, 214.
— Open letter to. Guiney. Goose-quill, 28.
— Surface of. Buckley, A. B. Through magic glass, 1.
— with bibliography. Todd, D. P. Stars & tel. 33.
Moon hoax. Proctor. Myths, 241.
Moonlight. Thoreau. Excursions, 307.
Moon-men. Soane. New curios. 1 : 80.
Moon-shapes; semi-lunar and crescent-shaped tools. (Ph. J. J. Valentini) Am. Antiq. Soc. Proc. n. s. 3 : 449.
Moor, James. Irving, D. Scot. writ. 2 : 288.
Moor Park, England. Timbs. Abbeys, 1 : 271.
— and Swift. Allingham. Varieties, 1 : 69.
Moore, Albert. (S. Colvin) Atkinson, J. B., et al. Eng. paint. 4. — Wedmore, F. Studies, 2 : 227.
Moore, Mrs. Clara J. Brockett. Woman's work, 599. — Hart, J. S. Fem. prose, 377.
Moore, E. Chalmers. Eng. poets, 14 : 193.
Moore, George, philanthropist. Blaikie, W. G. Leaders, 283. — Bosanquet. Ess. 1. — Cochrane, R. Gt. thinkers, 277. — Japp & Holmes. Succ. bus. men, 3. — Japp, A. H. Leaders of men, 179. — Smith, G. B. Chris. workers, 315.
Moore, George, author. Couch, A. T. Q. Adv. crit. 341. — Buchanan, R. Coming terr. 145. — Peck, H. T. Pers. equa. 89.
Moore, George Henry. Am. Antiq. Soc. Proc. n. s. 8 : 185.
Moore, Henry. Bate, P. H. Eng. Pre-Raph. 87. — Wesley & successors, 61, 102.
Moore, Jacob Bailey. (N. Crosby) N. E. Hist.-Gen. Soc. Biog. 2 : 75.
Moore, Jane Boswell. Moore, F. Women of the war, 554.
Moore, Dr. John. Carlyle, T. Montaigne, 39.
Moore, Sir John. Carlyle, T. Montaigne, 45. — Cole, J. W. Brit. generals, v. 1. — Gleig. Brit. mil. com. 3 : 251. — Johns. Nav. & mil. heroes. — Taylor, W. C. Mod. Brit. Plut. 242.
— Letter from, in Spain, 1808. Stanhope, Earl. Miscel. 1 : 51.
Moore, Mary. Ellet. Pioneer wom. 110.
Moore, Mollie E. Davidson, J. W. Writ. of South, 396. — Raymond, I. Southland wr. 2 : 959.

Moore, Thomas. Buchanan, R. Look round, 204. — Chambers's Miscel. no. 80. — Chorley. Authors of Eng. 65. — Devey. Mod. Eng. poets, 226. — Edgar. Footpr. 226. — Gilfillan. Mod. lit. 311. — Hannay. Satire, 204. — Hazlitt. Spirit. — Howitt. Homes Br. poets, 2 : 445. — Jones, W. A. Ess. on authors, 191. — Mason, E. T. Pers. traits, 3 : 141. — (R. H. Stoddard) Moore, T. Prose & v. — O'Hagan, T. Occ. pap. 163. — Oliphant, M. Lit. hist. v. 3. — Reed, H. Brit. poets, 2 : 54. — Saintsbury. Ess. Eng. lit. 170. — Saunders, F. Famous books, 160. — Tuckerman. Poets, 175. — (E. W. Gosse) Ward. Eng. poets, 4 : 309. — Wotton. Word portraits, 217. — Brooks, S. W. Eng. poets, 368. — Dixon, W. M. Engl. poetry, 125. — Duyckinck.. Portrait gall. 1 : 593. — Hall, S. C. Book of mem. 1. — Hatfield, E. F. Poets of church, 446. — Hunt, L. Byron, 1 : 279. — Grant, Jas. Port. pub. char. 2 : 120. — Miles, A. H. Poets of cent. 2 : 187. 9 : 133. 10 : 669. — Miller, Jos. Singers church, 2d ed. 363. — Minto. Georg. era, 224. — Mitchell, D. G. Eng. lands, 4 : 152. — Murray, J. O'K. Prose & poet. Irel. 502. — Ossoli. Art, 72. — Procter, B. W. Autob. 148. — Roscoe, W. C. Poems & ess. v. 2. — Russell, W. C. Book of au. 420. — With portrait. (T. Walsh) Warner Lib. 18 : 10271. — Williams, A. M. Poets of Irel.
— and Barry Cornwall. Willis. Fam. persons, 463.
— Duel with Jeffrey; a letter. Moore, T. Prose & v. 404.
— Haunts of. Winter. Gray days, 53.
— Lalla Rookh. Jeffrey, F. Contrib. Ed. Rev.
— Letters to Leigh Hunt. Moore, T. Prose & verse, 391.
— Political plagiaries. Maginn. Fras. papers, 130.
Moore, William, of Moore Hall. Pennypacker. Hist. sk. 229.
Moorman, Cornelius. Wallace, R. Anti-Trin. biog. 3 : 130.
Moors in France, The. Taylor, W. C. Revol. 1 : 144.
— in Spain. Chambers's Miscel. no. 196. — Taylor, W. C. Revol. 1 : 97.
Moorsom, Col. Robert. Rogers, C. Chr'n heroes, 100.
Moose. Murphy, J. M. Sport. adv. 244.
— and caribou hunting. (Lord Dunraven) Am. Geog. Soc. 11 : 334.
— Murder of. Thoreau. Selec. 103.
Moosehead Lake, Journal of a visit to, 1853. Lowell. Writ. 1 : 1.
Moot courts in law schools. Am. Bar Assoc. 22 : 494.
Moragne, Mary Elizabeth. Hart, J. S. Fem. prose, 453.
Moral and intellectual life, Analogy of. Hinton. Thinking, 245.
— and religious instruction in our public schools. Crooker, J. H. Problems, 197.
— and spiritual culture. Waterston. Culture, 129.
Moral code, Origin and nature of. Wilson, J. Thoughts sci. 128.
Moral condition of the people. Kempner, W. Common-sense soc. 45.
Moral conduct, Inattention to cause and effect in. Bailey, S. Essays, 152.
Moral controversies. Stephen, J. F. Horæ sabb. 359.
Moral education. Bryant, S. Short stud. 139. — Greenwood, F. W. P. Miscel. 256. — (H. Mann) Mass. Education, 9 : 62. 12 : 90.

Moral element in primary education. (W. H. Ruffner) Nat. Educa. Assoc. '76 : 39.

Moral government of the world. Goldsmith. Miscel. (N. Y. 4 v.) 1 : 361.

Moral ideals. Anderson, M. B. Papers, 1 : 173.

Moral law, The. Hinton. Thinking, 261.

Moral life, Influence of, on judgment in matters of faith. Wilks. Chr. ess. 322.

— Moral philosopher and. James, W. Will to bel. 184.

— Religious life and. (S. F. Scovel) Barrows, J. H. Parl. relig. 2 : 956.

Moral motive power. Shairp. Studies.

Moral philosophy, Sydney Smith's. Rogers, H. Ess. 3 : 195.

— Whewell on. Mill, J. S. Dissert. (N. Y.) 3 : 132.

Moral reform : an encouraging outlook. (J. J. Maclaren) Conf. char. & correc. '97 : 347.

Moral training in common schools, Methods of. (A. D. Mayo) Nat. Educa. Assoc. '72 : 11. 88 : 6.

— in elementary education. (Z. Richards) Nat. Educa. Assoc. '92 : 317. — (R. H. Rivers) Nat. Educa. Assoc. '77 : 180.

— in the public school. (E. E. White) Nat. Educa. Assoc. '86 : 128.

— in schools. (E. Bouton) N. Y. Regents, 101, app. : 79.

— Religious motives in, Importance of. (Robert Allyn) Nat. Educa. Assoc. '87 : 383.

— through the common branches. (C. De Garmo) Nat. Educa. Assoc. '94 : 165.

Moral virtues, Practical culture of. (Committee on Moral Education) Nat. Educa. Assoc. '92 : 759.

Morales, Luis de. Washburn, E. Span. mas. 31.

Moralists. Brown, J. Locke, etc. 360.

Moralities, The common. Holland, J. G. Every day, 1 : 204.

Morality. Webster, N. Ess. 233.

— and genius. Trail, F. Studies, 152.

— and sensibility. Stephen, J. F. Ess. by barr. 199.

— and theism. Smith, Goldw. Guesses, 189.

— Bad, is bad art. Patmore. Religio poetæ, 79.

— The church as teacher of. Seeley, J. R. Rom. imp. 259; or Lec. & ess. 245.

— Christian coöperation in maintaining. Evang. Alliance, '89 : 123.

— Comparative. Oxenham. Short stud. 181.

— Compulsory. Mathews. Conversers, 93.

— Conventional. Stephen, J. F. Ess. by barr. 31.

— Development of. Morris, C. Civilization, 1 : 420.

— in public schools. (J. W. Cook) Nat. Educa. Assoc. '88 : 127.

— Influence of, upon religion. Lyall. Asia, 54.

— Limitations of. Stephen, J. F. Ess. by barr. 107.

— Political. Lord, J. Beacon, 4 : 287.

— Public, and its teachers. Cobbe, F. P. Hours of work, 1.

— Right of the state to promote. Green, T. H. Works, 2 : 512.

— Sense of freedom in. Green, T. H. Works, 2 : 309.

— What have we left? Confl. of age, 43.

— Whewell's Elements of. Martineau, J. Ess. 2 : 1.

— Whewell's Systematic. Martineau, J. Ess. 2 : 52.

— without metaphysic. Tulloch. Mod. theories, 225.

Morality plays. Ulrici. Shakesp. dram. art, v. 1. — Ward, A. W. Eng. dram. 1 : 23. — Morley, H. Eng. writ. 7 : 72.

Morals and culture. Hamerton. Intellec. 68.

— and religion, The evolution of. Cobbe, F. P. Darwinism, 391.

— — Grounds of. Coleridge. Friend, 347.

— and science. Huxley. Ess. contro. 163.

— applied to business. (S. S. Packard) Nat. Educa. Assoc. '94 : 965.

— Bases of. Hinton. Thinking, 47.

— Instruction in, in schools and colleges. N. Y. Regents, 111 : 284.

— Lecky's European. Brownson. Works, 14 : 379.

— Mechanism in thought and. Holmes, O. W. Old vol. 260.

— Medicine and. Disraeli, I. Curios. (N. Y. 4 v.) 3 : 225.

— No sex in. (E. D. Cheney) Brackett, A. C. Educa. of girls, 129.

— of literature. Cobbe, F. P. Studies, 261.

— Principles of. Hume. Philos. works, 4 : 229.

— Public and private. Stephen, J. F. Ess. by barr. 208.

— Scientific basis of. Clifford. Lec. & ess. 287.

— Speculation on. Shelley. Ess. 1 : 197.

— taste and, Connection between. Hopkins, M. Miscel. ess. 101.

— Theory of. Brownson. Works, 14 : 236.

Moran, Edward. Sheldon, G. W. Amer. painters, 198.

Moran, Peter. Sheldon, G. W. Amer. painters, 23.

Moran, Thomas. Sheldon, G. W. Amer. painters, 122.

Morata, afterwards Grünthaler, Olympia Fulvia. Trollope, T. A. Dec. Ital. wom. — Gearey. Dau. of Italy, 1. — Yonge. Good wom. 1 : 1.

Moratin, L. F. Kennedy. Poets of Spain, 95.

Moravian Brethren. Hedge, F. H. Martin Luther, 38. — Ker, J. Lec. hist. preach. 229. — Chambers's Repos. no. 90. — Howells. Three villages, 117. — Howitt. Supernat. 2 : 426. — Winkworth. Chr. sing. Germ. 305.

— and the Wesleys. Larrabee, W. C. Wesley, 1 : 131.

— in Pennsylvania. Gibbons, P. E. Penn. Dutch.

Moray, James Stuart, earl of. Burke, S. H. Hist. portr. Tudor, 4 : 434.

Mordaunt, Chas. See Peterborough, Earl of.

Mordecai. Hills, O. A. Companion char. 205.

— Williams, H. L. Boys of Bible, 233.

More (or Moore), Sir Francis. Woolrych. Serjeants, 1 : 228.

More, Hannah. Balfour, C. L. Work. wom. 38. — Cone & Gilder. Pen-portr. 1 : 9. — De Quincey. Works (Masson), 14 : 94. — Fawcett, M. G. Em. wom. 211. — Kavanagh. Women of Christ. 257. — Lord, J. Beacon, 5 : 421. — Sprague, W. B. Europ. celeb. 64. — Walford, L. B. Four biog. 149. — Williams, Jane. Lit. wom. 313. — Wotton. Word portraits, 220. — Yonge. Good wom. 2 : 290. — Birrell. Men, women & books, 70. — Bethune, G. W. Brit. fem. poets, 141. — Duyckinck. Portrait gall. 1 : 43. — Griswold, R. W. Sac. poets.— Hale, S. J. Less. wom. lives, 110. — Hall, S. C. Book of mem. 67. — Hamilton, C. J. Women writers, 82. — Mitchell, D. G. Eng. lands, 3 : 171. — Pierce, B. K. Em. dead, 251. — Walford, L. B. Twelve Eng. authors, 1.

— Benevolence of. Starling, E. Noble deeds wom. 245.

— Memoirs of. Elwood. Lit. ladies, 1 : 259.

— Residence of. Hall, Mrs. S. C. Pilgr. Eng. shr. 1 : 49.

More, Henry. Benson, A. C. Ess. 35. — Creasy. Etonians, 137. — Macdonald, G. England's antiphon, 223. — Miller, Jos. Singers church, 2d ed. 78. — Tulloch. Rational theol. 17th cent. **2** : 303.

More, Henry. Theological works, 1708. Coleridge. Lit. rem. **3** : 156.

More, Sir John. Foss. Judges, **5** : 190. — Lodge. Portraits (Bohn), v. 1.

More, Sir Thomas. Brightwell. Gt. lawyers, 15. — Burke, S. H. Men of reforma. **1** : 182. — Campbell. Ld. chan. **2** : 1. — Collier, W. F. Hist. Eng. lit. 78. — Dawson, G. Shakesp. 209, — Foss. Judges, **5** : 203. — Foster, J. Crit. ess. (Bohn) **1** : 189, 217. — Fuller. Worthies, **2** : 361. — Gardiner, S. R. Hist. biog. 79. — Gilliat. Champions, 172. — Lodge. Portraits (Bohn), v. 1. — Macdiarmid. Brit. stat. **1** : 1.— Mackintosh, J. Miscel. 43. — Manning, J. A. Speakers, 161. — Wotton. Word portraits, 224. — Brink. Eng. lit. 2, pt. **2** : 144. — Burke, S. H. Hist. portr. Tudor, **1** : 337. — Choate, I. B. Wells of Eng. 73. — Morley, H. Eng. writ. **7** : 201. — Cooke, F. E. Three gt. lives. — Gibbins. Eng. soc. ref. 29. — Myers, F. Lec. gt. men, 172. — With portrait. (A. M. Sholl) Warner Lib. **18** : 10295. — Wordsworth, C. Eccles. biog. v. **2**. — Wrangham. Brit. Plutarch, v. 1.

— A characteristic of. Johnston, R. M. Stud. **2** : 44.

— Garden of. Hall, Mrs. S. C. Pilgr. Eng. shr. **2** : 114.

— Psychological character of. Disraeli, I. Amen. (N. Y. 4 v.) **1** : 331.

— Utopia. Adams, W. H. D. Famous books, 1. — Saunders, F. Famous books, 32. — Gibbins. Eng. soc. ref. 44. — Scudder, V. D. Soc. ideals, 46. — Tovey. Rev. & ess. 22.

— Wives of. Jeaffreson. Lawyers, 167.

Morecock, Edward. Ivimey. Eng. Bapt. **2** : 242.

Morell, Thomas. Hatfield, E. F. Poets of church, 449. — Jessie, J. H. Cel. Eton. v. 1. — Miller, Jos. Singers church, 2d ed. 370.

Morellet, Andrew. Haussonville. Salon of Necker, **1** : 127.

Morelli, Giovanni. (A. H. Layard) Morelli. Ital. paint. [1].

Morelos, Mex., Paludism in the state of. (A. Gavino) Am. Pub. Health, **22** : 224.

Morgagni, J. B. Pettigrew. Med. portr. gall. v. 1.

Morgan, Charles. Parton, J. Sk. of men of prog.

Morgan, Daniel. With portrait. [Amer.] Nat. portr. gall. v. **3**. — With portrait. Duyckinck. Nat. portr. gall. **1** : 272. — Headley, J. T. Washington, **2** : 366. — Lee, H. Memories, 579. — Lossing. Em. Amer. 222.

Morgan, Edwin D. With portrait. Stoddard, W. O. Men of bus. 111. — With portrait. Brockett. Men of our day, 371. — Parton, J. Sk. of men of prog. — Walker, C. D. Biog. Va. Mil. Inst. 390.

Morgan, Sir Henry. Pyle, H. Buccaneers, 131. — Whitehead. Highwaymen, **2** : 1.

Morgan, John H. Pollard. Life of Lee, 645. — Snow. So. Generals, 445.

Morgan, Mathew. Bell, R. Lit. & sci. men, **2** : 215.

Morgan, Nathan D., with portrait. (L. A. Hendrick) Rogers, A. C. Repres. men, 379.

Morgan, Lady Sydney Owenson. Adams, W. H. D. Wom. of fash. **1** : 265. — Chorley. Authors of Eng. 51. — Kavanagh. Eng. women, **2** : 285. — Redding. Pers. remin. **3** : 1. — Tartt. Ess. **2** : 148. — Thomson, K. Queens, 236. — Hall, S. C. Book of mem. 214. — Hamilton, C. J.

Women writers, 207. — Duyckinck. Portrait gall. **2** : 167. — Mayer, G. T. Wom. of lett. **2** : 115. — Smith, G. B. Women of renown, 321.

Morgan, William, bishop of St. Asaph. Parry. Cam. Plutarch, 318. — Tyerman. Oxf. Meth. 4.

Morgan, William H. Walker, C. D. Biog. Va. Mil. Inst. 392.

Moriarty, Ellen A. Raymond, I. Southland writ. **1** : 360.

Moriarty, Capt. Mortimer. Savage, J. Fenian heroes, 209.

Morier, James Justinian. Warner Lib. **18** : 10304.

Morier, Sir Robert. Em. persons, **6** : 74.

Mörike, Eduard, with portrait. Warner Lib. **18** : 10318.

Moriscan ballads. Bryant, W. C. Prose, v. 1.

Morison, Robert. Irving, D. Scot. writ. **2** : 177.

Moritz, Charles P. Brightwell. Byepaths of biog. 61.

Morland, George. Fairholt. Eng. artists, 58. — Thornbury. Brit. art. **2** : 142. — Wedmore. Studies, 2d ed. 25. — Wilson, H. Characters, 168.

Morley, George. Wesley & successors, 127.

Morley, John. Buchanan. Master-spirit, 110. — Davidson, J. M. Eng. lib. 169. — Hapgood, N. Lit. statesm. 19. — Smalley. Lond. lett. **1** : 199. — Stead. Char. sk. 39. — With portrait. Warner Lib. **18** : 10323.

Morley, Sir Robert. Edgar. Sea kings, 53.

Morley, Samuel. With portrait. Cochrane, R. Benef. lives, 160. — Hinton. Eng. radicals, 180. — Ritchie. Brit. sena. 218. — With photo. Cooper, T. Men of mark, **6** : 18.

Mormonism. (J. H. Anderson) Relig. systems, 657. — Bowles, S. Across cont. 79. — Bowles, S. Our new west, 207. — Chambers's Miscel. no. 14. — Codman, J. Round trip, 169. — Cook, J. Current perils, 188. — Cox, S. H. Interviews, 275. — Dilke. Greater Brit. 110. — Dixon, W. H. New America, 141. — Faithful, E. Three visits, 158. — Hardy, I. D. Thro' cities, 102. — Holst, H. von. Const. hist. **6** : 97. — Marshall, W. G. Thro' Amer. 146. — Pierrepont. Fifth ave. 17. — Prime, E. D. G. Around world, 25. — Rae. Westward, 98. — Strong, J. Our country, 59. — Todd, J. Sunset land, 162. — Dixon, W. H. White conquest, **1** : 182. — Thompson, H. M. Copy, 33.

— Educational cure of. (A. E. Winship) Nat. Educa. Assoc. '86 : 117.

Mormons. Brooks, J. Seven months, 10. — Prime, E. D. G. Around world, 25.

— in U. S.; J. Smith at Nauvoo. Quincy, J. Figures, 376.

— — Polygamy bill. McPherson. Handbk. pol. '82.

Morna. Montgomery, J. Prose, 1.

Mornay, Charlotte Arbaleste Du-Plessis, Mad. de, Memoirs of. Dempster. Ess. 115. — Yonge. Good. wom. **2** : 67.

Morning Post, London. Hatton. Jour. Lond. 240.

Morocco. Cust. Ling. studies, **3** : 555.

— Amer. trade opportunities in, 1891. (F. A. Mathews) U. S. Cons. Rept. **39** : 170.

— Bibliography. Meakin, B. Moorish empire.

— Commerce and industries of, 1891. (F. A. Mathews) U. S. Cons. Rept. **35** : 173.

— Historical survivals in. (T. Williams) Am. Hist. Assoc. **4** : 215.

— in 1890. Warner, C. D. Roundabout, 162.

Morot, Aimé. Child, T. Art & criticism, 56.

Morpeth, G. W. F. Howard, Lord. Francis, G.

H. Orators, 159. — Grant, J. Recoll. Ho. Comm. 217.

Morphology. Bibliography. Davenport, C. B. Experimental morphol.

— Physical. Hinton. Thinking, 319.

Morrill, Justin S. Johnston, A. Amer. ora. **4** : 296.

Morris, Ann E. Clement, J. Noble deeds, 311.

Morris, Capt. Arthur. Russell, W. Eccen. 262.

Morris, Clara. Matthews, B. Actors, **5** : 211. — (W. Holcomb) McKay, F. E. Fam. actors, 88. — Acting of. Winter, W. Shadows, **2** : 171.

Morris, Dick. Whitehead, C. Highwaymen, **1** : 189.

Morris, Dwight. Am. Bar Assoc. **18** : 497.

Morris, Eliza Fanny. Miller, Jos. Singers church, 2d ed. 557.

Morris, George P. Bungay. Off-hand, 43. — Griswold. Poets Am. 243. — Wallace, H. B. Lit. crit. 207. — Willis. Hurry-graphs, 253.

Morris, Gouverneur. Charles, P. Anglo-Amer. lit. 11. — With portrait. Duyckinck. Nat. portr. gall. **1** : 364. — Tuckerman. Ess. 412. — Lodge & Roosevelt. Hero-tales, 91. — Lodge, H. C. Hist. & pol. ess. — Lossing. Em. Amer. 202. — Moore, F. Am. eloq. **1** : 453. — Neven, D. R. B. Pennsylvanians, 209. — Perry, B. F. Biog. sketches, **1** : 428.

Morris, John Henry. Escott, T. H. S. Pillars emp. 214. — Laurie, W. F. B. Dist. Anglo-Ind. **2** : 73.

Morris, Lewis, 1702-65. Parry. Cam. Plutarch, 348.

Morris, Lewis, 1726-98. Dwight, N. Signers, 112. — Lossing. Signers, 44. — Sanderson. Signers, v. 9. — Lincoln, R. W. Signers, 48. — Field, R. S. Prov. courts N. J. 138.

Morris, Lewis. Songs of two worlds. Rees, J. R. With friend, 14.

Morris, Mrs. Margaret. Clement, J. Noble deeds, 316. — Ellet. Women of revol. **2** : 281.

Morris, Miss. Brockett. Woman's work, 496.

Morris, Robert. With portrait. [Amer.] Nat. portr. gall. v. **4**. — With portrait. Duyckinck. Nat. portr. gall. **1** : 240. — Hunt, F. Amer. merch. **2** : 595. — Dwight, N. Signers of decl. 147. — Lincoln, R. W. Signers, 49. — Lossing. Signers, 93. — Sanderson. Signers, v. **5**. — Lossing. Em. Amer. 90. — Neven, D. R. B. Pennsylvanians, 7. — Winslow, S. N. Biog. Phila. merch. 234.

— U. S. *versus.* Curtis, B. R. Mem. & writ. v. **2**.

Morris, Samuel D., with portrait. (W. L. Stone) Rogers, A. C. Repres. men, 385.

Morris, William. Austin, A. Poetry, 141. — Dawson, W. J. Mod. Eng. 363. — Forman. Liv. poets, 377. — Galton, A. Urbana, 132. — Pater. Appreciations, 213. — Sharp, A. Vic. poets, 157. — Stedman. Vic. poets, 366. — Bate, P. H. Eng. Pre-Raph. 79. — (H. B. Forman) Miles, A. H. Poets of cent. **6** : 1. — Saintsbury. Correc. imp. 178. — Scudder, V. D. Life of spirit, 274. — Symons, A. Stud. two lit. 150. — With portrait. (W. M. Payne) Warner Lib. **18** : 10337.

— Bibliography. (T. Scott) Vallance, A. Art of W. Morris. — Providence Pub. Lib. Bull. Dec. '96. — Salem (Mass.) Pub. Lib. Bull. Nov. '96.

— Life and death of Jason. Swinburne. Ess. 110.

— Story of Sigurd the Volsung. Hazeltine. Chats, 272. — Taylor, B. Crit. ess. 321.

Morris house, Germantown. Terhune. Colon. homes, 131.

Morrison, James. Famous boys, 262.

Morrison, John. Hatfield, E. F. Poets of church, 451. — Miller, Jos. Singers church, 2d ed. 300.

Morrison, Robert. Cust. Ling. & orient. ess. **4** : 550.

Morrison, William H. Woollen. Biog. sk. Indiana, 475.

Morscovius, Paul. Wallace, R. Anti-Trin. biog. **3** : 308.

Morscovius, Peter. Wallace, R. Anti-Trin. biog. **3** : 110.

Morse, Samuel F. B. Bolton, S. K. Fam. men of science, 202. — Bungay. Off-hand, 214. — Garfield. Works, **2** : 26. — Houghton. Kings, 377. — Howe, H. Adven. & achiev. 137. — McCabe. Great fortunes, 354. — With portr. Nicoll. Great move. 452. — Spalding, J. M. Miscellanea, **2** : 635. — Tuckerman. Artists, 163. — Tuckerman. Artist-life, 68. — Brooks, E. S. Hist. Amer. 305. — Duyckinck. Portrait gall. **2** : 363. — With portrait. Hubert, P. G., jr. Inventors, 111. — Jeans. Electricians, **1** : 231. — Munro, J. Heroes of Teleg. 45. — Thayer, W. M. Turn.-points, 194. — Youmans. Pioneers sci. 234.

— Address on statue of, 1871. Bryant. Orations, 361.

Morstinius, Andrew. Wallace, R. Anti-Trin. biog. **3** : 311.

Morstinius, Christopher. Wallace, R. Anti-Trin. biog. **2** : 426.

Morstinus, Faustus. Wallace, R. Anti-Trin. biog. **3** : 251.

Morstinus, Florian. Wallace, R. Anti-Trin. biog. **2** : 348.

Morstinus, John. Wallace, R. Anti-Trin. biog. **3** : 251.

Morstinus, Severin. Wallace, R. Anti-Trin. biog. **3** : 134.

Morstinus, Tobias. Wallace, R. Anti-Trin. biog. **3** : 310.

Morston, Little, A morning at. Croston. Hist. sites Lanc. 431.

Mortality, infant, Cause and prevention of. (E. Wende) Am. Pub. Health, **24** : 140.

— in U. S., Relations of race and nationality to. (F. A. Walker) Am. Pub. Health, **1** : 18.

— Influence of nationality upon. Bost. Health, '75 : 58.

Mortgages and foreclosure executions. N. J. Labor, '89 : 307.

— chattel, High rate of interest on. Kansas Labor, 1886.

— Farm, in Nebraska. Nebr. Labor, 1889.

— in foreign countries, 1889. U. S. Cons. Repts. nos. 110, 111.

— Occupational. N. J. Labor, '89 : 17, 167, 213.

— Real estate, in New Jersey. N. J. Labor, 1889.

— — in Russia, 1895. (R. H. D. Pierce) U. S. Cons. Rept. **49** : 410.

— Taxing. Hazard, T. R. Miscel. 144, 242.

Mortgage indebtedness in Illinois. Ill. Labor, 1888.

Mortier, Edouard Adolphe Casimir Joseph. Headley. Napoleon, **1** : 268.

Mortimer, Roger, Lord, favorite of Queen Isabella. Menzies, S. Roy. fav. **1** : 50.

Mortimer, Rev. Thomas. Grant, Jas. Metropol. pul. 232.

Morton, James Douglas, 4th earl of. Lodge. Portraits (Bohn), v. **2**.

Morton, John. Campbell. Ld. chan. **1** : 355. — Foss. Judges, 59. — Hook. Abps. Cant. **5** : 387. — Williams, R. F. Eng. Card. **2** : 152.

Morton, John, 1724-77. Dwight, N. Signers, 187. — Lincoln, R. W. Signers, 51. — Lossing.

Signers, 112. — Sanderson. Signers, v. **6.** — Neven, D. R. B. Pennsylvanians, 39.

Morton, Levi P., with portrait. Stoddard, W. O. Men. of bus. 94.

Morton, Nathaniel. New England's Memorial. Richardson. Amer. lit. **1** : 102.

Morton, Oliver Percy. With portrait. Brockett. Men of our day, 318. — With portrait. Woollen. Biog. sk. Indiana, 130.

Morton, Perez. Loring, J. S. Hundred Bost. ora. 127.

Morton, Samuel Geo. (S. B. Hunt) Gross. Lives physicians, 582.

Morton, Thomas, d. 1646, in Massachusetts. Adams, C. F. Three episodes, 1 : 162–343. — New England Canaan. Richardson. Amer. lit. 1 : 98.

Morton, Thomas, d. 1659. Fuller. Worthies, 8 : 465. — With portrait. Ollier, E. Brit. portr. paint. 74.

Morton, Dr. Wm. T. G. Bolton, S. K. Success, 195. — Cochrane, R. Benef. lives, 174.

Morton *vs.* Fenn. Erskine, T. Speeches, 84.

Morven, home of the Stocktons. Glenn, T. A. Colon. mans. 1 : 61. — Terhune, M. V. More colon. homes, 98.

Mosaic cosmogony, The. (C. W. Goodwin) Ess. & rev.

Mosaics. Woltmann & Woerman. · Hist. of painting, 1 : 165. — Florentine. Baxter, L. E. Tusc. stud. 110. — Manufactory of, at St. Petersburg. Atkinson, J. B. Art tour northern, 316. — Sketch of the history of. Parry, T. G. Min. of fine art, 114.

Mosarabic liturgy. Neale. Ess. liturgy.

Mosasaurus discovered. Adams, W. H. D. Fam. caves, 168.

Mosby, John S. Cooke, J. E. Wearing of the gray. — Wallace, F. T. Men & events, 119.

Moscheles, Felix, with portrait. Bie, O. Hist. of piano, 220.

Moscheles, Ignaz, German-Bohemian musician. Ferris, G. T. Great violinists, 196. — Keddie. Mus. comp. 354.

Moschion. Mills. Poets of Greece, 393.

Moschovius, John. Wallace, R. Anti-Trin. biog. 2 : 544.

Moschus. Arnold, E. Poets of Greece, 197. — Mills. Poets of Greece, 219. — Symonds. Greek poets, 2 : 247. — Warner Lib. **18** : 10360.

Moscow. Atkinson, J. B. Art tour northern, 357. — Brooks, E. S. Gt. cities, 58. — Curtis, W. E. Land of nihilist, 284. — Prime, S. I. Alhambra, 322. — Stoddard. Red letter, 161. — (A. Weir) Vaca. tourists, 2 : 1. — Wikoff, H. Reminis. 214. — French retreat from. Stanhope, P. H. French retreat.

Moscow. Kremlin. *See* Kremlin. — the magnificent. (W. Libbey, jr.) Am. Geog. Soc. **20** : 273.

Moscorovius, Andrew. Wallace, R. Anti-Trin. biog. **3** : 86.

Moscorovius, Jerome. Wallace, R. Anti-Trin. biog. 2 : 487.

Moselle, The. Bartley, G. C. D. Rhine, 270.

Moser, Mary. Clayton, E. C. Eng. fem. art. 1 : 295.

Moses. Geikie, C. Old Test. char. 93. — Headley, J. T. Sac. heroes, 85. — Hills, O. A. Compan. char. 50. — Lord, J. Beacon, 1 : 27. — Maurice. Patriarchs, 154. — Williams, H. L. Boys of Bible. 35. — Hundred greatest men,

118. — Wilberforce, S. Heroes Hebrew, 92. — Hahn-Hahn. Fathers, 231.

Moses, Greatness and influence of. (R. Gottheil) Barrows, J. H. Parl. relig. 1 : 673. — Historic personality of. (J. P. Thompson) Bost. lectures, '77 : 86.

Moses, Wm. Stainton. Lillie, A. Mod. mystics, 56. — Experiences of. (F. W. H. Myers) Soc. Psych. Res. **9** : 245. **11** : 24.

Mosheim, Johann Lorenz. Ker, J. Lec. hist. preach. 241.

Mosquito Coast, Nicaragua, Bibliography of. (C. De Kalb) Am. Geog. Soc. **26** : 241. — Language of. (W. D. Farrington) Am. Geog. Soc. **24** : 559. — Studies on. (C. De Kalb) Am. Geog. Soc. **25** : 236.

Mosquitoes ; De mosquitone. Guiney. Goosequill, 166.

Mossop, Henry. Fitzgerald, P. Rom. of stage, 228. — Matthews, B. Actors, 1 : 171.

Mote, Edward. Miller, Jos. Singers church, 2d ed. 448.

Mother Goose, Who was. Walsh, W. S. Paradox, 136. *See* Nursery rhymes.

Mother-right, Evidences of, in witchcraft customs. Pearson, K. Chances, 2 : 1.

Mothers, Duties of. Dodge, M. A. Gala, 267. — employment of, in factories, Infant mortality and. (W. C. Taylor *et al.*) Trans. Soc. Sci. Lond. **74** : 569. — (T. M. Dolan *et al.*) Trans. Soc. Sci. Lond. '82 : 357. — Modern. Linton, E. L. Girl of per. 1 : 10. — Responsibilities of. (Mrs. Sumner) Burdett-Coutts. Wom. miss. 65.

Motherwell, William. Deshler. Afternoons, 278. — (J. H. Ingram) Miles, A. H. Poets of cent. **3** : 185. — Mitford, M. R. Recollec. 540. — Stoddard, R. H. Under eve. lamp, 77. — With portrait. Warner Lib. **18** : 10365. — Wilson, J. G. Poets of Scot. 2 : 157.

Motion. Hunt, R. Poetry of sci. 7. — laws of, Galileo and. Morton, E. J. C. Heroes astron. 115.

Motive. Hazlitt. Sket. — in life, Effect of. Bulwer, E. Caxtoniana, 225.

Motley, John L. Anton. Masters in hist. — Fisher, M. Gen. sur. Am. lit. 276. — Lancaster, H. H. Ess. & rev. 141. — Nichol. Amer. lit. 150. — Whipple. Recol. 155. — Griswold. Prose writ. 642. — (O. W. Holmes) Mass. Hist. Proc. **16** : 404. — With portrait. (J. F. Jameson) Warner Lib. **18** : 10373. — Wright, H. C. Chil. sto. in Amer. lit. 174.

Mott, Alexander B. Francis. N. Y. surg. 105.

Mott, Lucretia. Bolton, S. K. Girls famous, 33. — With portrait. (M. Clemmer) Our fam. wom. 462. — With portrait. (E. C. Stanton) Parton. Em. wom. 371. — Hanaford. Wom. of cent. 150. — Holloway, L. C. Mothers of gt. men, 197.

Mott, Valentine. Francis. N. Y. surg. 13. — Gross, S. D. Autobiog. 2 : 308. — Parton. Peop. bk. biog. 227.

Motte, Rebecca. Ellet. Women of revol. 2 : 68. — Wister & Irwin. Women, 259. — Lossing. Em. Amer. 75.

Motte, Fort, Capture of. Dawson. Batt. of U. S. 1 : 689.

Mottey, Joseph. (D. Damon) Ware, W. Am. Unita. 1 : 193.

Mottoes and devices. Stirling-Maxwell. Miscel. ess. 201.

Moulton, John Carroll, with portrait. Sketches N. H. men, 114.

Moulton, Louise Chandler, with portrait. (H. P. Spofford) Our fam. wom. 498.

Moulton, William Fiddian. Wesley & successors, 257.

Moultrie, Gerard. Miller, Jos. Singers church, 2d ed. 583.

Moultrie, John. Griswold, R. W. Sac. poets. — Miles, A. H. Poets of cent. 10 : 745.

Moultrie, Mary Dunlap. Miller, Jos. Singers church, 2d ed. 584.

Moultrie, William. With portrait. [Amer.] Nat. portr. gall. v. 1. — With portrait. Duyckinck. Nat. portr. gall. 1 : 97. — With portrait. Headley, J. T. Washington, 2 : 78. — Lossing. Em. Amer. 262.

Mound-builders. (D. A. Robertson) Am. Geog. Soc. 5 : 256. — Chapin, J. H. Creation, 243. — Domenech. Seven years, 1 : 353. — Hubbard, B. Memo. of half cent. 199. — Joly, N. Man before metals, 166. — Lubbock, J. Prehistoric times, 250.
— of Michigan. Hubbard, B. Memorials, 201.
— Nationality of. Brinton. Ess. Amer. 67.
— Recently discov. relics of. (J. Campbell) Roy. Soc. Can. 2d. ser. 4, § 2 : 3.

Mounds, Ancient, in Clinton Co., Mich. (M. T. Leach) Smithson. Rept. '84:839.
— — in Illinois, and other States. (James Wickersham; J. P. MacLean) Smithson. Rept. '83: 825.
— burial, Aboriginal, in Ohio. (R. J. Thompson) Smithson. Rept. '92 : 571.
— of the Mississippi valley. (Lucien Carr) Smithson. Rept. '91 : 503.
— of Ohio, Iron from. (F. W. Putnam) Am. Antiq. Soc. Proc. n. s. 2 : 349.

Mounet-Sully. Henry, S. Hours w. Parisians, 169.

Mounsey, John. Redding. Misers, 2 : 58.

Mount, William S. Lanman, C. Haphazard, 168.

Mount Auburn cemetery. Drake, S. A. Hist. fields Mid. 326.
— and the burial of the dead. Bigelow, J. Mod. inq. 119.

Mount Carmel. Wilson, C. W. Pictur. Palest. 3 : 91.

Mount Desert. Drake. Nooks of N. E. 27.
— Sociological studies at. Eliot, C. W. Five Am. cont. 103.
— Geology of. (N. S. Shaler) U. S. Geol. Surv. Rept. '86–87.

Mount Edgcumbe. Jewitt, L. Stately homes, 1 : 54.

Mount Hermon and its temples. (S. B. Merrill) Wilson, C. W. Pictur. Palest. 2 : 121.

Mount Hoi and the cliffs of Edom. (Rogers) Wilson, C. W. Pictur. Palest. 3 : 217.

Mount Holyoke Seminary and College, South Hadley, Mass. (Sarah D. Stow) U. S. Bur. Ed. Circ. '91, no. 6 : 400. — (M. O. Nutting) Brackett, A. C. Educa. of girls, 318. — Pidgeon. Old world ques. 192.

Mt. Hope, R. I. Drake. Nooks of N. E. 407.

Mount Hor. Tweedie. Ruined cities, 32.

Mount Lebanon, N. Y. Pidgeon. Old world ques. 118.

Mount St. Mary's College, Emmitsburg, Md. (E. P. Allen) U. S. Bur. Ed. Circ. '94, no. 2 : 161.

Mt. Pleasant and the Macphersons. Glenn, T. A. Colon. mans. 2 ; 443.

Mount Vernon. Martineau. Retrosp. 1 : 311. — Silliman. Gallop, 12.

Mount Vernon and the Washingtons. Glenn, T. A. Colon. mans. 2 : 17.

Mountain, Col. Armine S. H. Rogers, C. Chr'n heroes, 94.

Mountain, T. (J. Strype) Wordsworth, C. Eccles. biog. v. 3.

Mountain combats. Fitchett. Deeds, 188.

Mountain flora. Allen, Gr. Science in Arc. 90.

Mountain form, Studies of. Ruskin. Miscel. v. 2.

Mountain whites of the South, The. (F. E. Jenkins) Evang. Alliance, '89 : 79.

Mountaineering, Episodes of. (E. L. Weeks) Wilson, E. L. Mt.-climbing, 65.

Mountains. Allen, Gr. Common-sense sci. 112. — Donnelly, I. Atlantis, 440. — Lanoye. Sublime, 49. — Ruskin. Mod. painters, v. 4.
— and history. (E. K. Alden) Am. Hist. Assoc. Rept. '94 : 519.
— and their origin. Agassiz. Geol. sk. 1 : 94.
— Japanese, In the. Arnold, E. Seas & l. 464.
— their origin, growth, and decay. Geikie, J. Frag. 36.
— Zach on the attraction of. Playfair, J. Works, v. 4.

Mountebanks, Wandering. Buckland, F. T. Curios. nat. hist. 4 : 71.

Mounteney, R. Jessie, J. H. Cel. Eton. v. 1.

Mountfort, William. Cook, D. Hours w. players, 1 : 2. — Galt. Players, 1 : 76.

Mourning worn for German emperor in London, 1888. Smalley. Lond. lett. 2 : 25.

Movement and mental status, Study of. (Francis Warner) Nat. Educa. Assoc. '93 : 750.

Moving. Dodge, M. A. Country, 3. — Howells. Sub. sk. 220.

Mowatt, Anna C. Matthews, B. Actors, 4 : 155.

Mowbray, Captain Philip. Russell, W. Eccen. 163.

Mowbray and Shelton-Place. (W. W. Smith) Charleston book, 375.

Mowlson (Lady) Scholarship at Cambridge. (A. McF. Davis) Am. Antiq. Soc. Proc. n. s. 8 : 274. — (W. W. Goodwin) Col. Soc. Mass. Trans. 1 : 158.

Moxom, Edward. Curwen. Booksellers, 347.
— Trial for blasphemy in publishing Shelley's works. Townsend, W. C. Mod. state trials, 2 : 363.

Moyle, Sir Thomas. Manning, J. A. Speakers, 191.

Mozambique, Province of, 1894. (W. S. Hollis) U. S. Cons. Rept. 46 : 163.

Mozart, W. A. Barnard, C. Tone-masters, 1 : 5. — Bourne, C. E. Gt. compos. 103. — Butterworth. Great compos. 50. — Crowest. Tone-poets, 139. — Edgar. Boyhood, 265. — Engel, L. Mozart, 1 : 254. — Ferris. Germ. composers, 94. — Hogarth. Mem. opera, 2 : 162. — Keddie. Mus. comp. 76. — Russell, W. Extraor. men, 116. — Upton, G. P. Stand. operas, 167. — With portrait. Bie, O. Hist. of piano, 151. — Bolton, S. K. Poor boys famous, 72. — Dole, N. H. Score, 175. — Hundred greatest men, 107. — With portrait. Elson, L. Gt. composers, 78. — Sharp, R. F. Makers of music. — Ossoli. Art, 243. — Parry, C. H. H. Gt. comp. — With portrait. Rowbotham. Priv. life compos. 33. — Statham. Music, 217.
— and Aloysia Weber. Hitchcock, T. Unhap. loves, 131.
— Centenary of. Krehbiel. Music & man, 115.
— Cherubini at the Scala theatre. Symonds, J. A. Ital. byways.

Mozart, W. A. Don Giovanni. Guerber. Stor. of operas, 84.

— — and the Requiem. Runciman, J. F. Old scores, 95.

— Letters of. Haweis. Music & mor. 263.

— Marriage of Figaro. Guerber. Stor. of operas, 211.

Mozley, Anne. Mozley, A. Ess. 7.

Mozley, James B., Biographical sketch of. Mozley. Ess. 1 : xi. — Davies, G. J. Suc. preach. 369.

Mucius Scævola. Malkin. Class. disq. 242.

Muckross Abbey. Silloway. Cathedral towns, 36.

Mud. Allen, Gr. Science in Arc. 123.

Mudge, Charles Redington. (J. T. Morse) Harvard mem. biog. 2 : 142.

Mudie, Chas. Edw., and the lending library. Curwen. Booksellers, 421. — Japp & Holmes. Succ. bus. men, 118.

Mueller, F. Max, with photo. Cooper, T. Men of mark, 3 : 23. — With portrait. (H. A. Stimson) Warner Lib. 18 : 10425.

— Chips from a German workshop. Cobbe, F. P. Darwinism, 235. — Whitney, W. D. Orient. 2 : 126.

Müller, Frederick Paludan. See Paludan-Müller, F.

Müller, Julius. Ker, J. Lec. hist. preach. 380.

Müller, Wilhelm. Müller. Chips, 3.

Müller, William J. Redgrave. Century of p. 2 : 450.

Mugeyer, Temple of. Tweedie. Ruined cities, 153.

Muggleton, Lodowick. Hain, J. Varia, 237. — Jessopp, A. Coming of friars, 302.

Muhlenberg, Gotthilf Heinrich Ernst. Youmans. Pioneers sci. 58.

Muhlenberg, Maj.-Gen. Peter. Lossing. Em. Amer. 210. — Neven, D. R. B. Pennsylvanians, 124.

Muhlenberg, Peter Gabriel. Headley, J. T. Chaplains Revol. 121.

Muhlenberg, William Augustus. Hatfield, E. F. Poets of church, 452. — Miller, Jos. Singers church, 2d ed. 465. — Scudder, H. E. Men & let. 106.

Muir, John, with portrait. Warner Lib. 18 : 10405.

Mulcaster, R. Quick. Educa. refor. 90.

Mulford, Elisha. Scudder, H. E. Men & let. 1. — Warner Lib. 18 : 10415.

Mulgrave, H. P. Phipps, Lord. Thornton. For. sec. v. 1.

Mullens, Mrs. Hannah Catherine, of Calcutta. Pitman, Mrs. Heroines mission. 81.

Mulliner, Abraham. Ivimey. Eng. Bapt. 2 : 393.

Muller. See Mueller.

Mullett, James. Proctor. Lawy. of N. Y. 84.

Mullins, Priscilla. Spofford, H. P. Three heroines, 15.

Mulready, William. Redgrave. Century of p. 2 : 213, 298.

Mulready exhibition at Kensington, 1864. Palgrave. Ess. on art, 125.

Mummies. Buckland, F. T. Curios. nat. hist. 4 : 40.

Munchin, St. Conyngham, D. P. Irish saints, 126.

Munday, Anthony. Minto, W. Eng. poets, 253. — Morley, H. Eng. writ. 9 : 154.

Mundella, Anthony John. Davidson, J. M. Eng. lib. 139. — Hinton. Eng. radicals, 121.

Munden, Joseph S. Matthews, B. Actors, 2 : 97. — Acting of. Lamb. Elia.

Munden, Joseph S., Autobiography of. Lamb. Elia.

Mumford, William. Griswold. Poets Am. 68.

Munich. Bellows. Old world, 1 : 123. — Fulton, C. C. Europe, 109. — Howe, J. W. Oak to olive, 275. — Guild. Over the ocean, 456. — Jameson. Visits, 1 : 111. — Taylor, B. Views, 271. — Warner, C. D. Saunterings, 96. — Brooks, E. S. Gt. cities, 125. — Child, T. Summ. holidays, 203. — Paladin. Glances, 251. — Temple, E. L. Old world, 1 : 65.

— Wiesbaden to. Haven, G. Pilgrim. 430.

Municipal affairs. Bibliography. Indiana State Lib. Bull. May 1, '98.

— Exclusion of partisan politics from. (G. E. Waring ; F. M. Loomis) Nat. Conf. City Govt. '96 : 267. '97 : 103.

Municipal control of heat, light, etc. (A. Jacobson and others) Sunset club echoes, 103.

— State boards of. (F. W. Holls) Nat. Conf. City Govt. '96 : 226.

Municipal corporations, Powers of. (F. J. Goodnow) Nat. Conf. City Govt. '97 : 63.

— Proposed act. Nat. Conf. City Govt. '98 : 25.

Municipal franchises. (C. Richardson) Nat. Conf. City Govt. '98 : 94.

— Public control of. (H. S. Pingree) Nat. Conf. City Govt. '96 : 216.

— Rela. of a municipality to corporations enjoying. (W. M. Salter) Nat. Conf. City Govt. '96 : 219.

Municipal government. Bibliography. Lowell. City Lib. Bull. Feb. '97. — (F. H. Hodder) Kansas Univ. Quar. Apr. '93, 1 : 179. — Nat. Conf. City Govt. '94. — (R. C. Brooks) Municip. affairs, v. 1. — San Francisco Mech. Inst. Lib. Bull. July, '97. — Providence Pub. Lib. Bull. Feb. '95, Nov. '96. — Wilcox, D. F. Stud. city govt.

— English. Bibliography. (M. R. Maltbie) Colum. Univ. Stud. 9 : no. 1.

— Place of Council and Mayor in. (F. J. Goodnow) Nat. Conf. City Govt. '98 : 71.

See Cities.

Municipal history, English, Study of. (C. Gross) Am. Hist. Assoc. 5 : 379.

Municipal Leagues and Good Government clubs. (H. Welsh) Nat. Conf. City Govt. 2-3 : 146.

Municipal monopolies. Commons, J. R. Soc. reform, 123.

Municipal ownership. (F. M. Loomis) Nat. Conf. City Govt. '96 : 207.

Municipal politics, Business man in. (F. MacVeagh) Nat. Conf. City Govt. '97 : 133.

Municipal reform. Bryant. Prose, 2 : 294.

— and the churches. (T. N. Strong) Nat. Conf. City Govt., '97 : 261.

— Closing work of 19th cent. (S. B. Capen) Nat. Conf. City Govt. '98 : 116.

— Commercial organizations and. (R. Ritchie) Nat. Conf. City Govt. '97 : 118.

— during '96-97. (C. R. Woodruff) Nat. Conf. City Govt. '97 : 45.

— in U. S., Advance of. (C. R. Woodruff) Nat. Conf. City Govt. '98 : 101.

Municipal voters. (C. Richardson) Nat. Conf. City Govt. '97 : 356.

Munkacsy, Michael. Child, T. Art & criticism, 155.

Munroe family, The. Muzzey, A. B. Prime movers, 130.

Munsell, Mrs. Jane R. Brockett. Woman's work, 522.

Munson, L. Drake, S. G. Trag. of wilderness, 352.

Giles, H. Lectures, **2** : 235. — Helmholtz. Pop. lec. 61. — Smith, Adam. Ess. phil. 179. — Tuckerman. Optimist, 60. — Véron. Æsthetics. — Thomson, E. Essays, 363. — (J. S. Dwight) Peabody, E. P. Æsthetic pap. 25.

Music and law. Elson. Realm of music, 58.
— and medicine. Elson. Realm of music, 123.
— and morals. Finck. Chopin, 141.
— and musicians. Jameson. Studies.
— — Grove's Dictionary of. Hueffer. Ital. stud. 126.
— and music study, Influence on character. (A. J. Gantvoort) Nat. Educa. Assoc. '98 : 390.
— and science. Apthorp. Musicians, 361.
— Art form of. Lanier. Music, 1.
— as an art, Modern churches and. Ritter. Music in Eng. 146.
— as a branch of school education. (D. B. Hagar) Nat. Educa. Assoc. '85 : 369.
— as a means of discipline and culture. (G. C. Young) Nat. Educa. Assoc. '92 : 515.
— Bibliography. Lavignac, A. Music and musicians. — Phila. Drexel Inst. Lib. Ref. List, no. 2. — Phila. Mercan. Lib. Bull. Apr. '94. — Providence Pub. Lib. Bull. Apr. '95, pt. 2. — Springfield (Mass.) Pub. Lib. Bull. Apr., May, '95. — Waltham (Mass.) Pub. Lib. Bull. Mar.-Apr. '96.
— Choral. Davis, L. S. Stud. mis. 45.
— Church. Wordsworth, C. Miscel. **2** : 229.
— — American. Mathews, W. S. B. Hundred years music, **7**.
— — and other parochials. Eagles. Ess. v. **1**.
— — A crisis in. Gurney. Tertium, **2** : 47.
— Color and thought in. Davis, L. S. Stud. mus. 103.
— Course of, for county institutes. (K. E. Stone) Nat. Educa. Assoc. '99 : 994.
— Different schools of. Goldsmith. Miscel. (N. Y. 4 v.) **1** : 183.
— Elementary, in public schools. (J. H. Elwood) Nat. Educa. Assoc. '88 : 651.
— — Teaching of. (W. F. Heath ; Mrs. M. E. Brand) Nat. Educa. Assoc. '88 : 637.
— emotion, and morals. (H. R. Haweis) Barrows, J. H. Parl. relig. **2** : 547.
— a factor in education. (Margaret Morris) Nat. Educa. Assoc. '90 : 815.
— Foreign schools of. Hueffer. Mus. stud. 68.
— Form and design in. Statham. Music, 1.
— Form in. Sully. Sensation and intuition.
— Function of; Cherubini at the Scala theatre. Symonds. Ital. byways.
— Good, makes good citizens. (F. Damrosch) Nat. Educa. Assoc. '96 : 722.
— Growth of, among the people. (E. O. Silver) Nat. Educa. Assoc. '91 : 813.
— harmony in, Physiolog. causes of. Helmholtz. Pop. lec. **1** : 61.
— Hebrew. Ewald. Comm. on Psalms, **2** : 328.
— How pupils learn to know and do in. (C. H. Congdon) Nat. Educa. Assoc. '95 : 778.
— Hungarian gipsy. Baddeley. Travel tide, 257.
— Imitative powers of. Hayward, A. Ess. **2** : 211.
— in ancient Greece. Mahaffy. Rambles Greece, 282.
— in the Calvinist church. Ritter. Music in Eng. 104.
— in education. (Emma A. Thomas) Nat. Educa. Assoc. '96 : 737.
— in England. Haweis. Music & mor. 409.
— in German schools. Bibliography. U. S. Bur. Educa. Rept. '95-96, **1** : 188.
— in the Lutheran church. Ritter. Music in Eng. 96.

Music in the new education. (D. M. Kelsey) Nat. Educa. Assoc. '94 : 928.
— in New England. Winthrop. Addresses, **2** : 225.
— in normal schools. (G. B. Loomis) Nat. Educa. Assoc. '70 : 65.
— in primary grades. (B. Jepson) Nat. Educa. Assoc. '85 : 384. — (W. G. McNaught) Internat. health exh. **13** : 417.
— in the public schools. Bryant. Orations, 283 ; or Prose, **2** : 203. — U. S. Bur. Educa. Circ. '86, no. 1. — (W. H. Dana) Nat. Educa. Assoc. '89 : 680. — (A. J. Gantvoort) Nat. Educa. Assoc. '92 : 524. — (H. Griggs) Nat. Educa. Assoc. '99 : 977. — (P. C. Hayden ; B. Jepson) Nat. Educa. Assoc. '92 : 530. — (O. E. McFadon) Nat. Educa. Assoc. '89 : 695. — (J. Mischka) Nat. Educa. Assoc. '96 : 730. — (T. J. Morgan) Nat. Educa. Assoc. '87 : 615. — (N. C. Stewart) Nat. Educa. Assoc. '89 : 668. '94 : 953.
— — Condition of. (E. O. Silver) Nat. Educa. Assoc. '89 : 684.
— — Influence of school superintendents in. (L. W. Day) Nat. Educa. Assoc. '88 : 658.
— — Teaching of. (E. W. Howson) Thirteen ess. educa.
— in the Roman Catholic Church. Ritter. Music in Eng. 84.
— in school. (Mari R. Hofer and others) Nat. Educa. Assoc. '98 : 833.
— in schools. (E. Mooney) Internat. health exh. **13** : 439.
— — Class-teaching. (W. A. Barrett) Internat. health exh. **13** : 400.
— in theatres and al fresco. Kingston, W. B. Music & manners, **1** : 272.
— Influence of. Two voices. Guiney. Goosequill, 148.
— Instruction in, in elementary schools. (J. Stainer) Internat. health exh. **13** : 394.
— — in kindergartens, primary and normal schools. (A. Larda) Internat. health exh. **13** : 467.
— Is it the type or measure of all art ? Symonds. Ess. **2** : 181.
— Italian and German styles of. Finck. Chopin, 183.
— Jewish, Spirit of. Davis, L. S. Stud. mus. 10.
— Legends of. Elson. Realm of music, 106.
— Magic of. Saunders. Mosaics, 302.
— a means of social elevation. Gurney. Tertium quid, **2** : 96.
— Medical. Disraeli, I. Curios. (N. Y. 4 v.) **1** : 358.
— Methods in teaching. (H. E. Holt) Nat. Educa. Assoc. '84 : 213.
— Ministry of. Potter, H. C. Scholar & state, 217.
— modern, Origin of. Symonds. Renais. Cath. reac. **2** : 315.
— Mystery of. Saunders. Stray leaves, 95.
— National education in. (Sir R. Stewart) Trans. Soc. Sci. Lond. '81 : 821.
— or the tone poetry. Cheney. Golden guess, 213.
— Organ. Davis, L. S. Stud. mus. 59.
— Philosophy of. Mazzini. Life, etc. **4** : 1.
— Physics of. Lanier. Music, 47.
— Popular cultivation of. Chambers's Papers, no. 7. — Ritter. Music in Amer. 385.
— Power of. Whiting, C. G. Saunterer, 277.
— — Poetical treatment of. Bain. On teaching English, 179.
— Progress of, during last thirty years. (C. Hallé) Trans. Soc. Sci. Lond. '79 : 768.

Music, Prosaic and poetic. Paget, V. Juvenilia. 1 : 149.
— Province of, in education. (W. A. Mowry) Nat. Educa. Assoc. '89 : 674.
— Psychology of. Gurney. Tertium, 2 : 251.
— Reformers in. Elson. Realm of music, 1.
— Religion and. (W. S. Pratt) Barrows, J. H. Parl. relig. 2 : 1005.
— Religious. Bushnell. Work, 440.
— Rise of. Keddie. Mus. comp. v. 1.
— Sacred. Cutts, E. L. Scenes mid. ages, 284.
— — Bibliography. (H. T. Henry) Am. Eccles. Rev. May, '95.
— — What is? Maitland, S. R. Eight ess. 34.
— school of, What constitutes a. (H. G. B. Hunt) Trans. Soc. Sci. Lond. '83 : 618.
— Standard of. Davis, L. S. Stud. mus. 1.
— Study of. (E. D. Cheney) Brackett, A. C. Educa. of girls, 139.
— — Against superficial. Craik, D. M. Plain speaking, 53.
— — in public schools, Purpose of. (F. Treudley) Nat. Educa. Assoc. '95 : 771.
— — in relation to mental development. (S. H. Preston) Nat. Educa. Assoc. '91 : 824.
— Teachers and taught. Davis, L. S. Stud. mus. 121.
— Teaching of. Mathews, W. S. B. Hundred years music, 536. — (A. T. Cringan) Nat. Educa. Assoc. '91 : 820.
— — and the public. Ehlert. Tone world, 117.
— — in German schools. U. S. Bur. Ed. Rept. '95-96, 1 : 187.
— Vocal, in public schools. (F. E. Chapman) Nat. Educa. Assoc. '94 : 939. — (H. Mann) Mass. Educa. Rept. 8 : 117. — (I. O. Best) N. Y. Regents, 90 : 584.
— Vocal, a necessary branch of education. Spark, W. Mus. mem. 411.
Music Hall, Boston. Curtis. From easy chair, 3 : 151.
Musical æsthetics, Historical summary of opinions on. Ritter. Mus. in Eng. 153.
Musical art, Decline of, under Puritan rule. Ritter. Music in Eng. 44.
Musical audiences. Kingston, W. B. Music & manners, 1 : 324.
Musical composers; how they work. Finck. Chopin, 59.
Musical conductors. Elson. Realm of music, 293.
— Letters on. Spark, W. Mus. mem. 371.
Musical conventions. Ritter. Music in Amer. 254.
Musical criticism. Apthorp. Musicians, 289. — Hueffer. Ital. stud. 213.
Musical development in the U. S. Ritter. Music in Amer. 342.
Musical education. Mathews, W. S. B. Hundred years music, 449.
— Bibliography. Eastman, E. V. Mus. educa. & art.
Musical festivals, The great. Mathews, W. S. B. Hundred years music, 306.
Musical humbugs. Elson. Realm of music, 200.
Musical instruction in public schools : what it should be. (N. C. Stewart) Nat. Educa. Assoc. '86 : 580.
— by the average teacher. (Sarah L. Dunning) Nat. Educa. Assoc. '86 : 574.
Musical instruments and their epochs. Elson. Realm of music, 163.
— and the music trade. Mathews, W. S. B. Hundred years music, 325.
Musical life in Italy in 18th cent. Paget, V. Study of 18th cent. 65.

Musical masterpieces, Fatal. Elson. Realm of music, 262.
Musical notation, Development of. Elson. Realm of music, 71.
— Learning to read. (C. H. Greene) Cong. Educa. Chic. '93, 510.
Musical novels. Elson. Realm of music. 244.
Musical romanticists, A study in. Paget, V. Belcaro, 106.
Musical societies and the oratorio in American cities. Ritter. Music in Amer. 112, 210, 263, 306.
Musician, The caste of. Elson. Realm of music, 209.
Musicians and amateurs. Apthorp. Musicians, 3.
— Bibliography. Bailey, A. L. Bibliog. of musicians.
— Fortunes of. Elson. Realm of music, 144.
— Manuscripts of. Elson. Realm of music, 260.
— Royal. Elson. Realm of music, 135.
— Wives of. Elson. Realm of music, 171.
Muskrat of Florida. (F. W. True) U. S. Nat. Mus. Rept. '84 : 325.
Musseeh, Abdool. Pierce, B. K. Em. dead, 335.
Musser, William. Winslow, S. N. Biog. Phila. merch. 39.
Musset, Alfred de. Harrison, J. A. Group of poets, 283. — Pellissier. Lit. move. Fr. 191. — Ste.-Beuve. Port. of men, 23. — With portrait. (A. Fortier) Warner Lib. 18 : 10487. — (P. E. de Musset) Gautier. Fam. Fr. au. 102. — James, H. French poets, 1. — (F. T. Palgrave) Oxf. ess. '55 : 80.
— and Heine. Buchanan, R. Poet's sk. book, 152; or Master-spir. 54.
— and Tennyson. Swinburne. Miscel. 219. — Trent. Authority, 269.
— Bibliography. Kuhns, L. O. (ed.). Alfred de Musset, poetry & comedies.
— " Lui et elle." Du Camp. Recol. 2 : 245.
— Poetry of. Hallard, J. H. Gallica, 95.
Mussey, Reuben D. Am. Bar Assoc. 15 : 431. — (S. D. Gross) Gross, S. D. Autobiog. 2 : 312.
Mustagh pass. Younghusband. Heart of cont. 188.
Mutabilities of life. Bushnell. Moral uses, 319.
Mutability. Montgomery, J. Prose, 1 : 272.
Mutations. Russell, A. P. Lit. notes, 214.
Mutiny of the Bounty. Chambers's Miscel. no. 122. See Bounty.
Mutual Benefit Societies, Fraternal. Conn. Bur. Lab. '91 : 61.
Myanoshita, Japan. Pidgeon. Engineer's holiday, 278.
Mycenæ. Gardner, P. New chap. Gr. hist. — Knox, T. W. Underground, 221. — Mahaffy. Rambles, 402.
— Acropolis of. Freeman. Studies Greece, 122.
— Excavations at, 1876-88. Diehl, C. Excursions, 2.
— Schliemann's discoveries at. Newton. Essays, 246.
— to Corinth. Freeman. Studies. Greece, 162.
— Treasuries and treasures of. Freeman. Studies Greece, 140.
Myddleton, Sir Hugh (1555-1631). Smiles. Engin. 1 : 85.
Myddletons and the Middletons of London, 1560-1631. Bourne, H. R. F. Eng. merch. 1 : 230.
Myers, Frederick William Henry. Warner Lib. 18 : 10511.
Mylne, James. McCosh. Scot. philos. 364.
Mylne, Robert. Walker, W., jr. Men of sci. 90.

Mynheer on his travels. Wraxall, C. F. L. Historic bye-ways, 1 : 313.

Myopia. (A. A. Foucher and others) Am. Pub. Health Assoc. 20 : 290.

Myslicius, Paul. Wallace, R. Anti-Trin. biog. 3 : 140.

Mysore, War in. Adams, W. H. D. Engl. at war, 1 : 223.

Mysteries. Lennox, W. P. Plays, 1 : 4. — Ward, A. W. Eng. dram. 1 : 18.

— Ancient. Duruy. Hist. of Greece, 2 : 351. — Heckethorn. Sec. soc. 1 : 47.

— and miracle plays in Italy. Symonds. Renais. It. lit. 1 : 311.

— Miracle plays. Moral plays. Dunham, S. A. Em. liter. men, 1 : 192.

Mysteries, On. Baring-Gould. Mod. diff. 22. — Hopkins, M. Miscel. ess. 9.

Mystery of Amaganset, The. Prime, W. C. I go a-fishing, 335.

Mystic, The, and the Puritan. Williams, W. R. Eras, 252.

— Evolution of a. Peck, H. T. Pers. equ. 135.

— history. Wyatt, W. J. Hunga. celeb. 3.

Mysticism. Cousin. True, beautiful, and good. — Lea. Chap. from relig. hist. of Spain. — (W. S. Lilly) Relig. systems, 631.

— Christian. Oxenham. Short stud. 359.

— German. Ueberweg. Hist. philos. 1 : 467.

— in all religions. Clarke, J. F. Events, 275.

— in Germany before the Reformation. Ullman. Reformers, 185.

— in Spain. Lea. Chap. relig. hist. Spain, 213.

— modern, Modern science and. Scoffern. Stray leaves, 274.

— Parodies of. Nordau. Degen. 214.

— Psychology of. Nordau. Degen. 45.

Mystics. Heckethorn. Sec. soc. 2 : 1. — Ullman. Reformers, 2 : 7. — Winkworth. Chr. singers Germ. 289.

— and illuminati. Lea. Rel. hist. Spain, 213.

— German. Trench. Lec. mediæval, 352.

— Preaching of the. Ker, J. Lec. hist. preach. 125.

— Vaughan's Hours with. Kingsley. Raleigh, 155; or Lit. lec. 299.

Myth. Chambers's Papers, no. 5.

— Algonkin, of Michabo. Brinton. Amer. hero-myths, 37.

— among the Hebrews. Clodd, E. Myths, 131.

— and ceremony, connec. between. (W. Matthews) Cong. Anthrop. Chic. '93, 246.

— Birth and growth of. Clodd, E. Myths, 3.

— in history, Survival of. Clodd, E. Myths, 114.

— Iroquois, of Ioskeha. Brinton. Amer. hero-myths, 53.

— of the four brothers. Brinton. Amer. hero-myths, 44, 73, 178.

— Origin and development of. Brinton. American, 20.

— Solar theory of. Clodd, E. Myths, 61.

Myth-hunting. Powell, G. H. Excurs. in Libr. 77.

Myth-making, Modern. Zangwill. Without prej. 131.

Mythological rites and mysteries. Chambers's Papers, no. 73.

Mythologies. Keary, C. F. Dawn of history, 254.

Mythology, Algonkian. Brinton. Ess. Amer. 130.

— Aryan, Cox's. Whitney, W. D. Orient. 2 : 149.

— Celtic. Rhys. Celtic heathendom.

— Classical. Bibliography. D'Ooge, B. L. Helps to study of class. mythol.

Mythology, Comparative. Lang. Lett. to dead au. 164. — Müller, M. Chips, 2. — Müller, M. Sel. ess. 1 : 299. — (Max Müller) Oxf. ess. '56 : 1. — Renan. Studies (N. Y.), 2 : 49.

— — of Egyptians, Aryans, and Aztecs. Brinton. Ess. Amer. 135.

— German. Keary. Vikings, 29.

— Greek. Müller. Chips, 2. — Müller, M. Sel. ess. 1 : 425. — Symonds. Greek poets, 1 : 51.

— heathen, Poetical uses of. Coleridge, H. Ess. 1 : 18.

— — Popular view of. Hunt. Day by fire, 47.

— Hottentot. Lang. Custom, 197.

— in English poetry. Bowd. Coll. Lib. Bull. no. 1.

— Norse. Budd, H. St. Mary's Hall lec. 72.

— Philosophy of. Müller. Chips, 5; or Sel. ess. 1 : 577.

— Value of, to modern art. Symonds. Ess. spec. 2 : 126.

— Scandinavian. Carlyle. Heroes.

Myths and allegories, Nature. Symonds. Ess. 2 : 126.

— and folk-lore of the Aryan peoples. (W. Sharp and E. Rhys) Warner Lib. 18 : 10522.

— The descent of fire. Fiske. Myths, 37.

— Divine, in India. Lyall. Asia, 30.

— A far-traveled tale. Lang. Custom, 87.

— Greek, Recent treatment of. Mahaffy. Prob. Gr. hist. 28.

— Light and darkness. Brinton. Amer. hero-myths, 64. — Fiske. Myths, 104.

— mediæval, Triad of. Scoffern. Stray leaves, 342.

— Nature. Clodd, E. Myths, 19.

— — in nursery rhymes. (T. Foster) Proctor, R. A. Leis. read. 231.

— of American Indians. Brinton. American, 37.

— of the barbaric world. Fiske. Myths, 141.

— of Plato. Westcott. Ess. relig. thought, 1.

— of the Quiches of Guatemala. Brinton. Ess. Amer. 104.

— popular, Interpretation of, with reference to Gk. mythology. Blackie, J. S. Horæ Helen. 167.

— Star. Lang. Custom, 121.

Mytton, John, of Halston. Burke, B. Viciss. of fam. 2 : 112.

Naaman the Syrian. Geikie, C. Old Test. char. 341.

— Story of, and its lesson. Manning, J. M. Sermons, 340.

Nablus. (G. Grove) Vaca. tourists, 2 : 337.

Nachez, Tivadar, with portrait. Buffen. Mus. celeb. 2 : 91.

Nachmanides. Schechter, S. Stud. Jud. 120.

Næranus, John. Wallace, R. Anti-Trin. biog. 3 : 139.

Næranus, Samuel. Wallace, R. Anti-Trin. biog. 3 : 71.

Nævius, Cneius. Dunlop, J. Rom. liter. 1 : 69.

Nævius, Gnæus. Sellar. Rom. poets repub. 52.

Nagas, The. Richards, W. Heroes, 197.

Nagasaki, Japan. Pidgeon. Engineer's holiday, 309.

Nagle, I. E. Davidson, J. W. Writ. of South, 399.

Nahant. Curtis, G. W. Lotus, 145. — Martineau. Retrosp. 3 : 140.

Naharro, B. de T. Ticknor. Span. lit. 1 : 295.

Nairne, Caroline Oliphant, Baroness. Fifty famous women, 307. — Hamilton, C. J. Women writers, 132. — Keddie. Songstresses, 2 : 108. — Robertson. Eng. poetesses, 162. — Wilson, J. G. Poets of Scot. 1 : 427. — (M. Bell) Miles,

A. H. Poets of cent. **7** : 17. — (T. Davidson)
Warner Lib. **18** : 10543.

Nairne, Caroline Oliphant, baroness, and her
songs. Williams, A. M. Stud. folk, 102.

— and Lady Wardlaw. Masson. Edinb. sketches,
110.

Nairs. Reclus. Prim. folk, 143.

Name, Cheapening one's. Curtis. From easy
chair, **3** : 214.

— Influence of a. Disraeli, I. Curios. (N. Y. 4 v.)
2 : 228.

Names. Peck, H. T. Good English, 91.

— and nicknames. Northcote. Lec. & ess. 286.

— and things, Barbaric confusion between. Clodd,
E. Myths, 154.

— Christian, Sterne's theory of. Ferrier. Ill. of
Sterne, **2** : 30.

— Geographic. Field, D. D. Speeches, **3** : 352.

— Influence of. Zangwill. Without prej. 219.

— of places in America. Irving. Biog. 440.

— of towns and cities in the U. S. (D. D. Field)
Am. Geog. Soc. **17** : 1.

— proper, Notes on. Saunders. Pastime, 1.

Nanak, Baba. Cust. Pic. Indian, 194.

Nancy's tryste, a reminiscence of Deeside.
Skelton, J. Ess. in romance, 257.

Nansen, Fridtjof, with portrait. Warner Lib.
18 : 10555.

— Expedition across Greenland, Scientific results
of. Geikie, J. Frag. 382.

— First crossing of Greenland. Montefiore, A.
Leaders, 271.

Nantasket, Mass., Settlement of. Adams, C. F.
Three episodes, **1** : 183.

Nantes. James, H. Little tour, 101.

— Edict of, Revocation of. Ker. Scot. national,
36.

Nantucket, Mass. Drake. Nooks of N. E. 324.

— Gov. Lincoln's visit to, in 1825. Quincy, J.
Figures, 174.

Naoel, St. Conyngham, D. P. Irish saints, 218.

Napier, Sir Charles James. Adams, W. H. D.
Em. soldiers, 245. — Foster, E. Heroes Ind.
emp. 126. — Ritchie. Brit. sena. 399. — Skelton. Impeach. of Mary, 259. — Skelton. Ess.
272. — Smiles. Self-help.

Napier, F., Lord. With photo. Cooper, T. Men
of mark, **3** : 25. — Escott, T. H. S. Pillars emp.
221.

Napier, John, inventor of logarithms. Craik.
Pursuit knowl. **2** : 43.

Napier, Macvey, and the Edinburgh Review.
Morley, J. Stud. in lit. 286.

Napier of Magdala, Robert C. Escott, T. H. S.
Pillars emp. 228. — Napier, Lord. Em. persons, **4** : 222.

— at the convent, Gibraltar. Yates, E. H. Celeb.
3 : 237.

Napier, Sir William F. P. Martineau, H. Biog.
sk. 193. — Redding. Pers. remin. **3** : 152.

Napiers, The. Lucas. Mornings, **2** : 258. —
Reed, W. B. Among books, 146.

Naples. Arnold, R. A. Levant, **1** : 1. — Bellows.
Old world, **2** : 58. — Benjamin, S. G. W.
World's paradises, 69. — Field, H. M. Killar-
ney, 272. — Fulton, C. C. Europe, 192. —
Hare. Cities of So. Italy, 81. — Howe, J. W.
Oak to olive, 80. — Howells. Ital. Jour. 75.
— Peabody, A. P. Rem. Eur. 174. — Taine.
Italy, **1** : 22. — Tuckerman. Ital. sk. 135. —
Child, T. Summ. holidays, 110. — Moulton, L.
L. Lazy tours, 49. — Sala. Journey south, 321.
— Pfirshing. Mem. Ital. 91.

— and Garibaldi. (W. G. Clark) Vaca. tourists,
1 : 1.

Naples, Campo Santo of. Arnold, H. P. Eur.
mosaic, 303.

— Caverns of. Knox, T. W. Underground, 205.

— during the renaissance. Symonds. Reviv. of
learn. 251.

— in revolution, 1820. Thayer, W. R. Dawn Ital.
1 : 215.

— Municipal government in. Shaw, A. Munic.
govt. Eur. 282.

— Paintings and sculpture in. Taine. Italy, **1** : 53.

— Poor in. (J. W. V. Mario) Woods, R. A. Poor,
300.

— Sieges of. Robson, W. Sieges, 357.

— Social state of. Taine. Italy, **1** : 65.

— State prosecution in, 1851–52. Gladstone.
Glean. **4** : 1, 45, 71.

— J. de Valdés in. Stoughton. Ital. reformers, 103.

Napoleon I. Alison. Ess. 2. — Bayne, P. Ess.
2 : 181. — Brougham. Works, **5** : 260. — Car-
lyle. Heroes. — Channing. Works, **1** : 69. —
Cormenin. Orators, 66. — Edgar. Boyhood,
246. — Emerson. Rep. men, 219. — Farmer,
L. H. Boys' book fam. rulers, 433. — Gilfillan.
Third gall. 38. — Headley. Napoleon, **1** : 9. —
Lord, J. Beacon, **4** : 411. — Nolan. Liber. of
Ita. 423. — Russell, W. Extraor. men, 195. —
Smith, G. B. Ambass. 197. — Wilson, J. G.
Illus. sol. 353. — Duyckinck. Portrait gall. **1** :
344. — (L. A. Thiers) Ferris, G. T. Gt. leaders, 423. — Gurney, J. H. Hist. sketches, **3** :
80. — Hundred greatest men, 445. — Mombert. Great lives, 253. — Wilson, J. Stud. mod.
mind. — Morris, W. O. Commanders, 102.

— and his marshals, Headley's. Ossoli. Life
without, 110.

— and Washington. Lieber, F. Reminis. 413.

— as a general. Dodge, T. A. Great. capt. 178.

— as subject of caricature. Everitt, G. Eng.
carica. 12.

— at St. Domingo. Adams, H. Hist. ess. 122.

— at St. Helena. Loomis, E. J. Eclipse party,
130. — Seaton, R. C. Sir Hudson Lowe & Napoleon.

— Bibliography. Providence Pub. Lib. Bull. Apr.
'95. — Bibliography. Sloane, W. J. N. Life
Napoleon Bona.

— the Bourbons, etc., Chateaubriand's. Jeffrey, F.
Contrib. Ed. Rev.

— Campaign in Poland, 1806. Baring, E. Staff-
coll. ess. 145.

— Campaign of 1815. Adams, W. H. D. Eng. at
war, **2** : 1.

— Character of. Croly. Hist. sket. 338. — Haven,
N. A. Remains, 86. — Mathews, W. Men, p.
& t. 1.

— Concordat with Pope Pius VII. (C. L. Wells)
Am. Hist. Assoc. Rept. '**95** : 469.

— Correspondence of. Parton. Topics, 316.

— Corsican traits of. Bryant. Prose, **2** : 370.

— Court of. Pearson, C. H. Reviews, 239.

— Lanfrey's Life of. Hayward, A. Ess. 3d ser.
194.

— the man of destiny. Wallace, S. E. Storied sea,
21.

— Memoirs of. Curran. Irish bar, **2** : 184.

— Mother of. Ellis, Mrs. S. S. Mothers. —
Mothers of great men, 348.

— Refusal of England to negotiate with, 1800.
(W. Pitt ; C. J. Fox) Adams, C. K. Rep. Brit.
orat. **2** : 19, 108.

— Remains of. Miller, H. Hist. ess. 34.

— Russian campaign. Chambers's Miscel. no. 97.

— Russian and German campaigns, 1806–13. Ellesmere. Ess. 394.

— The sin of. Baur. Relig. life Germ. **2** : 1.

Napoleon I., Surrender of. Archer. Decis. ev. 160.
— Was civil liberty in Europe promoted by? Hadley, J. Ess. 356.
— Duke of Wellington and. Dawson, G. Biog. ess. 534.
Napoleon II., the Forlorn. Brooks, E. S. Gt. men's sons, 286.
Napoleon III. Bernard, F. Escapes, 284. — Duyckinck. Portrait gall. **2** : 303. — Em. persons, **1** : 106. — Fairbanks, O. B. Aguecheek, 135. — Field, M. B. Memories, 47. — Forbes, A. Souvenirs, 48. — Kirwan, A. V. Mod. France, 331. — McCarthy, J. Mod. lead. 18. — Nolan. Liber. of Ita. 456. — Parton. Peop. bk. biog. 499. — Wilson, J. Stud. mod. mind.
— and Disraeli compared. Greg, W. R. Miscel. **1** : 149.
— and Eugénie. Tuckerman, C. K. Recollec. **2** : 105.
— and the republicans. Hillebrand. France, 171.
— at Wilhelmshöhe. Paladin. Glances, 141.
— Coup d'état, 1851, The week of. Bristed. Pieces, **3** : 126.
— Election of, as president. Simpson, J. P. Pic. revol. Paris, **2** : 254.
— three phases in his life. Everett, E. Mt. Vernon, 98.
Napoleon, Prince. Em. persons, **5** : 30.
Napoleonic ideas. Brownson. Works, **16** : 581.
Naramore, Gay. Hemenway. Poets of Vt. 98.
Narbonne. Baring-Gould. Troub.-land, 244. — James, H. Little tour, 154.
Narcotic stimulants. Dana, A. H. Eth. inq. 84.
Narcotics; it does pay to smoke. Fiske, J. Tobacco, 5.
Nardini, Pietro, with portrait. Ehrlich, A. Cel. violin. 171.
Nares, Sir G. S., with photo. Cooper, T. Men of mark, **3** : 3.
Nares, Robert. Jerdan. Men, 322.
Narraganset patent, 1643. (C. Deane) Mass. Hist. Proc. **5** : 399. — (T. Aspinwall) Mass. Hist. Proc. **6** : 41.
Narration. Bibliography. Brewster, W. T. (ed.). Specimens narration.
Naruszewicz, Adam Stanislaus. Soboleski. Poets of Poland, 92.
Narva, Battle of. King, C. Battles, 288.
Nasby, Petroleum V., *pseud. See* Locke, D. R.
Nash the miser. Redding. Misers, **1** : 272.
Nash, John W. Livingston, J. Dist. Amer. 458. — Livingston, J. Em. Am. lawy. 85.
Nash, Richard, "Beau." Doran. Habits, 344. — Hollingshead. Footlights, 115. — Russell, W. Eccen. 81.
— Goldsmith's Life of. Gosse, E. Gossip, 227.
— Life of. Goldsmith. Miscel. (N. Y. 4 v.) **3** : 266.
— Princess Amelia and. Doran. Queens Hanov. **2**.
Nash, Stephen P. Am. Bar Assoc. **21** : 689.
Nash, Thomas. Dunham. Lit. & sci. men, **2** : 70. — Jusserand. Eng. novel. 287. — Symonds. Shakesp. pred. 534. — Ward, A. W. Eng. dram. **1** : 229. — Minto, W. Eng. poets, 250.
Nashua river, Boating trip on. Fellows, H. P. Boating, 129.
Nashville, Battle of. King, C. Battles, 619. — Swinton. Twelve battles, 450.
— Municipal condition of. (A. V. S. Lindsley) Nat. Conf. City Govt. '96 : 102.
Naseby, Battle of. Adams, W. H. D. Memo. batt. **1** : 312.
Nasmith, David, founder of the city mission. Tillotson, J. Unit. nobil. 65.

Nasmyth, Alexander. Walker, W., jr. Men of sci. 91.
Nasmyth, James. Cochrane, R. Gt. thinkers, 73. — With photo. Cooper, T. Men of mark, **2** : 18. — Lewis, T. C. Mechanicians, 204. — Towle, G. M. Heroes of inven. 132.
— Inventions of. Smiles. Indus. biog.
Nasmyth, Patrick. Redgrave. Century of p. **2** : 450.
Nason, Elias. Am. Antiq. Soc. Proc. n. s. **5** : 16.
Nasr-ed-Deen, Shah of Persia, Reminiscences of. Kingston, W. B. Monarchs, **1** : 184.
Nast, Thomas. Parton. Triumphs, 363.
Natal, Am. trade with, 1892. (W. S. Hollis) U. S. Cons. Rept. **39** : 367.
— Imports of, coal and tea in, 1899. (J. G. Stowe) U. S. Cons. Rept. **60** : 371.
— Trade and commerce of, 1891. (W. S. Hollis) U. S. Cons. Rept. **37** : 13.
— Visit to, 1883. Hübner. Thro' Brit. empire, **1** : 91.
Nation, The, as an element in anthropology. (D. G. Brinton) Smithson. Inst. Rept. '93 : 589. — Same art. Cong. Anthrop. Chic. '93 : 19.
— as an organism in Shakespeare. Shackford. Soc. & lit. pap. 242.
— Flowering of a. Appleton, T. G. Sheaf of pap. 131.
— Place of, in civilization. (C. de Garmo) Factors Amer. civiliz. 3.
Nation-making, Roman and English idea of. Fiske. Beginnings of New England.
National Academy of Design, New York. Badeau. Vagabond, 151.
National banks. Sherman, J. Sel. speeches.
National characteristics. Hume. Philos. works, **3** : 217. — Senior. Hist. ess. **6** : 34.
National Council of Education, The. (T. W. Bicknell) Nat. Educa. Assoc. '82 : 77.
National crises. Arnold, F. Turning-points, 278.
National debts. Adams, H. C. Public debts. — Newman, F. W. Essays, 334. — Rogers. Econ. interp. 434.
— and indirect taxation. George, H. Soc. prob. 221.
— and national prosperity. Fawcett. Ess. & lec. 125.
— Justification of. Bristed. Pieces, **4** : 1.
— of the U. S. Greeley. Ess. pol. econ. 238.
— — National honor and. Blaine. Polit. discus. 77.
— — Specie payments and. Garfield. Works, **1** : 183.
— Perpetuity of. Bowen, F. Gleanings, 71.
— Social influence of. Ess. from Nation, 113.
National duties. Farrar. Soc. & p. day quest. 54.
National Educational Association, Historical sketch of. (Z. Richards) Nat. Educa. Assoc. '91 : 118.
— History of. (Zalmon Richards; W. T. Harris) U. S. Bur. Ed. Rept. '92–93 : 1495.
— Library department. (Melvil Dewey) Nat. Educa. Assoc. '96 : 998.
— Organization and functions of. (W. T. Harris) Nat. Educa. Assoc. '91 : 443.
— subjects considered by, Classified list of. U. S. Bur. Ed. Rept '92–93 : 1513.
National gallery, London. Beecher. Star papers, 77.
National guards, Military treason and. Alison. Ess. 1.
National Health Soc., of London, Objects of. (E. Hart) Am. Pub. Health, **19** : 71.
National heart. Holland, J. G. Plain talks, 195.

National Home Reading Union (Eng.). Cochrane, R. Benef. lives, 157.
National life and character. Roosevelt, T. Amer. ideals, 271.
— of Europe, Progress of our political culture in. Nicol, D. Polit. life, 1 : 167.
— The secret of. Vaughan, D. J. Questions, 12.
National literature, Effect of one, upon another. Gilman, S. Contrib. 93.
National perils. Farrar. Soc. & p. day quest. 26.
National politics. Winthrop. Addresses, 2 : 244.
National prejudices. Goldsmith. Miscel. (N. Y. 4 v.) 1 : 229.
National types, Survival of. Godkin. Reflections, 316.
National unity. Beecher, H. W. Patriotic add. 750. — Nicol, D. Polit. life, 2 : 349.
National university, A. (Andrew D. White ; W. T. Harris) Nat. Educa. Assoc. '74 : 58. — (C. W. Eliot) Nat. Educa. Assoc. '74 : 173. — (E. L. Gregory) N. Y. Regents' Rept. 107 : 386.
— and technical research. (R. H. Thurston) N.Y. Regents, 111 : 305.
— Creation of, by coöperation between existing universities. (S. G. Ashmore) N. Y. Regents, 111 : 319.
— in relation to common schools. (Mrs. S. P. Gage) N. Y. Regents, 111 : 313.
— in Washington, Proposals for. Gilman, D. C. Univ. prob. 313.
National views. (W. H. Simmons) Charleston book, 275.
Nationalism, Bellamy's. McClelland, J. Soc. sci. 171.
— and the Genevan church. (H. B. Wilson) Ess. & rev.
— as proposed by Edward Bellamy. (D. B. Jones and others) Sunset club echoes, 89.
Nationalist party. Walker, F. A. Discuss. in econ. 2 : 351.
Nationality. Birrell, A. Res Judicatæ, 274. — Linton, W. J. Eng. repub. 207.
Nationalization. Kempner, W. Commonsense soc. 109.
— of the land. Coan. Soc. prob. 229.
Nationals, the, Origin and aims of. Harrison, J. Dang. tend. 51.
Nations, Comparative morality of. Godkin. Reflections, 19.
— Decline of. Hare. Guesses, 2 : 15.
— Ideals of. Farrar. Sermons in Am. 219.
— True wealth or weal of. Bushnell. Words, 43.
Nativities of inmates of public institutions of N. Y. city. (B. C. Mathews)Conf. char. & correc. '97 : 282.
Nattier, Jean Marc. Dilke. Fr. painters 18th cent. 146.
Natural Bridge of Virginia. Lummis. Strange corners, 142. — Martineau. Retrosp. 2 : 270.
Natural history. Bibliography. Springfield (Mass.) Pub. Lib. Bull. Sept. '94.
— Education in. (N. S. Shaler) Nat. Educa. Assoc. '72 : 232.
— Moot points in. Wilson, A. Leisure, 239.
— nomenclature in, Some questions of. (Theodore Gill) Smithson. Rept. '96 : 457.
— Primitive. Romanes. Ess. 1.
— Study of. Goldsmith. Miscel. (N. Y. 4 v.) 2 : 491. — Greenwood, F. W. P. Miscel. 342. — Kingsley. Health, 150 ; or New miscel. 277 ; or Sci. lec.
Natural history sciences, Educational value of. Huxley. Lay sermons.

Natural phenomena, Continuity of. Shaler. Interpre. 50.
Natural science, Coördination in. (W. S. Jackman) Nat. Educa. Assoc. '95 : 97.
— for the common schools. (W. S. Jackman) Nat. Educa. Assoc. '91 : 581.
— in elementary education. (S. G. Williams) Nat. Educa. Assoc. '92 : 323.
— Place of, in a liberal course of study. (Elliot Whipple) Nat. Educa. Assoc. '70 : 27.
— Preparatory curriculum. (C. S. Palmer) Nat. Educa. Assoc. '97 : 917.
— Relation to art. (E. du Bois Reymond) Smithson. Rept. '91 : 661.
See Science.
Natural selection. *See* Selection, Natural.
Natural theology, *See* Theology, Natural.
Naturalism. Bartol. Rad. Prob. 153. — Mabie. Short stud. lit. 131.
— and æsthetic. Balfour, A. J. Founda. belief, 33.
— and ethics. Balfour, A. J. Founda. belief, 11.
— and reason. Balfour, A. J. Founda. belief, 67.
— Ethics of. Whittaker, T. Ess. & not. 211.
— on the stage. Zola. Exper. novel, 109.
— Philosophic basis of. Balfour A. J. Founda. belief, 89.
— Use of the term. Seth, A. Man's place, 289.
Naturalist abroad and at home, The. Forbes, E. Lit. papers, 278.
Naturalization in the American colonies. (J. Willard) Mass. Hist. Proc. 4 : 337.
Naturalization laws : No discrimination on account of color. Sumner. Works, 13 : 474.
Nature. Emerson. Nature, 13 ; *or* Ess. 2 : 161.
— Stevenson, R. L. Virgin. 262.
— and art. Friswell. Gentle life, 2 : 50.
— and childhood. Mabie. My study fire, 8.
— and God. Paget, J. Ess. 1 : 121.
— and law. Carpenter. Nature & man.
— and life, Laugel's problems of. Holland, H. Frag. papers, 311.
— and man. Brown, S. Atom, 2. — Whiting, C. G. Saunterer, 37.
— and the poets. Burroughs. Pepacton, 91.
— and providence. Mill, J. S. Three ess. 24.
— and religion. Mill, J. S. Three ess. 21.
— Appreciation of. Shaler. Interpre. 1.
— — by literary men. Symonds. Ess. spec. 2 : 78.
— as a standard of action. Mill, J. S. Three ess. 13.
— Bibliography. Hunt, C. W. Nat. study in prep. schools.
— Completeness and variety of. (S. Elliott) Charleston book, 5.
— Constitution of. Tyndall. Frag. sci. 9.
— Criticised by art. Willis. Fam. persons, 417.
— Enjoyment of. Wallace, H. B. Art, 319.
— The halfness of. Howe, J. W. Is polite soc. pol. 161.
— healing power of, Hippocrates on. Brown, J. Locke, etc. 161.
— in England. Burroughs. Fresh fields, 1.
— in literature. (J. Burroughs) Ess. from critic. 103. — Mabie. Short stud. lit. 56, 85.
— in old English poetry. Burton, R. Liter. likings, 183.
— in Roman poetry. Bibliography. Allen, Katharine. Nature in Lat. poetry.
— Indifference to. Jacox, F. Cues, 296.
— Interpreters of, and interpreters of the book of Genesis. Huxley. Ess. contro. 56.
— Lessons of. Rice, H. Nature & cel. 7.
— Love of. Waterston. Culture, 251.
— Lovers of. Burroughs, J. Riverby, 203.

Nature, Man the interpreter of. Carpenter, W. Benj. Nature, 185.
— Method of. Emerson. Nature, 181.
— a minister of happiness. Beecher. Star papers, 303.
— Night-side of. Abbott, C. C. Outings, 207.
— Oersted on the soul in. Martineau, J. Ess. 2 : 147. 3 : 83.
— On the study of [in art]. Poynter. Ten lec. 165.
— Poetic aspect of. Everett. Poetry, comedy, and duty.
— Primeval. Thoreau. Selec. 89.
— the prophecy of man. Wasson. Ess. 127.
— Relation of man to. Forster, J. Crit. ess. (Bohn) 2 : 223.
— Solitudes of. Alger. Solitudes, 19.
— Sympathy with. Ballantyne. Ess. 156.
— Touches of. Burroughs. Birds & poets, 51. — Matthews, A. Ruminations.
Nature-metaphors. Lanier. Music, 95.
Nature studies, Higher use of. (N. Cropsey) Nat. Educa. Assoc. '94 : 199.
Nature-study and moral culture. Jordan, D. S. Story, 245; also in Nat. Educa. Assoc. '96 : 130.
— Bibliography. Osterhout [Wilkesbarre] Free Lib. Newsletter, Aug. '95.
— in primary work, The place of. (Flora J. Cook) Nat. Educa. Assoc. '96 : 519.
— Value of. Clarke, J. F. Self-culture, 113.
Naucratis and the Greeks in Egypt. Gardner, P. New chap. Gr. hist.
Naugatuck valley. Pidgeon. Old world ques. 13.
Naur, Elias Eskildsen. Miller, Jos. Singers church, 2d ed. 577.
Nauvoo, Mormons at. Quincy, J. Figures, 376.
Navagero, Andrea. Symonds. Reviv. of learn. 485.
Navajo artist, A. (R. W. Shufeldt) Smithson. Rept. '86 : 240.
Navajo blanket. Lummis. Strange corners, 198.
Navajo dye-stuffs. (Washington Matthews) Smithson. Rept. '91 : 613.
Navajo Legends. Bibliography. (F. W. Hodge) Mathews, W. Navaho legends.
Navajo superstitions. Lummis. Strange corners, 58.
Naval academy, U. S. College book, 363.
Naval Administration. Bibliography. Hamilton, Sir R. V. Naval Administration.
Naval subjects, Current fallacies on. Mahan. Lessons war, 277.
Navarino, Battle of. Allen, Jos. Battles Brit. navy, 2 : 514. — Knox, T. W. Battles, 29. — Peel, R. Speeches, 1 : 531. — Valentine, L. J. Sea-fights, 271.
Navigation; Finding the way at sea. Proctor. Sci. byways, 194.
— Improvements in, 1785. Franklin. Works (1887), 9 : 155.
— of rivers. Bibliography. Johnson, E. R. Inland waterways. — Wheeler, W. H. Tidal rivers.
Navigation laws. Alison. Ess. 1. — (E. Channing) Am. Antiq. Soc. Proc. n. s. 6: 160.
Navigators, Dutch, 1593–1879. Markham. Sea-fathers, 68.
Navvies, Work among. (Miss Marsh) Burdett-Coutts. Wom. miss. 106.
Navy, The, as a motor in geographical and commercial progress. (G. W. Littlehales) Am. Geog. Soc. 31 : 123.
Navy mission society, Formation of. (Mrs. C. Garnett) Burdett-Coutts. Wom. miss. 92.

Naworth castle. Edwardes, C. Hist. houses. — Mackie, C. Castles of Mary.
Naxos. Tozer. Isl. Æg. 78.
Naylor, James. Whittier. Old portr. 71. — Baring-Gould. Yorks. odd. 1 : 86.
Nazareth. Buckley, J. M. Trav. 3 cont. 452. — Hoppin. Notes theol. stud. 211. — Kean, J. Among holy places, 207. — Little, W. J. K. Sketches, 328. — Lee, J. S. Sac. cities, 79. — Stuart-Glennie. Pilgrim. 386. — (H. B. Tristram) Wilson, C. W. Pictur. Palest. 2 : 25.
Neal, Alice Bradley, with portrait. Hart, J. S. Fem. prose, 363.
Neal, David, with portrait. Benjamin, S. G. W. Am. art. 1.
Neal, John. Griswold. Poets Am. 152. — Griswold. Prose writ. 313.
Neal, Joseph Clay. Clemens. Funny fellows, 123. — Griswold. Prose writ. 518.
Neale, Cornelius. Domestic hours. Drake, N. Winter nights, v. 2.
Neale, Henrietta. Burder. Pious wom. 585.
Neale, John Mason. Hatfield, E. F. Poets of church, 454. — Huntington, G. Random recol. 198. — (W. G. Horder) Miles, A. H. Poets of cent. 10 : 337. — Miller, Jos. Singers church, 2d ed. 537.
Neale, Leonard. Clarke, R. H. Cath. bishops, 1 : 116.
Nealy, Mary Elizabeth. Coggeshall. Poets of west, 477.
Nean, Elie. Agnew. Protes. exiles, 2 : 32.
Neander, Joachim. Hatfield, E. F. Poets of church, 457. — Miller, Jos. Singers church, 2d ed. 105. — Winkworth. Chr. singers Germ. 284.
Neander, J. A. W. Hurst. Rationalism, 249. — Lichtenberger. Hist. Ger. theol. 168. — Schaff, P. Germany, 261. — Sprague, W. B. Europ. celeb. 130.
Near-sightedness and school hygiene. (A. A. Foucher) Am. Pub. Health, 20 : 290.
Neate, Charles. Mozley. Reminis. 2 : 100.
Neaves, Charles, Lord. Skelton. Ess. 324. — Smith, J. Campbell. Writings, 468.
Nebraska and slavery. Parker, T. Add. sp. 1 : 295.
— — Question of. Parker, T. Add. speeches, 1 : 295.
— Climate of. U. S. Sen. Docs. '89–90, v. 10.
— Geography of. (G. K. Warren) Am. Geog. Soc. 1 : 257.
Nebula, Great, in Argo. Proctor, R. A. Univ. of suns, 112.
— in Orion. Proctor. Light sci. 2 : 53.
Nebulæ. Estes. Half-hour, 51.
Nebular hypothesis. Gall & Robertson. Pop. read. sci. 199.
— and the stability of the solar system. Lodge, O. J. Pioneers, 235.
Necessary truth, Mr. Mill's denial. Ward, W. G. Ess. theism, 1 : 33.
Necessity. Friswell. Gentle life, 2 : 36.
— and contingency. Leibnitz. Philos. works (1890), 170.
Neckam, Alexander, The works of. Lucas. Mornings, 2 : 172.
Necker, Jacques. Carlyle, T. Montaigne, 50. — Adolphus. Biog. Fr. rev. 2 : 140. — Brougham. Works, 5 : 119. — Edgar. Footpr. 68. — Crowe, E. E. For. statesmen, 5 : 240. — Haussonville. Salon of Necker, 2 : 69.
— Last views of, 1803. Smith, Syd. Ess. fr. Ed. R.
Necker, Madame Suzanne Curchod. Haussonville. Salon of Necker, 1 : 8. 2 : 1. — Hitch-

New England, Inhabitants of. Curtis, B. R. Mem. & wr. v. 2.
— of the ancients. Drake. Nooks of N. E. 17.
— Puritan England transplanted. Stebbing. Verdicts, 349.
— Puritan origin of. Alviella. Contemp. evol. 153.
— two centuries ago. Lowell. Writ. 2 : 1.
— Yankees at home. Parton. Topics, 30.
New England Anti-Slavery Society. Adams, J. G. Fifty years, 58.
New England Conference, The old. McClintock, J. Em. Meth. 361.
New England life. Bibliography. Salem (Mass.) Pub. Lib. Bull. Aug. '95.
New England philosophy. Tuckerman. Optimist, 1.
New England primer. Bibliography. Ford, P. L. (ed.). N. E. primer.
New England theocracy. Lucas. Secularia, 211.
New fields for American literature. Garland. Crumbling idols, 21.
New Forest, The. Wood, J. G. Out-of-doors, 156. — Allingham. Varieties, 1 : 1.
New Hall Manor. Timbs. Abbeys, 1 : 256.
New Hampshire. Everett. Orat. v. 3.
New Haven. (F. H. Cogswell) Powell, L. P. Hist. towns N. E. 553.
— An historic meeting-house. Deming. By-ways, 212.
— Municipal condition of. (G. L. Fox) Nat. Conf. City Govt. '97 : 164.
New Jersey and the great corporations. (E. Q. Keasbey) Am. Bar Assoc. 22 : 379.
— The buried forests of. Deming. By-ways, 162.
— Caché finds from ancient village sites in. (E. Volk) Cong. Anthr. Chic. '93, 140.
— Chancery, Court of. Field, B. S. Prov. courts N. J. 108.
— Climatology of. N. J. Labor, '78 : 211. '79 : 5.
— Geology of. (J. H. Cook) Am. Geog. Soc. 1 : 107.
— Slavery in. Field, R. S. Prov. courts N. J. 130.
New London, Conn. Drake. Nooks of N. E. 420.
New Mexico. (C. Pullen) Am. Geog. Soc. 19 : 22. — Brockett, L. P. Our west. empire, 1056. — Giddings. Speeches in Cong. 403. — Greg. Commerce of prairies, 122. — Powers, S. Afoot and alone. — Rideing, W. H. A-saddle in the wild west, 139. — Stephens, C. A. Knockabout club in tropics, 20.
— Conquest of. Dawson. Batt. of U. S. 2 : 454.
— Insurrection in. Dawson. Batt. of U. S. 2 : 483.
— pottery of, Prehistoric. (Henry Hales) Smithson. Rept. '92 : 535.
— Ruins in. (J. H. Simpson) Am. Geog. Soc. 5 : 194.
— The Spaniard in. (W. W. H. Davis) Am. Hist. Assoc. 3 : 164.
— Village Indians of. (E. Ingersoll) Am. Geog. Soc. 7 : 114.
New Orleans. Brooks, E. S. Gt. cities, 126. — Martineau. Retrosp. 2 : 120. — Sala. Amer. revis. 2 : 1. — Warner, C. D. Studies, 39.
— Battle of, 1815. Adams. Hist. U. S. 8 : 367. — Lodge & Roosevelt. Hero-tales, 137. — Roosevelt, T. Naval war 1812, 455.
— Batture at. Jefferson. Works, 8 : 503.
— Municipal affairs in. (C. Janvier) Nat. Conf. City Govt. '97 : 199.
— Municipal condition of. (W. B. Spencer) Nat. Conf. City Govt. 2-3 : 407.
— Sanitary protection of. (J. Holt) Am. Pub. Health, 11 : 89.
New South Wales. Dilke. Greater Brit. —

Hübner. Through Brit. empire, 1 : 280. — Jenks, E. Hist. Aust. col. 20.
New South Wales, Banking in, 1896. (G. W. Bell) U. S. Cons. Rept. 53 : 97.
— Fiscal changes in, 1895. (G. W. Bell) U. S. Cons. Rept. 51 : 293.
— Mineral products of, 1892. (A. Cameron) U. S. Cons. Rept. 41 : 163.
— Newcastle, Commerce of, 1892. (G. T. Baggs) U. S. Cons. Rept. 39 : 552.
— Tariff legislation, 1891. U. S. Cons. Rept. 39 : 27.
New Year, The. Curtis, G. W. Other ess. 1. — Gardner, S. J. Aut. leaves, v. 1.
— Thoughts for the. Rogers, H. Ess. from G. W. v. 1.
New Year's eve. Lamb. Elia. — Mabie. My study fire, 42.
New Year's night of an unhappy man. Richter. Campaner.
New York State, Agriculture of. Dix. Speeches, 2 : 360.
— and its press. Curtis, G. W. Orations, 1 : 287.
— Anti-rent, Episode in. (D. Murray) Am. Hist. Assoc. Rept. '96, 1 : 137.
— Census of, 1855. (B. Hough) Am. Geog. Soc. 1 : 205.
— Geological survey, Report on. Dix. Speeches, 2 : 181.
— Historical notes on. Seward. Works, 2 : 9.
— Historic glories of the Empire State. Winthrop. Addresses, 2 : 196.
— Mapping of. (H. Gannett) Am. Geog. Soc. 27 : 21.
— Physical geography of. (E. L. Viele) Am. Geog. Soc. 7 : 127. — (R. S. Tarr) Am. Geog. Soc. 28 : 99. 29 : 16. 30 : 28, 183, 375. 31 : 1-417.
— university of, Extension of. (M. Dewey) N. Y. Regents, 103, app. : 73.
— — Relations of, to colleges. N. Y. Regents, 98, app. : 167.
— Waterways of. (I. I. Hayes) Am. Geog. Soc. 13 : 93.
— — effect upon commerce. (T. C. Clarke) Deep waterways conven. 1 : 273.
New York city. Arnold, E. Seas & l. 78. — Brooks, E. S. Gt. cities, 23. — Dilke. Greater Brit. 40. — Hardy, I. D. Through cities, 59, 302. — Sala. Amer. revis. 1 : 19. — Pidgeon. Engineer's holiday, 1. — (J. B. Gilder) Powell, L. P. Hist. towns mid. states, 169. — Richardson. Amer. lit. 1 : 24. — Rousiers. Amer. life, 239. — Tuckerman, C. K. Recollec. 1 : 51.
— Amusements in. Willis. Hurry-graphs, 356.
— British in, How they left. McMasters. With Fathers, 271.
— Castle Garden theatre. Hutton, L. Plays, 214.
— Central Park, Glimpses of. Howells. Impressions, 224.
— Church street. Curtis. From easy chair, 3 : 127.
— Civic renaissance. Tolman, W. H. Munic. reform, 27.
— Draft riots and the Catholics. Brownson. Works, 17 : 413.
— East Side, Ramble in. Howells. Impressions, 127.
— Facts for the time. (C. H. Parkhurst) Tolman, W. H. Munic. reform, 17.
— Fifth Ave. Theatre. Hutton, L. Plays, 77.
— government of, Dishonesty in. Parton. Topics, 350.
— Growth of. Dix. Speeches, 2 : 337.

New York, harbor. Method of approaching, by sounding. (Trudelle) Am. Geog. Soc. 10 : 253.
— History of municipal land ownership on Manhattan Island. (G. A. Black) Colum. Univ. Stud. Hist. 1 : no. 3.
— in 1877. Vivian. Tour in Am. 47.
— in 1881. Hardy. Between two oceans, 56.— Russell, W. H. Hesper, 1 : 18.
— Invasion of. Dawson. Batt. of U. S. 2 : 312, 378.
— Literary haunts of. Wolfe, T. F. Lit. haunts, 1 : 80.
— May-day in. Willis. Hurry-graphs, 344.
— Mercantile Library, 50th anniversary, 1870. Bryant. Orations, 343.
— Metropolitan Art Museum, Address at founding of, Nov. 23, 1869. Bryant. Orations, 331.
— Niblo's garden. Badeau. Vagabond, 56.
— Old Broadway theatre. Hutton, L. Plays, 111.
— 'Short-hairs' and 'swallow-tails' of. Godkin. Reflections, 206.
— Society in. Bristed. Pieces, 1 : 220. — Willis. Hurry-graphs, 263, 282.
— Streets of. Curtis, G. W. Other ess. 69. — Howells. Impressions, 245.
— Tenement-house evil. (E. Flagg) Woods, R. A. Poor, 370.
— Tenement-houses, Life in. (W. T. Elsing) Woods, R. A. Poor, 42.
— Theatre-going in. Hutton, L. Plays, 1.
— Trinity church steeple, A dream of. Silliman. Gallop, 168.
— Vigilance League. Tolman, W. H. Munic. reform, 183.
New Zealand. Abercromby. Seas & skies, 142.
— (F. B. Passmore) Am. Geog. Soc. 7 : 378. — Barker, Lady. Travel. about, 46. — Dilke. Greater Brit. 228. — Froude. Oceana, 230. — Alexander, J. M. Isl. Pac. 353. — Jenks, E. Hist. Aust. col. 166. — Forbes, A. Souvenirs, 270. — Peel, R. Speeches, 4 : 534, 555.
— Aboriginal. McLennan. Stud. anc. 2 : 255.
— in 1887. Bates, E. K. Kaleidoscope, 61.
— Land and labor laws in, '99. (J. D. Connolly) U. S. Cons. Rept. 53 : 1.
— Land taxation in, 1894. (J. D. Connolly) U. S. Cons. Rept. 44 : 615.
— Legends of. Jones, W. Credulities, 96.
— Visit to, 1883. Hübner. Through Brit. empire, 1 : 167.
— Warrior chiefs of. Buckland, F. T. Curios. nat. hist. 4 : 57.
Newark, D. Lesley, Lord. Cust. Warriors 17th cent. v. 2. — Lodge. Portraits (Bohn), v. 6.
Newark, Priory of. Timbs. Abbeys, 1 : 276.
Newberry, J. S. Parton, J. Sk. of men of prog.
Newberry, John. Knight, C. Old booksel. 233.
Newbold, J. S. Collins, Stephen. Miscel.
Newburgh, N. Y. (A. Skeel) Powell, L. P. Hist. towns mid. states, 107.
Newbury, Eng. Silloway. Cathedral towns, 123.
Newbury, Mass., Old. Whittier. Prose works, v. 2.
Newcastle, Henry Pelham Clinton, 5th duke of. Martineau, H. Biog. sket. 360.
Newcastle, Margaret, duchess of. Bethune, G. W. Brit. fem. poets. — With portrait. Costello. Englishwomen, 3 : 211. — Darton. Fam. girls, 202. — Jeaffreson. Novelists, 1 : 28. — Robertson. Eng. poetesses, 14. — Williams, Jane. Lit. wom. 104. — Mayer, G. T. Wom. of lett. 1 : 1.
Newcastle, Thos. H. Pelham. duke of. Caulfield. Kit-cat, 53. — Earle, J. C. Eng. prem. 1 : 105. — Lodge. Portraits (Bohn), v. 7.

Newcastle, William Cavendish, 1st duke of. Lodge. Portraits (Bohn), v. 6.
Newcastle, N. H. Drake. Nooks of N. E. 196.
Newcastle House and its eccentric duchess. Timbs. Abbeys, 1 : 103.
Newcomb, Edgar Marshall. (J. C. Fernald) Harvard mem. biog. 2 : 153.
Newcomen, Thomas. Brightwell. Heroes of lab. 177.
Newdigate, Charles Newdigate. Reid, T. W. Cab. portr. 244. — Ritchie. Brit. sena. 197.
Newell, Harriet. Hanaford. Wom. of cent. 485. — Lossing. Em. Amer. 285. — Pitman, Mrs. Heroines mission. 300.
Newell, M. Alexander. (Sarah E. Richmond) Nat. Educa. Assoc. '94 : 234.
Newell, William. Putnam, A. P. Singers liberal, 177.
Newfoundland. Benjamin. Atlan. isl. 146. — Carlyle, T. Montaigne, 149. — Lanman. Recol. 257.
— and the Cod-fishers. Deming. By-ways, 75.
— and Labrador, Explorations in, connected with cruise of Grampus. U. S. Nat. Mus. Rept. '89 : 709.
— Bibliography. Prowse, D. W. Hist. Newfoundland.
— in 1855. Taylor, B. At home, 1 : 238.
— New tariff of, 1895. (S. Ryan) U. S. Cons. Rept. 49 : 53.
— Railway contract, 1898. (M. J. Carter) U. S. Cons. Rept. 57 : 201.
Newgate prison. Hatton, J. Old lamps, 162.
Newman, F. W. Phases of faith. Martineau, J. Ess. 3 : 1.
— The soul, Review of. Brownson. Works, 1 : 253.
Newman, John Henry. Birrell, A. Res judicatæ, 140. — Farrar. Soc. & p. day quest. 282. — Thomas, R. Lead. of thought, 48. — Church, R. W. Occ. pap. 2 : 379–479. — Lilly, W. S. Ess. 62. — Em. persons, 4 : 251. — Froude. Short stud. 4 : 179. — Hutton. Mod. guides, 47. — M'Carthy, J. Mod. leaders, 167. — Martineau, J. Ess. '91, 1 : 219. — Mozley. Reminis. 1 : 12. — Paul. Biog. sket. 171. — Rands, W. B. Henry Holbeach, 2 : 151. — Shairp, J. C. Aspects, 377. — Walsh, W. S. Pen-pic. mod. 68. — Gates, L. E. Three stud. 64. — (R. H. Hutton) Warner classics, 1 : 75. — Great mod. preachers. — Hatfield, E. F. Poets of church, 464. — Hutton, R. H. Criticisms, 1 : 270. — Jacobs, Jos. Ess. & rev. 119. — Miles, A. H. Poets of cent. 10 : 185. — Miller, Jos. Singers church, 2d ed. 470. — Smalley. Stud. 1. — With portrait. (R. H. Hutton) Warner Lib. 18 : 10597.
— and Emerson, as types. Mullany. Phases of thought, 13.
— and Francis William. McCarthy, J. Mod. lead. 167.
— Apologia. Wilberforce, S. Ess. Quar. 1 : 334.
— as a poet. Austin, A. Poetry, 170.
— at Birmingham. Yates, E. H. Celeb. 1 : 279.
— Dream of Gerontius. Doyle. Lec. Oxf. 91.
— Grammar of assent. Froude. Short stud. 2 : 86. — Mozley, J. B. Lec. 275.
— his influence on our present theology. Martineau, J. Ess. 1 : 329.
— on development. Thirlwall, C. Remains, 1 : 99.
— Prose poetry of. Shairp. Aspects.
Newmarket. Smythe, G. S. Hist. fancies, 75.
Newport, Christopher. Belknap. Amer. biog. 2 : 115.
Newport, Sir John. Hazlitt. Parl. portr. 195.

Newport, R. I. Badeau. Vagabond, 180. — Curtis, G. W. Lotus, 163. — Drake. Nooks of N. E. 356. — James, H. Portraits, 338. — (Susan Coolidge) Powell, L. P. Hist. towns N. E. 413.
— in September. Ames, M. C. Outlines, 29.
— Sanitary protection in. (H. R. Storer) Am. Pub. Health, 6 : 209. 8 : 42.
Newport, Game of. Curtis, G. W. Other ess. 31.
Newspaper, The, as an educator. (W. A. Cobb) N. Y. Regents, 101, app. : 153.
— A great national. Peck, H. T. Good English, 253.
Newspaper ethics. Curtis, G. W. Ars rec. viv. 93.
Newspaper literary criticism. Nadal, E. S. Ess. at home.
Newspaper press, The. Bryant. Prose, 2 : 208. — Garfield. Works, 2 : 575.
— of India. Escott, T. H. S. Pillars emp. 134.
Newspaper stamp, The first. Knight. Once on time, 2 : 1.
Newspaper writers, Advice to. Mathews. Men & bks. 256.
Newspaper-made man. Warner, C. D. As we go, 10.
Newspapers. Mansfield, E. D. Pers. mem. 329. Tuckerman. Collector, 246. — Tuckerman. Criterion, 252.
— and English. Traill. New fiction, 170.
— and people. Martin, E. S. Windfalls, 135.
— and periodicals. Porter, N. Books, 341.
— and their writers. (A. J. B. B. Hope) Camb. Ess. '58 : 1.
— a foe to eloquence. Higginson. Book & heart, 81.
— Good and evil of. Hamerton. Intellec. 272.
— in the U. S., 1833. McCulloch, H. Men & meas. 483.
— London. Hatton. Jour. Lond. 155.
— Origin of. Disraeli, I. Curios. (N. Y. 4 v.) 1 : 224.
— Ought young girls to read? (W. T. Harris) Nat. Educa. Assoc. '88 : 86.
— Our modern Mercury. Wynter, A. Our soc. bees, 1 : 304.
— Paris. Stuart, H. Paris days, 158.
— Provincial, London. Hatton. Jour. Lond. 27.
— Refuting misstatements of. Helps. Brevia.
— Rights and duties of. (J. H. Raymond ; Slason Thompson ; Williston Fish) Sunset club echoes, 18.
— thirty-five years ago [i. e. in 1788]. Lamb. Elia.
— Use and abuse of. Lunt. Three eras, 67. — Maurice. Friendship, 93.
Newstead abbey. Edwardes, C. Hist. houses. — Hawthorne. Eng. note-books, 2 : 217. — Hawthorne, Mrs. Eng. & It. 85.
Newton, Adelaide, L. Hack. Consec. wom. 269.
Newton, Gilbert Stuart. Eng. painters Georgian, 57. — Redgrave. Century of p. 2 : 326.
Newton, Sir Isaac. Bolton, S. K. Fam. men of science, 28. — Collier, W. F. Hist. Eng. lit. 266. — Craik. Pursuit. knowl. 1 : 1. — Edgar. Boyhood, 170. — Lodge. Portraits (Bohn), v. 7. — Morton, E. J. C. Heroes astron. 140. — Parton. Peop. bk. biog. 244. — Smith, J. Campbell. Writings, 161. — Stoughton, J. Worthies of sci. 209. — Ball, R. Great astron. 116. — Thayer, W. M. Turn.-points, 272. — Cooper, T. Triumphs of persev. 107. — Ewart, H. C. Heroes of sci. 146. — Hundred greatest men, 347. — Lodge, O. J. Pioneers, 161. — Nasmith. Mak. mod. thought, 2 : 250. — Russell, W. C. Book of au. 107. — Taylor, T.

Leicester Sq. 197. — Wallace, R. Anti-Trin. biog. 3 : 428. — With portrait. Warner Lib. 18 : 10619. — Wrangham. Brit. Plutarch, v. 5.
— and the law of gravitation. Lodge, O. J. Pioneers, 180.
— Darwin and. Proctor, R. A. Mysteries, 1 ; or Nat. stud. 9.
— Followers of. Morton, E. J. C. Heroes astron. 217.
— Principia. Lodge, O. J. Pioneers, 206. — Morton, E. J. C. Heroes astron. 166.
Newton, James. Ivimey. Eng. Bapt. 4 : 287. — Miller, Jos. Singers church, 2d ed. 260.
Newton, John. Crighton, A. Converts, 2 : 255. — Dale, T. P. Life's motto. — Hatfield, E. F. Poets of church, 469. — Miller, Jos. Singers church, 2d ed. 237. — Seeley, M. Later evang. 39.
Newton, Robert. Wesley & successors, 111, 131, 149, 169.
Newton, Thomas. Bell, R. Lit. & sci. men, 2 : 115.
Newton, Mrs. (mother of Rev. John). Holloway, L. C. Mothers of gt. men, 215.
Newton University, Baltimore, Md. U. S. Bur. Ed. Circ. '94, no. 2 : 260.
Ney, Michel. Headley. Napoleon, 2 : 274.
Niagara Falls. Arnold, E. Seas & l. 41. — Clark, W. G. Lit. rem. 154. — Curtis, G. W. Lotus, 75. — Greenwood, F. W. P. Miscel. 290. — Hardy. Between two oceans, 37. — James, H. Portraits, 364. — Marshall, W. G. Thro' Amer. 71. — Martineau. Retrosp. 1 : 151. — Silliman. Gallop, 137. — Pidgeon. Engineer's holiday, 61. — Sinclair, J. Sketches.
— and its visitors. Taylor, B. At home, 2 : 388.
— Utilization of. (T. C. Martin) Smithson. Rept. '96 : 223.
Niagara River, History of. (G. K. Gilbert) Smithson. Rept. '90 : 231.
Nibelungen, "Ring der," Study of. Henderson, W. J. Preludes.
Nibelungen Lied, The. Carlyle. Essays. — Chambers's Repos. no. 96. — Cox and Jones. Tales of Teutonic, 79. — Dippold. Great epics, 1. — Haweis. Mus. mem. 225. — Hosmer, J. K. Short hist. Ger. lit. 23. — Longfellow. Poets Eur. 217. — Ludlow. Epics, 1 : 105. — Taylor. Stud. Ger. 101. — Wagner, W. R. Epics, 229. — Scherer. Germ. lit. 1 : 101. — Warner Lib. 18 : 10627.
— epitomized. Dobson, W. T. Class. poets, 56.
Nica, Mareo de. Journey in Mexico. Frost, T. Explorers, 120.
Nicæa, Council of. Moxom. Jerus. to Nicæa, 393.
Nicænetus. Mills. Poets of Greece, 210.
Nicander. Arnold, E. Poets of Greece, 203. — Mills. Poets of Greece, 224.
Nicaragua and Monroe doctrine. Bibliography. Providence Pub. Lib. Bull. June, '95.
— Bibliography. (C. De Kalb) Amer. Geog. Soc. June, '94. — New Bedford (Mass.) Pub. Lib. Bull. June, '96.
— Bibliography of the Mosquito Coast. (C. De Kalb) Am. Geog. Soc. 26 : 241.
— Gold deposits in, 1896. (T. O'Hara) U. S. Cons. Rept. 52 : 126.
— Handbook of. Bur. Am. Rep. Bulletin, no. 51, pt. 2.
— Import duties of, 1891. Bur. Am. repub. no. 20.
— Market for U. S. goods in, 1896. (T. O'Hara) U. S. Cons. Rept. 51 : 423.
— natural resources, etc., 1896. (T. O'Hara) U. S. Cons. Rept. 51 : 410.

Nicaragua, R. R. extension in, 1891. (W. Newell) U. S. Cons. Rept. **37** : 23.
— Rubber industry of, 1896. (H. E. Lew) U. S. Cons. Rept. **52** : 241.
— Walker's filibustering in. Congdon, C. T. Trib. ess. 33.
See Mosquito Shore.
Nicaragua canal, Proposed. (T. B. Myers) Am. Geog. Soc. **8** : 210. — (H. C. Taylor) Am. Geog. Soc. **18** : 95.
— — Bibliography. (J. M. Baker) U. S. Sen. doc. 55th Cong. 3d Sess. no. 26.
Niccola del' Arca. Perkins, C. C. Tusc. sculp. **I** : III.
Niccoli, Niccolò de'. Symonds. Reviv. of learn. 178.
Niccolini, G. Howells. Mod. It. poets, 196.
Nice. Buckley, J. M. Trav. three cont. 139. — Sala. Journeys south, 51.
— Council of. Farrar. Lives of fathers, **1** : 353.
— Russell, J., earl. Ess. Chr. relig. in W. Eur. 61.
Nichol, Prof. John P. Gilfillan. Mod. lit. 207.
Nicholas, St., of Myra. Charles. Martyrs, 146.
Nicolas V., Pope. Oliphant. Makers Mod. Rome, 530. — Symonds. Age of despots, 378.
— Symonds. Reviv. of learning, 222. — Pastor, L. Hist. popes, **2** : 1.
Nicholas I., of Russia. Abbott. Kings & Queens, 147.
— and Stratford de Redcliffe. (C. Hamlin) Am. Antiq. Soc. Proc. n. s. **9** : 451.
— Last Birthday of. Martineau, H. Biog. sk. 405.
Nicholas II., of Russia, Coronation of. Davis, R. H. Year, 3.
Nicholas of Basle. Hodgson, Wm. Reformers, 51.
Nicholas, John. Johnston, A. Amer. ora. **1** : 131.
Nicholas, Tressilian George. Miller, Jos. Singers church, 2d ed. 566.
Nicholl, Mrs. Agnes Rose Bouvier. Clayton, E. C. Eng. fem. art. **2** : 34.
Nichols, Ichabod. Peabody. Harv. grad. 111.
Nichols, James R. Reminiscences of an experimenter. Nichols, J. R. Fireside sci. 245.
Nichols, John Gough. Smith, C. R. Retrospec. **2** : 112.
Nichols, Joseph Hulbert. Everest. Poets of Conn. 339.
Nichols, Rebecca S. Reed. Coggeshall. Poets of west, 290.
Nicholson, Anson A. Hemenway. Poets of Vt. 209.
Nicholson, A. O. P. Livingston, J. Em. Am. lawy. 572.
Nicholson, Gen. John. Kaye. Indian off. **2** : 417.
Nicholson, Margaret, Attempt to assassinate George III. Doran. Queens Hanov. v. **2**.
Nicholson, Nancy. Baring-Gould. Yorks. odd. **2** : 25.
Nicholson, William. Wilson, J. G. Poets of Scot. **2** : 43.
Nicias. Mills. Poets of Greece, 183.
Nicknames. Hazlitt. Sket. — Mathews. Words, 263.
— Names and. Northcote. Lec. & ess. 286.
— Political. Disraeli, I. Curios. (N. Y. 4 v.) **3** : 409.
Nicodé, Jean L. Maitland, J. A. F. Masters Ger. music, 265.
Nicodemus, Baldwin, G. C. Rep. men, 161.
Nicol, Erskine, with photo. Cooper, T. Men of mark, **4** : 9.
Nicol, James. Wilson, J. G. Poets of Scot. **1** : 441.

Nicolai, Henry. Wallace, R. Anti-Trin. biog. **3** : 251.
Nicolai, Henry L. Bartlett, J. R. R. I. officers, 450.
Nicolai, Philip. Miller, Jos. Singers church, 2d ed. 54. — Winkworth. Chr. singers Germ. 159.
Nicole, Pierre. Tollemache. French Jansen. 162.
Nicolette, Aucassin and. Pater. Stud. renais. 1.
Nicolini, C., Italian opera singer. Hogarth. Mem. opera, **1** : 195.
Nicoll, Robert. Smiles. Brief biog. 399. — Wilson, J. G. Poets of Scot. **2** : 370.
Nicomede, St. Charles. Martyrs, 26.
Niddry castle. Mackie, C. Castles of Mary.
Niebuhr, Barthold Geo., with portrait. Warner Lib. **18** : 10657.
— Reminiscences of. Lieber, F. Reminis. 45.
Niebuhr, Carsten. Edwards, B. B. Self-taught, 250. — St. John. Cel. travelers, **3** : 99. — Seymour, C. C. B. Self-made, 121.
Nieciecius, Samuel. Wallace, R. Anti-Trin. biog. **2** : 525.
Nielsen, Peter, bishop of Rithbe, Denmark. Baring-Gould. Oddities, **1** : 137.
Niemcewicz, Julian Ursin. Soboleski. Poets of Poland, 157.
Niemeyer, John C. Walker, C. D. Biog. Va. Mil. Inst. 406.
Niemiericius, George. Wallace, R. Anti-Trin. biog. **2** : 223.
Niemojevius, John. Wallace, R. Anti-Trin. biog. **2** : 215.
Nietzsche, Friedrich. Ellis, H. Affirmations, 1. — Nordau. Degen. 415. — Peck, H. T. Good English, 197.
Niger, Francis. Wallace, R. Anti-Trin. biog. **2** : 120.
Night and day. Saunders. Mosaics, 298. — Saunders. Stray leaves, 185.
— and sleep, Use of. Bushnell. Moral uses, 1.
Night-soil and garbage, Destruction of, by fire. (G. Baird) Am. Pub. Health, **12** : 119.
Nightingale, Florence. Bolton, S. K. Girls famous, 278. — Brocket. Woman's work, 69. — With portrait. Clarke, M. C. Noted wom. 377. — Fawcett, M. G. Em. wom. 69. — Hodder. Heroes, **2** : 51. — With portrait. Parton. Em. wom. 11. — Duyckinck. Portrait gall. **2** : 532. — Owen, Mrs. O. F. Heroines domes. 383. — Wallace, S. E. Bosphorus, 299.
Nightingale and musician, Contest between. Hunt. Day by fire, 308.
— A hunt for the. Burroughs. Fresh fields, 83.
Nightingale-catching. Buckland, F. T. Curios. nat. hist. **3** : 175.
Nightmare. Hunt, L. Seer, **2** : 166.
Nights, Summer. Lang. Leaders, 150.
Nigrinus, George. Wallace, R. Anti-Trin. biog. **3** : 104.
Nihilism, Administrative. Huxley. Critiques.
— Buddhist. Müller, M. Sel. ess. **2** : 292.
— Russian. Ewald, A. C. Paper, 322. — Rae, J. Contem. soc. 252.
Nihilists in Russia. Curtis, W. E. Land of nihilists, 264.
Nijni Novgorod and its great fair, in 1864. Forsyth, W. Essays, 346.
Nikko, Japan. Arnold, E. Seas & l. 188. — Pidgeon. Engineer's holiday, 295.
Nil nisi bonum. (W. M. Thackeray) Prose masterpieces, **1** : 177.
Nile, The. Hale, E. E. Sto. of discov. 188.
— Adventure on. Arnold, E. Wand. words, 47.
— Ascent of. Moore, Jos. Outl. Eur. 84.
— Battle of 1798. Allen, Jos. Battles Brit. navy,

Non-survival of the fittest. Greg. Enig. 111.

Noort, Oliver van, Circumnavigations of. Frost, T. Explorers, 219.

Norba. Freeman. Studies Italy, 131.

Norbury, John Toler, Lord. Russell, W. Eccen. 288. — Sheil, R. L. Sketches, 1 : 85. — Sheil. Sk. Irish bar, 2 : 5.

Norcott, John. Ivimey. Eng. Bapt. 3 : 295.

Norcross, Amasa, with portrait. Sketches N. H. men, 37.

Nordau, Max, Passing of. Peck, H. T. Pers. equa. 157.

Nordenskiöld, A. E., with portrait. Bolton, S. K. Fam. voyag. 443.
— Exploration of Arctic Asia. Frost, T. Mod. expl. 80.

Nordica, Lillian, with portrait. Buffen. Mus. celeb. 2 : 15.

Nore, Mutiny at. Burke, P. Cel. nav. & mil. trials, 229.

Norfolk, Thomas Howard, 2d duke of. Taylor, W. C. Rom. biog. v. 1. — Wrangham. Brit. Plutarch, v. 1. — Lodge. Portraits (Bohn), v. 1.

Norfolk, Thomas Howard, 3d duke of. Burke, S. H. Hist. portr. Tudor, 3 : 180.

Norfolk, Thomas Howard, 4th duke of. Burke, S. H. Hist. portr. Tudor, 4 : 428. — Lodge. Portraits (Bohn), v. 2.

Norfolk Broads. Bibliography. Goose, A. H. (publ.). Songs, Stories, etc., Norfolk.

Norfolk, Eng. Carlyle, T. Montaigne, 173.
— On the edge of the holy land of. Jessopp, A. Studies, 90.
— Village life in, 600 years ago. (A. Jessopp) Coan. Hist. stud. 1.

Norfolk islands. Alexander, J. M. Isl. Pac. 435.
— Visit to (1884). Hübner. Thro' Brit. empire, 2 : 259.

Norkott, Arthur, trial for murder, 1628. Craik, G. L. Eng. causes cél. 265.

Normal classes in academies. (W. D. Graves) N. Y. Regents, 96 : 403.

Normal departments in academies. (M. Weed) N. Y. Regents, 79, app. : 137.
— in State universities. (Grace C. Bibb) Nat. Educa. Assoc. '80 : 51.

Normal education, Practice work in. (J. W. Cook) Nat. Educa. Assoc. '95 : 501.

Normal instruction in academies. (N. T. Clarke) N. Y. Regents, 82 : 732.
— in college. (E. North) N. Y. Regents, 82 : 701. 95 : 390.
— Matter and method in. (G. P. Beard) Nat. Educa. Assoc. '72 : 214.

Normal school and the academy. (T. H. Kirke) Nat. Educa. Assoc. '88 : 503.
— Future of the. (W. T. Harris) Nat. Educa. Assoc. '99 : 395.
— The ideal. (E. Brooks) Cong. Educa. Chic. '93 : 451.
— Place of, in the educational system. Nat. Educa. Assoc. '82 : 175.
— What constitutes a? (J. C. Gilchrist) Nat. Educa. Assoc. '81 : 201.

Normal schools. Everett. Orat. v. 2. — (Anna C. Brackett) Nat. Educa. Assoc. '72 : 181. — (Louis Soldan; E. C. Hewitt) Nat. Educa. Assoc. '77 : 139.
— Academic function of. (J. M. Green) Nat. Educa. Assoc. '94 : 853.
— and training schools in France, Historical development of. (Eugene Martin) Nat. Educa. Assoc. '93 : 415.
— Attacks on. (C. C. Rounds) Nat. Educa. Assoc. '77 : 159.

Normal schools, Centennial thoughts on. (Edward Brooks) Nat. Educa. Assoc. '76 : 157.
— City. (L. H. Jones) Nat. Educa. Assoc. '91 : 324.
— Common school studies in. (J. C. Greenough) Nat. Educa. Assoc. '77 : 155.
— Condition and wants of. (S. H. White) Nat. Educa. Assoc. '70 : 5.
— Course of study for. (W. F. Phelps) Nat. Educa. Assoc. '70 : 11. — (John Ogden) Nat. Educa. Assoc. '74 : 216.
— Criticism in. (T. J. Gray) Nat. Educa. Assoc. '90 : 753.
— Curriculum of. (C. W. Hodgin ; Lucy M. Washburne) Nat. Educa. Assoc. '88 : 485. — (W. W. Parsons) Nat. Educa. Assoc. '90 : 718.
— Duties and Dangers of. (D. B. Hagar) Nat. Educa. Assoc. '73 : 164.
— Function of. (E. E. Sheib) Nat. Educa. Assoc. '85 : 235.
— German system of. (C. De Garmo) Nat. Educa. Assoc. '87 : 484.
— Gradation of. (T. Kirkland) Cong. Educa. Chic. '93, 410.
— How may they best accomplish their purpose ? (R. G. Boone) Nat. Educa. Assoc. '97 : 721.
— in France, History of. (E. Martin) Cong. Educa. Chic. '93, 415.
— in the state of New York. (F. J. Cheney) Cong. Educa. Chic. '93, 418.
— Mental habits fostered by. (C. A. Morey) Nat. Educa. Assoc. '76 : 192.
— Methods and courses in. (T. J. Gray, ed.) Nat. Educa. Assoc. '89 : 570.
— Methods of work in. (M. Macvicar) Cong. Educa. Chic. '93, 430.
— Necessity and growth of. (Thomas Hunter) Nat. Educa. Assoc. '84 : 238.
— New psychology in. (Lillie A. Williams) Nat. Educa. Assoc. '93 : 781.
— of the U. S., Methods of instruction in. (T. J. Gray) Nat. Educa. Assoc. '87 : 472.
— — Past, present, and future of. (Richard Edwards) Nat. Educa. Assoc. '76 : 48.
— open questions about. (T. J. Morgan) N. Y. Regents, 97, app. : 162.
— problem of. (S. S. Parr) Nat. Educa. Assoc. '88 : 465.
— Professional and academic studies in. (Committee on normal education) Nat. Educa. Assoc. '89 : 394.
— Professional course of study for. (John Ogden) Nat. Educa. Assoc. '76 : 203.
— Professional instruction in. (T. W. Harvey ; J. H. Hoose) Nat. Educa. Assoc. '72 : 196. — (Lewis McLouth) Nat. Educa. Assoc. '79 : 121. — (C. De Garmo) Nat. Educa. Assoc. '91 : 719.
— Proper work of. (J. C. Greenough ; A. G. Boyden) Nat. Educa. Assoc. '72 : 165.
— purpose of, Accomplishment of. (R. G. Boone) Nat. Educa. Assoc. '97 : 721.
— Relation of, to other schools. (Committee on Normal education) Nat. Educa. Assoc. '92 : 781.
— — to public schools. (E. O. Lyte) Nat. Educa. Assoc. '95 : 973.
— — to universities. (C. De Garmo) Nat. Educa. Assoc. '94 : 821.
— Sociological ideal view of. (D. Fulcomer) Cong. Educa. Chic. '93, 422.
— Special work of. (Larkin Dunton) Nat. Educa. Assoc. '74 : 234.
— Training of teachers in. (J. W. Cook) Nat. Educa. Assoc. '94 : 86.

Nottingham, Heneage Finch, earl of. Campbell. Ld. chan. 4 : 236. — Lodge. Portraits (Bohn), v. 6. — Welsby. Eng. judges.

Nottingham, Eng. Paladin. Glances, 195.

— rioters in, Trials of, 1817. Browne, G. L. Narr. state trials, 2 : 214.

Notton, James Sager. Am. Bar Assoc. 19 : 640.

Nova, Juan de, and Pedro Alvarez Cabral. Vogel. Cent. of discov. 87.

Nova Scotia, Constitution of the Legislative Council of. (J. G. Bourinot) Roy. Soc. Can. 2d ser. 2, § 2 : 141.

— currency of, Annals of. (R. W. McLachlan) Roy. Soc. Can. 10 : § 2.

Novalis (pseud.). See Hardenberg, Friedrich von.

Novara, Battle of, 1849. Adams, C. Gt. camp. 228.

Novatian. Evans, R. W. Biog. early church, 2 : 252.

Novel, The. Hunt, T. W. Rep. Eng. prose, 148. — Swing. Old pic. 2 : 39. — Zola. Exper. novel, 209.

— and the common school. Warner, C. D. Rela. of lit. 261.

— as a form of literature. Masson. Brit. novel. 11.

— Coming. Matthews, A. Ruminations.

— English, of 18th century. Texte, J. Rousseau, 142.

— — State of, 1892. Saintsbury. Miscel. ess. 388.

— Ethical. (R. K. Douglas) Art of writ. fiction, 109.

— The experimental. Zola. Exper. novel, 1.

— fashionable, The last. Lang. Ess. in lit. 93.

— The German. Boyesen, H. H. Ess. Ger. liter. 213.

— Historical. (A. J. Church) Art of writ. fiction, 98. — Saintsbury, G. Ess. Eng. lit. 2 : 303.

— The local. Garland. Crumbling idols, 69.

— The modern. Stearns, F. P. Real & ideal, 58.

— of incident, The. Repplier. Ess. in min. 207.

— of manners. (L. B. Walford) Art of writ. fiction, 22. — Traill. New fiction, 137.

— Political. Traill. New fiction, 27.

— Power of. Mabie. My study fire, 2 : 169.

— Predominance of the. Burton, R. Liter. likings, 61.

— The realistic. Zangwill. Without prej. 83.

— Tyranny of. Gosse, E. Questions, 1.

Novel party, A. Hunt, L. Men, wom. & books, 57.

Novel-reading. Gardner, S. J. Aut. leaves, 187.

Novel-writing. Rands, W. B. Holbeach, 1 : 256.

— and novel-reading. Brownson. Works, 19 : 221.

— in England. Moulton, L. C. Rambles, 127.

Novelist, American, and his public. Boyesen. Lit. silhouettes, 41.

Novelists and the table. Repplier, A. In dozy hours, 32.

— British. Friswell. Essays, 260.

— Contentiousness of. Repplier, A. Varia, 217.

— Lady. Eliot, Geo. Ess. 7.

— — False morality of. Greg. Lit. & soc. judg. 85.

— — Silly novels by. Eliot, Geo. Ess. 157.

— Lesser American. Richardson. Amer. lit. 2 : 390.

— Mistakes of. Walsh, W. S. Paradox, 61.

Novello, Clara Anastasia, Contessa Gigliucci. Clayton, E. C. Queens, 383. — Needham. Queens of song.

Novels. Paget, V. Baldwin, 187.

— and agnosticism. Hawthorne, J. Confess. 31.

— and novel-makers. Craik, D. M. Plain speaking, 121.

Novels and novel-readers. Burton, R. Liter. likings, 77.

— and novelists. Miller, H. Hist. ess. 469.

— British. Talfourd. Crit. writ.

— Conversation in. Repplier. Ess. in min. 59.

— Defoe to Thackeray. Reed, W. B. Among books, 182.

— 18th century. Dobson, A. 18th cent. vign. 3 : 83. — Perry, T. S. Eng. lit. 18th cent. 282, 337.

— Immoral. Mathews, W. Men, p. & t. 327.

— Realism and idealism of. Walsh, W. S. Paradox, 112.

— Relation of, to life. (F. Stephen) Camb. ess. '55 : 148.

— Religious. Brownson. Works, 19 : 143.

— Sensational. Mansel. Letters, 215.

— Women's. Brownson. Works, 19 : 595.

Novelty and familiarity. Hazlitt. Plain speaker, v. 2.

November, Customs and superstitions of. Soane. New curios. 2 : 234.

Noves, Laura de, with portrait. Clarke, M. C. Noted wom. 145.

— Petrarch and. Delepierre. Hist. diff. 93. — Jameson. Loves of poets.

Novikoff, Olga. Stead. Char. sket. 93.

"Now," Note on. Bax, E. B. Outlooks, 199.

Noxon, B. Davis. Proctor. Lawy. of N. Y. 672.

Noyes, G. R. Peabody. Harv. rem. 130.

Nuisances, Public. (R. S. Tracy) Buck, A. H. (ed.) Hygiene, 2 : 379.

Nullification. Clay. Life & speeches, 5 : 392. — Mansfield, E. D. Pers. mem. 236.

— Doctrine and history of. Foster, R. Comment. on Const. 1 : 123, 145, 293.

— Doctrine of. Madison, J. Letters, 4 : 95, 228, 263, 395.

— in South Carolina, 1832. Tilden, S. J. Writ. 1 : 1.

— — Bibliography. (D. F. Houston) Harv. Hist. stud. v. 3.

— — History of. Perry, B. F. Biog. sketches, 2 : 199.

Number systems, Primitive. (L. P. Conant) Smithson. Rept. '92 : 583.

Number-work, Short and rational method of. (F. B. Ginn) Nat. Educa. Assoc. '88 : 392.

Numbers, Fatality of. Baring-Gould. Myths, 647.

— Superstitions regarding. Jones, W. Credulities, 256.

Numerals, Arabic, On the antiquity of dates expressed in. Wright, T. Ess. archæol. 2 : 74.

Numismatics. Bibliography. Hazlitt, W. C. Coin Collector. — Hill, G. F. Handbook of Gr. & Roman coins.

— Greek. Newton. Essays, 404.

Nunneries, Mediæval. Burke, S. H. Men of reforma. 2 : 45.

Nuns, The Anglo-Saxon. Montalembert. Monks, 5 : 213.

Nuremberg. Bellows. Old world, 1 : 110. — Howard, B. W. One year, 85. — Jameson. Visits, 1 : 194. — Buckley, T. A. Great cities, 395.

— Heidelberg to, on foot. Taylor, B. At home, 1 : 66.

Nuremberg chronicle. Wood, J. G. Out-of-doors, 244.

Nurse, The trained. (S. F. Palmer) Conf. char. & correc. '95 : 259.

Nursery literature. Repplier. Ess. in min. 195.

Nursery rhymes, Nature myths in. (T. Foster) Proctor, R. A. Leis. read. 231.

Nursery tales, Problem of. Repplier. Ess. in min. 195.

Nursery work and child-hospital work. (Mrs. M. A. Du Bois) Conf. char. & correc. '85 : 181.

Nurses and nursing, Papers on. Cong. Char. Chic. '93, 5 : 444–624.

— in settlement work. (L. D. Wald) Conf. char. & correc. '95 : 264.

— Post-graduate school for. (C. B. Brown) Conf. char. & correc. '90 : 147.

— Trained, among sick poor in New York. (Mrs. A. H. Smith) Conf. char. & correc. '90 : 110.

— — Moral influence of, in hospitals. (L. Richards) Conf. char. & correc. '95 : 256.

— — Plea for, in almshouse hospitals. (G. H. M. Rowe) Conf. char. & correc. '95 : 276.

— Training of. (J. H. Packard) Phila. Soc. Sci. Assoc. '76.

— Training-schools for. Conf. char. & correc. '94 : 94. — (I. A. Hampton) Conf. char. & correc. '90 : 140. — Field, Mrs. H. M. Sket. France, 249. — U. S. Bur. Ed. Circ. '82, no. 1.

— — of the future. (E. Cowles) Conf. char. & correc. '90 : 115.

— Women as. Bolton, S. K. Soc. stud. in Eng. 93.

Nursing. (Hon. Mrs. Stuart Wortley) Burdett-Coutts. Wom. miss. 216.

— Care of the sick in their homes. (S. F. Palmer) Conf. char. & correc. '95 : 259.

— District, in London. (D. C. Kimber) Conf. char. & correc. '95 : 273.

— Hospital. (E. Garret) Trans. Soc. Sci. Lond. '66 : 472.

— Science of. (A. M. Fullerton) Conf. char. & correc. '90 : 130.

— Sick- and health-. (F. Nightingale) Burdett-Coutts. Wom. miss. 184.

"**Nurture,** Nature vs.," in the making of social careers. (C. H. Cooley) Conf. char. & correc. '96 : 399.

Nutrition, Decomposition and. Hinton. Thinking, 387.

Nuts as food in foreign countries, 1898. U. S. Cons. Rept. 58 : 537.

Nutt, Fannie W. Hemenway. Poets of Vt. 364.

Nuttall, Thomas. Youmans. Pioneers sci. 205.

Nyberg, L. T. Miller, Jos. Singers church, 2d ed. 227.

Nye, Edgar Wm., "Bill." Clemens. Funny fellows, 117.

Nye, James W. Brockett. Men of our day, 348.

Nymphs of antiquity and the poets. Hunt. Day by fire, 170.

Oahu college. Todd, M. L. Corona, 104.

Oak, live, Production and protection of. Woodbury, L. Writ. 3 : 332.

Oakford, Charles. Winslow, S. N. Biog. Phila. merch. 152.

Oakland College, Mississippi. U. S. Bur. Ed. Circ. '99, no. 2 : 63.

Oakley, Rev. Frederick, canon of Westminster. Oxenham. Stud. in eccl. hist. 325. — Miller, Jos. Singers church, 2d ed. 496.

Oastler, Richard. Gibbins. Eng. soc. ref. 119, 133.

Oates, Samuel. Ivimey. Eng. Bapt. 2 : 282.

Oates, Titus. Seccombe, T. Twelve bad men, 95.

Oath of allegiance, British. Pollock. Ess. in juris. 176.

Oaths, Consistency with Christianity. Rush, B. Ess. 125.

— of allegiance. Webster, N. Ess. 151.

— test, Constitutionality of. Field, D. D. Spee. 1 : 89.

Oatlands Palace. Timbs. Abbeys, 1 : 146.

Obedience, Christian. Wilks. Chr. ess. 100.

— Law of. Mabie. My study fire, 2 : 138.

Obelisk in Central Park, Misfortunes of. (A. A. Julien) Am. Geog. Soc. 25 : 66.

Obelisks, Egyptian. Macmillan, H. Rom. mosaics, 179.

Ober-Ammergau. Stoddard. Red letter, 63.

— Passion-play of, 1860. Stanley. Essays, 13.

— — 1880. Hall, G. S. Asp. Ger. 33.

— — 1890. Jordan, D. S. Story, 43.

Oberkampf, Christopher. Brightwell. Heroes of lab. 98.

Oberlin, John Frederic. Adams, W. H. D. Good Samar. 82. — Chambers's Miscel. no. 87. — Watson, Mrs. R. A. Poet-toilers, 137. — Miller, Jos. Singers church, 2d ed. 279.

Oberlin, Madame John Frederic (Madeleine Salome Witter; d. 1784). Child. Good wives, 141.

Oberlin College. (A. O. F. Johnston) Brackett, A. C. Educa. of girls, 329. — College book, 320. — (J. R. Commons) U. S. Bur. Ed. Circ. '91, no. 5 : 55.

Obesity, Comments on. Timbs. Doctors, 187.

Oblivion, or dead history, Use of. Bushnell. Moral uses, 73.

Object lessons, Place and value of. (Delia A. Lathrop) Nat. Educa. Assoc. '70 : 49.

Object-work, Educational value of. (L. S. Thompson) Nat. Educa. Assoc. '88 : 598.

Oblatio trium regum. Dunham, S. A. Em. liter. men, 1 : 353.

O'Brian, Patrick. Whitehead, C. Highwaymen, 1 : 122.

O'Brien, Fitz-James. Warner Lib. 18 : 10733.

O'Brien, Smith, Trial of, for high treason. Townsend, W. C. Mod. state trials, 1 : 474.

O'Brien, William. Cook, D. Hours w. players, 2 : 21. — Doran. Annals stage, 2 : 46.

Obscurity. Cowley. Ess. 34.

Observant Fathers of Greenwich, The. Burke, S. H. Men of reforma. 1 : 222.

Observation. Galton. Art of travel. — Herschel. Manual of sci. inquiry.

— Hasty. Burroughs, J. Riverby, 253.

Observational powers, Education of. Clarke, J. F. Self-culture, 113.

Observations, magnetic, General bearings of. (E. W. Creak) Smithson. Inst. Rept. '95 : 107.

Observatories, Astronomical, with bibliography. Todd, D. P. Stars & tel. 391.

— — American and foreign. (G. H. Boehmer) Smithson. Rept. '86 : 367.

— — Mountain, with bibliography. Todd, D. P. Stars & tel. 395.

— Meteorological. (R. Inwards) Smithson. Rept. '96 : 149.

Observatory, The first. Lodge, O. J. Pioneers, 33.

— Southern. (A. M. Clerke) Smithson. Rept. '91 : 115.

Observer, The enlightened. Curtis, G. W. Other ess. 88.

Obstruction, Parliamentary, in the U. S. Lodge, H. C. Hist. & pol. ess.

O'Carroll, Thomas. Burke, O. J. Cath. archb. 44.

Occleve, Thomas. Disraeli, I. Amen. (N. Y. 2 v.) 1 : 222. — (T. Arnold) Ward. Eng. poets, 1 : 124. — Minto, W. Eng. poets, 70.

Occom, Samson. Hatfield, E. F. Poets of church, 475.

Occupation, Loss of. Jacox, F. Cues, 218.

— Monotony in, a source of happiness. Bulwer, E. Caxtoniana.

Ogier of Denmark. Cox & Jones. Romances, 348. — Ludlow. Epics, **2** : 247.

Ogilvie, John. Hatfield, E. F. Poets of church, 477. — Wilson, J. G. Poets of Scot. **1** : 246.

Ogilvie, The ladies, of Airlie. Fittis. Heroines of Scot. 221.

Oglanders of Nunwell. Burke, B. Viciss. of fam. **3** : 4 6.

Oglesby, Richard J. Brockett. Men of our day, 359.

Oglethorpe, James Edward. Lossing. Em. Amer. 51.

— and Georgia. Japp, A. H. Master mission. 1.

— and the Wesleys. Larrabee, W. C. Wesley, **1** : 97.

Oglethorpe University, Midway, Ga. U. S. Bur. Ed. Circ. '88, no. **4** : 79.

O'Gorman, James Myles. Clarke, R. H. Cath. bishops, **3** : 626.

O'Grada, John. Burke, O. J. Cath. archb. 45.

O'Hely, James. Burke, O. J. Cath. archb. 94.

O'Higgins, Miler. Burke, O. J. Cath. archb. 93.

Ohio. Buckeyes in Amer. history. Swank. Notes, 206.

— Cities of, Municipal condition of. (A. C. Cassat) Nat. Conf. City Govt. '97 : 193.

— Early hist. of. Roosevelt. Winning west.

— Evolution of township government in. (J. A. Wilgus) Am. Hist. Assoc. Rept. '94 : 403.

— First fugitive slave case of record in. (W. H. Smith) Am. Hist. Assoc. Rept. '93 : 91.

— in 1803. Mansfield, E. D. Pers. mem. 3.

— Internal improvements in, 1825–50. (C. N. Morris) Am. Hist. Assoc. **3** : 351.

— Reform farm school. (B. W. Chidlaw) N. Y. Pris. Assoc. **26**, app. : 328.

— School laws of, Reforms in. Hinsdale, B. A. Schools & stud. 341.

— State board of commerce, Work of. (T. L. Johnson) Nat. Conf. City Govt. '96 : 192.

Ohio river. Bibliography. Thwaites, R. G. Afloat on Ohio.

Ohio State University, Athens, O. U. S. Bur. Ed. Circ. '91, no. **5** : 13.

Ohio State University, Columbus, O. U. S. Bur. Ed. Circ. '91, no. **5** : 36.

Ohio valle, First schools in. (W. A. Venable) Nat. Educa. Assoc. '89 : 231.

Ohio Wesleyan University, Delaware, O. U. S. Bur. Ed. Circ. '91, no. **5** : 79.

Ohm, Georg Simon. Munro, J. Pioneers elec. 179.

Ohnet, Georges. Van de Velde. Fr. fiction, **1** : 114.

O'Hoisin, Edan. Burke, O. J. Cath. archb. 13.

Oil, illuminating, Dangerous. (R. C. Redzie) Mich. Health, '73 : 34. '77 : 71.

— Stilling waves by. Franklin. Works ('87), **5** : 253.

Oil-cloth industry in Maine. Me. Bur. Lab. '95 : 122.

Oil tree, The Chinese, 1897. U. S. Cons. Rept. '54 : 477.

Oils, Vegetable, Manufacture of, 1892. (C. B. Trail) U. S. Cons. Rept. **39** : 475.

Ojéda, Alonzo de. Murray, J. O'K. Cath. heroes, 179.

"O. K." Origin of. Mansfield, E. D. Pers. mem. 324.

Okelevicius. Wallace, R. Anti-Trin. biog. **3** : 144.

O'Kelly, Maurice. Burke, O. J. Cath. archb. 49.

O'Kelly, Thomas. Burke, O. J. Cath. archb. 54.

Oklahoma. Dixon, W. H. White conquest, **1** : 302.

Olaf Haroldson, St. Maclear. Apostles, 190.

Olaf Tryggveson, king of Norway. Maclear. Apostles, 172. — (T. Carlyle) Ferris, G. T. Gt. leaders, 111.

Olavidé, Don Pablo. Brightwell. Byepaths of biog. 81.

Olcott, George. Am. Antiq. Soc. Proc. n. s. **10** : 26.

Old and rich, Born. Warner, C. D. As we go, 170.

Old, Growing. Friswell. Gentle life, **1** : 305. — Kaye. Essays of optimist, 140.

Old age. Boyd. Recreat. **1** : 408. — Holmes. Over the teacups, 25. — Parker, T. Add. sp. **2** : 413. — Emerson. Society, 295.

— and youth. Stevenson, R. L. Virginibus.

— Attention to nature in. Bulwer, E. Caxtoniana.

— Beautiful. Warner, C. D. As we go, 79.

— Hygiene of. (H. C. Wood) Penn. Health, '86 : 334.

— Light at evening; a sermon. Boyd. Graver tho'ts, 129.

Old age pensions. Mackay, T. Meth. soc. ref. 173. — Wagner, L. Mod. pol. ora. 194.

Old Bob, Story of. Chambers, W. Rem. pers. 60.

Old Catholics of Germany. Baring-Gould. Germany, 311.

— — and the Romish episcopate. Strauss, G. L. M. Men of Ger. **1** : 258.

Old Clothes Exchange. Wynter, A. Our soc. bees, **2** : 271.

Old corner, The. Fairbanks, O. B. Ague-cheek, 212.

Old maid, New. Tollemache. Ess. & mock-ess. 310.

Old maids, A new race of. Friswell. Gentle life, **2** : 46.

Old masters, Drawing by the. Carr, J. C. Papers, 1.

Old people, Cheerfulness of. Boyd. Our life, 194.

Old, Si., *pseud. See* Small, S. W.

Old world, Ruins of, as milestones of civilization. Dutt. Hist. stud. **2** : 409.

Oldcastle, Sir John. Gilpin, W. Lives, 91. — Ivimey. Eng. Bapt. **1** : 76. — Maurice, C. E. Eng. pop. leaders, v. **2**. — (J. Fox) Wrangham. Brit. Plutarch, v. 1.

Oldfield, Anne. (W. Oldys) Betterton. Hist. stage. — Doran. Annals stage, **1** : 288. — Galt. Players, **1** : 88.

Oldham, H. Espinasse. Lanc. worth. v. **1**.

Oldham, John. Poems. Bryant. Prose, **1** : 115.

Oldmixon, John. Lawrence. Brit. historians, **1** : 321.

Oldstyle, Jonathan, Gent., Letters of. Irving. Biog. 11.

Oldys, Wm., and his manuscripts. Disraeli, I. Curios. (N. Y. 4 v.) **4** : 425.

O'Leary, Ellen. (W. B. Yeats) Miles, A. H. Poets of cent. **7** : 449.

Oleo oil in the Netherlands, American, 1891. (W. E. Gardner) U. S. Cons. Rept. **36** : 289.

Oleomargarine. Mass. Health, '87 : 199.

— Bill of 1886 on. McPherson. Handbook pol. '86.

— Healthfulness of. (E. G. Brackett) Mass. Health, '87 : 248.

— Laws on, in the U. S. (E. Richards) Am. Pub. Health, **15** : 101.

— Manufacturing of, American methods. Am. Pub. Health, **15** : 107.

Olga, queen of Greece, with portrait. Crowned heads, 59.

Olga, queen of Württemberg, with portrait. Crowned heads, 17.

Olga the Dane. *See* Olgier.

Olin, Stephen. Gorrie. Em. Meth. 383. — Lossing. Em. Amer. 384. — (J. Floy) McClintock, J. Em. Meth. 317. — Sherman, D. N. Eng. divines, 414.

Oliphant, Caroline. *See* Nairne, Baroness.

Oliphant, Laurence. Smalley. Lond. lett. 1: 306.

Oliphant, Mrs. Margaret. Heywood, J. C. How they strike, 113. — With portrait. (H. W. Preston) Warner Lib. 19: 10819.

Oliva, Fernan Perez de. *See* Perez de Oliva.

Olivarez, Count (Gasparo de Guzman). Crowe, E. E. For. statesmen, 2: 220.

Oliver, Mrs. Emma (Eburne) Sedgwick. Clayton, E. C. Eng. fem. art. 2: 227.

Oliver, Fitch, E. (E. F. Slafter) Mass. Hist. Soc. Proc. 2d ser. 8: 474.

Oliver, Henry K. (J. H. Jones) Mass. Labor, '86: 3.

Oliver, James Edward. (Gustavus Hay) Am. Acad. A. & S. Proc. 31: 367.

Oliver, John M. Walker, C. D. Biog. Va. Mil. Inst. 410.

Oliver, Thomas, of Cambridge, Mass. Sabine. Loyalists, 492.

Olivers, Thomas. Hatfield, E. F. Poets of church, 479. — Jackson, T. Early Meth. 1: 193. — Miller, Jos. Singers church, 2d ed. 244.

Olives, Mount of. Little, W. J. K. Sketches, 308.

Olives and olive culture in maritime Alps. U. S. Cons. Repts. Special, v. 2.

Olivet College, Olivet, Mich. (J. S. Daniels) U. S. Bur. Ed. Circ. '91, no. 4: 138.

Olizavowski, Thomas. Soboleski. Poets of Poland, 456.

Ollivant, A., bishop of Llandaff. With photo. Cooper, T. Men of mark, 3: 11. — Morgan, J. Four biog. sk.

Ollivier, Olivier Emile. King, E. French pol. lead. 210.

Olmecas and the Tultecas. (Ph. J. J. Valentini) Am. Antiq. Soc. Proc. n. s. 2: 193.

Olmstead, Aaron Barlow. Am. Bar Assoc. 12: 360.

Olmsted, Asa, case of, against D. Wells. Curtis, B. R. Mem. & writ. v. 2.

Olmsted, Denison. Youmans. Pioneers sci. 250.

Olmsted, Frederick Law. Brockett. Woman's work, 299.

O'Loghlen, Sir Michael. Sheil, R. L. Sketches, 1: 157. 2: 106.

O'Loughlin, Marian. Burke, O. J. Cath. archb. 22.

Olympia and its church. Freeman. Studies Greece, 257.

— and the festival. Gardner, P. New chap. Gr. hist.

— Discoveries at. Newton. Essays, 321.

— — Recent. (T. Davidson) Am. Geog. Soc. 12: 217.

— Excavations at, 1875–81. Diehl, C. Excursions, 210.

Olympian register, Authenticity of. Huxley. Ess. contro. 217.

Olympias. Mahaffy, J. P. Greek life, ch. 4.

Olympic games. Bibliography. Providence Pub. Lib. Bull. Apr. '96.

Olympic Theatre, London. Lennox, W. P. Plays, 1: 142.

— in New York. Hutton, L. Plays, 18.

"Om," Practical significance of. (N. C. Paul) Five years theos. 540.

Omaha, Neb. Marshall, W. G. Thro' Amer. 113. — Sala. Amer. revis. 2: 145.

Omaha, Neb., Municipal condition of. (G. J. Powell) Nat. Conf. City Govt. 2–3: 418.

Omaha exposition, 1898. U. S. Bur. Ed. Rept. '97–98, 2: 1733.

Omaha Indians, Love songs of. (A. C. Fletcher) Cong. Anthrop. Chic. '93, 153.

O'Mahony, Francis S., with portrait. (J. Malone) Warner Lib. 19: 10845.

Omar Khayyám. (N. H. Dole) Warner Lib. 15: 8541. — Lang. Lett. to dead au. 216. — Palgrave. Ess. east. 271.

— Bibliography. Jackson, H. Edw. Fitzgerald.

— Rubáiyát. Bibliography. Heron-Allen, E. Rubáiyát of O. Khayyám.

O'Melaghlins of Meath. Burke, B. Viciss. of fam. 2: 365.

Omen, Days of good and evil. Lawrence, R. M. Magic, 239.

Omens. Aubrey, J. Miscel. — Jones, W. Credulities, 8. — Wynter, A. Fruit betw. leaves, 2: 96.

Ometepec, Nicaragua, Antiquities from. (C. C. Nutting) Smithson. Rept. '83: 908.

Omitlán, Mexico. (W. Niven) Am. Geog. Soc. 29: 217.

Omnibus, The inside of an. Hunt, L. Men, wom. & books, 8.

Omnibus-box, The. Cook, D. On stage, 2: 64.

Omnibuses, London. Wynter, A. Our soc. bees, 2: 9.

O'Moghan, Gregory. Burke, O. J. Cath. archb. 49.

O'Mullally, Thomas. Burke, O. J. Cath. archb. 68.

O'Murray, Donatus. Burke, O. J. Cath. archb. 54.

On, Egypt. Poole, R. S. Cities of Egypt, 131.

Onderdonk, Henry Ustick, Bishop. Hatfield, E. F. Poets of church, 483. — Miller, Jos. Singers church, 2d ed. 434.

Ondricek, Franz, with portrait. Ehrlich, A. Cel. violin. 184.

One idea, Men of. Hazlitt, W. Table-talk, 78. — Holland, J. G. Lessons, 208.

Oneby, Major, English gambler. Thornbury. Old stor. 20.

Oneida community. Hinds. Amer. commun. — Nordhoff. Commun. 259.

— and American socialism. Smith, G. Ess. on ques. of day, 337.

O'Neil, Henrietta, Lady. Williams, Jane. Lit. wom. 199.

O'Neil, James. With portrait. (H. G. Fiske) McKay, F. E. Fam. actors, 299.

O'Neill, Eliza. Matthews, B. Actors, 2: 285.

O'Neill, Gen. John. Savage, J. Fenian heroes, 383.

O'Neill family. Burke, B. Viciss. of fam. 1: 149.

Ongaro, F. dall'. Howells. Mod. It. poets, 30.

Onofrio, St., and Tasso. Macmillan, H. Rom. mosaics, 253.

Onomacritus. Arnold, E. Poets of Greece, 160. — Mills. Poets of Greece, 137.

Onomatology. (S. T. Frost) N. Y. Regents, 94: 606. *See also* Names.

Onomatopœia in language. Blackie, J. S. Horæ Hellen. 217.

Onslow, Arthur. Manning, J. A. Speakers, 435. — Woolrych. Serjeants, 2: 772.

Onslow, Phipps. Miller, Jos. Singers church, 2d ed. 561.

Onslow, Richard (1528–71). Manning, J. A. Speakers, 230.

Onslow, Sir Richard (1654–1717). Manning, J. A. Speakers, 412.

Ontario; Archæology. Bibliography. (A. F. Hunter) Toronto Mus. Archæ. Rept. '97-98.
— Educational system of. (G. W. Ross) Nat. Educa. Assoc. '91 : 143.
Ontario, Lake, Boat fight on. Silliman. Gallop, 67.
— Naval operations on, in 1812. Roosevelt, T. Naval war 1812, 139.
— — in 1813. Roosevelt, T. Naval war 1812, 221.
— An outing on. Abbott, C. C. Outings, 221.
Onyx marbles, Origin, composition, and uses of, ancient and modern. (G. P. Merrill) U. S. Nat. Mus. Rept. '93 : 539.
Oölogy, Comparative, of North American birds. (R. W. Shufeldt) U. S. Nat. Mus. Rept. '92 : 461.
Oom Keis, Ruins of. Tweedie. Ruined cities, 84.
Op Den Graeff, Abraham and Dirck. Pennypacker. Hist. sk. 201.
Open-air life. Guiney. Patrins, 13.
Opera, The. Carlyle. Essays.—Gurney. Power of sound.—Hazlitt. Lit. rem. 2 : 319.
— and opera singers, Italian. Hogarth. Mem. opera, 2 : 276.
— at Vauxhall. Goldsmith. Miscel. (N. Y. 4 v.) 1 : 211.
— Career of, to 1840. Mathews, W. S. B. Hundred yrs. music, 45.
— English, The chances of. Hueffer. Mus. stud. 233.
— — in New York. Ritter. Music in Amer. 144.
— — in present time. Hogarth. Mem. opera, 2 : 344.
— French, in New Orleans. Ritter. Music in Amer. 144, 287.
— Full dress at the. Willis. Hurry-graphs, 336.
— German, in New York. Finck. Chopin, 233.— Ritter. Music in Amer. 329.
— Heroes of. Adams, W. D. With poet, 103.
— in England. Goldsmith. Miscel. (N. Y. 4 v.) 1 : 159.
— Italian. Hogarth. Mem. opera, 1 : 6.
— — Dead and dying. Runciman, J. F. Old scores, 141.
— — Establishment of, in England. Hogarth. Mem. opera, 1 : 343.
— — in last century. Hogarth. Mem. opera, 1 : 156.
— — in middle of last century. Hogarth. Mem. opera, 2 : 62.
— — in New York. Ritter. Music in Amer. 181, 287, 329.
— — Metastasio and. Paget, V. Stud. of 18th cent. 141.
— — Modern. Hogarth. Mem. opera, 2 : 340.
— — State of, in early part of 18th century. Hogarth. Mem. opera, 1 : 271.
— Morality of. Willis. Hurry-graphs, 351.
Opera bouffe. Edwards, H. S. Prima don. 2 : 236.
Opera dancing, French. Hunt. Wishing-cap, 337.
Opera singers, Italian, last part of 18th century. Hogarth. Mem. opera, 2 : 119.
Opera writers, French. Hogarth. Mem. opera, 2 : 246, 261.
Operas, English and Italian, in first part of 18th century. Hogarth. Mem. opera, 1 : 353.
— Foreign, adapted to English stage. Hogarth. Mem. opera, 2 : 372.
— German. Hogarth. Mem. opera, 1 : 176.
Ophthalmia neonatorum, Prevention of. (A. Chacon) Am. Pub. Health, 18 : 176.
Opie, Amelia. Balfour, C. L. Women worth emu-

lating, 72. — Jeaffreson. Novelists, 2 : 15. — Kavanagh. Eng. women, 2 : 237. — Martineau, H. Biog. sk. 13. — Robertson. Eng. poetesses, 104.— Russell. Extr. women, 258. — Bethune, G. W. Brit. fem. poets, 315. — Hall, S. C. Book of mem. 167. — Hamilton, C. J. Wom. writers, 175. — Mayer, G. T. Wom. of lett. 2 : 59. — Miller, Jos. Singers church, 2d ed. 336.— Stanton, H. B. Reforms, 350.
Opie, John, English painter. Edwards, B. B. Self-taught, 191. — Spooner. Biog. fine arts, 2 : 630.
Opinion, Consistency of. Hazlitt. Sket.
— Influence of language on. Webster, N. Ess. 222.
— Sources of error in. Wilks. Chr. ess. 136.
— Treatment of people differing from us in. Boyd. Less. of mid. age, 180.
Opinions. Repplier, A. In dozy hours, 176.
— Formation of. Bailey, S. Essays, 15.—Thompson, D. G. Soc. prog.
— The free publication of. Bailey, S. Essays, 81.
— Legal, Great dissenting. (H. L. Carson) Am. Bar Assoc. 17 : 273.
— Poisonous. Stephen, L. Agnos. apol. 242; also in Coan. Ques. of belief, 129.
Opitz, Martin. Winkworth. Chr. singers Germ. 171.
Opium in China. DeQuincey. Works (Masson), 14 : 162.
— in India. Cust. Notes on missionary subj.
— Question of, Indo-Chinese, in 1893. Cust. Ling. & Orient. ess. 4 : 143.
— Sale and use of, in Massachusetts. (B. H. Hartwell) Mass. Health, '88 : 137.
— Use and abuse of. (F. E. Oliver) Mass. Health, '72 : 162.
Opium habit. Cumming, C. F. G. Wand. in China, 2 : 301. — (J. M. Hull) Iowa Health, '85 : 535.
— in Michigan. (O. Marshall) Mich. Health, '78 : 61.
Oporto. Crawfurd, O. Trav. in Portugal, 146.
Oppenheim, Joseph Suess, an early financial "operator." Baring-Gould. Oddities, 1 : 271.
— Wraxall. Remark. adv. 1 : 286.
Oppian. Arnold, E. Poets of Greece, 204.
Opportunities, Development of. Gray, E. C. Idle musings, 208.
Optics, Recent progress in. (W. LeC. Stevens) Smithson. Inst. Rept. '95 : 117.
Optimism. Pearson, C. H. Reviews, 99.
— L' Allegro. Watson, E. H. L. Uncon. humor, 37.
— Arrogance of. Fawcett, E. Agnost. 65.
— pessimism, and the moral order. Royce, J. Spir. mod. philos. 435.
— Rational. Dole, C. F. Theol. of civiliz. 121.
— Scientific bases of. Mallock. Stud. contemp. sup. 1.
O'Queely, Malachy. Burke, O. J. Cath. archb. 118.
Oracles. Aubrey, J. Miscel. — Davenport, R. A. Delusions, 5. — DeQuincey. Works (Masson), 7 : 44.
— Greek. (F. W. H. Myers) Abbott, E. Hellenica, 425.— Duruy. Hist. Greece, 2 : 318.— Dyer. Studies of Gods. — Myers. Ess. class. 1.
Oral teaching. (Larkin Dunton) Nat. Educa. Assoc. '82 : 63.— (J. W. Dickinson) Nat. Educa. Assoc. '84, app. : 13.
— and book teaching, Union of. (Mrs. N. S. Williams) Nat. Educa. Assoc. '87 : 364.
Oran, Algeria. Sala. Under sun, 175.
Orange, Mary, 2d princess of. Jesse. Court of Eng. Stuarts, 2 : 42.

Orange, France. Freeman. Hist. ess. 4 : 69.
Orange Free State. U. S. Cons. Rept. no. 154.
— in 1893. (E. R. Landgraf) U. S. Cons. Rept. 42 : 305.
Orator, Stump. Carlyle. Latter-day.
Oratorical success, Secret of. (T. S. Grimké) Charleston book, 42.
Oratorio, Musical societies and, in American cities. Ritter. Music in Amer. 112, 210, 263, 306.
— Progress of, to 1840. Mathews, W. S. B. Hundred years music, 55.
Oratorios. Hogarth. Mem. opera, 1 : 3.
— Hebrew. Butterworth. Great compos. 7.
Orators and oratory. Tuckerman. Charac. 239.
— young, Advice to. Butler, E. For good, 102.
Oratory. Walsh, R. Didactics, 1 : 129.
— American. Bryce. Amer. commonw. v. 2. — Nichol, J. Amer. lit. 97. — Bryce. Soc. institu. 212.
— Ancient and modern. Windsor. Ethica, 322.
— Anglican. Arnold, F. Our bishops, 2 : 139.
— Bibliography. Ringwalt, R. C. (ed.). Mod. Amer. oratory.
— English and American, compared. Burnap. Miscel.
— Political, Notes on. Peck, H. T. Pers. equa. 267.
— popular, Peculiarities of. (D. Sherlock) Afternoon lec. 5 : 181.
Orcagna, Andrea, di Cione. Perkins, C. C. Tusc. sculp. 1 : 77. — Stillman, W. J. Old Ital. mas. 62. — Symonds. Renais. fine arts, 124, 199.
— sonnet by ; trans. by W. W. Story. Perkins, C. C. Tusc. sculp. 2 : 190.
Orchard culture. Hoyt, J. G. Miscel. 256.
Orchard talk. Dodge, M. A. Summer rest. 3.
Orchards. Gray, J. C. Essays, 129.
Orchardson, Wm. Q. With photo. Cooper, T. Men of mark, 6 : 6. — Monkhouse, C. Brit. contemp. artists, 155.
Orchestra of to-day. Lanier. Music, 25.
Orchestras in theatres. Cook, D. Bk. of play, 1 : 172.
— Traveling. Ritter. Music in Amer. 314.
Orchids. Spence. Land of Bolivar, 2 : 192.
Orchomenus, Greece. Mahaffy. Rambles Greece, 195.
Ordeal, The. Lea. Supers. & force, 175. — Müller. Sac. books, 33 : 100, 247, 315.
— and duels. Mackay. Delusions, 1 : 160.
— by fire. Villari. Savonarola, 2 : 208.
Order of the Palm. Winkworth. Chr. singers Germ. 171.
Ordinance of 1787. (T. W. Bicknell) Nat. Educa. Assoc. '84 : 32.
— History of. (I. W. Andrews) Nat. Educa. Assoc. '87 : 120.
— Influence of. (B. A. Hinsdale ; T. A. Banning) Nat. Educa. Assoc. '87 : 135.
— Legislative history of. (J. M. Merriam) Am. Antiq. Soc. Proc. n. s. 5 : 303.
— Teaching of. (J. L. Pickard) Nat. Educa. Assoc. '87 : 129.
Ordinances. Dodge, M. A. Stumbl. 43.
Ordination : Holy orders. (C. Garrett) Church's ministry.
— Imposition of hands in. Hovey, A. Stud. in ethics, 429.
O'Regan, Anthony. Clarke, R. H. Cath. bishops, 3 : 162.
Oregon. (T. D. Hunt) Am. Geog. Soc. 1 : 137. — Brockett. Our west. emp. 1091. — Farnham. Trav. in Cal. 433. — Jackson, H. J. Three coasts, 129.

Oregon, Speeches on, 1845-46. Webster, D. Works, 5 : 60.
— Stone age of. (M. Eells) Smithson. Rept. '86 : 283.
— Title to. Senior. Hist. ess. 1.
Oregon question, The, 1845. Dix. Speeches, 1 : 1. — Field, D. D. Speeches, 2 : 3, 22. — Gallatin, A. Writ. 3 : 489. — Hilliard, H. W. Sp. 51. — Ludlow. Heart of contin. 445. — Murphy, J. M. Rambles, 43. — Winthrop, R. C. Addresses, 1 : 415, 460, 481.
Oregon territory, Languages of. Latham. Opuscula, 249.
— Government in. Dix. Speeches, 1 : 309.
— Territorial government for, 1848. Hilliard, H. W. Sp. 129.
O'Reilley, Bernard. Clarke, R. H. Cath. bishops, 2 : 391. — Jessie, J. H. Cel. Eton. v. 2. — Rogers, J. E. T. Gleanings, 1 : 47. — Wrangham. Brit. Plutarch, v. 6. See Walpole, Robert.
O'Reilly, Count Andrew. Grant, Jas. Cavaliers, 292.
O'Reilly, John Boyle, with portrait. Stoddard, R. H. Poets' homes, 196. — (M. F. Egan) Warner Lib. 19 : 10857.
Orford, Robert Walpole, earl of, with portrait. Caulfield. Kit-cat, 132.
Organ, About the. Statham. Music, 428.
— at Music Hall, Boston. Holmes. Soundings, 362.
— Old Italian organs and their builders. Baxter, L. E. Tusc. stud. 81.
Organ building, Bibliography. (F. E. Robertson) Eng. Mechanic, Feb. '97.
Organ question in Scotland, The. Boyd. Crit. ess. 320 ; or Leis. hours (Bost.), 274 ; or Less. of mid. age, 74.
Organs, Political. Godkin. Reflections, 242.
Organic life, Place of, in nature. Shaler. Interp. of nat. 103.
Organic nature, Riddle of. Mivart. Ess. 2 : 315.
Organisms, marine, Conditions and distribution of. (John Murray) Smithson. Rept. '96 : 397.
Organists. Mathews, W. S. B. Hundred years music, 236.
Organization. Gray, E. C. Idle musings, 246.
— (Parke Godwin) Peabody, E. P. Æsthetic pap. 50.
— Essentials of. (A. Johnson) Conf. char. & correc. '99 : 291.
— in daily life. Helps. Essays, 111.
— vs. originality. (Henry Sabin) Nat. Educa. Assoc. '90 : 228.
Organship. Miller, H. Lead. articles, 240.
Oriel College, Oxford, in 1823. Mozley. Reminis. 1 : 19.
Oriel school, Early, and its congeners. Tulloch. Movements 19th cent.
Oriental congresses, 1881-83. Cust. Ling. studies, 1 : 411. 2 : 40.
— 1889. Cust. Ling. studies, 3 : 195.
Oriental embassies. Wraxall, C. F. L. Hist. bye-ways, 2 : 272.
Oriental interiors. Stoddard, C. A. Span. cit. 216.
Oriental languages, study of, Influence of. Müller, M. Sel. ess. 2 : 1.
Oriental literature, Study of. Schlegel. Æsthet. (Bohn) 515.
Oriental masters, Old. Ellwanger. Sto. of house, 21.
Oriental religions. (Max Müller) Hundred greatest men, 115.
Oriental scholars. Cust. Ling. ess. 1 : 460.

Oriental scholarship in 19th century. (F. Max Müller) Smithson. Rept. '93 : 681.

Oriental science, Progress of, in America, during '88. (Cyrus Adler) Smithson. Rept. '88 : 675.

Oriental studies, Importance of. Müller. Chips, v. 4.

Oriental study, Stone-age basis for. (E. B. Tylor) Smithson. Rept. '93 : 701.

Orientation. (A. L. Lewis) Cong. Anthrop. Chic. '93, 113.

Origen of Alexandria. With portrait. Blakey, R. Prim. fathers, 108. — Broadus. Lec. hist. preach. 51. — Cave. Lives of fathers, 1 : 321. — Evans, R. W. Biog. early ch. 2 : 1. — Farrar. Lives of fathers, 1 : 291. — Pressensé. Martyrs, 282, 566. — Hort, F. J. A. Ante-N. fathers, 116. — Ker, J. Lec. hist. preach. 60. — (A. E. Brooke) Lefroy, W. Lec. eccl. hist. 299. — Vaughan, R. A. Ess. & rev. v. 1.

— and Celsus. Froude. Short stud. 4 : 237.

Origin. Bartol. Rad. prob. 262.

— and validity. Ritchie, D. G. Darwin.

Original sin. Mozley, J. B. Lec. 136, 148. — Newton, W. W. Ess. 227.

Originality. Hazlitt. Crit. on art, ser. 2. — Hopkins, M. Miscel. ess. 81. — Mabie. My study fire, 2 : 173.

— in literature. Mathews. Conversers, 211. — Mathews. Lit. style, 251.

"**Original,** L'," ship sunk at Quebec, 1750. (C. Würtell) Roy. Soc. Can. 2d ser. 4, § 2 : 67.

Orinda, The matchless. *See* Philips, Katherine Fowler.

Orkney Isles. Sinclair, J. Sketches.

— and Shetland. (C. S. Smith) Am. Geog. Soc. 23 : 131.

Orléans, Dukes of. Cook, T. D. Old Touraine, 1 : 92.

Orléans, Charles, duc d'. Besant. Fr. poetry, 54. — Cary. Fr. poets, 218. — Stevenson, R. L. Miscel. 2 : 221.

Orléans, Hélène Louise Elizabeth, duchesse d', and Queen Marie Amélie. Challice. Illus. wom. 213.

Orléans, Henrietta Maria, duchesse d'. Adams, W. H. D. Fam. beauties, 1 : 109. — Jesse. Court of Eng. Stuarts, 2 : 53.

Orléans, Louis P. J., duc d'. Adolphus. Biog. Fr. rev. 2 : 205. — Talleyrand. Memoirs, 1 : 109.

Orléans, Princess Palatine, duchess of. Imbert de St. A. Wom. Ct. Louis XIV, 167.

Orléans, House of. Field, Mrs. H. M. Sket. France, 176.

Orléans, Siege of. George, H. B. Battles, 80.

Orléans, Sieges of. Robson, W. Sieges, 297.

Orme, Robert. Lawrence. Brit. historians, 2 : 312.

Ormerod, E. A., Work of, in agricultural entomology. (Baroness Burdett-Coutts) Burdett-Coutts. Wom. miss. 323.

Ormond, James Butler, 1st duke of. Lodge. Portraits (Bohn), v. 9. — Wrangham. Brit. Plutarch, v. 4.

Ormond, James Butler, 2d duke of. Lodge. Portraits (Bohn), v. 7.

Ormuzd and Ahriman. Matheson. Distinc. mess. 171.

Ornament. Day, L. F. Every-day art, 1. — Maxwell, H. Post-mer. 86.

— Application of. Day, L. F. Every-day art, 85.

— Evolution in. (C. F. Hartt) N. Y. Regents, 87 : 689.

— Grammar of, Owen Jones's. Eliot, Geo. Ess. 189.

Ornament, past and present. Day, L. F. Every-day art, 20.

— Use in. Day, L. F. Every-day art, 68.

Ornamentation of nature. Taylor, I. Ult. civiliz. 314.

Orne, Caroline. Hart, J. S. Fem. prose, 436.

Orne, Henry. Loring, J. S. Hundred Bost. ora. 393.

Ornithology, Field study in. (H. B. Tristram) Smithson. Inst. Rept. '93 : 465.

— of North America, Audubon's. Peabody, W. B. O. Lit. rem. 137.

Orontea, Opera by M. A. Cesti. Hogarth. Mem. opera, 1 : 13.

O'Rorke, Capt. Michael. Savage, J. Fenian heroes, 223.

Orpheus and Eurydice : Lesson of a bas-relief. Paget, V. Belcaro, 49.

Orr, James L. Bartlett. Pres. candidates, 305. — Savage. Liv. rep. men, 382. — Livingston, J. Dist. Amer. 172.

Orsay, Alfred G. G., comte d'. Grant, Jas. Port. pub. char. 2 : 191.

Orseoli family. Oliphant. Makers Ven.

Orsini, Felice. Hodder, G. Memories, 293.

Orthodoxy. Brooks, P. Ess. & addr. 183. — Hutton. Ess. theol. 1 : 336.

— and heresy identical. Brownson. Works, 7 : 1.

— Rationalistic. Balfour, A. J. Founda. belief, 182.

Orthoepy of English speech. (W. C. Sawyer) Nat. Educa. Assoc. '76 : 134.

Orthography in high schools and colleges. (F. A. March) Nat. Educa. Assoc. '79 : 109.

Orthoptera. Bibliography. Scudder, S. H. Guide No. Amer. Orthoptera.

Ortiz, John. Drake, S. G. Trag. of wilderness, 11.

O'Ruadan, Felix. Burke, O. J. Cath. archb. 19.

Orvieto. Symonds. Sk. So. Eur. 1 : 257.

— Cathedral at, with plates. Perkins, C. C. Tusc. sculp. 1 : 89. — Symonds. Renais. fine arts, 56.

— Reformers in. Stoughton. Ital. reformers, 91.

— Shrine of the sacrament. Little, W. J. K. Sketches, 175.

Osage Indians ; were they mound-builders ? (J. F. Snyder) Smithson. Rept. '88 : 587.

Osaka, Japan, commercial museum, 1896. (J. F. Connelly) U. S. Cons. Rept. 53 : 372.

Osborn, A. C., with portrait. (E. L. Townsend) Rogers, A. C. Repres. men, 393.

Osborn, George. Wesley & successors, 199, 239.

Osborn, Selleck. Everest. Poets of Conn. 131.

Osborn, Sherard, Rear-admiral, Obituary of. Em. persons, 1 : 295.

Osborn, Thomas W., with portrait. (E. L. Townsend) Rogers, A. C. Repres. men, 401.

Osborne family. Sanford & Townsend. Gov. fam. 1.

Osborne, Bernal. Escott. Politics, 252. — Ritchie. Brit. sena. 261.

Osborne, Sir Edward. Bourne. Lond. merchants, 65.

Osborne's, Va., Action at. Dawson. Batt. of U. S. 1 : 687.

Oscar II., king of Sweden, with portrait. Crowned heads, 25.

Osceola. Lossing. Em. Amer. 357.

Osgood, Frances Sargent. Duyckinck. Portrait gall. 2 : 411. — Griswold. Fem. poets, 272. — Hart, J. S. Fem. prose, 229. — Poe. Works, 5 : 528. — Powell. Liv. authors (1850), 276.

Osgood, George. Putnam, A. P. Singers liberal, 383.

Osinski, Louis. Soboleski. Poets of Poland, 195.

Osler, Edward. Hatfield, E. F. Poets of church, 485. — Miller, Jos. Singers church, 2d ed. 451.

Osorius, John, 1542–94. Baring-Gould. Preachers, 177.

Osselles, Grottoes of. Adams, W. H. D. Fam. caverns, 95.

Ossian. Buchanan, R. Poet's sk. book, 141. — (W. Sharp and E. Rhys) Warner Lib. 19 : 10865.

— Blindness of. Drake, N. Evening, 2 : 170.

— Character of, as drawn by the Irish bards. Drake, N. Mornings, 2 : 37. — Darmesteter. Eng. stud. 195.

— Macpherson's Poems of. Cross lights, 33. — Montgomery, H. R. Impost. 38. — Davenport, R. A. Delusions, 185.

— See Macpherson, James.

— Poetry of. Schlegel. Æsthet. works, 243. — Shairp. Aspects, 210.

— Sir S. Ferguson and Celtic poetry. Williams, A. M. Stud. folk, 131.

Ossipee Falls. Dodge, N. S. Sk. of N. E. 79.

Ossoli, Margaret Fuller. Ames, M. C. Outlines, 77. — Cone & Gilder. Pen-portr. 2 : 131. — Crosland. Mem. women, 313. — Eliot, Geo. Ess. 91. — Griswold, H. T. Home-life, 302. — With portrait. Hart, J. S. Fem. prose, 266. — Griswold. Prose writ. 537. — (K. Sanborn) Our fam. wom. 295. — With portrait. (T. W. Higginson) Parton. Em. wom. 173. — Poe. Works, 5 : 506. — Powell. Liv. authors (1850), 287. — Russell, W. Eccen. 100. — Russell. Extr. women, 212. — Bolton, S. K. Girls famous, 68. — Duyckinck. Portrait gall. 2 : 273. — Fifty famous women, 207. — Frothingham. Transcend. 284. — Hanaford. Wom. of cent. 197. — With portrait. Mitchell, D. G. Am. lands, 2 : 177. — Richardson. Amer. lit. 1 : 431. — Smiles. Brief biog. 470.

— as a schoolgirl. Holmes, O. W. Old vol. 241.

— Extracts from letters and journals of. Ossoli. Women, 341.

— Homeward voyage and death of. Ossoli. At home, 443.

Ossuna, Pedro Tellez y Giron, duke of. Crowe, E. E. For. statesm. 1 : 282.

Ostade, Adrian van. Van Dyke, J. C. Dutch mast. 93. — Gower. Fig.-painters Holl. 21. — Wedmore. Masters of genre, 131.

Ostade, Isaak Jansz van. Gower. Fig.-painters Holl. 45.

Ostend. Kingston, W. B. Men, etc. 197.

— Siege of. Robson, W. Sieges, 501.

Ostend manifesto, 1854. Am. Hist. leafl. no. 2.

Ostendorfer, Michael. (A. Rosenberg) Dohme, R. Early mast. 173.

Ostens, Jacob. Wallace, R. Anti-Trin. biog. 3 : 317.

Osterley Park. Balch, E. Old Eng. homes, 210. — Timbs. Abbeys, 1 : 165.

Ostia. Freeman. Studies Italy, 96.

Ostler, William. Collier. Actors, 202.

Ostorod, Christopher. Wallace, R. Anti-Trin. biog. 2 : 390.

Ostrich, The. Morgan, C. L. Animal sk. 167.

Ostrida, queen of Ethelred. Hall. Queens before Conq. 256.

Ostrogoths. Grube, A. W. Heroes, 69.

— in Illyricum & Thrace. Bury. Later Rom. emp. 1 : 261.

Oswald, Henry Sigismund. Miller, Jos. Singers church, 2d ed. 303.

Oswald, James. McCosh. Scot. phil. 229.

Oswego, N. Y., Attack on. Dawson. Batt. of U. S. 2 : 339.

Oswego, N. Y., Loss of, 1756 : Pelham papers. (W. H. Smith) Am. Hist. Assoc. 4 : 369.

Otho I. the Great, History of. Lynam. Rom. emp. v. 2. — Peake, Eliz. Germ. emperors, 41.

Otho II. the Red, History of. Peake, Eliz. Germ. emperors, 46.

Otho III., History of. Peake, Eliz. Germ. emperors, 48.

Otho IV. of Brunswick, History of. Peake, Eliz. Germ. emperors, 107.

— Reign of. Busk, Mrs. Mediæv. popes, 3 : 123.

Otho, bishop of Pomerania. Maclear. Apostles, 217.

Otey, George G. Walker, C. D. Biog. Va. Mil. Inst. 412.

Otinovius, Erasmus. Wallace, R. Anti-Trin. biog. 2 : 353.

Otinovius, George. Wallace, R. Anti-Trin. biog. 2 : 356.

Otis, Harrison Gray. Loring, J. S. Hundred Bost. ora. 188. — Lossing. Em. Amer. 402. — Moore, F. Am. eloq. 1 : 557. — (A. T. Perkins) N. E. Hist.-Gen. Soc. Biog. 1 : 146.

Otis, Mrs. Harrison Gray, with portrait. Ellet. Queens Am. soc. 311.

Otis, J. M. P. Davidson, J. W. Writ. of South, 402.

Otis, James. Brooks, E. S. Hist. Amer. 34. — With portrait. Duyckinck. Nat. portr. gall. 1 : 45. — Magoon. Orators of rev. 61. — Johnston, A. Amer. ora. 1 : 11. — Knapp, S. L. Em. lawyers, 321. — Lossing. Em. Amer. 162. — Moore, F. Am. eloq. 1 : 1. — Richardson. Amer. lit. 1 : 182.

Otis, William Foster. Loring, J. S. Hundred Bost. ora. 493.

Otis family in U. S. history. Muzzey. Remin. 21.

Otley, Jona. Rawnsley. Lit. Assoc. Eng. lakes, 1 : 123.

O'Toole, St. Laurence. See Laurence O'Toole, St.

Otranto. Freeman. Subj. Venice, 313.

Ottacar of Bohemia. Utterton, F. A. Biog. sk. 106.

Ottawa, Can. Hardy, I. D. Thro' cities, 35.

Ottendorfer, Mrs. Anna. Bolton, S. K. Givers, 328.

Otterbein University, Westerville, O. U. S. Bur. Ed. Circ. '91, no. 5 : 140.

Ottery east hill. Watkins, M. G. In country, 116.

Otto, William Todd. Carson, H. L. Sup. Ct. of U. S. 569.

Ottoman empire, The. Wallace, S. E. Storied sea, 228.

Ottomans, Early. Church, R. W. Miscel. ess. 281.

Otway, Thomas. (S. Johnson) Chalmers. Eng. poets, 8 : 279. — Dunham. Lit. & sci. men, 3 : 123. — Gosse. 17th cent. stud. — Wotton. Word portraits, 231.

— The Orphan. Lennox, W. P. Plays, 1 : 25.

Ouananiche, Philology of the word. (E. T. D. Chambers) Roy. Soc. Can. 2d ser. 2, § 2 : 131.

Oudenarde, Battle of. Adams, W. H. D. Engl. at war, 1 : 142. — King, C. Battles, 339.

Oudinot, Nicolas Charles. Headley. Napoleon, 2 : 147.

Oughtred, William. Creasy. Etonians, 58.

Ouida, pseud. See La Ramée, L. de.

Ould, Robert. Am. Bar Assoc. 6 : 344.

"Our" Club. Jeaffreson, J. C. Book of recol 1 : 216.

Ousebridge, Kitcote, Notes by a prisoner in. Morris, J. Troub. of Cath. v. 3.

Oystermen, Chesapeake bay, Hardships of. (W. Wyman) Am. Pub. Health, **10** : 273.

Oysters. Barr, Mrs. Romances, 280. — De Vere. Wonders of the deep, 176. — Goodrich, F. B. Ocean's story, ch. 55. — Great fisheries, 238. — Mathews, W. Men, p. & t. 264. — Simmonds. Comm. prod. 131. — Morgan, C. L. Animal sk. 298. — Wood, J. G. Out of doors, 229.

— Bacteriologic study of. (C. J. Foote) Conn. Health, '95 : 189.

Oyster industry of Maryland. Maryland Labor, '90, '93.

Ozone. Andrews, T. Sci. papers, 240, 361. — Proctor. Pleas. ways, 347; also in Estes. Half-hour recre. 266.

— Atmospheric. (R. C. Kedzie) Mich. Health, '75 : 135. '80 : 277.

— Disinfection by. (J. D. Plunket) Am. Pub. Health, **4** : 297.

— Relation to public health. (J. D. Plunket) Tenn. Health, '80–84 : 389.

Paca, William. Dwight, N. Signers of decl. 252. — Lincoln, R. W. Signers, 53. — Lossing. Signers, 154. — Sanderson. Signers, v. **8.**

Pacchierotti, G., musician. Hogarth. Mem. opera, **2** : 121.

Pacericius, Samuel. Wallace, R. Anti-Trin. biog. **3** : 142.

Pachacamác, Peru, Explorations among ruins of. (J. Schumacher) Am. Geog. Soc. **5** : 248.

Paches, Death of. Thirlwall, C. Remains, **3** : 132.

Pachmann, Marguerite de, with portrait. Buffen. Mus. celeb. **2** : 61.

Pachmann, Vladimir de, with portrait. Buffen. Mus. celeb. **2** : 55.

Pachomius, abbot of Tabenna. Hahn-Hahn. Fathers, 174.

Pacific coast, The. (H. H. Bancroft) Shaler. The U. S. **1** . 341.

Pacific islands. Barker, Lady. Travel. about, 295.

Pacific ocean. Arnold, E. Seas and l. **1** : 1.

— Compulsory migrations in. Smithson. Inst. Rept. '95 : 519.

— Crossing. Brooks, J. Seven months, 24.

— Currents of. (T. Antisell) Am. Geog. Soc. **15** : 101.

— Fifteen days on. Todd, M. L. Corona, 30.

— Future of the. Alexander, J. M. Isl. of Pac. 461.

— the search for. Parkman. Half-cent. **2** : 24.

Pacific railroad. Marshall, W. G. Thro' Amer. 119. — Black, J. S. Ess. 172.

— U. S. *versus* U. P. R. R. Curtis, B. R. Men & writ. v. **2.**

Pacific slope, Journey of a dog and a man from Cariboo to California. Butler, W. F. Bar out, 68.

Packer, Asa. Cochrane, R. Benef. lives, 286.

— and Lehigh University. Bolton, S. K. Givers, 301.

Packer, John B. Am. Bar Assoc. **14** : 450.

Packer, William Fisher, with portrait. Armor. Gov. of Pa. 433.

Pacuvius, Marcus. Dunlop, J. Rom. liter. **1** : 314. — Sellar. Rom. poets repub. 134.

Paddock, Lovland. Livingston, J. Dist. Amer. 211.

Paderewski, Ignaz Jan, with portrait. Buffen. Mus. celeb. **2** : 11.

Padilla, Maria de, favorite of Pedro the Cruel. Menzies, S. Roy. fav. **1** : 71.

Padrone system. Stuart, J. M. Reminis. 85. — (J. Koren) U. S. Lab. Bull. **2** : 113.

Padua. Hare. Cities of No. Italy, **1** : 335. — Howells. Ital. jour. 196. — Taine. Italy, **2** : 198.

Pæstum. Fulton, C. C. Europe, 212. — Symonds. Sk. So. Eur. **1** : 368.

— and La Cava. Scollard. Und. sum. skies, 185.

Pagahn, Ancient. Shoemaker, M. M. Quaint corners, 91.

Pagan thought, Decay of. Bax, E. B. Outlooks, 39.

Pagani, G. Ottley. Ital. school.

Paganini, Nicolo, violinist. Dix, J. Lions, 248. — Engel, L. Mozart, **2** : 194. — With portrait. Ehrlich, A. Cel. violin. 264. — Ferris, G. T. Great violinists, 89. — Haweis. My mus. life, 339. — Haweis. Mus. memories, 105. — Phipson, T. L. Cel. violinists, 110.

— Secret of. Phipson. Violinists, 44.

Paganism, Best method of propagating. Hope. Ess. 199.

— compared with mediæval Christianity. Arnold, M. Ess. in crit. v. **1.**

— Decline of pagan thought. Bax, E. B. Outlooks, 39.

— History of. Renan. Studies (N. Y.), **2** : 33.

— Influence of, on Christianity. (C. F. Keary) Relig. systems, 246.

— to Christianity, Transition from. Bosanquet, B. Civil. of Christendom, 27.

— under the first Christian emperors. Cave. Lives of fathers, **2** : 1.

Page, Emily R. Hemenway. Poets of Vt. 349.

Page, Legh Richmond. Am. Bar Assoc. **16** : 448.

Page, Dame Mary. Ivimey. Eng. Bapt. **3** : 501.

Page, Thomas Nelson, with portrait. Warner Lib. **19** : 10937.

Page, William. Sheldon, G. W. Amer. painters, 221. — Tuckerman. Artists, 295.

Page family of Rosewell, Va. Glenn, T. A. Colon. mans. **1** : 171.

Pageants. Ward, A. W. Eng. dram. **1** : 79.

Pages, Training of. Doran. Knights, 30.

Paget, Sir E. Cole, J. W. Brit. generals, v. **1.**

Paget, Sir James. Bettany. Em. doctors, **2** : 167.

Paget, William, first Lord. Lodge. Portraits (Bohn), v. **2.**

Paget family. Sanford & Townsend. Gov. fam. **1.**

Pailleron, Edouard, with portrait. Warner Lib. **19** : 10961.

Pain. Stephen, J. F. Ess. by barr. 142.

— Ethics of. Gurney. Tertium, **1** : 151.

— Meaning of. Thompson, H. M. Copy, 322.

— Mystery of. Dixon, T. Liv. prob. 110. — Hinton. Thinking, 213.

— physical, Use of. Bushnell. Moral uses, 95.

— Probable uses of. Dana, A. H. Eth. inq. 236.

— Problem of. (J. R. Illingworth) Gore, C. Lux mundi, 113.

Paine, Charles. Loring, J. S. Hundred Bost. ora. 310.

Paine, Henry W. (N. Holmes) Am. Acad. A. & S. Proc. **29** : 432.

Paine, John K., Oratorio of St. Peter. Fiske, J. Unseen world, 266.

Paine, Martyn. Francis, S. W. N. Y. phys. 13.

Paine, Olive E. Hemenway. Poets of Vt. 252.

Paine, Robert Treat. Dwight, N. Signers of decl. 52. — Griswold. Poets Am. 65. — Irving. Biog. 303. — Lincoln, R. W. Signers, 53. — Lossing. Signers, 37. — Loring, J. S. Hundred Bost. ora. 283. — Sanderson. Signers, v. **2.** — Lossing. Em. Amer. 228.

Paine, Sumner. (F. C. Paine) Harvard mem. biog. 2 : 453.

Paine, Thomas. Adolphus. Biog. Fr. rev. 2 : 269. — Daly, J. B. Radicals. — Denslow. Mod. think. 131. — Ingersoll, R. G. Gods, 121. — Lossing. Em. Amer. 198. — With portrait. Mitchell, D. G. Am. lands, 112. — Stephen, J. F. Horæ sabb. 187. — With portrait. Warner Lib. 19 : 10975.

— Passages in the life of. Goddard, W. G. Pol. & mis. wr. 1 : 419.

— Trial of, for libel. Erskine, T. Speeches, 231.

— Works. Stephen, L. Eng. thought, 1 : 458.

Painter, William. Morley, H. Eng. writ. 8 : 288.

Painter and critic. Allingham. Varieties, 3 : 221.

Painters and engravers of New England, Early. (W. H. Whitmore) Mass. Hist. Proc. 9 : 197.

— Bolognese school of. Symonds. Renais. Cath. reac. 2 : 343.

— Dutch. Bibliography. Rooses, M. Dutch painters of 19th cent.

— Early, Anecdotes of. Chambers's Miscel. no. 154.

— modern, Chronological list of. Reynolds. Lit. works, 2 : 425.

— Modern French. Child, T. Art & criticism, 28.

— Spanish. Hay, J. Castil. days, 121.

Painting and its relation to sculpture. Guizot. Fine arts, 26.

— and painters, Spanish. Stirling-Maxwell. Ann. art. Spain, 1 : 1.

— and poetry, Parallel between. Reynolds. Lit. works, 2 : 377.

— and sculpture. (W. M. R. French) Cong. Educa. Chic. '93, 497. — Palgrave. Ess. on art, 264.

— and writing, Differences between. Hazlitt, W. C. Offspring, 130.

— Bibliography. Muther, R. Modern paint.

— British, Recent. Bayne, P. Ess. 1 : 211.

— British school of. Alison. Ess. v. 2.

— Continental, at Paris in 1878. Hamerton. Art ess. 2 : 43.

— Deceptions in. Davenport, R. A. Delusions, 209.

— Dutch genre painters. Fairholt. Homes Rubens, 165.

— Dutch landscape and flower painters. Fairholt. Homes Rubens, 209.

— English, Early. Buxton, H. J., et al. Eng. paint. 1.

— — 16th & 17th centuries. Buxton, H. J., et al. Eng. paint. 36.

— — in 18th century. Buxton, H. J., et al. Eng. paint. 36.

— — in 19th century. Buxton, H. J., et al. Eng. paint. 116.

— English and American. Hamerton. Art ess. 2 : 3.

— English school of, 1842. Eastlake. Contrib. 1 : 31.

— Epochs of. Thornbury. Brit. art. 2 : 185.

— Ferrarese school of. Morelli. Ital. paint. 200.

— from life. Fuseli. Life & writ. 2 : 371.

— Genre. Wedmore. Masters of genre, 3.

— history of, Prevailing method of treating. Fuseli. Life & writ. 3 : 1.

— Impressionist. Child, T. Art & criticism, 162.

— in America. Buxton, H. J., et al. Eng. paint. 187.

— in ancient Greece. Mahaffy. Rambles Greece, 282.

— in the dark ages. Crowe & Caval. Flem. painters, v. 1.

— in the 14th century. Ellesmere. Ess. 252.

Painting in the north, Rise of. Conway, W. M. Early Flem. artists, 1.

— in the renaissance. Symonds. Renais. Fine arts, 20, 180.

— Italian & French. Bibliography. Newark (N. J.) Pub. Lib. Spec. read. list, no. 4.

— Lombard school of. Morelli. Ital. paint. 151.

— Monumental. (W. B. Richmond) Poole, R. S. Lec. art, 26.

— Optics and. Helmholtz. Pop. lec. 2 : 73.

— Origin of. Jervis, Lady. Painting, 1 : 3.

— Pleasure of. Hazlitt. Crit. on art., ser. 2 ; or Table-talk.

— Practical work of. Hamerton. Art ess. 1 : 3.

— Principles and methods of critical study of. Morelli. Ital. paint. 1.

— Progress of, in England, in 18th century. Buxton, H. J., et al. Eng. paint. 60.

— — in Flanders. Crowe & Caval. Flem. painters, 337.

— The real in. Maitland, S. R. Eight ess. 96.

— Representation distinguished from description. Eastlake. Contrib. 1 : 53.

— Ruskin's views of. Patterson, R. H. Ess. hist. 340.

— Sacred. Maitland, S. R. Eight ess. 57.

— Schools of, in Italy. Symonds. Renais. Fine arts, 183.

— Self-explanatory quality in. Harrison, F. Choice of books, 301.

— Spanish. Washburn, E. Span. mas. 1.

— — Decline of. Washburn, E. Span. mas. 176.

— — School of Madrid. Washburn, E. Span. mas. 146.

— Temperament in. Appleton, T. G. Sheaf of pap. 242.

— Tuscan school of. Morelli. Ital. paint. 82.

— Venetian school of. Morelli. Ital. paint. 259.

Paintings in Paris and Netherlands, 1802–04. Schlegel. Æsthet. (Bohn) 1.

— Modern German. Schlegel. Æsthet. (Bohn) 283.

Paisiello, Giovanni. Ferris, G. T. Ital. & Fr. compos. 37. — Hogarth. Mem. opera, 2 : 97.

Pakenham, Gen. Sir E. Cole, J. W. Brit. generals, v. 2. — James. Mil. occur. v. 2.

Pakington, Lady Dorothy. Williams, Jane. Lit. wom. 115.

Pakington, Sir John. Kent, W. C. M. Derby min. 225. — Ritchie. Brit. sena. 34.

Pal, Krishnoo. Miller, Jos. Singers church, 2d ed. 368.

Palace tales. Wraxall, C. F. L. Hist. bye-ways, 1 : 265.

Palaces built by ministers. Disraeli, I. Curios. (N. Y. 4 v.) 4 : 71.

— Mediæval, of Italy. Symonds. Renais. Fine arts, 61.

Palæographic purism. Harrison, F. Mean. of hist. 456.

Palæography. Lacroix. Art in mid. ages, 328.

— Greek & Latin. Bibliography. Thompson, E. M. Hdbk. Greek & Lat. palæography.

Palæologus, James. Wallace, R. Anti-Trin. biog. 2 : 266.

Palæologus family. Burke, B. Viciss. of fam. 1 : 199.

Palæontology and the doctrine of evolution. Huxley. Critiques.

— Bibliography. Seward, A. C. Fossil plants.

— invertebrate, North American, Bibliography of. (J. B. Marcou) Smithson. Rept. '85 : 713.

— Progress in, 1846–96. (E. D. Cope) Goode. Smithson. Inst. 679.

— Rise and progress of. Huxley. Ess. contro. 41.

Palæontology vertebrate. Bibliography. Woodward, A. S. Outl. verteb. palæon.

Palais Royal, The. Challice. Fr. palaces, 173.
— in 1775. Houssaye. Men of 18th cent. **2** : 428.
— Men & wom. of France, **3** : 295.

Palatinate, Rhenish. Chambers's Repos. no. 31.

Palatines. Bibliography. Cobb, S. H. Palatines.

Paleario, Aonis, in Siena. Stoughton. Ital. reformers, 77.

Palenque. (E. H. Thompson) Am. Antiq. Soc. Proc. n. s. **10** : 191.
— Ancient tombs of. (E. H. Thompson) Am. Antiq. Soc. Proc. n. s. **10** : 418.
— tablets from, two, Analysis of pictorial text inscribed on. (P. J. J. Valentini) Am. Antiq. Soc. Proc. n. s. **9** : 429. **10** : 399.

Palermo. Hare. Cities of So. Italy, 481. — Symonds. Sk. So. Eur. **2** : 7. — Warner, C. D. Roundabout, 78.
— The Normans at. Freeman. Hist. ess. **3** : 437.
— Tombs of the kings. Little, W. J. K. Sketches, 59.

Palestine. Arnold, E. Wand. words, 73. — Bellows. Old world, **2** : 243. — Bonar, H. Days & nights, 163. — Greenwood, F. W. P. Miscel. 375. — Kinglake. Eothen, 84. — Moore, Jos. Outly. Eur. 152. — Stuart-Glennie. Pilgrim. 291. — Taylor, B. Lands of Sar. 17. — Warner, C. D. In Levant, v. **1**.
— as illustrating geological and geographical controls. (R. A. Daly) Am. Geog. Soc. **31** : 444.
— Aspect of, in 1883. Temple, R. Orient. exper. 435.
— Exploration of. (A. L. Rawson) Am. Geog. Soc. **7** : 101. — (C. P. Daly) Am. Geog. Soc. **5** : 166.
— — beyond the Jordan. (R. D. Hitchcock) Am. Geog. Soc. **8** : 204.
— in its physical aspects. (H. B. Tristram) Manch. Sci. lec. **11** : 27.
— in 1890. (H. Gillman) U. S. Cons. Rept. **34** : 683.
— in 1891. (S. Merrill) U. S. Cons. Rept. **38** : 337.
— in 1892. (S. Merrill) U. S. Cons. Rept. **41** : 307.
— Jews and Jewish colonies in, 1891. (S. Merrill) U. S. Cons. Rept. **38** : 26.
— Maritime cities and plains of. (Rogers) Wilson, C. W. Pictur. Palest. **3** : 109.
— Maundrel's travels in, 1700. St. John. Cel. travelers, **1** : 305.
— Modern researches in. (S. Merrill) Am. Geog. Soc. v. **9**.
— Physical geography of, and Hebrew thought. (F. Adler) Am. Geog. Soc. **7** : 149.
— Roman government of. Lord, J. Anc. states, 128.
— Routes of travel in. Temple, R. Cosmop. ess. 357.
— Ruins east of the Jordan. (W. H. Goodyear) Am. Geog. Soc. **8** : 266.
— Southern borderland of. (Palmer) Wilson, C. W. Pictur. Palest. **3** : 193.
— A tour in. Cust. Ling. ess. 252.
— Winter ride in. (H. B. Tristram) Vaca. tourists, **3** : 1.
— Witness of, to the Bible. (W. G. Blaikie) Liv. papers, v. **2**.

Palestine exploration society, Novel antiquities of. Rogers, H. Ess. fr. G. W. 31.

Palestrina, Giovanni Pierluigi da. Dole, N. H. Score, 9. — Elson, L. Gt. composers, 24. — Ferris, G. T. Ital. & Fr. compos. 7. — Ked-die. Mus. comp. 4. — Parry, C. H. H. Gt. compos.

Palestrina, Giovanni Pierluigi da, and the origins of modern music. Symonds. Renais. Cath. reac. **2** : 323.

Paley, William. Blunt. Ess. 133. — Georgian era, **1** : 255. — Groser, W. H. Men worth imita.
— and his school. Stephen, L. Eng. thought, **1** : 405.
— as a theologian. Foster, J. Crit. ess. (Bohn) **1** : 236.
— Memoirs by Meadley. Foster, J. Crit. ess. (Bohn) **1** : 315.

Palfrey, Cazneau. Peabody. Harv. grad. 207.

Palfrey, Francis W., with portrait. (J. C. Ropes) Mass. Hist. Proc. 2d ser. **7** : 39.

Palfrey, John Gorham. Griswold. Prose writ. 599. — Peabody. Harv. rem. 107. — Loring, J. S. Hundred Bost. ora. 485. — Richardson. Amer. lit. **1** : 474. — With portrait. Warner Lib. **19** : 10988.

Palfrey, Sara Hammond. Putnam, A. P. Singers liberal, 501.

Palgrave, Sir Francis. Quarrel with T. D. Hardy. Jeaffreson, J. C. Book of recol. **2** : 65.

Palgrave, Francis Turner. Miles, A. H. Poets of cent. **10** : 489. — Miller, Jos. Singers church, 2d ed. 566.

Palgrave, Wm. G., with photo. Cooper, T. Men of mark, **4** : 2. — With portrait. Warner Lib. **19** : 11001.
— Adventures in the Arabian desert. Adams, W. H. D. In perils, 334.

Palimpsest literature. (C. W. Russell) Afternoon lec. **4** : 95.

Palissy, Bernard. Bolton, S. K. Poor boys famous, 54. — Brightwell. Heroes of lab. 106. — Hundred greatest men, 465. — Lamartine. Cel. char. **1** : 233. — Pattison. Renais. in France, **2** : 239. — Towle, G. M. Heroes of inven. 43.

Palk, John. Baur. Relig. life Germ. **2** : 224.

Palladio, Andrea. Milizia. Lives arch. **2** : 30. — Symonds. Renais. fine arts, 94.

Palladus. Mills. Poets of Greece, 241.

Pallas, P. S. St. John. Cel. travelers, **3** : 65.

Palliano, Violante da Cardona, duchess of. Symonds. Renais. Cath. reac. **1** : 372.

Palma, Giovanni. Criticisms of his pictures. Guizot. Fine arts, 115.

Palmas, Cape, Maryland's colony at. Latimer. Eur. in Afr. in 19th cent. 290.

Palmer, Alice Freeman. Hanaford. Wom. of cent. 525.

Palmer, Anthony. Ivimey. Eng. Bapt. **3** : 374.

Palmer, Sir C. M., with portrait. Jones, E. R. Heroes of ind. 218.

Palmer, Prof. Edw. Henry. Adams, W. H. D. In perils, 441.

Palmer, Erastus D. Clarke, W. J. Amer. sculp. 117. — Tuckerman. Artists, 355.

Palmer, James Shedden. Headley, J. T. Farragut, 503.

Palmer, John, "Plausible Jack." Cook, D. Hours w. players, **1** : 139. — Doran. Annals stage, **2** : 232. — Fitzgerald, P. Rom. of stage, 273.

Palmer, Joseph. (G. Dexter) Mass. Hist. Proc. **19** : 224.

Palmer, Mrs. Mary E. Brockett. Woman's work, 640.

Palmer, Oliver H. Patton, J. Sk. of men of prog. — Rogers, A. C. Repres. men, 405.

Paper, Ancient Mexican. (Ph. J. J. Valentini) Am. Antiq. Soc. Proc. n. s. 1 : 58.
— fine, Manufacture of, in England in 18th cent. Garnett, R. Ess. in librarianship, 191.
— Vegetable parchment, 1894. U. S. Cons. Rept. 46 : 479.
Paper currency in America, History of. (N. Paine) Am. Antiq. Soc. Proc. n. s. 3 : 266.
Paper-hangings. See Wall paper.
Paper-mills, Dalton, Mass. Pidgeon. Old world ques. 104.
Paper-money. Turgot. Life & writ. 204. — Webster, N. Ess. 119.
— and banks. Elder, W. Questions, 133.
— Nature and necessity of. Franklin. Works ('87), 1 : 359.
— of U. S., 1781. Franklin. Works ('87), 7 : 339.
— Speech in opposition to. Madison, J. Letters, 1 : 255.
Paper-money inflation in France. (A. D. White) Econ. tracts, no. 7.
Paper trade in various foreign countries, 1897. U. S. Cons. Rept. 55 : 1.
Papias of Hierapolis. Lightfoot. Ess. "Super. relig." 142. — Moxom. Jerus. to Nicæa, 139.
— Yonge, C. M. Pupils of John, 201.
Papin, Denis. Ewart, H. C. Heroes of sci. 191.
— Sketch of. Agnew. Protes. exiles, 2 : 83.
Pappenheim, Godfrey Henry, Count von. Cust. Warriors 30 years, 1 : 223.
Papuan languages ; Vocabularies of the voyage of the "Rattlesnake." Latham. Opuscula, 223.
Papyrus, and mode of making paper from it. Abbot, E. Auth. 4th gosp. & ess. 137.
— from Herculaneum, Experiments on. Davy. Works, 6 : 160.
Papyri. Bibliography. Kenyon, F. G. Palæography of Gr. papyri.
Pará and the Amazons. (W. B. Ogden) Am. Geog. Soc. 21 : 459.
— Commerce of, 1898. U. S. Cons. Rept. 59 : 59.
— Rubber in, 1898. U. S. Cons. Rept. 59 : 65.
Parables of Christ, as illustrating Roman Catholic doctrine. Wiseman, N. Ess. 1 : 101.
Paracelsus, Aureolus Philippus Theophrastus. Bax. Ethics of socialism, 161. — Hain, J. Varia, 163. — Kingsley, C. Hist. lec. 361. — Soane. New curios. 1 : 134. — Vaughan. Hours w. mystics, 2 : 71.
Paradise, Law of. Barnes, A. Miscel. 2 : 290.
— Terrestrial. Baring-Gould. Myths, 250.
See also Eden.
Paradox and commonplace. Hazlitt. Table-talk.
Paradoxes. Russell, A. P. Lib. notes, 240.
— De Morgan on. Proctor. Light sci. 3 : 269.
Paraguay. Child. Spanish Amer. — Palgrave. Ulysses, 246. — Am. Geog. Soc. 1 : 11. — U. S. Cons. Rept. 38 : 556.
— Brazil and the Plate, Mansfield's. Kingsley, C. New miscel. 126.
— Hand-book of. Bur. Am. Repub., Bulletin no. 54, pt. 5.
— Republic of. Child, T. Span.-Amer. repub. 366. — (David Powell) Vaca. tourists, 3 : 311.
Paraguayan and Argentine bibliography. Garnett, R. Ess. in librarianship, 127.
Parallax, Stellar. Pritchard. Researches.
Paraná River. Child. Span. Amer. 343.
Parasites and their development. Wilson, A. Leisure, 183.
— and their strange uses. (T. S. Cobbold) Manch. Sci. lec. 5–6 : 40.
— Animal. (A. Wilson) Proctor, R. A. Nat. stud. 76.

Parasites, vegetable, Diseases caused by. (J. C. White) Mass. Health, '72 : 249.
Paray-le-Monial. Hare, A. J. C. Biog. sket. 183.
Parbeck, Sarah. Clement, J. Noble deeds, 331.
Parcel post, State. Jevons. Meth. soc. ref.
Parclesius, Stanislaüs. Wallace, R. Anti-Trin. biog. 2 : 229.
Pardee, Henry E. Am. Bar Assoc. 12 : 348.
Pardo-Bazán, Emilia. See Bazán.
Pardoning power. (G. Hoadly) Conf. char. & correc. '86 : 77. — (F. Wayland) Nat. Pris. Assoc. '85 : 35.
— of the President of the U. S. Sumner Works, 3 : 49.
Pardons, Executive. (E. L. Pierce) Mass. Charity, '69–70 : 46. — (J. L. Milligan) N. Y. Pris. Assoc. 26, app. : 422.
Parental duties. Friswell. Wick. world, 147.
Parenthood, Education of girls for. (Eudora L. Hailmann) Nat. Educa. Assoc. '89 : 455.
Parents as child students. (M. C. Bourland) Nat. Educa. Assoc. '97 : 859.
— as educators. Hamerton. Hum. int. 81.
— as judges of good and bad teaching. (Ella F. Young) Nat. Educa. Assoc. '87 : 245.
— Choice of. Zangwill. Without prej. 194.
— In behalf of. Repplier, A. In dozy hours, 42.
— Training of. Craik, D. M. Sermons, 75.
Parepa Rosa, Mad. Parton. Em. wom. 452.
Parini, Giuseppe. Howells. Mod. It. poets, 25.
— Stebbing. Ital. poets, v. 2. — Trollope. Ital. poets, 2 : 151. — Warner Lib. 19 : 11042.
Paris, Francis. Parton. Peop. bk. biog. 85.
Paris, Louis P. A. d'Orléans, Comte de. Em. persons, 6 : 135. — King, E. French pol. lead. 261.
Paris-Duverney, Joseph, French financier. Parton. Capt. indus. 332.
Paris. Bellows. Old world, 1 : 21. 2 : 503. — Fairbanks, O. B. Aguecheek, 113. — Field, Mrs. H. M. Sket. France, 65. — Fulton, C. C. Europe, 145. — Guild. Over the ocean, 246. — Guthrie, T. Out of harness, 59. — Haven, G. Pilgrim. 279. — Howard, B. W. One year, 24. — Howe, J. W. Oak to olive, 37. — James, H. Portraits, 75. — Peabody, A. P. Rem. Eur. 148. — Stowe. Sunny mem. 2 : 143, 389. — Taylor, B. Views, 464. — Thompson. Beaten paths, 228. — Warner, C. D. Saunterings, 9. — Willis. Pencillings. — Brooks, E. S. Gt. cities, 16. — Buckley, T. A. Great cities, 228. — Hillebrand. France, 94. — Howe, J. W. Is polite soc. pol. 37. — Tuckerman, C. K. Recollec. 2 : 69. — Temple, E. L. Old-world, 1 : 158. — Wikoff, H. Reminis. 79. — Zangwill. Without prej. 309.
— Aix to. Fairbanks, O. B. Aguecheek, 100.
— and Genoa. Moulton, L. C. Rambles, 23 : 235.
— and the provinces. Hillebrand. France, 72.
— Architecture ; new Paris. Palgrave. Ess. on art, 308.
— as an historic city. Harrison, F. Mean. of hist. 368.
— Aspects of life in. Bellows. Old world, 1 : 38.
— Bois de Boulogne. Wraxall. Scraps, 2 : 287.
— Boulevard des Italiens, Decline of. Stuart, H. Paris days, 78.
— Cafés of. Delille, E. Some French wr. 59.
— Catacombs of. Knox, T. W. Undergr. 314.
— Charities of. Bellows. Old world, 1 : 47. — Field, Mrs. H. M. Sk. France, 114.
— Churches of. Haven, G. Pilgrim. 286.
— Declaration of, 1861. Lubbock. Addresses, 129. — Adams, H. Hist. ess. 237.
— Education in. Bellows. Old world, 1 : 51.

Pastrana, Julia. Buckland, E. T. Curios. nat. hist. 4 : 40.

Patagonia. Curtis, W. E. Capitals, 516.

Patarines of Milan. Baring-Gould. Oddities, 2 : 146.

Patent causes, Preliminary injunctions in. (F. P. Fish) Am. Bar Assoc. 22 : 649.

Patent law. (J. H. Raymond) Am. Bar Assoc. 22 : 629.

— and practice. (R. S. Taylor) Am. Bar Assoc. 18 : 481.

Patent laws of the American republics. Bur. Am. repub. no. 3.

Patent medicines. (A. S. Huston) Indiana Health, '90 : 169.

— Medical by-ways. Wilson, A. Nat. note-book, 43.

— Relations of, to public health. (A. B. Prescott) Mich. Health, '81 : 151.

Pater, J. B. J. Dilke. Fr. painters 18th cent. 96. — Wedmore. Masters of genre, 191.

Pater, Walter. Gosse, E. Crit. kit-cats. — Symons, A. Stud. two lit. 169. — With portrait. (A. M. Sholl) Warner Lib. 19 : 11157.

— and prose. Zangwill. Without prej. 207.

Patera, Golden, of Rennes. (Thomas Wilson) U. S. Nat. Mus. Rept. '94 : 609.

Paternalism opposed. Bastiat. Ess. on pol. econ. 58, 63, 74, 97.

Paterson, William, of Dumfries, 1658-1719. Bourne, H. R. F. Eng. merch. 1 : 363.

Pathos. Bain. On teaching English, 157, 193. — Patmore. Principle in art, 94. — Schiller. Æsthetic letters, 211. — Meynell, A. Rhythm, 45.

— Uses of. Ess. from Sat. R. 307.

Patience and hopefulness. Bulwer, E. Caxtoniana, 157.

Patient, Thomas. Ivimey. Eng. Bapt. 2 : 326.

Patingham, Patrick. Wallace, R. Anti-Trin. biog. 2 : 127.

Patmore, Coventry. Forman. Liv. poets, 257. — Miles, A. H. Poets of cent. 10 : 485. — Symons, A. Stud. two lit. 158. — Tovey. Rev. & ess. 156. — With portrait. (M. F. Egan) Warner Lib. 19 : 11179.

— Angel in the house. Brimley, G. Ess. 204.

— Odes of. Meynell, A. Rhythm, 89.

— Poems. De Vere. Ess. 126.

— Sarum Close and. Rees, J. R. With friend, 72.

Patmore, Emily Augusta. Nicoll, W. R. Lit. anec. 2 : 375.

Patmos. Tozer. Islands of the Ægean.

— John at. Lee, J. S. Sac. cities, 157.

Paton, John G. Creegan. Gt. mission. 253.

Paton, Joseph Noel. Bate, P. H. Eng. Pre-Raph. 71. — Wilson, J. G. Poets of Scot. 2 : 428.

Paton-Wood, Mary Anne, English vocalist. Clayton, E. C. Queens, 274. — Needham. Queens of song.

Patrick, St. Burke, T. N. Lec. 9. — Charles. Martyrs, 391. — Kingsley. Hermits, 246. — Maclear. Apostles, 29. — Montalembert. Monks, 2 : 390. — Stokes, G. T. Ireland & Celtic church, 25. — Walsh, W. P. Heroes of mission. 45. — Conyngham, D. P. Irish saints, 25 : 559. — Maclear. Apostles, 29.

— Legends of. De Vere. Poetical works, v. 2.

— Purgatory of. Allingham. Varieties, 3 : 123. — Baring-Gould. Myths, 230.

Patrick, John. Holland, J. Psalmists, 2 : 78. — Miller, Jos. Singers church, 2d ed. 107.

Patriot, Advice to a. Hazlitt. Spirit.

— Duty of a. Bethune. Orations, 321.

Patriotism. Curtis, G. W. Orations, 1 : 37. — Giles, H. Lectures, 2 : 168. — Hazlitt. Round table. — Hamerton. French and English. — King, T. S. Patriotism, 29. — Lubbock. Use of life, 150. — Henry, C. S. Satan, 181. — Starling, E. Noble deeds wom. 438.

— and liberty. Beecher. New star papers, 264.

— danger in, On a certain. Fullerton, W. M. Patriotism, 13.

— Ethical element in. (A. P. Marble) Nat. Educa. Assoc. '95 : 142.

— local, Education and. Curtis, G. W. Orations, 1 : 457.

— Teaching of. (J. R. Preston) Nat. Educa. Assoc. '91 : 102.

— — in public schools. (G. W. F. Price) Nat. Educa. Assoc. '89 : 328.

Patronage and puffing. Hazlitt. Table-talk.

— Executive. Brownson. Works, 15 : 171.

— in offices un-American. Lodge, H. C. Hist. & pol. ess.

— Political. Curtis, G. W. Orations, 2 : 477.

Patrons of art, Royal. Robinson, F. S. Connois. 108.

Patrons of husbandry, Origin and purposes of. N. J. Labor, '86 : 333.

Patten, Henry Lyman. (G. E. Pond) Harvard mem. biog. 1 : 415.

Patten, John Wilson. Reid, T. W. Cab. portr. 100.

Pattern designing, History of. (W. Morris) Poole, R. S. Lec. art, 127.

Patterson, Angus. Livingston, J. Dist. Amer. 138.

Patterson, Mrs. Martha Johnson. With portrait. Holloway, L. C. Ladies, 573.

Patterson, Robert. Shenandoah Campaign. (T. L. Livermore) Dwight, T. F. Camp. Va. 3.

Patterson, Robert M. Lossing. Em. Amer. 396.

Patterson, William, and Alexander Hamilton. (C. Parker) Am. Bar Assoc. 3 : 149.

Patteson, John Coleridge. Adams, W. H. D. Heroes of cross, 441. — Blaikie, W. G. Leaders, 243. — Charles, E. Three martyrs. — Gladstone. Glean. 2 : 213. — Japp. Noble workers, 1. — Creegan. Gt. mission. 3. — Smith, G. B. Chris. workers, 55. — Smith, S. F. Noble workers, 7.

— and the South Pacific. Japp, A. H. Master mission. 294.

Patti, Adelina M. C. Edwards, H. S. Prima don. 2 : 64. — With portrait. Buffen, F. F. Mus. celeb. 9. — Engel, L. Mozart, 2 : 245. — Engel. Handel to Halle, 244. — Spark, W. Mus. mem. 324.

— at home. Kingston, W. B. Music & manners, 1 : 243.

Pattinson, H. L. Lonsdale. Worthies Cumb. v. 4.

Pattison, Dorothy W., "Sister Dora." Adams, W. H. D. Good Samar. 378. — Fawcett, M. G. Em. wom. 186. — Wise, D. Rem. women, 88.

Pattison, Mark. Church, R. W. Occ. pap. 2 : 351, 357. — Galton, A. Urbana, 187. — Morley. Crit. miscel. 3 : 133.

Patton, George S. Walker, C. D. Biog. Va. Mil. Inst. 422.

Patton, Walter T. Walker, C. D. Biog. Va. Mil. Inst. 425.

Patucket falls. Whittier. Lit. recre. 326.

Patuxent and the Prestons. Glenn, T. A. Colon. mans. 2 : 341.

Pau, Château of. Larned, W. C. Churches & C. 114.

Paul, St. Allen, J. H. Chr. hist. **1** : 21. — Baldwin, G. C. Rep. men, 313. — (G. P. Fisher) Bost. lectures, '**71** : 293. — Fisher, G. P. Discus. 487. — Giles, J. A. Apostle records, 317. — Hills, O. A. Companion char. 278. — Cave. Apostles, **1** : 187. **2** : **1.** — Hundred greatest men, 154. — Liddon. Ess. & add. 60. — Waterbury. Eloq. preach. 229.
— and his modern students. Martineau, J. Studies, 414.
— as a preacher. Broadus. Lec. hist. preach. 38.
— at Athens. Comegys. Tour. 72.
— at Malta. Merivale. Hist. stud. 450.
— at Puteoli. Macmillan, H. Rom. mosaics, 380.
— Bibliography. Stevens, G. B. Pauline theology.
— Character of. (B. Jowett) Noyes, G. R. Theol. ess. 341.
— Closing pæan of. Whedon. Ess. **1** : 103.
— Conversion of. Green, T. H. Works, **3** : 186. — Griffin, E. D. Rem. **2** : 445.
— Eloquence of. Bethune. Orations, 211.
— the first hermit. Kingsley. Hermits, 83.
— Nero and. Williams, W. R. Eras, 1.
— Renan's. Hutton. Ess. theol. **1** : 310.
— The teaching of, an integral part of Scripture. Mozley, J. B. Lec. 74.
— "Thorn in the flesh." Brown, J. Spare hours, 1.
Paul II., Pope. Oliphant. Makers mod. Rome, 558. — Pastor. Hist. popes, **4** : **1.** — Symonds. Age of despots, 383.
Paul III. [Alessandro Farnese], Pope. Ranke. Popes, **1** : 243. — Symonds. Renais. Cath. reac. **1** : 81.
Paul IV. [Giovanni Pietro Caraffa], Pope. Ranke. Popes, **1** : 286. — Symonds. Renais. Cath. reac. **1** : 102.
Paul V., Pope. Ranke. Popes, **2** : 330.
— The pope and the friar. Tartt. Ess. **1** : 172.
Paul I., emperor of Russia. Fowler, G. Sov. of Russ. 350.
Paul *silentiarius.* Browning, E. B. Ess. poets, 70.
Paul, bishop of Constantinople. Blakey, R. Prim. fathers, 233. — Cave. Lives of fathers, **3** : 385.
Paul of Samosata. Evans, R. W. Biog. early church, **2** : 322.
Paul the Simple. Hahn-Hahn. Fathers, 158.
Paul of Thebes. Hahn-Hahn. Fathers, 78.
Paul, Hamilton. Wilson, J. G. Poets of Scot. **1** : 498.
Paul, Jean (*pseud.*). *See* Richter, Jean P. F.
Paul, Lewis. Woodcroft, B. Biog. invent. 47.
Paul, Norman. Am. Bar Assoc. **17** : 536.
Paula, the friend of St. Jerome. Hahn-Hahn. Fathers, 436. — Kavanagh. Women of Chr. 32. — Lord, J. Beacon, **5** : 65. — Taylor, I. Logic in theol. 177.
Paulding, Hiram, with portrait. Headley, J. T. Farragut, 496.
Paulding, James Kirke. Griswold. Poets Am. 70. — Griswold. Prose writ. 143. — With portrait. Wilson, J. G. Bryant, 129. — With portrait. Mitchell, D. G. Am. lands, 295. — Richardson. Amer. lit. **2** : 292. — With portrait. Warner Lib. **19** : 11195.
Paulet, Amayas. Burke, S. H. Hist. portr. Tudor, **4** : 498.
Pauli, Gregory. Wallace, R. Anti-Trin. biog. **2** : 180.
Pauli, Stephen. Wallace, R. Anti-Trin. biog. **3** : 314.
Paulus Diaconus. Miller, Jos. Singers church, 2d ed. 18.
Paulus, Lucius Æmilius. Herbert, H. W. Capt. Rom.

Paulus Hook, N. J., Assault on. Dawson. Batt. of U. S. **1** : 543.
Pauper children, Boarding-out of. (Joanna M. Hill) N. Y. Pris. Assoc. **26,** app. : 394.
Pauper labor. Miller, H. Hist. ess. 245.
Pauperism. Haweis. Curr. coin. — Miller, H. Hist. ess. 240.
— and crime. (J. B. Weber) Cong. Char. Chic. '93, **1** : 131. — N. J. Labor, '**83** : 371.
— and old age pensions. (C. S. Loch) Bosanquet. Asp. soc. ques. 126.
— and organized charity. Anderson, M. B. Papers, **2** : 220.
— as produced by wealth. Davies, J. L. Theol. & mor. 244.
— Causes of, and the state. (A. O. Wright) Cong. Char. Chic. '93, **1** : 146.
— charity and the poor law. Fawcett. Ess. & lec. 70.
— The curse of. Holland, J. G. Every-day, **2** : 219.
— English. Rogers. Econ. interp. of history.
— in Brooklyn and New York, Problem of. (S. Low) Conf. char. & correc. '**79** : 200.
— in cities. (J. E. Monjaras) Am. Pub. Health, **21** : 280.
— in great cities, Four chief causes of. (R. T. Paine) Cong. Char. Chic. '93, **1** : 23.
— in Kansas. Kansas Labor, 1887.
— its diagnosis and treatment. (C. Lamport) Trans. Soc. Sci. Lond. '**70** : 527.
— Part which it plays in cities. (J. E. Monjaras) Am. Pub. Health, **21** : 280.
— Prevention of. (Mrs. C. R. Lowell) Conf. char. & correc. '**79** : 189. — (A. Reynolds) Conf. char. & correc. '**79** : 210. — (O. Craig) Woods, R. A. Poor, 339.
— Treatment of. Illinois charity, '**76** : 195.
Paupers, Classification of. (A. N. Lincoln) Conf. char. & correc. '**98** : 184.
— foreign, Relief from. Anderson, M. B. Papers, **2** : 241.
— Interstate migration of. (H. H. Hart) Conf. char. & correc. '**96** : 299.
See Poor ; Out-door relief ; In-door relief.
Pausanias. Cox, G. W. Gt. statesm. 195. — Herbert, H. W. Capt. old world. — (B. Perrin) Warner Lib. **19** : 11210.
Pavements from a sanitary standpoint. (L. E. Andrews) Iowa Health, '**87** : 253.
Pavia. Hare. Cities of No. Italy, **1** : 166.
— Sieges of. Robson, W. Sieges, 309.
Paving, street, Experiments in. Wynter, A. Peeps, **2** : 163.
— — in Australian cities. U. S. Cons. Rept. no. 154.
— — Sanitation in. (G. Baird) Am. Pub. Health, **12** : 142.
Paving stones, Natural history of. (A. W. Williamson) Manch. Sci. lec. **2** : 93.
Pawlovius, Christopher. Wallace, R. Anti-Trin. biog. **2** : 525.
Pawnbroking in Europe and U. S. (W. R. Patterson) U. S. Lab. Bull. **4** : 173.
— Pernicious influence of, in Scotland. (D. Macrae) Trans. Soc. Sci. Lond. '**62** : 619.
Pawn-shops. (W. R. Patterson) Conf. char. & correc. '**99** : 305.
Pawson, John. Jackson, T. Early Meth. **2** : 1. — Wesley & successors, 29, 55.
Paxton, Sir Joseph. Smiles. Self-help.
Payn, James. Wilman, G. Sk. liv. celeb. 77.
Payne, George, in Queen street. Yates, E. H. Celeb. **2** : 301.
Payne, John. Japp & Holmes. Succ. bus. men, 38.

Payne, John Howard. Dunlap. Am. theatre, 2 : 256. — Matthews, B. Actors, 3 : 37. — Lanman, C. Haphazard, 231. — Proctor, B. W. Autob. 132. — Richardson. Amer. lit. 2 : 19.
— Scenes of "Home, sweet home." Wolfe, T. F. Lit. haunts, 148.

Payne, Thomas. Jackson, T. Early Meth. 1 : 347.

Paynes, The two — Roger and Thomas. Dobson, A. 18th cent. vign. 199.

Payson, Edward. Pierce, B. K. Em. dead, 388. — Waterbury. Eloq. preach. 72.

Pazzi, The, Conspiracy of. Pastor, L. Hist. popes, 4 : 300.

Pea Ridge, Battle of. (E. A. Blodgett) Mil. ess. M. O. L. L. U. S. Ills. 289.

Peabody, Andrew Preston. (E. E. Hale) Am. Acad. A. & S. Proc. 28 : 351. — Am. Antiq. Soc. Proc. n. s. 8 : 281, 306. — With portrait. (E. J. Young) Mass. Hist. Soc. Proc. 2d ser. 11 : 25. — Vaille & Clark. Harv. book, v. 1.

Peabody, Charles A., with portrait. Sketches N. H. men, 209.

Peabody, Elizabeth Palmer. Hanaford. Wom. of cent. 220. — (W. E. Sheldon) Nat. Educa. Assoc. '94 : 231.

Peabody, Everett. (F. H. Peabody) Harvard mem. biog. 1 : 150.

Peabody, George. Bolton, S. K. Poor boys, 1. — Bourne. Lond. merchants, 267. — Everett. Orat. v. 3. — Houghton. Kings, 157. — McCabe, J. D. Great fortunes, 168. — Brockett. Men of our day, 540. — With portrait. Cochrane, R. Benef. lives, 38. — Duyckinck. Portrait gall. 2 : 291. — Thayer, W. M. Turningpoints, 24.
— Eulogy on. Winthrop, R. C. Addresses, 3 : 36.
— Life and character of. Wallis, S. T. Works, 1 : 63.

Peabody, Joseph, with portrait. (G. A. Ward) Hunt, F. Am. merch. 1 : 367.

Peabody, Oliver William Bourne. Putnam, A. P. Singers liberal, 152.

Peabody, Stephen, Reminiscences of. Gilman, S. Contrib. 190.

Peabody, William Bourne Oliver. Griswold, R. W. Sac. poets. — Hatfield, E. F. Poets of church, 461. — Miller, Jos. Singers church, 2d ed. 457. — Putnam, A. P. Singers liberal, 137.

Peabody, Mass. Bacon, E. M. Hist. pilgrim. 163.

Peabody Educational Fund, The. (A. D. Mayo) U. S. Bur. Ed. Rept. '93–94, 1 : 739.

Peabody homes in London. Bolton, S. K. Soc. Stud. in Eng. 121.

Peabody Institute, Baltimore, Sketch of. Kennedy, J. P. Occas. addr. 305.

Peabody Museum in Cambridge. (F. W. Putnam) Am. Antiq. Soc. Proc. n. s. 6 : 180.

Peace, Charles, Execution of. Buchanan, R. Coming terr. 302.

Peace. Cobden. Speeches, 509. — Friswell. Better self, 290. — Godkin. Reflections, 1. — Prime, W. C. I go a-fishing, 175.
— and happiness. Lubbock. Use of life, 281.
— Barbarities of. Friswell. About, 210.
— Bibliography of. Trueblood, B. F. Federation of the world.
— The evolution of, 1885. Lawrence. Ess. int. law, 234.
— in life and art. Patmore. Religio poetæ, 92.
— International. Stanton, H. B. Reforms, 346.
— Permanent. Newman, F. W. Miscel. 3 : 302.
— Perpetual. Kant. Politics ; tr. by Hastie.

Peace, the question of the age. Leslie, T. E. C. Ess. pol. econ. 62.

Peace conference, 1899. Mahan. Lessons war, 207.

Peace Jubilee at Boston, 1869. Howells. Sub. sket. 195.

Peace meetings. Miller, H. Hist. ess. 293.

Peacock, Sir Barnes. Em. persons, 4 : 293. — Escott, T. H. S. Pillars emp. 250.

Peacock, John. Hatfield, E. F. Poets of church, 493.

Peacock, Thomas Love. Buchanan, R. Look round, 162. — (E. W. Gosse) Ward. Eng. poets, 4 : 417. — Saintsbury. Studies Eng. liter. — Buchanan, R. Poet's sk. book, 93. — Stoddard, R. H. Under eve. lamp, 225. — (R. Garnett) Miles, A. H. Poets of cent. 2 : 331. — Miles, A. H. Poets of cent. 9 : 169. — Smith, G. B. Poets & nov. 111. — Warner Lib. 19 : 11223.
— Tales. Spedding. Reviews.

"Peacock," brig, Capture of. Dawson. Batt. of U. S. 2 : 206.

Peak, W. J. Parton, J. Sk. of men of prog.

Peale, Anna C. Ellet. Women artists, 288.

Peale, Charles Willson. Baker, W. S. Portr. of Wash. 11. — Boyle, E. Dist. Marylanders. — Lossing. Em. Amer. 176.

Peale, James. Baker, W. S. Portr. of Wash. 66.

Peale, Rembrandt. Baker, W. S. Portr. of Wash. 170. — Lester. Artists, 201.

Peanuts and peanut oil, 1894. U. S. Cons. Rept. 45 : 378.
— Manufacture of oil and food from, 1894. (F. H. Mason) U. S. Cons. Rept. 44 : 683.

Pearce, Samuel. Miller, Jos. Singers church, 2d ed. 334.

Pearce, Mrs. Samuel. Burder. Pious wom. 607.

Pearl button manufacture. Iowa Bur. Lab. '98 : 81.

Pearl fisheries and pearl supply in various countries, 1896. U. S. Cons. Rept. 51 : 622.

Pearl islands. Alexander, J. M. Isl. Pac. 116.

Pearl Lochs, Oahu, U. S. naval supply station. (G. W. Littlehales) Am. Geog. Soc. 30 : 277.

Pearl oysters, Parasites, commensals, and domiciliares in. (R. E. C. Stearns) Smithson. Rept. '86 : 339.

Pearls. Kunz. Gems, 211.
— and diamonds. Fields. Underbrush, 209.
— and pearl-fisheries. Chambers's Miscel. no. 67. — De Vere. Wonders of the deep, 75. — Goodrich, F. B. Ocean's story, ch. 55. — Japp. Days w. indus. 86. — Simmonds. Commercial products, 402.

Pearson, Chas. H., with portrait. (H. A. Strong) Pearson, C. H. Reviews, 1.

Pearson, John. (S. Cheetham) Barry, A. Masters theol. 213. — Creasy. Etonians, 151.

Pearson, Thomas Scott. (S. W. Boardman) N. E. Hist.- Gen. Soc. Biog. 3 : 126.

Pearson, Rev. W. Lonsdale. Worthies Cumb. v. 6.

Peary, R. E., Reception of. Am. Geog. Soc. 27 : 373.
— Plan of, and Capt. Sverdrup. (G. C. Hurlbut) Am. Geog. Soc. 29 : 453.

Peasant, Plea for, as soldier. Butler, W. F. Far out, 283.

Peasant life in old Germany. McLaughlin, E. T. Stud. mediæv. 71, 100.

Peasant proprietors in Germany. Baring-Gould. Germany, 71.

Peasant proprietorship. Kempner, W. Common-sense soc. 107.

Peters, Hugh, in literature. (W. S. Appleton) Mass. Hist. Soc. Proc. 2d ser. **8** : 118.

Peters, Jans. Brown, J. N. Bapt. martyrs, 222.

Peters, Mrs. Mary (Bowly). Hatfield, E. E. Poets of church, 496.

Peters, Mrs. Phillis Wheatley. Griswold. Fem. poets, 30.

Peters, Richard. Carson, H. L. Sup. Ct. of U. S. 566. — Lossing. Em. Amer. 169.

Peters, Samuel R., with portrait. Scott, H. W. Dist. Am. lawy. 569.

Petersburg, Va., Siege of. Stine, J. H. Army Poto. 660.

— Skirmish at. Dawson. Batt. of U. S. **1** : 687.

Peterson, Daniel. Wallace, R. Anti-Trin. biog. **3** : 128.

Peterson, Lawrence. Winslow, S. N. Biog. Phila. merch. 206.

Petigru, James Louis, and Hugh Swinton Legaré. (A. R. Lawton) Am. Bar Assoc. **5** : 180.

Petion, Jerome. Adolphus. Biog. Fr. rev. **2** : 328.

Petit, Lizzie. Freeman. J. D. Wom. of South, 425.

Petition, Right of. (Sir J. Eliot) Goodrich, C. A. Cel. Brit. eloq. — Phillips, W. Speeches, **2** : 1. — Winthrop, R. C. Addresses, 1 : 389.

— — J. Q. Adams and. Lodge and Roosevelt. Hero-tales, 149.

— — Maintenance of the. Archer. Decis. ev. 152.

Petitot, Jean. Brightwell. Byepaths of biog. 14.

Petofi, Alexander. Curwen. Sorrow, **1** : 197. — With portrait. (C. H. Genung) Warner Lib. **19** : 11347.

Petra. Gillett, E. H. Anc. cities, 121. — Martineau, H. Eastern life, 320. — Olin, S. Trav. in Egypt, 13. — Wright, W. B. Anc. cities, 97.

— Four days in. (W. B. Ogden) Am. Geog. Soc. **20** : 137.

— Ruins of. Twedie. Ruined cities, 26.

Petrarca, Francesco. Alger. Solitudes, 223. — Greene, G. W. Hist. stud. 1. — Longfellow. Poets Eur. 524. — Macaulay. Ess. **1** : 80. — Montgomery. Men of Ita. **1** : 61. — Oliphant, Mrs. Makers of Ven. 342. — Phillimore. Studies in Ital. liter. — Symonds. Renais. It. lit. **1** : 84. — Symonds. Reviv. of learn. 69. — Tuckerman. Poets, 7. — Vincent, G. E. Some Ital. au. 77. — Owen, J. Skeptics Ital. 107. — Shelley, Mrs. Lit. men Italy, v. **1**. — Snell, F. J. 14th cent. 236. — Stebbing. Ital. poets, v. **1**. — Swanwick, A. Poets, 141. — Trollope. Ital. poets, **1** : 51. — With portrait. (J. F. Bingham) Warner Lib. **19** : 11357. — Vincent, G. E. Ital. authors, 77.

— and Laura. Delepierre. Hist. diff. 93. — Jameson. Loves of poets.

— Bibliography. Cornell Univ. Lib. **1** : 42. — Rearden, T. H. Petrarch & oth. essays.

— Boccaccio and, Friendship of. Hueffer. Ital. stud. 31.

— Eight sonnets of. Symonds. Sk. So. Eur. **2** : 385.

— House of, at Arqua. Howells. Ital. jour. 216.

— Sentimentalism of. Lowell. Writ. **2** : 253.

— Sonnets of. Deshler. Afternoons, 21.

— Writings of. Knox. Essays, **2** : 206.

Petri, Henri W., with portrait. Ehrlich, A. Cel. violin. 176.

Petrie, Adam. Rules of good breeding. Maxwell, Sir H. Rainy days, 3.

Petrie, George. Allingham. Varieties, **3** : 161.

Petrified forest of Arizona. Lummis. Strange corners, 21.

— in California. Marshall, W. G. Thro' Amer. 319.

Petroleum. Hunt, J. S. Chem. & geol. ess. 168. — Knox, T. W. Underground, 331. — Japp. Days w. indus. 156.

— the light of the poor. Playfair. Sub. soc. 263.

Petroleum industry. Pa. Bur. Indus. Statis. '92.

Petroleum products for illuminating, Diphtheria and. (G. H. Wilson) Conn. Health, '86 : 309.

Petroleum trade, Russian, 1891–92. U. S. Cons. Rept. nos. 116, 152.

— — 1897–98. (J. C. Chambers) U. S. Cons. Rept. **54** : 185. **57** : 37. **60** : 209.

Petrolia and its marvels. Deming. Byways, 172.

Petronius Arbiter, with portrait. (H. W. Preston) Warner Lib. **19** : 11384.

— Quæstiones. (H. W. Hayley) Harv. stud. class. philol. **2** : 1.

Pets, Everybody's. Sanborn, Kate. Lit. zoo, **1** : 105.

— Old-world. Repplier. Ess. in min. 182.

— Queer, of Sailor Jack. Kelley, J. D. J. Ship's co. 207.

Pettes, Mary Dwight. Brockett. Woman's work, 385.

Pettibone lineage, The. Fields. Underbrush, 147.

Pettie, John, with photo. Cooper, T. Men of mark, **6** : 8.

Pettigrew, T. J. Pettigrew. Med. portr. gall. v. 4.

Pettingill, Almira H. Hemenway. Poets of Vt. 139.

Pettitt, Henry. Wilman, G. Sk. liv. celeb. 119.

Petty, Sir Wm. Arnold, F. Turning-points, 235. — Smiles. Self-help. — Wrangham. Brit. Plutarch, v. 4.

Petty-Fitzmaurice family. Sanford & Townsend. Gov. fam. 2.

Petty malignity and trickery. Boyd. Recreat. **1** : 65.

Pevensey Castle. Timbs. Abbeys, **1** : 355.

Pews. Coleridge, H. Ess. **2** : 351. — Ess. from Nation, 155.

— of the past. Bayly, J. A. S. New stud. 146.

Pew system. Hole, S. R. Addresses, 137.

Pfalz, The. Bartley, G. C. T. Rhine, 107.

Pfeiffer, Mrs. Emily Davis. Clayton, E. C. Eng. fem. art. **2** : 424. — (A. H. Japp) Miles, A. H. Poets of cent. **7** : 555. — Robertson. Eng. poetesses, 348.

Pfeiffer, Ida. Adams, W. H. D. Cel. wom. trav. 215. — With portrait. Fifty famous women, 169. — Miller. In ladies' comp. 167.

Phædimus. Mills. Poets of Greece, 183.

Phædo. Mills. Poets of Greece, 428.

Phædrus. Newbigging. Fables, 63.

Phaethon; or loose thoughts for loose thinkers. Kingsley. Raleigh, 276; or Lit. lec. 353.

Phalaris, and the brazen bull. Freeman. Sicily, **2** : 458.

— Epistles of, Bentley's pretended. Montgomery, H. R. Impost. 102.

Phallism. Bibliography. Howard, C. Sex worship.

— in ancient religions. Wake. Serpent wor. 8.

Phantasms. Mason, R. O. Telepathy, 224.

— of the dead. (Mrs. H. Sidgwick) Soc. Psych. Res. **3** : 69; (F. Podmore; F. W. H. Myers) **6** : 229, 314; (F. W. H. Myers) **8** : 170.

Phantom ship. Jones, W. Credulities, 82.

Pharamond, a romance. Gosse, E. Gossip, 79.

Pharaoh. Geikie, C. Old Test. char. 78.

— Daughter of. Geikie, C. Old Test. char. 86.

Pharisaism. Gladden, W. Ruling ideas, 217.

Pharisee, The. Curtis, G. W. Other ess. 149.

Photography, Applications of. Wynter, A. Peeps, 1 : 53.
— as an aid to local history. (G. E. Francis) Am. Antiq. Soc. Proc. n. s. 5 : 274.
— Astronomical, with bibliography. Todd, D. P. Stars & tel. 393.
— Bibliography. Providence Pub. Lib. Bull. Feb. '98.
— Doings of the sunbeam. Holmes. Soundings, 228.
— in colors. (F. E. Ives ; L. Warnerke) Smithson. Rept. '93 : 151, 163.
— in public libraries. Garnett, R. Ess. in librarianship, 234.
— in the service of astronomy. (R. Radau) Smithson. Rept. '89 : 469.
— Invisible image in. (Raphael Meldola) Smithson. Rept. '90 : 377.
— Scientific investigation by. Proctor, R. A. Univ. of suns, 124.
Photometry, Photographic. (M. J. Janssen) Smithson. Rept. '94 : 191.
Photo-sculpture. Wynter, A. Our soc. bees, 2 : 263.
Phrenology. Atkinson and Martineau. Letters on man's nature. — Brodie. Psychological inquiries, 225. — Combe. Constitution of man, 328. — Holland. Mental physiology, 203.
— Combe's System of. Brownson. Works, 9 : 235.
— Franz Joseph Gall. Lewes. Biog. phil.
— satirized. Walsh, R. Didactics, 2 : 56.
Phrontisterion ; or, Oxford in the 19th century ; a drama. Mansel. Letters, 302.
Phrygia. Gardner, P. New chap. Gr. hist.
Phthisis, On the prevention of. (E. M. Hunt) Am. Pub. Health, 15 : 136. — (B. F. Wyman) Am. Pub. Health, 16 : 94.
See Consumption.
Physical antipathies. Wynter, A. Our soc. bees, 1 : 453.
Physical culture. (A. G. Young) Maine Health, '91 : 216. — (T. Ward) N. Y. Regents, 90 : 563.
— Food and. Holland, J. G. Titcomb's let. 54.
— Scientific value of. (A. B. Poland) Nat. Educa. Assoc. '92 : 230.
Physical education. (Clara Conway) Nat. Educa. Assoc. '91 : 348. — (E. M. Hartwell) Cong. Educa. Chic. '93, 618. — (E. Hitchcock and others) N. Y. Regents, 105 : 340.
— and school life. (E. M. Hunt) N. J. Health, '91 : 57.
— for city people. Meath. Soc. arrows, 57.
— in Amherst College. (E. Hitchcock) Mass. Health, '79 (10th) : 65.
— in Denmark. (Joakim Larsen) Nat. Educa. Assoc. '93 : 664.
— in our schools. (R. Anna Morris) Nat. Educa. Assoc. '92 : 366.
— indispensable. (L. M. Törngren) Cong. Educa. Chic. '93, 54.
— Necessity of. (C. H. Horsch) Penn. Health, '86 : 313.
— Psychological aspect of exercises. (G. W. Fitz) Cong. Educa. Chic. '93, 626.
— Training of the human body. (A. Mosso) Cong. Educa. Chic. '93, 623.
— Unsolved problems in. (T. D. Wood) Cong. Educa. Chic. '93, 621.
— Warren on. Ossoli. Life without, 116. — (H. Mann) Mass. Educa. 6 : 56. 12 : 43. — Rosenkranz. Philos. educa. 63.
Physical exercises for school purposes. (J. G. Smith) Nat. Educa. Assoc. '93 : 631.

Physical geography. Bibliography. Salem (Mass.) Pub. Lib. Bull. Mar. '94.
— History of. (C. P. Daly) Am. Geog. Soc. 22 : 1.
— in secondary schools. (A. B. Brigham) Nat. Educa. Assoc. '97 : 923.
— its possibilities and difficulties. (E. L. Harris) Nat. Educa. Assoc. '95 : 615.
— Study of. (G. M. Ingalsbee) N. Y. Regents, 84 : 511.
Physical law and freedom. Royce, J. Spir. mod. philos. 381.
Physical science and theology. Mozley, J. B. Lec. 17.
— in common schools. (C. O. Thompson) Nat. Educa. Assoc. '72 : 149.
Physical sciences, Ancient and modern estimates of. (W. D. Wilson) N. Y. Regents, 92 : 499.
— Elementary teaching of. Cooke, J. P., jr. Sci. cul. 71.
— Speculations in. (A. White) N. Y. Regents, 85 : 577.
— Teaching, in academies. (L. R. C. Cooley) N. Y. Regents, 96 : 375.
Physical strength. Stephen, J. F. Ess. by barr. 69.
Physical-Technical Institute of Germany, 1897. (P. H. Mason) U. S. Cons. Rept. 54 : 412.
Physical training. (J. C. Boykin) U. S. Bur. Ed. Rept. '91-92 : 451. — (E. M. Hartwell) U. S. Bur. Ed. Rept. '97-98, 1 : 487. — (E. F. Hermanns) Nat. Educa. Assoc. '95 : 65. — (C. H. Raymond) N. J. Health, '91 : 91. — (D. A. Sargent ; J. M. Watson) Am. Pub. Health, 9 : 116.
— Development of will through. (W. O. Krohn) Nat. Educa. Assoc. '97 : 873.
— a factor in character building. (J. L. Hughes) Nat. Educa. Assoc. '96 : 911.
— in the colleges. (F. E. Leonard) Nat. Educa. Assoc. '97 : 909.
— in Germany. (E. M. Hartwell) Am. Pub. Health, 11 : 182.
— in the U. S. (E. M. Hartwell) Am. Pub. Health, 10 : 27.
— Status of, in the U. S. (R. Anna Morris) Nat. Educa. Assoc. '96 : 895.
— Testing, in civil service examinations. (H. Woodrow) Trans. Soc. Sci. Lond. '74 : 503.
Physicians and their relationship to the world. Richardson, B. W. Ministry, 186.
— as bon-vivants. Jeaffreson. Doctors, 90.
— as literary and scientific men. Winslow, F. Physic, 2 : 179.
— as poets. Winslow, F. Physic, 1 : 206.
— Eccentric. Winslow, F. Physic, 1 : 46.
— eminent, Early struggles of. Winslow, F. Physic, 1 : 130.
— English, abroad. Winslow, F. Physic, 2 : 193.
— Fees of. Jeaffreson. Doctors, 102.
— Notable. Timbs. Doctors, 12.
— Old. Timbs. Doctors, 1.
Physicists. Osborn. From Greeks, 36.
Physick, Philip Syng. With portrait. [Amer.] Nat. portr. gall. 4. — (John Bell) Gross. Lives physicians, 351. — Collins, Stephen. Miscel. — Lossing. Em. Amer. 330.
Physics, Ancient history of. Smith, Adam. Ess. phil. 95.
— Bibliography. Michigan Schoolmasters' Club, Proc. '99.
— Economical nature of. Mach. Pop. sci. lec. 186.
— Elementary. Bibliography. Norwich (Ct.) Otis Lib. Bull. Mar.-Apr. '96.

Physics, Importance of study of. (J. Tyndall) Youmans. Culture, 57.

— in college-entrance requirements. (E. H. Hall) Nat. Educa. Assoc. '97 : 937.

— in common schools. (C. K. Wead) Nat. Educa. Assoc. '85 : 114.

— Principle of comparison in. Mach. Pop. sci. lec. 236.

— Progress in, 1846–96. (T. C. Mendenhall) Goode. Smithson. Inst. 519.

— teaching of, Aims and methods of. (C. K. Wead) U. S. Bur. Ed. Circ. '84, no. 7.

— — in public schools. (C. K. Wead and others) Nat. Educa. Assoc. '87 : 41.

— — in the U. S. (F. W. Clarke) U. S. Bur. Ed. Circ. '80, no. 6.

Physiocrats. Bibliography. Higgs, H. Physiocrats.

Physiognomy. Saunders. Stray leaves, 84. — Schopenhauer. Relig. 73.

— Faces around us. Friswell. About, 104.

— "The human face divine." Saunders. Mosaics, 127.

Physiography, elementary, Laboratory work in. (R. H. Cornish) Nat. Educa. Assoc. '97 : 928.

Physiological station at Paris, Work of. (E. J. Marey) Smithson. Rept. '94 : 391.

Physiology, Comparative. Bibliography. Verworn, M. General physiology.

— Early teaching of. (E. D. Cheney) Brackett, A. C. Educa. of girls, 132.

— Elementary; four lectures. (J. E. Morgan) Manch. Sci. lectures, 1 : 117.

— the German science. Hall, G. S. Asp. Ger. 107.

— Method and aim of the study of. Carpenter, W. Benj. Nature, 155.

— problems in, Elementary. (J. S. Burdon Sanderson) Smithson. Rept. '89 : 423.

— Recent progress in. (M. Foster) Smithson. Rept. '97 : 437.

— Relations of, to chemistry and morphology. (Giulio Fano) Smithson. Rept. '94 : 377.

— study of, Importance of. (J. Paget) Youmans. Culture, 147.

— — in common schools. Mann. Works, 3 : 129.

— (G. Combe) Trans. Soc. Sci. Lond. '57 : 208.

Piacenza. Hare. Cities of No. Italy, 2 : 185.

Piano-forte, The. Hunt, L. Seer, 2 : 86.

— History of. Haweis. Music & mor. 337. — Parton. Triumphs, 323.

— Playing the. Kingston, W. B. Music & manners, 1 : 190.

Piano music, Evolution of. Henderson, W. J. Preludes.

Piano-playing and pianists. Mathews, W. S. B. Hundred yrs. music, 112.

Piatt, J. J. and S. M. B. Taylor, B. Crit. ess. 304. — Stoddard, R. H. Poets' homes.

Pi-beseth. Poole, R. S. Cities of Egypt, 150.

Picard, Louis Joseph Ernest. King, E. French pol. lead. 273. — Men of 3d repub. 147.

Picardy, Apollo in. Pater. Miscel. stud. 121.

Piccini, Nicolo, Italian musician. Ferris, G. T. Ital. & Fr. compos. 17. — Hogarth. Mem. opera, 2 : 83, 231.

Piccolomini, Alessandro. Badeau. Vagabond, 340.

Piccolomini, Marietta, later Marchesa Gaetani. Clayton, E. C. Queens, 493. — Needham. Queens of song.

Piccolomini, Octavio. Cust. Warriors thirty years, 2 : 489.

Picken, Andrew Belfrage. Wilson, J. G. Poets of Scot. 2 : 254.

Pickens, Andrew, with portrait. [Amer.] Nat. portr. gall. v. 3. — Lossing. Em. Amer. 194.

Pickens, Ezekiel. Livingston, J. Dist. Amer. 161.

Pickens, Fort, Reinforcement of. Keyes, E. D. Fifty years, 375.

Pickering, George. (Abel Stevens) McClintock, J. Em. Meth. 263.'— Pierce, B. K. Em. dead, 324. — Sherman, D. N. Eng. divines, 399.

Pickering, John. (W. H. Prescott) Mass. Hist. Coll. 3d ser. 10 : 204. — Peabody. Harv. grad. 42.

— Biographical sketch of. Sumner. Works, 1 : 214.

Pickering, Timothy. With portrait. [Amer.] Nat. portr. gall. v. 1. — Lodge, H. C. Studies, 182. — Lossing. Em. Amer. 165.

Pickersgill, F. R., with photo. Cooper, T. Men of mark, 6 : 36.

Pickett, George E. Pollard. Life of Lee, 509.

Pickett's cave, Colorado. Hovey, H. C. Cel. Am. Cav. 201.

Pickford, Joseph. Mozley. Reminis. 1 : 65.

Pickton, James Allanson. Davidson, J. M. Eng. lib. 253.

Pickton, Sir Thomas. Cole, J. W. Brit. generals, v. 2. — Johns. Nav. & mil. heroes.

— Trial of. Browne, G. L. Narr. state tri. 1 : 295.

Pico della Mirandola, Giovanni. Craik. Pursuit knowl. 1 : 83. — Pater. Stud. renais. 18. — Montgomery. Men of Ita. 1 : 161. — Symonds. Reviv. of learn. 329.

Pictor, Quintus Fabius. Dunlop, J. Rom. liter. 2 : 108.

Pictorial drawing in primary and grammar grades. (Wilhelmina Seegmiller) Nat. Educa. Assoc. '95 : 822.

Picts, Relation to the other tribes of Great Britain. Garnett. Philol. ess. 196.

Pictures. Tuckerman. Collector, 95. — Tuckerman. Criterion, 77.

— for the people. Barnett, S. A. Prac. socialism, 109.

— Gossip on. Thackeray. Early & late, 222.

— Judging of. Hazlitt. Crit. on art, ser. 2.

— Men and. Thackeray. Early & late, 188.

— their influence in the home. Hunt, L. Seer, 2 : 14.

Picturesque, The, and the ideal. Hazlitt. Table-talk.

— Taste for, among the Greeks. (E. M. Cope) Camb. ess. '56 : 115.

Picturesqueness. Rimmer, A. Country towns, 302.

Piedmont, Revolution in, 1821. Thayer, W. R. Dawn Ital. 1 : 253.

Piekarscius, Jerome. Wallace, R. Anti-Trin. biog. 2 : 366.

Pierce, Benjamin. Lossing. Em. Amer. 283.

Pierce, Edward Lillie. (G. F. Hoar) Am. Antiq. Soc. Proc. n. s. 12 : 197. — (Jas. F. Rhodes) Mass. Hist. Proc. 2d ser. 12 : 10.

Pierce, Franklin. Abbott. Lives of presidents, 332. — Duyckinck. Nat. portr. gall. 2 : 333. — Ellet. Court circles, 447. — Field, M. B. Memories, 157. — Frost. Presidents, 393. — Poore, B. P. Reminis. 424. — (B. Wadleigh) Wilson, J. G. Presidents, 262. — Thompson, R. W. Pers. recoll. 333.

— Social life during administration of. Ellet, E. F. Court circles, 447.

Pierce, Mrs. Franklin. Gordon, L. L. Lady Wash'n, 278.

Pierce, Henry L., with portrait. (J. M. Bugbee) Mass. Hist. Soc. Proc. 2d ser. 11 : 386.

Pierce, Henry Reuben. Bartlett, J. R. R. I. officers, 432.

Pierce, Mrs. Jane Appleton. Hanaford. Wom. of cent. 90. — Holloway, L. C. Ladies, 484.

Pierce, John. Peabody. Harv. grad. 27. — (T. B. Fox; G. Putnam) Ware, W. Am. Unita. 2 : 3. — (W. B. Trask) N. E. Hist.-Gen. Soc. Biog. 1 : 213.

Pierce, Thomas P., with portrait. Sketches N. H. men, 127.

Pierce, William. Jones, C. C., jr. Deleg. fr. Georgia, 155.

Pierpoint, Evelyn. See Kingston, Duke of.

Pierpoint, Folliott Sandford. Miles, A. H. Poets of cent. 10 : 757.

Pierpont, Rev. James. Bacon. Thirteen hist. discourses.

Pierpont, John. Bungay. Off-hand, 229. — Everest. Poets of Conn. 137. — Griswold. Poets Am. 85. — With portrait. Bungay. Pen-portr. 41. — Griswold, R. W. Sac. poets. — Miller, Jos. Singers church, 2d ed. 394. — Putnam, A. P. Singers liberal, 28.

Pierre de Blois, archdeacon of Bath. Neale. Mediæv. preachers.

Pierre de Celle, bp. of Chartres. Neale. Mediæv. preachers.

Pierre of Provence and the beautiful Maguelonne. (O. Flinch) Warner Lib. 20 : 11428.

Pierrepont, Edwards. Patten, J. Sket. of men of prog. — With portrait. (J. W. de Peyster) Rogers, A. C. Repres. men, 423.

Piers Plowman. Gibbins. Eng. soc. ref. 9. See Langland.

Pieterszoon, Jan. Wallace, R. Anti-Trin. biog. 3 : 279.

Pietism. Baring-Gould. Germany, 357. — Hurst, J. F. Hist. rationalism, 82. — Ker, J. Lec. hist. preach. 200.

— and mysticism. Ullman. Reformers, 178.

Pietist and Orthodox controversy. Ker, J. Lec. hist. preach. 218.

Pietists. Winkworth. Chr. singers Germ: 256.

Piety, Hereditary. Cobbe, F. P. Darwinism, 35.

Pig, Monster. Buckland, F. T. Curios. nat. hist. 4 : 146.

Pigs. Shaler. Dom. animals, 139.

Pigelius, John. Wallace, R. Anti-Trin. biog. 2 : 486.

Pigeons. (W. G. Barton) Essex Inst. Bull. 16 : 59.

— making love. Hunt, L. Men, wom. & books, 104.

Piggott, John. Ivimey. Eng. Bapt. 2 : 451. 3 : 565.

Pigmies. See Pygmies.

"Pigot," schooner, Capture of. Dawson. Batt. of U. S. 1 : 461.

Pii, The three deposed. Doran. Monarchs, 2 : 136.

Pike, Albert. Davidson, J. W. Writ. of South, 416. — Griswold. Poets Am. 368.

Pike, Austin F. Am. Bar Assoc. 10 : 413. — Long, J. D. After-dinner, 27.

Pike, Chester, with portrait. Sketches N. H. men, 123.

Pike, Robert, farmer. Parton. Capt. indus. 43.

Pike, Zebulon Montgomery. With portrait. Greely, A. W. Explorers, 163. — Lossing. Em. Amer. 191.

Pike's Peak. Pidgeon. Engineer's holiday, 141.

Pilate, Wife of. Hastings, F. Obscure charac. 231.

Pilgrimage to Parnassus. Hales. Folia litt. 165.

Pilgrimages of the middle ages. Cutts, E. L. Scenes mid. ages, 176. — Jusserand. Eng.

wayfaring life, 338. — Lacroix. Mil. and relig. life, 362.

Pilgrimages, Good and ill effect of. Evans, R. W. Biog. early church, 1 : 369.

Pilgrims of Grace, The. Burke, S. H. Men of Reforma. 1 : 264.

Pilgrims of New England. Bacon. Genesis N. Eng. churches. — Bacon. Thirteen historical discourses. — Coffin, C. C. Story of liberty, 383. — Doyle. Puritan colonies, 1 : 14. — Everett. Orat. v. 2. — Higginson, T. W. Amer. explor. 309. — Humphreys, H. Miscel. 79. — (W. Crafts) Charleston book, 22. — Phillips, Wend. Sp. 226. Stedman Lib. Amer. liter. v. 1. — Winthrop, R. C. Addresses, 1 : 1. — Stoughton, J. Spir. heroes, 61. — Whittier. Prose works, v. 2.

— Age of, the heroic period of our history. Choate. Addr. 74.

— and liberty. Seward. Works (1884), 4 : 179.

— at Leyden. (G. Sumner) Mass. Hist. Coll. 3d ser. 9 : 42.

— Bibliography. Brown, J. Pilgr. fathers. — Johnson, H. Scrooby to Plymouth Rock. — Winsor. Hist. Amer. 3 : 257.

— Character of. Vaughan, R. Ess. 1 : 1.

— — and purpose of. Richardson. Amer. lit. 1 : 11, 72.

— Departure of. Everett. Orat. v. 2.

— Exiles for conscience' sake. Blaxland. Mayflower ess. 1.

— Founders great in their unconsciousness. Bushnell. Work, 124.

— Landing of, 250th anniversary. Winthrop, R. C. Addresses, 3 : 79.

— Letter of John Robinson to. Blaxland. Mayflower ess. 35.

— Memory of our fathers. Beecher, L. Works, 1 : 315.

Pilkington, James, bp. of Durham. Croston. Hist. sites Lanc. 147.

Pilkington family. Croston. Hist. sites Lanc. 140.

Pillans, J. Defense of classical instruction. Hamilton. Discus.

Pillars, Isaiah. Am. Bar Assoc. 18 : 539.

Pillory, Reflections in the. Lamb. Elia.

Pillow, Gideon J. Livingston, J. Em. Am. lawy. 651.

Pillsbury, George Alfred, with portrait. Sk. N. H. men, 39.

Pillsbury, Oliver, with portrait. Sket. N. H. men, 191.

Pilon, Germain, sculptor, d. 1590. Pattison. Renais. of art in France, 1 : 218.

Pilot laws, The. Dix. Speeches, 2 : 1, 12.

Pilpay. (C. R. Lanman) Warner Lib. 20 : 11437.

Pilsbury, Charles A. Davidson, J. W. Writ. of South, 419.

Pinckney, Charles. Moore, F. Am. eloq. 1 : 361. — Perry, B. F. Biog. sketches, 1 : 447.

Pinckney, Charles Cotesworth. With portrait. [Amer.] Nat. portr. gall. v. 4. — With portrait. Duyckinck. Nat. portr. gall. 1 : 190. — Lossing. Em. Amer. 143. — Perry, B. F. Biog. sketches, 1 : 250.

Pinckney, Thomas. With portrait. [Amer.] Nat. portr. gall. v. 4. — Lossing. Em. Amer. 230.

Pindar. Arnold, E. Poets of Greece, 153. — Freeman. Hist. Sicily, 2 : 266. — Mills. Poets of Greece, 122. — Symonds. Greek poets, 1 : 340. — Hundred greatest men, 7. — With portrait. (B. L. Gildersleeve) Warner Lib. 20 : 11487.

Pindemonte, I. Stebbing. Ital. poets, v. 3.

Pine, Robert Edge. Baker, W. S. Portr. of Wash. 57.

Pinero, Arthur Wing. Archer. Eng. dram. 270. — Walkley, A. W. Playhouse, 149.

Piney, Marilla M. M. Hemenway. Poets of Vt. 346.

Pinhorne, William. Field, R. S. Prov. courts N. J. 73.

Pinkie Cleugh, Battle of. (J. A. Froude) Adams, W. H. D. Eng. at war, 1 : 16.

Pinkney, Edward Coate. Boyle, E. Dist. Marylanders. — Griswold. Poets Amer. 253.

Pinkney, F. Boyle, E. Dist. Marylanders.

Pinkney, William. With portrait. [Amer.] Nat. portr. gall. v. 3. — With portrait. Duyckinck. Nat. portr. gall. 1 : 476. — Magoon. Orators of rev. 343. — Walsh, R. Didactics, 2 : 158. — Boyle, E. Dist. Marylanders. — Browne, I. Stud. gt. lawyers, 238. — Johnston, A. Amer. ora. 2 : 63. — Lossing. Em. Amer. 237. — Mathews, W. Oratory, 359. — Moore, F. Em. Eloq. 2 : 93. — Perry, B. F. Biog. sketches, 1 : 329.

— Character of. Story, J. Miscel. 794.

Pin-money. Ames, M. C. Outlines, 193.

Pinney, Charles, Trial of, for neglect of duty when mayor of Bristol. Townsend, W. C. Mod. state trials, 2 : 283.

Pinney, Norman. Everest. Poets of Conn. 335.

Pinnock, William, and Maunder, Samuel. Jerdan. Men, 336.

Pins, ancient brooches, and dress fastenings. Fairholt. Rambles, 159.

Pinto, Alex. de Serpa. Cochrane, R. Famous trav. 221.

Pinturicchio, Bernardo. Symonds. Renais. fine arts, 301.

Pinwell, George John. Ewart, H. C. Toilers in art, 209.

Pinzon, Martin Alonzo, Duro's defense of. (G. C. Hurlbut) Am. Geog. Soc. 24 : 391.

Pio, Alberto. Symonds. Reviv. of learn. 375, 422.

Pioneers and pathfinders. Hodder. Heroes, 2 : 61.

Pionius, martyr of Smyrna. Yonge, C. M. Pupils of John, 255.

Piotrowski, Rufin. Bernard, F. Escapes, 267.

Piozzi, Mrs. Hester Lynch. Bethune, G. W. Brit. fem. poets, 124. — Autobiography of. Crosland. Mem. women, 53. — Elwood. Lit. ladies, 2 : 1. — Robertson. Eng. poetesses, 49. — Tartt. Ess. 1 : 199. — Thomson. Queens, 395. — Williams, Jane. Lit. wom. 267.

Piper, Pied, of Hameln. Baring-Gould. Myths, 417.

Pipes, and smokers, Old. Bayly, J. A. S. New stud. 122.

— and smoking customs of the American Indians. (J. D. McGuire) U. S. Nat. Mus. Rept. '97 : 351.

Piracy. Whymper, F. The sea.

— Slave trade and. Story, J. Miscel. 122.

Piræus; seaport of Athens. Arnold, R. A. Levant, 1 : 29.

— Commerce and industries of, 1891. (A. C. McDowall) U. S. Cons. Rept. 35 : 345.

Pirates, Chinese. Macfarlane, C. Banditti, 288. — Jamaica. Powell, G. H. Excurs. in Libr. 123.

Pirie, Alexander. Hatfield, E. F. Poets of church, 497.

Piron, Alexis. Houssaye. Men of 18th cent. 1 : 89. — Men and wom. of France, 1 : 87. — Saintsbury. Miscel. ess. 369. — With portrait. Warner Lib. **20** : 11506.

Piron, Alexis, and the French stage. Hawkins. Fr. stage 18th cent. v. 1.

Pirtle, Henry. Livingston, J. Em. Am. lawy. 129.

Pisa. Buckley, T. A. Great cities, 187. — Duffy, B. Tuscan repub. 11 : 106, 215. — Fulton, C. C. Europe, 190. — Guild. Over the ocean, 531. — Hare. Cities of No. Italy, 2 : 440. — Howells. Ital. jour. 251. — Howells. Tuscan cities, 195. — Michelet. Rome, 75. — Taine. Italy, 2 : 55. — Pfirshing. Mem. Ital. 45. — Sala. Journey South, 183.

— Council of 1409 at. Stoughton. Ital. reformers, 31.

— French at, in 15th century. Robinson, A. M. F. End of mid. ages.

— Synod of. Pastor, L. Hist. popes, 1 : 174.

Pisan, Christine de. Besant. Fr. poetry, 49.

Pisano, Andrea. Perkins, C. C. Tusc. sculp. 1 : 63. — Symonds. Renais. fine arts, 119.

Pisano, Giovanni. Perkins, C. C. Tusc. sculp. 1 : 37. — Symonds. Renais. fine arts, 110.

Pisano, Niccola. Perkins, C. C. Tusc. sculp. 1 : 8. — Symonds. Renais. fine arts, 100.

Pisano, Nino. Perkins, C. C. Tusc. sculp. 1 : 71.

Pisaroni, Rosamunda Benedetta, Italian vocalist. Clayton, E. C. Queens, 238. — Needham. Queens of song.

Pisecius, Thomas. Wallace, R. Anti-Trin. biog. 2 : 499.

Pisistratus. Mills. Poets of Greece, 436.

Pistoja. Howells. Tuscan cities, 237.

Pistorius, Simon. Wallace, R. Anti-Trin. biog. 2 : 497.

Pita, Maria. Bourne, H. R. F. Eng. seam. 2 : 254.

Pitcairn, Archibald. Irving, D. Scot. writ. 2 : 189.

Pitcairn, Major John. (C. Hudson) Mass. Hist. Proc. 17 : 315.

Pitcairn's Island. Fyfe. Enterprise beyond the seas, 233. — Hale. Stories of the sea, 192.

Pitcairn Islands. Alexander, J. M. Isl. Pac. 435.

Pitcairn Islanders. Van Santvoord, C. Disc. 373.

Pitchlynn, Peter. Lanman, C. Recoll. 67.

Piteglio, Italy. Mushroom merchants in the Apennines. Baxter, L. E. Tusc. stud. 235.

Pithom. Poole, R. S. Cities of Egypt, 102.

Pitkin, Hannah C. Hemenway. Poets of Vt. 331.

Pitkin, Timothy. (T. C. Pitkin) N. E. Hist.-Gen. Soc. Biog. 1 : 76.

Pitman, Robert C., with portrait. Bungay. Pen-portr. 55.

Pitt, Charles. (S. Johnson) Chalmers. Eng. poets, 12 : 365.

Pitt, Wm., the elder. See Chatham.

Pitt, Wm., the younger. Adams, C. K. Rep. Brit. orat. 2 : 1. — Adams, W. H. D. Eng. party, 1 : 421. 2 : 1. — Adams, W. H. D. Men at helm, 159. — Brougham. Works, 3 : 277. — Earle, J. C. Eng. prem. 2 : 3. — Edgar. Footpr. 82. — Ewald. Repr. statesm. 1 : 279. — Georgian era, 1 : 381. — Harsha. Orators, 256. — Lodge. Portraits (Bohn), v. 8. — Macaulay. Ess. 6 : 221. — Taylor, W. C. Mod. Brit. Plut. 269. — Trotter. Stud. biog. 223. — Arnold, F. Turning-points, 257. — Carlyle, T. Montaigne, 267. — (J. R. Green) Ferris, G. T. Gt. leaders, 417. — Goodrich, C. A. Sel. Brit. eloq. — Macaulay. Biog. Encyc. Brit. — Mathews, W. Oratory, 239. — Mitchell, D. G. Eng. lands, 3 : 192. — Nicoll, H. J. Great orators.

— Administration of. Lewis, G. C. Ess. on admin.

Pliny the younger, Country places of. Mitchell. Wet days, 60.
— Epistles of. Drake, N. Mornings, 1 : 13.
Plot, Need of. (L. Parr) Cody, A. S. Fiction, 16.
— Proposed abolition of the. Higginson. New world, 135.
Plotinus. Lang. Letter on lit. 92. — Lewes. Biog. phil.
— On theism. Whedon. Ess. 2 : 16.
Plow, Electric, in Germany, 1895. (O. Doederlein) U. S. Cons. Rept. 49 : 160.
Plowden, Edmund. Woolrych. Serjeants, 1 : 101.
Plumbers and physicians, Relations of. (A. Young) Am. Pub. Health, 17 : 48.
Plumbing. (J. N. Hughes and others) Am. Pub. Health Assoc. 331.
— Defective, in New York city. (A. L. Webster) Am. Pub. Health, 16 : 190.
— Domestic, during past thirty-five years. (J. W. Hughes) Am. Pub. Health, 20 : 331.
— Domestic sanitary. (E. C. Jordan) Maine Health, '87 : 267.
— in sanitation. (J. Mitchell) Am. Pub. Health, 20 : 336. — (W. P. Gerhard) R. I. Health, 4 : 257.
Plummer, Mrs. Eliza G. Brockett. Woman's work, 735.
Plummer, William. (A. P. Peabody) N. E. Hist.-Gen. Soc. Biog. 2 : 246.
Plummer, William S. Davidson, J. W. Writ. of South, 422.
Plumptre, Edward Hayes. (W. G. Horder) Miles, A. H. Poets of cent. 10 : 397.
Plumptre, James. Grant, J. Recoll. Lords & Comm. 2 : 397.
Plunket, William Conyngham, 1st lord. Brougham. Works, 4 : 355. — Curran. Irish bar, 1 : 127. — Grant, J. Recoll. Lords, 342. — Phillips, C. Irish eloq. — Sheil. Sk. Irish bar, 1 : 98. — Stanton, H. B. Reforms, 132. — Whiteside, J. Early sk. 157.
Plutarch. Emerson. Lec. & biog. sk. 275. — Hundred greatest men, 282. — Mahaffy. Greek world under Rom. — Mills. Poets of Greece, 483. — (E. B. Clapp) Warner Lib. 20 : 11601.
— Lives. Stephen, J. F. Ess. by barr. 280.
Plymouth, Mass. Drake. Nooks of N. E. 261. — (Ellen Watson) Powell, L. P. Hist. towns N. E. 299. — Bacon, E. M. Hist. pilgrim. 28.
— Pilgrimage to. Punshon. Lec. 295.
Plymouth Colony, Colonization of. Blaxland. Mayflower ess. 49.
— Site of. Blaxland. Mayflower ess. 82.
Pneumatic despatch ; suction-post. Wynter, A. Our soc. bees, 1 : 52.
Pneumonia, Causation of. (H. B. Baker) Mich. Health, '86 : 246.
— Checking of, by disinfection. (J. Cochran) Am. Pub. Health, 19 : 21.
Pocahontas. With portrait. Clarke, M. C. Noted wom. 283. — Clement, J. Noble deeds, 104. — Gilman. Pathfinders, 85. — Goodrich, F. B. Women, 211. — Parton. Triumphs, 451. — With portrait. Fifty famous women, 158. — Hale, S. J. Less. wom. lives, 41. — Lossing. Em. Amer. 16. — Owen, Mrs. O. F. Heroines domes. 137. — Terhune. Colon. homes, 432.
— Marriage of. Stedman. Lib. Amer. lit. 1 : 17.
— Myth of, exploded. (H. Adams) Adams, C. F. Erie, 192.
Poché, Felix Pierre. Am. Bar Assoc. 18 : 505.
Pocoke, Richard. St. John. Cel. travelers, 2 : 101.

Pococurantism. Ballantyne. Ess. 107.
Poe, Edgar Allan. Boyd. Crit. ess. 210. — Curwen. Sorrow, 2 : 93. — Gilfillan. Third gall. 325. — Griswold, H. T. Home-life, 312. — Griswold. Poets Am. 417. — Griswold. Prose writ. 523. — Higginson. Sh. stud. 12. — Lang. Lett. to dead au. 140. — Nichol, J. Amer. lit. 163, 217. — Ossoli. Life without, 86. — (R. H. Stoddard) Poe. Works, 1 : 1.. — (J. R. Lowell) Poe. Works, 1 : 201. — Powell. Liv. authors (1850), 108. — Salt. Lit. sk. 104. — Saunders, F. Famous books, 169. — Stedman. Poets Amer. 225. — Walsh, W. S. Pen pic. Vic. au. 240. — Willis. Hurry-graphs, 240. — Wilson, J. G. Bryant, 334. — Fisher, M. Gen. sur. Am. lit. 231. — With portrait. Mitchell, D. G. Am. lands, 2 : 373. — Howe, M. A. D. Am. bookm. 76. — With portrait. (F. W. H. Myers) Warner Lib. 20 : 11651. — Hutton, R. H. Criticisms, 2 : 59. — Richardson. Amer. lit. 1 : 402. 2 : 97. — Smiles. Brief biog. 334. — Wise, D. Vanq. victors, 180. — Wright, H. C. Chil. sto. in Am. lit. 137.
— Bibliography. Benton, J. B. In the Poe circle.
— Homes and haunts of. Wolfe, T. F. Lit. haunts, 104.
— The Raven. Rees, J. R. With friend, 46.
— Sonnets of. Deshler. Afternoons, 307.
Poet, The. Emerson. Ess. 2 : 7.
— and humorist. Walsh, W. S. Paradox, 81.
— and Philistine. Walsh, W. S. Paradox, 182.
— as a teacher. Cooke, G. W. Poets, 17.
— The crown of sorrow of. Mabie. My study fire, 21.
— Great, What is a ? Gosse, E. Questions, 91.
— or seer. Buchanan, R. Poet's sk. book, 1 ; or David Gray, 3.
— Popular conception of a. Couch, A. T. Q. Adv. crit. 235.
— vs. critic. Ossoli. Art, 21.
Poetesses, Early American. Wharton, A. H. Colon. days, 99.
Poetic expression, Theory of. Roscoe, W. C. Poems & ess. v. 2.
Poetic life, The. Taylor. Notes from life, 109.
Poetic morality. Paget, V. Belcaro, 230.
Poetic principle, The. Poe. Works, 1 : 227.
Poetic revelation. Shairp. Aspects.
Poetic style of modern England. Shairp. Aspects.
Poetical criticism. Foster, J. Crit. ess. Ecl. v. 1.
— and creation. Shairp. Aspects.
Poetical integrity. Patmore. Princ. in art. 56.
Poetical versatility. Hazlitt. Round table.
Poetry. Alford. Poets of Greece, 1. — Allen. Physiolog. æsthetics. — Day. Sci. æsthet. § 289. — Goldsmith. Miscel. (N. Y. 4 v.) 1 : 290. — Hazlitt. Eng. poets. — Humphrey, H. Miscel. 409. — Smith, Adam. Ess. phil. 179. — Allingham. Varieties, 3 : 253. — Brooks, P. Ess. & addr. 234.
— Æsthetic. Pater. Apprec. 213.
— American. Bristed. Pieces, 3 : 25. — Bryant. Prose, 1 : 45. — Stedman. Poets Amer. 1.
— — Tones and tendencies in. Richardson. Amer. lit. 2 : 219.
— American Indian. (J. Reade) Roy. Soc. Canada, v. 5.
— and criticism. Brimley, G. Ess. 184.
— and imagination. Emerson. Lec. & soc. aims, 7.
— and its varieties. Mill, J. S. Dissert. (N. Y.) 1 : 89 ; or Early ess. 201.
— and love. Patmore. Princ. in art, 72.

Poetry and painting, Parallel between. Reynolds. Lit. works, **2** : 377.
— and pessimism. Hutton, R. H. Criticisms, **1** : 174.
— and romance of the Italians. Prescott. Biog. miscel. 486.
— and science. Japp. Vers de soc. 164.
— Appreciation of. Gurney. Tertium, **2** : 191.
— Arte of English poesy. Disraeli, I. Amen. (N. Y. 2 v.) **2** : 48.
— as observation. Wordsworth, W. Prose works, v. **2**.
— Chinese. Johnson, S. Ori. relig. China, 509.
— Conjugal. Jameson. Loves of poets.
— Court, End of. Snell, F. J. Fourteenth cent. 1.
— A criticism of life ? Symonds. Essays speculative, **2** : 150.
— Defense of. Procter, B. W. Ess. **2** : 173. — (H. W. Longfellow) Rice, A. T. Ess. 303. — Shelley. Ess. **1** : 24.
— Definition of. Bain. On teaching English.
— Description in. Newman, F. W. Essays, 103.
— English. Browning, E. B. Life, etc. v. **2**. — Procter, B. W. Ess. **2** : 125. — Stedman. Vic. poets, v. **1**.
— — Cambridge poets. Birrell. Obiter dicta, v. **2**.
— — Century of. Swinburne. Miscel. 25.
— — Classical school. Cotterill. Introd. to study of poetry. — Gosse. From Shakespeare to Pope.
— — Elizabethan, compared with Victorian. Symonds. Ess. **2** : 225.
— — Fantastic. Jones, W. A. Ess. on authors, 103.
— — Humanitarian movement in. Dawson, W. J. Mod. Engl. 155.
— — in 1885. Galton, A. Urbana, 1.
— — in 18th century. Perry, T. S. Eng. lit. 18th cent. 370.
— — in 19th century. Bibliography. Buckingham, E. M. Reviv. Eng. poet cent. 19.
— — Lake school of. Brooks, S. W. Eng. poets, 298.
— — Lyrical. Dennis, J. Studies, 288.
— — Modern. Lang. Lett. on lit. 15.
— — of the Commonwealth and the Restoration. Brooks, S. W. Eng. poets, 156.
— — Rural. Dennis, J. Studies, 356.
— — Short notes on. Swinburne. Miscel. 1.
— — Spiritual ebb and flow in. Corson. Introd. to Browning.
— — Town-verse and folk-song. Snell, F. J. 14th cent. 60.
— — Two chief schools of. De Vere. Ess. **2** : 100.
— Epic. Very. Poems & ess. 3.
— Excursionists in. Couch, A. T. Q. Adv. crit. 229.
— for the people. Jones, W. A. Ess. on authors, 165.
— Formative arts and descriptive. Eastlake. Contrib. **2** : 331.
— Forms of. Newman, F. W. Essays, 82.
— higher than art. (Matthew Arnold) Hundred greatest men, 1.
— Influence of science on. Walker, H. Gt. Vic. poets, 231.
— Influence on working classes. Robertson, F. W. Lec. 93, 142.
— Integrity in. Patmore. Principle in art.
— Interpretation of nature. Noel. Essays on poetry. — Knight. Wordsworthiana, 179.
— Italian and English. Coleridge. Lit. rem. **1** : 79.
— — Mediæval out-door. Paget. Euphorion.
— — Narrative. Prescott. Biog. miscel. 410, 596.

Poetry, Jewish, Humor and love in. Karpeles. Jew. lit. 191.
— Lake school of. DeQuincey. Lit. rem. (Bost.) **2** : 115, 167.
— Lyric, and their critics. Salt. Lit. sk. 93.
— — Palgrave's Golden treasury. Haweis. Poets in pulpit, 261.
— — Rise of new. Snell, J. F. Fourteenth cent. 98.
— Modern, Dr. Johnson on. Watson, W. Excur. in crit. 140.
— — Heroines of. Jameson. Loves of poets.
— — Rise of. Lord, J. Beacon, **3** : 23.
— — Some tendencies of. McNicoll, T. Ess. Eng. lit. 171.
— Musical and picturesque elements in. Whittaker, T. Ess. & not. 95.
— My acquaintance with. Hazlitt. Sket.
— Mystery essential in. Hare. Guesses, **2** : 131.
— Native American. Brinton. Ess. Amer. 284.
— Nature in. Hare. Guesses, **1** : 53.
— Nature of. Brown, J. Locke, etc. 313. — Bryant. Prose, **1** : 3.
— — Prose and verse. Buchanan. Master-spir. 167.
— Norwegian, since 1814. Gosse. Northern stud. 1.
— of the Bible. Schaff. Lit. & poetry, 63.
— of intellect and fancy. Miller, H. Hist. ess. 448.
— of Ireland, Ballad and lyrical. (R. W. MacDonnell) Afternoon lec. **1** : 205.
— of the Jews. Matheson. Distinc. mess. 316.
— of nature. Brooke, S. Theol. Eng. poets, 29. — Walker, H. Gt. Vic. poets, 201.
— of the north of Europe. Schlegel. Æsthet. (Bohn) 243.
— of rude ages, Superiority of. Froude, R. H. Remains, **2** : 306.
— Office of. Jouffroy. Philos. miscel. **2** : 181.
— Old notion of. Cheney, J. V. Golden guess, 1.
— Origin of. Goldsmith. Miscel. (N. Y. 4 v.) **1** : 278. — Schlegel. Æsthet. (Bohn) 496.
— Originality and imitation in. Bryant. Prose, **1** : 35.
— ornament in, Use of. Newman, F. W. Essays, 123.
— outdoor, Mediæval. Paget, V. Euphorion, **1** : 111.
— Parties in. Coleridge, H. Ess. **1** : 3.
— Pastoral. Pope. Works (1871–89), v. **1**.
— — Greek. Alford. Poets of Greece, 205.
— Persian. Chambers's Repos. no. 24.
— Philosophy of. Everett. Poetry, comedy, and duty.
— Pleasures of. Dodge, M. A. Twelve miles, 113.
— Poet a revealer. Shairp. Aspects of poetry.
— Poet as a teacher. Cooke. Poets and problems.
— Poets on. Couch, A. T. Q. Adv. crit. 245.
— Position and prospects of. Austin. Human tragedy.
— Principles of. Wordsworth. Prose works, **2** : 77, 208.
— Principles of English verse. Hodgson. Outcast, 209.
— Prospects of. Courthope. Liberal movement in English literature.
— Prospects of, 1885. Courthope. Lib. mov't, 197.
— Provençal, Nostradamus on. Bryant. Prose writings, v. **1**.
— Province of. Shairp. Aspects.
— Provincial. Doyle. Lec. Oxf. 47.
— Public opinion of. Hare. Guesses, **2** : 185.

Poetry, Rainy-day. Hunt. Wishing-cap, 81.
— Relation to life. Cheney, J. V. That dome, 11.
— Relation to time and space. Bryant. Prose, 1 : 24.
— Roman Catholic. Austin, A. Poetry, 156.
— Romantic. Schlegel. Æsthet. (Bohn) 200.
— Scotch. Shairp. Aspects.
— — Early. Shairp. Sket. hist. & poetry, 202.
— — of the highlands. Shairp. Aspects.
— Scottish. Brooks, S. W. Eng. poets, 270.
— Shairp's Aspects of. Hutton, R. H. Criticisms, 1 : 159.
— Spanish South American. Spence. Land of Bolivar, 2 : 223.
— Spiritual side of. Shairp. Aspects.
— Studies in, Cheever's. Peabody, W. B. O. Lit. rem. 1.
— Study of. Arnold, M. Ess. 2 : 1. — Wordsworth. Prose, v. 2.
— Subjects proper to. Arnold, M. Irish ess. 8.
— Supernatural. Austin, A. Poetry, 224.
— Theories of. Masson. Wordsworth, 193 ; or Ess. 409.
— Theory of. Bunce, O. B. Bach. bluff, 31.
— — Contributions towards. Knight, W. Stud. 264.
— — Wordsworth's. Courthope. Liberal movement in English literature.
— Topics and essence of. Newman, F. W. Essays, 65.
— Trisyllabic feet in iambic measure. Bryant. Prose, 1 : 57.
— Untaught. Miller, H. Hist. ess. 457.
— Value and uses of. Bryant. Prose, 1 : 14.
— Versification. Goldsmith. Miscel. (N. Y. 4 v.) 1 : 324.
— Victorian, Characteristics of. Cooke, G. W. Poets, 57.
— — compared with Elizabethan. Symonds. Ess. 2 : 225.
— What is? Calvert. Ess. æsth. 36.
— with reference to Aristotle's Poetics. Newman, J. H. Ess. crit. 1 : 1.
— Writing. Holmes. Over the teacups, 75.
Poet's corner. Mabie. My study fire, 2 : 68.
Poet's love, A. Jameson. Loves of poets.
Poets. Disraeli, I. Curios. (N. Y. 4 v.) 2 : 107. — Zangwill. Without prej. 42.
— American. Chambers's Repos. no. 88.
— — Griswold's. Whipple. Ess. & rev. 1.
— and beauties. Jameson. Loves of poets.
— and critics. Clark, W. G. Lit. rem. 273. — Gurney. Tertium, 2 : 119.
— and poetry. Rees, J. R. With friend, 1.
— — of the English language. Bryant. Prose, 1 : 147.
— as religious teachers. Morison, J. H. Great poets, 39.
— at play. Mozley, A. Ess. fr. Blackw. 219.
— British, Campbell's. Jeffrey, F. Contrib. Ed. Rev.
— British female, Specimens of. Hunt, L. Men, wom. & books, 257.
— Children's. Repplier. Ess. in idle. 33.
— classic, Loves of the. Jameson. Loves of poets.
— Creeds of. Laing, S. Problems, 310.
— English. Coleridge, H. Ess. 2 : 3. — Friswell. Essays, 39.
— — The book of. Browning, E. B. Ess. poets, 121.
— — Cambridge and Oxford compared. Birrell. Obiter, 275.
— — Elizabethan. Browning, E. B. Ess. poets, 156.
— — — Minor. Whipple. Lit. Eliz. 221.

Poets, English, Elliott's Witty and humorous side of. Japp. Vers de soc. 127.
— — in 18th century. Stephen, L. Eng. thought, 2 : 348.
— — in Scotland. Knight. Once on time, 1 : 201.
— — Living. Chambers's Repos. no. 72.
— — Minor. Knox. Essays, 3 : 281.
— — Modern. Hazlitt. Eng. poets.
— — of the 19th century. Friswell. Essays, 305.
— — — Griswold's. Whipple. Ess. & rev. 1.
— — Winstanley's. Gosse, E. Gossip, 107.
— Great, who are the? Cheney, J. V. Golden guess, 43.
— Greek, Christian. Browning, E. B. Life, etc. v. 2.
— — Minor. Knox. Essays, 3 : 286.
— Hours with the. Appleton, T. G. Sheaf of pap. 302.
— Houses of. Hunt, L. Seer, 2 : 243.
— in obscurity. Buchanan. Master spir. 303.
— laureate. Birrell. Men, wom. & books, 157.
— Minor of the artificial school. Brooks, S. W. Eng. poets, 205.
— Modern, and cosmic law. Myers. Sci. & fut. life, 166.
— Nature and the. Burroughs. Pepacton, 91.
— Prose-style of. Hazlitt. Plain speaker, v. 1. — Jones, W. A. Lit. stud. 1 : 38.
— Victorian, Social, political, and religious aspects of. Walker, H. Gt. Vic. poets, 258.
— who flower but once. Jones, W. A. Lit. stud. 2 : 84.
Poey y Aloy, F. de. Jordan, D. S. Sci. sk. 160.
Poggio Bracciolini, Giovanni Francesco. Symonds. Age of despots, 274. — Symonds. Reviv. of learn. 230.
— Pickings from. Dasent. Jest & earnest, 2 : 354.
Poinsett, Joel Roberts, with portrait. [Amer.] Nat. portr. gall. v. 1.
Pointe-à-pitre, Guadeloupe, Guesde collection at. (O. T. Mason) Smithson. Rept. '84 : 731.
Poisoned cup ; a story. Hall, John. Papers, 129.
Poisoning, Trials for. Burton, J. H. Crim. trials, 2 : 1.
Poisonings. Timbs. Doctors, 233.
Poisonous lizard. (A. Wilson) Proctor, R. A. Nat. stud. 50.
Poisons. Wynter, A. Fruit betw. leaves, 1 : 67.
Poisons, Action of, on the animal system. Brodie. Works, 2 : 51.
— Domestic, from arsenic. Iowa Health, '85 : 64.
— Employment of, in agriculture and horticulture. (R. C. Kedzie) Am. Pub. Health, 2 : 82. — (R. C. Kedzie) Mich. Health, '75 : 11.
— Sale of. (C. M. Tidy ; G. L. Browne) Trans. Soc. Sci. Lond. '83 : 237.
Poitevent, Eliza Jane. Davidson, J. W. Writ. of South, 424. — Raymond, I. Southland writ. 2 : 631.
Poitiers. George, H. B. Battles, 54. — James, H. Little tour, 116.
— Battle of. Clinton, H. R. Crécy to Assye, 56.
— Churches of. Larned, W. C. Churches & C. 97.
— in 1866. Musgrave, G. Nooks of Fr. 2 : 233.
Poker-playing, History of. Matthews, B. Pen & ink, 187.
Pol, Vincent. Soboleski. Poets of Poland, 379.
Poland, Luke P. Am. Bar Assoc. 10 : 431.
Poland. Alison. Ess. 3. — Moore, Jos. Outl. Eur. 505. — (W. G. Clark) Vaca. tourists, 3 : 223.
— The cause of. Simpson, J. P. Pic. revol. Paris, 2 : 166.
— Expulsion of Socinians from. Wallace, R. Anti-Trin. biog. 3 : 580.

Political infidelity. Curtis, G. W. Orations, 1 : 123.

Political institutions in the U. S., Future of. Bryce. Soc. institu. 260.

Political morality, Causes of the decline of. Hazard, R. G. Econ. & pol. 1 ; or Ess. on lang. 264.

Political morals. Schurz, C. Speeches, 38.

Political notions. Bunce, O. B. Bach. bluff, 158.

Political obligation, Grounds of. Green, T. H. Works, 2 : 335.

Political opinions, Change of. Greg, W. R. Pol. prob. 172.

Political organization. Bright, J. Publ. add. 423.

Political parties in U. S., History of. Webster, N. Papers, 316.

Political philosophy. Coleridge. Friend, 154.

— Brougham's. Senior. Hist. ess. 1 : 276.

Political rectitude. White, C. Ess. 137.

Political rights, Evolution of. Putnam, J. O. Addresses, 45.

Political satire. Jones, W. A. Ess. on authors, 140.

— Twenty years of. Saintsbury, G. Ess. Eng. lit. 2 : 237.

Political science. Haven, N. A. Remains, 167.

— and history. (J. W. Burgess) Am. Hist. Assoc. Rept. '91, 1 : 201.

— Is there a science of government? Bisset, A. Ess. on hist. 1.

— Objects and advantages of. Brougham. Works, 7 : 373.

— Paris free school of. (E. Boutmy) Internat. Health exh. 15 : 409.

— Study of, in colleges. (I. W. Andrews) Nat. Educa. Assoc. '81 : 165.

Political sovereignty. Wilson, W. Old master, 61.

Political theories and experiments in 4th century, B. C. Huxley. Ess. contro. 110.

Political writers, English. Friswell. Essays, 239.

Politicians, Coffee-house. Hazlitt. Table-talk.

Politics. Bartol. Principles, 263. — Emerson. Ess. 2 : 189.

— Alienation of the educated class from. Diman. Orations, 41.

— Ancient and modern teacher of. Lieber, F. Reminis. 369.

— and the duty of the citizen. (T. F. Bayard) Butterfield. Lec. Un. Coll. 1 : 147.

— and industry. Whittaker, T. Ess. & not. 173.

— and political economy. Balfour, A. J. Ess. 225.

— and religion. Gladden. Ruling ideas, 163. — Vaughan, D. J. Questions, 154.

— and science. Pearson, K. Chances, 1 : 140.

— as a profession. Lorimer, Jas. Studies, nat'l & internat.

— at home and abroad, 1859. Brownson. Works, 16 : 548.

— Christian. Arnold, T. Miscel. 435.

— Christian aspect of. Vaughan, D. J. Questions, 1.

— Christianity and. Blackie, J. S. Lay serm. 191. — (W. J. H. Campion) Gore, C. Lux mundi, 437.

— Corruption in. Field, D. D. Speeches, 2 : 128.

— Criminal. Godkin. Problems, 123.

— Education in. (J. N. Pomeroy) N. Y. Regents, 82 : 815.

— Ethics in. Stryker. Hamilton, 102.

— The gentleman in. Holland, J. G. Every-day, 1 : 326.

— Machine, and the remedy. Curtis, G. W. Orations, 2 : 147.

— Morals and. Curtis, G. W. Orations, 2 : 121.

Politics, Personal. Hazlitt. Lit. remains, 1 : 97.

— Physical force in. Godkin. Reflections, 257.

— Practical, Manly virtues and. Roosevelt, T. Amer. ideals, 35.

— Reform principles and practice in. Mazzini. Ess. 1.

— The scholar in. Swing. Old pic. 2 : 57.

— a science. Hume. Philos. works, 3 : 11.

— Science and. Stephen, L. Soc. rights, 1 : 45.

— Study of. Wilson, W. Old master, 31.

— Teaching of. Seeley, J. R. Rom. imp. 306 ; or Lec. & ess. 290.

Poliziano, Angelo. Montgomery. Men of Ita. 1 : 162. — Symonds. Renais. It. lit. 1 : 399. — Symonds. Reviv. of learn. 345, 452. — Shelley, Mrs. Lit. men Italy, v. 1. — Stebbing. Ital. poets, v. 1.

— Poems. Symonds. Sk. So. Eur. 1 : 118.

Polk, James K. Abbott. Lives of presidents, 284. — With portrait. Duyckinck. Nat. portr. gall. 2 : 247. — Frost. Presidents, 323. — Lincoln. Lives of pres. 411. — Lossing. Em. Amer. 388. — (G. Bancroft) Wilson, J. G. Presidents, 216. — Thompson, R. W. Pers. Recoll. 241.

— Administration of. Schouler, Jas. Hist. briefs, 139.

— Diary of. Schouler, Jas. Hist. briefs, 121.

— Eulogy on. Woodbury, L. Writ. 3 : 378.

— Robespierre and Marat versus. Hazard, T. R. Miscel. 97.

— Social life during administration of. Ellet, E. F. Court circles, 368.

Polk, Mrs. James K. With portrait. Ellet. Queens Am. soc. 213. — With portrait. Holloway, L. C. Ladies, 400. — Gordon, L. L. Lady Wash'n, 217. — Hanaford. Wom. of cent. 86.

Polk, Leonidas. Pollard. Life of Lee, 587. — Snow. So. generals, 409.

Pollajuolo, Antonio. Perkins, C. C. Tusc. sculp. 1 : 223. — Symonds. Renais. fine arts, 145.

Pollard, Benjamin. Loring, J. S. Hundred Bost. ora. 365.

Pollard, Delia C. Hemenway. Poets of Vt. 362.

Pollard, Edward A. Davidson, J. W. Writ. of South, 427.

Pollio, Caius Asinius. Dunlop, J. Rom. liter. 3 : 45.

Pollock, Sir C. E., with photo. Cooper, T. Men of mark, 5 : 10.

Pollock, Frederick. Foss. Judges, 9 : 245. — Grant, J. Bench & bar, 2 : 56. — Grant, J. Recoll. Lords & Comm. 2 : 120. — (R. Garnett) Miles, A. H. Poets of cent. 9 : 585. — Em. persons, 1 : 28.

Pollock, James, with portrait. Armor. Gov. of Pa. 424.

Pollock, T. Benson. Miles, A. H. Poets of cent. 10 : 761.

Pollok, Robert. Brooks, S. W. Eng. poets, 491. — Gilfillan. First gall. 217. — McNicoll. Ess. Eng. lit. 65. — Wilson, J. G. Poets of Scot. 2 : 196. — Griswold, R. W. Sac. poets. — Miles, A. H. Poets of cent. 10 : 167.

— Course of time. Dana. P. & p. writ. 344. — McNicoll, T. Ess. Eng. lit. 93.

Polo, Marco. Adams, W. H. D. Heroes of travel, 1. — With portrait. Bolton, S. K. Fam. voyag. 73. — Goodrich, F. B. Man upon the sea, 99. — Haley, E. E. Stories of adven. — Oliphant, Mrs. Makers of Venice, 141. — St. John. Cel. travelers, 1 : 30. — Verne. Exploration, 43.

— Travels of. Frost, T. Explorers, 13.

Poor, Relief of, in Chicago. (C. G. Trusdell) Conf. char. & correc. '95: 66.
— — Indoor and outdoor. (C. G. Trusdell) Conf. char. & correc. '93: 94.
— — in Aberdeen, Scotland. (George Milne) Cong. Char. Chic. '93, 2 : 344.
— — in Manchester, Eng. (A. McDougall) Cong. Char. Chic. '93, 2 : 304.
— — New York methods. (Mrs. C. R. Lowell) Conf. char. & correc. '95 : 44.
— — official outdoor, Observations on. (E. Bicknell) Conf. char. & correc. '97 : 249.
— — Outdoor, in Mass. (T. F. Ring) Conf. char. & correc. '95 : 61.
— — Public. Conf. char. & correc. '94 : 106.
— — Public and private. (V. Böhmert) Cong. Char. Chic. '93, 2 : 210.
— Religious belief of. Jeune, Lady. Lesser ques. 2 : 73.
— Roman Catholic Church and. (C. F. Donnelley) Barrows, J. H. Parl. relig. 2 : 1032.
— The rural, improvement of their condition. Helps. Friends, 1st ser. v. 2.
    See also Pauperism.
— Some controverted points on. (C. S. Loch) Bosanquet. Asp. soc. ques. 226.
— Trials of. Farrar. Soc. & p. day quest. 82.
Poor colonies in Holland. (J. H. Gore) U. S. Lab. Bull. 1 : 113.
Poor law, American. (F. B. Sanborn) Trans. Soc. Sci. Lond. '74 : 878.
— and charity. Mackay, T. Meth. soc. ref. 259.
— as an obstacle to thrift. Mackay, T. Meth. soc. ref. 105.
— British. Bibliography. Twining, L. Workhouses, pauperism, adminis. poor law.
— English. (B. Fleming) Cong. Char. Chic. '93, 2 : 377.
— — its intention and results. (M. McCallum) Cong. Char. Chic. '93, 1 : 151.
— — Origin and history of. (H. Dendy) Bosanquet. Asp. soc. ques. 195.
— — Reform in. Mackay, T. Meth. soc. ref. 22.
— in English rural unions; tables. (H. G. Willink) Cong. Char. Chic. '93, 2 : 350.
— Pauperism, charity and. Fawcett. Ess. & lec. 70.
— Working classes and. Mackay, T. Meth. soc. ref. 149.
Poor law progress in an East London union. (W. Vallance) Cong. Char. Chic. '93, 1 : 158.
Poor law system, Austrian. (E. Sellers) Cong. Char. Chic. '93, 1 : 216.
Poor laws. Brougham. Works, 10 : 389.
— English. Browning. Polit. cond. Gt. Brit. 288. — Senior. Hist. ess. 45. — Wordsworth. Prose, 1 : 271.
— — in 1820. Smith, Syd. Ess. fr. Ed.
— — Philosophy of the. Cobbe, F. P. Studies, 145.
— of Ireland. Peel, R. Speeches, 4 : 788.
— of the U. S. (C. R. Henderson) Conf. char. & correc. '97 : 256.
— Scotch. Miller, H. Hist. ess. 227.
Poore, Benjamin Perley. Am. Antiq. Soc. Proc. n. s. 5 : 14.
Poorhouse, Discipline in. (E. Bicknell) Conf. char. & correc. '96 : 269.
Poorhouses and jails, Administration of. (A. G. Byers) Conf. char. & correc. '86 : 31.
— — in the Northwest. (C. S. Watkins) Conf. char. & correc. '79 : 96.
— Employment in. (A. O. Wright) Conf. char. & correc. '89 : 197.
— in Michigan. (H. C. Wyman) Conf. char. & correc. '89 : 203.

Poorhouses, in New England, Management of. (F. B. Sanborn) Conf. char. & correc. '84 : 300.
— Location, construction, and management of. (H. H. Giles) Conf. char. & correc. '84 : 295.
Pope, Alexander. (W. Rushton) Afternoon lec. 1 : 68. — Bell, R. Lit. & sci. men, 2 : 264. — Birrell. Obiter, 2 : 52. — (S. Johnson) Chalmers. Eng. poets, 12 : 51. — Coleridge, H. Ess. 2 : 79. — Collier, W. F. Hist. Eng. lit. 274. — Dana. P. & p. writ. 178. — Dennis, J. Studies, 1. — DeQuincey. Biog. ess. (Bost.) 95. — De Quincey. Ess. on poets (Bost.), 145. — Edgar. Boyhood, 26. — Gosse. 18th cent. liter. — Hannay. Satire, 130. — Hazlitt. Eng poets, 9, — Howitt. Homes Br. poets, 1 : 163. — Kingsley, C. New miscel. 72. — Lang. Lett. to dead au. 46. — Lowell. Writ. 4 : 1. — Oliphant. Hist. sketches, 166. — Reed, H. Brit. poets, 1 : 298. — Sanborn, K. Eng. poets, 139. — Saunders, F. Famous books, 68. — Taine. Eng. lit. 2 : 195. — Thackeray. Humorists. — Tuckerman. Poets, 73. — (Mark Pattison) Ward. Eng. poets, 3 : 55. — Williams, H. Eng. lett. 275. — Wotton. Word portraits, 234. — Brooke, S. Theol. Eng. poets, 3. — Brooks, S. W. Eng. poets, 205. — Dennis, J. Stud. Eng. lit. 1. — With portrait. Gostwick, J. Eng. poets, 89. — Howells. My lit. passions, 48. — Minto. Georg. era, 21. — Mitchell, D. G. Eng. lands, 3 : 30. — Hunt, L. Men, wom. & books, 203. — Lilly, W. S. Ess. 1. — Macdonald, G. England's antiphon, 285. — Miller, Jos. Singers church, 2d ed. 147. — Russell, W. C. Book of au. 180. — Swanwick, A. Poets, 247. — With portrait. (T. R. Lounsbury) Warner Lib. 20 : 11711. — Wrangham. Brit. Plutarch, v. 5.
— and Byron. Dawson, G. Biog. lec. 225.
— and his editors. Pattison. Ess. 2 : 350.
— and his friends. Jones, W. A. Lit. stud. 2 : 46.
— and Lord Bolingbroke. Thomson, Mrs. Cel. friend. 2 : 171.
— and Martha Blount. Jameson. Loves of poets.
— and Swift. Windsor. Ethica, 215.
— as a moralist. Stephen, L. Hours in libr. 1 : 90.
— as a poet. Ste.-Beuve. Eng. portr. 177.
— Biographical and critical sketch of. Drake, N. Ess. Tatler, 3 : 81.
— Carlisle on. DeQuincey. Theo. ess. (Bost.) 2 : 209.
— Elwin's edition of. Stephen, L. Hours in libr. 1 : 135.
— Essay on man, and Tennyson's In memoriam. Buchanan, R. Look round, 347.
— Infirmities of. Madden. Infirm. gen. 89.
— Letters of. Williams, H. Eng. lett. 351.
— Lady Montagu and. Jameson. Loves of poets.
— Poetry of. Carlisle, Earl. Lec. 7. — Conington. Miscel. 1 : 1; also in Oxf. ess. '58 : 1.
— The poetry of common sense. Noble, J. A. Sonnet in Eng. 134.
— Quarrels with Addison and others. Disraeli, I. Calam. 2.
— Retort upon Addison. DeQuincey. Notebook (Bost.), 286.
— A. Smith and. Kingsley, C. Lit. lec. 61.
— Sonnets of. Deshler. Afternoons, 167.
— Successors of. Swanwick, A. Poets, 250.
— Works. Perry, T. S. Eng. lit. 18th cent. 205. — Dilke. Papers, 1 : 93.
Pope, Benjamin, d. 1794. Redding. Misers, 2 : 68.
Pope, Jane. Doran. Annals stage, 2 : 339. — Cook, D. Hours w. players, 1 : 232.

Pope, Gen. John. Livingston, J. Dist. Amer. 432.
— Bibliography. Mass. Milit. Hist. Soc. Campaign of 1862, v. 2.
— Campaign of, 1862. Allen, W. Army of N. Va. 151.
Pope, Mrs. Mary E. Raymond, I. Southland writ. 2 : 728.
Pope, Thomas. Collier. Actors, 120.
Pope, William. Wesley & successors, 231.
Pope, the, Infallibility of, and civil allegiance. Brownson. Works, 13 : 370, 412, 483.
— Italian guarantees and 1871. Chatard. Occ. ess. 87.
— Office of, and how he is chosen. Fisher, G. P. Discuss. 141.
— Temporal power of. Chatard. Occ. ess. 283.
— — Lilly, W. S. Ess. 104.
Pope night in New England. Whittier. Lit. recre. 154.
Popes, The. Lawrence, E. Hist. stud. 9.
— Administration of. Ranke. Popes, 1 : 387.
— and the Hohenstaufen. Trench. Lec. mediæval, 168.
— Bibliography. Pastor, L. Hist. Popes from close mid. age. — Vincent, M. R. Age of Hildebrand.
— A characteristic of. Newman, J. H. Hist. sk. 3 : 130.
— Forged decretals of. Pennington. Epochs papacy, 65.
— Harper's Monthly on. Brownson. Works, 13 : 146.
— of the renaissance. Symonds. Age of despots, 371.
— of the 16th and 17th centuries. Ranke's History. — Milman. Savonarola, 149.
— Ranke's History of. Macaulay. Ess. 4 : 299.
— Small and great. Thompson, H. M. Copy, 68.
— Supremacy of. Gilbart. Lec. 145.
— Temporal kingdom of. Fisher, G. P. Discus. 68.
Popham, Edward William Leyborne. Mozley. Reminis. 2 : 135.
Popham, John. Campbell. Ch. just. 1 : 186. — Foss. Judges, 6 : 179. — Manning, J. A. Speakers, 245.
Popkin, John Snelling. Lowell. Writ. 1 : 91. — Peabody. Harv. rem. 40.
Popol Vuh. Müller. Chips, 1 ; or Sel. ess. 2 : 372.
Popular disaffection, Rise and progress of. Southey, R. Ess. 1832, 2 : 33.
Popular judgment in politics. Greg, W. R. Miscel. 1 : 161.
Popular rationalism. Shipley, O. Tracts, 429.
Popular sovereignty, Doctrine of. Schurz, C. Speeches, 76.
Popularity, Ethics of. Whipple. Success, 31.
Population. Jones, Rich. Lit. remains. — Laing, S. Problems, 389.
— and wealth in early New England. Adams, C. F. Three episodes, 2 : 689.
— Effects of increase of. Browning. Polit. condition of Gt. Brit.
— Growth of, in Europe, in excess of the productive powers of the soil. Coan. Soc. prob. 43.
— — World-crowding. (R. Giffen) Coan. Soc. prob. 1.
— Increase of. Proctor. Light sci. 3 : 287.
— — Law of. Elder, W. Questions, 70. — Patten. Premises of polit. econ.
— Malthus on. Graham. Soc. prob. 432.
— — Defense of. Macaulay. Ess. 2 : 268.

Population, Over-, its evils and remedies. Meath. Soc. arrows, 134.
— — Doctrine of. Kempner, W. Common-sense soc. 33.
— Principles of. Greg. Enig. 73.
— Sadler's Law of. Macaulay. Ess. 2 : 214.
Populist movement. Bibliography. (Frank L. McVey) Economic studies, 1 : no. 3.
Porcaro, Stefano, Conspiracy of. Pastor, L. Hist. popes, 2 : 215.
Porcelains, Chinese : catalogue of Hippisley collection in U. S. Nat. Mus., with historical sketch. — (A. E. Hippisley) U. S. Nat. Mus. Rept. '88 : 387.
Porcher, Francis Peyre. Davidson, J. W. Writ. of South, 429.
Porchester Castle. Timbs. Abbeys, 1 : 413.
Porden, Eleanor-Anne. Williams, Jane. Lit. wom. 279.
Porisms, Origin and investigation of. Playfair, J. Works, v. 3.
Porphyry. Pressensé. Martyrs, 521.
Porpoises, Adventures and journeys with. Buckland, F. T. Curios. nat. hist. 3 : 293.
Porpora, Nicolo, Italian opera writer. Hogarth. Mem. opera, 1 : 276.
Porsenna's country. Jarves. Ital. ramb. 132.
Porson, Richard. (H. R. Luard) Camb. ess. '57 : 125. — Creasy. Etonians, 466. — Jerdan. Men, 348. — Nicoll, H. J. Gt. scholars, 91. — Rogers, S. Recol. 139. — Timbs. Anec. biog. wits, v. 2.
— Eccentricities of. Timbs, J. Eng. eccen. 425.
Port Blair penal settlement, India. (F. A. de Roepstorff) N. Y. Pris. Assoc. 26, app. : 159.
Port Royal. Renan. Studies (N. Y.), 2 : 415.
— Literary salon at. Mason, A. G. Wom. of Fr. salons, 61.
Port-Royalists, The. Quick. Educa. ref. 172.
— Stephen. Ess. eccl. biog. 279.
See also Jansenists.
Porta, Baccio della, called Fra Bartolommeo. Oliphant. Makers of F. 337. — Symonds. Renais. fine arts, 304.
Portents. Aubrey, J. Miscel.
Porter, Andrew. Neven, D. R. B. Pennsylvanians, 131.
Porter, Ann Emerson. Hart, J. S. Fem. prose, 387.
Porter, Anna Maria. Hall, S. C. Book of mem. 128.
— Memoirs of. Elwood. Lit. ladies, 2 : 276.
Porter, Benjamin C. Sheldon, G. W. Amer. painters, 76.
Porter, David. With portrait. Duyckinck. Nat. portr. gall. 2 : 16. — Irving. Biog. 91. — Lossing. Em. Amer. 302. — Chesney. Ess. mil. biog. 136. — With portrait. Headley, J. T. Farragut, 320. — Brockett. Men of our day, 107.
Porter, David Rittenhouse, with portrait. Armor. Gov. of Pa. 379.
Porter, Elbert S., D. D. Bungay. Repr. men, 203.
Porter, Eliphalet. (G. Putnam) Ware, W. Am. Unita. 1 : 159.
Porter, Mrs. Eliza C. Brockett. Woman's work, 161.
Porter, Elizabeth L. Brockett. Woman's work, 792.
Porter, Fitz-John. Bibliography. Dwight, T. F. Va. campaign '62, under Gen. Pope.
Porter, Jane. Hall, S. C. Book of mem. 128. — Willis. Fam. persons, 471.
— Esher, Residence of. Hall, Mrs. S. C. Pilgr. Eng. shr. 2 : 129.

Pothnan, L. P. A. Men of 3d repub. 318.
Potocka, Claudine, countess. Starling, E. Noble deeds wom. 190.
Potomac, Army of. Oration at reunion, 1888. Curtis, G. W. Orations, 3 : 59.
Potomac marshes at Washington, D. C. (A. Y. P. Garnett) Am. Pub. Health, 7 : 186.
Potsdam and Sans-Souci. Guild. Abroad again, 434.
Pott, Francis. Miller, Jos. Singers church, 2d ed. 575.
Potter, Chandler E., with portrait. Sketches N. H. men, 302.
Potter, Cipriani. Keddie. Mus. comp 311.
Potter, Clarkson N. Am. Bar Assoc. 5 : 148.
Potter, Helen. Hanaford. Wom. of cent. 574.
Potter, Horatio, bishop. Wilson. Centen'l hist. P. E. church in N. Y.
Potter, Orlando Bronson. Am. Bar Assoc. 17 : 526. — Am. Geog. Soc. 26 : 118.
Potter, Paul. Cundall. Landsc. painters Holl. — Van Dyke, J. C. Dutch mast. 137.
— The bull. (E. Fromentin) Singleton, E. Great pic. 256.
— Home of. Fairholt. Homes Rubens, 145.
Potter, Thomas, of Manchester. Bourne, H. R. F. Eng. merch. 2 : 266.
Potter, Thomas J. Miller, Jos. Singers church, 2d ed. 576.
Pottery. Bibliography. Salem (Mass.) Pub. Lib. Bull. May, '95.
— Old china. Lamb. Elia.
— Origin of. Allen, G. Falling in l. 316.
— shore-land, Germ of. (F. H. Cushing) Cong. Anthrop. Chic. '93 : 217.
— Staffordshire vs. American, 1891. U. S. Cons. Rept. 37 : 41.
Pottery industry. (S. J. Thomas) Galton, F. W. Workers, 186.
— of Tunstall, 1894. (W. C. Warner) U. S. Cons. Rept. 44 : 635.
Pottinger, Eldred, the hero of Herat. Hodder. Heroes, 1 : 117. — Kaye. Indian off. 2 : 145.
Poulard inn, Mont St. Michel. Dodd, A. B. Three Norm. inns. 335.
Poule, Robert le. William, F. Eng. card. 1 : 141, 475.
Poultry. Dodge, M. A. Summer rest, 34.
— Bibliography. (E. B. Hawks) U. S. Dept. Agric. Lib. Bull. Oct. '97.
Poultry industry in Belgium, 1898. (H. C. Morris) U. S. Cons. Rept. 59 : 85.
— in various countries, 1893. U. S. Cons. Rept. 43 : 477.
Pounds, John. Hoare. Nota. workers, 11. — Lives of dist. shoemak. 331. — Winks. Illus. shoemakers, 175.
Poushkin, A. See Pushkin.
Pousset. Delille, E. Some French wr. 59.
Poussin, G. Ottley. Ital. school.
Poussin, Nicolas. (C. A. Regnet) Dohme, R. Early mast. 486. — Jervis, Lady. Painting, 2 : 259. — Ottley. Ital. school. — Spooner. Biog. fine arts, 2 : 726.
— Bibliography. Denio, Eliz. H. N. Poussin.
— Criticisms of his pictures. Guizot. Fine arts, 181.
— Landscape by. Hazlitt. Crit. on art ; or Table-talk, ser. 2.
Poverty. Friswell. Gentle life, 212. — (I. Steward) Hazlitt. Lit. rem. 2 : 227. — Mass. Labor, '73 : 411.
— Abolition of. (S. S. Craig) Conf. char. & correc. '97 : 272.

Poverty, Causes of. Hearn. Plutology, 447. — Walker, F. A. Discus. in econ. 2 : 455.
— Critical history of. Disraeli, I. Curios. (N. Y. 4 v.) 1 : 275.
— English. Hawthorne. Old home, 320.
— in N. Y. city : Possible methods of relief. (Mrs. C. R. Lowell) Conf. char. & correc. '95 : 44.
— Morality of. Jones, W. A. Lit. stud. 1 : 46.
— of the learned. Disraeli, I. Curios. (N. Y. 4 v.) 1 : 81.
— Pinch of. Payn. Private views, 57.
— That we all might be rich. George, H. Soc. prob. 101.
See also Pauperism ; Poor.
Powell, Foster, pedestrian. Baring-Gould. Yorks. odd. 1 : 20.
Powell, Richard. Pettigrew. Med. portr. gall. v. 4.
Powell, Walter, with portrait. Japp, A. H. Golden lives, 80.
Power, Thomas. Loring, J. S. Hundred Bost. ora. 586.
Power, Tyrone. Jones, W. A. Lit. stud. 1 : 13.
— acting in Philadelphia. Murdoch, J. E. Stage, 226.
Power. Emerson. Conduct, 43. — Friswell. Gentle life, 2 : 129.
Powers, Hiram. Clarke, W. J. Amer. sculp. 45. — Duyckinck. Portrait gall. 2 : 522. — Houghton. Kings, 501. — Mansfield, E. D. Pers. mem. 182. — Tuckerman. Artists, 276.
Powers, Ridgley C. (W. M. Compton) Rogers, A. C. Repres. men, 437.
Powle, Henry. Manning, J. A. Speakers, 389.
Powling, William. Wallace, R. Anti-Trin. biog. 2 : 128.
Poynder, John, Letters to. Wiseman, N. Ess. 1 : 245.
Poynter, Sir Edward J., with photo. Cooper, T. Men of mark, 4 : 17. — Monkhouse, C. Brit. contemp. artists, 231.
— Essay on. (S. Colvin) Atkinson, J. B., et al. Eng. paint. 1.
Pozzo, Conte Girolamo dal. Milizia. Lives arch. 2 : 359.
Pozzo di Biorgo, Count. Capefigue. Diplomats.
Prach, The root, in Greek. Hadley, J. Ess. 37.
Practical talent, Do our schools tend to destroy ? (G. W. Gillette) N. Y. Regents, 97, app. : 224.
Practice school, Professor Rein's, at Jena. (J. W. Hall) Nat. Educa. Assoc. '96 : 644.
Practice schools in connection with normal schools. (C. C. Rounds) Nat. Educa. Assoc. '85 : 429.
Practice work in model and training-schools. (F. S. Guptill) Nat. Educa. Assoc. '93 : 391.
Praed, Winthrop Mackworth. Creasy. Etonians, 497. — Saintsbury. Stud. Eng. liter. — Miles, A. H. Poets of cent. 3 : 425. 9 : 271. — Mitford, M. R. Recollec. 100. — Warner Lib. 20 : 11757.
— Country of. Collins, M. Pen sketches, 133.
Præmunire, Statute of. Sergeant, L. Wiclif, 130.
Prague. Haven, G. Pilgrim. 461. — Taylor, B. Views, 215.
— Battle of. Carlyle. Batt. Fred. the Gt. 70.
Prairie dog. Marshall, W. G. Thro' Amer. 125.
Prairies of the West. Marshall, W. G. Thro' Amer. 123.
— Origin of the. Caton. Miscell. 87.
Praise. Bacon. Ess. — Hare. Guesses, 2 : 359.
— Duty of. Mathews. Lit. style, 54.
— Efficacy of. Bulwer, E. Caxtoniana, 199.
— Influence of. Holland, J. G. Lessons, 265.

Prakrit versification, Laws of. Colebrooke. Miscel. essays, **2** : 62.

Praslin, Duke and duchess of. Burke, P. Romance of forum.

Prati, G. Howells. Mod. It. poets, 323.

Pratinas. Mills. Poets of Greece, 251.

Prato. Howells. Tuscan cities, 244.

Pratt, Benjamin. Knapp, S. L. Em. lawyers, 163.

Pratt, Lieut. C. S. Shea, J. G. Fallen brave.

Pratt, Charles. *See* Camden, 1st earl of.

Pratt, Charles, and Pratt Institute. Bolton, S. K. Givers, 108.

Pratt, Sir John, chief justice of England, 1718–25. Campbell. Ch. just. **2** : 143.

Pratt, Josiah. Seeley, M. Later evang. 329.

Pratt, Zadock. Patten, J. Sket. of men of prog.

Praxiteles. Hundred greatest men, 68.

Pray, Lewis Glover. Putnam, A. P. Singers liberal, 81.

Prayer. Conway, M. D. Idols, 63. — Dodge. Sermons to clergy, 227. — Greenwell, D. Ess. 114. — (H. A. Thomas) Faith & crit. : essays. — Ward, W. G. Ess. theism, **2** : 158.

— and nature. Davies, J. L. Theol. & mor. 108.

— and prayer-books. Wiseman, N. Ess. **1** : 375.

— and Science. Whedon. Ess. **1** : 269.

— Christian consciousness and. Phelps, A. Portfolio, 230.

— Faults in. Beecher. New star papers, 60.

— Function of. Knight, W. Stud. 340.

— in constitutional convention, 1787, Motion for. Franklin. Works ('87), **9** : 428.

— Intercessory. Phelps, A. Portfolio, 239.

— Liberty of. Beecher. New star papers, 54.

— Meditations of St. Ignatius. Brownson. Works, **14** : 577.

— Miracles and. Shipley, O. Tracts, 185.

— Morning and evening. Channing. Works, **5** : 321.

— Natural law and. Tyndall. Frag. sci. 35.

— The two spheres. Knight, W. Stud. 368.

— What is the use of ? Gladden. Burn. ques. 97.

— Why we pray. Thompson, H. M. Copy, 235.

Prayer-meetings. Dodge, M. A. Stumbl. 149.

Prayers. Emerson. Nat. hist. intel. 212.

— of mankind. Friswell. Silent hour, 63.

Praying. Dodge, M. A. Stumbl. 358.

— Fighting and. Thompson, H. M. Copy, 307.

— toward the East. Thompson, H. M. Copy, 212.

Praying machine. Conway, M. D. Idols, 63.

Praying smoke. Lummis. Strange corners, 228.

Preacher, The. Emerson. Lec. & biog. sk. 207.

Preachers. Tuckerman. Collector, 280 ; *or* Criterion, 292.

— and preaching. Holland, J. G. Every-day, **1** : 109.

— and what they should preach. Manning, J. M. Sermons, 262.

— English, in 18th century. Stephen, L. Eng. thought, **2** : 335.

— Itinerant. Story, A. T. Vagrom, 122.

— Jocular. Disraeli, I. Curios. (N. Y. 4 v.) **1** : 337.

— Popular. Goldsmith. Miscel. (N. Y. 4 v.) **1** : 339.

Preaching. Dods, M. Erasmus, 317. — Gilbart. Lec. 225. — Harrison, J. Dang. tend. 203.

— Ancient and modern. Oxenham. Stud. in eccl. hist. 269.

— and preachers. Kirkus. Miscel. 307.

— and sermon writers. Knox. Essays, **3** : 234.

— Calvinistic theory of. Phelps, A. Portfolio, 123.

— Decline of eloquence in. Jones, W. A. Lit. stud. **2** : 142.

Preaching, Evangelical, Sedgwick's Hints on. Coleridge. Lit. rem. **4** : 320.

— Extemporaneous, Hints on. Ware, H., jr. Works, **2** : 347.

— its adaptation to the present times. Alford, H. Ess. & addr. 23.

— Method of, adapted to the age. Blaikie, W. G. Preachers Scot. 325.

— Political. Black, J. S. Essays, 67.

— Practical. Barnes, A. Miscel. **2** : 232.

— Relation of theology to. Barnes, A. Miscel. **2** : 61.

— Training for the pulpit manward. Bushnell. Building eras, 221.

— University. Newman, J. H. Lec. univ. 187.

— Village. Blunt. Ess. 454.

See also Pulpit oratory.

Preble, Edward. Cooper, J. F. Am. nav. off. **1** : 171. — With portrait. [Amer.] Nat. portr. gall. v. 2. — Frost, J. Hist. Amer. navy, 135. — Waldo, S. P. Am. naval heroes, 143. — Lossing. Em. Amer. 199.

Preble, George Henry. Am. Antiq. Soc. Proc. n. s. **3** : 495.

Precedence, Perplexities of. Burke, B. Rise of gt. fam. 251.

Precious metals, Distribution & value of, in 16th and 19th centuries. Leslie, T. E. C. Ess. pol. econ. 264.

— Workers in. (W. A. Steward) Galton, F. W. Workers, 32.

Precious stones. Robinson, F. S. Connois. 222.

— Folk-lore of. (G. F. Kunz) Wynter, A. Our soc. bees, **2** : 383.

Precocity. Madden. Infirm. gen. 37.

Preconceptions. Butler, E. Gentle ways, 184.

Predatory classes, Plan for suppression of. (W. Pare) Trans. Soc. Sci. Lond. '63 : 473.

Predestination, Contest of Thomists and Molinists on. Renan. Studies (N. Y.), **2** : 380.

Pre-existence, The sense of. Walsh, W. S. Paradox, 147.

Preface, True theory of a. Matthews, B. Pen & ink, 50.

Prefaces and dedications. Jones, W. A. Lit. stud. **2** : 96.

Prehistoric America. Brinton. Ess. Amer. 20.

Prehistoric archæology. Brinton. Ess. Amer. 48. — Lubbock. Sci. lec. 138.

Prehistoric art, Origin of, manifested in prehistoric works. (Thomas Wilson) U. S. Nat. Mus. Rept. '96 : 325.

Prehistoric Europe. Fiske, J. Excurs. 7.

Prehistoric geography. Brinton. Races & peo. 86.

Prehistoric man and savage man. Mivart. Ess. **2** : 169.

— in Brit. Columbia, Later. (C. Hill-Tout) Roy. Soc. Can. 2d ser. **1,** § **2** : 103.

Prehistoric Mexico ; the Toltec myth. Brinton. Ess. Amer. 83.

Prehistoric races of Italy. (Isaac Taylor) Smithson. Rept. '90 : 489.

Prehistoric state of mankind. Newman, F. W. Essays, 146.

Prehistoric villages, Some. Thompson, H. M. Copy, 317.

Prejudices. Ess. from Sat. R. 163. — Hazlitt. Sket.

Prelatical power. Lord, J. Beacon, **2** : 291.

Premillennialism. Whedon. Ess. **2** : 359.

Premium lists, Newspaper. Thompson, H. M. Copy, 279.

Premonitions, Evidence of. (Mrs. H. Sidgwick) Soc. Psych. Res. **5** : 288.

Prenatal education. (F. C. Clark) R. I. Health, 4 : 233. — Derby, J. C. Fifty years, 419. — Griffin, G. W. Studies, 13.

Prentice, George Denison. Clarke, J. F. Memo. sket. 245. — Coggeshall. Poets of west, 121. — Everest. Poets of Conn. 321. — Derby, J. C. Fifty years, 419. — Griffin, G. W. Stud. in lit.

— and Kentucky forty years ago. Clarke, J. F. Memo. sketches, 243.

— Poems. Taylor, B. Crit. ess. 314.

Prentiss, Mrs. Elizabeth (Payson). Hatfield, E. F. Poets of church, 499. — (M. V. Terhune) Our fam. wom. 539. — Wise, D. Rem. women, 60.

Prentiss, Sergeant Smith. Lossing. Em. Amer. 397. — Moore, F. Am. eloq. 2 : 579. — Sparks, W. H. Memories, 350.

Prentiss, Thomas, Biographical notice of. Ware, H., jr. Works, 2 : 85.

Preparatory schools. (J. P. Gulliver) Nat. Educa. Assoc. '70 : 19.

— for college and university life. (Noah Porter) Nat. Educa. Assoc. '74 : 42.
  See Fitting schools.

Pre-Raphaelite brotherhood. Quilter. Preferences, 30, 60.

Pre-Raphaelite magazine; The Germ. Noble, J. A. Sonnet in Eng. 64.

Pre-Raphaelite mansion in London. Child, T. Art and criticism, 305.

Præ-Raphaelites. Nordau. Degen. 67.

Pre-Raphaelitism. Badeau. Vagabond, 235. — Ruskin. Arrows, v. 1.

Presbyterian Church. Bibliography. Thompson, R. E. Hist. Presby. churches in U. S.

Presbyterian confession of faith. Brownson. Works, 6 : 160.

Presbyterianism. (D. Fotheringham) Relig. systems, 521.— (C. S. Robinson) Why I am, 18. — English. White, Jos. Blanco. Life, 3 : 403.

Presbyterians and Congregationalists; a plea for union. Phelps, A. Portfolio, 191.

— English. Alviella. Contemp. evol. 75.

Prescott, Benjamin F., with portrait. Sketches N. H. men, 281.

Prescott, Edward Goldsborough. Loring, J. S. Hundred Bost. ora. 500.

Prescott, Henry A., with portrait. Bartlett, J. R. R. I. officers, 131.

Prescott, James, Defense of, 1821. Webster, D. Works, 5 : 502.

Prescott, William. Lossing. Em. Amer. 175.

Prescott, William Hickling. Bolton, S. K. Amer. au. 82. — With portrait. Duyckinck. Nat. portr. gall. 2 : 221. — Everett, E. Mt. Vernon, 268. — Everett. Orat. v. 4. — With portrait. Griswold. Prose writ. 369. — Powell. Liv. authors (1850), 169. — Saunders, F. Famous books, 171. — Cranbourne. Hist. sk. 1 : 87. — Fisher, M. Gen. sur. Am. lit. 99. — Howe, M. A. D. Am. bookm. 125. — With portrait. (F. N. Thorpe) Warner Lib. 20 : 11767; also in Warner classics, 4 : 169. — (G. S. Hillard) Hubbard, E. Little jour. 2 : 725. Also in Homes of Amer. authors, 1 : 169. — With portrait. Mitchell, D. G. Am. lands, 357. — (R. Wolcott) N. E. Hist.-Gen. Soc. Biog. 3 : 322. — Nichol. Amer. lit. 147.— Powell, T. Liv. auth. Am. — Richardson. Amer. lit. 1 : 494. — With portrait. Stirling-Maxwell. Miscel. ess. 55. — Wright, H. C. Chil. sto. in Am. lit. 82.

— at college. (E. P. Whipple) Parton. Princes, 297.

Prescott, William Hickling. Bibliography. Salem (Mass.) Pub. Lib. Bull. June, '96.

— Conquest of Peru. Whipple. Ess. & rev. v. 2.

— historical works. Whipple. Ess. & rev. v. 2.

Presence of mind. DeQuincey. Lett. to young, Bost. 287.

— Causes of. Helps. Brevia.

Present age, The. Channing. Works, 6 : 147.

Present time, The. Carlyle. Latter-day.

Presentiments. Gray, E. C. Idle musings, 252.

Presents, Rules in making. Hunt, L. Seer, 2 : 127.

Presidency in Yale Coll., Powers and duties of. (F. B. Dexter) Am. Antiq. Soc. Proc. n. s. 12 : 27.

Presidency of the U. S., Fitness of the candidates for, 1861. Lyon, N. Last pol. writ. 161.

— Third-term question. Black, J. S. Ess. & sp. 366.

President of the U. S. Warner, C. D. As we go, 3.

— appointing power of, History of. (L. M. Salmon) Am. Hist. Assoc. 1 : 293.

— election of, Congress and. Garfield. Works, 2 : 393.

— — Defects of mode of. Madison. Lett. 3 : 332.

— Nomination of. Parton. Triumphs, 419.

— Third-term tradition. McMaster. With fathers, 55.

"President," U. S. S., capture of. Roosevelt, T. Naval war 1812, 401. — Dawson. Batt. of U. S. 2 : 420.

Presidential election, Mode of. Hart. Am. govt. 58.

— of 1860. Winthrop addresses, 2 : 491.

— of 1864. Winthrop addresses, 2 : 600.

— of 1876. Black, J. S. Ess. & sp. 312.

— — The electoral count. Field, D. D. Speeches, 2 : 88.

— — The electoral commission. Monroe, Jas. Oberlin lec. 254.

— — The returns. Garfield. Works, 2 : 435, 449.

Presidential elections and civil service reform. Sumner, W. G. Essays, 140.

— Reform in. Schouler, Jas. Hist. briefs, 160.

Presidential etiquette. Hamilton. Ed. by Lodge, 7 : 43.

Presidential government. Freeman. Hist. ess. 1 : 373.

Presidential inauguration, A. Tuckerman. Optimist, 212.

Press and the pulpit, compared. Payne, P. Ess. 2 : 322.

— The anonymous. Congreve, R. Ess. 165.

— as it is. (M. M. Trumbull) Sunset club echoes, 31.

— as teacher. Friswell. Gentle life, 281.

— British, American complaints of. Curran. Irish bar, 2 : 29.

— Censorship of, in Spain. Lea. Chap. relig. hist. Spain, 15.

— — in France, Feb. 17, 1851. Du Camp. Recol. 2 : 28.

— duties and privileges of the public. (C. C. Bonney) Sunset club echoes, 12.

— Freedom of, in England. Routledge, J. Pop. prog. in Eng. 493.

— in France, Power of. Hillebrand. France, 162.

— in our civilization. (H. Gilzean-Reid) Samuelson, Jas. Civiliz'n, 276.

— Liberty of. Hall, R. Miscell. 157.— Coleridge. Friend, 69. — Hume. Philos. works, 3 : 6.

— Licensers of. Disraeli, I. Curios. (N. Y. 4 v.) 2 : 399.

— Licentiousness of. Brownson. Works, 19 : 133.

Prime, William Cowper, with portrait. Warner Lib. 20 : 11820.

Primitive peoples, Relation of, to environment. (J. W. Powell) Smithson. Rept. '95 : 625.

Primogeniture. Baring-Gould. Germany, 56.
— Law and custom of. Brodrick. Pol. stud. 394. Same in Cobden Club ess. 2 : 57.
— Laws of settlement and. (J. E. T. Rogers) Trans. Soc. Sci. Lond. '64 : 117.

Prince, John. (C. W. Upham) Ware, W. Am. Unita. 1 : 101 ; also in Mass. Hist. Coll. 3d ser. 5 : 271.

Prince, John Critchley. Ossoli. Art, 186.

Prince, Joseph Hardy. Loring, J. S. Hundred Bost. ora. 453.

Prince, Thomas. Holland, J. Psalmists, 2 : 186.
— Moore, J. B. Am. gov. 139. — Richardson. Amer. lit. 1 : 112.

Prince Edward Island. Benjamin. Atlan. isl. 188.

Princess Theatre. Lennox, W. P. Plays, 1 : 142.

Princeton, N. J. (W. M. Sloane) Powell, L. P. Hist. towns mid. states, 251.
— Battle of. Dawson. Batt. of U. S. 1 : 204.

Princeton College. College book, 95. — Richardson. Amer. lit. 1 : 295.
— in 1820. Mansfield, E. D. Pers. mem. 92.

Princeton Theolog. Sem. (J. H. Dulles) U. S. Bur. Ed. Circ. '99, no. 1 : 322.

Princeton University. (W. M. Sloane) Norton, C. E. Four Am. univ. 93. — (J. DeWitt) U. S. Bur. Ed. Circ. '99, no. 1 : 199.
— University ideals at. (A. T. Ormond) Nat. Educa. Assoc. '97 : 346.

Principle and practice. Rands, W. B. Holbeach, 1 : 218.

Principles, Great, and small duties. King, T. S. Patriotism, 100.

Pring, Martin. Belknap. Amer. biog. 2 : 229.

Pringle, Sir John. Crichton, A. Converts, 1 : 235. — Grant, J. Recoll. Lords & Comm. 2 : 226. — McCosh. Scot. phil. 109. — Pettigrew. Med. portr. gall. v. 2.

Pringle, Thomas. Redding. Pers. remin. 3 : 235. — Wilson, J. G. Poets of Scot. 2 : 100.

Prinsep, James. Laurie, W. F. B. Dist. Anglo-Ind. 1 : 171.

Prinsep, Val. Bate, P. H. Eng. Pre-Raph. 87.

Printer, Country. Howells. Impressions, 1.

Printers, Ancient. Saunders. Pastime, 210.

Printers, First. Gurney, J. H. Hist. sketches, 1 : 1.

Printing. Head, F. B. Descr. ess. 1 : 257. — (W. Morris ; E. Walker) Morris, W. Arts & crafts, 111.
— an aid to preaching Broadus. Lec. hist. preach. 133.
— and paper, Repeal of taxes on, in England. Nicoll. Great move. 291.
— art of. Knox. Essays, 3 : 81.
— Early. Disraeli, I. Curios. (N. Y. 4 v.) 1 : 130.
— Early Spanish and Portuguese. Bibliography. Haebler, K. Early printers Spain & Portug.
— Establishment of, in Italy. Symonds. Reviv. of learn. 368.
— European, Introduc. into East. Garnett, R. Ess. in librarianship, 115.
— First, in America. Bancroft, H. H. Essays, 481.
— Invention of. Blades. Books in chains, 165. — Disraeli, I. Amen. (N. Y. 4 v.) 1 : 233. — Morley. Eng. writ. 6 : 266.
— Who invented ? Blades. Books in chains, 133.

Printing-press, First, in England. Blades. Books in chains, 209.

Printing trade, Benefit and relief assoc. in. (W. S. Waudby) U. S. Lab. Bull. 3 : 829.

Prints. Bibliography. Wedmore, F. Fine prints.

Printup, Daniel S. Livingston, J. Dist. Amer. 80.

Prinzenraub, a glimpse of Saxon history. Carlyle. Essays.

Prior, F. Hemenway. Poets of Vt. 345.

Prior, Margaret. Clement, J. Noble deeds, 388.

Prior, Matthew. Bell, R. Lit. & sci. men, 2 : 232.
— (S. Johnson) Chalmers. Eng. poets, 10 : 105. — Dennis, J. Studies, 109. — Thackeray. Humorists. — (A. Dobson) Ward. Eng. poets, 3 : 17. — Dobson, A. 18th cent. vign. 3 : 223.
— With portrait. Warner Lib. 20 : 11837. — Stebbing. Verdicts, 82. — Wrangham. Brit. Plutarch, v. 5.

Prison, Authors in. Jones, W. A. Ess. on authors, 152.
— Evolution of the. (H. M. Hoyt) Conf. char. & correc. '85 : 286.
— Woman's, at Sherborn. Blanc, T. Wom. in U. S. 225.

Prison associations, State, Organization of. (W. M. F. Round) Nat. Pris. Assoc. '86 : 281.

Prison diet. (A. A. Brush) Nat. Pris. Assoc. '86 : 61.
— scheme of, Principles involved in. (E. Smith) Trans. Soc. Sci. Lond. '57 : 293.

Prison discipline. Martineau, H. Miscel. 2 : 281.
— (F. B. Sanborn) Mass. Charity, '66 : 113. — (F. Hill) Nat. Pris. Assoc. '85 : 419. — (Z. R. Brockway) Nat. Pris. Assoc. '88 : 122. — (Sir J. Jebb) Trans. Soc. Sci. Lond. '63 : 425.
— Bibliography of. N. Y. Pris. Assoc. 26, app. : 117.
— Improvements in. Everett. Orat. v. 2.
— in Denmark. (F. Bruün) N. Y. Pris. Assoc. 26, app. : 117.
— in U. S., Outlook of [1870]. (E. C. Wines) N. Y. Pris. Assoc. 26, app. : 15.
— international congress on, History of movement for. (E. C. Wines) N. Y. Pris. Assoc. 26, app. : 253.
— Irish system of. (Sir W. Crofton) N. Y. Pris. Assoc. 26, app. : 66.
— national and international congresses on, History of. (M. B. Scalia) N. Y. Pris. Assoc. 26, app. : 267.
— Proper purpose of. (Sir J. Bowring) N. Y. Pris. Assoc. 26, app. : 75.
— Reformatory. (J. W. Edmonds) N. Y. Pris. Assoc. 26, app. : 165.
— — as applied to adults. (G. B. Hubbell) N. Y. Pris. Assoc. 26, app. : 169.
— Rival systems of. Sumner. Works, 1 : 486.

Prison ethics. Spencer, H. Ess. (N. Y.) 210.

Prison heroines. Hodder. Heroes, 1 : 177.

Prison industry. (J. F. Mouat) Trans. Soc. Sci. Lond. '73 : 289.

Prison labor. (C. E. Felton) Nat. Pris. Assoc. '86 : 216. — (H. H. Tucker) Nat. Pris. Assoc. '86 : 245. — (G. J. Holyoake ; H. Manton) Trans. Soc. Sci. Lond. '84 : 232.
— and discipline. (Sir J. Bowring) Trans. Soc. Sci. Lond. '69 : 246.
— and reformatory labor. (J. C. Thomson) Trans. Soc. Sci. Lond. '77 : 262.
— in Canada. (J. G. Moylan) Nat. Pris. Assoc. '86 : 238.

Prison-life, Female. Lucas. Mornings, 1 : 260.
— of literary men. Saunders. Pastime, 126.

Prison management. (J. H. Patterson) Nat. Pris. Assoc. '88 : 298.
— Personnel of. (W. H. Mills) Conf. char. & correc. '89 : 50.

Prison newspaper, Question of a. (J. R. Chandler) N. Y. Pris. Assoc. **26**, app. : 299.

Prison physicians, Duties and influences of. (J. Morris) Nat. Pris. Assoc. '86 : 77.

Prison punishments. (A. A. Brush) Nat. Pris. Assoc. '85 : 101. — (W. D. Patterson) Nat. Pris. Assoc. '86 : 181.

Prison reform. Illinois Charity, '72 : 199. — (A. G. Haygood) Nat. Pris. Assoc. '86 : 30. — Nicoll. Great move. 23. — (R. Brinkerhoff) Conf. char. & correc. '86 : 90.

— Education as a factor in. (C. D. Warner) Nat. Pris. Assoc. '85 : 232.

— Indeterminate sentences. (W. F. Spalding) Conf. char. & correc. '97 : 46.

— a measure of political economy. (E. Smith) Nat. Pris. Assoc. '84 : 12.

— Necessity for radical. (P. C. Garrett) Conf. char. & correc. '97 : 26.

— Probation system. (C. J. Lewis) Conf. char. & correc. '97 : 38.

— Progress of. (W. F. Spalding) Conf. char. & correc. '96 : 406.

— The sighing prisoner. Dodge. Sermons to clergy, 347.

Prison schools. (H. S. Tarbell) N. Y. Pris. Assoc. **26**, app. : 193.

Prison science, Modern. (C. A. Collin) Conf. char. & correc. '91 : 214.

Prison statistics in U. S. for 1888. (R. P. Falkner) Univ. Pa. Publ. Pol. Econ. **1** : no. 5.

Prison system, Ideal of a true. (Z. R. Brockway) N. Y. Pris. Assoc. **26**, app. : 38.

— Irish, in American prisons. (F. B. Sanborn) N. Y. Pris. Assoc. **26**, app. : 406.

— of the Southern States. (P. D. Sims) Nat. Pris. Assoc. '86 : 130.

Prison systems, Humanity and humanitarianism in. (W. Tallack) N. Y. Pris. Assoc. **26**, app. : 204.

— Present, and their effect. (R. Vaux) Nat. Pris. Assoc. '88 : 161.

Prisoner's right to reform, The State's protection of. (J. W. Clemmer) Nat. Pris. Assoc. '88 : 235.

Prisoners, Counsel for. Smith, Syd. Ess. fr. Ed.

— Discharged. (J. J. Lytle) Nat. Pris. Assoc. '87 : 290. — (Howland) Nat. Pris. Assoc. '86 : 286. — (W. M. F. Round) Nat. Pris. Assoc. '88 : 221.

— — Aid to. (J. W. Henry) Conf. char. & correc. '83 : 230.

— — Employment of. (C. W. Eddy) Trans. Soc. Sci. Lond. '59 : 496.

— — Prisoners' aid societies. (T. L. M. Browne et al.) Trans. Soc. Sci. Lond. '80 : 281. — (W. R. Crofton et al.) Trans. Soc. Sci. Lond. '81 : 298. — (C. Goldney et al.) Trans. Soc. Sci. Lond. '82 : 263.

— of war in England, French. Chambers's Miscel. no. 116.

— — Exchange of, during American revolution. Mass. Hist. Proc. **5** : 325.

— Our duty to. (P. Brooks) Nat. Pris. Assoc. '88 : 30.

— Paroling of. (F. H. Wines) Nat. Pris. Assoc. '86 : 114.

— United States. (R. Brinkerhoff) Nat. Pris. Assoc. '85 : 388.

— untried, Cruel treatment of. Smith, Syd. Ess. fr. Ed.

Prisons and penitentiaries in France. (F. Desportes) Conf. char. & correc. '84 : 276.

— and prison discipline. (F. B. Sanborn) Mass. charity, '65 : supp. — Sumner. Works, **1** : 163.

Prisons and prisoners, G. Minshall on. Jones, W. A. Lit. stud. **2** : 135.

— and reformatories for adults. (T. E. Ellison) Conf. char. & correc. '99 : 331.

— — Labor in. (Z. R. Brockway) Conf. char. & correc. '86 : 113.

— — Officers of, Special training for. (J. Woodworth) N. Y. Pris. Assoc. **26**, app. : 384.

— Centralization of. (T. B. L. Baker) Nat. Pris. Assoc. '85 : 382.

— Construction of. (W. D. Patterson) Nat. Pris. Assoc. '86 : 43.

— County. (E. Smith) Trans. Soc. Sci. Lond. '57 : 306.

— District, for minor criminals. (A. G. Byers) N. Y. Pris. Assoc. **26**, app. : 219.

— English, 1821–22. Smith, Syd. Ess. fr. Ed.

— — Buxton's inquiry. Jeffrey, F. Contrib. Ed. Rev.

— in Europe. (S. J. Barrows) Conf. char. & correc. '97 : 52.

— in U. S. in 1880. (F. H. Wines) Nat. Pris. Assoc. '88 : 251.

— Industrial and art education in. (N. A. Wells) Nat. Pris. Assoc. '85 : 93.

— Model. Carlyle. Latter-day.

— Moral and religious instruction in. (G. Tufts) Nat. Pris. Assoc. '86 : 98.

— Moral education in. (C. A. Collin) Nat. Pris. Assoc. '85 : 299.

— progress, 1873–93. (R. Brinkerhoff) Conf. char. & correc. '93 : 148.

— Religious forces in, Importance and power of. (C. C. Foote) N. Y. Pris. Assoc. **26**, app. : 185.

— State, Construction of. (A. Woodbury) Conf. char. & correc. '79 : 129.

— Sunday in. (R. Brinkerhoff) Conf. char. & correc. **190** : 309.

Pritchard, George Frederick. Smith, C. R. Retrospec. **3** : 149.

Pritchard, Hannah. Doran. Their maj. serv. **2** : 78.

Pritchard, John. Jackson, T. Early Meth. **3** : 445.

Pritchard, Mrs. (wife of John L.). Doran. Annals stage, **2** : 59.

Private institutions, State aid to. (R. Prendergast) Conf. char. & correc. '86 : 161.

Private judgment. Newman, J. H. Ess. crit. **2** : 336.

— Right of. Rogers, H. Ess. **2** : 1 ; or Reason, 290.

Privateer, The " General Armstrong." Lodge & Roosevelt. Hero-tales, 122.

Privateering, American. (A. B. Ellis) Mass. Hist. Proc. 2d ser. **1** : 15.

— and declaration of Paris, with bibliog. (F. R. Stark) Colum. Univ. Stud. Hist. **8** : no. 3.

— Injustice of. Franklin. Works, 1887, **9** : 80. — Laughton. Stud. nav. hist. 194.

Privy Council judgments. Church, R. W. Occ. pap. **2** : 32.

Prize-fights. Hutton, L. Other times, 11.

Prize-system in colleges. (J. H. Carlisle) Nat. Educa. Assoc. '82 : 46.

— in education. (D. Melville) Trans. Soc. Sci. Lond. '58 : 249.

Prizes for art students, Value of. Poynter. Ten lec. 172.

— in schools, as usually distributed. (M. P. Cavert) N. Y. Regents, **90** : 527.

Prjevalsky, The Russian traveler. (E. Schuyler) Am. Geog. Soc. **21** : 87.

Pro, Latin preposition. Key, T. H. Philol. ess. 74.

Public schools, Has the people's heart changed towards ? (C. G. Pearse) Nat. Educa. Assoc. '97 : 143.
— Hygiene and health in. (A. P. Marble) Iowa Health, '97 : 207.
— in colonial period of the U. S. (A. D. Mayo) U. S. Bur. Ed. Rept. '93-94, 1 : 639.
— in France, Curriculum in. (B. Buisson) Cong. Educa. Chic. '93, 262.
— in Italy. (E. Rossi) Cong. Educa. Chic. '93, 907.
— in New England, 1790-1840. (A. D. Mayo) U. S. Bur. Ed. Rept. '94-95, 2 : 1551.
— in Ohio. Hinsdale, B. A. Schools & stud. 341.
— in rela. to the community. (J. S. Whitney) Phila. Soc. Sci. Assoc. '80.
— in Sweden. Cong. Educa. Chic. '93, 289.
— Influence of, nationally and internationally. (G. M. Grant) Nat. Educa. Assoc. '91 : 244.
— Labor question and. (A. Johnston) Conv. Labor Bur. '86 : 57. — N. J. Labor, '86 : 245.
— Legal status of. (A. S. Draper) Nat. Educa. Assoc. '89 : 180.
— Light in. Mich. Health, '80 : 20.
— Mission of. Hinsdale, B. A. Schools & stud. 150.
— Moral and literary training in. (J. B. Peaslee) Nat. Educa. Assoc. '81 : 104.
— Moral and religious instruction in. Crooker, J. H. Problems, 197.
— Moral influence of. Mann, H. Lec. 2 : 539.
— Morality in. Wilson, J. M. Ess. & addr. 30.
— — Relation of, to religion. Wilson, J. M. Ess. 30.
— of Mass. Mann, H. Lec. v. 2.
— The public library and. Adams, C. F. New dep. Quincy, 5.
— Public opinions of. Hinsdale, B. A. Schools & stud. 296.
— Reasonable expectations of. (N. C. Dougherty) Nat. Educa. Assoc. '96 : 75.
— Relation of, to labor. (W. N. Ackley) Nat. Educa. Assoc. '88 : 238.
— Religion in. Wood, W. C. Five prob. 115.
— Sanitation of, in Massachusetts. (D. F. Lincoln) Mass. Health, '78 : 229.
— True function of. (R. E. Sears) Nat. Educa. Assoc. '97 : 983.
— What they should teach American laborers. (G. H. Howison) Nat. Educa. Assoc. '88 : 243.
Public service, Duty of. Rosebery. Apprec. 173.
Public speakers, Rules for. Helps. Brevia.
Public speaking, Relation of high-school training to. (F. S. Fosdick) Nat. Educa. Assoc. '94 : 773.
Public works, *quasi*, Modern municipalities and. Am. Econ. Assoc. v. 2.
Publicans of England, a religious sect. Brown, J. N. Bapt. martyrs, 165.
Publicity, Over-. Helps. Soc. pressure, 172.
Publisher, Trials of a. Repplier. Ess. in min. 28.
Publishers and authors. Payn. Lit. recol. 176.
— Thomson, K. B. Recoll. v. 2.
Publishing business in Maine. Me. Bur. Lab. '94 : 124.
Publishing societies, religious, Duties of. Beecher. New star papers, 351.
Puccini, Giacomo. Streatfeild. Masters Ital. mus. 189.
Puckering, Sir John. Campbell. Ld. chan. 2 : 297. — Manning, J. A. Speakers, 250.
Puckle's Club. Dobson, A. 18th cent. vign. 3 : 270.
Pudlodovius, Stanislaüs. Wallace, R. Anti-Trin. biog. 3 : 85.

Pueblo child, Education of the. (F. C. Spencer) Colum. Univ. Contrib. Philos. 7 : no. 1.
Pueblo prayer sticks. Lummis. Strange corners, 62.
Pueblo ruins near Winslow, Arizona, Expedition to, in '96. (J. W. Fewkes) Smithson. Rept. '96 : 517.
Pueblos at home. Lummis. Strange corners, 255.
— of S. W. No. America. (J. Stevenson) Am. Geog. Soc. 18 : 329.
— of Zuñi. Lummis. Strange corners, 21.
Puerperal fever, Contagiousness of. Holmes, O. W. Med. ess. 103 ; also in his Currents, 189.
Puffing. Hazlitt. Table talk.
Pugh, Eliza Lofton. Raymond, I. Southland writ. 1 : 294.
Pugnani, Gaetano, with portrait. Ehrlich, A. Cel. violin. 65.
Pulaski's legion, Massacre of. Dawson. Batt. of U. S. 1 : 457.
Pulcheria, Augusta, empress. Kavanagh. Women of Chris. 45.
Pulcherius, St. Conyngham, D. P. Irish saints, 371.
Pulci, Bernardo. Montgomery. Men of Ita. 1 : 167.
Pulci, Luigi. Montgomery. Men of Ita. 1 : 168.
— Symonds. Renais. It. lit. 1 : 440. — Owen, J. Skeptics Ital. 147. — Stebbing. Ital. poets, v. 1. — Warner Lib. 20 : 11891.
— Stories from. Hunt, L. Stories from Ital. poets, 1 : 281.
Pullain, John. Holland, J. Psalmists, 1 : 134.
Pullman, George M. Houghton. Kings, 212.
— With portrait. Stoddard, W. O. Men of bus. 246.
Pullman, Illinois. (D. Doty) Am. Pub. Health, 14 : 191. — Iowa Labor, 1884. — Mass. Labor, '85 : 3. — Wis. Labor, 1883. — Missouri Labor, 1884. — Penna. Labor, 1884.
— An attractive industrial experiment. N. J. Labor, '84 : 297.
— from a medical point of view. (I. C. DeWolf) Am. Pub. Health, 9 : 290.
Pulmonary consumption, Prevention of. (P. H. Kretzschmar) Am. Pub. Health, 15 : 128.
Pulmonary disease, Inheritance of. (H. Gibbons) Calif. Health, '79-80 : 74.
Pulp and paper making in Maine. Me. Bur. Lab. '94 : 111.
Pulpit, The. Farrar. Soc. & p. day quest. 190.
— Phillips, W. Speeches, 2 : 252.
— and politics. Thomson, E. Essays, 254.
— and popular skepticism. Brooks, P. Ess. & addr. 61.
— and the press compared. Bayne, P. Ess. 2 : 322
— British, 1840. Rogers, H. Ess. 1 : 405 ; or Reason, 197.
— Influence of the. Giles, H. Lectures, 2 : 112.
— Is it iosing its power ? Friswell. Wick. world, 244.
— Scotch. Boyd. Recreat. 2 : 364.
Pulpit at Pisa, with plates. Perkins, C. C. Tusc. sculp. 1 : 16.
— at San Andrea. Perkins, C. C. Tusc. sculp. 1 : 45.
— at Siena. Perkins, C. C. Tusc. sculp. 1 : 23.
Pulpit eloquence. Bethune. Orations, 212. — Brougham. Works, 7 : 256. — Goldsmith. Miscel. (N. Y. 4 v.) 1 : 123.
Pulpit fortune-tellers. Kirkus. Miscel. 265.
Pulpit oratory. Mathews. Conversers, 200. — Talfourd. Crit. writ.

Pulpit talent. Bushnell. Building eras, 182.
Pulque and scurvy in prisons. (F. M. Baca) Am. Pub. Health, **22**: 287.
— Manufacture of, in Mexico, 1896. (T. T. Crittenden) U. S. Cons. Rept. **51**: 396.
Pulteney, William. *See* Bath, Earl of.
Pultowa, Battle of. Creasy. Fifteen battles, 270. — King, C. Battles, 298.
Pulvis et umbra. Stevenson, R. L. Across pl. 289.
Puma, or American lion. (F. W. True) U. S. Nat. Mus. Rept. '**89**: 591.
Punch, London. Hatton. Jour. Lond. 12. — Reid, T. W. Politicians, **2**: 143.
— Cartoons of John Leech in. Everitt, G. Eng. carica. 294.
— Origin of. Hodder, G. Memories, 39.
— Writers for. Taylor, B. At home, **2**: 416.
Punchard, George. (H. M. Dexter) Mass. Hist. Proc. **19**: 262.
Punic wars. Lord, J. Anc. states, 429.
Punishment. Combe. Constitution of man. — Stephen, L. Soc. rights, **2**: 55.
— as seen by children. (Earl Barnes) Nat. Educa. Assoc. '**95**: 914.
— Corporal. Newman, F. W. Miscel. **3**: 134.
— Nature and due extent of. Hope. Ess. 161.
— Right of the state to inflict. Green, T. H. Works, **2**: 486.
Punjab, Civil justice in. Cust. Linguistic essays, **1**: 198.
— Jalandhar. Cust. Linguistic essays, **2**: 86.
— Visit to, 1884. Hübner. Thro' Brit. empire, **2**: 104.
— War of. Gleig. Ess. **1**: 378.
Punshon, William M. Great mod. preachers. — Wesley & successors, 223.
Punsters, asylum for, Visit to. Holmes. Soundings, 348.
Pupil, The, as a social factor. (Earl Barnes) Nat. Educa. Assoc. '**96**: 184.
Pupils, Classification of. (H. S. Jones) Nat. Educa. Assoc. '**86**: 276.
— — according to ability. (F. L. Barnard) Nat. Educa. Assoc. '**99**: 163.
— Early withdrawal of. (W. T. Harris) Nat. Educa. Assoc. '**72**: 260.
— Progress of, before leaving school to go to work. (C. W. Hill; J. H. Shinn) Nat. Educa. Assoc. '**92**: 645.
Pupper, Johann (John of Goch). Ullmann. Reformers, **1**: 15.
Puppets for grown gentlemen. Doran. Habits, 205.
Puppy, The; a portrait. Guiney. Patrins, 73.
Purcell, Henry. Dole, N. H. Score, 30. — Keddie. Mus. comp. 8. — Runciman, J. F. Old scores, 19. — Sharp, R. F. Makers of music.
— Musical works of. Hogarth. Mem. opera, **1**: 91, 125.
Purcell, John Baptist. Clarke, R. H. Cath. bishops, **3**: 196.
Purchas case, Sir J. Coleridge on. Church, R. W. Occ. pap. **2**: 48.
Purdue University, La Fayette, Ind. U. S. Bur. Ed. Circ. '91, no. **1**: 102.
Purgatory. Shipley, O. Tracts, 49.
Puritan, The, and the mystic. Williams, W. R. Eras, 252.
— and cavalier England transplanted. Stebbing. Verdicts, 349.
Puritan boy, Puzzles of. Rands, W. B. Holbeach, **1**: 77.
Puritan character. Shedd. Lit. ess. 229.
Puritan colony, An obscure. Rands, W. B. Holbeach, **1**: 1.
Puritan commonwealth, The. Wasson. Ess. 305.
Puritan poets, A group of. Ward, May A. Old col. 235.
Puritan principle and John Brown. Phillips, W. Speeches, **2**: 294.
Puritan principle and Puritan pluck. Curtis, G. W. Orations, **1**: 251.
— and the modern world. (A. H. Bradford) Abbott, L. New purit. 75.
— Liberty under the law. Curtis, G. W. Orations, **1**: 239.
Puritan spirit, The. Curtis, G. W. Orations, **1**: 367. — Pierce, E. L. Addresses, 279.
Puritanism. Carlyle. Heroes.
— Benefits and dangers of. Keyes, E. D. Fifty years, 83.
— in Old and New England. Lowell. Writ. **2**: 1.
— Rise of. Tulloch. Eng. purit. v. 7.
Puritans, The. Bacon, L. Genesis N. Eng. churches. — Gleig. Ess. **2**: 1. — Rands, H. Holbeach, **1**: 31, 77. — Lodge, H. C. Speeches, 31. — Stanton, H. B. Reforms, 118. — Stryker. Hamilton, 36.
— and the restoration. Lodge, H. C. Studies, 1.
— and Viscount Falkland. Smith, Gold. Lec. & ess. 219.
— in New England. Higginson. Atlan. Ess. 189.
— Independent spirit of. Lodge, H. C. Speeches, 1.
— Neal's History of. Whipple. Ess. & rev. 1.
— of England. Brigham, C. H. Mem. 368.
— of 17th century and English drama. Kingsley. Plays and p. 1.
— of New England, History and influence of. Story, J. Miscel. 408.
— — Neglected characteristics of. Wendell, B. Stelligeri, 45.
— Virtue and vices of the. Richardson. Amer. lit. **1**: 11.
— Why we honor the. Eliot, C. W. Five Am. cont. 355.
Purity. (R. Bourne) Wace, H. Lond. mission. 88.
— Ancient and modern ideas of. Patmore. Religio poetæ, 102.
— Social, A plea for. Ossoli. Woman, 131.
Purpose. Munger. On threshold, 1.
Pusey, Edward Bouverie. Davies, G. J. Suc. preach. 398. — Horne. New spirit, **1**: 199. — Em. persons, **3**: 42.
— and the Oxford movement. Oxenham. Stud. in eccl. hist. 367.
— Sermon, Feb. 1, 1846. Mozley. Ess. **2**: 149.
Pusey, Philip. Miles, A. H. Poets of cent. **10**: 668.
Pushkin, Alex. S. Panin. Lectures on Russian literature. — With portrait. (I. F. Hapgood) Warner Lib. **20**: 11904. — Wolkonsky. Lowell lec. 184.
Pushmatahaw. Lanman, C. Recoll. 205.
Pustule, Malignant, in Livingston county, N. Y., 1875. (J. Law) Am. Pub. Health, **2**: 465.
Putnam, George. Peabody. Harv. rem. 159.
Putnam, George Palmer. Derby, J. C. Fifty years, 299.
Putnam, Harvey. Putnam, J. O. Addresses, 228.
Putnam, Gen. Israel. With portrait. [Amer.] Nat. portr. gall. v. 1. — Duyckinck. Nat. portr. gall. **1**: 228. — Glazier, W. Heroes, 74. — With portrait. Headley, J. T. Washington, **1**: 92. — Parton. Capt. indus. 96. — With portrait. Seymour, C. C. B. Self-made, 258. — Lossing. Em. Amer. 226.
— Headquarters at Cambridge. Drake, S. A. Hist. fields Mid. 187.
Putnam, Rufus. Lossing. Em. Amer. 182.

Putnam, Rufus, and his pioneer life in the Northwest. (S. Crawford) Am. Antiq. Soc. Proc. n. s. **12** : 431.

Putnam, Lieut. Wm. Lowell. (J. F. Clarke) Shea, J. G. Fallen brave.

Puttenham, Geo. Choate, I. B. Wells of Eng. 110.

— Arte of English poesy. Disraeli, I. Amen. (N. Y. 2 v.) **2** : 48.

Puvis de Chavannes. Child, T. Art & criticism.

— (K. Cox) VanDyke, J. C. Mod. Fr. mast. 17.

Pydna, Battle of. King, C. Battles, 144.

Pye, Henry James. Austin & Ralph. Laureates, 333. — Hamilton, Wal. Poets laur.

Pyer, John. Miller, Jos. Singers church, 2d ed. 413.

Pygmies. Flower, W. H. Ess. on museums, 290.

— of equatorial Africa. (P. B. Du Chaillu) Am. Geog. Soc. **2**, pt. 2 : 99.

— Stories of. Ferrier. Ill. of Sterne, **2** : 73.

— Who discovered the ? (C. P. Daly) Am. Geog. Soc. **24** : 18.

Pym, Sir Charles, Manslaughter of. Burke, P. Cel. trials.

Pym, John. Adams, C. K. Rep. Brit. orat. **1** : 27.

— (J. R. Green) Ferris, G. T. Gt. leaders, 280.

— With portrait. Forster. Brit. statesm. **3** : 1.

— Smith, G. Three statesm. 7.

— *versus* Falkland. Bulwer. Ess. 317.

Pyne, Louisa Fanny, vocalist. Clayton, E. C. Queens, 502. — Hutton, L. Plays, 167. — Needham. Queens of song.

Pyramid of Cheops. Proctor, R. A. Univ. of suns, 288. — Estes. Half-hour recr. 132.

— Observatory, tomb, and temple. Proctor, R. A. Pyramid, 1.

— Problem of. Proctor, R. A. Fam. sci. 104.

— Religion of. Proctor. Myths, 52.

Pyramid builders, Early. (J. N. Lockyer) Smithson. Inst. Rept. **'93** : 95.

Pyramids of Egypt. Buckley, J. M. Trav. 3 cont. 221. — Kinglake. Eothen, 176. — Pidgeon. Engineer's holiday, 447. — Proctor, R. A. Fam. sci. 143.

— Lady's adventure in. Cobbe, F. P. Hours of work, 147.

— Mystery of. Proctor. Myths, 77.

Pyrenees, The, and western France. Moore, Jos. Outl. Eur. 365.

— Bibliography. Spender, H. Through high Pyrenees.

Pyrrho. Diog. Laertius. Lives, 402. — Lewes. Biog. phil. — Mills. Poets of Greece, 433. — Fénélon. Philosophers, 252.

Pyrrhus. Mahaffy, J. P. Greek life, ch. 4.

Pytchley hunt, The. Sinclair, J. Sketches.

Pythagoras. Bruce, J. Classic portr. 15. — Diog. Laertius. Lives, 338. — Fénélon. Philosophers, 113. — Lewes. Biog. phil. — Mills. Poets of Greece, 423. — Fairbanks, A. Philos. of Greece, 142. — Hundred greatest men, 199.

— as a geologist. Duncan, P. M. Botanists, 209.

Quackery and the medical profession. Bigelow, J. Mod. inq. 199.

— Illustrations of. Winslow, F. Physic, **1** : 304.

Quacks and quackery. Brodie. Works, **1** : 616.

— Timbs. Doctors, 91.

— Medical. Jeaffreson. Doctors, 50.

— of the 18th century. Ashton. 18th cent. waifs, 287.

See Empiricism.

Quad, M., *pseud. See* Lewis, C. B.

Quadratus, St., bishop of Athens. Blakey, R.

Prim. fathers, 76. — Cave. Lives of fathers, **1** : 219. — Yonge, C. M. Pupils of John, 172.

Quadrupeds and their lives. Goldsmith. Miscel. (N. Y. 4 v.) **2** : 498.

— Great extinct. (P. M. Duncan) Manch. Sci. lec. **7** : 73.

Quain, Sir John R. Gener. of judges, 30.

Quaker and Baptist controversy. Ivimey. Eng. Bapt. **1** : 388.

Quaker Christmas. Abbott, C. C. Outings, 41.

Quakerism, Clarkson's Portraiture of. Jeffrey, F. Contrib. Ed. Rev.

— Literature of. Jones, W. A. Ess. on authors, 159.

Quakers. (W. Pollard) Relig. systems, 575. — (J. J. Cornell) Why I am, 120.

— Bibliography. Weeks, S. B. South. Quakers & slav.

— in New England. Ferguson, H. Ess. Am. hist. 9.

— Rise and principles of. Burnap. Miscel.

Quakers' meeting, A. Lamb. Elia.

Quantity in English verse. (C. K. Gaines) N. Y. Regents, **'94** : 544.

Quarantine. (S. R. Oliphant) Am. Pub. Health, **19** : 107. — Iowa Health, **'95** : 186.

— and U. S. marine hospital service. (A. N. Bell) Am. Pub. Health, **18** : 349.

— as it is, and as it ought to be. (G. Milroy) Trans. Soc. Sci. Lond. **'58** : 521.

— Cholera and. (J. H. Rauch) Am. Pub. Health, **13** : 242.

— Effectual external regulations without delay to commerce. (A. W. Perry) Am. Pub. Health, **1** : 437.

— Greek, Experience in. Stillman, W. J. Old Rome.

— in Boston. (S. H. Durgin) Am. Pub. Health, **13** : 134.

— in Canada. (F. Montizambert) Am. Pub. Health, **19** : 92.

— in Mexico, Difficulties of. (D. Orvañanos) Am. Pub. Health, **19** : 104.

— in Texas. (R. M. Swearingen) Am. Pub. Health, **19** : 111.

— — from 1878 to 1888. (R. Rutherford) Am. Pub. Health, **14** : 125.

— Inland. (S. S. Herrick) Buck, A. H. (ed.). Hygiene, **2** : 497.

— Inner regulations, Modification of. (D. B. Blake) Am. Pub. Health, **18** : 320.

— International. (B. W. James) Am. Pub. Health, **5** : 145.

— New York establishment. (W. M. Smith) Am. Pub. Health, **15** : 201.

— of the future. (W. C. Van Bibber) Am. Pub. Health, **18** : 313.

— on the Gulf Coast. (G. B. Thornton) Tenn. Health, **'80–84** : 437.

— Organization and practice of. (S. O. Vanderpoel) Am. Pub. Health, **1** : 402.

— Sea-port. (S. O. Vanderpoel) Buck, A. H. (ed.). Hygiene, **2** : 471.

— Yellow fever. (J. T. Tyner) Am. Pub. Health, **5** : 147. — (G. M. Sternberg) Am. Pub. Health, **6** : 351.

— — in Arkansas, 1879. (R. G. Jennings ; J. B. Cummings) Am. Pub. Health, **5** : 121.

— — of the future. (H. F. Campbell) Am. Pub. Health, **5** : 131.

See also Sanitation, Maritime.

Quarantine appliances. (F. Montizambert and others) Am. Pub. Health Assoc. **20** : 345.

Quarantine legislation, International aspect of. (G. Milroy) Trans. Soc. Sci. Lond. **'63** : 869.

Quarantine stations of Middle Atlantic coast, Visit to. (B. Lee) Am. Pub. Health, 14 : 97.

Quarantine system, Canadian. (F. Montizambert) Am. Pub. Health, 19 : 92.

— in Louisiana. (L. F. Salmon) Am. Pub. Health, 14 : 110.

Quarles, Francis. Adams, W. H. D. Worthies Church Eng. 105. — Gosse, E. Jacobean poets, 188. — Griswold, R. W. Sac. poets. — Macdonald, G. England's antiphon, 171.

— Brevity of life. Jones, W. A. Ess. on authors, 104.

— Emblems. Adams, W. D. Famous books, 170. — Saunders, F. Famous books, 51.

Quarles, J. Griswold, R. W. Sac. poets.

Quarreling. Helps. Conv. on war, 220.

Quarrels, The Christian in. Butler, E. For good, 125.

Quarter, William. Clarke, R. H. Cath. bishops, 2 : 240.

Quartley, Arthur. With portrait. Benjamin, S. G. W. Am. art. 2 : 12. — Sheldon, G. W. Amer. painters, 80.

Quartz fibers. (C. V. Boys) Smithson. Rept. '90 : 315.

Quatre Bras, Battle of. Adams, W. H. D. Eng. at war, 2 : 7.

Quebec, Berry, C. B. The other side, 261. — Hardy, I. D. Thro' cities, 13. — James, H. Portraits, 350. — Taylor, B. At home, 2 : 366.

— and its environs in 1881. Hardy. Between two oceans, 22.

— Arnold's expedition to, Diary of. (E. Wild) Mass. Hist. Proc. 2d ser. 2 : 265.

— Historical, etc., literature of, 1764–1830. (B. Sulte) Roy. Soc. Can. 2d ser. 3 : § 2, 269.

— in 1877. Vivian. Tour in Amer. 17.

— Siege of. Clinton, H. R. Crécy to Assye, 547.

— Wolfe's attack on. Fitchett. Deeds, 13.

See also Plains of Abraham.

Queen Anne's war. Parkman. Half-cent. 1 : 32.

"Queen Charlotte," Wreck of. Senior, W. Shipwrecks, 36.

Queens, Tiring bowers of. Doran. Habits, 89.

— unqueened, A group of. Doran. New pic. 247.

Queensborough, England, Hogarth's visit to. Mahaffy. Holl. & Germ. 264.

Queensland. Jenks, E. Hist. Aust. col. 108.

— Sugar in, 1895. (G. W. Bell) U. S. Cons. Rept. 50 : 340.

— Visit to, 1883. Hübner. Thro' Brit. empire, 1 : 304.

Queenstown. Silloway. Cathedral towns, 3.

— Battle of. Dawson. Batt. of U. S. 2 : 143.

Quendrida-Petronilla, queen of Offa, "the proud." Hall. Queens bef. Conq. 296.

Quendrida II. Hall. Queens bef. Conq. 312.

Quercia, Giacomo della. Perkins, C. C. Tusc. sculp. 1 : 103. — Symonds. Renais. Fine arts, 127.

Quesnay, Jules de Beaurepaire. Warner Lib. 20 : 11925.

Quesnel, Pasquier. Tollemache. French Jansen. 229.

Quetzalcoatl, God of the Aztecs. Brinton. Amer. hero-myths, 64.

Quevedo, Francisco Gomez de. Hain, J. Varia. 105. — Montgomery. Men of Ita. 3 : 255. — Ticknor. Span. lit. 2 : 255.

— Writings of. Curran. Irish bar, 2 : 80.

Quichuas, Hero-god of the. Brinton. Amer. hero-myths, 169.

Quicksilver. Nichols, J. R. Fireside sci. 222.

Quietism. Astie. Louis XIV, 161. — Lea. Chap.

from the relig. hist. of Spain. — Vaughan, R. A. Mystics, 2 : 201.

Quietism, Madame Guyon and. Hain, J. Varia. 137.

Quietists in Spain. Lea. Chap. relig. hist. Spain, 384.

Quillinan, E., Wordsworth's son-in-law. Rawnsley. Lit. assoc. Eng. lakes, 2 : 115.

Quin, James. Baker, H. B. Eng. actors, 1. 117. — Doran. Annals stage, 1 : 242, 320, 393. — Galt. Players, 1 : 183. — Matthews, B. Actors, 1 : 25. — Russell, W. Rep. actors, 70.

Quinault, Philip, his works. Hogarth. Mem. opera, 1 : ??

Quinby's Creek Bridge, S. C., Battle of. Dawson. Batt. of U. S. 1 : 705.

Quincy, Josiah, b. 1744. Loring, J. S. Hundred Bost. ora. 258. — Magoon. Orators of rev. 121. — Lossing. Em. Amer. 187. — Moore, F. (ed.). Am. eloq. 1 : 331. — Richardson. Amer. lit. 1 : 186.

Quincy, Josiah, b. 1772, Pres. Harv. Univ. Everett. Orat. v. 4. — Griswold. Prose writ. 129. — Johnston, A. Amer. ora. 1 : 180. — Loring, J. S. Hundred Bost. ora. 418. — Lowell. Writ. 2 : 272. — (J. Walker) Mass. Hist. Proc. 9 : 83. — Peabody. Harv. rem. 20.

Quincy, Josiah, jr., b. 1802. Loring, J. S. Hundred Bost. ora. 495. — Parton. Triumphs, 311.

Quincy family, The. Muzzey, A. B. Prime movers, 77.

— in U. S. history. Muzzey. Remin. 77.

Quincy, Mass., Public school system of. Adams, C. F. Three episodes, 2 : 933.

Quinet, Edgar. Dowden. Studies, 357. — With portrait. (H. Bérenger) Warner Lib. 20 : 11961.

— Paradox on. Saintsbury. Miscel. ess. 274.

Quinine. Drury. Useful plants of India. — Japp. Days w. indus. 1.

Quinlan, John. Clarke, R. H. Cath. bishops, 3 : 378.

Quintana. Kennedy. Poets of Spain, 141.

Quintard, Geo. W. Patten, J. Sk. of men of prog. — With portrait. Rogers, A. C. Repres. men, 445.

Quintilian. (H. W. Preston) Warner Lib. 20 : 11980.

Quintin's Bridge, Skirmish at. Dawson. Batt. of U. S. 1 : 379.

Quist, Sören, Trial of. Phillips, S. M. Famous cases, 14.

Quitman, John Anthony, with portrait. Duyckinck. Nat. portr. gall. 2 : 263. — Sparks, W. H. Memories, 343.

Quito, capital of Ecuador. Curtis, W. E. Capitals, 298.

— in 1867. Orton. Andes, 56.

Quodlibets. Disraeli, I. Curios. (N. Y. 4 v.) 1 : 115.

Quotation and originality. Emerson. Lett. & soc. aims, 167.

— Lessons by. Walsh, R. Didactics, 1 : 235.

— Literary. Mathews, W. Men, p. & t. 345.

Quotation books. Reed, W. B. Among books, 40.

Rabanus, Maurus. Miller, Jos. Singers church, 2d ed. 20. — Neale. Mediæv. preachers. — Hatfield, E. F. Poets of church, 501.

Rabbet, Michael. McClure. Translators, 184.

Rabbinical stories. Disraeli, I. Curios. (N. Y. 4 v.) 1 : 185.

Rabbins, Traditions of. DeQuincey. Avenger. Bost. 265.

Rabelais, François. Besant. Fr. humor. 99. — Lang. Lett. to dead au. 66. — Quick. Educa. ref. 63. — Shelley, M. W. Lit. men Fr. 1. — Henley. Views, 97. — Nasmith. Mak. mod. thought, 1 : 70. — Hundred greatest men, 35. — Shelley, Mrs. Fr. authors, v. 1.— Thomson, Jas. (B. V.). Biog. ess. 1.— With portrait. (H. Bérenger) Warner Lib. 21 : 12001.
— at Rome. Powell, G. H. Excurs. in Libr. 207.
— Imitation of, by Sterne. Ferrier. Ill. of Sterne, 1 : 41.

Rabies : its prevention and treatment. (J. J. Kinyoun) Am. Pub. Health, 17 : 162.
— suspected, Report on diagnosis of. (F. F. Wesbrook and L. B. Wilson) Am. Pub. Health, 23 : 219.

Rabotean refugees, Sketch of. Agnew. Protes. exiles, 2 : 262.

Raby Castle. Jewitt, L. Stately homes, 2 : 242.

Race and civilization. (W. M. F. Petrie) Smithson. Rept. '95 : 589.
— and language. Freeman. Hist. ess. 3 : 173; also in Prose masterpieces, 3 : 55.
— and tradition. Darmesteter. Sel. ess. 155.
— Asian. Brinton. Races & peo. 194.
— Austafrican. Brinton. Races & peo. 174.
— Eurafrican. Brinton. Races & peo. 140.
— European. Brinton. Races & peo. 104.

Race acclimation. Brinton. Races & peo. 278.

Race distinctions. Brinton. Races & peo. 29.

Race element in literature. Mabie. Short stud. lit. 46.

Race extermination. Brinton. Races & peo. 292.

Race migration. Grube, A. W. Heroes, 43. — Brinton. Races & peo. 113, 152.

Race problem, General statement of. (A. A. Gunby) Nat. Educa. Assoc. '90 : 254.
— solution of, by education. (J. C. Price) Nat. Educa. Assoc. '90 : 267.

Racecourse, Roman. Buckland, F. T. Curios. nat. hist. 3 : 40.

Races of men. Dana, A. H. Eth. inq. 8.
— Conflict of, in America. Dixon, W. H. White conquest, 1 : 336. 2 : 283.
— Classification of. Brinton. Races & peo. 97. — Flower, W. H. Ess. on museums, 274.
— Insular. Brinton. Races & peo. 220.
— Migration of. (J. Bryce) Smithson. Inst. Rept. '93 : 567.
— Mingled, in the U. S. Higginson. Book & heart, 154.

Rachel. Smith, G. B. Wom. of renown, 377.
— and Leah. Geikie, C. Old Test. char. 47.

Rachel Felix, Eliza. Badeau. Vagabond, 263. — Lewes. Actors, 23. — Wraxall. Scraps, 1 : 312. — Cook, D. Hours w. players, 2 : 206. — Curtis, G. W. Lit. & soc. ess. 95. — Marston, J. W. Rec. actors, 2 : 279.
— and the new world, Beauvallet's. Bristed. Pieces, 1 : 331.
— in "Phèdre." Stuart, H. Paris days, 224.

Racial deterioration. (L. Irwell) Am. Pub. Health, 22 : 264.

Racial experience. Mabie. Books and cul. 165.

Racine, Jean. Beard. Port Royal, 2 : 326-397. — Shelley, M. W. Lit. men. Fr. v. 1. — Hallard, J. H. Gallica, 40. — With portrait. (F. M. Warren) Warner Lib. 21 : 12027.
— Corneille and. Astié. Louis xiv, 289.

Racine, Louis, 1692-1763. Vinet. Fr. lit. 18th cent. 84.

Racine College, Racine, Wis. U. S. Bur. Ed. Circ. '89, no. 1 : 58.

Rackam, John. Whitehead, C. Highwaymen, 2 : 48.

Radcliffe, Mrs. Anne. Adams, W. H. D. Fam. beauties, 2 : 3. — Hamilton, C. J. Women writers, 144. — Jeaffreson. Novelists, 2 : 1. — Kavanagh. Eng. women, 2 : 235. — Scott, W. Biog. mem. v. 1. — Wotton. Word portraits, 243.
— Gaston de Blondeville, or the court of Henry III. Dana. P. & p. writ. 314.
— Memoirs of. Elwood. Lit. ladies, 2 : 155.
— Pedigree of. (A. McF. Davis) Col. Soc. Mass. Trans. 1 : 351.

Radcliffe, Charles. Thomson, Mrs. Jacobites, 3 : 480.

Radcliffe, James. See Derwentwater, J. Radcliffe, earl of.

Radcliffe, Jeremiah. McClure. Translators, 189.

Radcliffe, John, M. D. Georgian era, 2 : 363. — Jeaffreson. Doctors, 69. — Pettigrew. Med. portr. gall. v. 1.

Radcliffe, William. Woodcroft, B. Biog. invent. 32.

Radecius, Matthew. Wallace, R. Anti-Trin. biog. 2 : 357.

Radegonde, Queen. Bush, A. F. Queens of F. 1 : 32.

Radewins, Florentius. Ullman. Reformers, 81.

Radiation. Tyndall. Frag. sci. 167.
— Chemical. Hunt, R. Poe. of sci. 166.

Radical and conservative. Stryker. Hamilton, 138.

Radicalism. Bartol. Rad. prob. 98.
— and conservatism. Bunce, O. B. Bach. bluff, 266.
— versus conservatism. Brownson. Works, 4 : 542.

Radiometer, The. Cooke, J. P., jr. Sci. cul. 86.

Radisson, Pierre E., Further history of. (G. Bryce) Roy. Soc. Can. 2d ser. 4 : § 2, 53.

Radnor, William P. Bouverie, Earl. Francis, G. H. Orators, 172.— Grant, J. Recoll. Lords, 290.

Radowitz, Gen. von. Hayward, A. Ess. 1 : 269.

Radzivil, Princess Anne. Wallace, R. Anti-Trin. biog. 2 : 237.

Radzivil, Prince Nicholas. Wallace, R. Anti-Trin. biog. 2 : 232.

Rae, John. Am. Geog. Soc. 25 : 479.

Rae, Robert, with portrait. Bungay. Pen-portr. 221.

Raeburn, Sir Henry. Brown, J. J. Leech, 415.
— Cunningham, A. Brit. painters, 4 : 172.
— Some portraits by. Stevenson, R. L. Virgin. 205.

Raffaelle. See Raphael.

Raffles, Sir Stamford. Chambers's Miscel. no. 53.

Raffles, Thomas. Hatfield, E. F. Poets of church, 502. — Miller, Jos. Singers church, 2d ed. 404.

Rafinesque, Constantine Samuel. Jordan, D. S. Sci. sk. 143.— Youmans. Pioneers sci. 182.
— Bibliography. Call, R. E. Life of Rafinesque.

Rafn, C. C. (T. H. Webb) Mass. Hist. Proc. 8 : 175.

Ragged-schools and the educational movement. (Mary Carpenter) Trans. Soc. Sci. Lond. '57 : 226.
— at Naples. Howells. Ital. jour. 136.

Raglan, James Henry Fitzroy Somerset, Baron. Martineau, H. Biog. sk. 187.

Raglan castle. Hutton, B. Castles, 155.
— Siege of. Thomson, K. B. Recoll. 1.

Rags, Disinfection of. Am. Pub. Health, 12 : 170.
— Transmission of infectious diseases by. (C. F. Withington) Mass. Health, '86 : 3.

Ragusa, Architecture of. Freeman. Subj. Venice, 240.

Raikes, Robert. Adams, W. H. D. Good Samar. 37. — Tillotson, J. Untit. nobil. 47.

Rail and track, American. (J. E. Watkins) U. S. Nat. Mus. Rept. '89 : 651.

— Romance of the. Grahame, K. Pagan papers, 21.

Railroad, Intercontinental, A plea for. Helper, H. R. Andean diplom. 275.

Railroad accidents. Rogers, H. Ess. from G. W. 276. — (H. Brougham) Trans. Soc. Sci. Lond. '57 : 505.

— Chief securities against. Rogers, H. Ess. fr. G. W. 276.

Railroad by-laws, Passengers and. Williams, Syd. Forensic, 118.

Railroad cars, Cleaning of. (D. Orvañanos) Am. Pub. Health, 21 : 300.

— Hygiene of. (T. Noriega) Am. Pub. Health, 21 : 80.

— Sanitation in. (W. W. Daniells) Am. Pub. Health, 17 : 67. — (J. Pattison ; G. P. Conn) Am. Pub. Health, 20 : 236. 21 : 61, 285.

— Ventilation of. (J. S. Buist) Am. Pub. Health, 16 : 147. — (S. H. Woodbridge) Am. Pub. Health, 21 : 75. — (T. W. Fisher ; W. R. Nichols) Mass. Health, '75 : 227. — (R. C. Kedzie) Mich. Health, '76 : 133.

— Water supply on. (S. W. Latta) Am. Pub. Health, 15 : 145.

Railroad conductor, city, Musings of a. Siegvolk. Papers, 145.

Railroad consolidation. Adams, C. F. Erie, 380.

Railroad employees, Brotherhood relief and insurance of. (E. R. Johnson) U. S. Lab. Bull. 3 : 552.

— Protective legislation for. N. J. Labor, '88 : 27, 32.

Railroad insurance and relief associations. N. J. Labor, '88 : 140, 188.

Railroad labor in Europe, Condition of. (W. E. Weyl) U. S. Lab. Bull. 4 : 1.

Railroad literature. Phillips, S. Ess. from Times, 1 : 311.

— on the continent. Wraxall. Scraps, 2 : 15.

Railroad morals and railroad policy. Spencer, H. Ess. (N. Y.) 251.

Railroad rates. Adams, C. F. Erie, 355.

Railroad relief departments. U. S. Lab. Bull. 2 : 39.

Railroad sanitation. (W. T. Parker) Am. Pub. Health, 10 : 335. — (T. J. Dunott) Am. Pub. Health, 4 : 123.

— Need of. (T. P. Wilson) Am. Pub. Health, 8 : 142.

— Objects and advantages of. (S. S. Herrick) Am. Pub. Health, 7 : 218.

Railroad system, History and development of. Adams, C. F. Erie, 333.

Railroad traveling in America. Marshall, W. G. Thro' Amer. 60 : 107.

Railroad wages. N. J. Labor, '78 : 257. '88 : 78.

Railroads. Head, F. B. Descr. ess. 1 : 170.

— American inventions. (H. G. Prout) Shaler. The U. S. 2 : 163.

— and the state. (E. J. James) Am. Econ. Assoc. v. 2. — (W. S. Jevons) Owens College essays, '74 : 465. — Hoffman, F. S. Sphere, 88.

— — in Europe. (S. Sterne) U. S. Sen. miscel. docs. '86–87, v. 2.

— — State ownership. (W. Todd) Adams, C. F. Erie, 414. — Trans. Soc. Sci. Lond. '70 : 450.

— Benefits of. Everett. Orat. v. 3.

Railroads. Bibliography. Larrabee, W. Railroad question.

— English, Early. Smiles. Engin. 3 : 5.

— — Management of. (W. A. Hunter ; E. J. Watherston) Trans. Soc. Sci. Lond. '82 : 492.

— the farmer, and the public. (E. Atkinson) Econ. tracts, no. 19.

— Higher laws of. Dodge, M. A. Twelve miles, 135.

— in Europe, 1894. U. S. Cons. Rept. 46 : 309.

— in Natal, 1892. U. S. Cons. Rept. no. 149.

— in the U. S. Bryce. Soc. institu. 32. — (T. M. and C. H. Cooley) Shaler. The U. S. 2 : 65.

— Locking-in passengers on. Smith, Syd. Wits & wis. 345.

— Management of. Ruskin. Arrows, v. 2.

— mortgages on, Rights of employees as against. (G. T. Bispham) Am. Bar Assoc. 3 : 167.

— of the west. Barrows, W. U. S. of yester. 314.

— Relations of, to the public. Hazard, R. G. Econ. & pol. 32.

— Speeches on act to equalize charges for carrying freight. Hazard, R. G. Econ. & pol. 45, 74.

— State and. Arnold, A. Soc. pol. — Jevons. Meth. soc. ref.

— State control of. Lusk, H. H. Foes at home, 169.

— Stephenson and. Boyd. Crit. ess. 249.

— Strict regulations on. Guild. Abroad again, 92.

— vs. waterways. (L. M. Haupt) Deep waterways conven. 1 : 118.

Railway book-stalls. Wynter, A. Our soc. bees, 1 : 304.

Railway profits and deep waterways. (E. R. Johnson) Deep waterways conven. 1 : 112.

Railway routes, Choice of. Moltke. Ess. 1 : 221.

Railway season-tickets. Wynter, A. Peep, 2 : 55.

Raimbach, Abraham, An English engraver in Paris. Dobson, A. Miscel. 144.

Raimondi, Marc' Antonio, Italian engraver. Spooner. Biog. fine arts, 2 : 760.

Rain. Proctor. Sci. by-ways, 243.

— Beneficial effects of. Kingsley, C. San. lec. 131.

— Forcing power of. Proctor. Light sci. 1 : 225.

— how formed. (H. F. Blanford) Smithson. Rept. '89 : 287.

— Is it going to rain ? Burroughs, J. Locusts, 77.

— Leveling power of. Proctor. Pleas. ways, 367 ; also in Estes. Half-hour recre. 428.

Rain-water in streets, Strainers for. (M. Uribe) Am. Pub. Health, 18 : 169.

Rainaldi, Carlo. Milizia. Lives arch. 2 : 199.

Rainbow, The. (H. E. Roscoe) Manch. Sci. lec. 3–4 : 145.

— and its congeners. Tyndall. New frag. 199.

"Rainer," ship, Wreck of. Kelley, J. D. J. Ship's co. 187.

Rainy day. Hunt. Day by fire, 292 ; or Seer, 1 : 154.

Raisin River, Battle and massacre. Dawson. Batt. of U. S. 2 : 194.

Rájendralála Mitra, Raja. Cust. Ling. & orient. ess. 4 : 73.

Rajpútána. Lyall. Asia, 181.

— Visit to, 1884. Hübner. Thro' Brit. empire, 2 : 45.

Rakóczy II. Wyatt, W. J. Hunga. celeb. 95.

Rale, Sebastian, patriarch of Norridgewock. Gilman. Pathfinders, 176. — Parkman. Half-cent. 1 : 204.

Raleigh, Sir Walter. Barrow, J. Nav. worthies, 377. — With portrait. Bolton, S. K. Fam.

voyag. 154. — Bourne, H. R. F. Eng. seam, 1 : 180, 260. 2 : 298. — Collier, W. F. Hist. Eng. lit. 150. — Edgar. Sea-kings, 154. — Ewald. Studies, 164. — Fuller. Worthies, 1 : 419. — Gilman. Pathfinders, 54. — Langford. Prison books, 83. — Lawrence. Brit. historians, 1 : 31. — Lodge. Portraits (Bohn), v. 3. — Mitchell, D. G. English lands, 2 : 19. — Ross, G. Studies, 118. — Strickland. Queens Eng. v. 7. — (J. W. Hales) Ward. Eng. poets, 1 : 486. — Wotton. Word portraits, 244. — Choate, I. B. Wells of Eng. 117. — Farrar. Soc. & p. day quest. 228. — Deshler. Afternoons, 89. — Macdonald, G. England's antiphon, 71. — Parker, H. F. Morning stars, 137. — Southey & Bell. Brit. adm. v. 4. — Winthrop. Addresses, 3 : 263. — Wrangham. Brit. Plutarch, v. 2.

Raleigh, Sir Walter, and his time. Kingsley, C. Plays and p. 81 ; *or* Raleigh, 1.

— and Queen Elizabeth. Menzies, S. Roy. fav. 1 : 271.

— and Richard Grenville. Belknap. Amer. biog. 1 : 289.

— and Spenser. Morley, H. Eng. writ. 9 : 92, 373.

— Confession and execution of. Winthrop, R. C. Addresses, 3 : 263.

— Explorations in Guiana. Frost, T. Explorers, 192.

— Last hours of. Disraeli, I. Curios. (N. Y. 4 v.) 3 : 459.

— Psychological history of. Disraeli, I. Amen. (N. Y. 2 v.) 2 : 254.

— Secret history of. Disraeli, I. Curios. (N. Y. 4 v.) 3 : 445.

— Sidney and. Whipple. Lit. Eliz. 250.

Raleigh's Colony, Surroundings and site of. (T. Williams) Am. Hist. Assoc. Rept. '95 : 47.

"Raleigh," frigate, Loss of. Dawson. Batt. of U. S. 1 : 455.

Ralph of Escures, 1114–22. Hook. Abps. Cant. 2 : 277.

Ralph, James. Lawrence. Brit. historians, 2 : 232.

Rama, the Indian hero. Cust. Pic. of Indian life, 150.

Ramabai Sarasvati. Chapman, E. F. Sk. Ind. wom. 26.

Ramapo valley. Willis. Hurry-graphs, 124.

Ramáyana, The ; a Sanskrit epic. Cust. Ling. ess. 56. — Reed. Hindu literature, 153. — Williams. Indian wisdom, 337.

Rambaldoni, Vittorino de. *See* Feltre, Vittorino.

Rambaud, Alfred. Warner Lib. 21 : 12041.

Rambler, Sketches of occasional contributors to the. Drake, N. Ess. Rambler, 2 : 35.

Rambouillet, House of. Doran. Knights, 263.

— Hôtel de. Mason, A. G. Wom. of Fr. salons, 10.

Ramcke, J. H. Senior. Biog. sk. 313.

Rameau, Jean Philippe. Ferris, G. T. Ital. & Fr. compos. 126.

— Works of. Hogarth. Mem. opera, 2 : 207.

Rameses. *See* Zoan.

Rameswaram, and its temple. Shoemaker, M. M. Quaint corners, 1.

Ramie industry in France. U. S. Cons. Rept. no. 158.

Ramie spinning machinery, 1895. (C. Meeker) U. S. Cons. Rept. 49 : 172.

Ramillies, Battle of. Adams, W. H. D. Engl. at war, 1 : 137. — Adams, W. H. D. Battle sto. 186. — King, C. Battles, 329. — Lowe, C. R. Great battles, 90.

Rammohun Roy, Rajah. Müller. Biog. ess. 1.

Ramsay, Allan. Irving, D. Scot. poets, 2 : 309. — (W. Minto) Oliphant. Royal Edinburgh, 435. — Veitch. Feeling for nature in Scottish poetry, 2 : 24. — Ward. Eng. poets, 3 : 159. — Wilson, J. G. Poets of Scot. 1 : 101. — Masson. Edinb. sk. 88. — With portrait. Warner Lib. 21 : 12061.

Ramsay, Allan (K.), painter, a rival of Reynolds. Dobson, A. 18th cent. vign. 3 : 148. — Cook, D. Art in Eng. 123.

Ramsay, David. With portrait. [Amer.] Nat. portr. gall. v. 3. — Lossing. Em. Amer. 167. — Moore, F. Am. eloq. 1 : 308. — Perry, B. F. Biog. sketches, 1 : 496.

Ramsay, M. J. Boyle, E. Dist. Marylanders.

Ramsay family. Taylor, J. Fam. of Scot. 1 : 308.

Ramsden, Jesse, English optician. Craik. Pursuit knowl. 2 : 278. — Howe, H. Em. mech. 313.

Ramsden dividing engine. (J. E. Watkins) Smithson. Rept. '90 : 721.

Ramsgate, A holy voyage to, 1787. Ashton. 18th cent. waifs, 278.

Ramsgate lifeboat, The. Treanor, T. S. Heroes Goodw. sands, 213.

Ramsour's Mill, Battle of. Dawson. Batt. of U. S. 1 : 592.

Ramus, Peter. Owen, J. Skeptics French, 493.

Rance, Chevalier de, and the Trappists. Doran. Knights, 94.

Randall, Andrew. (A. M. Alger) N. E. Hist.-Gen. Soc. Biog. 3 : 70.

Randall, Henry S. Davidson, J. W. Writ. of South, 438.

Randall, James Ryder. Davidson, J. W. Writ. of South, 439. — Derby, J. C. Fifty years, 661.

Randolph, Edmund. Lossing. Em. Amer. 170. — Moore, F. Am. eloq. 1 : 163.

Randolph, George Engs. Bartlett, J. R. R. I. officers, 408.

Randolph, Innis. Davidson, J. W. Writ. of South, 449.

Randolph, Jacob, 1796–1848. (J. Aitken Meigs) Gross. Lives physicians, 512.

Randolph, John. With portrait. [Amer.] Nat. portr. gall. v. 4. — Baldwin. Party leaders, 135. — With portrait. Duyckinck. Nat. portr. gall. 2 : 88. — Magoon. Orators of rev. 421. — Parton. Fam. Amer. 173. — Russell, H. P. Charac. 195. — Johnston, A. Amer. ora. 1 : 164. — Lossing. Em. Amer. 292. — Moore, F. Am. eloq. 2 : 155. — Nichol. Amer. lit. 100. — Perry, B. F. Biog. sketches, 1 : 382. — Richardson. Amer. lit. 1 : 212. — Trent. South. statesm. 89.

— Visits to. Quincy, J. Figures, 209.

Randolph, Mrs. Martha Jefferson. With portrait. Holloway, L. C. Ladies, 136. — (S. H. Randolph) Wister & Irwin. Women, 9.

Randolph, Peyton. Lossing. Em. Amer. 84.

— Biographical sketch of. Jefferson. Works, 8 : 477.

Randolph, Theodore F., with portrait. Rogers, A. C. Repres. men, 449.

Randolph, Thomas. Bell, R. Lit. & sci. men, 2 : 183. — (E. W. Gosse) Ward. Eng. poets, 2 : 219. — Choate, I. B. Wells of Eng. 236. — Griswold, R. W. Sac. poets.

— at the court of Mary, queen of Scots. Strickland. Queens Scot. 3 : 4.

Randolph, Thomas. Woollen. Biog. sk. Indiana, 391.

Randolph family of Virginia. Glenn, T. A. Colon. mans. 1 : 433.

"Randolph," frigate, Loss of. Dawson. Batt. of U. S. 1 : 374.

Randolph-Macon College, Boydton, Va. U. S. Bur. Ed. Circ. '88, no. 1 : 240.

Ranelagh. Dobson, A. 18th cent. vign. 269.

Ranelegh, Katharine (Boyle) Jones, Lady. Anderson, Jas. Mem. wom. Pur. 2 : 108.

Rangoon. Shoemaker, M. M. Quaint corners, 101.

Rank. Schopenhauer. Wisdom, 72.

Ranke, Leopold von. (E. G. Bourne) Am. Hist. Assoc. Rept. '96, 1 : 65. — Am. Hist. Assoc. Papers, 3 : 101. — With portrait. Warner Lib. 21 : 12074.
— Bibliography. (W. Price) Am. Hist. Assoc. Ann. Rept. '96, 1 : 1263.

Rankin, J. E. Hemenway. Poets of Vt. 126.

Rankin, John H. Am. Bar Assoc. 9 : 536.

Rankin, Thomas. Jackson, T. Early Meth. 3 : 1.

Ranney, Rufus P. Am. Bar Assoc. 15 : 459.

Rantoul, R., jr., Tribute to. Sumner. Works, 3 : 76.

Rantoul family. Essex Inst. Hist. Coll. v. 21.

Raoul of Cambray. Ludlow. Epics, 2 : 142.

Raper, James H., with portrait. Bungay. Penportr. 202.

Raphael. Bolton, S. K. Fam. Europ. art. 105. — Eastlake, C. L. Contrib. 1 : 182. — Eastlake, E. R. Five painters, 2 : 89. — Gebhart, E. Rom. cameos, 181. — Jameson. Ital. painters, 228. — Knox, R. Great artists, 187. — Lee, H. F. Old painters, 121. — Milizia. Lives arch. 1 : 218. — Symonds. Renais. fine arts, 327. — With portrait. Sharp, W. Great minds, 129. — Spooner. Biog. fine arts, 2 : 750. — Taine. Italy, 1 : 150. — Wallace, H. B. Art, 268. — Hundred greatest men, 79. — Jarves. Art stud. 439. — Jervis, Lady. Painting, 1 : 145. — Ottley. Ital. school. — Pastor, L. Hist. popes, 6 : 540. — Pater. Miscel. stud. 26. — Rose, G. B. Renais. masters, 18. — Stillman, W. J. Old Ital. mas. 225.
— Criticisms of his pictures. Guizot. Fine arts, 53.
— Dramatic pictures by. Stearns, F. P. Midsum. Ital. art, 225.
— Drawings by, in the university galleries, Oxford. (G. Butler) Oxf. ess. '55 : 137.
— Evolution of. Stearns, F. P. Midsum. Ital. art. 169.
— in Rome. Fairholt. Homes Rubens, 245.
— Scholars of. Jameson. Ital. painters, 280.
— School of. Symonds. Renais. fine arts, 490.
— Sistine Madonna. (F. A. Gruyer) Singleton, E. Great pic. 45.
— The Transfiguration. (Anna Jameson) Singleton, E. Great pic. 249.
— Virgil, and Tasso. Alison. Ess. 3.

Rapin, Paul de, Sieur de Thoyras. Lawrence. Brit. historians, 2 : 226.

Rappe, Louis Amedeus. Clarke, R. H. Cath. bishops, 3 : 235.

Rappelye, Miss Julia A. (Alice D. Jewett) Haydn, H. C. Am. miss. heroes, no. 10.

Rappoldi, Eduard, with portrait. Ehrlich, A. Cel. violin. 174.

Raree show. Story, A. T. Vagrom, 43.

Rascality, Romance of. Whipple. Ess. & rev. 2.

Raspe, R. A. Baron Munchausen. Saunders, F. Famous books, 63.

Rassam, H., with photo. Cooper, T. Men of mark, 5 : 27.

Rastall, John. Dunham. Lit. & sci. men, 1 : 281.

Ratcliff, Philip, Barbarous punishment of, at Salem, Mass., 1631. Adams, C. F. Three episodes, 1 : 259.

Ratcliff highway, Murders in, 1811. Thornbury. Old stor. 185.

Ratcliffe, Mrs. Jane. Burder. Pious wom. 158.

Rathbone, W., with portrait. Jones, E. R. Heroes of ind. 35.

Rational irregularities, Hygienic value of. (J. F. Hibberd) Am. Pub. Health, 16 : 183.

Rationalism. Balfour, A. J. Founda. belief, 163. Fisher, G. P. Discus. 439 ; also in Bost. lectures, '70 : 240.
— and traditionalism. Brownson. Works, 1 : 490.
— From, to faith. (Egbert C. Smyth) Bost. lectures, '70 : 276.
— German. Lichtenberger. Hist. Ger. theol. 18. — Moore, T. Prose & v. 177.
— in religion. Newman, J. H. Ess. crit. 1 : 30.
— Lecky's History of. Eliot, G. Ess. 160.
— Popular. Shipley, O. Tracts, 429.

Rationality, Sentiment of. James, W. Will to bel. 63.

Ratke, W. Quick. Educ. ref. 103.

Ratlecius, Valentin. Wallace, R. Anti-Trin. biog. 2 : 494.

Rats. Buckland, F. T. Curios. nat. hist. 1 : 56.
— and their doings. Wynter. Fruit, 1 : 207.

Rattan industry in various foreign countries, 1898. U. S. Cons. Rept. 56 : 1.

Rattenbury, John. Wesley & successors, 195.

Rattlesnake dance. Lummis. Strange corners, 42.

Rau, Charles. Am. Antiq. Soc. Proc. n. s. 5 : 18.

Raucourt, Mdlle. Françoise, and the French stage. Hawkins. Fr. stage 18th cent. v. 2.

Raulin, Jean, 1443–1514. Baring-Gould. Preachers, 69.

Rauschmaier, G., Trial of. Feuerbach. Crim. trials.

Ravello. Little, W. J. K. Sketches, 273.

Ravenna. Child, T. Summ. holidays, 177. — Hare. Cities of No. Italy, 2 : 295. — James. Transatl. sketches. — Jarves. Ital. ramb. 155. — Symonds. Sk. So. Eur. 2 : 110. — Tuckerman. Ital. sk. 335. — Warner, C. D. Saunterings, 169.
— Goths at. Freeman. Hist. ess. 3 : 121.
— Sieges of. Robson, W. Sieges, 315.

Ravens, Ralph. McClure. Translators, 170.

Ravenscroft, Edward. Dunham. Lit. & sci. men, 3 : 198.

Ravensworth, H. G. Liddell, earl of. Jones, E. R. Heroes of ind. 51.

Ravis, Thomas. McClure. Translators, 148.

Ravogli, Sofia and Giulia, with portraits. Buffen. Mus. celeb. 2 : 115. — Sala, Mrs. Fam. peop. 194.

Rawle, William, 1759–1832. Brown, D. P. Forum, 1 : 499.

Rawle, William Henry. Am. Bar Assoc. 12 : 369.

Rawle family, of Laurel Hill. Glenn, T. A. Colon. mans. 2 : 123.

Rawlinson, Sir H. C. With photo. Cooper, T. Men of mark, 6 : 4. — Laurie, W. F. B. Dist. Anglo-Ind. 1 : 185.

Rawson, A. Richmond. Bartlett, J. R. R. I. officers, 157.

Rawson, George. Miles, A. H. Poets of cent. 10 : 704. — Miller, Jos. Singers church, 2d ed. 551.

Rawson, Guillermo. Am. Antiq. Soc. Proc. n. s. 7 : 8.

Ray, James Brown. Woollen. Biog. sk. Indiana, 56.

Ray, John. Macgillivray, W. Em. zoöl. — Stoughton, J. Worthies of sci. 175. — Jardine, W. Nat. lib. v. 33.

Ray, John Mead. Morison, J. Fathers of Lond. Miss. Soc. 2 : 558.

Ray, Miss. Fitzgerald, P. Rom. of stage, 259.

Ray, William, b. 1771, d. 1827. Everest. Poets of Conn. 113.

Raymond, George. Barrow, J. Nav. worthies, 484.

Raymond, Henry J. Brockett. Men of our day, 491. — Derby, J. C. Fifty years, 352. — Johnston, A. Amer. ora. 4 : 168. — Mansfield, E. D. Pers. mem. 342.

Raymond, John T. Matthews, B. Actors, 5 : 229. — With portrait. (F. Fyles) McKay, F. E. Fam. actors, 361.

— in Wolfert's Roost. Winter, W. Shadows, 2 : 200.

Raymond, Sir Robert, chief justice of England, 1725-31. Campbell. Ch. just. 2 : 150.

Raynal, Guillaume Thomas François, 1713-96. Vinet. Fr. lit. 18th cent. 350.

Rayner sisters. Clayton, E. C. Eng. fem. art. 2 : 235.

Raynsford, Sir Richard, chief justice of England, 1676-78. Campbell. Ch. just. 2 : 17.

Re, and pro, Latin prepositions. Key, T. H. Philol. ess. 74.

Rea, Mason Archelaus. (H. N. Fisher) Harvard mem. biog. 2 : 38.

Read, George. Dwight, N. Signers of decl. 231. — Lincoln, R. W. Signers, 55. — Lossing. Signers, 137. — Sanderson. Signers, v. 4.

Read, John. Knapp, S. L. Em. lawyers, 153.

Read, John M. Savage. Liv. rep. men, 397.

Read, Mary. Whitehead, C. Highwaymen, 2 : 51.

Read, Thomas Buchanan. Griswold. Poets Amer. 495. — With portrait. Warner Lib. 21 : 12094.

Reade, Charles. Buchanan, R. Look round, 308. — Friswell. Mod. men of l. 77. — Hazeltine. Chats, 326. — McCarthy, J. Mod. lead. 192. — Swinburne. Miscel. 271. — Courtney. Stud. 150. — Wotton. Word portraits, 248. — Coleman, G. Players, 2 : 3. — Couch, A. T. Q. Adv. crit. 124. — Field, R. S. Prov. courts N. J. 158. — Howells. My lit. passions, 191. — With portrait. Warner Lib. 21 : 12103.

— as a dramatist. Archer. Eng. dram. 27.

— Why Dickens more famous novelist than ? (E. Cumpston) Moulton, R. G. Four years' novel, 43.

Reade, Sir William. Jeaffreson. Doctors, 58.

Reader, The desultory. Burton, J. H. Bookhunter, 108.

Readers and reading. Martin, E. S. Cousin Anthony, 15.

Reading. Hare. Guesses, 1 : 209. — Helps. Friends, 1st ser. v. 1. — Lowell. Democ. 105. — Munger. On threshold, 155. — Lubbock. Use of life, 139. — Mabie. My study fire, 2 : 1, 6.

— Abuse of. Quincy, J. P. Protec. 109.

— and spelling, Association tracks in. (T. M. Balliet) Nat. Educa. Assoc. '93 : 756.

— and writing, Exaggerated estimates of. (W. B. Hodgson) Trans. Soc. Sci. Lond. '67 : 393.

— Art of. Ballantyne. Ess. 1.

— between the lines. Arnold, F. Three-cor. ess. 224.

— children's, Observations on. (R. W. Bullock) Nat. Educa. Assoc. '90 : 1015.

Reading, Desultory. Northcote. Lec. & ess. 118.

— Elementary. (G. L. Farnham ; Edwin Leigh) Nat. Educa. Assoc. '73 : 199.

— expression in, Philosophy and application of. (Mary F. Hendrick) N. Y. Regents, 91 : 454.

— for the young. Burnap. Miscel.

— How to read. (A. B. Whipple) N. Y. Regents, 81 : 655.

— in common schools. (T. D. P. Stone) N. Y. Regents, 93 : 529.

— Leigh's method of teaching. (W. M. Bryant) Nat. Educa. Assoc. '73 : 262.

— of new books. Hazlitt. Sket.

— old books. Hazlitt. Plain speaker, v. 2.

— Pleasures of. Balfour, A. J. Ess. 1.

— Private. (E. W. Mundy) N. Y. Regents, 101, app. : 123.

— Sunday. Porter, N. Books, 322.

— Teaching of, by synthetic sound system. (F. B. Gault) Nat. Educa. Assoc. '91 : 572.

— Use and abuse of. Brownson. Works, 19 : 517.

— What shall we read ? Mathews, W. Men, p. & t. 335.

Reading exercise, Object of. (E. O. Vaile) Nat. Educa. Assoc. '80 : 203.

Reading public, The. Mabie. My study fire, 2 : 107.

Reading, Eng. Silloway. Cathedral towns, 121, 127.

Ready writers. Jacox. Aspects, 256.

Real and the ideal. Finlayson, T. C. Ess. 111. — Stearns, F. P. Real, 1.

— and the sham. Mabie. My study fire, 2 : 57.

Real estate, Valuation of. (T. Cochran) Phila. Soc. Sci. Assoc. '74.

Real presence, The. Shipley, O. Tracts, 217.

Real property, Devolution of personal and. (M. Whyte) Trans. Soc. Sci. Lond. '82 : 127.

— Record of title to. (R. D. Urlin ; J. H. Gregson) Trans. Soc. Sci. Lond. '84 : 131.

Realism. Nordau. Degen. 473.

— and idealism. Symonds. Ess. 1 : 168.

— and nominalism. (W. D. Wilson) N. Y. Regents, 96 : 359. — Ullman. Reformers, 299.

— and truth. Jones, H. A. Renascence, 85.

— Dilemma of. Archer, W. Theatre, 329.

— in art. Badeau. Vagabond, 235.

— in fiction, Limits of. Gosse, E. Questions. 135.

— in French literature. Pellissier. Lit. move. Fr. 321.

— Perigot. Paget, V. Juvenilia, 2 : 19.

— Physical. Whittaker, T. Ess. & not. 291.

— Romance, humor, and. Stearns, F. P. Real & ideal, 40.

— Scientific and pseudo-scientific. Huxley. Ess. contro. 184.

Reality and idealism. Royce, J. Spir. mod. philos. 341.

— Appearance and, Bradley on. Seth, A. Man's place, 129.

— as a phenomenon. Whittaker, T. Ess. & not. 298.

— its place in philosophy. (J. McCosh) Cong. Educa. Chic. '93, 682.

— What is ? Ritchie, D. G. Darwin. — Stock. Attempts, 169.

Rearden, Timothy H. Rearden. Petrarch, ix.

Reason and faith. Rands, W. B. Holbeach, 2 : 108.

— — Claims and conflicts of. Rogers, H. Ess. 2 : 250 ; or Reason, 339.

— — Theism of. Hedge, F. H. Martin Luther, 306.

— and the understanding distinguished. Coleridge. Friend, 143.

Reason, Bailey's theory of. Martineau, J. Ess. 2 : 318.
— Descartes on use of. Huxley. Method, 166.
— Dignity of. Brownson. Works, 1 : 439.
— Influence of, on the feelings. Bailey, S. Essays, 140.
— Philosophic and catholic. Brownson. Works, 3 : 180.
— What it can do. Brownson. Works, 1 : 306.
Réaumur, R. A. F. de. Cooper, T. Triumphs of persev. 115. — Duncan, P. M. Botanists, 137. — Macgillivray, W. Em. zoöl.
Reay, Miss, Assassination of. Burke, P. Cel. trials.
Rebekah. Hastings, F. Obscure charac. 176.
Rebellion, right of, Christian teaching on. Oxenham. Stud. in eccl. hist. 171.
Récamier, Madame. Adams, W. H. D. Fam. beauties, 2 : 273. — Bolton. Famous types, 62. — Mason, A. G. Women of Fr. salons, 264. — Lord, J. Beacon, 5 : 349. — Maceuen. Celeb. 125. — Russell. Extr. women, 205. — Thomson, K. & J. C. Queens, 289.
— Souvenirs and correspondence of. Cranbourne. Hist. sk. 1 : 303.
Recanati. Jarves. Ital. ramb. 113.
Recess or no recess in schools. (Committee on hygiene) Nat. Educa. Assoc. '84, app. : 9. — (J. H. Hoose) Nat. Educa. Assoc. '85 : 414.
Rechabites. Guthrie, T. Out of harness, 338.
Reciprocity. Cleveland, R. E. Eliot, 27. — Internat. Amer. conference, 1889–90, Reports, 1 : 103.
Recitation. (George Howland) Nat. Educa. Assoc. '89 : 240.
Recitation estimates. (A. R. Taylor) Nat. Educa. Assoc. '90 : 744.
Recke, Matilda Volmerstein, Countess von der. Hack. Consec. wom. 169.
Reclus, E., on the United States. (G. C. Hurlbut) Am. Geog. Soc. 24 : 379.
Recluses ; Anchoresses or female recluses. Cutts, E. L. Scenes mid. ages, 120.
Recognition [in international law], Letters on. Harcourt, W. V. Letters fr. Times.
Recollections as a source of history. (E. L. Pierce) Mass. Hist. Soc. Proc. 2d ser. 10 : 473 ; or Pierce, E. L. Addresses, 375.
Reconstruction of the Southern States. Blaine. Twenty years in Congress, 2 : 34. — Dixon, W. H. White conquest, v. 2. — Garfield. Works, 1 : 95, 243, 390. — Tilden. Writings, 1 : 341, 394.
Recording laws of the U. S. (T. M. Cooley) Am. Bar Assoc. 4 : 199.
Recreation. Arnold, F. Three-cor. ess. 239. — Helps. Friends, 1st ser. v. 1. — Haweis. Curr. coin. — Lubbock. Use of life, 62. — Mabie. Ess. on work, 170. — Romanes. Ess. 164.
— and literature, Duty of the church toward. Meath. Soc. arrows, 369.
— as a sanitary agent. (J. W. Hageman) Wisc. Health, '80 : 18.
— Bodily repairs. Wynter. Curios. of toil, 1 : 170.
— Christian, and amusement. (T. L. Cuyler) Graham & Collar. Pulpit and rost. v. 1.
— Ethics of. (R. Eyton) Wace, H. Lond. mission. 109.
— Healthful. (C. H. Brigham) Mich. Health, '77 : 29. See Relaxation.
Reculver. Timbs. Abbeys, 1 : 291.
Recusants. Baring-Gould. Yorks. odd. 2 : 229.
— Hampshire, temp. Q. Elizabeth. Gasquet, F. A. Old Eng. Bible, 319.

Red Cross Society. (J. Turley) Cong. Char. Chic. '93, 5 :657.
— Bibliography. Waltham (Mass.) Pub. Lib. Bull. Sept. '98.
Red-disease among swine in Mexico. (J. L. Gomez) Am. Pub. Health, 16 : 168.
Red Jacket. Lossing. Em. Amer. 264. — Moore, F. Am. cloq. 1 : 423
Red men, Books about. Lang. Lett. on lit. 182.
Red race, Antiquity of, in America. (Thomas Wilson) U. S. Nat. Mus. Rept. '95 : 1039.
Red Sea. Field, H. M. Egypt to Japan, 106.
Red-tape, British official. Butler, E. Gentle ways, 161.
Reddish, Samuel. Doran. Annals stage, 2 : 217.
Redemption, Philosophy of. Whittaker, T. Ess. & not. 218.
Redemptioners. Ashton. 18th cent. waifs, 112.
Redemptive work, Power of personality in. (A. Mackay-Smith) Conf. char. & correc. '90 : 16.
Redesdale, J. F. Mitford, Lord. With photo. Cooper, T. Men of mark, 1 : 29. — Townsend. Twelve judges, 2 : 145. — Grant, J. Recoll. Lords & Comm. 1 : 118.
Redfield, Isaac F. (W. G. Veazey) Memo. of judges fr. Dartm. 95.
Redfield, J. S. Derby, J. C. Fifty years, 585.
Redgrave, Frances. Clayton, E. C. Eng. fem. art. 2 : 239.
Redgrave, R. With photo. Cooper, T. Men of mark, 3 : 5. — Wilman, G. Sk. liv. celeb. 141.
Redi, F. Macgillivray, W. Em. zöol.
Redmond, Charles P. Am. Bar Assoc. 12 : 347.
Redmond, Mary. Clement, J. Noble deeds, 134.
Redoch, Wilhelm Davidsz. Wallace, R. Anti-Trin. biog. 3 : 317.
Reece, Richard. Wesley & successors, 91, 137.
Reece, Robert. Archer. English dramatists. — Wilman, G. Sk. liv. celeb. 110.
Reed, Andrew. Blaikie, W. G. Leaders, 161. — Grant, Jas. Metropol. pul. 345. — Hatfield, E. F. Poets of ch. 505. — Japp, A. H. Leaders of men, 331. — Miles, A. H. Poets of cent. 10 : 675. — Miller, Jos. Singers church, 2d ed. 400.
Reed, Sir Charles, with photo. Cooper, T. Men of mark, 4 : 13. — Ritchie. Brit. sen. 212.
Reed, Elizabeth. Miller, Jos. Singers church, 2d ed. 439.
Reed, Mrs. Esther. Clement, J. Noble deeds, 80. — Ellet. Women of revol. 1 : 36.
Reed, Henry. Am. Bar Assoc. 19 : 677. — Reed, W. B. Among books, 256.
Reed, Joseph. Lossing. Em. Amer. 207. — Neven, D. R. B. Pennsylvanians, 138.
Reed, Peter Fiske. Coggeshall. Poets of west, 413.
Reedy, Sallie Ada. Freeman, J. D. Wom. of South, 435.
Rees, David. Ivimey. Eng. Bapt. 3 : 526.
Reeve, Clara. Jeaffreson. Novelists, 1 : 269. — Scott, W. Biog. mem. v. 1.
Reeve, John. Jessopp, A. Coming of friars, 306.
Reeves, Helen B. (Mathers), with portrait. Black, H. C. Wom. authors, 68.
Reeves, Sims, with portrait. Buffen, F. F. Mus. celeb. 87.
— at Beulah Hill. Yates, E. H. Celeb. 3 : 55.
Reference books, Practical use of. (Mary W. Hinman) Nat. Educa. Assoc. '80 : 194.
Referendum in America. (E. P. Oberholtzer) Univ. Pa. Publ. Pol. Econ. 4 : no. 12.
— of Switzerland. Bibliography. Deploige, S. Referendum of Switz.
Reflection, Powers of. Clarke, J. F. Self-culture, 131.

Renaissance, The, in Italy, skepticism of, Causes of. Owen, J. Skeptics Ital. 3.
— — Symonds's. Hueffer. Ital. stud. 62.
— in literature and art. Pastor, L. Hist. popes, 2 : 163.
— in Spain. Washburn, E. Span. mast. 15.
— Manners and customs of. Taine. Italy, 1 : 170.
— Meaning and value of. Symonds. Renais. It. lit. 2 : 488.
— Mediæval spirit and. Cotterill. Introd. to study of poetry.
— Michael Angelo and. Lilly. Chapters, 2 : 1.
— Nature of. Paget, V. Euphorion, 1 : 27.
— Paul II. and. Pastor, L. Hist. popes, 4 : 36.
— Spirit of. Symonds. Age of despots, 1.
Renan, Ernest. Church, R. W. Occ. pap. 2 : 190, 237. — Pellissier. Lit. move. Fr. 396. — Darmesteter. Sel. ess. 178. — Em. persons, 5 : 263. — Stuart, H. Paris days, 131. — Griswold, H. T. Personal sk. 32. — With portrait. (F. Brunetière) Warner Lib. 21 : 12149. — Hutton, R. H. Criticisms, 2 : 227. — Rogers, H. Ess. fr. G. W. 511. — With portrait. Brandes. Em. auth. 147. — Myers. Ess. mod. 163. — Saintsbury. Miscel. ess. 114.
— and his criticism of Christ. (W. G. Elmslie) Liv. papers, v. 4.
— and Marcus Aurelius. Smalley. Lond. lett. 1 : 332.
— The apostles. Deutsch. Lit. rem. 197.
— Early life of. Pearson, C. N. Reviews, 289.
— Renanism. Tollemache. Ess. & mock-ess. 50.
Rendu, Jeanne Marie, afterwards Sister Rosalie. Belloc. Vignettes, 51.
Renée, duchess of Ferrara. Chapman, W. Women of ref. 239. — Wittenmeyer. Women reform. 99. — Stoughton. Ital. reformers, 193.
Rennell, Thomas. Smith, Syd. Ess. fr. Ed.
Rennequin, Swalm. Brightwell. Heroes of lab. 203.
Rennie, George and John. Smith, G. B. Leaders mod. ind. 442.
Rennie, Sir John. Brightwell. Heroes of lab. 124. — Parton. Capt. indus. 372. — Smiles. Engin. 2 : 93. — Walker, W., jr. Men of sci. 96.
Rensselaer Polytechnic Institute. (P. C. Ricketts) U. S. Bur. Ed. Rept. '91–92 : 757.
Rent, Doctrine of. Walker, F. A. Discuss. in econ. 1 : 417.
— price and, Early history of. Maine. Vill.-com. 175.
Rents, Ground, in Phila. (E. P. Allinson; B. Penrose) Univ. Pa. Publ. Pol. Econ. 1 : no. 3.
Renwick, James. Blaikie, W. G. Preachers Scot. 178.
Repentance, Fruits meet for. Boyd. Towards sunset, 191.
— The great voice from Heaven; a sermon. Boyd. Graver tho'ts, 289.
— Place of, in the experience of a Christian. Hall, John. Papers, 238.
Repingdon, Philip, cardinal priest. Williams, R. F. Eng. card. 2 : 3.
Reporting, Parliamentary. Hatton. Jour. Lond. 179.
Repose in activity. Warner, C. D. As we go, 117.
Representation, American on. Fawcett. Ess. & lec. 318.
— and misrepresentation. Boyd. Recreat. 1 : 25.
— of the people, 1866. Gladstone. Speeches (1869), 17.
— Proportional. Commons, J. R. Soc. reform, 155. — De Vere. Ess. 162. — Fawcett. Ess. &

lec. 336. — Field, D. D. Speeches, 2 : 71. — (S. D. Horton) Phila. Soc. Sci. Assoc. '73.
Representation, Proportional, and municipal reform. (J. W. Jenks) Nat. Conf. City Govt. 2–3 : 129. — (W. D. Foulke) Nat. Conf. City Govt. 4 : 135.
— — Bibliography. Providence Pub. Lib. Bull. Dec. '96. See Minority representation.
— Quality the prevailing element in. (W. B. Weeden) Am. Antiq. Soc. Proc. n. s. 9 : 339.
Representative government. Brodrick. Pol. stud. 1. — Spencer, H. Ess. (N. Y.) 163.
— Abuse of. (S. H. Perkins) Peabody, E. P. Æsthetic pap. 174.
Representative men. Froude. Short stud. 1 : 465.
Representatives, Popular choice of. (L. Stephen) Ess. on reform, '67 : 85.
Repression at long range. Higginson. Conc. all, 204.
Reproduction in kind. Holland, J. G. Lessons, 54.
Repton Club. (H. Legge) Knapp, J. M. Univ. 131.
Republic, The, Influence of, in literature. Zola. Exper. novel, 373.
— Pillars of the. Higginson. Conc. all, 1.
Republican party. Thompson, D. G. Politics in dem. 52.
— and secession. Seward. Works (1884), 4 : 410.
— arraigned. Black, J. S. Essays, 300.
— Beginning of. Birney, J. G., and his times.
— Principles of. Putnam, J. O. Addresses, 349.
Republicanism, Is Europe tending to? Hadley, J. Ess. 361.
— monarchy and democracy. Lorimer, Jas. Studies, nat'l & internat.
— Triumph of, 1861. Lyon, N. Last pol. writ. 204.
Republics, Ancient. Newman, F. W. Essays, 219.
— Minor American. Higginson. Book & heart, 97.
— Thoughts on. Saintsbury. Miscel. ess. 161.
Repudiation. (G. W. Green) Econ. tracts, no. 11.
— in the U. S. Smith, Syd. Wit & miscel. 353.
Repulsive, Attraction of the. Warner, C. D. As we go, 85.
Reputation. Schopenhauer. Wisdom, 59.
— Desire of. Barnes, A. Miscel. 2 : 167.
— Honor and. Bacon. Ess.
— Posthumous. Bulwer, E. Caxtoniana, 331.
Requier, Augustus Julian. Davidson, J. W. Writ. of South, 454.
Resaca de la Palma, Battle of. Dawson. Batt. of U. S. 2 : 451.
Resé, Frederick. Clarke, R. H. Cath. bishops, 3 : 266.
Research and general study. (R. Virchow) Smithson. Rept. '94 : 653.
— as a means of education. (H. E. Roscoe) Owens College essays, '74 : 21.
— Endowment of. (Mark Pattison) Ess. end. research, 3. — (R. Hamilton) Trans. Soc. Sci. Lond. '82 : 319.
— — as a form of productive expenditure. (C. E. Appleton) Ess. end. research, 86.
— Original, in college education. (J. H. Wright) Nat. Educa. Assoc. '82 : 91.
— Spirit of. Schouler, Jas. Hist. briefs, 22.
— Unencumbered. (H. C. Sorby) Ess. end. research, 149.
Resentment as a virtue. Oxenham. Short stud. 38.

Rimini, Malatestas of. Robinson, A. M. F. End of mid. a. 273.
— Sieges of. Robson, W. Sieges, 258.
Rimmon, House of. (E. D. A. Morshead) Tollemache. Ess. & mock-ess. 166.
Rindge, Frederick H., and his gifts. Bolton, S. K. Givers, 283.
Rinehart, W. J. Boyle, E. Dist. Marylanders.
Rings, finger, Facts about. Fairholt. Rambles, 71.
— Superstitions concerning. Jones, W. Credulities, 195.
Ringwaldt, Bartholomew. Hatfield, E. F. Poets of church, 507. — Miller, Jos. Singers church, 2d ed. 53. — Winkworth. Chr. singers Germ. 148.
Ringwood, Ralph, Early experiences of. Irving. Crayon pap. 110.
Rinkart, Martin. Miller, Jos. Singers church, 2d ed. 56. — Winkworth. Chr. singers Germ. 182.
Rio Grande, Lower, Resources of. U. S. Cons. Rept. no. 151.
— Commerce of, 1891. (C. Negley) U. S. Cons. Rept. **38** : 51.
Rio Grande College, Rio Grande, O. (J. M. Davis) U. S. Bur. Ed. Circ. '91, no. **5** : 235.
Rio de Janeiro. Brooks, E. S. Gt. cities, 98.
— capital of Brazil. Curtis, W. E. Capitals, 660.
— harbor of, Three years in. Ingram. Hearts of oak, 219.
— in 1846. Wise. Los Gringos, 9.
— in 1854. Hadfield. Brazil, 136.
Rio Tularosa, Prehistoric ruins of the. (U. F. Duff) Am. Geog. Soc. **29** : 261.
Riobujo, Italy. Giostra ; or, Open-air plays in the Apennines. Baxter, L. E. Tusc. stud. 217.
Rion, James Henry. Am. Bar Assoc. **10** : 429.
Rion, Mrs. Mary C. Davidson, J. W. Writ. of South, 470.
Riots at Bristol, Eng., 1831. Thornbury. Old stor. 433.
— O. P., in London, 1809. Mackay. Delusions, **1** : 226. — Thornbury. Old stor. 162.
Ripley, Ezra, D. D. Emerson. Lec. & biog. sk. 355. — (J. B. Thayer) Harvard mem. biog. **1** : 99. — (B. Frost) Ware, W. Am. Unita. **1** : 119.
Ripley, George. Derby, J. C. Fifty years, 193.
— Frothingham, O. B. Transcendentalism, 322. — Richardson. Amer. lit. **1** : 426.
Ripley, Sarah Alden. (E. Hoar) Wister & Irwin. Women, 113.
Ripon, Frederick John Robinson, earl of. Hazlitt. Parl. portr. 173.
Ripon, G. F. S. R., Lord. Grant, J. Recoll. Lords, 367. — Jerdan. Men, 350.
— and India. Smalley. Lond. lett. **1** : 214.
Ripon Cathedral, Bone-house at. Buckland, F. T. Curios. nat. hist. **4** : 174.
Ripon College, Ripon, Wis. (N. S. Fuller and others) U. S. Bur. Ed. Circ. '89, no. **1** : 55.
Ripperda, John William, duke of. Crowe, E. E. For. statesmen, **4** : 268. — Moore, Geo. Lives.
— Wraxall. Remark. adv. **1** : 73.
Rippon, John. Hatfield, E. F. Poets of church, 508. — Miller, Jos. Singers church, 2d ed. 302.
Rist, Johann von. Winkworth. Chr. singers Germ. 188.
Ristori, Adelaide. Elliot, F. Rom. gossip, 319.
— Lewes. Actors, 165. — With portrait. (W. Winter) Parton. Em. wom. 440. — Winter, W. Shadows, **2** : 229.
Ritchie, Andrew, Jr. Loring, J. S. Hundred Bost. ora. 325.
Ritchie, Mrs. Anna Cora Mowatt. Davidson,

J. W. Writ. of South, 471. — Griswold. Fem. poets, 267. — Freeman, J. D. Wom. of South, 80.
Ritchie, Anne Thackeray, with portrait. Warner Lib. **21** : 12273.
Ritchie, Edward Samuel. (A. E. Dolbear) Am. Acad. A. & S. Proc. **31** : 359.
Ritchie, John Stanton, H. B. Reforms, 224.
Ritchie, Montgomery. (S. Eliot) Harvard mem. biog. **1** : 108.
Ritchie, Thomas. Mansfield, E. D. Pers. mem. 338.
Ritner, Joseph, with portrait. Armor. Gov. of Pa. 361.
Ritschl, A. Bibliography. Orr, J. Ritschlian theol.
Rittenhouse, David, with portrait. [Amer.] Nat. portr. gall. v. **2**. — Pennypacker. Hist. sk. 59. — With portrait. Seymour, C. C. B. Seif-made, 114. — Edwards, B. B. Self-taught, 131. — Lossing. Em. Amer. 35. — Wynne. Lit. men Amer. — Youmans. Pioneers sci. 47.
— Eulogium on. Rush, B. Ess. 335.
Ritter, Karl. (A. H. Guyot) Am. Geog. Soc. **2**, pt. **1** : 25.
Ritual as dramatization of myth. (W. W. Newell) Cong. Anthrop. Chic. '93 : 237.
Ritualism. Arnold, F. Our bishops, **2** : 64. — Stanley. Essays, 6. — Thirlwall, C. Remains, **2** : 145, 231.
— and ritual. Gladstone. Glean. **6** : 108.
— in the Church of England. Martineau, J. Studies, 46.
Rivarol, Antoine de. Houssaye. Men of 18th cent. **1** : 197. — Men & women of France, **1** : 206.
— and Chamfort. Saintsbury. Miscel. ess. 42.
Rivas, Duke de. Kennedy. Poets of Spain, 203.
River and harbor bill, Biography of a. Hart. Am. govt. 206; also in Am. Hist. Assoc. **3** : 180.
Rivers, R. H. Davidson, J. W. Writ. of South, 478.
Rivers, William James. Davidson, J. W. Writ. of South, 479.
Rivers and evolution of geographical forms. (A. P. Brigham) Am. Geog. Soc. **24** : 23.
— and valleys. Shaler. Aspects, 143.
— Conservancy boards of. (P. H. Bryce) Am. Pub. Health, **21** : 35. — Am. Pub. Health, **21** : 316.
— Land from deposit of. Allen, Grant. Science in Arc. 123.
— Pollution of. (R. Hering) Am. Pub. Health, **13** : 272. — (S. S. Kilvington) Am. Pub. Health, **15** : 56. — Am. Pub. Health, **13** : 254. — (J. B. Olcott) Conn. Health, '86 : 248. — (S. W. Williston et al.) Conn. Health, '87 : 173. '88 : 237. — (S. Macadam) Trans. Soc. Sci. Lond. '66 : 443. — (S. Macadam et al.) Trans. Soc. Sci. Lond. '80 : 565.
— — in America. (E. Playter) Am. Pub. Health, **12** : 124.
— — in Connecticut. (S. W. Williston) Am. Pub. Health, **13** : 267.
— — in Massachusetts. (S. W. Abbott) Am. Pub. Health, **13** : 259. — (J. P. Kirkwood) Mass. Health, '76 : 23. — (C. F. Folsom) Mass. Health, '77 : 21. — Mass. Health, '78 : 5. — (C. F. Folsom ; W. R. Nichols) Mass. Health, '79 (1st) : 3. — (W. E. Hoyt) Mass. Health, '80 : 3. — (F. P. Stearns) Mass. Health, '90 : 785.
— — Legislation for restraint of. (H. Y. D. Scott) Trans. Soc. Sci. Lond. '74 : 675.

Robertson, Frederick William, and Bp. Ewing. Tulloch. Movements 19th cent.
— Life and letters of. Cobbe, F. P. Darwinism, 95.
— Verny and. Pressensé. Contem. portr. 283.
Robertson, James. (G. Wilson) St. Giles lec. 3 : 316. — Skelton. Ess. 312.
Robertson, John. Espinasse. Lit. recol. 124.
Robertson, Struan. Brown, J. J. Leech, 383.
Robertson, Thomas William. Archer. Eng. dram. 21 — Friswell. Mod. men of l. 345. — Coleman, G. Players, 2 : 140.
Robertson, Walter. Baker, W. S. Portr. of Wash. 105.
Robertson, William. Brougham. Works, 2 : 231. — Collier, W. F. Hist. Eng. lit. 329. — Lawrence. Brit. historians, 1 : 327. — (F. L. Robertson) St. Giles lec. 3 : 189. — Hatfield, E. F. Poets of church, 512. — Miller, Jos. Singers church, 2d ed. 144.
Robertson, William B. Graham, W. Ess. 263. — Ker. Scot. national, 239.
Robeson, Thomas Rodman. (J. C. Davis) Harvard mem. biog. 2 : 250.
Robespierre, M. M. I. Adolphus. Biog. Fr. rev. 2 : 365. — Brougham. Works, 5 : 46. — Morley. Crit. miscel. 1 : 1. — (H. A. Taine) Ferris, G. T. Gt. leaders, 410. — Smythe, G. S. Hist. fancies, 303.
— Speeches of. Stephens, H. M. Ora. Fr. Rev. 2 : 287.
Robethon, John, Sketch of. Agnew. Protes. exiles. 2 : 70.
Robin Hood. Radford, G. H. Shylock, 29.— Stone, J. S. Heart of Eng. 390. — Whitehead, C. Highwaymen, 1 : 1.
— Ballads of. Saunders, F. Famous books, 55. — Wheeler, D. H. By-ways, 69.
Robins, George. Grant, Jas. Portr. pub. char. 2 : 261.
Robins, Rev. Sanderson. Grant. Jas. Metropol. pul. 175.
Robins. Whiting, C. G. Saunterer, 23.
Robinson Crusoe, of Portsmouth. Buckland, F. T. Curios. nat. hist. 3 : 1.
Robinson, Agnes Mary Frances. Bethune, G. W. Brit. fem. poets, 85. — Robertson. Eng. poetesses, 376. — Warner Lib. 21 : 12315.
— Poetry of. Darmesteter. Eng. stud. 171.
Robinson, Alfred Peter. Am. Bar Assoc. 16 : 415.
Robinson, Anastasia. Edwards, H. S. Prima don. 1 : 13. — Hogarth. Mem. opera, 1 : 347. — Clayton, E. C. Queens. 26.
Robinson, Beverly, of New York. Sabine. Loyalists, 562.
Robinson, Charles, Gov. of Kansas, Chapter in life of. (F. W. Blackmar) Am. Hist. Assoc. Rept. '94 : 213.
Robinson, Charles Seymour. Hatfield, E. F. Poets of church, 514.
Robinson, Edward. Griswold. Prose writ. 382.
Robinson, Ezekiel Gilman. Am. Acad. A. & S. Proc. 30 : 572.
Robinson, Frederick. Loring, J. S. Hundred Bost. ora. 524.
Robinson, Frederick John. See Ripon, Earl of.
Robinson, Henry Crabb. Mitchell, D. G. Eng. lands, 4 : 24.
Robinson, Sir Hercules G. R. Escott, T. H. S. Pillars emp. 271.
Robinson, Jack. Burke, B. Viciss. of fam. 2 : 151.
Robinson, James. Redding. Misers, 2 : 91.

Robinson, Jasper. Jackson, T. Early Meth. 3 : 239.
Robinson, Rev. John. (R. Ashton) Mass. Hist. Coll. 4th ser. 1 : 111. — Belknap. Amer. biog. 2 : 254.
Robinson, John, Biogr. acc. of. Playfair, J. Works, v. 4.
Robinson, John L. Woollen. Biog. sk. Indiana, 315.
Robinson, Rev. John T. Grant, J. S. Metropol. pul. 126.
Robinson, Mary D. ("Perdita"). Baker, H. B. Eng. actors, 2 : 79. — Cook, D. Hours w. players, 1 : 61. — Doran. Annals stage, 2 : 212. — Fitzgerald, P. Rom. of Stage, 291. — Williams, Jane. Lit. wom. 204.
Robinson, Richard. Collier. Actors, 268.
Robinson, Robert, 1735-90. Georgian era, 1 : 451. — Broadus. Lec. hist. preach. 223. — Hatfield, E. F. Poets of church, 515. — Ivimey. Eng. Bapt. 4 : 452. — Miller, Jos. Singers church, 2d ed. 263.
Robinson, Solon. Bungay. Off-hand, 186.
Robinson, Stuart. Davidson, J. W. Writ. of South, 483.
Robinson, Thérèse Louise Albertine. Hart, J. S. Fem. prose, 224.
Robinson, William Stevens. Robinson, W. S. Pen-portr. 1.
Robson, Frederick. Matthews, B. Actors, 4 : 189.
Robson, George, and Copley Fielding. Ruskin. Art of Engl. 137.
Robson, Stuart, with portrait. (C. M. Skinner) McKay, F. E. Fam. actors, 352.
Roby, Wm., with portrait. Morison, J. Fathers of Lond. Miss. Soc. 2 : 240.
Rochdale, Eng.; industries, poor laws, and charities. (R. A. Leach) Cong. Char. Chic. '93, 2 : 319.
Roche, Captain. Whitehead, C. Highwaymen, 2 : 127.
Rochefort-Luçay, Victor Henri. Clarétie. Fr. celeb. 2 : 59. — King, F. French pol. lead. 279 — Rae, W. F. Men of 3d repub. 257.
Rochefoucault, Mme. de la. See La Rochefoucault.
Rochelle. See La Rochelle.
Rochester, Henrietta Boyle, Countess of, with portrait. Jameson. Beauties, 201.
Rochester, John Wilmot, earl of. Burnett, G. Lives ; also in Wrangham. Brit. Plutarch, v. 4.— (S. Johnson) Chalmers. Eng. poets, 8 : 231.— Crichton, A. Converts, 1 : 1. — Jesse. Court of Eng. Stuarts, 3 : 254.— Rogers, C. Chr'n heroes, 205. — Street, G. S. Miniatures, 22.
Rochester, N. Y., Municipal reforms in. (J. T. Alling) Nat. Conf. City Govt. '97 : 175.
Rochester Castle. Timbs. Abbeys, 1 : 286.
Rochlitz, Countess von. Wraxall, F. C. L. Remark. adv. 2 : 89.
Rochois, Marthe le, French vocalist. Clayton, E. C. Queens, 43. — Needham. Queens of song.
Rock Hill College, Ellicott City, Md. U. S. Bur. Ed. Circ. '94, no. 2 : 186.
Rockefeller, J. D. Bolton, S. K. Givers, 357.
Rockhill, Daniel H. Winslow, S. N. Biog. Phila. merch. 91.
Rockingham, Chas. W. Wentworth, 2d marquis of. Earle, J. C. Eng. prem. 1 : 289. — Lodge. Portraits (Bohn), v. 8. — Jesse, J. H. Cel. Eton. v. 2.
— Administration of. Lewis, G. C. Ess. on admin.

Rockwell, James Otis. Everest. Poets of Conn. 357. — Griswold. Poets Am. 298.

Rockwell, O. P., a Mormon. Marshall, W. G. Thro' Amer. 214.

Rocky Mount, S. C., Attack on. Dawson. Batt. of U. S. 1 : 604.

Rocky Mountains. Am. Geog. Soc. 1 : 33. — Barker, Lady. Travel. about, 112. — Bryant, E. What I saw, 92. — Dilke. Greater Brit. 104, 142. — Marshall, W. G. Thro' Amer. 131.
— Canadian. Muir. Pic. Calif. 465.
— En route for. Pidgeon. Engineer's holiday, 99.
— Explorations in. (W. H. Brewer) Am. Geog. Soc. 3 : 193.
— In the. Pidgeon. Engineer's holiday, 110.
— Mid-winter excursion in. Rutgers, L. On saddle, 57.
— Mining camps of the. Pidgeon. Engineer's holiday, 129.
— A month in the, 1887. Bates. Year in Gt. Repub. 2 : 234.
— Over the. Rae. Westward, 70.
— Picnic to the. White, John. Sk. Amer. 203.
— Winter grazing in. (B. Alvord) Am. Geog. Soc. 15 : 257.

Rocky Mountain railroads. (J. Douglas) Am. Geog. Soc. 17 : 299.

Rocky Mountain region, Influence of, upon health and disease. (B. E. Fryer) Am. Pub. Health, 2 : 141.

Rod, Edouard. (Grace King) Warner Lib. 21 : 12335.

Rodda, Richard. Jackson, T. Early Meth. 2 : 113.

Rode, Jacques P. J., with portrait. Ehrlich, A. Cel. violin. 94.

Roden, Lord. Grant, J. Recoll. Lords, 143.

Rodenbach, Georges. Crawford, V. M. Stud. for. lit. 175.

Roderick, the pretended Christ, of St. Kilda. Ashton. 18th cent. waifs, 1.

Rodes, Robert E. Pollard. Life of Lee, 524. — Walker, C. D. Biog. Va. Mil. Inst. 440.

Rodger, Alexander. Wilson, J. G. Poets of Scot, 2 : 57.

Rodgers, John, Comm. Headley, J. T. Farragut, 542. — Lossing. Em. Amer. 372.

Rodin, Auguste. Child, T. Art & criticism, 261.

Rodman, Isaac Peace, with portrait. Bartlett, J. R. R. I. officers, 257.

Rodman, William Logan. (T. W. Higginson) Harvard mem. biog. 1 : 59.

Rodney, Cæsar. Dwight, N. Signers of decl. 222. — Lincoln, R. W. Signers, 56. — Lossing. Signers, 133. — Sanderson. Signers, v. 8.

Rodney, George B. Rodney, first Lord. Lodge. Portraits (Bohn), v. 8. — Edgar. Sea-kings, 272. — Johns. Nav. & mil. heroes. — With portrait. Laughton, J. K. Twelve sailors, 275. — Yonge, C. D. Our nav. comm.
— Sea-fight of. Valentine, L. J. Sea-fights, 104.

Rodolph of Hapsburg. Utterton, F. A. Biog. sk. 106.

Rodrigo Dias de Bivar. Utterton, F. A. Biog. sk. 64.

Rodriguez, Simon. Rose. Loyola.

Rodway Manor. Hodges, Eliz. Anc. Eng. homes, 72.

Roe, Marion H. Hemenway. Poets of Vt. 335.

Roebling, John Augustus. Stuart, C. B. Am. engineers, 301.

Roebuck, Benjamin. Perry, B. F. Biog. sketches, 1 : 502.

Roebuck, John, Inventions of. Smiles. Indus. biog.

Roebuck, John A. Reid, T. W. Politicians, 2 : 83. — With photo. Cooper, T. Men of mark, 5 : 6. — Ritchie. Brit. sena. 249. — Em. persons, 2 : 197. — Francis, G. H. Orators, 272.
— at Ashley place. Yates, E. H. Celeb. 3 : 201.

Roemor, Olaus, and the velocity of light. Lodge, O. J. Pioneers, 233.

Roentgen rays. Bibliography. Salem (Mass.) Pub. Lib. Bull. May, '96.

Roger, bishop of Salisbury. Foss. Judges, 1 : 153.

Rogers, Arthur L. Walker, C. D. Biog. Va. Mil. Inst. 458.

Rogers, Henry. Gilfillan. Third gall. 391.

Rogers, Hester Ann. Wise, D. Heroic Meth. 194. — Stevens, A. Women of Meth. 98.

Rogers, Horatio, with portrait. Bartlett, J. R. R. I. officers, 305.

Rogers, James. Jackson, T. Early Meth. 2 : 355.

Rogers, Jas. Blythe. Youmans. Pioneers sci. 368.

Rogers, James E. Thorold. Em. persons, 4 : 283.

Rogers, John, the martyr. (J. Fox) Wrangham. Brit. Plutarch, v. 2.
— Genealogy of. (J. L. Chester) Mass. Hist. Proc. 5 : 486.

Rogers, John, Rev. Headley, J. T. Chaplains Revol. 347.

Rogers, John. Houghton. Kings, 489.

Rogers, Loula Kendall. Raymond, I. Southland wr. 1 : 413.

Rogers, Nathaniel Peabody. Bartlett, D. W. Mod. agit. v. 7. — Whittier. Old portr. 250.

Rogers, Randolph. Clarke, W. J. Amer. sculp. 62.

Rogers, Robert. Drake, S. G. Trag. of wilderness, 109. — Lossing. Em. Amer. 77.

Rogers, Samuel. Brooks, S. W. Eng. poets, 486. — Devey. Mod. Eng. poets, 145. — Hayward, A. Ess. 1 : 60. — Howitt. Homes Br. poets, 2 : 420. — Jerdan. Men, 375. — Martineau, H. Biog. sk. 51. — Mason, E. T. Pers. traits, 3 : 167. — Oliphant. Lit. hist. 3 : 1. — Reed, H. Brit. poets, 2 : 52. — Saunders, F. Famous books, 145. — Wotton. Word portraits, 254. — (H. Taylor) Ward. Eng. poets, 4 : 89. — Hall, S. C. Book of mem. 432. — Miles, A. H. Poets of cent. 1 : 123. — Mitchell, D. G. Eng. lands, 3 : 301. — Procter, B. W. Autob. 148. — With portrait. Warner Lib. 21 : 12345.
— Conversation and poetry of. Roscoe, W. C. Poems and ess. v. 2.
— Human life. Jeffrey, F. Contrib. Ed. Rev.
— Poems. Mackintosh, J. Miscel. 254.
— Sonnet of. Deshler. Afternoons, 223.

Rogers, Wm. Barton. Youmans. Pioneers sci. 410.

Rogers, William Matticks. (J. T. Morse) Harvard mem. biog. 2 : 158.

Roget, P. M. Pettigrew. Med. portr. gall. v. 4.

Rokh the Intrepid. Brooks, E. S. Gt. men's sons, 207.

Roland, Madame. Adams, W. H. D. Noble women, 214. — Chambers's Miscel. no. 91. — Cox & Jones. Romances, 320. — Russell. Extr. women, 39. — Ste.-Beuve. Cel. wom. 93. — Shelley, M. W. Lit. men Fr. v. 2. — Underwood, S. A. Heroines, 11. — Wilson, H. S. Stud. in hist. 266. — Dobson, A. Four Frenchwomen. — Mason, A. G. Wom. of Fr. salons, 235. — Fifty famous women, 121. — Starling, E. Noble deeds wom. 286.
— Bibliography. Tarbell, I. M. Mme. Roland.

Roland, Song of. Ludlow. Epics, 1 : 362. — Symonds. Renais. Ital. lit. **1** : 433. — Mackaye. Abbess Pt. Royal, 44.

Rolando the Paladin. Utterton, F. A. Biog. sk. 49.

Rolfe, Sir Robert. Grant, Jas. Bench & bar, **2** : 40.

Rolica, Battle of. Adams, W. H. D. Engl. at war, **1** : 266.

Rolle, Sir Henry, chief justice of England, 1648–1654. Ch. just. **1** : 340.

Rolleston, George. Flower, W. H. Ess. on museums, 357.

Rollin, Charles, 1661–1741. Vinet. Fr. lit. 18th cent. 71.

Rollins, Edward Ashton, with portrait. Sketches N. H. men, 143.

Rollins, Edward H., with portrait. Sketches N. H. men, 217.

Rollins College, Winter Park, Fla. U. S. Bur. Ed. Circ. '88, no. **7** : 47.

Rollo the Norman. Edgar. Sea-kings, 11. — Utterton, F. A. Biog. sk. 52.

Rollock, Robert. Blaikie, W. G. Preachers Scot. 74.

— and the beginnings of Edinburgh University. Masson. Edinb. sk. 35.

Romaine, William. Kyle, J. C. Chr. leaders, 149.

Roman antiquities in Gaul and Britain. Freeman. Hist. ess. **4** : 49.

Roman Catholic Bar. Sheil, R. L. Sketches, **1** : 119.

Roman Catholic Church. Bellows. Old world, **2** : 40. — (W. Elliott) Why I am, 48. — (B. F. C. Costelloe) Relig. systems, 442.

— accredits herself. Brownson. Works, **8** : 399.

— and the Bible. (R. Seton) Barrows, J. H. Parl. relig. **1** : 662.

— and liberalism. Brownson. Works, **13** : 1.

— and monarchy. Brownson. Works, **18** : 107.

— and paganism. Middleton. Miscel. works, 1752, v. **3**.

— and reason, an imaginary contradiction. Brownson. Works, **3** : 391.

— and slavery. Brownson. Works, **17** : 317.

— and the state. Brownson. Works, **10** : 328.

— Battle of the churches. Martineau, J. Essays, **2** : 119.

— Bibliography. O'Gorman, T. Hist. Roman Ch. in U. S.

— Conversations on. Brownson. Works, **10** : 267. **11** : 165.

— Dangers to. Brownson. Works, **12** : 136.

— Derby's Letters on. Brownson. Works, **7** : 335.

— Errors of. Brownson. Works, **7** : 304.

— in England, Erection of dioceses. Robertson, F. W. Lec. 302.

— — Organization of. Wiseman, N. Ess. **1** : 337.

— in France. Hillebrand. France, 91. — Wilberforce, S. Ess. Quar. **2** : 42.

— in Germany. Pastor, L. Hist. popes, **2** : 105.

— — The Culturkampf. Pressensé. Contem. port. 103. — Spalding, J. L. Ess. & rev. 190.

— — under Emperor Ludwig. Döllinger. Stud. hist. 119.

— in Quebec. Hatton, J. To-day in Amer. **2** : 65.

— in the U. S. Brownson. Works, **20** : 40.

— — 1776-1877. Spalding, J. L. Ess. & rev. 9.

— Independence of. Brownson. Works, **13** : 86.

— Infallibility of. Brownson. Works, **6** : 427.

— The mass. Davis, L. S. Stud. mus. 22.

— Minor rites and offices of. Wiseman, N. Ess. **1** : 469.

— Morality of, during the renaissance. Symonds. Age of despots, 447.

Roman Catholic Church, No salvation outside of. Brownson. Works, **5** : 572.

— not anti-republican. Brownson. Works, **12** : 1.

— not a despotism. Brownson. Works, **20** : 215.

— not hostile to literature and science. Brownson. Works, **6** : 520.

— The only true Christianity. Brownson. Works, **5** : 527.

— "Papal conspiracy exposed." Brownson. Works, **7** : 543.

— The path to. Brownson. Works, **20** : 93.

— Plea for honest treatment of. Brownson. Works, **8** : 299.

— Reformation of: Letter to Gregory XVI. Bushnell. Building to eras, 356.

— Rights of laymen in. Brownson. Works, **12** : 376.

— Dr. Stone's conversion to. Bacon, L. W. Irenics, 59.

Roman Catholic civilization and Protestant. Brownson. Works, **12** : 305.

Roman Catholic Congress at Malines, 1891. Cust. Ling. & orient. ess. **4** : 476.

Roman Catholic disabilities, Removal of, 1822. Canning. Speeches, **4** : 382. — Peel, R. Speeches, **1** : 698. — Grattan, H., sr. Speeches, **3** : 43, 63, 87. — Arnold, T. Miscel. 160. — Gladstone. Speeches, **10** : 309.

Roman Catholic emancipation. Peel, R. Speeches, **1** : 467. — Stanton, H. B. Reforms, 134.

Roman Catholic literature, English. Newman, J. H. Lec. univ. 67.

Roman Catholic philosophy. Brownson. Works, **2** : 468.

Roman Catholic polemics. Brownson. Works, **20** : 107.

Roman Catholic press in the U. S. Brownson. Works, **20** : 50.

Roman Catholic publications, Morality of. Bridgett, T. E. Blunders, 114.

Roman Catholic question. Brownson. Works, **18** : 418.

— in England, 1809-28. Peel, R. Speeches, **1** : 74. — Smith, Syd. Ess. fr. Ed. — Southey, R. Ess. 1832, **2** : 277.

Roman Catholic religion, Needs of humanity supplied by. (J. Gibbons) Barrows, J. H. Parl. relig. **1** : 485.

Roman Catholic secular literature. Brownson. Works, **19** : 293, 575.

Roman Catholic societies. Chatard. Occ. ess. 166.

Roman Catholicism. Hare. Guesses, **1** : 29.

— and the American people. Brownson. Works, **3** : 219.

— and naturalism. Brownson. Works, **8** : 339.

— and non-Catholics. Brownson. Works, **3** : 205.

— and Protestantism. Brownson. Works, **5** : 241. **6** : 244. — Lowell. Writ. **1** : 194. — Spalding, J. L. Ess. & re. 80.

— and reason. Brownson. Works, **3** : 298.

— and the world. Brownson. Works, **3** : 324.

— at home and abroad, 1873. Brownson. Works, **18** : 535.

— Attacks on. Brownson. Works, **12** : 270.

— both Celtic and Germanic. Brownson. Works, **12** : 238.

— Four years' experience of. Brownson. Works, **20** : 1.

— in America. Brownson. Works, **7** : 509.

— in Ireland, and British liberalism. Arnold, M. Mixed ess. 3.

— in Maryland. Kennedy, J. P. Occas. addr. 192.

Roman Catholicism in So. America; authority of the Pope. Wiseman, N. Ess. 1 : 299.
— in U. S. Should we fear? Godwin, P. Pol. ess. 210.
— Prof. Park against. Brownson. Works, 6 : 353.
— Philosophy of. Froude. Short stud. 1 : 155.
— Protestantism, Anglicanism. Hutton. Ess. theol. 1 : 375.
— Relation of, to modern civilization. Fisher, G. P. Discus. 161.
— Restoration of. Ranke. Popes, 2 : 373.
— Revival of. Froude. Short stud. 3 : 93.
— Triumphs of. Ranke. Popes, 2 : 452.
Roman Catholics, Are they right on the school question? Chatard. Occ. ess. 291.
— Claims of. Peel, R. Speeches, 1 : 12, 337, 612.
— in Great Britain, Laws concerning, 1827. Canning. Speeches, 6 : 144.
— — Liberal party and. Arnold, A. Soc. pol.
— — Question of. Lewis, G. C. Ess. on admin.
— in Ireland. Burke. Works (Bohn), 3 : 282.
— — Claims of, 1812. Canning. Speeches, 3 : 293.
— — Laws affecting, 1794. Burke. Works (Bohn), 6 : 5.
— — Petition of, 1805. Grattan, H., sr. Speeches, 4 : 37, 142, 271.
— in Scotland under Mary and James VI. Scott, Mrs. M. M. Abbotsf. 227.
— in the U. S. Brownson. Works, 20 : 23. — Channing. Works, 2 : 261.
— — Rights of. Woodbury, L. Writ. 1 : 495.
— of England and Ireland. Brownson. Works, 16 : 390.
— Our Roman Catholic brethren. Parton. Topics, 132.
— Persecution of. Brownson. Works, 10 : 395.
— Proceedings against. Burton, J. H. Crim. tri. 2 : 117.
— Treatment of English establishment by. Croly. Hist. sk. 120.
Roman city, Buried, in England. Wynter. Subtle brains, 1.
Roman colonies. Brodwick. Pol. stud. 47.
Roman drama. Dunlop, J. Rom. liter. 1 : 328.
Roman emperors and Christianity. Grube, A. W. Heroes, 15.
— Insanity of. Ireland, W. W. Blot, 92.
Roman empire, Holy. Trench. Lec. mediæval, 77.
— — Bryce's history of. Freeman. Hist. ess. 1 : 126.
— Western, Revival of. Lord, J. Beacon, 2 : 58.
Roman history. Dunlop, J. Rom. liter. 2 : 88.
Roman imperialism: three lectures. Seeley, J. R. Lec. & ess. 1.
Roman law and legal education. (H. J. S. Maine) Camb. ess. '56 : 1 ; also in Maine. Vill.-com. 330.
— The family under. Villari. Two 1st cent. Flor. 2 : 6.
— in collegiate education. (W. C. Morey) N. Y. Regents, 91 : 391.
Roman legislation, Origin, history, and influence of. Legaré. Writ. 1 : 502.
Roman literature. Griffin, E. D. Rem. 2 : 272.
— Legaré. Writ. 2 : 52.
See also Latin literature.
Roman oratory. Dunlop, J. Rom. liter. 2 : 177.
Roman poets of the later empire. (H. W. Preston) Warner Lib. 21 : 12357.
Roman Question, About's. Cranbourne. Hist. sk. 1 : 203.
Roman race, Origin of the. Sinclair, T. Humanities, 39.

Roman religion, The. Bettany. World's relig. 418.
Roman theatre. Dunlop, J. Rom. liter. 1 : 516.
Roman tragedy and epic poetry, Early. Conington. Miscel. 294.
Roman wall in Britain. (H. W. Haynes) Am. Geog. Soc. 22 : 157.
— in North of England. Smith, C. R. Retrospec. 1 : 169.
Romance. Scott, W. Ess. on chiv. 127.
— A gossip on. Stevenson, R. L. Mem. 247 ; or Miscel. 1 : 248.
Romance, humor, and realism. Stearns, F. P. Real & ideal, 40.
— mediæval, The three cycles of. MacCallum. Stud. Ger. 131.
— of real life. Howells. Sub. sk. 171.
— Persistence of the. Burton, R. Liter. likings, 70.
— Revival of, in Eng. literature. Courthope. Lib. movem't, 111.
Romance of the rose, French, Analysis of. Besant. Fr. humor. 44.
Romances. Disraeli, I. Curios. (N. Y. 4 v.) 2 : 119.
— English metrical. Morley. English writers, v. 3, 6.
— Mediæval. Lacroix. Science and literature, 363. — Perry, T. S. Eng. lit. 18th cent. 282.
— — in Italy. Symonds. Renais. Ital. lit. 1 : 17.
— Metrical. Minto, W. Eng. poets, 61.
— — Old English. Hales. Folia litt. 1.
Romano, G. Pippi, called. Ottley. Ital. school.
Romanoffs, Insanity of. Ireland, W. W. Blot, 145.
Romans, Greatness of. Smith, Gold. Lec. & ess. v. 1.
— in Greece. Huxley. Ess. contro. 187.
Romantic, Application of the epithet. Foster, J. Dec. of char. 127.
— and classic. Hedge, F. H. Martin Luther, 184. — Stearns, F. P. Real & ideal, 19.
— and classical school in literature. Pater. Apprec. 243.
Romantic movement in French dramatic literature. Matthews, J. B. Fr. dram. 1.
Romantic school, Fiction of the. Wells, B. W. Cent. Fr. fic. 44.
— in German literature. Wells, B. W. Mod. Ger. lit. 290. — Hillebrand. Ger. thought, 228.
— — Literary aspects of. Boyesen, H. H. Ess. Ger. liter. 332.
— — Social aspects of. Boyesen, H. H. Ess. Ger. liter. 281.
Romanticism. Pellissier. Lit. move. Fr. 99.
— Early. Mitchell, D. G. Eng. lands, 3 : 281.
— English. Bibliography. Beers, H. A. Eng. romant. in 18th cent.
— Gautier and. Vincent, L. H. Bibliotaph, 192.
— German. Heine. The romantic school. — Hillebrand. German thought. — Japp. German life, 469.
— Howells and. Trent. Authority, 257.
— Musical. Paget, V. Belcaro, 106.
Rome, Ancient, and modern London. Escott. Politics, 109.
— — Bibliography. Clarke, G. Educa. childr. Rome. — Salem (Mass.) Pub. Lib. Bull. Mar. '95.
— — Home life in. Allen, W. F. Essays, 25.
— — Lex curiata de imperio. Allen, W. F. Essays, 183.
— — Monetary crisis in, A. D. 33. Allen, W. F. Essays, 200.
— and Germany in middle ages. Döllinger. Stud. hist. 58.

Roper, Margaret More. Darton. Fam. girls, 1.
— Williams, Jane. Lit. wom. 40. — Yonge.
Good wom. 2 : 36. — With portrait. Fifty
famous women, 53. — Owen, Mrs. O. F. Heroines domes. 53.

Roper, Mary. Williams, Jane. Lit. wom. 56.

Ropes, Henry. (H. M. Rogers) Harvard mem.
biog. 2 : 304.

Rosa, Parepa. See Parepa.

Rosa, Salvator. Cooper, T. Triumphs of perse-
verance, 60. — Urbino, Mrs. S. R. Princes. —
Hazlitt. Crit. on art. ser. 2. — Ottley. Ital.
school. — Jervis, Lady. Painting, 2 : 12.
— Criticisms of his pictures. Guizot. Fine arts,
171.

Rosalie, Sister. See Rendu, J. M.

Rosalind, Shakespeare's. Martin. Shakesp. female, 227.
— Spenser's. Jameson. Loves of poets.

Rosati, Joseph. Clarke, R. H. Cath. bishops,
1 : 353.

Roscher, Wm. Principles of political economy.
Leslie, T. E. C. Ess. pol. & mor. 95.

Roscoe, Wm. Espinasse. Lanc. worth. v. 2. —
Coleridge. Nor. worthies, 3 : 1. — Tuckerman.
Charac. 1 : 105.

Roscommon, W. Dillon, earl of. (S. Johnson)
Chalmers. Eng. poets, 8 : 255. — Miller, Jos.
Singers church, 2d ed. 96.

Rose, St., of Lima, with portrait. Murray, J.
O'K. Cath. heroes, 311.

Rosé, Arnold, with portrait. Ehrlich, A. Cel.
violin. 180.

Rose, Ernestine L. Underwood, S. A. Heroines,
255.

Rose, George. Hazlitt. Parl. portr. 181.

Rose, Hugh J. Burgon. Twelve men, 1 : 116.

Rose, Samuel Patrick. Am. Bar Assoc. 16 : 411.

Rose, Susan Penelope. Clayton, E. C. Eng. fem.
art. 1 : 54.

Rose family of Kilravock. Skelton. Ess. 100.

Rose, The, in poetry, Pathos of. Symonds. Ess.
2 : 197.

Rose castle. Venables, E. Episc. palaces, 209.

Rose Polytechnic Institute, Terre Haute, Ind.
U. S. Bur. Ed. Circ. '91, no. 1 : 130.

Rosebery, A. Primrose, Lord. Barrie. Edinburgh eleven, 7. — Hapgood, N. Lit. statesm.
3. — Smalley. Stud. 194, 270.
— as public speaker. Smalley. Lond. lett. 1 : 205.
— at the Durdans. Yates, E. H. Celeb. 3 : 287.

Rosecrans, Sylvester Horton. Clarke, R. H.
Cath. bishops, 3 : 250.

Rosecrans, Gen. William Starke. Duyckinck.
Nat portr. gall. 2 : 451. — Shanks. Rec. of gen-
erals, 258. — (J. W. de Peyster) Rogers, A. C.
Repres. men, 459.

Rosenroth, Christian Knorr von. Hatfield, E. F.
Poets of church, 518.

Roses of Kilravock. Skelton, J. Ess. in hist.
100.
— War of. George, H. B. Battles, 101. — Warner, B. E. Eng. hist. 169.

Rosewell, Gloucester Co., Va. Glenn, T. A.
Colon. mans. 1 : 171. — Page. Old South. 211.

Rosicrucian philosophy, The. Wallace, H. B.
Lit. crit. 173.

Rosicrucianism and Freemasonry. Soane.
New curios. 2 : 35.

Rosicrucians. DeQuincey. Works (Masson),
13 : 384. — Heckethorn. Sec. soc. 1 : 224. —
King. Gnostics. — Vaughan. Hours with
mystics, 2 : 128.

Rosier, Prudent, Trial of, 1846. Clinton, H. L.
Extraor. cases, 29.

Roslyn, Alex. Wedderburn, earl of. Foss.
Judges, 8 : 385.

Ross, Alexander. Irving, D. Scot. poets, 2 : 343.
— Wilson, J. G. Poets of Scot. 1 : 137.

Ross, Anna Maria. Brockett. Woman's work,
343. — Moore, F. Women of the war, 341.

Ross, Charles H. Wilman, G. Sk. liv. celeb. 85.

Ross, George. Dwight, N. Signers of decl. 219.
— Lincoln, R. W. Signers, 57. — Lossing.
Signers, 130. — Sanderson. Signers, v. 8. —
Neven, D. R. B. Pennsylvanians, 85.

Ross, Sir Hew D., Maj.-Gen. Cole, J. W. Brit.
generals, v. 2.

Ross, Sir James Clark. Jerdan. Men, 381.

Rossbach, Battle of. Carlyle. Batt. Fred. the
Gt. 106.

Rossburgh, John. Headley, J. T. Chaplains
Revol. 158.

Rosse, Earl of. Ball, R. Great astron. 272.

Rossellino, Antonio. Symonds. Renais. fine
arts, 153.

Rosser, Leonidas. Davidson, J. W. Writ. of
South, 484.

Rossetti, Christina G. Benson, A. C. Ess. 268.
— Forman. Liv. poets, 231. — Robertson.
Eng. poetesses, 338. — Taylor, B. Crit. ess.
330. — Gosse, E. Crit. kit-kats. — Griswold,
H. T. Personal sk. 281. — With portrait. (W.
M. Payne) Warner Lib. 21 : 12397. — With
portrait. Hubbard, E. Little journeys, 3 : 145.
— Symons, A. Stud. two lit. 135. — (A. Symons)
Miles, A. H. Poets of cent. 7 : 417. — Miles,
A. H. Poets of cent. 10 : 597. — Miller, Jos.
Singers church, 2d ed. 578.
— Bibliography. Bell, H. T. M. C. Rossetti.
— Burden of. Noble, J. A. Impressions, 55.

Rossetti, Dante Gabriel. (P. W. Nicholson)
Baildon. Round table. — Buchanan, R. Look
round, 152. — Dawson, W. J. Mod. Engl. 341.
— Pater. Apprec. 228. — Sharp. Vic. poets,
157. — Stedman. Vic. poets, 357. — Wotton.
Word portraits, 256. — Bate, P. H. Pre-Raph.
41. — Quilter. Preferences, 15 : 80. — Scudder, V. D. Life of spirit, 269. — Skelton, J.
Table-talk, 74. — With portrait. (W. M.
Payne) Warner Lib. 21 : 12411.
— and the religion of beauty. Myers. Ess. mod.
312.
— and W. Holman Hunt. Ruskin. Art of Engl. 3.
— as a poet. Patmore. Princ. in art, 103.
— Bibliography. Knight. Life of R. — Hodgkins. 19th cent. au.
— Influence of, in art. Carr, J. C. Papers, 196.
— Lilith. (A. C. Swinburne) Singleton, E. Great
pic. 212.
— pictures by, Exhibitions of. Hueffer. Ital. stud.
83.
— Poems of. Mabie. Ess. lit. interp. — Patmore.
Poetry in art. — Swinburne. Ess. 60.

Rossetti, Mrs. Lucy Madox (Brown). Clayton,
E. C. Eng. fem. art. 2 : 116.

Rossetti, Wm. M. Bate, P. H. Eng. Pre-Raph.
53.

Rossettis, The. Bibliography. Salem (Mass.)
Pub. Lib. Bull. Nov. '96.

Rossi, Ernesto, as Hamlet. Winter. Shad.
stage, 3 : 235.
— Home of. Kingston, W. B. Music & manners,
2 : 275.

Rossi, Marcello, with portrait. Ehrlich, A. Cel.
violin. 63.

Rossini, Gioacchino Antonio. Badeau. Vagabond, 315. — Bourne, C. E. Gt. compos. 219.
— Butterworth. Great compos. 102. — Crowest. Tone-poets, 257. — Engel, L. Mozart, 2 :

42. — Hogarth. Mem. opera, **2** : 108, 301. — Keddie. Mus. comp. 262. — Dole, N. H. Score, 237. — Elliot. Rom. gossip, 253. — Elson, L. Gt. composers, 210. — Ferris, G. T. Ital. & Fr. compos. 48. — With portrait. Rowbotham. Priv. life compos. 231.

Rossini, Gioacchino Antonio. Barber of Seville. Guerber. Stor. of operas, 102.

Rossiter, Mrs. Frances Fripp (Seares). Clayton, E. C. Eng. fem. art. **2** : 316.

Rosslyn, A. Wedderburn, Earl of. Brougham. Works, **3** : 167. — Campbell. Lord chan. **7** : 334.

Rost, Pierre Adolphe. Livingston, J. Dist. Amer. 461. — Livingston, J. Em. Am. lawy. 118.

Rostand, E. Cyrano de Bergerac. Crawford, V. M. Stud. for. lit. 27.

Rotch, Charity. Clement, J. Noble deeds, 136.

Rothe, John A. Miller, Jos. Singers church, 2d ed. 145.

Rothe, Richard. Lichtenberger. Hist. German theology, 492. — Schaff, P. Germany, 360.

Rotheram, Thomas, abp. Campbell. Ld. chan. **1** : 337. — Creasy. Etonians, 23.

Rothes, John Leslie, Duke of. Lodge. Portraits (Bohn), v. **6.**

Rothes, House of. Burke, B. Viciss. of fam. **2** : 165.

"Rothsay Castle," Wreck of the. Senior, W. Shipwrecks, 82.

Rothschild, Nathan Meyer, of Lond. Bourne, H. R. F. Eng. merch. **2** : 234. — Bourne. Lond. merchants, 231. — Francis, J. Stock exch. 109. — Parton. Triumphs, 405.

Rothwell, Bone-house at. Buckland, F. T. Curios. nat. hist. **4** : 189.

Rotterdam. Amicis. Holland, 37. — Brooks, E. S. Gt. cities, 168.

Rottmann, Bernard, the Anabaptist of Münster. Baring-Gould. Oddities, **2** : 195.

Roubillac, Louis Francis. Dobson, A. 18th cent. vign. 84.

— A sculptor's life in the last century. Cook, D. Art in Eng. 28.

Roubo, Jacques. Brightwell. Heroes of lab. 133.

Rouen. Buckley, T. A. Great cities, 211. — James, H. Portraits, 130.

Rouen, Churches and other buildings of. Larned, W. C. Churches & C. 37.

Rough House ; Wichern's reformatory. Stevenson. Praying & w. 84.

Rough it, How to. Fields. Underbrush, 179.

Rouher, Eugène. King, E. French pol. lead. 160. — Rae, W. F. Men of 3d repub. 70.

Roulette, Monte Carlo, Scientific aspect of. Pearson, K. Chances, **1** : 42.

Roumania in 1887. Laveleye. Balkan peninsula.

Roumanian music. Kingston, W. B. Music & manners, **1** : 112.

Roumelia in 1887. Laveleye. Balkan peninsula.

Round Hill school, Northampton, Mass. Appleton, T. G. Sheaf of pap. 9.

Round towers of Ireland. Davis, T. Prose, 90. — Moore, T. Prose & v. 204.

Rouquette, Adrian. Davidson, J. W. Writ. of South, 484.

Rouquette, François Dominique. Davidson, J. W. Writ. of South, 490.

Rouse, Francis. Holland, J. Psalmists, **2** : 31.

Rouse, Rebecca. Ellet. Pioneer wom. 199. — Brockett. Woman's work, 544.

Rousseau, Jean Jacques. Alger. Solitudes, 255. — Brougham. Works, **2** : 122. — Carlyle. Heroes. — Clarke, J. F. Memo. sket. 345. — Compayre. Hist. pedagog. 278. — Curran.

Irish bar, **2** : 118. — Dawson, G. Shakes. 254. — Hale, E. E. Lights two cent. 189. — Quick. Educa. ref. 239. — Ste.-Beuve. Monday chats, 141. — Shelley, M. W. Lit. men Fr. v. **2.** — Vinet. Fr. lit. 18th cent. 369. — Caird. Ess. on lit. & p. **1** : 105. — Clarke, J. F. Memo. sketches, 343. — Forster. Fr. & Span. genius, 57. — Green, T. H. Works, **2** : 386, — Pellissier. Lit. move. Fr. 24. — Shelley, Mrs. Fr. authors, v. **2.** — With portrait. (E. Rod) Warner Lib. **21** : 12435.

Rousseau, Jean Jacques, and the French stage. Hawkins. Fr. stage 18th cent. v. **1.**

— and the Genevans, Gaberel's. Cranborne. Hist. sket. **1** : 229.

— and the religion of nature. (Mrs. F. Macdonald) Relig. systems, 724.

— and the sentimentalists. Lowell. Writ. **2** : 232.

— Bibliography. Bost. Pub. Lib. Bull. **10** : 81.

— Character of. Hazlitt. Round table.

— Controversy with Hume. Hume. Philos. works, **1** : xliii.

— Cowper and. Stephen, L. Hours in libr. **3** : 93.

— Life of. Everett, A. H. Ess. **2** : 301.

— Pygmalion. Hunt. Wishing-cap, 202.

— Social contract. Coleridge. Friend, 177. — Lowell. Essays on government. — Pollock. History of science of politics.

— Voltaire, Goethe and. Merivale. Hist. stud. 130.

Rousseau, Gen. Lovell H. Shanks. Rec. of generals, 193.

Rousseau, Théodore. Mollett, J. W. Paint. of Barbizon, **1** : 47. — (W. A. Coffin) Van Dyke, J. C. Mod. Fr. mast. 119.

Routh, Martin Joseph. Bailey, J. B. Methuselahs, 392. — Burgon. Twelve men, **1** : 1. — Mozley. Reminis. **1** : 318.

Rover families, Rise of. Pastor, L. Hist. popes, **4** : 231.

Rovezzano, Benedetto da. Perkins, C. C. Tusc. sculp. **1** : 257.

Row, John. Woolrych. Serjeants, **1** : 92.

Rowan, Archibald Hamilton. Curran. Irish bar, **2** : 241. — Sheil. Sk. Irish bar, **2** : 230.

Rowan, Stephen Clegg. Headley, J. T. Farragut, 401.

Rowe, Mrs. Elizabeth. Burder. Pious wom. 221. — Pierce, B. K. Em. dead, 134. — Williams, Jane. Lit. wom. 157.

Rowe, John. Hatfield, E. F. Poets of church, 519.

Rowe, John, Diary of, 1764-79. Mass. Hist. Soc. Proc. 2d ser. **10** : 11.

Rowe, Nicholas. Austin & Ralph. Laureates, 223. — (S. Johnson) Chalmers. Eng. poets, **9** : 457. — Hamilton, Wal. Poets laur. — Lennox, W. P. Plays, **1** : 27.

Rowena, 2d queen of Vortigern. Hall. Queens bef. Conq. 178.

Rowing at Oxford and Cambridge. Whitney, C. W. Sport. pilgr. 114.

— — Styles of. Proctor, R. A. Rough ways, 148, 169. — Proctor. Light sci. **1** : 269.

— on the Thames. Whitney, C. W. Sport. pilgr. 157.

Rowlands, Daniel. Ryle, J. C. Chr. leaders, 180.

Rowlands, Samuel. Alden, R. M. Rise of satire, 165. — Gosse. 17th cent. stud. 71.

Rowlandson, Mary. Clement, J. Noble deeds, 299. — Drake, S. G. Trag. of wilderness, 20.

— Removes of. (H. S. Nourse) Am. Antiq. Soc. Proc. n. s. **12** : 401.

Rowles, Samuel. Ivimey. Eng. Bapt. **4** : 446.

Rowley, William. Gosse, E. Jacobean poets, 129.

Rowson, Mrs. Susannah Haswell. Griswold. Fem. poets, 33. — Richardson. Amer. lit. 2 : 128.

Roxburghe Club. Burton, J. H. Book-hunter, 265. — Hitchman. 18th cent. 272.

Roxbury Latin School; its history. (J. E. Greene) Am. Antiq. Soc. Proc. n. s. 4 : 348.

Royal Academy, 1863–65. Palgrave. Ess. on art, 1.

— 1872–90. Quilter. Preferences, 297.

— Influence of. Buxton, H. J., et al. Eng. paint. 44.

— Rise of. Cook, D. Art in Eng. 55.

"**Royal** Arch," Wreck of the. Treanor, T. S. Heroes Good. sands, 158.

Royal Asiatic society. Cust. Linguistic essays, 2 : 1.

— Improvement of, Suggestions for. Cust. Ling. & orient. ess. 64.

Royal authorship. Wilberforce, S. Ess. Quar. 2 : 115.

"**Royal** Charter," Wreck of the. Senior, W. Shipwrecks, 221.

Royal college of surgeons of England. Flower, W. H. Ess. on museums, 74, 97.

— Reform of. Mackenzie, M. Ess. 132.

Royal family, Grants for. Gladstone. Speeches, 10 : 103.

"**Royal** George," Wreck of. Senior, W. Shipwrecks, 27.

Royal house, Medford, Mass. Drake, S. A. Hist. fields Mid. 119.

Royal pretenders. Wraxall. Remark. adv. 1 : 1. See Pretenders.

Royal proclamations. Disraeli, I. Curios. (N. Y. 4 v.) 4 : 284.

Royal progresses, Recent and remote. Miller, H. Hist. ess. 16.

Royal Society, The. Disraeli, I. Calam. v. 2.

Royal Society of Literature. Macaulay. Ess. 1 : 20.

Royal succession and the Salic law. Maine. Early laws, 125.

Royal supremacy in England. Brewer. Eng. stud. 293. — Gladstone. Glean. 5 : 173.

— Gladstone on. Church, R. W. Occ. pap. 2 : 1.

Royalston, Mass., History of. Bullock, A. H. Addresses, 108.

Royalties, English. Tuckerman, C. K. Recollec. 1 : 298.

Royalty, Military courage of. Forbes, A. Camps, 298.

Royer-Collard, Pierre Paul. Cormenin. Orators, 133, 365.

Rôze, Marie, with portrait. Buffen. Mus. celeb. 2 : 29.

Rozgonyi, Cecily. Wyatt, W. J. Hunga. celeb. 191.

Ruarus, Joachim. Wallace, R. Anti-Trin. biog. 3 : 7.

Ruarus, Martin. Wallace, R. Anti-Trin. biog. 2 : 571.

Rubattino, R., with portrait. Jones, E. R. Heroes of ind. 255.

Rubens, Peter Paul. Bolton, S. K. Fam. Europ. art. 246. — Hamerton. Art ess. 1 : 54. — Lee, H. F. Old painters, 233. — Spooner. Biog. fine arts, 2 : 815. — With portrait. Hubbard, E. Little jour. 5 : 113. — Hundred greatest men, 91. — Jervis, Lady. Painting, 2 : 129. — Van Dyke, J. C. Dutch mast. 163.

— Contributions to the life of. Dempster. Ess. 138.

Rubens, Peter Paul. Descent from the cross. (E. Fromentin) Singleton, E. Great pic. 62.

— Homes, haunts and works of. Fairholt. Homes Rubens, 139.

— Visit to the château of. King, R. J. Sket. 443.

Rubinstein, Anton, with portrait. Bie, O. Hist. of piano, 295. — With portrait. Buffen, F. F. Mus. celeb. 45.

Rubric, The, and the celebration of pub. service. Thirlwall, C. Remains, 1 : 53.

Rubruquis, Guillaume de Rysbroeck. St. John. Cel. travelers, 1 : 17.

Rucellai, Giovanni. Symonds. Renais. Ital. lit. 2 : 128, 236. — Jarves. Ital. ramb. 364.

Ruchrath (or Richrath), Johann (John of Wesel). Hodgson, Wm. Reformers, 202. — Ullman. Reformers, 1 : 159.

Ruddiman, T. Nicoll, H. J. Gt. scholars, 191.

Rude, François. Hamerton. Mod. French, 168.

Rudnicius, Christopher. Wallace, R. Anti-Trin. biog. 2 : 422.

Rudnicius, T. Nicoll, H. J. Gr. scholars, 191.

Rudolph of Hapsburg. Hewlett. Heroes, 141.

— Peake, Eliz. Germ. emperors, 131.

Rudolph II., 1576–1612, History of. Peake, Eliz. Germ. emperors, 315.

Rueckert, Friedrich. Gostwick. Ger. poets, 215. — Taylor, B. Crit. ess. 92. — With portrait. Warner Lib. 21 : 12457. — Winkworth. Chr. sing. Germ. 336.

Ruego, Frances De. Wallace, R. Anti-Trin. biog. 2 : 118.

Ruffini, Giovanni Domenico. Warner Lib. 21 : 12471.

Rugby school. Cochrane, R. Benef. lives, 212. — Corbin, J. Schoolboy, 147. — Staunton, H. Schools, 350.

— Use of classics in. Arnold, T. Miscel. 340.

Ruggiero, Count de, alchemist. Wraxall. Remark. adv. 1 : 168.

Ruggles, Timothy. Knapp, S. L. Em. lawyers, 331. — Lossing. Em. Amer. 73. — Sabine. Loyalists, 583.

Ruim, Island of. Allen, Gr. Science in Arc. 230.

Ruisdael, Jacob van. Cundall. Landsc. painters Holl. — Van Dyke, J. C. Dutch mast. 121.

Ruiz de Hita, J. Ticknor. Span. lit. 1 : 78.

Rumbold, Thomas. Whitehead, C. Highwaymen, 1 : 125.

Rumford, Benjamin Thompson, count. Bigelow, J. Mod. inq. 90. — Chambers's Miscel. no. 161. — Garnett. Physicists, 148. — Parton. Triumphs, 669. — Seymour, C. C. B. Selfmade, 238. — Edwards, B. B. Self-taught, 310. — Tyndall. New frag. 94. — Walker, W., jr. Men of sci. 102.

— Home of. Drake, S. A. Hist. fields Mid. 427.

Rūmī, Jalāl-Ad-Dīn. (A. V. W. Jackson) Warner Lib. 21 : 12487.

Rumsey, Mary Ann. Ellet. Pioneer wom. 376.

Runciman, Alexander; Widow Hogarth and her lodger. Cook, D. Art in Eng. 104.

Runeberg, Johan Ludvig, Swedish poet. Gosse. Stud. lit. No. Eur. 98. — With portrait. (W. M. Payne) Warner Lib. 21 : 12495.

Runes. Du Chaillu. Viking age, 1 : 154.

Rupert von Pfalz, Prince. Cust. Warriors civ. 2 : 319. — Edgar. Sea-kings, 227. — Higginson. Atlan. ess. 125. — Lodge. Portraits (Bohn), v. 6. — With portrait. Jesse. Court of Eng. Stuarts, 3 : 32. — Smith, H. G. Romance of hist. 29.

— Inventions of. Timbs. Inventors, 146.

Rupnovius, Joachim. Wallace, R. Anti-Trin. biog. 3 : 18.

Russia, and the United States. Everett. Orat. v. 4.

— and the western powers. Brownson. Works, 16 : 427.

— as it is, Dolgoruki's. Cranbourne. Hist. sk. 1 : 167.

— Bibliography. Krausse, A. Russia in Asia, 1558-1899. — Morse, A. L. Univ. N. Y. State Lib. Bull. Jan. '99. — Providence Pub. Lib. Bull, June, '96. — Salem (Mass.) Pub. Lib. Bull. Dec. '94. — Waltham (Mass.) Pub. Lib. Bull. July, '96.

— Commerce of, 1891. U. S. Cons. Rept. 39 : 735.

— Custom-houses of. Curtis, W. E. Land of nihilist, 15.

— Education in. Curtis, W. E. Land of nihilist, 125.

— Farm products in 1891. (J. M. Crawford) U. S. Cons. Rept. 38 : 321.

— history of, Karamsin's. Alison. Ess. v. 3.

— Journey through southeastern. (G. Kennan) Am. Geog. Soc. 15 : 289.

— Local transportation in, 1891. U. S. Cons. Rept. '38 : 661.

— Old times in. Wraxall, C. F. L. Historic bye-ways, 337.

— on the Caspian sea. Cust. Ling. studies, 2 : 211.

— on the Pacific, Position of. Norman, H. Far East, 151.

— Origin and political character of. Bancroft, G. Miscel. 318.

— Pallas's travels in. St. John. Cel. travelers, 3 : 65.

— Police of. Curtis, W. E. Land of nihilist, 249.

— Politics ; bibliography. Thompson, H. M. Russian politics.

— Politics and prospects of, in 1829. Croly. Hist. sk. 17.

— Press in, and censor. Curtis, W. E. Land of nihilist, 142.

— Royal family, Insanity in. Ireland, W. W. Blot, 129.

— Sunflower industry of, 1891. (J. M. Crawford) U. S. Cons. Rept. 38 : 233.

— Thumb-nail sketches in. Hollingshead. Foot-lights, 299.

— A visit in 1864. Forsyth, W. Essays, 346.

Russian America, Ethnography of. Latham. Opuscula, 266. See Alaska.

Russian artists. Atkinson, J. B. Art tour north-ern, 271, 437.

Russian church. Curtis, W. E. Land of nihilist, 177. — Fowler, G. Sov. of Russ. 1 : 378. — (N. Orloff) Relig. systems, 418.

— Relation to arts. Atkinson, J. B. Art tour northern, 415.

Russian Empire. Bibliography. Providence Pub. Lib. Bull. June, '96.

Russian literature, Epochs in. Vogüé. Rus. nov. 19.

Russian lyric poetry. Warner Lib. 21 : 12583.

Russian Magna Charta. Wraxall, C. F. L. Hist. bye-ways, 1 : 140.

Russian moujik [peasant]. Chambers's Repos. no. 848.

Russian policy and deeds in Turkestan. Gladstone. Bulga. 71.

Russian sculpture. Atkinson, J. B. Art tour northern, 158.

Russian village, Economics of. (J. A. Hourwich) Col. Univ. Hist. 2 : 7.

Rust, George. Tulloch. Rational theol. 17th cent. 2 : 433.

Rustem, Story of. Church, A. J. Stories of magic, 119.

Rutebeuf, the Trouvère. Besant. Fr. humor. 25.

Rutgers College. College Book, 151. — (D. D. Demarest) U. S. Bur. Ed. Circ. '99, no. 1 : 287.

Ruth. Geikie, C. Old Test. char. 176. — Owen, Mrs. O. F. Heroines domes. 1.

Rutherford, Daniel. Walker, W., jr. Men of sci. 107.

Rutherford, R. Miller, S. F. Bench of Ga. v. 2.

Rutherford, Samuel. Blaikie, W. G. Preachers Scot. 112. — Grosart. Nonconf. 195. — (P. McA. Muir) St. Giles lec. 3 : 73. — Innes, A. T. Studies, 3. — Taylor, W. M. Scot. pulpit, '88 : 109.

Rutherfurd, Andrew, Lord. Grant, Jas. Port. pub. char. 1 : 67.

Ruthven, Edw. Southwell. Grant, J. Recoll. Ho. Comm. 339.

Ruthven family. Taylor, J. Fam. of Scot. 1 : 147.

Ruthwell cross, The. Scott, Mrs. M. M. Abbotsf. 352.

Rutkorius, Andrew. Wallace, R. Anti-Trin. biog. 3 : 126.

Rutland, John H. M., Duke of. Grant, J. Recoll. Lords & comm. 1 : 77.

— Poems. Gosse, E. Gossip, 293.

Rutland, John James Robert Manners, earl of. Kent, W. C. M. Derby min. 247.

Rutland, Mass. (S. T. Pickard) Powell, L. P. Hist. towns N. E. 53.

Rutledge, Edward. Dwight, N. Signers of decl. 336. — Lincoln, R. W. Signers, 60. — Lossing. Signers, 211. — Sanderson. Signers, v. 3.

Rutledge, John. With portrait. [Amer.] Nat. portr. gall. v. 4. — With portrait. Barnes, W. H. Sup. ct. 21. — Flanders. Ch. just. 1 : 431. — Lossing. Em. Amer. 153. — Moore, F. Am. eloq. 1 : 118. — Perry, B. F. Biog. sketches, 1 : 254. — Van Santvoord. Ch. just.

Ruvigny, Henri and Pierre de. Agnew. Protes. exiles.

Ruysbroek, John. Ullmann. Reformers, 31.

Ruysch, F. Pettigrew. Med. portr. gall. v. 1.

Ruyter, Michiel Adrianszoon de. De Liefde. Dutch adm. 148.

Ryan, Abram J. Davidson, J. W. Writ. of South, 491.

Ryan, Lacy. Galt. Players, 1 : 215.

Ryan, Richard. Doran. Annals stage, 2 : 41.

— the theatrical tailor. Doran. Habits, 298.

Rydal. Rawnsley. Lit. Assoc. Eng. lakes, 2 : 123.

Ryder, Sir Dudley, chief justice of England, 1754-56. Campbell. Ch. just. 2 : 183.

Ryder, D. F. S. See Sandon, Viscount.

Ryder, John. Coleman, G. Players, 1 : 300.

Ryder, John Adam, Biog. sketch of. (H. Allen) Smithson. Rept. '96: 673.

Ryder, Richard. Hazlitt. Parl. portr. 99.

Rye house plot, 1682. Ewald. Studies, 225.

Ryland, John, D. D. Foster, J. Crit. ess. (Bohn) 2 : 446. — Hatfield, E. F. Poets of church, 520. — Ivimey. Eng. Bapt. 4 : 281. — Miller, Jos. Singers church, 2d ed. 312.

Rynievicius, James. Wallace, R. Anti-Trin. biog. 3 : 118.

Rynievicius, Paul. Wallace, R. Anti-Trin. biog. 3 : 120.

Saa de Miranda, F. Montgomery. Lit. men Italy, v. 3.

Sabbath, The. Cook, Jos. Curr. relig. perils, 28. — Dodge, M. A. Summer rest, 130, 153. — Everett, A. H. Crit. ess. 458. — Hall, John. Questions, 192. — Parsons, T. Ess. 2 : 149. — Thompson, J. P. Man in Genesis. — (J. W.

St. **Michel**, Mont, By land to.   Dodd, A. B.
Three Norm. inns, 318.
— Insulation of.   Müller. Chips, v. 3.
— Legends of.   Mackaye. Abbess Pt. Royal, 115.
St. **Monica's** convent.   Morris, J. Troub. of
Cath. v. 1.
St. **Nicholas**, John.   Ivimey. Eng. Bapt. 2 : 257.
St. **Osyth**, Priory of.   Timbs. Abbeys, 1 : 216.
Saint-Ouen, Artificial ice-cave of.   Adams,
W. H. D. Fam. caverns, 150.
St. **Palais**, James Maurice de.   Clarke, R. II.
Cath. bishops, 3 : 313.
St. **Patrick's** day   Allingham, Varieties, 3 : 111.
St. **Paul**, Minn., City government of.   (W. H.
Lightner) Nat. Conf. City Govt. 2–3 : 105.
— Disposal of garbage, etc., at.   (H. F. Hoyt)
Am. Pub. Health, 18 : 115.
— Outdoor relief as provided in.   (J. F. Jackson)
Conf. char. & correc. '96 : 264.
— Sanitation in.   (H. F. Hoyt) Am. Pub. Health,
14 : 33.
St. **Paul's** Cathedral.   (H. H. Milman) Farrar,
F. W. Westmin. 61. — Guild. Over the ocean,
212. — Howe, J. W. Oak to olive, 23. — Moul-
ton, L. C. Rambles, 172.
— Wonders of.   Timbs. Abbeys, 1 : 1.
St. **Paul's** school, London.   Staunton, H.
Schools, 164.
St. **Peter's**, Rome.   Guild. Abroad again, 128.
— Symonds. Renais. fine arts, 88.
St. **Peter's** chains; old Congleton custom.   (R.
Head) Andrews, W. Bygone Ches. 137.
St. **Petersburg**.   Atkinson, J. B. Art tour
northern, 149. — Brooks, E. S. Gt. cities, 47.
— Curtis, W. E. Land of nihilist, 22. —
Prime, S. I. Alhambra, 284. — Stoddard. Red
letter, 105. — (A. Weir) Vaca. tourists, 2 : 1.
— Wikoff, H. Reminis. 203.
— Founding of.   Schuyler. Peter the Great, 2 : 1.
— Technical school.   U. S. Cons. Rept. no. 153.
— Winter life in.   Taylor, B. Byways, 85.
Saint-Pierre, Charles Irenee Castel de.   Mac-
call. For. biog. 1 : 114.
St. **Pierre**, Mr.   Redding. Misers, 1 : 118.
St. **Pierre**, Battle of, bloodiest fight in the penin-
sula ; map.   Fitchett. Deeds, 199.
St. **Regis**, Affair at.   Dawson. Batt. of U. S. 2 :
173.
St. **Regis** waters.   Prime, W. C. I go a-fishing,
122.
Saint-Saens, Camille.   Hervey, A. Masters Fr.
music, 107. — Elson, L. Gt. composers, 209.
St. **Sebastian**, Siege of.   Robson, W. Sieges,
585.
Saint-Simon, L. de R., duc de.   Hayward, A.
Sket. em. statesm. 2 : 67. — Thomson, K. &
J. C. Wits and beaux, 257. — Warner Lib.
22 : 12709.
— at Versailles.   Richards, L. E. Glimpses, 72.
— Memoirs.   Richards, L. E. Glimpses, 102. —
Ste.-Beuve. Port. of men, 77.
Saint-Simonians, Account of.   Robertson, J.
B. Lec. mod. hist. 498.
St. **Thome**.   Malleson, G. B. Battles of India, 1.
Saint Victor, Adam de.   (M. F. Egan) Warner
Lib. 22 : 12727.
St. **Vincent**, John Jervis, earl of.   Brougham.
Works, 4 : 141. — Edgar. Boyhood, 221. —
Edgar. Sea-kings, 308. — Lodge. Portraits
(Bohn), v. 8. — Johns. Nav. & mil. heroes. —
With portrait.   Laughton, J. K. Twelve
sailors, 397.
St. **Vincent**, Cape, Fight off.   Allen, Jos. Battles
Brit. navy, 1 : 441. — Fitchett. Deeds, 1. —
Valentine, L. J. Sea-fights, 140.

St. **Weonard**, Tumulus at.   Wright, T. Ess.
archæol. 1 : 48.
Sainte-Beuve, Charles Augustin.   Birrell, A.
Res judicatæ, 298. — Calvert. Ess. æsth. 158.
— (E. C. J. B. Jacquot) Gautier. Fam. Fr. au.
27. — Kirwan, A. V. Mod. France, 284. —
Mauris, M. Fr. men of lett. 108. — Ste.-Beuve.
Monday chats, ix. — With portrait. (B. W.
Wells) Warner Lib. 22 : 12659.
— as a critic.   Pellissier. Lit. move. Fr. 281.
— as a poet.   Pellissier. Lit. move. Fr. 184.
— Critical memoir of.   (Wm. Sharp) Ste.-Beuve.
Port. of men, vii.
— Life and writings of.   Ste.-Beuve. Engl. portr.
vii.
Sainthill, Richard.   Smith, C. R. Retrospec. 2 :
183.
Saintine, Joseph X. B., with portrait.   Warner
Lib. 22 : 12678.
Sainton, Prosper P. C., with portrait.   Ehrlich,
A. Cel. violin. 206.
Saints, and their bodies.   Higginson. Out-door, 1.
— Barbour's Legends of.   Scott, Mrs. M. M.
Abbotsf. 23.
— Communion of.   Boyd. Towards sunset, 213.
— Early northern.   Burton, J. H. Book-hunter, 352.
— Lives and miracles of.   Wright, T. Ess. ar-
chæol. 1 : 227.
— Lives of.   Froude. Short stud. 1 : 440. 4 : 207.
— Superstitions of sailors concerning.   Jones, W.
Credulities, 36.
— Syrian.   Nöldeke, T. Sk. from east. hist. 207.
— Worship of.   Brownson. Works, 8 : 117.
Saints' days, Superstitions connected with.
Jones, W. Credulities, 107.
Saiovicius, Andrew.   Wallace, R. Anti-Trin.
biog. 3 : 258.
Saker, Alfred.   Watson, Mrs. R. A. Poet-toilers,
181.
Sakhalin and Vladivostock, Prisons in.   (B.
Howard) Am. Geog. Soc. 30 : 135.
Sakkara, Egypt.   Buckley, J. M. Trav. 3 cont.
247.
Sakya Muni, Place of, in history.   Five years
theos. 365.
Sala, George Augustus.   Friswell. Mod. men of
lett. 159. — Hodder, G. Memories, 362. —
Sala, Mrs. Fam. peop. 1.
— in Gower street.   Yates, E. H. Celeb. 2 : 157.
Salad, Literature of.   Adams, W. D. With poet,
72.
Saladin.   (E. Gibbon) Ferris, G. T. Gt. leaders,
135. — Hutton, B. Heroes crusades, 267. —
Utterton, F. A. Biog. sk. 94.
Salamanca, Battle of.   Adams, W. H. D. Engl.
at war, 1 : 327.
Salamanders, Myths of.   Scoffern. Stray leaves,
359.
Salamis, Battle of.   Duruy. Hist. Greece, 2 :
460. — Rawson, E. K. Twenty nav. batt. 1 : 3.
Salamona.   Owen, Mrs. O. F. Heroines hist. 22.
Saldanha, Duc de.   Em. persons, 2 : 8.
Sale, Florentia (Wynch), Lady Robert (d. 1853).
Crosland. Mem. women, 370.
Salel, Hugues.   Cary. Fr. poets, 40.
Salem, Mass.   Bacon, E. M. Hist. pilgrim. 125.
— (G. D. Latimer) Powell, L. P. Hist. towns
N. E. 121. — Drake. Nooks of N. E. 208.
— Day of disappointment in.   Gilman, S. Con-
trib. 474.
— Literary.   Wolfe. Lit. shr. Am. auth. 128.
— Old sea-captains of.   Higginson, T. W. Travel-
ers, 11.
— Vegetation about.   Peabody, E. P. Æsthetic
pap. 224.

Saleri, A., musical composer. Hogarth. Mem. opera, 2 : 252.

Salerno, Walter de. Burke, O. J. Cath. archb. 26.

Salic law, Royal succession and. Maine. Early laws, 125.

Salimbene, Fra. Oliphant, T. L. K. Duke, 84.

Salisbury, Alicia de Lacy, countess of. Holt, E. S. Roy. ladies, v. 1.

Salisbury, Charles Babcock. Am. Antiq. Soc. Proc. n. s. 8 : 22.

Salisbury, Ela de Rosmar, countess of. Holt, E. S. Roy. ladies, v. 1.

Salisbury, James B. W. G. Cecil, marquis of. Kent, W. C. M. Derby min. 87.

Salisbury, Margaret Plantagenet, countess of. Burke, S. H. Hist. portr. Tudor, 2 : 176.

— and her execution. Burke, S. H. Men of reforma. 2 : 130.

Salisbury, R. A. T. Gascoyne-Cecil, marquis of. With photo. Cooper, T. Men of mark, 2 : 10. — Forster. Brit. statesm. 5 : 1. — Higginson, T. W. Engl. statesm. 232. — Hill, F. H. Polit. portr. 76. — Hutton, R. H. Stud. in parl. 73. — Lodge. Portraits (Bohn), v. 3. — Reid, T. W. Cab. portr. 199. — Reid, T. W. Politicians, 1 : 151. — Smith, G. Barnett. Prime min. 385. — Escott, T. H. S. Pillars emp. 277.

— at Hatfield. Yates, E. H. Celeb. 1 : 187.

Salisbury, Robert Cecil, 1st earl of. With portrait. Jesse. Court of Eng. Stuarts, 1 : 189. — Wrangham. Brit. Plutarch, v. 2.

Salisbury, Stephen. (A. P. Peabody) Am. Antiq. Soc. Proc. n. s. 3 : 211, 227. — (J. D. Washburn) Mass. Hist. Proc. 2d ser. 2 : 89. — Peabody. Harv. grad. 181.

Salisbury, Eng. Allingham. Varieties, 1 : 166. — Silloway. Cathedral towns, 106. — Temple, E. L. Old-world, 2 : 280.

Salisbury Cathedral. (H. T. Armfield) Farrar, F. W. Westmin. 199. — James. Transatl. 52. — Van Rensselaer, M. G. Eng. cath. 107.

Salisbury palace. Venables, E. Episc. palaces, 165.

Salkeld, William. Woolrych. Serjeants, 2 : 482.

Sallust, with portrait. Dunlop, J. Rom. liter. 2 : 131. — Warner Lib. 21 : 12743.

Salmon, Natural history of. Buckland, F. T. Curios. nat. hist. 4 : 249.

Salmon family, The. Jordan, D. S. Sci. sk. 35.

Salmon-fishing. Lang. Leaders, 9.

— on the Jacques Cartier river. Lanman, C. Recollec. 147.

Salmon-flies. Maxwell, H. Post-mer. 321.

Salomon, Mrs. Eliza. Brockett. Woman's work, 613.

Salon, The, in America. Howe, J. W. Is polite soc. pol. 113.

Salon Helvétique, The. Mason, A. G. Wom. of Fr. salons, 223.

Salonica. Arnold, R. A. Levant, 1 : 321.

Salons. Hayward, A. Ess. 2d ser. 1 : 350.

Salpétrière, La, Paris. Field, Mrs. H. M. Sk. France, 134.

Salsette, Temples of. Adams, W. H. D. Fam. caves, 60.

Salt, Sir Titus. Blaikie, W. G. Leaders, 261. — Bolton, S. K. Poor boys. — Japp. Good men, 375. — Cochrane, R. Gt. thinkers, 129. — Em. persons, 2 : 15. — Fortunes made in bus. 1 : 289. — Japp. Labor, 175.

— & Sons. Japp & Holmes. Succ. bus. men, 98.

Salt. Carey, A. Autob. of a lump of coal, 24. — De Vere, M. S. Wonders of deep, 145. — Jones, Wm. Treasures, 327. — Knox, T. W.

Underground, 930. — Simmonds. Comm. prod. of the sea, 339.

Salt, common, Mining and manufacture of. Japp. Days w. indus. 112.

— Folk-lore of. Lawrence, R. M. Magic, 154.

Salt industry in Michigan. Winchell. Sparks geol. ham. 255.

Salt Lake City. Bridges, F. D. Lady's trav. 387. — Coffin, C. C. Our new way, 491. — Hardy, I. D. Thro' cities, 102. — Marshall, W. G. Thro' Amer. 189. — Rusling, J. F. Gt. west, 164. — Sala. Amer. revis. 2 : 289. — Jackson, H. H. Bits trav. home, 17. — Marshall, W. G. Thro' Amer. 163. — Pidgeon. Engineer's holiday, 157.

— and Mormonism in 1877. Vivian. Tour in Am. 98.

— and the Mormons. Forbes, E. Lit. papers, 263. — Pierrepont. Fifth ave. 17.

— in 1881. Hardy. Between two oceans, 117.

Salt tax in southern India. Hobart, V. H. H. Ess. & mis. 2 : 462.

Salt wells, The great, at Tsz-Liu-Ching, China. (G. F. Smither) U. S. Cons. Rept. 55 : 384.

Saltillo, Infectious diseases in. (D. G. Fuertes) Am. Pub. Health, 18 : 389.

Saltmarsh, John. Holland, J. Psalmists, 1 : 280.

Salton Sea. Lummis. Strange corners, 37.

Saltonstall, Leverett. Mass. Hist. Soc. Proc. 2d ser. 10 : 139. — With portrait. (C. R. Codman) Mass. Hist. Soc. Proc. 2d ser. 11 : 337.

Saltonstall, Wye. Bell, R. Lit. & sci. men, 2 : 178.

Saltwood Castle. Timbs. Abbeys, 1 : 317.

Salutati, Coluccio de'. Symonds. Reviv. of learn. 103.

Salutation, Modes of. Disraeli, I. Curios. (N. Y. 4 v.) 2 : 165.

Salutations, Social. Saunders. Stray leaves, 132.

Salvador, Hand-book of. Bur. Am. Rep. no. 58.

— Import duties of, 1891. Bur. Am. Rep. no. 23.

Salvation. Godwin, W. Ess. 129.

— by the cross. Brownson. Works, 8 : 280.

— natural and supernatural. Brownson. Works, 3 : 1.

Salvation army. Adams, F. W. L. Australian essays, 27. — Jeune. Lesser ques. 246.

Salvi, Niccolo. Milizia. Lives arch. 2 : 322.

Salviani, Hippolito. Jardine, W. Nat. lib. v. 35. — Macgillivray, W. Em. zoöl.

Salvini, Alex., with portrait. (J. A. Waldron) McKay, F. E. Fam. actors, 292.

Salvini, Tommaso. Elliot, F. Rom. gossip, 324. — as King Saul and King Lear. Winter. Shadows, 339.

— First impressions of. Lewes. Actors, 264.

Salzburg. Bellows. Old world, 1 : 135.

Samaria. Gillett, E. H. Anc. cities, 226. — Wright, W. B. Anc. cities, 184. — (Rogers) Wilson, C. W. Pictur. Palest. 2 : 1.

— Ruins of. Tweedie. Ruined cities, 79.

— Sieges of. Robson, W. Sieges, 55.

Samaritan, Better. Quincy, J. P. Protec. 127.

Samaritan pentateuch, On the. Deutsch. Lit. rem. 404.

Sameness and identity. (G. S. Fullerton) Univ. Pa. Publ. Philos. no. 1.

Samnium, Glimpse of. Freeman. Studies Italy, 251.

Samoa. Alexander, J. M. Isl. Pac. 274.

— Aboriginal. McLennan. Stud. anc. 2 : 232.

— Government, Commerce, etc., 1895. (J. H. Mulligan) U. S. Cons. Rept. 51 : 656.

Samoa, Great hurricane at, March 15, 1889. God-
bey. Great disasters, 195.
Samos island. Holland, J. E. Europ. concert,
70. — Tozer. Islands of the Ægean.
Samothrace. Tozer. Isl. Ægean, 310.
Sampson, Ellen H. Hemenway. Poets of Vt.
276.
Sampson, Richard. Ivimey. Eng. Bapt. **2**:
131.
Samson. Chapin, E. H. Less. of faith, 182. —
Headley, J. T. Sac. heroes, 202. — Williams,
H. L. Boys of Bible, 85. — Wilberforce, S.
Heroes Hebrew, 161.
— and Delilah. Geikie, C. Old Test. char. 167.
Samuel the prophet. Geikie, C. Old Test. char.
193. — Wilberforce, S. Heroes Hebrew, 198.
Samworth, Joanna. Clayton, E. C. Eng. fem.
art. **2** : 290.
San Blas coast, Trade with, 1891. (J. T. Abbott)
U. S. Cons. Rept. **38** : 217.
Sanborn, Francis G., 1838–84. Worcester Soc.
Antiquity Coll. v. **6**.
Sancerre, France, Sieges of. Davenport. Narr.
peril, **2** : 270.
Sanchez, Miguel. Owen, J. Skeptics French,
617.
— Two plays of. (H. A. Rennert) Univ. Pa. Publ.
Philol. v. **5**.
Sancho II. of Portugal. Doran. Monarchs, **2** :
350.
Sancroft, William, archbishop of Canterbury.
Fowler, M. Some abps. Cant. 126. — Strick-
land. Bishops, 1.
Sancta Clara, Abraham à. *See* Abraham à
Sancta Clara.
Sanctification, or Christian perfection. Whe-
don. Ess. **1** : 141.
Sand, George. Arnold, M. Mixed ess. — Chal-
lice. Fr. authors, **1** : 193. — Cone & Gilder.
Pen-portr. **2** : 59. — With portr. (E. C. J. B.
Jacquot) Gautier. Fam. Fr. au. 85. — Gris-
wold, H. T. Home-life, 164. — James, H.
French poets, 190. — Loménie. Liv. charac-
ters, 293. — McCarthy, J. Mod. lead. 144. —
Mazzini. Life, etc. **6** : 33. — Myers. Ess. mod.
70. — Ossoli. Woman, 228. — Taylor, B. Crit.
ess. 280. — Thorne, W. H. Mod. idols, 168. —
Underwood, S. A. Heroines, 117. — Zimmern.
For. novelists, **1** : 1. — Smith, G. B. Women
of renown, 221. — Walsh, R. M. Liv. char.
France. — Pellissier. Lit. move. Fr. 297. —
With portrait. (Th. Bentzon) Warner Lib.
22 : 12759. — Wells, B. W. Cent. Fr. fic. 219.
— Correspondence, 1812–47. Coan. Stud. biog.
193.
Sand filter, Lawrence, Mass., Work of the. (H.
W. Clark) Am. Pub. Health, **23** : 189.
Sand filtration of water. (G. W. Fuller) Maine
Health, '94–95 : 242.
Sand quarry in winter. Wood, J. G. Out-of-
doors, 29.
Sandbach over sixty years ago. (Mrs. G. L.
Banks) Andrews, W. Bygone Ches. 159.
Sandeau, Jules. Saintsbury. French novelists,
263. — Thorne, W. H. Mod. idols, 168. —
Zimmern. For. novelists, **2** : 341.
Sandeau, Léonard S. J., with portrait. War-
ner Lib. **22** : 12806.
Sanderson, John. Griswold. Prose writ. 239.
Sanderson, Dr. Robert. Walton, I. Lives;
also in Wrangham. Brit. Plutarch, v. **4**.
Sandford, David. Headley, J. T. Chaplains
Revol. 361.
Sandford, Samuel. Galt. Players, **1** : 81.
Sandgate Castle. Timbs. Abbeys, **1** : 327.

Sandius, Christopher, jr. Wallace, R. Anti-
Trin. biog. **3** : 243, 318.
Sandon, D. F. S. Ryder, Viscount. With photo.
Cooper, T. Men of mark, **3** : 14. — Francis,
G. H. Orators, 303.
Sandown Castle. Timbs. Abbeys, **1** : 326.
Sands, Robt. C. Griswold. Poets Am. 213.
Sands, Physical and chemical properties of.
(H. W. Clark) Mass. Health, '94 : 701.
Sandwich, Edward Montagu, 1st earl of.
Lodge. Portraits (Bohn), v. **5**. — Southey &
Bell. Brit. adm. v. **5**.
Sandwich, John George Montague, earl of.
Creasy. Etonians, 394. — Jesse, J. H. Cel.
Eton. v. **2**.
Sandy Creek, N. Y., Action at. Dawson. Batt.
of U. S. **2** : 342.
Sandys, Sir Edwin. Holland, J. Psalmists, **1** :
270.
Sandys, Frederick. Bate, P. H. Eng. Pre-Raph.
59.
Sandys, George. Bell, R. Lit. & sci. men, **2** :
169. — (G. A. Simcox) Ward. Eng. poets, **2** :
192. — Willmott. Early Eng. sac. poets, 52. —
Gosse, E. From Shakesp. 231. — Griswold,
R. W. Sac. poets. — Hatfield, E. F. Poets of
church, 526. — Holland, J. Psalmists, **1** : 282.
— Macdonald, G. England's antiphon, 127. —
Miller, Jos. Singers church, 2d ed. 55.
San Francisco. Arnold, E. Seas and l. 127. —
Brooks, E. S. Gt. cities, 105. — Hardy, I. D.
Thro' cities, 142. — Jackson, H. H. Bits trav.
home, 77. — Keyes, E. D. Fifty years, 223.
— Knox, T. W. Underground, 768. — Mar-
shall, W. G. Thro' Amer. 260. — Pierrepont.
Fifth ave. 41, 90. — Rae. Westward, 259. —
Rusling, J. F. Gt. west, 276. — Sala. Amer.
revis. **2** : 184. — Vincent, F. Thro' tropics, 41.
— Pidgeon. Engineer's holiday, 181.
— The bay of. (J. T. Doyle) Am. Antiq. Soc.
Proc. n. s. **6** : 78.
— Chinatown. Marshall, W. G. Thro' Amer.
286. — Jackson, H. H. Bits trav. home, 62.
— in 1846. Wise. Los Gringos, 60, 97.
— in 1849 and 1859. Taylor, B. At home, **2** : 37.
— in 1857–89. Bancroft. Hist. Calif. **7** : 682.
— in 1866. Dilke. Greater Britain, v. **2**.
— in 1881. Russell, W. H. Hesper, **2** : 44.
— Municipal affairs in. (J. R. Freud) Nat. Conf.
City Govt. '97 : 249.
— Municipal condition of. (I. T. Milliken) Nat.
Conf. City Govt. **2–3** : 449.
San Francisco river. Barker, Lady. Travel.
about, 157.
Sangallerie, Marquis de. *See* Gentils.
Sangallo, Antonio. Milizia. Lives arch. **1** : 231.
Sangallo, Francesco di. Perkins, C. C. Tus.
sculp. **1** : 253.
Sangallo, Giuliano di. Milizia. Lives arch. **1** :
210.
San Gemignano. Baxter, L. E. Tusc. stud. 306.
— Hare. Cities of No. Italy, **3** : 304.
Sanger, Ralph. (G. P. Sanger) N. E. Hist.-Gen.
Soc. Biog. **4** : 76.
Sangreal. Baring-Gould. Myths, 604.
Sanitary administration. (C. A. Lindsley) Conn.
Health, '93 : 178.
— good, Essential conditions of. (D. B. Eaton)
Am. Pub. Health, **2** : 498.
— in unincorporated districts. (H. Mitchell) Am.
Pub. Health, **22** : 143.
Sanitary arrangements, Domestic, of Metropol.
poor. Internat. Health Ex. Sanita.
— of metropol. houses, Improvement of. Inter-
nat. Health Ex. Sanita.

Sanitary association, Ladies', Speech in behalf of, 1859. Kingsley, C. New miscel. 241.

Sanitary associations, Organization of. (J. H. Kellogg) Mich. Health, '79 : 81.

Sanitary bureau, national, Necessity for. (C. C. Cox) Am. Pub. Health, 1 : 522.

Sanitary bureaus, Importance of. (J. E. Monjaras) Am. Pub. Health, 19 : 69.

Sanitary education in public schools. (Mrs. E. H. Richards) Am. Pub. Health, 24 : 100.

Sanitary houses for working classes in urban districts. Internat. Health Ex. Sanita.

Sanitary inspection. (A. N. Bell) Am. Pub. Health, 8 : 34.

Sanitary jurisprudence. (J. B. Sommerville) Penn. Health, 60 : 419.

— National and international. (T. J. Turner) Am. Pub. Health, 7 : 32.

Sanitary knowledge, Progress of, among women of Eng. (Lady Priestley) Am. Pub. Health, 19 : 172.

Sanitary law, A uniform. (N. E. Wordin) Am. Pub. Health, 23 : 375.

Sanitary laws, Objections of evolutionists against. (S. E. Chaillé) Am. Pub. Health, 6 : 279.

Sanitary legislation. (U. O. B. Wingate) Am. Pub. Health, 22 : 138.

— in Gt. Brit., Progress of. Internat. Health Ex. Sanita.

— in London. (E. Lankester) Trans. Soc. Sci. Lond. '60 : 666.

Sanitary matters, Federal intervention in. (J. M. Gamboa) Am. Pub. Health, 18 : 125.

Sanitary movement, The. Chambers's Papers, no. 9.

Sanitary nomenclature. (E. M. Hunt) Am. Pub. Health, 11 : 31.

Sanitary organization. (A. W. Suiter) Am. Pub. Health, 22 : 133.

— in villages and rural districts. (E. M. Hunt) Am. Pub. Health, 1 : 491.

Sanitary problems of Chicago, 1877. (J. H. Rauch) Am. Pub. Health, 4 : 3.

Sanitary protection in Newport, R. I. (H. R. Storer) Am. Pub. Health, 6 : 209. 8 : 42.

— of New Orleans. (J. Holt) Am. Pub. Health, 11 : 89.

Sanitary reform in England, 1858. Kingsley, C. San. lec. 271.

— Need of. Kingsley, C. New miscel. 1.

— Obstacles to. (C. Kingsley) Trans. Soc. Sci. Lond. '58 : 428.

Sanitary regulations of buildings. (J. Gowans ; F. Jenkin) Trans. Soc. Sci. Lond. '80 : 529.

Sanitary requirements in factories. (L. F. C. Garvin) Am. Pub. Health, 3 : 69.

Sanitary science. Gibbins. Eng. Soc. ref. 173.

— and the medical profession. (N. Allen) Am. Pub. Health, 12 : 85.

— and public hygiene. (W. S. Robertson ; R. J. Farquharson) Iowa Health, '85 : 429.

— Eminent domain of. (J. E. Reeves) Am. Pub. Health, 9 : 171.

— in schools, Popularization of. (E. W. Claypole) Am. Pub. Health, 3 : 208.

— — Plea for teaching of. (D. Fall) Mich. Health, 96 : 131.

— Progress of. (H. E. Roscoe) Manch. Sci. lec. 3–4 : 126.

— Relations of, to public instruction. (A. D. White) Am. Pub. Health, 1 : 139.

— What our schools may do for. (E. T. Nelson) Ohio Health, '89 : 345.

Sanitary service, Maritime. (S. Smith) Am. Pub. Health, 7 : 70.

Sanitary survey of St. Louis. (G. Homan, ed.) Am. Pub. Health, 10 : 297.

— of U. S., Plan for. Am. Pub. Health, 3 : 106. 4 : 27.

— Report on. Am. Pub. Health, 2 : 41.

Sanitary work in Brooklyn, N. Y. Am. Pub. Health, 13 : 56.

— in Memphis, Tenn. (G. B. Thornton) Am. Pub. Health, 12 : 109.

— The state and. (E. Brook) Am. Pub. Health, 8 : 23.

Sanitary works in the U. S., Progress of. (E. Harris) Am. Pub. Health, 2 : 151.

Sanitation. (J. A. Skilton) Brooklyn Eth. Assoc. Life, 361.

— and education. (J. Eaton) Am. Pub. Health, 6 : 248.

— Border-land of. (J. Hartzell) Ohio Health, '95 : 343.

— Car. (G. P. Conn) Am. Pub. Health, 21 : 61, 285. — (S. H. Woodbridge) Am. Pub. Health, 24 : 218.

— Census in its relation to. (J. S. Billings) Am. Pub. Health, 15 : 43.

— Church and, Relation of. (T. R. Beeber) Penn. Health, '90 : 541.

— Does it pay ? (E. T. Nelson) Ohio Health, '91 : 306.

— Domestic, in rural districts. Internat. Health Ex. Sanita.

— Economic. (A. L. Gihon) Penn. Health, '86 : 256.

— general, Plea for better methods of. Mich. Health, '80 : 120.

— House. (W. K. Newton) Am. Pub. Health, 10 : 159. — (J. H. Raymond) Am. Pub. Health, 9 : 211. — (J. L. Leal) Am. Pub. Health, 23 : 401.

— Ideal. (B. O. Reynolds) Wisc. Health, '87 : 117.

— in 1890. (H. B. Baker) Am. Pub. Health, 16 : 1.

— in St. Paul. (H. F. Hoyt) Am. Pub. Health, 14 : 33.

— Maritime. (S. T. Armstrong) Am. Pub. Health, 11 : 98.

— — at ports of arrival. (H. B. Horlbeck) Am. Pub. Health, 16 : 110.

— — Canadian system of. (F. Montizambert) Am. Pub. Health, 14 : 116.

— Municipal. (S. H. Stevenson) Am. Pub. Health, 19 : 242.

— of armies in barracks and field, Necessity of. (R. Rawlinson) Trans. Soc. Sci. Lond. '57 : 488.

— of the Mississippi valley. (G. B. Thornton) Am. Pub. Health, 10 : 214.

— Public. (S. H. Durgin) Am. Pub. Health, 19 : 1.

— — How can women best promote ? (Sarah H. Brayton) Am. Pub. Health, 19 : 178.

— Railroad. (W. T. Parker) Am. Pub. Health, 10 : 335.

— — Need of. (T. P. Wilson) Am. Pub. Health, 8 : 142.

— — Objects and advantages of. (S. S. Herrick) Am. Pub. Health, 7 : 218.

— Report on. (J. W. Hughes) Am. Pub. Health, 23 : 399. 24 : 192.

— Sanitary condition of towns in Eng. and Scot. (T. C. Orr) Trans. Soc. Sci. Lond. '58 : 450.

— School and college. (D. F. Lincoln) N. Y. Regents, 97, app. : 153.

— Steamboat and steamship. (F. Montizambert) Am. Pub. Health, 21 : 309. 23 : 239.

— Theatre. (W. P. Gerhard) Am. Pub. Health, 24 : 103.

Sanitation, Value of, from an economic stand-point. (J. M. Keating) Am. Pub. Health, **6** : 266.

Sanity of true genius. Lamb. Elia.

San José, capital of Costa Rica. Curtis, W. E. Capitals, 196.

San José, California, Valley of. Taylor, B. At home, **2** : 50.

San Juan de Nicaragua Rio. (R. E. Peary) Am. Geog. Soc. **21** : 57.

Sânkhya system. Johnson, S. Ori. relig. India, 375.

San Marco, Monks of. Oliphant. Makers of F. 183.

San Marino. Hare. Cities of No. Italy, **2** : 377. — Tuckerman. Ital. sk. 99.

Sanmicheli, Michele. Milizia. Lives arch. **1** : 249.

San Miniato Cemetery. Festival of the dead. Baxter, L. E. Tusc. stud. 181.

Sannazzaro, Jacopo. Stebbing. Ital. poets, v. **2**. — Symonds. Renais. Ital. lit. **2** : 197. — Symonds. Reviv. of learn. 468.

San Pedro, D. de. Ticknor. Span. lit. **1** : 424.

San Remo. Green, J. R. Stray studies, 79.

San Salvador, capital of San Salvador. Curtis, W. E. Capitals, 171.

Sansavino, Andrea and Jacopo. Perkins, C. C. Tusc. sculp. **1** : 241.

Sanskrit grammars, List of. Colebrooke, H. T. Miscel. ess. v. **2**.

Sanskrit inscriptions, ancient, Description of. Colebrooke. Miscel. essays, **2** : 238.

Sanskrit language. Colebrooke. Miscel. essays, **2** : 1. — Schlegel. Æsthet. (Bohn) 428.

— Accent in. Whitney, W. D. Orient. **2** : 318.

— Grammatical forms of. Müller. Chips, v. **4**.

— Is it the proper basis of ling. science? Key, T. H. Philol. ess. 248.

Sanskrit literature. Foster, J. Crit. ess. (Bohn) **1** : 400.

— Chinese translations of. Müller. Chips, v. **1**.

— Human interest in. Müller, M. India, 95.

— Objections to. Müller, M. India, 135.

— Study of. Schlegel. Æsthetic works, 515.

Sanskrit poetry. Colebrooke, H. T. Miscel. ess. v. **2**.

Sanskrit texts discovered in Japan. Müller. Chips, v. **5**; or Sel. ess. **2** : 313.

Sanskrit versification, Laws of. Colebrooke. Miscel. essays, **2** : 62.

Sanskritic Indians, early, Religion of. Rawlinson. Religions, 123.

Sanson, Charles. Brightwell. Byepaths of biog. 251.

Sansovino, Jacopo. Symonds. Renais. fine arts, 85, 167.

Sansovino, Michael Angelo Andrea Contucci da. Symonds. Renais. fine arts, 166.

Sant, James, with photo. Cooper, T. Men of mark, **2** : 23.

Santa Anna, A. L. de. Calderon de la Barca. Life in Mexico.

Santa Fé trade; its route and character. (J. E. Greene) Am. Antiq. Soc. Proc. n. s. **8** : 324.

Santa Rosa, Santorre, Conti di. Redding. Pers. remin. **1** : 38.

Santerre, Jean Baptiste. Criticisms of his pictures. Guizot. Fine arts, 200.

Santeuil, Claude de. Hatfield, E. F. Poets of church, 528. — Miller, Jos. Singers church, 2d ed. 97.

Santeuil, Jean Baptiste de. Hatfield, E. F. Poets of church, 529. — Miller, Jos. Singers church, 2d ed. 97.

Santiago, Cuba, Battle of. Rawson, E. K. Twenty nav. batt. **2** : 643.

Santiago, capital of Chili. Curtis, W. E. Capitals, 454.

Santillana, I. L. de M., Marquis of. Ticknor. Span. lit. **1** : 366.

Santley, Charles, at St. John's Wood. Yates, E. H. Celeb. **2** : 183.

Santo Domingo. Hill, R. T. Cuba, 236. — Kelley, W. D. Speeches, 427.

— Commercial directory of, 1891. Bur. Am. re-pub. no. 29.

— Dominican Republic in 1898. U. S. Cons. Rept. 57 : 403.

— Handbook of. Bur. Am. Rep., Bulletin no. 52, pt. 3.

— Import duties of, 1891. Bur. Am. Rep. no. 12.

Santo Domingo city. (N. Appleton) Am. Geog. Soc. **23** : 535.

Santolius Maglorianus, Santolius Victorinus. *See* Santeuil.

Santo Niño de la Guardia. Lea. Rel. hist. Spain, 437.

Santorin. Tozer. Isl. Æg. 94.

San Yuste, Convent of. Stoughton. Span. ref. 168.

Saporta, Gaston, Marquis de. Am. Acad. A. & S. Proc. **30** : 598.

Sappho. Arnold, E. Poets of Greece, 105. — With portrait. Clarke, M. C. Noted wom. 9. — Higginson. Atlan. ess. 299. — Holland, J. G. Every-day, 301. — Mills. Poets of Greece, 91. — Symonds. Greek poets, **1** : 309. — With portrait. (T. Davidson) Warner Lib. **22** : 12817.

— Bibliography. Wharton, H. W. (tr.). Sappho.

Saracen's head, The. DeQuincey. Lit. rem. (Bost.) **2** : 101.

Saracens at Tours, Defeat of the. Archer. Decis. ev. 68.

— Bibliography. Ameer Ali. Short hist. of Saracens.

— Conquests of. Lord, J. Beacon, **2** : 23.

Saragossa. Stoddard, C. A. Span. cit. 43. — Hale, E. E. Seven Spanish cit. 247.

— Lerida to. Stoddard, C. A. Span. cit. 37.

— Shrines of Lourdes and. Cust. Ling. & orient. ess. 568.

— Siege of. Robson, W. Sieges, 561. — Stanhope, Earl. Miscel. **1** : 55.

Sarasate, Pablo de. With portrait. Buffen, F. F. Mus. celeb. 79. — With portrait. Ehrlich, A. Cel. violin. 191.

Sarasin, Jean-Fra. Besant. Fr. humor. 214.

Saratoga. Badeau. Vagabond, 180. — Curtis, G. W. Lotus, 105. — James, H. Portraits, 324. — (E. H. Walworth) Powell, L. P. Hist. towns mid. States, 39.

— Battle of. Creasy. Fifteen battles, 285. — King, C. Battles, 400. — Dawson. Batt. of U. S. **1** : 284.

— in 1877. Vivian. Tour in Amer. 32.

Saravia, Hadrian. McClure. Translators, 93.

Sarbiewski, Mathew Casimir. Soboleski. Poets of Poland, 81.

Sarcey, Francisque. Matthews, B. Books & play-books. — Matthews, B. Stud. stage, 126. With portrait. Warner Lib. **22** : 12825.

Sardinia. Vuillier. Forgot. isles, 261.

Sardis, Ruins of. Tweedie. Ruined cities, 18.

— Sieges of. Robson, W. Sieges, 111.

Sardou, Victorien. Henry, S. Hours w. Parisians, 21. — Matthews, J. B. Fr. dram. 172. — Mauris, M. de. Fr. men of lett. 199. — Men of 3d repub. 309. — Walkley, A. B. Playhouse, 80.

Schamyl, Country of. (W. Marshall) Vaca. tourists, **2** : 51.

Scharnhorst, Gerhard D. Baur. Relig. life Germ. **1** : 76.

Schäufelin, Hans Leonard. (A. Rosenberg) Dohme, R. Early mast. 158.

Schauffler, Mrs. Clara E. (Mrs. Douglas Putnam) Haydn, H. C. Am. miss. heroes, no. 1.

Schauffler, William G. Creegan. Gt. mission. 59. — With portrait. Haydn, H. C. Am. miss. heroes, no. 12.

Scheele, Carl Wilhelm. Thorpe, T. E. Ess. hist. chem. 53.

Scheffel, Joseph Victor von, with portrait. Warner Lib. **22** : 12837.

Scheffer, Ary. Appleton, J. G. Chequer-work, 303. — Q. You have heard of them, 164. — Hamerton. Contem. Fr. painters. — With portrait. Hubbard, E. Little jour. **5** : 321.

Scheffler, Johannes. Hatfield, E. F. Poets of church, 530.

Schellenberg, Battle of. Adams, W. H. D. Engl. at war, **1** : 122. — Low, C. R. Gt. battles, 63.

Schelling, Frederick W. J. Lewes. Biog. phil. — Erdmann. Hist. philos. **2** : 559. — Heine. Romantic school. — Hedge. Prose Ger. 509. — Frothingham. Transcend. 40.

Schenck, Robert C., with portrait. Carroll, H. Twelve Amer. 219.

Schenck, William Rogers. Coggeshall. Poets of west, 74.

Schenectady. (J. S. Landon) Powell, L. P. Hist. towns mid. states, 71.

Schenk, H. Theodore. Miller, Jos. Singers church, 2d ed. 155.

Schepler, Louise. Hack. Consec. wom. 231. — Owen, Mrs. O. F. Heroines domes. 285.

Schérer, Edmond. Dowden. New stud. 355. — Fisher, M. Group of Fr. crit. 40. — (V. Charbonnel) Warner Lib. **22** : 12865.

Schiller, J. C. Friedrich von. Bancroft, G. Miscel. 180. — Bryant. Prose, **2** : 215. — Bulwer. Ess. 387. — Carlyle. Essays. — DeQuincey. Biog. ess. (Bost.) 261. — Gostwick. Ger. poets, 153. — Hale, E. E. Lights two cent. 435. — With portrait. Hedge. Prose Ger. 365. — Longfellow. Poets Eur. 305. — Taylor. Stud. Ger. 266. — Duyckinck. Portr. gall. **1** : 310. — Roscoe. Germ. novel. **3** : 106. — Scherer. Germ. lit. **2** : 199. — Selss. Lit. Germ. 123. — Swankwick, A. Poets, 341. — With portrait. (E. P. Evans) Warner Lib. **22** : 12877. — Wells, B. W. Mod. Ger. lit. 219.

— Æsthetic letters, etc. Brownson. Works, **19** : 100.

— and Goethe. Scherer. Germ. lit. **2** : 170.

— Bibliography. Carruth, W. H. (ed.). Schiller's Wm. Tell. — Nevinson. Life of S.

— Cottage of, at Gohlis. Hoppin. Notes theol. stud. 71.

— Don Carlos. Jameson. Studies.

— Festival of; Address at Cooper Inst. Nov. 11, 1859. Bryant. Orations, 293.

— Kant, and Goethe, Triumvirate of. Hillebrand. Ger. thought, 173.

— Life and works of. Boyesen, H. H. Ess. Ger. liter. 177. — Everett, A. H. Crit. ess. **1** : 102.

— Life of. Müller. Chips, v. **3**.

— Poems of, translated. Herschel, J. F. W. Essays, 685.

Schimberg, Theodosius. Wallace, R. Anti-Trin. biog. **2** : 368.

Schinder-Hannes. See Buckler, Johann.

Schism in the modern church. Gladstone. Later gl. 280.

— of 1378. Sergeant, L. Wiclif, 219.

Schlechtweg, Hugo. Wraxall, F. C. L. Remark. adv. **2** : 48.

Schlegel, Friedrich von, with portrait. Warner Lib. **22** : 12913.

— and A. W. von. Hedge. Prose Ger. 472. — Heine. Romantic school.

Schleiermacher, Friedrich D. E. Baur. Relig. life Germ. **1** : 259. — Frothingham. Transcend. 48. — Hedge. Prose Ger. 441. — Lichtenberger. Hist. German theology, 46. — Martineau, J. Essays, **1** : 283. — Pfleiderer, O. Philos. of relig. 302. — Vaughan, R. A. Ess. & rev. v. **1**.

— Appearance of. Ker, J. Lec. hist. preach. 304.

— From Lessing to. (Egbert C. Smyth) Bost. lectures, '70 : 276.

— Preaching of. Ker, J. Lec. hist. preach. 288.

Schleswig-Holstein. Sybel. German empire, **1** : 247. **3** : 3. **4** : 3. — Walpole. Life of Russell, v. **2**.

— Language and poetry of. Müller. Chips, v. **3**.

— Question of. Disraeli. Sel. spee. **2** : 81.

Schley, Bradley G. Am. Bar Assoc. **18** : 549.

Schlichtingius, Jonas. Wallace, R. Anti-Trin. biog. **3** : 39.

Schlichtingius, Paul. Wallace, R. Anti-Trin. biog. **3** : 309.

Schlichtingius, Wolfgang. Wallace, R. Anti-Trin. biog. **2** : 424.

Schliemann, H., with photo. Cooper, T. Men of mark, **2** : 29.

— and his discoveries. (T. Chase) Am. Antiq. Soc. Proc. n. s. **7** : 257.

— Discoveries at Mycenæ. Newton. Essays, 246.

Schmidt, Christopher, Trial of. Phillips, S. M. Famous cases, 97.

Schmohling, Elizabeth, the child violinist. Phipson. Violinists, 150.

Schmolke, Benjamin. Hatfield, E. F. Poets of church, 532. — Miller, Jos. Singers church, 2d ed. 125. — Winkworth. Chr. singers Germ. 276.

Schnorr, Ludwig, Painting of St. Cecilia. Schlegel. Æsthet. (Bohn) 407.

Schoening, Maria Eleonora, Tale of. Coleridge. Friend, 312.

Scholar, The. Emerson. Lec. & biog. sk. 247.

— and the state, The. (R. H. Webster) Nat. Educa. Assoc. '99 : 143.

— Dream of a. Mabie. My study fire, 47.

— The ideal. (N. Porter) Phillips Ex. lec. '85–86 : 145.

— in American life. Potter, H. C. Scholar & state, 47.

— in politics, The. Swing. Old pic. **2** : 59.

— in a republic. Phillips, W. Speeches, **2** : 330.

— Mission of the. Brownson. Works, **19** : 65.

— Relation of, to practical life. Anderson, M. B. Papers, **1** : 121.

Scholars, Oriental. Cust. Ling. ess. **1** : 460.

— Shyness of. Hazlitt. Liter. rem. **2** : 397.

— Some old. Mabie. My study fire, 89.

Scholarship and service. Potter, H. C. Scholar and state, 71.

— Average, of the average pupil. (F. Rigler) Nat. Educa. Assoc. '99 : 86.

— Purposes of. Brooks, P. Ess. & addr. 247.

— Spontaneous element in. (S. C. Bartlett) Phillips Ex. lec. '85–86 : 79.

Scholarships. (J. L. Pickard) Nat. Educa. Assoc. '80 : 159.

School hygiene and school-houses. (A. G. Young) Maine Health, '91 : 83.

— Bibliography. (W. H. Burnham) Nat. Educa. Assoc. '98 : 505. — Kotelmann, L. School hygiene.

School incentives. (J. E. Bradley) N. Y. Regents, 89 : 575.

School influences. Osgood, S. Amer. leaves, 55.

School inspection, Scope and limitations. (Gerard) Internat. health exh. 13 : 301.

School law; recent decisions. U. S. Bur. Ed. Circ. '83, no. 4.

School legislation of Massachusetts, Features of. (J. White) Mass. Education, 29 : 70.

School life, Physical deterioration in. (J. H. Kellogg) Nat. Educa. Assoc. '96 : 899.

School management, Ethics of. (C. B. Gilbert) Nat. Educa. Assoc. '88 : 528.

School museums, libraries, and exhibitions of appliances for teaching. U. S. Bur. Ed. Rept. '91–92 : 247.

Schoolmaster, The. Johnston, R. M. Studies, 1.

— country, Sufferings of. Austin, W. Lit. papers, 99.

— The ideal. (T. J. Morgan) Nat. Educa. Assoc. '85 : 69.

School museums. (T. W. J. Blake) Internat. health exh. 14 : 548.

School organization in large cities. (A. S. Draper) Nat. Educa. Assoc. '94 : 298.

School privileges. Mann, H. Lec. 2 : 419.

School punishments. Mann, H. Lec. 1 : 333.

School question, Protestant and Catholic. Brownson. Works, 13 : 241.

School reminiscence. Beecher. Star papers, 189.

School savings-banks. (W. Oulton) Internat. health exh. 14 : 623.

— in France. (G. Serrurier) Cong. Educa. Chic. '93, 287.

— in the U. S. (J. H. Thiry) Cong. Educa. Chic. '93, 286.

School-ship Massachusetts. (M. M. Eldridge) N. Y. Pris. Assoc. 26, app. : 350.

School statistics. (W. T. Harris) Nat. Educa. Assoc. '91 : 361.

— as basis of legislative or official action. (H. M. Lafollette) Nat. Educa. Assoc. '90 : 377.

— Uniformity of. (Andrew McMillan) Nat. Educa. '81, app. : 17.

School superintendence. (T. C. Mendenhall) Nat. Educa. Assoc. '99 : 355.

— County. (J. W. Holcombe) Nat. Educa. Assoc. '85 : 162.

— Development of. (C. F. Adams) Nat. Educa. Assoc. '80 : 61 ; also in Adams, C. F. New dep. Quincy, 52.

— in cities. (E. E. White ; B. A. Hinsdale ; J. C. Dougherty) Nat. Educa. Assoc. '90 : 309.

— Popular criticisms of. (M. E. Gates) Nat. Educa. Assoc. '90 : 468.

School superintendent, Authority of. (E. E. White) Nat. Educa. Assoc. '99 : 314.

School superintendents and good literature. (O. H. Cooper) Nat. Educa. Assoc. '87 : 530.

— city, Duties of. (Aaron Gove) Nat. Educa. Assoc. '84 : 26.

— County, Duties of, to teachers. (E. B. McElroy) Nat. Educa. Assoc. '86 : 337.

— State, Powers and duties of. (N. C. Schaeffer) Nat. Educa. Assoc. '95 : 350.

School supervision. (John Hancock ; J. W. Akers) Nat. Educa. Assoc. '87 : 512. — (H. Sabin) Nat. Educa. Assoc. '97 : 127. — (J. W.

Chandler) N. Y. Regents, 93 : 569. — (L. S. Packard) N. Y. Regents, 88 : 685.

School supervision. (Committee on city school systems) Nat. Educa. Assoc. '84 : 19.

— and State aid. (W. W. Dowley) N. Y. Regents, 90 : 610.

— as viewed by the supervised. (S. L. Brooks) Nat. Educa. Assoc. '97 : 225.

— City and town. (R. W. Stevenson) Nat. Educa. Assoc. '84 : ?83.

— Efficient. (J. M. Greenwood) Nat. Educa. Assoc. '88 : 519.

— Extent, methods, and value of. Nat. Educa. Assoc. '72 : 245.

— The kind needed. (H. Sabin) Nat. Educa. Assoc. '97 : 127.

— State. (J. H. Smart and others) Nat. Educa. Assoc. '85 : 439.

— Teacher's side. (S. L. Brooks) Nat. Educa. Assoc. '97 : 225.

— True function of. (C. A. Babcock) Nat. Educa. Assoc. '96 : 242.

School supervisor, Duties and privileges of. (Sarah L. Arnold) Nat. Educa. Assoc. '98 : 228.

— Province of. (L. H. Jones) Nat. Educa. Assoc. '97 : 217.

School supplies, Relation of state to. (John Swett) Nat. Educa. Assoc. '88 : 198. — (R. W. Stevenson) Nat. Educa. Assoc. '88 : 211.

School system, Essentials of a. (D. F. De Wolf) Nat. Educa. Assoc. '81 : 55.

— of New England. Pidgeon. Old-world ques. 80.

— of the U. S. Brownson. Works, 10 : 564.

School systems, City. (W. T. Harris) Nat. Educa. Assoc. '89 : 437. — (W. H. Maxwell) Nat. Educa. Assoc. '90 : 447. — (Aaron Gove) Nat. Educa. Assoc. '96 : 464.

— Best, for a state. (J. H. Smart) Nat. Educa. Assoc. '80, app. : 31.

— — Business side of. (B. A. Hinsdale and H. M. James) Nat. Educa. Assoc. '88 : 310.

School training, early, True object of. (C. E. Meleney) Nat. Educa. Assoc. '85 : 313.

School war. Dixon, T. Liv. prob. 211.

School-work, Unsanitary methods and results of. Mich. Health, '82 : 61.

Schoolcraft, Henry Rowe. Griswold. Prose writ. 298. — Lanman, C. Haphazard, 365. — Youmans. Pioneers sci. 300.

Schoolmen, The. Newman, J. H. Hist. sk. 3 : 163. — Russell, J., Earl. Ess. Chris. relig. in W. Eur. 126.

— The age of. Newton, W. W. Ess. 30.

— and the mendicants. Trench. Lec. mediæval, 263.

— Earlier. Trench. Lec. mediæval, 200.

— Wiclif and the. Sergeant, L. Wiclif, 59. *See* Scholastic philosophy.

Schools and school life. Northcote. Lec. & ess. 185.

— art and literature, Why studied in. (W. T. Harris) Nat. Educa. Assoc. '97 : 261.

— Art in. (D. Farrar) Tollemache. Ess. & mock-ess. 99.

— Art teaching in. (W. H. Maxwell) Nat. Educa. Assoc. '97 : 268.

— Can their programmes be shortened ? Eliot, C. W. Educa. reform.

— city, Improved systems of. (H. P. Emerson) Nat. Educa. Assoc. '94 : 121.

— — Supervision of. (W. H. Maxwell) Nat. Educa. Assoc. '94 : 310.

— compulsory attendance of pupils. (T. B. Stockwell and others) Cong. Educa. Chic. '93, 82.

Schools, elementary, Curriculum of. (C. J. Lawson; B. Lambert) Trans. Soc. Sci. Lond. '79 : 399.
— — Essential studies in, and industrial needs. (C. M. Woodward, A. P. Marble, and others) Cong. Educa. Chic. '93, 266, 268.
— Special preparation for citizenship. (W. A. Mowry; C. H. Spence) Cong. Educa. Chic. '93, 273.
— — Use of works of art in. (T. C. Horsfall) Internat. health exh. 13 : 54.
— endowed, British. (G. B. Davis et al.) Trans. Soc. Sci. Lond. '84 : 335.
— English. Corbin, J. Schoolboy, 189.
— European. Mann, H. Lec. 2 : 230.
— evening, Adult. (J. C. Miller) Trans. Soc. Sci. Lond. '57 : 194.
— Factory, in England. (H. S. Tremenheere) Trans. Soc. Sci. Lond. '65 : 291.
— for neglected children. (J. S. Small) Cong. Educa. Chic. '93, 315.
— Foundation, of England. (J. D. Collis) Trans. Soc. Sci. Lond. '57 : 122.
— Free, and free governments. Winthrop, R. C. Addresses, 1 : 137.
— German, V. Cousin on. Hamilton. Discus.
— Girls'. (Louisa O. Hope) Trans. Soc. Sci. Lond. '60 : 397.
— — Structure, fitting and equipment of. (Canon Holland) Internat. Health exh. 13 : 25.
— Grading and classification of. (E. F. Young) Cong. Educa. Chic. '93, 83.
— grammar, Reform in. Hart, A. B. Stud. Am. educa. 20 : 22.
— half-time, English. Mass. Labor, '71 : 622.
— Health in. (J. S. Goodman) Mich. Health, '74 : 63.
— Heart of people towards. (C. G. Pearse) Nat. Educa. Assoc. '97 : 143.
— infant, British, under code of 1884. (A. Bourne) Internat. health exh. 13 : 120.
— — in France. (Mad. Dillon) Internat. health exh. 13 : 136.
— Mastery of studies in. (Lillie J. Martin) Nat. Educa. Assoc. '88 : 135.
— Medical inspection of. (S. H. Durgin) Am. Pub. Health, 21 : 149. — (W. B. Powell) Nat. Educa. Assoc. '98 : 454. — (D. Fall) Nat. Educa. Assoc. '98 : 534.
— middle-class, Curriculum of. (A. S. Wilkins ; H. J. Roby) Trans. Soc. Sci. Lond. '79 : 369.
— New demands upon, by the industries. (C. M. Woodward) Nat. Educa. Assoc. '93 : 594.
— of the 19th century. (F. L. Soldan) Nat. Educa. Assoc. '81 : 143.
— of Prussia. (J. W. Dickinson) Nat. Educa. Assoc. '70 : 152.
— of Switzerland, System of. (L. R. Klemm) U. S. Bur. Ed. Rept. '91–'92 : 197.
— Parochial : have they a proper place in America? (E. D. Mead; J. J. Keane) Nat. Educa. Assoc. '89 : 123.
— Preparation for active life in. (J. P. Irish ; W. E. Sheldon) Nat. Educa. Assoc. '88 : 144.
— Preparation for citizenship. (Duncan Brown) Nat. Educa. Assoc. '88 : 102.
— private, State or municipal supervision of. (J. C. Mackenzie) Nat. Educa. Assoc. '93 : 183.
— Roman Catholic, and education. Brownson. Works, 12 : 496.
— rural, Agriculture, chemistry, and botany in. (E. de Koralevsky) Nat. Educa. Assoc. '93 : 304.
— — Classification and instruction in. (W. T. Harris) Nat. Educa. Assoc. '97 : 121.

Schools, rural, Improv. of instruc. in. (A. T. Smith) U. S. Bur. Ed. Circ. '84, no. 6.
— — Instruction in, in Europe. (E. de Koralevsky) Cong. Educa. Chic. '93, 304.
— — Intellectual needs of. (D. L. Kiehle) Nat. Educa. Assoc. '97 : 132.
— — Need of more material support for. (B. A. Hinsdale) Nat. Educa. Assoc. '97 : 113.
— — Problem of. (E. E. White) Nat. Educa. Assoc. '94 : 669.
— — Report of committee of twelve on. Nat. Educa. Assoc. '97 : 385. — U. S. Bur. Ed. Rept. '96–97, 1 . 811.
— Sanitary legislation affecting. U. S. Bur. Ed. Rept. '93–94, 2 : 1301.
— Sanitation of. (W. A. Mowry) Nat. Educa. Assoc. '96 : 449.
See School hygiene.
— Secondary. (C. H. Verrill) N. Y. Regents, 99, app. : 153.
— — Colleges and. (C. F. P. Bancroft) N. Y. Regents, 88 : 695.
— — of England, Reform needed. Arnold, M. Mixed ess. 4.
— — of France, compared with English. Arnold, M. Mixed ess. 4.
— — Teachers for. (J. E. Russell) Nat. Educa. Assoc. '90 : 285.
See Secondary education, etc.
— State and parish, Union between. (John Ireland) Nat. Educa. Assoc. '90 : 179.
— State supervision of. (J. W. Patterson) Nat. Educa. Assoc. '90 : 432.
— Supervision of. See School supervision, above.
— Technical and trade. U. S. Cons. Rept. 45 : 530.
— — in Germany, 1894. U. S. Cons. Rept. 47 : 360.
See Technical education.
— Thrift in. (Prof. Laurent) Internat. health exh. 14 : 603.
— Uniformity in. Eliot, C. W. Educa. reform.
— — Undesirable and desirable. (C. W. Eliot) Nat. Educa. Assoc. '92 : 82.
— Upper. (James McCosh) Hamerton. Higher educa. 33.
— Village. Blunt. Ess. 475.
— Voluntary and school-board. (W. Hughes) Trans. Soc. Sci. Lond. '79 : 344.
— workhouse, Public schools and. (J. Wood) Trans. Soc. Sci. Lond. '82 : 335.
Schoonmaker, Augustus. Am. Bar Assoc. 17 : 530.
Schopenhauer, Arthur. Alger. Solitudes, 358. — Hedge. Atheism, 51. — Hueffer. Mus. stud. 85. — Saltus, E. E. Philos. of disench. — Royce, J. Spir. mod. philos. 228. — With portrait. (W. M. Payne) Warner Lib. 22 : 12923.
— Bibliography. Wallace. Life of S.
— Life and philosophy of. (E. B. Bax) Schopenhauer. Selec. ess. 9.
— Literary aspects of work of. Hueffer. Ital. stud. 173.
— Pessimism and. Cobbe, F. P. Peak in Darien, 93.
Schouler, James, Life of. Schouler, Jas. Hist. briefs, 169.
Schradieck, Henry, with portrait. Ehrlich, A. Cel. violin. 34.
Schreiner, Olive, with portrait. Warner Lib. 22 : 12957.
Schroder, J. H. Miller, Jos. Singers church, 2d ed. 119.
Schroeder, John Frederick. (J. G. White) N. E. Hist.-Gen. Soc. Biog. 3 : 168.

Schroeder-Devrient, Wilhelmina, German vocalist. Clayton, E. C. Queens, 288. — Ferris, G. T. Gt. singers, 2 : 67. — Needham. Queens of song.

Schubert, Franz, with portrait. Bie, O. Hist. of piano, 224. — Runciman, J. F. Old scores, 119. — Bourne, C. E. Gt. compos. 191. — Crowest. Tone-poets, 288. — Ferris. Germ. composers, 135. — Hale, E. E. Lights two cent. 343. — Haweis. Mus. & mor. 227. — Hueffer, F. Wagner, 125. — Keddie. Mus. composers, 329. — Parry, C. H. H. Gt. compos. 235. — Dole, N. H. Score, 283. — With portrait. Elson, L. Gt. composers, 128. — Sharp, R. F. Makers of music. — With portrait. Rowbotham. Priv. life compos. 192. — Statham. Music, 314.

— Bibliography. Paterson (N. J.) Pub. Lib. Bull. Feb., March, '97. — Providence Pub. Lib. Bull. Feb. '97.

Schulze-Delitzsch. Tuttle, H. Ger. pol. lead. 148.

Schumann, Clara, German pianist. Ferris, G. T. Great violinists, 216. — Maitland, J. A. F. Masters Ger. music, 228.

Schumann, Robert, with portrait. Bie, O. Hist. of piano, 231. — Bourne, C. E. Gt. compos. 299. — Crowest. Tone-poets, 347. — Engel, L. Mozart to Mario, 1 : 217. — Ferris. Germ. composers, 150. — Ferris, G. T. Great violinists, 216. — Hale, E. E. Lights two cent. — Hueffer. Wagner, 193. — Keddie. Mus. comp. 342. — Parry, C. H. H. Gt. composers, 289. — Dole, N. H. Score, 375. — With portrait. Elson, L. Gt. composers, 180. — Sharp, R. F. Makers of music. — Hadow. Stud. mod. mus. v. 1. — With portrait. Rowbotham. Priv. life compos. 251.

— and his school. Ehlert. Tone-world, 209.
— and the programme-symphony. Henderson, W. J. Preludes.
— Bibliography. Paterson (N. J.) Pub. Lib. Bull. Feb., March, '97.
— in his letters. Finck. Chopin, 111.

Schuppach, Michael. Brightwell. Byepaths of biog. 20.

Schurmann, Anna Maria. Ellet. Women artists, 99.

Schurz, Carl. Johnston, A. Amer. ora. 4 : 400. — With portrait. (J. F. Rhodes) Warner Lib. 22 : 12974.

Schurz, Carl, Tribute to. Pierce, E. L. Addresses, 246.

Schuyler, Catherine V. R. Ellet. Women of revol. 1 : 57. — (S. F. Cooper) Wister & Irwin. Women, 71.

Schuyler, Eugene. Richardson. Amer. lit. 1 : 507.

Schuyler, Montgomery, with portrait. Butterfield. Lec. Un. Coll. 1 : 169.

Schuyler, Philip. With portrait. [Am.] Nat. portr. gall. v. 2. — With portrait. Duyckinck. Nat. portr. gall. 1 : 264. — With portrait. Headley, J. T. Washington, 1 : 229. — Lossing. Em. Amer. 189.

Schuyler family and home. Glenn, T. A. Colon. mans. 2 : 395. — Terhune, M. V. More colon. homes, 187.

Schuyler house, Pompton, N. J. Terhune. Colon. homes, 141.

Schuyler, Fort, and Oriskany. Dawson. Batt. of U. S. 1 : 237.

Schwartz, Christian Friedrich. Yonge. Pioneers.

Schwarz, Karl. Ker, J. Lec. hist. preach. 374.

Schwatka, Lieut. F. Adams, W. H. D. In perils, 216.
— Reception to, 1880, by Am. Geog. Soc. of N. Y. Am. Geog. Soc. 12 : 237.

Schweidnitz, Sieges of. Robson, W. Sieges, 522.

Schweinichen, H. von. Memoirs. Baring-Gould. Oddities, 1 : 67.

Schweinitz, Lewis David von. Youmans. Pioneers sci. 167.

Schwenkfelders. Gibbons, P. E. Penn. Dutch.

Sciarra, Marco. Macfarlane, C. Banditti, 19.

Science. Bartol. Principles, 108. — Kingsley. Health, 259; or Sci. lec. — Lubbock. Pleas. 153.
— Advance of, in last half century. (T. H. Huxley) Smithson. Rept. '87 : 57.
— — Three English bishops on. Huxley. Ess. contro. 232.
— American, Literature of. Richardson. Amer. lit. 1 : 510.
— and Christianity. Newman, J. H. Lec. univ. 221. — Oxenham. Stud. in eccl. hist. 1.
— and the church. Godkin. Reflections, 138.
— and crime. Wilson, A. Nat. note-bk. 1.
— and culture. Huxley. Sci. & cul. 7. — (C. E. Bessey) Nat. Educa. Assoc. '96 : 939.
— and education. (W. L. Bryan) Nat. Educa. Assoc. '95 : 161.
— and faith. Hedge, F. H. Martin Luther, 173. — (F. Guizot) Noyes, G. R. Theol. ess. v. 1.
— and the French Revolution. Mallock. Stud. contemp. sup. 201.
— and literature. Arnold, M. Disc. Amer. 72. — Burroughs, J. Indoor, 43.
— — Relations between. Nettleship, H. Lec. 2d ser. 235. — Thirlwall, C. Remains, 3 : 284.
— and man, Tyndall's. Porter, N. Sci. & sent. 192.
— and modern life. Potter, H. C. Scholar and state, 111.
— and morals. Huxley. Ess. contro. 163.
— and orthodoxy in England. McCarthy, J. Mod. lead. 233.
— and philosophy. Rands, W. B. Holbeach, 2 : 197.
— — Relations of. Hinton. Thinking, 131.
— and poetry. Japp. Vers de soc. 164. — Wilson, A. Leisure, 360.
— and the poets. Burroughs, J. Indoor, 67.
— and pseudo-science. Huxley. Ess. contro. 206.
— and religion. Martineau, J. Ess. 1 : 121. — Proctor, R. A. Fam. sci. 30. — Mozley, J. B. Lec. 17.
— — Draper on conflict of. Brownson. Works, 9 : 547. — Fiske, J. Unseen world, 138.
— and revelation. Stephen, L. Eng. thought, 1 : 389.
— and the sciences. Brownson. Works, 9 : 254.
— and sentiment. Porter, N. Sci. & sent. 11.
— and the state. Playfair. Subj. soc. 225.
— and theism. Hutton. Ess. theol. 1 : 45.
— and theology. Balfour, A. J. Founda. belief, 298. — Hinton. Thinking, 119.
— and war. (H. B. Pritchard) Estes. Half-hour, v. 2.
— Awakening of. Osborn. From Greeks, 86.
— Beginnings of, in the U. S. Parton. Triumphs, 97.
— Bibliography. Nottingham (Eng.) Pub. Lib. Aug. '95.
— culture, acquirement. Hudson. Studies Wordsworth, 259.
— Culture in, for the masses. Wilson, A. Leisure, 27.

Scudder, Isaac Williamson. Am. Bar Assoc. 5 : 146.

Scudéry, Madeleine de. Kavanagh. Fr. wom. 21. — Mason, A. G. Wom. of Fr. salons, 34.

Scuderys, The. Disraeli, I. Curios. (N. Y. 4 v.) 1 : 167.

Sculptors, French. Perkins, C. C. Tusc. sculp. 2 : 127.

Sculpture. Day. Science of æsthetics. — East-lake. Contrib. 1 : 63. — Lacroix. Arts in middle ages, 253. — Patterson, R. II. Ess. hist. 102. — Sampson. Elem. of art criticism.
— American. Badeau. Vagabond, 221.
— American school of, An. Partridge, W. W. Art. for Amer. 33.
— and its relation to painting. Guizot. Fine arts, 4.
— and painting. Palgrave. Ess. on art, 264.
— Bibliography. Marquand and Frothingham. Textbk. hist. sculp. — Partridge, W. O. Technique sculp. — Radcliffe, A. G. Schools & masters sculp.
— Flaxman on. Hazlitt. Crit. on art, ser. 1.
— French, 1600–1700. Dilke. Art in the mod. state.
— Giants at the gates. Baxter, L. E. Tusc. stud. 13.
— Greek. Duruy. Hist. Greece, 3 : 116. — Newton. Essays, 73.
— — Beginnings of. Pater. Greek stud. 194.
— in America, Outlook for. Partridge, W. O. Art for Amer. 60.
— in England, Position of. Palgrave. Ess. on art, 245.
— Modern French. Child, T. Art & criticism, 216.
— Moral effects of. Knox. Essays, 2 : 47.
— Religious aspects of. Stanley, A. P. Ser. spec. occ. 57.

Scurvy, Pulque as a prophylaxis of, in prisons. (F. M. Baca) Am. Pub. Health, 22 : 287.

Scythe out of fashion. Whiting, C. G. Saunterer, 86.

Sea, The. Arnold, E. Wand. words, 311. — Bushnell. Moral uses, 344. — Greenwood, F. W. P. Miscel. 227.
— At. Burroughs. Fresh fields, 287.
— Chapter on. Hobart, V. H. H. Ess. & miscel. 1 : 188.
— deep, Deposits of. (A Daubrée) Smithson. Inst. Rept. '93 : 545.
— — Explorations in. Dunman. Talks sci. 185.
— Carpenter, W. B. Nature, 316.
— — Temperature and animal life of. (W. B. Carpenter) Manch. sci. lec. 2 : 111.
— in early English literature. Brooke, S. A. Hist. early Eng. lit. 162.
— Jurisdiction over. (S. Amos and H. Young) Trans. Soc. Sci. Lond. '77 : 165.
— Leaves from my journal. Lowell. Writ. 1 : 100.
— Lessons of. Parsons, T. Ess. 3 : 180.
— Life at, Preservation of. (T. B. M. Mason) Am. Geog. Soc. 11 : 59.
— Loss of life at. Chamberlain, J. Speeches, 172.
— Plant life in. (L. Kny) Estes. Half-hour, v. 2.
— Plants of. Forbes, E. Lit. papers, 293.
— Religion of. Greenwood, F. W. P. Miscel. 278.
— Superstitions of. Jones, W. Credulities, 1. — Kelley, J. D. J. Ship's co. 101.

Sea-birds, Amongst the. Watkins, M. G. In country, 211.

Sea-cow, great northern, Extermination of. (L. Stejneger) Am. Geog. Soc. 18 : 317.

Sea creatures, Strange. Proctor, R. A. Pleas. ways, 199; *or* Nat. stud. 90.

Sea-duels, Great. Fitchett. Deeds, 74.

Sea-elephants, Hunters of. Lanman, C. Recoll. 55.

Sea-lions and seals. Morgan, C. L. Animal sk. 108.

Seamanship, Hardships of. Kelley, J. D. J. Ship's co. 149.

Sea-serpents of science. Wilson, A. Leisure, 95.

Sea-shore. Whiting, C. G. Saunterer, 101.
— Hunt on. Buckland, F. T. Curios. nat. hist. 2 : 213.
— Inland *vs.* Beecher. Star papers, 110.

Seaside, At the. Watkins, M. G. In country, 13.
— By the. Boyd. Aut. holid. 1.

Sea-songs, American. Williams, A. M. Stud. folk, 1.

Sea studies. Froude. Short stud. 3 : 147.

Sea-voyage on an Indiaman. Chambers's Papers, no. 52.

Seaweed. Simmonds. Comm. prod. 311.

Seabury, Samuel. Lossing. Em. Amer. 110.

Seafield, Anna Ogilvie, countess of. Burder. Pious wom. 335.

Seaforth, Fate of. Burke, B. Viciss. of fam. 3 : 266.

Seagar, Francis. Holland, J. Psalmists, 1 : 165.

Seagrave, Robert. Hatfield, E. F. Poets of church, 542. — Miller, Jos. Singers church, 2d ed. 152.

Seal, Joseph H. Winslow, S. N. Biog. Phila. merch. 43.

Seal, Roderick. Livingston, J. Dist. Amer. 299.

Seal, The great, of England. Jeaffreson. Lawyers, 1.
— — Changes in. Foss. Judges, 3 : 315.
— — of New England. (J. Appleton) Mass. Hist. Proc. 6 : 79.

Seals of Massachusetts, State. (T. C. Amory) Mass. Hist. Proc. 10 : 94.
— — Provincial. (A. C. Goodell, jr.) Mass. Hist. Proc. 20 : 157.
— Scottish, Ancient. Stirling-Maxwell. Miscel. ess. 215.

Seals of the West Indies. (F. W. True and F. A. Lucas) U. S. Nat. Mus. Rept. '84 : 331.
— Fur, and the Behring Sea arbitration. (J. S. Brown) Am. Geog. Soc. 26 : 326.

Search, Right of. Brougham. Works, 8 : 385.
— Harcourt, W. V. Letters fr. Times.

Searle, John. Campbell. Ld. chan. 1 : 263.

Sears, Dr. Barnas, Services rendered to Southern schools by. Winthrop. Addresses, 4 : 206.

Sears, David. (R. C. Winthrop, jr.) Mass. Hist. Proc. 2d ser. 2 : 405.

Sears, Edmund Hamilton. Hatfield, E. F. Poets of church, 546. — (C. Robbins) Mass. Hist. Proc. 18 : 224. — Miller, Jos. Singers church, 2d ed. 507. — Putnam, A. P. Singers liberal, 305.

Sears, Isaac. Lossing. Em. Amer. 251.

Sears, Philip Howes. Am. Bar Assoc. 21 : 673.

Seasons, The. Holmes, O. W. Old vol. 132. — Mitchell, D. G. Bound toge. 61.
— and their change. Saunders. Stray leaves, 69.

Seaton, W. W. Lanman, C. Haphazard, 41.

Seaton castle and palace. Mackie, C. Castles of Mary.

Seattle, Municipal condition of. (E. O. Graves) Nat. Conf. City Govt. 2–3 : 439.

Sebastian, Don (1554–78). Utterton, A. A. Biog. sk. 197.

Sebastiano, Fra. Jervis, Lady. Painting, 1 : 230.

Sebastopol, Siege of. Arnold, R. A. Levant, 2 : 166. — Great sieges, 600. — Knox, T. W. Decis. battles, 133. — Robson, W. Sieges, 600. — Valentine, L. J. Sea-fights, 280.
See also Crimean war.
Secession. Buchanan, J. Messages, 136. — Seward. Works (1884), 4 : 644.
— Against. Davis, H. W. Speeches, 187.
— Legality of, and History of. Foster, R. Comment. on Const. 1 : 110, 163.
— northern, Proposed, 1814. Roosevelt. Life of G. Morris.
— Oration on. Phillips, Wend. Speeches, 396.
— Orations for and against. (T. L. Clingman and others) Johnston, A. Amer. ora. v. 3.
— Republican party and. Seward. Works (1884), 4 : 410.
— Right of. Lyon, N. Last pol. writ. 224.
— — Early assertions of. Foster, R. Comment. on Const. 1 : 116.
Secluded life. Gardner, S. J. Aut. leaves, 228.
Second Advent, The. Whedon. Ess. 2 362.
— Edward Irving's Ben-Ezra. Coleridge. Lit. rem. 4 : 399.
Second-sight in Scotland. Aubrey, J. Miscel.
Second University of Maryland, Baltimore, Md. U. S. Bur. Ed. Circ. '94, no. 2 : 118.
Secondary education. (E. E. Brown) Butler, N. M. Educa. in U. S. 141.
— and the university problem. (A. F. West) Nat. Educa. Assoc. '85 : 195.
— Bibliography. (E. F. Brown) School R. Feb.-Mar. '97 : 84.
— English Royal Commission, 1894. U. S. Bur. Ed. Rept. '94-95, 1 : 583.
— in Great Britain. U. S. Bur. Ed. Rept. '90-91 : 135.
— in New Zealand. (Robert Stout) U. S. Bur. Ed. Rept. '90-91 : 45.
— in the U. S., Reform of. (N. M. Butler) U. S. Bur. Ed. Rept. '92-93 : 1448.
— of girls in France. (Marie Dugard) Nat. Educa. Assoc. '93 : 211.
— Reform of, in U. S. Butler, N. M. Meaning of educa. 187.
Secondary school and higher education. Walker, F. A. Discus. in educa. 323.
Secondary school, courses in, Modifications of. (C. H. Keyes) Nat. Educa. Assoc. '95 : 731.
— Differentiation of the American. (C. H. Keyes) Nat. Educa. Assoc. '99 : 412.
— Function of. Butler, N. M. Meaning of educa. 151.
— What is a? (E. W. Coy) Nat. Educa. Assoc. '96 : 613.
Secondary schools, Algebra and geometry in. (W. N. Hailmann and others) Cong. Educa. Chic. '93, 221.
— are they defective? (C. P. Lynch) Nat. Educa. Assoc. '94 : 845.
— Changes in. (O. T. Bright) Nat. Educa. Assoc. '95 : 259.
— College requirements of. N. Y. Regents' Rept. 108 : 787.
— Course of study in. (G. N. Carman) Cong. Educa. Chic. '93, 193.
— Curriculum for. (W. T. Harris) U. S. Bur. Ed. Rept. '92-93 : 1457. '94 : 496.
— — Organization of. Laurie, S. S. Educa. add. 59.
— Languages and sciences in. (D. W. Abercrombie ; C. F. P. Bancroft) Cong. Educa. Chic. '93, 196, 199.
— Latin and modern languages. (C. W. Pearson ;

W. W. Smith) Cong. Educa. Chic. '93, 234, 235.
Secondary schools, Relation of, to college or university. (W. R. Webb ; R. B. Warder) Nat. Educa. Assoc. '77 : 70.
— Studies in. Bibliography. U. S. Comm. Educa. Rept. '92-93, 2 : 1491.
— — Report of Committee of Ten. U. S. Bur. Ed. Rept. '92-93 : 1415.
— teachers for, Training of. (E. P. Hughes) Cong. Educa. Chic. '93, 217.
Soorooy. Helps, Essays, 51
Secret societies. DeQuincey. Hist. ess. (Bost.) 2 : 285. — Elder, W. Questions, 264. — Robertson, J. B. Lec. mod. hist. 321.
— and sacred mysteries. (S. D. Peet) Cong. Anthrop. Chic. 1893, 176.
— in France. (J. de Paris) Coan. Soc. prob. 75.
— in the middle ages. Chambers's Papers, no. 33.
— in modern Europe. Chambers's Papers, no. 15.
— of modern times. Robertson, J. B. Lec. mod. hist. 405.
Sects. Bushnell. Building eras, 387.
— in the U. S. Fisher, G. P. Hist. of the church, 559.
— New affinities. Martineau, J. Ess. 2 : 449.
— of the middle ages. Trench. Lec. mediæval, 213.
— Tendency of. Hazlitt. Round table, 6.
Secular, The, and the sacred. Gladden. Ruling ideas, 97.
Secularism. (G. W. Foote) Relig. systems, 794.
— Vaughan, D. J. Questions, 188.
Secularists. Alviella. Contemp. evol. 147.
Secularization, Era of. Stillé. Stud. med. 440.
Securinus, John. Wallace, R. Anti-Trin. biog. 2 : 209.
Sedan, Battle of. Knox, T. W. Battles, 344.
Sedgmoor, Battle of. Adams, W. H. D. Eng. at war, 1 : 102.
— and Monmouth rebellion. (K. Parkes) Walters, J. C. Bygone Som. 6.
Sedgwick, Adam. Stoughton, J. Worthies of sci. 314.
Sedgwick, Catharine Maria. Duyckinck. Portrait gall. 2 : 80. — Hart, J. S. Fem. prose, 17.
— With portrait. [Amer.] Nat. portr. gall. 1.
— Griswold. Prose writ. 357. — With portrait. Mitchell, D. G. Am. lands, 349.
Sedgwick, Gen. John. Curtis, G. W. Orations, 3 : 1.
Sedgwick, William Dwight. (L. T. Sedgwick) Harvard mem. biog. 1 : 167.
Sedimentation in water. (W. Johnston) Am. Pub. Health Assoc. 20 : 37.
Seditions and troubles. Bacon. Ess.
Sedley, Catharine. Macaulay. Biog. sk. 149.
Sedley, Sir Chas. Dunham. Lit. & sci. men, 3 : 171. — Jesse. Court of Eng. Stuarts, 3 : 325.
Sedulius, Cœlius. Miller, Jos. Singers church, 2d ed. 10.
Seeds. Japp & Holmes. Succ. bus. men, 142.
— Dispersal of. Allen, Grant. Science in Arc. 40.
— — Bibliography. Beal, W. J. Seed dispersal.
— Germination of. Bibliography. (F. Escombe) Science Prog. Oct. '97.
Seeing life. Butler, E. Gentle ways, 146.
Seeley, John Robert. Natural religion. Myers. Ess. mod. 289.
Seeming and the actual, The. Parsons, T. Ess. 2 : 1.
Seers, thinkers, and talkers. Patmore. Princ. in art, 14.
Segerson, Jeronimus, and his wife. Brown, J. N. Bapt. martyrs, 123.

Segethus, Thomas. Wallace, R. Anti-Trin. biog. **2** : 541.

Seghers, Charles John. Clarke, R. H. Cath. bishops, **3** : 509.

Segui. Freeman. Studies Italy, 150.

Segura, J. L. Ticknor. Span. lit. **1** : 56.

Seidelius, George. Wallace, R. Anti-Trin. biog. **3** : 4.

Seidelius, Martin. Wallace, R. Anti-Trin. biog. **3** : 575.

Sejour, Victor. Davidson, J. W. Writ. of South, 501.

Selborne, R. Palmer, Lord. With portrait. Cooper, T. Men of mark, **1** : 22. — Hill, F. H. Polit. portr. 156. — Reid. Cab. portr. 251.

Selby, Eng. Freeman. Eng. towns, 302.

Selden, John. Adams, W. H. D. Learned in law, 75. — Fuller. Worthies, **3** : 259. — Lodge. Portraits (Bohn), v. 5. — Roscoe, H. Em. lawyers, **1** : 61. — Morley, H. Eng. writ. **11** : 160. — With portrait. Warner Lib. **22** : 13099. — Wrangham. Brit. Plutarch, v. 3.

— Table talk. Adams, W. D. Famous books, 251.

Selden, William B. Walker, C. D. Biog. Va. Mil. Inst. 463.

Selection, Color in animals and. Wallace, A. R. Trop. nat. 158.

— From natural to Christian. (J. C. Kimball) Brooklyn Eth. Assoc. Life, 333.

— Literary. Couch, A. T. Q. Adv. crit. 198.

— Natural. Mivart. Less. fr. nature, 280.

— — Evolution by. Wright, C. Philos. dis. 168.

— — Civilization antagonistic to. Greg. Enig. 111.

— — Limits of. Wright, C. Philos. disc. 97.

— — Primeval vegetation and. (W. C. Williamson) Owens College essays, '74 : 199.

— — Socialism and. (B. Bosanquet) Bosanquet. Asp. soc. **9** : 289.

— Reproductive. Pearson, K. Chances, **1** : 63.

— Sexual. Mivart. Less. fr. nature, 302.

— Socialism and. Pearson, K. Chances, **1** : 103.

Seleucus Nicator. Mahaffy, J. P. Greek life, ch. 3.

Self. Friswell. Wick. world, 93.

— My lost. Boyesen. Lit. silhouettes, 194.

— The subliminal. (F. W. H. Myers) Soc. Psych. Res. **11** : 334.

— Talking of. Ess. from Sat. R. 259.

Self-activity in education. (J. G. Schurman and others) Cong. Educa. Chic. '93, 703.

Self-advancement, The arts of. Helps. Friends, 2d ser. v. **1**.

Self-consciousness, Evolution of. Wright, C. Philos. dis. 199.

— Freedom from. Mabie. Ess. on work, 231.

— in education. (E. T. Jeffers) Nat. Educa. Assoc. '82 : 8.

Self-control. Bulwer, E. Caxtoniana, 209. — Starling, E. Noble deeds wom. 356.

Self-culture. Channing. Works, **2** : 347. — Hoyt, J. G. Miscel. 299.

Self-denial. Channing. Works, **4** : 105.

— Christian ; a sermon. Boyd. Graver tho'ts, 274.

Self-depreciation, The trick of. Higginson. New world, 206.

Self-destruction. Rands, W. B. Holbeach, **2** : 275.

Self-development and self-abnegation. Cobbe, F. P. Studies, 49.

— and self-surrender. Bryant, S. Short stud. 97.

Self-discipline. Helps. Essays, 15.

Self-education. Thirlwall, C. Remains, **3** : 257.

Self-education, Necessity of. Lieber, F. Reminis. 281.

Self-extinction, Pleasing art of. Higginson. Conc. all, 176.

Self-help. Holland, J. G. Plain talks, 9.

Self-knowledge. Clarke, J. F. Self-culture, 93. — Genin, T. H. Selec. writ. — Thomson, E. Essays, 168.

Self-love. Bacon. Ess. — Rands, W. B. Holbeach, **1** : 176. — Hazlitt. Lit. rem. **2** : 1.

— and benevolence. Hazlitt. Sket.

Self-made men. Gardner, S. J. Aut. leaves, 156. — Holland, J. G. Plain talks, 9. — (E. G. Robinson) Phillips. Ex. lec. '85–86 : 125.

Self-reliance. Burke, B. Viciss. of fam. **3** : 246. — Emerson. Ess. **1** : 45.

— and courage. Munger. On threshold, 99.

Self-sacrifice, Law of. Anderson, M. B. Papers, **1** : 179.

— What is ? Craik, D. M. Sermons, 9.

Selfishness. Hazlitt. Table talk.

— Hidden. Friswell. Wick. world, 67.

— Proverbs of. Henry, C. S. About men, 184.

Selkirk, Alex. Scott, W. Biog. mem. v. **2**. — Chambers's Miscel. no. 140.

Selkirks, glaciers of, Scenes among. Rutgers, L. On saddle, 166.

Sellar, William Y. Barrie. Edinburgh eleven, 77.

Sellon, Baker John. Woolrych. Serjeants, **2** : 806.

Sellwood, Sir Andrew. Russell, W. Eccen. 50.

Selnecker, Nicholas. Winkworth. Chr. singers Germ. 151.

Selover, A. A. Parton, J. Sk. of men of prog.

Selves, Our two. Friswell. Wick. world, 80.

Selwyn, George. Hayward, A. Ess. **1** : 149. — Thomson, K. & J. C. Wits & beaux, 307. — Street, G. S. Miniatures, 57.

Selwyn, George Augustus, bp. Japp. Labor, 100. — Jesse, J. H. Cel. Eton. v. **2**. — Smith, G. B. Chr. workers, 391.

Semble, Henry C. Am. Bar Assoc. **17** : 497.

Sembrich, Marcella, with portrait. Buffen, F. F. Mus. celeb. 49.

Seminole war, The. Clay. Life & speeches, **5** : 179.

Seminoles, The. Drake, F. S. Indian hist. 405. — Irving. Crayon pap. 137.

Semiramis. Goodrich, F. B. Women, 13. — Hewitt, M. E. Illus. women. — Jameson. Fem. sov. **1**. — Owen, Mrs. O. F. Heroines hist. 41.

Semitic contributions to the history of civilization. Renan. Studies (N. Y.), **1** : 149.

Semitic culture. Deutsch, E. Lit. rem. 159.

Semitic languages. Deutsch, E. Lit. rem. 293.

Semitic palæography. Deutsch, E. Lit. rem. 153.

Semitic race, Characteristics of. Nöldeke, T. Sk. fr. east. hist. **1**.

Semler. Ker, J. Lec. hist. preach. 224.

Semmes, Raphael. Davidson, J. W. Writ. of South, 502.

Semmes, Thomas Jenkins. Am. Bar Assoc. **22** : 680.

Sempill, Francis. Wilson, J. G. Poets of Scot. **1** : 81.

Semple, Gabriel. Blaikie, W. G. Preachers Scot. 166.

Senancour, Etienne P. de. Warner Lib. **22** : 13111.

Senate, U. S. Foster, R. Comment. on Const. **1** : 355, 457, 499, 512, 529, 612.

— Basis of. Webster, D. Works, **3** : 8.

— in the Federal Convention. Foster, R. Comment. on Const. **1** : 466.

Senate, U. S., Officers of.   Foster, R. Comment. on Const. 1 : 499.
— Origin of.   Foster, R. Comment. on Const. 1 : 459.
— Roll of members, 1789–89. (W. S. Appleton) Mass. Hist. Soc. Proc. 2d ser. 10 : 9.
Sendigovius, Michael.   Waite, A. E. Lives of alchem. 175.
Seneca, L. A., with portrait.   Warner Lib. 22 : 13119.
— and his writings.   Malkin. Class. disq. 285.
— and the later Roman tragedy.   Conington. Miscel. 385.
— Biography of.   Farrar. Seekers, v. 1.
Seneca Indians, Expedition against.   Dawson. Batt. of U. S. 1 : 533.
Senegal.   Norman. Colonial France, 23.
Senesino, F. B., Italian singer.   Hogarth. Mem. opera, 1 : 313.
Senior, Henry.   Charles Vernon.   Senior. Ess. on fic. 189.
Senior, Job.   Baring-Gould. Yorks. odd. 2 : 18.
Senkrah, Arma, with portrait.   Ehrlich, A. Cel. violin. 193.
Sennefelder, Alois.   Brightwell. Heroes of lab. 141.
Sensation and the sensiferous organs.   Huxley. Sci. & cul. 253.
— Mechanism of.   Dunman. Talks sci. 1.
— Metaphysics of.   Huxley. Critiques.
Sensational, The, in literature and life.   Whipple. Outlooks, 63.
Sensational school.   Lewes. Biog. phil.
Senses, The.   Le Pileur, A. Wonders of human body. — (C. Robertson) Manch. sci. lec. 5–6 : 97. — Parsons, T. Ess. 2 : 49.
— External, of man.   Smith, Adam. Ess. phil. 195.
— Gateways of knowledge.   Thomson, Sir W. Popular lec. 1.
— Higher.   Gurney. Power of sound.
— Limits and fallacies of.   Scoffern. Stray leaves, 311.
— Missing, and new ones.   Martin, E. S. Windfalls, 167.
— Perfection of, important to the intellect.   Hamerton. Intellec. 36.
— Relation to art.   Samson. Art criticism.
Sensibilities, Education of.   (J. W. Dowd) Nat. Educa. Assoc. '81 : 231.
Sensibility in French literature.   Saintsbury. Ess. Fr. nov. 112.
Sensitiveness to criticism, Folly of.   Mathews. Lit. style, 100.
Sentences, Indeterminate penal.   (Z. R. Brockway) Nat. Pris. Assoc. '87 : 184. — (E. Smith) Nat. Pris. Assoc. '87 : 199. — (F. Wayland) Trans. Soc. Sci. Lond. '81 : 322.
— — a necessity.   (G. W. Burchard) Conf. char. & correc. '82 : 189.
— limited, Objections to.   (M. D. Hill) N. Y. Pris. Assoc. 26, app. : 105.
— Terms of.   (R. Pitman) N. Y. Pris. Assoc. 26, app. : 95.
Sentiment and pretension.   Friswell. Better self, 267.
— Decay of.   Repplier. Books, 94.
Sentimental, Decline of the.   Higginson. New world, 178.
Sentimentalism.   Finlayson, T. C. Ess. 203.
— in literature.   Lowell. Writ. 2 : 250.
Sentimentality in American verse.   Richardson. Amer. lit. 2 : 219.
Seoul and its inhabitants.   Norman, H. Far East, 341.

Seoul, Trip from, to Peng Yang.   (S. B. Bernerston) Am. Geog. Soc. 16 : 234.
Sepoy mutiny.   See India, Mutiny in.
September, Customs and superstitions of.   Soane. New curios. 2 : 156.
Sepulchres.   Tuckerman. Collector, 203. — Tuckerman. Criterion, 202.
— Curious forms of, in East Yorkshire.   Wright, T. Ess. archæol. 1 : 37.
— Pagan and Christian.   Milman. Savonarola, 446.
Sequoia.   Gray, A. Darwiniana, 205.
Serao, Matilde.   Warner Lib. 22 : 13133.
Serapion the Sindonite.   Hahn-Hahn. Fathers, 210.
Serapis, Temple of.   Adams, W. H. D. Fam. caves, 40.
"Serapis," frigate, Capture of.   Dawson. Batt. of U. S. 1 : 554.
Seres, On the existence of a nation called.   Latham. Opuscula, 89.
Serf, St.   Kingsley. Hermits, 255.
Serfdom in England.   Allen, W. F. Essays, 240.
— — 14th century.   Mackay. English poor.
Sergeant, Adeline, with portrait.   Black, H. C. Wom. authors, 157.
Sergeant, John.   Brown, D. P. Forum, 2 : 205.
— Moore, F. Am. eloq. 2 : 506.
Sergeant, Thomas.   (T. S. Perry) N. E. Hist.-Gen. Soc. Biog. 4 : 69.
Seringapatam, Siege of.   Robson, W. Sieges, 559.
Serle, Ambrose.   Miller, Jos. Singers church, 2d ed. 283.
Sermons.   Boyd. Graver tho'ts, 14.
— Barrow to Manning.   Reed, W. B. Among books, 129.
— Length of.   Phelps, A. Portfolio, 117.
Serpa-Pinto, Alexander de.   See Pinto.
Serpents, Anecdotes of.   Chambers's Miscel. no. 80.
Serpent-worship and tree-worship, Fergusson on.   Cobbe, F. P. Darwinism, 175.
— Origin of.   Wake. Serpent wor. 81.
Serra in the Apennines.   Jarves. Ital. ramb. 41.
Serre, Pierre François Hercule, Comte de.   Cormenin. Orators, 102.
Serres, Mrs. Olivia.   Thomson, K. B. Recoll. v. 2.
Sertorius, Quintus.   (Plutarch) Ferris, G. T. Gt. leaders, 44.
Servants and houses.   Ruskin. Arrows, v. 1.
— and masters, Relation between.   Craik, D. M. Sermons, 145.
— Maid-.   Payn. Private views, 149.
— Man-.   Payn. Private views, 165.
— Our.   Friswell. Gentle life, 1 : 164.
See Domestics.
Servetus, Michel.   Burke, S. H. Hist. portr. Tudor, 3 : 100. — Wallace, R. Anti-Trin. biog. 1 : 420.
— Burning of, 1553.   Bacon, L. W. Irenics, 205.
Servia, Church and people of.   (W. T. Greive) Vaca. tourists, 3 : 417.
— in 1887.   Laveleye. Balkan peninsula. — Minchen. Balkan peninsula.
Servian princes and the tragedy of Topchiderch.   Kingston, W. B. Music & manners, 2 : 235.
Servile war in the East, in the 9th century.   Nöldeke, T. Sk. fr. east. hist. 146.
Serving one another.   (Miss Petrie) Burdett-Coutts. Wom. miss. 300.
Setchel, Sarah.   Clayton, E. C. Eng. fem. art. 2 : 124.

Seton, Elizabeth Ann, with portrait. Murray, J. O'K. Cath. heroes, 659.

Seton, Mary. Miller. In ladies' comp. 1.

Seton family. Taylor, J. Fam. of Scot. 1 : 126.

Seton Hall College. U. S. Bur. Ed. Circ. '99, no. 1 : 303.

Sette Comuni, The. (W. D. McCrackan) Am. Geog. Soc. 29 : 168.

Settle, Elkanah. Dunham. Lit. & sci. men, 3 : 182.

Settlement and primogeniture, Laws of. (J. E. T. Rogers) Trans. Soc. Sci. Lond. '64 : 117.

— Law of. (E. L. Pierce) Mass. Charity, '70–71 : 8.

— — and right to public relief. (F. H. Wines) Conf. char. & correc. '98 : 223.

— strict, Advantages of. (F. B. Sanborn) Conf. char. & correc. '98 : 231.

Settlement, Social, and education. (J. J. Abt) Conf. char. & correc. '96 : 117.

— — and the labor movement. (G. Taylor) Conf. char. & correc. '96 : 143.

— — and municipal reform. (J. B. Reynolds) Conf. char. & correc. '96 : 138.

— — and organized charity. (M. E. M'Dowell) Conf. char. & correc. '96 : 123.

Settlements, Social. (C. S. Loch) Conf. char. & correc. '96 : 128.

— — Civic efforts of. (K. B. Davis) Conf. char. & correc. '96 : 131.

— English and Scotch. (W. Caldwell) Conf. char. & correc. '96 : 110.

Settlement idea, The. (R. E. Ely) Conf. char. & correc. '97 : 332.

Settlement work : What it stands for. (J. C. Lathrop) Conf. char. & correc. '96 : 106.

Sevastopol. See Sebastopol.

Seven ; luck of odd numbers. Lawrence, R. M. Magic, 312.

— The number. Hadley, J. Ess. 325.

Seven churches of Asia. Gillett, E. H. Anc. cities, 254.

— in 1845. Ingram. Hearts of oak, 43.

Seven days' battles to Malvern Hill. (F. W. Palfrey) Dwight, T. F. Camp. Va. 217.

Seven Pines, Battle of. Allan, W. Army of N. Va. 36.

Seven sleepers of Ephesus. Baring-Gould. Myths, 93.

Seven years' war. Adams, W. H. D. Engl. at war, 1 : 187. — Galt, J. Lit. life, 2 : 1. — Goldsmith. Miscel. (N. Y. 4 v.) 1 : 474. — Macaulay. Ess. 5 : 217.

— and the American revolution. Everett. Orat. v. 1.

— Diplomatic prelude to. (H. E. Mills) Am. Hist. Assoc. 3 : 29.

Sevenfold principle in esotericism. (H. P. Blavatsky) Five years theos. 187.

— in man, Brahmanism on. (T. S. Row) Five years theos. 153.

1775, Spirit of. Long, J. D. After-dinner, 161.

Seventeenth century. Ducoudray. Modern civilization, 247.

Severance, Caroline M. (E. C. Stanton) Parton. Em. wom. 379.

Severine, Madame. Van de Velde. Fr. fic. 2 : 182.

Severinus of Vienna, St. Kingsley. Hermits, 224.

Sevier, Catharine. Ellet. Pioneer wom. 29.

Sevier, John. Lossing. Em. Amer. 331. — Roosevelt. Winning of the west, 1 : 166.

Sévigné, Madame de. Chambers's Repos. no. 4. — Cracroft. Ess. 2 : 255. — Everett, A. H. Crit. ess. 1 : 1. — Hayward, A. Em. statesm.

2 : 1. — Lamartine. Cel. char. 2 : 38. — Russell. Extr. women, 92. — Ste.-Beuve. Cel. wom. 1. — Shelley, M. W. Lit. men Fr. 1. — Tuckerman. Charac. 78. — Mason, A. G. Wom. of Fr. salons, 78. — With portrait. Warner Lib. 22 : 13153.

Sévigné, Madame de. Life and letters. Hunt, L. Men, wom. & books, 368.

Seville. Buckley, J. M. Trav. three cont. 43. — Finck, H. T. Spain & Morocco. — Thomas, M. Scamper thr. Spain, 127. — Hale, E. E. Seven Spanish cit. 56. — Lathrop, G. P. Span. vistas, 103. — Prime, S. I. Alhambra, 92. — Stoddard. Red letter, 21.

— and its environs. Stoddard. C. A. Span. cit. 129.

— Casa de Contratacion of. (B. Moses) Am. Hist. Assoc. Rept. '94 : 93.

— Impressions of. Disraeli, B. Home letters, 30.

— Moorish mementoes in. Stoddard, C. A. Span. cit. 114.

— Religious persecutions in. Stoughton. Span. ref. 129.

Sewage. (H. I. Bowditch) Mass. Health, '71 : 233.

— Bibliography. Rafter, G. W. Sewage irrigation.

— Chemical disposition of. (W. J. Harris) Am. Pub. Health, 10 : 266.

— Disposal of. (G. E. Waring) Am. Pub. Health, 10 : 174. — (C. F. Folsom) Mass. Health, '76 : 276. '77 : 21. — (S. M. Gray) R. I. Health, 7 : 271.

— — at Asylum for Insane at London, Ontario. (R. M. Bucke) Am. Pub. Health, 24 : 27.

— — from isolated country houses. (W. P. Gerhard) Indiana Health, '90 : 211.

— — in England. U. S. Cons. Rept. no. 154.

— — in U. S. (C. G. Horetzky) Am. Pub. Health, 24 : 51.

— — Prevailing methods of. (C. A. Lindsley) Conn. Health, '80 : 205.

— — problem in Am. cities. (A. Hazen) Am. Pub. Health, 19 : 44.

— Filtration of. (W. F. Van Buskirk) Am. Pub. Health, 24 : 60.

— of inland towns, Disposal of. (A. Smee et al.) Trans. Soc. Sci. Lond. '73 : 436.

— of large cities. (W. L. Richardson) Bost. Health, '75 : 81.

— rural, Disposal of. Iowa Health, '93 : 183.

— town, Disposal of. (E. Pritchard et al.) Trans. Soc. Sci. Lond. '84 : 419. — (R. Rawlinson) Trans. Soc. Sci. Lond. '64 : 486.

— Treatment of. (J. H. Raymond) Am. Pub. Health, 16 : 132.

Sewage irrigation works, Influence of, upon health. (B. Latham) Trans. Soc. Sci. Lond. '79 : 524.

Sewall, Jonathan, Letters of. Mass. Hist. Soc. Proc. 2d ser. 10 : 407.

Sewall, Hon. Joseph. (S. E. Sewall) N. E. Hist.-Gen. Soc. Biog. 1 : 252.

Sewall, Judge Samuel. Knapp, S. L. Em. lawyers, 219. — With portrait. Mitchell, D. G. Am. lands, 90. — Richardson. Amer. lit. 1 : 105.

— Diary of. Ward, May A. Old col. 129.

— a puritan Pepys. Lodge, H. C. Studies, 21.

Seward, Mrs. Anna. Bethune, G. W. Brit. fem. poets, 98. — Dawson, G. Biog. ess. 191. — Oliphant, M. Lit. hist. 1 : 217. — Robertson. Eng. poetesses, 98. — Scott, W. Biog. mem. v. 2. — Williams, Jane. Lit. wom. 239.

— Memoirs of. Elwood. Lit. ladies, 1 : 242.

Shadwell, Sir Launcelot.   Grant, J. Bench & bar, **2** : 7.

Shadwell, Thomas.   Austin & Ralph. Laureates, 183. — Dunham. Lit. & sci. men, **3** : 155. — Hamilton, Wal. Poets laur.

Shafter, O. L. Hemenway. Poets of Vt. 245.

Shaftesbury, Anthony Ashley-Cooper, 1st earl of.   Campbell. Ld. chan. **4** : 154. — Foss. Judges, **7** : 70. — Stebbing. Verdicts, 23. — Wrangham. Brit. Plutarch, v. **4**.

— and Mandeville.   Stephen, L. Eng. thought, **2** : 15.

Shaftesbury, Anthony, 3d earl of, Characteristics.   McCosh. Scot. phil. 29. — Stephen, L. Ess. freeth. 198.

Shaftesbury, A. Ashley-Cooper, 7th earl of. With photo. Cooper, T. Men of mark, **1** : 28. — Horne. New spirit, **1** : 91. — Bolton, S. K. Fam. Eng. statesm. — With portrait. Cochrane, R. Benef. lives, 7. — Em. persons, **3** : 262. — Smith, G. B. Chr. workers, 99. — Gibbins. Eng. soc. ref. 138. — Grant, J. Recoll. Lords & Comm. **1** : 90. — Smalley. Lond. lett. **1** : 286. — Thayer, W. M. Turn.-points, 13.

— at St. Giles's house. Yates, E. H. Celeb. **1** : 225.

Shaftesbury House.   Hall, Mrs. S. C. Engl. shrines, 194.

Shaftesbury Nunnery and prize Bezant. Timbs. Abbeys, **1** : 446.

Shah Jahan. Adams, W. H. D. Warriors of crescent, 250.

Shâh-Nâmeh, The ; or book of Kings. Johnson, S. Ori. relig. Persia, 711.

Shairp, J. C. (W. Y. Sellars) Shairp. Portraits, 11. — Veitch. Scot. poetry, **2** : 281. — Wilson, J. G. Poets of Scot. **2** : 424.

Shaker Village, Mount Lebanon. Pidgeon. Old world ques. 118.

Shakers, The. Hinds. Amer. commun. — Nordhoff. Commun. 117.

— in New York state, Demands of, in 1839. Tilden, S. J. Writ. **1** : 88.

Shakespeare, Anne H., Sketch of. Holloway, L. C. Mothers of gt. men, 329.

Shakespeare, Hamnet.   Brooks, E. S. Gt. men's sons, 259.

Shakespeare, Mary A.   Holloway, L. C. Mothers of gt. men, 329.

Shakespeare, William.   Brewer. Eng. stud. 208. — Browning, E. B. Ess. poets, 169. — Bryant. Prose, **2** : 300. — Calvert. Brief essays, 140. — Canning. Literary infl. in Brit. history. — Carlyle. Heroes. — Chalmers. Eng. poets, **5** : 3. — Collier, W. F. Hist. Eng. lit. 140. — Craik. Pursuit knowl. **1** : 383. — Crofts, S. Chap. Eng. lit. 195. — DeQuincey. Biog. ess. (Bost.) **1**. — Disraeli, I. Amen. (N. Y. 2 v.) **2** : 186. — Dunham. Lit. & sci. men, **2** : 1. — Emerson. Rep. men, 187. — Gilfillan. Third gall. 434. — Hazlitt. Comic. — Hazlitt. Eng. poets. — Howitt. Homes Brit. poets, **1** : 45. — Lowell. Writ. **3** : 1. — Mitchell, D. G. Eng. lands, v. **2**. — Morris, G. S. Brit. tho't, 80. — Müller. Chips, v. **3**. — Neele. Lec. on Eng. poetry, 85. — Parton. Peop. bk. biog. 559. — Reed, H. Brit. poets, **1** : 160. — (J. R. Lowell) Rice, A. T. Ess. 377. — Russell, W. Extraor. men, 27. — Sanborn, K. Eng. poets, 45. — Saunders, F. Famous books, 57. — Taine. Eng. lit. **1** : 296. Ward, A. W. Eng. dram. **1** : 271. — (E. Dowden) Ward. Eng. poets, **1** : 435. — Whipple. Lit. Eliz. 31. — Wotton. Word portraits, 267. — (J. K. Ingram) Afternoon lec. **1** : 93. — Brooks, S. W. Eng. poets, 133. — Clarke, J. F. Memo. sketches, 301. — Crawfurd, O.

Eng. com. dram. **1**. — Dunham, S. A. Em. liter. men, **2** : 1. — With portrait. Gostwick, J. Eng. poets, 17. — Henley. Views, 101. — Nasmith. Mak. mod. thought, **1** : 188. — Sherer. Ess. Eng. lit. 36. — Swanwick, A. Poets, 183. — Hubbard, E. Lit. jour. 339. — Hundred greatest men, 41. — Lanier. Music. — Farrar, F. W. Great books, 72. — With portrait. (E. Dowden) Warner Lib. **22** : 13167. — Minto, W. Eng. poets, 210, 257, 371. — Morison, J. H. Great poets, 83. — Russell, W. C. Book of au. 35. — Smith, C. R. Retrospec. **1** : 46, 55. — Symons, A. Stud. two lit. 3. — Very. Poems & ess. 26.

Shakespeare, William, and Aristophanes. Hope. Ess. 143.

— and the Bible. Japp. Vers de soc. 214.

— and criticism. Scherer. Ess. Eng. lit. 96.

— and Goethe. Masson. Ess. **1** ; *or* Three devils, 61.

— and his contemporaries. Coleridge, H. Ess. **1** : 353.

— and his Spanish prototypes. (A. R. Frey) N. Y. Shakesp. Soc. pap. v. **3**.

— and his time. Morley, H. Eng. writ. 10.

— — Bibliography. Morley, H. Eng. writers, v. **11**.

— Antony. Hazlitt. Char. Shakesp.

— Antony and Cleopatra. Winter. Old shrines, 219.

— Art of, as revealed by himself. Macdonald, G. Orts, 141.

— as actor and critic. Lewes. Actors, 88.

— As you like it. Winter. Old shrines, 133.

— Authorship of. Ingleby. Ess. **1**. — Spedding. Reviews.

— — Baconian. Clarke, J. F. 19th cent. ques. 38. — Fiske, J. Cent. of science, 350.

— Bibliography. New Bedford (Mass.) Pub. Lib. Bull. Oct. '96. — (A. Morgan) N. Y. Shakesp. Soc. pap. v. **4, 7**.

— Blank verse of. Mayor. English metre.

— Commentators on. Bowen, F. Gleanings, 457.

— Comments on. Holland, H. Frag. papers, 238.

— Critics of. Whipple. Ess. & rev. v. **2**.

— Delicacy of. Johnston, R. M. Studies, 184.

— Doubtful plays of. Hazlitt. Char. Shakesp.

— Early dramatic works. Schlegel. Æsthet. (Bohn) 272.

— Eclipse of. Cook, D. On stage, **1** : 90.

— English critics of. Hare. Guesses, **1** : 266.

— English kings of. Pater. Apprec. 192.

— First ride to London. Knight. Once on time, **1** : 169.

— Future of. Scudder, H. E. Men & let. 215.

— Genius of. Hare. Guesses, **2** : 87.

— Hamlet. Owen, J. Five skep. dramas, 279. — Calvert. Brief essays. — Dawson, G. Shakesp. 6. — Reed, H. Lec. Eng. hist. 406. — Very. Poems & ess. 53.

— — and the commentators. Fairbanks, O. B. Aguecheek, 282.

— — Character of. Maginn. Fras. papers, 236.

— — Ecclesiastical law in. (R. S. Guernsey) N. Y. Shakesp. Soc. pap. v. **1**.

— — Hamlet, the Elder. Macdonald, G. Orts, 170.

— — Lectures on. Conington. Miscel. 105.

— — A new reading. (F. Leifchild) Coan. Stud. lit. 67.

— — Time in. (E. P. Vining) N. Y. Shakesp. Soc. pap. v. **5**.

— Historical plays. Pater. Apprec. 192.

— Iago, Actors' Criticism of. Woodberry. Stud. in lett. 167.

Sharp, Granville. Smiles. Self-help. — Stanton, H. B. Reforms, 80.
— The slave trade and. Gibbins. Eng. soc. ref. 100.
Sharp, Tom. Whitehead, C. Highwaymen, 1 : 179.
Sharp, William, "Three Laps." Baring-Gould. Yorks. odd. 1 : 102.
Sharpe, Charles K. Masson. Edinb. sk. 359.
Sharpless, Hattie R. Brockett. Woman's work, 741.
Sharpless, James. Baker, W. S. Portr. of Wash. 180.
Sharpsburg, Battle of. Allan, W. Army of N. Va. 362.
Sharswood, George. Brown, D. P. Forum, 2 : 154.
Shattuck, A. D. Sheldon, G. W. Amer. painters, 174.
Shattuck, George C. (S. Eliot) Am. Acad. A. & S. Proc. 28 : 356. — (G. C. Shattuck) N. E. Hist.-Gen. Soc. Biog. 2 : 164. — Vaille & Clark. Harv. book, v. 1.
Shattuck, George Otis. Am. Bar Assoc. 20 : 540.
Shattuck, Lemuel. (J. W. Dean) N. E. Hist.-Gen. Soc. Biog. 3 : 290.
Shaving. Lang. Leaders, 92.
Shaw, Albert M., with portrait. Sketches N. H. men, 267.
Shaw, E. M., Captain, in Watling street. Yates, E. H. Celeb. 1 : 265.
Shaw, F. Grant, J. Recoll. Ho. Comm. 151.
Shaw, F. G. Curtis, G. W. Other ess. 222.
Shaw, H. W. [Josh Billings]. Clemens. Funny fellows, 49.
Shaw, Henry, and his botanical garden. Bolton, S. K. Givers, 247.
Shaw, James, with portrait. Bartlett, J. R. R. I. officers, 185.
Shaw, John. Cooper, J. F. Am. nav. off. 1 : 123.
Shaw, John P. Bartlett, J. R. R. I. officers, 155.
Shaw, Lemuel. Loring, J. S. Hundred Bost. ora. 375. — (B. F. Thomas) Mass. Hist. Proc. 10 : 50. — (S. S. Shaw; P. E. Aldrich) N. E. Hist.-Gen. Soc. Biog. 4 : 200.
Shaw, Col. Robert Gould. (S. B. Shaw) Harvard mem. biog. 2 : 172. — Lodge & Roosevelt. Hero-tales, 249. — (F. G. Shaw) N. E. Hist.-Gen. Soc. Biog. 2 : 38.
Shaw, Samuel, with portrait. Hunt, F. Am. merch. 2 : 201.
Shaw, Thomas. St. John. Cel. travelers, 2 : 19.
Shaw, William. Wesley & successors, 203.
— Trial of. Phillips, S. M. Famous cases, 85.
Shawl, Art of wearing a. Willis. Hurry-graphs, 332.
Shays's rebellion, 1786–87. Egleston. Gen. Paterson, 156.
Sheads, Carrie. Brockett. Woman's work, 776.
— Moore, F. Women of the war, 238.
Sheas, Burning of the. Sheil, R. L. Sketches, 1 : 253.
Sheba, Queen of. Geikie, C. Old Test. char. 268.
Shechem. Kean, J. Among holy places, 190.
— and Jacob's well. Lee, J. S. Sac. cities. 63.
Sheep. Shaler. Dom. animals, 114.
— and wool in Asia, 1891. (H. M. Jewett and others) U. S. Cons. Rept. 35 : 566.
— Our, and the tariff. (W. D. Lewis) Univ. Pa. Publ. Pol. Econ. 2 : no. 9.
Sheffield, Mary E. Brockett. Woman's work, 714.
Sheffield. Guild. Over the ocean, 96.

Sheffield castle and manor. Mackie, C. Castles of Mary.
— Mary Queen of Scots at. Strickland. Queens Scot. v. 7.
Sheffield Scientific School. Gilman, D. C. Univ. prob. 109.
Sheil, Richard Lalor. Francis, G. H. Orators, 187. — Grant, J. Recoll. Ho. Comm. 328. — Mathews, W. Oratory, 299. — Stanton, H. B. Reforms, 143. — Murray, J. O'K. Prose & poet. Irel. 483.
Shelburne, Lord, Administration of. Lewis, G. C. Ess. on admin.
Shelby, Isaac. With portrait. [Amer.] Nat. portr. gall. v. 1. — Lossing. Em. Amer. 98.
Shelby, Sarah. Ellet. Pioneer wom. 162.
Sheldon, Edward Austin. (C. R. Skinner) Nat. Educa. Assoc. '98 : 63.
Shell-money. (R. E. C. Stearns) U. S. Nat. Mus. Rept. '87 : 297.
Shell-mounds of Denmark (Mrs. Lubbock) Vaca. tourists, 3 : 357.
Shelley, Harriet, In defense of. Clemens. How to tell, 15.
Shelley, Mary Wollstonecraft. Cone & Gilder. Pen-portr. 1 : 109. — Gilfillan. Mod. lit. 251. — Underwood, S. A. Heroines, 89. — Wotton. Word portraits, 275. — Horne, R. H. New spirit, 317. — With portrait. Hubbard, E. Little journeys, 3 : 393. — Mayer, G. T. Wom. of lett. 2 : 207.
Shelley, Percy B. Alger. Solitudes, 272. — Arnold, M. Ess. 2 : 205. — Bagehot. Estimates, 274. — Caine, T. H. Cobwebs. — Calvert. Coleridge, 129. — Chorley. Authors of Eng. 56. — Cotterill. Introd. study of poetry. — Courthope. Liberal move. in Eng. liter. — Creasy. Etonians, 481. — Dawson, W. J. Mod. Engl. 36. — DeQuincey. Ess. on poets (Bost.), 49; or Works (Masson), 11 : 354. — De Vere. Ess. 2 : 124. — Devey. Mod. Eng. poets, 239. — Dowden. Transcripts, 75. — Gilfillan. First gall. 49. — Godwin, P. Out of past, 111. — Griswold, H. T. Home-life, 102. — Howitt. Homes Br. poets, 1 : 489. — Johnson, C. F. Three Amer. 88. — Lang. Lett. to dead au. 173. — Macdonald, G. Orts, 264. — Mason, E. T. Pers. traits, 3 : 73. — Noel. Ess. on poetry. — Oliphant, M. Lit. hist. v. 3. — Patmore. Princ. in art. — Thompson, Jas. (B. V.). Biog. ess. 270. — Trent. Authority, 35. — Tuckerman. Poets, 137. — (T. W. H. Myers) Ward. Eng. poets, 4 : 348. — With portrait. (G. E. Woodberry) Warner Lib. 23 : 13265. — Armstrong, R. A. Faith and doubt, 1. — Wotton. Word portraits, 277. — Brooks, S. W. Eng. poets, 456. — Deshler. Afternoons, 226. — Dixon, W. M. Engl. poetry, 137. — With portrait. Gostwick, J. Eng. poets, 191. — Griffin, G. W. Stud. in lit. — Hoyt, J. G. Miscel. 173. — Kinsley, W. W. Views, 255. — (H. G. Groser) Miles, A. H. Poets of cent. 2 : 515. — Minto. Georg. era, 292. — Mitchell, D. G. Eng. lands, 4 : 216, 225, 233. — Mitford, M. R. Recollec. 315. — Ossoli. Art, 78. — Russell, W. C. Book of au. 448. — Swanwick, A. Poets, 300. — Wise, D. Vanq. victors, 248.
— Alleged infidel passages in works of. Talfourd. Crit. wr.
— and Byron, Thoughts on. Kingsley, C. Lit. lec. 35.
— and Crabbe. Patmore. Princ. in art, 134.
— and Thomson compared. Brooke, S. Theol. Eng. poets, 34.

Personal recoll. 17. — Stowe. Men of time, 423. — Wilson, J. G. Illus. sol. 447. — With portrait. Brockett. Men of our day, 78. — Duyckinck. Portrait gall. **2** : 563. — (J. C. Ropes) Dwight, T. F. Fed. & confed. comm. 125. — Long, J. D. After-dinner, 107. — Em. persons, **5** : 19.

Sherman, Gen. Wm. T., Cavalry of. (S. D. Atkins) Mil. ess. M. O. L. L. U. S. Ills. 383.

Sherwin, John Keyse, engraver. Cook, D. Art in Eng. 230.

— and Cosway. Thornbury. Brit. art. **1** : 111.

Shetland and the Orkneys. (C. S. Smith) Am. Geog. Soc. **23** : 131.

— Visit to. Chambers's Miscel. no. 75.

Shewell, Joseph B. Winslow, S. N. Biog. Phila. merch. 239.

Shields, Fred. Bate, P. H. Eng. Pre-Raph. 95.

— Ewart, H. C. Toilers in art, 153.

Shields, James. Duyckinck. Nat. portr. gall. **2** : 428. — Glazier, W. Heroes, 227.

Shillaber, B. P. Bungay. Off-hand, 372. — Derby, J. C. Fifty years, 407.

Shindler, Mrs. Mary S. B. Dana. Davidson, J. W. Writ. of South, 504. — Hart, J. S. Fem. prose, 153. — Freeman, J. D. Wom. of South, 369. — Hatfield, E. F. Poets of church. — Raymond, I. Southland wr. **2** : 875.

Shinto burial mounds, and relics in Japan. (Romeyn Hitchcock) U. S. Nat. Mus. Rept. '90 : 489.

— Myths and ritual. Griffis. Relig. Japan, 35.

Shintoism. (R. Shibata) Barrows, J. H. Parl. relig. **1** : 451. — Bettany. World's relig. 167. — (Dagors Goh ; Mrs. I. B. Bishop) Relig. systems, 99.

Ship-building. (W. C. Steadman) Galton, F. W. Workers, 56.

— American. Blaine. Polit. discus. 300.

— — and foreign commerce. Greeley. Ess. pol. econ. 214.

— and deep waterways. (G. Tunell) Deep waterways conven. **1** : 203.

— British, in 1890–91. (E. R. Jones) U. S. Cons. Rept. **35** : 349.

— — in 1892. U. S. Cons. Rept. no. 149.

— of the world, 1891. (H. Metcalf) U. S. Cons. Rept. **38** : 281.

— Prehistoric. (G. H. Boehmer) U. S. Nat. Mus. Rept. '91 : 527.

Ship canal across American isthmus. (D. Ammen) Am. Geog. Soc. **10** : 142. *See* Interoceanic.

— Florida, Sanitary urgency of. (J. Gamgee) Am. Pub. Health, **6** : 336.

— from Lakes to ocean, Necessities and advantages of. (D. B. Smith) Deep waterways conven. **1** : 81.

Ship canals, Modern. (C. Francis) Deep waterways conven. **1** : 100.

Ship-life, Need of sanitary reform in. (A. L. Gihon) Am. Pub. Health, **3** : 85.

Shipley, Lieut. W. Shea, J. G. Fallen brave.

Shipley, Rev. William Davies, Trial of, for libel. Erskine, T. Speeches, 90.

Shipman, Jehiel G. Am. Bar Assoc. **16** : 432.

Shipp, Barnard. Davidson, J. W. Writ. of South, 506.

Shippen, Edward, with portrait. [Amer.] Nat. portr. gall. v. **1**.

Shipping, American. Garfield. Works, **1** : 118.

— and shipbuilding, British, 1899. (J. Boyle) U. S. Cons. Rept. **60** : 274.

Ships, Air and moisture on. (T. J. Turner) Am. Pub. Health, **4** : 103.

Ships, Genealogy of. Winchell. Sparks geol. ham. 301.

— iron, Fairbairn's. Smiles. Indus. biog.

— Lake and ocean combined. (J. R. Oldham ; A. McDougall) Deep waterways conven. **1** : 176, 182.

— passenger, Marine hygiene on. (A. N. Bell) Am. Pub. Health, **3** : 98.

— Safety of, and of those who travel in them. (J. M. Woodworth) Am. Pub. Health, **3** : 79.

— Sanitation of. (S. T. Armstrong) Am. Pub. Health, **11** : 98.

— Scandinavian, Ancient. Du Chaillu. Viking age, v. **2**.

— territoriality of the merchant vessel. Harcourt, W. V. Letters fr. Times.

Shipston-on-Stour. Stone, J. S. Heart of Eng. **25** : 52.

Shipton, Anna. Miller, Jos. Singers church, 2d ed. 582.

Shipwreck. Thoreau. Selec. 124.

Shipwrecks. Chambers's Repos. no. 69.

— Narratives of. Senior, W. Shipwrecks, 198.

Shire, The, and the Gá. Freeman. Eng. towns, 103.

— Colonial. Hart. Am. govt. 147.

Shire river, South Africa. (D. Livingstone) Am. Geog. Soc. **2**, pt. **1** : 64.

Shirking. Ess. from Sat. R. 176.

Shirlaw, Walter, with portrait. Benjamin, S. G. W. Am. art. v. **1**. — Sheldon, G. W. Amer. painters, 96.

Shirley, James. Choate, I. B. Wells of Eng. 223. — Griswold, R. W. Sac. poets. — Minto, W. Eng. poets, 366. — Dunham. Lit. & sci. men, **3** : 1. — Ward, A. W. Eng. dram. **2** : 309. — (W. Minto) Ward. Eng. poets, **2** : 215.

— Masque ; Triumph of peace. Hogarth. Mem. opera, **1** : 55.

Shirley, John M. Am. Bar Assoc. **10** : 418.

Shirley, Walter, 1725–86. Hatfield, E. F. Poets of church, 555. — Miller, Jos. Singers church, 2d ed. 246.

Shirley homestead, Va. Terhune. Col. homes, 63.

Shoals, Isles of. Benjamin. Atlantic, 205. — De Costa. Mt. Desert, 179. — Drake, N. E. coast, 153.

Shoddy. Whipple. Success, 273.

Shoemaker, Lazarus Denison. Am. Bar Assoc. **17** : 534.

Shoemaker, Murray Colegate. Am. Bar Assoc. **9** : 538.

Shoemakers, Anecdotes of. Chambers's Miscel. no. 115. *See also* Cobblers.

Shoemaking in the U. S., History of. (H. P. Fairfield) Shaler. The U. S. **2** : 178.

Shofar, The. (Cyrus Adler) U. S. Nat. Mus. Rept. '92 : 437.

Shop windows. Wynter, A. Our soc. bees, **1** : 123.

Shopping in the east. Wallace, S. E. Storied sea, 83.

Shops and shop-windows. Wynter. Curios. of toil, **2** : 68.

— and shopping. Curtis. From easy ch. 27.

Short story, The. (L. Falconer) Art of writ. fic. 75.

— Philosophy of. Matthews, B. Pen & ink, 67.

Shorter, E. S. Miller, S. F. Bench of Ga. v. **2**.

Shorthand and typewriting. (W. A. Woodworth) Nat. Educa. Assoc. '95 : 882.

— Bibliography. (J. E. Rockwell) U. S. Bur. Educa. Circ. '93 : no. 1.

Shorthand, Teaching, practice, and literature of. (J. E. Rockwell) U. S. Bur. Ed. Circ. '84 : no. 2.

Shorthouse, John H., with portrait. Warner Lib. 23 : 13363.

Shovel, Sir Cloudesley. Edgar. Sea-kings, 247. — Winks. Illus. shoemakers, 1. — Lives of dist. shoemak. 228.

Shreve, Thomas H. Coggeshall. Poets of west, 174.

Shrewsbury, Earl of. Grant, J. Recoll. Lords & Comm. 1 : 147.

Shrewsbury, Charles Talbot, duke of. Lodge. Portraits (Bohn), v. 7.

Shrewsbury, Elizabeth Talbot, countess of, with portrait. Costello. Englishwomen, 1 : 9.

Shrewsbury, Eng. Hawthorne. Engl. note-bks. 1 : 262. — Silloway. Cathedral towns, 85.

Shrewsbury school. Staunton, H. Schools, 404.

Shrine of San Donato. Perkins, C. C. Tusc. sculp. 1 : 43.

Shrines, English. King, R. J. Sket. 197.

Shrubsole, Wm., with portrait. Morison, J. Fathers of Lond. Miss. Soc. 1 : 419.

Shrubsole, William, jr. Hatfield, E. F. Poets of church, 558. — Miller, Jos. Singers church, 2d ed. 325.

Shubrick, John Templer. Cooper, J. F. Am. nav. off. 1 : 147.

Shulze, John Andrew, with portrait. Armor. Gov. of Penn. 343.

Shunk, Francis Rawn, with portrait. Armor. Gov. of Penn. 392.

Shurtleff, Benj. (H. S. Shurtleff) N. E. Hist.-Gen. Soc. Biog. 1 : 32.

Shurtleff, Nathaniel Bradstreet. (W. R. Dimmock) Harvard mem. biog. 2 : 42. — (C. C. Smith) Mass. Hist. Proc. 13 : 389.

Shurtleff, R. M. Sheldon, G. W. Amer. painters, 211.

Shurtleff, Stephen C. Am. Bar Assoc. 21 : 709.

Shurtleff, Wm. S. (G. S. Merriam) Mass. Hist. Soc. Proc. 2d ser. 10 : 447. — With portrait. (G. S. Merriam) Mass. Hist. Soc. Proc. 2d ser. 11 : 234.

Shuswap Indians, Dawson on. Am. Geog. Soc. 24 : 591.

Shuter, Edward. Doran. Annals stage, 2 : 116.

Shylock. Radford, G. H. Shylock, 9. — and David as interpreters of life. Quayle, W. A. Poet, 326.

Shyness. Bulwer, E. Caxtoniana.

Siam. (T. G. G. D'Abain) Am. Geog. Soc. 7 : 336. — Earl, G. W. East. seas, 147. — Malcolm, H. S. E. Africa, 111. — Thomson, J. Straits of Malacca, 78. — Wood, W. M. Fankwei, 149.
— and the Siamese. Chambers's Papers, no. 79.
— Foreign trade of, 1895. (J. Barrett) U. S. Cons. Rept. 51 : 21.
— France and. Norman, H. Far East, 468.
— Government of. Norman, H. Far East, 434.
— Life in. Keating. With Grant, 137.
— Notes on. (D. O. King) Am. Geog. Soc. 1 : 193.
— Trade opportunities in, 1898. (J. Barrett) U. S. Cons. Rept. 57 : 55.
— Travels in. Helms. Pioneering, 94.

Sibbald, Robert. Jardine, W. Nat. lib. v. 1.

Siberia. Hartwig. Polar world, 191. — Pumpelly. Amer. & As. 388. — Whymper, F. Alaska, 286.
— and the penal settlements. Chambers's Papers, no. 74.

Siberia, the exiles' abode. (G. Kennan) Am. Geog. Soc. 14 : 13. — Knox, T. W. Underground, 599.
— Northeastern, Dog-sledge journey in. (G. Kennan) Am. Geog. Soc. 8 : 96.
— Railway across. Norman, H. Far East, 159.
— — 1894. (J. M. Crawford) U. S. Cons. Rept. 45 : 425.

Sible, Eng. Barrett, C. R. B. Essex, 56.

Sibley, John Langdon. Peabody. Harv. rem. 146. — (A. P. Peabody) Mass. Hist. Proc. 2d ser. 2 : 487. — Vaille & Clark. Harv. book, v. 1.

Sibley, Sarah. Ellet. Pioneer wom. 225.

Sibthorpe, Colonel. Grant, J. Recoll. Ho. Comm. 141.

Sibylla of Cleves. Chapman, W. Wom. of ref. 109.

Sibyls, The. Neale. Ess. liturg.

Sicilian literature. Symonds. Renais. It. lit. 1 : 21.

Sicily. Bennett, J. H. Winter on Medit. 339. — Browne, J. R. Yusef, 13. — Moore, Jos. Outl. Eur. 257. — (M. E. G. Duff) Oxf. ess. '57 : 57. — Symonds. Sk. So. Eur. v. 2.
— Essential oils from, 1894. (C. M. Caughy) U. S. Cons. Rept. 45 : 70.
— History of. Freeman. Hist. ess. 3 : 428.
— Early. Hare. Cities of So. Italy, 371.
— A month in. (A. T. Bacon) Murphy, Lady B. On Rhine, 147.
— Sulphur-mining in, 1891. (C. Heath) U. S. Cons. Rept. 37 : 363.
— Through. Lee, A. E. Europ. days, 253.

Sick and injured, Carriage and removal of. Internat. Health Exh. Sanita.
— Prayer for the. Shipley, O. Tracts, 341.

Sick calls. Brownson. Works, 10 : 585.

Sicklemore, James. Ivimey. Eng. Bapt. 2 : 567.

Sickles, Gen. Daniel E. Fiske. Off-hand, 284.

Sickness. Stevenson, R. L. Virgin. 128.
— and its lessons. Manning, J. M. Sermons, 395.
— Consolations of. Bulwer. Student, 1 : 157.
— Conversations with a student in. Bulwer. Student, 2 : 13.

Siculus, Camillus. Wallace, R. Anti-Trin. biog. 2 : 13.

Siddons, Sarah Kemble. Baker, H. B. Engl. actors, 2 : 11. — DeQuincy. Lit. rem. (Bost.) 2 : 218. — Doran. Annals stage, 2 : 241. — Galt. Players, 2 : 294. — Hunt, L. Crit. ess. on performers, 16. — Matthews, B. Actors, 2 : 23. — Russell. Extr. women, 174. — Russell, A. P. Charac. 23. — Russell, W. Rep. actors, 225. — Thomson, K. B. Recoll. v. 2. — Yonge. Good wom. 2 : 428. — Duyckinck. Portrait gall. 1 : 446. — Fifty famous women, 311. — Hazlitt. Crit. & dram. ess. — Lennox, W. P. Plays, 1 : 211.
— as Lady Macbeth, etc. Jenkin, Fl. Papers, 1 : 45.

Sidell, William H. Shanks. Rec. of generals, 300.

Sidney, Algernon. Lodge. Portraits (Bohn), v. 6. — Parton. Triumphs, 601. — Tweedie, W. K. Earnest men, 266. — Winthrop, R. C. Addresses, 2 : 140. — Taylor, T. Leicester Sq. 62.
— Wrangham. Brit. Plutarch, v. 4.

Sidney, Mary. See Pembroke, Countess of.

Sidney, Sir Philip. Adams, W. H. D. Records, 11. — Bourne, H. R. F. Eng. seam. 1 : 209. 2 : 159. — (W. Stigant) Camb. ess. '58 : 81. — Collier, W. F. Hist. Eng. lit. 116. — Disraeli, I. Amen. N. Y. 2 v.) 2 : 99. — Lodge. Portraits (Bohn), v. 2. — Mitchell, D. G. English lands, 1 : 230. — Sanborn, K. Eng. poets, 34.

— Taine. Eng. lit. 1 : 164. — (M. A. Ward) Ward. Eng. poets, 1 : 341. — Wotton. Word portraits, 284. — Curtis, G. W. Lit. & soc. ess. 147. — Henley. Views, 104. — Morley, H. Eng. writ. 8 : 394. 9 : 329. — Holland, J. Psalmists, 1 : 194. — Macdonald, G. England's antiphon, 76. — Minto, W. Eng. poets, 185, 368. — Russell, W. C. Book of au. 30. — Simson, Jas. Em. men of Kent, 111. — Utterton, F. A. Biog. sk. 202. — With portrait. (P. Duffield) Warner Lib. 23 : 13385. — Wrangham. Brit. Plutarch, v. 2.

Sidney, Sir Philip, and Fulke Greville. Knight. Once on time, 1 : 162. — Thomson, Mrs. Cel. friend. 2 : 1.

— and his sister, Memoirs of. Drake, N. Mornings, 1 : 113.

— and Raleigh. Whipple. Lit. Eliz. 250.

— Arcadia. Mitford, M. R. Recollec. 196. — Saunders, F. Famous books, 29. — Adams, W. D. Famous books, 114.

— Death of. Adams, W. H. D. Engl. at war, 1 : 24.

— Defense of poesy. Jones, W. A. Ess. on authors, 79.

— — Text from. Mabie. My study fire, 71.

— Miscellanies. Legaré. Writ. 2 : 334.

— Pastoral romance. Jusserand. English novel. 217.

— Sonnets of. Deshler. Afternoons, 46. — Lamb. Elia.

— Stella and. Jameson. Loves of poets.

Sidney family, Genealogical sketch of. Jewitt, L. Stately homes, 1 : 176.

Sidon. Gillett, E. H. Anc. cities, 218.

Siedlecius, James. Wallace, R. Anti-Trin. biog. 3 : 84.

Siemichovia, Sophia. Wallace, R. Anti-Trin. biog. 2 : 351.

Siemens, Ernst Werner. Munro, J. Heroes of Teleg. 281.

Siemens, Sir William. Jeans. Creators, 131. — Munro, J. Heroes of Teleg. 115. — Smith, G. B. Leaders mod. ind. 379.

Siena. (S. J. Capper) Coan. Hist. stud. 54. — Hare. Cities of No. Italy, 3 : 253. — Howells. Tuscan cities, 125. — James. Transatl. 254. — Norton, C. E. Church building, 87. — Symonds. Sk. So. Eur. 1 : 178. — Taine. Italy, 2 : 40. — Scollard. Und. sum. skies, 151.

— Cathedral of. Norton, C. E. Church bldg. — Symonds. Renais. fine arts, 54.

— Reformers in. Stoughton. Ital. reformers, 77.

— War of Florence with. Duffy, B. Tuscan repub. 81.

Sienese School. Perkins, C. C. Tusc. sculp. 1 : 85.

Sienese sculptors. Perkins, C. C. Tusc. sculp. 1 : 93.

Sienicius, Nicholas. Wallace, R. Anti-Trin. biog. 2 : 214.

Sieninius, James. Wallace, R. Anti-Trin. biog. 2 : 440.

Sienkiewicz, Charles. Soboleski. Poets of Poland, 441.

Sienkiewicz, Henryk. Crawford, V. M. Stud. for. lit. 248. — With portrait. (C. H. Genung) Warner Lib. 23 : 13399.

Sierra Leone. Forde, H. A. Black & white. — Williams, G. W. Negro race, 1 : 85.

— Commerce, population, etc., 1894. (R. P. Pooley) U. S. Cons. Rept. 46 : 238.

— Industrial resources and trade, 1895. (R. P. Pooley) U. S. Cons. Rept. 49 : 401.

— Mission to. Gurney, J. H. Hist. sketches, 3 : 315.

Sierra Nevada Mts., Across the. Rae. Westward, 216.

— Traveling in. Taylor, B. At home, 2 : 144.

Sieveking, Amelia. Adams, W. H. D. Good Samar. 360. — Japp. Wise words, 221. — Hack. Consec. wom. 41. — Yonge. Good wom. 1 : 458.

Sievers, Jacob Johann von, Sketch of. Wraxall, C. F. L. Hist. bye-ways, 2 : 168.

Siéyes, Emmanuel Joseph, comte. Brougham. Works, 5 : 98.

Sigel, Gen. Franz. Glazier, W. Heroes, 368.

Sight, Berkeley's theory. Case. Physical realism.

— Defective, Control of. (B. J. Jeffries) Am. Pub. Health, 7 : 225.

— in school-children, Deterioration of. (S. O. Richey) Am. Pub. Health, 10 : 51.

— Sense of. Allen, G. Physiolog. æsthetics.

Sight-seeing. Appleton, T. G. Chequer-work, 367.

Sight singing, Eye and ear training for. (F. A. Lyman) Nat. Educa. Assoc. '97 : 778.

Sigismund, king of Hungary, History of. Peake, Eliz. Germ. emperors, 176.

Sigismund, John. Wallace, R. Anti-Trin. biog. 2 : 214.

Signatures in books, Use and development of. Blades. Books in chains, 85.

Signboards, Curiosities of. Wynter. Curios. of toil, 2 : 1.

Signorelli, Luca d'. (R. Vischer) Dohme, R. Early mast. 448. — Ottley. Ital. school. — Stillman, W. J. Old Ital. mast. 167. — Symonds. Renais. fine arts, 278.

— Cortona and. E. E. Vari. of fortune, 133.

Signs of the times. Carlyle. Essays.

— How to read. Vaughan, D. J. Questions, 123.

Sigourney, Lydia Huntley. With portrait. [Amer.] Nat. portr. gall. v. 4. — Everest. Poets of Conn. 195. — Griswold. Fem. poets, 91. — Hart, J. S. Fem. prose, 76. — With portrait. (E. B. Huntington) Parton. Em. wom. 85. — Parton. Peop. bk. biog. 601. — Duyckinck. Portrait gall. 1 : 605. — Griswold, R. W. Sac. poets. — Hatfield, E. F. Poets of church, 560. — Miller, Jos. Singers church, 2d ed. 422. — With portrait. Mitchell, D. G. Am. lands, 1 : 335. — Phelps, A. L. Rev. & ess. 210.

Sikh wars. Adams, W. H. D. Eng. at war, 2 : 99.

Sikhism. (F. Pincott) Relig. systems, 301.

Sikhland, or the country of Baba-Nának. Cust. Ling. est. 24.

Sikhs, The. Barth, A. Relig. India, 242.

Sikinos. Tozer. Isl. Æg. 90.

Sikkim, Visit to (1884). Hübner. Thro' Brit. empire, 2 : 182.

Silchester, Eng. Freeman. Eng. towns, 157.

— Roman city of. Timbs. Abbeys, 1 : 407.

Silence an element of repute. Bulwer, E. Caxtoniana.

— meditation, and rest. Friswell. Silent hour, 1.

— Power of. Oxenham. Short stud. 72.

Silesius, Angelus. Winkworth. Chr. singers Germ. 246.

Silex in certain vegetables. Davy. Works, 2 : 133.

Silistria, Siege of. Knox, T. W. Battles, 47.

Silk and silk-worms in China, 1897. (G. F. Smithers) U. S. Cons. Rept. 56 : 523.

Silk culture. N. J. Labor, '79 : 173, 275. '81 : xx. 83 : 198.

— and home industry. (S. Chamberlaine) Phila. Soc. Sci. Assoc. '75.

Silk culture in Chin-Kiang. U. S. Cons. Rept. no. 122.
— in Siam, 1891. (J. T. Child) U. S. Cons. Rept. 45 : 303.
— in the U. S. Pidgeon. Old world ques. 203.
Silk farming. Bibliography. Bailey, L. H. Sketch evol. native fruits.
Silk industry. Pa. Bur. Indus. Statis. '98.
— in France, 1891. (C. A. Hansman) U. S. Cons. Rept. 36 : 307.
— in Russia, 1896. (J. Karel) U. S. Cons. Rept. 53 : 244.
Silkville Prairie home, Kansas. Nordhoff. Commun. 375.
Sill, Edward Rowland, with portrait. Warner Lib. 23 : 13439.
Sillar, David, Burns and. Stoddard, R. H. Under eve. lamp, 7.
Silliman, Benjamin, the elder. Youmans. Pioneers sci. 140. — Griswold. Prose writ. 584.
Silsbee, Nathaniel. Peabody. Harv. grad. 202.
Silurian beach, The. Agassiz. Geol. sk. 1 : 29.
Silver. Bourne, S. Trade, population, and food, 199. — Bowles, S. Across the continent. — Knox, T. W. Underground, 82.
— Century's struggle for. McMaster. With fathers, 222.
— Free coinage of. Walker, F. A. Discus. in econ. 1 : 175.
— gold and, Decline in value of. Bolles. Chap. pol. econ. 101.
— Notes on depreciation of. Giffen. Ess. finance, 198.
— Question of. Blaine. Twenty years, 2 : 595. — Farquhar. Econ. delusions, 356. — McPherson. Handbk. pol. '78, '86, '90. — Garfield. Works, 2 : 329.
— — Bibliography. (C. Warden) U. S. 55th C. 2d sess. Ho. Docs. 286.
— — Minority report on. Bowen, F. Gleanings, 33.
— Remonetization of. Blaine. Polit. discus. 163.
Silver dollar, Standard. (W. C. Ford) Econ. tracts, no. 13.
Silvestre, Armand. Zola. Exper. novel. 299.
Simeon, Bishop of Jerusalem. Cave. Lives of fathers, 1 : 164.
Simeon, Bishop of Persepolis. Yonge, C. M. Pupils of John, 272.
Simeon Stylites, St. Hahn-Hahn. Fathers, 308.
— Kingsley. Hermits, 167.
Simeon, Charles. Seeley, M. Later evang. 234.
— Dale, T. P. Life's motto.
Simmias. Mills. Poets of Greece, 149.
Simmons, Charles Francis. (T. W. Higginson) Harvard mem. biog. 1 : 50.
Simmons, Franklin. Clarke, W. J. Amer. sculp. 128.
Simms, John. Wallace, R. Anti-Trin. biog. 2 : 129.
Simms, W. Gilmore. Bungay. Off-hand, 386. — Davidson, J. W. Writ. of South, 508. — Griswold. Poets Am. 323. — Griswold. Prose writ. 503. — (W. C. Bryant) Hubbard, E. Little jour. 2 : 149. Same art. Homes Am. authors. — Richardson. Amer. lit. 2 : 398. — With portrait. Warner Lib. 23 : 13445.
Simon, St., the Zealot. Cave. Apostles, 2 : 175.
Simon, the Cyrenian. Hastings, F. Obscure charac. 239.
Simon, Henry. Bartlett, J. R. R. I. officers, 220.
Simon, John. Bettany. Em. doctors, 2 : 304.
Simon, Jules. Claretie. French celeb. 2 : 93. — King, E. French pol. lead. 98. — Men of 3d repub. 295.

Simon, Jules, in the Place de la Madeleine. Yates, E. H. Celeb. 2 : 145.
Simond, G. G. Pettigrew. Med. portr. gall. v. 3.
Simonds, Artemas. (A. Simonds) N. E. Hist.-Gen. Soc. Biog. 2 : 288.
Simonides of Amorgos. Arnold, E. Poets of Greece, 86. — Symonds. Greek poets, 1 : 280.
Simonides of Ceos. Arnold, E. Poets of Greece, 124. — Mills. Poets of Greece, 122. — Sterling, J. Ess. 1 : 188. — Symonds. Greek poets, 1 : 327. — (W. Miller) Warner Lib. 23 : 13462.
Simonin process with garbage. (I. M. Simonin) Am. Pub. Health, 18 : 405.
Simonis, Theodore. Wallace, R. Anti-Trin. biog. 3 : 123.
Simonius, Simon. Wallace, R. Anti-Trin. biog. 2 : 341.
Simplicity. Patmore. Religio poetæ, 98. — Warner, C. D. Rela. of lit. 43.
Simplification of life. Carpenter, E. Eng. ideal, 79.
Simpson, Sir James Y. Bettany. Em. doctors, 2 : 83. — Japp. Noble workers, 272. — With portrait. Cochrane, R. Benef. lives, 185. — Japp. Labor, 259.
Simpson, Mrs. Jane Cross. Miller, Jos. Singers church, 2d ed. 486. — Wilson, J. G. Poets of Scot. 2 : 351.
Simpson, Jonathan. Whitehead, C. Highwaymen, 1 : 114.
Simpson, Palgrave. Coleman, G. Players, 2 : 165.
Simpson, Robert. With portrait. Morison, J. Fathers of Lond. Miss. Soc. 2 : 222. — Pierce, B. K. Em. dead, 232.
Simpson, Robert H. Walker, C. D. Biog. Va. Mil. Inst. 475.
Simpson, Thomas, English mathematician. Craik. Pursuit knowl. 1 : 89. — Davenport, R. A. Dives, 395.
Simpson, Thomas, of R. I. Bartlett, J. R. R. I. officers, 412.
Simpson College, Indianola, Ind. U. S. Bur. Ed. Circ. '93, no. 6 : 156.
Sims, George Robert. Archer. Eng. dram. 294.
Sims, Thomas, Kidnapping of, in Boston, 1851. Parker, T. Add. speeches, 1 : 19. — Phillips, Wend. Sp. 55, 77.
Simsbury caverns, Conn. Hovey, H. C. Cel. Am. cav. 197.
Simson, Martin Eduard. Tuttle, H. Ger. pol. lead. 101.
Simson, Robert. Brougham. Works, 1 : 123.
Simulation and dissimulation. Bacon. Ess.
Sin, Egyptian city. Poole, R. S. Cities of Egypt, 166.
Sin. Maurice, F. D. Theol. ess. 18.
— Evil of. Channing. Works, 4 : 151.
— Original, Augustinian and Federal theories of, compared. Fisher, G. P. Discus. 355.
— — Doctrine of. Birks. Diffic. of belief, 117. — Shedd. Theo. ess. 211.
— What it is, what it is not. Martineau, J. Studies, 466.
Sinai. Kitto, J. Scrip. lands, 64. — Lepsius. Lett. from Egypt, 290. — Loring, W. W. Confed. soldier, 208. — Martineau, H. Eastern life, 261. — Olin, S. Travels in Egypt, 373. — Stuart-Glennie. Pilgrim. 137. — (R. St. J. Tyrwhitt) Vaca. tourists, 3 : 327. — (Clarke) Wilson, C. W. Pictur. Palest. 4 : 1.
— Geography of. (M. K. Kellogg) Am. Geog. Soc. 3 : 379.
— wilderness of, Four weeks in. (H. C. Bolton) Am. Geog. Soc. 22 : 575.

Smellie, Wm. Jardine, W. Nat. lib. v. 2.
Smet, Peter John de, with portrait. Murray, J. O'K. Cath. heroes, 835.
Smibert, Thomas. Wilson, J. G. Poets of Scot. 2 : 323.
Smile on faces after death. Jacox, F. Cues, 328.
Smiles, Samuel. Ritchie, J. E. City men, 227.
Smiles and tears. Saunders. Stray leaves, 173.
Smillie, George H. Sheldon, G. W. Amer. painters, 184.
Smillie, James D. Sheldon, G. W. Amer. painters, 187.
Smith, Adam. Brougham. Works, 1 : 166. — Denslow. Mod. think. 71. — Edgar. Footpr. 348. — McCosh. Scot. phil. 162. — Price. Hist. pol. econ. in Eng. — Rogers, J. E. T. Gleanings, 1 : 93. — With portrait. (R. T. Ely) Warner Lib. 23 : 13519. — Wilson, W. Old master, 3.
— and D. Hartley. Stephen, L. Eng. thought, 2 : 63.
— and his precursors. Sargant. Ess. 2 : 288.
— Bibliography. Haldane. Life of S.
— Life of. (Dugald Stewart) Smith, Adam. Ess. phil. ix.
— The political economy of. Leslie, T. E. C. Ess. pol. econ. 148.
— Works. Stephen, L. Eng. thought, 2 : 315.
Smith, Albert. Hodder, G. Memories, 88.
Smith, Albert L. Bartlett, J. R. R. I. officers, 451.
Smith, Alexander. Gilfillan. Third gall. 130. — Wilson, J. G. Poets of Scot. 2 : 467. — Smetham. Lit. works, 195. — (P. P. Alexander) Smith, Alex. Last leaves, v.
— and Pope. Kingsley, C. Lit. lec. 61.
— Poems of. Kingsley, C. New miscel. 72. — Clough. Prose rem. 355.
Smith, Ariana. (A. W. Fiske) Wister & Irwin. Women, 246.
Smith, Asa D. Hemenway. Poets of Vt. 289.
Smith, Mrs. Caroline (Sprague). Hatfield, E. F. Poets of church, 564.
Smith, Charitie Lees. Miller, Jos. Singers ch. 2d ed. 579.
Smith, Charles H., "Bill Arp." Clemens. Funny fellows, 104. — Davidson, J. W. Writ. of South, 530.
Smith, Mrs. Charlotte. Bethune, G. W. Brit. fem. poets, 88.
— Memoirs of. Elwood. Lit. ladies, 1 : 284. — Jeaffreson. Novelists, 1 : 306. — Kavanagh. Eng. women, 1 : 187. — Robertson. Eng. poetesses, 64. — Scott, W. Biog. mem. v. 2. — Williams, Jane. Lit. wom. 217.
— Sonnets of. Deshler. Afternoons, 253.
Smith, Cotton Mather. Headley, J. T. Chaplains Revol. 305.
Smith, E. Delafield. Parton, J. Sk. of men of prog. — With portrait. (G. P. Andrews) Rogers, A. C. Repres. men, 473.
Smith, Edmund. (S. Johnson) Chalmers. Eng. poets, 9 : 165.
Smith, Gen. Edmund Kirby. Pollard. Life of Lee, 761. — Snow. So. generals, 437.
Smith, Elihu Hubbard. Everest. Poets of Conn. 105.
Smith, Elizabeth. Balfour, C. L. Women, 57. — Burder. Pious wom. 577. — Elwood. Lit. ladies, 2 : 187.
Smith, Elizabeth Oakes. Derby, J. C. Fifty years, 545. — Griswold. Fem. poets, 177. — Hart, J. S. Fem. prose, 189.
— Poems. Poe. Works, 6 : 13.
Smith, Emma W. Hemenway. Poets of Vt. 44.

Smith, F. Hopkinson. Sheldon, G. W. Amer. painters, 120.
Smith, Francis W. Walker, C. D. Biog. Va. Mil. Inst. 484.
Smith, Frederick E. Am. Bar Assoc. 13 : 372.
Smith, George. Hoare. Nota. workers, 184.
Smith, Dr. George. Miller, Jos. Singers church, 2d ed, 552.
Smith, Gerrit. With portrait. Brockett. Men of our day, 607. — Bungay. Pen-portr. 81. — Bungay. Off-hand, 330. — Parton. Capt. indus. 133.
Smith, Gervase. Wesley & successors, 227.
Smith, Goldwin. With photo. Cooper, T. Men of mark, 3 : 20. — With portrait. Warner Lib. 23 : 13537.
— at home. (C. G. D. Roberts) Gilder. Authors, 263.
Smith, Gen. Gustavus W. Pollard. Life of Lee, 482.
Smith, Henry Barney. Loring, J. S. Hundred Bost. ora. 483.
Smith, Henry K. Proctor. Lawy. of N. Y. 104.
Smith, Horace. Hall, S. C. Book of mem. 257. — (W. Whyte) Miles, A. H. Poets of cent. 9 : 139. — Timbs. Anec. biog. wits, v. 2. — Wotton. Word portraits, 286.
— and James, Recollections of. Patmore. My friends, 2 : 205.
— — Rejected addresses. Jeffrey, F. Contrib. Ed. Rev.
Smith, Isaac Wm. Am. Bar Assoc. 22 : 692.
Smith, James. Hall, S. C. Book of mem. 257. — Hayward, A. Ess. 1 : 131. — Timbs. Anec. biog. wits, v. 2. — Wilson, J. G. Poets of Scot. 2 : 445. — (W. Whyte) Miles, A. H. Poets of cent. 9 : 101.
Smith, James, Signer of the Declaration of Independence. — Dwight, N. Signers, 198. — Sanderson. Signers, v. 7. — Lincoln, R. W. Signers, 62. — Lossing. Signers, 119. — Neven, D. R. B. Pennsylvanians, 60.
Smith, Col. James. Drake, S. G. Trag. of wilderness, 178.
Smith, James Edward. Miller, Jos. Singers church, 2d ed. 324.
Smith, James Y., with portrait. Bartlett, J. R. R. I. officers, 161.
Smith, Jerome V. C. Loring, J. S. Hundred Bost. ora. 551.
Smith, Capt. John. Adams, H. Hist. ess. 42. — Chambers's Repos. no. 36. — Coffin, C. C. Story of liberty, 362. — Fuller. Worthies, 1 : 275. — Higginson, T. W. Amer. explorers, 229. — Kennedy, J. P. At home, 9. — Richardson, C. F. Amer. liter. 63. — With portrait. Seymour, C. C. B. Self-made, 479. — Lossing. Em. Amer. 34. — Mass. Hist. Proc. 11 : supp. — Parker, H. F. Morning stars, 249.
— and his works. Morley, H. Eng. writ. 11 : 184.
— unreliable as an authority. (H. Adams) Adams, C. F. Erie, 192.
Smith, Capt. John (b. 1759). Brightwell. Bye-paths of biog. 105.
Smith, John (1618–52). Tulloch. Rational theol. 17th cent. 2 : 117.
Smith, John Gregory. Parton, J. Sk. of men of prog.
Smith, Joseph, Founder of Mormonism. Timbs, J. Eng. eccen. 210.
— at Nauvoo. Quincy, J. Figures, 376.
Smith, Joseph Denham. Miller, Jos. Singers church, 2d ed. 534.
Smith, Joshua Hett, 1780. Chandler, P. W. Am. crim. trials, 2 : 183.

Smuggling. Forbes, A. Souvenirs, 183.

Smyrna. Benjamin, S. G. W. World's paradises, 31. — Buckley, J. M. Trav. three cont. 504. — Kinglake. Eothen, 37. — Taylor, B. At Home, 1 : 113. — Wallace, S. E. Storied sea, 201. — Warner, C. D. Levant, 255. — Wikoff, E. Reminis. 293.

— Polycarp and. Lee, J. S. Sac. cities, 188.

Smyth, Clement. Clarke, R. H. Cath. bishops, 2 : 536.

Smyth, Frederick. Field, R. S. Prov. courts N. J. 159. — With portrait. Sketches N. H. men, 106.

Smyth, Hugh. Ivimey. Eng. Bapt. 2 : 175.

Smyth, Rev. John Brownist. Ivimey. Eng. Bapt. 1 : 113.

Smyth, Miles. Holland, J. Psalmists, 2 : 56.

Smyth, Thomas. Davidson, J. W. Writ. of South, 533.

Smythe, Clement Taylor. Smith, C. R. Retrospec. 1 : 147.

Smythe, Sir Thomas. Bourne. Lond. merchants, 98.

Smyths of Ashton court. Burke, B. Viciss. of fam. 3 : 387.

Smyth's channel, South America. Child, T. Span.-Amer. repub. 227.

Smyttan, George Hunt. Miller, Jos. Singers church, 2d ed. 554.

Snake-eater, The. Clark, W. G. Lit. rem. 350.

Snakes. Morgan, C. L. Animal sk. 183.

— Poisonous, of North America. (Leonhard Stejneger) U. S. Nat. Mus. Rept. '93 : 337.

Snead, John Claiborne. Livingston, J. Em. Amer. lawy. 584.

Sneezing, Omens of. Lawrence, R. M. Magic, 206.

Snell, Hannah, *called* Amazon, 1723–79. Dowie, M. M. Wom. adv. 57. — Russell, W. Eccen. 152.

Snelling, Abigail. Ellet. Pioneer wom. 305.

Snelus, George James. Jeans. Creators, 318.

Snider, Denton, J., with portrait. Warner Lib. 25 : 13601.

Snobs. Friswell. Gentle life, 232.

Snow, E. L. Bungay. Off-hand, 286.

Snow, Mrs. Ellet. Pioneer wom. 303.

Snow, Rev. Thomas. Grant, Jas. Metropol. pul. 119.

Snow. Higginson. Out-door, 339.

Snow-birds. Abbott, C. C. Outings, 243.

Snow-crystals, Shower of. Proctor. Light sci. 1 : 230.

Snow-storm traveling. Beecher. Star papers, 348.

Snubbing. Ess. from Sat. R. 13. — Friswell. Better self, 221.

Snuff, A pinch of. Hunt, L. Seer, 1 : 187.

— Taking. Mathews. Men & bks. 347.

Snyder, Sicke, or Frecks. Brown, J. N. Bapt. martyrs, 65.

Snyder, Simon, with portrait. Armor. Gov. of Pa. 308.

Snydor, Richard D. B. Walker, C. D. Biog. Va. Mil. Inst. 506.

Soap bubbles. (A. W. Rücker) Manch. Sci. lec. 7 : 33.

Soaring. (E. C. Huffaker) Smithson. Rept. '97 : 183.

— Practical experiments in. (O. Lilienthal) Smithson. Inst. Rept. '93 : 195.

Sobieski, Princess Clementina Maria. Jesse. Pretenders, 54.

Sobieski, John. *See* John I. Sobieski.

Sobraon. Malleson, G. B. Battles of India, 337.

Social affairs in England, 1763–89. Routledge, J. Pop. prog. in Eng. 137.

Social aims. Emerson. Lett. & soc. aims, 77.

Social amelioration. Farrar. Soc. & p. day quest. 7.

Social and industrial revolution. Smith, G. Ess. on ques. of day, 1.

Social architects, The. Greeley. Hints ref. 272.

Social circles, Little. Higginson. Conc. all, 30.

"Social classes ; " Is the term a scientific category? (F. H. Giddings) Conf. char. & correc. '05 : 110.

Social compact, Theory of the. Lowell, A. L. Ess. gov't, 136.

Social condition of the operative classes. Arnold, T. Miscel. 404.

Social conditions, Wrong in existing. George, H. Soc. prob. 74.

Social consciousness of children, Development of. (W. S. Monroe) Nat. Educa. Assoc. '98 : 921.

Social contract, Rousseau on. Coleridge. Friend, 177.

Social contract theory, History of. Ritchie, D. G. Darwin.

Social democracy in Germany. Baring-Gould. Germany, 400.

Social distinctions. Hamerton. Hum. int. 131.

Social duties. Bryant, S. Short stud. 30.

Social economy of the future. (A. R. Wallace) Reid, A. New party, 177.

— Teaching of. (W. M. Williams) Trans. Soc. Sci. Lond. '57 : 509.

Social element in churches, Cultivating the. Thompson, H. M. Copy, 141.

Social equality. Stephen, L. Soc. rights, 1 : 175.

Social evolution, Kidd on. Roosevelt, T. Amer. ideals, 303.

— A new method of. Oliphant, L. Traits, 268.

Social formula and social freedom. Dodge, M. A. Twelve miles, 246.

Social forms and forces of the Hindus. Johnson, S. Ori. relig. India, 237.

Social freedom community. Nordhoff. Commun. 357.

Social future and economic future of the U. S. Bryce. Soc. institu. 275.

Social graces. Wilde, Lady. Soc. stud. 53.

Social grievances. Collins, W. W. Miscel. 24.

Social hints and studies. Matthews, A. Rumina.

Social hyperbole. Mozley, A. Ess. 1.

Social intercourse. Holland, J. G. Every-day, 1 : 291.

Social life. Tuckerman. Optimist, 112. — Vaughan, D. J. Questions, 43.

— in early New England. Adams, C. F. Three episodes, 2 : 699.

— in past centuries. Tartt. Ess. 1 : 63.

— of workingmen. Mass. Labor, '80 : 239.

Social mentor, in London. Smalley. Lond. lett. 2 : 21.

Social organism. (H. Jones) Seth & Haldane. Ess. 187.

Social organization and Christianity. Blackie, J. S. Ess. 1.

Social philosophers, Some of our. Ess. from Nation, 89.

Social philosophy, Unsound. Greg. Ess. pol. 1 : 207.

Social plans and problems. Shackford. Soc. & lit. pap. 198.

Social pressure, Increase of. George, H. Soc. prob. 36.

Social problems. Rosebery. Speeches, 64.

— first principles. George, H. Soc. prob. 116.

Social problems, Modern, Æschylus on. Shackford. Soc. & lit. pap. 9.
— of the future. (W. Gladden) Abbott L. New purit. 173.
Social productiveness, Conditions of. Wasson. Ess. 257.
Social progress. Carpenter, E. Eng. ideal, 45.
— Shackford. Soc. & lit. pap. 180.
— Ethics of. (F. H. Giddings) Addams. Philanth.
— of states. Arnold, T. Miscel. 306.
— Psychology of. Bosanquet, Mrs. Standard, 114.
— Science and. (R. A. Smith) Trans. Soc. Sci. Lond. '57 : 517.
Social question, Christianity and. (F. G. Peabody) Barrows, J. H. Parl. relig. 2 : 1024.
Social questions. Turgot. Life & writ. 193.
— Importance of. George, H. Soc. prob. 9.
Social reconstruction, Outlines of. Robertson, J. M. Mod. humanists, 261.
Social reform. Bibliography. Bost. Pub. Lib. Bull. May, June, '98.
— W. H. Channing on. Brownson. Works, 10 : 137.
— Christian ethics and. Potter, H. C. Scholar & state, 183.
— How not to promote. Roosevelt, T. Amer. ideals, 214.
— Sensationalism in. (S. A. Barnett) Barnett, S. A. Prac. socialism, 173.
Social reformers. Platt, J. Excelsior, 89.
Social reforms. Henry, C. S. About men, 148.
— Holland, J. G. Every-day, 2 : 261.
— The common reason in. Shackford. Soc. & lit. pap. 260.
Social restoration. Brownson. Works, 14 : 197.
Social science in elementary schools. (W. C. Taylor) Trans. Soc. Sci. Lond. '71 : 384.
— in England. Temple, R. Cosmop. ess. 109.
— Relation of fine art to. (T. G. Parry) Trans. Soc. Sci. Lond. '78 : 135.
Social settlements. Addams, Jane. Philanth. — (J. Addams) Conf. char. & correc. '97 : 338. — (F. G. Peabody) Conf. char. & correc. '97 : 329. See also Settlements.
Social tendencies. Shackford. Soc. & lit. pap. 220.
Social texture. Wasson. Ess. 221.
Social up-draught, Developing the. (F. G. Peabody) Conf. char. & correc. '97 : 225.
Social Utopias. Chambers's Papers, no. 18.
Social work of the church. Woods, R. A. Eng. soc. move. 142.
Socialism. Gladden. Tools, 242. — (F. A. Walker) Phillips. Ex. lec. '85–86 : 47. — Rae, J. Contem. soc. 1. — Woods, R. A. Eng. soc. move. 38.
— and Christianity. (M. Kaufman) Liv. papers, v. 10.
— and the church. Brownson. Works, 10 : 79.
— and liberty. Pembroke, Earl. Polit. lett. 185.
— and natural selection. Bosanquet. Asp. soc. ques. 289.
— and religion. Bax. Relig. of socialism, 48.
— and the social question. Rae, J. Contem. soc. 319.
— Bibliography. Bliss, W. D. P. Hdbk. socialism. — Ely, R. T. Socialism. — Menger, A. Right to whole prod. of labor, 6. — Salem (Mass.) Pub. Lib. Bull. Aug. '94, Aug. '96.
— Elements of truth in. Brownson. Works, 10 : 526.
— English. Greg. Ess. pol. 1 : 458.

Socialism, Evolution of. Mallock. Stud. contemp. spu. 274, 278.
— Fundamental error of. Mallock. Stud. contemp. sup. 245.
— Impracticability of. (E. S. Robertson) Plea for liberty, 29.
— in ancient society. Bosanquet. Ess. 48.
— in England. (S. Webb) Am. Econ. Assoc. v. 4.
— in Europe; The European terror. (E. de Laveleye) Coan. Soc. prob. 138.
— in public libraries. Garnett, R. Ess. librarianship, 234.
— in the U. S.; Oneida community. Smith, G. Ess. on ques. of day, 337.
— Individual rights under. Bax, E. B. Outlooks, 143.
— Liberalism vs. Bax, E. B. Outlooks, 67.
— Modern. Fawcett. Ess. & lec. 1.
— Progress and hopes of. Greg. Ess. pol. 1 : 505.
— Progress toward ; From freedom to bondage. (H. Spencer) Plea for liberty, 1.
— Sophisms of. Bastiat. Ess. on pol. econ. 74, 173.
— State, in the antipodes. (C. Fairfield) Plea for liberty, 145.
— Strength and weakness of. Gladden. Appl. Chr. 53.
— True line of deliverance. (A. Herbert) Plea for liberty, 379.
— Unscientific. Bax. Relig. of socialism, 92.
— What is ? Mallock. Stud. contemp. sup. 232, 235, 244.
— Who will pay the bills of ? Godkin. Problems, 225.
Socialist ethics. Bax, E. B. Outlooks, 109.
Socialists, Account of. Robertson, J. B. Lec. mod. hist. 490.
— Christian. Rae, J. Contem. soc. 222.
— of the chair. Rae, J. Contem. soc. 193.
Socializing of consumption. Smart, W. Stud. econ. 249.
Societies. Learned and educational, in the U. S. (S. B. Weeks) U. S. Bur. Ed. Rept. '93–94, 2 : 1493.
— to found. Zangwill. Without prej. 171.
Society. Clarke, J. F. Self-culture, 415.
— American. (M. E. Beedy) Brackett, A. C. Educa. of girls, 246.
— and the individual. Gladden. Ruling ideas, 63.
— and solitude. Emerson. Society, 7. — Hamerton. Intellec. 300.
— Christ's idea of, Brook Farm interpretation of. Peabody, E. P. Last evening, 181.
— Christianization of. Gladden. Tools, 1.
— Distinction between, and the state. Ritchie, D. G. State interf. 155.
— English and French, Spirit of. Bulwer. Student, 2 : 143.
— — not exciting. (M. E. Beedy) Brackett, A. C. Educa. of girls, 239.
— Formation of. Elder, W. Questions, 14.
— Good, and the best. Higginson. Conc. all, 8.
— Influence of Christianity upon. Oxenham. Stud. in eccl. hist. 120.
— Literary. Jacox. Lit. life, 128.
— Married women in. Willis. Hurry-graphs, 268.
— Men in. Willis. Hurry-graphs, 311.
— Modern. Clarke, J. F. Self-culture, 221.
— — Evolution of. (R. D. Melville) Smithson. Rept. '94 : 507.
— natural, Vindication of. Burke. Works (Bohn), 1 : 1.
— Parisian. Hillebrand. France, 95.
— polite, Future of. Higginson. Book & heart, 129.

Solitude and retirement. Ballantyne. Ess. 136.
— and society. Martineau, H. Miscel. **2** : 42.
— Dangers of. Alger. Solitudes, 91.
— in crowds. Jacox, F. Cues, 84.
— Morals of. Alger. Solitudes, 91.
— Uses of. Alger. Solitudes, 140. — Gray, E. C. Idle musings, 262.
Solomon, King. Geikie, C. Old Test. char. 260.
— Williams, H. L. Boys of the Bible, 154.
— Character and history of. Keble. Occas. pap.
— in Europe. MacCallum. Stud. Ger. 87.
Solomon, Rabbi, of St. Goar. Schlechter, S. Stud. Jud. 173.
Solomon, Rebecca. Clayton, E. C. Eng. fem. art. **2** : 129.
Solomon, Simeon. Bate, P. H. Eng. Pre-Raph. 59.
— Essay on, (S. Colvin) Atkinson, J. B., et al. Eng. paint. 13.
Solon, the Athenian. Cox, G. W. Gt. statesm. 1. — Diog. Laertius. Lives, 23. — Duruy. Hist. Greece, **1** : 504. — Fénélon. Philosophers, 44. — Mombert. Great lives, 15. — With portrait. Warner Lib. **23** : 13642.
— as a poet. Arnold, E. Poets of Greece, 91.
— Mills. Poets of Greece, 89. — Symonds. Greek poets, **1** : 247.
Solution, gaseous theory of, Deduction from. (Orme Masson) Smithson. Rept. '92 : 289.
Solutions, Suggestions regarding. (William Ramsay) Smithson. Rept. '92 : 299.
Somerby, Horatio G. (W. S. Appleton) Mass. Hist. Proc. 2d ser. **1** : 132.
Somercote, Robert, cardinal deacon. Williams, R. F. Eng. card. **1** : 252.
Somerleyton. Jewitt, L. Stately homes, **2** : 201.
Somers, Sir George. Belknap. Amer. biog. **2** : 115.
Somers, John, Lord. Adams, W. H. D. Learned in law, 104. — Campbell. Ld. chan. **5** : 54. — Foss. Judges, **7** : 348. — Lodge. Portraits (Bohn), v. **7**. — Roscoe, H. Em. lawyers, **1** : 169.
Somers, Richard. Cooper, J. F. Am. nav. off. **1** : 73.
Somerset, Charles Seymour, sixth duke of. Caulfield. Kit-cat, 9. — Lodge. Portraits (Bohn), v. **7**.
Somerset, Edward. See Worcester, Marquis of.
Somerset, Edward Seymour, duke of. Burke, S. H. Men of reforma. **2** : 178, 247. — Lodge. Portraits (Bohn), v. **1**. — Johns. Nav. & mil. heroes. — Wrangham. Brit. Plutarch, v. **1**.
Somerset, Elizabeth Percy, duchess of. Costello. Englishwomen, **3** : 130. — With portrait. Jameson. Beauties, 167.
Somerset, Frances Howard, countess of. With portrait. Costello. Englishwomen, **2** : 186. — Jesse. Court of Eng. Stuarts, **1** : 229. — (G. Martin) Vincent, A. Twelve bad women, 63.
Somerset, Frances Thynne, duchess of. Bethune, G. W. Brit. fem. poets, 51. — Elwood. Lit. ladies, **1** : 61. — Williams, Jane. Lit. wom. 189.
Somerset, Lady Henry. Bolton. Fam. lead. wom. 250.
Somerset, Robert Carr, 1st earl of. Jesse. Court of Eng. Stuarts, **1** : 198. — Ewald. Stories fr. st. pap. **2** : 42. — Menzies, S. Roy. fav. v. **1**.
— Trial of. Wright, T. Nar. sorcery, **2** : 15.
Somerset family. Sanford & Townsend. Gov. fam. v. **2**. — Thomson, K. B. Recoll. v. **1**.
Somerset House, Old, Stories of. Timbs. Abbeys, **1** : 85.

Somersetshire, England, Baptists of. Ivimey. Eng. Bapt. **2** : 521.
— Walk through. Collins, M. Pen sketches, **1** : 145.
Somerville, John, Lord. Scott, W. Biog. mem. v. **2**.
Somerville, Mary. Adams, W. H. D. Cel. Eng. wom. Vict. **2** : 1. — Bailey, J. B. Methuselahs, 297. — Balfour, C. L. Women worth emula. 1. — Chambers, W. Rem. pers. 24. — Fawcett, M. G. Em. wom. 35. — Japp. Wise words, 1. — Proctor. Light sci. **2** : 1. — Queens of liter. 3. — Walford, L. B. Four. biog. 229. — Duyckinck. Portrait gall. **2** : 219. — Fifty famous women, 204. — Smith, G. B. Women of renown, 173. — Walford, L. B. Twelve Eng. auth. 103.
Somerville, W. (S. Johnson) Chalmers. Eng. poets, **11** : 149.
Somerville, Mass., Old landmarks of. Drake, S. A. Hist. fields Mid. 141.
— Old powder house. Drake, S. A. Hist. fields Mid. 110.
Somewhere else. Zangwill. Without prej. 339.
Sommer, Hans. Maitland, J. A. F. Masters Ger. music, 276.
Sommer, John. Wallace, R. Anti-Trin. biog. **2** : 263.
Somnambulism. Boismont, A. B. de. Hallucina. 188. — Dendy, N. F. Philos. of mystery. — Ennemoser. Hist. magic, **2** : 429. — Elam. Phys. prob. 333. — Mason, R. O. Telepathy, 129.
— Artificial. Proctor, R. A. Rough ways, 178.
Sonata, Rise of the. Elson. Realm of music, 42.
Song, Faculty and ministry of. (W. L. Tomlins) Nat. Educa. Assoc. '95 : 551.
— German. Whitman, S. Teuton. stud. 70.
— in the kindergarten. (Constance Mackenzie) Nat. Educa. Assoc. '93 : 331.
— The modern. Davis, L. S. Stud. mus. 108.
— Provençal. Mackaye. Abbess Pt. Royal, 129.
Song-books, Elizabethan, Lyrics from. Symonds. Key of blue, 265.
Songs, American national. Butterworth. Great compos. 134.
— from the dramatists. Donne, W. B. Ess. on drama, 89.
— Mediæval Norman. Symonds. Key of blue, 133.
— morning talks, and stories. (Emilie Poulsson) Nat. Educa. Assoc. '92 : 292.
— of the sea, American. Williams, A. M. Stud. folk. 1.
— of trades, or songs for the people. Disraeli, I. Curios. (N. Y. 4 v.) **2** : 315.
— of Tuscany, Popular. Symonds. Sk. So. Eur. **1** : 228.
— Popular, Migration of. Peck, H. T. Pers. equa. 173.
— Scotch, before Burns. Shairp. Sk. hist. & poetry, 282.
Sonnemann, Leopold. Tuttle, H. Ger. pol. lead. 192.
Sonnet, The. Deshler. Afternoons, 6.
— The English. Dennis, J. Studies, 392. — Jones, W. A. Lit. stud. **1** : 56. — Milton. Sonnets, ed. by Pattison ; introd. — Reed, H. Brit. poets, **2** : 235.
— — History of. (R. C. French) Afternoon lec. **4** : 133.
Sonora and Arizona. (S. Mowry) Am. Geog. Soc. **1** : 66.
— Commerce and mines of, 1891. (A. Willard) U. S. Cons. Rept. **39** : 122.

South, Robert. Broadus. Lec. hist. preach. 217.
— Mathews. Men & bks. 58.
South, The. Dilke. Greater Brit. 35.
— after the war. Godkin. Reflections, 173.
— and its problems. (L. B. Evans; J. M. Carlisle) Nat. Educa. Assoc, '94 : 567.
— Authorship at the. Bocock. Writings, 445.
— — before the war. Page. Old South, 57.
— Black ascendency in. Dixon, W. H. White conquest, 2 : 134.
— Education in. (J. C. Gibbs) Nat. Educa. Assoc. '73 : 80.
— — since 1865. (W. A. Candler) Nat. Educa. Assoc. '89 : 339.
— Educational necessities of. (Leon Trousdale) Nat. Educa. Assoc. '75 : 77.
— Educational needs and natural resources of. (Alexander Hogg) Nat. Educa. Assoc. '76 : 76.
— Educational outlook in. (Booker T. Washington) Nat. Educa. Assoc. '84 : 125.
— Higher education in. (E. A. Alderman) Nat. Educa. Assoc. '95 : 979. — (G. T. Winston) Nat. Educa. Assoc. '97 : 183.
— Impressions of, in 1885. Warner, C. D. Studies, 3.
— Industrial education in. (A. D. Mayo) U. S. Bur. Ed. Circ. '88, no. 5.
— Last words from. (A. D. Mayo) Nat. Educa. Assoc. '84 : 117.
— Life in, 1838. Martineau. Retrospec. 2 : 36.
— New. Grady, H. W. Writings & speech. 83. — (Robert Bingham) Nat. Educa. Assoc. '84 : 76.
— — Society in. Warner, C. D. Studies, 18.
— Problem of. Grady, H. W. Writings & speech. 94.
— A recollection of. Nadal, E. S. Ess. 232.
— Reign of anarchy in. Dixon, W. H. White conquest, 2 : 11.
— revisited, 1887. Warner, C. D. Studies, 99.
— Tour in. Bryant. Prose, 2 : 23.
— Two studies of. Matthews, B. Aspects fic. 25.
— University and State in. (E. A. Alderman) Nat. Educa. Assoc. '96 : 278.
South America, Local transportation in, 1891. U. S. Cons. Rept. 38 : 700.
— Mining province of. Barker, Lady. Travel. about, 147.
— Railroads to. Helper, H. R. Andean diplom. 275. — Am. Geog. Soc. 24 : 409.
— Social and polit. development of. (C. De Kalb) Am. Geog. Soc. 26 : 1.
— tribes of, Characteristics of. Brinton. Races & peo. 267.
— Ulloa's travels in. St. John. Cel. travelers, 2 : 320.
— west coast, Journey along. (J. Douglas) Am. Geog. Soc. 10 : 197.
South Carolina. (O. M. Lieber) Am. Geog. Soc. 1 : 252. — Campbell, G. White & black, 312. — Doyle, J. A. Eng. colonies, 328. — Lodge, H. C. Eng. colonies, 158. — Olmsted. Seaboard, 377.
— Bibliography. McCrady, E. Hist. of So. Carolina.
— — of Colonial Hist. of. (E. L. Whitney) Am. Hist. Assoc. Rept. '94 : 563.
— Collegiate education in. U. S. Bur. Ed. Circ. '88, no. 3 : 52.
— colony of, Education in. U. S. Bur. Ed. Circ. '88, no. 3 : 13.
— Denominational education in. U. S. Bur. Ed. Circ. '88, no. 3 : 87.
— higher education in, Bibliography of. U. S. Bur. Ed. Circ. '88, no. 3 : 193.

South, Invasion of. Dawson. Batt. of U. S. 1 : 495.
— Nullification in, History of. Perry, B. F. Biog. sketches, 2 : 199.
— Provisional governorship of, 1865. Perry, B. F. Biog. sketches, 2 : 242.
— Slavery in, 1670–1770. (E. McCrady) Am. Hist. Assoc. Rept. '95 : 631.
South Carolina College, Columbia, S. C. U. S. Bur. Ed. Circ. '88, no. 3 : 127.
— History of. (W. J. Rivers) Nat. Educa. Assoc. '76 : 91.
South Carolina Military Academy, Charleston, S. C. U. S. Bur. Ed. Circ. '88, no. 3 : 69.
South Carolina State Board of Health, Report from. (J. R. Bratton) Am. Pub. Health, 16 : 176.
South Downs, The. Lower. Contrib. 146.
South Kensington, Museum at, Art treasures. Gibson, W. S. Miscel. 235.
South Kentucky College, Hopkinsville. U. S. Bur. Ed. Circ. '99, 3 : 169.
South Mountain, Battle of. Stine, J. H. Army Poto. 154.
South Sea bubble, The. Chambers's Miscel. no. 172. — Davenport, R. A. Delusions, 261. — Mackay. Delusions, 1 : 58.
South-sea house, The. Lamb. Elia.
South Sea islands, 1st missionaries to. Gurney, J. H. Hist. sketches, 3 : 337.
South Seas, Discoveries in. Jenks, E. Hist. Aust. col. 1.
South Wales tin-plate trade, 1896. (A. Howells) U. S. Cons. Rept. 51 : 67.
Southampton, Henry Wriothesley, earl of. Lodge. Portraits (Bohn), v. 3.
Southampton, Thomas Wriothesley, 4th earl of. Lodge. Portraits (Bohn), v. 5.
Southampton, Eng. Winter. Old shrines, 13.
— Castle and ancient houses in. Timbs. Abbeys, 1 : 394.
Southcote family, The. Morris, J. Troub. of Cath. v. 1.
Southcott, Joanna. Davenport, R. A. Delusions, 47.
— an extraordinary fanatic. Wilson, H. Characters, 186.
Southern Baptist Theological Seminary, Louisville, Ky. U. S. Bur. Ed. Circ. '99, 3 : 279.
Southern confederacy. Morton, O. P. So. Empire, 1.
Southern continent, The. Galt, J. Lit. life, 2 : 175.
Southern literature, Necessity of. (D. K. Whittaker) Charleston book, 313.
Southern people, history of, Want of. Page. Old South, 253.
Southern railroad. Mansfield, E. D. Pers. mem. 296.
Southern University, Greensborough, Ala. U. S. Bur. Ed. Circ. '89, no. 3 : 179.
Southern women, Needs of. (Clara Conway) Nat. Educa. Assoc. '84 : 169.
Southerne, J. Oroonoko. Lennox, W. P. Plays, 1 : 26.
Southesk, Anne Hamilton, countess of, with portrait. Jameson. Beauties, 223. — Jesse. Court of Eng. Stuarts, 3 : 295.
Southey, Mrs. Caroline. Bethune, G. W. Brit. fem. poets, 327. — Miles, A. H. Poets of cent. 7 : 39. — Miller, Jos. Singers church, 2d ed. 396. — Robertson. Eng. poetesses, 248.
Southey, Robert. Austin & Ralph. Laureates, 346. — Brooks, S. W. Eng. poets, 336. — Caine, T. H. Cobwebs, 30. — Carlyle. Remi-

nis. 513. — Chorley. Authors of Eng. 27. — Collier, W. F. Hist. Eng. lit. 447. — Dawson, W. J. Mod. Engl. 81. — Dennis, J. Studies, 250. — Devey. Mod. Eng. poets, 112. — Dixon, W. M. Eng. poetry, 167. — Edgar. Footpr. 200. Gilfillan. 1st gall. 287. — Griswold, R. W. Sac. poets. — Hall, S. C. Book of mem. 185. — Hamilton, Wal. Poets laur. — Hatton, J. Old lamps, 245. — Hazlitt. Spirit. — Howitt. Homes Br. poets, 2 : 255. — Jerdan. Men, 406. — Mason, E. T. Pers traits, 3 : 209. — Miles, A. H. Poets of cent. 2 : 1. 9 : 93. — Mitchell, D. G. Eng. lands, 4 : 5. — Mitford, M. R. Recollec. 392. — Ossoli. Art, 91. — Phillips, S. Ess. from Times, 1 : 163. — Reed, H. Brit. poets, 2 : 132. — Saunders, F. Famous books, 148. — Tuckerman. Ess. 59. — (H. Taylor) Ward. Eng. poets, 4 : 155. — Wotton. Word portraits, 290. — Procter, B. W. Autob. 137. — Saintsbury, G. Ess. Eng. lit. 2 : 1, 415. — With portrait. Warner Lib. 23 : 13677.

Southey, Robert, and Landor. Oliphant, M. Lit. hist. 1 : 343.
— at Greta Hall. Rawnsley. Lit. Assoc. Eng. lakes, 1 : 39.
— Cottle's Reminiscences of. Phillips, S. Ess. from Times, 1 : 237.
— Curse of Kehama. Foster, J. Crit. ess. (Bohn) 1 : 453.
— Roderick. Jeffrey, F. Contrib. Ed. Rev.
— Sonnets of. Deshler. Afternoons, 215.
— Wordsworth, and Coleridge. DeQuincey. Lit. rem. (Bost.) 2 : 44.

Southwark. Wolfe. Lit. pilg. Brit. au. 24.
— in olden time. (E. Boger) Clinch, G. Bygone Surrey, 114.

Southwell, Robert. Macdonald, G. England's antiphon, 97. — Langford. Prison books, 124. — (J. W. Hales) Ward. Eng. poets, 1 : 479.
— Turnbull's edition of. Lowell. Writ. 1 : 255.

Southwestern Presbyterian University, Clarksville, Tenn. U. S. Bur. Ed. Circ. '93, no. 5 : 214.

Southwick, Stephen Henry. Bartlett, J. R. R. I. officers, 438.

Southworth, Mrs. Emma D. E. N. Davidson, J. W. Writ. of South, 535. — Hart, J. S. Fem. prose, 211. — Freeman, J. D. Wom. of South, 216.

Souvestre, Emile. Warner Lib. 23 : 13693.

Souza-Botelho, Adélaïde Marie Emilie. Moore, T. Prose & v. 75. — Ste.-Beuve. Cel. wom. 70.

Sovereigns of olden time. Doran. Monarchs, 1 : 43.
— Submission due to. Hume. Philos. works, 3 : 518.

Sovereignty and the general will. Green, T. H. Works, 2 : 399.
— Conception of. Ritchie, D. G. Darwin.
— Hobbes's doctrine of. Stephen, J. F. Horæ Sabb. 2 : 54.
— Limits of. Lowell. Essays on government.
— Modern theories of. Pollock. History of science of politics, 93.
— Nature of. Ritchie, D. G. State interf. 161.

Space. Laing. Mod. sci. 3.
— Idea of. Hume. Philos. works, 1 : 44.
— Motion in. Holland, H. Frag. papers, 48.
— Muscular perception of. Hall, G. S. Asp. Ger. 208.

Spagnoletto, Jose Ribera. Jervis, Lady. Painting, 2 : 55.

Spain. Bennett, J. H. Winter on Medit. 526. — Champney, L. W. Three Vassar girls abroad,

92. — Cox, S. S. Winter sunbeams, 283. — Disraeli, B. Home letters, 14. — Longfellow, H. W. Outre-mer, 165. — Prime, S. I. Alhambra, 1. — Taylor, B. Lands of Sar. 383. — Warner, C. D. Roundabout, 191. — Kingston, W. B. Music & manners, 2 : 149.

Spain and Cuba. Bibliography. Providence Pub. Lib. Bull. Mar. '98.
— and England (1823). Brougham. Works, 9 : 262.
— and U. S., Commerce of, 1891. (R. W. Turner) U. S. Cons. Rept. 37 : 182.
— Andalusian. Moore, Jos. Outl. Eur. 292.
— Bibliography. Paterson (N. J.) Pub. Lib. Bull. Apr. '98. — St. Louis Pub. Lib. Magazine, May, '98. — Salem (Mass.) Pub. Lib. Bull. Apr. '98.
— Borders of. Stoddard, C. A. Span. cit. 1.
— Buckle's essay on. Robertson, J. B. Lec. mod. hist. 164.
— Carlist struggle in. Alison. Ess. v. 2.
— Carthagena, 1892. (C. Molina) U. S. Cons. Rept. 39 : 329.
— Castilian. Moore, Jos. Outl. Eur. 343.
— Commerce of, in 1895. U. S. Cons. Rept. 51 : 47.
— Cortes, A field-night in. Hay, J. Castil. days, 313.
— Economic conditions of, in 16th cent. (B. Moses) Am. Hist. Assoc. Rept. '93, 123.
— Evangelization of, Modern efforts for. Stoughton. Span. ref. 301.
— in 1809. Foster, J. Crit. ess. (Bohn) 1 : 264.
— Industries of, 1895. (H. W. Bowen) U. S. Cons. Rept. 50 : 310.
— Institutions of, in 18th cent. Robertson, J. B. Lec. mod. hist. 96.
— Judicial and criminal statistics of, 1891. (R. W. Turner) U. S. Cons. Rept. 37 : 224.
— Letters from. Putnam, J. O. Addresses, 390.
— Local transportation in, 1891. U. S. Cons. Rept. 38 : 665.
— National ballads of ; Moriscan romances. Bryant. Prose, 1 : 93.
— Naturalist's impressions of. (P. L. Sclater) Vaca. tourists, 2 : 189.
— North, Visit to. (Francis Galton) Vaca. tourists, 1 : 422.
— Notes on. Mivart. Ess. 1 : 168.
— Political and intellectual development of, 1884. Döllinger. Stud. hist. 243.
— Politics in, 1883. Hale, E. E. Seven Spanish cit. 166.
— — Moral of. Hay, J. Castil. days, 347.
— Reciprocity with, 1891. (J. G. Blaine & Señor Guanes) U. S. Cons. Rept. 38 : 481.
— Religious condition of, 1844. Wiseman, N. Ess. 3 : 1.
— Religious exiles from. Stoughton. Span. ref. 281.
— Republican government needed for. Hay, J. Castil. days, 389.
— Royal family, Insanity in. Ireland, W. W. Blot, 151.
— Through Andalusia. Lee, A. E. Europ. days, 342.
— Two peeps into. Arnold, F. Arm-chair, 118.
— War against Napoleon I., 1807–14. Sterling, J. Ess. 1 : 120.
— War of succession. Robertson, J. B. Lec. mod. hist. 1.
— Worship in. Hale, E. E. Seven Spanish cit. 118.

Spalato. Freeman. Subj. Venice, 137.

Spalding, Edward, with portrait. Sketches N. H. men, 81.

Spalding, George Burley, with portrait. Sketches N. H. men, 291.

Spalding, Johann Joachim. Ker, J. Lec. hist. preach. 248, 260.

Spalding, John. Burton, J. H. Book-hunter, 330.

Spalding, Archbishop M. J. Brownson. Works, 14 : 500. — Clarke, R. H. Cath. bishops, 3 : 11. — Davidson, J. W. Writ. of South, 539. — Gross, S. D. Autobiog. 2 : 361.

Spalding, Rufus Paine. Livingston, J. Em. Am. lawy. 579.

Spangenberg, Augustus G. Miller, Jos. Singers church, 2d ed. 178.

Spangenberg, Everhard. Wallace, R. Anti-Trin. biog. 2 : 378.

Spaniard, The, in New Mexico. (W. W. H. Davis) Am. Hist. Assoc. 3 : 164.

Spaniards, Last discoveries of. Vogel. Cent. of discov. 346.

Spanish-American war. Bibliography. Wilkesbarre (Pa.) Osterhout Lib. Newsletter, Aug. '98.

Spanish Armada. Allen, Jos. Battles Brit. navy, 1 : 27. — Bagwell. Ireland under the Tudors, 3 : 172. — Bayly, J. A. S. New stud. 94. — Ewald. Stories fr. st. pap. 1 : 225.— Hale, E. E. Stories of sea, 52. — Hopkins, S. Puritans, 3 : 183.— Motley. Un. Neth. v. 3. — Strickland. Queens Eng. 7 : 76. — Tillotson, J. Stories of wars, 125. — Froude. Eng. seamen, 176. — Low, G. R. Gt. battles, 15.
— Coming of. Lucas. Secularia, 131.
— Defeat of. Archer. Decis. ev. 138. — Creasy. Fifteen battles, 218. — Valentine, L. J. Seafights.
— England's preparation for. Adams, W. H. D. Eng. at war, 1 : 32.
— Evolution of. Hume, M. A. S. Year after Armada, 175.
— The second. Hayward, A. Ess. 3d ser. 384.
— Spanish story of. Froude, J. A. Span. Armada, 1.
— Year after. Hume, M. A. S. Year after Armada, 1.

Spanish ballads. Mitford, M. R. Recollec. 204.
— Early. Legaré. Writ. 2 : 299.

Spanish language and poetry. Longfellow. Poets Eur. 621.
— Origin of. Ticknor. Span. lit. 2 : 358.

Spanish literature. Bibliography. Clarke, H. B. Element. hdbk. Spanish lit. — Kelly, J. F. Hist. Spanish lit. — Underhill, J. G. Sp. lit. in Eng. of the Tudors.

Spanish match, The. Doran. Knights, 364.

Spanish peaks. Wahatoya ; or before the graders. Jackson, H. H. Bits trav. home, 351.

Spanish Protestants in Germany and the Netherlands. Stoughton. Span. ref. 73.

Spanish revolution. Causes of. Robertson, J. B. Lec. mod. hist. 132.

Spanish rule in America. Vogel. Cent. of discov. 356.

Spankie, Serjeant. Grant, J. Bench & bar, 2 : 190.

Sparhawk, George. (Miss F. C. Sparhawk) N. E. Hist.-Gen. Soc. Biog. 3 : 195.

Sparhawk family in New England. (C. H. C. Howard) Essex Inst. Hist. Coll. v. 25.

Sparks, Mrs. Catherine Adeline (Edwards). Clayton, E. C. Eng. fem. art. 2 : 130.

Sparks, Jared. Griswold. Prose writ. 307.— (G. E. Ellis) Mass. Hist. Proc. 10 : 211. — Peabody. Harv. grad. 137. — Powell. Liv. authors, 1850, 355.— Parton. Triumphs, 131. —

Richardson. Amer. lit. 1 : 459. — (F. Bowen) Vaille & Clark. Harv. book, v. 1.

Sparks, Ruth. Ellet. Pioneer wom. 153.

Sparks, Thomas. Winslow, S. N. Biog. Phila. merch. 141.

Sparrow, English. Morgan, C. L. Animal sket. 148.
— in N. America. (Barrows) U. S. Dept. Agric., Div. Econ. Ornith. Bull. 1.

Sparrows. Story, A. T. Vagrom, 34.

Sparta, Constitution of, and the agrarian laws of Lycurgus. Blackie, J. S. Horæ Hellen. 235.

Spartan tombs. Gardner, P. New chap. Gr. hist.

Spas. Bibliography. Weber, H. and F. P. Spas & min. waters Europe.

Spaulding, Mrs. Daniel. Clement, J. Noble deeds, 186.

Spaulding, Jennie Tileston. Brockett. Woman's work, 789.

Spaulding, John. Am. Bar Assoc. 17 : 510.

Spaulding, Robert. McClure. Translators, 119.

Speaker of the House of Representatives as premier. Hart. Am. govt. 1.

Speakers, General Epistle to. Butler, E. For furth. consid. 96.

Speaking, Extempore. Osgood, S. Amer. leaves, 193.
— Public. Mathews. Men & books, 279.
— Timidity in. Mathews. Conversers, 249.

Special training. Mabie. Ess. on work, 108.

Specialism in medicine. Mackenzie, M. Ess. 1.
— Reynolds, J. R. Ess. 194.

Specialist, The. Watson, E. H. L. Uncon. humor, 123.

Specialists, General culture needed by. Bowen, F. Gleanings, 8.

Specialization in studies. (M. G. Glazebrook) Thirteen ess. educa.

Specie payments, The public debt and. Garfield. Works, 1 : 183.
— Suspension and resumption of. Garfield. Works, 2 : 609.

Species, genesis of, Huxley on. Mivart. Less. fr. nature, 422.
— — Chauncey Wright on. Mivart. Less. fr. nature, 332.
— Origin of. Huxley. Sci. & cul. 317. — Wright, C. Philos. dis. 126.
— — Darwin's. Huxley. Lay sermons. — Jenkin, H. C. F. Papers, 1 : 215. — Wilberforce, S. Ess. Quar. 1 : 52.

Specimens in museums, Preservation of, from insects and dampness. (Walter Hough) U. S. Nat. Mus. Rept. '87 : 549.

Spectacles, Protective, for working men. (A. Alt) Am. Pub. Health, 10 : 262.

Spectator, Sketches of occasional contributors to the. Drake, N. Ess. Tatler, 3 : 1.

Spectra, Ocular. Herschel. Famil. lec. 400.

Spectral and dream testimony. Burton, J. H. Crim. tri. 2 : 79.

Spectral illusions. Chambers's Miscel. no. 70.

Spectroscope, The. Buckley, A. B. Thro' magic glass, 50. — Gall & Robertson. Pop. read. sci. 299.

Spectroscopy, Astronomical. Bibliography. Scheiner, J. Astron. spectroscopy. — (W. Huggins) Smithson. Rept. '91 : 69.

Spectrum analysis. (H. E. Roscoe) Manch. Sci. lec. 2 : 19.
— Applied to the heavenly bodies. (W. Huggins) Manch. Sci. lec. 2 : 33.
— Bibliography. Brit. Assoc. Adv. Sci. '84, '89.
— Discoveries in. Estes. Half-hour, v. 1.

Spenser, Edmund, and Sir W. Raleigh. Morley, H. Eng. writ. 9 : 92–373.
— as a philosophic poet. De Vere. Ess. 1 : 48.
— An evening with. Thomson, J. Ess. 177.
— Faerie queene. Maurice. Friendship, 219. — Mitchell, D. G. English lands, 1 : 217.
— — Epitomized. Dobson, W. T. Class. poets, 327.
— — Spirit of. Chambers's Repos. no. 40.
— Heroines of. Dowden. Transcripts, 305.
— poems, Characteristics of. De Vere. Ess. 1 : 1.
— the poet and teacher. Dowden. Transcripts, 269.
— Rosalind. Jameson. Loves of poets.
— Sonnets of. Deshler. Afternoons, 54.
— Spenseriana. Hales. Folia litt. 155
Speratus, Paul. Winkworth. Chr. singers Germ. 123.
Spermaceti candle, Song of. Maginn. Fras. papers, 184.
Sperone, Speron. Symonds. Renais. It. lit. 2 : 130.
Spey, My native salmon river. Forbes, A. Camps, 153.
— Naturalist on the. Wilberforce, S. Ess. Quar. 1 : 1.
Sphinx, The. Buckley, J. M. Trav. three cont. 231. — Kinglake. Eothen, 179.
— Riddle of. DeQuincey. Memo. (Bost.) 2 : 235; or Writings (Masson), v. 6.
Spice islands. Chambers's Miscel. no. 53.
Spicer, James. Ritchie, J. E. City men, 216.
Spiders. Allen, Grant. Science in Arc. 105. — Morgan, C. L. Animal sk. 273.
— Anecdotes of. Chambers's Miscel. no. 100.
— Sagacity of. Goldsmith. Miscel. (N. Y. 4 v.) 1 : 76.
Spielhagen, Friedrich. With portrait. Warner Lib. 23 : 13772. — Zimmern. For. novelists, 1 : 189.
Spies and informers in England, in 1817. Routledge, J. Pop. prog. in Eng. 315.
Spine, curvature of, School life and. (R. T. McKenzie) Nat. Educa. Assoc. '98 : 939.
Spinner, Francis Elias. Bungay. Repr. men, 248. — Derby, J. C. Fifty years, 644.
Spinola, Ambrosio, Marquis de. Cust. Warriors 30 years, 1 : 53.
Spinoza, B. Arnold, M. Ess. in crit. 1 : 237. — Buchanan, J. Mod. atheism, 142. — Erdmann. History of philosophy, 2 : 52. — Froude. Short stud. 1 : 274. — Lewes. Biog. phil. — Maccall. For. biog. 1 : 299. — Manning, J. M. Half-truths, 37. — Pfleiderer. Philos. relig. 31. — Pünjer. Christian philos. religion, 407. — Renan. Studies (N. Y.), 2 : 453. — Caird. Ess. on lit. & p. 2 : 332. — Nasmith. Mak. mod. thought, 2 : 138. — (Sir F. Pollock) Relig. systems, 709. — Green, T. H. Works, 2 : 355. — Hundred greatest men, 232. — Maccall, W. For. biog. 1 : 299. — Renan. Leaders, 47. — With portrait. (J. Royce) Warner Lib. 23 : 13785.
— on the interpretation of Scripture. Arnold, M. Ess. in crit. v. 1.
— System of. Thompson, J. Ess. 303.
— to Kant. Royce, J. Spir. mod. philos. 68.
Spinozism, Religious aspect of. Royce, J. Spir. mod. philos. 27.
Spinster, discontented, Myth of. Higginson. Conc. all, 161.
Spirit and non-spirit, Discrimination of. (Sankara-Acharva) Five years theos. 394.
Spirit of the age. (H. L. Pinckney) Charleston book, 96. — Mabie. Short stud. lit. 63.

Spirit-knockings. Aubrey, J. Miscel.
Spirit-rappers. Brownson. Works, 9 : 1.
— Fair play to the. Willis. Hurry-graphs, 360.
Spirit-rapping. Stephen, J. F. Ess. by barr. 224.
Spirit world, The, and its literature. Hain, J. Varia. 323.
Spiritiana. Silliman. Gallop, 198.
Spiritism, Modern spiritualism and. Wake. Serpent wor. 233.
Spirits, Converse with. Aubrey, J. Miscel.
— Science and. Tyndall. Frag. sci. 402.
Spiritual appeal, Courts of, Joyce on. Church, R. W. Occ. pap. 2 : 21.
Spiritual body, The. Hall, J. A. Glimpses, 191.
Spiritual forces in human progress. (E. E. Hale) Barrows, J. H. Parl. relig. 1 : 523.
Spiritual laws. Emerson. Ess. 1 : 123.
Spiritual life, Succession of. Stanley, A. P. Addr. St. And. 107.
Spiritual sense, Culture of. Mullany. Phases of tho't, 72.
Spiritualism. Appleton, T. G. Chequer-work, 139. — Appleton, T. G. Sheaf of pap. 289. — Bartol. Rad. prob. 195. — Brownson. Works, 9 : 1, 332. — Buchanan, R. Look round, 227. — Edgar, S. Autob. notes, 211. — Hazard, T. R. Miscel. 162. — Conway, M. D. Idols, 34. — Laing, S. Problems, 163. — Romanes. Mind & motion, 47, 119.
— and the philosophy of force. Stock. Attempts, 60.
— Bearings of. Stock. Attempts, 140.
— Bibliography. Evans, H. R. Hours with ghosts.
— Confessions of a medium. Taylor, B. At home, 2 : 432.
— Davey's imitations by conjuring. (R. Hodgson) Soc. Psych. Res. 8 : 253.
— W. A. Hammond on. Fiske, J. Darwin, 119.
— in Germany. Hall, G. S. Asp. Ger. 128.
— in London. Jeaffreson, J. C. Book of recol. 2 : 43.
— in the U. S., 1881. Hatton, J. To-day in Amer. 1 : 162.
— — 1887. Bates. Year in Gt. Rep. 1 : 157.
— investigation, Experimental. (S. J. Davey) Soc. Psych. Res. 4 : 405.
— McDonald on. Whedon. Ess. 1 : 323.
— Mediæval. Lilly. Chapters, 1 : 197.
— Modern. Mansel. Letters, 255.
— — and spiritism. Wake. Serpent wor. 233.
— — Materialism and. Stock. Attempts, 157.
— The pulpit and. Phelps, A. Portfolio, 150.
— Witchcraft and. Oxenham. Short stud. 414.
Spiritualistic phenomena. (F. W. H. Myers; W. F. Barrett; Mrs. H. Sidgwick) Soc. Psych. Res. 2 : 217. 4 : 25, 45.
Spiritualistic seances, Accounts of. (H. C. Lewis) Soc. Psych. Res. 4 : 338.
Spitta, Carl Johann Philipp. Hatfield, E. F. Poets of church, 569. — Miller, Jos. Singers church, 2d ed. 468.
Spitzbergen. Dufferin. Lett. from high lat. 182. — Hartwig. Polar world, 131. — Kingsley, H. Tales of old trav. 142. — Nature's wonders, 110.
Spitzbergen seas. (A. H. Van Der Horck) Am. Geog. Soc. 8 : 214.
Spofford, Ainsworth Rand. Derby, J. C. Fifty years, 648.
Spofford, Harriet Prescott. With portrait. (R. T. Cooke) Our fam. wom. 521. — Richardson. Amer. lit. 2 : 443. — Stoddard, R. H. Poets' homes, 196. — With portrait. Warner Lib. 23 : 13805.

Spohr, Ludwig. Crowest. Tone-poets, 190. — Ferris, G. T. Great violinists, 58. — Keddie. Mus. comp. 322. — Dole, N. H. Score, 305. — With portrait. Ehrlich, A. Cel. violin. 223. — Spark, W. Mus. mem. 47.

— Dramatic works. Hogarth, Mem. opera, 2 : 205.

Spoils system, The. (C. Schurz) Conf. char. & correc. '98 : 247. — Curtis, G. W. Orations, 2 : 171.

Dangers of the. (L. D. Swift) Conf. char. & correc. '96 : 391.

Sponge trade of the Bahamas, 1891. (T. J. McLain) U. S. Cons. Rept. 36 : 411.

Sponges. Deming, C. By-ways, 143. — Simmonds. Comm. products, 155.

— Canadian fresh-water. (A. H. MacKay) Roy. Soc. Canada, v. 7.

— Marine, of British Columbia. (L. M. Lambe) Roy. Soc. Can. 10 : § 4.

— New Brunswick fossil. (J. W. Dawson) Roy. Soc. Canada, v. 7.

Sponsorship. Thompson, H. M. Copy, 84.

Spontaneous generation. Huxley. Lay sermons.

Spontini, Gasparo Luigi Pacifico. Ferris, G. T. Ital. & Fr. compos. 180. — Keddie. Mus. comp. 262.

Spooner, Bathsheba, and others, 1778. Chandler, P. W. Am. crim. trials, 2 : 1.

Spooner, William Brown, with portrait. Bungay. Pen-portr. 244.

Spoopendyke, Mr. & Mrs., *pseud*. *See* Huntley, Stanley.

Sport. Rosebery. Apprec. 307.

— American big-game. Bibliography. Roosevelt, T., and Grinnell, G. B. Amer. big-game hunt.

— Big game. Bibliography. Woolley, C. P. Big-game shooting.

Sporting Magazine, 1793. Maxwell, Sir H. Rainy days, 25.

Sporting spirit, English. Whitney, C. W. Sport. pilgr. 3.

Sports in America, 1881. Hatton, J. To-day in Amer. 1 : 117.

Sportsmen, Affectation of character of. Knox. Essays, 1 : 287.

Spottiswoode, William. Ritchie, J. E. City men, 236.

Spottsylvania, Battle of. Stine, J. H. Army Poto. 613.

Sprague, A. W. Hemenway. Poets of Vt. 398.

Sprague, Charles. Griswold. Poets Amer. 125. — (E. Quincy) Mass. Hist. Soc. Proc. 14 : 39. — Loring, J. S. Hundred Bost. ora. 408. — Putnam, A. P. Singers liberal, 64.

Sprague, Eben Carlton. Am. Bar Assoc. 18 : 529.

Sprague, Horatio J. Buckley, J. M. Trav. three cont. 105.

Sprague, John. Knapp, S. L. Em. lawyers, 335.

Sprague, Peleg. Knapp, S. L. Em. lawyers, 337.

Sprague, William, with portrait. Bartlett, J. R. R. I. officers, 105.

Sprague, William B. Lanman, C. Haphazard, 226.

Sprat, T. (S. Johnson) Chalmers. Eng. poets, 9 : 309.

Spriggs, Captain. Whitehead, C. Highwaymen, 2 : 126.

Spring, Samuel, D. D. Headley, J. T. Chaplains Revol. 89.

Spring. Burroughs, J. Signs & seasons, 179. —

Greenwood, F. W. P. Miscel. 387. — Holmes, O. W. Old vol. 132. — Hunt, L. Seer, 1 : 28 ; *or* Wishing-cap, 74. — Mitchell, D. G. Bound toge. 79. — Whiting, C. G. Saunterer, 11, 16.

Spring as seen from a city window. Woolson. Browsing, 168.

— Associations connected with. Drake, N. Mornings, 1 : 1.

— Footsteps of. Ellwanger. Sto. of nouse, 168.

— Glimpse of. Mabie. My study fire, 127.

Spring in winter, Round a. Abbott, C. C. Outings, 51.

Spring pictures. Curtis, G. W. Other ess. 176.

Spring poems. Burroughs. Birds & poets, 125.

Spring poets, A company of. (E. M. Thomas) Ess. from Critic, 91.

Springs. Burroughs. Pepacton, 43.

— and solitudes. Beecher. Star paper, 314.

— Origin and nature of. Nichols, J. R. Fireside sci. 1.

Springer, Mrs. C. R. Brockett. Woman's work, 639.

Springett, Sir William. Brightwell. Byepaths of biog. 235.

Springfield, Illinois. Warner, C. D. Studies, 234.

Springfield, Mass., Municipal condition of. (G. A. Dennison) Nat. Conf. City Govt. '96 : 128.

— Settlement of. Everett. Orat. v. 2.

Springfield, N. J., Action at. Dawson. Batt. of U. S. 1 : 597.

Springinklee, Hans. (A. Rosenberg) Dohme, R. Early mast. 137.

Sproule, Samuel. Rogers, C. Chr'n heroes, 263.

Spurgeon, Charles Haddon. Bolton, S. K. Fam. leaders, 333. — Great mod. preachers. — With photo. Cooper, T. Men of mark, 4 : 14. — Davidson, J. M. Eng. lib. 217. — Field, H. M. Summer pic. 47. — Hood, E. P. Lamps, pitchers & trumpets, 2 : 185. — Mathews. Men & bks. 81. — (L. C. Moulton) Parton. Princes, 242. — Em. persons, 5 : 203. — Miller, Jos. Singers church, 2d ed. 580. — Smalley. Stud. 55. — Tyler, M. C. Glimpses Eng. 42.

— in Nightingale Lane. Yates, E. H. Celeb. 1 : 79.

— Marriage of. Hardy, E. J. Love aff. 186.

Spurgeon, Mrs. C. H. Bolton, S. K. Soc. stud. in Eng. 106.

Spurr, Thomas Jefferson. (S. S. Green) Harvard mem. biog. 1 : 440.

Spurrier, Aaron, jr. Ivimey. Eng. Bapt. 3 : 529.

Squanto, Pokánoket Indian, Story of. Adams, C. F. Three episodes, 1 : 23.

Squarcialupees, Marcellus. Wallace, R. Anti-Trin. biog. 2 : 339.

Squarcione, Francesco. Symonds. Renais. fine arts, 236.

Square men in round holes, and round in square. Jacox, F. Cues, 151.

Squatter sovereignty ; Sovereign squattereignty. Lyon, N. Last pol. writ. 129.

Squirrels, Intelligence of. (T. W. Mills) Roy. Soc. Canada, v. 5.

Staal, Marguerite Cordier, Baroness. Vinet. Fr. lit. 18th cent. 126.

Stabat Mater, with English and German translations. Schaff. Lit. & poetry, 187, 218.

Stacy, William R. Bungay. Off-hand, 327.

Staël-Holstein, Anne L. G., Madame de. Adams, W. H. D. Fam. beauties, 2 : 109. — Alison. Ess. v. 3. — Bolton, S. K. Girls who became famous, 158. — Brougham. Works, 5 : 132. — Chambers's Repos. no. 71. — Darton. Fam. girls, 150. — Everett, A. H. Ess. 2 : 95.

— Greg. Lit. & soc. judg. 7. — Griswold, H. T. Home-life, 34. — Hale, S. J. Less. from women, 131. — Japp. Vers de soc. 203. — Kavanagh. Fr. women, 275. — Lord, J. Beacon, 5 : 387. — Russell. Extr. women, 184. — Ste.-Beuve. Cel. wom. 151. — Shelley, M. W. Lit. men Fr. v. 2. — Thomson, K. & J. C. Queens of soc. 354. — Vinet. Fr. lit. 18th cent. 126. — Duyckinck. Portrait gall. 1 : 368. — With portrait. Fifty famous women, 146. — Hamilton, C. J. Women writers, 46. — Haussonville. Salon of Necker, 2 : 19. — With portrait. Hubbard, E. Little journeys, 3 : 213. — Pellissier. Lit. move. Fr. 52. — Johnston, R. M. Studies, 130. — Mason, A. G. Wom. of Fr. salons, 250. — With portrait. Warner Lib. 23 : 13823.

Staël-Holstein, Anne L. G., Madame de, and Eng. literature. Texte, J. Rousseau, 355.

— L'Allemagne. Mackintosh, J. Miscel. 260.

— Literature and society. Jeffrey, F. Contrib. Ed. Rev.

— Schiller, Goethe and. Carlyle. Essays.

— Works. Jeffrey, F. Contrib. Ed. Rev.

Stafford, A. Pettigrew. Med. portr. gall. v. 4.

Stafford, Edward. *See* Buckingham, Duke of.

Stafford, E., English physician, 1643, Recipes of. (O. W. Holmes) Mass. Hist. Proc. 5 : 379.

Stafford, John. Campbell. Ld. chan. 1 : 297. — Hook. Abps. Cant. 5 : 130.

Stafford, Philip. Whitehead, C. Highwaymen, 1 : 72.

Stafford, William Howard, viscount. Lodge. Portraits (Bohn), v. 6.

Staffordshire, Eng. Rimmer, A. Country towns, 169.

Stage, Ancient, mediæval, and modern. Coan. Art & lit. 70.

— and religion. Jones, H. A. Renascence, 26.

— as it is. Irving, H. Drama, 1. — Morris, M. Ess. theat. crit. 40.

— as it once was. Kingsley, C. Lit. lec. 3 ; *or* Lec. Amer. 32.

— The Bible on. Jones, H. A. Renascence, 119.

— Censorship on. Archer, W. Theatre, 101.

— Costume on, and stage tricks. Doran. Their maj. serv. 2 : 419.

— English, Distortions of. Story, W. W. Excur. 232.

— — Historical sketch of. Doran. Drury Lane, 1 : 136.

— — immediately prior to Shakespeare. Dunham. Lit. & sci. men, 2 : 1.

— — in Shakespeare's time. Dunham. Lit. & sci men, 2 : 22.

— — in the 17th century. Dunham. Lit. & sci. men, 3 : 70.

— — Origin and early history of. Dunham. Lit. & sci. men, 1 : 173.

— French. Lennox, W. P. Plays, 2 : 151.

— — Some eccentricities of the. Doran. Drury Lane, 1 : 189.

— in the U. S., 1881. Hatton, J. To-day in Amer. 2 : 1.

— Indecency on the English. Zangwill. Without prej. 175.

— Influence of. Winter. Shad. stage. 3 : 338.

— Jewish. Karpeles. Jew. lit. 229.

— Marriages from the. Hunt, L. Men, wom. & books, 287.

— Naturalism on. Zola. Exper. novel. 109.

— of Germany. Baring-Gould. Germany, 243.

— Prologues, epilogues, etc. Doran. Their maj. serv. 2 : 442.

Stage alarums and excursions. Cook, D. Bk. of play, 2 : 69.

Stage banquets. Cook, D. Bk. of play, 2 : 38.

Stage doors. Cook, D. On stage, 1 : 185.

Stage furniture. Adams, W. D. With poet, 10.

Stage illusions. Lamb. Elia.

Stage properties. Cook, D. On stage, 1 : 207.

Stage storms. Cook, D. Bk. of play, 2 : 84.

Stage tradition. Cook, D. On stage, 1 : 229.

Stage wigs. Cook, D. Bk. of play, 2 : 49.

Stagnant lakes, Sanitary improvement of, at Virginia Beach. (J. H. Raymond) Am. Pub. Health, 16 : 57.

Stainer, John, with photo. Cooper, T. Men of mark, 3 : 30.

Stair, John Dalrymple, 1st earl. Georgian era, 2 : 36. — Lancaster, H. H. Ess. & rev. 90.

Stamners, Joseph. Miller, Jos. Singers church, 2d ed. 468.

Stamp, William W. Wesley & successors, 193.

Stamp act. Lossing. Signers, 371.

Stampede pass, Cascade Range, Washington. (V. G. Bogue) Am. Geog. Soc. 27 : 239.

Stamps. Bibliography. Hardy, W. J., & Bacon, E. D. Stamp collector.

Standard (London newspaper). Hatton. Jour. Lond. 141.

Standard weights and measures. Bibliography. U. S. Coast Geod. Surv. 1898.

Standards. Russell, A. P. Lib. notes, 90.

Standing committees, Origin of. (J. F. Jameson) Am. Hist. Assoc. Rept. '93 : 391.

Standish, Miles. Belknap. Amer. biog. 3 : 116. — Lossing. Em. Amer. 13. — Parker, H. F. Morning stars, 275.

— Bibliography. Johnson, H. Exploits Myles Standish.

Standsfield, Philip, trial for treason and murder, 1688. Craik, G. L. Eng. causes cél. 369.

Stanford, Chas. V., with portrait. Willeby, C. Mast. Eng. mus. 281.

Stanford, Leland. Cochrane, R. Benef. lives, 283. — (W. S. Monroe) Nat. Educa. Assoc. '94 : 236. — With portrait. Stoddard, W. O. Men of bus. 295.

— and his university. Bolton, S. K. Givers, 201.

Stanford, Mrs. Mary. Raymond, I. Southland writ. 2 : 616.

Stanhope, Charles, 3d earl. Walker, W., jr. Men of sci. 112.

Stanhope, Hester, Lady. Adams, W. H. D. Cel. wom. trav. 302. — Kinglake. Eothen, 62. — Russell, W. Eccen. 74. — Russell. Extr. women, 222. — Fifty famous women, 287. — Smith, G. B. Women of renown, 421.

Stanhope, James, earl of, with portrait. Caulfield. Kit-cat, 112.

Stanhope, Philip Dormer. *See* Chesterfield, 4th earl of.

Stanhope, Lord P. H. Miscellanies. Tartt. Ess. 2 : 183.

Stanhope, Spencer. Bate, P. H. Eng. Pre-Raph. 111.

Stanhope family. Sanford & Townsend. Gov. fam. 1.

Staniforth, Samson. Jackson, T. Early Meth. 2 : 145.

Stanislas, King, and Voltaire. Wolff. Odd bits, 181.

Stanislaus Augustus, king of Poland, Seizure of. Davenport. Narr. peril. 1 : 220.

Stanislaus Leczinski, king of Poland, Perils of. Davenport. Narr. peril. 1 : 155. — Doran. Monarchs, 1 : 387.

Stanislaus Poniatowski, the last king of Poland. Doran. Monarchs, 1 : 411.

Stanley, Arthur Penrhyn. Arnold, F. Our bishops, 2 : 237. — Brooks, P. Ess. & addr. 341. — Hutton, R. H. Criticisms, 1 : 129. — Comegys. Tour, 39. — With photo. Cooper, T. Men of mark, 4 : 4. — Davis, G. J. Suc. preach. 342. — With portrait. Japp. Good men, 291. — Lowell. Democ. 57 ; or Writ. 6 : 47. — Myers. Ess. mod. 276. — Oxenham. Stud. in eccl. hist. 344. — (F. W. Farrar) Parton. Princes, 1. — Wotton. Word portraits, 296. — Em. persons, 2 : 325. — With portrait. (R. H. Story) Ewart, H. C. Leaders, 63. — Farrar. Men, 93. — Farrar. Soc. & p. day quest. 269. — With portrait. Hare, A. J. C. Biog. sk. 1. — Miles, A. H. Poets of cent. 10 : 721. — Miller, Jos. Singers church, 2d ed. 525.

— on eccles. history. Church, R. W. Occ. pap. 1 : 66.

Stanley, Clinton Warrington. Am. Bar Assoc. 8 : 459.

Stanley, Edward, bishop of Norwich. Croston. Hist. sites Lanc. 79. — With portrait. Japp. Good men, 273.

Stanley, Lord Edward Henry. See Derby, E. H. S., 15th earl Derby.

Stanley, Henry M. Bolton, S. K. How success is won, 74. — With photo. Cooper, T. Men of mark, 4 : 22. — Frost, T. Mod. explorers, 57. — Cochrane, R. Famous trav. 146. — With portrait. Greely, A. W. Explorers, 349. — Sala, Mrs. Fam. peop. 24. — Tuckerman, C. K. Recoll. 2 : 149.

— and Livingstone. Latimer. Eur. in Afr. in 19th cent. 130.

— and the map of Africa. (J. S. Keltie) Smithson. Rept. '90 : 277.

— Critical review of his work. (R. F. Burton) Am. Geog. Soc. 7 : 329.

— Descent of the Congo. Montefiore, A. Leaders, 215.

— in darkest Africa. Latimer. Eur. in Afr. in 19th cent. 153.

— Reception to, 1872. Am. Geog. Soc. 4 : 453.

— Search for Livingstone. Frost, T. Mod. expl. 57.

— Verification of Ptolemy's geography. (C. P. Daly) Am. Geog. Soc. 7 : 290.

— Verification of Speke's discoveries. (J. A. Grant) Am. Geog. Soc. 7 : 311.

— Visit to King M'Tsé's capital. (L. de Bellefonds) Am. Geog. Soc. 7 : 283.

Stanley, Jacob. Wesley & successors, 163.

Stanley, Thomas. Gosse, E. From Shakesp. 174. — (E. Gosse) Ward. Eng. poets, 2 : 286.

Stanley family. Croston. Hist. sites Lanc. 50. — Thomson, K. B. Recollec. v. 2.

— of Knowsley. Sanford & Townsend. Gov. fam. v. 1.

Stannard, Eloise Harriet. Clayton, E. C. Eng. fem. art. 2 : 293.

Stannard, Mrs. H. E. V., with portrait. Black, H. C. Wom. authors, 45.

Stannon, Richard Boyle, Viscount, with portrait. Caulfield. Kit-cat, 131.

Stano, Francis. Wallace, R. Anti-Trin. biog. 3 : 312.

Stano, Samuel. Wallace, R. Anti-Trin. biog. 3 : 359.

Stansfeld, James. Hutton, R. H. Stud. in parl. 127. — Ritchie. Brit. sena. 68.

Stansfield, Philip, parricide. Burke, P. Cel. trials.

Stanton, Edwin M. Black, J. S. Ess. 245. — Piatt, D. Memories, 50. — Reid, W. Ohio in the war, 1027. — Stowe. Men of time, 363. — Tilton, J. Sanctum, 213. — With portrait. Brockett. Men of our day, 199.

Stanton, Elizabeth Cady. Hanaford. Wom. of cent. 348. — (L. C. Bullard) Our fam. wom. 602. — With portrait. (T. Tilton) Parton. Em. wom. 332. — Tilton, T. Sanctum, 250.

Stanton Drew, Tradition of. Timbs. Abbeys, 1 : 541.

Stanyan, Abraham, with portrait. Caulfield. Kit-cat, 207.

Stanyhurst, Richard. Bell, R. Lit. & sci. men, 2 : 105. — Holland, J. Psalmists, 1 : 187.

Staoueli, Battle of. Knox, T. W. Battles, 64.

Staples, Hamilton Barclay. Am. Antiq. Soc. Proc. n. s. 7 : 309.

Staples, Mrs. Mary Ellen (Edwards). Clayton, E. C. Eng. fem. art. 2 : 75.

Stapp, Milton. Woollen. Biog. sk. Indiana, 168.

Star of Bethlehem ; what was it ? Proctor, R. A. Univ. of suns, 186.

Star unto star. Proctor, R. A. Mysteries, 402.

Star-clouds and star-mist. Proctor, R. A. Mysteries, 334.

Star-craft, leechdoms, and wort-cunning of early England. Lucas. Mornings, 1 : 165.

Star-depths, The. Proctor, R. A. Mysteries, 287 ; also in Manch. Sci. lec. 3-4 : 248.

Star-grouping, star-drift, and star-mist. Proctor. Pleas. ways, 136.

Star showers. Proctor. Borderland, 188.

Star surveys. Proctor, R. A. Other suns, 24.

Star Chamber, Stories of the. Timbs. Abbeys, 1 : 201.

Starch industry in Aroostook Co. Me. Bur. Lab. '96 : 83.

Staring. Gray, E. C. Idle musings, 195.

Stark, George, with portrait. Sketches N. H. men, 9.

Stark, Gen. John. With portrait. Duyckinck. Nat. portr. gall. 1 : 166. — Glazier, W. Heroes, 160. — With portrait. Headley, J. T. Washington, 1 : 200. — Lossing. Em. Amer. 248.

Starkey, Captain. Lamb. Elia.

Starkey, Thos. Brink. Eng. lit. 2, pt. 2 : 202.

Starr, Louisa. Clayton, E. C. Eng. fem. art. 2 : 133.

Starr, Mrs. Lucy E. Brockett. Woman's work, 728.

Stars, The. Buckley, A. B. Thro' magic glass. 145.

— Distances of. Lodge, O. J. Pioneers, 305.

— distribution of, Herschel and. Morton, E. J. C. Heroes astron. 269.

— Ever-widening world of. Proctor. Light sci. 2 : 15.

— fixed, Herschel on motion of. Lodge, O. J. Pioneers, 274.

— — with bibliography. Todd, D. P. Stars & tel. 311.

— Geology of. (A. Winchell) Estes. Half-hour, v. 1.

— History of two, appearing in 1866 and 1876. Proctor. Pleas. ways, 106.

— Motions of the. Proctor. Light sci. 2 : 30.

— Numbers and distances of. (A. M. Clerke). Smithson. Rept. '91 : 103.

— Occultation by the moon. (W. F. King) Roy. Soc. Canada, v. 6.

— Photographing. Proctor, R. A. Other suns, 73.

— Shooting. Laing, S. Problems, 33.

— The starlit sky. Dunman. Talks sci. 17. — Proctor, R. A. Leis. read. 1.

Stars, Variable. (C. A. Young) Smithson. Inst. Rept. '93 : 107.

Stasinus. Arnold, E. Poets of Greece, 73.

State, The, and religion. Hovey, A. Stud. in ethics, 346.

— Aristotle's conception of. (A. C. Bradleigh) Abbott, E. Hellenica, 181.

— Being of. Henry, C. S. Satan, 197.

— Greek idea of. Butcher, S. H. Greek genius, 46.

— Has the citizen rights against. Green, T. H. Works, 2 : 448.

— Interference of, with private contracts. Bolles. Chap. pol. econ. 170.

— — in spiritual matters. Froude, R. H. Remains, pt. 2, 1 : 184.

— — with individual duty. Hazard. Ess. on lang. 256.

— — with corporation and church property. Mill, J. S. Dissert. (N. Y.) 1 : 28.

— its functions and duties. (C. S. Darrow and others) Sunset club echoes, 155.

— origin of, Theories on. Henry, C. S. Satan, 206.

— Power of, developed by mental culture. Choate. Add. 106.

— Rights of. Green, T. H. Works, 2 : 466. — Hinsdale, B. A. Schools & stud. 200.

— Herbert Spencer's conception of. Ritchie, D. G. State interf. 53.

— Sphere, powers, and duties of. Greeley. Ess. pol. econ. 120.

— Will the basis of. Green, T. H. Works, 2 : 427.

State-action, Individualism and. Whittaker, T. Ess. & not. 111.

State activities and politics. (W. F. Willoughby) Am. Hist. Assoc. 5 : 113.

State board of health, Plea for a. (B. Lee) Phila. Soc. Sci. Assoc. '78.

State Boards of Control. (C. Snyder) Conf. char. & correc. '95 : 37.

State charities, Organization of. (F. H. Wines) Conf. char. & correc. '97 : 163.

State debts. Bibliography. Scott, W. A. Repudiation State debts.

State interference and individual liberty. Ritchie, D. G. State interf. 83.

State intervention, General aspects of. Fawcett. Ess. & lec. 31.

State laws, Uniform. (L. D. Brewster) Am. Bar Assoc. 21 : 315.

— — Rept. of committee on. Am. Bar Assoc. 14 : 365.

State legislation, Phases of. Roosevelt, T. Amer. ideals, 63.

State organization. Mivart. Ess. 1 : 151.

State papers, Neglect of, in England. Ewald. Stories fr. st. pap. 1 : 1.

State politics. Goddard, W. G. Pol. & mis. wr. 2 : 24.

State rights and state sovereignty. Black, J. S. Ess. 212, 590. — Madison, J. Letters, 3 : 217. 4 : 18, 61, 289, 290.

State school federation, Plan of. U. S. Bur. Ed. Rept. '91–92 : 753.

State sovereignty, National sovereignty against. Blaine. Polit. discus. 260.

— Revived doctrine of. Garfield. Works, 2 : 708.

State university, The. (J. H. Baker) Nat. Educa. Assoc. '97 : 357.

States, decay of; Is it inevitable ? Northcote. Lec. & ess. 1.

— of the U. S. Are they equal under the constitution ? Dunning, W. A. Ess. on civ. war, 304.

States of the U. S., names of, Origin of. (H. B. Stappes) Am. Antiq. Soc. Proc. n. s. 1 : 366.

— — Sovereignty of. Foster, R. Comment. on Const. 1 : 63.

— True greatness of. Bacon. Ess.

Statesman, The. Lecky. Map of life, 136.

Statesmanship. Ballantyne. Ess. 95. — Osgood, S. Amer. leaves, 165.

— British, Prospects of. Greg. Ess. pol. 2 : 364.

— Character in. Potter, H. C. Scholar & state, 33.

— Constitutional and autocratic. Greg, W. R. Pol. prob. 1.

— Physical basis of. Ames, M. C. Outlines, 155.

Statesmen, On. Foster, J. Crit. ess. Eccl. v. 1.

— Philosophers and. Ames, M. C. Outlines, 164.

— who have written verses. Hunt, L. Men, wom. & books, 171.

Statistical Congress, International, 1891. (J. Goldschmidt) U. S. Cons. Rept. 38 : 175.

Statistical inquiry, Development of, in the U. S. N. J. Labor, 1890.

Statistics, Abuse of. Mackay, T. Meth. soc. ref. 213.

— and economic science. Duff, M. E. G. Miscel. 1. — (R. M. Smith) Am. Econ. Assoc. v. 3.

— Educational. (J. M. Greenwood, ed.) Nat. Educa. Assoc. '89 : 431.

— Educational lessons of. (John Eaton, jr.) Nat. Educa. Assoc. '72 : 41.

— in rela. to economics and sociology. Penn. Bur. Indus. Statis. '97.

— Lies of. Sargant. Ess. 2 : 56.

— Origin and progress of. (J. C. G. Kennedy) Am. Geog. Soc. 2, pt. 1 : 92.

— Relation of, to social science. (W. F. Willcox) Conf. char. & correc. '94 : 86.

— Study of. (D. R. Dewey) Am. Econ. Assoc. v. 4. — Walker, F. A. Discus. in educa. 289.

— — in colleges. (C. D. Wright) Am. Econ. Assoc. v. 3.

— Tabulation of, by machinery. (C. F. Pidgin) Conv. Labor Bur. '89 : 70.

— Utility of. Giffen. Essays in finance, 2 : 275, 315.

Statius. (W. C. Lawton) Warner Lib. 24 : 13845.

— and the later Roman epic. Conington. Miscel. 348.

Statorius, Peter, 3d. Wallace, R. Anti-Trin. biog. 3 : 17.

Statues. Tuckerman. Collector, 309; or Criterion, 325.

— in Central park, N. Y., 1889. Curtis, G. W. Other ess. 186.

Statutes, Titles of. (U. M. Rose) Am. Bar Assoc. 5 : 221.

Staunton, Henry de, chief justice of England, 1323–30. Campbell. Ch. just. 1 : 95.

Staupitz, John. Ullman. Reformers, 234.

Stavenhagen, B., with portrait. Buffen, F. F. Mus. celeb. 95.

Stead, William T., with portraits. Lynch, A. Hum. doc's, 138.

Steam. (O. Reynolds) Owens College essays, '74 : 161.

— Utilization of. Neil, S. Epoch men, 273.

Steamboats. Head, F. B. Descr. ess. 1 : 151.

Steam engine and its application to locomotion. Nicoll. Great move. 390.

— Bibliography. Bost. Pub. Lib. Bull. Jan. '94.

— Birth of. Wynter, A. Our soc. bees, 2 : 424.

— The inventor of. Delepierre. Hist. diff. 139.

— The story of. Wynter, A. Peeps, 2 : 65.

Steam engine, Watt's invention of. Smiles. Indus. biog.

Steam-engines, First. Lewes, T. C. Mechanicians, 1.

Steam-hammer, Invention of the. Nasmyth, Ja. Autobiog. 235, 270. — Smiles. Indus. biog.

Steam heat as germicide in maritime sanitation. Am. Pub. Health, 18 : 363.

Steam heating. Rumford, S. 3 : 475.

Steam navigation, Early. Hazard, T. R. Miscel. 272.

Steamship crews, Wages of, 1894. U. S. Cons. Rept. 46 : 289.

Steamship service, Australian subsidy to, 1893. (W. Kapus) U. S. Cons. Rept. 42 : 41.

Steamship subsidies, British. Swank. Notes, 65.

Steamships, Life on. Kelley, J. D. J. Ship's co. 3.
— Sanitation on. (F. Montizambert) Am. Pub. Health, 21 : 309.

Stearns, Asahel. Peabody. Harv. rem. 51.

Stearns, Charles. (C. W. Stearns) N. E. Hist.-Gen. Soc. Biog. 4 : 55.

Stearns, John N., with portrait. Bungay. Penportr. 267.

Stearns, Oliver. Peabody. Harv. rem. 163. — Vaille & Clark. Harv. book, v. 1.

Stearns, Mrs. S. Burger. Brockett. Woman's work, 760. — Moore, F. Women of the war, 382.

Stedman, Edmund C. Bolton, S. K. Amer. au. 232. — Derby, J. C. Fifty years, 530. — Rideing, W. H. Boyhood of liv. authors, 195. — Richardson. Amer. lit. 1 : 444. 2 : 256. — Stoddard, R. H. Poet's homes, 253. — Vedder, H. C. Amer. writers, 3. — With portrait. Warner Lib. 24 : 13857.
— at home. (A. B. Dodd) Gilder. Authors, 273.
— Sonnets of. Deshler. Afternoons, 301.
— Victorian poets. Taylor, B. Crit. ess. 284.

Steedman, Gen. James B. Reid, W. Ohio in the war, 784. — Shanks. Rec. of generals, 276.

Steel, cast, Invention of. Smiles. Indus. biog.
— Manufacture of, in Pennsylvania. Penna. Labor, 1884.

Steele, Anne. Griswold, R. W. Sac. poets. — Hatfield, E. F. Poets of church, 570. — Holland, J. Psalmists, 2 : 223. — Miller, Jos. Singers church, 2d ed. 213.

Steele, Elizabeth. Eliot. Women of revol. 1 : 297.

Steele, Sir Richard. Portrait. Caulfield. Kit-cat, 158. — Collier, W. F. Hist. Eng. lit. 269. — Dennis, J. Studies, 148. — Drake, N. Ess. Tatler, 1 : 41. — Forster, J. Hist. ess. 2 : 105. — Thackeray. Humorists. — Timbs. Anec. biog. wits, v. 1. — Wotton. Word portraits, 299. — Murray, J. O'K. Prose & poet. Irel. 89. — Russell, W. C. Book of au. 147. — With portrait. Warner Lib. 24 : 13875. — Wrangham. Brit. Plutarch, v. 5.
— and Addison. Jones, W. A. Lit. stud. 1 : 1. — Thomson, Mrs. Cel. friend. 1 : 227.
— as an essayist. Drake, N. Ess. Tatler, 1 : 185. — Purnell. Liter. 192.
— Bibliography. Aitken. Life of S. 2 : 387.
— Censor. Tuckerman. Charac. 38.
— Latest life of. Dobson, A. Miscel. 57.
— The Tatler. Adams, W. D. Famous books, 274.

Steele, Tom. Burke, B. Rise of gr. fam. 277.

Steen, Jan. Gower. Fig. painters Holl. 49. — Wedmore. Masters of genre, 106. — Van Dyke, J. C. Dutch mast. 101.

Steere, Edward. Cust. Ling. & orient. ess. 4 : 560.

Steere, William H. P. Bartlett, J. R. R. I. officers, 199.

Steevens, George. Jesse, J. H. Cel. Eton. v. 2.
— Puck the commentator. Disraeli, I. Curios. (N. Y. 4 v.) 4 : 197.

Steffanoni. Willis. Hurry-graphs, 218.

Steffens, H. Baur. Relig. life Germ. 1 : 316.

Stegmann, Christopher. Wallace, R. Anti-Trin. biog. 3 : 64, 257.

Stegmann, Joachim. Wallace, R. Anti-Trin. biog. 3 : 58, 281.

Stegmann, Laurence. Wallace, R. Anti-Trin. biog. 3 : 65.

Stegmann, Peter. Wallace, R. Anti-Trin. biog. 3 : 66.

Stein, Heinrich Friedrich Karl, Baron von. Bartley, G. C. D. Rhine, 251. — Baur. Relig. life Germ. 1 : 147.

Steiner, L. Feuerbach. Crim. trials.

Steinmetz, Karl Friedrich von. Strauss, G. L. M. Men of Ger. 2 : 151.

Stella. See Johnson, Esther.

Stella, Sidney's. Jameson. Loves of poets.
— Swift's. Jameson. Loves of poets.

Stendal, M. de, pseud. See Beyle, H.

Stennett, Edward. Ivimey. Eng. Bapt. 2 : 70.

Stennett, Joseph. Hatfield, E. F. Poets of church, 573. — Ivimey. Eng. Bapt. 2 : 446. 3 : 70, 221, 242, 271, 580. — Miller, Jos. Singers church, 2d ed. 117.

Stennett, Joseph, jr. Ivimey. Eng. Bapt. 2 : 481.

Stennett, Samuel. Hatfield, E. F. Poets of church, 577. — Ivimey. Eng. Bapt. 4 : 351. — Miller, Jos. Singers church, 2d ed. 249.

Stenography and typewriting in business education. (I. S. Dement) Cong. Educa. Chic. '93, 798.

Stephen, St. Baldwin, G. C. Rep. men, 211. — Blakey, R. Prim. fathers, 27. — Cave. Lives of Fathers, 1 : 47.

Stephen the Sabaite. Miller, Jos. Singers church, 2d ed. 17.

Stephen I. of Hungary. Wyatt, W. J. Hunga. celeb. 52.

Stephen, Sir J. F., with photo. Cooper, T. Men of mark, 6 : 14. — Escott, T. H. S. Pillars emp. 293. — Hazlitt. Parl. portr. 192. — Laurence, P. M. Collect. 71.
— Liberty, equality, fraternity. Hutton, R. H. Criticisms, 2 : 110–164.

Stephen, James Kenneth. Miles, A. H. Poets of cent. 9 : 599.

Stephen, Leslie. Hours in a library. Birrell. Men, women & books, 190.

Stephen, Holdfast, Passage in the ministry of. Skelton, J. Ess. in romance, 277.

Stephens, Alexander H. Savage. Liv. rep. men, 451. — Bartlett. Pres. candidates, 179. — Bolton, S. K. How success is won, 152. — With portrait. Carroll, H. Twelve Amer. 429. — Davidson, J. W. Writ. of South, 540. — Derby, J. C. Fifty years, 500. — Lanman, C. Haphazard, 342. — Johnston, A. Amer. ora. 4 : 39. — (J. F. McLaughlin) Rogers, A. C. Repres. men, 509. — Trent. South. statesm. 197.

Stephens, Andrew. Redding. Misers, 1 : 267.

Stephens, Ann Sophia. With portrait. Hart, J. S. Fem. prose, 204. — (Winterbotham) Everest. Poets of Conn. 383.

Stephens, Catharine. See Capell, C.

Stephens, Frederick G. Bate, P. H. Eng. Pre-Raph. 53.

Stuart, Simmeren. Townsend. Descend. Stuarts, 96.

Stuart, Villiers. Grant, J. Recoll. Lords & Comm. **2**: 261.

Stuart, William D. Walker, C. D. Biog. Va. Mil. Inst. 502.

Stuart books, The. Reed, W. B. Among books, 155.

Stuart family. Burke, B. Viciss. of fam. **1**: 83.

Stuarts, The, of England. Brewer. Eng. stud. 162.

— Characters of. Townsend. Descend. Stuarts, 325.

— England under. Phelps, A. L. Rev. & ess. 50.

— Genealogies of. Townsend. Descend. Stuarts, 304.

Stubbs, William. (E. S. Nadal) Warner Lib. 24 : 14139.

Stucco and Gesso. (G T. Robinson) Morris, W. Arts & crafts, 172.

Stuckey, Nathaniel. Wallace, R. Anti-Trin. biog. **3** : 326.

Student, The, and his vocation. Buchanan. David Gray, 177.

— in American life. Crooker, J. H. Problems, 11.

Students, Pecuniary aid for, in universities and colleges. U. S. Bur. Ed. Rept. '92–93 : 1573.

Studies. Bacon. Ess.

— Concentration of, to develop character. (C. DeGarmo) Nat. Educa. Assoc. '96 : 309.

— Conflict of. Wright, C. Philos. dis. 267.

— Constant, in higher education. (J. M. Green) Nat. Educa. Assoc. '98 : 702.

— Coördination of. (C. DeGarmo) Nat. Educa. Assoc. '95 : 87.

— Correlation of. DeGarmo. Herbart, 215, 240. — (W. T. Harris ; J. M. Greenwood) Nat. Educa. Assoc. '95 : 287. — (E. E. White ; G. H. Howison) U. S. Bur. Ed. Rept. '96–97, **1** : 929.

— — advisable. (C. B. Gilbert) Nat. Educa. Assoc. '96 : 299.

— — in normal schools. (N. C. Schaeffer) Nat. Educa. Assoc. '95 : 709.

— in academies, Relative value of. (C. S. Halsey) N. Y. Regents, 81 : 675.

— Organic relations of, in human development. (W. N. Hailman) Nat. Educa. Assoc. '96 : 325.

— Specialization of. Hinsdale, B. A. Schools & stud. 68.

Study a corrective of morbid notions. (C. H. Dall) Brackett, A. C. Educa. of girls, 166, 228.

— Art of. Bain, A. Prac. ess. 203.

— Course of, from primary school to university. (W. T. Harris) Nat. Educa. Assoc. '76 : 58.

— courses of, Basis of. (J. H. Hoose) N. Y. Regents, 91 : 463.

— — Overcrowded. (G. A. Bacon) N. Y. Regents, 101, app. : 107.

— general divisions of, Classification of. (H. C. Kirk) N. Y. Regents, 85 : 522.

— Isolation and unification as bases of. (E. E. White) Nat. Educa. Assoc. '96 : 316.

— A plea for. Bethune. Orations, 345.

— Practical course of. (E. A. Singer) Nat. Educa. Assoc. '80 : 108.

Study, The ; The ideal haven. Ellwanger. Sto. of house, 54.

Stukeley, Thos. Simpson. School of Shakespeare, v. 1.

Stump-orator. Carlyle. Latter-day.

Stupidity, Instances of. Butler, E. For furth. consid. 71.

Sturge, Joseph. Blaikie, W. G. Leaders, 141. — Famous boys, 283. — Grant, Jas. Port.

pub. char. **2** : 84. — Stanton, H. B. Reforms, 217.

Sturgeon-hunting. Whiting, C. G. Saunterer, 171.

Sturgis, William. (C. G. Loring) Mass. Hist. Proc. **7** : 420.

Sturgis, Mrs. Moore, F. Women of the war, 478.

Sturm, Joseph. Quick. Educa. ref. 27.

Sturmi, St., of Fulda. Maclear. Apostles, 132.

Stutfall Castle. Timbs. Abbeys, **1** : 292.

Stuttering, Prevention and cure of. (E. M. Hartwell) Nat. Educa. Assoc. '93 : 739.

Stuttgart. Howard, B. W. One year, 44.

Stuyvesant, Peter. Lossing. Em. Amer. 22.

Style. Calvert. Ess. æsth. 94. — DeQuincey. Hist. ess. (Bost.) **2** : 61.

— and diction. Bulwer, E. Caxtoniana.

— bespeaks the man. Jacox. Lit. life, 417.

— Clearness of. Hare. Guesses, **2** : 228.

— English prose, Progress of. Drake, N. Ess. Tatler, **2** : 1.

— Familiar. Hazlitt. Table talk.

— The genteel, in writing. Lamb. Elia.

— in art. Hamerton. Portfo. pap. 249.

— — Hints on the formation of. Poynter. Ten lec. 115.

— in fiction. (W. E. Norris) Art of writ. fiction, 1.

— Literary. Coleridge. Lit. rem. **1** : 230. — Forsyth, W. Essays, 162. — Pater. Apprec. v. 1. — Symonds. Ess. **1** : 256. **2** : 1. — Hill, G. B. Writers & readers, 125.

— — good, Value and characteristics of. Mathews. Lit. style, 5.

— — Mystery of. Watson, W. Excur. in crit. 104.

— Philosophy of. Spencer, H. Ess. (N. Y.) 9.

— Poetic. Gummere. Handbook of poetics.

— — Modern. Shairp. Aspects poetry.

— Simplicity in. Hare. Guesses, **1** : 290.

— Spell of. Mabie. My study fire, **2** : 91.

Suarez. Osborn. From Greeks, 83.

Sub-conscious reasoning. (W. R. Newbold) Soc. Psych. Res. **12** : 11.

Subiaco, Visit to, from Rome. Lowell. Writ. **1** : 152.

Subjective of it, The. Stillman, W. J. Old Rome.

Sublime, The. Bain. On teaching English, 145. — Begg. Development of taste, 273. — Harris. Theory of the arts, **1** : 267. — Knight. Principles of taste.

— and beautiful in nature, Relig. teaching of. (H. C. Rawlinson) Liv. Papers, v. 4.

Sublime Porte. Tuckerman, C. K. Recollec. **2** : 107.

Subliminal messages, Apparent sources of. Soc. Psych. Res. **11** : 114.

Subraon, Battle of. Adams, W. H. D. Engl. at war, **2** : 108.

Subscription, Clerical. Wilberforce, S. Ess. Quar. **2** : 1.

— to creeds. Stanley. Essays, v. 4. — Knight, W. Stud. 318.

Subsidies and the tariff. (E. S. Taylor ; F. H. Scott) Sunset club echoes, 77.

Submersion of ancient cities, Traditions of. Thirlwall, C. Remains, **3** : 189.

Subterranean chambers in Cornwall, Eng. Timbs. Abbeys, **1** : 506.

Sub-treasury system, 1839. Hilliard, H. W. Sp. 9. — Winthrop, R. C. Addresses, **1** : 227.

Subjunctive in Latin. Hadley, J. Ess. 215.

Suburb, Growth of a. Arnold, F. Arm-chair, 101.

Success. Bancroft, H. H. Essays, 165; *or* Works, **38** : 165. — Boyd. Recreat. **2** : 19. — Dodge, M. A. Gala, 391. — Emerson. Society, 267. — Gladden, W. Plain thoughts, 121. — Kaye. Essays of optimist, 77. — Mowry, W. A. Talks, 57. — Friswell. Gentle life, **1** : 77, 144. — Lecky. Map of life, 316.
— Business. (A. Carnegie) Cochrane, R. Benef. lives, 114.
— Conditions of. Bosanquet. Ess. 271.
— Elements of. Anderson, M. B. Papers, **1** : 145.
— in life. Henry, C. S. About men, 1.
— — Qualifications for. Hazlitt. Plain speaker, v. **2.**
— Key to. Kinsley. Views, 231.
Succession, Law of. Maine, H. Life & sp. 192.
Suchet, Louis Gabriel. Headley. Napoleon, **2** : 218. — Redding. Pers. remin. **2** : 167.
Suckling, Sir J. Chalmers. Eng. poets, **6** : 485. — Hazlitt. Comic. — (E. W. Gosse) Ward. Eng. poets, **2** : 170. — Wotton. Word portraits, 304. — Hunt, L. Men, wom. & books, 194. — Jesse. Court of Eng. Stuarts, **2** : 215. With portrait. Warner Lib. **24** : 14155.
Sudbury, Simon, 1375–81. Hook. Abps. **4** : 244.
Sudbury, Mass. Drake, S. A. Hist. fields Mid. 410.
Sudermann, Hermann, with portrait. Warner Lib. **24** : 14163.
Sue, Eugene. Miller, H. Hist. ess. 482. — With portrait. Warner Lib. **24** : 14181.
— and Emile Zola. Foster. Fr. & Span. genius, 245.
Suetonius, with portrait. Warner Lib. **24** : 14202.
Suez to Gaza. Kinglake. Eothen, 188.
Suez canal. Adams, W. H. D. Land of the Nile, 323. — Coffin, C. C. Our new way, 47. — Loring, W. W. Confed. soldier, 241. — Buckley, J. M. Trav. three cont. 334.
— in international law. Lawrence. Ess. int. law, 41.
— Traffic of, 1893–95. U. S. Cons. Rept. **51** : 543.
Suffering. Parsons, T. Mystery, 98.
— Philosophy of. Fairbanks, O. B. Aguecheek, 247.
— Privilege of. Manning, J. M. Sermons, 369.
Sufferings of the world. Schopenhauer. Stud. pess. 11.
Suffield, Lord. Grant, J. Recoll. Lords, 74.
Suffixes, False division of. Key, T. H. Philol. ess. 225.
Suffolk, Charles Brandon, duke of. Burke, S.H. Hist. portr. Tudor, 222. — Burke, S. H. Men of reforma. **2** : 154. — Lodge. Portraits (Bohn), v. **1**.
— Marriage to Mary, queen of France. Ewald. Stories fr. st. pap. **1** : 96.
Suffolk, Henrietta, countess of. Willing. Dames, 17.
Suffolk, Henry Gray, duke of. Lodge. Portraits (Bohn), v. **1**.
Suffolk, Susanna, countess of. Burder. Pious wom. 75.
Suffolk, Thomas Howard, earl of. Barrow, J. Nav. worthies, 419. — Bourne, H. R. F. Eng. seam. **2** : 268. — Lodge. Portraits (Bohn), v. **3**.
Suffolk family vicissitudes. Burke, B. Viciss. of fam. **3** : 427.
Suffolk, Mass., County of, Early recorders. (J. T. Hassam) Mass. Hist. Soc. Proc. 2d ser. **12** : 203.
Suffrage. Linton, W. J. Eng. repub. 68.
— and safety. Garfield. Works, **1** : 85.
— Constitutional right of. Foster, R. Comment. on Const. **1** : 319.

Suffrage, Exercise of. Hart. Am. govt. 20.
— Household. Fawcett. Sp. pol. ques. 172.
— in Rhode Island. Goddard, W. G. Pol. & mis. wr. **2** : 51.
— Manhood. Eliot, C. W. Five Am. cont. 21.
— parliamentary, Right of. Mackintosh, J. Miscel. 472.
— Right of. Curtis, G. W. Orations, **1** : 179. — Greene, W. B. Soc. frag. 19.
— universal, Necessity of. Davis, H. W. Spee. 585.
— Women's. *See* Women, Suffrage for.
Suffren Saint-Tropès, P. A. de. Laughton. Stud. nav. hist. 94.
Sufiism. (E. G. Browne) Relig. systems, 314.
Sugar. Hazard, S. Cuba, 337. — Johnston, J. F. Chem. comm. life, **1** : 197.
— Beet-root. Scoffern. Stray leaves, 259. — U. S. Cons. Rept. no. 113 ; also, Spec. rept. **2** : 392.
— Chemistry of. Nichols, J. R. Fireside sci. 90.
— Culture of. Hooker. Botanical miscel. **1** : 95.
— from sorghum. N. J. Labor, '81 : 279. '82 : 210. '83 : 321. '84 : 361. '85 : 327.
— History of. Galt, J. Lit. life, **2** : 209.
— Production of, and its protection. Greeley. Ess. pol. econ. 186.
— Tariff on. Garfield. Works, **2** : 637.
Sugar-beet, German, Legislation on, 1891. (A. H. Washburn) U. S. Cons. Rept. **35** : 253.
Sugar industry of Santiago de Cuba, 1891. (O. E. Reimer) U. S. Cons. Rept. **37** : 8.
Sugar production in Egypt, 1894. (F. C. Penfield) U. S. Cons. Rept. **46** : 38.
Sugar refining in Pennsylvania. Penn. Bur. Indus. Statis. '90.
Sugden, Sir Edward. Grant, J. Bench & bar, **2** : 28. — Grant, J. Recoll. Lords & Comm. **2** : 78. — Em. persons, **1** : 279.
Suggestion without hypnotism. (C. M. Barrows) Soc. Psych. Res. **12** : 21.
Suicide. DeQuincey. Note-book (Bost.), 260 ; *or* Works (Masson), **8** : 398. — Hume. Philos. works, **4** : 535. — Leopardi. Ess. 182. — (H. H. Henson) Oxf. Ho. papers, **3** : 64. — Schopenhauer. Stud. pess. 43. — Schopenhauer. Selec. ess. 257.
— Cooper's Purgatory of suicides. Longford. Prison books, 334.
— Ethics of. Oxenham. Short stud. 170.
— Fear of death and. Dana, A. H. Eth. inq. 166.
— Frequency of. Chatard. Occ. ess. 182.
— Impulses to. Wynter. Borderl. of insan. 240.
— in England. Wynter. Curios. of toil, **2** : 245.
— in New York city. (J. T. Nagle) Am. Pub. Health, **7** : 247.
— Man's property in himself. Rands. Henry Holbeach, **2** : 275.
— Prevalence of. (J. N. Radcliffe) Trans. Soc. Sci. Lond. '63 : 461.
Suicides, Burial of ; Eccles. law and Ophelia. (R. S. Guernsey) N. Y. Shakes. Soc. pap. v. **1**.
Suitors. Bacon. Ess.
Suleiman Pasha. Houghton, Lord. Monog. 1.
Suliotes. DeQuincey. Logic of p. e. (Bost.) 256 ; *or* Works (Masson), v. **7**.
Sulla, Lucius Cornelius. Dunlop, J. Rom. liter. **2** : 125. — (J. A. Froude) Ferris, G. T. Gt. leaders, 37. — Freeman. Hist. ess. **2** : 271. — Herbert, H. W. Capt. Rom. — Ihne. Hist. Rome, v. **5**.
Sullivan, Algernon Sydney. Am. Bar Assoc. **11** : 339.
Sullivan, Sir Arthur. Engel. Handel to Hallé, 95. — With portraits. Willeby, C. Mast. Eng. mus. 1.

Sullivan, Sir Arthur. Bibliography. Lawrence, A. Sir Arthur Sullivan.

Sullivan, George. Loring, J. S. Hundred Bost. ora. 381.

Sullivan, James. Knapp, S. L. Em. lawyers, 291.

Sullivan, Jeremiah. Woollen. Biog. sk. Indiana, 366.

Sullivan, Gen. John. With portrait. Headley, J. T. Washington, 2 : 180. — (T. C. Amory) Mass. Hist. Proc. 0 : 380, — Lossing. Em. Amer. 347.

Sullivan, Richard. (T. C. Amory) N. E. Hist.-Gen. Soc. Biog. 4 : 384.

Sullivan, William. Loring, J. S. Hundred Bost. ora. 313. — (T. C. Amory) Mass. Hist. Proc. 2 : 150.

Sullivant, William Starling. Youmans. Pioneers sci. 394.

Sulloway, Alvah W., with portrait. Sketches N. H. men, 119.

Sully, Maximilien de Bethune, Duc de. Crowe, E. E. For. statesm. 1 : 211.

Sully, T. Tuckerman. Artists, 158 ; or Artist-life, 99.

Sully-Prudhomme. See Prudhomme.

Sulphur, phosphorus and, Combinations of. Davy. Works, 5 : 358.

Sulphur dioxide as a disinfectant. (G. M. Sternberg) Am. Pub. Health, 11 : 238.

Sulphur war in Sicily, 1840. Ingram. Hearts of oak, 20.

Sulpicius Rufus, Publius. Dunlop, J. Rom. liter. 2 : 198.

Sultans of Ghazni. Adams, W. H. D. Warriors of crescent, 3.

— Three. Tuckerman, C. K. Recollec. 2 : 236.

Sumatra. Adams, W. H. D. Eastern archipelago, 24. — Bickmore, A. S. East. I. archipel. 384. — Bock, C. Head-hunters, 257. — Forbes, H. O. Naturalist's wand. 125. — Thomson, J. Straits of Malacca, 1. — Wallace, A. R. Malay archipel. 132.

Sumelas, Monastery of. Palgrave. Ess. east. 225 ; or Ulysses, 24.

Summer. Ho'm s, O. W. Old vol. 150. — Mitchell, D. G. bound toge. 98. — Whiting, C. G. Saunterer, 49.

— gone. Dodge, M. A. Country, 317.

— in England. Jefferies, R. Toilers, 289.

— The passing of. Whiting, C. G. Saunterer, 136.

— Torrid. Lang. Leaders, 173.

Summer business of the Maine woods. Me. Bur. Lab. 97 : 124.

Summer days. Boyd. Recreat. 2 : 127.

Summer homes and sanitaria near large cities. (C. L. Brace) Conf. char. & correc. '84 : 150.

Summer reading. Jones, W. A. Ess. on authors, 120.

Summer resort, Evolution of the. Godkin. Reflections, 295.

Summer resorts. Bibliography. Salem (Mass.) Pub. Lib. Bull. June, '94.

— for debilitated city children. (J. Walker) Am. Pub. Health, 3 : 188.

— in Maine. Me. Bur. Lab. '93 : 1.

Summer rest. Godkin. Reflections, 309.

Summer schools and their relation to higher education. (J. F. Mullany) N. Y. Regents' Rept. 107 : 484.

— and university extension. (H. B. Adams) Butler, N. M. Educa. in U. S. 821.

— Bibliography. U. S. Comm. Educa. Rept. 1894-95, 2 : 1486.

Summer schools in foreign countries. (H. B. Adams) U. S. Bur. Ed. Rept. '97-98, 1 : 83.

— in the U. S., History of. (W. W. Willoughby) U. S. Bur. Ed. Rept. '91-92 : 893.

— Training of teachers in. (E. E. White) Nat. Educa. Assoc. '94 : 100.

Summer travel in America. Wallace, H. B. Art, 343.

Summer's day, A. Wilson, A. Leisure, 346.

Summers, Charles, sculptor. Parton. Capt. indus. 300.

Summers, Thomas O. Davidson, J. W. Writ of South, 545.

Summerfield, J. Collins, Stephen. Miscel.

Summerfield, John. Waterbury. Eloq. preach. 23.

Sumner, Bradford. Loring, J. S. Hundred Bost. ora. 449.

Sumner, Charles, with portrait. Brockett. .Men of our day, 375. — Bungay. Off-hand, 273. — Clarke, J. F. Memo. sketches, 93. — Forney. Anec. 2 : 173, 253. — Headley, P. C. Mass. in rebel. 29. — Loring, J. S. Hundred Bost. ora. 617. — Parton. Capt. indus. 300. — Stowe. Men of time, 214. — Whipple. Recol. 204. — With portrait. Brooks, N. Statesmen, 223. — Curtis, G. W. Orations, 3 : 199. — Higginson, T. W. Contemp. 280. — Johnston, A. Amer. ora. 2 : 268. 3 : 88. — Nichol. Amer. lit. 141. — Richardson. Amer. lit. 1 : 251. — With portrait. Warner Lib. 24 : 14221.

— and the State Dept. Whittier. Prose, v. 3.

— Assault upon, May 22, 1856. Emerson. Miscel. 231. — Sumner. Works, 4 : 257. — Gammel. Writ. 364. — Putnam, J. O. Addresses, 331.

— Censure of. Whittier. Prose, v. 3.

— Fame and glory. Whittier. Lit. recre. 98.

— Home of. Ames, M. C. Outlines, 43.

Sumner, Charles Pinckney. Loring, J. S. Hundred Bost. ora. 325.

Sumner, Charles Richard, bp. of Winchester. Arnold, F. Our bishops, 1 : 154.

Sumner, Edwin Vose. Duyckinck. Nat. portr. gall. 2 : 308.

Sumner, George. (R. C. Waterston) Mass. Hist. Proc. 18 : 189.

Sumner, Increase. Knapp, S. L. Em. lawyers, 79.

Sumner, John Bird, abp. of Canterbury. Arnold, F. Our bishops, 1 : 142. — Fowler, M. Some abps. Cant. 154. — Jesse, J. H. Cel. Eton. v. 1.

Sumner, Samuel Barrett. Putnam, A. P. Singers liberal. 130.

Sumner, William H. (A. H. Quint) Mass. Hist. Proc. 18 : 282. — (O. B. Stebbins) N. E. Hist.-Gen. Soc. Biog. 4 : 329.

Sumroo, Begum. Brightwell. Byepaths of biog. 126.

Sumter, Thomas, with portrait. [Amer.] Nat. portr. gall. v. 4. — Lossing. Em. Amer. 236. — Perry, B. F. Biog sketches, 1 : 570.

Sumter, Fort, First attack on. Keyes, E. D. Fifty years, 367.

Sumptuary laws. Mathews. Conversers, 107.

Sun, The. Herschel. Famil. lec. 47. — (H. E. Roscoe) Manch. Sci. lec. 10 : 25. — (J. N. Lockyer) Manch. Sci. lec. 2 : 157. — Meynell, A. Rhythm, 17.

— and the earth. (B. Stewart) Estes. Half-hour recre. 73 ; also in Manch. Sci. lec. 3-4 : 177.

— and the weather. Proctor. Sci. byways, 169.

— as a perpetual machine. Proctor, R. A. Mysteries, 80.

— Atmosphere of. Proctor. Light sci. 2 : 70.

Table-turning. Faraday. Researches in chem. 382.
— Theory of. Zangwill. Without prej. 153.
Tabley, Lord de. *See* De Tabley.
Tabor, Mt. Buckley, J. M. Trav. three cont. 449.
Taborites, The, *or* Hussites. MacCrie, T. Miscel. writ.
Tacitus, C. C. Hundred greatest men, 278. — Vincent, G. E. Ital. authors, 62. — With portrait. (C. E. Bennett) Warner Lib. **24** : 14369.
— A translation of. Cracroft. Ess. **2** : 112.
Tact. Friswell. Better self, 157. — Lubbock. Use of life, 23.
Tadda, Cecco del. Perkins, C. C. Tusc. sculp. **1** : 235.
Tadema, Lawrence Alma. *See* Alma-Tadema.
Taft, Alphonso. Am. Antiq. Soc. Proc. n. s. **7** : 303.
Taggart, Cynthia. Griswold. Fem. poets, 133.
Tagliacozzi, Gasparo. Brightwell. Byepaths of biog. 75.
Taglioni. Willis. Pencillings.
Tahiti. Kelley, J. D. J. Ship's co. 113.
— in 1892–93. (J. L. Doty) U. S. Cons. Rept. **40** : 634. **44** : 265.
Tahitian literature. (J. LaFarge) Warner Lib. **24** : 14389.
Tahoe, Lake. Jackson, H. H. Bits trav. home, 148.
Tailoresses, Dressmakers and. (F. Hicks) Galton, F. W. Workers, 13.
Tailors. Saunders. Pastime, 106.
— distinguished in other pursuits. Doran. Habits, 219.
— measured by the poets, The. Doran. Habits, 231.
— Patron saint of. Doran. Habits, 221.
Tails, Men with. Baring-Gould. Myths, 145. — Ferrier. Ill. of Sterne, **2** : 82.
Taine, Hippolyte A. Pellissier. Lit. move. Fr. 387. — Ém. persons, 611. — Ste.-Beuve. Engl. portr. 239. — With portrait. (F. Brunetière) Warner Lib. **24** : 14399.
— History of English literature. Ste.-Beuve. Sel. ess. 210.
— On intelligence. Mill, J. S. Dissert. (N. Y.) **5** : 122.
Taiping rebellion, "Chinese" Gordon and. Chesney. Ess. mil. biog. 350.
Tait, Archibald Campbell, abp. of Canterbury. Arnold, F. Our bishops, **1** : 281. — With photo. Cooper, T. Men of mark, **1** : 35. — Oxenham. Stud. in eccl. hist. 385. — Em. persons, **3** : 65. — Smith, G. B. Chr. workers, 5. — Ewart, H. C. Leaders, 123. — With portrait. Fowler, M. Some abps. Cant. 187.
Tait, Catherine. Charles, E. R. Women of Christendom, 258. — Japp. Wise words, 311.
Tait, Peter G. Barrie. Edinburgh eleven, 45.
Taj Mahal. Field, H. M. Egypt to Japan, 157. — Prime, E. D. G. Around world, 299. — Pidgeon. Engineer's holiday, 400.
Take, Emma. Miller, Jos. Singers church, 2d ed. 573.
Taking leave, On. Friswell. Gentle life, **2** : 292.
Taking ourselves seriously. Higginson. New world, 35.
Talavera, Battle of. Adams, W. H. D. Engl. at war, **1** : 282.
Talbot, Catherine. Burder. Pious wom. 497. — Elwood. Lit. ladies, **1** : 127.
— and Mrs. Elizabeth Carter. Thomson, Mrs. Cel. friend. **2** : 145.

Talbot, Charles, Baron. Campbell. Ld. chan. **6** : 126.
Talbot, Mary A. Dowie, M. M. Wom. adv. 137.
Talbot, Silas. Lossing. Em. Amer. 211.
Talbot, Mrs. William. Burder. Pious wom. 406.
Talbot de Malahide, James, Baron. (Photo.) Cooper, T. Men of mark, **1** : 12.
Talbot family. Sanford & Townsend. Gov. fam. v. 1.
Talcott papers, Remarks on. (M. Chamberlain) Mass. Hist. Soc. Proc. 2d ser. **8** : 123.
Talent and genius. Siegvolk. Papers, 108.
Talfourd, Thomas Noon. DeQuincey. Writings (Masson), **3** : 126. — Foss. Judges, **9** : 270. — Horne. New spirit of the age, **1** : 245. — Redding. Pers. remin. **2** : 129. — Whipple. Ess. & rev. **1** : 181. — Grant, Jas. Bench & bar, **2** : 108. — Miles, A. H. Poets of cent. **3** : 107. — Lennox, W. P. Plays, **2** : 106. — Stanton, H. B. Reforms, 387.
— as a dramatist. Tuckerman. Charac. 144.
— Sonnets of. Deshler. Afternoons, 251.
Taliesin. Parry. Camb. Plutarch, 41.
Talismans. Jones, W. Credulities, 186.
Talk. *See* Conversation.
— and talkers. Stevenson, R. H. Mem. 144.
Talk, Everyday. Matthews, A. Ruminations.
Talkative folk. Henry, C. S. About men, 68.
Tall girls. Warner, C. D. As we go, 148.
Talladega, Battle of. Dawson. Batt. of U. S. **2** : 303.
Tallemant des Réaux. Historiettes. Maxwell, Sir H. Rainy days, 81.
Talley, Susan Archer (Mrs. Von Weiss). Davidson, J. W. Writ. of South, 547. — Griswold. Fem. poets, 311. — Freeman, J. D. Wom. of South, 309.
Talleyrand-Perigord, Charles Maurice. Brougham. Works, **5** : 211. — Bulwer, H. L. Hist. char. **1** : 3. — Everett. Mt. Vernon, 352. — Holland, H. R. For. reminis. 33. — Neale, E. Closing scene, **2** : 299. — Rogers, S. Recollec. 177. — Smith, G. B. Ambass. 53. — (A. Alison) Ferris, G. T. Gt. leaders, **1** : 400. — Capefigue. Diplomats.
Tallien, Jean Lambert. Brougham. Works, **5** : 225. — Smythe, G. L. Hist. fancies, 262.
Tallien, Madame. *See* Chimay, T. C., Princesse de.
Tallmadge, Benjamin, with portrait. [Amer.] Nat. portr. gall. v. 3.
Tallushatches, Battle at. Dawson. Batt. of U. S. **2** : 301.
Talma, François Joseph, and the French stage. Hawkins. Fr. stage 18th cent. v. 2.
— Conversations with. Irving. Biog. 151.
Talmage, T. DeWitt. With portrait. Bungay. Pen-portr. 148. — Griswold. Prose writ. 697. — Parton, J. Sk. of men of prog.
Talmud, The. Disraeli, I. Curios. (N. Y. 4 v.) **1** : 177. — Deutsch, E. Lit. remains, v. 1. — Hearn, L. Stray leaves, 191. — (T. Theodores) Owens College essays, '74 : 329. — Karpeles. Jew. lit. 52. — (M. Margolis) Warner Lib. **24** : 14453.
— Bibliography. Mielziner, M. Introd. Talmud.
— Education and. (N. H. Imber) U. S. Bur. Ed. Rept. '94-95, **2** : 1795.
— Notes of a lecture on. Deutsch, E. Lit. rem. 135.
Talomei, Bernardo. Symonds, J. A. Ital. byways.
Tamaulipas, State of, 1891. (J. B. Richardson) U. S. Cons. Rept. **35** : 600.
Tamerlane. (E. Gibbon) Ferris, G. T. Gt. lead-

Tassoni, Allessandro. Montgomery. Men of Ita. **2** : 169. — Symonds. Renais. Cath. reac. **2** : 297. — Stebbing. Ital. poets, v. **3**.

Taste. Bridge, N. Penalties of taste, 1. — Day, L. F. Every-day art, 30. — Hazlitt. Sket. — Northcote. Lec. & ess. 41.

— Alison on. Jeffrey, F. Contrib. Ed. Rev.

— and morals, Connection between. Hopkins, M. Miscel. ess. 101.

— Cultivation of. Goldsmith. Miscel. (N. Y. 4 v.) **1** : 268.

— literary, Revolutions in. Hill, G. B. Writers & leaders, 11.

— Standard of. Hume. Philos. works, **3** : 249.

Tastes, Why they differ. Mivart. Ess. **1** : 400.

Taszycki, Daniel. Wallace, R. Anti-Trin. biog. **3** : 9.

Taszycki, Stanislaüs. Wallace, R. Anti-Trin. biog. **2** : 345.

Tate, Nahum. Austin & Ralph. Laureates, 196. — Dunham. Lit. & sci. men, **3** : 194. — Hamilton, Wal. Poets laur. — Hatfield, E. F. Poets of church, 593. — Holland, J. Psalmists, **2** : 109. — Miller, Jos. Singers church, 2d ed. 111.

— Dido and Æneas. Hogarth. Mem. opera, **1** : 93.

Tatian. Evans, R. W. Biog. early church, **1** : 161.

— Diatessaron. (J. R. Harris) Haverford stud. no. 5. — Lightfoot. Ess. " Super relig." 272.

Tatler, The. Hazlitt. Round table.

— Sketches of occasional contributors to. Drake, N. Ess. Tatler, **3** : 26.

Tatti, Jacopi. Milizia. Lives arch. **1** : 302.

Tattini, Giuseppe, with portrait. Ehrlich, A. Cel. violin. 155.

Tatwine, 731-734. Hook. Abps. Cant. **1** : 194.

Tauler, Johann. Broadus. Lec. hist. preach. 110. — Hodgson, Wm. Reformers, 62. — Miller, Jos. Singers church, 2d ed. 36. — Ullman. Reformers, 203.

— and the mystics. Herrick, S. E. Heretics, 1. — Vaughan. Hours with mystics, **1** : 226.

— History and life. Kingsley, C. New miscel. 319.

Taunton, Eng., and the Bloody Assize. (J. T. Page) Walters, J. C. Bygone Som. 22.

Taunton Castle. Timbs. Abbeys, **1** : 547.

Taunus, The. Bartley, G. C. D. Rhine, 162.

Tausig, Aloïs. Fay. Music study in Germany.

Tausig, Carl. Ehlert. Tone-world, 7. — Lenz. Gt. piano virtuosos, 77.

Taussig, Chas. Sumner. Am. Bar Assoc. **21** : 685.

Taverner, Samuel. Ivimey. Eng. Bapt. **2** : 250.

Tavernier, J. B. St. John. Cel. travelers, **1** : 180.

Tavistock, Abbey of. Timbs. Abbeys, **1** : 471.

Tax, Income. Peel, R. Speeches, **4** : 8, 468, 753.

— inheritance. (Max West) Col. Univ. Stud. Hist. **4** : 171.

— Single, on land. George, H. Soc. prob. 264. — Mich. Bur. Lab. '93 : 325.

— Succession. (Cyrus D. Roys) Sunset club echoes, 206.

Tax system of Pennsylvania. (C. Elder) Phil. Soc. Sci. Assoc. '73.

Taxation. Bolles. Chap. pol. econ. 200. — (J. H. Caulfield) Econ. tracts, no. **9**. — Filangieri. Sci. legis. **2** : 173. — Hume. Philos. works, **3** : 374. — Proudhon. Works, **4** : 319. — Hoffman, F. S. Sphere, 112. — Laing, S. Problems, 365.

— and assessment. Maryland Labor, '**93** : 85.

Taxation, Basis of. Atkinson. Indust. prog. 253. — Walker, F. A. Discus. in econ. **1** : 79.

— Bibliography. Cossa. Taxation, 184. — Indianapolis State Lib. Bull. March 1, '98.

— Budgets of, 1852-62. Disraeli. Sel. spee. **1** : 345.

— Cumulative. Worthington. Pol. & prop. 90.

— Direct. Alison. Ess. v. **3**. — Foster, R. Comment. on Const. **1** : 413.

— — and indirect. Greeley. Ess. pol. econ. 264. — Greg, W. R. Pol. prob. 291.

— Double, in U. S. (F. Walker) Colum. Univ. Stud. Hist. **5** : no. 1.

— Early methods in England. Francis, J. Stock exch. 1.

— Exemption from. Eliot, C. W. Five Am. cont. 299.

— False theories of. Bastiat. Ess. on pol. econ. 58.

— Incidence of. Walker, F. A. Discus. in econ. **1** : 71. — Jones, Rich. Lit. remains.

— — Regulation of. Jenkin, H. C. F. Papers, **2** : 107.

— Indirect, and public debts. George, H. Soc. prob. 221.

— in England, 1833. Browning. Polit. cond. of Gt. Brit. 531.

— — its bearing on the social conditions. (C. F. Macqueen) Trans. Soc. Sci. Lond. '**58** : 672.

— in Vermont, History of. (F. A. Wood) Colum. Univ. Stud. Hist. **4** : no. 3.

— Local. Disraeli. Sel. spee. **1** : 208. — (J. J. Colman *et al.*) Trans. Soc. Sci. Lond. '**73** : 522. — (T. Cochran) Phila. Soc. Sci. Assoc. '71.

— " no tyranny." Disraeli, I. Curios. (N. Y. 4 v.) **4** : 78.

— of church property. *See* Church property.

— of land. Field, D. D. Speeches, **3** : 147. — Worthington. Pol. & prop. 59.

— of the people. Lusk, H. H. Foes at home, 111.

— Principles of. Greg. Ess. pol. **1** : 237. — Jenkin. Papers, **2** : 107.

— — True. Hazard, T. R. Miscel. 167.

— Profitable. Lusk, H. H. Foes at home, 127.

— Progressive. Bibliography. (E. R. A. Seligman) Am. Econ. Assoc. **9** : no. 1.

— rational, Methods of. (S. N. Patten) Phila. Soc. Sci. Assoc. '89.

— — Principles of. (S. N. Patten) Univ. Pa. Publ. Pol. Econ. **1** : no. 6.

— Right use of a surplus. Greg, W. R. Miscel. **1** : 112.

— Vulgar errors concerning. Coleridge. Friend, 208.

Taxidermy. Bibliography. Browne, M. Art. & scient. taxidermy.

— Methods of, in Leyden Museum, Holland. (R. W. Shufeldt) U. S. Nat. Mus. Rept. '**95** : 1031.

— Scientific, for museums. (R. W. Shufeldt) U. S. Nat. Mus. Rept. '**92** : 369.

Tayler, John James. Martineau, J. Ess. '91, **1** : 381.

Taylor, Alfred S. Bettany. Em. doctors, **2** : 291.

Taylor, Alice. Brockett. Woman's work, 168.

Taylor, Mrs. Ann (Martin). Hatfield, E. F. Poets of church, 596. — Japp. Wise words, 92.

— and Jane. Miles, A. H. Poets of cent. **10** : 670.

Taylor, Bayard. Bolton, S. K. Poor boys, 13. — Griswold. Poets Am. 511. — Griswold. Prose writ. 687. — Harris, A. B. Amer. authors, 141. — Stedman. Poets Amer. 396. — Walsh, W. S. Pen pic. mod. 178. — Wilson, J. G. Bryant, 348. — Griswold, H. T. Personal sk. 216. —

Tea-meetings : Theology of the tea-pot. Oxenham. Short stud. 341.
Tea-party salvation. Dodge. Sermons to clergy.
Teach, Edward, " Black-beard." Macfarlane, C. Banditti, 264. — Pyle, H. Buccaneers, 239. — Whitehead, C. Highwaymen, **2** : 32.
Teacher and parent. (Jennie S. M'Lauchlan) Nat. Educa. Assoc. '**90** : 608.
— and the school. (J. L. Spalding) Nat. Educa. Assoc. '**96** : 162.
— as an intellectual force. (T. J. Backus) N. Y. Regents' Rept. **108** : 916.
— as a moral force. (J. M. Milne) N. Y. Regents' Rept. **108** : 912.
— Character in the. (N. L. Andrews) N. Y. Regents, **92** : 555.
— Has the, a profession ? Hart, A. B. Stud. Am. educa. 1.
— Nervous force of the. (Mara L. Pratt) Nat. Educa. Assoc. '**96** : 929.
— The new, in new America. (A. D. Mayo) Nat. Educa. Assoc. '**79** : 57.
— Obligations and duties of. (Edward Brooks) Nat. Educa. Assoc. '**94** : 186.
— Profession of. (W. R. Abbott) Nat. Educa. Assoc. '**74** : 23.
— Substitution of, for textbook. (J. M. Rice) Nat. Educa. Assoc. '**95** : 562.
Teachers and teaching. Greeley. Hints ref. 206.
— Appointment and nomination of. (H. S. Tarbell) Cong. Educa. Chic. '**93**, 78.
— as experts. (R. G. Boone) Nat. Educa. Assoc. '**94** : 857.
— common-school, Instruction of. (L. D. Miller) N. Y. Regents, **87** : 595.
— — Licensing of. (E. Bouton) N. Y. Regents, **93** : 537.
— diplomas, Certificates and registration of. (T. Storr) Internat. health exh. **16** : 136.
— Education of. Dix. Speeches, **2** : 72.
— Efficient and inefficient. (F. L. Soldan) Nat. Educa. Assoc. '**99** : 298.
— Employment and dismissal of. (E. E. Rosling) Nat. Educa. Assoc. '**99** : 1118.
— Ethics for. Hinsdale, B. A. Schools & stud. 296.
— Examination of. (John Swett) Nat. Educa. Assoc. '**72** : 71.
— — and licensing of, Laws concerning. U. S. Bur. Ed. circ. '**83**, no. 1.
— for city public schools, Supply of. (W. E. Anson ; A. B. Blodgett) Nat. Educa. Assoc. '**91** : 422.
— good, How to make, out of poor ones. (W. T. Harris) Nat. Educa. Assoc. '**99** : 310.
— inefficient, How to improve work of. (F. A. Fitzpatrick) Nat. Educa. Assoc. '**93** : 71.
— Influence, duties and rewards of. Boutwell. Educa. topics, 241.
— Influence of, in favor of education. (Henry Sabin) Nat. Educa. Assoc. '**87** : 238.
— Instruction and improvement of. (A. S. Olin ; Earl Barnes ; L. H. Jones) Nat. Educa. Assoc. '**95** : 165.
— Licensure of. (N. C. Dougherty, ed.) Nat. Educa. Assoc. '**89** : 366.
— Literary responsibility of. White, C. Ess. 433.
— New. Friswell. Gentle life, **2** : 281.
— Non-progressive and retrogressive. (J. M. Greenwood) Nat. Educa. Assoc. '**94** : 383.
— of elementary schools, Normal training for. (Kate N. T. Tupper) Nat. Educa. Assoc. '**88** : 369.
— of kindergartens ; things they should know. (W. E. Sheldon) Nat. Educa. Assoc. '**91** : 554.

Teachers, of teachers. Verses. (O. W. Holmes) Nat. Educa. Assoc. '**94** : 260.
— Pastors and. Hall, John. Papers, 318.
— Pensions for. U. S. Bur. Ed. Rept. '**94–95**, **1** : 1079.
— Professional training of. (S. H. White) Nat. Educa. Assoc. '**70** : 29. — (D. J. Goggin) Nat. Educa. Assoc. '**91** : 193. — (Eudora L. Hailmann) Nat. Educa. Assoc. '**92** : 272. — E. A. Sheldon) Cong. Educa. Chic. '**93**, 387. — (W. Jolly) Trans. Soc. Sci. Lond. '**74** : 490.
— — in Sweden. · (E. Osternberg) Cong. Educa. Chic. '**93**, 60.
— professionally trained, Demand for. (W. W. Parsons) Nat. Educa. Assoc. '**87** : 250.
— Qualifications of. (W. T. Harris) Nat. Educa. Assoc. '**82**, app. : 98.
— Relation of, to reforms of the day. (Frances E. Willard) Nat. Educa. Assoc. '**75** : 181.
— Relations of citizens and. (I. C. Bender) Nat. Educa. Assoc. '**97** : 248.
— rural, Improvement of. (S. S. Parr) Nat. Educa. Assoc. '**94** : 527.
— salaries of, Economic aspect of. (C. B. Dyke) Colum. Univ. Contrib. Philos. **7** : no. 2.
— Scholarship and methods of. (H. B. Buckham) Nat. Educa. Assoc. '**73** : 190.
— secondary, Professional spirit in. (Ida B. Haslop) Nat. Educa. Assoc. '**94** : 758.
— Tenure of office of. Eliot, C. W. Educa. reform, 49. — (E. E. Higbee) Nat. Educa. Assoc. '**87** : 307.
— Training of. (B. A. Hinsdale) Butler, N. M. Educa. in U. S. 359. — (C. C. Mansford) Internat. health exh. **16** : 1. — (G. B. Emerson) Mass. education, **17** : 29. — (Dr. Stoy) Internat. health exh. **16** : 81. — (W. F. Phelps and others) Nat. Educa. Assoc. '**72** : 28. — (Delia A. Lathrop) Nat. Educa. Assoc. '**75** : 138. — (E. A. Sheldon) Nat. Educa. Assoc. '**93** : 387. — (H. S. Tarbell) Nat. Educa. Assoc. '**95** : 238. — (F. W. Parker) Nat. Educa. Assoc. '**95** : 969.
— — Academical and professional. (B. A. Hinsdale) Nat. Educa. Assoc. '**91** : 713.
— — at Westminster Training College, England. (J. H. Cowham) Nat. Educa. Assoc. '**93** : 401.
— — Coördination of normal school and university in. (C. De Garmo) Nat. Educa. Assoc. '**92** : 411.
— — for elementary schools. (G. B. Davis ; Miss S. A. Miller) Internat. health exh. **16** : 14.
— — for elementary schools in Gt. Brit. and on the continent. (Canon Cromwell) Internat. health exh. **16** : 59.
— — for secondary schools. (Miss E. P. Hughes) Nat. Educa. Assoc. '**93** : 217.
— — for ungraded country schools. (E. A. Sheldon) N. Y. Regents, **102**, app. : 37.
— — in actual service. (T. M. Balliet) Nat. Educa. Assoc. '**94** : 377.
— — in colleges. (S. G. Williams) Nat. Educa. Assoc. '**94** : 93.
— — in Germany. U. S. Bur. Ed. Circ. '**78**, no. 1.
— — in Germany, Austria, and Switzerland. (L. R. Klemm) U. S. Bur. Ed. Rept. '**91–92** : 139.
— — in high schools in Sweden. (E. Osterberg) Nat. Educa. Assoc. '**93** : 60.
— — in the South. (A. D. Mayo) Nat. Educa. Assoc. '**89** : 597.
— — — Means available for. (Henry Sabin) Nat. Educa. Assoc. '**91** : 505.
— — Relation of universities to. (R. H. Quick) Internat. health exh. **16** : 74.

Teachers, Training of, to coöperate with librarians. (M. E. Schreiber) Nat. Educa. Assoc. '97 : 1008.
— value of practice work in training-school. (F. S. Guptill) Cong. Educa. Chic. '93, 391.
— What makes — what mars. (Corinne Harrison) Nat. Educa. Assoc. '94 : 136.
— work of, How to test. (W. C. Warfield) Nat. Educa. Assoc. '95 : 218.
— — in development of mental and moral power. (N. A. Calkins) Nat. Educa. Assoc. '81 : 69.
Teachers' Aid societies, Workings of. (Nellie E. Owens) Nat. Educa. Assoc. '88 : 671.
Teachers' College, Columbia University. Gilman, D. C. Univ. prob. 265.
Teachers' Institutes. (D. C. Tillotson) Nat. Educa. Assoc. '86 : 346. — (E. C. Hewett and others) Nat. Educa. Assoc. '87 : 292. — U. S. Bur. Ed. circ. '85, no. 2.
Teaching. Dodge, M. A. Country, 80.
— Acquirement of methods of. (G. O. Bomaféde) Cong. Educa. Chic. '93, 399.
— and examining boards in a university, Relation between. (Sir G. Young) Internat. health exh. 15 : 247.
— and teachers. Friswell. Gentle life, 1 : 45.
— art of, Art of analysis and. (F. S. Jewell) N. Y. Regents, 80 : 629.
— as a profession for women. (G. Butler) Butler. Woman's work, 49.
— Bibliography. Boyer, C. C. Princ. & meth. of teaching.
— a business for men. (C. W. Bardeen) Nat. Educa. Assoc. '85 : 138.
— for light and power. (Merrill E. Gates) Nat. Educa. Assoc. '91 : 180.
— Graphical methods of. (R. H. Richards) Cong. Educa. Chic. '93, 567.
— Infant; apparatus needed for play and instruction. (C. Ellis) Internat. health exh. 13 : 128.
— Method and manner in. (Louis Soldan) Nat. Educa. Assoc. '74 : 245.
— Method in. (J. W. Dickinson) Nat. Educa. Assoc. '84 : 185.
— Methods of. (J. W. Dickinson) Nat. Educa. Assoc. '80 : 95.
— — A basis of. N. Y. Regents, 95 : 353.
— Natural method of. Clarke, J. F. Self-culture, 3.
— objective, Value of. (N. A. Calkins ; A. B. Alcott) Nat. Educa. Assoc. '72 : 126.
— Objective element in. (J. W. Dickinson) Nat. Educa. Assoc. '87 : 70.
— Personal and acquired gifts of. (H. B. Buckham) Nat. Educa. Assoc. '76 : 196.
— Physiological influence of certain methods of. Trans. Soc. Sci. Lond. '57 : 219.
— Preparation for. Mann, H. Lec. 1 : 89.
— Principles of, and common errors in. (Agnes I. Rounds) Nat. Educa. Assoc. '86 : 538.
— Some errors in. (L. R. Klemm ; J. M. Greenwood) Nat. Educa. Assoc. '86 : 149.
— Some fundamentals in. (L. D. Harvey) Nat. Educa. Assoc. '99 : 93.
— Tact in. (Bro. Noah) N. Y. Regents, 100, app. : 100.
Teaching spirit, The. (W. K. Wickes) N. Y. Regents' Rept. 107 : 403.
Teaching of the Twelve. Moxom. Jerus. to Nicæa, 123.
Teall, Oliver. Livingston, J. Dist. Amer. 111.
Tears and smiles. Saunders. Stray leaves, 173.
Teaziehs, Persian, Analysis of. Renan. Studies (N. Y.), 2 : 183.

Tebbetts, Ezra Martin. (J. Batchelder) Harvard mem. biog. 2 : 52.
Technical education. (T. C. Mendenhall) Butler, N. M. Educa. in U. S. 551. — Huxley. Sci. & cul. 73. — (W. Garnett) Internat. health exh. 14 : 106. — Jenkin, Fl. Papers, 2 : 157. — Playfair. Subj soc 307. — (S. P. Thompson et al.) Trans. Soc. Sci. Lond. '82 : 289. — (A. C. Rembaugh) Phila. Soc. Sci. Assoc. '78. — Rosebery. Speeches, 416. — Walker, F. A. Discus. in educa. 31 ; also in Nat. Educa. Assoc. '93 : 528.
— and art education in public schools. (Felix Adler) Nat. Educa. Assoc. '84 : 308.
— Assistance by government to. Bright, Jo. Publ. add. 58.
— for women. Jeune, Lady. Lesser ques. 201.
— in American schools. (E. E. White) U. S. Bur. Ed. circ. '81, no. 2.
— in Central Europe. U. S. Bur. Ed. Rept. '90-91 : 165.
— in Europe. Bolton, S. K. Soc. stud. in Eng. 190. — (C. O. Thompson) U. S. Bur. Ed. circ. '85, no. 3.
— — 1893. U. S. Cons. Rept. no. 157.
— in France. U. S. Bur. Ed. circ. '82, no. 6.
— in Great Britain. U. S. Bur. Ed. Rept. '90-91 : 135. — (A. T. Smith) U. S. Bur. Ed. Rept. '91-92 : 105.
— in Institucion libre de ensenanza, Madrid. (G. del Rios) Internat. health exh. 14 : 275.
— International Congress on, London, 1897. (C. P. Brooks) U. S. Bur. Ed. Rept. '97-98, 1 : 295.
— Need and value of. (C. T. Millis) Galton, F. W. Workers, 1.
— Problems in. (P. Magnus) Internat. health exh. 14 : 2.
— Relation of, to elementary schools. (J. P. Philbrick) Nat. Educa. Assoc. '80 : app. 49. *See* Industrial schools.
Technical instruction in Land-grant colleges. (J. M. Gregory) Nat. Educa. Assoc. '80 : 229.
Technical school and the university. Walker, F. A. Discus. in educa. 39.
Technical schools. N. Y. Labor, '86.
— in the U. S. (A. Riedler) U. S. Bur. Ed. Rept. '92-93 : 657.
— Place of. (F. A. Walker) N. Y. Regents, 105 : 375.
— Purpose of. (R. H. Thurston) Nat. Educa. Assoc. '93 : 534.
— — and accomplishment of. (R. H. Thurston and others) Cong. Educa. Chic. '93, 534.
— Relation of, to public education. (I. I. Hopkins) Nat. Educa. Assoc. '87 : 158.
— Workshop instruction in. (E. M. Dixon) Internat. health exh. 14 : 16.
Technical training in American schools. (E. E. White) Nat. Educa. Assoc. '80 : 222.
Technology and civilization. (F. Reuleaux) Smithson. Rept. '90 : 705.
Tecumseh. James. Mil. occur. v. 1. — Moore, F. Am. eloq. 2 : 354.
Teerlinck, Lavinia. Clayton, E. C. Eng. fem. art. 1 : 7.
Teese, Frederick H. Am. Bar Assoc. 17 : 514.
Teeth, Children's. (J. C. Adams and others) Am. Pub. Health Assoc. 20 : 339.
— degeneracy of, Causes of. (H. S. Chase) Estes. Half-hour recr. 127.
Tegetthoff, Wilhelm von. Laughton. Stud. nav. hist. 148.
Tegg, Thomas. Curwen. Booksellers, 379. — Grant, Jas. Portr. pub. char. 2 : 24.
Tegner, Esaias. Boyesen. Scand. lit. 219. —

Temple, R. Grenville, 1st earl. Jesse, J. H. Cel. Eton. v. 1.

Temple, Sir Wm. Wrangham. Brit. Plutarch, v. 4.

— as a gardener. Hazlitt, W. C. Gleanings, 182.

— Courtenay's Memoirs of. Macaulay. Ess. 4 : 1.

Temple, William James. (W. W. Swan) Harvard mem. biog. 2 : 334.

Temple and pyramid builders, Early. (J. N. Lockyer) Smithson. Inst. Rept. '93 : 95.

Temple, Inner and Middle. Foss, Judges, 5 : 431. 7 : 43.

Temple Bar, London, Stories of. Timbs. Abbeys, 1 : 107.

Temporal and spiritual powers. Stephen, J. F. Horæ sabb. 343.

Temptation. Parsons, T. Mystery, 108.

Ten-hours day, M. T. Sadler and the. Gibbins. Eng. soc. ref. 123.

Tenant, Contract between landlord and. (W. A. Hunter) Trans. Soc. Sci. Lond. '77 : 189.

Tenant right. Kempner, W. Common-sense soc. 105.

Tench, Watkin. Redding. Pers. remin. 3 : 259.

Tencin, Mad. de. Kavanagh. Fr. women, 136. — Mason, A. G. Wom. of Fr. salons, 155.

Tenement-house census of Boston. Mass. Bur. Lab. '91 : 1. '92 : 1.

Tenement-house problem, The. (C. F. Wingate) Conv. Labor Bur. '86 : 34.

Tenement-house reform in New York city. (J. Gallatin) Am. Pub. Health, 6 : 309.

Tenement houses. (W. L. Richardson) Bost. Health, '74 : 58.

— in foreign cities, 1895. U. S. Cons. Rept. 48 : 381.

— residents in, Place of birth, occupations, etc. Mass. Bur. Lab. '92 : 167.

— Sanitary drainage of. (W. P. Gerhard) Conn. Health, '83 : 99.

Tenement populations, Health of. (E. H. Janes) Am. Pub. Health, 2 : 115.

Teneriffe. Benjamin. Atlan. isl. 121. — Benjamin, S. G. W. World's paradises, 188. — Chambers's Miscel. no 64.

— as a health resort. Mackenzie, M. Ess. 49.

Teniers, David. Wedmore. Masters of genre, 140.

— Visit to the château of. King, R. J. Sket. 443.

Teniers, David, the younger. Van Dyke, J. C. Dutch mast. 189.

Tennant, Charles. Walker, W., jr. Men of sci. 122.

Tennant, Thomas. Jackson, T. Early Meth. 3 : 425.

Tennant, Wm. Miles, A. H. Poets of cent. 2 : 285. — Wilson, J. G. Poets of Scot. 2 : 48.

Tenneman, W. G. History of Philosophy. Hamilton. Discus.

Tennent, Emerson. Grant, J. Recoll. Lords & Comm. 2 : 243.

Tennent, William. Headley, J. T. Chaplains Revol. 115. — Lossing. Em. Amer. 116.

Tennessee, Secession and reconstruction of. Bibliography. Fertig, J. W. Secess. & reconstruc. Tenn.

Tennessee river, Scenery on the. Mansfield, E. D. Pers. mem. 301.

Tenney, Tabitha. Richardson. Amer. lit. 2 : 285.

Tenniel, John, and John Leech. Ruskin. Art of Eng. 111.

— and Punch. Ewart, H. C. Toilers in art, 19.

Tennis. Hutton, L. Other times, 22.

Tennis Court oath. (J. H. Robinson) Am. Hist. Assoc. Rept. '94 : 541.

Tennyson, Alfred. (E. J. Lowell) Am. Acad. A. & S. Proc. 28 : 420. — Armstrong, R. A. Faith and doubt, 67. — Griswold, H. T. Personal sk. 11. — Rearden. Petrarch, 43. — With portrait. (H. Van Dyke) Warner Lib. 25 : 14581 ; also in Warner Classics, 3 : 113. — Austin, A. Poetry, 1. — Cochrane, R. Gt. thinkers, 50. — Collier, W. F. Hist. Eng. lit. 472. — Cooke. Poets and problems, 55. — Dawson, W. J. Mod. Eng. 169. — Devey. Mod. Eng. poets, 275. — Duyckinck. Portrait gall. 2 : 537. — Farrar. Men, 1. — Fields, A. Authors, 335. — Em. persons, 5 : 272. — Forman. Liv. poets, 29. — Friswell. Mod. men of l. 147. — Galton, A. Urbana, 36. — Gilfillan. Mod. lit. 192. — Gladstone. Glean. 2 : 131. — With portrait. Gostwick, J. Eng. poets, 221. — Graham, P. A. Nature, 44. — Griswold, H. T. Home-life, 197. — Hayward, A. Em. statesm. 2 : 305. — Hamilton, Wal. Poets laur. — Henley. Views, 154. — Horne, R. H. New spirit, 193. — Howitt. Homes Brit. poets, 2 : 513. — Japp. Three great teachers. — Kingsley, C. Lit. lec. 103. — Macdonald, G. England's antiphon, 329. — (A. H. Japp) Miles, A. H. Poets of cent. 4 : 67. — Roscoe, W. C. Poems & ess. v. 2. — Russell, W. C. Book of au. 484. — Saunders, F. Famous books, 199. — Sharp, A. Vic. poets, 1. — Stedman. Vic. poets, 150. — Stirling, J. H. Jerrold, 50. — Swanwick, A. Poets, 380. — Taine. Eng. lit. 2 : 518. — Taylor, B. Crit. ess. 1. — Tuckerman. Poets, 273. — Walsh, W. S. Pen pic. mod. 74. — Howells. My lit. passions, 150. — Saintsbury. Correc. imp. 21. — Smalley. Stud. 66. — Walker, H. Gt. Vic. poets, 16, 70, 150. — Innes, A. D. Seers & s. — Stewart, Geo. Ess. 2 : 9. — Winter, W. Shadows, 2 : 359.

— and after. Gosse, E. Questions, 175.

— and Browning. (E. Dowden) Afternoon lec. 5 : 139. — Dowden. Studies, 191.

— and Charles, Hallam as advocate of. Nicoll, W. R. Lit. anec. 1 : 21.

— and Heine, and De Musset. Buchanan. Master-spir. 54.

— and his critics. Cheney, J. V. Golden guess, 161.

— and his teachers. Bayne, P. Ess. 1 : 50.

— and Longfellow. Hatton, J. Old lamps, 176.

— and A. de Musset. Swinburne. Miscel. 219. — Trent. Authority, 269.

— and politics. Dawson, W. J. Mod. Eng. 214.

— Art of. Robertson. Ess. toward crit. meth.

— as a dramatist. Archer. Eng. dram. 334. — Cooke, G. W. Poets, 138.

— as a lyrical and idyllic poet. Cooke, G. W. Poets, 127.

— as a moralist. Cooke, G. W. Poets, 144.

— as prophet. Myers. Sci. and fut. life, 127.

— as a religious poet. Dawson, W. J. Mod. Eng. 236.

— at Haslemere. Yates, E. H. Celeb. 1 : 21.

— at Mirehouse. Rawnsley. Lit. Assoc. Eng. Lakes, 1 : 169.

— Ballads and poems. Mallock. Atheism, 83.

— Bibliography. Dixon, W. M. Tennyson primer. — Van Dyke, H. Poetry of Tennyson.

— Blank verse of. Mayor. Eng. metre.

— Characteristics of his poetry. Haweis. Poets in pulpit, 33.

— Despair. Hutton, R. H. Criticisms, 1 : 197.

— Dramas. Archer. Eng. dram.

— Early poems of. Hallam. Remains, 424. — Stirling, J. Ess. 1 : 422.

— The England of. Bibliography. Ward, W. G. Tennyson's debt to environment.

Tennyson, Alfred. Enoch Arden. Dawson, G. Shakesp. 481.
— The Foresters. Winter. Shadows, 269.
— Home of. Haven, G. Pilgrim. 209.
— Human side of. Peck, H. T. Good English, 169.
— Idylls of the king. Dawson, G. Shakesp. 471.
— — Building of the. Nicoll, W. R. Lit. anec. 2 : 222.
— — Christian life and character in. Butler, E. For furth. consid. 1.
— In memoriam. Finlayson, T. C. Ess. 1. — Haweis. Poets in pulpit, 87. — Scudder, V. D. Life of spirit, 281.
— — and Pope's Essay on man. Buchanan, R. Look round, 347.
— — Spiritual sense of. Mullany. Phases of tho't, 183.
— Life of. Stephen, L. Stud. biog. 2 : 196.
— Locksley Hall in youth and age. Hutton, R. H. Criticisms, 1 : 204.
— the moodist. Mather, J. M. 19th cent. poets, 125.
— An opinion on. (E. B. Browning) Nicoll, W. R. Lit. anec. 1 : 33.
— or Darwin? Swinburne. Stud. prose & p. 141.
— over-rated poet. Heywood, J. C. How they strike, 126.
— Palace of art. O'Conor. Ess. 25.
— Philosophy of. Lindsay, J. Ess. 79. — Salt. Lit. sk. 39.
— Poems. Brimley, G. Ess. 1 ; also in Camb. ess. '55 : 226. — Devey. Mod. Eng. poets, 275. — Haweis. Poets in the pulpit. — Horne. New spirit, 2 : 1. — McNicoll. Ess. on Eng. lit. — Noel. Ess. on poetry. — Kingsley. Raleigh. 177. — Mill. Early ess. 239. — Spedding. Reviews.
— Poetic style of. Cooke, G. W. Poets, 88.
— Poetry of. McNicoll, T. Ess. Eng. lit. 248.
— — Subjective qualities of. Cooke, G. W. Poets, 98.
— The Princess. Bristed. Pieces, 1 : 171. — Hadley, J. Ess. 296.
— Religious teachings of. Cooke, G. W. Poets, 153.
— Sonnets of. Deshler. Afternoons, 281.
— The supernatural in. Hodgson. Outcast, 157.
— Vision of sin and Palace of art. Haweis. Poets in pulpit, 65.
— Works. (J. K. Ingram) Afternoon lec. 4 : 47.
Tennyson, Lady Emily. Fields, A. Authors, 349.
Tennyson, Frederick. (A. H. Japp) Miles, A. H. Poets of cent. 4 : 1.
Tennysoniana. Nicoll, W. R. Lit. anec. 2 : 421.
Tenos. Tozer. Isl. Æg. 15.
Tense, Future. Hadley, J. Ess. 184.
Tent life. Arnold, E. Wand. words, 363.
Tenterden, Chas. Abbott, Baron. Arnold, F. Turning-points, 196. — Grant, J. Bench & bar, 1 : 81. — Townsend. Twelve judges, 2 : 234.
Te Papa, Battle of. Richards, W. Heroes, 24.
Tepic and the Pacific coast of Mexico, Hygienic conditions of. (J. Revueltas) Am. Pub. Health, 18 : 101.
Terburg, or Ter Borch, Gerard. (K. Lemcke) Dohme, R. Early mast. 274. — Gower. Fig.-painters Holl. 14. — Van Dyke, J. C. Dutch mast. 79. — Wedmore. Masters of genre, 72.
Terentius Afer, Publius. Dunlop, J. Rom. liter. 1 : 257. — Sellar. Rom. poets repub. 201. — With portrait. (T. B. Lindsay) Warner Lib. 25 : 14643.
— and Plautus compared. Malkin. Class. disq. 1.

Teresa, St. Coleridge. Lit. rem. 4 : 65. — Kavanagh. Women of Chr. 114. — Lord, J. Beacon, 5 : 187. — Froude, J. A. Span. Armada, 155.
— and the Catholic mystics. Brigham, C. H. Mem. 277.
Terhune, Mrs. Mary V. With portrait. Bolton, S. K. Succ. women, 90. — Davidson, J. W. Writ. of South, 552. — With portrait. (K. Sanborn) Our fam. wom. 624. — Derby, J. C. Fifty years, 563. — Freeman, J. D. Wom. of South, 195.
Terpander. Arnold, E. Poets of Greece, 100.
— Mills. Poets of Greece, 83.
— and the lyre of Greece. Butterworth. Great compos. 19.
Terrill, Edward. Ivimey. Eng. Bapt. 2 : 538.
Terrill, James B. Walker, C. D. Biog. Va. Mil. Inst. 512.
Terriss, William, with portrait. Goddard, A. Players, 2 : 207.
Territorial sovereignty. Black, J. S. Ess. & sp. 212.
Territories, Federal jurisdiction in. Black, J. S. Ess. & sp. 595.
— Governments in the. Dix. Speeches, 1 : 346. — Hilliard, H. W. Sp. 196.
Territory, New, in the U. S., How it is opened. Rousiers. Amer. life, 19.
Terror, Reign of, and secret police. Wilson, J. Stud. mod. mind.
Terry, Edward, with portrait. Goddard, A. Players, 2 : 61.
Terry, Ellen. Matthews, B. Actors, 5 : 247. — Brockett. Woman's work, 546.
— and Irving, in "Macbeth." Winter, W. Shadows, 2 : 277.
— — in "Merchant of Venice." Winter. Shadows, 1 : 178, 286.
— — in "Olivia." Winter. Shadows, 1 : 119.
— — in "Ravenswood." Winter. Shadows, 1 : 226.
— as Portia. Winter. Shadows, 3 : 242.
— as Queen Katharine. Winter. Shadows, 3 : 199.
— Henry Irving and. Winter. Shadows, 3 : 148.
Terry, Mary. Burder. Pious wom. 353.
Tersteegen, Gerhard. Baillie, J. Life-stud. 134.
— Hatfield, E. F. Poets of church, 605. — Miller, Jos. Singers church, 2d ed. 157. — Winkworth. Chr. sing. Germ. 297.
Tertiary age, Characteristic animals of. Agassiz. Geol. sk. 1 : 181.
Tertiary man. Laing, S. Problems, 92.
Tertullian, presbyter of Carthage. Blakey, R. Prim. fathers, 102. — Cave. Lives of fathers, 1 : 305. — Evans, R. W. Biog. early church, 1 : 325. — Farrar. Lives of fathers, 1 : 118, — Pressensé. Martyrs, 375, 591. — Hort, F. J. A. Ante-N. fathers, 93. — (G. A. Schneider) Lefroy, W. Lec. eccl. hist. 181.
Tesimond, Father, landing in England. Morris, J. Troub. of Cath. v. 1.
Tessie, Vittoria, Italian singer. Hogarth. Mem. opera, 1 : 295.
Test, Ultimate. Mabie. Ess. on work, 53.
Test act. Hall, R. Miscel. 147.
Test laws. Webster, N. Ess. 151.
Test-oaths, Constitutionality of. Field, D. D. Speeches, 1 : 89.
Testi, F. Stebbing. Ital. poets, v. 3.
Testimony, Historical. (J. Schouler) Am. Hist. Assoc. Rept. '95 : 435.
Tête Noire, Over the. Scollard. Und. Sum. skies, 199.
Tetuan. Finck, H. T. Spain & Morocco. — Warner, C. D. Roundabout, 178.

Thicknesse, R. Jesse, J. H. Cel. Eton. v. 1.

Thierry, Augustin. Pellissier. Lit. move. Fr. 242. — With portrait. (F. Loliée) Warner Lib. 25 : 14803.

Thiers, Louis Adolphe. Castelar. Byron, 295. — Cormenin. Orators, 286, 376. — Hayward, A. Em. statesm. 1 : 1. — King, E. French pol. lead. 55. — Loménie. Liv. characters, 25. — Men of 3d repub. 1. — McCarthy, J. Mod. lead. 66. — Parton. Princes, 331. — Pressensé. Contemp. portr. 3. — Duyckinck. Portrait gall. 2 : 427. — Em. persons, 2 : 22. — Walsh, R. M. Liv. char. France. — With portrait. (A. Cohn) Warner Lib. 25 : 14821.

— as a historian. Pellissier. Lit. move. Fr. 257.

— as Warwick of 2d Empire. Malortie. Here, there, 167.

— Dictatorship of. Hillebrand. France, 201.

— Evenings with. Stuart, J. M. Reminis. 50.

Thieves. Jacox, F. Cues, 132.

— great, Popular admiration for. Mackay. Delusions, 1 : 138.
See also Predatory classes.

Thieving the leading profession. Knight. Once on time, 2 : 168.

Things-in-themselves, Nature of. Clifford. Lec. & ess. 274.

— slowly learnt. Boyd. Leis. hours (Bost.), 57.

— which cannot go on. Boyd. Every-day, 255.

Thinker in some of his relations to the community. Hoyt, J. G. Miscel. 87.

Thinking. Azarias. Phases of tho't, 5.

— Art of. Ballantyne. Ess. 15. — Hinton. Thinking, 15. — Martineau, H. Miscel. 1 : 57.

Thinking sounds directly or indirectly. (S. W. Cole) Nat. Educa. Assoc. '96 : 741.

Thirlmere. Rawnsley. Lit. assoc. Eng. lakes, 2 : 213.

Thirlwall, Connop. Huntington, G. Random recol. 79. — Hutton, R. H. Criticisms, 1 : 288. — Morgan, J. Four biog. sket.

— Eulogy on. Stanley, A. P. Ser. spec. occ. 212.

— Obituary of. Em. persons, 1 : 303.

Thirnynge, Sir William, chief justice of England, 1390–97. Campbell. Ch. just. 1 : 117.

Thirteenth century, Survey of. Harrison, F. Mean. of hist. 139.

Thirty-nine articles. Bibliography. Green, E. T. Thirty-nine art. & the Reforma.

— Bishop Forbes on. Conington. Miscel. 502.

Thirty Years' War. Chambers's Miscel. no. 120. — Lord, J. Beacon, 4 : 23. — Winkworth. Chr. singers Germ. 165.

— An episode of. Smith, Gold. Lec. & ess. 42.

Thistlewood, Arthur, and others. Browne, G. L. State trials 19th cent. 2 : 309.

Thoburn, James M. Creegan. Gt. mission. 109.

Tholuck, Frederick August. Ker, J. Lec. hist. preach. 316.

Thom, William, weaver poet. Miles, A. H. Poets of cent. 3 : 249. — Ossoli. Art, 177. — Williams, A. M. Stud. folk. 166. — Wilson, J. G. Poets of Scot. 2 : 202. — Kennedy, J. P. Occas. addr. 216.

Thomas Didymus. Baldwin, G. C. Rep. men, 137. — Cave. Apostles, 2 : 147.

Thomas Aquinas, St. Broadus. Lect. hist. preach. 106. — Ker, J. Lect. hist. preach. 124. — Miller, Jos. Singers of church, 2d ed. 33. — Hundred greatest men, 217. — Lord, J. Beacon, 2 : 256. — Townsend, W. J. Schoolmen, 199. — With portrait. (E. A. Pace) Warner Lib. 2 : 613.

— The angelic doctor. Hain, J. Varia, 1.

— Pelagianism of. Ullman. Reformers, 95.

Thomas à Becket, St. Adams, W. H. D. Gt. churchm. 62. — Campbell. Ld. chan. 1 : 56. — Froude, J. A. Short stud. 4 : 1. — Hook. Abps. Cant. 2 : 354. — Lord, J. Beacon, 2 : 291. — Trotter. Stud. biog. 37. — Brown, J. B. Stoics, 171. — Simson, Jas. Em. men of Kent, 55. — (D. Hume) Ferris, G. T. Gt. leaders, 130. — Fowler, M. Some abps. Cant. 48. — Marshall, W. Men of mark. — Williams, F. Eng. card. 1 : 173.

— and Henry II., Contest between. Froude, R. H. Remains, pt. 2, 2 : 1.

— and his shrine, Canterbury. Bayly, J. A. S. New stud. 53, 65.

— Biographies of. Freeman. Hist. ess. 1 : 79.

— Life and times of. Froude. Short stud. 4 : 1.

Thomas of Celano. Hatfield, E. F. Poets of church, 610. — Miller, Jos. Singers church, 2d ed. 34.

Thomas of Erceldowne. Choate, I. B. Wells of Eng. 11.

Thomas à Kempis. Neale. Mediæv. preachers.

— and the Imitatio Christi. Hain, J. Varia. 59.

Thomas the Rhymer. Wilson, J. G. Poets of Scot. 1 : 1.

Thomas, Antoine Léonard. Haussonville. Salon of Necker, 1 : 307.

Thomas, Charles Ambroise. Ferris, G. T. Ital. & Fr. compos. 248. — Hervey, A. Masters Fr. music, 1.

— Mignon. Guerber. Stor. of operas, 189.

Thomas, Mrs. E. Brockett. Woman's work, 496.

Thomas, Edith Matilda, with portrait. Warner Lib. 25 : 14845.

Thomas, Father, Murder of. Baring-Gould. Oddities, 2 : 86.

Thomas, Frederick William. Coggeshall. Poets of west, 184. — Davidson, J. W. Writ. of south, 554.

Thomas, George, 1756–1802. Davenport, R. A. Lives of indiv. 97.

Thomas, George Dudley. Am. Bar Assoc. 18 : 498.

Thomas, Gen. George H., with portrait. Brockett. Men of our day, 150. — Brockett. Gt. capt. 163. — Garfield. Works, 1 : 643. — Glazier, W. Heroes, 304. — Headley, J. T. Grant and Sherman, 261. — Piatt, D. F. Memories, 172. — (H. Stone & T. L. Livermore) Dwight, T. F. Fed. & Confed. comm. 163.

— as a tactician. Shanks. Rec. of generals, 58.

— in Grant's Memoirs. (J. H. Sherratt) Mil. ess. M. O. L. L. U. S. Ills. 499.

Thomas, Goring, with portrait. Buffen, F. F. Mus. celeb. 113.

Thomas, Isaiah. Lossing. Em. Amer. 149. — Mass. Hist. Proc. 1 : 440.

Thomas, Jane. Clement, J. Noble deeds, 188. — Ellet. Women of revol. 1 : 250.

Thomas, Joshua. Mass. Hist. Coll. 2d ser. 10 : 1.

Thomas, Lewis Foulke. Coggeshall. Poets of west, 243.

Thomas, Lewis M. Walker, C. D. Biog. Va. Mil. Inst. 516.

Thomas, Margaret. Clayton, E. C. Eng. fem. art. 2 : 259.

Thomas, Seth J. Am. Bar Assoc. 19 : 661.

Thomas, Sidney Gilchrist. Jeans. Creators, 300.

Thomas, Theodore, master of music. Bungay. Repr. men, 26.

Thomas, Timothy. Ivimey. Eng. Bapt. 4 : 557.

Thomas, William B. Winslow, S. N. Biog. Phila. merch. 75.

Tindal, Nicholas C., Lord chief justice. Grant, J. Bench & bar, **1** : 174, 255.

Tindale, John. *See* Tyndale.

Tinkers. Story, A. T. Vagrom, 140.

Tinnè, Alexina. Adams, W. H. D. Cel. wom. trav. 184. — Adams, W. H. D. Heroes of trav. 229. — Edwards, M. B. Six women, 41.

Tintagel Castle. Timbs. Abbeys, **1** : 499.

Tintoretto, Giacomo. Jameson. Ital. painters, 339. — Oliphant. Makers of Venice, 324. — Spooner. Biog. fine arts, **2** : 971. — Symonds. Renais. fine arts, 369. — Taine. Italy, **2** : 312. — Jervis, Lady. Painting, **1** : 236. — Stillman, W. J. Old Ital. mas. 269. — Ruskin. Miscel. v. 1.

— Bacchus and Ariadne. (H. A. Taine) Singleton, E. Great pic. 273.

— Marriage in Cana. (J. Ruskin) Singleton, E. Great pic. 172.

— Paradise. (J. Ruskin) Singleton, E. Great pic. 106.

— Venice and. Greene, J. R. Stray studies, 300.

Tinworth, George. Ewart, H. C. Toilers in art, 301.

Tiodas. Milizia. Lives arch. **1** : 130.

Tippecanoe, Battle of. Dawson. Batt. of U. S. **2** : 73.

Tiptoft, Sir John. Manning, J. A. Speakers, 39.

Tipton, John. Woollen. Biog. sk. Indiana, 185.

Tirel, Walter, and his wife. Round, J. H. Feudal Eng. 468.

Tiring-room, The. Cook, D. Book of play, **1** : 238.

Tirro di Carnaino. Perkins, C. C. Tusc. sculp. **1** : 96.

Tiryns. Freeman. Studies Greece, 85.

— Excavations at, 1884–85. Diehl, C. Excursions, 46.

— Palace at. Gardner, P. New chap. Gr. hist.

Tischendorf, L. F. C. Abbot, E. Auth. 4th gosp. & ess. 155.

Tissot, James. Bate, P. H. Eng. Pre-Raph. 87.

Titchbourne, Chidiock. Disraeli, I. Curios. (N. Y. 4 v.) **2** : 346.

Titcomb, Louise. Brockett. Woman's work, 461.

Tithes and church. Peel, R. Speeches, **3** : 286, 331.

— in England. Grattan, H., sr. Speeches, **2** : 25, 82.

— in Ireland. Grattan, H., sr. Speeches, **2** : 163. — Peel, R. Speeches, **3** : 62, 549.

Tithing, Town, township and. Allen, W. F. Essays, 263.

Tithingmen. (H. B. Adams) Am. Antiq. Soc. Proc. n. s. **1** : 398.

Titian Vecelli. Bolton, S. K. Fam. Europ. art. 155. — Eastlake, E. R. Five painters, **1** : 215. **2** : 1. — Jameson. Ital. painters, 319. — Lee, H. F. Old painters, 177. — Oliphant. Makers of Venice, 291. — Spooner. Biog. fine arts, **2** : 977. — Symonds. Renais. fine arts, 379. — Taine. Italy, **2** : 301. — With portrait. Hubbard, E. Little jour. **5** : 209. — Hundred greatest men, 87. — Jervis, Lady. Painting, **1** : 214. — Rose, G. B. Renais. masters, 104. — Stillman, W. J. Old Ital. mas. 238.

— and Giuglini. Spark, W. Mus. mem. 253.

— and his times. Mitchell, D. G. Bound toge. 19.

— as a man and a painter. Bailey, J. B. Methuselahs, 113, 145.

— Assumption of the Virgin. (T. Gautier) Singleton, E. Great pic. 119.

— Bacchus and Ariadne. (C. Lamb ; E. T. Cook) Singleton, E. Great pic. 71.

Titian Vecelli, House of. Jameson. Mem. & ess. **1** ; *or* Studies.

— Story of the Venus and Adonis. Smythe, G. S. Hist. fancies, 39.

Title-pages, Old French. Lang. Books & bookm. 109.

Titles. Marshall, F. Internat. van. 95.

— of rank and office. Jones, W. A. Lit. stud. **2** : 119.

— of books. Disraeli, I. Curios. (N. Y. 4 v.) **1** : 379.

Titus, St., bishop of Crete. Blakey, R. Prim. fathers, 50. — Cave. Lives of Fathers, **1** : 118.

— and Berenice. Malkin. Class. disq. 157.

Titus, Emperor. Lynam. Rom. emp. v. 2.

— and apostle John. Williams, W. R. Eras, 21.

Tivoli, Trip to. Scollard. Und. sum. skies, 161.

— Visit to. Lowell. Writ. **1** : 132.

Tixhall, England, Historical notice of. Drake, N. Evenings, **1** : 139.

— Mary Queen of Scots at. Strickland. Queens Scot. v. 7.

Toads. Buckland, S. T. Curios. nat. hist. **1** : 1. — Wood, J. G. Out-of-doors, 146.

— enclosed in stone. Franklin. Works ('87), **8** : 184.

Tobacco. Field, Kate. Haphazard, 65. — Fothergill, J. M. Health, 144. — Greeley. Hints ref. 357. — Higginson. Out-door, 177. — Johnston, J. F. Chem. common life, **2** : 5. — Richardson, B. W. Diseases mod. life, 273. — Hutton, L. Other times, 70.

— and health. Curtis, G. W. Ars rec. viv. 65.

— and its effects on youth. (L. Dennis) N. J. Health, '92 : 107. — (A. C. Gorgas) Am. Pub. Health, **7** : 230.

— and manners. Curtis, G. W. Ars rec. viv. 69.

— Bibliography of. Fiske, J. Tobacco, 159.

— Culture of, in Nicaragua. U. S. Cons. Rept. no. 148.

— It does pay to smoke. Fiske, J. Tobacco, 5.

— Use and abuse of. Brodie. Works, **1** : 652.

Tobacco lands, Fertilizing, in Germany. U. S. Cons. Rept. no. 159.

Tocqueville, Alexis C. H. C. de. Allison. Ess. v. 3. — Dodge, M. A. Skirmish, 318. — Greg. Lit. & soc. judg. 241.

— Democracy in America. Mill, J. S. Dissert. **2** : 79.

Todd, Andrew J. Am. Bar Assoc. **17** : 532.

Todd, Major D'Arcy. Kaye. Indian off. **2** : 209.

Todd, John. Comegys. Tour, 34.

— Character of. Story, J. Miscel. 817.

Todd, Col. John, jr., 1750–82. Chicago Hist. Soc. Coll. **4** : 285.

Toebbe, Augustus Maria. Clarke, R. H. Cath. bishops, **3** : 261.

Tofts, Katharine, vocalist. Clayton, E. C. Queens, 15. — Hogarth. Mem. opera, **1** : 185. — Needham. Queens of song.

Tohopaka, Battle of. Dawson. Batt. of U. S. **2** : 327.

Toil as a boon to sorrow. Jacox, F. Cues, 174.

Tojal, Baron de. Sinclair, J. Sketches.

Tokio, Japan. Arnold, E. Seas & l. 173. — Brooks, E. S. Gt. cities, 42. — Brooks, J. Seven months, 52. — Pidgeon. Engineer's holiday, 267.

— Fires in. Arnold, E. Seas & l. 337.

— National industrial exhibition of 1890. Arnold, E. Seas & l. 314.

Tökölyi, Emerich. Wyatt, W. J. Hunga. celeb. 101.

Toland, J., and Locke. Stephen, L. Eng. thought, **1** : 94.

Told, Silas, English sailor and preacher. Dobson, A. 18th cent. vign. 168. — Thornbury. Old stor. 1. — Withrow. Makers of Meth. 113.

Toledo, Spain. Buckley, T. A. Great cities, 324. — Finck, H. T. Spain & Morocco. — Stoddard, C. A. Span. cit. 73. — Thomas, M. Scamper thr. Spain, 65. — Hale, E. E. Seven Spanish cit. 206. — Hay, J. Castil. days, 182. — Lathrop, G. P. Span. vistas, 34. — Lee, A. E. Europ. days, 334. — Prime, S. I. Alhambra, 53. — Stoddard. Red letter, 2,

— Religious persecutions in. Stoughton. Span. ref. 118.

Tolerance, The need for. Helps. Friends, 2d ser. v. 2.

Toleration. Disraeli, I. Curios. (N. Y. 4 v.) **4** : 139. — Kaye. Essays of optimist, 175. — Newman, F. W. Miscel. **3** : 162.

— and indifferentism in religion. Oxenham. Stud. in eccl. hist. 140.

— Civil and religious. Brownson. Works, 10 : 207.

— Locke on. Stephen, J. F. Horæ Sabb. **2** : 157.

— Petition of the Thugs for. (W. S. Landor) Prose masterpieces, 1 : 109.

— Religious. Stanton, H. B. Reforms, 117. — Walsh, R. Didactics, 2 : 41. — Foster, J. Crit. ess. (Bohn) **2** : 251.

— — in the U. S. Eliot, C. W. Five Am. cont. 18.

Toller, John. Woolrych. Serjeants, **2** : 502.

Tollet, Elizabeth. Williams, Jane. Lit. wom. 191.

Tolmen, The great, of Cornwall, Eng. Timbs. Abbeys, **1** : 512.

Tolstoi, Lyof, Count. Arnold, M. Ess. **2** : 253. — Panin. Lec. on Russian lit. — Vogüé. Rus. nov. 209. — Ellis, H. New spirit. — Farrar. Soc. & p. day quest. 345. — Henley. Views, 223. — Gosse, E. Crit. kit-kats. — Griswold, H. T. Personal sket. 251. — With portrait. (W. D. Howells) Warner Lib. **25** : 14985. — Howells. My lit. passions, 250. — Wolkonsky. Lowell lec. 263.

— War and peace. Crawford, V. M. Stud. for. lit. 276.

Tolstoism. Nordau. Degen. 144.

Toltecs, Who were the? Brinton. Amer. heromyths, 86.

Tom o' Bedlam's. Disraeli, I. Curios. (N. Y. 4 v.) **3** : 46.

Tomb, Egyptian, and the future state. Poole, R. S. Lec. art, 1.

Tombes, John. Ivimey. Eng. Bapt. **2** : 589.

Tombstone, Arizona, Around, on burro-back. Scollard. Und. sum. skies, 219.

Tomkins, Charles H., with portrait. Bartlett, J. R. R. I. officers, 373.

Tomkins, Cornelia M. Brockett. Woman's work, 489.

Tomkins, Daniel D., with portrait. [Amer.] Nat. portr. gall. v. 1. — Jenkins. Gov. of N. Y. 109.

Tomkins, Henry Clay. Am. Bar Assoc. **21** : 641.

Tomkins, Henry George. Miller, Jos. Singers church, 2d ed. 575.

Tomkins, John A. Bartlett, J. R. R. I. officers, 391.

Tomlinson, Russell, with portrait. (J. A. Patten) Rogers, A. C. Repres. men, 555.

Tommas, John. Ivimey. Eng. Bapt. **4** : 283.

Tompson, Benjamin. (S. A. Green) Mass. Hist. Soc. Proc. 2d ser. **10** : 263.

Toms, Robert P. Am. Bar Assoc. **7** : 317.

Tomson, Giles. McClure. Translators, 163.

Toner, Jos. M., Memorial of. (A. R. Spofford) Smithson. Rept. '96 : 637.

Tonga Islands. Alexander, J. M. Isl. Pac. 343.

— Aboriginal. McLennan. Stud. anc. **2** : 241.

Tongues, Gift of. (A. P. Stanley) Noyes, G. R. Theol. ess. 453.

Tonic Sol-Fa system. (S. M'Burney) Nat. Educa. Assoc. '88 : 633.

— Educational value of. (Daniel Bachelor) Nat. Educa. Assoc. '87 : 630.

— Notation of. (H. E. Holt; T. F. Seward) Nat. Educa. Assoc. '86 : 596.

Tonna, Mrs. Charlotte Elizabeth. Bethune, G. W. Brit. fem. poets, 311. — Hack. Consec. wom. 73. — Miles, A. H. Poets of cent. **10** : 676.

Tonsilitis, Acute specific. (S. H. Collins) Indiana Health, '90 : 201.

Tonson, Jacob. With portrait. Caulfield. Kitcat, 233. — Curwen. Booksellers, 24. — Knight, C. Old booksel. 48.

Toogood, Thomas. Drake, S. G. Trag. of wilderness, 112.

Tooke, John Horne. Brougham. Works, **4** : 95. — Foster, J. Crit. ess. (Bohn) **2** : 156. — Hazlitt. Spirit. — Rogers, J. E. T. Gleanings, **2** : 187. — Rogers, S. Recol. 151. — Tuckerman. Charac. 107. — Jesse, J. H. Cel. Eton. v. 2. — Stanton, H. B. Reforms, 36.

— Diversions of Purley. Hazlitt. Lit. rem. **1** : 331.

— In defense of. Erskine, T. Speeches, 442.

— Oddities of. Timbs, J. Eng. eccen. 444.

Tool or man? Mabie. Ess. on work, 7.

Tool-makers, Machine. Wynter, A. Our soc. bees, **2** : 171.

Tool-work, Intellectual value of. (W. T. Harris) Nat. Educa. Assoc. '89 : 92.

— Teacher of. (C. M. Woodward) Nat. Educa. Assoc. '91 : 749.

Toole, John L. With portrait. Goddard, A. Players, **1** : 337. — Matthews, B. Actors, **5** : 265. — Wilman, G. Sk. liv. celeb. 15.

— at Orme square. Yates, E. II. Celeb. **2** : 65.

Tooley, Nicholas. Collier. Actors, 233.

Toombs, Robert. Johnston, A. Amer. ora. **3** : 294. — Trent. South. statesm. 197.

— and Governor Brown. Grady, H. W. Writings & speech. 245.

Topham, Capt. Letters from Edinburgh, 1774–1775. Maxwell, Sir H. Rainy days, 101.

Toplady, Augustus Montague. Griswold, R. W. Sac. poets. — Hatfield, E. F. Poets of church, 615. — Larrabee, W. C. Wesley, **2** : 245. — Miller, Jos. Singers church, 2d ed. 274. — Pierce, B. K. Em. dead, 246. — Ryle, J. C. Chr. leaders, 358.

Topographic forms, Composite origin of. (A. P. Brigham) Am. Geog. Soc. **27** : 161.

Topsy-Turveydom, Philosophy of. Zangwill. Without prej. 137.

Torbett, Miss Allie. Raymond, I. Southland writ. **1** : 192.

Tordenskiold, Peter Wessell, *called* (1691–1720). Davenport, R. A. Lives of indiv. 188.

Torgan, Battle of. King, C. Battles, 386. — Carlyle. Batt. Fred. the Gt. 212.

Tories under Gen. Pyle, Defeat of. Dawson. Batt. of U. S. **1** : 658.

Torlonia, Alessandro, Prince. Elliot, F. Rom. gossip, 292.

Tornado, Louisville. Godbey. Great disasters, 65.

Tornadoes. Proctor. Light sci. **1** : 153. — Shaler. Aspects of earth, 197.

Toronto. Hardy, I. D. Thro' cities, 51.

Toronto, Montreal and. Arnold, E. Seas & l. 28.
— Sewerage in. (A. Macdougall) Am. Pub.
Health, 12 : 41.
Torotszkai, Matthew. Wallace, R. Anti-Trin.
biog. 2 : 454.
Torpedo (Animal), Experiments on. Davy.
Works, 6 : 359.
Torralva, Eugene, the magician. Wright, T.
Nar. sorcery, 2 : 1.
Torrance, W. H. Miller, S. F. Bench of Ga.
v. 2.
Torrens, Colonel. Grant, J. Recoll. of Ho.
Comm. 188.
Torrens system. Bibliography. Providence Pub.
Lib. Bull. March, '96.
Torres Naharro, Bartolomé. Montgomery. Men
of Ita. 3 : 97.
Torrey, Ebenezer. Am. Antiq. Soc. Proc. n. s.
5 : 372.
Torrey, Henry W. (W. Everett) Am. Acad.
A. & S. Proc. 29 : 448. — (W. W. Goodwin)
Mass. Hist. Soc. Proc. 2d ser. 6 : 197.—Vaille
& Clark. Harv. book, v. 1.
Torrey, John. Youmans. Pioneers sci. 327.
Torrington and Appledore, Eng. Timbs. Ab-
beys, 1 : 480.
Torstenson, Leonard von. Cust. Warriors
thirty years, 2 : 391.
Torture. Lea. Supers. & force, 281.
Toru Dutt. Chapman, E. F. Sk. Ind. wom. 91.
Total depravity. Dodge, M. A. Summer rest,
255.
Totem, Import of, in Omaha tribe. (Alice C.
Fletcher) Smithson. Rept. '97 : 577.
Totem-clans in the Old Testament, Are there?
Jacobs, J. Stud. bibl. arch. 64.
Totems and Totemism. McLennan. Stud. anc.
2 : 489. — Wake. Serpent wor. 247.
— belief in descent from animal to plant. Clodd,
E. Myths, 99.
Totnes, George Carew, earl of. Lodge. Por-
traits (Bohn), v. 3.
Totness Castle. Timbs. Abbeys, 1 : 479.
Tottel's Miscellany. Morley, H. Eng. writ. 8 :
212.
Touch, Lightness of. Mabie. My study fire, 2 :
63.
Touching for the evil. Smythe, G. S. Hist. fan-
cies, 88.
Tougaloo University. U. S. Bur. Ed. Circ. '99,
no. 2 : 259.
Toulmouche, A. Hamerton. Contem. Fr.
painters.
Toulouse. James, H. Little tour, 130.
— Battle of. Adams, W. H. D. Eng. at war, 1 :
357.
— Siege of. Robson, W. Sieges, 233.
Touraine, Early history of. Cook, T. D. Old
Touraine, 1 : 10.
— Grottoes of. Adams, W. H. D. Fam. caverns,
47.
Tourgénieff. See Turgénieff.
Tourists, European, Hints to. Fulton, C. C.
Europe, 311.
Tournai, Sieges of. Robson, W. Sieges, 289.
Tournaments. Cutts, E. L. Scenes mid. ages,
423.
Tournefort, J. P. de. St. John. Cel. travelers,
2 : 7.
Tourneur, Cyril. Choate, I. B. Wells of Eng.
159. — Henley. Views, 106. — Gosse, E. Jaco-
bean poets, 159. — Minto, W. Eng. poets,
357.
Tourneux, Nicholas le. Miller, Jos. Singers
church, 2d ed. 106.

Touro, Judah. (A. Walker) Hunt, F. Am. merch.
2 : 441.
Tours. James, H. Little tour, 2.
— and its surroundings. Cook, T. D. Old Tou-
raine, 2 : 215.
— Battle of. Creasy. Fifteen battles, 152. —
King, C. Battles, 178. — Archer. Decis. ev. 68.
— Cathedral of. Larned, W. C. Churches & C.
25.
Toussaint l'Ouverture. See L'Ouverture, T.
Tovey, Mary S. Clayton, E. C. Eng. fem. art.
2 : 143.
Tower, Levi. With portrait. Bartlett, J. R.
R. I. officers, 127. — Shea, J. G. Fallen brave.
Tower of London. Guild. Over the ocean, 202.
— Harrison, F. Choice of bks. 275. — Wal-
lace, S. C. Bosphorus, 129.
— and its memories. Timbs. Abbeys, 1 : 15.
Towle, Edwin R. Hemenway. Poets of Vt. 328.
Towles, Catherine W. Raymond, I. Southland
writ. 2 : 594.
Town and gown. Higginson. New world, 161.
— township, and tithing. Allen, W. F. Essays,
263.
Town councils and social reform. (S. A. Bar-
nett) Barnett, S. A. Prac. socialism, 62.
— in Scotland. Miller, H. Lead. articles, 378.
Town government and church government in
New England, Study of. Adams, C. F. Three
episodes, 2 : 581.
Town histories, New England. Bibliography.
Springfield (Mass.) Lib. Bull. May, June, '94.
Town improvement, Central and local action in.
(T. Taylor) Trans. Soc. Sci. Lond. '57 : 473.
Town meeting, Colonial. Hart. Am. govt. 133.
— The New England. Adams, C. F. Three epi-
sodes, 2 : 810, 965.
Town meetings in New England. Pidgeon. Old
world ques. 91.
— Origin and character of. Fiske. Am. polit.
ideas, 17.
Town Records, Great Britain. Bibliography.
Am. Hist. Rev. Oct. '96 : 191.
Towneley, Charles. Edwards, E. Founders
Brit. Mus. 1 : 369.
Towneleys of Towneley. Espinasse. Lanc.
worth. v. 2.
Townley, James. Wesley & successors, 125.
— High life below stairs. Goldsmith. Miscel.
(N. Y. 4 v.) 1 : 101.
Towns, G. W. Miller, S. F. Bench of Ga. v. 2.
Towns, British, Rise of. Shaw, A. Munic. govt.
Gt. Brit. 20.
— English, Origin and growth of. Jessopp, A.
Studies, 112.
— French and English. Freeman. Hist. ess. 4 : 25.
— in Massachusetts, Origin of. (M. Chamber-
lain) Mass. Hist. Proc. 2d ser. 5 : 265. — (A.
C. Goodell, jr.) Mass. Hist. Proc. 2d ser. 5 :
320. — (C. F. Adams) Mass. Hist. Proc. 2d
ser. 7 : 174, 441.
— in New England, Origin, organization, and in-
fluence of. (J. Parker) Mass. Hist. Proc. 9 :
14.
— may be too large. Helps. Soc. pressure, 7.
— Political activity of Mass., in Revolution. (H.
A. Cushing) Am. Hist. Assoc. Rept. '95 : 105.
— Small country, Future of. Higginson. Conc.
all, 67.
— Trees in. Beecher. Star papers, 129.
Townsend, Alexander. Loring, J. S. Hundred
Bost. ora. 349.
Townsend, Eliza. Griswold. Fem. poets, 38.
Townsend, Geo. Morison, J. Fathers of Lond.
Miss. Soc. 2 : 451.

Townsend, Mrs. Gideon. Raymond I. Southland writ. 1 : 381.

Townsend, John. Morison, J. Fathers of Lond. Miss. Soc. 2 : 309.

Townsend, Mrs. Mary Ashley. Derby, J. C. Fifty years, 667.

Townshend, Charles, Viscount. Creasy. Etonians, 196.

Townshend, T. Jesse, J. H. Cel. Eton. v. 1.

Townson, Thomas, Discourses of. Blunt. Ess. 293.

Toynbee, Arnold. Cochrane, R. Benef. lives, 133. — With portrait. Japp. Good men, 139. — Price. Hist. pol. econ. in Eng. 183.

Toynbee, Joseph. Bettany. Em. doctors, 2 : 272.

Toynbee Hall. Cochrane, R. Benef. lives, 141. — Woods, R. A. Eng. social movements, 79.

Toys, How and where made. Wynter. Fruit, 1 : 173.

— of the day. Wynter, A. Fruit, 2 : 118.

Trabea, Quintus. Dunlop, J. Rom. liter. 1 : 255.

Tracks, John. Winslow, S. N. Biog. Phila. merch. 225.

Tract XC. and its consequences. Froude. Short stud. 4 : 193.

Tractarian controversy. Thirlwall, C. Remains, 1 : 24.

Tractarian school, The Oxford. Rogers, H. Ess. 2 : 58.

Tractarianism, Recent developments of (1844). Rogers, H. Ess. 2 : 150.

Tractarians. Froude. Short stud. 4 : 166.

Tracts for the Times. Hunt, J. Rel. thought 19th cent. 115. — Mozley. Reminis. 1 : 312. — Wiseman, N. Ess. 2 : 27, 161.

Tracts, On. Haven, N. A. Remains, 69.

Tracy, Albert H. Proctor. Lawy. of N. Y. 466.

Tracy, Frederick Palmer. (R. W. Allen) N. E. Hist.-Gen. Soc. Biog. 4 : 125.

Tracy, Uriah. Moore, F. Am. eloq. 1 : 431.

Tracy, Mme. Victor de. Cracroft. Ess. 2 : 243.

Trade, American, Regulation of, before 1789. — (W. C. Fisher) Am. Hist. Assoc. 3 : 467.

— Balance of. Greeley. Ess. pol. econ. 60. — Haven, N. A. Remains, 147.

— Depression of. Kempner, W. Common sense soc. 185.

— — Social aspect of. (S. Bourne) Trans. Soc. Sci. Lond. '79 : 673.

— — Why greater in material producing countries than in manufacturing. Giffen. Ess. finance, 133.

— Foreign, and reciprocity. (Franklin MacVeagh; R. W. Dunham) Sunset club echoes, 195.

— — Policies of various countries in regard to, 1898. U. S. Cons. Rept. 59 : 161.

— International. Elder, W. Questions, 176.

— is over-manned. Kempner, W. Common-sense soc. 249.

— Morals of. Smalley. Lond. lett. 2 : 373. — Spencer, H. Ess. (N. Y.) 107.

Trade dollars. (J. C. Hallock) Phila. Soc. Sci. Assoc. '86.

Trade journals. Hatton. Jour. Lond. 212.

Trade life, Duration of. N. J. Labor, '83 : 81. '84 : 205. '85 : 112. '89 : 3.

Trade-mark laws of the American republics. Bur. Am. repub. no. 3.

Trade-marks, Fraudulent imitations of. (A. Ryland) Trans. Soc. Sci. Lond. '59 : 229.

Trade organizations in Illinois. Ills. Labor, '86.

Trade reform. Greeley. Hints ref. 342.

Trade schools. N. Y. Labor, '86.

— their place in industry, educa., and philanthropy. (C. R. Richards) Conf. char. & correc. '95 : 195.

Trade union label, The. (J. G. Brooks) U. S. Lab. Bull. 3 : 197.

Trades and professions. Hamerton. Intellec. 395.

— Effect of certain Sheffield, on life and health. (J. C. Hall) Trans. Soc. Sci. Lond. '65 : 382. See Occupations.

Trades teaching in juvenile reformatories. (T. J. Charlton) Conf. char. & correc. '97 : 115.

Trades-unionism. Vaughan, D. J. Questions, 77.

Trades-unions. Baring-Gould. Germany, 388.

— Address to. Bax. Relig. of socialism, 154.

— and the relations of capital and labor. (J. Gostick) Cobden Cl. ess. 2 : 357.

— Agricultural. Davies, J. L. Theol. & mor. 260.

— and labor organizations. N. J. Labor, '81 : 109. '87 : 3, 65, 101, 153.

— and their tendencies. (E. Potter) Trans. Soc. Sci. Lond. '60 : 755.

— Benevolent features of. (J. D. Flanigan) Conf. char. & correc. '96 : 154.

— Bibliography. (R. A. Peddie) Webb, S. & B. Hist. trade unionism. — Springfield (Mass.) Pub. Lib. Bull. March, '94. — Webb, S. & B. Indust. democracy.

— Evil of. Greg, W. R. Pol. prob. 110.

— Fellow-crafts. Heckethorn. Sec. soc. 2 : 61.

— Guilds and. Mass. Labor, '71 : 12.

— History of. Ohio Labor, '85–86.

— in England, 1838–60. Nat. Assoc. Soc. Sci. Rept. on strikes, 1860.

— — Rise and progress of. Bosanquet. Ess. 215.

— in Great Britain. U. S. Lab. Bull. 1 : 166.

— Legitimacy of. Jenkin, H. C. F. Papers, 2 : 3.

— John Stuart Mill on. (J. Stirling) Grant, A. Recess, 309.

— Social effect of. (J. Watts; J. Grey) Trans. Soc. Sci. Lond. '77 : 592.

— Statistics of membership. N. J. Labor, '87 : 3.

Tradition. Arnold, T. Miscel. 272.

— Abandonment of. Hamerton. Intellec. 200.

— and race. Darmesteter. Sel. ess. 155.

— Game of. Rands, W. B. Holbeach, 1 : 133.

— Philosophy of. Morell, J. D. Philos. tend.

— Religious. Clough. Prose rem. 415.

Trafalgar, Battle of. Allen, Jos. Battles Brit. navy, 2 : 119. — Fitchett. Deeds, 290. — Low, C. R. Gt. battles, 337. — Rawson, E. K. Twenty nav. batt. 1 : 311. — Thornbury. Old stor. 138. — Valentine, L. J. Sea-fights, 218.

Trafalgar Square, The lions in. Jefferies, R. Toilers, 321.

Tragedians. See Actors.

Tragedy. Hume. Philos. works, 3 : 237.

— Ancient and modern. Symonds. Greek poets, 2 : 145.

— Domestic, in England. Symonds. Shakesp. pred. 412.

— English. Procter, B. W. Ess. 2 : 82.

— Ethics of. Hudson. Studies Wordsworth, 296.

— The first English. Adams, W. D. Famous books, 57.

— Greek and French compared. Astié. Louis XIV, 224.

— — Nature of. (A. W. Schlegel) Donaldson. Theatre of Greeks, 330.

— Moral effects of a good. Knox. Essays, 3 : 23.

— Rise of, in England. Symonds. Shakesp. pred. 211.

— Rymer on. Talfourd. Crit. writ.

— Sensational, in England. Symonds. Shakesp. pred. 485.

Tragic, The. Emerson. Nat. hist. intel. 260.

— and comic, Essence of. (A. W. Schlegel) Donaldson. Theatre of Greeks, 304.

Treago, and the large tumulus at St. Weonard's. Wright, T. Ess. archæol. **1** : 48.

Treason, High, Trials for, in England, in 1817. Routledge, J. Pop. prog. in Eng. 343.

Treasure, Supposed buried, and magic. Jessopp, A. Rand. roam. 84.

Treaties and the law of nations. Thompson, J. P. Amer. com. 132.

— Obligation of. Barnard. Four lec. on diplom.

Treaty of Berlin, 1878. Disraeli. Sel. spee. **2** : 179.

— of Paris, 1763. Am. hist. leafl. no. 5.

— — 1856, an unholy alliance. Brownson. Works, **16** : 450.

— of San Stefano, 1878. Disraeli. Sel. spee. **2** : 161.

— of Washington, 1842. Peel, R. Speeches, **4** : 213, 240.

Treaty-making power, The. (H. W. Rogers) Am. Bar Assoc. **16** : 243.

Treaty obligations. Mill, J. S. Dissert. (N. Y.) **5** : 131.

Trebizond, in 1890. U. S. Cons. Rept. no. 113.

Tree, Ellen. *See* Kean, Ellen T.

Tree, H. Beerbohm, with portrait. Goddard, A. Players, **1** : 185.

Tree growth, Notes on. (A. Gray) Estes. Half-hour recr. 406.

Tree-planting for sanitary effects. (W. H. Brewer) Am. Pub. Health, **4** : 42.

Tree worship and serpent worship, Fergusson on. Cobbe, F. P. Darwinism, 175.

Trees. Whiting, C. G. Saunterer, 62. — Zangwill. Without prej. 90.

— Big, of California. Marshall, W. G. Thro' Amer. 322. — Prime, E. D. G. Around world, 46. — Taylor, B. At home, **2** : 176. — Pidgeon. Engineer's holiday, 210.

— cultivation of, Health interests in. (F. B. Hough) Am. Pub. Health, **3** : 176.

— Growth of. Abbott, C. C. Outings, 257.

— Physiology of. Allen, Gr. Science in Arc. 140.

— Sacred. King, R. J. Sket. 34.

— Shade ; overshading of houses. (W. T. Parker) Am. Pub. Health, **15** : 36.

— Towns and. Beecher. Star papers, 129.

— Uses of. Hubbard, B. Memorials, 371.

— Walk among. Beecher. Star papers, 271.

— Wayside. Abbott, C. C. Outings, 183.

Trees of liberty. Carlyle. Resc. ess. 107.

Tregelles, S. P. Abbott, E. Auth. 4th gosp. & ess. 175.

Tregian, Francis, Imprison't of. Morris, J. Troub. of Cath. v. 1.

Treitschke, Heinrich Gotthard. Tuttle, H. Ger. pol. lead. 233.

Trelawny, Jonathan, lord bishop of Bristol, etc. Strickland. Bishops, 364.

Tremaine, Sir John. Woolrych. Serjeants, **1** : 416.

Tremazzi, Ambrogio. Symonds. Renais. Cath. reac. **1** : 405.

Trembecki, Stanislaus. Soboleski. Poets of Poland, 151.

Trench, Richard Chenevix. Miles, A. H. Poets of cent. **4** : 137. **10** : 225. — Miller, Jos. Singers church, 2d ed. 489.

— Journal of. Lucas. Mornings, **1** : 300.

— Poems. De Vere. Ess. 58. — Myers. Ess. mod. 235.

Trench, Mrs. Richard, Remains of. Lucas. Mornings, **1** : 319.

Trenchard, Sir John. Woolrych. Serjeants, **1** : 421.

Trenck, Frederick, Baron. Bernard, F. Escapes, 122. — Chambers's Miscel. no. 76.

Trenck, Frederick, Baron, Adventures of. Davenport. Narr. peril. **1** : 235.

Trend, Henry. Miller, Jos. Singers ch. 2d ed. 479.

Trendelenburg, F. Adolf. Erdmann. Hist. of philos. **3** : 268.

Trent, William. Field, R. S. Prov. courts N. J. 105.

Trent, Council of. Russell, J., Earl. Ess. Chris. relig. in W. Eur. 224. — Stoughton. Ital. reformers, 277. — Symonds. Renais. Cath. reac. **1** : 97, 118.

"**Trent**" affair, The. Harcourt, W. V. Letters fr. Times.

— Bibliography. Harris, T. L. Trent Affair.

Trentham. Jewitt, L. Stately homes, **2** : 32.

Trentham Hall. Edwardes, C. Hist. houses.

Trenton, Battle of. Dawson. Batt. of U. S. **1** : 196. — Lodge & Roosevelt. Hero-tales, 43.

— Bibliography. Stryker, W. S. Battles Trenton & Princeton.

Trenton falls, N. Y. Curtis, G. W. Lotus, 59. — Taylor, B. At home, **2** : 396.

Trescot, William Henry. Davidson, J. W. Writ. of South, 576.

Tresilian, Sir Robert, chief justice of England, 1380–88. Campbell. Ch. just. **1** : 103. — Foss. Judges, **4** : 102.

Trets and Gardanne. Baring-Gould. Troubland, 156.

Trèves. Bartley, G. C. D. Rhine, 273. — Freeman. Hist. ess. **3** : 68.

— Holy coat of. Cust. Ling. & orient. ess. 465.

Treviranus, Gottfried Rheinhold. Osborn. From Greeks, 187.

Trevisanus, Julius. Wallace, R. Anti-Trin. biog. **2** : 118.

Trévison, Bernard. Waite, A. E. Lives of alchem. 124.

Trevithick, Richard. Walker, W., jr. Men of sci. 126.

Trevor, Arthur. Grant, J. Recoll. Lords & Comm. **2** : 101.

Trevor, Sir John. Campbell. Ld. chan. **5** : 36. — Foss. Judges, **8** : 64. — Manning, J. A. Speakers, 383.

Trevoux, Dictionary of. Disraeli, I. Curios. (N. Y. 4 v.) **4** : 120.

Trial, An extraordinary. Cumming, C. F. G. Wand. in China, **1** : 356.

— proper mode of, An inquiry into. (G. W. Biddle) Am. Bar Assoc. **8** : 201.

Trials and proofs of guilt in superstitious ages. Disraeli, I. Curios. (N. Y. 4 v.) **1** : 232.

— Pitcairn's Criminal. Maxwell, Sir H. Rainy days, 111.

Triangle, Properties of the. (Morley) Haverford Coll. Stud. no. 3.

Trianon, The Little, and La Malmaison. Challice. Fr. palaces, 283.

Tribolo, Niccolo Braccini. Perkins, C. C. Tusc. sculp. **2** : 164.

Trichinæ. (A. Hazlewood) Mich. Health, '75 : 29.

— at New Orleans abattoir. (C. B. White) Am. Pub. Health, **7** : 135.

— at San Antonio, Tex. (J. R. Smith) Am. Pub. Health, **7** : 145.

— History, pathology and diagnosis of. (J. M. Partridge) Am. Pub. Health, **7** : 140.

— in Massachusetts in 1870. Mass. Health, '71 : 46.

— in relation to public health. (F. S. Billings) Mass. Health, '79 (1st) : 25.

— in swine. (E. L. Mark) Mass. Health, '88 : 13.

Trichinæ, Natural history of. (N. Cressy) Conn. Health, '81 : 245.

Trichinosis. Mass. Health, '83 : 179. — (M. G. Motter) Penn. Health, '92 : 325.

— Prophylaxis of. (A. Abrams) California Health, '84–86 : 149.

Trichotomy. Whedon. Ess. 2 : 70.

Trieste. Freeman. Subj. Venice, 85. — Fulton, C. C. Europe, 78. — Howells. Ital. jour. 264.

— and general politics in that quarter. Burton, Isabella. Arabia, 30.

— Vienna to, Road from. Taylor, B. At home, 1 : 102.

Treffry, Richard, sr. Wesley & successors, 133.

Trifle-blindness. Tollemache. Ess. & mock ess. 19.

Trifles, Exaggeration of the power of. Mathews. Conversers, 100.

Trigonometry of the Brahmins. Playfair, J. Works, v. 3.

Trimmer, Mrs. Sarah K. Burder. Pious wom. 514. — Elwood. Lit. ladies, 1 : 202. — Yonge. Good wom. 2 : 268.

Trinidad and Tobago, Affairs in, 1891. (W. P. Pierce) U. S. Cons. Rept. 37 : 246.

— Trade of, 1893. (W. P. Pierce) U. S. Cons. Rept. 42 : 395.

Trinity a practical truth. Bushnell. Building eras, 106.

— Bushnell on. Brownson. Works, 7 : 22.

— Controversy on. Martineau, J. Ess. 2 : 525.

— Doctrine of, Oxlee on. Coleridge. Lit. rem. 4 : 308.

— — Sherlock's vindication of. Coleridge. Lit. rem. 4 : 184.

— The Hindu. Barth, A. Relig. India, 179.

— in unity. Maurice, F. D. Theol. ess. 410.

Trinity Church, York, Ghost at. Baring-Gould. Yorks. odd. 1 : 1.

Trinity College, Hartford, Conn. College book, 263. — U. S. Bur. Ed. Circ. '93, no. 2 : 237.

Trinity College, Randolph Co., N. C. U. S. Bur. Ed. Circ. '88, no. 2 : 113.

Tripataka, The. Barth, A. Relig. India, 102.

— Teachings of. Alviella. Contemp. evol. 297, 309.

Tripoli, Bombardments of. Dawson. Batt. of U. S. 2 : 38.

— War with. Dix. Speeches, 2 : 383.

"Tripoli," ship, Capture of. Dawson. Batt. of U. S. 2 : 35.

Triqueti, Henri, Baron de. Marmor Homericum. Palgrave. Ess. on art, 273.

Trissino, Gian Giorgio. Stebbing. Ital. poets, v. 2. — Symonds. Renais. It. lit. 2 : 126, 300.

Tristan. Dippold. Great epics.

Tristram, T. H., with photo. Cooper, T. Men of mark, 6 : 23.

Tristrem, Sir. Cox & Jones. Romances, 245.

Tritons and men of the sea. Hunt. Day by fire, 206.

Troas. Gardner, P. New chap. Gr. hist. — Kinglake. Eothen, 31.

Troglodytes, Home of. (E. T. Hamy) Smithson. Rept. '91 : 425.

Trollope, Anthony, with photo. Cooper, T. Men of mark, 3 : 2. — Friswell. Mod. men of l. 135. — Hawthorne, J. Confess. 140. — James, H. Par. portr. 97. — Wotton. Word portraits, 313. — Harrison, F. Stud. early Vict. 183. — Saintsbury. Correc. imp. 172. — Heywood, J. C. How they strike, 78. — Paladin. Glances, 100. — With portrait. (J. G. Cooke) Warner Lib. 25 : 15031. — Wilman, G. Sk. liv. celeb. 60.

Trollope, Frances Milton. Holloway, L. C. Mothers of gt. men, 375. — Horne, R. H. New spirit, 141.

Tromp, Cornelis van. De Liefde. Dutch adm. 296.

Tromp, Marten Harperts (van). De Liefde. Dutch adm. 60.

Troop-ship Bombay (dismasted), Life on, in 1858. Ingram. Hearts ot oak, 172.

Troost, Gerard. Youmans. Pioneers sci. 119.

Tropical America, Economic importance of geological and physical conditions in. (F. C. Nicholas) Am. Geog. Soc. 29 : 55.

Tropics, Educational value of the. Allen, Grant. Science in Arc. 21.

Troppmann, Case of. Morse, J. T., jr. Famous trials.

Trotter, John. Jerdan. Men, 421.

Troubadours. Mitchell. Wet days, 87.

— Ancient and modern. Hueffer. Ital. stud. 106.

— Bibliography. Smith, J. H. Troub. at home.

— Female. Bryant. Prose, 1 : 103.

— Jewish. Karpeles. Jew. lit. 169.

— Literature of. Wright, T. Ess. archæol. 2 : 194.

— Loves of. Jameson. Loves of poets.

Troubles and adversity. Friswell. Gentle life, 2 : 36.

Troughton, Edward. Lonsdale. Worthies Cumb. v. 6. — Walker, W., jr. Men of sci. 132.

Troup, Gov. George M. Sparks, W. H. Memories, 124.

Trouson du Coudray, Guillaume A. Senior. Biog. sk. 94.

Trout, Speckled. Burroughs, J. Locusts, 107.

Trout fishing with the dry fly. Lang. Leaders, 197.

Trouting. Beecher. Star papers, 144, 161.

Trouting tattle. Maxwell, H. Post-mer. 297.

Troy, Daniel Shipman. Am. Bar Assoc. 19 : 619.

Troy, Jean-Francis de. Dilke. Fr. painters 18th cent. 29.

Troy, Ancient, Modern siege of. Barrows, S. J. Isles of Greece, 357.

— Siege of. Robson, W. Sieges, 10, 433.

Troyon, Constant. Hamerton. Contem. Fr. painters. — (W. H. Howe) Van Dyke, J. C. Mod. Fr. mast. 143.

Trowbridge, J. T. Rideing. Boyhood. — Stoddard, R. H. Poets' homes, 45.

Trowbridge, Wm. Petit. (G. Lanza) Am. Acad. A. & S. Proc. 28 : 398.

Truancy. See Absenteeism.

Truants and incorrigibles, Care of. (E. P. Seaver) U. S. Bur. Ed. Rept. '91–92 : 775.

Trublet, Nicolas Charles Joseph. Houssaye. Men of 18th cent. 2 : 185. — Men & wom. of France, 3 : 28.

Truck system. Missouri Labor, 1889.

— in England. Mass. Labor, '72 : 568.

— in New Jersey. N. J. Labor, '82 : 81. '85 : 278, 284, 365. '87 : 186.

Truedel, Frau. Hack. Consec. wom. 55.

Trueman, Rev. (d. between 1780 and 1790). Redding. Misers, 1 : 39.

Trumbull, Benjamin. Headley, J. T. Chaplains Revol. 233.

Trumbull, James Hammond. Am. Antiq. Soc. Proc. n. s. 12 : 16.

Trumbull, John. With portrait. [Amer.] Nat. portr. gall. v. 1. — Baker, W. S. Portr. of Wash. 84. — Everest. Poets of Conn. 35. — Griswold. Poets Am. 36. — Lester. Artists, 137. — Spooner. Biog. fine arts, 2 : 994. —

Tuckerman. Artists, 82.—Tuckerman. Artist-life, 36.—Lanman, C. Haphazard, 379.—Lossing. Em. Amer. 196, 259.—With portrait. Mitchell, D. G. Am. lands, 152.—Nichol. Amer. lit. 88.

Trumbull, John. McFingal. Mitchell, D. G. Amer. lands, 147, 152.—Richardson. Amer. lit. 2 : 11.

Trumbull, Jonathan. With portrait. [Amer.] Nat. portr. gall. v. 4.—Duyckinck. Nat. portr. gall. 1 : 102.—Lossing. Em. Amer. 43.

Trumbull, Lyman. Am. Bar Assoc. 19 : 641. — With portrait. Brockett. Men of our day, 420.—With portrait. Scott, H. W. Dist. Am. lawy. 671.

" Trumbull," frigate, and " Watt," Action between. Dawson. Batt. of U. S. 1 : 586.

Truro, T. Wilde, Lord. With portrait. Bennett, W. H. Sel. biog. 97.—Francis, G. H. Orators, 298.—Grant, J. Bench & bar, 2 : 152.—Jerdan. Men, 431.

Truscott, Sir Francis Wyatt. Ritchie, J. E. City men, 106.

Trust. Parsons, T. Mystery, 45.

— in God. Beecher. New star papers, 156.

Trustee, Whole duty of a. Williams, Syd. Forensic, 162.

Trusts and combinations. Ohio Labor, 1888–1889.

— and strikes, Law of. (U. M. Rose) Am. Bar Assoc. 16 : 287.

— Bibliography. Halle, E. V. Trusts or indust. combin. in U. S.

— charitable, Perpetual. (P. W. Bunting) Trans. Soc. Sci. Lond. '66 : 195.

— Concerning. (R. E. Thompson) Phila. Soc. Sci. Assoc. '89.

— in the U. S., Some great. (C. A. Chase) Am. Antiq. Soc. Proc. n. s. 11 : 291.

Truth. Bacon. Ess.—Helps. Friends, 1st ser. v. 1.

— and honor. Rands, W. B. Holbeach, 1 : 190.

— and truthfulness. Holland, J. G. Lessons, 68.

— and truths. Thompson, H. M. Copy, 292.

— Authoritative. Rands, W. B. Holbeach, 2 : 151.

— Departures from. Friswell. Gentle life, 2 : 157.

— Discrimination in teaching the. Hall, John. Papers, 274.

— Equilibrium bet. physical and moral. (Theo. D. Woolsey) Bost. lectures, '70 : 145.

— A fragment on. Jenkin, Fl. Papers, 1 : 264.

— Imperiousness of. Dodge. Sermons to clergy, 9 : 1.

— Love of. Burton, N. J. Yale lec. 480.—Thomson, E. Essays, 191.

— Mysterious. Mozley, J. B. Lec. 102.

— of intercourse. Stevenson, R. L. Virgin. 63.

— Pursuit of. Martineau, H. Miscel. 2 : 174.

— Some guessers at. Stevenson. Lives & deeds, 290.

— Test of; Mill vs. Hamilton. Spencer, H. Ess. (N. Y.) 383.

— versus edification. Greg. Lit. & soc. judg. 309.

"Truth," London. Hatton, J. Jour. Lond. 96.

Truth-hunting, disparaged as an occupation. Birrell. Obiter, 1 : 96.

Truths, First. Mivart. Lessons from Nature, 29.

Tschaikowsky and his Pathetic symphony. Runciman, J. F. Old scores, 257.

Tshimsian language. (J. Campbell) Roy. Soc. Can. 2d ser. 4 : § 2, 23.

Tua, Teresina, with portrait. Ehrlich, A. Cel. violin. 28.

Tubercular bacilli. (C. S. Bond) Indiana Health, '90 : 176.

Tuberculosis. (N. E. Wordin and others) Am. Pub. Health, 20 : 130.

— and the food supply. (D. E. Salmon) Am. Pub. Health, 19 : 196.

— and insanity. (L. Irwell) Am. Pub. Health, 22 : 264.

— and milk supply. (M. P. Ravenel) Am. Pub. Health, 23 : 289.

— — in New York. (F. O. Donohue) Am. Pub. Health, 20 : 156.

— Bovine. Iowa Health, '97 : 266.—(A. G. Young) Maine Health, '86 : 219.—(C. Curtice) N. C. Health, '97–98 : 178.

— — and public health. (D. H. Bergey) Am. Pub. Health, 23 : 310.

— — in New Hampshire. (I. A. Watson) Am. Pub. Health, 24 : 147.

— Cause and prevention of. (J. M. Emmert) Iowa Health, '97 : 128.

— Dangers of. (B. F. Lyle) Conf. char. & correc. '99 : 129.

— 4th Congress of, at Paris, 1898. (E. A. de Schweinitz) Am. Pub. Health, 24 : 287.

— in cattle. Iowa Health, '95 : 112.

— in Guadalajara, Mexico. (J. M. Benitez) Am. Pub. Health, 18 : 210.

— in milch cows, Tuberculin test for. (D. S. White) Ohio Health, '96 : 5.

— in relation to industry and public health. (J. Law) Iowa Health, '95 : 126.

— Influence of habitation in development of. (M. Gutierrez) Am. Pub. Health, 19 : 202.

— Municipal responsibility in the spread of. (G. F. Keene) Conf. char. & correc. '99 : 118.

— Origin and prevention of. (D. E. Salmon) Am. Pub. Health, '14 : 92.

— Place of the state in dealing with. (P. H. Bryce) Am. Pub. Health, 23 : 277.

— Prevention of. Am. Pub. Health, 16 : 60. 19 : 208.

— — and restriction of, in man. (E. Playter) Am. Pub. Health, 15 : 122.—(N. E. Wordin) Am. Pub. Health, 20 : 130.—(J. M. O'Donnell) Am. Pub. Health, 20 : 137.

— Pulmonary. N. H. Health, '93 : 121.

— — in Mexico. (A. J. Carbajal) Am. Pub. Health, 18 : 43.

— Transmission of, from meat and milk. (N. Cressy) Conn. Health, '80 : 219.

— transmitted by syphilitic contagion. (M. Carmona y Valle) Am. Pub. Health, 19 : 204.

Tuckahoe, estate of the Randolphs. Glen, T. A. Colon. mans. 1 : 433.

Tuckahoe or Indian bread. (J. H. Gore) Smithson. Rept. '81 : 687.

Tucker, Abraham. Light of nature. Stephen, J. F. Horæ sabb. 57.

Tucker, Charlotte [A. L. O. E.] (Emily Marshall) Oliphant. Wom. novelists, 293.

Tucker, George Herriot. (W. B. Trask) N. E. Hist.-Gen. Soc. Biog. 4 : 441.

Tucker, John. Carson, H. L. Sup. Ct. of U. S. 571.

Tucker, John Henry. (J. W. Cotton) Harvard mem. biog. 2 : 348.

Tucker, John Randolph. Am. Bar Assoc. 20 : 553.—With portrait. Scott, H. W. Dist. Am. lawy. 671.

Tucker, Mrs. Mary E. Davidson, J. W. Writ. of South, 577.—Raymond, I. Southland writ. 1 : 393.

Tucker, Rhoda P. Hemenway. Poets of Vt. 38.

Tuckerman, Edward. Am. Antiq. Soc. Proc. n. s. 4 : 83.

Tuckerman, Henry Theo. Griswold. Poets Am. 433. — Griswold. Prose writ. 531.

Tuckerman, Joseph. Channing. Works, 6 : 91. — (Mary Carpenter) Ware, W. Am. Unita. 2 : 31.

Tudor, Frederick, ice exporter. Parton. Capt. indus. 156.

Tudor, Lady Mary. With portrait. Costello. Englishwomen, 3 : 303. — Burke, S. H. Hist. portr. Tudor, 1 : 127.

Tudor, William. Loring, J. S. Hundred Bost. ora. 135, 229. — Mass. Hist. Coll. 2d ser. 8 : 285.

Tudor, William, jr. (C. C. Smith) Mass. Hist. Proc. 1 : 429.

Tudor Exhibition, Impressions from. Guiney. Patrins, 39.

Tudors, Plantagenets and. Forster, J. Hist. ess. 1 : 177.

Tufton, Sackville, earl of Thanet, Proceedings against. Erskine, T. Speeches, 541.

Tufts, Henry, a New England vagabond. Higginson, T. W. Travelers, 88.

Tufts College, Medford, Mass. (E. H. Capen) U. S. Bur. Ed. Circ. '91, no. 6 : 271.

Tuileries. Smythe, A. S. Hist. fancies, 50.
— The Louvre and the. Challice. Fr. palaces, 95.
— Night in the garden of. Warner, C. D. Rela. of lit. 297.

"Tulchan" bishops. Taylor, W. M. Scot. pulpit, 16.

Tulipomania. Mackay. Delusions, 1 : 98.

Tull, Jethro. Mitchell. Wet days, 195.

Tullibardine, William Murray, marquis of. Thomson, Mrs. Jacobites, 2 : 92.

Tullock, John. (D. Macleod), with portrait. Ewart, H. C. Leaders, 315.

Tully's Head. Dobson, A. Eighteenth cent. vign. 28.

Tunbridge Castle. Timbs. Abbeys, 1 : 301.

Tunbridge Wells. Moulton, L. C. Lazy tours, 359.

Tung-chow, From, to Peking. Cumming, C. F. G. Wand. in China, 2 : 153.

Tunis. Baddeley. Travel-tide, 232. — Norman. Colonial France, 264.
— Algeria and, A look at. (F. A. Ober) Am. Geog. Soc. 21 : 287.
— In and about. Wallace, S. E. Storied sea, 46.
— Sieges of. Robson, W. Sieges, 197.

Tunnell, John. Wakeley. Heroes Meth. 201.

Tunnels and tunneling. Wynter, A. Fruit betw. leaves, 1 : 259.

Tuotilo of St. Gall. (A. Schultz) Dohme, R. Early mast. 21.

Tupper, Almon Pinney. Am. Bar Assoc. 21 : 712.

Tupper, Martin F. Lanman, C. Haphazard, 339.

Turberville, George. Bell, R. Lit. & sci. men, 2 : 121. — Chalmers. Eng. poets, 2 : 577. — Morley, H. Eng. writ. 9 : 30.

Turchin, Mme. Brockett. Woman's work, 770.

Turck, Eliza. Clayton, E. C. Eng. fem. art. 2 : 146.

Turco-Russian war. Forbes, A. Souvenirs, 199.

Turenne, Henri de la Tour D'Auvergne, Vicomte de. Cust. Warriors civ. 1 : 5. — James, G. P. R. Commanders, 2 : 9. — Wilson, J. G. Illus. sol. 151. — Morris, W. O. Commanders, 12. — Richards, L. E. Glimpses, 130.

Turgénieff, Ivan S. Heywood, J. C. How they strike, 265. — James, H. Par. portr. 291. — James, H. French poets, 269. — Panin. Lec.

on Russ. literature. — Zimmern. For. novelists, 2 : 3. — Vogüé. Russ. nov. 88. — Monkhouse, A. Books, 118. — With portrait. (H. James) Warner Lib. 25 : 15057. — Wolkonsky. Lowell lec. 249.

Turgot, Anne Robert Jacques, Baron de l'Aulne. Morley. Crit. miscel. 2 : 41.

Turin. Hare. Cities of No. Italy, 1 : 74. — Tuckerman. Ital. sk. 122.
— and vicinity, Reformers in. Stoughton. Ital. reformers, 1.
— Siege of. Robson, W. Sieges, 507.

Turkestan, Chinese. Younghusband. Heart of cont. 123.

Turkey. Moore, Jos. Outl. Eur. 224.
— and the east, in 1851. Forbes, E. Lit. papers, 46.
— and Greece in 1869. (C. E. Trevelyan) Grant, A. Recess, 55.
— Decline of. Alison. Ess. v. 2.
— Empire of. Cust. Ling. studies, 2 : 244. — Everett. Orat. v. 3.
— — Dismemberment of. (E. K. Alden) Am. Hist. Assoc. Rept. '95 : 501.
— European. Kinglake. Eothen, 1.
— in Asia. Taylor, B. Lands of Sar. 215.
— in European politics, 1863. Strangford. Selec. writ. 1 : 1.
— Lady Montagu in, 1715-40. St. John. Cel. travelers, 2 : 72.
— Occasional notes on, 1866-68. Strangford. Selec. writ. 1 : 69.
— Politics and customs in. Arnold, R. A. Levant, 2 : 113.
— Recollections of. Everett. Orat. v. 3.
— Russia, England and. Cobden. Polit. writ. 1 : 155.
— sultans of, Reminiscences of. Kingston, W. B. Monarchs, 2 : 1.

Turkey, The, as an American emblem. Franklin. Works ('87), 8 : 438.
— Wild, and its domestication. Caton. Miscel. 176.

Turkeys. Wood, J. G. Out-of-doors, 223.
— Rhode Island. Hazard, T. R. Miscel. 126, 308.

Túrki language, a branch of the Ural-Altaic family. Cust. Ling. & orient. ess. 4 : 17.

Turkish bath. Wynter, A. Our soc. bees, 1 : 273.
— Sanitary advantages of the. (C. H. Shepard) Am. Pub. Health, 16 : 202. — (E. Wilson) Trans. Soc. Sci. Lond. '60 : 705.
— The working class and the. (R. Monteith) Trans. Soc. Sci. Lond. '74 : 730.

Turkomans, The, and other tribes of the Northeast Turkish frontier. Palgrave. Ess. east, 142.

Turks, History of. Newman, J. H. Hist. sk. 1 : 1.
— of Constantinople. (C. M. Kennedy) Vaca. tourists, 3 : 77.

Turnbull, George. McCosh. Scot. phil. 95.

Turner, Charles Tennyson. (A. H. Japp) Miles, A. H. Poets of cent. 4 : 45. — With portrait. Warner Lib. 25 : 14638.
— Sonnet of. Deshler. Afternoons, 309.

Turner, Daniel. Hatfield, E. F. Poets of church, 619. — Ivimey. Eng. Bapt. 4 : 421. — Miller, Jos. Singers church, 2d ed. 202.

Turner, Dawson. Smith, C. R. Retrospec. 1 : 235.

Turner, Ely, James, and John. Trial for felony and burglary. Craik, G. L. Eng. causes cél. 86.

Turner, Francis, bishop of Ely. Strickland. Bishops, 150.

Turner, George F. Bartlett, J. R. R. I. officers, 263.

Turner, Joseph M. W. Bolton, S. K. Fam.
Europ. art. 396. — Buxton, H. J., *et al.* Eng.
paint. 127. — Eng. painters Georgian, 89. —
Fairholt. Eng. artists, 71. — Knight, W.
Wordsworthiana, 267. — Redgrave. Century
of p. **2** : 80. — Rossetti, W. M. Fine art, 291.
— Russell, W. Eccen. 276. — Smiles. Self-
help. — Spooner. Biog. fine arts, **2** : 997. —
Timbs. Anec. liv. painters, 309. — Hubbard,
E. Lit. jour. **1** : 109 — With portrait. Ollier,
E. Brit. portr. paint. 90. — Ruskin. Arrows,
v. **1**.
— and Ruskin. Cook, D. Art in Eng. 316.
— Fighting Témeraire. (J. Ruskin) Singleton, E.
Great pic. 306.
— Liber studiorum. Wedmore. Studies, 2d ed.
165.
Turner, Nat., Insurrection of. Higginson, T. W.
Travelers, 276.
Turner, Sharon. Jerdan. Men, 441.
Turner, "Squire." Livingston, J. Em. Am.
lawy. 634.
Turner, William. Trial for felony and burglary.
Craik, G. L. Eng. causes cél. 86.
Turner, William Wilberforce. Davidson, J. W.
Writ. of South, 580.
Turner-bund, North American. (H. Muench
and L. Garde) Cong. Educa. Chic. '93, 657.
Turpin, Chronicle of. Ludlow. Epics, **1** : 423.
Turpin, Richard. Whitehead, C. Highwaymen,
2 : 154.
Turton, David. Baring-Gould. Yorks. odd. **1** :
109.
Tusayan ritual, The. (J. W. Fewkes) Smithson.
Rept. '**95** : 683.
Tuscan cities. James. Transatl. 314.
Tuscany, Mountaineers of. Jarves. Ital. ramb.
87.
— Olive tree and olive oil in, '95. (A. S. Rosen-
thal) U. S. Cons. Rept. **50** : 317.
Tushi language, The. Latham. Opuscula, 168.
Tussaud's wax works. Guild. Over the ocean,
185.
Tusser, Thomas. Choate, I. B. Wells of Eng.
95. — Mitchell. Wet days, 138.
Tutbury castle. Mackie, C. Castles of Mary.
— Mary, Queen of Scots, at. Strickland. Queens
Scot. **6** : 7.
Tuthill, Louisa Caroline. Hart, J. S. Fem.
prose, 111.
Tuttiett, Laurence. Miles, A. H. Poets of cent.
10 : 738. — Miller, Jos. Singers church, 2d ed.
570.
Tuttle, Charles W. (E. F. Slafter) Mass. Hist.
Proc. 2d ser. **1** : 406.
Tuttle, Prof. Herbert, Historical work of. (H.
B. Adams) Am. Hist. Assoc. Rept. '**95** : 29.
Tuttle, Hiram A., with portrait. Sketches N. H.
men, 14.
Tuxpan, Mex., The city of. (E. Alcazar) Am.
Pub. Health, **18** : 215.
Twain, Mark, *pseud. See* Clemens, S. L.
Twardochleb, Matthias. Wallace, R. Anti-
Trin. biog. **2** : 517.
Tweed, W. M., Contempt proceedings in case of.
Field, D. D. Speeches, **2** : 322.
"**Tweed**," Wreck of the. Senior, W. Ship-
wrecks, 98.
Tweed ring, Rise and fall of. Tilden, S. J.
Writ. **1** : 550.
Twelfth night. Hunt, L. Seer, **2** : 115. — Win-
ter. Shad. stage, **3** : 20.
Twells, H. Miles, A. H. Poets of cent. **10** : 734.
Twentieth century. Nordau. Degen. 536.
— Therapeutics for. Nordau. Degen. 550.

Twilight accused and defended. Hunt. Wish-
ing-cap, 266.
Twinham, Eng. Freeman. Eng. towns, 165.
Twiss, Horace. Grant, J. Recoll. Lords & Com.
2 : 45.
Two brothers, The, or, Why are you a protestant ?
Brownson. Works, **6** : 244.
Two sides, The, of a thing. Hinton. Thinking,
157.
Tycho, the great lunar crater. (A. C. Ranyard)
Smithson. Rept. '**93** : 89.
Tycho Brahe. Brewster. Martyrs sci.
Tyler, Mrs. Adaline. Brockett. Woman's work,
241.
Tyler, Edward Griswold. (N. T. Clarke) N. Y.
Regents, **105** : 492.
Tyler, James Endell. Mozley. Reminis. **1** : 82.
Tyler, Joel W. Am. Bar Assoc. **17** : 533.
Tyler, John. Abbott. Lives of presidents, 274.
— Duyckinck. Nat. portr. gall. **2** : 322. —
Frost. Presidents, 305. — Lincoln. Lives of
pres. 393. — (R. A. Brock) N. E. Hist.-Gen.
Soc. Biog. **4** : 414. — (J. Fiske) Wilson, J. G.
Presidents, 195. — Thompson, R. W. Pers.
Recoll. 203.
— Inaugural message. Brownson. Works, **15** :
186.
— Social life during administration of. Ellet, E. F.
Court circles, 296.
Tyler, Mrs. John (Julia Gardiner). Gordon, L. L.
Lady Wash'n, 202.
Tyler, Mrs. John (Letitia). Gordon, L. L. Lady
Wash'n, 202. — With portrait. Holloway,
L. C. Ladies, 366.
Tyler, John Eugene. Vaille & Clark. Harv.
book, v. **1**.
Tyler, Moses Coit, with portrait. Warner Lib.
26 : 15131.
Tyler, Royall. Hemenway. Poets of Vt. 5. —
With portrait. Mitchell, D. G. Am. lands,
220.
Tyler, Samuel. Lanman, C. Haphazard, 304.
Tyler, Wat. Maurice, C. E. Eng. pop. leaders,
v. **2**. — Sergeant, L. Wiclif, 285.
Tyler, William. Clarke, R. H. Cath. bishops, **2** :
272.
Tymnes. Mills. Poets of Greece, 226.
Tyndal, John. Ivimey. Eng. Bapt. **1** : 92.
Tyndale, Wm. Adams, W. H. D. Gt. churchm.
343. — Collier, W. F. Hist. Eng. lit. 84. —
Tweedie, W. K. Earnest men, 62. — Brink.
Eng. lit. **2**, pt. **2** : 173. — Morley, H. Eng. writ.
7 : 221, 314.
— Language of. Oliphant. New Eng. **1** : 408.
Tyndall, John. With photo. Cooper, T. Men of
mark, **2** : 3. — Porter, N. Sci. & sent. 192. —
Em. persons, **6** : 79. — Jeans. Electricians, **1** :
1. — Skelton, J. Table-talk, 95. — Smalley.
Stud. 167. — With portrait. Warner Lib. **26** :
15141.
— and the theologians. Godkin. Reflections,
129.
— Belfast address. Clarke, J. F. 19th cent. ques.
128.
— in Albemarle street. Yates, E. H. Celeb. **2** :
121.
— Inaugural address. Brownson. Works, **9** : 528.
— on the religious emotions. Hinton. Thinking,
74.
Tyng, Dudley A. (J. Lowell) Mass. Hist. Coll.
3d ser. **2** : 280.
Tyng, William. Sabine. Loyalists, 655.
Types. Russell, A. P. Lit. notes, 295.
— Tricks of. Mathews, W. Men, p. & t. 295.
— Worn-out. Birrell. Obiter, **2** : 265.

Typhoid fever. (J. F. Kennedy) Iowa Health, '89 : 141. — Iowa Health, '97 : 145.

— and dysenteric diseases, Spread of. (M. A. Veeder) Am. Pub. Health, **24**: 260.

— and impure milk. (L. H. Taylor) Penn. Health, '92 : 353.

— Causation and prevention of. (V. C. Vaughan) N. H. Health, '93 : 267.

— Causes of, in Massachusetts. Mass. Health, '71 : 110.

— Depth of water in wells and. (H. B. Baker) Am. Pub. Health, **10** : 184.

— Diagnosis of, by Widal's blood reaction. (A. H. Stewart) Am. Pub. Health, **23** : 151.

— due to infected water supply. (J. L. Leal) Am. Pub. Health, **24** : 70.

— An epidemic of, in Madison, Conn., 1884. (C. A. Lindsley) Am. Pub. Health, **11** : 38.

— — in Plymouth, Pa., 1885. (B. Lee) Am. Pub. Health, **11** : 283.

— Epidemics of. (W. T. Sedgwick) Mass. Health, '92 : 667.

— Etiology of. (J. H. Kellogg) Am. Pub. Health, **18** : 296.

— — and pathology of. (H. B. Baker) Mich. Health, '96 : 142.

— How to prevent it in rural districts. (H. B. Bashore) Am. Pub. Health, **23** : 156.

— of America. (R. J. Farquharson) Iowa Health, '85 : 547.

— Origin and dissemination of. (W. T. Sedgwick) Am. Pub. Health, **19** : 235.

— Practical remarks about. (R. S. Goodwin) Conn. Health, '90 : 253.

— Preventable causes of. (R. Bartholow) Iowa Health, '87 : 33. — (R. Bartholow) Wisc. Health, '88 : 125.

— Prophylaxis of. (J. E. Woodbridge) Am. Pub. Health, **22** : 254.

— Questions concerning. (A. G. Young) Maine Health, '89 : 209.

— Recurrence of, as an endemic. (N. S. Everhord) Ohio Health, '86 : 210.

— Relation to water supplies. Mass. Health, '90 : 525.

— Serum diagnosis of. (W. Johnston) Am. Pub. Health, **22** : 248. — (F. F. Wesbrook and L. B. Wilson) Am. Pub. Health, **23** : 139.

— sporadic, Sanitary significance of. (P. Dudley) Penn. Health, '86 : 274.

— Well-pollution in relation to. (J. Hartzell) Ohio Health, '94 : 315.

Typhoid infection. (H. M. Bracken) Am. Pub. Health, **23** : 158.

Typhus fever, Etiology and prophylaxis of. (N. R. de Arellano) Am. Pub. Health, **18** : 81.

— exanthematic, Etiology of. (N. R. DeArellano) Am. Pub. Health, **18** : 81.

— in City of Mexico. (A. Martinez) Am. Pub. Health, **18** : 189.

— in Mexican Central plateau, Etiology of. (J. Chico) Am Pub. Health, **23** : 476.

— in New York city, 1881. (E. H. Janes) Am. Pub. Health, **9** : 301.

— in San Luis Potosi, Mexico. (J. E. Monjaras) Am. Pub. Health, **24**: 83.

— Mexican, as a communicable disease. (J. Chico) Am. Pub. Health, **18** : 130.

— Notes on etiology of. (J. Brena) Am. Pub. Health, **24** : 206.

— Study of pathogeny, etiology, and prophylaxis of. (F. de P. Bernaldez) Am. Pub. Health, **22** : 171.

Typography, Early schools of. Blades. Books in chains, 125.

Tyrannicide, Ethics of. Oxenham. Short stud. 406.

Tyranny of things. Martin, E. S. Windfalls, 89.

Tyrconnel, Frances Jennings, duchess of. Jesse. Court of Eng. Stuarts, **3** : 231. — Costello. Englishwomen, **3** : 286.

Tyre. Gillett, E. H. Anc. cities, 196.

— Ruins of. Tweedie. Ruined cities, 70.

— Sieges of. Robson, W. Sieges, 90.

Tyrol, The. Alison. Ess. v. 2. — Bellows. Old world, **1** : 147. — Field, H. M. Killarney, 194. — Guild. Abroad again, 317. — Temple, E. L. Old-world, **1** : 82.

— A tramp through. Lee, A. E. Europ. days, 192.

Tyrone, H. O'Neill, earl of. Taylor, W. C. Rom. biog. v. **1**.

Tyrotoxicon. Iowa Health, '89 : 26. — (V. C. Vaughan) Mich. Health, '86 : 154.

— Chemistry of. (V. C. Vaughan) Mich. Health, '87 : 177.

— Poisoning from. (V. C. Vaughan) Mich. Health, '87 : 12.

Tyrrell, Anthony, Fall of. Morris, J. Troub. of Cath. v. 2.

Tyrtæus, A. Arnold, E. Poets of Greece, 79. — Mills. Poets of Greece, 77. — Warner Lib. **26** : 15161.

Tyscovicius, John. Wallace, R. Anti-Trin. biog. **2** : 528.

Tyson, Job Roberts. (C. S. Tyson) N. E. Hist.-Gen. Soc. Biog. **3** : 226.

Tyson, Miss. Brockett. Woman's work, 663.

Tzetza, John. Browning, E. B. Ess. poets, 108.

Uberti, Bonifacio *or* Fazio degli. Symonds. Renais. It. lit. **1** : 160.

Ucello, Paolo. Symonds. Renais. fine arts, 231.

Udalism and feudalism. Davis, T. Prose, 44.

Udall, Nicholas. Dunham. Lit. & sci. men, **1** : 295. — Minto, W. Eng. poets, 139. — Morley, H. Eng. writ. **8** : 98, 153.

— Plays of. Adams, W. D. Famous books, 73.

Uganda. Latimer. Eur. in Afr. in 19th cent. 188.

— and the White Nile. (C. C. Long) Am. Geog. Soc. **8** : 285.

— Annexation of. Cust. Ling. & or. ess. **4** : 237.

— in 1890–92. Am. Geog. Soc. **24**: 613.

Ugliness, Advantages of. Mathews, W. Men, p. & t. 237.

Uhland, Johann Ludwig. Gostwick. Ger. poets, 225. — Heine. Romantic school. — With portrait. (C. H. Genung) Warner Lib. **26** : 15185.

Ujejski, Kornel. Soboleski. Poets of Poland, 425.

Ulloa, Antonio de. St. John. Cel. travelers, **2** : 320.

Ulloa, Francisco de, Discoveries of. Frost, T. Explorers, 110.

Ullswater. Rawnsley. Lit. Assoc. Eng. lakes, **2** : 42.

Ulm, Battle of, 1805. Adams, C. Gr. camp. 79.

— Campaign of. Baring, E. Staff-coll. ess. 77.

Ulman, H. Charles, with portrait. Rogers, A. C. Repres. men, 559.

Ulrich, Anton. Winkworth. Chr. singers Germ. 224.

Ulrici, Hermann. Erdmann. Hist. of philos. **3** : 256.

Ultramontane doubts. Rogers, H. Ess. **3** : 295.

Ultramontanism, Pascal and. Church, R. W. Ess. & rev.

— Rise and growth of. Oxenham. Stud. in eccl. hist. 64.

Ulu or woman's knife of the Eskimo. (O. T. Mason) U. S. Nat. Mus. Rept. '90 : 411.

U. S. Grant University, Athens and Chattanooga Tenn. U. S. Bur. Ed. Circ. '93, no. 5 : 239.

Umbrellas. Baring-Gould, S. Survivals, 129.

Umbria. Symonds, J. A. Ital. byways, 2.

Umfraville family. Burke, B. Viciss. of fam. 1 : 193.

Unbelief, Modern. DeVere. Ess. 239.

— Origin, results, and remedies of. Hole, S. R. Addresses, 82, 101, 118.

— Responsibilities of, Paget, V. Baldwin, 15; also in Coan. Ques. of belief, 1.

Uncas. Lossing. Em. Amer. 37.

Uncle Remus, *pseud. See* Harris, Joel Chandler.

Uncle Tom's Cabin in Liverpool. Peck, H. T. Good English, 299.

Unconditioned, Philosophy of the. Hamilton. Discus.

Unconscious cerebration. (W. B. Carpenter) Estes. Half-hour, v. 1.

Unction. (C. C. Grafton) Church's ministry.

— of the sick. Shipley, O. Tracts, 341.

Undenominational religious instruction. (C. W. Gent) Oxf. Ho. papers, 3 : 146.

Undergraduate life of American students. (B. P. Raymond) Nat. Educa. Assoc. '93 : 142.

"Underground Railroad." (W. H. Siebert) Am. Hist. Assoc. Rept. '95 : 395.

— Bibliography. Siebert, W. H. Underground R. R. from slav. to freedom.

Underground waters as sources of public water-supplies in Ontario. (P. H. Bryce) Am. Pub. Health, 16 : 209.

Understanding, Full assurance of. Wilks. Chr. ess. 39.

Understood, On being. Ess. from Sat. R. 140.

Undertaker, A royal. Malortie. Here, there, 252.

Underwood, John. Collier. Actors, 224.

Undwah Nálá. Malleson, G. B. Battles of India, 125.

Unemployed. Bibliography. Mass. Board on Unemp. Rept. pt. 1, '95.

— Emergency relief by work for. (P. W. Ayres) Conf. char. & correc. '95 : 96.

— How dealt with, 1893–94. Conf. char. & correc. '94 : 21.

— in Massachusetts, 1885, Statistics of. Mass. Labor, '87.

— What to do with. (W. Gladden) Conf. char. & correc. '99 : 141.

Unemployment. Mass. Bur. Lab. 93 : 1.

— and its remedies. Samuelson, Jas. Civiliz'n, 167.

Unexpected, The. Arnold, F. Three-cor. ess. 200.

Unger, William. Etchings. Hamerton. Art. ess. 1 : 88.

Ungraded schools, Report on. (Henry Sabin) Nat. Educa. Assoc. '95 : 459.

Uniformity, Act of. Disraeli. Sel. spee. 2 : 581.

Union is strength. Humphrey, H. Miscel. 9.

Union of the Colonies, Coxe's plan for. Field, R. S. Prov. courts N. J. 134.

Union of England and Ireland, Repeal of. Carlyle. Resc. ess. 15.

Union College. College book, 186.

Union Pacific railroad. Dilke. Greater Brit. 75.

— Hazard, R. G. Econ. & pol. 302.

Unionism, True. Vaughan, D. J. Questions, 242.

Unitarian Christianity. Channing. Works, 3 : 59.

Unitarian Church. (H. W. Crosskey) Relig. systems, 602.

Unitarian movement in the U. S. Renan. Studies (N. Y.), 1 : 298.

Unitarian principles and doctrines. Brigham, C. H. Mem. 392.

Unitarian protests. Lamb. Elia.

Unitarianism. Martineau, Ja. Essays, 2 : 371, 381. — Lorimer. Isms, 182. — Maurice, F. D. Kingdom of Christ, 131. — Reynolds, G. Papers, 474. — (J. W. Chadwick) Why I am, 85.

— Bibliography. Allen, J. H., & Eddy, R. Hist. Unitarians & Universalists in U. S.

— English. Alviella. Contemp. evol. 81.

— — In 1830. Taylor, I. Logic in theol 77

— in New England. Richardson. Amer. lit. 1 : 285, 308, 475.

— in the United States. Alviella. Contemp. evol. 155.

— most favorable to piety. Channing. Works, 3 : 163.

— Objections to, considered. Channing. Works, 5 : 393.

— Rise of. Stephen, L. Eng. thought, 1 : 421.

Unitarians in England, Designs of (1792). Burke. Works (Bohn), 6 :.113.

— of New England. Frothingham. Transcend. 109.

United brethren. Ker, J. Lec. hist. preach. 234.

— Bibliography. Berger, D. Hist. Unit. Breth.

United Kingdom Alliance, The. Jevons. Meth. soc. ref.

United States. Froude. Oceana, 354.

— Agriculture. (J. Jay) Am. Geog. Soc. 1 : 50, 76.

— and Canada : an historical retrospect. (J. G. Bourinot) Am. Hist. Assoc. 5 : 275.

— and Christianity. Anderson, M. B. Papers, 1 : 252.

— and England : Kin beyond sea. (W. E. Gladstone) Prose masterpieces, 3 : 151.

— and Great Britain, 1856. Brownson. Works, 471.

— — Comparison of institutions of. Gladstone. Glean. 1 : 203.

— — Walsh's appeal from judgments of Gt. Brit. Jeffrey, F. Contrib. Ed. Rev.

— and Macedonian. Roosevelt, T. Naval war 1812, 108.

— and new dependencies, Relation of. Mahan. Lessons war, 241.

— and Peru, Trade between, 1892. U. S. Cons. Rept. no. 148.

— and the States, Partition of powers. (R. M. Venable) Am. Bar Assoc. 8 : 235.

— Anti-slavery struggle. Johnston, A. Amer. ora. 2 : 3.

— Are they a nation ? Brownson. Works, 17 : 560. — Sumner. Works, 12 : 187.

— Army during civil war. (J. C. Black) Mil. ess. M. O. L. L. U. S. Ills. 443.

— — in Mexico, Memorials of officers of. Dix. Speeches, 2 : 35.

— — Lieut.-Gen. of, On bill to appoint a. Dix. Speeches, 1 : 163.

— — President's relations to. Field, D. D. Speeches, 2 : 165.

— — Reports and letters on. Hamilton. Ed. by Lodge, 6 : 71.

— Art in (1840). Bethune. Orations, 159.

— Articles of confederation, 1777. Lossing. Signers, 310.

— before the revolution. Foster, J. Crit. ess. (Bohn) 1 : 251.

— Bold diplomacy in, in 1861. (M. J. Wright) Am. Hist. Assoc. Rept. '95 : 405.

— boundary, N. E., Twenty unsettled miles in. (T. C. Mendenhall) Am. Antiq. Soc. Proc. n. s. 11 : 188.

Value. Böhm-Bawerk. Positive theory of capital. — Clark, J. B. Philosophy of wealth. — Macleod. Theory of credit, v. 1. — Marx. Capital.
— Meaning and causes of. Bolles. Chap. pol. econ. 48.
— A measure of. Bolles. Chap. pol. econ. 73. — DeQuincey. Uncollected writings, 1 : 134 ; or Writings (Masson), 9 : 32, 68. — Proudhon. Works, 1 : 73.

Vámbéry, Arminius. Adams, W. H. D. In perils, 112.
— Travels in Central Asia. Frost, T. Mod. expl. 9.

Vampires, with bibliog. Tozer. Highl. Turk. 3 : 80.
— Myths of. Scoffern. Stray leaves, 346.

Vampyrism. Davenport, R. A. Delusions, 273.

Van Alstyne, Nancy. Clement, J. Noble deeds, 223.

Van Anden, I. Parton, J. Sk. of men. of prog.

Vanbrugh, Sir John. Birrell. Men, women & books, 96. — With portrait. Caulfield. Kitcat, 147. — Crawfurd, O. Eng. com. dram. 83. — Dunham. Lit. & sci. men, 3 : 213. — Hazlitt. Comic.

Van Buren, Mrs. Angelica Singleton, with portrait. Holloway, L. C. Ladies, 339.

Van Buren, Evert. Proctor. Lawy. of N. Y. 424.

Van Buren, Mrs. Hannah Hoes. With portrait. Holloway, L. C. Ladies, 333. — Gordon, L. L. Lady Wash'n, 168.

Van Buren, John. Bungay. Off-hand, 127. — Field, M. B. Memories, 181.

Van Buren, Martin. Abbott. Lives of presidents, 241. — With portrait. [Amer.] Nat. portr. gall. v. 3. — Baldwin. Party leaders, 343. — Duyckinck. Nat. portr. gall. 310. — Frost. Presidents, 257. — Jenkins. Gov. of N. Y. 346. — Lincoln. Lives of pres. 325. — Maury, S. M. Statesm. of Am. 67. — (J. C. Welling) Wilson, J. G. Presidents, 169. — Thompson, R. W. Pers. recoll. 166.
— Administration of. Mansfield, E. D. Pers. mem. 312.
— Electors of, and electoral college for senate of Maryland. (B. C. Steiner) Am. Hist. Assoc. Rept. '95 : 129.
— Social life during administra. of. Ellet, E. F. Court circles, 234.

Van Buren, William H. Francis. N. Y. surg. 37.

Vance, Mrs. Ada Reedy. Davidson, J. W. Writ. of South, 585. — Raymond, I. Southland wr. 2 : 609.

Vance, Mary. Brockett. Woman's work, 429.

Van Cortlandt manor house. Terhune. Colon. homes, 171.

Van Cott, Maggie N. Hanaford. Wom. of cent. 460.

Vancouver Island, Coal mines of, 1892. (L. W. Myers) U. S. Cons. Rept. 40 : 23.

Van Curler, Arent. Journal, 1634-35. (J. G. Wilson) Am. Hist. Assoc. Rept. '95 : 81.

Vandals. Hodgkin. Dynasty of Theodosius, 204.

Vandeleur, Major Arthur. Rogers, C. Chr'n heroes, 104.

Vanderbilt, Cornelius, with portrait. Brockett. Men of our day, 504. — Houghton. Kings, 193. — Parton. Fam. Amer. 373. — Rogers, A. C. Repres. men, 565. — With portrait. Stoddard, W. O. Men of bus. 31.
— and Vanderbilt Univ. Bolton, S. K. Givers, 306.
— Erie railway war in 1868. Adams, C. F. Erie, 1.

Vanderbilt, Wm. H. Houghton. Kings, 253. — Parton, J. Sk. of men of prog.

Vanderbilt University, Nashville, Tenn. U. S. Bur. Ed. Circ. '93, no. 5 : 107.

Van der Helst, B. Banquet of the Arquebusiers. (W. M. Thackeray) Singleton, E. Great pic. 33.

Vanderkemp, John Theodore. Carne, J. Em. mission. 2 : 85. — Thompson, A. Gt. mission. 103.

Vanderlyn, John. Tuckerman. Artist-life, 61 ; or Artists, 126.

Van der Meire, Gerard. Crowe & Cav. Flem. painters, 147.

Van der Mey, ——. Brightwell. Heroes of lab. 209.

Vanderpoel, Aaron J. Am. Bar Assoc. 10 : 421. — Parton, J. Sk. of men of prog.

Vanderpoel, S. Oakley, with portrait. Rogers, A. C. Repres. men, 561.

Van der Weyden, Roger. Crowe & Cav. Flem. painters, 182.

Van Devanter, Isaac. Am. Bar Assoc. 22 : 678.

Van de Velde, James Oliver. Clarke, R. H. Cath. bishops, 2 : 372.

Van de Weyer, M. Sylvain, Obituary of. Em. persons, 1 : 237.

Van Dieman's Land. Chambers's Papers, no. 45.

Van Doran, Earl. Pollard. Life of Lee, 627.

Van Dyck, Antoon. Fairholt. Homes Rubens, 39. — Houssaye. Philos. 2 : 229. — Lee, H. F. Old painters, 253. — Spooner. Biog. fine arts, 2 : 1012. — With portrait. Hubbard, E. Little jour. 5 : 245. — Jervis, Lady. Painting, 2 : 157. — Van Dyke, J. C. Dutch mast. 177.
— and Sir Kenelm Digby. Thomson, Mrs. Cel. friend. 1 : 319.
— Children of Charles I. (J. Guiffrey) Singleton, E. Great pic. 300.
— Portrait of English lady by. Hazlitt. Crit. on art. ser. 2.

Van Dyke, Henry, with portrait. Warner Lib. 26 : 15237.

Vane, Charles. Whitehead, C. Highwaymen, 2 : 41.

Vane, Sir Henry. Bayne. Pur. revol. 347. — Diman. Orations, 168. — With portrait. Moore, J. B. Am. gov. 313.

Vane, Sir Henry, the younger. Fiske, J. Cent. of science, 154. — Forster. Brit. statesm. 4 : 1. — Forster. Statesm. of Comm.

Vane family. Sanford & Townsend. Gov. fam. 1.

Van Elten, Kruseman. Sheldon, G. W. Amer. painters, 196.

Vanessa, Swift's. Jameson. Loves of poets.

Van Eyck, The brothers. Conway, W. M. Early Flem. artists, 125. — Jervis, Lady. Painting, 2 : 113. — (O. Eisenmann) Dohme, R. Early mast. 209.
See also Eyck, H. van.

Van Flekwyk, Hermann. Wallace, R. Anti-Trin. biog. 2 : 272.

Van Horn, Maj., Defeat of. Dawson. Batt. of U. S. 2 : 96.

Vanini, Lucilio. Owen, J. Skeptics Ital. 345.

Vanity. Cracroft. Ess. 1 : 211.

Vanloo, Carle. Criticisms of his pictures. Guizot. Fine arts, 209.

Vanloo family, The. Houssaye. Men of 18th cent. 2 : 236. — Men & wom. of France, 3 : 85.

Van Ness, Mrs. John P. Ellet. Queens Am. soc. 264.

Van Ness, Mrs. Marcia, with portrait. [Amer.] Nat. portr. gall. v. 2.

Van Parris, George. Wallace, R. Anti-Trin. biog. **2** : 124.

Van Rensselaer, Stephen, with portrait. [Amer.] Nat. portr. gall. v. **3**. — Lossing. Em. Amer. 260.

— Funeral sermon on. Bethune. Orations, 37.

Van Rensselaers of Albany, Patroonship of. Glenn, T. A. Colon. mans. **1** : 141.

Vansittart, Nicholas. Hazlitt. Parl. portr. 34.

Van Slyck, Nicholas. Am. Bar Assoc. **16** : 445.

Vanuxem, Lardner. Youmans. Pioneers sci. 270.

Van Valkenburg, John. Am. Bar Assoc. **14** : 417.

Vanvitelli, Luigi. Milizia. Lives arch. **2** : 337.

Van Winkle, Edgar S. Am. Bar Assoc. **6** : 341.

Vapors, Latent heat of. Malloy, G. Gleanings, 28.

— noxious, Legislation relative to. (R. A. Smith) Trans. Soc. Sci. Lond. '**76** : 495.

Varchi, Benedetto. Symonds. Age of despots, 279.

Vardarelli, The, Neapolitan brigands. Macfarlane, C. Banditti, 36.

Varela, Jos. P., and education in Uruguay. Cong. Educa. Chic. '93, 56.

Varelst, Maria. Clayton, E. C. Eng. fem. art. **1** : 71.

Variation in man and woman. Pearson, K. Chances, **1** : 256.

Variations, structural, Origin of. (E. D. Cope) Brooklyn. Eth. Assoc. Life, 159.

Varina, home of Pocahontas. Terhune. Colon. homes, 432.

Varnhagen von Ense. Carlyle. Essays.

Varro Reatinus, Marcus Terentius. Dunlop, J. Rom. liter. **2** : 33.

— a Roman farmer. Mitchell. Wet days, 30.

Varus, Defeat of, by Arminius, A. D. 9. Creasy. Fifteen battles, 113.

Vasari, Giorgio, with portrait. Warner Lib. **26** : 15248.

— Lives of painters. Robinson, F. S. Connois. 185.

Vasey, George. (B. L. Robinson) Am. Acad. A. & S. Proc. **28** : 401.

Vashti, Queen. Finlayson, T. C. Ess. 175. — Hastings, F. Obscure charac. 146.

Vassar, Matthew. Brockett. Men of our day, 629. — (J. H. Raymond) N. Y. Regents, **82** : 785. — Parton. Triumphs, 90.

Vassar College. (A. C. Avery) Brackett, A. C. Educa. of girls, 346. — College book, 372. — Marshall, W. G. Thro' Amer. 56.

— Educational influence of. (C. H. Dall) Brackett, A. C. Educa. of girls, 163.

— Four years in. (James Orton) Nat. Educa. Assoc. '74 : 109.

Vatican, The. Guild. Abroad again, 179. — Hazlitt. Lit. rem. **2** : 421. — Hazlitt. Crit. on art, ser. 2.

— The child in. Paget, V. Belcaro, 17.

— In the. Sala. Journey south, 268.

Vatican Council, 1870. Thirlwall, C. Remains, **2** : 260, 290. — Mozley. Lett. fr. Rome. — Wordsworth, C. Miscel. **1** : 312. — Chatard. Ecc. ess. 41. — Deutsch. Lit. rem. 211.

— Antecedents of. Pressensé. Contem. port. 39.

— Council of Constance and. Fisher, G. P. Discus. 101.

Vatke, Wilhelm. Cheyne. Founders O. T. crit. 131.

Vattemare, Alexandre. (J. P. Quincy) Mass. Hist. Proc. 2d ser. **1** : 260.

Vauban, Sébastien le Prestre. Lloyd, E. M. Vauban.

Vaucanson, Jacques. Brightwell. Heroes of lab. 166.

Vaucluse. James, H. Little tour, 222. — Warner, C. D. Roundabout, 10.

— Fountain of. Adams, W. H. D. Fam. caverns, 60.

Vaudemont, Louise de, and Henry III. Imbert de St. A. Wom. Valois ct. 293.

Vaudois, The. Lawrence, E. Hist. stud. 198.

— Perrin's History of. Maitland, S. R. Eight ess. 187.

Vaughan, Charles John, with photo. Cooper, T. Men of mark, **6** : 2.

Vaughan, Henry, poet. Griswold, R. W. Sac. poets. — Holland, J. Psalmists, **2** : 100. — Macdonald, G. England's antiphon, 251. — Miller, Jos. Singers church, 2d ed. 92, 534. — Warner Lib. **26** : 15257. — Shairp. Sk. hist. & poetry, 350. — (G. A. Simcox) Ward. Eng. poets, **2** : 192.

Vaughan, Henry, silurist. Brown, J. Locke, etc. 309.

Vaughan, Sir John, 1769–1839. Grant, J. Bench & bar, **1** : 302.

Vaughan, Thomas ; a skeleton for a novelist. Rees, J. R. With friend, 51.

Vaughn, John. *See* Carberry, Earl of.

Vauquelin, Fresnaie. Cary, H. F. Early Fr. poets, 245.

Vauvenargues, Luc de Clapiers, marquis de. Maccall. For. biog. **1** : 99. — Morley. Crit. miscel. **2** : 1. — Vinet. Fr. lit. 18th cent. 175.

Vaux, Richard. Am. Bar Assoc. **18** : 541.

Vayringe, Philip. Davenport, R. A. Lives, 28. — Seymour, C. C. B. Self-made, 330.

Vazoff, Ivan, with portrait. (L. C. Bull) Warner Lib. **26** : 15263.

Veal, Concerning ; a discourse of immaturity. Boyd. Leis. hours (Bost.), 16.

Vecchietta, Il. Perkins, C. C. Tusc. sculp. **1** : 112.

Veda and Vedanta. Müller, M. India, 221.

— Lessons of. Müller, M. India, 161.

— Rig-. Barth, A. Relig. India, 1. — Hopkins. Relig. of India, 37.

— — Religious system of. Cook, F. C. Origins, 1.

— — Müller's translation of. Whitney, W. D. Orient, **1** : 133.

— Translation of. Whitney, W. D. Orient, **1** : 100.

Vedas, The. Colebrooke. Miscel. essays, **1** : 9. — Müller. Chips, v. **1** ; *or* Sel. ess. **2** : 109. — Müller. Phys. relig. 22. — Müller. Relig. of India, 128. — Whitney, W. D. Orient, **1** : 1. — Williams, D. Ind. wisdom. — Johnson, S. Ori. relig. India, 305.

Vedantism and the Bruhmu Subhá. Dutt. Ess. 49.

Vedder, David. Wilson, J. G. Poets of Scot. **2** : 117.

Vedder, Elihu. Sheldon, G. W. Amer. painters, 216.

Vedic deities. Müller, M. India, 195.

Vedic literature, Müller's history of. Whitney, W. D. Orient, **1** : 64.

Vedic religions. Barth, A. Relig. India, 1.

Vega, Garcilaso de la. Montgomery. Men of Ita. **3** : 36. — Ticknor. Span. lit. **1** : 486.

Vega Carpio, Lope Felix de. Montgomery. Men of Ita. **3** : 189. — Ticknor. Span. lit. **2** : 120. — Swanwick, A. Poets, 202. — With portrait. (M. F. Egan) Warner Lib. **26** : 15287.

— and Cervantes. Foster. Fr. & Span. genius, 269.

Vidal, Pierre. Rutherford. Troubadours.
Vido; a Greek quarantine. Barrows, S. J. Isles of Greece, 13.
Vidocq, Eugene F. Smith, H. G. Romance of hist. 218.
Vienna. Arnold, R. A. Levant, 2 : 291. — Bellows. Old world, 1 : 419. — Bliss, O. J. Three months in Orient, 189. — Brace, C. L. Home life, 383. — Fulton, C. C. Europe, 25. — Guild. Over the ocean, 469. — Moore, Jos. Outl. Eur. 513. — Brooks, E. S. Gt. cities, 39. — Kingston, W. B. Music & mann. 2 : 1.
— Commercial academy at, 1893. (J. Goldschmidt) U. S. Cons. Rept. 42 : 50.
— Congress of. Talleyrand. Memoirs, v. 2, 3. — Thayer, W. R. Dawn Ital. 1 : 116.
— Handels-Akademie. U. S. Cons. Rept. no. 152.
— Sieges of. Robson, W. Sieges, 451.
— by the Turks, A. D. 1683. King, C. Battles, 279.
— to Trieste, Road from. Taylor, B. At home, 1 : 102.
— Transformation of. Shaw, A. Munic. govt. Eur. 410.
Vienne. Baring-Gould. Troub. land, 294.
Vienne, Jean de. Laughton. Stud. nav. hist. 1.
Vieuxtemps, Henri, with portrait. Ehrlich, A. Cel. violin. 203.
— Personal recollections of. Phipson. Violinists, 240.
Vieyra, A. Neale. Mediæv. preachers.
Vigée Le Brun, Madame. Bolton. Fam. lead. wom. 92.
Vigilius, Bartholomew. Wallace, R. Anti-Trin. biog. 2 : 527.
Vignaud, Henri. Davidson, J. W. Writ. of South, 593.
Vigny, Alfred Victor, Count de. Mill, J. S. Dissert. (N. Y.) 1 : 312. — Pellissier. Lit. move. Fr. 165, 235, 294. — With portrait. (G. King) Warner Lib. 26 : 15341.
Vigo. Crawfurd, O. Trav. in Portugal, 1.
— Sea-fight off. Valentine, L. J. Sea-fights, 84.
Vikings ; invasions of France, England & Ireland. Taylor, W. C. Revol. 1 : 200.
— Raid of. Lanier. Music, 68.
Vilas of the South Slavs. (F. S. Krauss) Cong. Anthrop. Chic. '93, 367.
Village communities. Allen, W. F. Essays, 231.
— among early Germans. Allen, W. F. Essays, 215.
— and feudal manor. Allen, W. F. Essays, 257.
— in England. Allen, W. F. Essays, 240.
— Maine on. Mill, J. S. Dissert. (N. Y.) 5 : 143.
— Theory of. (C. M. Andrews) Am. Hist. Assoc. 5 : 47.
Villages, English community. Mackay. Engl. poor.
— English manor and. Ashley. Introduc. econ. hist.
— Religious destitution of. Crooker, J. H. Problems, 245.
Villains, Short defense of. Repplier. Ess. in min. 70.
Villani, Giovanni. Symonds. Age of despots, 253.
Villari, Pasquale. Warner Lib. 26 : 15354.
Villegas, Estéban Manuel de. Montgomery. Men of Ita. 3 : 240.
Villemain, A. F., as a critic. Pellissier. Lit. move. Fr. 272.
Villemarqué, Hersart de la. (Wm. Sharp) Warner Lib. 26 : 15377.
Villena, Henry, Marquis of. Ticknor. Span. lit. 1 : 357.

Villenage and slavery, Extinction of, in England. (E. Washburn) Mass. Hist. Proc. 7 : 308.
— in England in 1282. Jessopp, A. Coming of friars, 66.
Villerville, France. Dodd, A. B. Three Norm. inns, 1.
Villiers, Barbara. See Cleveland, Duchess of.
Villiers, Charles Pelham. Francis, G. H. Orators, 221. — Grant, J. Recoll. Lords & Comm. 2 : 189.
Villiers, Frederic. Forbes, A. Souvenirs, 141.
Villiers, George. See Buckingham, Duke of.
Villiers, George W. F. See Clarendon, Earl of.
Villiers family. Sandford & Townsend. Gov. fam. v. 2.
Villon, François. Besant. Fr. poetry, 114. — Cary. Fr. poets, 236. — Stevenson, R. L. Fam. stud. 192. — Cary, H. F. Early Fr. poets, 236. — Stevenson, R. L. Miscel. 2 : 182. — With portrait. Warner Lib. 26 : 15392.
— student, poet and housebreaker. Stevenson, R. L. Famil. stud. 191.
Vimeira, Battle of. Adams, W. H. D. Engl. at war, 1 : 268.
Vincennes University, Vincennes, Ind. U. S. Bur. Ed. Circ. '91, no. 1 : 29.
Vincent, Ferrer, St. Allies, M. H. Three cath. ref. 3. — Adams, W. H. D. Good Samar. 339.
Vincent de Paul, St. Adams, W. H. D. Good Samar. 339. — Adams, W. H. D. Heroes Chr. 385. — Maccall. For. biog. 1 : 69.
Vincent of Serius, View of Christianity. Newman, J. H. Hist. sk. 1 : 375.
Vincent of Spain, St. Charles. Martyrs, 103.
Vincent, Frank, jr. Derby, J. C. Fifty years, 701.
Vincent, Henry. Stanton, H. B. Reforms, 315.
Vincent, John Heyl, D. D. Bolton, S. K. Success, 221. — Cochrane, R. Benef. lives, 147.
Vincent, Mrs. Mary Ann, with portrait. (Geo. P. Baker) McKay, F. E. Fam. actors, 194.
Vincent, Nicholas, admiral. Redding. Pers. remin, 3 : 55.
Vincent, Samuel. Maccall. For. biog. 1 : 60.
Vincent, Strong. (W. W. Swan) Harvard mem. biog. 2 : 62.
Vincente, Gil. Montgomery. Men of Ita. 3 : 292.
Vinci, Leonardo da. Bolton, S. K. Fam. Europ. art. 66. — Eastlake, E. R. Five painters, 1 : 1. — Jameson. Ital. painters, 170. — Kent, C. Footprints, v. 1. — Knox, R. Great artists, 133. — Lee, H. F. Old painters, 50. — Pater. Stud. renais. 90. — Schlegel. Æsthetic works. — Spooner. Biog. fine arts, 2 : 1053. — Symonds. Renais. fine arts, 312. — Taine. Italy, 2 : 350. — Wallace, H. B. Art, 231. — Hundred greatest men, 71. — Jarves. Art. stud. 376. — Jervis, Lady. Painting, 1 : 85. — Ottley. Ital. school. — Perkins, C. C. Tusc. sculp. 1 : 184. — Rose, G. B. Renais. masters, 71. — Stearns, F. P. Midsum. Ital. art, 37. — Stillman, W. J. Old Ital. mas. 175.
— Last Supper. Child, T. Summ. holidays, 140. — Fuseli. Life and writ. 3 : 1. — (J. W. von Goethe) Singleton, E. Great pic. 289.
— Madonna of the rocks. (T. Gautier) Singleton, E. Great pic. 234.
— Monna Lisa. (W. Pater) Singleton, E. Great pic. 142.
— School of. Symonds. Renais. fine arts, 482.
Vinci, Leonardo, Italian opera writer. Hogarth. Mem. opera, 1 : 275.
Vinegar hill, Battle of, 1798. Thornbury. Old stor. 99.

Vitoni, Ventura. Symonds. Renais. fine arts, 83.

Vitrelinus, Alexander. Wallace, R. Anti-Trin. biog. **2** : 195.

Vitruvius. Milizia. Lives arch. **1** : 83.

— Influence of, on Italian architecture. Symonds. Renais. fine arts, 96.

Vittoria, Battle of. Adams, W. H. D. Eng. at war, **1** : 338.

Viturgia, empress of Proculus. Hall. Queens bef. conq. 100.

Vivian, Sir H. H., with portrait. Jones, E. R. Heroes of Ind. 111.

Vivian, Sir R. J. H. Laurie, W. F. B. Dist. Anglo-Ind. **2** : 16.

Vivisection. Gurney. Tertium, **1** : 204. — Hall, G. S. Asp. Ger. 18. — Japp. Vers de soc. 176. — Newman, F. W. Miscel. **3** : 369, 395. — Proctor. Light sci. **3** : 238. — Scoffern. Stray leaves, 431.

— Defense of. Playfair. Subj. soc. 82. — Wynter. Subtle brains, 55.

— Ethics of. Paget, V. Baldwin, 129.

Vladivostok. Norman, H. Far East, 141.

— and Sakhalin, Prisons in. (B. Howard) Am. Geog. Soc. **30** : 135.

Vocabularies, Pocket. Meynell, A. Rhythm, 40.

Vocal harmony : Plea for oral language in music. (H. E. Holt) Nat. Educa. Assoc. '**95** : 802.

Vocal music in public schools. (Eben Tourjee) Nat. Educa. Assoc. '**70** : 133. — (T. H. Brand) Nat. Educa. Assoc. '**85** : 376. — (O. S. Westcott) Nat. Educa. Assoc. '**87** : 610.

— Methods of teaching. (H. E. Holt) Nat. Educa. Assoc. '**85** : 396.

— a necessary branch of education. Spark, W. Mus. mem. 411.

Vocal organs, Physiology and hygiene of. (J. Howard) Nat. Educa. Assoc. '**93** : 514.

Vogel, Catherine. Wallace, R. Anti-Trin. biog. **2** : 139.

Vogel, Sir Julius. Escott, T. H. S. Pillars emp. 322.

Vogüé, Eugène Melchior de. Blaze de Bury, Y. French lit. 133. — (G. King) Warner Lib. **26** : 15439.

Voice, fervent, Nature and influence of. (W. L. Tomlins) Nat. Educa. Assoc. '**87** : 643.

— How affected by smoking. Mackenzie, M. Ess. 159.

— in speech and song. Mackenzie. Ess. 71.

— of children. (F. E. Howard) Nat. Educa. Assoc. '**97** : 784.

— Physiology and hygiene of. (J. Howard) Cong. Educa. Chic. '**93**, 514.

Voice culture in primary and elementary schools. (Z. Richards) Nat. Educa. Assoc. '**91** : 606.

Voice training and singing. (F. W. Root) Nat. Educa. Assoc. '**87** : 621.

Voiture, Vincent. Besant. Fr. humor. 199.

Voke, Mrs. Miller, Jos. Singers church, 2d ed. 349.

Volcanoes. Kingsley, C. Madame How, 54. — Kneeland. Amer. in Iceland, 247. — Lanoye. Sublime, 179. — Reclus. The earth, 505.

— and coral reefs. Dunman. Talks sci. 54.

— and earthquakes. (T. E. Hunt) Am. Geog. Soc. **2** : pt. 2, 89. — Herschel. Famil. lec. **1**. — (W. C. Williamson) Manch. sci. lec. **5–6** : 220. — Shaler. Aspects.

— in Ecuador. Orton. Andes and Amazon, 127.

— in Southern Europe. Proctor, R. A. Univ. of suns, 237.

— Mallet's theory of. Proctor. Pleas. ways, 151.

— of the Pacific coast. (S. F. Emmons) Am. Geog. Soc. **9** : 45.

Volcanoes, Phenomena of. Davy. Works, **6** : 344. **8** : 223.

Volkelius, John. Wallace, R. Anti-Trin. biog. **2** : 428.

Volkmann, Robert. Ehlert. Tone-world, 235. — Kingston, W. B. Music & manners, **1** : 90.

Volmerstein, Matilda. See Recke, Countess van der.

Volney, C. T. C., Count. St. John. Ccl. travelers, **3** : 219.

Volo. Arnold, R. A. Levant, **1** : 314.

Volsunga Saga. Dippold. Epics, 59.

Volta, Alessandro. Munro, J. Pioneers elec. 89.

— Galvanic apparatus of. Davy. Works, **2** : 139.

Voltaire. Brougham. Works, **2** : 1. — Carlyle. Essays. — Dawson, G. Shakesp. 269. — Hale, E. E. Lights of two cent. 161. — Houssaye. Philos. **1** : 29. — Pressensé. Contemp. portraits. — Schlegel. Dram. art, 153. — Shelley, M. W. Lit. men Fr. 9. — Vinet. Fr. lit. lec. 254. — Clarke, J. F. 19th cent. ques. 235. — Hundred greatest men, 293. — Shackford. Soc. & lit. pap. 61. — With portrait. (A. Cohn) Warner Lib. **26** : 15449. — Wilson, J. Stud. mod. mind.

— and the Calas tragedy. Pattison. Ess. **2** : 199.

— and Frederick the Great. Grimm, H. Liter. 93. — Macaulay. Ess. **5** : 160. — Wraxall, C. F. L. Hist. bye-ways, **2** : 25.

— and the French stage. Hawkins. Fr. stage 18th cent. v. **1**.

— and King Stanislas. Wolff. Odd bits, 181.

— and Mad. Du Chatelet. Jameson. Loves of poets.

— and M'lle de Livry. Houssaye. Philos. **1** : 109.

— and France. Grimm, H. Liter. 44.

— and Strauss. Pressensé. Contem. portr. 79.

— as a theologian, moralist, and metaphysician. Stephen, J. F. Horæ Sabb. **2** : 211.

— His visit to England, 1726. Jusserand. Eng. Ess. 193.

— Influence in England. Texte, J. Rousseau, 56.

— Memoirs of. Goldsmith. Miscel. (N. Y. 4 v.) **3** : 217.

— Private life of. Everett, A. H. Crit. ess. **1** : 172.

— Rousseau and Goethe. Merivale. Hist. stud. 130.

Volterra. Hare. Cities of No. Italy, **2** : 482.

— and the Borax springs. Baxter, L. E. Tusc. stud. 275.

Volumnian tomb. Freeman. Studies Italy, 34.

Voluntary movements, Automatic execution of. Carpenter, W. Benj. Nature, 164.

Voluntaryism in higher education. Anderson, M. B. Papers, **1** : 102.

"**Vomito Prieto**," Yellow coloration of persons attacked by. (M. C. y Valle) Am. Pub. Health, **19** : 89.

Von Bora, Catherine. Wittenmeyer. Women reform. 361.

Von Brederode, Lancelot. Wallace, R. Anti-Trin. biog. **3** : 68.

Vondel, Joost Van der, with portrait. Warner Lib. **26** : 15491.

— Bibliography. Van Noppen, L. C. (tr.). Vondel's Lucifer.

Voorhees, Daniel W., with portrait. Scott, H. W. Dist. Am. lawy. 91.

Vordovius, Andrew. Wallace, R. Anti-Trin. biog. **2** : 402.

Vorstius, Conrad. Wallace, R. Anti-Trin. biog. **2** : 444.

Vorstius, William Henry. Wallace, R. Anti-Trin. biog. **3** : 129.

Vortices, Descartes's theory of. Lodge, O. Pioneers, 137.

Vose, Frank. (A. Redington) N. E. Hist.-Gen. Soc. Biog. 4 : 26.

Vosgos country, The. Bartley, G. C. T. Rhine, 68.

Voudoo dance, A. Warner, C. D. Studies, 64.

Vowel quantity. Hadley, J. Ess. 263.

Vowels and consonants, Relation of. Whitney, W. D. Orient, 2 : 277.

Voyagers, early, Chronological table of. Belknap. Amer. biog. 59.

Voyages and travels. Ess. from Nation, 177.

Voysey, C. Alviella. Contemp. evol. 104.

Vulcano Island, Past history of. (E. Chaix) Am. Geog. Soc. 20 : 463.

Vulgarity. Hazlitt. Table-talk.

— and affectation. Hazlitt, W. Table-talk, 214.

— Lack of self-confidence a cause of. Helps. Soc. pressure, 146.

— Social standard of. Curtis, G. W. Other ess. 137.

— universal, Theory of. Higginson. Conc. all, 52.

Wabash College, Crawfordsville, Ind. U. S. Bur. Ed. Circ. '91, no. 1 : 152.

Wace, Master. Round, J. H. Feudal Eng. 399.

Wachs, G. Feuerbach. Crim. trials.

Wachusett, Mt., A walk to. Thoreau. Excursions, 73.

Waddell, Mrs. William Coventry, with portrait. Ellet. Queens Am. soc. 382.

Waddington, M. Em. persons, 6 : 93.

Waddy, Samuel D. Wesley & successors, 191.

Wade, Benjamin Franklin, with portrait. Brockett. Men of our day, 233. — Johnston, A. Amer. ora. 3 : 246.

Wade, James Addison. Bartlett, J. R. R. I. officers, 444.

Wade, Mrs. Jennie. Brockett. Woman's work, 775.

Wade, John, jr. Loring, J. S. Hundred Bost. ora. 507.

Wade, Mrs. Mary B. Brockett. Woman's work, 736.

Wade, Thomas. (H. B. Forman) Miles, A. H. Poets of cent. 3 : 597.

— and his surroundings. (H. B. Forman) Nicoll, W. R. Lit. anec. 1 : 43.

Wadsworth, Rev. Charles. Bungay. Off-hand, 378.

Wadsworth, James Samuel. (W. J. Hoppin) Harvard mem. biog. v. 1.

Wâdy, Barada. (H. H. Jessup) Wilson, C. W. Pictur. Palest. 2 : 206.

Waelder, Jacob. Am. Bar Assoc. 11 : 353.

Wage, A living. Smart, W. Stud. econ. 33.

Wage-fund theory, Literary history of. Walker, F. A. Discus. in econ. 1 : 289.

Wager of battle. Lea. Supers. & force, 73.

Wager of law. Lea. Supers. & force, 13.

Wagers, Winning. Proctor, R. A. Leis. read. 290.

Wages. Bolles. Chap. pol. econ. 15. — Elder, W. Questions, 85. — Greeley. Ess. pol. econ. 83. — Ills. Labor, '84. — Sumner, W. G. Essays, 36.

— and coöperation. (H. K. Oliver) Mass. Labor, '73 : 440.

— and cost of living in Germany, 1892. (A. H. Washburn) U. S. Cons. Rept. 41 : 96.

— and cost of production in Massachusetts, 1888. Mass. Labor, '89 : 1.

— and expenses. Minn. Labor, 2 : 301.

— and prices in Kansas. Kansas Labor, 1891.

Wages and profits. Conn. Labor, '85 : 1.

— and work. U. S. Lab. Rept. 1895–96.

— and working hours. N. Y. Labor, '88.

— Dictation of. (C. S. Byrkit) Conv. Labor Bur. '87 : 52.

— Effect of protection on. Playfair. Subj. soc. 164.

— Fluctuations in, and movements of population. Jones, Rich. Lit. remains.

— Graded weekly. Mass. Bur. Lab. '95 : 417.

— in Great Britain and Pennsylvania. Penn. Labor, 1884.

— in Massachusetts, 1870. Mass. Labor, '71 : 154.

— — in 1882. Mass. Labor, '83 : 181.

— — in 1888, Statistics of. Mass. Labor, '89 : 403.

— in Mass. and Gt. Britain, Comparative, 1860–1883. Mass. Labor, '84 : 135.

— in New Jersey. N. J. Labor, '78 : 105.

— in the United Kingdom. Bibliography. (A. Hopkinson & A. L. Bowley) Econom. Rev. Oct. 15, '98 : 504.

— in U. S. and Europe, 1870–98. U. S. Lab. Bull. 3 : 665.

— Increase of. Bolles. Chap. pol. econ. 28.

— Living, and strikes. Wagner, L. Mod. pol. ora. 1.

— Manner of payment of. Conn. Labor, '85 : 70. '86 : xxxi.

— Natural rate of. Carpenter, E. Eng. ideal, 100.

— of labor. Nicol, D. Polit. life, 2 : 230.

— Purchasing power of, 1860, 1872, 1878. (C. D. Wright) Mass. Labor, '79 : 61.

— — Historical review of, 1752–1860. (C. D. Wright) Mass. Labor, '85 : 161.

— — in England. (H. K. Oliver) Mass. Labor, '72 : 469.

— — in Massachusetts, 1630–1870. (H. K. Oliver) Mass. Labor, '72 : 500.

— — in Massachusetts and Europe. Mass. Labor, '74 : 161.

— — in Massachusetts and Gt. Britain, 1860–83. (C. D. Wright) Mass. Labor, '85 : 105.

— regulating themselves reasonably. Kempner, W. Common-sense soc. 221.

— scientific law of, Possibility of. (J. B. Clark) Am. Econ. Assoc. v. 4.

— Sliding scale of. Smart, W. Stud. econ. 63.

— Theory of. (S. Wood) Am. Econ. Assoc. v. 4. See also Labor and capital.

— — German. (J. W. Crook) Colum. Univ. Stud. Hist. 9 : no. 2.

Waghorn, Thomas Fletcher. Smith, C. R. Retrospec. 1 : 136.

Waghorn, Thomas ; pioneer of the overland route. Tillotson, J. Untit. nobil. 26.

Wagner, George. Brown, J. N. Bapt. martyrs, 55.

Wagner, Richard. Dole, N. H. Score, 517. — Engel. Mozart to Mario, 2 : 1. — Ferris. Germ. composers, 198. — Hadow. Stud. mod. mus. v. 1. — Hale, E. E. Lights of two cent. 387. — Haweis. My mus. life, 393. — Haweis. My mus. memories, 144. — Keddie. Mus. comp. 416. — Parry. Stud. gt. compos. 322. — Upton. Stan. operas, 243. — Kingston, W. B. Music & manners, 1 : 288. — Paladin. Glances, 109. — With portrait. Rowbotham. Priv. life compos. 316. — Sharp, R. F. Makers of music. — With portrait. (C. H. Genung) Warner Lib. 26 : 15499. — Statham. Music, 359.

— and his enemies. Elson. Realm of music, 282.

— and his music in America. Butterworth. Great compos. 175.

— and Hugo. Archer, W. Theatre, 321.

Wagner, Richard, and Wagnerism. Gurney. Tertium, **2** : **1** ; also in Coan. Art and lit. 152.
— and Weber. Runciman, J. F. Old scores, 131.
— Bibliography. Paterson (N. J.) Pub. Lib. Bull. Feb.–March, '97.— Providence Pub. Lib. Bull. Mar. '95.
— Cult of. Nordau. Degen. 171.
— The Dusk of the Gods. Runciman, J. F. Old scores, 201.
— Festival at Bayreuth. Ehlert. Tone-world, 181.
— The Flying Dutchman. Runciman, J. F. Old scores, 163.
— in Bayreuth. Yates, E. H. Celeb. **2** : 197.
— Intellectuality of. Elson. Realm of music, 269.
— Life and theories of. Elson, L. Gt. composers, 221.
— Lohengrin. Runciman, J. F. Old scores, 171.
— Music dramas of. Bibliography. (E. Singleton, tr.) Lavignac, A. Mus. dramas R. Wagner.
— Parsifal. Runciman, J. F. Old scores, 211.— Warner, C. D. Roundabout, 333.
— Ring of the Nibelung. Hueffer. Mus. stud. 130.
— Siegfried. Runciman, J. F. Old scores, 191.
— Tristan and Isolde. Ehlert. Tone-world, 87.— Runciman, J. F. Old scores, 181.
— Wagneriana. Henderson, W. J. Preludes.
Wahab's Plantation, Affair at. Dawson. Batt. of U. S. **1** : 624.
Wainwright, Thomas Griffiths. Procter, B. W. Autob. 188.— (A. G. Allen) Seccombe, T. Twelve bad men, 292.
Waireka Hill, Battle of. Richards, W. Heroes 15.
Wait, Luther. (A. D. Wait) N. E. Hist.-Gen. Soc. Biog. **1** : 60.
Wake Forest College, Wake Co., N. C. U. S. Bur. Ed. Circ. '88, no. **2** : 101.
Wakefield, Mrs. Rebecca, of Ribé, East Africa. Pitman, Mrs. Heroines mission. 221.
Wakefield, Eng., Battle of. Freeman. Hist. ess. **4** : 275.
Wakelee, Kate C. Raymond, I. Southland wr. **1** : 459.
Wakley, Thomas. Francis, G. H. Orators, 229.
— Grant, J. Recoll. Ho. Comm. 262.
Waldegrave, Sir Richard. Manning, J. A. Speakers, 10.
Walden Water. Guiney. Goose-quill, 156.
Waldenses, The. Hare. Cities of No. Italy, **1** : 96.— Headley, J. T. Rambles, 202.— Lawrence, E. Hist. stud. 198.— Merson. Heroic days, 30.— Smiles, S. Huguenots in France, 287.— Trench. Lec. mediæval, 247.— Ivimey. Eng. Bapt. **1** : 19, 24, 55.— Pennington. Epochs papacy, 158.
— and Albigenses. Maitland, S. R. Eight ess. 154.
— Arnaud and the. Chambers's Repos. no. 28.
Waldhauser, Conrad. Hodgson, Wm. Reformers, 106.
Waldhere, Poem of. Brooke, S. A. Hist. early Eng. lit. 93.
Waldo, Peter de. Hodgson, Wm. Reformers, 45.— Pennington. Epochs papacy, 157.
Waldric. Round, J. H. Feudal Eng. 480.
Wales, Leonard Eugene. Am. Bar Assoc. **20** : 530.
Wales. Allingham. Varieties, **2** : 1.
— Celtic church of. Bibliography. Bund, J. W. W. Celt. ch. Wales.
— Church in, Disestablishment of. Rosebery. Speeches, 300.
— North, A fortnight in. Wynter, A. Our soc. bees, **1** : 346.

Wales, Kings of. Doran. Monarchs, **1** : 172.
— South. Freeman. Eng. towns, 3.
Walford, Lucy B., with portrait. Black, H. C. Wom. authors, 26.
Walker, Adeline. Brockett. Woman's work, 457.
Walker, Amanda L. Hemenway. Poets of Vt 155.
Walker, Amasa. Loring, J. S. Hundred Bost. ora. 508.
Walker, Mrs. D. M. F. Hemenway. Poets of Vt. 196.
Walker, Elizabeth. Williams, Jane. Lit. wom. 128.
Walker, Francis A. (C. F. Dunbar) Am. Acad. Proc. **32** : 344.— (G. F. Hoar and C. D. Wright) Smithson. Rept. '97 : 635.
— Educational discussions by. U. S. Bur. Ed. Rept. '96–97, **1** : 695.
Walker, Frederick. Ewart, H. C. Toilers in art, 171.— Wedmore. Studies, 2d ed. 227.
— Essay on. (S. Colvin) Atkinson, J. B. Eng. paint. 15.
Walker, George, commodore. Laughton. Stud. nav. hist. 225.
Walker, George Leon. Hemenway. Poets of Vt. 260.
Walker, George Rivers. Am. Bar Assoc. **5** : 162.
Walker, George Washington, and the convicts. Japp, A. H. Master mission. 162.
Walker, Helen (Jeanie Deans). Owen, Mrs. O. F. Heroines domes. 235.
Walker, Sir Hovenden, Expedition to Canada, 1711. Parkman. Half-cent. **1** : 150.
Walker, James, with portrait. (O. B. Frothingham) Mass. Hist. Proc. 2d ser. **6** : 443.— Peabody. Harv. grad. 123.— (J. Lovering) Vaille & Clark. Harv. book, v. 1.
Walker, John. Jardine, W. Nat. lib. v. **3.**— Lonsdale. Worthies Cumb. v. **6.**
Walker, Mrs. Margaret. Burder. Pious wom. 445.
Walker, Mary Jane. Miller, Jos. Singers church, 2d ed. 556.
Walker, Rev. Robert, called "Wonderful." Parton. Capt. indus. 355.
Walker, Samuel. Pierce, B. K. Em. dead, 140.
— Ryle, J. C. Chr. leaders, 306.
Walker, Sears Cook. Youmans. Pioneers sci. 428.
Walker, Thomas, English actor. Hogarth. Mem. opera, **2** : 9.
Walker, Thomas, and six others, Trial of. Erskine, T. Speeches, 325.
Walker, Timothy. Livingston, J. Em. Am. lawy. 559.
Walker, Wilhelmina Augusta. Clayton, E. C. Eng. fem. art. **2** : 152.
Walker, William, filibuster. Buchanan, J. Messages, ed. by Henry, 172.— Holst. Const. history of U. S. v. **5.**— Wraxall, F. C. L. Remark. adv. **2** : 257.
Walkers, Thomas, The two. Espinasse. Lanc. worth v. **2.**
Walking. Thoreau. Selec. 198. — Thoreau. Excursions, 161.— Tuckerman. Optimist, 135.
— Physiology of. Holmes, O. W. Old vol. 121.
Walking parties. Arnold, F. Arm-chair, 219.
Walking tours. Stevenson. Virginibus.
Wall, Joseph, Trial of. Browne, G. L. Narr. state trials, **1** : 28.— Burke, P. Cel. nav. & mil. trials, 264.
Wall papers. (W. Crane) Morris, W. Arts & crafts, 52.

Wall papers, Arsenic in. (F. C. Robinson) Maine Health, '89 : 284.
— Poisonous. Iowa Health, '85 : 64. — (G. Derby) Mass. Health, '72 : 33. — (R. C. Kedzie) Mich. Health, '73 : 60. '74 : 53. — (E. S. Wood) Mass. Health, '83 : 213. — Mass. Health, '91 : 701.
Wall street. Bryce. Soc. institu. 46.
Walls, Henry J. Ohio Labor, '88.
Wallace, Alfred Russell With portrait. Clodd. Pioneers evol. 134. — With portrait. Warner Lib. **26** : 15517.
— and the Malay Archipelago. Montefiore, A. Leaders, 159.
Wallace, David. Woollen. Biog. sk. Indiana, 70.
Wallace, Horace Binney. Godwin, P. Out of past, 302.
Wallace, John William. Carson, H. L. Sup. Ct. of U. S. 568.
Wallace, Julia. Hemenway. Poets of Vt. 140.
Wallace, Lew, with portrait. Warner Lib. **26** : 15531.
— Ben Hur. Richardson. Amer. lit. **2** : 441.
Wallace, Rodney, with portrait. Sketches N. H. men, 56.
Wallace, Thomas, barrister. Curren. Irish bar, **1** : 325. — Grant, J. Recoll. Ho. Comm. 304. — Sheil. Sk. Irish bar, **1** : 269.
Wallace, Gen. W. H. L. Caton. Miscel. 15.
Wallace, Sir Wm. Tytler. Scot. worth. v. **1**. — Chambers's Miscel. no. 31.
Wallace, Wm. Rosebery. Apprec. 73.
Wallace, Wm., Amer. poet. Griswold. Poets Am. 477.
Wallace, William Ross. Coggeshall. Poets of west, 227.
Wallace, William Vincent. Hodder, G. Memories, 313. — Spark, W. Mus. mem. 178.
Wallack, James W. Matthews, B. Actors, **3** : 55.
Wallack, Lester. Matthews, B. Actors, **5** : 283. — McKay, F. E. Fam. actors, 119.
Wallacks, The. Hutton. Plays.
Walladmor. DeQuincey. Lit. rem. (Bost.) **1** : 137.
Wallcut, Thomas. Mass. Hist. Proc. **2** : 193.
Wallenstein, A. W. E. von. Adams, W. H. D. Em. sol. **1**. — Ellesmere. Ess. 55. — Hewlett. Heroes, 340. — James, G. P. R. Dark sce. — Wilson, J. G. Illus. sol. 87. — (F. von Schiller) Ferris, G. T. Gt. leaders, 291.
— Was he guilty? Wraxall, C. F. L. Hist. byeways, **2** : 151.
Waller, Edmund. Bell, R. Lit. & sci. men, **1** : 91. — (S. Johnson) Chalmers. Eng. poets, **8** : 3. — Creasy. Etonians, 110. — Gosse. Shakes. to Pope. — (E. W. Gosse) Ward. Eng. poets, **2** : 270. — Wotton. Word portraits, 317. — Burke, B. Viciss. of fam. **1** : 241. — Deshler. Afternoons, 153. — Griswold, R. W. Sac. poets. — Macdonald, G. England's antiphon, 212. — Tovey. Rev. & ess. 88. — With portrait. Warner Lib. **26** : 15555. — Wrangham. Brit. Plutarch, v. **4**.
— and Sacharissa. Jameson. Loves of poets.
Waller, John Green. Smith, C. R. Retrospec. **2** : 20.
Waller, Sir William. Cust. Warriors civ. **2** : 633.
Waller, William M., jr. Walker, C. D. Biog. Va. Mil. Inst. 526.
Walley, Samuel H. Peabody. Harv. grad. 214.
Wallin, Benjamin. Hatfield, E. F. Poets of church, 624. — Ivimey. Eng. Bapt. **3** : 472. — Miller, Jos. Singers church, 2d ed. 203.

Wallin, Edward. Ivimey. Eng. Bapt. **3** : 462.
Wallingford, Zimri S., with portrait. Sketches N. H. men, 70.
Wallingford community. Hinds. Amer. commun. — Nordhoff. Commun. 259.
Wallis, Henry Bate, P. H. Eng. Pre-Raph. 87.
Wallis, S. Teackle. Davidson, J. W. Writ. of South, 594.
Walmer Castle. Timbs. Abbeys, **1** : 328.
Waln, Robert. Winslow, S. N. Biog. Phila. merch. 129.
Walpole, Horace. Creasy. Etonians, 339. — Dawson, G. Shakesp. 223. — Galton, A. Urbana, 211. — Hayward, A. Em. statesm. **2** : 243. — Lodge. Portraits (Bohn), v. **8**. — Mitchell. Wet days, 235. — Scott, W. Biog. mem. **1**. — Stephen, L. Hours in libr. **2** : 154. — Wotton. Word portraits, 319. — Mitchell, D. G. Eng. lands, **3** : 83. — With portrait. Warner Lib. **27** : 15565.
— As a connoisseur. Robinson, F. S. Connois. 175.
— as a gardener. Hazlitt, W. C. Gleanings, 186.
— Era of. Stephen, L. Eng. thought, **2** : 167.
— Letters to Sir Horace Mann. Macaulay. Ess. **3** : 143.
— Private press of. Dobson, A. 18th cent. vign. **3** : 206.
— world of fashion. Knight. Once on time, **2** : 53.
— world of letters. Knight. Once on time, **2** : 67.
Walpole, Horatio, 1st Lord. Lodge. Portraits (Bohn), 7.
Walpole, Sir Robert, 1st earl of Orford. Adams, W. H. D. Eng. party, **1** : 3. — Adams, W. H. D. Men at helm, 105. — Brougham. Wks. **4** : 441. — Creasy. Etonians, 157. — Earle, J. C. Eng. prem. **1** : 3. — Ewald. Repr. statesmen, **1** : 121. — Georgian era, **1** : 272. — Lodge. Portraits (Bohn), v. **7**. — Oliphant, Hist. sketches, 46. — Rogers, J. E. T. Gleanings, **1** : 47. — With portrait. Caulfield. Kit-cat, 132. — (W. E. H. Lecky) Ferris, G. T. Gt. leaders, 351. — Goodrich, C. A. Sel. Brit. eloq. — (R. Peel) Stanhope, Earl. Miscel. **1** : 66.
— at the court of England. Doran. Queens Hanov. **1** : 2.
Walpole, Spencer H., with photo. Cooper, T. Men of mark, **1** : 5. — Ritchie. Brit. sena. 42. — Kent, W. C. M. Derby min. 113.
Walrus, The. Morgan, C. L. Animal sk. 122.
Walsh, Mike, Trial of, 1848. Clinton, H. L. Extraor. cases, 42.
Walsh, Robert. Griswold. Prose writ. 197. — Mansfield, E. D. Pers. mem. 340.
Walsh, William, with portrait. Caulfield. Kit-cat, 211. — (S. Johnson) Chalmers. Eng. poets, **8** : 401.
Walsingham, Sir Francis. Lodge. Portraits (Bohn), v. **2**. — Wrangham. Brit. Plutarch, v. **2**.
Walsingham, Mary. Davidson, J. W. Writ. of South, 595.
Walter, Benno, with portrait. Ehrlich, A. Cel. violin. 102.
Walter, Emma. Clayton, E. C. Eng. fem. art. **2** : 299.
Walter, Hubert, 1193-1205. Hook. Abps. Cant. **2** : 584.
Walter, John, editor of the "Times." Ashton. 18th cent. waifs, 203. — Reid, T. W. Politicians, **1** : 95. — Smalley. Stud. 334. — Em. persons, **6** : 178.
— Three John Walters and their newspaper. Parton. Capt. indus. 275.

Walters, Lucy. Jesse. Court of Eng. Stuarts, 3 : 362.

Waltham Abbey, burial place of Harold. Timbs. Abbeys, 1 : 243.

Walthar of Aquitain. Ludlow. Epics, 1 : 45.

Walther, John. Miller, Jos. Singers church, 2d ed. 52.

Walther von der Vogelweide. Gosse. Stud. lit. No. Eur. 197. — Taylor. Stud. Ger. 37 — With portrait. (C. H. Genung) Warner Lib. 26 : 15580.

Walton, George, 1740–1804. Dwight, N. Signers of decl. 366. — Jones, C. C., jr. Deleg. fr. Georgia, 168. — Lincoln, R. W. Signers, 66. — Lossing. Signers, 233. — Sanderson. Signers, v. 4.

Walton, Izaak. Choate, J. B. Wells of Eng. 217. — Henley. Views, 108. — Lowell. Latest ess. 57. — Lang. Lett. to dead au. 86. — Wotton. Word portraits, 323. — Teale, W. H. Laymen, 137. — With portrait. (H. van Dyke) Warner Lib. 26 : 15601. — Mitford, M. R. Recollec. 198.

— Complete angler. Saunders, F. Famous books, 73.

— Grave of. Hall, Mrs. S. C. Pilgr. Eng. shr. 2 : 1.

— Lives. Jones, W. A. Lit. stud. 1 : 104.

— Wand of. Ellwanger. Idyllists, 9.

Walton, John. Jones, C. C., jr. Deleg. fr. Georgia, 199.

Walton, John. Wesley & successors, 252.

Walton, N. Y. Willis. Hurry-graphs, 72.

Walworth, Mrs. John. Ellet. Pioneer wom. 271.

Walworth, Reuben Hyde. Browne, I. Stud. gt. lawyers, 341. — Livingston, J. Dist. Amer. 17. — Livingston, J. Em. Am. lawy. 513.

Wampanoag Indians, Notes on. (H. E. Chase) Smithson. Rept. '83 : 878.

Wanamaker, John. Bolton, S. K. How success is won, 59. — Pierson, A. T. Evangelistic work, 302.

Wanborough. (Lady West) Clinch, G. Bygone Surrey, 163.

Wandering, Idyl of. Mabie. My study fire, 189.

— Year of. Mabie. Ess. on work, 44.

Wandering Jew. Baring-Gould. Myths, 1.

Wanstead House. Timbs. Abbeys, 1 : 238.

Want and waste, Use of. Bushnell. Moral uses, 29.

War. Channing. Works, 3 : 29. 4 : 237. 5 : 107. — DeQuincey. Mis. pap. (Bost.) 2 : 191 ; or Works (Masson), 8 : 369. — Emerson. Miscel. 177. — Franklin. Works (1887), 10 : 60. — Hall, R. Miscel. 299. — Helps. Brevia. — Helps. Friends, 2d ser. 1. — Wood, J. G. Nature's teaching, 50. — Maurice, F. D. Soc. morality, 171. — (R. W. Emerson) Peabody, E. P. Æsthetic pap. 36. — Vaughan, D. J. Questions, 100.

— Abolition of. Maine. Internat. law, 207.

— and armor in poetry. Brooke, S. A. Hist. early Eng. lit. 120.

— and culture. Godkin. Reflections, 11.

— and loyalty. Brownson. Works, 16 : 1.

— and peace. Montgomery, J. Prose, 2 : 1.

— and progress. (L. G. James) Factors Amer. civiliz. 85.

— art of, Changes in, 1792–1812. Baring, E. Staff coll. ess. 3.

— Barbarities of. Friswell. About, 199.

— Benefits of. Morris. Civiliz. 1 : 233.

— Bibliography. Lib. Jour. 23 : 191.

War, Causes of, and means of reducing them. (E. De Laveleye) Cobden Cl. ess. 2 : 1.

— Cost of. Giles, H. Lec. & ess. 342.

— Ethics of. Newman, F. W. Miscel. 3 : 54.

— Future of. Forbes, A. Camps, 233.

— Implements of. Bayly, J. A. S. New stud. 1.

— In peace prepare for. Roosevelt, T. Amer. ideals, 247.

— in the world. Friswell. About, 189.

— Influence of U. S. against. Eliot, C. W. Five Am. cont. 2.

— Laws and usages of. (M. Bernard) Oxf. ess. '56 : 88.

— Moral aspect of. Mahan. Lessons war, 207.

— Negotiation *versus*. Bryant. Prose, 2 : 284.

— Praise of. Repplier. Ess. in idle. 65.

— Prevention of. Rogers, J. E. T. Cobden, 109.

— Right of the state over the individual in. Green, T. H. Works, 2 : 466.

— severity in, Limitations to. (C. Buxton) Camb. ess. '55 : 110.

— Workingmen and. Hobart, V. H. H. Ess. & mis. 2 : 210.

War correspondent, How I became a. Forbes, A. Souvenirs, 47.

War powers of U. S. Congress. Sumner. Works, 7 : 128.

War prayers, German. Forbes, A. Camps, 39.

Warships, Distinguishing qualities of. Mahan. Lessons war, 257.

War-songs, English. Saintsbury, G. Ess. Eng. lit. 2 : 171.

— Period of the. Mathews, W. S. B. Hundred yrs. music, 66.

Warbeck, Perkin. James, G. P. R. Dark sce.

Warboys, England, Witches of. Wright, T. Nar. sorcery, 1 : 254.

Warburton, Colonel E., Travels of. Adams, W. H. D. Heroes of trav. 293.

Warburton, Wm., bishop. Georgian era, 1 : 229. — Stephen, L. Ess. freeth. 279.

— and his quarrels. Disraeli, I. Calam. 2.

— Divine legation. Stephen, J. F. Horæ Sabb. 2 : 315.

— Letters. Jeffrey, T. Contrib. Ed. Rev.

— Minor works. Stephen, J. F. Horæ Sabb. 2 : 333.

— Watson's Life of. Pattison. Ess. 2 : 119.

— Works. Stephen, L. Eng. thought, 1 : 344.

Ward, Artemus, *pseud. See* Browne, Chas. F.

Ward, Artemus, Jr., *pseud. See* Williams, J. H.

Ward, E. M., with photo. Cooper, T. Men of mark, 3 : 12.

Ward, Elizabeth S. P., with portrait. Warner Lib. 26 : 15623.

Ward, F. William Orde. *See* Williams, F. Harald.

Ward, Genevieve, in " Forget me not." Winter. Shadows, 1 : 315.

Ward, Henrietta. Clayton, E. C. Eng. fem. art. 2 : 161.

Ward, Sir Henry George. Francis, G. H. Orators, 268.

Ward, Mrs. Humphry. James, H. Ess. in Lond. 253. — Smalley. Stud. 227. — With portrait. Warner Lib. 26 : 15641. — Wilson, S. L. Theol. mod. liter.

— Robert Elsmere ; the battle of belief. Gladstone. Later gl. 77.

— — and miracles. Dixon, T. Liv. prob. 83.

— — Theology of. Hutton, R. H. Criticisms, 1 : 263.

Ward, Capt. J. H. Shea, J. G. Fallen brave.

Ward, James. (R. B. Ward) N. E. Hist.-Gen. Soc. Biog. 3 : 91.

Ward, James Warner. Coggeshall. Poets of west, 255.

Ward, John. McClure. Translators, 208.

Ward, John Q. A. Clarke, W. J. Amer. sculp. 114.

Ward, Mrs. Julia Rush. Griswold. Fem. poets, 90.

Ward, R. Plumer, Recollections of. Patmore. My friends, 2 : 1.

Ward, Samuel. McClure. Translators, 190.

Ward, Samuel, governor of Rhode Island. Gammel. Writ. 99.

Ward, Samuel, merchant. Fiske, S. Off-hand, 351. — (C. King) Hunt, F. Am. merch. 1 : 295. — Keyes. Fifty years' observ. 70.

Ward, Thomas, Baron. Burke, B. Viciss. of fam. 2 : 218.

Ward, Thomas, Amer. poet. Griswold. Poets Am. 313. — Poe. Works, 6 : 57.

Ward, William George. Church. Oxf. move. 292. — Oxenham. Stud. in eccl. hist. 358. — Hutton, R. H. Criticisms, 1 : 213.

Wardlaw, David L. Perry, B. F. Biog. sketches, 2 : 166.

Wardlaw, Lady Elizabeth. Wilson, J. G. Poets of Scot. 1 : 96.

— and the Baroness Nairne. Masson. Edinb. sk. 110.

Wardlaw, Ralph. Hatfield, E. F. Poets of church, 626. — McCosh. Scot. phil. 461. — Miller, Jos. Singers church, 2d ed. 365. — Stanton, H. B. Reforms, 223. — Taylor, W. M. Scott. pulpit, 287.

Wardrop, J. Pettigrew. Med. portr. gall. v. 2.

Ware, Ashur. Loring, J. S. Hundred Bost. ora. 382.

Ware, Darwin E. Am. Bar Assoc. 20 : 544.

Ware, Henry. Miller, Jos. Singers church, 2d ed. 430. — Peabody. Harv. rem. 2. — (J. G. Palfrey) Ware, W. Am. Unita. 1 : 227. — Richardson. Amer. lit. 1 : 293.

Ware, Henry, jr. (C. C. Smith) Mass. Hist. Proc. 2 : 278. — Peabody. Harv. rem. 97. — Griswold. Poets Am. 142. — Putnam, A. P. Singers liberal, 103.

Ware, J. Pettigrew. Med. portr. gall. v. 3.

Ware, Mrs. Katharine A. Rhodes. Griswold. Fem. poets, 102.

Ware, Mary L. [Mrs. Henry]. Crosland. Mem. women, 203.

Ware, Robert. Brockett. Woman's work, 299. — (C. E. Stedman) Harvard mem. biog. 1 : 221.

Ware, Robert, Forgeries of. Bridgett, T. E. Blunders, 209.

Ware, William. Griswold. Prose writ. 398. — Richardson. Amer. lit. 2 : 405.

Wareham, Eng., and Corfe Castle. Freeman. Eng. towns, 149.

Warehouse system, The. Dix. Speeches, 1 : 104, 124.

Warfare, modern, Influence of science upon. (H. B. Pritchard) Estes. Half-hour recr. 412.

— Bibliography. Lib. Jour. 23 : 191.

Warfield, Mrs. Catherine Ann. Coggeshall. Poets of west, 319. — Davidson, J. W. Writ. of South, 600. — Freeman, J. D. Wom. of South, 114. — Raymond, I. Southland writ. 1 : 25.

Warham, John. Sherman, D. N. Eng. divines, 111.

Warham, William, archbishop. Campbell. Ld. chan. 1 : 365. — Hook. Abps. Cant. 6 : 155. — Lodge. Portraits (Bohn), v. 1. — Towler, M. Some abps. Cant. 76.

Waring, Anna Lætitia. (W. G. Horder) Miles, A. H. Poets of cent. 10 : 387. — Miller, Jos. Singers church, 2d ed. 553.

Warka, Ruins of. Tweedie. Ruined cities, 156.

Warlike armaments, Continuance of. Helps. Brevia.

Warne, Charles, with portrait. Smith, C. R. Retrospec. 1 : 85. 3 : 176.

Warner, Andrew Ferdinando. (E. L. Sage) N. E. Hist.-Gen. Soc. Biog. 3 : 74.

Warner, Charles, with portrait. Goddard, A. Players, 2 : 113. — Wilman, G. Sk. liv. celeb. 25.

Warner, Charles Dudley. Bolton, S. K. Amer. au. 387. — Rideing, W. H. Boyhood, 204. — Richardson. Amer. lit. 1 : 395. — Vedder, H. C. Amer. writers, 87.

— as a writer of fiction. Matthews, B. Aspects fic. 206 ; or Books & play-books.

— at home. (J. H. Twichell) Gilder. Authors, 323.

Warner, Helen M. L. Hemenway. Poets of Vt. 386.

Warner, Mrs. (née Huddart). Marston, J. W. Rec. actors, 1 : 274.

Warner, Seth. Lossing. Em. Amer. 206.

Warner, Susan. Hart, J. S. Fam. prose, 421.

Warner, William. Bell, R. Lit. & sci. men, 2 : 116. — Chalmers. Eng. poets, 4 : 501. — (G. Saintsbury) Ward. Eng. poets, 1 : 431.

Warnham Court. Jewitt, L. Stately homes, 2 : 280.

Warren, John. Loring, J. S. Hundred Bost. ora. 156. — (Buckminster Brown) Gross. Lives physicians, 86.

Warren, John Collins. (E. Warren) Gross. Lives physicians, 796. — (H. P. Arnold) N. E. Hist.-Gen. Soc. Biog. 3 : 28.

Warren, Joseph. With portrait. [Amer.] Nat. portr. gall. v. 2. — Duyckinck. Nat. portr. gall. 1 : 87. — Everett. Orat. v. 3. — Glazier, W. Heroes, 43. — Loring, J. S. Hundred Bost. ora. 45, 59. — Magoon. Orators of rev. 155. — Knapp, S. L. Em. lawyers, 107. — Lossing. Em. Amer. 190. — Moore, F. Am. eloq. 1 : 57.

Warren, Mrs. Mercy Otis. Ellet. Women of revol. 1 : 74. — Griswold. Fem. poets, 21. — Lossing. Em. Amer. 85.

Warren, Samuel. Jeaffreson. Novelists, 2 : 399.

Warren, Sophy S. Clayton, E. C. Eng. fem. art. 2 : 247.

Warren, Wm. Jefferson, J. Autob. — With portrait. (Mrs. E. G. Sutherlandy) McKay, F. E. Fam. actors, 178.

Wars of the Roses. Reed, H. Lec. Eng. hist. 278. *See* Roses, Wars of.

Warsaw. Brooks, E. S. Gt. cities, 85. — Prime, S. I. Alhambra, 273.

Wart, Gertrude von der. Owen, Mrs. O. F. Heroines domes. 41.

Warth, Sally. Ellet. Pioneer wom. 191.

Warton, Joseph. Chalmers. Eng. poets, 18 : 145.

— and Thos. Dennis, J. Studies, 192.

Warton, Thomas. Austin & Ralph. Laureates, 316. — Chalmers. Eng. poets, 18 : 75. — Dennis, J. Stud. Eng. lit. 192. — Hamilton, Wal. Poets laur.

— Sonnets of. Deshler. Afternoons, 178.

Warwick, Ambrose Dudley, earl of. Lodge. Portraits (Bohn), v. 2.

Warwick, Barksdale. Walker, C. D. Biog. Va. Mil. Inst. 527.

Warwick, Mary Rich, countess of. Burder. Pious wom. 93. — Williams, Jane. Lit. wom.

115. — With portrait. Johnstone, G. Lead. women, 91.

Warwick, Robert Rich, 2d earl of. Lodge. Portraits (Bohn), v. 5.

Warwick, England. Guild. Over the ocean, 125. — Hawthorne. Old home, 77. — Silloway. Cathedral towns, 167. — Winter, W. Shakesp. Eng.

Warwick castle. Edwardes, C. Hist. houses. — Jewitt, L. Stately homes, 1 : 192. — (Countess of Warwick) Malan, A. H. Famous homes, 327. — Stowe. Sunny mem. 1 : 224.

— the Earls of Warwick. Hutton, B. Castles, 224.

Warwick Congress. Smith, C. R. Retrospec. 1 : 45.

Warwick Hall college of physicians, Chronicles of. Winslow, F. Physic. 2 : 1.

Warwickshire. James, H. Portraits, 247. — Stone, J. S. Heart of Eng. 301. — Temple, E. L. Old world, 2 : 73. — Wolfe. Lit. pilg. Brit. au. 91.

— Baptists of. Ivimey. Eng. Bapt. 2 : 573.

— Rambles in, 1851. Taylor, B. At home, 1 : 51. — Shrines of. Winter, W. Shakesp. Eng.

— Staunton collection relating to. Dawson, G. Shakesp. 170.

Warwickshire dialect, a study in. (A. Morgan) N. Y. Shakesp. Soc. pap. v. 2.

Warwickshire homes. Hodges, Eliz. Anc. Eng. homes, 126.

Washburn, Emory. (A. P. Peabody) Mass. Hist. Proc. 17 : 23. — Vaille & Clark. Harv. book, v. 1.

Washburn, Mrs. H. B. Hemenway. Poets of Vt. 167.

Washburn, Ichabod, wiremaker. Parton. Capt. indus. 18.

Washburn, James. Knapp, S. L. Em. lawyers, 346.

Washburne, Elihu Benjamin. With portrait. Carroll, H. Twelve Amer. 395. — (G. W. Smith) Chic. Hist. Coll. 4 : 78.

Washerwomen. Hunt, L. Seer, 2 : 157.

Washington, Bushrod, 1761-1829. Brown, D. P. Forum, 1 : 350.

— Character of. Story, J. Miscel. 808.

Washington, George. Abbott. Lives of presidents, 9. — With portrait. [Amer.] Nat. portr. gall. v. 1. — Benson & Tatham. Men of might, 164. — Brooks, E. S. Hist. Amer. 46. — Chambers's Miscel. no. 60. — With portrait. Duyckinck. Nat. portr. gall. 1 : 59. — Edgar. Footpr. 9. — Forney. Anec. 10. — Frost. Presidents, 9. — Glazier, W. Heroes, 21. — With portrait. Headley, J. T. Washington, 1 : 15. — Lincoln. Lives of pres. 1. — Mackay. Founders Amer. v. 1. — Parker, T. Hist. Amer. 73. — Parton. Peop. bk. biog. 9. — Tuckerman. Ess. 5. — Wallace, H. B. Art, 443. — Wilson, J. G. Illus. sol. 305. — (W. E. H. Lecky) Ferris, G. T. Gt. leaders, 378. — Genin, T. H. Selec. writ. — (T. S. Bocock) Graham & Collar. Pulpit & rost. v. 1. — Gurney, J. H. Hist. sketches, 3 : 156. — With portrait. Hubbard, E. Lit. jour. 4 : 1. — With portrait. Warner Lib. 26 : 15665. — Hundred greatest men, 434. — Lodge & Roosevelt. Hero-tales, 1. — Lossing. Em. Amer. 55. — Mombert. Great lives, 222. — Moore, F. Am. eloq. 1 : 251. — Myers, F. Lec. gt. men, 434. — Richardson. Amer. lit. 1 : 203, 243, 468. — Sinclair, J. Sketches. — (W. E. Gladstone) Smalley. Lond. lett. 2 : 297. — Sparks, W. H. Memories, 188. — Thompson, R. W. Pers. recoll. 1. — (R. C. Winthrop)

Wilson, J. G. Presidents, 1. — Trent. South. statesm. 3. — Upton, Mrs. H. T. Our early pres. 19.

Washington, George, abroad and at home. Everett. Orat. v. 3.

— Address at unveiling statue of. Curtis, G. W. Orations, 3 : 169.

— Address, Memorial Arch. N. Y. Curtis, G. W. Orations, 3 : 191.

— Address on 100th anniv. of birth of. Curtis, B. R. Mem. & writ. v. 2.

— Ancestors of. Sumner. Works, 5 : 357.

— and the American Revolution. Whipple. Charac.

— — Bibliography. Indianapolis Pub. Lib. '95.

— and his contemporaries. Chambers's Papers, no. 10.

— and Lafayette. Clark, W. G. Lit. rem. 387.

— and Napoleon I. Lieber, F. Reminis. 413.

— Bibliography. Baker, W. S. Early sketches G. Washington. — Providence Pub. Lib. Bull. Jan. '98.

— Birthday of. Everett. Orat. v. 3.

— Character of. Everett. Orat. v. 4. — Webster, D. Works, 1 : 217.

— Critical occasions in the life of. Everett, E. Mt. Vernon, 323.

— Diary of. Everett, E. Mount Vernon, 81.

— Erskine's testimony to. Everett, E. Mt. Vernon, 155.

— Eulogy on. Ames, F. Works, 115.

— Greatness of. King, T. S. Patriotism, 55.

— Headquarters of, at Cambridge, Mass. Drake, S. A. Hist. fields Mid. 289.

— Home of. (C. M. Kirkland) Homes Am. statesm. 1.

— in domestic life. Rush, R. Occ. prod. 31.

— Inauguration of. McMaster. With fathers, 150.

— influence of, Secret of. Clarke, J. F. Memo. sketches, 281.

— Intention to retire from the presidency in 1792. Madison, J. Letters, 1 : 554, 563.

— National monument to, at Washington, D. C. Winthrop, R. C. Addresses, 1 : 70.

— on Capture of Cornwallis. Webster, N. Papers, 166.

— Portrait of, Lansdowne. Smalley. Lond. lett. 2 : 308.

— — Peale's. (C. H. Hart) Am. Hist. Assoc. Rept. '96, 1 : 189.

— Social life during administration of. Ellet, E. F. Court circles, 15.

— Statue of, Crawford's. Everett. Orat. v. 3.

— — Greenough's. Everett, A. H. Ess. 2 : 224.

— Washingtoniana. Bibliography. (A. P. C. Griffin) Bost. Athenæum Wash. coll. '97.

Washington, Jane. Ellet. Women of revol. 2 : 89.

Washington, Martha. With portrait. [Amer.] Nat. portr. gall. v. 1. — Clement, J. Noble deeds, 33. — Ellet. Women of revol. 2 : 7. — With portrait. Holloway, L. C. Ladies, 39. — Duyckinck. Portr. gall. 1 : 182. — Gordon, L. L. Lady Wash'n, 1. — Hanaford. Wom. of cent. 66. — Lossing. Em. Amer. 119. — Upton, Mrs. H. T. Our early pres. 19.

Washington, Mary. Clement, J. Noble deeds, 25. — Ellet. Women of revol. 1 : 24. — Holloway, L. C. Mothers of gt. men, 25.

Washington, William Augustine. With portrait. [Amer.] Nat. portr. gall. v. 3.

Washington family. Glen, T. A. Colon. mans. 2 : 17. — Rimmer, A. Old towns, 73.

Washington, D. C. Arnold, E. Seas & l. 58. — Brooks, E. S. Gt. cities, 141. — Pidgeon. Engineer's holiday, 13.—Tuckerman, C. K. Recollec. 1 : 80.

Washington, D. C., as a camp in 1861. Winthrop, T. Open air, 255.

— at time of first battle of Bull Run. (A. N. Waterman) Mil. ess. M. O. L. L. U. S. Ills. 21.

— Attack on, in 1814. (G. W. Cullum) Am. Hist. Assoc. **2** : 54.

— Capture of, 1814. Dawson. Batt. of U. S. **2** : 371.

— Defense of, July, 1864. (M. D. Hardin) Mil. ess. M. O. L. L. U. S. Ills. 121.

— in 1867. Curtis. From easy chair, **3** : 94.

— in 1877. Vivian. Tour in Am. 201.

— in 1881. Hardy. Between two oceans, 250.— Russell, W. H. Hesper, **1** : 70.

— Municipal condition of. (F. L. Siddons) Nat. Conf. City Govt. **2–3** : 358.

— Society in. Badeau. Vagabond, 228.

— — in 1826. Quincy, J. Figures, 254.

Washington, State of. (T. D. Hunt) Am. Geog. Soc. **1** : 137.

Washington, Fort, Capture of. Dawson. Batt. of U. S. **1** : 188.

Washington, Mt. Dodge, N. S. Sk. of N. E. 97.

— Ascent of. Taylor, B. At home, **2** : 355.

— in winter. (E. L. Wilson) Wilson, E. L. Mt.-climbing, 3.

— summit of, Glacial action upon. (C. H. Hitchcock) Estes. Half-hour recre. 422.

Washington monument. Winthrop. Addresses, **4** : 134.

Washington and Lee University. Gilman, D. C. Univ. prob. 277. — (Profs. White and Harris) U. S. Bur. Ed. Circ. '88, no. **1** : 293.

— Bibliography of. (H. B. Adams) U. S. Bur. Ed. Circ. '88, no. **1** : 301.

Washington University, Baltimore, Md. U. S. Bur. Ed. Circ. '94, no. **2** : 286.

Washington University, St. Louis, Mo. (M. S. Snow) U. S. Bur. Ed. Circ. '98, no. **2** : 129.

— Polytechnic department of. Missouri Labor, 1881.

Wasilewski, Edmund. Soboleski. Poets of Poland, 314.

Wason, Rigby. Grant, J. Recoll. Lords & Comm. **2** : 61.

"**Wasp**" and "Frolic." Roosevelt, T. Naval war 1812, 100.

— Cruise of the. Lodge & Roosevelt. Hero-tales, 115.

Wasps, Lubbock on. Hutton, R. R. Criticisms, **1** : 363.

Wasson, David A. Allen, J. H. Sequel, 152.

— Frothingham. Transcend. 349. — Stearns, F. P. Sk. Concord, 134. — Warner Lib. **26** : 15683. — (O. B. Frothingham) Wasson. Ess. 1.

Waste. Ess. from Nation, 97. — Kempner, W. Common-sense soc. 255.

— of cities and towns, Destruction of, by fire. (W. F. Morse) Ohio Health, '92 : 307.

— Reclamation of. Leslie, T. E. C. Ess. pol. econ. 254.

— Use of. Bushnell. Moral uses, 29.

Waste products, Disposal of. (J. Hartzell) Ohio Health, '86 : 198.

Watches, Waterbury. Pidgeon. Old world ques. 29.

Watch-night. Guthrie, T. Out of harness, 316.

Water. Gall & Robinson. Pop. read. sci. 357.— Tyndall. New frag. 331. — Iowa Health, '97 : 308.

— analysis of, chemical, Value of. (T. M. Stevens) Am. Pub. Health, **10** : 96.

Water, analysis of, sanitary, Present and future of. (C. Smart) Am. Pub. Health, **10** : 79.

— and air, Relations to life. (G. G. Hubbard) Smithson. Inst. Rept. '93 : 265.

— and ice. Iowa Health, '93 : 144.

— Bibliography. Whipple, G. C. Microscopy of water.

— composition of, Discovery of. Davy. Works, **7** : 129.

— Conservation of, in New South Wales. U. S. Cons. Rept. no. 140.

— Deterioration of, in reservoirs. (G. W. Rafter) N. J. Health, '90 : 111.

— Drinking. (E. J. Bartlett) N. H. Health, '94–95 : 196.

— — and public water-supplies. (W. R. Nichols) Buck, A. H. (ed.). Hygiene, **1** : 209.

— — Impure, Dangers of. (M. T. Runnels) Am. Pub. Health, **7** : 283.

— — Impurities in. (F. P. Venable) N. C. Health, '95–96 : 164.

— — — caused by vegetable growths. (W. G. Farlow) Mass. Health, '79 (1st) : 131.

— — — Organic. (C. W. Chamberlain) Conn. health, '82 : 257.

— in its relation to health. (J. L. Ludlow) N. C. Health, '97–98 : 163.

— — of Chilpancingo, Mexico. (L. Viramontes) Am. Pub. Health, **18** : 118.

— — of the City of Mexico. (J. Ramirez) Am. Pub. Health, **18** : 57.

— — Removal of bacteria from, by sand filtration. (G. W. Fuller) Am. Pub. Health, **19** : 152.

— — Sanitary examination of. (A. J. Wolff) Conn. Health, '85 : 249.

— Filtration of. (C. J. Foote) Conn. Health, '92 : 217.

— — by sand. (T. H. McKenzie) Conn. Health, '94 : 221.

— — — at Lawrence, Mass. (G. W. Fuller) Am. Pub. Health, **20** : 64.

— — Mechanical. (H. E. Ames) Am. Pub. Health, **18** : 94.

— — — Bacteriological results from. (G. T. Swarts) Am. Pub. Health, **21** : 154.

— Hardness of, and how determined. (E. H. Richards) Mass. Health, '95 : 435.

— History of. (R. W. Raymond) Brooklyn Eth Assoc. Life, 95.

— in agriculture. Nichols, J. R. Fireside sci. 156.

— of Lake Ontario, Bacteriological work on. (E. B. Shuttleworth) Am. Pub. Health, **20** : 58.

— polluted, Origin of ammonias in. (E. G. Horton) Am. Pub. Health, **23** : 199.

— Potable. (F. Davis) Iowa Health, '87 : 213.

— Properties, etc. of, and natural theology. Wilson, Jas. M. Ess. 1.

— Purification of, by metallic iron, 1896. (C. W. Chancellor) U. S. Cons. Rept. **51** : 571.

— Relation of, to health. Kingsley. Health, 89.

— — to propagation of fever. (A. Flint) Am. Pub. Health, **1** : 164.

— Sanitary chemistry of. (C. F. Chandler) Am. Pub. Health, **1** : 533.

— Sedimentation in. (W. Johnston) Am. Pub. Health, **20** : 37.

Water-closets at railway stations. (H. O. Hitchcock) Mich. Health, '79 : 15.

Water colors, English painters in. Buxton, H. J., et al. Eng. paint. 100.

Water-cure at Malvern, Life at the. Boyd. Crit. ess. 344.

Water-cure establishments, Life at. Boyd. Recreat. **2** : 300.

Water-lilies. Higginson. Out-door, 269.

Water-pipes, What shall we use for? Nichols, J. R. Fireside sci. 135.

Water-spouts and whirlwinds. Franklin. Works ('87), 2 : 267.

Water-supplies of the U. S., Relations of geology to. (E. Orton) Am. Pub. Health, 2 : 292.

— Pollution of. Am. Pub. Health, 14 : 62. — (C. Smart) Am. Pub. Health Assoc. 20 : 72. 21 : 312. — Am. Pub. Health, 19 : 191. — Maine Health, '88 : 170. — Penn. Health, '92 : 385.

— — in Mass. (S. W. Abbott) Am. Pub. Health, 13 : 259.

— — Report on. Am. Pub. Health, 23 : 56.

— Purification of. (C. W. Chancellor) Penn. Health, '90 : 508.

— Underground sources of, in Ontario. (P. H. Bryce) Am. Pub. Health, 16 : 209.

Water supply. Am. Pub. Health, 20 : 361. — Arnold, A. Soc. pol.

— and its relation to health and disease. (W. H. Dickenson) Iowa Health, '81 : 197.

— and natural drainage of North Carolina. (W. C. Kerr) Am. Pub. Health, 2 : 348.

— and public health. (A. Hazen) Am. Pub. Health, 17 : 74.

— and sewerage. (E. L. Vielé) Am. Pub. Health, 2 : 331.

— — in Mass. (W. R. Nichols; G. Derby) Mass. Health, '73 : 20. — (J. P. Kirkwood) Mass. Health, '76 : 23. — (F. Winsor) Mass. Health, '76 : 175. '87 : 2.

— Bibliography. Nichols. Water-supply, 216.

— Domestic. (S. Macadam) Trans. Soc. Sci. Lond. '97 : 536.

— for large and small towns. (G. J. Symons et al.) Trans. Soc. Sci. Lond. '76 : 542.

— for large institutions and small communities. (J. H. Shedd) Am. Pub. Health, 3 : 109.

— for towns. (A. P. Reid) Am. Pub. Health Assoc. 20 : 53.

— in Chicago. (A. R. Reynolds) Am. Pub. Health, 19 : 146.

— in Michigan. (A. Hazlewood; R. C. Kedzie) Mich. Health, '76 : 71.

— Investigations of. (F. H. Newell) Am. Pub. Health, 23 : 184.

— of Cambridge, Mass. (E. S. Wood) Mass. Health, '79 (1st) : 69.

— of England. (A. T. Atchinson; D. T. Ansted) Trans. Soc. Sci. Lond. '79 : 488.

— of London. Kingsley, C. New miscel. 203. — Wynter, A. Fruit. betw. leaves, 1 : 218. 2 : 249.

— of towns. Chambers's Papers, no. 49. — (W. R. Nichols) Mass. Health, '74 : 63.

— of towns and cities, Selection of. (C. F. Chandler) Am. Pub. Health, 1 : 533.

— of towns and vessels, Juniper water as. (T. W. Wood) Am. Pub. Health, 11 : 109.
See Rivers, Pollution of.

— on railroads. (S. W. Latta) Am. Pub. Health, 15 : 145.

— Public and domestic. (J. O. Webster) Maine Health, '86 : 197.

— Pure vs. purified. (D. W. Mead) Am. Pub. Health, 20 : 49.

— Should companies furnish? Wynter. Fruit, 2 : 249.

Waters, Chemical analysis of, etc. (T. M. Drown) Mass. Health, '90 : 519.

— Circulation of. (H. W. Dove) Estes. Half-hour, v. 1.

— Well, of our farm homesteads. (F. T. Shutt) Am. Pub. Health, 20 : 44.

Waterbury, Jared Bell. Miller, Jos. Singers church, 2d ed. 546.

Waterbury, Kate E. Brockett. Woman's work, 658.

Wateree (S. C.) Ford, Affair at. Dawson. Batt. of U. S. 1 : 611.

Waterford, Lady Louisa Stuart, marchioness. Clayton, E. C. Eng. fem. art. 2 : 338.

Waterford, Ireland. Silloway. Cathedral towns, 57.

Waterhouse, Dr. Benjamin. Lowell. Writ. 1 : 94.

Waterhouse, Sir Edward. Fuller. Worthies, 2 : 44.

Watering-place, A Pomeranian. Hall, G. S. Asp. Ger. 80.

Watering-places. Badeau. Vagabond, 180.

— American, Sanitary condition of. (H. Hartshorne) Am. Pub. Health, 2 : 55.

— French. Moulton, L. C. Rambles, 225.

— German. Fulton, C. C. Europe, 85. — Prime, S. I. Alhambra, 232.

— Health of. (J. Macpherson et al.) Trans. Soc. Sci. Lond. '75 : 494.

— Progress of. Arnold, F. Arm-chair, 107.

Waterloo, Battle of. Adams, C. Gr. camp. 202. — Adams, W. H. D. Battle stories, 224. — Adams, W. H. D. Eng. at war, 2. 11. — Adams, W. H. D. Memo. battles, 373. — Creasy. Fifteen battles, 329. — Guild. Over the ocean, 314. — King, C. Battles, 494. — Low, C. R. Great battles, 410. — Mathews. Conversers, 272. — Thackeray. Early & late, 181. — Fitchett. Deeds, 224. — George, H. B. Battles, 237. — Head, F. B. Descr. ess. 2 : 63.

— — Personal reminiscences of. Lieber, F. Reminis. 149.

— Campaign of. Morris, W. O. Commanders, 315.

— — Inner history of. Forbes, A. Camps, 321.
See also Napoleon I.; Wellington.

Waterlow, Herbert Jameson. Ritchie, J. E. City men, 148.

Waterlow, Sir Sidney. Ritchie, J. E. City men, 62.

Waterman, Richard. Bartlett, J. R. R. I. officers, 400.

Waterston, Anna C. L. Putnam, A. P. Singers liberal, 406.

Waterston, Robert Cassie. Putnam, A. P. Singers liberal, 390.

— Memoir of. (J. P. Quincy) Mass. Hist. Soc. Proc. 2d ser. 8 : 292.

Waterton, Charles. Hatton, J. Old lamps, 315.

— Home of. Wood, J. G. Out-of-doors, 290.

Watlington, England. Stone, J. S. Heart of Eng. 154.

— to Thame, From. Stone, J. S. Heart of Eng. 178.

Watrous, George H. Am. Bar Assoc. 12 : 349.

Watson, Asa Rogers. Davidson, J. W. Writ. of South, 604.

Watson, B. M. Memoir of, with portrait. (E. E. Hale) Mass. Hist. Soc. Proc. 2d ser. 12 : 253.

Watson, J. D. Bate, P. H. Eng. Pre-Raph. 87.

Watson, John [Ian Maclaren]. With portrait. Warner Lib. 26 : 15692. — Wilson, S. L. Theol. mod. liter.

Watson, Joshua. Arnold, F. Turning-points, 216.

Watson, Musgrave L., sculptor. Lonsdale. Worthies Cumb. v. 6.

Watson, Richard. Gorrie. Em. Meth. 136. — Pierce, B. K. Em. dead, 350. — Walker, W., jr. Men of sci. 134. — Wesley & successors, 117.

Watson, Thomas. Bell, R. Lit. & sci. men, **2** : 101. — (T. H. Ward) Ward. Eng. poets, **1** : 389. — Bettany. Em. doctors, **2** : 148. — Minto, W. Eng. poets, 203. — Morley, H. Eng. writ. 9 : 162.

Watson, William, with portrait. Warner Lib. **27** : 15705.

Watson, William Stuart. Stuart, C. B. Am. engineers, 293.

Watson, Fort, Capture of. Dawson. Batt. of U. S. **1** : 671.

Watt, James. Arago. Sci. men, **2** : 351. — Bolton, S. K. Poor boys, 33. — Brightwell. Heroes of lab. 178. — Brougham. Works, **1** : 25. — Chambers's Miscel. no. 136. — Cooper, T. Triumphs of persev. 99. — Craik. Pursuit knowl. **2** : 295. — Edgar. Footpr. 340. — Edwards, B. B. Self-taught, 446. — Hale, E. E. Lights of two cent. 525. — Howe, H. Em. mech. 279. — Jeffrey, F. Contrib. Ed. Rev. — Hundred greatest men, 485. — Lewis, T. C. Mechanicians, 14. — Neil, S. Epoch men, 271. — Nicoll. Great move. 396. — Parton. Peop. bk. biog. 140. — With portr. Seymour, C. C. B. Self-made, 531. — Smiles. Brief biog. 1. — Smiles. Self-help, 3. — Smiles. Indus. biog. — Taylor, W. C. Mod. Brit. Plut. 315. — Tweedie. Earnest men, 434. — Towle, G. M. Heroes of inven. 103. — Walker, W., jr. Men of sci. 137.

Watt, Linnie. Clayton, E. C. Eng. fem. art. **2** : 249.

Watteau, Antoine. Dilke. Fr. painters 18th cent. 74. — Houssaye. Men of 18th cent. **2** : 203. — Pater. Imag. port. 1. — Wedmore. Masters of genre, 155. — Men & wom. of France, **3** : 48.

— L'embarquement pour l'île de Cythère. (E. and J. de Goncourt) Singleton, E. Great pic. 38.

Watts, Alaric A. Miller, Jos. Singers church, 2d ed. 446.

Watts, George F. With photo. Cooper, T. Men of mark, **6** : 20. — Monkhouse, C. Brit. contemp. artists, 1. — Quilter. Preferences, 201. — Smalley. Lond. lett. **1** : 347.

— and E. Burne-Jones. Ruskin. Art of Engl. 29.

— Essay on. (J. B. Atkinson) Atkinson, J. B., et al. Eng. paint. 25.

Watts, Isaac. Griswold, R. W. Sac. poets. — Hatfield, E. F. Poets of church, 629. — Holland, J. Psalmists, **2** : 146. — Macdonald, G. England's antiphon, 280. — Miller, Jos. Singers church, 2d ed. 126. — Mitchell, D. G. Eng. lands, **3** : 12. — With portrait. Warner Lib. **27** : 15717. — (S. Johnson) Chalmers. Eng. poets, **13** : 3.

— and the Baptists. Ivimey. Eng. Bapt. **3** : 221.

— Letters of. (H. F. Jenks and others) Mass. Hist. Soc. Proc. 2d ser. **9** : 331.

— Residence of. Hall, Mrs. S. C. Engl. shrines, 224.

— Unpublished letters. (S. A. Green) Mass. Hist. Soc. Proc. 2d ser. **12** : 149.

Watts, Theodore. (M. Bell) Miles, A. H. Poets of cent. **6** : 255.

Waugh, Alex., D. D. Grant, Jas. Metropol. pul. 35. — With portrait. Morison, J. Fathers of Lond. Miss. Soc. **2** : 1.

Waugh, Edwin. Espinasse. Lit. recollec. 349. — Watson, W. Excur. in crit. 46.

Wave, sea, Greatest ever known. Proctor. Light sci. **1** : 194.

Wavellite, Experiments on. Davy. Works, **2** : 297.

Waverley Abbey. Timbs. Abbeys, **1** : 268.

Waves, Stilling by oil. Franklin. Works ('87), **5** : 253.

Waxhaws, S. C., Action at. Dawson. Batt. of U. S. **1** : 582.

Wayland, Francis. Griswold. Prose writ. 364.

Waymouth, George. Bourne, H. R. F. Eng. seam. **1** : 299.

Wayne, Gen. Anthony. With portrait. [Amer.] Nat. portr. gall. v. **1**. — With portrait. Duyckinck. Nat. portr. gall. **1** : 280. — Glazier, W. Heroes, 153. — With portrait. Headley, J. T. Washington, **1** : 314. — With portrait. Seymour, C. C. B. Self-made, 94. — Lossing. Em. Amer. 286. — Neven, D. R. B. Pennsylvanians, 94.

— and Wayneborough. Glenn, T. A. Colon. mans. **2** : 279.

Wayne, James Moore. Livingston, J. Em. Am. lawy. 158.

Wayne, Fort, Siege of. Dawson. Batt. of U. S. **2** : 125.

Waynflete, William. Campbell. Ld. chan. **1** : 309. — Foss. Judges, **4** : 370.

Wayside Inn, Sudbury, Mass. Drake, S. A. Hist. fields Mid. 420.

Wealth. Denslow. Mod. think. 363. — Emerson. Conduct, 71.

— and character. Warner, C. D. As we go, 62.

— and free government. Hoyt, J. G. Miscel. 204.

— and its uses. (A. Carnegie) Butterfield Lec. Un. Coll. **1** : 319.

— Antidote to. Higginson. Book & heart, 182.

— as means of education. Clarke, J. F. Self-culture, 263.

— Bibliography. (I. Fisher) Cournot, A. Mathemat. prin. wealth.

— Christianity and. Gladden. Appl. Chris. 1.

— Consumption of. (S. N. Patten) Univ. Pa. Publ. Pol. Econ. **1** : no. 4.

— Democracy and. Walker, F. A. Discus. in econ. **2** : 399.

— Disadvantages of. Eliot, C. W. Five Am. cont. 291.

— Distribution of. Mass. Bur. Lab. '94 : 49.

— Duties of. Carpenter, E. Eng. ideal, 139.

— Flux of; its effect on families. Hamerton. Hum. int. 119.

— Gospel for. Potter, H. C. Scholar & state, 233.

— growth of, Laws and conditions of. Elder, W. Questions, 40.

— in England, Unequal distribution of. Greg, W. R. Pol. prob. 157.

— Liberalism and. Ess. in liberalism, 31.

— National, Sources of. Burnap. Miscel.

— New and old. Smart, W. Stud. econ. 217.

— of Protestant and Catholic nations. Brownson. Works, **18** : 184.

— Poetry of. Green, J. R. Stray studies, 93.

— Religion and. (W. Gladden) Barrows, J. H. Parl. relig. **2** : 1068.

— Right use of. Anderson, M. B. Papers, **1** : 217. — Farrar. Soc. & p. day quest. 95.

— Sources of advancement in. Elder, W. Questions, 53.

— Transplantation of. Higginson. Conc. all, 74.

— Uses of. Bristed. Pieces, **4** : 4.

— Way to. Franklin. Works ('87), **1** : 441.

Weapon ointment. Holmes, O. W. Currents, 61.

Weare, Meshech. Lossing. Em. Amer. 183.

Weare, William, Murder of, 1823. Thornbury. Old stor. 340.

Weather, The. Tuckerman. Optimist, 224.

— and weather prophets. Herschel. Famil. lec. 142.

West Indies and Florida. (F. A. Ober) Am. Geog. Soc. **18** : 183.
— Danish, 1891. (S. B. Horne) U. S. Cons. Rept. 37 : 369.
— Expedition to, 1585. Froude. Eng. seamen, 130.
— Slavery in, J. Stephen on. Macaulay. Ess. **6** : 303.
West Point Military Academy. (P. S. Michie) Butterfield lec. Un. Coll. **1** : 13.
— Early days at. Mansfield, E. D. Pers. mem. 64. — Willis. Hurry-graphs, 134. — College book, 210. — Keyes, E. D. Fifty years, 188.
West Roxbury, Mass., Heroes of, in the civil war. Clarke, J. F. Memo. sketches, 383.
Westbury, Richard Bethell, 1st baron. Reid, T. W. Cab. portr. 217. — Smith, J. Campbell. Writings, 397.
— and Bishop Wilberforce. (H. D. Traill) Coan. Stud. biog. 176.
— Obituary of. Em. persons, **1** : 162.
Westchester, N. Y. Willis. Hurry-graphs, 129.
Western Maryland College, Westminster, Md. (T. H. Lewis) U. S. Bur. Ed. Circ. '94, no. **2** : 189.
Western Reserve, Settlement of. Garfield. Works, **2** : 70.
Western Reserve University, Cleveland, O. U. S. Bur. Ed. Circ. '91, no. **5** : 116.
Westmeath, Marquis of. Grant, J. Recoll. Lords & Comm. **1** : 86.
Westmeath committee. Disraeli. Sel. spee. **2** : 363.
Westminster Abbey. Farrar, F. W. Our Eng. minsters, 25. — Guild. Over the ocean, 170. — Irving. Sk.-book, 130. — Kingsley, C. Lec. Amer. **1**. — Moulton, L. C. Rambles, 162. — Thompson. Beaten paths, 65. — Wallace, S. E. Bosphorus, 305. — Winter, W. Shakesp. Eng.
— Building of. Timbs. Abbeys, **1** : 7.
— Dedication of. Stanley, A. P. Ser. spec. occ. 16.
— Tombs in. Lamb. Elia.
Westminster Assembly of divines. Stoughton, J. Spir. heroes, 116.
— Bibliography. Memor. vol. Westminster Assem. 1647–1897.
Westminster College, Fulton, Mo. (W. R. Dobyns) U. S. Bur. Ed. Circ. '98, no. **2** : 93.
Westminster Palace. Winter, W. Shakesp. Eng.
Westminster School, London. Staunton, H. Schools, 116.
Westmoreland, Maria Jourdan. Raymond, I. Southland wr. **1** : 447.
Westmoreland, Priscilla Anne (Pole), Countess. Clayton, E. C. Eng. fem. art. **2** : 340.
Weston, Agnes E. Bolton, S. K. Soc. stud. in Eng. 101.
Weston, Edward, 1703-70. Jesse, J. H. Cel. Eton. v. **1**.
Weston, George. (H. A. Clapp) Harv. mem. biog. **2** : 199.
Weston, James Adams, with portrait. Rogers, A. C. Repres. men, 593. — With portrait. Sketches N. H. men, 85.
Weston, Mrs. Mary Pillsbury. Ellet. Women artists, 332.
Weston, Thomas. Galt. Players, **1** : 232.
Weston, Thomas, English adventurer, and his followers. Adams, C. F. Three episodes, **1** : 45.
Weston, Father William, Life of. Morris, J. Troub. of Cath. v. **2**.

Westover homestead, Va. Glenn, T. A. Colon. mans. **1** : 17. — Terhune. Colon. homes, 33.
Westphalia, Congress of. Bernard. Four lectures on diplomacy.
— Peace of. Cust. Warriors thirty years, **2** : 589.
Westward ho! (1887.) Bates. Year in gt. rep. **2** : 1.
Westwood, Thomas. Miles, A. H. Poets of cent. **4** : 435.
Westwood Park. Jewitt, L. Stately homes, **2** : 160.
Wetherell, Sir Charles. Grant, Jas. Bench & bar, **2** : 136. — Grant, J. Recoll. Ho. Comm. 91. — Whiteside, J. Early sk. 46.
Wetherill, John P. Winslow, S. N. Biog. Phila. merch. 137.
Wetherill, William D. Am. Bar Assoc. **10** : 427.
Wetmore, Prosper Montgomery. Everest. Poets of Conn. 299.
Wette, W. M. L. de. Cheyne. Founders O. T. crit. 31.
Wetzell's Mill, Skirmish at. Dawson. Batt. of U. S. **1** : 661.
Wexford, Memorials of. Davis, T. Prose, 116.
Weyden, Roger van der. Conway, W. M. Early Flem. artists, 161.
Weyer, S. van de. Hayward, A. Ess. 2d ser. **1** : 281.
Weymouth, George. Belknap. Amer. biog. **2** : 239.
Whale, Night on a. Wraxall. Scraps, **2** : 168.
Whale fisheries in Arctic and Pacific oceans. Seward. Works, **1** : 236.
Whaleman and the whale. Forbes, E. Lit. papers, 145.
Whales and their neighbors. Wilson, A. Nat. note-book, 118.
— and the whale fishery. Flower, W. H. Ess. on museums, 185.
— and whale fishing. Weeden. New England, **1** : 430.
Whalley, George H. Ritchie. Brit. sena. 205.
Wharncliffe, Lord. Grant, J. Recoll. Lords, 197.
Wharton, Anne. Williams, Jane. Lit. wom. 125.
Wharton, Lucy, Marchioness of. Williams, Jane. Lit. wom. 126.
Wharton, Margaret. Baring-Gould. Yorks. odd. **1** : 173.
— Abduction of. Burke, P. Cel. trials. — Morse, J. T., jr. Famous trials.
Wharton, Philip, duke of (1699-1731). Russell, W. Eccen. 331.
Wharton, Thomas, marquis of, 1640-1716, with portrait. Caulfield. Kit-cat, 70. — Macaulay. Biog. sk. 312. — Russell, W. Eccen. 324. — (O. Wister) Warner Lib. **27** : 15819.
Whatcoat, Richard. Gorrie. Em. Meth. 212. — Jackson, T. Early Meth. **3** : 261.
Whately, Richard, abp. of Dublin. Arnold, F. Our bishops, **1** : 168. — Hunt, J. Rel. thought 19th cent. 103. — Martineau, H. Biog. sk. 169. — Mozley. Reminis. **1** : 267.
Whateley, Thomas. Mitchell. Wet days, 230.
Wheat, Z. Livingston, J. Em. Am. lawy. 139.
Wheat in the Argentine Republic, Transportation of, '95. (E. L. Baker) U. S. Cons. Rept. **49** : 460.
Wheathill, Anne. Williams, Jane. Lit. wom. 63.
Wheatland, Henry. (F. W. Putnam) Am. Acad. A. & S. Proc. **31** : 363. — (W. P. Upham) Mass. Hist. Soc. Proc. 2d ser. **9** : 276.
Wheatley, Francis. Wedmore. Studies, 2d ed. 41.

White, Hugh Lawson. With portrait. [Amer.] Nat. portr. gall. v. 4.

White, James. Ritchie. Brit. sena. 140.

White, James, author of history of France. Payn. Lit. recol. 163.

White, James Clark. Vaille & Clark. Harv. book, v. 1.

White, Mrs. James W. With portrait. Ellet. Queens Am. soc. 342.

White, Jeremiah W., with portrait. Sketches N. H. men, 149.

White, John, bishop of Winchester. Burke, S. H. Hist. portr. Tudor, 3 : 284. — Holland, J. Psalmists, 2 : 67.

White, John, voyager. Bourne, H. R. F. Eng. seam. 1 : 232.

White, Joseph Blanco. Gladstone. Glean. 2 : 1. — Mozley. Reminis. 1 : 53. — Thomson, K. B. Recoll. v. 2. — Redding. Pers. remin. 3 : 173. — Miles, A. H. Poets of cent. 10 : 667.

— Arguments of, criticised. Froude, R. H. Remains, pt. 2, 1 : 315.

— Autobiography of. Mozley. Ess. 2 : 68.

— Sonnets of. Deshler. Afternoons, 310.

White, Lydia E. Hemenway. Poets of Vt. 233.

White, Nathaniel, with portrait. Sketches N. H. men, 172.

White, Philip S. Bungay. Off-hand, 267.

White, Richard. Tayler. Eng. martyrs.

White, Richard Grant. Richardson. Amer. lit. 1 : 142. — With portrait. Warner Lib. 27 : 15876.

White, Robert. Wilson, J. G. Poets of Scot. 2 : 257.

White, Thomas, bishop of Peterborough. Strickland. Bishops, 132.

White, William, D. D. With portrait. [Amer.] Nat. portr. gall. v. 1. — Headley, J. T. Chaplains Revol. 171. — Lossing. Em. Amer. 53.

White, William, H. R. N., with portrait. Jones, E. R. Heroes of ind. 236.

White, Sir William A. Em. persons, 5 : 173.

White, William Charles. Loring, J. S. Hundred Bost. ora. 344.

White and colored races in the U. S., Comparative vital movement of. (S. S. Herrick) Am. Pub. Health, 7 : 266.

White-Cross movement in education. (Frances E. Willard) Nat. Educa. Assoc. '90 : 159.

White-hoods, The. Taylor, W. C. Revol. 2 : 284.

White-horse hill, Berkshire. Buckland, F. T. Curios. nat. hist. 3 : 182.

"White House" inn. Baring-Gould. Yorks. odd. 1 : 183.

White Mountains, The. Martineau. Retrosp. 3 : 56.

— Bibliography. Providence Pub. Lib. Bull. Sept. '95.

— The Notch. Dodge, N. S. Sk. of N. E. 86.

White Plains, Battle of. Dawson. Batt. of U. S. 1 : 176.

White race, Cradle of. Brinton. Races & peo. 109.

White Sea, The. Helms. Pioneering, 329.

Whitefield, George. Broadus. Lect. hist. preach. 222. — Foster, J. Crit. ess. (Bohn) 2 : 62. — Georgian era, 1 : 443. — Pierson, A. T. Evangelistic work, 169. — Ryle, J. C. Christian leaders, 30. — Stephen, J. Ess. — Larrabee, W. C. Wesley, 2 : 87. — Mathews, W. Oratory, 379. — Waterbury. Eloq. preach. 163. — With portrait. Withrow. Makers of Meth. 127. — Wise, D. Heroic Meth. 66.

Whitefield, George, in Boston. Cook, J. Transcendentalism, 193-217.

— Last meeting of John Wesley with. Larrabee, W. C. Wesley, 1 : 356.

— Marriage of. Hardy, E. J. Love aff. 176.

Whitehall. Thomson, K. B. Recoll. v. 1.

— Old. Dobson, A. Miscel. 183.

— Palace of. Timbs. Abbeys, 1 : 168.

Whitehead, Charles. Hodder, G. Memories, 354. — (M. Bell) Miles, A. H. Poets of cent. 3 : 559.

Whitehead, James. Ritchie, J. E. City men, 159.

Whitehead, Paul, the poet tailor. Chalmers. Eng. poets, 16 : 199. — Doran. Habits, 304.

Whitehead, William. Austin & Ralph. Laureates, 287. — Chalmers. Eng. poets, 17 : 189. — Hamilton, Wal. Poets laur.

Whitelamb, John. Tyerman. Oxf. meth. 374.

Whitelock, Sir Bulstrode. Campbell. Ld. chan. 3 : 328. — Foss. Judges, 6 : 498. — Woolrych. Serjeants, 1 : 263. — Welsby. Eng. Judges.

Whiteside, James. Ritchie. Brit. sena. 287.

Whitfield, Frederick. Miller, Jos. Singers church, 2d ed. 579.

Whitfield, James. Clarke, R. H. Cath. bishops, 1 : 456.

Whitgift, John, abp. Burke, S. H. Hist. portr. Tudor, 4 : 306. — Hook. Abps. Cant. 10 : 121. — Tulloch. Eng. purit. 19. — Taylor, W. C. Rom. biog. v. 2. — (G. Paul) Wrangham. Brit. Plutarch, v. 3.

Whiting, Harold. (J. Trowbridge) Am. Acad. A. & S. Proc. 31 : 356.

Whiting, William. Livingston, J. Em. Am. lawy. 640.

Whiting, William, poet. Miles, A. H. Poets of cent. 10 : 737. — Miller, Jos. Singers church, 2d ed. 573.

Whitman, Marcus. Creegan. Gt. mission. 341.

Whitman, Sarah Helen. Griswold. Fem. poets, 166.

Whitman, Walt. Austin, A. Poetry, 192. — Buchanan. David Gray, 203. — Burroughs. Birds & poets, 213. — Lanier, S. Eng. novel. — Noel. Ess. on poetry. — Stedman. Poets Amer. 349. — Stevenson, R. L. Fam. stud. 91. — Walsh, W. S. Pen pic. mod. 161. — Chapman, J. J. Emerson, 111. — Howe, M. A. D. Am. bookm. 222. — With portrait. (J. Burroughs) Warner Lib. 27 : 15885. — Cheney, J. V. That dome, 144. — Ellis, H. New spirit. — Em. persons, 5 : 226. — Gosse, E. Crit. kitcats. — Higginson, T. W. Contemp. 72. — Hubbard, E. Little jour. 2 : 167. — Nichol. Amer. lit. 207. — Richardson. Amer. lit. 2 : 268. — Stevenson, R. L. Miscel. 2 : 95. — Stoddard, R. H. Poets' homes, 35.

— American Socrates. Buchanan, R. Look round, 341.

— and democratic art. Symonds. Ess. 2 : 30.

— at home. (George Selwyn) Gilder. Authors, 333.

— at Whitestone. Wolfe, T. F. Lit. haunts, 129.

— Bibliography. Triggs, O. L. (ed.). Selec. W. Whitman.

— Day with. Wolfe. Lit. shr. Am. auth. 201.

— Poems. Nichol, J. Amer. lit. 207.

— poet and democrat. (J. Robertson) Baildon. Round table.

— the poet of democracy. Dowden. Studies, 468.

— Works of. Swinburne. Stud. prose & p. 129.

Whitmarsh, Skirmish at. Dawson. Batt. of U. S. 1 : 368.

Whitney, Adeline Dutton Train. With portrait. (H. B. Stowe) Our fam. wom. 652. — Stoddard, R. H. Poets' homes, 28. — Vedder, H. C. Amer. writers, 201.

Whitney, Anne. (M. A. Livermore) Our fam. wom. 668.

Whitney, Eli. Brooks, E. S. Hist. Amer. 218. — Edwards, B. B. Self-taught, 468. — Howe, H. Em. mech. 101. — Seymour, C. C. B. Self-made, 420. — Parton. Peop. bk. biog. 159. — With portrait. Hubert, P. G., jr. Inventors, 69. — Lossing. Em. Amer. 132. — Thayer, W. M. Turn.-points, 235. — Towle, G. M. Heroes of inven. 93. — Wynne. Lit. men Amer.

Whitney, Frederick Augustus. Putnam, A. P. Singers liberal, 331.

Whitney, Henry A., with portrait. (E. Bangs) Mass. Hist. Proc. 2d ser. **5** : 424.

Whitney, Jos. Dwight. Vaille & Clark. Harv. book, v. **1**.

Whitney, William Dwight. Am. Acad. A. & S. Proc. **30** : 579. — Am. Antiq. Soc. Proc. n. s. **9** : 369.

— On the origin of language. Müller. Chips, 4.

Whittelsea, Cambridgeshire. Rimmer, A. Old towns, 138.

Whittemore, Amos. Howe, H. Em. mech. 147. — With portrait. Seymour, C. C. B. Self-made, 553.

Whittemore, George. (T. B. Fox) Harvard mem. biog. **1** : 379.

Whittemore, Thomas. Livingston, J. Dist. Amer. 300.

Whittier, John Greenleaf. (B. Wendell) Am. Acad. A. & S. Proc. **28** : 357. — Bartlett, D. W. Mod. agita. 240. — Bolton, S. K. Success, 42. — Bungay. Off-hand, 132. — Griswold, H. T. Home-life, 238. — Griswold. Poets Am. 337. — Griswold. Prose writ. 617. — Hazeltine. Chats, 212. — Rideing. Boyhood. — Saunders, F. Famous books, 197. — Stedman. Poets Amer. 95. — Walsh, W. S. Pen pic. mod. 119. — Cheney, J. V. That dome, 91. — Stearns, F. P. Sket. Concord, 253. — Wright, H. C. Chil. sto. in Am. lit. 96. — Em. persons, **5** : 255. — Fisher, M. Gen. sur. Am. lit. 216. — Higginson, T. W. Contemp. 60. — With portrait. Mitchell, D. G. Am. lands, **2** : 305. — Griswold, R. W. Sac. poets. — Howe, M. A. D. Am. bookm. 242. — Lawton, W. C. N. E. poets, 155. — With portrait. (G. R. Carpenter) Warner Lib. **27** : 15911. — Miller, Jos. Singers church, 2d ed. 498. — Mitford, M. R. Recollec. 334. — Nichol. Amer. lit. 240. — (R. H. Stoddard) Powers, H. N. Homes of eld. poets, 105. — Richardson. Amer. lit. **1** : 415. **2** : 173. — Stewart, G. Ess. from Rev. — Stewart, Geo., jr. Evenings in lib. 130. — Stoddard, R. H. Poets' homes, 19. — Wendell, B. Stelligeri, 147.

— at home. (H. E. P. Spofford) Gilder. Authors, 343.

— Bibliography. Hodgkins. 19th cent. authors.

— Home of. (H. Butterworth) Parton. Princes, 319. — Wolfe. Lit. shr. Am. auth. 117.

— Life and friendships of. Fields, A. Authors, 263.

— Mabel Martin. Taylor, B. Crit. ess. 294.

— Poems. Nichol, J. Amer. lit. 240.

— Sonnets. Deshler. Afternoons, 294.

Whittingham, William. Holland, J. Psalmists, **1** : 115.

— and the Puritans. Taylor, W. C. Rom. biog. v. **2**.

Whittington, Richard, of London. Bourne, H. R. F. Eng. merch. **1** : 71. — Bourne. Lond. merchants, 15.

— and his cat. Tartt. Ess. **1** : 187.

Whittlesey, Charles. Am. Antiq. Soc. Proc. n. s. **4** : 187.

Whittlesey, Sarah J. Ç. Davidson, J. W. Writ. of South, 614. — Raymond, I. Southland writ. **2** : 808.

Whittlesey, William, 1368–74. Hook. Abps. Cant. **4** : 221.

Whittredge, Worthington. Sheldon, G. W. Amer. painters, 98.

Whitwell, Benjamin. Loring, J. S. Hundred Bost. ora. 368.

Whitwell, Samuel. Loring, J. S. Hundred Bost. ora. 228.

Whitworth, Sir Joseph. Em. persons, **4** : 10. — Jeans. Creators, 213. — Lewis, T. C. Mechanicians, 266.

— at Stancliffe. Yates, E. H. Celeb. **2** : 335.

Whytehead, Thomas. Miller, Jos. Singers church, 2d ed. 527.

Wiborg. Atkinson, J. B. Art tour northern, 144.

Wichern, Immanuel. Stevenson. Praying & w. 61.

— Theories of, illustrated in Indiana House of refuge. (F. B. Ainsworth) N. Y. Pris. Assoc. **26**, app. : 322.

Wick, William W. Woollen. Biog. sk. Indiana, 252.

Wickersham, John. (E. Brooks) Nat. Educa. Assoc. '92 : 598.

Wiclif, John. Brown, J. B. Stoics, 265. — Coffin, C. C. Story of liberty, 30. — Collier, W. F. Hist. Eng. lit. 46. — Fuller. Worthies, **1** : 479. — Gilliat, E. Champions, 120. — Graham, W. Ess. 45. — Herrick, S. E. Heretics, 23. — Lord, J. Beacon, **2** : 434. — (J. Corbet) Reformers. Paisley lec. 1. — Rogers, J. E. T. Gleanings, **2** : 1. — Sterling, J. Ess. **1** : 30. — Tayler, C. B. Memorials of Eng. martyrs, 40. — Gilpin, W. Lives, 11. — Gurney, J. H. Four eccl. biog. — Leake, F. Hist. bub. 201. — Marshall, W. Men of mark. — Wittenmeyer. Women reform. 16. — With portrait. Warner Lib. **27** : 16235. — (J. Fox) Wrangham. Brit. Plutarch, v. **1**. — Broadus. Lec. hist. preach. 188. — Hodgson, Wm. Reformers, 80. — Ivimey. Eng. Bapt. **1** : 67. — Myers, F. Lec. gt. men, 143. — Pennington. Epochs papacy, 197. — Williams, F. Eng. card. **2** : 5.

— and the Lollards. Merson. Heroic days, 57. — Trench. Lec. mediæval, 306.

— English version of the Bible. Hunt, T. W. Rep. Eng. prose, 33.

— Portraits of. Sergeant, L. Wiclif, 17.

— Savonarola, and Huss. Williams, W. R. Eras, 110.

Wickliffe, Robert. Livingston, J. Em. Am. lawy. 568.

Wicklow, Earl of. Grant, J. Recoll. Lords, 133.

Widows. Linton, E. L. Girl of per. **1** : 223.

— Consecrated, of middle ages. Cutts, E. L. Scenes mid. ages, 152.

— with dependent children, Treatment of. (L. Wolcott) Conf. char. & correc. '88 : 137.

Widsith, Deor, and the scôp. Brooke, S. A. Hist. early Eng. lit. 1.

Widvilles, Fortunes of the. Burke, B. Viciss. of fam. **3** : 355.

Wieck, Clara. *See* Schumann, Clara.

Wieland, Christoph Martin. Bancroft, G. Miscel. 146. — Gostwick. Ger. poets, 81. — Hedge. Prose Ger. 128. — Taylor. Stud. Ger. 245. —

With portrait. Warner Lib. **27** : 15954. — Wells, B. W. Mod. Ger. lit. 38.
Wieniawski, with portrait. Ehrlich, A. Cel. violin. 208.
Wiesbaden. Moulton, L. C. Lazy tours, 323.
— to Munich. Haven, G. Pilgrim. 430.
Wietrowetz, Gabrielle, with portrait. Ehrlich, A. Cel. violin. 259.
Wife, Choosing a. Holland, J. G. Titcomb's let. 22.
— The literary. Disraeli, I. Curios. (N. Y. 4 v.) **1** : 423.
Wife-beating as a crime. (R. Adams, jr.) Phila. Soc. Sci. Assoc. '86.
Wife's mother, The. Friswell. Better self, 35.
Wigan, Alfred. Marston, J. W. Rec. actors, **2** : 251.
— and Horace Wigan. Coleman, G. Players, **1** : 263.
Wigglesworth, Michael. Mitchell, D. G. Amer. lands, 42. — Nichol. Amer. lit. 58. — Richardson. Amer. lit. **2** : 5.
— and his Day of doom. (S. A. Green) Mass. Hist. Soc. Proc. 2d ser. **9** : 269.
— Day of doom. Ward, May A. Old col. 259.
— a warm writer. Mitchell, D. G. Am. lands, 42.
Wight, Isle of. Benjamin, S. G. W. Atlan. isl. 234. — Sterling, J. Ess. **2** : 64. — Benjamin, S. G. W. World's paradises, 152. — Timbs. Abbeys, **1** : 417.
Wightman, Edward. Brown, J. N. Bapt. martyrs, 240. — Wallace, R. Anti-Trin. biog. **2** : 534.
— Warrant for the execution of. Wallace, R. Anti-Trin. biog. **3** : 568.
Wightman, William. Foss. Judges, **9** : 292.
Wignell, Thomas. Dunlap. Am. theatre, v. **1**.
Wigs and gowns of lawyers. Jeaffreson. Lawyers, 280.
— and their wearers. Doran. Habits, 138.
Wigton martyrs, The. Paget, J. Paradoxes, 253.
Wikes, Mr., of Leascholme. Baring-Gould. Yorks. odd. **2** : 10.
Wikoff, Henry, "chevalier." Derby, J. C. Fifty years, 368. — Forney. Anec. 366.
Wilberforce, Samuel, bp. of Winchester. Arnold, F. Our bishops, **1** : 217. — Bayne, P. Chr. life, 158. — Burgon. Twelve men, **2** : 1. — (Sir G. W. Dasent) Coan. Stud. biog. 140. — Davies, G. J. Suc. preach. **1**. — Church, R. W. Occ. pap. **2** : 334. — Em. persons, **1** : 168. — Paladin. Glances, 28. — Huntington, G. Random recol. 58. — Smith, G. B. Chr'n workers, 241.
— and Henry. Mozley. Reminis. **1** : 99.
— and Lord Westbury. (H. D. Traill) Coan. Stud. biog. 176.
Wilberforce, William. Adams, W. H. D. Good Samar. 147. — Adams, W. H. D. Worthies Church Eng. 201. — Blaikie, W. G. Leaders, 41. — Brougham. Works, **3** : 343. — Child, L. M. Oasis, v. **1**. — Edgar. Boyhood, 110. — Hazlitt. Spirit. — With portrait. Nicoll. Great move. 48. — Seeley, M. Later evang. 188. — Stephen. Ess. eccl. biog. 469. — Taylor, W. C. Mod. Brit. Plut. 333. — Duyckinck. Portrait gall. **1** : 416. — Hazlitt. Parl. portr. 70. — Stanton, H. B. Reforms, 81.
— and John Wesley. Gibbins. Eng. soc. ref. 65.
Wilberforce, William. Thayer, W. M. Turn.-points, 184.
Wilberforce University, Xenia, O. U. S. Bur. Ed. Circ. '91, no. 5 : 214.
Wilbor, Otis. (Miss A. M. Wilbor) N. E. Hist.-Gen. Soc. Biog. **3** : 285.

Wilbur, Anne Tappan. Hart, J. S. Fem. prose, 402.
Wilcox, Cadmus M. Pollard. Life of Lee, 496.
Wilcox, Carlos. Griswold. Poets Am. 145. — Griswold, R. W. Sac. poets. — Hemenway. Poets of Vt. 21.
Wild, Jonathan. Whitehead, C. Highwaymen, **2** : 151.
Wild, Robert. Bell, R. Lit. & sci. men, **2** : 181. — Gosse, E. From Shakesp. 163.
Wild children. Chambers's Miscel. no. 48.
Wild lands in New Jersey. N. J. Labor, '78 : 85.
Wildbad and its water. Dasent. Jest & earnest, **1** : 105.
Wilde, J. P. See Penzance, Lord.
Wilde, Oscar. Walsh, W. S. Pen pic. mod. 202. — Intentions. Repplier. Ess. in min. 121.
Wilde, Richard Henry. Griswold. Poets Am. 109. — Griswold. Prose writ. 258. — Miller, S. F. Bench of Ga. v. **2**. — Richardson. Amer. lit. **2** : 33.
Wilde, Samuel S. (N. Crosby) Memo. of judges fr. Dartm. **1**. — (J. G. White) N. E. Hist.-Gen. Soc. Biog. **2** : 368.
Wilde, Sir Thomas. See Truro, Thomas W., Baron.
Wilder, Marshall P., with portrait. Sketches N. H. men, 25.
Wilderness, Battle of. Swinton. Twelve battles, 356.
Wilderness campaign. (S. Prentice) Mil. ess. M. O. L. L. U. S. Ills. 99. — Stine, J. H. Army Poto. 593.
Wilderspin, S. Leitch, J. Prac. educa.
Wildgoose lodge, Burning of, 1816. Thornbury. Old stor. 226.
Wiley, Calvin H. Davidson, J. W. Writ. of South, 617.
— and southern common schools. Weeks, S. B. Beginning comm. sch. syst. in South.
Wiley, John. Derby, J. C. Fifty years, 292.
Wiley, Mrs. Mary. Raymond, I. Southland wr. **2** : 777.
Wilfrid, St., and suppression of the Cetic heresy. Montalembert. Monks, **4** : 129.
— Contemporaries and successors of. Montalembert. Monks, **4** : 375. **5** : 1.
Wilhelm, Martin. Wallace, R. Anti-Trin. biog. **2** : 443.
Wilhelmine von Bayreuth. Warner Lib. **27** : 15969.
Wilhelmj, August, with portrait. Ehrlich, A. Cel. violin. 38.
Wilkes, Charles. Duyckinck. Nat. portr. gall. **2** : 298. — With portrait. Headley, J. T. Farragut, 103. — With portrait. Greely, A. W. Explorers, 194.
Wilkes, John. Collins, Stephen. Miscel. — Brougham. Works, **3** : 425. — Daly, J. B. Radicals. — Dilke. Papers, **2** : 229. — Hitchman. 18th cent. **1**. — Rogers, E. T. Gleanings, **2** : 129.
Wilkie, Sir David. Edgar. Boyhood, 286. — Eng. painters. Georgian, 49. — Jerdan. Men, 449. — Redgrave. Century of p. **2** : 213, 256. — Russell, W. Extraor. men, 185. — With portrait. Sharp, W. Great minds, 287. — Smiles. Self-help. — Spooner. Biog. fine arts, **2** : 1095. — Taylor, W. C. Mod. Brit. Plut. 338. — Thomson, K. B. Recoll. — Tuckerman. Ess. 379. — Wedmore. Masters of genre, 225. — With portrait. Ollier, E. Brit. portr. paint. 80. — Thayer, W. M. Turn.-points, 216.
Wilkie, William. Chalmers. Eng. poets, **16** : 109.

William Frederick, king of Holland. Doran. Monarchs, **1** : 289.

William Frederick, 2d duke of Gloucester, 1776–1833. Fitzgerald, P. Royal dukes, **2** : 303.

William Henry, Duke of Gloucester, son of George II., 1743–1805. Fitzgerald, P. Royal dukes, **1** : 191.

William and Mary College. College book, 54. — (H. B. Adams) U. S. Bur. Ed. Circ. '87, no. 1. — Richardson. Amer. lit. **1** : 137. — U. S. Bur. Ed. Circ. '88, no. **1** : 41.

— Facts from records of. (L. G. Tyler) Am. Hist. Assoc. **4** : 455.

William Jewell College, Liberty, Mo. (J. G. Clark) U. S. Bur. Ed. Circ. '98, no. **2** : 67.

Williams, Anna. Bethune, G. W. Brit. fem. poets, 62. — Williams, Jane. Lit. wom. 195.

Williams, Mrs. Bessie W. Raymond, I. Southland wr. **1** : 494.

Williams, Charles. Bettany. Em. doctors, **2** : 178.

Williams, Charles, with portrait. Sketches N. H. men, 47.

Williams, Sir Charles Hanbury. Creasy. Etonians, 279. — Jesse, J. H. Cel. Eton. v. **1**.

Williams, Charles Kilborn. (S. Williams) N. E. Hist.-Gen. Soc. Biog. **2** : 17.

Williams, Edw., with portrait. Morison, J. Fathers of Lond. Miss. Soc. **2** : 344.

Williams, Edward Calvin. Am. Bar Assoc. **17** : 504.

Williams, Eleazer. (D. T. V. Huntoon) N. E. Hist.-Gen. Soc. Biog. **3** : 252.

Williams, F. Harold, *pseud.* Miles, A. H. Poets of cent. **9** : 575.

Williams, George. Ritchie, J. E. City men, 250.

Williams, Helen Maria. Bethune, G. W. Brit. fem. poets, 138. — Hatfield, E. F. Poets of church, 676. — Miller, Jos. Singers church, 2d ed. 330. — Williams, Jane. Lit. wom. 303.

Williams, Henry Willard. Vaille & Clark. Harv. book, v. **1**.

Williams, Isaac. Griswold, R. W. Sac. poets. — Miller, Jos. Singers church, 2d ed. 474.

Williams, J. H. Clemens. Funny fellows, 94.

Williams, James D. Woollen. Biog. sk. Indiana, 147.

Williams, Jesse Lynch. With portrait. Stuart, C. B. Am. engineers, 141.

Williams, Sir John. Grant, J. Bench & bar, **1** : 193. — Gurney, J. H. Hist. sketches, **3** : 351. — Brougham. Works, **4** : 312. — Campbell. Ld. chan. **3** : 147. — Foss. Judges, **6** : 379. — Woolrych. Serjeants, **2** : 680.

Williams, John, Archbishop. Stephen, J. F. Horæ Sabb. **1** : 286. — Wrangham. Brit. Plutarch, v. **3**.

Williams, John, Archdeacon. Sinclair, J. Sketches.

Williams, John, the martyr of Erromango. Yonge. Pioneers, 240. — Adams, W. H. D. Good Samar. 237. — Creegan. Gt. mission. 179. — Thompson, A. Gt. mission. 61.

Williams, John Ambrose, Trial of, for libel on the Durham clergy. Townsend, W. C. Mod. state trials, **2** : 237.

Williams, John Fletcher. Am. Antiq. Soc. Proc. n. s. **10** : 208.

Williams, Jonathan, with portrait. [Amer.] Nat. portr. gall. v. **1**.

Williams, Mrs. Marie Bushnell. Davidson, J. W. Writ. of South, 619. — Raymond, I. Southland wr. **1** : 224.

Williams, Mrs. Mary, of the South Seas. Pitman, Mrs. Heroines mission. 121.

Williams, Montagu. Sala, Mrs. Fam. peop. 110.

Williams, Otho Holland. With portrait. [Amer.] Nat. portr. gall. v. **2**. — Boyle, E. Dist. Marylanders.

Williams, Rebecca. Ellet. Pioneer wom. 171.

Williams, Robert. Wakeley. Heroes Meth. 169.

Williams, Roger. Caldwell, S. L. Cities of faith, 212. — Diman. Orations, 108. — Doyle. Pur. colonies, **1** : 151. — Purnell. Liter. 164. — With portrait. Seymour, C. C. B. Self-made, 275. — Tuckerman. Ess. 181. — Ivimey. Eng. Bapt. **1** : 217. **2** : 575. — Lossing. Em. Amer. 18. — Mitchell, D. G. Amer. lands, 18. — Nichol. Amer. lit. 46. — Richardson. Amer. lit. **1** : 121. — Sherman, D. N. Eng. divines, 34.

— as a statesman. Purnell. Liter. 164.

— Freeman of Massachusetts. (R. A. Guild) Am. Antiq. Soc. Proc. n. s. **5** : 140.

— a liberal Puritan. Mitchell, D. G. Am. lands, 18.

Williams, Rowland. Paul. Biog. sk. 93. — Thirlwall, C. Remains, **1** : 290.

Williams, Samuel Wells. Am. Geog. Soc. **16** : 186. — With portrait. (Rev. E. W. Gilman) Hayden, H. C. Am. miss. heroes, no. 8.

Williams, Sarah. (A. H. Japp) Miles, A. H. Poets of cent. **7** : 573.

Williams, Stephen West. (Mrs. H. M. Huntington) N. E. Hist. Gen. Soc. Biog. **2** : 389.

Williams, Thos. Manning, J. A. Speakers, 223.

Williams, Thomas. Miles, A. H. Poets of cent. **10** : 691.

Williams, Watkin. Gener. of judges, 211.

Williams, Sir William. Manning, J. A. Speakers, 378.

Williams, William. Miller, Jos. Singers church, 2d ed. 220. — Hatfield, E. F. Poets of church, 679.

Williams, William. Dwight, N. Signers of decl. 90. — Lincoln, R. W. Signers, 68. — Lossing. Signers, 56. — Sanderson. Signers, v. **4**.

Williams College. College book, 167. — (E. B. Parsons) U. S. Bur. Ed. Circ. '91, no. **6** : 225.

— Inaugural at, 1836. Hopkins, M. Misc. ess. 232.

— Semi-centennial address, 1843. Hopkins, M. Misc. ess. 256.

Williamsburg, Va. Terhune. Colon. homes, 471.

Williamson, Hugh. Lossing. Em. Amer. 156. — Neven, D. R. B. Pennsylvanians, 194.

Williamson, Sir J. Lonsdale. Worthies Cumb. v. **6**.

Williamson, Peter. Drake, S. G. Trag. of wilderness, 147.

Williamson, William D. (J. Williamson) N. E. Hist. Gen. Soc. Biog. **1** : 13.

Williamson's plantation, Affair at. Dawson. Batt. of U. S. **1** : 601.

Williamstown, Mass. Pidgeon. Old World ques. 152.

Willibrod, St. Maclear. Apostles, 99.

Willimantic, Conn., Thread mills at. Pidgeon. Old World ques. 217.

Willing, Jennie F. Hanaford. Women of cent. 440.

Willis, Benj. A. Am. Bar Assoc. **10** : 423.

Willis, Nathaniel Parker. Howe, M. A. D. Am. bookm. 99. — With portrait. Warner Lib. 27 : 16001. — Bungay. Off-hand, 43. — Cobb, J. B. Leisure labors, 301. — Griswold. Poets Am. 301. — Griswold. Prose writ. 483. — Par-

Winlock, Joseph. Vaille & Clark. Harv. book, v. 1.

Winmarleigh, J. Wilson-Patten, Lord, with photo. Cooper, T. Men of mark, 2 : 6.

Winslow, Gov. Edward. (W. C. Winslow) Am. Hist. Assoc. Rept. '95 : 65. — Belknap. Amer. biog. 3 : 85. — With portrait. Moore, J. B. Am. gov. 93. — Lossing. Em. Amer. 23. — Richardson. Amer. lit. 1 : 81.

Winslow, Hubbard. Loring, J. S. Hundred Bost. ora. 576.

Winslow, John, of Marshfield, Mass. Sabine. Loyalists, 713.

Winslow, John Ancrum, with portrait. Headley, J. T. Farragut, 288.

Winslow, Josias. Moore, J. B. Am. gov. 175.

Winslow, Mary. Baillie, J. Life-stud. 321.

Winsor, Justin. (A. L. Lowell) Am. Acad. A. & S. Proc. 34 : 641. — Am. Antiq. Soc. Proc. n. s. 12 : 229.

— Memoir of. (H. E. Scudder) Mass. Hist. Soc. Proc. 2d ser. 12 : 457.

— Tribute to, with portrait. (S. A. Green and others) Mass. Hist. Soc. Proc. 2d ser. 12 : 30.

Winsted, Conn. Pidgeon. Old world ques. 45.

Winter, Sir William. Bourne, H. R. F. Eng. seam. 2 : 13.

Winter, William, with portrait. Warner Lib. 27 : 16061.

Winter. Dodge, M. A. Country, 335. — Holmes, O. W. Odd. vol. 174. — Mitchell, D. G. Bound toge. 61. — Walsh, R. Didactics, 1 : 57. — Guthrie, T. Out of harness, 258. — Whiting, C. G. Saunterer, 249.

— Duties of. Greenwood, F. W. P. Miscel. 363.

— Good word for. Lowell. Writ. 3 : 255.

— An open. Abbott, C. C. Outings, 82.

— Supposed change in temperature of. Webster, N. Papers, 119.

— Use of. Bushnell. Moral uses, 188.

— Word for. Skelton, J. Ess. in romance, 7.

Winter spirit. Whiting, C. G. Saunterer, 231.

Winter sports. Lang. Leaders, 17.

Winter sunrise, A. Abbott, C. C. Outings, 1.

Winter walk, A. Thoreau. Excursions, 109.

Winterbotham, Henry Self Page. Ritchie. Brit. sena. 171.

Winters, cold, Notable. Proctor, R. A. Rough ways, 125.

— English. Proctor, R. A. Fam. sci. 201.

Winterslow Hutt, Eng., and Hazlitt. Rees, J. R. With friend, 38.

Winthrop, John, Gov. Belknap. Amer. biog. 3 : 148. — Bryant. Prose, 2 : 221. — With portrait. Moore, J. B. Am. gov. 237. — Brooks, E. S. Hist. Amer. 1. — Lossing. Em. Amer. 9 : 44. — Mitchell, D. G. Amer. lands, 28. — Richardson. Amer. lit. 1 : 90. — Whittier. Prose works, v. 2.

— Estate of. (M. Chamberlain) Mass. Hist. Soc. Proc. 2d ser. 7 : 127.

Winthrop, John, jr. (F. G. Kingsbury) Am. Antiq. Soc. Proc. n. s. 12 : 295. — Belknap. Amer. biog. 3 : 185.

Winthrop, John, Prof. Youmans. Pioneers sci. 40.

Winthrop, Margaret (Tindal), wife of Gov. John. Anderson, J. Mem. wom. Pur. 1 : 120. — Belloc. Vignettes, 257. — Child. Good wives, 243. — Clement, J. Noble deeds, 404. — Chapman, W. Wom. of Purit. 9. — Earle. Colon. dames, 110.

Winthrop, Robert C. Am. Acad. A. & S. Proc. 30 : 566. — Mass. Hist. Soc. Proc. 2d ser. 9 : 211. — Am. Antiq. Soc. Proc. n. s. 10 : 14. —

Loring, J. S. Hundred Bost. ora. 638. — Maury, S. M. Statesm. of Am. 79. — Smalley. Stud. 307.

Winthrop, Robert C., and the Peabody Education Fund. (A. D. Mayo) U. S. Bur. Ed. Rept. '93–94, 1 : 739.

— Tribute to. (J. G. Wilson) Am. Hist. Assoc. Rept. '94 : 55.

Winthrop, Theodore. Griswold. Prose writ. 692. — Nichol. Amer. lit. 370. — Shea, J. G. Fallen brave. — With portrait. Warner Lib. 27 : 16075.

— Novels. Nichol, J. Amer. lit. 370.

— Writings. Hawthorne, J. Confess. 172.

Winthrop, Thomas L. (W. Jenks) Mass. Hist. Coll. 4th ser. 2 : 202.

Winthrop papers. Lowell. Writ. 2 : 21.

Winthrops of early New England. Mitchell, D. G. Am. lands, 28.

Winton, Andrew. Irving, D. Scot. poets, 1 : 275.

Winzel, Ninian. Irving, D. Scot. writ. 1 : 98.

Wire-mills at Ansonia, Conn. Pidgeon. Old World ques. 16.

Wirt, William. With portrait. [Amer.] Nat. portr. gall. v. 1. — With portrait. Duyckinck. Nat. portr. gall. 1 : 423. — Griswold. Prose writ. 121. — Magoon. Orators of rev. 368. — Mathews, W. Men, p. & t. 20. — Browne, I. Stud. gt. lawyers, 256. — Lossing. Em. Amer. 218. — Moore, F. Am. eloq. 2 : 439. — With portrait. Scott, H. W. Dist. Am. lawy. 709. — With portrait. Warner Lib. 27 : 16090.

— Character of. Kennedy, J. P. Occas. addr. 78.

Wisby. Buckley, T. A. Great cities, 93.

Wisconsin, Early lead mining in. (R. G. Thwaites) Am. Hist. Assoc. Rept. '93 : 189.

— Economic and social aspects of. Warner, C. D. Studies, 157.

Wisdom, Robert. Holland, J. Psalmists, 1 : 127.

Wisdom. Taylor. Notes from life, 74.

— Excellence of ; a sermon. Thirlwall, C. Remains, 3 : 339.

— Practical. Helps. Essays, 3.

— Simulated. Bacon. Ess.

Wise, Henry A. Bartlett. Pres. candidates, 233. — Pollard. Life of Lee, 559. — Savage. Liv. rep. men, 473. — Willis. Hurry-graphs, 224.

Wiseman, Cardinal Nicholas. Houghton, Ld. Monog. 37.

— Essays. Brownson. Works, 10 : 450.

Wiseman, Luke H. Wesley & successors, 217.

Wishart, George. Pierce, B. K. Em. dead, 38.

— P. Hamilton and. (J. Kidd) Reformers. Paisley lec. 344.

Wismar, Germany. Mahaffy. Holl. & Germ. 201.

Wisnovius, Stanislaus. Wallace, R. Anti-Trin. biog. 2 : 229.

Wissowatius, Andrew. Wallace, R. Anti-Trin. biog. 2 : 523.

Wissowatius, Andrew, jr. Wallace, R. Anti-Trin. biog. 2 : 225.

Wissowatius, Benedict. Wallace, R. Anti-Trin. biog. 2 : 524.

Wistar, Casper. With portrait. [Amer.] Nat. portr. gall. v. 2. — (C. Morris) Gross. Lives physicians, 116.

Wister, Owen, with portrait. Warner Lib. 27 : 16101.

Wiswall, Hattie. Brockett. Woman's work, 725.

Wit. Hare. Guesses, 1 : 23.

— and humor. Coleridge. Lit. rem. 1 : 131. — Hazlitt. Comic, 1. — Whipple. Lit. & life. — Repplier. Ess. in idle. 168.

Women, working, Boarding homes and clubs for. (Mary S. Ferguson) U. S. Lab. Bull. **3** : 141.
— — in Chicago. Illinois Labor, '**92** : iii, 3.
— — in Germany. U. S. Cons. Rept. no. 153.
— — in large cities of U. S. U. S. Labor, v. **4**.
— — in Missouri. Missouri Labor, '91.
— — in New York. N. Y. Labor, '85.
— — Organization of. (L. M. Hubbard) Burdett-Coutts. Wom. miss. 273.
Women agriculturists, Hanaford. Wom. of cent. 700.
Women artists. Hanaford. Wom. of cent. 271.
Women convicts and convict prisons. Wynter, A. Fruit betw. leaves, **1** : 88.
Women educators. Hanaford. Wom. of cent. 496.
Women historians. Hanaford. Wom. of cent. 710.
Women inventors. Hanaford. Wom. of cent. 621.
Women journalists. Hanaford. Wom. of cent. 661.
Women lawyers. Hanaford. Wom. of cent. 635.
Women lecturers. Hanaford. Wom. of cent. 305.
Women librarians. Hanaford. Wom. of cent. 697.
Women missionaries. Hanaford. Wom. of cent. 477.
Women physicians. Hanaford. Wom. of cent. 531.
Women poets. Hanaford. Wom. of cent. 229.
Women preachers. Hanaford. Wom. of cent. 415.
Women printers. Hanaford. Wom. of cent.
Women reformers. Hanaford. Wom. of cent. 331.
Women scientists. Hanaford. Wom. of cent. 256.
Women students in Scottish universities. (L. Stevenson) Cong. Educa. Chic. '93, 877.
Women teachers, University Association of. (C. Elder) Cong. Educa. Chic. '93, 865.
Women travellers. Hanaford. Wom. of cent. 715.
Women wage-earners. Me. Bur. Lab. '**92** : 9.
Women's Club, New England. Blanc, T. Wom. in U. S. 105.
Women's clubs as an educational factor. (Margaret J. Evans) Nat. Educa. Assoc. '98 : 237.
— Coöperation of, in public schools. (Ellen M. Henrotin) Nat. Educa. Assoc. '**97** : 73.
— in Chicago. Blanc, T. Wom. in U. S. 43.
Women's work at Cotton Centennial Exposition, New Orleans, 1885. Nat. Educa. Assoc. '**85** : 534.
— in the mission field. Pitman, Mrs. Heroines mission.
Wood, Sir Andrew. Edgar. Sea-kings, 98. — Grant, Jas. Constable of Fr. 187.
Wood, Edward Stickney. Vaille & Clark. Harv. book, v. **1**.
Wood, George B. Gross, S. D. Autobiog. **2** : 393.
Wood, Mrs. Henry. (A. Sergeant) Oliphant. Wom. novelists, 176. — Wotton. Word portraits, 330.
Wood, Isaac. Francis, S. W. N. Y. phys. 159.
Wood, J. Riddall. Miller, Jos. Singers church, 2d ed. 574.
Wood, James. Wesley & successors, 53, 75.
Wood, James, 1756–1836. Redding. Misers, **1** : 20.
Wood, James Frederic. Clarke, R. H. Cath. bishops, **3** : 533.

Wood, James K. Francis. N. Y. surg. 83.
Wood, Joseph. Jones, C. C., jr. Deleg. fr. Georgia, 201.
Wood, Nathaniel. Peabody. Harv. grad. 196.
Wood, Thomas, Trial of. Phillips, S. M. Famous cases, 53.
Wood, Thomas J. Shanks. Rec. of generals, 289.
Wood, Thomas Waterman. With portrait. Benjamin, S. G. W. Am. art. 1. — Sheldon, G. W. Amer. painters, 109.
Wood, William Page. Foss. Judges, **9** : 316.
Wood-carving. Bibliography. Providence Pub. Lib. Bull. May, '95.
Wood-cutting and wood-cut printing in Japan. (T. Tokuno and S. R. Koehler) U. S. Nat. Mus. Rept. '**92** : 221.
Wood-engraving. Chambers's Miscel. no. 85. — (H. Crossfield) Galton, F. W. Workers, 67.
Wood pulp, Manufacture of, in Germany. U. S. Cons. Rept. no. 152.
Woodberry, George Edward, with portrait. Warner Lib. **27** : 16145.
Woodburne, John, Crime of. Burke, P. Romance of forum.
Woodbury, Levi. With portrait. [Amer.] Nat. portr. gall. v. **2**. — Loring, J. S. Hundred Bost. ora. 660. — (C. L. Woodbury) N. E. Hist.-Gen. Soc. Biog. **1** : 295.
Woodchucks. Whiting, C. G. Saunterer, 7.
Woodcocke, John. Stone, J. M. Faithful, 209.
Woodd, Basil. Holland, J. Psalmists, **2** : 296. — Miller, Jos. Singers church, 2d ed. 328.
Woodd, Mrs. Hannah. Burder. Pious wom. 437.
Wooden statue of Baron Ii Kamon-no-Kami Naosuké, of Japan. (A. Satoh, tr.) U. S. Nat. Mus. Rept. '**94** : 619.
Woodford, James Russell, bishop of Ely. With photo. Cooper, T. Men of mark, **4** : 10. — Miller, Jos. Singers church, 2d ed. 548.
Woodford, Samuel. Holland, J. Psalmists, **2** : 69.
Woodhouse, James. Lives of dist. shoemak. 272. — Southey. Uned. poets, 114.
Woodhull, Alfred Alexander. Hatfield, E. F. Poets of church, 684.
Woodlands. Maxwell, H. Post-mer. 230.
Woodman, Richard. Brown, J. N. Bapt. martyrs, 169.
Woodpile, An old farm's. Abbott, C. C. Outings, 96.
Woodrow, Henry. Laurie, W. F. B. Dist. Anglo-Ind. **2** : 137.
Woodrow, Robert. Burton, J. H. Book-hunter, 338.
Woods, Andrew S. (H. Bingham) Memo. of judges fr. Dartm. 25.
Woods, Leonard. Lossing. Em. Amer. 390.
Woods, Mrs. Margaret L. Couch, A. T. Q. Adv. crit. 349. — Warner Lib. **27** : 16153.
Woods and other materials. (S. Webb) Morris, W. Arts & crafts, 345.
Woods in winter. Abbott, C. C. Outings, 22.
Woodville, Elizabeth. Russell. Extr. women, 67.
Woodville, R. C. Tuckerman. Artists, 408.
Woodville, W. Lonsdale. Worthies Cumb. v. **6**.
Woodward, Ashbel. Am. Antiq. Soc. Proc. n. s. **4** : 66.
Woodward, George W. Brown, D. P. Forum, **2** : 134.
Woodward, Harry. Doran. Annals stage, **2** : 113.
Woodward, Mrs. Ellet. Pioneer wom. 402.

Workingmen in England. Carlyle. Past and present.
— in Massachusetts, Families of. (C. D. Wright) Mass. Labor, '75 : 191.
— Institutes of. Robertson, F. W. Lec. 1.
— Opportunities of. Gladstone. Speeches, 10 : 123.
— Party of. Everett. Orat. v. 1.
— Sanitary condition of. Mass. Labor, '74 : 29.
— Three typical. Harrison, J. Dang. tend. 77.
— Wives of. Harrison, J. Dang. tend. 107.
Workingmen's clubs. (A. F. W. Ingram) Knapp, J. M. Univ. 31.
Works and days. Emerson. Society, 149.
Workshop instruction in schools, Value of. (J. F. Moss) Internat. health exh. 14 : 24.
Workshops, Large, in Europe. Bolton, S. K. Soc. stud. in Eng. 154.
— school, Equipment of. (J. F. Moss) Internat. health exh. 14 : 31.
World, The, as an educator. (F. Temple) Ess. & rev.
— as an eject. Romanes. Mind & motion, 88.
— as injured by man. Swing. Old pic. 2 : 173.
— as it goes. Friswell. Wick. world, 267.
— End of. Proctor, R. A. Mysteries, 229.— Stephen, J. F. Ess. by barr. 134. — Whittier. Lit. recre. 364.
— The external. Mivart. Less. fr. nature, 55.
— history of, Introduction to. Goldsmith. Miscel. (N. Y. 4 v.) 1 : 533.
— of commerce in 1492, The. (W. B. Weeden) Am. Antiq. Soc. Proc. n. s. 8 : 246.
— Progress of. Lowell. Latest ess. 160.
World, The London. Hatton. Jour. Lond. 85.
Worldliness. Hazlitt. Sket.
— and other worldliness. Eliot, G. Ess. 7.
Worldlings, Great loss of the. (R. Baxter) Friswell. Silent hour, 56.
Worlds, Birth and death of. Proctor, R. A. Mysteries, 55.
— organic and inorganic, Relation between. Hinton. Thinking, 91.
— Other, and other universes. Proctor. Myths, 134.
— physical and spiritual, Oneness of. Hinton. Thinking, 145.
— Plurality of. (H. J. S. Smith) Oxf. ess. '55 : 105.
Worley, Captain. Whitehead, C. Highwaymen, 2 : 117.
Wormeley, Katherine P. Brockett. Woman's work, 318.
Worms to Mayence. Bartley, G. C. D. Rhine, 133.
Woronicz, John Paul. Soboleski. Poets of Poland, 117.
Worry. Boyd. Our life, 11. — Helps. Friends, 2d ser. 1. — Mathews, W. Men, p. & t. 247.
Worsaae, Jens Jacob Asmussen. Smith, C. R. Retrospec. 2 : 150.
Worship. Burton, N. J. Yale lec. 465. — Emerson. Conduct, 173. — Friswell. Silent hour, 9.
— Acceptable. Hopkins, M. Miscel. ess. 356.
— Celebration of public. Thirlwall, C. Remains, 1 : 53.
— Christian. Channing. Works, 4 : 303.
— — Bibliography. Hall, C. C. & oth. Christian worship.
— — Early. Ker, J. Lec. hist. preach. 44.
— National. Maurice, F. D. Soc. morality, 192.
— The rule of. Shipley, O. Tracts, 381.
— Social public. Drake, N. Evenings, 2 : 316.
Worsley, C. Espinasse. Lanc. worth. v. 1.
Worsley, Philip Stanhope. Miles, A. H. Poets of cent. 10 : 751.

Worsted yarn, Manufacture of, in Pennsylvania. Penna. Labor, 1888.
Wort-cunning, leechdoms, and starcraft of early England. Lucas. Mornings, 1 : 165.
Worth, William Jenkins. Duyckinck. Nat. portr. gall. 2 : 301. — Glazier, W. Heroes, 203.
Worthington, John. Tulloch. Rational theol. 17th cent. 2 : 427.
Wortley, Lady Emmeline Stuart. Bethune, G. W. Brit. fem. poets, 376.
Wortley, Sir Francis. Bell, R. Lit. & sci. men, 2 : 172.
Wotton, Sir Henry. Adams, W. H. D. Worthies Church Eng. 26. — Creasy. Etonians, 88. — Lodge. Portraits (Bohn), v. 4. — (J. W. Hales) Ward. Eng. poets, 2 : 108. — Wotton. Word portraits, 335. — Griswold, R. W. Sac. poets. — Holland, J. Psalmists, 1 : 296. — Walton, I. Lives ; also in Wrangham. Brit. Plutarch, v. 4.
Wotton, Nicholas. Burke, S. H. Hist. portr. Tudor, 3 : 160.
Wotton-under-Edge and Bradley Court. Hodges, Eliz. Anc. Eng. homes, 15.
Woulfe, Serjeant. Grant, J. Recoll. Lords & Comm. 2 : 294.
Wouwerman, Philips. Gower. Fig.-painters Holl. 40.
Wrangel, Friedrich Heinrich Ernst von. Strauss, G. L. M. Men of Ger. 2 : 19.
Wrangel, Karl Gustaf. Cust. Warriors thirty years, 2 : 503.
Wrangel Island, First landing on. (I. C. Rosse) Am. Geog. Soc. 15 : 163.
Wrangham, William. Miller, Jos. Singers church, 2d ed. 300.
Wray, Cecil D. Huntington, G. Random recol. 283.
Wray, Sir Christopher. Campbell. Ch. just. 1 : 180. — Manning, J. A. Speakers, 235.
Wray, William, Last, of Ards. Burke, B. Viciss. of fam. 2 : 57.
Wrecks and wreckers on the English coast. Wynter, A. Peeps, 2 : 236.
Wreford, J. Reynell. Miles, A. H. Poets of cent. 10 : 687. — Miller, Jos. Singers church, 2d ed. 461.
Wren, Sir Christopher. Edgar. Footpr. 289. — Milizia. Lives arch. 2 : 270. — Parton. Capt. indus. 363. — Spooner. Biog. fine arts, 2 : 1109. — Wrangham. Brit. Plutarch, v. 5.
— Monument of. Hall, Mrs. S. C. Pilgr. Eng. shr. 2 : 52.
Wrestlers, Japanese. Arnold, E. Wand. words, 147.
Wright, Benjamin. Lossing. Em. Amer. 363. — With portrait. Stuart, C. B. Am. engineers, 48.
Wright, Chauncey. Fiske, J. Darwin, 78. — Wright, C. Philos. dis. 7.
Wright, Duncan. Jackson, T. Early Meth. 1 : 247.
Wright, Fortunatus. Laughton. Stud. nav. hist. 194.
Wright, George G. Am. Bar Assoc. 19 : 650.
Wright, Joseph. Baker, W. S. Portr. of Wash. 46. — Redgrave. Century of p. 1 : 231.
Wright, Joseph. Ivimey. Eng. Bapt. 2 : 237.
Wright, Joseph A., with portrait. Woollen. Biog. sk. Indiana, 94.
Wright, Sir Nathan. Campbell. Ld. chan. 5 : 203.
Wright, Philip James. Miller, Jos. Singers church, 2d ed. 507.

Yang-tze Kiang, Region of the, 1897. (A. C. Jones) U. S. Cons. Rept. **54** : 9.

Yard, pendulum, and metre, The. Herschel. Famil. lec. 419.

Yarmouth, England. Hatton, J. Old lamps, 46.

Yarranton, Andrew, iron-worker. Smiles. Indus. biog.

Yate Court. Hodges, Eliz. Anc. Eng. homes, 100.

Yates, Edmund. Sala, Mrs. Fam. peop. 87.

Yates, Frederick. Imitations. Lennox, W. P. Plays, **2** : 61.

Yates, Joseph C. Jenkins. Gov. of N. Y. 319.

Yates, Richard. Brockett. Men of our day, 332. — Cook, D. Hours w. players, **1** : 258.

Yazoo land companies. (C. H. Haskins) Am. Hist. Assoc. **5** : 395.

Year, The Pueblo "doctoring" of. Lummis. Strange corners, 243.

Yeardley, Sir George. Belknap. Amer. biog. **2** : 148.

Yearsley, Mrs. Anna (Sactilla). Bethune, G.W. Brit. fem. poets, 152. — Southey. Uned. poets, 125.

Yeast. (T. H. Huxley) Estes. Half-hour, v. 1. — Huxley. Critiques. — (T. H. Huxley) Manch. sci. lec. **3–4** : 7.

Yedo. *See* Tokio.

Yellow fever. (W. Wyman and others) Am. Pub. Health Assoc. 203. — (W. Nelson) Calif. Health, '84–86 : 220.

— causes of, New method of investigation into. (B. F. Gibbs) Am. Pub. Health, **6** : 358.

— Coloration of persons attacked by. (M. Carmona y Valle) Am. Pub. Health, **19** : 89.

— Contribution to the study of. (E. Liceaga) Am. Pub. Health, **19** : 122.

— Disinfection in. (C. B. White) Am. Pub. Health, **3** : 154.

— Distribution and natural history of, in U. S. (J. M. Toner) Am. Pub. Health, **1** : 358.

— early cases of, How to deal with. (J. Chandler) Am. Pub. Health, **5** : 108.

— Epidemic of 1839. (W. G. Austin) Am. Pub. Health, **4** : 231.

— — in 1864. (D. W. Hand) Am. Pub. Health, **4** : 293.

— — in U. S., 1878, Significance of. (E. Harris) Am. Pub. Health, **4** : 158.

— Etiology of. (J. T. Tyner) Am. Pub. Health, **5** : 147. — (G. M. Sternberg) Am. Pub. Health, **15** : 170. — (H. B. Horlbeck) Am. Pub. Health, **24** : 116. — (E. Liceaga) Am. Pub. Health, **24** : 128.

— — and treatment of. (G. M. Sternberg) Am. Pub. Health, **23** : 426.

— Fallacies of personal quarantine. (A. N. Bell) Am. Pub. Health, **14** : 55.

— Importation of, into the U. S., 1693–1876. (S. Choppin) Am. Pub. Health, **4** : 190.

— in Baltimore, 1876. (J. Morris) Am. Pub. Health, **4** : 243.

— in Chattanooga, 1878. (J. H. Vandeman) Am. Pub. Health, **4** : 210.

— in Cordova, Mex. (G. Mendizabal) Am. Pub. Health, **22** : 167.

— in Florida, 1873–75. (G. M. Sternberg) Am. Pub. Health, **2** : 468.

— in Georgia, 1876. (E. M'Clellan) Am. Pub. Health, **4** : 249.

— in Jackson, Miss., 1888. (W. Johnston) Am. Pub. Health, **14** : 51.

— in Key West, 1880. (F. W. Lester) Am. Pub. Health, **6** : 354.

Yellow fever in Memphis, 1879. (G. B. Thornton) Am. Pub. Health, **5** : 111. — (J. F. Cameron) Am. Pub. Health, **5** : 152. — Mich. Health, '80 : 72.

— — Sanitation and quarantine against. (G. B. Thornton) Am. Pub. Health, **6** : 189.

— in Mexico. (G. Mendizabal) Am. Pub. Health, **17** : 193.

— — Study of. (E. Liceaga) Am. Pub. Health, **21** : 164. **22** : 162.

— in Mobile, Ala., Measures to prevent spread of. (T. S. Scales) Am. Pub. Health, **6** : 176.

— in Pensacola, 1882. (R. B. S. Hargis) Am. Pub. Health, **9** : 306.

— in Puebla, Mexico, 1892. (A. Contreras) Am. Pub. Health, **18** : 221.

— in the state of Tabasco. (A. Castanares) Am. Pub. Health, **18** : 217.

— in the U. S., 1873. (J. H. Erskine *et al.*) Am. Pub. Health, **1** : 385, 430.

— in Vera Cruz. (N. Del Rio) Am. Pub. Health, **18** : 292.

— Infection of vessels with, at Havana. (D. M. Burgess) Am. Pub. Health, **7** : 205.

— International committee on. Am. Pub. Health, **19** : 120.

— May it not originate in the U. S.? (A. A. Woodhull) Am. Pub. Health, **5** : 80.

— Medico-geographical view of. (E. Liceaga and J. Ramirez) Am. Pub. Health, **23** : 422.

— Observations on. (A. N. Bell) Am. Pub. Health, **14** : 55.

— Panics about. (J. H. Rauch) Am. Pub. Health, **14** : 136.

— Parasitism in. (M. Carmona y Valle) Am. Pub. Health, **18** : 265.

— Prevention of. (W. Selden) Am. Pub. Health, **4** : 286. — Am. Pub. Health, **22** : 156.

— — of the spread of. (F. Formento) Am. Pub. Health, **20** : 217. — (W. Wyman) Am. Pub. Health, **20** : 203.

— — Problems in. (J. Cochran) Am. Pub. Health, **14** : 41.

— Prophylaxis of. (M. Carmona y Valle) Am. Pub. Health, **21** : 169.

— Seventh report on. (E. Liceaga) Am. Pub. Health, **24** : 135.

— Study of. (E. Liceaga) Am. Pub. Health, **20** : 227. **22** : 162.

— What to do against. (H. Hartshorne) Am. Pub. Health, **1** : 396.

Yellow races, The. (E. T. Hamy) Smithson. Inst. Rept. '65 : 505.

Yellowstone Park. Brockett. Our west. emp. 1227. — Pierrepont. Fifth ave. 237. — (W. I. Marshall) Nat. Educa. Assoc. '81 : 132.

— Autumn in. Rutgers, L. On saddle, 1.

— Bibliography. Chittenden, H. M. Yellowstone nat. park.

— Geological history of. (Arnold Hague) Smithson. Rept. '92 : 133.

Yellowstone river, Wonders of the. (J. Gibbon) Am. Geog. Soc. **5** : 112. — Raymond, R. W. Comp. 153.

Yelverton, Sir Christopher. Manning, J. A. Speakers, 267.

Yeoman, R. Tayler. Eng. martyrs.

Yew-trees in churchyards. Lower. Contrib. 193.

— of Great Britain & Ireland. Bibliography. Lowe, J. Yew-trees.

Yezo, Japan, pit-dwellers of, Ancient. (Romyn Hitchcock) U. S. Nat. Mus. Rept. '90 : 417.

Yiddish literature. Bibliography. Wiener, Leo. Hist. of Yid. lit. in 19th cent.

Yojoa Lake, Honduras. (E. G. Squier) Am. Geog. Soc. **2** : pt. **1**, 19.

Yokohama. Pidgeon. Engineer's holiday, 238. — Pumpelly. Amer. & Asia, 78.

Yonge, Charlotte M. Bethune, G. W. Brit. fem. poets, 487.

York, Anne Hyde, Duchess of. With portrait. Jesse. Court of Eng. Stuarts, **3** : 471. — Costello. Eng. women, **3** : 315. — Lodge. Portraits (Bohn), v. **5**. — With portrait. Oliphant. Hist. char. Q. Anne, 43.

York, Frederick Augustus, Duke of. Georgian era, **1** : 129. — Scott, W. Biog. mem. v. **2**.

— and Mary Ann Clarke. Browne, G. L. Narr. state trials, **1** : 243.

York, England. Baur. Relig. life Germ. **1** : 71. — Buckley, T. A. Great cities, 271. — Guild. Over the ocean, 89. — Hawthorne. Eng. notebks. **2** : 56, 182. — Rimmer, A. Country towns, 51. — Silloway. Cathedral towns, 254. — Temple, E. L. Old-world, **2** : 181.

— and Lincoln, Minsters of. Freeman. Eng. towns, 222.

— Capture of. Dawson. Batt. of U. S. **2** : 214.

— Literary school of. Brooks, S. A. Hist. early Eng. lit. 444.

— Old. Winter. Gray days, 38.

York cathedral. Van Rensselaer, M. G. Eng. cath. 328. — (C. Anderson) Farrar, F. W. Westmin. 125.

— Incendiary of. Baring-Gould. Yorks. odd. **2** : 139.

York, Me. Drake. Nooks of N. E. 109.

York, Cape, Greenland, Ironstone of. (R. E. Peary) Am. Geog. Soc. **26** : 447.

Yorke, Charles. Hazlitt. Parl. portr. 189. — Campbell. Ld. chan. **7** : 53.

Yorke, Charles P. *See* Hardwicke, 4th earl of.

Yorke, Philip, lord chancellor, 1737. Foss. Judges, **8** : 178.

Yorkshire, Ancient barrows in East. Wright, T. Ess. archæol. **1** : 22.

— A Glimpse of. Moulton, L. C. Lazy tours, 357.

— North Riding. Freeman. Eng. towns, 309.

— Remains of primitive people in S. E. Wright, T. Ess. archæol. **1** : 1.

Yorkshire butcher, A. Baring-Gould. Yorks. odd. **1** : 229.

Yorkshire dale, A. Heath, R. Eng. peasants, 91.

Yorkshire recusants. Baring-Gould. Yorks. odd. **2** : 229.

Yorkshire shrines. Wolfe. Lit. pilg. Brit. au. 106.

Yorkshire tyke, Old [Verses]. Baring-Gould. Yorks. odd. **1** : 243.

Yorktown, Va., Old. Page. Old South, 189.

— Siege of, 1781. Dawson. Batt. of U. S. **1** : 733.

— Siege of, 1862. Allan, W. Army of N. Va. 7. — (J. C. Palfrey) Dwight, T. F. Camp. Va. 89.

Yosemite Valley. Bridges, F. D. Lady's trav. 376. — Butler, W. F. Far out, 137. — Cumming, C. F. G. Granite crags, 75. — Jackson, H. H. Bits trav. home, 87, 134. — Marshall, W. G. Thro' Amer. 334. — Pierrepont. Fifth ave. 52. — Prime, E. D. G. Around world, 46. — Russell, W. H. Hesper, **2** : 19. — Pidgeon. Engineer's holiday, 218. — Tiffany, O. H. Pulpit & p.

— and its origin, The. Caton. Miscel. 335.

— Camping in. Rutgers, L. On saddle, 48.

Yoshida-Torajiro. Stevenson, R. L. Fam. stud. 172; *or* Miscel. **2** : 165.

Youmans, Edward L. Fiske, J. Cent. of science, 64.

Young, Alexander (born 1798). Winslow, S. N. Biog. Phila. merch. 163.

Young, Andrew. Miller, Jos. Singers church, 2d ed. 506.

Young, Arthur. Edwards, B. B. Self-taught, 237. — Mitchell. Wet days, 248. Stephen, L. Stud. biog. **1** : 188. — With portrait. Warner lib. **27** : 16261.

Young, Brigham. Dilke. Greater Brit. 110. — McCarthy, J. Mod. lead. 96.

— and his home. Marshall, W. G. Thro' Amer. 172.

— Will of. Marshall, W. G. Thro' Amer. 499.

Young, Charles, and his times. Doran. Drury Lane, **1** : 54.

Young, Charles M. Baker, H. B. Eng. actors, **1** : 175. — Matthews, B. Actors, **2** : 269.

Young, Edward. Griswold, R. W. Sac. poets. — Bell, R. Lit. & sci. men, **2** : 327. — (S. Johnson) Chalmers. Eng. poets, **13** : 339. — Eliot, G. Ess. 7. — Eliot, G. Ess. & leaves, 3. — Hazlitt. Eng. poets. — Sanborn, K. Eng. poets, 155. — Tuckerman. Poets, 101. — (G. Saintsbury) Ward. Eng. poets, **3** : 222. — Brooks, S. W. Eng. poets, 233. — Davidson, J. W. Writ. of South, 630. — Deshler. Afternoons, 168. — Mitchell, D. G. Eng. lands, **3** : 15. — With portrait. Warner Lib. **27** : 16277. — Wrangham. Brit. Plutarch, v. **6**.

— Night thoughts. Saunders, F. Famous books, 86.

Young, Edward James. Vaille & Clark. Harv. book, v. **1**.

Young, Edmond Stafford. Am. Bar Assoc. **11** : 343.

Young, Henry C. Perry, B. F. Biog. sketches, **2** : 173.

Young, John. McCosh. Scot. phil. 367. — Jenkins. Gov. of N. Y. 793. — Proctor. Lawy. of N. Y. 152.

Young, Josué Maria. Clarke, R. H. Cath. bishops, **2** : 514.

Young, Miss M. A. B. Brockett. Woman's work, 459.

Young, Mrs. Maud J. Raymond, I. Southland writ. **2** : 952.

Young, Robert. Macaulay. Biog. sk. 268. — Wesley & successors, 185.

Young, Robert Newton. Wesley & successors, 249.

Young, Thomas. Arago. Sci. men, **2** : 280. — Garnett. Physicists, 194. — Loring, J. S. Hundred Bost. ora. 24. — Tyndall. New frag. 248. — Walker, W., jr. Men of sci. 145.

Young, the, Exaggerated importance of, in modern literature. Stephen, J. F. Ess. by barr. 190.

Young Italy, Society of. Heckethorn. Sec. soc. **2** : 272.

Young men, association for, Form of. Webster, N. Papers, 305.

— in history. Whipple. Success, **1**.

Young Men's Christian Association, Some duties of. Meath. Soc. arrows, 93.

Young's House, Affair at. Dawson. Batt. of U. S. **1** : 579.

Youth and age. Bacon. Ess. — Saunders, F. Mosaics, 76.

— and revolutions. (W. R. Thayer) Mass. Hist. Soc. Proc. 2d ser. **11** : 226.

— Crabbed age and. Stevenson, R. L. Virgin. 81.

— Departure of. Bulwer. Student, **1** : 47.

— Pain of. Mabie. Ess. on work, 35.

Yriarte, Don Tomas de. Newbigging. Fables, 117. — Kennedy. Poets of Spain, 37.

Ysaye, Eugene, with portrait. Ehrlich, A. Cel. violin. 201.

Yucatan, Ancient structures of. (E. H. Thompson) Am. Antiq. Soc. Proc. n. s. **8** : 263.
— and Central America, Bibliography of. (Ad. F. Bandelier) Am. Antiq. Soc. Proc. n. s. **1** : 82.
— Archæological research in. (E. H. Thompson) Am. Antiq. Soc. Proc. n. s. **4** : 248.
— at the time of its discovery. (E. H. Thompson) Am. Antiq. Soc. Proc. n. s. **8** : 270.
— Bill to take temporary military possession of, 1849. Dix. Speeches, **1** : 284.
— Explorations in. (E. H. Thompson) Am. Antiq. Soc. Proc. n. s. **4** : 379.
— Myths of. Brinton. Amer. hero-myths, 143.
— resources, commerce, etc., 1895. (C. Smyth) U. S. Cons. Rept. **49** : 495.
— Statue called Chac-mool. (S. Salisbury, jr.) Am. Geog. Soc. **9** : 142.

Yukon gold-fields, The, 1898. (L. E. Dudley) U. S. Cons. Rept. **56**: 315.
— Copper River as a route to. (C. W. Hayes) Am. Geog. Soc. **30** : 127.
— Mining regulations, 1897. (C. E. Turner) U. S. Cons. Rept. **55** : 145.

Yukon river, Exploration of, in 1883. (F. Schwatka) Am. Geog. Soc. **16** : 345.
— Journey up. (I. C. Russell) Am. Geog. Soc. **27** : 143.

Yung-ho-Kung temple. Cumming, C. F. G. Wand. in China, **2** : 191.

Yuste. Buckley, T. A. Great cities, 362.

Zaandam. Amicis. Holland, 301.

Zacatecas, Mex., as a sanitary station. (J. Brena) Am. Pub. Health, **18** : 68.

Zachaire, Denis. Waite, A. E. Lives of alchem. 140.

Zadig, Method of. Huxley. Sci. & cal. 135.

Zajic, Florian, with portrait. Ehrlich, A. Cel. violin. 99.

Zaleski, Joseph Bohdan. Soboleski. Poets of Poland, 295.

Zama, Battle of. King, C. Battles, 116.

Zambo village. Dixon, W. H. White conquest, **1** : 272.

Zan, Thomas. Soboleski. Poets of Poland, 323.

Zane, Elizabeth. Ellet. Women of revol. **2** : 275.

Zante, Island of. Arnold, R. A. Levant, **1** : 207.
— Barrows, S. J. Isles of Greece, 70.

Zanzibar. Latimer. Eur. in Afr. in 19th c. 250.
— Loanda to. Malortie. Here, there, 227.
— Slavery in. Wagner, L. Mod. pol. ora. 222.

Zappi, The two. Jameson. Loves of poets.

Zaragoza. *See* Saragossa.

Zarini, Princess. Tuckerman, C. K. Recollec. **2** : 280.

Zarzerius, Philip Audactus. Wallace, R. Anti-Trin. biog. **2** : 385.

Zeal. Friswell. Gentle life, **2** : 222.

Zealand. Amicis. Holland, 17.
— Spanish troops in, Daring of. Davenport. Narr. peril. **2** : 309.

Zehir-ed-din Muhammed Baber. Memoirs. Jeffrey, F. Contrib. Ed. Rev.

Zeisberger, David. Carne, J. Em. mission. **2** : 1.
— and the Indians. Japp, A. H. Master mission. 82.

Zelich, Gerasime. Brightwell. Byepaths of biog. 201.

Zell, Catherine. Stevenson. Lives & deeds, 116.

Zenana mission. Pitman. Mrs. Heroines mission. 21.

Zend-Avesta, The. Müller. Chips, v. **1**.

Zend-Avesta, and Persian cuneiform inscriptions. Cook, F. C. Origins, 105.
— and Zoroaster. Clarke, J. F. Ten relig. 171.
— Study of, in India. Müller. Chips, v. **1**.
See Avesta.

Zend scholarship, Progress of. Müller. Chips, v. **1**.

Zenger, John Peter, 1735. Chandler, P. W. Am. crim. trials, **1** : 151.

Zeno, the stoic. Belknap. Amer. biog. **1** : 138. — Diog. Laertius. Lives, 259. — Fénélon. Philosophers, 287. — Lewes. Biog. phil. — Mills. Poets of Greece, 428. — Fairbanks, A. Philos. of Greece, 119.

Zeno, A. Stebbing. Ital. poets, v. **3**.
— Dramatic works of. Hogarth. Mem. opera, **1** : 172.

Zeno brothers, Voyages of. (R. H. Major) Mass. Hist. Proc. **13** : 352.

Zeno, Carlo. Oliphant. Makers of Venice, 166.

Zenobia. (E. Gibbon) Ferris, G. T. Gt. leaders, 60. — Goodrich, F. B. Women, 57. — Jameson. Fem. sov. v. **1**. — Owen, Mrs. O. F. Heroines hist. 120.

Zerbolt, Gerhard. Ullman. Reformers, 105.

Zermatt. Coolidge. Swiss travel.

Zeus, Pheidian, at Olympia, Group of gods on front of base of. Davidson, T. Parthenon, 129.

Zglobicius. Wallace, R. Anti-Trin. biog. **2** : 361.

Ziegenbalg, Bartholomew. Thompson, A. Gt. mission. 189.

Ziller, Tuiskon. DeGarmo. Herbart, 101.

Zimmerman, Bettie M. Raymond, I. Southland wr. **1** : 480.

Zimmermann, J. G. von. Alger. Solitudes, 262.

Zimorowicz, Simeon. Soboleski. Poets of Poland, 69.

Zingarelli, N. A., musical composer. Hogarth. Mem. opera, **2** : 106.

Zinzendorf, Count Nikolaus Ludwig. Hatfield, E. F. Poets of ch. 689. — Miller, Jos. Singers church, 2d ed. 160.
— and the Moravians. Hedge, F. H. Martin Luther, 38. — Winkworth. Chr. sing. Germ. 306. — Ker, J. Lec. hist. preach. 229. — Pierce, B. K. Em. dead. 247.— Larrabee, W. C. Wesley, **1** : 147.

Zinzendorf, Philip Louis, Count. Crowe, E. E. For. statesmen, **5** : 62.

Zisca, J. Gilpin, W. Lives, 216. — Mears, J. W. Heroes Bohem. — Pennington. Epochs papacy, 233. — Wittenmeyer. Women Reform. 65. — Gilpin. Reformers, v. **1**.

Zmichowska, Narcissa. Soboleski. Poets of Poland, 448.

Zmorski, Roman. Soboleski. Poets of Poland, 445.

Zoan. Poole, R. S. Cities of Egypt, 64.

Zoar, Community of. Hinds. Amer. commun. — Nordhoff. Commun. 99.

Zodiac, Indian and Arabian divisions of the. Colebrooke. Miscel. essays, **2** : 321.
— Lunar, of India, Arabia, and China. Whitney, W. D. Orient, **2** : 341.
— Signs of the. (T. S. Row) Five years theos. 103.

Zola, Emile. Couch, A. T. Q. Adv. crit. 192. — With portraits. Lynch, A. Hum. doc's, 176. — Amicis. Stud. Paris, 108. — Buchanan, R. Look round, 303. — Hazeltine. Chats, 188. — Ellis, H. Affirmations, 131. — With portrait. (R. Vallier) Warner Lib. **27** : 16283. — Wells, B. W. Cent. Fr. fic. 283. — Pellissier. Lit. mov. Fr. 432. — Henry S. Hours w.

Parisians, 27. — Van de Velde. Fr. fic. 2 : 107.

Zola, Emile, and his school. Nordau. Degen. 473.
— and the present tendencies of French drama. Matthews, J. B. Fr. dram. 264.
— as an evolutionist. Blaze de Bury, Y. French lit. 37.
— La bête humaine. Symonds. Key of blue, 111.
— Method of, Note on. Symons, A. Stud. two lit. 204.
— Prosecution of Vizetelly for pub. works of. Buchanan, R. Coming terr. 99.

Zollicoffer, Felix K. Pollard. Life of Lee, 705.
Zollikofer, Georg Joachim, Preaching of. Ker, J. Lec. hist. preach. 250, 260.
— Sermons. Foster, J. Crit. ess. (Bohn) 2 : 123.
Zollverein, The. (J. Bowring) Rand. Selec. econ. hist. 170.

Zonas. Mills. Poets of Greece, 237.
Zoölogical collections in education. (W. A. Conklin) N. Y. Regents, 97, app. : 196.
Zoölogical gardens. Wynter, A. Peeps, 2 : 83.
— of London. Wood, J. G. Out-of-doors, 1.
— — Visit to. Hunt, L. Men, wom. & books, 36.

Zoölogy. Bibliography. Salem (Mass.) Pub. Lib. Bull. July, '97.
— Century's progress in. Flower, W. H. Ess. on museums, 153.
— Elementary. (T. Alcock) Manch. Sci. lec. 1 : 49.
— a factor in mental culture. (S. H. Gage) Nat. Educa. Soc. '96 : 960.
— Facts and fictions of. Wilson, A. Leisure, 72.
— Heroes of. Duncan, P. M. Botanists, 122.
— History and scope of. Lankester. Advan. sci. 287.
— in the high school curriculum. (H. B. Ward) Nat. Educa. Assoc. '97 : 952.
— Marine. Bibliography. Salem (Mass.) Pub. Lib. Bull. June, '94.
— Pedagogical content of. (N. A. Harvey) Nat. Ed. Assoc. '99 : 1106.
— Progress in, 1846-96. (T. Gill) Goode. Smithso. Inst. 711.
— since Darwin. (L. von Graff) Smithson. Inst. Rept. '95 : 477.
— Study of. Huxley. Lay sermons.

Zorndorf, Battle of. Carlyle. Batt. Fred. the Gt. 138.

Zoroaster. Bettany. World's relig. 343. — Hundred greatest men, 125. — Matheson. Distinc. mess. 167.
— and the Zend-Avesta. Clarke, J. F. Ten relig. 171. — (J. Milne) St. Giles lec. 2 : 100.
— Bibliography. Jackson, A. V. W. Zoroaster.
— The Gâthâs of. Cook, F. C. Origins, 203.
— a protestant. Matheson. Distinc. mess. 176.

Zoroastrianism. (L. H. Mills) Relig. systems, 180.
— Sacred books of. Cobbe, F. P. Studies, '89.

Zorrilla, José y Moral. Kennedy. Poets of Spain, 323. — Warner Lib. 27 : 16325.

Zrinyi, Helen. Wyatt, W. J. Hunga. celeb. 181.

Zschokke, Johann Heinrich Daniel. Hedge. Prose Ger. 459.

Zubly, John J. Jones, C. C., jr. Deleg. fr. Georgia, 203.

Zulu nursery tales. Müller. Chips, v. 2.
Zulu war, 1879; Sir B. Frere's policy. Pembroke, Earl. Polit. lett. 416. — Richards, W. Heroes, 36. — Latimer. Eur. in Afr. in 19th c. 331.

Zulus. Butler, W. F. Far out, 175.

Zunz, Leopold. Karpeles. Jew lit. 318.

Zurbaran, Francisco de. Stirling-Maxwell. Ann. art. Spain, 3 : 918. — Washburn, E. Span. mas. 96.

Zuyder Zee. Amicis. Holland, 342. — Mahaffy, Holl. & Germ. 64.

Zwanziger, A. M. Feuerbach. Crim. trials.

Zwiartovius, Christopher. Wallace. R. Anti-Trin. biog. 3 : 144.

Zwicker, Daniel. Wallace, R. Anti-Trin. biog. 3 : 258.

Zwinger, Theodore. Hatfield, E. F. Poets of church, 694.

Zwingli, Anna Reinhard, wife of Ulrich. Chapman, W. Wom. of ref. 176.

Zwingli, Ulrich. Broadus. Lect. hist. preach. 127. — Croly. Hist. sk. 153. — Dawson, G. Biog. lec. 465. — Pünjer. Chr. philos. relig. 145. — Tagart. Sk. ref. 16th c. 47.

Zymotics. Bost. Health, '75 : 82.

Zytnius, Nicholas. Wallace, R. Anti-Trin. biog. 2 : 238.

LIST OF BOOKS INDEXED.

This list contains the names of the books indexed throughout for this work. But there will be found in the Index many references to other books, which have been added from various sources. (*See* Preface.)

In the imprints, L = London, B = Boston, P = Philadelphia.

Where imprints are omitted, it is because the books appear in various editions, and the references in the index apply equally well to either one.

The titles are spaced apart to give room for the insertion of library numbers by such librarians as care to affix them.

Abbot, Ezra. Authorship of the Fourth Gospel, and other essays. Boston, 1888.

Abbott, Charles C. Outings at odd times. New York, 1890.

Abbott, Evelyn. Hellenica. London, 1880.

Abbott, John S. C. Kings and queens. New York, 1848.

—— Lives of presidents. Boston, 1867.

Abbott, Lyman, *and others.* The new puritanism. New York, 1898.

Abel, Carl. Linguistic essays. Boston, 1882.

Abercromby, Ralph. Seas and skies. London, 1888.

Adams, Charles. Great campaigns. London, 1878.

Adams, Chas. Francis. New departure. Boston, 1881.

—— *and* Henry. Chapters of Erie. Boston, 1871.

Adams, Chas. Kendall. Representative British orations. New York, 1884.

Adams, George B. Civilization during the middle ages. New York, 1895.

Adams, Henry. Historical essays. New York, 1891.

Adams, John. Works. Boston, 1850-56. 10 v.

Adams, John G. Fifty notable years. Boston, 1882.

Adams, Wm. Davenport. Famous books. N. Y. 1881.

—— With poet and player. London, 1891.

—— Worthies of Church of England. London, 1880.

Adams, Wm. H. D. Anecdotal memoirs of English princes. London, 1863. 2 v.

—— Celebrated Englishwomen of the Victorian era. London, 1884. 2 v.

—— Celebrated women travellers. London, 1883.

—— England at war. London, 1886. 2 v.

—— English party leaders. London, 1878. 2 v.

—— Famous beauties. London, 1865. 2 v.

—— Famous caves and catacombs. London, 1886.

—— Famous caverns and grottoes. London, 1886.

—— Good Samaritans. London, 1883.

—— Great English churchmen. London, 1879.

—— Great names in European history. Edinburgh, 1879.

—— Heroes of the Cross. London, 1880.

—— In perils oft. New York, 1886.

Adams, Wm. H. D. Learned in the law. London, 1882.

—— Memorable battles. London, 1879.

—— Men at the helm. Edinburgh, 1862.

—— Noble women. London, 1882.

—— Old English worthies. Edinburgh, 1862.

—— Records of noble lives. London, n. d.

—— Some heroes of travel. London, 1880.

—— Warriors of the Crescent. New York, 1892.

—— Women of fashion. London, 1878. 2 v.

—— Worthies of the Church of England. New York, n. d.

Addams, Jane, *and others.* Philanthropy and social progress. New York, 1893.

Addison, Joseph. Works. (Bohn) London, 1854-56. 6 v.

Adolphus, John. French revolution. London, 1799. 2 v.

Afternoon Lectures. London, 1863-69. 5 v.

Agassiz, Louis. Geological sketches. Boston, 1876. 2 v.

Agnew, D. C. A. Protestant exiles. L. 1871. 2 v.

Aguilar, Grace. Women of Israel. New York, 1879.

Alexander, Jas. M. Islands in the Pacific; missions. New York, 1895.

Alford, Henry. Essays and addresses. London, 1869.

Alger, Wm. R. Solitudes. Boston, 1867.

Alison, Sir Archibald. Essays. Edinburgh, 1850. 3 v.

Allan, Wm. Army of Northern Virginia in 1862. B. 1892.

—— Battlefields of Virginia. New York, 1867.

Allen, Grant. Falling in love. London, 1889.

—— Science in Arcady. London, 1892.

Allen, James Lane. Blue-grass region of Kentucky. New York, 1892.

Allen, Joseph. Battles of the British navy. L. 1883. 2 v.

Allen, Joseph H. Sequel to "Our liberal movement." Boston, 1897.

Allen, Wm. F. Essays. Boston, 1890.

Allies, M. H. Three Catholic reformers. London, 1878.

Allingham, Wm. Varieties in Prose. London, 1892. 3 v.

Altgeld, John P. Live questions. Chicago, 1890.

Alviela, Goblet d'. Contemporary evolution of religious thought. New York, 1886.